The Longman Anthology
of British Literature

VOLUME 2C

THE TWENTIETH CENTURY

David Damrosch
COLUMBIA UNIVERSITY

Christopher Baswell
BARNARD COLLEGE

Clare Carroll
QUEENS COLLEGE, CITY UNIVERSITY OF NEW YORK

Kevin J. H. Dettmar
CLEMSON UNIVERSITY

Heather Henderson
MOUNT HOLYOKE COLLEGE

Constance Jordan
CLAREMONT GRADUATE UNIVERSITY

Peter J. Manning
UNIVERSITY OF SOUTHERN CALIFORNIA

Anne Howland Schotter
WAGNER COLLEGE

William Chapman Sharpe
BARNARD COLLEGE

Stuart Sherman
FORDHAM UNIVERSITY

Jennifer Wicke
UNIVERSITY OF VIRGINIA

Susan J. Wolfson
PRINCETON UNIVERSITY

The Longman Anthology of British Literature

David Damrosch

General Editor

VOLUME 2C

THE TWENTIETH CENTURY
Kevin Dettmar *and* Jennifer Wicke

LONGMAN

An imprint of Addison Wesley Longman, Inc.

New York • Reading, Massachusetts • Menlo Park, California • Harlow, England
Don Mills, Ontario • Sydney • Mexico City • Madrid • Amsterdam

Editor-in-Chief: *Patricia Rossi*
Senior Editor: *Lisa Moore*
Development Editor: *Mark Getlein*
Marketing Manager: *Melanie Goulet*
Supplements Editor: *Donna Campion*
Project Coordination and Text Design: *York Production Services*
Cover Designer: *Kay Petronio*
Cover Design Manager: *Nancy Danahy*
On the cover: *Tom Phillips, A Document (Thames & Hudson, revised edition, 1987), p. 185.*
    This work is a copy of a Victorian novel, A Human Document by W.H. Mallock; Phillips has
    made paintings and drawings on every page, leaving some words exposed. Reprinted by permis-
    sion of the artist.
Photo Researcher: *Julie Tesser*
Full Service Production Manager: *Valerie Zaborski*
Publishing Services Manager: *Al Dorsey*
Senior Print Buyer: *Hugh Crawford*
Electronic Page Makeup: *York Production Services*
Printer and Binder: *R.R. Donnelley and Sons Company*
Cover Printer: *The Lehigh Press, Inc.*

For permission to use copyrighted material, grateful acknowledgment is made to the copyright
holders on pages 2945–2947, which are hereby made part of this copyright page.

Library of Congress Cataloging-in-Publication Data

The Longman anthology of British literature. The twentieth century/ David Damrosch,
    general editor; [complied by] Kevin Dettmar and Jennifer Wicke.
        p.   cm.
    Includes bibliographical references and indexes.
    ISBN 0-321-06767-3
        1. English literature—20th century.   2. Great Britain—Civilization—
20th century Literary collections.   I. Damrosch, David.   II. Dettmar, Kevin J. H.,
1958–   .   III. Wicke, Jennifer.   IV. Title: Anthology of British literature.
V. Title: Twentieth century.
PR1148.L66   1999
820.8'0091—dc21   99-35640
                                                                                   CIP

ISBN 0-321-06767-3

1234567890–DOC–010099

CONTENTS

PREFACE

This is an exciting time to be reading British literature. Literary studies are experiencing a time of transformation, involving lively debate about the nature of literature itself, its relations to the wider culture, and the best ways to read and understand it. These questions have been sharpened by the "culture wars" of recent years, in which traditionalists have debated advocates of fundamental reform, close readers have come up against cultural theorists who may seem more interested in politics than in aesthetic questions, and lovers of canonical texts have found themselves sharing the stage with multiculturalists who typically focus on ethnic and minority literatures, usually contemporary and often popular in nature, rather than on earlier and more elite literary productions.

The goal of this anthology is to present the wealth of British literature, old and new, classic and newly current, in ways that will respond creatively to these debates. We have constructed this anthology in the firm belief that it is important to attend both to aesthetic and to cultural questions as we study literature, and to continue to read the great classics even as we discover or rediscover new or neglected works. Admittedly, it is difficult to do all this at once, especially within the pages of a single anthology or the time constraints of a survey course. To work toward these goals, it has been necessary to rethink the very form of an anthology. This preface can serve as a kind of road map to the pages that follow.

A NEW LITERARY GEOGRAPHY

Let us begin by defining our basic terms: What is "British" literature? What is literature itself? And just what is the function of an anthology at the present time? The term "British" can mean many things, some of them contradictory, some of them even offensive to people on whom the name has been imposed. If the term has no ultimate essence, it does have a history. The first British were Celtic people who inhabited the British Isles and the northern coast of France (still called Brittany), before various Germanic tribes of Angles and Saxons moved onto the islands in the fifth and sixth centuries. Gradually the Angles and Saxons amalgamated into the Anglo-Saxon culture that became dominant in the southern and eastern regions of Britain and then spread outward; the old British people were pushed west, toward what became known as Cornwall, Wales, and Ireland, which remained independent kingdoms for centuries, as did Celtic Scotland to the north. By an ironic twist of linguistic fate, the Anglo-Saxons began to appropriate the term British from the Britons they had displaced, and they took as a national hero the legendary Welsh King Arthur. By the seventeenth century, English monarchs had extended their sway over Wales, Ireland, and Scotland, and they began to refer to their holdings as "Great Britain." Today, Great Britain includes England, Wales, Scotland, and Northern Ireland, but does not include the Republic of Ireland, which has been independent from England since 1922.

This anthology uses "British" in a broad sense, as a geographical term encompassing the whole of the British Isles. For all its fraught history, it seems a more satisfactory term than to speak simply of "English" literature, for two reasons. First: most speakers of English live in countries that are not the focus of this anthology; second, while the English language and its literature have long been dominant in the British Isles, other cultures in the region have always used other languages and have produced great literature in these languages. Important works by Irish, Welsh, and Scots writers appear regularly in the body of this anthology, some of them written directly in their languages and presented here in translation, others written in an English inflected by the rhythms, habits of thought, and modes of expression characteristic of these other languages and the people who use them. Important works, moreover, have often been written in the British Isles by recent arrivals, from Marie de France in the twelfth century to T. S. Eliot and Salman Rushdie in the twentieth; in a very real sense, their writings too are part of British literary production.

We use the term "literature" itself in a similarly capacious sense, to refer to a range of artistically shaped works written in a charged language, appealing to the imagination at least as much as to discursive reasoning. It is only relatively recently that creative writers have been able to make a living composing poems, plays, and novels purely "for art's sake," and only in the past hundred years or so have "belles lettres" or works of high literary art been thought of as sharply separate from other sorts of writing that the same authors would regularly produce. Sometimes, Romantic poets wrote sonnets to explore the deepest mysteries of individual perception and memory; at other times, they wrote sonnets the way a person might now write an Op-Ed piece, and such a sonnet would be published and read along with parliamentary debates and letters to the editor on the most pressing contemporary issues.

Great literature is double in nature: it is deeply rooted in its cultural moment, and yet it transcends this moment as well, speaking to new readers in distant times and places, long after the immediate circumstances of its production have been forgotten. The challenge today is to restore our awareness of cultural contexts without trapping our texts within them. Great writers create imaginative worlds that have their own compelling internal logic, built around the stories they tell using formal patterns of genre, literary reference, imagery, and style. At the same time, as Virginia Woolf says in A Room of One's Own, the gossamer threads of the artist's web are joined to reality "with bands of steel." To understand where a writer is taking us imaginatively, it is helpful to know where we are supposed to be starting from in reality: any writer assumes a common body of current knowledge, which this anthology attempts to fill in by means of detailed period introductions, full introductions to the individual authors, and notes and glosses to each text. Many of the greatest works of literature, moreover, have been written in response to the most sharply contested issues of the authors' own times. This anthology presents and groups selections in such a way as to suggest the literary and cultural contexts in which, and for which, they were created.

WOMEN'S WRITING, AND MEN'S

Literary culture has always involved an interplay between central and marginal regions, groups, and individuals. At a given time, some will seem dominant; in retrospect, some will remain so and others will be eclipsed, for a time or permanently, while formerly neglected writers may achieve a new currency. A major emphasis in literary study in recent years has been the recovery of writing by a range of women writers, some of them little read until recently, others major figures in their time and now again fascinating to read. Attending to the voices of such compelling writers as Margery Kempe, Elizabeth Cary, Mary Wollstonecraft, Mary Shelley, and Edith Nesbit often involves a shift in our understanding of the literary landscape, giving a new and lively perspective on much-read works. Thus, Shakespeare's *Othello* can fruitfully be read together with Elizabeth Cary's *Tragedy of Mariam, the Fair Queen of Jewry*, which tells a tale of jealousy and betrayal from a woman's point of view. On a larger scale, the first third of the nineteenth century can be defined more broadly than as a "Romantic Age" dominated by six male poets; looking closely at women's writing as well as men's, and at prose writing as well as poetry, we can deepen our understanding of the period as a whole—including the specific achievements of Blake, William Wordsworth, Coleridge, Keats, Percy Shelley, and Byron, all of whom continue to have a major presence in these pages as most of them did during the nineteenth century.

HISTORICAL PERIODS IN PERSPECTIVE

Overall, we have sought to give a varied presentation of the major periods of literary history, as customarily construed by scholars today: the Middle Ages (punctuated by the Norman Conquest in 1066); the early modern period or Renaissance; the Restoration and the eighteenth century; the era of the Romantics and their contemporaries; the Victorian age; and the twentieth century. These names mix chronology, politics, and literary movements: each period is of course a mixture of all of these elements and many others. Further, the boundaries of all these periods are fluid. Milton should be thought of in the context of Restoration politics as well as of early modern humanism; what is more, selections from *Paradise Lost* will also be found in Volume 2, in a Context section showing Milton's influence on the Romantics and their contemporaries. Reflecting the division of Thomas Hardy's literary life, Hardy appears in the Victorian section as a prose writer, and in the Twentieth Century as a poet. In general, one of the great pleasures of a survey of centuries of British literary production is the opportunity to see the ways texts speak to one another both across periods and within them, and indeed several layers of time may coexist within a single era: many writers consciously or unconsciously hearken back to earlier values (there were medievalists in the nineteenth century), while other writers cast "shadows of futurity" before them, in Percy Shelley's phrase.

Within periods, we have sought a variety of means to suggest the many linkages that make up a rich literary culture, which is something more than a sequence of individual writers all producing their separate bodies of work. In this anthology, each period includes several groupings called "Perspectives," with texts that address an important literary or social issue of the time. These Perspective sections typically illuminate underlying issues in a variety of the major works of their time, as with a section on Government and Self-Government that relates broadly to Sir Thomas More's *Utopia*, to Spenser's *Faerie Queene*, and to Milton's *Paradise Lost*. Most of the writers included in Perspective sections are important period figures, less well known today, who might be neglected if they were listed on their own with just a few pages each; grouping them together should be useful pedagogically as well as intellectually. Perspective sections may also include writing by a major author whose primary listing appears elsewhere in the period: thus, a Perspective section on the abolition of slavery and the slave trade—a hotly debated issue in England from the 1790s through the 1830s—includes poems and essays by Wordsworth, Byron, and Barbauld, so as to give a rounded presentation of the issue in ways that can inform the reading of those authors in their individual sections.

WORKS IN CONTEXT

Periodically throughout the anthology we also present major works "In Context," to show the terms of a specific debate to which an author is responding. Thus Sir Philip Sidney's great *The Apology for Poetry* is accompanied by a context section to show the controversy that was raging at the time concerning the nature and value of poetry. Similarly, Thomas Dekker and Thomas Middleton's hilarious seventeenth-century comedy *The Roaring Girl: Or, Moll Cut-Purse* is accompanied by a Context section giving several readings on the virtues and vices of city life. Some of the writers in that context section are not classically literary figures, but all have produced lively and intriguing works, from King James I's *Counterblast to Tobacco* to Thomas Deloney's satiric account of *How Simon's Wife . . . Being Wholly Bent to Pride and Pleasure, Requested Her Husband to See London.*

Additionally, we include "Companion Readings" to present specific prior texts to which a work is responding: when Sir Thomas Wyatt creates a beautiful poem, *Whoso List to Hunt,* by making a free translation of a Petrarch sonnet, we include Petrarch's original (and a more literal translation) as a companion reading. For Conrad's *Heart of Darkness,* companion texts include Conrad's diary of the Congo journey on which he based his novella, and a bizarre lecture by Sir Henry Morton Stanley, the explorer-adventurer whose travel writings Conrad parodies.

ILLUSTRATING VISUAL CULTURE

Literature has always been a product of cultures that are visual as well as verbal. We include a hundred illustrations in the body of the anthology, presenting artistic and cultural images that figured importantly for literary creation. Sometimes, a poem refers to a specific painting, or more generally emulates qualities of a school of visual art. At other times, photographs, advertisements, or political cartoons can set the stage for literary works. In some cases, visual and literary creation have merged, as in Hogarth's series *A Rake's Progress,* included in Volume 1, or Blake's engravings of his *Songs of Innocence and Experience,* several of whose plates are reproduced in Volume 2.

AIDS TO UNDERSTANDING

We have tried to contextualize our selections in a suggestive rather than an exhaustive way, wishing to enhance rather than overwhelm the experience of reading the texts themselves. Our introductions to periods and authors are intended to open up ways of reading rather than dictating a particular interpretation, and the suggestions presented here should always be seen as points of departure rather than definitive pronouncements. We have striven for clarity and ease of use in our editorial matter.

Thus, when difficult or archaic words need defining in poems, we use glosses in the margins, in all periods, so as to disrupt the reader's eye as little as possible; footnotes are intended to be concise and informative, rather than massive or interpretive. Spelling and punctuation are modernized in Volume 1, except when older forms are important for meter or rhyme, and with general exceptions for certain major writers, like Chaucer and Spenser, whose specific usages are crucial to their understanding. Important literary and social terms are defined when they are used; for convenience of reference, there is also an extensive glossary of literary and cultural terms at the end of each volume, and we provide summaries of British political and religious orders, and of money, weights, and measures. For further reading, we give carefully selected bibliographies for each period and for each author.

A NEW AND VARIED FORMAT

For this printing, we introduce a choice of form: the anthology is available in the classic two-volume version, and also in six separate parts, one for each of the historical periods into which the anthology is divided. To preserve full freedom of choice, we have kept the paging the same in both versions, so that either can be used within a single course. The three sections of Volume 1 are thus available separately as Volumes 1A, 1B, and 1C, and the individual sections of Volume 2 can similarly be purchased as Volumes 2A, 2B, and 2C. When bought together, these sets are available at the same price as the two-volume version. The two-volume format keeps more material together, for ease of comparison and cross-reference; the six-volume version greatly increases the portability of the individual sections, and also enables them to be purchased individually for use in period courses. We hope that this innovative format will greatly increase the convenience and flexibility of the anthology; it is a physical embodiment of the variousness of British literature itself.

VARIETIES OF LITERARY EXPERIENCE

Above all, we have striven to give as full a presentation as possible to the varieties of great literature produced over the centuries in the British Isles, by women as well as by men, in outlying regions as well as in the metropolitan center of London, and in prose, drama, and verse alike. This is, in fact, the most capacious anthology of British literature ever assembled in a form suited to a survey course.

We hope that this anthology will show that the great works of earlier centuries can also speak to us compellingly today, their value only increased by the resistance they offer to our views of ourselves and our world. To read and reread the full sweep of this literature is to be struck anew by the degree to which the most radically new works are rooted in centuries of prior innovation. Even this preface can close in no better way than by quoting the words written eighteen hundred years ago by Apuleius—both a consummate artist and a kind of anthologist of extraordinary tales—when he concluded the prologue to his masterpiece *The Golden Ass*: Attend, reader, and pleasure is yours.

David Damrosch

Tom Phillips. Illustration to Canto 10 of Dante's *Inferno*, 1983.

The Twentieth Century

BURYING VICTORIA

Writing in 1928, Virginia Woolf described the cultural atmosphere of the Victorian era in the following way:

> Damp now began to make its way into every house. . . . The damp struck within. Men felt the chill in their hearts; the damp in their minds. . . . The life of the average woman was a succession of childbirths. She married at nineteen and had fifteen or eighteen children by the time she was thirty; for twins abounded. Thus the British Empire came into existence; and thus—for there is no stopping damp; it gets into inkpots as it gets into the wood-work—sentences swelled, adjectives multiplied, lyrics became epics, and little trifles that had been essays a column long were now encyclopedias in ten or twenty volumes.

Woolf of course exaggerates here for her own effect; yet this passage does capture nicely the stereotypical view of the Victorians that flourished during the modern period—and helped make it possible. Ezra Pound, for instance, called the later nineteenth century "a rather blurry, messy sort of period, a rather sentimentalistic, mannerish sort of period." Whether accurate or not, polemical descriptions like these served the rhetorical purposes of writers at the start of the new century as they attempted to stake out their terrain and to forge a literature and a perspective of their own.

The opening decade of the new century was a time of transition. Woolf later suggested, her tongue perhaps in her cheek, that as a result of a Post-Impressionist exhibition of paintings in London, "on or about December, 1910, human character changed." Almost no one, however, seems to have maintained that anything changed very decisively on the morning of 1 January 1900. Queen Victoria, at that time on the throne for nearly sixty-five years and in mourning for Prince Albert for almost forty, lived and ruled on into the following year; the subsequent reign of Edward VII (1901–1910) differed only slightly from that of his mother in many respects, the entire nation mourning the loss of their queen as she had the loss of her husband. But Woolf, in a 1924 essay, saw a gulf between herself and the Edwardians: Edwardian novelists, she writes, "established conventions which do their business; and that business is not our business." Edward VII himself, in fact, was clearly not a Victorian. He had a reputation as a playboy and implicitly rebelled against the conventions that his mother had upheld. During his reign, the mannered decadence of the 1890s modulated into a revived social realism seen in ambitious novels like Joseph Conrad's *Nostromo* and H. G. Wells's darkly comic masterpiece *Tono-Bungay*, while poets like Yeats and Hardy produced major poems probing the relations of self, society, and history. Writers in general considered themselves to be voices of a nation taking stock of its place in the world in a new century. They saw their times as marked by accelerating social and technological change and by the burden of a worldwide empire, which achieved its greatest extent in the years between 1900 and 1914—encompassing as much as a quarter of the world's population and dominating world trade through a global network of ports.

This period of consolidation and reflection abruptly came to an end four years into the reign of George V, with the start of World War I in August 1914; the relatively tranquil prewar years of George's early reign were quickly memorialized, and nostalgized, in the wake of the war's disruption to the traditionally English way of life. This first Georgian period was abruptly elevated into a cultural "golden age" by the British public and British publishers, a process that was typified by the pastoral poetry gathered by Edward Marsh in his hugely popular series of five anthologies called *Georgian Poetry*, the first of which was published in 1912. As a consequence of Marsh's skill as a tastemaker, this brief period before the war is frequently known as the Georgian period in British literature, though George V himself remained on the throne until 1936, when the distant rumble of World War II was to be heard by those with ears to hear.

The quarter century from 1914 until the start of the war in 1939 is now conventionally known as the modernist period. To be modern was, in one respect, to rebel openly and loudly against one's philosophical and artistic inheritance, in much the same way that the Romantic writers of the late eighteenth and early nineteenth centuries had sought to distinguish themselves from their Augustan forebears. This gesture—the way in which a new artistic movement seeks to define itself through caricature of the movement(s) that gave it birth—is a recurrent feature in literary history, but it took on a particular urgency and energy among the modernists, who advanced the view summarized in Pound's bold slogan, "Make It New." A great modernist monument to this anti-Victorian sentiment was Lytton Strachey's elegantly ironic *Eminent Victorians* (1918), whose probing biographical portraits punctured a series of Victorian pieties. Much of Bernard Shaw's writing (including *Major Barbara*) is animated by anti-Victorian animus as well, taking the theatrical wit of Oscar Wilde and turning it against specific targets. Exaggerated though it was, the ritualized slaughter performed by modernists like Woolf, Strachey, and Shaw seems to have achieved a clearing of the literary and artistic terrain that formed a necessary prelude to further innovation. The modernists' "Victorians" were oversimplified, sometimes straw figures, but the battle that was waged against them was real indeed, and the principles of modernism were forged and refined in the process.

THE FOUNDATIONS OF MODERN SKEPTICISM

The best Victorian writers had not been afraid to ask difficult, unsettling questions. Tennyson's restless skepticism in *In Memoriam*, for example, exemplifies the spirit of Victorian inquiry. But the conclusion of that poem foresees an ongoing progress toward future perfection, guided by "One God, one law, one element, / And one far-off divine event, / To which the whole creation moves." Tennyson himself doubted that such unities could be embodied in the present; twentieth-century writers found increasing fragmentation around them and became more and more suspicious of narratives of historical progress and of social unity. It makes sense that in 1832 Tennyson would make a representative man of Ulysses—the wanderer who, though his journey be long and convoluted, will ultimately find his way back to Ithaca, his faithful wife waiting, in the concluding lines of *Ulysses*:

> Though much is taken, much abides; and though
> We are not now that strength which in old days
> Moved earth and heaven, that which we are, we are—
> One equal temper of heroic hearts,

Made weak by time and fate, but strong in will
To strive, to seek, to find, and not to yield.

Leopold Bloom, the modern Odysseus in Joyce's novel *Ulysses* (1922), also finds his way home, but to a wife who has not remained faithful (though his journey has taken just twenty hours, rather than twenty years); his symbolic victory over his wife's suitor lies precisely in the fact that he knows when to yield. In the modern period the certainty associated with the Victorian exploration of values has vanished; modern explorations are undertaken with absolutely no confidence as to the results that will be discovered, still less that a public exists who could understand the writers' discoveries. For that reason Thomas Hardy's ruthless skepticism now seems quintessentially modern. This new attitude is quite clear in Ford Madox Ford's *The Good Soldier* (1915), the first installment of which was published in the inaugural issue of Wyndham Lewis's violently modern magazine *Blast*. John Dowell, the narrator/protagonist of Ford's novel, worries for 250 pages about his sense that the "givens" of civil society seem to have been knocked out from under him, and that he has been left to create values and meaning on his own. Struggling to extract the moral of the story he tells us—the story of his wife's long-standing affair with his best friend, and their consequent deaths—Dowell can only conclude: "I don't know. And there is nothing to guide us. And if everything is so nebulous about a matter so elementary as the morals of sex, what is there to guide us in the more subtle morality of all other personal contacts, associations, and activities? Or are we meant to act on impulse alone? It is all a darkness." In Conrad's *Heart of Darkness*, the narrator Charlie Marlow suffers from a similar moral vertigo. When, at the novella's close, he resolves to perform an action he finds deeply repugnant—to tell a lie—he worries that his willful violation of the moral order will provoke an immediate act of divine retribution. None, however, is forthcoming: "It seemed to me that the house would collapse before I could escape, that the heavens would fall upon my head. But nothing happened. The heavens do not fall for such a trifle." In works like these, a voyage is undertaken into a vast, unknown, dark expanse. Those few who come out alive have seen too much ever to be the same.

Similar perceptions underlie modern humor. The Theater of the Absurd that flourished in the 1950s and 1960s, in the work of playwrights like Samuel Beckett and Harold Pinter, had roots in Wilde and Shaw and their comic explorations of the arbitrary conventionality of long-held social values. Throughout the twentieth century, writers devoted themselves to unfolding many varieties of irony—from the severe ironies of Conrad and Yeats to the more tender ironies of Woolf and Auden, to the farcical absurdities of Tom Stoppard and Joe Orton. Joyce described his mixture of high and low comedy as "jocoserious"; asked the meaning of his dense book *Finnegans Wake*, he replied, "It's meant to make you laugh."

Whether seen in comic or tragic light, the sense of a loss of moorings was pervasive. Following the rapid social and intellectual changes of the previous century, the early twentieth century suffered its share of further concussions tending to heighten modern uncertainty. It was even becoming harder to understand the grounds of uncertainty itself. The critiques of Marx and Darwin had derived new messages from bodies of evidence available in principle to all literate citizens; the most important paradigm shifts of the early twentieth century, on the other hand, occurred in the fields of philosophy, psychology, and physics, and often rested on evidence invisible to the average citizen. The German philosopher Friedrich Nietzsche (1844–1900) was, as his dates suggest, wholly a nineteenth-century man, yet his ideas had their most profound impact in the twentieth century. Nietzsche described his lifelong philosophical project as "the revaluation of all values"; in his 1882 treatise *The Joyful Science,* he went so far as to assert that "God is dead." This deliberately provocative statement came as the culmination of a long and complicated argument, and did not mean simply that Nietzsche was an atheist (though he was). Nietzsche was suggesting that traditional religion had been discredited by advances in the natural and physical sciences, and as transcendent standards of truth disappeared, so logically must all moral and ethical systems depending on some faith for their force. It was from this base that Nietzsche created the idea of the *Übermensch,* the "superman" who because of his intellectual and moral superiority to others must not be bound by social conventions. Conrad's tragic figure Kurtz and Shaw's comic antihero Undershaft represent two very different takes on this idea, building on Nietzsche's interest in showing how all values are "constructed" rather than given—at some level arbitrary, all truths being merely opinions or superstitions.

The new psychology, whose earliest stirrings are to be found in the last decades of the nineteenth century, came of age at the turn of the twentieth. Sigmund Freud's *The Interpretation of Dreams* (1900) and *Psychopathology of Everyday Life* (1901) together illustrate in an especially vivid way his evolving theories about the influence of the unconscious mind, and past (especially childhood) experience, on our daily lives. The whole of Freud's work was translated into English by James Strachey (Lytton's brother), and was published in conjunction with the Hogarth Press, owned and run by Leonard and Virginia Woolf; for this reason, among others, the Freudian revolution was felt early, and strongly, among the London intelligentsia. The new psychology in general, and the theories of Freud in particular, were frequently distorted and misunderstood by the larger public, over whom they exercised a real fascination; among the artistic community Freud provoked a wide range of response, from the enthusiastic adoption of his theories by the Surrealists (a movement founded in Paris in 1924 by André Breton) to nervous rejection by writers like Joyce. This response is complicated, in part, by the fact that Freud himself took an interest in artistic and creative processes, and presumed to explain to writers the psychopathology at the heart of their own genius; as the Freudian literary critic Lionel Trilling succinctly put it, "the poet is a poet by reason of his sickness as well as by reason of his power." As Freud's supporter W. H. Auden wrote in his elegy *In Memory of Sigmund Freud* (1939): "If often he was wrong and at times absurd, / To us he is no more a person / Now but a whole climate of opinion / Under whom we conduct our different lives."

A further intellectual shock wave was the revolution in physics that was spearheaded by Albert Einstein's *Special Theory of Relativity* (1905). In both this theory (dealing with motion) and later in the General Theory of Relativity (dealing with gravity), Einstein shook the traditional understanding of the universe and our relationship to it; the certainty and predictability of the Newtonian description of the universe had been undone. The "uncertainty" of Einstein's universe was seemingly reinforced by developments in quantum physics, such as the work of Niels Bohr (who won the Nobel Prize in physics in 1922) and Werner Heisenberg, author of the famous "Uncertainty Principle" and the principle of complementarity, which together assert that the movement of subatomic particles can only be predicted by probability and not measured, as the very act of measurement alters their behavior. Ironically enough, the true import of these ideas is not, as the truism has it, that "everything is relative"—in fact, Einstein says almost the exact opposite. In Einstein's vision of the world, *nothing* is relative: everything is absolute, and absolutely fixed—except for us, fallible and limited observers, who have no secure standpoint from which "to see the thing as in itself it really is," to quote Matthew Arnold's 1867 formulation of the critic's goal. The only way to experience the truth, it would seem, would be to find what T. S. Eliot called "the still point of the turning world," an "unmoved mover" outside the flux and change of our day-to-day world. Einstein himself never really rejected the idea of transcendent truth; he once said to an interviewer that to him, the idea of our universe without a Creator was inconceivable. In this case, however, the popular fiction has been more influential than the facts, and the work of Einstein, Heisenberg, and Bohr has been used to support the widespread sense that, as Sean O'Casey's character Captain Jack Boyle puts it in *Juno and the Paycock* (1924), "the whole worl's in a state o' chassis!"

The philosophical and moral upheavals of these years were given added force by the profound shock of World War I—"The Great War," as it came to be known. The British entered the conflict against Germany partly in order to preserve their influence in Europe and their dominance around the globe, and partly out of altruistic notions of gallantry and fair play—to aid their weaker allies against German aggression. The conflict was supposed to take a few weeks; it lasted four grueling years and cost hundreds of thousands of British lives. Notions of British invincibility, honor, even of the viability of civilization all weakened over the years of vicious trench warfare in France. The progress of technology, which had raised Victorian standards of living, now led to a mechanization of warfare that produced horrific numbers of deaths—as many as a million soldiers died in the single protracted battle of the Somme in 1916. As poets discovered as they served in the trenches, and as the people back home came to learn, modernity had arrived with a vengeance.

REVOLUTIONS OF STYLE

The end of the war was accompanied by a sense of physical and moral exhaustion. To be modern has been defined as a persistent sense of having arrived on the stage of history after history has finished. The critic Perry Meisel, for instance, describes modernism as "a structure of compensation, a way of adjusting to the paradox of belatedness." Behind Ezra Pound's struggle to reinvent poetry lay a nagging suspicion that there was nothing new left to make or say, and Pound claimed that the very slogan "Make It New" was taken off the bathtub of an ancient Chinese emperor. As T. S. Eliot explains in his essay *Tradition and the Practice of Poetry,* "The perpetual task of poetry is to *make all things new.* Not necessarily to make new things. . . . It is always partly a revolution, or a reaction, from the work of the previous generation."

That revolution was carried out both on the level of subject matter and often on the level of style as well. Some important early twentieth-century fiction writers, like John Galsworthy, Arnold Bennett, H. G. Wells, and George Moore, felt no real need to depart from inherited narrative models, and hewed more or less to a realist or naturalist line, carrying on from the French naturalists like Emile Zola and the Norwegian dramatist Henrik Ibsen. But for those writers we now call modernist, these conventions came to seem too limiting and lifeless. The modern writer was faced with an enormous, Nietzschean task: to create new and appropriate values for modern culture, and a style appropriate to those values. As a consequence, there is often a probing, nervous quality in the modernist explorations of ultimate questions. This quality can be seen at the very start of the century in Conrad's *Heart of Darkness,* a novel about psychological depth and social disintegration that simultaneously implicates its readers in the moral ambiguities of its events. These ambiguities, moreover, are

Soldiers of the 9th Cameronians division prepare to go "over the top" during a daylight raid near Arras, France, 24 March 1917. During such an offensive, troops would make their way quickly across the contested territory between the opposing armies' trenches—the area known as No Man's Land—and attempt to take control of an enemy trench in order to conduct bombing raids and gain whatever intelligence might be found in the abandoned foxholes. The pace of this warfare—where a week's progress might be measured in yards, rather than miles—was, according to troops on both sides, the most salient feature of trench warfare. The human costs included diseases caused by standing water (like infamous "trench foot") and emotional disorders caused by the stress of waiting and constant shelling ("shell shock").

reflected in the very presentation of the narrative itself. In the modern novel, we are no longer allowed to watch from a safe distance while our protagonists mature and change through their trials; instead, we are made to undergo those trials ourselves, through the machinations of the narrative. This technique had already been employed in the nineteenth century, as for instance in the dramatic monologues of Robert Browning; but this narrative of process becomes pervasive in modernist texts, where the uncertainties of the form, the waverings and unpredictability of the narrative, mirror similar qualities in the mind of the narrator or protagonist. Often the reader is drawn into the story's crisis by a heightened use of the technique of plunging the narrative suddenly *in medias res*: "There was no hope for him this time: it was the third stroke" (Joyce, *The Sisters*); "A sudden blow:" (Yeats, *Leda and the Swan*); "'Yes, of course, if it's fine tomorrow,' said Mrs. Ramsay" (Woolf, *To the Lighthouse*). The customary preliminary information—the sort of dossier about the characters that we expect—isn't given; the reader is put in the position of a detective who has to sort all this information out unaided. This narrative decontextualization reaches its culmination in the theater of Beckett and Pinter, who typically withhold any and all background information about characters. "Confusion," Samuel Beckett told an interviewer in 1956, "is all around us and our only chance now is to let it in. The only chance of renovation is to open our eyes and see the mess. It is not a mess you can make sense of."

Early in the century, a number of poets began to dispense with the frames of reference provided by conventional poetic forms. The first real Anglo-American poetic movement of the century was Imagism, a reaction against the expansive wordiness of Victorian poetry like Tennyson's *Idylls of the King* or Browning's *The Ring and the Book*. Imagists like Pound and H. D. wrote short, spare poems embodying a revelatory image or moment. The most memorable Imagist poems have the concentrated impact of a haiku. But the form leaves little scope for narrative development; that path seems to have been opened by a rediscovery of the seventeenth-century metaphysical poets, notably by T. S. Eliot. The techniques of metaphysical poets like John Donne suggested to Eliot a means for expanding the technical repertory of Imagist poetry, which he used to good effect in poems like *The Love Song of J. Alfred Prufrock*, which opens with a thoroughly modernized metaphysical conceit: "Let us go then, you and I, / when the evening is spread out against the sky / Like a patient etherized upon a table."

One strategy for making literature new was to make it difficult; this notion was, in part, a response to the huge proliferation of popular entertainments during the early twentieth century, a proliferation that both disturbed and intrigued many artists, writers, and cultural critics. In such a context, "difficult" literature (such as the densely allusive poetry of Eliot, or the multilayered prose of Joyce) was seen to be of greater artistic merit than the products of an easily consumable mass culture—even as both Eliot and Joyce drew on popular culture and diction as they reshaped the norms of their literary art. Thus, while one of the primary targets of modernist renovation was Victorian literary manners, another was the complacent taste and sensibility of a large, and growing, middle class. Artists had been declaring the need to shock the bourgeoisie since time immemorial; Matthew Arnold worried publicly, and at length, about the dilution of a natural aristocracy of taste by the pseudoculture of newly educated British philistines, at the same time that he campaigned for greatly expanded public education. The Education Act of 1870 resulted in the explosive growth of elementary education, which meant that the reading class grew exponentially. Within the art world, the most obvious result of this anxiety was the "art for art's sake" movement associated with Walter Pater that began in the 1870s. Art was becoming its own material—as, for instance, in French artist Marcel Duchamp's mustache on the Mona Lisa.

In some ways modernist art and literature turned inward, becoming cannibalistic and self-referential. This is demonstrated well in Joyce's novel *A Portrait of the Artist as a Young Man*, whose protagonist is autobiographical in genesis yet critical in intent; the way Joyce accomplishes this is by moving Stephen Dedalus, his artist-protagonist, through various prose poses—writing now like Gustave Flaubert, now like Cardinal Newman, now like Pater. Stephen can only mimic—not create—a style; such is the situation of the modern writer, Joyce suggests, and his novel *Ulysses* dramatizes this by adopting a kaleidoscopic array of styles in its eighteen chapters. It thus becomes increasingly difficult to think of "style" as the achievement of an individual, and more and more it becomes the culmination of a cultural, national, ethnic project or history. As the French critic Roland Barthes has written, the text in the modern period becomes a "multidimensional space in which a variety of writings, none of them original, blend and clash," "a tissue of quotations drawn from innumerable centres of culture"—an apt and dramatic description of modernist texts like Eliot's *The Waste Land,* Joyce's *Ulysses,* and Pound's *Cantos.* To be textual is, during this period, to be intertextual and interdisciplinary as well.

The stylistic experimentation of modernist writers was fueled by the era's technological advances. From the mid-nineteenth century on, Britain had prided itself on its industrial strength and leadership; with the electrification of Britain at the turn of the century, however, the Industrial Revolution was gradually overtaken by a technological revolution. If the sinking of the Titanic on her maiden voyage in 1912 stands as a symbol of the vulnerability of progress—a sort of watery funeral for traditional British industry—the first transatlantic flight in 1919 pointed toward the future. Advances in photographic technology made documentary photographs a part of daily life and brought a heightened visual dimension to political campaigns and to advertising; the advent of quick and inexpensive newspaper photographs put vivid images of the carnage of World War I on Britain's breakfast tables. The texture and pace of daily life changed in the early years of the century to such a degree that average men and women were comfortable referring to themselves by that hopelessly awkward designation, "modern" (from the Latin *modo,* "just now"). And clearly, the London inhabited by the denizens of Eliot's *Waste Land* is a profoundly different place from the London of Dickens. Eliot portrays a woman who works in an office, composes letters on a typewriter, talks to clients on the telephone, plays records on the phonograph at her flat after having casual sex with a co-worker, and eats her evening meal from tins.

The advent of technology had far-reaching effects on the writing of the period. Beckett, famously, imagined a tape recorder before he had ever seen one in order to make possible the memory play of his *Krapp's Last Tape* (1959); more generally, the technology of the transistor radio, and government sponsorship of radio and television by the British Broadcasting Corporation, made possible wholly new literary genres. Beckett and Dylan Thomas were among the first to take advantage of the new media, writing plays for radio and then for television. A generation earlier, Joyce made use of early art film strategies in his "Circe" episode of *Ulysses.* In the most advanced writing of the modernist period we find an increasing sense that the technologies of print affect the text itself. Pound's *Cantos* were composed, not just transcribed, on a typewriter, and cannot be imagined in their current form composed with pen and ink; Joyce plays with the typographic conventions of newspaper headlines in the "Aeolus" chapter of *Ulysses* to create an ironic running commentary on the action. A crucial scene in Joyce's *Finnegans Wake* features a television broadcast (which was not available commercially when the novel was published), blending with a nuclear explosion (also several years before the fact). The scene culminates in "the abnihilisation of the etym"—both a destruction of atom/Adam/etym and its recovery *from* ("ab") nothingness.

MODERNISM AND THE MODERN CITY

Paralleling the new social and artistic opportunities of the twentieth century was a kind of anomie or alienation created by the rush towards industrialization. Vast numbers of human figures remained undifferentiated and the mass-manufactured hats and clothing worn by British industrial workers served only to heighten the monotony of their daily routines. Newspapers eagerly published photographs of thousands of sooty-faced miners. The members of the workforce, which Marx had called "alienated labor," were seen to be estranged not just from their work but from one another as well, as they themselves became mass products. This situation is dramatized especially vividly in the silent films of the period—from the dystopian vision of Fritz Lang's *Metropolis* (1926) to the more comic vision presented by the British-American Charlie Chaplin in *Modern Times* (1936). The sense of major cities being overrun by crowds of nameless human locusts recurs in the poetry of the period:

> A crowd flowed over London Bridge, so many,
> I had not thought death had undone so many.
> Sighs, short and infrequent, were exhaled,
> And each man fixed his eyes before his feet.

> (Eliot, *The Waste Land*)

> I have met them at close of day
> Coming with vivid faces
> From counter or desk among grey
> Eighteenth-century houses.

> (Yeats, *Easter 1916*)

The Victorian concern over huge numbers of urban poor was seconded by a fear of large numbers of restive urban lower-middle class workers and their families.

The critic Hugh Kenner has described modernism as both metropolitan and also international in character. While the bulk of Victorian British literary production is associated in some way or another with London, writing in the modern period is spread not just throughout England but throughout the Empire (and later the Commonwealth). To this day, London still serves as a spiritual and economic center of British writing, and many of the best British writers, regardless of their provenance, come to London at some point in their career. Modernist literary production was further stimulated by close cross-pollination between writers and other artists in other nations, and much of the most important writing in the modern "British" canon was undertaken in cities as far-flung as Dublin, Paris, Zurich, New York, and Johannesburg. Conversely, much of the important literature written in Britain itself during the twentieth century was produced by immigrants from abroad, from the Polish Joseph Conrad and the American Henry James at the start of the century to V. S. Naipaul, Salman Rushdie, and Hanif Kureishi in recent decades. As a result, the distinctions between "British" and "American" writing often blurred in this period of easy and relatively inexpensive transatlantic travel. Henry James based novels like *The American* and *Portrait of a Lady* on the adventures of Americans living in Europe; James himself was an American who lived most of the last thirty-five years of his life in London, and was naturalized as a British citizen three months before his death. T. S. Eliot moved to London in 1915 and lived there until his death in 1965, becoming a British subject, a communicant of the Church of England, and being knighted along the way. The great comic writer P. G. Wodehouse commuted back and forth across the Atlantic in the 1920s and 1930s as his plays and musical comedies were staged in New York and London. In many ways, New York and London had never been so close. This artistic diaspora has inevitably resulted in a richer, more complex and urbane literature.

PLOTTING THE SELF

The Freudian revolution grew from and reinforced an intense interest in the workings of the individual psyche, and modernists like Woolf and Joyce devoted themselves to capturing the mind's modulations. Both Woolf and Joyce employed versions of what came to be known as the "stream-of-consciousness" technique, in which fragmentary thoughts gradually build up a portrayal of characters' perceptions and of their unstated concerns. Consider this passage from the "interior monologue" of Joyce's protagonist Leopold Bloom, as he prepares a saucer of milk for his cat:

> They call them stupid. They understand what we say better than we understand them. She understands all she wants to. Vindictive too. Wonder what I look like to her. Height of a tower? No, she can jump me. . . . Cruel. Her nature. Curious mice never squeal. Seem to like it.

On the surface, Bloom's staccato thoughts reflect on the cat; at the same time, he identifies the cat with his unfaithful wife Molly, and—without admitting it to himself—he reflects on the cat's foreign psyche as a way of coming to terms with Molly's needs and desires. The development of stream-of-consciousness narrative grows out of a sense that the self is not "natural" or "given" but a construction—specifically a social construction—and that, consequently, traditional methods for depicting character no longer suffice. We are all the products of our own past and we are also, powerfully, products of larger social forces that shape the stories we tell about ourselves, and which others tell about us.

In the Victorian novel, plot crises were typically resolved in some definitive way, such as by a marriage or a change in the financial status of the protagonist. In the modern novel, lasting resolutions growing out of a common vision are few and far between. Walter Pater had counseled his readers, at the conclusion of *The Renaissance*, that "to burn always with a hard, gemlike flame, to maintain this ecstasy" was "success in life"; in the modern period, everyone wants that ecstasy, but no one is sure quite what it looks like amid the ruthless individualism of modern life. "We live as we dream, alone," Conrad's narrator Marlow mutters despondently; "Only connect," the epigraph to E. M. Forster's *Howards End* (1910) implores. On the eve of the London Blitz, however, the characters in Woolf's *Between the Acts* (still the most powerful British novel of World War II) are united only as they sing the refrain, "Dispersed are we." The texts of the modern period, bookended as they are by two world wars, represent a real, agonized meditation on how modern individuals can become united as community again. Woolf herself was skeptical of the possibility and her last novel remains unfinished—or finished only by her husband Leonard—because she took her own life before she could complete it. In the novels of Woolf and Joyce, and in the poetry of Yeats and Auden, community is the glimpsed prospect, the promised land: seen as a possibility but never realized, or embodied precariously in a gesture, a moment, a metaphor, and above all in art itself.

After the modernist high-water mark of the 1920s, the atmosphere darkened amid the international financial depression of the 1930s triggered by the U.S. stock market crash of 1929. The decade saw the growth of British Marxism and widespread labor agitation. The decade also witnessed the international growth of fascism and totalitarianism; writers like Shaw, Wyndham Lewis, Eliot, Yeats, Pound, and Lawrence for a time saw the order and stability promised by authoritarian governments as the only antidote to the "mere anarchy" Yeats decries in his poem *The Second Coming*. In the late thirties, however, intellectual sentiment turned increasingly against the fascist movements being led in Germany by Hitler, in Italy by Mussolini and in Spain by Franco. During Spain's brutal civil war (1936–1939), many writers supported the democratic Republicans against the ultimately victorious fascist General Franco. Meanwhile a series of weak British governments did little to oppose

Hitler's increasing belligerence and extremism; the failure to stand up for democratic principles, coupled with worldwide economic depression, led many young intellectuals and artists to became Leftists.

Compared to the stylistic experiments of the previous two decades, British writing of the 1930s sometimes looks rather flat, neutral. This can be attributed in part to the disillusionment that followed World War I, and the very real sense throughout the thirties that things were building up to another war, that art had become something of an irrelevancy. The German cultural critic Theodor Adorno was to write after the war, "no poetry after Auschwitz"; writers of the thirties seem to have had this sense well in advance of Auschwitz. Yeats admired the character in Auguste de Villiers de L'Isle-Adam's drama *Axël* who said, "As for living, we let the servants do that for us"; the young writers of the thirties, however, were concerned that (in Auden's phrase) "poetry makes nothing happen," and were committed to the idea that it must.

THE RETURN OF THE REPRESSED

Modern British literature is characterized by the increasing presence of women's voices, working-class voices, and voices expressing varied ethnic, religious, and sexual perspectives which, whether methodically or inadvertently, had often been excluded from the British literary tradition. The writings of an author like Woolf made England think hard about who she really was, as did, in another sense, the writings of the former colonial administrator George Orwell. In the modern period, Britain begins to deal in a fully conscious way with its human rights problems—most significantly, its treatment of women and the diverse ethnic groups of its colonial possessions.

The gradual enfranchisement and political and economic liberation of British women in the early years of the twentieth century comprised a fundamental social change; the novelist D. H. Lawrence, a rather equivocal friend of the women's movement, called it "perhaps the greatest revolution of modern times." The Women's Property Act—passed in 1882, the year of Woolf's birth—for the first time allowed married women to own property. Decades of sometimes violent suffragist agitation led finally to full voting rights for women in 1928 and to the gradual opening up of opportunities in higher education and the professions.

The quick pace of these changes naturally made many men uneasy. In their monumental three-volume study *No Man's Land: The Place of the Woman Writer in the Twentieth Century*, critics Sandra Gilbert and Susan Gubar suggest that this "war between the sexes" was one of the primary driving forces behind the modernist literary movement. Having emphasized the revolutionary force of the women's movement, Lawrence goes on to warn that the movement, "is even going beyond, and becoming a tyranny of woman, of the individual woman in the house, and of the feminine ideas and ideals in the world." In a half-serious essay titled *Cocksure Women and Hensure Men*, Lawrence complained of women "more cocky, in their assurance, than the cock himself. . . . It is really out of scheme, it is not in relation to the rest of things. . . . They find, so often, that instead of having laid an egg, they have laid a vote, or an empty ink-bottle, or some other absolutely unhatchable object, which means nothing to them." On the level of literary principles, a masculinist emphasis can be seen in Ezra Pound's insistence that modern poetry should "move against poppy-cock," "be harder and saner . . . 'nearer the bone' . . . as much like granite as it can be."

Other writers, male and female, supported women's rights; almost all writers sought to rebel against Victorian sexual norms and gender roles. Joyce battled with censors beginning in 1906, and his *Ulysses* was put on trial in New York on obscenity charges in 1933 (and cleared of those charges in the same week that the United States repealed Prohibition). Defending his sexual and scatological scenes, Joyce put the modernists' case for frankness this way: "The modern writer has other problems facing him, problems which are more intimate and unusual. We prefer to search in the corners for what has been hidden, and moods, atmospheres and intimate relationships are the modern writers' theme. . . . The modern theme is the subterranean forces, those hidden tides which govern everything and run humanity counter to the apparent flood: those poisonous subtleties which envelop the soul, the ascending fumes of sex." In defense of his "dirty" book *Lady Chatterley's Lover* (1928), whose full text was banned as obscene until 1960, Lawrence wrote: "In spite of all antagonism, I put forth this novel as an honest, healthy book, necessary for us today. . . . We are today, as human beings, evolved and cultured far beyond the taboos which are inherent in our culture. . . . The mind has an old groveling fear of the body and the body's potencies. It is the mind we have to liberate, to civilize on these points." In a rich irony, Joyce and Lawrence hated one another's writing: Joyce insisted on calling Lawrence's best-known novel "Lady Chatterbox's Lover," for he felt the characters talked too much. He dismissed the novel as "a piece of propaganda in favour of something which, outside of D. H. L.'s country at any rate, makes all the propaganda for itself." Lawrence, for his part, thought the last chapter of *Ulysses* (Molly Bloom's famous soliloquy) "the dirtiest, most indecent, obscene thing ever written."

Sexuality of all stripes was on trial. The lesbian writer Radclyffe Hall was tried for obscenity in 1928 for her novel *The Well of Loneliness*—whose most obscene sentence is, "That night they were not divided." The trial became a public spectacle, and was a rallying point for writers like Woolf and E. M. Forster, who spoke valiantly in favor of Hall's right to explore her subject, which was primarily the loneliness, rather than the fleshly joys, of same-sex love. Forster's overtly homosexual writings, including his novel *Maurice*, were not published until after his death in 1970. Woolf was somewhat more open in her novel *Orlando* (1928), whose protagonist changes sex from male to female. In Joyce's *Ulysses*, Leopold Bloom fantasizes about becoming a "new womanly man" and dreams of being chastised by a dominatrix who appears first as Bella and then as Bello Cohen. It was not only sexual taboos that were challenged in the writing of the period; in practice there began to be a loosening of the strict gender and sexual roles, which had been reinforced by the homophobia resulting from Oscar Wilde's trial for homosexual offenses in 1895. Gay, lesbian, and bisexual writers like Forster, Woolf, Hall, Stein, Natalie Barney, Djuna Barnes, H. D., Ronald Firbank, and Carl Van Vechten pushed the comfort level of the British reading public; even the "healthy" version of sexuality celebrated by D. H. Lawrence in his greatest novel *Women in Love* begins to suggest that heterosexuality and homosexuality are boundaries, not immutable categories.

The growing independence of the individual subject began to be matched by drives for independence among imperial subjects as well. In "John Bull's other island," as Bernard Shaw called Ireland in his play of that title, agitations for independence grew widespread from the late nineteenth century onward, culminating in the Easter Rising of 1916 and the 1922 partitioning of Ireland, when the Irish Republic became an independent nation while Northern Ireland remained part of Great Britain. No match for England militarily, the Irish used words as their chief weapon in the struggle for independence. Yeats and Joyce, among other writers, reflected on this war of words in such important works as Yeats's *Easter 1916* and Joyce's *Ivy Day in the Committee Room* and the "Aeolus" chapter from *Ulysses*.

The liberation of Britain's overseas colonial holdings began in the early decades of the century and gathered momentum thereafter. The history of Great Britain in the twentieth century is, in some ways, the story of the centrifugal forces that have largely stripped Britain of its colonial possessions. Britain suffered humiliating losses in the Boer War (1899–1902), fought by the British to take possession of the Boer Republic of South Africa. Half a million British troops were unable to win outright victory over eighty thousand Boers; finally the British adopted a scorched-earth policy that entailed massive arrests and the deaths of thousands of captives in unsanitary camps. This debilitating and unsavory conquest marked the low point of British imperialism, and public disgust led to a reaction against empire itself. Independence movements sprang up in colonies around the world, most notably in India, Britain's largest colony, "the jewel in the crown" of Queen Victoria, where Mohandas Gandhi's Congress Party struggled through nonviolent resistance to force Britain to grant its independence.

WORLD WAR II AND ITS AFTERMATH

The year 1939 and the start of World War II closed the modernist era. It was the year that saw the publication of Joyce's *Finnegans Wake,* which the critic Ihab Hassan calls a "monstrous prophecy" of postmodernity. The seminal modernist careers of Joyce, Woolf, Yeats, Ford, and Freud all came to an end—as did the social and political order of the previous decades. Throughout the late thirties, the government had engaged in futile efforts at diplomacy as Hitler expanded German control in central Europe. Prime Minister Neville Chamberlain finally denounced Hitler when the Germans invaded Czechoslovakia early in 1939; on September 1, Germany invaded Poland, and within days Britain declared war. In contrast to the "Great War," this conflict began with few illusions—but with the knowledge that Britain was facing an implacable and better-armed enemy. Unlike the Great War, fought on foreign soil, the new war hit home directly; during "the Blitz" from July 1940 through 1941, the German Luftwaffe carried out massive bombing raids on London and many other targets around Britain.

During these years, Winston Churchill emerged as a pivotal figure both strategically and morally. First as commander in chief of the navy, and starting in May 1940 as prime minister, he directed British military operations while rallying popular support through stirring speeches and radio addresses. The war had profound effects throughout British society, as almost every man—and many women—between the ages of 14 and 64 came to be involved in the war effort, in conditions that weakened old divisions of region and class and that provided the impetus for new levels of government involvement in social planning. At the war's end in September of 1945, Britain emerged victorious, in concert with its allies. In contrast with the United States, though, Britain had suffered enormous civilian casualties and crushing economic losses, both within Great Britain and throughout its far-flung colonies. As much as a quarter of Britain's national wealth had been consumed by the war. The great city of London had undergone horrific bombing during the the Blitz, whose attacks left the face of this world capital as scarred as had the Great Fire three centuries before. Although morally and socially triumphant in its defeat of Nazism and fascism, Britain was left shattered economically and exhausted spiritually. Its people had come through the war gallantly, only to face grim conditions at home and political unrest throughout the empire.

London during the Blitz, seen from the north transept of St. Paul's Cathedral.

The global effort of that war, whose battles were fought not only in Europe but in Africa, Asia, Latin America, the Middle East, and the Pacific, had forced Britain to draw massively on its colonies for raw materials, money, and soldiers. Since the resistance to the British empire had begun long before World War II, the drafting of millions of already restive colonial subjects into the armed forces intensified the tensions and the conflicts running beneath the surface of the empire. One of the most important political phenomena of the twentieth century was about to hit a depleted Britain with a vengeance: the decolonization of most of the conquered globe in the great wave of independence movements that swept the world after 1945. One by one, with greater and lesser degrees of violence and agony, colonies slipped out of Britain's imperial net. From the independence of India (1947) to the independence struggles of Kenya, Nigeria, Zaire, Palestine, Egypt, and many others, Britain experienced the accelerated loss of the largest empire in Western history. Retaining only a handful of Caribbean, Latin American, and Pacific Rim possessions, the empire had radically shrunk. India, Pakistan, Canada, Australia, and a few other countries adopted commonwealth status, remaining commercially linked but becoming essentially independent politically. The empire on which the sun never set was fast becoming largely confined to England, Scotland, Wales, and Northern Ireland—an ongoing area of tension and conflict to the present day.

The dizzying pace of decolonization after the war put Britain in a paradoxically modern position ahead of many other Western countries: the unquestioned ability, and the rarely questioned right, of Western societies to dominate the globe had finally encountered decisive opposition. Within fifty years Britain found itself transformed from the dominant global power into a relatively small and, for a time, impoverished island nation, no longer a dictator of the world's history, but merely part of it. This dislocation was profoundly registered in British culture, and British writers strove to assess these losses—and to define the new possibilities for a freer and more open society that might emerge from the wreckage of empire.

A new generation of writers took on the task of evaluating English culture and the tradition of English literature itself from inside. John of Gaunt's beautiful paean to "this sceptered isle, this England," in Shakespeare's *Henry IV* had to be rewritten now: what was "this England" to be? In the absence of its colonial possessions, and in the general misery of shortages and rationing after the war, there was suddenly a sharp new scrutiny of British society. Its class-bound hierarchies appeared in an even harsher light, and its failures at home, in addition to its failure as an empire abroad, became the source of profound self-examination. Rage and anger accompanied this process of self-awareness, and a generation of literary artists dubbed the "angry young men" arose to meet the failures head-on, often in realist drama so faithful to its shabby subjects it was called "kitchen sink" drama, after the cold-water flat settings where the characters played out their rage. Playwrights such as John Osborne (as in the aptly titled *Look Back in Anger*) and novelists such as Anthony Burgess (*A Clockwork Orange*) angrily or satirically probed the discrepancy between England's glorious past and its seemingly squalid present.

A sense of diminishment in the world's eyes led to a passionate critique of British institutions, particularly its class structure, even where the literature produced was conservative in its looking backward. The extraordinary poet Philip Larkin might be seen as a key figure in this generation of writers. Larkin was a librarian in a rural town for most of his adult life. His poetry takes on the sardonic voice of the disenfranchised and the dispossessed—speaking not for the poor or the downtrodden but instead articulating the sense of loss and fury of middle and upper-class England, bereft of its historical prestige, impoverished by modern culture. He sings of nature, home, and country in a voice that is lacerating and self-mocking. Larkin's often jazzy and colloquial poetic diction, and his effective use of Anglo-Saxon expletives—he brought "fuck" into the opening of a major poem—offered a rebarbative retort to pastoral poetry. Larkin also wrote several notable novels at this time, among them *A Girl in Winter*, which explores from a surprisingly feminine and even feminist point of view the struggles of an emigré to Britain who must conceal the traumas her family experienced during the war, in order to "fit in" with a blithe and cavalier aristocratic British family. Larkin's artistry joins that of a host of other postwar writers, mostly male, who write from the center of an England now put off-kilter by the wrenching changes after the war.

Profound historical changes were to continue after the war with the commencement of the Cold War, in which the new world superpowers, the United States and the former Soviet Union, became locked in an intense battle for ideological, political, and economic dominance. Human beings now possessed the technological means to destroy the planet and its inhabitants, and these weapons of destruction were amassed by two societies with sharply conflicting goals. Britain along with Western Europe unequivocally aligned itself on the side of the United States, joining in the long fight against communism and Soviet socialism. While not itself a superpower, Britain had to shape its own social goals in light of the Cold War raging around it. A supremely eloquent voice in the articulation of what was at stake was that of the British writer George Orwell, known for his lucid essays on politics and language, including *The Politics of the English Language*, to cite one of his classic works. Immediately after the war Orwell crafted *1984*, an enduring parable of Cold War culture. This book envisions a future society in the year 1984 when the infamous "Big Brother" is watching everyone. That tale of a society of totalitarian surveillance was a thinly veiled allegory of the possibilities inherent not only in a Soviet takeover but even in Western societies and their implicit tendencies toward control and bureaucracy. It may be that Orwell was able to be prophetic about the cultural touchstones of the next several decades because as a British writer he wrote from an oblique angle: the colonial relationship of Britain to the United States had become reversed, with Britain almost becoming an outpost of the United States in terms of its Cold War dominance, reminiscent of Britain's dominance of the fate of the American colonies in the centuries leading up to the American Revolution. It is sometimes possible to see more clearly from a position outside the exact center—and Britain was, in this sense, no longer the center of English-speaking Western civilization. Strangely enough, that ex-centricity granted its literary writers a certain kind of insight.

The British novel after World War II made a retreat from modernist experimentalism. One explanation for a return to the realism that Woolf had so passionately argued against comes, paradoxically, from feminism of the very sort Woolf espouses in *A Room of One's Own* and *Three Guineas*. For as women began to write in large numbers, the novel with characters and a plot became a kind of room these writers needed to make their own. A host of important women writers emerged who revived the novel—which had been declared dead by the French, at least, around 1950—by using its traditions to incorporate their experiences as women, "making it new" not by formal experiments, but by opening that familiar, even a little shabby, room to new voices and new stories. Among the practitioners of this "feminist realism"— although some of them would vehemently deny the label "feminist"—are Jean Rhys, Doris Lessing, Margaret Drabble, A. S. Byatt, Muriel Spark, Iris Murdoch, Nadine Gordimer, and Buchi Emecheta. In every case these are writers who ring changes on ostensibly traditional forms.

A particularly vibrant arena of British literary innovation after the postwar period was British drama; the dramatic form seemed to lend itself to the staging of new social and aesthetic experiments which, with the exception of women's writing as noted above, largely bypassed the British novel of this period. The most innovative of all British dramatists of the twentieth century after World War I was indubitably the Irishman Samuel Beckett. Living in a form of self-imposed exile in France, and a further self-imposed exile within the French language, Beckett moved from being the writer of mordant novels (*Molloy; Malone Dies*) to becoming an extraordinary dramatist. He often wrote his plays first in French, later translating them into English, so that English was their "secondary" language, leading to multiple puns in both English and French. Beckett's contribution to dramatic form, for which he received the Nobel Prize, is nonetheless a creation within British literature. Beckett sculpted his plays out of silence, paring down lines of dialogue until their short sentences and sometimes single words reverberate with the unspoken. Samuel Beckett, more than any other dramatist in English, found the pockets of silence in English speech, and made those silences speak. His characters do not inhabit a real place, like England, for example, but instead occupy an abstract space of human existence, where the human predicaments of longing and desire for redemption, the failures of understanding, and the bafflement of death are experienced in their purest form.

Within England a host of dramatic luminaries gave vital energy to the British stage after 1945. While John Osborne created realist dramas of rage and dispossession, Harold Pinter emphasized the careful chiseling of language, bringing out the full ambiguity hidden in seemingly innocuous social conversation. Tom Stoppard joins

Harold Pinter in his postwar longevity as a master of the British drama, despite or perhaps because of being an immigrant—"a bounced Czech," as he has called himself. Stoppard employs a brilliant rhetorical surface in his plays, which are often modernist puzzle boxes in their annihilation of the rules of time and space. In his meteoric but short dramatic career the playwright Joe Orton took a reverse tack to that of Beckettian silence and economy, or Pinterian ordinary language, and returned to the example of Oscar Wilde. Using a wildly baroque vocabulary and an epigrammatic wit, Orton brought an explicit gay drama and gay sensibility to the postwar theater, in works like *Loot,* which revolves around a seductive lower-class character who wreaks sexual havoc with all the inhabitants of a country estate, male and female, young and old. In *What the Butler Saw*, Orton imagines a monumental statue, bearing the national "phallus," which is hilariously blown to bits.

Many of the themes and techniques of postwar drama come together in the work of the novelist, playwright, and screenwriter Hanif Kureishi, who draws on experiences and sources from both England and the Indian subcontinent. His screenplay for *My Beautiful Laundrette* is indebted to the intricate fictional experiments of Salman Rushdie, playing with time and with illusion. At the same time, he can be seen as a contemporary version of the "angry young men" who wrote in the British postwar period, since *My Beautiful Laundrette* is replete with those kitchen-sink details, and with all the struggles faced by the unemployed and socially unwanted. To add another facet to this literary mosaic, Kureishi's writing also adopts the transgressive energies shown by Britain's feminist and gay writers, producing a convincing love story between two men separated by race and class, and giving a portrait of an assertive and able young woman who finds her freedom in feminism.

Kureishi came of age during the sixties, as the Beatles and the Rolling Stones held sway in the world of rock and roll. The impoverishment of the fifties abated in the sixties, at least for the middle class, as British banking and finance reinvigorated the economy. "Swinging London" became a household phrase, as British urban culture set the pace in music, fashion, and style. The Carnaby Street mode of dress and fashion mavens like Mary Quant, Jean Muir, and Zandra Rhodes were copied all over the world, worn by Jean Shrimpton and Twiggy, who were among the first supermodels. British film came out of a postwar slump and movies like *Morgan* and *Georgy Girl* had huge audiences at home and in the United States. A delirious excitement invested British popular culture, and London became a hub of the new once more. The critique of British society mounted by Joe Orton's work found its double in the youth culture of "Mods" and "Rockers." Asked which he was, the Beatles' drummer Ringo Starr claimed to synthesize both: "I'm a mocker."

Amid the cultural ferment of the sixties and seventies, successive British governments struggled with intractable problems of inflation and unemployment, punctuated by frequent strikes by Britain's powerful unions, and rising violence in Northern Ireland. The generally pro-union government of Harold Wilson (1964–1970) was followed by the Conservative government of Edward Heath, who put new stress on private enterprise. A major shift away from the "welfare state," however, came only at the end of the decade, when Heath was succeeded by the formidable Margaret Thatcher, the prime minister of Britain for a record twelve years. The daughter of a lower middle-class family, Thatcher vaulted into politics when that was an exceptionally rare opportunity not only for a woman, but for a person whose father was a shop-keeper. Trained as a chemist, Thatcher worked long and hard for the (Tory) Conservative Party, even as Britain was ruled by a succession of Labour and Socialist

The Beatles landing at Heathrow Airport, 29 October 1963.

governments. When her chance came to lead England as its Tory prime minister, Thatcher and her political and ideological colleagues began a governmental revolution by adopting free-market policies similar to those identified with the Ronald Reagan school of U.S. Republicanism. Thatcher set about dismantling as much of the welfare state of postwar modern Britain as she could—and that was a considerable amount.

Margaret Thatcher had an enormous impact on British identity, as well as on British society. Among the very small number of women worldwide who have ever wielded such substantial political power—Golda Meir and Indira Gandhi come to mind as others—Thatcher's polished good looks, her extreme toughness, and her uncompromising political dictates combined to produce a caricature of her as the domineering English governess, laying down the rules of what would be good for Britain's unruly citizens. Thatcher's economic policies emphasized productivity as never before; under her rule, an entrepreneurial culture began to flourish at the expense of once-sacred British social entitlements, in education, health care, and civic subsidy of the arts and culture. Margaret Thatcher's most breathtaking quotation, and the one summing up her philosophy of government, was uttered in response to complaints about what was happening to the fabric of British society and, especially, to its poor, elderly, immigrants, and the mass numbers of the unemployed. "There is no such thing as society," she declared. What she meant was that government had no role to play in creating a unitary, egalitarian society. The forces of the unleashed free market, and the will of private individuals, would replace any notion of a social contract or social compact between and among British citizens. There was irony, of course, in Thatcher's seeming to turn her back on members of her own class and those below it, and despite the power and immense reputation she acquired worldwide, there was always scathing and vocal opposition to her within Britain, as she privatized the universities and abolished tenure, made inroads on the National Health Service, dissolved city councils and established poll taxes. Prime Minister Thatcher declared and fought Britain's last imperial war of modern times, against Argentina over the control of the Falkland Islands, and she was fierce opponent of nationalist sentiment among the Scottish and the Welsh, a firm upholder of Britain's right to control Northern Ireland in perpetuity, and strongly against the move toward joining the European Community. Thatcher became an icon in Britain, as well as its longest-governing Prime Minister: an icon for her certainty, confidence, and her personification of the huge changes she brought about. Though she provoked sharp opposition, her brilliance and energy were never in question, nor was her international influence.

Equally large changes have occurred in the last several years of the twentieth century, however, changes sweeping enough to have diminished Margaret Thatcher's iconic stature, and to have partially reversed the social revolution she began. The historian Simon Schama points out, in an essay analyzing the British reaction to the death of Princess Diana in 1997, that the Thatcher era was simultaneous with the early Diana years. "For, by the time Charles Philip Arthur George and Diana Frances stepped out of the nave of Saint Paul's Cathedral into the sunlight and the cheers of millions, it was Margaret Thatcher who had annexed the idea of a revolutionized "new" Britain within her steely grip. This was to be a Britain in which the worst thing was not, as Diana would later say, 'to feel unloved' but to be unproductive." At the turn of the century, though, the Labour Party has reclaimed countrol of the country, changing course economically and emphasizing the very social contract Thatcher had set aside. Britain is an increasingly pivotal member of the European Community alliance, and its own internal divisions have come productively to the fore. Diana's vision of the need for society to take account for all those who are "unloved" within it can be said to have prevailed over the views of the now-titled Baroness Thatcher, productive in her retirement as a writer and political pundit, although in many ways now a prophet without honor—in the sense of followers—in her own land.

Surprisingly, the twentieth century is ending in much the same way as did the nineteenth century for Britain, with a nationwide debate on home rule. In 1886 and again in 1893 the eminent British prime minister William Gladstone fought for the establishment of a separte Irish parliament—thus the term "home rule"—to allow the Irish colony, with its differing religion of Roman Catholicism and its unique Gaelic culture, to have control over its own internal affairs. Gladstone and his Liberal Party formed an alliance with the Irish National Party's members of Parliament, who were led by the great Charles Steward Parnell, a Protestant Irishman known as "the uncrowned king of Ireland." Parnell's political fall due to an extramarital scandal removed a key player in Gladstone's strategy, and his final attempt in 1893 at voting in home rule failed. This failure led to the Irish revolution, the Irish Civil War, and the continuing violence within Northern Ireland, the six counties still belonging to Britain and occupied by their army.

Britain's new prime minister, Anthony Blair, was elected in 1997 from the Labour Party, breaking the Conservative Party's eighteen-year hold on the position, for twelve years of which the redoubtable Margaret Thatcher ruled, followed by her chosen successor, the rather low-key John Major. One of Blair's main campaign promises was bringing home rule to both Scotland and Wales, regions of Britain with their own language and dialect, their own cultural mores, and a long history of armed conflict with England. The referendum on the Scottish parliament, with the power to raise and lower income taxes within Scotland, and a considerable budget to operate as Scotland chooses, for its schools, health, housing and transport, overwhelmingly passed the popular vote, and is likely to be a reality by 1999; Wales has voted as well for the creation of a Welsh assembly with many of the same powers and responsibilities. While the Republic of Ireland is now a nation in its own right, Tony Blair's commitment to the peace talks in Northern Ireland, and to the inclusion of Sinn Fein in those thalks, has also provided the first stirrings of political momentum in resolving the century-old conflict between Northern Irish Protestants who largely wish to remain attached to Britain, and the Northern Irish Catholics who have fought for the autonomy of this part of Ireland.

LANGUAGE AND IDENTITY

Complicated questions of language and identity have increasingly come to dominate the most recent phase of twentieth-century British literature. A great paradox of the British postwar period, in its time of imperial shrinkage, involves the fate of the English language. Britain may have been "kicked out" of many of its former colonies as a governing presence, but English was rarely shown the door at the same time. For economic and cultural reasons English as a global language became even more widely dispersed and dominant after World War II. Of course, the spread of U.S. interests has played a role in the hegemony of English. However, the old contours of the British empire continue to shape much of the production of English literature today. In this way, the former British empire has become part of the fabric of British literature. V. S. Naipaul, for example, has long resided in England, but he was born to Indian parents in Trinidad, where the British had deployed Indian labor. His writing is as much in dialog with the British literary tradition, and an extension of it, as that of any native-born British author.

Salman Rushdie, who is of Pakistani parentage, is another intriguing example of this process of crossing the increasingly porous boundaries of Britishness, as well as a cautionary tale of how powerful literature can be. Rushdie's novels are part of British literature at its modernist best, drawing on the entire English literary tradition, yet informed by a cosmopolitan and a non-Western literary tradition as well. Eight years after he achieved great acclaim for his novel *Midnight's Children* (1980), a book that adapted the "magic realism" of Latin American fiction to the history of Indian independence, Rushdie published *The Satanic Verses*. This novel recounts a magical mystery tour of sorts, the arrival of two South Asian refugees to modern London: one a film star from Bombay, the other a kind of trickster figure. Embedded in this complex tale of migration and identity is a brief dream sequence satirizing the prophet Mohammed. In response to this tiny dream-within-a-dream passage, the Iranian theocratic government delivered a *fatwa*—an edict sentencing Rushdie to death in absentia for treachery to the religion of Islam. Rushdie did not write the book in Arabic, nor did he write it for a Muslim audience, but that was irrelevant to the clerics who pronounced sentence on him before millions of devout adherents. From that time, Rushdie has been forced to live in a form of self-imposed house arrest, guarded by the British government. In an ironic twist, British literature itself has become his prison house of language, his internal exile. It is this tradition that "protects" him as a great writer, and, because of its porous literary borders, is responsible for his predicament. These issues and more underlie his striking story *Chekhov and Zulu*.

In recent years British literature has been infused with new life both from foreign-born writers and from new voices bubbling up from within the British Isles, in the shape of Welsh, Scottish, and Irish literary prose and poetry. The Nobel Prize–winning Irish poet Seamus Heaney is a kind of internal outsider, since, as he has written, he does not consider himself to be part of "British" literature as ordinarily defined, while he nonetheless writes English poetry deeply influenced by English poets from Milton to Wordsworth to Eliot. Some writers have deliberately taken themselves out of British literature for political and literary reasons, using the strongest means possible: they have decided to write in a language other than English. For example, the Kenyan writer Ngugi wa-Thiongo, educated by British missionaries and then at a British university, whose first memorized poem was Wordsworth's *Daffodils*, now writes in the Kikuyu language, and translates his work into English. The Irish poet Nuala Ní Dhomhnaill has made a similar decision: she writes and publishes her poetry first in Irish, and only later translates it into English as a "second" language.

In recent years British writing has been invigorated from "below," as well as from "outside": there has been a profusion of working-class or lower-middle-class novelists, poets, and screenwriters, many of whom adopt the dialect or argot of lower-class Welsh, Scottish, and Irish English. When James Kelman won the Booker Prize for the best novel published in England in 1994, there was widespread outrage: the working-class, expletive-laced speech of his Scottish protagonist was deemed unliterary by many, or at least unreadable and not in conformity with what was revered as the Queen's English. Poetry too has become a vehicle for a range of literary experiments, linking music and film to rhymed and unrhymed, and often performed, verse, connecting the popular and the literary. This upsurge of vivacious and often provocative writing is primarily the work of younger writers, and in many instances the novels are almost immediately being turned into films with international audiences.

In the past hundred years British literature has seen upheavals of aesthetic form, of geographic location, and of linguistic content. What is no longer in question, oddly enough, despite the current age of cyberspace and interactive media, is whether literature itself will survive. As Mark Twain once commented dryly after reading his own obituary in the newspaper: "The reports of my death are greatly exaggerated." The reports of literature's inevitable eclipse at the hands of media and mass culture have, it seems, been greatly exaggerated too. At this moment, British literary creativity is fed from many streams, welling up unpredictably, located in unexpected places. British literature has not merely survived; it remains a vital index of contemporary social and cultural life, and a crucial indication of the shape of things to come.

Joseph Conrad
1857–1924

One of the ironies of twentieth-century British literature is that many of its greatest writers were not conventionally "British." In the case of Joseph Conrad, arguably the first modern British writer, the irony is even more extreme, because Conrad was born a Pole, and learned English only when he was in his twenties. The transformation of Josef Konrad Nalecz Korzeniowski into "Joseph Conrad" is as fascinating and mysterious a story as the transforming journeys at the heart of his fiction.

Joseph Conrad was a lifelong exile from a country that no longer existed on the map of Europe as a separate country. At the time of Conrad's birth in 1857, Poland was divided between Russia and the Austro-Hungarian empire. His parents, Apollo and Eva, were Polish patriots, and after an uprising against Russia in 1863, the family was exiled to a village in the far north of Russia. Eva died when Josef was seven years old; Apollo when he was twelve. Apollo had been both a political activist and a man of letters, a poet and a translator of French and English literature into Polish. In a sense, by becoming a British novelist writing in English, Conrad was carrying on a project of translation begun by his father, a translation across cultures and literatures as well as languages. Hidden within Conrad's poetic and impressionistic literary language is a secret language—Polish—and a secret history of exile from his homeland.

After Conrad's parents died, he was raised by a cosmopolitan uncle, Tadeusz Bobrowski, who was also imbued with patriotic political leanings and a deep love of literature. Josef was sent to school in Cracow, Poland, where he was bored and restless. His uncle then sent him to Switzerland with a private tutor; they argued constantly for a year, and the tutor resigned. Not quite seventeen years old, Conrad proceeded to Marseilles and joined the French merchant navy. He spent twenty years as a sailor and as a ship's captain, spending four years sailing under the French flag, and then sixteen years with British trading ships. In 1894 Josef Korzeniowski completed his transformation into the writer Joseph Conrad by changing his name and settling in England to become a full-time writer.

By the end of the nineteenth century, the nationalistic wars that had led to a divided Poland had been followed by another historical phenomenon: the dividing-up of the globe by the nations of Europe as these powers consolidated empires. The oceans were crucial pathways in these struggles, not simply vast, watery landscapes outside of history. The seafaring Conrad, who had wanted to leave the frustrations of school behind him and see the world, became intimately involved in the everyday business of the making of empires, playing a minor role behind the scenes of the major political forces of the age. Merchant ships of the kind he served on traced the routes of trade and commerce, which now had become the routes of colonization and political conquest as well. As he came to realize he was an eyewitness to modern history in the making, Joseph Conrad discovered his abiding subject as a writer.

Conrad's voyages during this twenty-year odyssey took him East and West, to Indonesia and the Philippines, to Venezuela, the West Indies, and Africa. Working all the while, he watched as bit by bit the patchwork quilt of empire was put together. Wishing to avoid conscription in the French navy when he came of age, in 1878 Conrad joined the British merchant navy. The British empire had become the most extensive and mighty of any imperial power, and in his capacity as seaman Conrad worked in the main ports of call of the empire upon which the sun supposedly never set. He adopted British citizenship in 1886; after his uncle Tadeusz's death in 1894, Conrad made the final decision to become a writer, and to write in English rather than in French. At the age of thirty-seven, Joseph Conrad was newly born.

As a British writer, Conrad was a sort of ventriloquist. On the surface, he was as English as any other writer in his circle: he married an Englishwoman, Jessie George, and became a recognized part of British literary life, forming friendships with other major writers like Henry James and Ford Madox Ford, and achieving great popularity with the British reading public. A stranger from an exotically foreign place, by British standards, a newcomer to the English language, he nonetheless spoke through an English "voice" he created. From his distanced perspective, he was able to make English do things it had not done in the past for native writers of English. Language in Conrad's writing is always a bit off kilter, reading as if it had been translated instead of being, as it was, originally written in English. His prose has a hallucinatory effect, and a poetic intensity linked to his approaching the words of the English language afresh. The most famous of Conrad's narrators is the character Marlow, who appears in several of his major works as an elusive commentator on the action. His Englishness is as real as it can be, for an imitation. Marlow is perhaps even more British than the British, lapsing often into British slang like "By Jove!" as if to authenticate the reality of Conrad's vision of the British world. Through narrative voices like that of Marlow, Conrad can tell stories that may appear to be familiar and ordinary but are in fact anything but that. If modernist writers succeed in making us doubt that we can truly be at home in the world, Conrad can be said to have been the first writer to convey this homelessness in English.

There is another paradox at the heart of Joseph Conrad's work. His writing straddles the nineteenth and the twentieth centuries, with the five major works he wrote in the years before 1900— *Almayer's Folly, The Nigger of the "Narcissus," Heart of Darkness, Lord Jim,* and *Typhoon*—thought of by many critics as more modernist and experimental than later novels he wrote in the twentieth century—*Nostromo, The Secret Agent, Under Western Eyes, Chance,* and *Victory.* The critic Ian Watt claims that the "intense experimentation which began in 1896 and ended in 1900" resulted from Conrad's concentration in those five earlier works on his own personal experience, a personal experience of travel, exile, and solitude that was a radical premonition of the conditions of modernity. Works like *Heart of Darkness,* written during Queen Victoria's reign, for Watt present "the obdurate incompatibility of the self and the world in which it exists." In book after book, he sets a lone individual into confrontation with the complexities of the modern world, whether the world be that of European imperialism, or political anarchism, or the secret world of spies, or the world of political revolution. His heroes and (much less often) heroines have to find their bearings as society crumbles around them, and Conrad usually depicts them at a moment of choice, when they have to act on their lonely knowledge without any guarantee that they have chosen rightly.

A reliance on personal experience might seem to be a recipe for a straightforward, realist style, but Conrad's prose throughout his work is complex and symbolic, relying on images that are spun into complicated and ambiguous webs of symbolism. What stands out prominently in Conrad's style is its visual nature, the emphasis on making the reader "see." Critcs of Conrad's writing early on seized on the strikingly visual aspect of his effects, and his friend and fellow modernist writer Ford Madox Ford wrote an essay in 1913, *On Impressionism,* which put Conrad in a newly invented camp of impressionist writers. Conrad never fully agreed with this description of his style, nor did he have any special fondness for impressionist painting or the works of its greatest practitioners, Monet and Cézanne. Nonetheless, his own preface to *The Nigger of the "Narcissus"* describes all successful art as based on "an impression conveyed through the senses," and in each of his first five books narrators recount what they have *seen.* The narrator goes back over an experience in retelling it to an audience, an experience whose significance is not necessarily clear even to the narrator but whose meaning is revealed through the accumulation of imagistic details. The powers of sight are directly related to the powers of insight, or self-knowledge. A famous passage from *Heart of Darkness* explains the storytelling technique of the narrator Marlow, but also explains a philosophical conviction at the core of Conrad's writing: "The yarns of seamen have a direct simplicity, the whole meaning of which lies within the shell of a cracked nut. But Marlow was not typical (if his propensity to spin yarns be excepted), and to him the meaning of an episode was not inside like a kernel but outside, enveloping the tale which brought it out only as a glow brings out a haze, in the likeness of one of these misty halos that are sometimes made visible by the spectral illumination of moonshine." Events cast a visual glow and haze where meaning can be found only in the most subtle shades and ambiguous highlights of language. The reader must participate in the gradual, and partial, process of accumulating meaning.

Heart of Darkness is a work at the heart of modern British literature. First published serially in *Blackwood's Magazine* in 1899, it was reprinted as a complete work along with a companion novella, *Youth*, in 1902, and writers have returned to it again and again, in the form of quotations and allusions and imitations of its style; its story has been rewritten by each successive generation, in novels, films like *Apocalypse Now*, and even rock lyrics. Almost mythic in resonance, *Heart of Darkness* itself is structured around a mythical core—that is, the hero's quest. The journey or quest motif pervades world literature and English literature alike, from the *Odyssey* and the *Epic of Gilgamesh* to Dante's *Divine Comedy*, Bunyan's *Pilgrim's Progress*, and Byron's *Childe Harold*. *Heart of Darkness* condenses in its pages an epic range of theme and experience, both the social themes of empire and cultural clash, and the personal theme of the hero's quest for self-discovery.

As with all his early work, Conrad based *Heart of Darkness* on his own experience, in this case a trip he took up the Congo River in 1890 in order to become captain of a small steamship. The trip was an unusual one even by Conrad's standards, as he had been sailing the major oceans of the world on large ships. Conrad had reasons for choosing the assignment, however; he had been fascinated by maps since boyhood, and the blank space on the continent of Africa represented by the then-unexplored interior impelled him on. He was curious to see for himself the scandalous imperial practices of the Belgian King Leopold II in the Congo, who possessed what he called the Congo Free State (now Zaire) as his own private property, draining it of raw materials like ivory, while claiming to be suppressing savagery and spreading European civilization. After traveling two hundred miles upriver to Kinshasa to join his ship, however, he found it was undergoing repairs. He traveled as a passenger on a trip to Stanley Falls, to bring back an ailing company agent, Georges Klein, who died on the return trip to Kinshasa. These events provided the germ of Conrad's novella, which transformed Klein ("Little," in German) into the uncanny figure of Kurtz.

A diary Conrad kept during his journey (excerpted as a Companion Reading following *Heart of Darkness*) records his dawning awareness that King Leopold's policy in the Congo was nothing other than slave labor, ultimately causing the deaths of more than a million Africans. Initially an observer, Conrad became a passionately informed partisan, and made known his findings in the form of journalism and essays in the attempt to halt the King's genocidal policies. *Heart of Darkness* records these evils, and the ravages of Belgian colonialism on the African tribal societies it encountered and uprooted. Scholars of African history have shown how accurate his descriptions are, from the bit of white thread worn around the neck of a certain tribal group, to the construction of the railroad to Kinshasa and its devastating human impact. Conrad never names the Congo, nor the places and landmarks his character Marlow visits, yet he himself later called the book a "Kodak," or a snapshot, of the Congo.

The location is left unnamed in part because Conrad wishes to show that the heart of this darkness can shift on its axis. Marlow is telling the tale to several anonymous Englishmen as they sail the Thames on their yacht. Under the Roman empire, Britain had itself been thought of as a savage wilderness, a dark continent. The journey upriver, as Marlow points out, has been a reverse journey as well, a journey back from Africa to the darkness that lies at the heart of an England that claims to be civilizing those whom it is merely conquering. The seemingly clear-cut boundaries of light and dark, black and white, have blurred and even reversed themselves, and the nested narrative of the story itself challenges our understanding and even our sense of self. In this narrative, as in Conrad's other works, we are confronted with the tragic irony that human knowledge always comes too late.

Preface to *The Nigger of the "Narcissus"*[1]

A work that aspires, however humbly, to the condition of art should carry its justification in every line. And art itself may be defined as a single-minded attempt to render the highest kind of justice to the visible universe, by bringing to light the truth, manifold and one, underlying its every aspect. It is an attempt to find in its forms, in its colours, in its light, in its shadows, in the aspects of matter, and in the facts of life what of each is fundamental, what is enduring and essential—their one illuminating and convincing quality—the very truth of their existence. The artist, then, like the thinker or the scientist, seeks the truth and makes his appeal. Impressed by the aspect of the world the thinker plunges into ideas, the scientist into facts—whence, presently, emerging they make their appeal to those qualities of our being that fit us best for the hazardous enterprise of living. They speak authoritatively to our common sense, to our intelligence, to our desire of peace, or to our desire of unrest; not seldom to our prejudices, sometimes to our fears, often to our egoism—but always to our credulity. And their words are heard with reverence, for their concern is with weighty matters: with the cultivation of our minds and the proper care of our bodies, with the attainment of our ambitions, with the perfection of the means and the glorification of our precious aims.

It is otherwise with the artist.

Confronted by the same enigmatical spectacle the artist descends within himself, and in that lonely region of stress and strife, if he be deserving and fortunate, he finds the terms of his appeal. His appeal is made to our less obvious capacities: to that part of our nature which, because of the warlike conditions of existence, is necessarily kept out of sight within the more resisting and hard qualities—like the vulnerable body within a steel armour. His appeal is less loud, more profound, less distinct, more stirring—and sooner forgotten. Yet its effect endures for ever. The changing wisdom of successive generations discards ideas, questions facts, demolishes theories. But the artist appeals to that part of our being which is not dependent on wisdom; to that in us which is a gift and not an acquisition—and, therefore, more permanently enduring. He speaks to our capacity for delight and wonder, to the sense of mystery surrounding our lives; to our sense of pity, and beauty, and pain; to the latent feeling of fellowship with all creation—and to the subtle but invincible conviction of solidarity that knits together the loneliness of innumerable hearts, to the solidarity in dreams, in joy, in sorrow, in aspirations, in illusions, in hope, in fear, which binds men to each other, which binds together all humanity—the dead to the living and the living to the unborn.

It is only some such train of thought, or rather of feeling, that can in a measure explain the aim of the attempt, made in the tale which follows, to present an unrestful episode in the obscure lives of a few individuals out of all the disregarded multitude of the bewildered, the simple, and the voiceless. For, if any part of truth dwells in the belief confessed above, it becomes evident that there is not a place of splendour or a dark corner of the earth that does not deserve, if only a passing glance of wonder and pity. The motive, then, may be held to justify the matter of the work; but this preface, which is simply an avowal of endeavour, cannot end here—for the avowal is not yet complete.

---

1. Conrad's novella *The Nigger of the "Narcissus"* deals with the tragic death of a black seaman aboard a merchant ship named the *Narcissus*; Conrad had served as first mate on a ship of that name in the Indian Ocean in 1883. He published the novella in *The New Review* in 1897, then added this preface when it came out in book form in 1898.

Fiction—if it at all aspires to be art—appeals to temperament. And in truth it must be, like painting, like music, like all art, the appeal of one temperament to all the other innumerable temperaments whose subtle and resistless power endows passing events with their true meaning, and creates the moral, the emotional atmosphere of the place and time. Such an appeal to be effective must be an impression conveyed through the senses; and, in fact, it cannot be made in any other way, because temperament, whether individual or collective, is not amenable to persuasion. All art, therefore, appeals primarily to the senses, and the artistic aim when expressing itself in written words must also make its appeal through the senses, if its high desire is to reach the secret spring of responsive emotions. It must strenuously aspire to the plasticity of sculpture, to the colour of painting, and to the magic suggestiveness of music—which is the art of arts. And it is only through complete, unswerving devotion to the perfect blending of form and substance; it is only through an unremitting never-discouraged care for the shape and ring of sentences that an approach can be made to plasticity, to colour, and that the light of magic suggestiveness may be brought to play for an evanescent instant over the commonplace surface of words: of the old, old words, worn thin, defaced by ages of careless usage.

The sincere endeavour to accomplish that creative task, to go as far on that road as his strength will carry him, to go undeterred by faltering, weariness, or reproach, is the only valid justification for the worker in prose. And if his conscience is clear, his answer to those who, in the fullness of a wisdom which looks for immediate profit, demand specifically to be edified, consoled, amused; who demand to be promptly improved, or encouraged, or frightened, or shocked, or charmed, must run thus: My task which I am trying to achieve is, by the power of the written word to make you hear, to make you feel—it is, before all, to make you see. That—and no more, and it is everything. If I succeed, you shall find there according to your deserts: encouragement, consolation, fear, charm—all you demand—and, perhaps, also that glimpse of truth for which you have forgotten to ask.

To snatch in a moment of courage, from the remorseless rush of time, a passing phase of life, is only the beginning of the task. The task approached in tenderness and faith is to hold up unquestioningly, without choice and without fear, the rescued fragment before all eyes in the light of a sincere mood. It is to show its vibration, its colour, its form; and through its movement, its form, and its colour, reveal the substance of its truth—disclose its inspiring secret: the stress and passion within the core of each convincing moment. In a single-minded attempt of that kind, if one be deserving and fortunate, one may perchance attain to such clearness of sincerity that at last the presented vision of regret or pity, of terror or mirth, shall awaken in the hearts of the beholders that feeling of unavoidable solidarity; of the solidarity in mysterious origin, in toil, in joy, in hope, in uncertain fate, which binds men to each other and all mankind to the visible world.

It is evident that he who, rightly or wrongly, holds by the convictions expressed above cannot be faithful to any one of the temporary formulas of his craft. The enduring part of them—the truth which each only imperfectly veils—should abide with him as the most precious of his possessions, but they all: Realism, Romanticism, Naturalism, even the unofficial sentimentalism (which, like the poor, is exceedingly difficult to get rid of), all these gods must, after a short period of fellowship, abandon him—even on the very threshold of the temple—to the stammerings of his conscience and to the outspoken consciousness of the difficulties of his work. In that uneasy solitude the supreme cry of Art for Art itself, loses the exciting ring of its apparent immorality. It sounds far off. It has ceased to be a cry, and is heard only as a whisper, often incomprehensible, but at times and faintly encouraging.

Sometimes, stretched at ease in the shade of a roadside tree, we watch the motions of a labourer in a distant field, and after a time, begin to wonder languidly as to what the fellow may be at. We watch the movements of his body, the waving of his arms, we see him bend down, stand up, hesitate, begin again. It may add to the charm of an idle hour to be told the purpose of his exertions. If we know he is trying to lift a stone, to dig a ditch, to uproot a stump, we look with a more real interest at his efforts; we are disposed to condone the jar of his agitation upon the restfulness of the landscape; and even, if in a brotherly frame of mind, we may bring ourselves to forgive his failure. We understood his object, and, after all, the fellow has tried, and perhaps he had not the strength—and perhaps he had not the knowledge. We forgive, go on our way—and forget.

And so it is with the workman of art. Art is long and life is short, and success is very far off. And thus, doubtful of strength to travel so far, we talk a little about the aim—the aim of art, which, like life itself, is inspiring, difficult—obscured by mists. It is not in the clear logic of a triumphant conclusion; it is not in the unveiling of one of those heartless secrets which are called the Laws of Nature. It is not less great, but only more difficult.

To arrest, for the space of a breath, the hands busy about the work of the earth, and compel men entranced by the sight of distant goals to glance for a moment at the surrounding vision of form and colour, of sunshine and shadows; to make them pause for a look, for a sigh, for a smile—such is the aim, difficult and evanescent, and reserved only for a very few to achieve. But sometimes, by the deserving and the fortunate, even that task is accomplished. And when it is accomplished—behold!—all the truth of life is there: a moment of vision, a sigh, a smile—and the return to an eternal rest.

Heart of Darkness

1

The *Nellie*, a cruising yawl,[1] swung to her anchor without a flutter of the sails, and was at rest. The flood had made, the wind was nearly calm, and being bound down the river, the only thing for it was to come to and wait for the turn of the tide.

The sea-reach of the Thames stretched before us like the beginning of an interminable waterway. In the offing the sea and the sky were welded together without a joint, and in the luminous space the tanned sails of the barges drifting up with the tide seemed to stand still in red clusters of canvas sharply peaked, with gleams of varnished sprits. A haze rested on the low shores that ran out to sea in vanishing flatness. The air was dark above Gravesend, and farther back still seemed condensed into a mournful gloom, brooding motionless over the biggest, and the greatest, town on earth.[2]

The Director of Companies was our captain and our host. We four affectionately watched his back as he stood in the bows looking to seaward. On the whole river there was nothing that looked half so nautical. He resembled a pilot, which to a seaman is trustworthiness personified. It was difficult to realise his work was not out there in the luminous estuary, but behind him, within the brooding gloom.

1. A two-masted ship.

2. London. Gravesend is the last major town on the Thames estuary, from which the river joins the North Sea.

Between us there was, as I have already said somewhere, the bond of the sea. Besides holding our hearts together through long periods of separation, it had the effect of making us tolerant of each other's yarns—and even convictions. The Lawyer—the best of old fellows—had, because of his many years and many virtues, the only cushion on deck, and was lying on the only rug. The Accountant had brought out already a box of dominoes, and was toying architecturally with the bones. Marlow sat cross-legged right aft, leaning against the mizzen-mast.[3] He had sunken cheeks, a yellow complexion, a straight back, an ascetic aspect, and, with his arms dropped, the palms of hands outwards, resembled an idol. The Director, satisfied the anchor had good hold, made his way aft and sat down amongst us. We exchanged a few words lazily. Afterwards there was silence on board the yacht. For some reason or other we did not begin that game of dominoes. We felt meditative, and fit for nothing but placid staring. The day was ending in a serenity of still and exquisite brilliance. The water shone pacifically; the sky, without a speck, was a benign immensity of unstained light; the very mist on the Essex marshes was like a gauzy and radiant fabric, hung from the wooded rises inland, and draping the low shores in diaphanous folds. Only the gloom to the west, brooding over the upper reaches, became more sombre every minute, as if angered by the approach of the sun.

And at last, in its curved and imperceptible fall, the sun sank low, and from glowing white changed to a dull red without rays and without heat, as if about to go out suddenly, stricken to death by the touch of that gloom brooding over a crowd of men.

Forthwith a change came over the waters, and the serenity became less brilliant but more profound. The old river in its broad reach rested unruffled at the decline of day, after ages of good service done to the race that peopled its banks, spread out in the tranquil dignity of a waterway leading to the uttermost ends of the earth. We looked at the venerable stream not in the vivid flush of a short day that comes and departs for ever, but in the august light of abiding memories. And indeed nothing is easier for a man who has, as the phrase goes, "followed the sea" with reverence and affection, than to evoke the great spirit of the past upon the lower reaches of the Thames. The tidal current runs to and fro in its unceasing service, crowded with memories of men and ships it has borne to the rest of home or to the battles of the sea. It had known and served all the men of whom the nation is proud, from Sir Francis Drake to Sir John Franklin, knights all, titled and untitled—the great knights-errant of the sea.[4] It had borne all the ships whose names are like jewels flashing in the night of time, from the *Golden Hind* returning with her round flanks full of treasure, to be visited by the Queen's Highness and thus pass out of the gigantic tale, to the *Erebus* and *Terror*, bound on other conquests—and that never returned. It had known the ships and the men. They had sailed from Deptford, from Greenwich, from Erith—the adventurers and the settlers; kings' ships and the ships of men on 'Change; captains, admirals, the dark "interlopers" of the Eastern trade, and the commissioned "generals" of East India fleets.[5] Hunters for gold or pursuers of fame, they all had gone out on that stream, bearing the sword, and often the torch, messengers

3. A secondary mast at the stern of the ship.
4. Sir Francis Drake (1540–1596) was captain of *The Golden Hind* in the service of Queen Elizabeth I; his reputation came from the successful raids he mounted against Spanish ships returning laden with gold from the New World (South America). In 1845 Sir John Franklin led an expedition in the *Erebus* and *Terror* in search of the Northwest Passage (to the Pacific); all perished.

5. Deptford, Greenwich, and Erith lie on the Thames between London and Gravesend; "men on 'Change" are brokers on the Stock Exchange; the East India Company, a commercial and trading concern, became *de facto* ruler of large tracts of India in the 18th and 19th centuries.

though I had got a heavenly mission to civilise you. It was very fine for a time, but after a bit I did get tired of resting. Then I began to look for a ship—I should think the hardest work on earth. But the ships wouldn't even look at me. And I got tired of that game too.

"Now when I was a little chap I had a passion for maps. I would look for hours at South America, or Africa, or Australia, and lose myself in all the glories of exploration. At that time there were many blank spaces on the earth, and when I saw one that looked particularly inviting on a map (but they all look that) I would put my finger on it and say, When I grow up I will go there. The North Pole was one of these places, I remember. Well, I haven't been there yet, and shall not try now. The glamour's off. Other places were scattered about the Equator, and in every sort of latitude all over the two hemispheres. I have been in some of them, and . . . well, we won't talk about that. But there was one yet—the biggest, the most blank, so to speak—that I had a hankering after.

"True, by this time it was not a blank space any more. It had got filled since my boyhood with rivers and lakes and names. It had ceased to be a blank space of delightful mystery—a white patch for a boy to dream gloriously over. It had become a place of darkness. But there was in it one river especially, a mighty big river, that you could see on the map, resembling an immense snake uncoiled, with its head in the sea, its body at rest curving afar over a vast country, and its tail lost in the depths of the land. And as I looked at the map of it in a shop-window, it fascinated me as a snake would a bird—a silly little bird. Then I remembered there was a big concern, a Company for trade on that river. Dash it all! I thought to myself, they can't trade without using some kind of craft on that lot of fresh water—steamboats! Why shouldn't I try to get charge of one. I went on along Fleet Street, but could not shake off the idea. The snake had charmed me.

"You understand it was a Continental concern, that Trading Society; but I have a lot of relations living on the Continent, because it's cheap and not so nasty as it looks, they say.

"I am sorry to own I began to worry them. This was already a fresh departure for me. I was not used to get things that way, you know. I always went my own road and on my own legs where I had a mind to go. I wouldn't have believed it of myself; but, then—you see—I felt somehow I must get there by hook or by crook. So I worried them. The men said 'My dear fellow,' and did nothing. Then—would you believe it?—I tried the women. I, Charlie Marlow, set the women to work—to get a job. Heavens! Well, you see, the notion drove me. I had an aunt, a dear enthusiastic soul. She wrote: 'It will be delightful. I am ready to do anything, anything for you. It is a glorious idea. I know the wife of a very high personage in the Administration, and also a man who has lots of influence with,' &c., &c. She was determined to make no end of fuss to get me appointed skipper of a river steamboat, if such was my fancy.

"I got my appointment—of course; and I got it very quick. It appears the Company had received news that one of their captains had been killed in a scuffle with the natives. This was my chance, and it made me the more anxious to go. It was only months and months afterwards, when I made the attempt to recover what was left of the body, that I heard the original quarrel arose from a misunderstanding about some hens. Yes, two black hens. Fresleven—that was the fellow's name, a Dane—thought himself wronged somehow in the bargain, so he went ashore and started to hammer the chief of the village with a stick. Oh, it didn't surprise me in the least to hear this, and at the same time to be told that Fresleven was the gentlest, quietest creature that ever walked on two legs. No doubt he was; but he had been a couple of years already out there engaged in the noble cause, you know, and he probably felt the need at last of asserting his self-respect in some way. Therefore he whacked the old nigger mercilessly, while a big crowd of his people watched him, thunderstruck, till some man,—I was told the chief's son,—in desperation at hearing the old chap yell, made a tentative jab with a spear at the white man—and of course it went quite easy between the shoulder-blades. Then the whole population cleared into the forest, expecting all kinds of calamities to happen, while, on the other hand, the steamer Fresleven commanded left also in a bad panic, in charge of the engineer, I believe. Afterwards nobody seemed to trouble much about Fresleven's remains, till I got out and stepped into his shoes. I couldn't let it rest, though; but when an opportunity offered at last to meet my predecessor, the grass growing through his ribs was tall enough to hide his bones. They were all there. The supernatural being had not been touched after he fell. And the village was deserted, the huts gaped black, rotting, all askew within the fallen enclosures. A calamity had come to it, sure enough. The people had vanished. Mad terror had scattered them, men, women, and children, through the bush, and they had never returned. What became of the hens I don't know either. I should think the cause of progress got them, anyhow. However, through this glorious affair I got my appointment, before I had fairly begun to hope for it.

"I flew around like mad to get ready, and before forty-eight hours I was crossing the Channel to show myself to my employers, and sign the contract. In a very few hours I arrived in a city that always makes me think of a whited sepulchre.[8] Prejudice no doubt. I had no difficulty in finding the Company's offices. It was the biggest thing in the town, and everybody I met was full of it. They were going to run an over-sea empire, and make no end of coin by trade.

"A narrow and deserted street in deep shadow, high houses, innumerable windows with venetian blinds, a dead silence, grass sprouting between the stones, imposing carriage archways right and left, immense double doors standing ponderously ajar. I slipped through one of these cracks, went up a swept and ungarnished staircase, as arid as a desert, and opened the first door I came to. Two women, one fat and the other slim, sat on straw-bottomed chairs, knitting black wool. The slim one got up and walked straight at me—still knitting with downcast eyes—and only just as I began to think of getting out of her way, as you would for a somnambulist, stood still, and looked up. Her dress was as plain as an umbrella-cover, and she turned round without a word and preceded me into a waiting-room. I gave my name, and looked about. Deal table in the middle, plain chairs all round the walls, on one end a large shining map, marked with all the colours of a rainbow. There was a vast amount of red—good to see at any time, because one knows that some real work is done in there, a deuce of a lot of blue, a little green, smears of orange, and, on the East Coast, a purple patch, to show where the jolly pioneers of progress drink the jolly lager-beer.[9] However, I wasn't going into any of these. I was going into the yellow. Dead in the centre. And the river was there—fascinating—deadly—like a snake. Ough! A door opened, a white-haired secretarial head, but wearing a compassionate expression, appeared, and a skinny forefinger beckoned me into the sanctuary. Its light was dim, and a heavy writing-desk squatted in the middle. From behind that structure

8. Brussels was the headquarters of the Société Anonyme Belge pour le Commerce du Haut-Congo (Belgian Corporation for Trade in the Upper Congo), with which Conrad obtained his post through the influence of his aunt, Marguerite Poradowska.
9. British territories were traditionally marked in red on colonial maps; lager was originally a continental beer, not much drunk in England.

came out an impression of pale plumpness in a frock-coat. The great man himself. He was five feet six, I should judge, and had his grip on the handle-end of ever so many millions. He shook hands, I fancy, murmured vaguely, was satisfied with my French. *Bon voyage.*

"In about forty-five seconds I found myself again in the waiting-room with the compassionate secretary, who, full of desolation and sympathy, made me sign some document. I believe I undertook amongst other things not to disclose any trade secrets. Well, I am not going to.

"I began to feel slightly uneasy. You know I am not used to such ceremonies, and there was something ominous in the atmosphere. It was just as though I had been let into some conspiracy—I don't know—something not quite right; and I was glad to get out. In the outer room the two women knitted black wool feverishly. People were arriving, and the younger one was walking back and forth introducing them. The old one sat on her chair. Her flat cloth slippers were propped up on a foot-warmer, and a cat reposed on her lap. She wore a starched white affair on her head, had a wart on one cheek, and silver-rimmed spectacles hung on the tip of her nose. She glanced at me above the glasses. The swift and indifferent placidity of that look troubled me. Two youths with foolish and cheery countenances were being piloted over, and she threw at them the same quick glance of unconcerned wisdom. She seemed to know all about them and about me too. An eerie feeling came over me. She seemed uncanny and fateful. Often far away there I thought of these two, guarding the door of Darkness, knitting black wool as for a warm pall, one introducing, introducing continuously to the unknown, the other scrutinising the cheery and foolish faces with unconcerned old eyes. *Ave!* Old knitter of black wool. *Morituri te salutant.*[1] Not many of those she looked at ever saw her again—not half, by a long way.

"There was yet a visit to the doctor. 'A simple formality,' assured me the secretary, with an air of taking an immense part in all my sorrows. Accordingly a young chap wearing his hat over the left eyebrow, some clerk I suppose,—there must have been clerks in the business, though the house was as still as a house in a city of the dead,—came from somewhere upstairs, and led me forth. He was shabby and careless, with ink-stains on the sleeves of his jacket, and his cravat was large and billowy, under a chin shaped like the toe of an old boot. It was a little too early for the doctor, so I proposed a drink, and thereupon he developed a vein of joviality. As we sat over our vermouths he glorified the Company's business, and by-and-by I expressed casually my surprise at him not going out there. He became very cool and collected all at once. 'I am not such a fool as I look, quoth Plato to his disciples,' he said sententiously, emptied his glass with great resolution, and we rose.

"The old doctor felt my pulse, evidently thinking of something else the while. 'Good, good for there,' he mumbled, and then with a certain eagerness asked me whether I would let him measure my head. Rather surprised, I said Yes, when he produced a thing like calipers and got the dimensions back and front and every way, taking notes carefully. He was an unshaven little man in a threadbare coat like a gaberdine, with his feet in slippers, and I thought him a harmless fool. 'I always ask leave, in the interests of science, to measure the crania of those going out there,' he said. 'And when they come back too?' I asked. 'Oh, I never see them,' he remarked; 'and moreover, the changes take place inside, you know.' He smiled, as if at some quiet joke. 'So you are going out there. Famous. Interesting too.' He gave me a searching glance, and made another note. 'Ever any madness in your family?' he asked, in a

---

1. Hail! . . . Those who are about to die salute you!—traditional cry of Roman gladiators.

matter-of-fact tone. I felt very annoyed. 'Is that question in the interests of science too?' 'It would be,' he said, without taking notice of my irritation, 'interesting for science to watch the mental changes of individuals, on the spot, but . . .' 'Are you an alienist?'[2] I interrupted. 'Every doctor should be—a little,' answered that original, imperturbably. 'I have a little theory which you Messieurs who go out there must help me to prove. This is my share in the advantages my country shall reap from the possession of such a magnificent dependency. The mere wealth I leave to others. Pardon my questions, but you are the first Englishman coming under my observation . . .' I hastened to assure him I was not in the least typical. 'If I were,' said I, 'I wouldn't be talking like this with you.' 'What you say is rather profound, and probably erroneous,' he said, with a laugh. 'Avoid irritation more than exposure to the sun. Adieu. How do you English say, eh? Good-bye. Ah! Good-bye. Adieu. In the tropics one must before everything keep calm.' . . . He lifted a warning forefinger. . . . 'Du calme, du calme. Adieu.'

"One thing more remained to do—say good-bye to my excellent aunt. I found her triumphant. I had a cup of tea—the last decent cup of tea for many days—and in a room that most soothingly looked just as you would expect a lady's drawing-room to look, we had a long quiet chat by the fireside. In the course of these confidences it became quite plain to me I had been represented to the wife of the high dignitary, and goodness knows to how many more people besides, as an exceptional and gifted creature—a piece of good fortune for the Company—a man you don't get hold of every day. Good heavens! and I was going to take charge of a twopenny-half-penny river-steamboat with a penny whistle attached! It appeared, however, I was also one of the Workers, with a capital—you know. Something like an emissary of light, something like a lower sort of apostle. There had been a lot of such rot let loose in print and talk just about that time, and the excellent woman, living right in the rush of all that humbug, got carried off her feet. She talked about 'weaning those ignorant millions from their horrid ways,' till, upon my word, she made me quite uncomfortable. I ventured to hint that the Company was run for profit.

"'You forget, dear Charlie, that the labourer is worthy of his hire,' she said, brightly.[3] It's queer how out of touch with truth women are. They live in a world of their own, and there had never been anything like it, and never can be. It is too beautiful altogether, and if they were to set it up it would go to pieces before the first sunset. Some confounded fact we men have been living contentedly with ever since the day of creation would start up and knock the whole thing over.

"After this I got embraced, told to wear flannel, be sure to write often, and so on—and I left. In the street—I don't know why—a queer feeling came to me that I was an impostor. Odd thing that I, who used to clear out for any part of the world at twenty-four hours' notice, with less thought than most men give to the crossing of a street, had a moment—I won't say of hesitation, but of startled pause, before this commonplace affair. The best way I can explain it to you is by saying that, for a second or two, I felt as though, instead of going to the centre of a continent, I were about to set off for the centre of the earth.

"I left in a French steamer, and she called in every blamed port they have out there, for, as far as I could see, the sole purpose of landing soldiers and custom-house officers. I watched the coast. Watching a coast as it slips by the ship is like thinking about an enigma. There it is before you—smiling, frowning, inviting, grand, mean, insipid, or savage, and always mute with an air of whispering, Come and find out.

2. A psychologist.   3. 1 Timothy 5.18.

This one was almost featureless, as if still in the making, with an aspect of monotonous grimness. The edge of a colossal jungle, so dark-green as to be almost black, fringed with white surf, ran straight, like a ruled line, far, far away along a blue sea whose glitter was blurred by a creeping mist. The sun was fierce, the land seemed to glisten and drip with steam. Here and there greyish-whitish specks showed up, clustered inside the white surf, with a flag flying above them perhaps—settlements some centuries old, and still no bigger than pin-heads on the untouched expanse of their background. We pounded along, stopped, landed soldiers; went on, landed customhouse clerks to levy toll in what looked like a Godforsaken wilderness, with a tin shed and a flag-pole lost in it; landed more soldiers—to take care of the customhouse clerks, presumably. Some, I heard, got drowned in the surf; but whether they did or not, nobody seemed particularly to care. They were just flung out there, and on we went. Every day the coast looked the same, as though we had not moved; but we passed various places—trading places—with names like Gran' Bassam, Little Popo,[4] names that seemed to belong to some sordid farce acted in front of a sinister backcloth. The idleness of a passenger, my isolation amongst all these men with whom I had no point of contact, the oily and languid sea, the uniform sombreness of the coast, seemed to keep me away from the truth of things, within the toil of a mournful and senseless delusion. The voice of the surf heard now and then was a positive pleasure, like the speech of a brother. It was something natural, that had its reason, that had a meaning. Now and then a boat from the shore gave one a momentary contact with reality. It was paddled by black fellows. You could see from afar the white of their eyeballs glistening. They shouted, sang; their bodies streamed with perspiration; they had faces like grotesque masks—these chaps; but they had bone, muscle, a wild vitality, an intense energy of movement, that was as natural and true as the surf along their coast. They wanted no excuse for being there. They were a great comfort to look at. For a time I would feel I belonged still to a world of straightforward facts; but the feeling would not last long. Something would turn up to scare it away. Once, I remember, we came upon a man-of-war anchored off the coast. There wasn't even a shed there, and she was shelling the bush. It appears the French had one of their wars going on thereabouts. Her ensign dropped limp like a rag; the muzzles of the long eight-inch guns stuck out all over the low hull; the greasy, slimy swell swung her up lazily and let her down, swaying her thin masts. In the empty immensity of earth, sky, and water, there she was, incomprehensible, firing into a continent. Pop, would go one of the eight-inch guns; a small flame would dart and vanish, a little white smoke would disappear, a tiny projectile would give a feeble screech—and nothing happened. Nothing could happen. There was a touch of insanity in the proceeding, a sense of lugubrious drollery in the sight; and it was not dissipated by somebody on board assuring me earnestly there was a camp of natives—he called them enemies!—hidden out of sight somewhere.

"We gave her letters (I heard the men in that lonely ship were dying of fever at the rate of three a day) and went on. We called at some more places with farcical names, where the merry dance of death and trade goes on in a still and earthy atmosphere as of an overheated catacomb;[5] all along the formless coast bordered by danger-

---

4. Grand Bassam and Grand Popo are the names of ports where Conrad's ship called on its way to the Congo.
5. In a letter in May 1890 Conrad wrote: "What makes me rather uneasy is the information that 60 per cent. of our Company's employés return to Europe before they have completed even six months' service. Fever and dysentery! There are others who are sent home in a hurry at the end of a year, so that they shouldn't die in the Congo." According to a 1907 report, 150 out of every 2,000 native Congolese laborers died each month while in company employ; "All along the [railroad] track one would see corpses."

ous surf, as if Nature herself had tried to ward off intruders; in and out of rivers, streams of death in life, whose banks were rotting into mud, whose waters, thickened into slime, invaded the contorted mangroves, that seemed to writhe at us in the extremity of an impotent despair. Nowhere did we stop long enough to get a particularised impression, but the general sense of vague and oppressive wonder grew upon me. It was like a weary pilgrimage amongst hints for nightmares.

"It was upward of thirty days before I saw the mouth of the big river. We anchored off the seat of the government. But my work would not begin till some two hundred miles farther on. So as soon as I could I made a start for a place thirty miles higher up.

"I had my passage on a little sea-going steamer. Her captain was a Swede, and knowing me for a seaman, invited me on the bridge. He was a young man, lean, fair, and morose, with lanky hair and a shuffling gait. As we left the miserable little wharf, he tossed his head contemptuously at the shore. 'Been living there?' he asked. I said, 'Yes.' 'Fine lot these government chaps—are they not?' he went on, speaking English with great precision and considerable bitterness. 'It is funny what some people will do for a few francs a month. I wonder what becomes of that kind when it goes up country?' I said to him I expected to see that soon. 'So-o-o!' he exclaimed. He shuffled athwart, keeping one eye ahead vigilantly. 'Don't be too sure,' he continued. 'The other day I took up a man who hanged himself on the road. He was a Swede, too.' 'Hanged himself! Why, in God's name?' I cried. He kept on looking out watchfully. 'Who knows? The sun too much for him, or the country perhaps.'

"At last we opened a reach. A rocky cliff appeared, mounds of turned-up earth by the shore, houses on a hill, others, with iron roofs, amongst a waste of excavations, or hanging to the declivity. A continuous noise of the rapids above hovered over this scene of inhabited devastation. A lot of people, mostly black and naked, moved about like ants. A jetty projected into the river. A blinding sunlight drowned all this at times in a sudden recrudescence of glare. 'There's your Company's station,' said the Swede, pointing to three wooden barrack-like structures on the rocky slope. 'I will send your things up. Four boxes did you say? So. Farewell.'

"I came upon a boiler wallowing in the grass, then found a path leading up the hill. It turned aside for the boulders, and also for an undersized railway-truck lying there on its back with its wheels in the air. One was off. The thing looked as dead as the carcass of some animal. I came upon more pieces of decaying machinery, a stack of rusty rails. To the left a clump of trees made a shady spot, where dark things seemed to stir feebly. I blinked, the path was steep. A horn tooted to the right, and I saw the black people run. A heavy and dull detonation shook the ground, a puff of smoke came out of the cliff, and that was all. No change appeared on the face of the rock. They were building a railway. The cliff was not in the way or anything; but this objectless blasting was all the work going on.

"A slight clinking behind me made me turn my head. Six black men advanced in a file, toiling up the path. They walked erect and slow, balancing small baskets full of earth on their heads, and the clink kept time with their footsteps. Black rags were wound round their loins, and the short ends behind wagged to and fro like tails. I could see every rib, the joints of their limbs were like knots in a rope; each had an iron collar on his neck, and all were connected together with a chain whose bights swung between them, rhythmically clinking. Another report from the cliff made me think suddenly of that ship of war I had seen firing into a continent. It was the same kind of ominous voice; but these men could by no stretch of imagination be called enemies. They were called criminals, and the outraged law, like the bursting shells, had come to them, an insoluble mystery from over the sea. All their meagre breasts panted together, the violently dilated nostrils quivered, the eyes stared stonily up-hill. They passed me within six inches, without a glance, with that complete, death-like indifference of unhappy savages. Behind this raw matter one of the reclaimed, the product of the new forces at work, strolled despondently, carrying a rifle by its middle. He had a uniform jacket with one button off, and seeing a white man on the path, hoisted his weapon to his shoulder with alacrity. This was simple prudence, white men being so much alike at a distance that he could not tell who I might be. He was speedily reassured, and with a large, white, rascally grin, and a glance at his charge, seemed to take me into partnership in his exalted trust. After all, I also was a part of the great cause of these high and just proceedings.

"Instead of going up, I turned and descended to the left. My idea was to let that chain-gang get out of sight before I climbed the hill. You know I am not particularly tender; I've had to strike and to fend off. I've had to resist and to attack sometimes—that's only one way of resisting—without counting the exact cost, according to the demands of such sort of life as I had blundered into. I've seen the devil of violence, and the devil of greed, and the devil of hot desire; but, by all the stars! these were strong, lusty, red-eyed devils, that swayed and drove men—men, I tell you. But as I stood on this hillside, I foresaw that in the blinding sunshine of that land I would become acquainted with a flabby, pretending, weak-eyed devil of a rapacious and pitiless folly. How insidious he could be, too, I was only to find out several months later and a thousand miles farther. For a moment I stood appalled, as though by a warning. Finally I descended the hill, obliquely, towards the trees I had seen.

"I avoided a vast artificial hole somebody had been digging on the slope, the pur-pose of which I found it impossible to divine. It wasn't a quarry or a sandpit, anyhow. It was just a hole. It might have been connected with the philanthropic desire of giv-ing the criminals something to do. I don't know. Then I nearly fell into a very narrow ravine, almost no more than a scar in the hillside. I discovered that a lot of imported drainage-pipes for the settlement had been tumbled in there. There wasn't one that was not broken. It was a wanton smash-up. At last I got under the trees. My purpose was to stroll into the shade for a moment; but no sooner within than it seemed to me I had stepped into the gloomy circle of some Inferno. The rapids were near, and an uninterrupted, uniform, headlong, rushing noise filled the mournful stillness of the grove, where not a breath stirred, not a leaf moved, with a mysterious sound—as though the tearing pace of the launched earth had suddenly become audible.

"Black shapes crouched, lay, sat between the trees, leaning against the trunks, clinging to the earth, half coming out, half effaced within the dim light, in all the attitudes of pain, abandonment, and despair. Another mine on the cliff went off, fol-lowed by a slight shudder of the soil under my feet. The work was going on. The work! And this was the place where some of the helpers had withdrawn to die.

"They were dying slowly—it was very clear. They were not enemies, they were not criminals, they were nothing earthly now,—nothing but black shadows of dis-ease and starvation, lying confusedly in the greenish gloom. Brought from all the recesses of the coast in all the legality of time contracts, lost in uncongenial sur-roundings, fed on unfamiliar food, they sickened, became inefficient, and were then allowed to crawl away and rest. These moribund shapes were free as air—and nearly as thin. I began to distinguish the gleam of eyes under the trees. Then, glancing down, I saw a face near my hand. The black bones reclined at full length with one shoulder against the tree, and slowly the eyelids rose and the sunken eyes looked up at me, enormous and vacant, a kind of blind, white flicker in the depths of the orbs, which died out slowly. The man seemed young—almost a boy—but you know with them it's hard to tell. I found nothing else to do but to offer him one of my good Swede's ship's biscuits I had in my pocket. The fingers closed slowly on it and held—there was no other movement and no other glance. He had tied a bit of white worsted round his neck—Why? Where did he get it? Was it a badge—an ornament—a charm—a propitiatory act? Was there any idea at all connected with it? It looked startling round his black neck, this bit of white thread from beyond the seas.

"Near the same tree two more bundles of acute angles sat with their legs drawn up. One, with his chin propped on his knees, stared at nothing, in an intolerable and appalling manner: his brother phantom rested its forehead, as if overcome with a great weariness; and all about others were scattered in every pose of contorted collapse, as in some picture of a massacre or a pestilence. While I stood horror-struck, one of these creatures rose to his hands and knees, and went off on all-fours towards the river to drink. He lapped out of his hand, then sat up in the sunlight, crossing his shins in front of him, and after a time let his woolly head fall on his breastbone.

"I didn't want any more loitering in the shade, and I made haste towards the station. When near the buildings I met a white man, in such an unexpected elegance of get-up that in the first moment I took him for a sort of vision. I saw a high starched collar, white cuffs, a light alpaca jacket, snowy trousers, a clear silk necktie, and varnished boots. No hat. Hair parted, brushed, oiled, under a green-lined parasol held in a big white hand. He was amazing, and had a penholder behind his ear.

"I shook hands with this miracle, and I learned he was the Company's chief accountant, and that all the book-keeping was done at this station. He had come out for a moment, he said, 'to get a breath of fresh air.' The expression sounded wonderfully odd, with its suggestion of sedentary desk-life. I wouldn't have mentioned the fellow to you at all, only it was from his lips that I first heard the name of the man who is so indissolubly connected with the memories of that time. Moreover, I respected the fellow. Yes; I respected his collars, his vast cuffs, his brushed hair. His appearance was certainly that of a hairdresser's dummy; but in the great demoralisation of the land he kept up his appearance. That's backbone. His starched collars and got-up shirt-fronts were achievements of character. He had been out nearly three years; and, later on, I could not help asking him how he managed to sport such linen. He had just the faintest blush, and said modestly, 'I've been teaching one of the native women about the station. It was difficult. She had a distaste for the work.' Thus this man had verily accomplished something. And he was devoted to his books, which were in apple-pie order.

"Everything else in the station was in a muddle,—heads, things, buildings. Strings of dusty niggers with splay feet arrived and departed; a stream of manufactured goods, rubbishy cottons, beads, and brass-wire set into the depths of darkness, and in return came a precious trickle of ivory.

"I had to wait in the station for ten days—an eternity. I lived in a hut in the yard, but to be out of the chaos I would sometimes get into the accountant's office. It was built of horizontal planks, and so badly put together that, as he bent over his high desk, he was barred from neck to heels with narrow strips of sunlight. There was no need to open the big shutter to see. It was hot there too; big flies buzzed fiendishly, and did not sting, but stabbed. I sat generally on the floor, while, of faultless appearance (and even slightly scented), perching on a high stool, he wrote, he wrote. Sometimes he stood up for exercise. When a truckle-bed with a sick man (some invalided agent from up-country) was put in there, he exhibited a gentle annoyance. 'The groans of this sick person,' he said, 'distract my attention. And without that it is extremely difficult to guard against clerical errors in this climate.'

"One day he remarked, without lifting his head, 'In the interior you will no doubt meet Mr Kurtz.' On my asking who Mr Kurtz was, he said he was a first-class agent; and seeing my disappointment at this information, he added slowly, laying down his pen, 'He is a very remarkable person.' Further questions elicited from him that Mr Kurtz was at present in charge of a trading-post, a very important one, in the true ivory-country, at 'the very bottom of there. Sends in as much ivory as all the others put together . . .' He began to write again. The sick man was too ill to groan. The flies buzzed in a great peace.

"Suddenly there was a growing murmur of voices and a great tramping of feet. A caravan had come in. A violent babble of uncouth sounds burst out on the other side of the planks. All the carriers were speaking together, and in the midst of the uproar the lamentable voice of the chief agent was heard 'giving it up' tearfully for the twentieth time that day. . . . He rose slowly. 'What a frightful row,' he said. He crossed the room gently to look at the sick man, and returning, said to me, 'He does not hear.' 'What! Dead?' I asked, startled. 'No, not yet,' he answered, with great composure. Then, alluding with a toss of the head to the tumult in the station-yard, 'When one has got to make correct entries, one comes to hate those savages—hate them to the death.' He remained thoughtful for a moment. 'When you see Mr Kurtz,' he went on, 'tell him from me that everything here'—he glanced at the desk—'is very satisfactory. I don't like to write to him—with those messengers of ours you never know who may get hold of your letter—at that Central Station.' He stared at me for a moment with his mild, bulging eyes. 'Oh, he will go far, very far,' he began again. 'He will be a somebody in the Administration before long. They, above—the Council in Europe, you know—mean him to be.'

"He turned to his work. The noise outside had ceased, and presently in going out I stopped at the door. In the steady buzz of flies the homeward-bound agent was lying flushed and insensible; the other, bent over his books, was making correct entries of perfectly correct transactions; and fifty feet below the doorstep I could see the still tree-tops of the grove of death.

"Next day I left that station at last, with a caravan of sixty men, for a two-hundred-mile tramp.

"No use telling you much about that. Paths, paths, everywhere; a stamped-in network of paths spreading over the empty land, through long grass, through burnt grass, through thickets, down and up chilly ravines, up and down stony hills ablaze with heat; and a solitude, a solitude, nobody, not a hut. The population had cleared out a long time ago. Well, if a lot of mysterious niggers armed with all kinds of fearful weapons suddenly took to travelling on the road between Deal[6] and Gravesend, catching the yokels right and left to carry heavy loads for them, I fancy every farm and cottage thereabouts would get empty very soon. Only here the dwellings were gone too. Still, I passed through several abandoned villages. There's something pathetically childish in the ruins of grass walls. Day after day, with the stamp and shuffle of sixty pair of bare feet behind me, each pair under a 60-lb. load. Camp, cook, sleep, strike camp, march. Now and then a carrier dead in harness, at rest in the long grass near the path, with an empty water-gourd and his long staff lying by his

6. An English port.

side. A great silence around and above. Perhaps on some quiet night the tremor of far-off drums, sinking, swelling, a tremor vast, faint; a sound weird, appealing, suggestive, and wild—and perhaps with as profound a meaning as the sound of bells in a Christian country. Once a white man in an unbuttoned uniform, camping on the path with an armed escort of lank Zanzibaris,[7] very hospitable and festive—not to say drunk. Was looking after the upkeep of the road, he declared. Can't say I saw any road or any upkeep, unless the body of a middle-aged negro, with a bullet-hole in the forehead, upon which I absolutely stumbled three miles farther on, may be considered as a permanent improvement. I had a white companion too, not a bad chap, but rather too fleshy and with the exasperating habit of fainting on the hot hillsides, miles away from the least bit of shade and water. Annoying, you know, to hold your own coat like a parasol over a man's head while he is coming-to. I couldn't help asking him once what he meant by coming there at all. 'To make money, of course. What do you think?' he said, scornfully. Then he got fever, and had to be carried in a hammock slung under a pole. As he weighed sixteen stone I had no end of rows with the carriers. They jibbed, ran away, sneaked off with their loads in the night—quite a mutiny. So, one evening, I made a speech in English with gestures, not one of which was lost to the sixty pairs of eyes before me, and the next morning I started the hammock off in front all right. An hour afterwards I came upon the whole concern wrecked in a bush—man, hammock, groans, blankets, horrors. The heavy pole had skinned his poor nose. He was very anxious for me to kill somebody, but there wasn't the shadow of a carrier near. I remembered the old doctor,—'It would be interesting for science to watch the mental changes of individuals, on the spot.' I felt I was becoming scientifically interesting. However, all that is to no purpose. On the fifteenth day I came in sight of the big river again, and hobbled into the Central Station. It was on a back water surrounded by scrub and forest, with a pretty border of smelly mud on one side, and on the three others enclosed by a crazy fence of rushes. A neglected gap was all the gate it had, and the first glance at the place was enough to let you see the flabby devil was running that show. White men with long staves in their hands appeared languidly from amongst the buildings, strolling up to take a look at me, and then retired out of sight somewhere. One of them, a stout, excitable chap with black moustaches, informed me with great volubility and many digressions, as soon as I told him who I was, that my steamer was at the bottom of the river. I was thunderstruck. What, how, why? Oh, it was 'all right.' The 'manager himself' was there. All quite correct. 'Everybody had behaved splendidly! splendidly!'—'You must,' he said in agitation, 'go and see the general manager at once. He is waiting!'

"I did not see the real significance of that wreck at once. I fancy I see it now, but I am not sure—not at all. Certainly the affair was too stupid—when I think of it—to be altogether natural. Still. . . . But at the moment it presented itself simply as a confounded nuisance. The steamer was sunk. They had started two days before in a sudden hurry up the river with the manager on board, in charge of some volunteer skipper, and before they had been out three hours they tore the bottom out of her on stones, and she sank near the south bank. I asked myself what I was to do there, now my boat was lost. As a matter of fact, I had plenty to do in fishing my command out of the river. I had to set about it the very next day. That, and the repairs when I brought the pieces to the station, took some months.

7. Africans from Zanzibar, in East Africa; they were widely used as mercenaries.

"My first interview with the manager was curious. He did not ask me to sit down after my twenty-mile walk that morning. He was commonplace in complexion, in feature, in manners, and in voice. He was of middle size and of ordinary build. His eyes, of the usual blue, were perhaps remarkably cold, and he certainly could make his glance fall on one as trenchant and heavy as an axe. But even at these times the rest of his person seemed to disclaim the intention. Otherwise there was only an indefinable, faint expression of his lips, something stealthy—a smile—not a smile—I remember it, but I can't explain. It was unconscious, this smile was, though just after he had said something it got intensified for an instant. It came at the end of his speeches like a seal applied on the words to make the meaning of the commonest phrase appear absolutely inscrutable. He was a common trader, from his youth up employed in these parts—nothing more. He was obeyed, yet he inspired neither love nor fear, nor even respect. He inspired uneasiness. That was it! Uneasiness. Not a definite mistrust—just uneasiness—nothing more. You have no idea how effective such a . . . a . . . faculty can be. He had no genius for organising, for initiative, or for order even. That was evident in such things as the deplorable state of the station. He had no learning, and no intelligence. His position had come to him—why? Perhaps because he was never ill . . . He had served three terms of three years out there . . . Because triumphant health in the general rout of constitutions is a kind of power in itself. When he went home on leave he rioted on a large scale—pompously. Jack ashore—with a difference—in externals only. This one could gather from his casual talk. He originated nothing, he could keep the routine going—that's all. But he was great. He was great by this little thing that it was impossible to tell what could control such a man. He never gave that secret away. Perhaps there was nothing within him. Such a suspicion made one pause—for out there there were no external checks. Once when various tropical diseases had laid low almost every 'agent' in the station, he was heard to say, 'Men who come out here should have no entrails.' He sealed the utterance with that smile of his, as though it had been a door opening into a darkness he had in his keeping. You fancied you had seen things—but the seal was on. When annoyed at meal-times by the constant quarrels of the white men about precedence, he ordered an immense round table to be made, for which a special house had to be built. This was the station's mess-room. Where he sat was the first place—the rest were nowhere. One felt this to be his unalterable conviction. He was neither civil nor uncivil. He was quiet. He allowed his 'boy'—an overfed young negro from the coast—to treat the white men, under his very eyes, with provoking insolence.

"He began to speak as soon as he saw me. I had been very long on the road. He could not wait. Had to start without me. The up-river stations had to be relieved. There had been so many delays already that he did not know who was dead and who was alive, and how they got on—and so on, and so on. He paid no attention to my explanations, and, playing with a stick of sealing-wax, repeated several times that the situation was 'very grave, very grave.' There were rumours that a very important station was in jeopardy, and its chief, Mr Kurtz, was ill. Hoped it was not true. Mr Kurtz was . . . I felt weary and irritable. Hang Kurtz, I thought. I interrupted him by saying I had heard of Mr Kurtz on the coast. 'Ah! So they talk of him down there,' he murmured to himself. Then he began again, assuring me Mr Kurtz was the best agent he had, an exceptional man, of the greatest importance to the Company; therefore I could understand his anxiety. He was, he said, 'very, very uneasy.' Certainly he fidgeted on his chair a good deal, exclaimed, 'Ah, Mr Kurtz!' broke the stick of sealing-wax and seemed dumbfounded by the accident. Next thing he wanted to know 'how long it would take to' . . . I interrupted him again. Being hungry, you know, and kept on my feet too, I was getting savage. 'How can I tell?' I said. 'I haven't even seen the wreck yet—some months, no doubt.' All this talk seemed to me so futile. 'Some months,' he said. 'Well, let us say three months before we can make a start. Yes. That ought to do the affair.' I flung out of his hut (he lived all alone in a clay hut with a sort of verandah) muttering to myself my opinion of him. He was a chattering idiot. Afterwards I took it back when it was borne in upon me startlingly with what extreme nicety he had estimated the time requisite for the 'affair.'

"I went to work the next day, turning, so to speak, my back on that station. In that way only it seemed to me I could keep my hold on the redeeming facts of life. Still, one must look about sometimes; and then I saw this station, these men strolling aimlessly about in the sunshine of the yard. I asked myself sometimes what it all meant. They wandered here and there with their absurd long staves in their hands, like a lot of faithless pilgrims bewitched inside a rotten fence. The word 'ivory' rang in the air, was whispered, was sighed. You would think they were praying to it. A taint of imbecile rapacity blew through it all, like a whiff from some corpse. By Jove! I've never seen anything so unreal in my life. And outside, the silent wilderness surrounding this cleared speck on the earth struck me as something great and invincible, like evil or truth, waiting patiently for the passing away of this fantastic invasion.

"Oh, those months! Well, never mind. Various things happened. One evening a grass shed full of calico, cotton prints, beads, and I don't know what else, burst into a blaze so suddenly that you would have thought the earth had opened to let an avenging fire consume all that trash. I was smoking my pipe quietly by my dismantled steamer, and saw them all cutting capers in the light, with their arms lifted high, when the stout man with moustaches came tearing down to the river, a tin pail in his hand, assured me that everybody was 'behaving splendidly, splendidly,' dipped about a quart of water and tore back again. I noticed there was a hole in the bottom of his pail.

"I strolled up. There was no hurry. You see the thing had gone off like a box of matches. It had been hopeless from the very first. The flame had leaped high, driven everybody back, lighted up everything—and collapsed. The shed was already a heap of embers glowing fiercely. A nigger was being beaten near by. They said he had caused the fire in some way; be that as it may, he was screeching most horribly. I saw him, later on, for several days, sitting in a bit of shade looking very sick and trying to recover himself: afterwards he arose and went out—and the wilderness without a sound took him into its bosom again. As I approached the glow from the dark I found myself at the back of two men, talking. I heard the name of Kurtz pronounced, then the words, 'take advantage of this unfortunate accident.' One of the men was the manager. I wished him a good evening. 'Did you ever see anything like it—eh? it is incredible,' he said, and walked off. The other man remained. He was a first-class agent, young, gentlemanly, a bit reserved, with a forked little beard and a hooked nose. He was stand-offish with the other agents, and they on their side said he was the manager's spy upon them. As to me, I had hardly ever spoken to him before. We got into talk, and by-and-by we strolled away from the hissing ruins. Then he asked me to his room, which was in the main building of the station. He struck a match, and I perceived that this young aristocrat had not only a silver-mounted dressing-case but also a whole candle all to himself. Just at that time the manager was the only man supposed to have any right to candles. Native mats covered the clay walls; a collection of spears, assegais,[8] shields, knives was hung up in trophies. The business intrusted to this fellow was the making of bricks—so I had been informed; but there wasn't a fragment of a brick anywhere in the station, and he had been there more than a year—waiting. It seems he could not make bricks without something, I don't know what—straw maybe. Anyway, it could not be found there, and as it was not likely to be sent from Europe, it did not appear clear to me what he was waiting for. An act of special creation perhaps. However, they were all waiting—all the sixteen or twenty pilgrims of them—for something; and upon my word it did not seem an uncongenial occupation, from the way they took it, though the only thing that ever came to them was disease—as far as I could see. They beguiled the time by backbiting and intriguing against each other in a foolish kind of way. There was an air of plotting about that station, but nothing came of it, of course. It was as unreal as everything else—as the philanthropic pretence of the whole concern, as their talk, as their government, as their show of work. The only real feeling was a desire to get appointed to a trading-post where ivory was to be had, so that they could earn percentages. They intrigued and slandered and hated each other only on that account,—but as to effectually lifting a little finger—oh, no. By heavens! there is something after all in the world allowing one man to steal a horse while another must not look at a halter. Steal a horse straight out. Very well. He has done it. Perhaps he can ride. But there is a way of looking at a halter that would provoke the most charitable of saints into a kick.

"I had no idea why he wanted to be sociable, but as we chatted in there it suddenly occurred to me the fellow was trying to get at something—in fact, pumping me. He alluded constantly to Europe, to the people I was supposed to know there—putting leading questions as to my acquaintances in the sepulchral city, and so on. His little eyes glittered like mica discs—with curiosity,—though he tried to keep up a bit of superciliousness. At first I was astonished, but very soon I became awfully curious to see what he would find out from me. I couldn't possibly imagine what I had in me to make it worth his while. It was very pretty to see how he baffled himself, for in truth my body was full of chills, and my head had nothing in it but that wretched steamboat business. It was evident he took me for a perfectly shameless prevaricator. At last he got angry, and, to conceal a movement of furious annoyance, he yawned. I rose. Then I noticed a small sketch in oils, on a panel, representing a woman, draped and blind-folded, carrying a lighted torch. The background was sombre—almost black. The movement of the woman was stately, and the effect of the torchlight on the face was sinister.

"It arrested me, and he stood by civilly, holding a half-pint champagne bottle (medical comforts) with the candle stuck in it. To my question he said Mr Kurtz had painted this—in this very station more than a year ago—while waiting for means to go to his trading-post. 'Tell me, pray,' said I, 'who is this Mr Kurtz?'

"'The chief of the Inner Station,' he answered in a short tone, looking away. 'Much obliged,' I said, laughing. 'And you are the brickmaker of the Central Station. Every one knows that.' He was silent for a while. 'He is a prodigy,' he said at last. 'He is an emissary of pity, and science, and progress, and devil knows what else. We want,' he began to declaim suddenly, 'for the guidance of the cause intrusted to us by Europe, so to speak, higher intelligence, wide sympathies, a singleness of purpose.'

8. Spears.

'Who says that?' I asked. 'Lots of them,' he replied. 'Some even write that; and so *he* comes here, a special being, as you ought to know.' 'Why ought I to know?' I interrupted, really surprised. He paid no attention. 'Yes. To-day he is chief of the best station, next year he will be assistant-manager, two years more and . . . but I daresay you know what he will be in two years' time. You are of the new gang—the gang of virtue. The same people who sent him specially also recommended you. Oh, don't say no. I've my own eyes to trust.' Light dawned upon me. My dear aunt's influential acquaintances were producing an unexpected effect upon that young man. I nearly burst into a laugh. 'Do you read the Company's confidential correspondence?' I asked. He hadn't a word to say. It was great fun. 'When Mr Kurtz,' I continued severely, 'is General Manager, you won't have the opportunity.'

"He blew the candle out suddenly, and we went outside. The moon had risen. Black figures strolled about listlessly, pouring water on the glow, whence proceeded a sound of hissing; steam ascended in the moonlight; the beaten nigger groaned somewhere. 'What a row the brute makes!' said the indefatigable man with the moustaches, appearing near us. 'Serve him right. Transgression—punishment—bang! Pitiless, pitiless. That's the only way. This will prevent all conflagrations for the future. I was just telling the manager . . .' He noticed my companion, and became crestfallen all at once. 'Not in bed yet,' he said, with a kind of servile heartiness; 'it's so natural. Ha! Danger—agitation.' He vanished. I went on to the river-side, and the other followed me. I heard a scathing murmur at my ear, 'Heap of muffs—go to.' The pilgrims could be seen in knots gesticulating, discussing. Several had still their staves in their hands. I verily believe they took these sticks to bed with them. Beyond the fence the forest stood up spectrally in the moonlight, and through the dim stir, through the faint sounds of that lamentable courtyard, the silence of the land went home to one's very heart,—its mystery, its greatness, the amazing reality of its concealed life. The hurt nigger moaned feebly somewhere near by, and then fetched a deep sigh that made me mend my pace away from there. I felt a hand introducing itself under my arm. 'My dear sir,' said the fellow, 'I don't want to be misunderstood, and especially by you, who will see Mr Kurtz long before I can have that pleasure. I wouldn't like him to get a false idea of my disposition. . . .'

"I let him run on, this papier-mâché Mephistopheles, and it seemed to me that if I tried I could poke my forefinger through him, and would find nothing inside but a little loose dirt, maybe. He, don't you see, had been planning to be assistant-manager by-and-by under the present man, and I could see that the coming of that Kurtz had upset them both not a little. He talked precipitately, and I did not try to stop him. I had my shoulders against the wreck of my steamer, hauled up on the slope like a carcass of some big river animal. The smell of mud, of primeval mud, by Jove! was in my nostrils, the high stillness of primeval forest was before my eyes; there were shiny patches on the black creek. The moon had spread over everything a thin layer of silver—over the rank grass, over the mud, upon the wall of matted vegetation standing higher than the wall of a temple, over the great river I could see through a sombre gap glittering, glittering, as it flowed broadly by without a murmur. All this was great, expectant, mute, while the man jabbered about himself. I wondered whether the stillness on the face of the immensity looking at us two were meant as an appeal or as a menace. What were we who had strayed in here? Could we handle that dumb thing, or would it handle us? I felt how big, how confoundedly big, was that thing that couldn't talk, and perhaps was deaf as well. What was in there? I could see a little ivory coming out from there, and I had heard Mr Kurtz was in there. I had heard enough about it too—God knows! Yet somehow it didn't bring any image with it—no more than if I had been told an angel or a fiend was in there. I believed it in the same way one of you might believe there are inhabitants in the planet Mars. I knew once a Scotch sailmaker who was certain, dead sure, there were people in Mars. If you asked him for some idea how they looked and behaved, he would get shy and mutter something about 'walking on all-fours.' If you as much as smiled, he would—though a man of sixty—offer to fight you. I would not have gone so far as to fight for Kurtz, but I went for him near enough to a lie. You know I hate, detest, and can't bear a lie, not because I am straighter than the rest of us, but simply because it appals me. There is a taint of death, a flavour of mortality in lies,—which is exactly what I hate and detest in the world—what I want to forget. It makes me miserable and sick, like biting something rotten would do. Temperament, I suppose. Well, I went near enough to it by letting the young fool there believe anything he liked to imagine as to my influence in Europe. I became in an instant as much of a pretence as the rest of the bewitched pilgrims. This simply because I had a notion it somehow would be of help to that Kurtz whom at the time I did not see—you understand. He was just a word for me. I did not see the man in the name any more than you do. Do you see him? Do you see the story? Do you see anything? It seems to me I am trying to tell you a dream—making a vain attempt, because no relation of a dream can convey the dream-sensation, that commingling of absurdity, surprise, and bewilderment in a tremor of struggling revolt, that notion of being captured by the incredible which is of the very essence of dreams. . . ."

He was silent for a while.

". . . No, it is impossible; it is impossible to convey the life-sensation of any given epoch of one's existence,—that which makes its truth, its meaning—its subtle and penetrating essence. It is impossible. We live, as we dream—alone. . . ."

He paused again as if reflecting, then added—

"Of course in this you fellows see more than I could then. You see me, whom you know. . . ."

It had become so pitch dark that we listeners could hardly see one another. For a long time already he, sitting apart, had been no more to us than a voice. There was not a word from anybody. The others might have been asleep, but I was awake. I listened, I listened on the watch for the sentence, for the word, that would give me the clue to the faint uneasiness inspired by this narrative that seemed to shape itself without human lips in the heavy night-air of the river.

". . . Yes—I let him run on," Marlow began again, "and think what he pleased about the powers that were behind me. I did! And there was nothing behind me! There was nothing but that wretched, old, mangled steamboat I was leaning against, while he talked fluently about 'the necessity for every man to get on.' 'And when one comes out here, you conceive, it is not to gaze at the moon.' Mr Kurtz was a 'universal genius,' but even a genius would find it easier to work with 'adequate tools—intelligent men.' He did not make bricks—why, there was a physical impossibility in the way—as I was well aware; and if he did secretarial work for the manager, it was because 'no sensible man rejects wantonly the confidence of his superiors.' Did I see it? I saw it. What more did I want? What I really wanted was rivets, by heaven! Rivets. To get on with the work—to stop the hole. Rivets I wanted. There were cases of them down at the coast—cases—piled up—burst—split! You kicked a loose rivet at every second step in that station yard on the hillside. Rivets had rolled into the grove of death. You could fill your pockets with rivets for the trouble of stooping down—

and there wasn't one rivet to be found where it was wanted. We had plates that would do, but nothing to fasten them with. And every week the messenger, a lone negro, letter-bag on shoulder and staff in hand, left our station for the coast. And several times a week a coast caravan came in with trade goods,—ghastly glazed calico that made you shudder only to look at it, glass beads value about a penny a quart, confounded spotted cotton handkerchiefs. And no rivets. Three carriers could have brought all that was wanted to set that steamboat afloat.

"He was becoming confidential now, but I fancy my unresponsive attitude must have exasperated him at last, for he judged it necessary to inform me he feared neither God nor devil, let alone any mere man. I said I could see that very well, but what I wanted was a certain quantity of rivets—and rivets were what really Mr Kurtz wanted, if he had only known it. Now letters went to the coast every week. . . . 'My dear sir,' he cried, 'I write from dictation.' I demanded rivets. There was a way—for an intelligent man. He changed his manner; became very cold, and suddenly began to talk about a hippopotamus; wondered whether sleeping on board the steamer (I stuck to my salvage night and day) I wasn't disturbed. There was an old hippo that had the bad habit of getting out on the bank and roaming at night over the station grounds. The pilgrims used to turn out in a body and empty every rifle they could lay hands on at him. Some even had sat up o' nights for him. All this energy was wasted, though. 'That animal has a charmed life,' he said; 'but you can say this only of brutes in this country. No man—you apprehend me?—no man here bears a charmed life.' He stood there for a moment in the moonlight with his delicate hooked nose set a little askew, and his mica eyes glittering without a wink, then, with a curt Good night, he strode off. I could see he was disturbed and considerably puzzled, which made me feel more hopeful than I had been for days. It was a great comfort to turn from that chap to my influential friend, the battered, twisted, ruined, tin-pot steamboat. I clambered on board. She rang under my feet like an empty Huntley & Palmer[9] biscuit-tin kicked along a gutter; she was nothing so solid in make, and rather less pretty in shape, but I had expended enough hard work on her to make me love her. No influential friend would have served me better. She had given me a chance to come out a bit—to find out what I could do. No, I don't like work. I had rather laze about and think of all the fine things that can be done. I don't like work—no man does—but I like what is in the work,—the chance to find yourself. Your own reality—for yourself, not for others—what no other man can ever know. They can only see the mere show, and never can tell what it really means.

"I was not surprised to see somebody sitting aft, on the deck, with his legs dangling over the mud. You see I rather chummed with the few mechanics there were in that station, whom the other pilgrims naturally despised—on account of their imperfect manners, I suppose. This was the foreman—a boiler-maker by trade—a good worker. He was a lank, bony, yellow-faced man, with big intense eyes. His aspect was worried, and his head was as bald as the palm of my hand; but his hair in falling seemed to have stuck to his chin, and had prospered in the new locality, for his beard hung down to his waist. He was a widower with six young children (he had left them in charge of a sister of his to come out there), and the passion of his life was pigeon-flying. He was an enthusiast and a connoisseur. He would rave about pigeons. After work hours he used sometimes to come over from his hut for a talk about his children and his pigeons; at work, when he had to crawl in the mud under the bottom of the

9. A brand of English cookies.

steamboat, he would tie up that beard of his in a kind of white serviette[1] he brought for the purpose. It had loops to go over his ears. In the evening he could be seen squatted on the bank rinsing that wrapper in the creek with great care, then spreading it solemnly on a bush to dry.

"I slapped him on the back and shouted 'We shall have rivets!' He scrambled to his feet exclaiming 'No! Rivets!' as though he couldn't believe his ears. Then in a low voice, 'You . . . eh?' I don't know why we behaved like lunatics. I put my finger to the side of my nose and nodded mysteriously. 'Good for you!' he cried, snapped his fingers above his head, lifting one foot. I tried a jig. We capered on the iron deck. A frightful clatter came out of that hulk, and the virgin forest on the other bank of the creek sent it back in a thundering roll upon the sleeping station. It must have made some of the pilgrims sit up in their hovels. A dark figure obscured the lighted doorway of the manager's hut, vanished, then, a second or so after, the doorway itself vanished too. We stopped, and the silence driven away by the stamping of our feet flowed back again from the recesses of the land. The great wall of vegetation, an exuberant and entangled mass of trunks, branches, leaves, boughs, festoons, motionless in the moonlight, was like a rioting invasion of soundless life, a rolling wave of plants, piled up, crested, ready to topple over the creek, to sweep every little man of us out of his little existence. And it moved not. A deadened burst of mighty splashes and snorts reached us from afar, as though an ichthyosaurus had been taking a bath of glitter in the great river. 'After all,' said the boiler-maker in a reasonable tone, 'why shouldn't we get the rivets?' Why not, indeed! I did not know of any reason why we shouldn't. 'They'll come in three weeks,' I said, confidently.

"But they didn't. Instead of rivets there came an invasion, an infliction, a visitation. It came in sections during the next three weeks, each section headed by a donkey carrying a white man in new clothes and tan shoes, bowing from that elevation right and left to the impressed pilgrims. A quarrelsome band of footsore sulky niggers trod on the heels of the donkey; a lot of tents, camp-stools, tin boxes, white cases, brown bales would be shot down in the courtyard, and the air of mystery would deepen a little over the muddle of the station. Five such instalments came, with their absurd air of disorderly flight with the loot of innumerable outfit shops and provision stores, that, one would think, they were lugging, after a raid, into the wilderness for equitable division. It was an inextricable mess of things decent in themselves but that human folly made look like the spoils of thieving.

"This devoted band called itself the Eldorado Exploring Expedition,[2] and I believe they were sworn to secrecy. Their talk, however, was the talk of sordid buccaneers: it was reckless without hardihood, greedy without audacity, and cruel without courage; there was not an atom of foresight or of serious intention in the whole batch of them, and they did not seem aware these things are wanted for the work of the world. To tear treasure out of the bowels of the land was their desire, with no more moral purpose at the back of it than there is in burglars breaking into a safe. Who paid the expenses of the noble enterprise I don't know; but the uncle of our manager was leader of that lot.

"In exterior he resembled a butcher in a poor neighbourhood, and his eyes had a look of sleepy cunning. He carried his fat paunch with ostentation on his short legs, and during the time his gang infested the station spoke to no one but his nephew. You could see these two roaming about all day long with their heads close together in an everlasting confab.

---

1. Napkin.
2. Eldorado, legendary land of gold in South America and the object of many fruitless 16th-century Spanish expeditions.

"I had given up worrying myself about the rivets. One's capacity for that kind of folly is more limited than you would suppose. I said Hang!—and let things slide. I had plenty of time for meditation, and now and then I would give some thought to Kurtz. I wasn't very interested in him. No. Still, I was curious to see whether this man, who had come out equipped with moral ideas of some sort, would climb to the top after all, and how he would set about his work when there."

2

"One evening as I was lying flat on the deck of my steamboat, I heard voices approaching—and there were the nephew and the uncle strolling along the bank. I laid my head on my arm again, and had nearly lost myself in a doze, when somebody said in my ear, as it were: 'I am as harmless as a little child, but I don't like to be dictated to. Am I the manager—or am I not? I was ordered to send him there. It's incredible.' . . . I became aware that the two were standing on the shore alongside the forepart of the steamboat, just below my head. I did not move; it did not occur to me to move: I was sleepy. 'It *is* unpleasant,' grunted the uncle. 'He has asked the Administration to be sent there,' said the other, 'with the idea of showing what he could do; and I was instructed accordingly. Look at the influence that man must have. Is it not frightful?' They both agreed it was frightful, then made several bizarre remarks: 'Make rain and fine weather—one man—the Council—by the nose'—bits of absurd sentences that got the better of my drowsiness, so that I had pretty near the whole of my wits about me when the uncle said, 'The climate may do away with this difficulty for you. Is he alone there?' 'Yes,' answered the manager; 'he sent his assistant down the river with a note to me in these terms: "Clear this poor devil out of the country, and don't bother sending more of that sort. I had rather be alone than have the kind of men you can dispose of with me." It was more than a year ago. Can you imagine such impudence?' 'Anything since then?' asked the other, hoarsely. 'Ivory,' jerked the nephew; 'lots of it—prime sort—lots—most annoying, from him.' 'And with that?' questioned the heavy rumble. 'Invoice,' was the reply fired out, so to speak. Then silence. They had been talking about Kurtz.

"I was broad awake by this time, but, lying perfectly at ease, remained still, having no inducement to change my position. 'How did that ivory come all this way?' growled the elder man, who seemed very vexed. The other explained that it had come with a fleet of canoes in charge of an English half-caste clerk Kurtz had with him; that Kurtz had apparently intended to return himself, the station being by that time bare of goods and stores, but after coming three hundred miles, had suddenly decided to go back, which he started to do alone in a small dug-out with four paddlers, leaving the half-caste to continue down the river with the ivory. The two fellows there seemed astounded at anybody attempting such a thing. They were at a loss for an adequate motive. As to me, I seemed to see Kurtz for the first time. It was a distinct glimpse: the dug-out, four paddling savages, and the lone white man turning his back suddenly on the headquarters, on relief, on thoughts of home—perhaps; setting his face towards the depths of the wilderness, towards his empty and desolate station. I did not know the motive. Perhaps he was just simply a fine fellow who stuck to his work for its own sake. His name, you understand, had not been pronounced once. He was 'that man.' The half-caste, who, as far as I could see, had conducted a difficult trip with great prudence and pluck, was invariably alluded to as 'that scoundrel.' The 'scoundrel' had reported that the 'man' had been very ill—had recovered imperfectly.

. . . The two below me moved away then a few paces, and strolled back and forth at some little distance. I heard: 'Military post—doctor—two hundred miles—quite alone now—unavoidable delays—nine months—no news—strange rumours.' They approached again, just as the manager was saying, 'No one, as far as I know, unless a species of wandering trader—a pestilential fellow, snapping ivory from the natives.' Who was it they were talking about now? I gathered in snatches that this was some man supposed to be in Kurtz's district, and of whom the manager did not approve. 'We will not be free from unfair competition till one of these fellows is hanged for an example,' he said. 'Certainly,' grunted the other; 'get him hanged! Why not? Any-thing—anything can be done in this country. That's what I say; nobody here, you understand, *here*, can endanger your position. And why? You stand the climate—you outlast them all. The danger is in Europe; but there before I left I took care to—' They moved off and whispered, then their voices rose again. 'The extraordinary series of delays is not my fault. I did my possible.' The fat man sighed, 'Very sad.' 'And the pestiferous absurdity of his talk,' continued the other; 'he bothered me enough when he was here. "Each station should be like a beacon on the road towards better things, a centre for trade of course, but also for humanising, improving, instructing." Conceive you—that ass! And he wants to be manager! No, it's—' Here he got choked by excessive indignation, and I lifted my head the least bit. I was sur-prised to see how near they were—right under me. I could have spat upon their hats. They were looking on the ground, absorbed in thought. The manager was switching his leg with a slender twig: his sagacious relative lifted his head. 'You have been well since you came out this time?' he asked. The other gave a start. 'Who? I? Oh! Like a charm—like a charm. But the rest—oh, my goodness! All sick. They die so quick, too, that I haven't the time to send them out of the country—it's incredible!' 'H'm. Just so,' grunted the uncle. 'Ah! my boy, trust to this—I say, trust to this.' I saw him extend his short flipper of an arm for a gesture that took in the forest, the creek, the mud, the river,—seemed to beckon with a dishonouring flourish before the sunlit face of the land a treacherous appeal to the lurking death, to the hidden evil, to the profound darkness of its heart. It was so startling that I leaped to my feet and looked back at the edge of the forest, as though I had expected an answer of some sort to that black display of confidence. You know the foolish notions that come to one some-times. The high stillness confronted these two figures with its ominous patience, waiting for the passing away of a fantastic invasion.

"They swore aloud together—out of sheer fright, I believe—then, pretending not to know anything of my existence, turned back to the station. The sun was low; and leaning forward side by side, they seemed to be tugging painfully uphill their two ridiculous shadows of unequal length, that trailed behind them slowly over the tall grass without bending a single blade.

"In a few days the Eldorado Expedition went into the patient wilderness, that closed upon it as the sea closes over a diver. Long afterwards the news came that all the donkeys were dead. I know nothing as to the fate of the less valuable animals. They, no doubt, like the rest of us, found what they deserved. I did not inquire. I was then rather excited at the prospect of meeting Kurtz very soon. When I say very soon I mean it comparatively. It was just two months from the day we left the creek when we came to the bank below Kurtz's station.

"Going up that river was like travelling back to the earliest beginnings of the world, when vegetation rioted on the earth and the big trees were kings. An empty stream, a great silence, an impenetrable forest. The air was warm, thick, heavy, sluggish. There was no joy in the brilliance of sunshine. The long stretches of the water-way ran on, deserted, into the gloom of overshadowed distances. On silvery sand-banks hippos and alligators sunned themselves side by side. The broadening waters flowed through a mob of wooded islands; you lost your way on that river as you would in a desert, and butted all day long against shoals, trying to find the channel, till you thought yourself bewitched and cut off for ever from everything you had known once—somewhere—far away—in another existence perhaps. There were moments when one's past came back to one, as it will sometimes when you have not a moment to spare to yourself; but it came in the shape of an unrestful and noisy dream, remembered with wonder amongst the overwhelming realities of this strange world of plants, and water, and silence. And this stillness of life did not in the least resemble a peace. It was the stillness of an implacable force brooding over an inscrutable intention. It looked at you with a vengeful aspect. I got used to it afterwards; I did not see it any more; I had no time. I had to keep guessing at the channel; I had to discern, mostly by inspiration, the signs of hidden banks; I watched for sunken stones; I was learning to clap my teeth smartly before my heart flew out, when I shaved by a fluke some infernal sly old snag that would have ripped the life out of the tin-pot steamboat and drowned all the pilgrims; I had to keep a look-out for the signs of dead wood we could cut up in the night for next day's steaming. When you have to attend to things of that sort, to the mere incidents of the surface, the reality—the reality, I tell you—fades. The inner truth is hidden—luckily, luckily. But I felt it all the same; I felt often its mysterious stillness watching me at my monkey tricks, just as it watches you fellows performing on your respective tight-ropes for—what is it? half-a-crown a tumble—"

"Try to be civil, Marlow," growled a voice, and I knew there was at least one listener awake besides myself.

"I beg your pardon. I forgot the heartache which makes up the rest of the price. And indeed what does the price matter, if the trick be well done? You do your tricks very well. And I didn't do badly either, since I managed not to sink that steamboat on my first trip. It's a wonder to me yet. Imagine a blindfolded man set to drive a van over a bad road. I sweated and shivered over that business considerably, I can tell you. After all, for a seaman, to scrape the bottom of the thing that's supposed to float all the time under his care is the unpardonable sin. No one may know of it, but you never forget the thump—eh? A blow on the very heart. You remember it, you dream of it, you wake up at night and think of it—years after—and go hot and cold all over. I don't pretend to say that steamboat floated all the time. More than once she had to wade for a bit, with twenty cannibals splashing around and pushing. We had enlisted some of these chaps on the way for a crew. Fine fellows—cannibals—in their place. They were men one could work with, and I am grateful to them. And, after all, they did not eat each other before my face: they had brought along a provision of hippo-meat which went rotten, and made the mystery of the wilderness stink in my nostrils. Phoo! I can sniff it now. I had the manager on board and three or four pilgrims with their staves—all complete. Sometimes we came upon a station close by the bank, clinging to the skirts of the unknown, and the white men rushing out of a tumble-down hovel, with great gestures of joy and surprise and welcome, seemed very strange,—had the appearance of being held there captive by a spell. The word 'ivory' would ring in the air for a while—and on we went again into the silence, along empty reaches, round the still bends, between the high walls of our winding way, reverberating in hollow claps the ponderous beat of the stern-wheel. Trees, trees, millions of trees, massive, immense, running up high; and at their foot, hugging the bank against the stream, crept the little begrimed steamboat, like a sluggish beetle crawling on the floor of a lofty portico. It made you feel very small, very lost, and yet it was not altogether depressing that feeling. After all, if you were small, the grimy beetle crawled on—which was just what you wanted it to do. Where the pilgrims imagined it crawled to I don't know. To some place where they expected to get something, I bet! For me it crawled towards Kurtz—exclusively; but when the steam-pipes started leaking we crawled very slow. The reaches opened before us and closed behind, as if the forest had stepped leisurely across the water to bar the way for our return. We penetrated deeper and deeper into the heart of darkness. It was very quiet there. At night sometimes the roll of drums behind the curtain of trees would run up the river and remain sustained faintly, as if hovering in the air high over our heads, till the first break of day. Whether it meant war, peace, or prayer we could not tell. The dawns were heralded by the descent of a chill stillness; the woodcutters slept, their fires burned low; the snapping of a twig would make you start. We were wanderers on a prehistoric earth, on an earth that wore the aspect of an unknown planet. We could have fancied ourselves the first of men taking possession of an accursed inheritance, to be subdued at the cost of profound anguish and of excessive toil. But suddenly, as we struggled round a bend, there would be a glimpse of rush walls, of peaked grass-roofs, a burst of yells, a whirl of black limbs, a mass of hands clapping, of feet stamping, of bodies swaying, of eyes rolling, under the droop of heavy and motionless foliage. The steamer toiled along slowly on the edge of a black and incomprehensible frenzy. The prehistoric man was cursing us, praying to us, welcoming us—who could tell? We were cut off from the comprehension of our surroundings; we glided past like phantoms, wondering and secretly appalled, as sane men would be before an enthusiastic outbreak in a madhouse. We could not understand, because we were too far and could not remember, because we were travelling in the night of first ages, of those ages that are gone, leaving hardly a sign—and no memories.

"The earth seemed unearthly. We are accustomed to look upon the shackled form of a conquered monster, but there—there you could look at a thing monstrous and free. It was unearthly, and the men were—No, they were not inhuman. Well, you know, that was the worst of it—this suspicion of their not being inhuman. It would come slowly to one. They howled, and leaped, and spun, and made horrid faces; but what thrilled you was just the thought of their humanity—like yours—the thought of your remote kinship with this wild and passionate uproar. Ugly. Yes, it was ugly enough; but if you were man enough you would admit to yourself that there was in you just the faintest trace of a response to the terrible frankness of that noise, a dim suspicion of there being a meaning in it which you—you so remote from the night of first ages—could comprehend. And why not? The mind of man is capable of anything—because everything is in it, all the past as well as all the future. What was there after all? Joy, fear, sorrow, devotion, valour, rage—who can tell?—but truth—truth stripped of its cloak of time. Let the fool gape and shudder—the man knows, and can look on without a wink. But he must at least be as much of a man as these on the shore. He must meet that truth with his own true stuff—with his own inborn strength. Principles? Principles won't do. Acquisitions, clothes, pretty rags—rags that would fly off at the first good shake. No; you want a deliberate belief. An appeal to me in this fiendish row—is there? Very well; I hear; I admit, but I have a voice too, and for good or evil mine is the speech that cannot be silenced. Of course, a fool, what with sheer fright and fine sentiments, is always safe. Who's that grunting? You wonder I didn't go ashore for a howl and a dance? Well, no—I didn't. Fine sentiments, you say? Fine sentiments be hanged! I had no time. I had to mess about with white-lead and strips of woollen blanket helping to put bandages on those leaky steam-pipes—I tell you. I had to watch the steering, and circumvent those snags, and get the tin-pot along by hook or by crook. There was surface-truth enough in these things to save a wiser man. And between whiles I had to look after the savage who was fireman. He was an improved specimen; he could fire up a vertical boiler. He was there below me, and, upon my word, to look at him was as edifying as seeing a dog in a parody of breeches and a feather hat, walking on his hind-legs. A few months of training had done for that really fine chap. He squinted at the steam-gauge and at the water-gauge with an evident effort of intrepidity—and he had filed teeth too, the poor devil, and the wool of his pate shaved into queer patterns, and three ornamental scars on each of his cheeks. He ought to have been clapping his hands and stamping his feet on the bank, instead of which he was hard at work, a thrall to strange witch-craft, full of improving knowledge. He was useful because he had been instructed; and what he knew was this—that should the water in that transparent thing disappear, the evil spirit inside the boiler would get angry through the greatness of his thirst, and take a terrible vengeance. So he sweated and fired up and watched the glass fearfully (with an impromptu charm, made of rags, tied to his arm, and a piece of polished bone, as big as a watch, stuck flatways through his lower lip), while the wooded banks slipped past us slowly, the short noise was left behind, the interminable miles of silence—and we crept on, towards Kurtz. But the snags were thick, the water was treacherous and shallow, the boiler seemed indeed to have a sulky devil in it, and thus neither that fireman nor I had any time to peer into our creepy thoughts.

"Some fifty miles below the Inner Station we came upon a hut of reeds, an inclined and melancholy pole, with the unrecognisable tatters of what had been a flag of some sort flying from it, and a neatly stacked wood-pile. This was unexpected. We came to the bank, and on the stack of firewood found a flat piece of board with some faded pencil-writing on it. When deciphered it said: 'Wood for you. Hurry up. Approach cautiously.' There was a signature, but it was illegible—not Kurtz—a much longer word. Hurry up. Where? Up the river? 'Approach cautiously.' We had not done so. But the warning could not have been meant for the place where it could be only found after approach. Something was wrong above. But what—and how much? That was the question. We commented adversely upon the imbecility of that telegraphic style. The bush around said nothing, and would not let us look very far, either. A torn curtain of red twill hung in the doorway of the hut, and flapped sadly in our faces. The dwelling was dismantled; but we could see a white man had lived there not very long ago. There remained a rude table—a plank on two posts; a heap of rubbish reposed in a dark corner, and by the door I picked up a book. It had lost its covers, and the pages had been thumbed into a state of extremely dirty softness; but the back had been lovingly stitched afresh with white cotton thread, which looked clean yet. It was an extraordinary find. Its title was, 'An Inquiry into some Points of Seamanship,' by a man Tower, Towson—some such name—Master in his Majesty's Navy. The matter looked dreary reading enough, with illustrative diagrams and repulsive tables of figures, and the copy was sixty years old. I handled this amazing antiquity with the greatest possible tenderness, lest it should dissolve in my hands. Within, Towson or Towser was inquiring earnestly into the breaking strain of ships' chains and tackle, and other such matters. Not a very enthralling book; but at the first glance you could see there a singleness of intention, an honest concern for the right way of going to work, which made these humble pages, thought out so many years ago, luminous with another than a professional light. The simple old sailor, with his talk of chains and purchases, made me forget the jungle and the pilgrims in a delicious sensation of having come upon something unmistakably real. Such a book being there was wonderful enough; but still more astounding were the notes pencilled in the margin, and plainly referring to the text. I couldn't believe my eyes! They were in cipher! Yes, it looked like cipher. Fancy a man lugging with him a book of that description into this nowhere and studying it—and making notes—in cipher at that! It was an extravagant mystery.

"I had been dimly aware for some time of a worrying noise, and when I lifted my eyes I saw the wood-pile was gone, and the manager, aided by all the pilgrims, was shouting at me from the river-side. I slipped the book into my pocket. I assure you to leave off reading was like tearing myself away from the shelter of an old and solid friendship.

"I started the lame engine ahead. 'It must be this miserable trader—this intruder,' exclaimed the manager, looking back malevolently at the place we had left. 'He must be English,' I said. 'It will not save him from getting into trouble if he is not careful,' muttered the manager darkly. I observed with assumed innocence that no man was safe from trouble in this world.

"The current was more rapid now, the steamer seemed at her last gasp, the stern-wheel flopped languidly, and I caught myself listening on tiptoe for the next beat of the float, for in sober truth I expected the wretched thing to give up every moment. It was like watching the last flickers of a life. But still we crawled. Sometimes I would pick out a tree a little way ahead to measure our progress towards Kurtz by, but I lost it invariably before we got abreast. To keep the eyes so long on one thing was too much for human patience. The manager displayed a beautiful resignation. I fretted and fumed and took to arguing with myself whether or no I would talk openly with Kurtz; but before I could come to any conclusion it occurred to me that my speech or my silence, indeed any action of mine, would be a mere futility. What did it matter what any one knew or ignored? What did it matter who was manager? One gets sometimes such a flash of insight. The essentials of this affair lay deep under the surface, beyond my reach, and beyond my power of meddling.

"Towards the evening of the second day we judged ourselves about eight miles from Kurtz's station. I wanted to push on; but the manager looked grave, and told me the navigation up there was so dangerous that it would be advisable, the sun being very low already, to wait where we were till next morning. Moreover, he pointed out that if the warning to approach cautiously were to be followed, we must approach in daylight—not at dusk, or in the dark. This was sensible enough. Eight miles meant nearly three hours' steaming for us, and I could also see suspicious ripples at the upper end of the reach. Nevertheless, I was annoyed beyond expression at the delay, and most unreasonably too, since one night more could not matter much after so many months. As we had plenty of wood, and caution was the word, I brought up in the middle of the stream. The reach was narrow, straight, with high sides like a railway cutting. The dusk came gliding into it long before the sun had set. The current ran smooth and swift, but a dumb immobility sat on the banks. The living trees, lashed together by the creepers and every living bush of the undergrowth, might have been changed into stone, even to the slenderest twig, to the lightest leaf. It was not sleep—it seemed unnatural, like a state of trance. Not the faintest sound of any kind could be heard. You looked on amazed, and began to suspect yourself of being deaf—

then the night came suddenly, and struck you blind as well. About three in the morning some large fish leaped, and the loud splash made me jump as though a gun had been fired. When the sun rose there was a white fog, very warm and clammy, and more blinding than the night. It did not shift or drive; it was just there, standing all round you like something solid. At eight or nine, perhaps, it lifted as a shutter lifts. We had a glimpse of the towering multitude of trees, of the immense matted jungle, with the blazing little ball of the sun hanging over it—all perfectly still—and then the white shutter came down again, smoothly, as if sliding in greased grooves. I ordered the chain, which we had begun to heave in, to be paid out again. Before it stopped running with a muffled rattle, a cry, a very loud cry, as of infinite desolation, soared slowly in the opaque air. It ceased. A complaining clamour, modulated in savage discords, filled our ears. The sheer unexpectedness of it made my hair stir under my cap. I don't know how it struck the others: to me it seemed as though the mist itself had screamed, so suddenly, and apparently from all sides at once, did this tumultuous and mournful uproar arise. It culminated in a hurried outbreak of almost intolerably excessive shrieking, which stopped short, leaving us stiffened in a variety of silly attitudes, and obstinately listening to the nearly as appalling and excessive silence. 'Good God! What is the meaning—?' stammered at my elbow one of the pilgrims,—a little fat man, with sandy hair and red whiskers, who wore side-spring boots, and pink pyjamas tucked into his socks. Two others remained open-mouthed a whole minute, then dashed into the little cabin, to rush out incontinently and stand darting scared glances, with Winchesters at 'ready' in their hands. What we could see was just the steamer we were on, her outlines blurred as though she had been on the point of dissolving, and a misty strip of water, perhaps two feet broad, around her— and that was all. The rest of the world was nowhere, as far as our eyes and ears were concerned. Just nowhere. Gone, disappeared; swept off without leaving a whisper or a shadow behind.

"I went forward, and ordered the chain to be hauled in short, so as to be ready to trip the anchor and move the steamboat at once if necessary. 'Will they attack?' whispered an awed voice. 'We will all be butchered in this fog,' murmured another. The faces twitched with the strain, the hands trembled slightly, the eyes forgot to wink. It was very curious to see the contrast of expressions of the white men and of the black fellows of our crew, who were as much strangers to that part of the river as we, though their homes were only eight hundred miles away. The whites, of course greatly discomposed, had besides a curious look of being painfully shocked by such an outrageous row. The others had an alert, naturally interested expression; but their faces were essentially quiet, even those of the one or two who grinned as they hauled at the chain. Several exchanged short, grunting phrases, which seemed to settle the matter to their satisfaction. Their headman, a young, broad-chested black, severely draped in dark-blue fringed cloths, with fierce nostrils and his hair all done up artfully in oily ringlets, stood near me. 'Aha!' I said, just for good fellowship's sake. 'Catch 'im,' he snapped, with a bloodshot widening of his eyes and a flash of sharp teeth— 'catch 'im. Give 'im to us.' 'To you, eh?' I asked; 'what would you do with them?' 'Eat 'im!' he said, curtly, and, leaning his elbow on the rail, looked out into the fog in a dignified and profoundly pensive attitude. I would no doubt have been properly horrified, had it not occurred to me that he and his chaps must be very hungry: that they must have been growing increasingly hungry for at least this month past. They had been engaged for six months (I don't think a single one of them had any clear idea of time, as we at the end of countless ages have. They still belonged to the beginnings of time—had no inherited experience to teach them, as it were), and of course, as long as there was a piece of paper written over in accordance with some farcical law or other made down the river, it didn't enter anybody's head to trouble how they would live. Certainly they had brought with them some rotten hippo-meat, which couldn't have lasted very long, anyway, even if the pilgrims hadn't, in the midst of a shocking hullabaloo, thrown a considerable quantity of it overboard. It looked like a high-handed proceeding; but it was really a case of legitimate self-defence. You can't breathe dead hippo waking, sleeping, and eating, and at the same time keep your precarious grip on existence. Besides that, they had given them every week three pieces of brass wire, each about nine inches long; and the theory was they were to buy their provisions with that currency in river-side villages. You can see how *that* worked. There were either no villages, or the people were hostile, or the director, who like the rest of us fed out of tins, with an occasional old he-goat thrown in, didn't want to stop the steamer for some more or less recondite reason. So, unless they swallowed the wire itself, or made loops of it to snare the fishes with, I don't see what good their extravagant salary could be to them. I must say it was paid with a regularity worthy of a large and honourable trading company. For the rest, the only thing to eat—though it didn't look eatable in the least—I saw in their possession was a few lumps of some stuff like half-cooked dough, of a dirty lavender colour, they kept wrapped in leaves, and now and then swallowed a piece of, but so small that it seemed done more for the looks of the thing than for any serious purpose of sustenance. Why in the name of all the gnawing devils of hunger they didn't go for us—they were thirty to five—and have a good tuck-in for once, amazes me now when I think of it. They were big powerful men, with not much capacity to weigh the consequences, with courage, with strength, even yet, though their skins were no longer glossy and their muscles no longer hard. And I saw that something restraining, one of those human secrets that baffle probability, had come into play there. I looked at them with a swift quickening of interest—not because it occurred to me I might be eaten by them before very long, though I own to you that just then I perceived—in a new light, as it were—how unwholesome the pilgrims looked, and I hoped, yes, I positively hoped, that my aspect was not so—what shall I say?—so—unappetising: a touch of fantastic vanity which fitted well with the dream-sensation that pervaded all my days at that time. Perhaps I had a little fever too. One can't live with one's finger everlastingly on one's pulse. I had often 'a little fever,' or a little touch of other things—the playful paw-strokes of the wilderness, the preliminary trifling before the more serious onslaught which came in due course. Yes; I looked at them as you would on any human being, with a curiosity of their impulses, motives, capacities, weaknesses, when brought to the test of an inexorable physical necessity. Restraint! What possible restraint? Was it superstition, disgust, patience, fear—or some kind of primitive honour? No fear can stand up to hunger, no patience can wear it out, disgust simply does not exist where hunger is; and as to superstition, beliefs, and what you may call principles, they are less than chaff in a breeze. Don't you know the devilry of lingering starvation, its exasperating torment, its black thoughts, its sombre and brooding ferocity? Well, I do. It takes a man all his inborn strength to fight hunger properly. It's really easier to face bereavement, dishonour, and the perdition of one's soul—than this kind of prolonged hunger. Sad, but true. And these chaps too had no earthly reason for any kind of scruple. Restraint! I would just as soon have expected restraint from a hyena prowling amongst the corpses of a battlefield. But there was the fact facing me—the fact dazzling, to be seen, like the foam on the depths of the sea, like a ripple on an unfathomable enigma, a mystery greater—when I thought of it—than the curious, inexplicable note of desperate grief in this savage clamour that had swept by us on the river-bank, behind the blind whiteness of the fog.

"Two pilgrims were quarrelling in hurried whispers as to which bank. 'Left.' 'No, no; how can you? Right, right, of course.' 'It is very serious,' said the manager's voice behind me; 'I would be desolated if anything should happen to Mr Kurtz before we came up.' I looked at him, and had not the slightest doubt he was sincere. He was just the kind of man who would wish to preserve appearances. That was his restraint. But when he muttered something about going on at once, I did not even take the trouble to answer him. I knew, and he knew, that it was impossible. Were we to let go our hold of the bottom, we would be absolutely in the air—in space. We wouldn't be able to tell where we were going to—whether up or down stream, or across—till we fetched against one bank or the other,—and then we wouldn't know at first which it was. Of course I made no move. I had no mind for a smash-up. You couldn't imagine a more deadly place for a shipwreck. Whether drowned at once or not, we were sure to perish speedily in one way or another. 'I authorise you to take all the risks,' he said, after a short silence. 'I refuse to take any,' I said shortly; which was just the answer he expected, though its tone might have surprised him. 'Well, I must defer to your judgment. You are captain,' he said, with marked civility. I turned my shoulder to him in sign of my appreciation, and looked into the fog. How long would it last? It was the most hopeless look-out. The approach to this Kurtz grubbing for ivory in the wretched bush was beset by as many dangers as though he had been an enchanted princess sleeping in a fabulous castle. 'Will they attack, do you think?' asked the manager, in a confidential tone.

"I did not think they would attack, for several obvious reasons. The thick fog was one. If they left the bank in their canoes they would get lost in it, as we would be if we attempted to move. Still, I had also judged the jungle of both banks quite impenetrable—and yet eyes were in it, eyes that had seen us. The river-side bushes were certainly very thick; but the undergrowth behind was evidently penetrable. However, during the short lift I had seen no canoes anywhere in the reach—certainly not abreast of the steamer. But what made the idea of attack inconceivable to me was the nature of the noise—of the cries we had heard. They had not the fierce character boding of immediate hostile intention. Unexpected, wild, and violent as they had been, they had given me an irresistible impression of sorrow. The glimpse of the steamboat had for some reason filled those savages with unrestrained grief. The danger, if any, I expounded, was from our proximity to a great human passion let loose. Even extreme grief may ultimately vent itself in violence—but more generally takes the form of apathy. . . .

"You should have seen the pilgrims stare! They had no heart to grin, or even to revile me; but I believe they thought me gone mad—with fright, maybe. I delivered a regular lecture. My dear boys, it was no good bothering. Keep a look-out? Well, you may guess I watched the fog for the signs of lifting as a cat watches a mouse; but for anything else our eyes were of no more use to us than if we had been buried miles deep in a heap of cotton-wool. It felt like it too—choking, warm, stifling. Besides, all I said, though it sounded extravagant, was absolutely true to fact. What we afterwards alluded to as an attack was really an attempt at repulse. The action was very far from being aggressive—it was not even defensive, in the usual sense: it was undertaken under the stress of desperation, and in its essence was purely protective.

"It developed itself, I should say, two hours after the fog lifted, and its commencement was at a spot, roughly speaking, about a mile and a half below Kurtz's station. We had just floundered and flopped round a bend, when I saw an islet, a mere grassy hummock of bright green, in the middle of the stream. It was the only thing of the kind; but as we opened the reach more, I perceived it was the head of a long sandbank, or rather of a chain of shallow patches stretching down the middle of the river. They were discoloured, just awash, and the whole lot was seen just under the water, exactly as a man's backbone is seen running down the middle of his back under the skin. Now, as far as I did see, I could go to the right or to the left of this. I didn't know either channel, of course. The banks looked pretty well alike, the depth appeared the same; but as I had been informed the station was on the west side, I naturally headed for the western passage.

"No sooner had we fairly entered it than I became aware it was much narrower than I had supposed. To the left of us there was the long uninterrupted shoal, and to the right a high, steep bank heavily overgrown with bushes. Above the bush the trees stood in serried ranks. The twigs overhung the current thickly, and from distance to distance a large limb of some tree projected rigidly over the stream. It was then well on in the afternoon, the face of the forest was gloomy, and a broad strip of shadow had already fallen on the water. In this shadow we steamed up—very slowly, as you may imagine. I sheered her well inshore—the water being deepest near the bank, as the sounding-pole informed me.

"One of my hungry and forbearing friends was sounding in the bows just below me. This steamboat was exactly like a decked scow.[3] On the deck there were two little teak-wood houses, with doors and windows. The boiler was in the fore-end, and the machinery right astern. Over the whole there was a light roof, supported on stanchions. The funnel projected through that roof, and in front of the funnel a small cabin built of light planks served for a pilot-house. It contained a couch, two camp-stools, a loaded Martini-Henry[4] leaning in one corner, a tiny table, and the steering-wheel. It had a wide door in front and a broad shutter at each side. All these were always thrown open, of course. I spent my days perched up there on the extreme fore-end of that roof, before the door. At night I slept, or tried to, on the couch. An athletic black belonging to some coast tribe, and educated by my poor predecessor, was the helmsman. He sported a pair of brass earrings, wore a blue cloth wrapper from the waist to the ankles, and thought all the world of himself. He was the most unstable kind of fool I had ever seen. He steered with no end of a swagger while you were by; but if he lost sight of you, he became instantly the prey of an abject funk, and would let that cripple of a steamboat get the upper hand of him in a minute.

"I was looking down at the sounding-pole, and feeling much annoyed to see at each try a little more of it stick out of that river, when I saw my poleman give up the business suddenly, and stretch himself flat on the deck, without even taking the trouble to haul his pole in. He kept hold on it though, and it trailed in the water. At the same time the fireman, whom I could also see below me, sat down abruptly before his furnace and ducked his head. I was amazed. Then I had to look at the river mighty quick, because there was a snag in the fairway. Sticks, little sticks, were flying about—thick: they were whizzing before my nose, dropping below me, striking behind me against my pilot-house. All this time the river, the shore, the woods, were very quiet—perfectly quiet. I could only hear the heavy splashing thump of the stern-wheel and the patter of these things. We cleared the snag clumsily. Arrows, by Jove!

---

3. A flat-bottomed boat.   4. A rifle.

We were being shot at! I stepped in quickly to close the shutter on the landside. That fool-helmsman, his hands on the spokes, was lifting his knees high, stamping his feet, champing his mouth, like a reined-in horse. Confound him! And we were staggering within ten feet of the bank. I had to lean right out to swing the heavy shutter, and I saw a face amongst the leaves on the level with my own, looking at me very fierce and steady; and then suddenly, as though a veil had been removed from my eyes, I made out, deep in the tangled gloom, naked breasts, arms, legs, glaring eyes,—the bush was swarming with human limbs in movement, glistening, of bronze colour. The twigs shook, swayed, and rustled, the arrows flew out of them, and then the shutter came to. 'Steer her straight,' I said to the helmsman. He held his head rigid, face forward; but his eyes rolled, he kept on lifting and setting down his feet gently, his mouth foamed a little. 'Keep quiet!' I said in a fury. I might just as well have ordered a tree not to sway in the wind. I darted out. Below me there was a great scuffle of feet on the iron deck; confused exclamations; a voice screamed, 'Can you turn back?' I caught sight of a V-shaped ripple on the water ahead. What? Another snag! A fusillade burst out under my feet. The pilgrims had opened with their Winchesters, and were simply squirting lead into that bush. A deuce of a lot of smoke came up and drove slowly forward. I swore at it. Now I couldn't see the ripple or the snag either. I stood in the doorway, peering, and the arrows came in swarms. They might have been poisoned, but they looked as though they wouldn't kill a cat. The bush began to howl. Our wood-cutters raised a warlike whoop; the report of a rifle just at my back deafened me. I glanced over my shoulder, and the pilot-house was yet full of noise and smoke when I made a dash at the wheel. The fool-nigger had dropped everything, to throw the shutter open and let off that Martini-Henry. He stood before the wide opening, glaring, and I yelled at him to come back, while I straightened the sudden twist out of that steamboat. There was no room to turn even if I had wanted to, the snag was somewhere very near ahead in that confounded smoke, there was no time to lose, so I just crowded her into the bank—right into the bank, where I knew the water was deep.

"We tore slowly along the overhanging bushes in a whirl of broken twigs and flying leaves. The fusillade below stopped short, as I had foreseen it would when the squirts got empty. I threw my head back to a glinting whizz that traversed the pilot-house, in at one shutter-hole and out at the other. Looking past that mad helmsman, who was shaking the empty rifle and yelling at the shore, I saw vague forms of men running bent double, leaping, gliding, distinct, incomplete, evanescent. Something big appeared in the air before the shutter, the rifle went overboard, and the man stepped back swiftly, looked at me over his shoulder in an extraordinary, profound, familiar manner, and fell upon my feet. The side of his head hit the wheel twice, and the end of what appeared a long cane clattered round and knocked over a little camp-stool. It looked as though after wrenching that thing from somebody ashore he had lost his balance in the effort. The thin smoke had blown away, we were clear of the snag, and looking ahead I could see that in another hundred yards or so I would be free to sheer off, away from the bank; but my feet felt so very warm and wet that I had to look down. The man had rolled on his back and stared straight up at me; both his hands clutched that cane. It was the shaft of a spear that, either thrown or lunged through the opening, had caught him in the side just below the ribs; the blade had gone in out of sight, after making a frightful gash; my shoes were full; a pool of blood lay very still, gleaming dark-red under the wheel; his eyes shone with an amazing lustre. The fusillade burst out again. He looked at me anxiously, gripping the spear like something precious, with an air of being afraid I would try to take it away from him. I had to make an effort to free my eyes from his gaze and attend to the steering. With one hand I felt above my head for the line of the steam-whistle, and jerked out screech after screech hurriedly. The tumult of angry and warlike yells was checked instantly, and then from the depths of the woods went out such a tremulous and prolonged wail of mournful fear and utter despair as may be imagined to follow the flight of the last hope from the earth. There was a great commotion in the bush; the shower of arrows stopped, a few dropping shots rang out sharply—then silence, in which the languid beat of the stern-wheel came plainly to my ears. I put the helm hard astarboard at the moment when the pilgrim in pink pyjamas, very hot and agitated, appeared in the doorway. 'The manager sends me—' he began in an official tone, and stopped short. 'Good God!' he said, glaring at the wounded man.

"We two whites stood over him, and his lustrous and inquiring glance enveloped us both. I declare it looked as though he would presently put to us some question in an understandable language; but he died without uttering a sound, without moving a limb, without twitching a muscle. Only in the very last moment, as though in response to some sign we could not see, to some whisper we could not hear, he frowned heavily, and that frown gave to his black death-mask an inconceivably sombre, brooding, and menacing expression. The lustre of inquiring glance faded swiftly into vacant glassiness. 'Can you steer?' I asked the agent eagerly. He looked very dubious; but I made a grab at his arm, and he understood at once I meant him to steer whether or no. To tell you the truth, I was morbidly anxious to change my shoes and socks. 'He is dead,' murmured the fellow, immensely impressed. 'No doubt about it,' said I, tugging like mad at the shoelaces. 'And, by the way, I suppose Mr Kurtz is dead as well by this time.'

"For the moment that was the dominant thought. There was a sense of extreme disappointment, as though I had found out I had been striving after something altogether without a substance. I couldn't have been more disgusted if I had travelled all this way for the sole purpose of talking with Mr Kurtz. Talking with . . . I flung one shoe overboard, and became aware that that was exactly what I had been looking forward to—a talk with Kurtz. I made the strange discovery that I had never imagined him as doing, you know, but as discoursing. I didn't say to myself, 'Now I will never see him,' or 'Now I will never shake him by the hand,' but, 'Now I will never hear him.' The man presented himself as a voice. Not of course that I did not connect him with some sort of action. Hadn't I been told in all the tones of jealousy and admiration that he had collected, bartered, swindled, or stolen more ivory than all the other agents together. That was not the point. The point was in his being a gifted creature, and that of all his gifts the one that stood out pre-eminently, that carried with it a sense of real presence, was his ability to talk, his words—the gift of expression, the bewildering, the illuminating, the most exalted and the most contemptible, the pulsating stream of light, or the deceitful flow from the heart of an impenetrable darkness.

"The other shoe went flying unto the devil-god of that river. I thought, By Jove! it's all over. We are too late; he has vanished—the gift has vanished, by means of some spear, arrow, or club. I will never hear that chap speak after all,—and my sorrow had a startling extravagance of emotion, even such as I had noticed in the howling sorrow of these savages in the bush. I couldn't have felt more of lonely desolation somehow, had I been robbed of a belief or had missed my destiny in life. . . . Why do you sigh in this beastly way, somebody? Absurd? Well, absurd. Good Lord! mustn't a man ever—Here, give me some tobacco." . . .

There was a pause of profound stillness, then a match flared, and Marlow's lean face appeared, worn, hollow, with downward folds and dropped eyelids, with an aspect of concentrated attention; and as he took vigorous draws at his pipe, it seemed to retreat and advance out of the night in the regular flicker of the tiny flame. The match went out.

"Absurd!" he cried. "This is the worst of trying to tell . . . Here you all are, each moored with two good addresses, like a hulk with two anchors, a butcher round one corner, a policeman round another, excellent appetites, and temperature normal—you hear—normal from year's end to year's end. And you say, Absurd! Absurd be—exploded! Absurd! My dear boys, what can you expect from a man who out of sheer nervousness had just flung overboard a pair of new shoes? Now I think of it, it is amazing I did not shed tears. I am, upon the whole, proud of my fortitude. I was cut to the quick at the idea of having lost the inestimable privilege of listening to the gifted Kurtz. Of course I was wrong. The privilege was waiting for me. Oh yes, I heard more than enough. And I was right, too. A voice. He was very little more than a voice. And I heard—him—it—this voice—other voices—all of them were so little more than voices—and the memory of that time itself lingers around me, impalpable, like a dying vibration of one immense jabber, silly, atrocious, sordid, savage, or simply mean, without any kind of sense. Voices, voices—even the girl herself—now—"

He was silent for a long time.

"I laid the ghost of his gifts at last with a lie," he began suddenly. "Girl! What? Did I mention a girl? Oh, she is out of it—completely. They—the women I mean—are out of it—should be out of it. We must help them to stay in that beautiful world of their own, lest ours gets worse. Oh, she had to be out of it. You should have heard the disinterred body of Mr Kurtz saying, "My Intended." You would have perceived directly then how completely she was out of it. And the lofty frontal bone of Mr Kurtz! They say the hair goes on growing sometimes, but this—ah—specimen was impressively bald. The wilderness had patted him on the head, and, behold, it was like a ball—an ivory ball; it had caressed him, and—lo!—he had withered; it had taken him, loved him, embraced him, got into his veins, consumed his flesh, and sealed his soul to its own by the inconceivable ceremonies of some devilish initiation. He was its spoiled and pampered favourite. Ivory? I should think so. Heaps of it, stacks of it. The old mud shanty was bursting with it. You would think there was not a single tusk left either above or below the ground in the whole country. 'Mostly fossil,' the manager had remarked disparagingly. It was no more fossil than I am; but they call it fossil when it is dug up. It appears these niggers do bury the tusks sometimes—but evidently they couldn't bury this parcel deep enough to save the gifted Mr Kurtz from his fate. We filled the steamboat with it, and had to pile a lot on the deck. Thus he could see and enjoy as long as he could see, because the appreciation of this favour had remained with him to the last. You should have heard him say, 'My ivory.' Oh yes, I heard him. 'My Intended, my ivory, my station, my river, my—' everything belonged to him. It made me hold my breath in expectation of hearing the wilderness burst into a prodigious peal of laughter that would shake the fixed stars in their places. Everything belonged to him—but that was a trifle. The thing was to know what he belonged to, how many powers of darkness claimed him for their own. That was the reflection that made you creepy all over. It was impossible—it was not good for one either—trying to imagine. He had taken a high seat amongst the devils of the land—I mean literally. You can't understand. How could you?—with solid pavement under your feet, surrounded by kind neighbours ready to cheer you or to fall on you, stepping delicately between the butcher and the policeman, in the holy terror of scandal and gallows and lunatic asylums—how can you imagine what particular region of the first ages a man's untrammelled feet may take him into by the way of solitude—utter solitude without a policeman—by the way of silence—utter silence, where no warning voice of a kind neighbour can be heard whispering of public opinion? These little things make all the great difference. When they are gone you must fall back upon your own innate strength, upon your own capacity for faithfulness. Of course you may be too much of a fool to go wrong—too dull even to know you are being assaulted by the powers of darkness. I take it, no fool ever made a bargain for his soul with the devil: the fool is too much of a fool, or the devil too much of a devil—I don't know which. Or you may be such a thunderingly exalted creature as to be altogether deaf and blind to anything but heavenly sights and sounds. Then the earth for you is only a standing place—and whether to be like this is your loss or your gain I won't pretend to say. But most of us are neither one nor the other. The earth for us is a place to live in, where we must put up with sights, with sounds, with smells too, by Jove!—breathe dead hippo, so to speak, and not be contaminated. And there, don't you see? your strength comes in, the faith in your ability for the digging of unostentatious holes to bury the stuff in—your power of devotion, not to yourself, but to an obscure, back-breaking business. And that's difficult enough. Mind, I am not trying to excuse or even explain—I am trying to account to myself for—for—Mr Kurtz—for the shade of Mr Kurtz. This initiated wraith from the back of Nowhere honoured me with its amazing confidence before it vanished altogether. This was because it could speak English to me. The original Kurtz had been educated partly in England, and—as he was good enough to say himself—his sympathies were in the right place. His mother was half-English, his father was half-French. All Europe contributed to the making of Kurtz; and by-and-by I learned that, most appropriately, the International Society for the Suppression of Savage Customs had intrusted him with the making of a report, for its future guidance. And he had written it too. I've seen it. I've read it. It was eloquent, vibrating with eloquence, but too high-strung, I think. Seventeen pages of close writing he had found time for! But this must have been before his—let us say—nerves went wrong, and caused him to preside at certain midnight dances ending with unspeakable rites, which—as far as I reluctantly gathered from what I heard at various times—were offered up to him—do you understand?—to Mr Kurtz himself. But it was a beautiful piece of writing. The opening paragraph, however, in the light of later information, strikes me now as ominous. He began with the argument that we whites, from the point of development we had arrived at, 'must necessarily appear to them [savages] in the nature of supernatural beings—we approach them with the might as of a deity,' and so on, and so on. 'By the simple exercise of our will we can exert a power for good practically unbounded,' &c., &c. From that point he soared and took me with him. The peroration was magnificent, though difficult to remember, you know. It gave me the notion of an exotic Immensity ruled by an august Benevolence. It made me tingle with enthusiasm. This was the unbounded power of eloquence—of words—of burning noble words. There were no practical hints to interrupt the magic current of phrases, unless a kind of note at the foot of the last page, scrawled evidently much later, in an unsteady hand, may be regarded as the exposition of a method. It was very simple, and at the end of that moving appeal to every altruistic sentiment it blazed at you, luminous and terrifying, like a flash of lightning in a serene sky: 'Exterminate all the brutes!' The curious part was that he had apparently forgotten all about that valuable postscriptum, because, later on, when he in a sense came to himself, he repeatedly entreated me to take good care of 'my pamphlet' (he called it), as it was sure to have in the future a good influence upon his career. I had full information about all these things, and, besides, as it turned out, I was to have the care of his memory. I've done enough for it to give me the indisputable right to lay it, if I choose, for an everlasting rest in the dust-bin of progress, amongst all the sweepings and, figuratively speaking, all the dead cats of civilisation. But then, you see, I can't choose. He won't be forgotten. Whatever he was, he was not common. He had the power to charm or frighten rudimentary souls into an aggravated witch-dance in his honour; he could also fill the small souls of the pilgrims with bitter misgivings: he had one devoted friend at least, and he had conquered one soul in the world that was neither rudimentary nor tainted with self-seeking. No; I can't forget him, though I am not prepared to affirm the fellow was exactly worth the life we lost in getting to him. I missed my late helmsman awfully,—I missed him even while his body was still lying in the pilot-house. Perhaps you will think it passing strange this regret for a savage who was no more account than a grain of sand in a black Sahara. Well, don't you see, he had done something, he had steered; for months I had him at my back—a help—an instrument. It was a kind of partnership. He steered for me—I had to look after him, I worried about his deficiencies, and thus a subtle bond had been created, of which I only became aware when it was suddenly broken. And the intimate profundity of that look he gave me when he received his hurt remains to this day in my memory—like a claim of distant kinship affirmed in a supreme moment.

"Poor fool! If he had only left that shutter alone. He had no restraint, no restraint—just like Kurtz—a tree swayed by the wind. As soon as I had put on a dry pair of slippers, I dragged him out, after first jerking the spear out of his side, which operation I confess I performed with my eyes shut tight. His heels leaped together over the little doorstep; his shoulders were pressed to my breast; I hugged him from behind desperately. Oh! he was heavy, heavy; heavier than any man on earth, I should imagine. Then without more ado I tipped him overboard. The current snatched him as though he had been a wisp of grass, and I saw the body roll over twice before I lost sight of it for ever. All the pilgrims and the manager were then congregated on the awning-deck about the pilot-house, chattering at each other like a flock of excited magpies, and there was a scandalised murmur at my heartless promptitude. What they wanted to keep that body hanging about for I can't guess. Embalm it, maybe. But I had also heard another, and a very ominous, murmur on the deck below. My friends the woodcutters were likewise scandalised, and with a better show of reason—though I admit that the reason itself was quite inadmissible. Oh, quite! I had made up my mind that if my late helmsman was to be eaten, the fishes alone should have him. He had been a very second-rate helmsman while alive, but now he was dead he might have become a first-class temptation, and possibly cause some startling trouble. Besides, I was anxious to take the wheel, the man in pink pyjamas showing himself a hopeless duffer at the business.

"This I did directly the simple funeral was over. We were going half-speed, keeping right in the middle of the stream, and I listened to the talk about me. They had given up Kurtz, they had given up the station; Kurtz was dead, and the station had been burnt—and so on—and so on. The red-haired pilgrim was beside himself with the thought that at least this poor Kurtz had been properly revenged. 'Say! We must have made a glorious slaughter of them in the bush. Eh? What do you think? Say?' He positively danced, the bloodthirsty little gingery beggar. And he had nearly fainted when he saw the wounded man! I could not help saying, 'You made a glorious lot of smoke, anyhow.' I had seen, from the way the tops of the bushes rustled and flew, that almost all the shots had gone too high. You can't hit anything unless you take aim and fire from the shoulder; but these chaps fired from the hip with their eyes shut. The retreat, I maintained—and I was right—was caused by the screeching of the steam-whistle. Upon this they forgot Kurtz, and began to howl at me with indignant protests.

"The manager stood by the wheel murmuring confidentially about the necessity of getting well away down the river before dark at all events, when I saw in the distance a clearing on the river-side and the outlines of some sort of building. 'What's this?' I asked. He clapped his hands in wonder. 'The station!' he cried. I edged in at once, still going half-speed.

"Through my glasses I saw the slope of a hill interspersed with rare trees and perfectly free from undergrowth. A long decaying building on the summit was half buried in the high grass; the large holes in the peaked roof gaped black from afar; the jungle and the woods made a background. There was no enclosure or fence of any kind; but there had been one apparently, for near the house half-a-dozen slim posts remained in a row, roughly trimmed, and with their upper ends ornamented with round carved balls. The rails, or whatever there had been between, had disappeared. Of course the forest surrounded all that. The river-bank was clear, and on the water-side I saw a white man under a hat like a cart-wheel beckoning persistently with his whole arm. Examining the edge of the forest above and below, I was almost certain I could see movements—human forms gliding here and there. I steamed past prudently, then stopped the engines and let her drift down. The man on the shore began to shout, urging us to land. 'We have been attacked,' screamed the manager. 'I know—I know. It's all right,' yelled back the other, as cheerful as you please. 'Come along. It's all right. I am glad.'

"His aspect reminded me of something I had seen—something funny I had seen somewhere. As I manoeuvred to get alongside, I was asking myself, 'What does this fellow look like?' Suddenly I got it. He looked like a harlequin. His clothes had been made of some stuff that was brown holland[5] probably, but it was covered with patches all over, with bright patches, blue, red, and yellow,—patches on the back, patches on front, patches on elbows, on knees; coloured binding round his jacket, scarlet edging at the bottom of his trousers; and the sunshine made him look extremely gay and wonderfully neat withal, because you could see how beautifully all this patching had been done. A beardless, boyish face, very fair, no features to speak of, nose peeling, little blue eyes, smiles and frowns chasing each other over that open countenance like sunshine and shadow on a wind-swept plain. 'Look out, captain!' he cried; 'there's a snag lodged in here last night.' What! Another snag? I confess I swore shamefully. I had nearly holed my cripple, to finish off that charming trip. The harlequin on the bank turned his little pug nose up to me. 'You English?' he asked, all smiles. 'Are you?' I shouted from the wheel. The smiles vanished, and he shook his head as if sorry for my disappointment. Then he brightened up. 'Never mind!' he cried encouragingly. 'Are we in time?' I asked. 'He is up there,' he replied, with a toss of the head up the hill, and becoming gloomy all of a sudden. His face was like the autumn sky, overcast one moment and bright the next.

5. A smooth linen fabric.

"When the manager, escorted by the pilgrims, all of them armed to the teeth, had gone to the house, this chap came on board. 'I say, I don't like this. These natives are in the bush,' I said. He assured me earnestly it was all right. 'They are simple people,' he added; 'well, I am glad you came. It took me all my time to keep them off.' 'But you said it was all right,' I cried. 'Oh, they meant no harm,' he said; and as I stared he corrected himself, 'Not exactly.' Then vivaciously, 'My faith, your pilot-house wants a clean-up!' In the next breath he advised me to keep enough steam on the boiler to blow the whistle in case of any trouble. 'One good screech will do more for you than all your rifles. They are simple people,' he repeated. He rattled away at such a rate he quite overwhelmed me. He seemed to be trying to make up for lots of silence, and actually hinted, laughing, that such was the case. 'Don't you talk with Mr Kurtz?' I said. 'You don't talk with that man—you listen to him,' he exclaimed with severe exaltation. 'But now—' He waved his arm, and in the twinkling of an eye was in the uttermost depths of despondency. In a moment he came up again with a jump, possessed himself of both my hands, shook them continuously, while he gabbled: 'Brother sailor . . . honour . . . pleasure . . . delight . . . introduce myself . . . Russian . . . son of an arch-priest . . . Government of Tambov[6] . . . What? Tobacco! English tobacco; the excellent English tobacco! Now, that's brotherly. Smoke? Where's a sailor that does not smoke?'

"The pipe soothed him, and gradually I made out he had run away from school, had gone to sea in a Russian ship; ran away again; served some time in English ships; was now reconciled with the arch-priest. He made a point of that. 'But when one is young one must see things, gather experience, ideas; enlarge the mind.' 'Here!' I interrupted. 'You can never tell! Here I have met Mr Kurtz,' he said, youthfully solemn and reproachful. I held my tongue after that. It appears he had persuaded a Dutch trading-house on the coast to fit him out with stores and goods, and had started for the interior with a light heart, and no more idea of what would happen to him than a baby. He had been wandering about that river for nearly two years alone, cut off from everybody and everything. 'I am not so young as I look. I am twenty-five,' he said. 'At first old Van Shuyten would tell me to go to the devil,' he narrated with keen enjoyment; 'but I stuck to him, and talked and talked, till at last he got afraid I would talk the hind-leg off his favorite dog, so he gave me some cheap things and a few guns, and told me he hoped he would never see my face again. Good old Dutch-man, Van Shuyten. I sent him one small lot of ivory a year ago, so that he can't call me a little thief when I get back. I hope he got it. And for the rest, I don't care. I had some wood stacked for you. That was my old house. Did you see?'

"I gave him Towson's book. He made as though he would kiss me, but restrained himself. 'The only book I had left, and I thought I had lost it,' he said, looking at it ecstatically. 'So many accidents happen to a man going about alone, you know. Canoes get upset sometimes—and sometimes you've got to clear out so quick when the people get angry.' He thumbed the pages. 'You made notes in Russian?' I asked. He nodded. 'I thought they were written in cipher,' I said. He laughed, then became serious. 'I had lots of trouble to keep these people off,' he said. 'Did they want to kill you?' I asked. 'Oh no!' he cried, and checked himself. 'Why did they attack us?' I pursued. He hesitated, then said shamefacedly, 'They don't want him to go.' 'Don't

6. A province of Western Russia.

they?' I said, curiously. He nodded a nod full of mystery and wisdom. 'I tell you,' he cried, 'this man has enlarged my mind.' He opened his arms wide, staring at me with his little blue eyes that were perfectly round."

3

"I looked at him, lost in astonishment. There he was before me, in motley, as though he had absconded from a troupe of mimes, enthusiastic, fabulous. His very existence was improbable, inexplicable, and altogether bewildering. He was an insoluble problem. It was inconceivable how he had existed, how he had succeeded in getting so far, how he had managed to remain—why he did not instantly disappear. 'I went a little farther,' he said, 'then still a little farther—till I had gone so far that I don't know how I'll ever get back. Never mind. Plenty time. I can manage. You take Kurtz away quick—quick—I tell you.' The glamour of youth enveloped his particoloured rags, his destitution, his loneliness, the essential desolation of his futile wanderings. For months—for years—his life hadn't been worth a day's purchase; and there he was gallantly, thoughtlessly alive, to all appearance indestructible solely by the virtue of his few years and of his unreflecting audacity. I was seduced into something like admiration—like envy. Glamour urged him on, glamour kept him unscathed. He surely wanted nothing from the wilderness but space to breathe in and to push on through. His need was to exist, and to move onwards at the greatest possible risk, and with a maximum of privation. If the absolutely pure, uncalculating, unpractical spirit of adventure had ever ruled a human being, it ruled this be-patched youth. I almost envied him the possession of this modest and clear flame. It seemed to have consumed all thought of self so completely, that, even while he was talking to you, you forgot that it was he—the man before your eyes—who had gone through these things. I did not envy him his devotion to Kurtz, though. He had not meditated over it. It came to him, and he accepted it with a sort of eager fatalism. I must say that to me it appeared about the most dangerous thing in every way he had come upon so far.

"They had come together unavoidably, like two ships becalmed near each other, and lay rubbing sides at last. I suppose Kurtz wanted an audience, because on a certain occasion, when encamped in the forest, they had talked all night, or more probably Kurtz had talked. 'We talked of everything,' he said, quite transported at the recollection. 'I forgot there was such a thing as sleep. The night did not seem to last an hour. Everything! Everything! . . . Of love too.' 'Ah, he talked to you of love!' I said, much amused. 'It isn't what you think,' he cried, almost passionately. 'It was in general. He made me see things—things.'

"He threw his arms up. We were on deck at the time, and the headman of my wood-cutters, lounging near by, turned upon him his heavy and glittering eyes. I looked around, and I don't know why, but I assure you that never, never before, did this land, this river, this jungle, the very arch of this blazing sky, appear to me so hopeless and so dark, so impenetrable to human thought, so pitiless to human weakness. 'And, ever since, you have been with him, of course?' I said.

"On the contrary. It appears their intercourse had been very much broken by various causes. He had, as he informed me proudly, managed to nurse Kurtz through two illnesses (he alluded to it as you would to some risky feat), but as a rule Kurtz wandered alone, far in the depths of the forest. 'Very often coming to this station, I had to wait days and days before he would turn up,' he said. 'Ah, it was worth waiting for!—sometimes.' 'What was he doing? exploring or what?' I asked. 'Oh yes, of course'; he had discovered lots of villages, a lake too—he did not know exactly in what direction; it was dangerous to inquire too much—but mostly his expeditions had been for ivory. 'But he had no goods to trade with by that time,' I objected. 'There's a good lot of cartridges left even yet,' he answered, looking away. 'To speak plainly, he raided the country,' I said. He nodded. 'Not alone, surely!' He muttered something about the villages round that lake. 'Kurtz got the tribe to follow him, did he?' I suggested. He fidgeted a little. 'They adored him,' he said. The tone of these words was so extraordinary that I looked at him searchingly. It was curious to see his mingled eagerness and reluctance to speak of Kurtz. The man filled his life, occupied his thoughts, swayed his emotions. 'What can you expect?' he burst out; 'he came to them with thunder and lightning, you know—and they had never seen anything like it—and very terrible. He could be very terrible. You can't judge Mr Kurtz as you would an ordinary man. No, no, no! Now—just to give you an idea—I don't mind telling you, he wanted to shoot me too one day—but I don't judge him.' 'Shoot you!' I cried. 'What for?' 'Well, I had a small lot of ivory the chief of that village near my house gave me. You see I used to shoot game for them. Well, he wanted it, and wouldn't hear reason. He declared he would shoot me unless I gave him the ivory and then cleared out of the country, because he could do so, and had a fancy for it, and there was nothing on earth to prevent him killing whom he jolly well pleased. And it was true too. I gave him the ivory. What did I care! But I didn't clear out. No, no. I couldn't leave him. I had to be careful, of course, till we got friendly again for a time. He had his second illness then. Afterwards I had to keep out of the way; but I didn't mind. He was living for the most part in those villages on the lake. When he came down to the river, sometimes he would take to me, and sometimes it was better for me to be careful. This man suffered too much. He hated all this, and somehow he couldn't get away. When I had a chance I begged him to try and leave while there was time; I offered to go back with him. And he would say yes, and then he would remain; go off on another ivory hunt; disappear for weeks; forget himself amongst these people—forget himself—you know.' 'Why! he's mad,' I said. He protested indignantly. Mr Kurtz couldn't be mad. If I had heard him talk, only two days ago, I wouldn't dare hint at such a thing. . . . I had taken up my binoculars while we talked, and was looking at the shore, sweeping the limit of the forest at each side and at the back of the house. The consciousness of there being people in that bush, so silent, so quiet—as silent and quiet as the ruined house on the hill—made me uneasy. There was no sign on the face of nature of this amazing tale that was not so much told as suggested to me in desolate exclamations, completed by shrugs, in interrupted phrases, in hints ending in deep sighs. The woods were unmoved, like a mask—heavy, like the closed door of a prison—they looked with their air of hidden knowledge, of patient expectation, of unapproachable silence. The Russian was explaining to me that it was only lately that Mr Kurtz had come down to the river, bringing along with him all the fighting men of that lake tribe. He had been absent for several months—getting himself adored, I suppose—and had come down unexpectedly, with the intention to all appearance of making a raid either across the river or down stream. Evidently the appetite for more ivory had got the better of the—what shall I say?—less material aspirations. However, he had got much worse suddenly. 'I heard he was lying helpless, and so I came up—took my chance,' said the Russian. 'Oh, he is bad, very bad.' I directed my glass to the house. There were no signs of life, but there was the ruined roof, the long mud wall peeping above the grass, with three little square window-holes, no two of the same size; all this brought within reach of my hand, as it were. And then I made a brusque movement, and one of the remaining posts of that vanished fence leaped up in the field of my glass. You remember I told you I had been struck at the distance by certain attempts at ornamentation, rather remarkable in the ruinous aspect of the place. Now I had suddenly a nearer view, and its first result was to make me throw my head back as if before a blow. Then I went carefully from post to post with my glass, and I saw my mistake. These round knobs were not ornamental but symbolic; they were expressive and puzzling, striking and disturbing—food for thought and also for the vultures if there had been any looking down from the sky; but at all events for such ants as were industrious enough to ascend the pole. They would have been even more impressive, those heads on the stakes, if their faces had not been turned to the house. Only one, the first I had made out, was facing my way. I was not so shocked as you may think. The start back I had given was really nothing but a movement of surprise. I had expected to see a knob of wood there, you know. I returned deliberately to the first I had seen—and there it was, black, dried, sunken, with closed eyelids,—a head that seemed to sleep at the top of that pole, and, with the shrunken dry lips showing a narrow white line of the teeth, was smiling too, smiling continuously at some endless and jocose dream of that eternal slumber.

"I am not disclosing any trade secrets. In fact the manager said afterwards that Mr Kurtz's methods had ruined the district. I have no opinion on that point, but I want you clearly to understand that there was nothing exactly profitable in these heads being there. They only showed that Mr Kurtz lacked restraint in the gratification of his various lusts, that there was something wanting in him—some small matter which, when the pressing need arose, could not be found under his magnificent eloquence. Whether he knew of this deficiency himself I can't say. I think the knowledge came to him at last—only at the very last. But the wilderness had found him out early, and had taken on him a terrible vengeance for the fantastic invasion. I think it had whispered to him things about himself which he did not know, things of which he had no conception till he took counsel with this great solitude—and the whisper had proved irresistibly fascinating. It echoed loudly within him because he was hollow at the core. . . . I put down the glass, and the head that had appeared near enough to be spoken to seemed at once to have leaped away from me into inaccessible distance.

"The admirer of Mr Kurtz was a bit crestfallen. In a hurried, indistinct voice he began to assure me he had not dared to take these—say, symbols—down. He was not afraid of the natives; they would not stir till Mr Kurtz gave the word. His ascendancy was extraordinary. The camps of these people surrounded the place, and the chiefs came every day to see him. They would crawl . . . 'I don't want to know anything of the ceremonies used when approaching Mr Kurtz,' I shouted. Curious, this feeling that came over me that such details would be more intolerable than those heads drying on the stakes under Mr Kurtz's windows. After all, that was only a savage sight, while I seemed at one bound to have been transported into some lightless region of subtle horrors, where pure, uncomplicated savagery was a positive relief, being something that had a right to exist—obviously—in the sunshine. The young man looked at me with surprise. I suppose it did not occur to him Mr Kurtz was no idol of mine. He forgot I hadn't heard any of these splendid monologues on, what was it? on love, justice, conduct of life—or what not. If it had come to crawling before Mr Kurtz, he crawled as much as the veriest savage of them all. I had no idea of the conditions, he said: these heads were the heads of rebels. I shocked him excessively by laughing. Rebels! What would be the next definition I was to hear? There had been enemies, criminals, workers—and these were rebels. Those rebellious heads looked very subdued to me on their sticks. 'You don't know how such a life tries a man like Kurtz,' cried Kurtz's last disciple. 'Well, and you?' I said. 'I! I! I am a simple man. I have no great thoughts. I want nothing from anybody. How can you compare me to . . . ?' His feelings were too much for speech, and suddenly he broke down. 'I don't understand,' he groaned. 'I've been doing my best to keep him alive, and that's enough. I had no hand in all this. I have no abilities. There hasn't been a drop of medicine or a mouthful of invalid food for months here. He was shamefully abandoned. A man like this, with such ideas. Shamefully! Shamefully! I—I—haven't slept for the last ten nights . . . .'

"His voice lost itself in the calm of the evening. The long shadows of the forest had slipped down-hill while we talked, had gone far beyond the ruined hovel, beyond the symbolic row of stakes. All this was in the gloom, while we down there were yet in the sunshine, and the stretch of the river abreast of the clearing glittered in a still and dazzling splendour, with a murky and overshadowed bend above and below. Not a living soul was seen on the shore. The bushes did not rustle.

"Suddenly round the corner of the house a group of men appeared, as though they had come up from the ground. They waded waist-deep in the grass, in a compact body, bearing an improvised stretcher in their midst. Instantly, in the emptiness of the landscape, a cry arose whose shrillness pierced the still air like a sharp arrow flying straight to the very heart of the land; and, as if by enchantment, streams of human beings—of naked human beings—with spears in their hands, with bows, with shields, with wild glances and savage movements, were poured into the clearing by the dark-faced and pensive forest. The bushes shook, the grass swayed for a time, and then everything stood still in attentive immobility.

"'Now, if he does not say the right thing to them we are all done for,' said the Russian at my elbow. The knot of men with the stretcher had stopped too, half-way to the steamer, as if petrified. I saw the man on the stretcher sit up, lank and with an uplifted arm, above the shoulders of the bearers. 'Let us hope that the man who can talk so well of love in general will find some particular reason to spare us this time,' I said. I resented bitterly the absurd danger of our situation, as if to be at the mercy of that atrocious phantom had been a dishonouring necessity. I could not hear a sound, but through my glasses I saw the thin arm extended commandingly, the lower jaw moving, the eyes of that apparition shining darkly far in its bony head that nodded with grotesque jerks. Kurtz—Kurtz—that means 'short' in German—don't it? Well, the name was as true as everything else in his life—and death. He looked at least seven feet long. His covering had fallen off, and his body emerged from it pitiful and appalling as from a winding-sheet. I could see the cage of his ribs all astir, the bones of his arm waving. It was as though an animated image of death carved out of old ivory had been shaking its hand with menaces at a motionless crowd of men made of dark and glittering bronze. I saw him open his mouth wide—it gave him a weirdly voracious aspect, as though he had wanted to swallow all the air, all the earth, all the men before him. A deep voice reached me faintly. He must have been shouting. He fell back suddenly. The stretcher shook as the bearers staggered forward again, and almost at the same time I noticed that the crowd of savages was vanishing without any perceptible movement of retreat, as if the forest that had ejected these beings so suddenly had drawn them in again as the breath is drawn in a long aspiration.

"Some of the pilgrims behind the stretcher carried his arms—two shot-guns, a heavy rifle, and a light revolver-carbine—the thunderbolts of that pitiful Jupiter. The manager bent over him murmuring as he walked beside his head. They laid him down in one of the little cabins—just a room for a bed-place and a camp-stool or two, you know. We had brought his belated correspondence, and a lot of torn envelopes and open letters littered his bed. His hand roamed feebly amongst these papers. I was struck by the fire of his eyes and the composed languor of his expression. It was not so much the exhaustion of disease. He did not seem in pain. This shadow looked satiated and calm, as though for the moment it had had its fill of all the emotions.

"He rustled one of the letters, and looking straight in my face said, 'I am glad.' Somebody had been writing to him about me. These special recommendations were turning up again. The volume of tone he emitted without effort, almost without the trouble of moving his lips, amazed me. A voice! a voice! It was grave, profound, vibrating, while the man did not seem capable of a whisper. However, he had enough strength in him—factitious no doubt—to very nearly make an end of us, as you shall hear directly.

"The manager appeared silently in the doorway; I stepped out at once and he drew the curtain after me. The Russian, eyed curiously by the pilgrims, was staring at the shore. I followed the direction of his glance.

"Dark human shapes could be made out in the distance, flitting indistinctly against the gloomy border of the forest, and near the river two bronze figures, leaning on tall spears, stood in the sunlight under fantastic head-dresses of spotted skins, warlike and still in statuesque repose. And from right to left along the lighted shore moved a wild and gorgeous apparition of a woman.

"She walked with measured steps, draped in striped and fringed cloths, treading the earth proudly, with a slight jingle and flash of barbarous ornaments. She carried her head high; her hair was done in the shape of a helmet; she had brass leggings to the knee, brass wire gauntlets to the elbow, a crimson spot on her tawny cheek, innumerable necklaces of glass beads on her neck; bizarre things, charms, gifts of witchmen, that hung about her, glittered and trembled at every step. She must have had the value of several elephant tusks upon her. She was savage and superb, wild-eyed and magnificent; there was something ominous and stately in her deliberate progress. And in the hush that had fallen suddenly upon the whole sorrowful land, the immense wilderness, the colossal body of the fecund and mysterious life seemed to look at her, pensive, as though it had been looking at the image of its own tenebrous and passionate soul.

"She came abreast of the steamer, stood still, and faced us. Her long shadow fell to the water's edge. Her face had a tragic and fierce aspect of wild sorrow and of dumb pain mingled with the fear of some struggling, half-shaped resolve. She stood looking at us without a stir, and like the wilderness itself, with an air of brooding over an inscrutable purpose. A whole minute passed, and then she made a step forward. There was a low jingle, a glint of yellow metal, a sway of fringed draperies, and she stopped as if her heart had failed her. The young fellow by my side growled. The pilgrims murmured at my back. She looked at us all as if her life had depended upon the unswerving steadiness of her glance. Suddenly she opened her bared arms and threw them up rigid above her head, as though in an uncontrollable desire to touch the sky, and at the same time the swift shadows darted out on the earth, swept around on the river, gathering the steamer in a shadowy embrace. A formidable silence hung over the scene.

"She turned away slowly, walked on, following the bank, and passed into the bushes to the left. Once only her eyes gleamed back at us in the dusk of the thickets before she disappeared.

"'If she had offered to come aboard I really think I would have tried to shoot her,' said the man of patches, nervously. 'I had been risking my life every day for the last fortnight to keep her out of the house. She got in one day and kicked up a row about those miserable rags I picked up in the storeroom to mend my clothes with. I wasn't decent. At least it must have been that, for she talked like a fury to Kurtz for an hour, pointing at me now and then. I don't understand the dialect of this tribe. Luckily for me, I fancy Kurtz felt too ill that day to care, or there would have been mischief. I don't understand. . . . No—it's too much for me. Ah, well, it's all over now.'

"At this moment I heard Kurtz's deep voice behind the curtain, 'Save me!—save the ivory, you mean. Don't tell me. Save *me!* Why, I've had to save you. You are interrupting my plans now. Sick! Sick! Not so sick as you would like to believe. Never mind. I'll carry my ideas out yet—I will return. I'll show you what can be done. You with your little peddling notions—you are interfering with me. I will return. I . . . .'

"The manager came out. He did me the honour to take me under the arm and lead me aside. 'He is very low, very low,' he said. He considered it necessary to sigh, but neglected to be consistently sorrowful. 'We have done all we could for him— haven't we? But there is no disguising the fact, Mr Kurtz has done more harm than good to the Company. He did not see the time was not ripe for vigorous action. Cautiously, cautiously—that's my principle. We must be cautious yet. The district is closed to us for a time. Deplorable! Upon the whole, the trade will suffer. I don't deny there is a remarkable quantity of ivory—mostly fossil. We must save it, at all events—but look how precarious the position is—and why? Because the method is unsound.' 'Do you,' said I, looking at the shore, 'call it "unsound method"?' 'Without doubt,' he exclaimed, hotly. 'Don't you?' . . . 'No method at all,' I murmured after a while. 'Exactly,' he exulted. 'I anticipated this. Shows a complete want of judgment. It is my duty to point it out in the proper quarter.' 'Oh,' said I, 'that fellow—what's his name?—the brickmaker, will make a readable report for you.' He appeared confounded for a moment. It seemed to me I had never breathed an atmosphere so vile, and I turned mentally to Kurtz for relief—positively for relief. 'Nevertheless, I think Mr Kurtz is a remarkable man,' I said with emphasis. He started, dropped on me a cold heavy glance, said very quietly, 'He was,' and turned his back on me. My hour of favour was over; I found myself lumped along with Kurtz as a partisan of methods for which the time was not ripe: I was unsound! Ah! but it was something to have at least a choice of nightmares.

"I had turned to the wilderness really, not to Mr Kurtz, who, I was ready to admit, was as good as buried. And for a moment it seemed to me as if I also were buried in a vast grave full of unspeakable secrets. I felt an intolerable weight oppressing my breast, the smell of the damp earth, the unseen presence of victorious corruption, the darkness of an impenetrable night. . . . The Russian tapped me on the shoulder. I heard him mumbling and stammering something about 'brother seaman—couldn't conceal—knowledge of matters that would affect Mr Kurtz's reputation.' I waited. For him evidently Mr Kurtz was not in his grave; I suspect that for him Mr Kurtz was one of the immortals. 'Well!' said I at last, 'speak out. As it happens, I am Mr Kurtz's friend—in a way.'

"He stated with a good deal of formality that had we not been 'of the same profession,' he would have kept the matter to himself without regard to consequences. He suspected 'there was an active ill-will towards him on the part of these white men that—' 'You are right,' I said, remembering a certain conversation I had overheard. 'The manager thinks you ought to be hanged.' He showed a concern at this intelligence which amused me at first. 'I had better get out of the way quietly,' he said, earnestly. 'I can do no more for Kurtz now, and they would soon find some excuse. What's to stop them? There's a military post three hundred miles from here.' 'Well, upon my word,' said I, 'perhaps you had better go if you have any friends amongst the savages near by.' 'Plenty,' he said. 'They are simple people—and I want nothing, you know.' He stood biting his lip, then: 'I don't want any harm to happen to these whites here, but of course I was thinking of Mr Kurtz's reputation—but you are a brother seaman and—' 'All right,' said I, after a time. 'Mr Kurtz's reputation is safe with me.' I did not know how truly I spoke.

"He informed me, lowering his voice, that it was Kurtz who had ordered the attack to be made on the steamer. 'He hated sometimes the idea of being taken away—and then again . . . But I don't understand these matters. I am a simple man. He thought it would scare you away—that you would give it up, thinking him dead. I could not stop him. Oh, I had an awful time of it this last month.' 'Very well,' I said. 'He is all right now.' 'Ye-e-es,' he muttered, not very convinced apparently. 'Thanks,' said I; 'I shall keep my eyes open.' 'But quiet—eh?' he urged, anxiously. 'It would be awful for his reputation if anybody here—' I promised a complete discretion with great gravity. 'I have a canoe and three black fellows waiting not very far. I am off. Could you give me a few Martini-Henry cartridges?' I could, and did, with proper secrecy. He helped himself, with a wink at me, to a handful of my tobacco. 'Between sailors—you know—good English tobacco.' At the door of the pilot-house he turned round—'I say, haven't you a pair of shoes you could spare?' He raised one leg. 'Look.' The soles were tied with knotted strings sandal-wise under his bare feet. I rooted out an old pair, at which he looked with admiration before tucking it under his left arm. One of his pockets (bright red) was bulging with cartridges, from the other (dark blue) peeped 'Towson's Inquiry,' &c., &c. He seemed to think himself excellently well equipped for a renewed encounter with the wilderness. 'Ah! I'll never, never meet such a man again. You ought to have heard him recite poetry—his own too it was, he told me. Poetry!' He rolled his eyes at the recollection of these delights. 'Oh, he enlarged my mind!' 'Good-bye,' said I. He shook hands and vanished in the night. Sometimes I ask myself whether I had ever really seen him—whether it was possible to meet such a phenomenon! . . .

"When I woke up shortly after midnight his warning came to my mind with its hint of danger that seemed, in the starred darkness, real enough to make me get up for the purpose of having a look round. On the hill a big fire burned, illuminating fitfully a crooked corner of the station-house. One of the agents with a picket of a few of our blacks, armed for the purpose, was keeping guard over the ivory; but deep within the forest, red gleams that wavered, that seemed to sink and rise from the ground amongst confused columnar shapes of intense blackness, showed the exact position of the camp where Mr Kurtz's adorers were keeping their uneasy vigil. The monotonous beating of a big drum filled the air with muffled shocks and a lingering vibration. A steady droning sound of many men chanting each to himself some weird incantation came out from the black, flat wall of the woods as the humming of bees comes out of a hive, and had a strange narcotic effect upon my half-awake senses. I believe I dozed off leaning over the rail, till an abrupt burst of yells, an overwhelming outbreak of a pent-up and mysterious frenzy, woke me up in a bewildered wonder. It was cut short all at once, and the low droning went on with an effect of audible and soothing silence. I glanced casually into the little cabin. A light was burning within, but Mr Kurtz was not there.

"I think I would have raised an outcry if I had believed my eyes. But I didn't believe them at first—the thing seemed so impossible. The fact is, I was completely unnerved by a sheer blank fright, pure abstract terror, unconnected with any distinct shape of physical danger. What made this emotion so overpowering was—how shall I define it?—the moral shock I received, as if something altogether monstrous, intolerable to thought and odious to the soul, had been thrust upon me unexpectedly. This lasted of course the merest fraction of a second, and then the usual sense of commonplace, deadly danger, the possibility of a sudden onslaught and massacre, or something of the kind, which I saw impending, was positively welcome and composing. It pacified me, in fact, so much, that I did not raise an alarm.

"There was an agent buttoned up inside an ulster[7] and sleeping on a chair on deck within three feet of me. The yells had not awakened him; he snored very slightly; I left him to his slumbers and leaped ashore. I did not betray Mr Kurtz—it was ordered I should never betray him—it was written I should be loyal to the nightmare of my choice. I was anxious to deal with this shadow by myself alone,—and to this day I don't know why I was so jealous of sharing with any one the peculiar blackness of that experience.

"As soon as I got on the bank I saw a trail—a broad trail through the grass. I remember the exultation with which I said to myself, 'He can't walk—he is crawling on all-fours—I've got him.' The grass was wet with dew. I strode rapidly with clenched fists. I fancy I had some vague notion of falling upon him and giving him a drubbing. I don't know. I had some imbecile thoughts. The knitting old woman with the cat obtruded herself upon my memory as a most improper person to be sitting at the other end of such an affair. I saw a row of pilgrims squirting lead in the air out of Winchesters held to the hip. I thought I would never get back to the steamer, and imagined myself living alone and unarmed in the woods to an advanced age. Such silly things—you know. And I remember I confounded the beat of the drum with the beating of my heart, and was pleased at its calm regularity.

"I kept to the track though—then stopped to listen. The night was very clear: a dark blue space, sparkling with dew and starlight, in which black things stood very still. I thought I could see a kind of motion ahead of me. I was strangely cocksure of everything that night. I actually left the track and ran in a wide semicircle (I verily believe chuckling to myself) so as to get in front of that stir, of that motion I had seen—if indeed I had seen anything. I was circumventing Kurtz as though it had been a boyish game.

"I came upon him, and, if he had not heard me coming, I would have fallen over him too, but he got up in time. He rose, unsteady, long, pale, indistinct, like a vapour exhaled by the earth, and swayed slightly, misty and silent before me; while at my back the fires loomed between the trees, and the murmur of many voices issued from the forest. I had cut him off cleverly; but when actually confronting him I seemed to come to my senses, I saw the danger in its right proportion. It was by no means over yet. Suppose he began to shout? Though he could hardly stand, there was still plenty of vigour in his voice. 'Go away—hide yourself,' he said, in that profound tone. It was very awful. I glanced back. We were within thirty yards from the nearest fire. A black figure stood up, strode on long black legs, waving long black arms, across the glow. It had horns—antelope horns, I think—on its head. Some sorcerer, some witch-man, no doubt: it looked fiend-like enough. 'Do you know what you are doing?' I whispered. 'Perfectly,' he answered, raising his voice for that single word: it sounded to me far off and yet loud, like a hail through a speaking-trumpet. If he makes a row we are lost, I thought to myself. This clearly was not a case for fisticuffs, even apart from the very natural aversion I had to beat that Shadow—this wandering and tormented thing. 'You will be lost,' I said—'utterly lost.' One gets sometimes such a flash of inspiration, you know. I did say the right thing, though indeed he could not have been more irretrievably lost than he was at this very moment, when the foundations of our intimacy were being laid—to endure—to endure—even to the end—even beyond.

7. Long overcoat.

"'I had immense plans,' he muttered irresolutely. 'Yes,' said I; 'but if you try to shout I'll smash your head with—' there was not a stick or a stone near. 'I will throttle you for good,' I corrected myself. 'I was on the threshold of great things,' he pleaded, in a voice of longing, with a wistfulness of tone that made my blood run cold. 'And now for this stupid scoundrel—' 'Your success in Europe is assured in any case,' I affirmed, steadily. I did not want to have the throttling of him, you understand—and indeed it would have been very little use for any practical purpose. I tried to break the spell—the heavy, mute spell of the wilderness—that seemed to draw him to its pitiless breast by the awakening of forgotten and brutal instincts, by the memory of gratified and monstrous passions. This alone, I was convinced, had driven him out to the edge of the forest, to the bush, towards the gleam of fires, the throb of drums, the drone of weird incantations; this alone had beguiled his unlawful soul beyond the bounds of permitted aspirations. And, don't you see, the terror of the position was not in being knocked on the head—though I had a very lively sense of that danger too—but in this, that I had to deal with a being to whom I could not appeal in the name of anything high or low. I had, even like the niggers, to invoke him—himself—his own exalted and incredible degradation. There was nothing either above or below him, and I knew it. He had kicked himself loose of the earth. Confound the man! he had kicked the very earth to pieces. He was alone, and I before him did not know whether I stood on the ground or floated in the air. I've been telling you what we said—repeating the phrases we pronounced,—but what's the good? They were common everyday words,—the familiar, vague sounds exchanged on every waking day of life. But what of that? They had behind them, to my mind, the terrific suggestiveness of words heard in dreams, of phrases spoken in nightmares. Soul! If anybody had ever struggled with a soul, I am the man. And I wasn't arguing with a lunatic either. Believe me or not, his intelligence was perfectly clear—concentrated, it is true, upon himself with horrible intensity, yet clear; and therein was my only chance—barring, of course, the killing him there and then, which wasn't so good, on account of unavoidable noise. But his soul was mad. Being alone in the wilderness, it had looked within itself, and, by heavens! I tell you, it had gone mad. I had—for my sins, I suppose—to go through the ordeal of looking into it myself. No eloquence could have been so withering to one's belief in mankind as his final burst of sincerity. He struggled with himself, too. I saw it,—I heard it. I saw the inconceivable mystery of a soul that knew no restraint, no faith, and no fear, yet struggling blindly with itself. I kept my head pretty well; but when I had him at last stretched on the couch, I wiped my forehead, while my legs shook under me as though I had carried half a ton on my back down that hill. And yet I had only supported him, his bony arm clasped round my neck—and he was not much heavier than a child.

"When next day we left at noon, the crowd, of whose presence behind the curtain of trees I had been acutely conscious all the time, flowed out of the woods again, filled the clearing, covered the slope with a mass of naked, breathing, quivering, bronze bodies. I steamed up a bit, then swung down-stream, and two thousand eyes followed the evolutions of the splashing, thumping, fierce river-demon beating the water with its terrible tail and breathing black smoke into the air. In front of the first rank, along the river, three men, plastered with bright red earth from head to foot, strutted to and fro restlessly. When we came abreast again, they faced the river, stamped their feet, nodded their horned heads, swayed their scarlet bodies; they shook towards the fierce river-demon a bunch of black feathers, a mangy skin with a pendent tail—something that looked like a dried gourd; they shouted periodically together strings of amazing words that resembled no sounds of human language; and the deep murmurs of the crowd, interrupted suddenly, were like the responses of some satanic litany.

"We had carried Kurtz into the pilot-house: there was more air there. Lying on the couch, he stared through the open shutter. There was an eddy in the mass of human bodies, and the woman with helmeted head and tawny cheeks rushed out to the very brink of the stream. She put out her hands, shouted something, and all that wild mob took up the shout in a roaring chorus of articulated, rapid, breathless utterance.

"'Do you understand this?' I asked.

"He kept on looking out past me with fiery, longing eyes, with a mingled expression of wistfulness and hate. He made no answer, but I saw a smile, a smile of indefinable meaning, appear on his colourless lips that a moment after twitched convulsively. 'Do I not?' he said slowly, gasping, as if the words had been torn out of him by a supernatural power.

"I pulled the string of the whistle, and I did this because I saw the pilgrims on deck getting out their rifles with an air of anticipating a jolly lark. At the sudden screech there was a movement of abject terror through that wedged mass of bodies. 'Don't! don't! you frighten them away,' cried some one on deck disconsolately. I pulled the string time after time. They broke and ran, they leaped, they crouched, they swerved, they dodged the flying terror of the sound. The three red chaps had fallen flat, face down on the shore, as though they had been shot dead. Only the barbarous and superb woman did not so much as flinch, and stretched tragically her bare arms after us over the sombre and glittering river.

"And then that imbecile crowd down on the deck started their little fun, and I could see nothing more for smoke.

"The brown current ran swiftly out of the heart of darkness, bearing us down towards the sea with twice the speed of our upward progress; and Kurtz's life was running swiftly too, ebbing, ebbing out of his heart into the sea of inexorable time. The manager was very placid, he had no vital anxieties now, he took us both in with a comprehensive and satisfied glance: the 'affair' had come off as well as could be wished. I saw the time approaching when I would be left alone of the party of 'unsound method.' The pilgrims looked upon me with disfavour. I was, so to speak, numbered with the dead. It is strange how I accepted this unforeseen partnership, this choice of nightmares forced upon me in the tenebrous land invaded by these mean and greedy phantoms.

"Kurtz discoursed. A voice! a voice! It rang deep to the very last. It survived his strength to hide in the magnificent folds of eloquence the barren darkness of his heart. Oh, he struggled! he struggled! The wastes of his weary brain were haunted by shadowy images now—images of wealth and fame revolving obsequiously round his unextinguishable gift of noble and lofty expression. My Intended, my station, my career, my ideas—these were the subjects for the occasional utterances of elevated sentiments. The shade of the original Kurtz frequented the bedside of the hollow sham, whose fate it was to be buried presently in the mould of primeval earth. But both the diabolic love and the unearthly hate of the mysteries it had penetrated fought for the possession of that soul satiated with primitive emotions, avid of lying fame, of sham distinction, of all the appearances of success and power.

"Sometimes he was contemptibly childish. He desired to have kings meet him at railway-stations on his return from some ghastly Nowhere, where he intended to accomplish great things. 'You show them you have in you something that is really profitable, and then there will be no limits to the recognition of your ability,' he would say. 'Of course you must take care of the motives—right motives—always.' The long reaches that were like one and the same reach, monotonous bends that were exactly alike, slipped past the steamer with their multitude of secular[8] trees looking patiently after this grimy fragment of another world, the forerunner of change, of conquest, of trade, of massacres, of blessings. I looked ahead—piloting. 'Close the shutter,' said Kurtz suddenly one day; 'I can't bear to look at this.' I did so. There was a silence. 'Oh, but I will wring your heart yet!' he cried at the invisible wilderness.

"We broke down—as I had expected—and had to lie up for repairs at the head of an island. This delay was the first thing that shook Kurtz's confidence. One morning he gave me a packet of papers and a photograph,—the lot tied together with a shoe-string. 'Keep this for me,' he said. 'This noxious fool' (meaning the manager) 'is capable of prying into my boxes when I am not looking.' In the afternoon I saw him. He was lying on his back with closed eyes, and I withdrew quietly, but I heard him mutter, 'Live rightly, die, die . . .' I listened. There was nothing more. Was he rehearsing some speech in his sleep, or was it a fragment of a phrase from some newspaper article? He had been writing for the papers and meant to do so again, 'for the furthering of my ideas. It's a duty.'

"His was an impenetrable darkness. I looked at him as you peer down at a man who is lying at the bottom of a precipice where the sun never shines. But I had not much time to give him, because I was helping the engine-driver to take to pieces the leaky cylinders, to straighten a bent connecting-rod, and in other such matters. I lived in an infernal mess of rust, filings, nuts, bolts, spanners, hammers, ratchet-drills—things I abominate, because I don't get on with them. I tended the little forge we fortunately had aboard; I toiled wearily in a wretched scrap-heap—unless I had the shakes too bad to stand.

"One evening coming in with a candle I was startled to hear him say a little tremulously, 'I am lying here in the dark waiting for death.' The light was within a foot of his eyes. I forced myself to murmur, 'Oh, nonsense!' and stood over him as if transfixed.

"Anything approaching the change that came over his features I have never seen before, and hope never to see again. Oh, I wasn't touched. I was fascinated. It was as though a veil had been rent. I saw on that ivory face the expression of sombre pride, of ruthless power, of craven terror—of an intense and hopeless despair. Did he live his life again in every detail of desire, temptation, and surrender during that supreme moment of complete knowledge? He cried in a whisper at some image, at some vision,—he cried out twice, a cry that was no more than a breath—

"'The horror! The horror!'

"I blew the candle out and left the cabin. The pilgrims were dining in the mess-room, and I took my place opposite the manager, who lifted his eyes to give me a questioning glance, which I successfully ignored. He leaned back, serene, with that peculiar smile of his sealing the unexpressed depths of his meanness. A continuous shower of small flies streamed upon the lamp, upon the cloth, upon our hands and faces. Suddenly the manager's boy put his insolent black head in the doorway, and said in a tone of scathing contempt—

"'Mistah Kurtz—he dead.'

8. Ancient.

"All the pilgrims rushed out to see. I remained, and went on with my dinner. I believe I was considered brutally callous. However, I did not eat much. There was a lamp in there—light, don't you know—and outside it was so beastly, beastly dark. I went no more near the remarkable man who had pronounced a judgment upon the adventures of his soul on this earth. The voice was gone. What else had been there? But I am of course aware that next day the pilgrims buried something in a muddy hole.

"And then they very nearly buried me.

"However, as you see, I did not go to join Kurtz there and then. I did not. I remained to dream the nightmare out to the end, and to show my loyalty to Kurtz once more. Destiny. My destiny! Droll thing life is—that mysterious arrangement of merciless logic for a futile purpose. The most you can hope from it is some knowledge of yourself—that comes too late—a crop of unextinguishable regrets. I have wrestled with death. It is the most unexciting contest you can imagine. It takes place in an impalpable greyness, with nothing underfoot, with nothing around, without spectators, without clamour, without glory, without the great desire of victory, without the great fear of defeat, in a sickly atmosphere of tepid scepticism, without much belief in your own right, and still less in that of your adversary. If such is the form of ultimate wisdom, then life is a greater riddle than some of us think it to be. I was within a hair's-breadth of the last opportunity for pronouncement, and I found with humiliation that probably I would have nothing to say. This is the reason why I affirm that Kurtz was a remarkable man. He had something to say. He said it. Since I had peeped over the edge myself, I understand better the meaning of his stare, that could not see the flame of the candle, but was wide enough to embrace the whole universe, piercing enough to penetrate all the hearts that beat in the darkness. He had summed up—he had judged. 'The horror!' He was a remarkable man. After all, this was the expression of some sort of belief; it had candour, it had conviction, it had a vibrating note of revolt in its whisper, it had the appalling face of a glimpsed truth—the strange commingling of desire and hate. And it is not my own extremity I remember best—a vision of greyness without form filled with physical pain, and a careless contempt for the evanescence of all things—even of this pain itself. No! It is his extremity that I seem to have lived through. True, he had made that last stride, he had stepped over the edge, while I had been permitted to draw back my hesitating foot. And perhaps in this is the whole difference; perhaps all the wisdom, and all truth, and all sincerity, are just compressed into that inappreciable moment of time in which we step over the threshold of the invisible. Perhaps! I like to think my summing-up would not have been a word of careless contempt. Better his cry—much better. It was an affirmation, a moral victory paid for by innumerable defeats, by abominable terrors, by abominable satisfactions. But it was a victory! That is why I have remained loyal to Kurtz to the last, and even beyond, when a long time after I heard once more, not his own voice, but the echo of his magnificent eloquence thrown to me from a soul as translucently pure as a cliff of crystal.

"No, they did not bury me, though there is a period of time which I remember mistily, with a shuddering wonder, like a passage through some inconceivable world that had no hope in it and no desire. I found myself back in the sepulchral city resenting the sight of people hurrying through the streets to filch a little money from each other, to devour their infamous cookery, to gulp their unwholesome beer, to dream their insignificant and silly dreams. They trespassed upon my thoughts. They were intruders whose knowledge of life was to me an irritating pretence, because I felt so sure they could not possibly know the things I knew. Their bearing, which was simply the bearing of commonplace individuals going about their business in the assurance of perfect safety, was offensive to me like the outrageous flauntings of folly in the face of a danger it is unable to comprehend. I had no particular desire to enlighten them, but I had some difficulty in restraining myself from laughing in their faces, so full of stupid importance. I daresay I was not very well at that time. I tottered about the streets—there were various affairs to settle—grinning bitterly at perfectly respectable persons. I admit my behaviour was inexcusable, but then my temperature was seldom normal in these days. My dear aunt's endeavours to 'nurse up my strength' seemed altogether beside the mark. It was not my strength that wanted nursing, it was my imagination that wanted soothing. I kept the bundle of papers given me by Kurtz, not knowing exactly what to do with it. His mother had died lately, watched over, as I was told, by his Intended. A clean-shaved man, with an official manner and wearing gold-rimmed spectacles, called on me one day and made inquiries, at first circuitous, afterwards suavely pressing, about what he was pleased to denominate certain 'documents.' I was not surprised, because I had had two rows with the manager on the subject out there. I had refused to give up the smallest scrap out of that package, and I took the same attitude with the spectacled man. He became darkly menacing at last, and with much heat argued that the Company had the right to every bit of information about its 'territories.' And, said he, 'Mr Kurtz's knowledge of unexplored regions must have been necessarily extensive and peculiar—owing to his great abilities and to the deplorable circumstances in which he had been placed: therefore—' I assured him Mr Kurtz's knowledge, however extensive, did not bear upon the problems of commerce or administration. He invoked then the name of science. 'It would be an incalculable loss if,' &c., &c. I offered him the report on the 'Suppression of Savage Customs,' with the postscriptum torn off. He took it up eagerly, but ended by sniffing at it with an air of contempt. 'This is not what we had a right to expect,' he remarked. 'Expect nothing else,' I said. 'There are only private letters.' He withdrew upon some threat of legal proceedings, and I saw him no more; but another fellow, calling himself Kurtz's cousin, appeared two days later, and was anxious to hear all the details about his dear relative's last moments. Incidentally he gave me to understand that Kurtz had been essentially a great musician. 'There was the making of an immense success,' said the man, who was an organist, I believe, with lank grey hair flowing over a greasy coat-collar. I had no reason to doubt his statement; and to this day I am unable to say what was Kurtz's profession, whether he ever had any—which was the greatest of his talents. I had taken him for a painter who wrote for the papers, or else for a journalist who could paint—but even the cousin (who took snuff during the interview) could not tell me what he had been—exactly. He was a universal genius—on that point I agreed with the old chap, who thereupon blew his nose noisily into a large cotton handkerchief and withdrew in senile agitation, bearing off some family letters and memoranda without importance. Ultimately a journalist anxious to know something of the fate of his 'dear colleague' turned up. This visitor informed me Kurtz's proper sphere ought to have been politics 'on the popular side.' He had furry straight eyebrows, bristly hair cropped short, an eye-glass on a broad ribbon, and, becoming expansive, confessed his opinion that Kurtz really couldn't write a bit—'but heavens! how that man could talk! He electrified large meetings. He had faith—don't you see?—he had the faith. He could get himself to believe anything—anything. He would have been a splendid leader of an extreme party.' 'What party?' I asked. 'Any party,' answered the other. 'He was an—an—extremist.' Did I not think so? I assented. Did I know, he asked, with a sudden flash of curiosity, 'what it was that had induced him to go out there?' 'Yes,' said I, and forthwith handed him the famous Report for publication, if he thought fit. He glanced through it hurriedly, mumbling all the time, judged 'it would do,' and took himself off with this plunder.

"Thus I was left at last with a slim packet of letters and the girl's portrait. She struck me as beautiful—I mean she had a beautiful expression. I know that the sunlight can be made to lie too, yet one felt that no manipulation of light and pose could have conveyed the delicate shade of truthfulness upon those features. She seemed ready to listen without mental reservation, without suspicion, without a thought for herself. I concluded I would go and give her back her portrait and those letters myself. Curiosity? Yes; and also some other feeling perhaps. All that had been Kurtz's had passed out of my hands: his soul, his body, his station, his plans, his ivory, his career. There remained only his memory and his Intended—and I wanted to give that up too to the past, in a way,—to surrender personally all that remained of him with me to that oblivion which is the last word of our common fate. I don't defend myself. I had no clear perception of what it was I really wanted. Perhaps it was an impulse of unconscious loyalty, or the fulfilment of one of those ironic necessities that lurk in the facts of human existence. I don't know. I can't tell. But I went.

"I thought his memory was like the other memories of the dead that accumulate in every man's life,—a vague impress on the brain of shadows that had fallen on it in their swift and final passage; but before the high and ponderous door, between the tall houses of a street as still and decorous as a well-kept alley in a cemetery, I had a vision of him on the stretcher, opening his mouth voraciously, as if to devour all the earth with all its mankind. He lived then before me; he lived as much as he had ever lived—a shadow insatiable of splendid appearances, of frightful realities; a shadow darker than the shadow of the night, and draped nobly in the folds of a gorgeous eloquence. The vision seemed to enter the house with me—the stretcher, the phantom-bearers, the wild crowd of obedient worshippers, the gloom of the forests, the glitter of the reach between the murky bends, the beat of the drum, regular and muffled like the beating of a heart—the heart of a conquering darkness. It was a moment of triumph for the wilderness, an invading and vengeful rush which, it seemed to me, I would have to keep back alone for the salvation of another soul. And the memory of what I had heard him say afar there, with the horned shapes stirring at my back, in the glow of fires, within the patient woods, those broken phrases came back to me, were heard again in their ominous and terrifying simplicity. I remembered his abject pleading, his abject threats, the colossal scale of his vile desires, the meanness, the torment, the tempestuous anguish of his soul. And later on I seemed to see his collected languid manner, when he said one day, 'This lot of ivory now is really mine. The Company did not pay for it. I collected it myself at a very great personal risk. I am afraid they will try to claim it as theirs though. H'm. It is a difficult case. What do you think I ought to do—resist? Eh? I want no more than justice.' . . . He wanted no more than justice—no more than justice. I rang the bell before a mahogany door on the first floor, and while I waited he seemed to stare at me out of the glassy panel—stare with that wide and immense stare embracing, condemning, loathing all the universe. I seemed to hear the whispered cry, 'The horror! The horror!'

"The dusk was falling. I had to wait in a lofty drawing-room with three long windows from floor to ceiling that were like three luminous and bedraped columns. The bent gilt legs and backs of the furniture shone in indistinct curves. The tall marble fireplace had a cold and monumental whiteness. A grand piano stood massively in a corner, with dark gleams on the flat surfaces like a sombre and polished sarcophagus. A high door opened—closed. I rose.

"She came forward, all in black, with a pale head, floating towards me in the dusk. She was in mourning. It was more than a year since his death, more than a year since the news came; she seemed as though she would remember and mourn for ever. She took both my hands in hers and murmured, 'I had heard you were coming.' I noticed she was not very young—I mean not girlish. She had a mature capacity for fidelity, for belief, for suffering. The room seemed to have grown darker, as if all the sad light of the cloudy evening had taken refuge on her forehead. This fair hair, this pale visage, this pure brow, seemed surrounded by an ashy halo from which the dark eyes looked out at me. Their glance was guileless, profound, confident, and trustful. She carried her sorrowful head as though she were proud of that sorrow, as though she would say, I—I alone know how to mourn for him as he deserves. But while we were still shaking hands, such a look of awful desolation came upon her face that I perceived she was one of those creatures that are not the playthings of Time. For her he had died only yesterday. And, by Jove! the impression was so powerful that for me too he seemed to have died only yesterday—nay, this very minute. I saw her and him in the same instant of time—his death and her sorrow—I saw her sorrow in the very moment of his death. Do you understand? I saw them together—I heard them together. She had said, with a deep catch of the breath, 'I have survived'; while my strained ears seemed to hear distinctly, mingled with her tone of despairing regret, the summing-up whisper of his eternal condemnation. I asked myself what I was doing there, with a sensation of panic in my heart as though I had blundered into a place of cruel and absurd mysteries not fit for a human being to behold. She motioned me to a chair. We sat down. I laid the packet gently on the little table, and she put her hand over it. . . . 'You knew him well,' she murmured, after a moment of mourning silence.

"'Intimacy grows quickly out there,' I said. 'I knew him as well as it is possible for one man to know another.'

"'And you admired him,' she said. 'It was impossible to know him and not to admire him. Was it?'

"'He was a remarkable man,' I said, unsteadily. Then before the appealing fixity of her gaze, that seemed to watch for more words on my lips, I went on, 'It was impossible not to—'

"'Love him,' she finished eagerly, silencing me into an appalled dumbness. 'How true! how true! But when you think that no one knew him so well as I! I had all his noble confidence. I knew him best.'

"'You knew him best,' I repeated. And perhaps she did. But with every word spoken the room was growing darker, and only her forehead, smooth and white, remained illumined by the unextinguishable light of belief and love.

"'You were his friend,' she went on. 'His friend,' she repeated, a little louder. 'You must have been, if he had given you this, and sent you to me. I feel I can speak to you—and oh! I must speak. I want you—you who have heard his last words—to know I have been worthy of him. . . . It is not pride. . . . Yes! I am proud to know I understood him better than any one on earth—he told me so himself. And since his mother died I have had no one—no one—to—to—'

"I listened. The darkness deepened. I was not even sure whether he had given me the right bundle. I rather suspect he wanted me to take care of another batch of his papers which, after his death, I saw the manager examining under the lamp. And the girl talked, easing her pain in the certitude of my sympathy; she talked as thirsty men drink. I had heard that her engagement with Kurtz had been disapproved by her people. He wasn't rich enough or something. And indeed I don't know whether he had not been a pauper all his life. He had given me some reason to infer that it was his impatience of comparative poverty that drove him out there.

"'. . . Who was not his friend who had heard him speak once?' she was saying. 'He drew men towards him by what was best in them.' She looked at me with intensity. 'It is the gift of the great,' she went on, and the sound of her low voice seemed to have the accompaniment of all the other sounds, full of mystery, desolation, and sorrow, I had ever heard—the ripple of the river, the soughing of the trees swayed by the wind, the murmurs of wild crowds, the faint ring of incomprehensible words cried from afar, the whisper of a voice speaking from beyond the threshold of an eternal darkness. 'But you have heard him! You know!' she cried.

"'Yes, I know,' I said with something like despair in my heart, but bowing my head before the faith that was in her, before that great and saving illusion that shone with an unearthly glow in the darkness, in the triumphant darkness from which I could not have defended her—from which I could not even defend myself.

"'What a loss to me—to us!'—she corrected herself with beautiful generosity; then added in a murmur, 'To the world.' By the last gleams of twilight I could see the glitter of her eyes, full of tears—of tears that would not fall.

"'I have been very happy—very fortunate—very proud,' she went on. 'Too fortunate. Too happy for a little while. And now I am unhappy for—for life.'

"She stood up; her fair hair seemed to catch all the remaining light in a glimmer of gold. I rose too.

"'And of all this,' she went on, mournfully, 'of all his promise, and of all his greatness, of his generous mind, of his noble heart, nothing remains—nothing but a memory. You and I—'

"'We shall always remember him,' I said, hastily.

"'No!' she cried. 'It is impossible that all this should be lost—that such a life should be sacrificed to leave nothing—but sorrow. You know what vast plans he had. I knew of them too—I could not perhaps understand,—but others knew of them. Something must remain. His words, at least, have not died.'

"'His words will remain,' I said.

"'And his example,' she whispered to herself. 'Men looked up to him,—his goodness shone in every act. His example—'

"'True,' I said; 'his example too. Yes, his example. I forgot that.'

"'But I do not. I cannot—I cannot believe—not yet. I cannot believe that I shall never see him again, that nobody will see him again, never, never, never.'

"She put out her arms as if after a retreating figure, stretching them black and with clasped pale hands across the fading and narrow sheen of the window. Never see him! I saw him clearly enough then. I shall see this eloquent phantom as long as I live, and I shall see her too, a tragic and familiar Shade, resembling in this gesture another one, tragic also, and bedecked with powerless charms, stretching bare brown arms over the glitter of the infernal stream, the stream of darkness. She said suddenly very low, 'He died as he lived.'

"'His end,' said I, with dull anger stirring in me, 'was in every way worthy of his life.'

"'And I was not with him,' she murmured. My anger subsided before a feeling of infinite pity.

"'Everything that could be done—' I mumbled.

"'Ah, but I believed in him more than any one on earth—more than his own mother, more than—himself. He needed me! Me! I would have treasured every sigh, every word, every sign, every glance.'

"I felt like a chill grip on my chest. 'Don't,' I said, in a muffled voice.

"'Forgive me. I—I—have mourned so long in silence—in silence. . . . You were with him—to the last? I think of his loneliness. Nobody near to understand him as I would have understood. Perhaps no one to hear. . . .'

"'To the very end,' I said, shakily. 'I heard his very last words. . . .' I stopped in a fright.

"'Repeat them,' she said in a heart-broken tone. 'I want—I want—something—something—to—to live with.'

"I was on the point of crying at her, 'Don't you hear them?' The dusk was repeating them in a persistent whisper all around us, in a whisper that seemed to swell menacingly like the first whisper of a rising wind. 'The horror! the horror!'

"'His last word—to live with,' she murmured. 'Don't you understand I loved him—I loved him—I loved him!'

"I pulled myself together and spoke slowly.

"'The last word he pronounced was—your name.'

"I heard a light sigh, and then my heart stood still, stopped dead short by an exulting and terrible cry, by the cry of inconceivable triumph and of unspeakable pain. 'I knew it—I was sure!' . . . She knew. She was sure. I heard her weeping; she had hidden her face in her hands. It seemed to me that the house would collapse before I could escape, that the heavens would fall upon my head. But nothing happened. The heavens do not fall for such a trifle. Would they have fallen, I wonder, if I had rendered Kurtz that justice which was his due? Hadn't he said he wanted only justice? But I couldn't. I could not tell her. It would have been too dark—too dark altogether. . . ."

Marlow ceased, and sat apart, indistinct and silent, in the pose of a meditating Buddha. Nobody moved for a time. "We have lost the first of the ebb," said the Director, suddenly. I raised my head. The offing was barred by a black bank of clouds, and the tranquil waterway leading to the uttermost ends of the earth flowed sombre under an overcast sky—seemed to lead into the heart of an immense darkness.

COMPANION READINGS

Joseph Conrad: from *Congo Diary*

Arrived at Matadi[1] on the 13th of June, 1890.

Mr Gosse, chief of the station (O.K.) retaining us for some reason of his own.

Made the acquaintance of Mr Roger Casement,[2] which I should consider as a great pleasure under any circumstances and now it becomes a positive piece of luck.

Thinks, speaks well, most intelligent and very sympathetic.

Feel considerably in doubt about the future. Think just now that my life amongst the people (white) around here cannot be very comfortable. Intend avoid acquaintances as much as possible. * * *

---

1. Colonial station near the mouth of the Congo River. Conrad arrived there on his way to take up his command of a steamship upriver at Kinshasa.
2. Casement (1864–1916) and Conrad were employed at the time by the same company. Casement later served as British consul in various parts of Africa, and was the author of a report on the Congo (1904) that did much to make public the terrible conditions there. He was knighted in 1912. In 1916 he was executed by the British for his part in the Easter Rebellion in Ireland.

24th. Gosse and R.C. gone with a large lot of ivory down to Boma. On G.['s] return to start to up the river. Have been myself busy packing ivory in casks. Idiotic employment. Health good up to now. * * *

Prominent characteristic of the social life here: people speaking ill of each other.

* * *

Friday, 4th July.

Left camp at 6h a.m. after a very unpleasant night. Marching across a chain of hills and then in a maze of hills. At 8:15 opened out into an undulating plain. Took bearings of a break in the chain of mountains on the other side. * * *

Saw another dead body lying by the path in an attitude of meditative repose.

In the evening three women of whom one albino passed our camp. Horrid chalky white with pink blotches. Red eyes. Red hair. Features very Negroid and ugly. Mosquitos. At night when the moon rose heard shouts and drumming in distant villages. Passed a bad night.

Saturday, 5th July. go.

Left at 6:15. Morning cool, even cold and very damp. Sky densely overcast. Gentle breeze from NE. Road through a narrow plain up to R. Kwilu. Swift-flowing and deep, 50 yds. wide. Passed in canoes. After[war]ds up and down very steep hills intersected by deep ravines. Main chain of heights running mostly NW-SE or W and E at times. Stopped at Manyamba. Camp[in]g place bad—in hollow—water very indifferent. Tent set at 10:15.

Section of today's road. NNE Distance 12 m. [a drawing]

Today fell into a muddy puddle. Beastly. The fault of the man that carried me. After camp[in]g went to a small stream, bathed and washed clothes. Getting jolly well sick of this fun.

Tomorrow expect a long march to get to Nsona, 2 days from Manyanga. No sunshine today.

* * *

Saturday, 26th.

Left very early. Road ascending all the time. Passed villages. Country seems thickly inhabited. At 11h arrived at large market place. Left at noon and camped at 1h p.m.

[section of the day's march with notes]

a camp—a white man died here—market—govt. post—mount—crocodile pond—Mafiesa. * * *

Sunday, 27th.

Left at 8h am. Sent luggage carriers straight on to Luasi and went ourselves round by the Mission of Sutili.

Hospitable reception by Mrs Comber. All the missio[naries] absent.

The looks of the whole establishment eminently civilized and very refreshing to see after the lots of tumble-down hovels in which the State and Company agents are content to live—fine buildings. Position on a hill. Rather breezy.

Left at 3h pm. At the first heavy ascent met Mr Davis, miss[ionary] returning from a preaching trip. Rev. Bentley away in the South with his wife. * * *

Tuesday, 29th.

Left camp at 7h after a good night's rest. Continuous ascent; rather easy at first. Crossed wooded ravines and the river Lunzadi by a very decent bridge.

At 9h met Mr Louette escorting a sick agent of the Comp[an]y back to Matadi. Looking very well. Bad news from up the river. All the steamers disabled. One wrecked. Country wooded. At 10:30 camped at Inkissi. * * *

Today did not set the tent but put up in Gov[ernmen]t shimbek.[3] Zanzibari in charge—very obliging. Met ripe pineapple for the first time. On the road today passed a skeleton tied up to a post. Also white man's grave—no name. Heap of stones in the form of a cross.

Health good now.

Wednesday, 30th.

Left at 6 a.m. intending to camp at Kinfumu. Two hours' sharp walk brought me to Nsona na Nsefe. Market. ½ hour after, Harou arrived very ill with billious [sic] attack and fever. Laid him down in Gov[ernmen]t shimbek. Dose of Ipeca.[4] Vomiting bile in enormous quantities. At 11h gave him 1 gramme of quinine and lots of hot tea. Hot fit ending in heavy perspiration. At 2 p.m. put him in hammock and started for Kinfumu. Row with carriers all the way. Harou suffering much through the jerks of the hammock. Camped at a small stream.

At 4h Harou better. Fever gone. * * *

Up till noon, sky clouded and strong NW wind very chilling. From 1h pm to 4h pm sky clear and very hot day. Expect lots of bother with carriers tomorrow. Had them all called and made a speech which they did not understand. They promise good behaviour. * * *

Friday, 1st of August 1890.

* * * Row between the carriers and a man stating himself in Gov[ernmen]t employ, about a mat. Blows with sticks raining hard. Stopped it. Chief came with a youth about 13 suffering from gunshot wound in the head. Bullet entered about an inch above the right eyebrow and came out a little inside. The roots of the hair, fairly in the middle of the brow in a line with the bridge of the nose. Bone not damaged apparently. Gave him a little glycerine to put on the wound made by the bullet on coming out. Harou not very well. Mosquitos. Frogs. Beastly. Glad to see the end of this stupid tramp. Feel rather seedy. Sun rose red. Very hot day. Wind S[ou]th.

Sir Henry Morton Stanley: from *Address to the Manchester Chamber of Commerce*[1]

There is not one manufacturer here present who could not tell me if he had the opportunity how much he personally suffered through the slackness of trade; and I dare say that you have all some vague idea that if things remain as they are the future of the cotton manufacture is not very brilliant. New inventions are continually cropping up, so that your power of producing, if stimulated, is almost incalculable; but new markets for the sale of your products are not of rapid growth, and as other nations, by prohibitive tariffs, are bent upon fostering native manufacturers to the

3. A group of huts.
4. A medicine.
1. The journalist and adventurer Henry Morton Stanley wrote best-selling accounts of his exploits in Africa; an excerpt from his *Through the Dark Continent* begins on page 1839. He delivered this address to the textile manu-

facturers of Manchester in 1886, seeking their support for the commercial exploitation of the Congo. This speech gives a striking example of the outlook—and rhetoric—of the people who created the conditions Conrad encountered when he went to the Congo in 1890.

exclusion of your own, such markets as are now open to you are likely to be taken away from you in course of time. Well, then, I come to you with at least one market where there are at present, perhaps, 6,250,000 yards of cheap cottons sold every year on the Congo banks and in the Congo markets.[2]

I was interested the other day in making a curious calculation, which was, supposing that all the inhabitants of the Congo basin were simply to have one Sunday dress each, how many yards of Manchester cloth would be required; and the amazing number was 320,000,000 yards, just for one Sunday dress! (Cheers.) Proceeding still further with these figures I found that two Sunday dresses and four everyday dresses would in one year amount to 3,840,000,000 yards, which at 2d. [two pence] per yard would be of the value of £16,000,000. The more I pondered upon these things I discovered that I could not limit these stores of cotton cloth to day dresses. I would have to provide for night dresses also—(laughter)—and these would consume 160,000,000 yards. (Cheers.) Then the grave cloths came into mind, and, as a poor lunatic, who burned Bolobo Station,[3] destroyed 30,000 yards of cloth in order that he should not be cheated out of a respectable burial, I really feared for a time that the millions would get beyond measurable calculation. However, putting such accidents aside, I estimate that, if my figures of population are approximately correct, 2,000,000 die every year, and to bury these decently, and according to the custom of those who possess cloth, 16,000,000 yards will be required, while the 40,000 chiefs will require an average of 100 yards each, or 4,000,000 yards. I regarded these figures with great satisfaction, and I was about to close my remarks upon the millions of yards of cloth that Manchester would perhaps be required to produce when I discovered that I had neglected to provide for the family wardrobe or currency chest, for you must know that in the Lower Congo there is scarcely a family that has not a cloth fund of about a dozen pieces of about 24 yards each. This is a very important institution, otherwise how are the family necessities to be provided for? How are the fathers and mothers of families to go to market to buy greens, bread, oil, ground nuts, chickens, fish, and goats, and how is the petty trade to be conducted? How is ivory to be purchased, the gums, rubber, dye powders, gunpowder, copper slugs, guns, trinkets, knives, and swords to be bought without a supply of cloth? Now, 8,000,000 families at 300 yards each will require 2,400,000,000. (Cheers.) You all know how perishable such currency must be; but if you sum up these several millions of yards, and value all of them at the average price of 2d. per yard, you will find that it will be possible for Manchester to create a trade—in the course of time—in cottons in the Congo basin amounting in value to about £26,000,000 annually. (Loud cheers.) I have said nothing about Rochdale savelist, or your own superior prints, your gorgeous handkerchiefs, with their variegated patterns, your checks and striped cloths, your ticking and twills.[4] I must satisfy myself with suggesting them; your own imaginations will no doubt carry you to the limbo of immeasurable and incalculable millions. (Laughter and cheers.)

2. The Congo Free State (later Zaire), a vast area of central Africa around the Congo River, was formally brought under the ownership of Leopold II of Belgium and other investors in the International Association of the Congo by the Berlin West Africa Conference of 1884–1885. Stanley's expeditions there (from 1876) had been financed by Leopold, and from 1879 Stanley had set up trading stations along the river to facilitate the exploita-

tion of the area's natural resources.
3. The London *Times* carried frequent reports of disturbances in the Congo at this time; in March 1884, for example, Congolese attacks on foreign trading establishments at Nokki in the Lower Congo had caused the Europeans to "declare war against the natives."
4. Savelist is cheap fabric; ticking is a strong cotton or linen fabric; twill is a kind of textile weave.

Now, if your sympathy for yourselves and the fate of Manchester has been excited sufficiently, your next natural question would be as follows: We acknowledge, sir, that you have contrived by an artful array of imposing millions to excite our attention, at least, to this field; but we beg to ask you what Manchester is to do in order that we may begin realising this sale of untold millions of yards of cotton cloth? I answer that the first thing to do is for you to ask the British Government to send a cruiser to the mouth of the Congo to keep watch and ward over that river until the European nations have agreed among themselves as to what shall be done with the river, lest one of these days you will hear that it is too late. (Hear, hear.) Secondly, to study whether, seeing that it will never do to permit Portugal to assume sovereignty over that river[5]—and England publicly disclaims any wish to possess that river for herself—it would not be as well to allow the International Association to act as guardians of international right to free trade and free entrance and exit into and out of the river. (Hear, hear.) The main point, remember, always is a guarantee that the lower river shall be free, that, however the Upper Congo may be developed, no Power, inspired by cupidity, shall seize upon the mouth of the river and build custom houses. (Hear, hear.) The Lower Congo in the future will only be valuable because down its waters will have to be floated the produce of the rich basin above to the ocean steamships. It will always have a fair trade of its own, but it bears no proportion to the almost limitless trade that the Upper Congo could furnish. If the Association could be assured that the road from Europe to Vivi[6] was for ever free, the first steps to realise the sale of those countless millions of yards of cotton cloth would be taken. Over six millions of yards are now used annually; but we have no means of absorbing more, owing to the difficulties of transport. Every man capable and willing to carry a load is employed. When human power was discovered to be not further available we tested animal power and discovered it to be feebler and more costly than the other; and we have come to the conclusion that steam power must now assist us or we remain *in statu quo* [as things now stand]. But before having recourse to this steam power, and building the iron road along which your bales of cotton fabrics may roll on to the absorbing markets of the Upper Congo unceasingly, the Association pauses to ask you, and the peoples of other English cities, such as London, Liverpool, Glasgow, Birmingham, Leeds, Preston, Sheffield, who profess to understand the importance of the work we have been doing, and the absorbing power of those markets we have reached, what help you will render us, for your own sakes, to make those markets accessible? (Hear, hear.) The Association will not build that railway to the Upper Congo, nor invest one piece of sterling gold in it, unless they are assured they will not be robbed of it, and the Lower Congo will be placed under some flag that shall be a guarantee to all the world that its waters and banks are absolutely free. (Cheers.)

You will agree with me, I am sure, that trade ought to expand and commerce grow, and if we can coax it into mature growth in this Congo basin that it would be a praiseworthy achievement, honoured by men and gods; for out of this trade, this intercourse caused by peaceful barter, proceed all those blessings which you and I enjoy. The more trade thrives, the more benefits to mankind are multipled, and nearer to gods do men become. (Hear, hear.) The builders of railroads through wilder-

---

5. The mouth of the Congo River had been discovered by the Portuguese in 1482.
6. A town on the Upper Congo river; from 1882 Stanley

had been arguing that a railway should be built between the Lower and Upper Congo to facilitate the exploitation of the interior. It was completed in 1898.

nesses generally require large concessions of lands; but the proposed builders of this railway to connect the Lower with the Upper Congo do not ask for any landed concessions; but they ask for a concession of authority over the Lower Congo in order that the beneficent policy which directs the civilising work on the Upper Congo may be extended to the Lower River, and that the mode of government and action may be uniform throughout. The beneficent policy referred to is explained in the treaty made and concluded with the United States Government.[7] That treaty says: "That with the object of enabling civilisation and commerce to penetrate into Equatorial Africa the Free States of the Congo have resolved to levy no customs duties whatever. The Free States also guarantee to all men who establish themselves in their territories the right of purchasing, selling, or leasing any land and buildings, of creating factories and of trade on the sole condition that they conform to the law. The International Association of the Congo is prepared to enter into engagements with other nations who desire to secure the free admission of their products on the same terms as those agreed upon with the United States."

Here you have in brief the whole policy. I might end here, satisfied with having reminded you of these facts, which probably you had forgotten. Obedience to the laws—that is, laws drawn for protection of all—is the common law of all civilised communities, without which men would soon become demoralised. Can anybody object to that condition? Probably many of you here recollect reading those interesting letters from the Congo which were written by an English clerk in charge of an English factory. They ended with the cry of "Let us alone." In few words he meant to say, "We are doing very well as we are, we do not wish to be protected, and least of all taxed—therefore, let us alone. Our customers, the natives, are satisfied with us. The native chiefs are friendly and in accord with us; the disturbances, if any occur, are local; they are not general, and they right themselves quickly enough, for the trader cannot exist here if he is not just and kind in his dealings. The obstreperous and violent white is left to himself and ruin. Therefore, let us alone." Most heartily do I echo this cry; but unfortunately the European nations will not heed this cry; they think that some mode of government is necessary to curb those inclined to be refractory, and if there is at present a necessity to exhibit judicial power and to restrict evil-minded and ill-conditioned whites, as the Congo basin becomes more and more populated this necessity will be still more apparent. At the same time, if power appears on the Congo with an arbitrary and unfeeling front—with a disposition to tax and levy burdensome tariffs just as trade begins to be established—the outlook for enterprise becomes dismal and dark indeed.[8] (Hear, hear.) * * *

No part of Africa, look where I might, appeared so promising to me as this neglected tenth part of the continent. I have often fancied myself—when I had nothing to do better than dream—gazing from some lofty height, and looking down upon this square compact patch of 800,000,000 acres, with its 80,000 native towns, its population of 40,000,000 souls, its 17,000 miles of river waters, and its 30,000 square miles of lakes, all lying torpid, lifeless, inert, soaked in brutishness and bestiality, and I have never yet descended from that airy perch in the empyrean and

7. The United States was the first country to recognize the right of the International Association to govern the Congo territories in April 1884.

8. The right of the International Association to govern the Congo was eventually ended in 1908, following widespread protests against the regime's brutality.

touched earth but I have felt a purpose glow in me to strive to do something to awaken it into life and movement, and I have sometimes half fancied that the face of aged Livingstone,[9] vague and indistinct as it were, shone through the warm, hazy atmosphere, with a benignant smile encouraging me in my purpose. * * *

Yet, though examined from every point of view, a study of the Upper Congo and its capabilities produces these exciting arrays of figures and possibilities, I would not pay a two-shilling piece for it all so long as it remains as it is. It will absorb easily the revenue of the wealthiest nation in Europe without any return. I would personally one hundred times over prefer a snug little freehold in a suburb of Manchester to being the owner of the 1,300,000 English square miles of the Congo basin if it is to remain as inaccessible as it is to-day, or if it is to be blocked by that fearful tariff-loving nation, the Portuguese. (Hear, hear.) But if I were assured that the Lower Congo would remain free, and the flag of the Association guaranteed its freedom, I would if I were able build that railway myself—build it solid and strong—and connect the Lower Congo with the Upper Congo, perfectly satisfied that I should be followed by the traders and colonists of all nations. * * * The Portuguese have had nearly 400 years given them to demonstrate to the world what they could do with the river whose mouth they discovered, and they have been proved to be incapable to do any good with it, and now civilisation is inclined to say to them, "Stand off from this broad highway into the regions beyond—(cheers); let others who are not paralytic strive to do what they can with it to bring it within the number of accessible markets. There are 40,000,000 of naked people beyond that gateway, and the cotton spinners of Manchester are waiting to clothe them. Rochdale and Preston women are waiting for the word to weave them warm blue and crimson savelist. Birmingham foundries are glowing with the red metal that shall presently be made into ironwork in every fashion and shape for them, and the trinkets that shall adorn those dusky bosoms; and the ministers of Christ are zealous to bring them, the poor benighted heathen, into the Christian fold." (Cheers.)

Mr JACOB BRIGHT, M.P., who was received with loud cheers, said: I have listened with extreme interest to one of the ablest, one of the most eloquent addresses which have ever been delivered in this city—(cheers); and I have heard with uncommon pleasure the views of a man whose ability, whose splendid force of character, whose remarkable heroism, have given him a world-wide reputation. (Cheers.) * * *

Mr GRAFTON, M.P., moved:—

> That the best thanks of this meeting be and are hereby given to Mr H. M. Stanley for his address to the members of the Chamber, and for the interesting information conveyed by him respecting the Congo and prospects of international trade on the West Coast and interior of Africa.

He remarked that Mr Stanley's name was already enrolled in the pages of history, and would be handed down to posterity with the names of the greatest benefactors of our species, such as Columbus, who had opened out the pathways of the world. Long might Mr Stanley be spared to witness the benefit of his arduous and beneficent labours. (Cheers.)

---

9. David Livingstone (1813–1873), Scottish explorer and missionary. His expeditions into central Africa, in search of the source of the Nile River, were heavily publicized; when Livingstone "disappeared" in the course of what proved to be his last expedition, Stanley, then a correspondent for the *New York Herald*, was sent to find him. The two men met on the banks of Lake Tanganyika in East Africa in 1871; Stanley published an account of their meeting in *How I Found Livingstone* (1872).

Gang of Four: We Live As We Dream, Alone[1]

Everybody is in too many pieces
No man's land surrounds our desires
To crack the shell we mix with others
Some lie in the arms of lovers

The city is the place to be
With no money you go crazy
I need an occupation
You have to pay for satisfaction

We live as we dream, alone
To crack this shell we mix with others
Some flirt with fascism
Some lie in the arms of lovers

We live as we dream, alone
(repeat)

Everybody is in too many pieces
No man's land surrounds me
Without money we'll all go crazy

Man and woman need to work
It helps to define ourselves
We were not born in isolation
But sometimes it seems that way

We live as we dream, alone
(repeat)

We live as we dream, alone
The space between our work and its product
Some fall into fatalism
As if it started out this way

We live as we dream, alone
(repeat)

We live as we dream, alone
We were not born in isolation
But sometimes it seems that way
The space between our work and its product
As if it must always be this way

With our money we'll . . .

---

1. In 1976 the Sex Pistols set off the British punk revolution with their first single, "Anarchy in the U.K." The Gang of Four is one of many bands that arose during the early years of punk, when a wide range of musical possibilities seemed open to anyone with a guitar. The Gang of Four's music combines the assaultive sound of punk bands with an infectious dance sensibility—lacing this unlikely hybrid with neo-Marxist lyrics about consumerism and labor. "We Live As We Dream, Alone," from their 1982 album *Songs of the Free*, takes a famous line from *Heart of Darkness* and makes it the cry of alienated labor, thereby reframing Conrad's message for a nation dominated by the conservative policies of Thatcherism.

Thomas Hardy
1840–1928

Thomas Hardy led a double life: one of the great Victorian novelists, he abandoned fiction in 1896 and reinvented himself as a poet. In a series of volumes published from 1898 through the early decades of the twentieth century, Hardy emerged as one of the most compelling voices in modern poetry. How should this strangely bifurcated literary career be read? There are continuities as well as divergences between Hardy's fiction and his poetry, and the shifts in his work provide a telling instance of the interwoven links and discontinuities between the Victorian era and the new modernism of the twentieth century.

Hardy was born and reared in the village of Higher Bockhampton, Stinsford, in the rural county of Dorset in southern England. He left home in his early twenties and worked as a church architect in London for five years, then returned to the family home in 1867; he continued to accept architectural commissions while trying his hand at fiction and poetry. In early poems such as *Hap* and *Neutral Tones* Hardy revealed his abiding sense of a universe ruled by a blind or hostile fate, a world whose landscapes are etched with traces of the fleeting stories of their inhabitants. He was not able to find a publisher for such works, and he largely stopped writing poetry, but his first novel, *Desperate Remedies,* was published in 1871. By 1874 he was earning a steady income from his writing and was able to marry Emma Lavinia Gifford, the sister-in-law of a rector whose church he had been restoring. He produced twenty novels within a twenty-five year period, achieving fame, popularity, and no little controversy for the provocative and dark worlds he created. In *Far from the Madding Crowd, The Return of the Native, Tess of the d'Urbervilles,* and *Jude the Obscure,* Hardy transformed the realist novel of manners into tragic accounts of the industrialization of rural Britain, the bankruptcy of religious faith, and irreconcilable tensions between social classes and between men and women. Though he had become a master of characterization and plot, in his later novels Hardy grew increasingly preoccupied with fundamentally lyrical questions of interiority, subjective perception, and personal voice. After the sexual frankness of *Jude the Obscure* provoked shocked reviews—the Bishop of Wakefield went so far as to burn the book—Hardy decided to abandon his prose writing altogether and to mine his chosen territory with the tools of a poet.

He began by recreating in poetry the landscape of his fiction. Hardy's first poetry collection, published when he was fifty-eight, was *Wessex Poems* (1898), its title referring to the imaginary countryside that he had created in his novels, loosely based on regions in the south of England but named for a long-vanished medieval kingdom. Hardy's "Wessex" was a place whose towns and roads and forests and fields were breathed into life by the novelist. The Wessex novels were published with maps of the territory, and the landmarks were to remain constant throughout the disparate books. The region took such a hold on readers' imaginations that a Wessex tourist industry emerged, one which is still in place today. Hardy was as painstaking in giving the precise (although imaginary) coordinates of a village pathway as he was in tracing the path of a character's destiny.

Many of Hardy's poems take root in this same creative landscape, now viewed by an intensely self-aware speaker who retraces his personal history, himself "tracked by phantoms having weird detective ways," as he says in *Wessex Heights.* Burning logs, a photograph, a diminishing figure on a train platform, a deer at a window all provide "moments of vision" (the title of one of his collections) that foreshadow the modernist "epiphanies" of Joyce and Woolf. Like the major modernists, Hardy explored the workings of memory, of perception, and of individual vision. In other poems, he focused on contemporary events, most notably in a series of poems written during World War I, unsparing in their presentation both of the necessity of waging the conflict and of its horrifying waste.

In his poetry as in his prose, Hardy's modern themes are typically set in a rural landscape with ancient roots. A constant feature of the Wessex novels involves characters setting off on one of the myriad footpaths connecting obscure villages and solitary cottages with one another. Hardy invented his own geography for Wessex, but the footpaths really existed and were the most important trails carved into the landscape by travelers over many years. Called "ley lines" in folk culture, such footpaths are thought to gather their energy over time, as hundreds of people gradually wear down a shared path and leave traces of themselves in the form of memory and tradition. Hardy's poems move between personal, historical, and natural levels of experience, but it is the landscape above all that conveys the power of these events.

Hardy embodied his moments of vision in poems that recall old oral and religious forms of verse, especially those of ballads and hymns. Like Wordsworth, Burns, and Kipling, Hardy was fascinated by the power of popular verse forms to convey deep truths in seemingly simple meters and diction; like his predecessors, Hardy brought his traditional forms to life by subtle modulations of their elements. The lines of Hardy's poetry are measured with extreme care and precision—not in any way approaching "free verse." As W. H. Auden wrote of Hardy's poetry: "No English poet, not even Donne or Browning, employed so many and so complicated stanza forms. Anyone who imitates his style will learn at least one thing, how to make words fit into a complicated structure." With architectural care, Hardy built up his words into complicated structures, lines, and stanzas following well-used poetic paths. With its compelling mixture of tradition and modernity, stoic calm and deep emotional intensity, Hardy's poetry has become a touchstone for modern poets writing in English, from Ezra Pound, who said he "needed no other poet," to Philip Larkin, Seamus Heaney, and Derek Walcott. "Auden worshiped his honesty, Eliot disliked his heresy," the critic Irving Howe has commented; "but Hardy prepared the ground for both."

Hardy mined his native landscape, and his own memory, until his death, composing many of his best poems in his seventies and eighties. He had built a house on the outskirts of Dorchester in 1885, and he lived there for the rest of his life, with his wife Emma until her death in 1912, and subsequently with his secretary, Florence Dugdale, whom he married in 1914. When he died, his body was buried in Westminster Abbey; but his heart, as he had directed, was buried in the grave of his wife Emma, next to his father's grave, in the Stinsford churchyard.

Hardy's short story *The Withered Arm* appears on page 1476.

Hap°   *chance*

If but some vengeful god would call to me
From up the sky, and laugh: "Thou suffering thing,
Know that thy sorrow is my ecstasy,
That thy love's loss is my hate's profiting!"

5   Then would I bear it, clench myself, and die,
Steeled by the sense of ire unmerited;
Half-eased in that a Powerfuller than I
Had willed and meted° me the tears I shed.   *given*

But not so. How arrives it joy lies slain,
10 And why unblooms the best hope ever sown?
—Crass Casualty obstructs the sun and rain,
And dicing° Time for gladness casts a moan. . . .   *gambling*
These purblind° Doomsters had as readily strown   *half-blind*
Blisses about my pilgrimage as pain.

1866   1898

Neutral Tones

We stood by a pond that winter day,
And the sun was white, as though chidden° of God,   *rebuked*
And a few leaves lay on the starving sod;
   —They had fallen from an ash, and were gray.

5   Your eyes on me were as eyes that rove
Over tedious riddles of years ago;
And some words played between us to and fro
   On which lost the more by our love.

The smile on your mouth was the deadest thing
10   Alive enough to have strength to die;
And a grin of bitterness swept thereby
   Like an ominous bird a-wing . . . .

Since then, keen lessons that love deceives,
And wrings with wrong, have shaped to me
15   Your face, and the God-curst sun, and a tree,
   And a pond edged with grayish leaves.

1867   1898

Wessex Heights

There are some heights in Wessex,[1] shaped as if by a kindly hand
For thinking, dreaming, dying on, and at crises when I stand,
Say, on Ingpen Beacon eastward, or on Wylls-Neck westwardly,
I seem where I was before my birth, and after death may be.

5   In the lowlands I have no comrade, not even the lone man's friend—
Her who suffereth long and is kind;[2] accepts what he is too weak to mend:
Down there they are dubious and askance; there nobody thinks as I,
But mind-chains do not clank where one's next neighbour is the sky.

In the towns I am tracked by phantoms having weird detective ways—
10   Shadows of beings who fellowed with myself of earlier days:
They hang about at places, and they say harsh heavy things—
Men with a wintry sneer, and women with tart disparagings.

Down there I seem to be false to myself, my simple self that was,
And is not now, and I see him watching, wondering what crass cause
15   Can have merged him into such a strange continuator as this,
Who yet has something in common with himself, my chrysalis.

I cannot go to the great grey Plain; there's a figure against the moon,
Nobody sees it but I, and it makes my breast beat out of tune;
I cannot go to the tall-spired town, being barred by the forms now passed
20   For everybody but me, in whose long vision they stand there fast.

1. An imaginary county in southwest England that forms the setting for Hardy's writings; the place names that follow are in "Wessex."

2. Cf. Corinthians 13.4: "Charity suffereth long, and is kind."

There's a ghost at Yell'ham Bottom chiding loud at the fall of the night,
There's a ghost in Froom-side Vale, thin-lipped and vague, in a shroud
    of white,
There is one in the railway train whenever I do not want it near,
I see its profile against the pane, saying what I would not hear.

25   As for one rare fair woman, I am now but a thought of hers,
I enter her mind and another thought succeeds me that she prefers,
Yet my love for her in its fulness she herself even did not know;
Well, time cures hearts of tenderness, and now I can let her go.

So I am found on Ingpen Beacon, or on Wylls-Neck to the west,
30   Or else on homely Bulbarrow, or little Pilsdon Crest,
Where men have never cared to haunt, nor women have walked with me,
And ghosts then keep their distance; and I know some liberty.

1898

The Darkling Thrush[1]

I leant upon a coppice° gate   *wood*
   When Frost was spectre-gray,
And Winter's dregs made desolate
   The weakening eye of day.
5 The tangled bine-stems° scored the sky   *stems of bushes*
   Like strings of broken lyres,
And all mankind that haunted nigh
   Had sought their household fires.

The land's sharp features seemed to be
10   The Century's corpse outleant[2],
His crypt the cloudy canopy,
   The wind his death-lament.
The ancient pulse of germ° and birth   *seed*
   Was shrunken hard and dry,
15 And every spirit upon earth
   Seemed fervourless as I.

At once a voice arose among
   The bleak twigs overhead
In a full-hearted evensong
20   Of joy illimited;
An aged thrush, frail, gaunt, and small,
   In blast-beruffled plume,
Had chosen thus to fling his soul
   Upon the growing gloom.

25 So little cause for carolings
   Of such ecstatic sound
Was written on terrestrial things
   Afar or nigh around,
That I could think there trembled through

---

1. The poem was published on 31 December 1900.   2. As if leaning out from a coffin.

30   His happy good-night air
    Some blessed Hope, whereof he knew
        And I was unaware.

On the Departure Platform

We kissed at the barrier; and passing through
She left me, and moment by moment got
Smaller and smaller, until to my view
    She was but a spot;

5   A wee white spot of muslin fluff
That down the diminishing platform bore
Through hustling crowds of gentle and rough
    To the carriage door.

Under the lamplight's fitful glowers,
10   Behind dark groups from far and near,
Whose interests were apart from ours,
    She would disappear,

Then show again, till I ceased to see
That flexible form, that nebulous white;
15   And she who was more than my life to me
    Had vanished quite . . . .

We have penned new plans since that fair fond day,
And in season she will appear again—
Perhaps in the same soft white array—
20   But never as then!

—"And why, young man, must eternally fly
A joy you'll repeat, if you love her well?"
—O friend, nought happens twice thus; why,
    I cannot tell!

                                  1909

The Convergence of the Twain
(Lines on the loss of the "Titanic")[1]

1

In a solitude of the sea
Deep from human vanity,
And the Pride of Life that planned her, stilly couches she.

2

Steel chambers, late the pyres
    Of her salamandrine° fires,   *white-hot*
5   Cold currents thrid°, and turn to rhythmic tidal lyres.   *thread*

3

Over the mirrors meant
    To glass the opulent
The sea-worm crawls—grotesque, slimed, dumb, indifferent.

---

1. The largest ocean-liner of its day, the supposedly unsinkable *Titanic* sank on 15 April 1912 on its maiden voyage after colliding with an iceberg; two thirds of its 2,200 passengers died.

4

10   Jewels in joy designed
To ravish the sensuous mind
Lie lightless, all their sparkles bleared and black and blind.

5

Dim moon-eyed fishes near
Gaze at the gilded gear
15   And query: "What does this vaingloriousness down here?" . . .

6

Well: while was fashioning
This creature of cleaving wing,
The Immanent Will that stirs and urges everything

7

Prepared a sinister mate
20   For her—so gaily great—
A Shape of Ice, for the time far and dissociate.[2]

8

And as the smart ship grew
In stature, grace, and hue,
In shadowy silent distance grew the Iceberg too.

9

25   Alien they seemed to be:
No mortal eye could see
The intimate welding of their later history,

10

Or sign that they were bent
By paths coincident
30   On being anon twin halves of one august event,

11

Till the Spinner of the Years
Said "Now!" And each one hears,
And consummation comes, and jars two hemispheres.

1912   1912

At Castle Boterel[1]

As I drive to the junction of lane and highway,
And the drizzle bedrenches the waggonette,°   *cart*
I look behind at the fading byway,
And see on its slope, now glistening wet,
5   Distinctly yet

Myself and a girlish form benighted
In dry March weather. We climb the road
Beside a chaise.° We had just alighted   *carriage*
To ease the sturdy pony's load
10   When he sighed and slowed.

---

2. According to Hardy, the Immanent Will is that which secretly guides events.
1. Hardy's first wife Emma died in November 1912; in 1913 the poet revisited scenes of their courtship in Cornwall in southwest England.

What we did as we climbed, and what we talked of
    Matters not much, nor to what it led,—
Something that life will not be balked of
    Without rude reason till hope is dead,
15   And feeling fled.

It filled but a minute. But was there ever
    A time of such quality, since or before,
In that hill's story? To one mind never,
    Though it has been climbed, foot-swift, foot-sore,
20   By thousands more.

Primaeval rocks form the road's steep border,
    And much have they faced there, first and last,
Of the transitory in Earth's long order;
    But what they record in colour and cast
25   Is—that we two passed.

And to me, though Time's unflinching rigour,
    In mindless rote, has ruled from sight
The substance now, one phantom figure
    Remains on the slope, as when that night
30   Saw us alight.

I look and see it there, shrinking, shrinking,
    I look back at it amid the rain
For the very last time; for my sand is sinking,
    And I shall traverse old love's domain
35   Never again.
March 1913   1914

Channel Firing[1]

That night your great guns, unawares,
Shook all our coffins as we lay,
And broke the chancel window-squares,
We thought it was the Judgment-day

5   And sat upright. While drearisome
Arose the howl of wakened hounds:
The mouse let fall the altar-crumb,
The worms drew back into the mounds,
The glebe° cow drooled. Till God called, "No;   *field*
10   It's gunnery practice out at sea
Just as before you went below;
The world is as it used to be:

"All nations striving strong to make
Red war yet redder. Mad as hatters
15   They do no more for Christés sake
Than you who are helpless in such matters.

1. The poem refers to military exercises in the English Channel prior to World War 1.

"That this is not the judgment-hour
For some of them's a blessed thing,
For if it were they'd have to scour
20   Hell's floor for so much threatening . . . .

"Ha, ha. It will be warmer when
I blow the trumpet (if indeed
I ever do; for you are men,
And rest eternal sorely need)."

25   So down we lay again. "I wonder,
Will the world ever saner be,"
Said one, "than when He sent us under
In our indifferent century!"

And many a skeleton shook his head.
30   "Instead of preaching forty year,"
My neighbour Parson Thirdly said,
"I wish I had stuck to pipes and beer."

Again the guns disturbed the hour,
Roaring their readiness to avenge,
35   As far inland as Stourton Tower,
And Camelot, and starlit Stonehenge.[2]

April 1914   1914

In Time of "The Breaking of Nations"[1]

1

Only a man harrowing clods
In a slow silent walk
With an old horse that stumbles and nods
Half asleep as they stalk.

2

5   Only thin smoke without flame
From the heaps of couch-grass;
Yet this will go onward the same
Though Dynasties pass.

3

Yonder a maid and her wight°   *man*
10   Come whispering by:
War's annals will cloud into night
Ere their story die.

1915   1916

I Looked Up from My Writing

I looked up from my writing,
And gave a start to see,

---

2. The town of Stour Head, which Hardy calls Stourton, is in the county of Dorset. According to legend, Camelot was the site of King Arthur's court; Stonehenge is a prehistoric site in southwest England.

1. Cf. Jeremiah 51.20: "Thou art my battle axe and weapons of war: for with thee will I break in pieces the nations, and with thee will I destroy kingdoms."

As if rapt in my inditing,
    The moon's full gaze on me.

5   Her meditative misty head
        Was spectral in its air,
    And I involuntarily said,
        "What are you doing there?"

    "Oh, I've been scanning pond and hole
10   And waterway hereabout
For the body of one with a sunken soul
        Who has put his life-light out.

    "Did you hear his frenzied tattle?
        It was sorrow for his son
15   Who is slain in brutish battle,
        Though he has injured none.

    "And now I am curious to look
        Into the blinkered mind
Of one who wants to write a book
20   In a world of such a kind."

Her temper overwrought me,
    And I edged to shun her view,
For I felt assured she thought me
    One who should drown him too.

1917

"And There Was a Great Calm"[1]
(On the Signing of the Armistice, 11 Nov. 1918)[2]

1

There had been years of Passion—scorching, cold,
And much Despair, and Anger heaving high,
Care whitely watching, Sorrows manifold,
Among the young, among the weak and old,
5   And the pensive Spirit of Pity whispered, "Why?"

2

Men had not paused to answer. Foes distraught
Pierced the thinned peoples in a brute-like blindness,
Philosophies that sages long had taught,
And Selflessness, were as an unknown thought,
10 And "Hell!" and "Shell!" were yapped at Lovingkindness.

3

The feeble folk at home had grown full-used
To "dug-outs," "snipers," "'Huns,'"[3] from the war-adept
In the mornings heard, and at evetides perused;

1. A phrase from Mark 4.39, after Jesus has calmed a storm at sea.
2. The armistice ending World War I was signed by Germany and the Allies on this date.
3. Slang for "Germans" during the war.

15 To day-dreamt men in millions, when they mused—
   To nightmare-men in millions when they slept.

4

   Waking to wish existence timeless, null,
   Sirius[4] they watched above where armies fell;
   He seemed to check his flapping when, in the lull
   Of night a boom came thencewise, like the dull
20 Plunge of a stone dropped into some deep well.

5

   So, when old hopes that earth was bettering slowly
   Were dead and damned, there sounded "War is done!"
   One morrow. Said the bereft, and meek, and lowly,
   "Will men some day be given to grace? yea, wholly,
25 And in good sooth,° as our dreams used to run?"   *truth*

6

   Breathless they paused. Out there men raised their glance
   To where had stood those poplars lank and lopped,
   As they had raised it through the four years' dance
   Of Death in the now familiar flats of France;
30 And murmured, "Strange, this! How? All firing stopped?"

7

   Aye; all was hushed. The about-to-fire fired not,
   The aimed-at moved away in trance-lipped song.
   One checkless regiment slung a clinching shot
   And turned. The Spirit of Irony smirked out, "What?
35 Spoil peradventures° woven of Rage and Wrong?"   *perhaps*

8

   Thenceforth no flying fires inflamed the gray,
   No hurtlings shook the dewdrop from the thorn,
   No moan perplexed the mute bird on the spray;
   Worn horses mused: "We are not whipped to-day;"
40 No weft-winged engines° blurred the moon's thin horn.   *early airplanes*

9

   Calm fell. From Heaven distilled a clemency;
   There was peace on earth, and silence in the sky;
   Some could, some could not, shake off misery:
   The Sinister Spirit sneered: "It had to be!"
45 And again the Spirit of Pity whispered, "Why?"
1918   1919, 1922

Logs on the Hearth
A Memory of a Sister[1]

   The fire advances along the log
        Of the tree we felled,
   Which bloomed and bore striped apples by the peck°   *basketful*
        Till its last hour of bearing knelled.

---

4. The brightest star in the night sky.   1. Hardy's sister Mary died in November 1915.

5   The fork that first my hand would reach
        And then my foot
    In climbings upward inch by inch, lies now
      Sawn, sapless, darkening with soot.

      Where the bark chars is where, one year,
10   It was pruned, and bled—
    Then overgrew the wound. But now, at last,
      Its growings all have stagnated.

      My fellow-climber rises dim
        From her chilly grave—
15   Just as she was, her foot near mine on the bending limb,
      Laughing, her young brown hand awave.

1915   1917

The Photograph

  The flame crept up the portrait line by line
  As it lay on the coals in the silence of night's profound,
    And over the arm's incline,
  And along the marge° of the silkwork superfine,   *margin*
5 And gnawed at the delicate bosom's defenceless round.

  Then I vented a cry of hurt, and averted my eyes;
  The spectacle was one that I could not bear,
    To my deep and sad surprise;
  But, compelled to heed, I again looked furtivewise
10 Till the flame had eaten her breasts, and mouth, and hair.

  "Thank God, she is out of it now!" I said at last,
  In a great relief of heart when the thing was done
    That had set my soul aghast,
  And nothing was left of the picture unsheathed from the past
15 But the ashen ghost of the card it had figured on.

  She was a woman long hid amid packs of years,
  She might have been living or dead; she was lost to my sight,
    And the deed that had nigh drawn tears
  Was done in a casual clearance of life's arrears;
20 But I felt as if I had put her to death that night! . . .

        . . .

  —Well; she knew nothing thereof did she survive,
  And suffered nothing if numbered among the dead;
    Yet—yet—if on earth alive
  Did she feel a smart, and with vague strange anguish strive?
25 If in heaven, did she smile at me sadly and shake her head?

                            1917

The Fallow Deer at the Lonely House

  One without looks in to-night
    Through the curtain-chink

From the sheet of glistening white;
One without looks in to-night
    As we sit and think
    By the fender-brink.

We do not discern those eyes
    Watching in the snow;
Lit by lamps of rosy dyes
We do not discern those eyes
    Wondering, aglow,
    Fourfooted, tiptoe.

1922

Afterwards

When the Present has latched its postern° behind my tremulous stay,   *gate*
    And the May month flaps its glad green leaves like wings,
Delicate-filmed as new-spun silk, will the neighbours say,
    "He was a man who used to notice such things"?

5   If it be in the dusk when, like an eyelid's soundless blink,
    The dewfall-hawk comes crossing the shades to alight
Upon the wind-warped upland thorn, a gazer may think,
    "To him this must have been a familiar sight."

If I pass during some nocturnal blackness, mothy and warm,
10   When the hedgehog travels furtively over the lawn,
One may say, "He strove that such innocent creatures should come to no harm,
    But he could do little for them; and now he is gone."

If, when hearing that I have been stilled at last, they stand at the door,
    Watching the full-starred heavens that winter sees,
15   Will this thought rise on those who will meet my face no more,
    "He was one who had an eye for such mysteries"?

And will any say when my bell of quittance is heard in the gloom,
    And a crossing breeze cuts a pause in its outrollings,
Till they rise again, as they were a new bell's boom,
20   "He hears it not now, but used to notice such things"?

1917

Epitaph

I never cared for Life: Life cared for me,
And hence I owed it some fidelity.
It now says, "Cease; at length thou hast learnt to grind
Sufficient toll for an unwilling mind,
And I dismiss thee—not without regard
That thou didst ask no ill-advised reward,
Nor sought in me much more than thou couldst find."

1922

Bernard Shaw

1856–1950

Few writers so dominate their times that their names become household words, let alone, as with (George) Bernard Shaw, their initials: three letters as identifiable during his lifetime as a brand name or a logo is today. G.B.S. was the shorthand code for one of the most celebrated and controversial writers of the twentieth century—a novelist, music critic, playwright, pamphleteer, political theorist, educator, and essayist. Shaw's life arc stretched a venerable ninety-four years from the midpoint of the nineteenth century to the midpoint of the twentieth. In his very long and almost unbelievably prolific career Shaw articulated most of the new ideas associated with modernity, whether in the dramatic form of the plays he is best remembered for today, or in the philosophical and political essays for which he was equally famed during his lifetime. He was awarded the Nobel Prize for literature in 1925, although in characteristically defiant fashion, he refused to accept the money, saying that the honor "is greater than is good for my spiritual health." By the same token, when the British government tried to award him the Order of Merit, he riposted, "I have already conferred it upon myself." So well known was he, and so influential as an iconoclast, that the adjective "Shavian" sprang from his last name, denoting a world view of exuberant and profound contradictions, where opposing ideas are brought into comic, and ultimately serious, artistic and social synthesis.

A major force on the London stage and in British cultural life, Shaw was not conventionally British. He was Irish, born in Dublin in 1856, the third child of George Carr Shaw and Bessie Gurly. Brought up in "an awful little kennel with primitive sanitary arrangements" on Synge Street in Dublin, Shaw had a startlingly unusual childhood: his father, an alchoholic clerk on his way down the social scale, had permitted Shaw's mother Bessie to bring her vocal coach and lover, Vandeleur Lee, to live in the family house. As Shaw once remarked, Bessie "was simply not a wife or mother at all." Bessie's brother Walter Gurly, a ship's surgeon, was another part of the menage; an ebullient man who electrifyingly proclaimed his idiosyncratic views of the Bible, Gurly became Shaw's "third father." The eccentricities of his upbringing, with three fathers and an absentee mother, led to Shaw's firm belief that parents and children were inevitably mismatched, and to his strong activism for equal rights for all members of the family constellation.

Shaw's experiments with schooling were abysmal failures, largely because only vocational training was available to a family of his means, and by the age of fifteen he had seen his last of school, which he likened to a jail designed "to keep the little devils locked up where they cannot drive their mothers mad." What took the place of formal schooling was Shaw's self-education as a voracious reader of Homer, Shakespeare, Shelley, Dickens, and much popular literature—"all normal people require both classics and trash," he wrote—and his constant immersion in the rich musical life of Dublin. In 1873 his "father" Vandeleur Lee left for London to become a musical impresario, followed soon after by Bessie Shaw and young Bernard's two sisters, leaving Shaw essentially abandoned in Dublin. Thrown back on his own resources, he worked miserably as a clerk and lived in a rooming house, teaching himself to play the piano and organizing musicales with other clerks in their off hours. So acute did his misery grow that in 1876 he decided to go to London himself, and moved in with his mother, Lee, and his sister Lucy.

The move to London altered everything for Shaw. London was the cornucopia that the deprived and impoverished colonial city of Dublin was not, and Shaw was simultaneously intoxicated with its grandeur and disillusioned by its poverty and inequalities. He recognized London as "the literary center of the English language," and he quickly established himself as a budding essayist and critic, and a would-be playwright, while also writing four novels that received rejection notices labeling them "sordid" and "perverse." The hub of Shaw's endeavors was the British Museum's famous reading room and library. Sitting at his assigned carrel (unbeknownst to him, Lenin sat nearby), Shaw read large numbers of books, among them Karl Marx's *Das Kapital*, a book that ironically had been written in that very same reading room. "It was the only book that ever turned me upside down," Shaw confessed, and he began attending meetings of every radical society he could find, until the Fabian Society claimed his loyalty. He delivered a paper before the group in 1884, beginning a long career as a political theorist and polemicist, writing essays such as *The Intelligent Woman's Guide to Socialism and Capitalism*.

Shaw became a charismatic public lecturer on social and political topics, and he began to write art and music criticism. In vivid essays he argued that the innovations of such radical composers as Wagner were parallel to the radical changes in politics and social arrangements Shaw also championed. Like James Joyce, he fervently admired Henrik Ibsen, the Norwegian playwright whose plays seemed to sound the death knell for Victorian social certainties. Ibsen's *The Doll House*, for example, dramatized the growing movement for the emancipation of women, a cause Shaw adamantly supported. Ibsen's drama pointed the way for Shaw's own development into a great playwright: he realized through Ibsen's example that he need not adopt an "art for art's sake" philosophy, as the reigning vision of the *fin de siècle* described its ideal; instead, art could be fully engaged in ideas, and could have as its mission nothing less than changing the world.

Shaw struggled for seven years to break free of Victorian dramatic constraints and the rigid structures of nineteenth-century drama, until in 1895 he had created his first play, *Widower's Houses*. While the play is not particularly memorable, its subtitle does give a sense of the special goals of Shavian drama at this early stage: "An Original Didactic Realist Play in Three Acts, Designed to Induce People to Vote on the Progressive Side at the Next County Council in London." Art for art's sake, indeed. "Why would art if it was just for art's sake interest me at all?" Shaw asked.

The political play of ideas was the form Shaw crafted and perfected over the next thirty years, drawing on a rich history of political thought and philosophical inquiry. He borrowed from British thinkers like Carlyle and from the German philosopher Friedrich Nietzsche, whose controversial writings argued that human beings make their own truth and thus create their own values. In plays like *Man and Superman, Androcles and the Lion, Arms and the Man,* and *The Doctor's Dilemma*, Shaw staged debates over values that only seem to be universal or eternal, likening the contemporary values of Edwardian Britain to outmoded garments that his society should change. Shaw was a political iconoclast whose democratic ideals were meshed with an unsentimental acknowledgment of human nature. He wanted the best cultural goods—education, art, freedom from drudgery—to be distributed equally to all without regard to sex, class, or race. However, he never romanticized the working class nor any other political group, and, never a utopian, Shaw always argued that lasting change should gradually be pressed with pragmatism, common sense, and energetic wit.

The "Shavian" element of all the plays, and of Shaw's essays and reviews, resides in an unwillingness to propose a simple answer to social problems, or to establish a clear-cut "right" and "wrong." Shaw's thinking is dialectical in style: ideas bounce and ricochet off one another, and things happen in his plays by means of a quicksilver collision of ideas that yields a new and unexpected synthesis. Shaw's characters are not simply ideas dressed up to look like people; instead, the characters embody the ever-changing and often arbitrary flow of ideas as these come to life in real, quirky, individual human beings, embroiled in verbal duels. One of his characters puts it this way: "I want to be an active verb." There are no outright villains, and no pure heroes or heroines, in a Shaw play: for example, while ruthless capitalism is a social evil in Shaw's universe, his plays are full of capitalist *characters* who are wise and winning, as is Andrew Undershaft in *Major Barbara*.

It is helpful—if somewhat dizzying—to remember that Bernard Shaw and Sigmund Freud were born in the same year, and that each man was a powerful voice in transforming modern ideas of sex, gender, and "the woman question." Shaw in fact commented on this unexpected affinity when he first stumbled on Freud's writings in 1911, and pronounced "I have said it all before him." For Freud, the Rosetta Stone of understanding was sex, and his great discovery was that women are also sexual beings. For Shaw, too, sex is everywhere, but it is never the problem—sex is liberating for men and women alike. Shaw was an ardent proponent of free love, and had many romances and affairs, although most of them appear to have been limited to the pages of his torrid correspondence. In 1898, at the age of forty-two, he married Charlotte Payne-Townshend, a wealthy supporter of Fabian socialist causes, but he remained attached, at least on paper, to several other women.

In his famous essay *The Quintessence of Ibsenism* Shaw used his commentary on Ibsen's plays as a way of proclaiming his own discoveries about the New Woman: "There is no such species in creation as 'Woman, lovely Woman,' the woman being simply the female of the human species, and to have one conception of humanity for the woman and another for the man, or one law for the woman and another for the man, or one artistic convention for the woman and another for the man, or, for that matter, a skirt for the woman and a pair of breeches for the man . . . is unnatural and unworkable." Shaw was dedicated to tearing down what he saw as the oppressive veil of Victorian ideals of womanhood—that women are self-sacrificing, pure, noble, and passive. Women are usually the social visionaries in his plays, not because he thought of women as "better," or even as fundamentally different, but because their struggles with orthodoxy were basic. The modern woman can change into "modern dress"— the radical costumes of the mind—with much more ease and enthusiasm, indeed, more light-heartedly and playfully, than can men. By allying women with the newest of the new ideas, in plays including *Major Barbara*, *Mrs. Warren's Profession*, *Pygmalion*, *Misalliance*, and *Saint Joan*, Shaw indicates the excitement, the vitality, and the innovation behind women who have burst out of the confines of domestic duty.

Shaw's plays employ classic comic situations, with elements drawn from Roman comedy and from Shakespeare—whom the puppet Shav overcomes in Shaw's last play, *Shakes Versus Shav*, written when he was ninety-two. For all their classical economy, Shaw's plays feel experimental, perhaps because they are constructed musically rather than dramatically. Shaw, who is still considered to be the most distinguished music critic of modern times, loves to draw on the musical style of a harmony of voices rather than singling out one or two main protagonists, often creating a kind of chamber play that is reliant on its ensemble. *Major Barbara* has this ensemble structure—we don't get a "full" portrait of any single character in the play, since the characters, like the colored glass bits of a kaleidoscope, change in relation to one another and form new patterns from scene to scene.

Produced in 1907, *Major Barbara* was written during Shaw's most fruitful period as a dramatist; like *Pygmalion* (1916) and *Heartbreak House* (1919), it deals with poverty, social class, war, and the fraying society of England, in a comic mode laced with rapier repartee. A moving force in the play is Andrew Undershaft, an arms merchant; though his trade might ordinarily symbolize all that is evil and destructive in modern life, he is revealed in the dialogue to be a home-grown version of a Nietzschean philosopher, a man who has followed his "will to power" beyond the moral pieties of his time. His family hates the source of his money, but nonetheless relies on him for their material comfort and their secure futures. His daughter Barbara has followed her own will to power into the Salvation Army, becoming Major Barbara as she tries to lead the poor and downtrodden toward faith in God. Barbara's fiancé, the young classics professor Adolphus Cusins, is a kind of stand-in for Shaw himself; he is drawn into the Undershaft family and business in unexpected ways that upset his own sense of self and his idea of the proper place of intellectuals in society. By the play's end, all roles are reversed, all values and ideals turned on their heads.

Bernard Shaw is at once a brilliant comic dramatist—in his essays and his letters as in his plays—and one of the great political playwrights of modern British literature, infusing all his work with the conviction that our social, economic, and sexual lives need transformation. For

Shaw, it is comedy and laughter that draw an audience into a generous, collective ensemble—one rather like the ensemble of characters in his plays, none of whom could exist as a full-fledged human being without the others. Shaw disarms us with laughter, dismantling our expectations about what is natural, necessary, or inevitable. In his comedy, words are deeds and gestures speak, always pointedly.

Preface to *Major Barbara*
First Aid to Critics

Before dealing with the deeper aspects of Major Barbara, let me, for the credit of English literature, make a protest against an unpatriotic habit into which many of my critics have fallen. Whenever my view strikes them as being at all outside the range of, say, an ordinary suburban church-warden, they conclude that I am echoing Schopenhauer, Nietzsche, Ibsen, Strindberg, Tolstoy, or some other heresiarch in northern or eastern Europe.

I confess there is something flattering in this simple faith in my accomplishment as a linguist and my erudition as a philosopher. But I cannot countenance the assumption that life and literature are so poor in these islands that we must go abroad for all dramatic material that is not common and all ideas that are not superficial. I therefore venture to put my critics in possession of certain facts concerning my contact with modern ideas.

About half a century ago, an Irish novelist, Charles Lever, wrote a story entitled A Day's Ride: A Life's Romance. It was published by Charles Dickens in Household Words, and proved so strange to the public taste that Dickens pressed Lever to make a short work of it.[1] I read scraps of this novel when I was a child; and it made an enduring impression on me. The hero was a very romantic hero, trying to live bravely, chivalrously, and powerfully by dint of mere romance-fed imagination, without courage, without means, without knowledge, without skill, without anything real except his bodily appetites. Even in my childhood I found in this poor devil's unsuccessful encounters with the facts of life, a poignant quality that romantic fiction lacked. The book, in spite of its first failure, is not dead: I saw its title the other day in the catalogue of Tauchnitz.[2]

Now why is it that when I also deal in the tragic-comic irony of the conflict between real life and the romantic imagination, critics never affiliate me to my countryman and immediate forerunner, Charles Lever, whilst they confidently derive me from a Norwegian author of whose language I do not know three words, and of whom I knew nothing until years after the Shavian *Anschauung* [world view] was already unequivocally declared in books full of what came, ten years later, to be perfunctorily labelled Ibsenism? I was not Ibsenist even at second hand; for Lever, though he may have read Henri Beyle, *alias* Stendhal,[3] certainly never read Ibsen. Of the books that made Lever popular, such as Charles O'Malley and Harry Lorrequer, I know nothing but the names and some of the illustrations. But the story of the day's ride and life's romance of Potts (claiming alliance with Pozzo di Borgo) caught me and fascinated

1. Lever's popular novels include *The Confessions of Harry Lorrequer* (1837); typically, they recount the picaresque adventures of Irishmen in Napoleonic Europe. *Household Words* (1850–1859) was one of several weekly periodicals edited by Dickens; Lever's *A Day's Ride: A Life's Romance* (1861) was serialized in another of Dickens's periodicals *All the Year Round*. Dickens's novel *The Pickwick Papers*

(1837), referred to later in the *Preface*, describes the adventures of Mr. Pickwick, an honest fool, and his side-kick, Sam Weller.
2. A publishing house.
3. Pen name of French novelist Marie-Henri Beyle (1783–1842), noted for his acute psychological and political insight.

me as something strange and significant, though I already knew all about Alnaschar and Don Quixote and Simon Tappertit and many another romantic hero mocked by reality.[4] From the plays of Aristophanes to the tales of Stevenson that mockery has been made familiar to all who are properly saturated with letters.

Where, then, was the novelty in Lever's tale? Partly, I think, in a new seriousness in dealing with Pott's disease. Formerly, the contrast between madness and sanity was deemed comic: Hogarth shews us how fashionable people went in parties to Bedlam to laugh at the lunatics.[5] I myself have had a village idiot exhibited to me as something irresistibly funny. On the stage the madman was once a regular comic figure: that was how Hamlet got his opportunity before Shakespear touched him. The originality of Shakespear's version lay in his taking the lunatic sympathetically and seriously, and thereby making an advance towards the eastern consciousness of the fact that lunacy may be inspiration in disguise, since a man who has more brains than his fellows necessarily appears as mad to them as one who has less. But Shakespear did not do for Pistol and Parolles what he did for Hamlet.[6] The particular sort of madman they represented, the romantic make-believer, lay outside the pale of sympathy in literature: he was pitilessly despised and ridiculed here as he was in the east under the name of Alnaschar, and was doomed to be, centuries later, under the name of Simon Tappertit. When Cervantes relented over Don Quixote, and Dickens relented over Pickwick, they did not become impartial: they simply changed sides, and became friends and apologists where they had formerly been mockers.

In Lever's story there is a real change of attitude. There is no relenting towards Potts: he never gains our affections like Don Quixote and Pickwick: he has not even the infatuate courage of Tappertit. But we dare not laugh at him, because, somehow, we recognize ourselves in Potts. We may, some of us, have enough nerve, enough muscle, enough luck, enough tact or skill or address or knowledge to carry things off better than he did; to impose on the people who saw through him; to fascinate Katinka (who cut Potts so ruthlessly at the end of the story); but for all that, we know that Potts plays an enormous part in ourselves and in the world, and that the social problem is not a problem of story-book heroes of the older pattern, but a problem of Pottses, and of how to make men of them. To fall back on my old phrase, we have the feeling—one that Alnaschar, Pistol, Parolles, and Tappertit never gave us—that Potts is a piece of really scientific natural history as distinguished from funny story telling. His author is not throwing a stone at a creature of another and inferior order, but making a confession, with the effect that the stone hits each of us full in the conscience and causes our self-esteem to smart very sorely. Hence the failure of Lever's book to please the readers of Household Words. That pain in the self-esteem nowadays causes critics to raise a cry of Ibsenism. I therefore assure them that the sensation first came to me from Lever and may have come to him from Beyle, or at least out of the Stendhalian atmosphere. I exclude the hypothesis of complete originality on Lever's part, because a man can no more be completely original in that sense than a tree can grow out of air.

Another mistake as to my literary ancestry is made whenever I violate the romantic convention that all women are angels when they are not devils; that they are better looking than men; that their part in courtship is entirely passive; and that

---

4. Cervantes' Don Quixote (1605, 1615) is a comic satire; in it an elderly knight, Don Quixote, and his assistant Sancho Panza, set out to seek adventure. Simon Tappertit is a character in Dickens's novel Barnaby Rudge (1841).
5. William Hogarth (1697–1764), painter best known for

his satirical engravings and caricatures; Bedlam is the popular name of the Royal Bethlehem Hospital in London, an asylum for the insane.
6. Pistol is a low-life character appearing in Shakespeare's Henry IV, Part II, Henry V, and The Merry Wives of Windsor; Parolles is a character in All's Well that Ends Well.

the human female form is the most beautiful object in nature. Schopenhauer wrote a splenetic essay which, as it is neither polite nor profound, was probably intended to knock this nonsense violently on the head. A sentence denouncing the idolized form as ugly has been largely quoted. The English critics have read that sentence; and I must here affirm, with as much gentleness as the implication will bear, that it has yet to be proved that they have dipped any deeper. At all events, whenever an English playwright represents a young and marriageable woman as being anything but a romantic heroine, he is disposed of without further thought as an echo of Schopenhauer. My own case is a specially hard one, because, when I implore the critics who are obsessed with the Schopenhauerian formula to remember that playwrights, like sculptors, study their figures from life, and not from philosophic essays, they reply passionately that I am not a playwright and that my stage figures do not live. But even so, I may and do ask them why, if they must give the credit of my plays to a philosopher, they do not give it to an English philosopher? Long before I ever read a word by Schopenhauer, or even knew whether he was a philosopher or a chemist, the Socialist revival of the eighteen-eighties brought me into contact, both literary and personal, with Ernest Belfort Bax,[7] an English Socialist and philosophic essayist, whose handling of modern feminism would provoke romantic protests from Schopenhauer himself, or even Strindberg. As a matter of fact I hardly noticed Schopenhauer's disparagements of women when they came under my notice later on, so thoroughly had Bax familiarized me with the homoist attitude,[8] and forced me to recognize the extent to which public opinion, and consequently legislation and jurisprudence, is corrupted by feminist sentiment.

Belfort Bax's essays were not confined to the Feminist question. He was a ruthless critic of current morality. Other writers have gained sympathy for dramatic criminals by eliciting the alleged "soul of goodness in things evil"; but Bax would propound some quite undramatic and apparently shabby violation of our commercial law and morality, and not merely defend it with the most disconcerting ingenuity, but actually prove it to be a positive duty that nothing but the certainty of police persecution should prevent every right-minded man from at once doing on principle. The Socialists were naturally shocked, being for the most part morbidly moral people; but at all events they were saved later on from the delusion that nobody but Nietzsche had ever challenged our mercanto-Christian morality. I first heard the name of Nietzsche from a German mathematician, Miss Borchardt, who had read my Quintessence of Ibsenism, and told me that she saw what I had been reading: namely, Nietzsche's Jenseits von Gut und Böse.[9] Which I protest I had never seen, and could not have read with any comfort, for want of the necessary German, if I had seen it.

Nietzsche, like Schopenhauer, is the victim in England of a single much quoted sentence containing the phrase "big blonde beast." On the strength of this alliteration it is assumed that Nietzsche gained his European reputation by a senseless glorification of selfish bullying as the rule of life, just as it is assumed, on the strength of the single word Superman (Übermensch) borrowed by me from Nietzsche, that I look for the salvation of society to the despotism of a single Napoleonic Superman,

7. Bax published *Socialism: Its Growth and Outcome* in 1893, which he wrote in collaboration with William Morris, as well as the antifeminist *The Fraud of Feminism* (1913).
8. One giving priority to men.
9. In his *Beyond Good and Evil* (1886), Nietzsche rejected most forms of morality and religious thought on the grounds that they fostered weakness and "resentment," arguing instead for an understanding of the world free of metaphysical categories such as "God." He argued that a higher humanity would evolve, producing an elite type of *Übermensch* ("Over-Man"), described as the "big blond beast" by some of Nietzsche's followers.

in spite of my careful demonstration of the folly of that outworn infatuation. But even the less recklessly superficial critics seem to believe that the modern objection to Christianity as a pernicious slave-morality was first put forward by Nietzsche. It was familiar to me before I ever heard of Nietzsche. The late Captain Wilson, author of several queer pamphlets, propagandist of a metaphysical system called Comprehensionism, and inventor of the term "Crosstianity" to distinguish the retrograde element in Christendom, was wont thirty years ago, in the discussions of the Dialectical Society, to protest earnestly against the beatitudes of the Sermon on the Mount as excuses for cowardice and servility, as destructive of our will, and consequently of our honor and manhood. Now it is true that Captain Wilson's moral criticism of Christianity was not a historical theory of it, like Nietzsche's; but this objection cannot be made to Stuart-Glennie, the successor of Buckle as a philosophic historian, who devoted his life to the elaboration and propagation of his theory that Christianity is part of an epoch (or rather an aberration, since it began as recently as 6000 B.C. and is already collapsing) produced by the necessity in which the numerically inferior white races found themselves to impose their domination on the colored races by priestcraft, making a virtue and a popular religion of drudgery and submissiveness in this world not only as a means of achieving saintliness of character but of securing a reward in heaven.[1] Here was the slave-morality view formulated by a Scotch philosopher of my acquaintance long before we all began chattering about Nietzsche.

As Stuart-Glennie traced the evolution of society to the conflict of races, his theory made some sensation among Socialists—that is, among the only people who were seriously thinking about historical evolution at all—by its collision with the class-conflict theory of Karl Marx. Nietzsche, as I gather, regarded the slave-morality as having been invented and imposed on the world by slaves making a virtue of necessity and a religion of their servitude. Stuart-Glennie regarded the slave-morality as an invention of the superior white race to subjugate the minds of the inferior races whom they wished to exploit, and who would have destroyed them by force of numbers if their minds had not been subjugated. As this process is in operation still, and can be studied at first hand not only in our Church schools and in the struggle between our modern proprietary classes and the proletariat, but in the part played by Christian missionaries in reconciling the black races of Africa to their subjugation by European Capitalism, we can judge for ourselves whether the initiative came from above or below. My object here is not to argue the historical point, but simply to make our theatre critics ashamed of their habit of treating Britain as an intellectual void, and assuming that every philosophical idea, every historic theory, every criticism of our moral, religious and juridical institutions, must necessarily be either a foreign import, or else a fantastic sally (in rather questionable taste) totally unrelated to the existing body of thought. I urge them to remember that this body of thought is the slowest of growths and the rarest of blossomings, and that if there be such a thing on the philosophic plane as a matter of course, it is that no individual can make more than a minute contribution to it. In fact, their conception of clever persons parthenogenetically bringing forth complete original cosmogonies by dint of sheer "brilliancy" is part of that ignorant credulity which is the despair of the honest philosopher, and the opportunity of the religious impostor.

1. Henry Thomas Buckle, author of the *History of Civilization in England* (1857, 1861), attempted to put the study of history on scientific foundations; John Stuart-Glennie wrote works on folklore, Christianity, and sociology.

THE GOSPEL OF ST ANDREW UNDERSHAFT

It is this credulity that drives me to help my critics out with Major Barbara by telling them what to say about it. In the millionaire Undershaft I have represented a man who has become intellectually and spiritually as well as practically conscious of the irresistible natural truth which we all abhor and repudiate: to wit, that the greatest of our evils, and the worst of our crimes is poverty, and that our first duty, to which every other consideration should be sacrificed, is not to be poor. "Poor but honest," "the respectable poor," and such phrases are as intolerable and as immoral as "drunken but amiable," "fraudulent but a good after-dinner speaker," "splendidly criminal," or the like. Security, the chief pretence of civilization, cannot exist where the worst of dangers, the danger of poverty, hangs over everyone's head, and where the alleged protection of our persons from violence is only an accidental result of the existence of a police force whose real business is to force the poor man to see his children starve whilst idle people overfeed pet dogs with the money that might feed and clothe them.

It is exceedingly difficult to make people realize that an evil is an evil. For instance, we seize a man and deliberately do him a malicious injury: say, imprison him for years. One would not suppose that it needed any exceptional clearness of wit to recognize in this an act of diabolical cruelty. But in England such a recognition provokes a stare of surprise, followed by an explanation that the outrage is punishment or justice or something else that is all right, or perhaps by a heated attempt to argue that we should all be robbed and murdered in our beds if such stupid villainies as sentences of imprisonment were not committed daily. It is useless to argue that even if this were true, which it is not, the alternative to adding crimes of our own to the crimes from which we suffer is not helpless submission. Chickenpox is an evil; but if I were to declare that we must either submit to it or else repress it sternly by seizing everyone who suffers from it and punishing them by inoculation with smallpox, I should be laughed at; for though nobody could deny that the result would be to prevent chickenpox to some extent by making people avoid it much more carefully, and to effect a further apparent prevention by making them conceal it very anxiously, yet people would have sense enough to see that the deliberate propagation of smallpox was a creation of evil, and must therefore be ruled out in favor of purely humane and hygienic measures. Yet in the precisely parallel case of a man breaking into my house and stealing my wife's diamonds I am expected as a matter of course to steal ten years of his life, torturing him all the time. If he tries to defeat that monstrous retaliation by shooting me, my survivors hang him. The net result suggested by the police statistics is that we inflict atrocious injuries on the burglars we catch in order to make the rest take effectual precautions against detection; so that instead of saving our wives' diamonds from burglary we only greatly decrease our chances of ever getting them back, and increase our chances of being shot by the robber if we are unlucky enough to disturb him at his work.

But the thoughtless wickedness with which we scatter sentences of imprisonment, torture in the solitary cell and on the plank bed, and flogging, on moral invalids and energetic rebels, is as nothing compared to the silly levity with which we tolerate poverty as if it were either a wholesome tonic for lazy people or else a virtue to be embraced as St. Francis[2] embraced it. If a man is indolent, let him be

---

2. Founder of the Franciscan monastic order, St. Francis was known for his humility and love of absolute poverty.

poor. If he is drunken, let him be poor. If he is not a gentleman, let him be poor. If he is addicted to the fine arts or to pure science instead of to trade and finance, let him be poor. If he chooses to spend his urban eighteen shillings a week or his agricultural thirteen shillings a week[3] on his beer and his family instead of saving it up for his old age, let him be poor. Let nothing be done for "the undeserving": let him be poor. Serve him right! Also—somewhat inconsistently—blessed are the poor!

Now what does this Let Him Be Poor mean? It means let him be weak. Let him be ignorant. Let him become a nucleus of disease. Let him be a standing exhibition and example of ugliness and dirt. Let him have rickety children. Let him be cheap, and drag his fellows down to his own price by selling himself to do their work. Let his habitations turn our cities into poisonous congeries of slums. Let his daughters infect our young men with the diseases of the streets, and his sons revenge him by turning the nation's manhood into scrofula, cowardice, cruelty, hypocrisy, political imbecility, and all the other fruits of oppression and malnutrition. Let the undeserving become still less deserving; and let the deserving lay up for himself, not treasures in heaven, but horrors in hell upon earth. This being so, is it really wise to let him be poor? Would he not do ten times less harm as a prosperous burglar, incendiary, ravisher or murderer, to the utmost limits of humanity's comparatively negligible impulses in these directions? Suppose we were to abolish all penalties for such activities, and decide that poverty is the one thing we will not tolerate—that every adult with less than, say, £365 a year, shall be painlessly but inexorably killed, and every hungry half naked child forcibly fattened and clothed, would not that be an enormous improvement on our existing system, which has already destroyed so many civilizations, and is visibly destroying ours in the same way?

Is there any radicle[4] of such legislation in our parliamentary system? Well, there are two measures just sprouting in the political soil, which may conceivably grow to something valuable. One is the institution of a Legal Minimum Wage. The other, Old Age Pensions.[5] But there is a better plan than either of these. Some time ago I mentioned the subject of Universal Old Age Pensions to my fellow Socialist Cobden-Sanderson,[6] famous as an artist-craftsman in bookbinding and printing. "Why not Universal Pensions for Life?" said Cobden-Sanderson. In saying this, he solved the industrial problem at a stroke. At present we say callously to each citizen "If you want money, earn it" as if his having or not having it were a matter that concerned himself alone. We do not even secure for him the opportunity of earning it: on the contrary, we allow our industry to be organized in open dependence on the maintenance of "a reserve army of unemployed" for the sake of "elasticity." The sensible course would be Cobden-Sanderson's: that is, to give every man enough to live well on, so as to guarantee the community against the possibility of a case of the malignant disease of poverty, and then (necessarily) to see that he earned it.

Undershaft, the hero of Major Barbara, is simply a man who, having grasped the fact that poverty is a crime, knows that when society offered him the alternative of poverty or a lucrative trade in death and destruction, it offered him, not a choice between opulent villainy and humble virtue, but between energetic enterprise and

---

3. About a dollar a day at the time.
4. Root.
5. The Liberal government of 1906–1916 enacted a program of welfare legislation, which included similar measures.

6. Thomas James Cobden-Sanderson (1840–1922), British book-designer.

cowardly infamy. His conduct stands the Kantian test,[7] which Peter Shirley's does not. Peter Shirley is what we call the honest poor man. Undershaft is what we call the wicked rich one: Shirley is Lazarus, Undershaft Dives.[8] Well, the misery of the world is due to the fact that the great mass of men act and believe as Peter Shirley acts and believes. If they acted and believed as Undershaft acts and believes, the immediate result would be a revolution of incalculable beneficence. To be wealthy, says Undershaft, is with me a point of honor for which I am prepared to kill at the risk of my own life. This preparedness is, as he says, the final test of sincerity. Like Froissart's medieval hero, who saw that "to rob and pill was a good life," he is not the dupe of that public sentiment against killing which is propagated and endowed by people who would otherwise be killed themselves, or of the mouth-honor paid to poverty and obedience by rich and insubordinate do-nothings who want to rob the poor without courage and command them without superiority. Froissart's knight, in placing the achievement of a good life before all the other duties—which indeed are not duties at all when they conflict with it, but plain wickedness—behaved bravely, admirably, and, in the final analysis, public-spiritedly. Medieval society, on the other hand, behaved very badly indeed in organizing itself so stupidly that a good life could be achieved by robbing and pilling. If the knight's contemporaries had been all as resolute as he, robbing and pilling would have been the shortest way to the gallows, just as, if we were all as resolute and clearsighted as Undershaft, an attempt to live by means of what is called "an independent income" would be the shortest way to the lethal chamber. But as, thanks to our political imbecility and personal cowardice (fruits of poverty, both), the best imitation of a good life now procurable is life on an independent income, all sensible people aim at securing such an income, and are, of course, careful to legalize and moralize both it and all the actions and sentiments which lead to it and support it as an institution. What else can they do? They know, of course, that they are rich because others are poor. But they cannot help that: it is for the poor to repudiate poverty when they have had enough of it. The thing can be done easily enough: the demonstrations to the contrary made by the economists, jurists, moralists and sentimentalists hired by the rich to defend them, or even doing the work gratuitously out of sheer folly and abjectness, impose only on those who want to be imposed on.

The reason why the independent income-tax payers are not solid in defence of their position is that since we are not medieval rovers through a sparsely populated country, the poverty of those we rob prevents our having the good life for which we sacrifice them. Rich men or aristocrats with a developed sense of life—men like Ruskin and William Morris and Kropotkin[9]—have enormous social appetites and very fastidious personal ones. They are not content with handsome houses: they want handsome cities. They are not content with bediamonded wives and blooming daughters: they complain because the charwoman[1] is badly dressed, because the laundress smells of gin, because the sempstress is anemic, because every man they meet is not a friend and every woman not a romance. They turn up their noses at their

7. In the moral philosophy of the German philosopher Immanuel Kant (1724–1804), the "categorical imperative" is proposed as a test of rules of conduct: "Act only on that maxim which you can at the same time will to be a universal law."

8. In the biblical story of Dives and Lazarus (Luke 16), Lazarus is a beggar at the gate of the rich man Dives's house. Both die, Lazarus going to Heaven and Dives to Hell, since he had refused Lazarus assistance. Dives subsequently asks of Abraham that Lazarus might be permitted to give him water and is refused.

9. Pyotr Alekseyevich Kropotkin (1842–1921), Russian anarchist leader and theorist.

1. Cleaning woman.

neighbor's drains, and are made ill by the architecture of their neighbor's houses. Trade patterns made to suit vulgar people do not please them (and they can get nothing else): they cannot sleep nor sit at ease upon "slaughtered" cabinet makers' furniture. The very air is not good enough for them: there is too much factory smoke in it. They even demand abstract conditions: justice, honor, a noble moral atmosphere, a mystic nexus to replace the cash nexus.[2] Finally they declare that though to rob and pill with your own hand on horseback and in steel coat may have been a good life, to rob and pill by the hands of the policeman, the bailiff, and the soldier, and to underpay them meanly for doing it, is not a good life, but rather fatal to all possibility of even a tolerable one. They call on the poor to revolt, and, finding the poor shocked at their ungentlemanliness, despairingly revile the proletariat for its "damned wantlessness" (verdammte Bedürfnislosigkeit).

So far, however, their attack on society has lacked simplicity. The poor do not share their tastes nor understand their art-criticisms. They do not want the simple life, nor the esthetic life; on the contrary, they want very much to wallow in all the costly vulgarities from which the elect souls among the rich turn away with loathing. It is by surfeit and not by abstinence that they will be cured of their hankering after unwholesome sweets. What they do dislike and despise and are ashamed of is poverty. To ask them to fight for the difference between the Christmas number of the Illustrated London News and the Kelmscott Chaucer is silly:[3] they prefer the News. The difference between a stock-broker's cheap and dirty starched white shirt and collar and the comparatively costly and carefully dyed blue shirt of William Morris is a difference so disgraceful to Morris in their eyes that if they fought on the subject at all, they would fight in defence of the starch. "Cease to be slaves, in order that you may become cranks" is not a very inspiring call to arms; nor is it really improved by substituting saints for cranks. Both terms denote men of genius; and the common man does not want to live the life of a man of genius: he would much rather live the life of a pet collie if that were the only alternative. But he does want more money. Whatever else he may be vague about, he is clear about that. He may or may not prefer Major Barbara to the Drury Lane pantomime;[4] but he always prefers five hundred pounds to five hundred shillings.

Now to deplore this preference as sordid, and teach children that it is sinful to desire money, is to strain towards the extreme possible limit of impudence in lying and corruption in hypocrisy. The universal regard for money is the one hopeful fact in our civilization, the one sound spot in our social conscience. Money is the most important thing in the world. It represents health, strength, honor, generosity and beauty as conspicuously and undeniably as the want of it represents illness, weakness, disgrace, meanness and ugliness. Not the least of its virtues is that it destroys base people as certainly as it fortifies and dignifies noble people. It is only when it is cheapened to worthlessness for some and made impossibly dear to others, that it becomes a curse. In short, it is a curse only in such foolish social conditions that life itself is a curse. For the two things are inseparable: money is the counter that enables life to be distributed socially: it is life as truly as sovereigns[5] and bank notes are money. The first

2. Marx had argued that money was the "nexus," or link, between people in industrial society; 19th-century socialists argued for a different kind of link, perhaps a "mystic nexus" instead of a "cash" one.
3. The Illustrated London News was a popular weekly paper; The Kelmscott Chaucer was an edition of Chaucer's works produced at William Morris's Kelmscott Press

(founded 1891), which aimed to produce traditionally made and beautifully designed books.
4. Drury Lane in central London is the site of many popular theaters; pantomime is a traditional Christmas entertainment, primarily for children.
5. A gold coin worth one pound.

duty of every citizen is to insist on having money on reasonable terms; and this demand is not complied with by giving four men three shillings each for ten or twelve hours' drudgery and one man a thousand pounds for nothing. The crying need of the nation is not for better morals, cheaper bread, temperance, liberty, culture, redemption of fallen sisters and erring brothers, nor the grace, love and fellowship of the Trinity, but simply for enough money. And the evil to be attacked is not sin, suffering, greed, priestcraft, kingcraft, demagogy, monopoly, ignorance, drink, war, pestilence, nor any other of the scapegoats which reformers sacrifice, but simply poverty.

Once take your eyes from the ends of the earth and fix them on this truth just under your nose; and Andrew Undershaft's views will not perplex you in the least. Unless indeed his constant sense that he is only the instrument of a Will or Life Force which uses him for purposes wider than his own, may puzzle you.[6] If so, that is because you are walking either in artificial Darwinian darkness, or in mere stupidity. All genuinely religious people have that consciousness. To them Undershaft the Mystic will be quite intelligible, and his perfect comprehension of his daughter the Salvationist and her lover the Euripidean republican natural and inevitable. That, however, is not new, even on the stage. What is new, as far as I know, is that article in Undershaft's religion which recognizes in Money the first need and in poverty the vilest sin of man and society.

This dramatic conception has not, of course, been attained *per saltum* [in one attempt]. Nor has it been borrowed from Nietzsche or from any man born beyond the Channel. The late Samuel Butler, in his own department the greatest English writer of the latter half of the XIX century, steadily inculcated the necessity and morality of a conscientious Laodiceanism in religion and of an earnest and constant sense of the importance of money.[7] It drives one almost to despair of English literature when one sees so extraordinary a study of English life as Butler's posthumous Way of All Flesh making so little impression that when, some years later, I produce plays in which Butler's extraordinarily fresh, free and future-piercing suggestions have an obvious share, I am met with nothing but vague cacklings about Ibsen and Nietzsche, and am only too thankful that they are not about Alfred de Musset and Georges Sand.[8] Really, the English do not deserve to have great men. They allowed Butler to die practically unknown, whilst I, a comparatively insignificant Irish journalist, was leading them by the nose into an advertisement of me which has made my own life a burden. In Sicily there is a Via Samuele Butler. When an English tourist sees it, he either asks "Who the devil was Samuele Butler?" or wonders why the Sicilians should perpetuate the memory of the author of Hudibras.[9]

Well, it cannot be denied that the English are only too anxious to recognize a man of genius if somebody will kindly point him out to them. Having pointed myself out in this manner with some success, I now point out Samuel Butler, and trust that in consequence I shall hear a little less in future of the novelty and foreign origin of the ideas which are now making their way into the English theatre through plays

6. A reference to the philosophy of Schopenhauer and Nietzsche.

7. Samuel Butler's *Erewhon* (1871) and *Erewhon Revisited* (1901) brought him fame as a satirist, as did his autobiographical novel *The Way of All Flesh* (1903), which poked fun at many aspects of Victorian life, especially its piety. To be Laodicean is to be lukewarm about religion.

8. Louis Charles Alfred de Musset (1810–1857), French poet, dramatist and fiction writer, had a famous liaison with the novelist George Sand (pen name of Aurore Dupin), an unconventional woman and early feminist.

9. *Hudibras* (three parts, 1663–1678), a long satirical poem by the English poet Samuel Butler, directed chiefly against religious Puritanism.

written by Socialists. There are living men whose originality and power are as obvious as Butler's and when they die that fact will be discovered. Meanwhile I recommend them to insist on their own merits as an important part of their own business.

THE SALVATION ARMY

When Major Barbara was produced in London, the second act was reported in an important northern newspaper as a withering attack on the Salvation Army, and the despairing ejaculation of Barbara deplored by a London daily as a tasteless blasphemy. And they were set right, not by the professed critics of the theatre, but by religious and philosophical publicists like Sir Oliver Lodge and Dr Stanton Coit, and strenuous Nonconformist journalists like William Stead,[1] who not only understood the act as well as the Salvationists themselves, but also saw it in its relation to the religious life of the nation, a life which seems to lie not only outside the sympathy of many of our theatre critics, but actually outside their knowledge of society. Indeed nothing could be more ironically curious than the confrontation Major Barbara effected of the theatre enthusiasts with the religious enthusiasts. On the one hand was the playgoer, always seeking pleasure, paying exorbitantly for it, suffering unbearable discomforts for it, and hardly ever getting it. On the other hand was the Salvationist, repudiating gaiety and courting effort and sacrifice, yet always in the wildest spirits, laughing, joking, singing, rejoicing, drumming, and tambourining: his life flying by in a flash of excitement, and his death arriving as a climax of triumph. And, if you please, the playgoer despising the Salvationist as a joyless person, shut out from the heaven of the theatre, self-condemned to a life of hideous gloom; and the Salvationist mourning over the playgoer as over a prodigal with vine leaves in his hair, careering outrageously to hell amid the popping of champagne corks and the ribald laughter of sirens![2] Could misunderstanding be more complete, or sympathy worse misplaced?

Fortunately, the Salvationists are more accessible to the religious character of the drama than the playgoers to the gay energy and artistic fertility of religion. They can see, when it is pointed out to them, that a theatre, as a place where two or three are gathered together, takes from that divine presence an inalienable sanctity of which the grossest and profanest farce can no more deprive it than a hypocritical sermon by a snobbish bishop can desecrate Westminster Abbey. But in our professional playgoers this indispensable preliminary conception of sanctity seems wanting. They talk of actors as mimes and mummers, and, I fear, think of dramatic authors as liars and pandars,[3] whose main business is the voluptuous soothing of the tired city speculator when what he calls the serious business of the day is over. Passion, the life of drama, means nothing to them but primitive sexual excitement: such phrases as "impassioned poetry" or "passionate love of truth" have fallen quite out of their vocabulary and been replaced by "passional crime" and the like. They assume, as far as I can gather, that people in whom passion has a larger scope are passionless and therefore uninteresting. Consequently they come to think of religious people as people who are not interesting and not amusing. And so, when Barbara cuts the regular

---

1. Lodge (1851–1940), a physicist, made efforts to reconcile science with religion; Coit (1857–1944) wrote on ethics, religion, and philosophy; Stead (1849–1912), a journalist, pressed for welfare legislation and social reform.

2. The first of many references to Dionysus, the ancient Greek god of wine. "Sirens" are seductive women.
3. Go-betweens for prostitutes.

Salvation Army jokes, and snatches a kiss from her lover across his drum, the devotees of the theatre think they ought to appear shocked, and conclude that the whole play is an elaborate mockery of the Army. And then either hypocritically rebuke me for mocking, or foolishly take part in the supposed mockery!

Even the handful of mentally competent critics got into difficulties over my demonstration of the economic deadlock in which the Salvation Army finds itself. Some of them thought that the Army would not have taken money from a distiller and a cannon founder: others thought it should not have taken it: all assumed more or less definitely that it reduced itself to absurdity or hypocrisy by taking it. On the first point the reply of the Army itself was prompt and conclusive. As one of its officers said, they would take money from the devil himself and be only too glad to get it out of his hands and into God's. They gratefully acknowledged that publicans[4] not only give them money but allow them to collect it in the bar—sometimes even when there is a Salvation meeting outside preaching teetotalism. In fact, they questioned the verisimilitude of the play, not because Mrs Baines took the money, but because Barbara refused it.

On the point that the Army ought not to take such money, its justification is obvious. It must take the money because it cannot exist without money, and there is no other money to be had. Practically all the spare money in the country consists of a mass of rent, interest, and profit, every penny of which is bound up with crime, drink, prostitution, disease, and all the evil fruits of poverty, as inextricably as with enterprise, wealth, commercial probity, and national prosperity. The notion that you can earmark certain coins as tainted is an unpractical individualist superstition. None the less the fact that all our money is tainted gives a very severe shock to earnest young souls when some dramatic instance of the taint first makes them conscious of it. When an enthusiastic young clergyman of the Established Church first realizes that the Ecclesiastical Commissioners[5] receive the rents of sporting public houses, brothels, and sweating dens;[6] or that the most generous contributor at his last charity sermon was an employer trading in female labor cheapened by prostitution as unscrupulously as a hotel keeper trades in waiter's labor cheapened by tips, or commissionaires' labor cheapened by pensions; or that the only patron who can afford to rebuild his church or his schools or give his boys' brigade a gymnasium or a library is the son-in-law of a Chicago meat King,[7] that young clergyman has, like Barbara, a very bad quarter hour. But he cannot help himself by refusing to accept money from anybody except sweet old ladies with independent incomes and gentle and lovely ways of life. He has only to follow up the income of the sweet ladies to its industrial source, and there he will find Mrs Warren's profession[8] and the poisonous canned meat and all the rest of it. His own stipend has the same root. He must either share the world's guilt or go to another planet. He must save the world's honor if he is to save his own. This is what all the Churches find just as the Salvation Army and Barbara find it in the play. Her discovery that she is her father's accomplice; that the Salvation Army is the accomplice of the distiller and the dynamite maker; that they can no more escape one another than they can escape the air they breathe; that there is no salvation for them through personal righteousness, but only through the

4. Proprietors of public houses (bars).
5. Church officials responsible for finances.
6. Betting parlors, houses of prostitution, and sweatshops.
7. The first of several references to Upton Sinclair's *The*

Jungle (1906), a novel that exposed conditions in the Chicago meat-packing industry and led to legal reforms.
8. Shaw's *Mrs Warren's Profession* (1898) deals with the economic aspects of prostitution.

redemption of the whole nation from its vicious, lazy, competitive anarchy: this discovery has been made by everyone except the Pharisees[9] and (apparently) the professional playgoers, who still wear their Tom Hood shirts and underpay their washerwomen without the slightest misgiving as to the elevation of their private characters, the purity of their private atmospheres, and their right to repudiate as foreign to themselves the coarse depravity of the garret and the slum. Not that they mean any harm: they only desire to be, in their little private way, what they call gentlemen. They do not understand Barbara's lesson because they have not, like her, learnt it by taking their part in the larger life of the nation.

BARBARA'S RETURN TO THE COLORS

Barbara's return to the colors may yet provide a subject for the dramatic historian of the future. To get back to the Salvation Army with the knowledge that even the Salvationists themselves are not saved yet; that poverty is not blessed, but a most damnable sin; and that when General Booth chose Blood and Fire for the emblem of Salvation instead of the Cross, he was perhaps better inspired than he knew:[1] such knowledge, for the daughter of Andrew Undershaft, will clearly lead to something hopefuller than distributing bread and treacle at the expense of Bodger.

It is a very significant thing, this instinctive choice of the military form of organization, this substitution of the drum for the organ, by the Salvation Army. Does it not suggest that the Salvationists divine that they must actually fight the devil instead of merely praying at him? At present, it is true, they have not quite ascertained his correct address. When they do, they may give a very rude shock to that sense of security which he has gained from his experience of the fact that hard words, even when uttered by eloquent essayists and lecturers, or carried unanimously at enthusiastic public meetings on the motion of eminent reformers, break no bones. It has been said that the French Revolution was the work of Voltaire, Rousseau and the Encyclopedists. It seems to me to have been the work of men who had observed that virtuous indignation, caustic criticism, conclusive argument and instructive pamphleteering, even when done by the most earnest and witty literary geniuses, were as useless as praying, things going steadily from bad to worse whilst the Social Contract and the pamphlets of Voltaire were at the height of their vogue. Eventually, as we know, perfectly respectable citizens and earnest philanthropists connived at the September massacres[2] because hard experience had convinced them that if they contented themselves with appeals to humanity and patriotism, the aristocracy, though it would read their appeals with the greatest enjoyment and appreciation, flattering and admiring the writers, would none the less continue to conspire with foreign monarchists to undo the revolution and restore the old system with every circumstance of savage vengeance and ruthless repression of popular liberties.

The nineteenth century saw the same lesson repeated in England. It had its Utilitarians, its Christian Socialists, its Fabians (still extant): it had Bentham, Mill, Dickens, Ruskin, Carlyle, Butler, Henry George,[3] and Morris. And the end of all

9. An ancient Jewish sect described in the Gospels as having pretensions to superior sanctity.

1. In 1865 William Booth founded the East London Revival Society, or Christian Mission, which in 1878 became the Salvation Army. The organization featured military-style titles and uniforms, the better to wage "warfare against evil." In 1890 General Booth set out his idea in In Darkest England and the Way Out. The first U.S. branch of the organization was set up in Pennsylvania in 1880.

2. A series of preemptive strikes against counterrevolutionary suspects that took place in 1792 during the French Revolution.

3. American economist and tax reformer.

their efforts is the Chicago described by Mr Upton Sinclair and the London in which the people who pay to be amused by my dramatic representation of Peter Shirley turned out to starve at forty because there are younger slaves to be had for his wages, do not take, and have not the slightest intention of taking, any effective step to organize society in such a way as to make that everyday infamy impossible. I, who have preached and pamphleteered like any Encyclopedist, have to confess that my methods are no use, and would be no use if I were Voltaire, Rousseau, Bentham, Marx, Mill, Dickens, Carlyle, Ruskin, Butler, and Morris all rolled into one, with Euripides, More, Montaigne, Molière, Beaumarchais, Swift, Goethe, Ibsen, Tolstoy, Jesus and the prophets all thrown in (as indeed in some sort I actually am, standing as I do on all their shoulders). The problem being to make heroes out of cowards, we paper apostles and artist-magicians have succeeded only in giving cowards all the sensations of heroes whilst they tolerate every abomination, accept every plunder, and submit to every oppression. Christianity, in making a merit of such submission, has marked only that depth in the abyss at which the very sense of shame is lost. The Christian has been like Dickens' doctor in the debtor's prison,[4] who tells the newcomer of its ineffable peace and security: no duns; no tyrannical collectors of rates, taxes, and rent; no importunate hopes nor exacting duties; nothing but the rest and safety of having no farther to fall.

Yet in the poorest corner of this soul-destroying Christendom vitality suddenly begins to germinate again. Joyousness, a sacred gift long dethroned by the hellish laughter of derision and obscenity, rises like a flood miraculously out of the fetid dust and mud of the slums; rousing marches and impetuous dithyrambs[5] rise to the heavens from people among whom the depressing noise called "sacred music" is a standing joke; a flag with Blood and Fire on it is unfurled, not in murderous rancor, but because fire is beautiful and blood a vital and splendid red; Fear, which we flatter by calling Self, vanishes; and transfigured men and women carry their gospel through a transfigured world, calling their leader General, themselves captains and brigadiers, and their whole body an Army: praying, but praying only for refreshment, for strength to fight, and for needful MONEY (a notable sign, that); preaching, but not preaching submission; daring ill-usage and abuse, but not putting up with more of it than is inevitable; and practising what the world will let them practise, including soap and water, color and music. There is danger in such activity; and where there is danger there is hope. Our present security is nothing, and can be nothing, but evil made irresistible.

WEAKNESSES OF THE SALVATION ARMY

For the present, however, it is not my business to flatter the Salvation Army. Rather must I point out to it that it has almost as many weaknesses as the Church of England itself. It is building up a business organization which will compel it eventually to see that its present staff of enthusiast-commanders shall be succeeded by a bureaucracy of men of business who will be no better than bishops, and perhaps a good deal more unscrupulous. That has always happened sooner or later to great orders founded by saints; and the order founded by St William Booth is not exempt from the same danger. It is even more dependent than the Church on rich people who would cut off

---

4. Dickens's *Little Dorrit* (1855–1857) centers around Marshalsea debtors' prison in London; William Dorrit has been incarcerated there for so long that he has adopted the title "Father of the Marshalsea."

5. Hymns in praise of Dionysus.

supplies at once if it began to preach that indispensable revolt against poverty which must also be a revolt against riches. It is hampered by a heavy contingent of pious elders who are not really Salvationists at all, but Evangelicals of the old school.[6] It still, as Commissioner Howard affirms, "sticks to Moses," which is flat nonsense at this time of day if the Commissioner means, as I am afraid he does, that the Book of Genesis contains a trustworthy scientific account of the origin of species, and that the god to whom Jephthah sacrificed his daughter is any less obviously a tribal idol than Dagon or Chemosh.[7]

Further, there is still too much other-worldliness about the Army. Like Frederick's grenadier,[8] the Salvationist wants to live for ever (the most monstrous way of crying for the moon); and though it is evident to anyone who has ever heard General Booth and his best officers that they would work as hard for human salvation as they do at present if they believed that death would be the end of them individually, they and their followers have a bad habit of talking as if the Salvationists were heroically enduring a very bad time on earth as an investment which will bring them in dividends later on in the form, not of a better life to come for the whole world, but of an eternity spent by themselves personally in a sort of bliss which would bore any active person to a second death. Surely the truth is that the Salvationists are unusually happy people. And is it not the very diagnostic of true salvation that it shall overcome the fear of death? Now the man who has come to believe that there is no such thing as death, the change so called being merely the transition to an exquisitely happy and utterly careless life, has not overcome the fear of death at all: on the contrary, it has overcome him so completely that he refuses to die on any terms whatever. I do not call a Salvationist really saved until he is ready to lie down cheerfully on the scrap heap, having paid scot and lot and something over, and let his eternal life pass on to renew its youth in the battalions of the future.

Then there is the nasty lying habit called confession, which the Army encourages because it lends itself to dramatic oratory, with plenty of thrilling incident. For my part, when I hear a convert relating the violences and oaths and blasphemies he was guilty of before he was saved, making out that he was a very terrible fellow then and is the most contrite and chastened of Christians now, I believe him no more than I believe the millionaire who says he came up to London or Chicago as a boy with only three halfpence in his pocket. Salvationists have said to me that Barbara in my play would never have been taken in by so transparent a humbug as Snobby Price; and certainly I do not think Snobby could have taken in any experienced Salvationist on a point on which the Salvationist did not wish to be taken in. But on the point of conversion all Salvationists wish to be taken in; for the more obvious the sinner the more obvious the miracle of his conversion. When you advertize a converted burglar or reclaimed drunkard as one of the attractions at an experience meeting, your burglar can hardly have been too burglarious or your drunkard too drunken. As long as such attractions are relied on, you will have your Snobbies claiming to have beaten their mothers when they were as a matter of prosaic fact habitually beat-

---

6. Term applied from the 18th century on to a school of Protestants maintaining that salvation came through faith and emphasizing the literal truth of the Bible.

7. In the Book of Judges (ch. 11), the Israelite general Jephthah vows that if he is victorious in war he will sacrifice the first of his household to meet him on his return;

the first to do so is his daughter. Dagon and Chemosh were Near Eastern gods.

8. Frederick William I of Prussia (1688–1740) formed an elite corps of grenadiers, all of them at least 6 feet tall; an expensive luxury, the king described this group as his "one and only vice."

en by them, and your Rummies of the tamest respectability pretending to a past of reckless and dazzling vice. Even when confessions are sincerely autobiographic we should beware of assuming that the impulse to make them was pious or that the interest of the hearers is wholesome. As well might we assume that the poor people who insist on shewing disgusting ulcers to district visitors are convinced hygienists, or that the curiosity which sometimes welcomes such exhibitions is a pleasant and creditable one. One is often tempted to suggest that those who pester our police superintendents with confessions of murder might very wisely be taken at their word and executed, except in the few cases in which a real murderer is seeking to be relieved of his guilt by confession and expiation. For though I am not, I hope, an unmerciful person, I do not think that the inexorability of the deed once done should be disguised by any ritual, whether in the confessional or on the scaffold.

And here my disagreement with the Salvation Army, and with all propagandists of the Cross (which I loathe as I loathe all gibbets) becomes deep indeed. Forgiveness, absolution, atonement, are figments: punishment is only a pretence of cancelling one crime by another; and you can no more have forgiveness without vindictiveness than you can have a cure without a disease. You will never get a high morality from people who conceive that their misdeeds are revocable and pardonable, or in a society where absolution and expiation are officially provided for us all. The demand may be very real; but the supply is spurious. Thus Bill Walker, in my play, having assaulted the Salvation Lass, presently finds himself overwhelmed with an intolerable conviction of sin under the skilled treatment of Barbara. Straightway he begins to try to unassault the lass and deruffianize his deed, first by getting punished for it in kind, and, when that relief is denied him, by fining himself a pound to compensate the girl. He is foiled both ways. He finds the Salvation Army as inexorable as fact itself. It will not punish him: it will not take his money. It will not tolerate a redeemed ruffian: it leaves him no means of salvation except ceasing to be a ruffian. In doing this, the Salvation Army instinctively grasps the central truth of Christianity and discards its central superstition: that central truth being the vanity of revenge and punishment, and that central superstition the salvation of the world by the gibbet.

For, be it noted, Bill has assaulted an old and starving woman also; and for this worse offence he feels no remorse whatever, because she makes it clear that her malice is as great as his own. "Let her have the law of me, as she said she would," says Bill: "what I done to her is no more on what you might call my conscience than sticking a pig." This shews a perfectly natural and wholesome state of mind on his part. The old woman, like the law she threatens him with, is perfectly ready to play the game of retaliation with him: to rob him if he steals, to flog him if he strikes, to murder him if he kills. By example and precept the law and public opinion teach him to impose his will on others by anger, violence, and cruelty, and to wipe off the moral score by punishment. That is sound Crosstianity. But this Crosstianity has got entangled with something which Barbara calls Christianity, and which unexpectedly causes her to refuse to play the hangman's game of Satan casting out Satan. She refuses to prosecute a drunken ruffian; she converses on equal terms with a blackguard to whom no lady should be seen speaking in the public street: in short, she imitates Christ. Bill's conscience reacts to this just as naturally as it does to the old woman's threats. He is placed in a position of unbearable moral inferiority, and strives by every means in his power to escape from it, whilst he is still quite ready to meet the abuse of the old woman by attempting to smash a mug on her face. And that is the triumphant justification of Barbara's Christianity as against our system of judicial punishment and the vindictive villain-thrashings and "poetic justice" of the romantic stage.

For the credit of literature it must be pointed out that the situation is only partly novel. Victor Hugo long ago gave us the epic of the convict and the bishop's candlesticks, of the Crosstian policeman annihilated by his encounter with the Christian Valjean.[9] But Bill Walker is not, like Valjean, romantically changed from a demon into an angel. There are millions of Bill Walkers in all classes of society today; and the point which I, as a professor of natural psychology, desire to demonstrate, is that Bill, without any change in his character or circumstances whatsoever, will react one way to one sort of treatment and another way to another.

In proof I might point to the sensational object lesson provided by our commercial millionaires today. They begin as brigands: merciless, unscrupulous, dealing out ruin and death and slavery to their competitors and employees, and facing desperately the worst that their competitors can do to them. The history of the English factories, the American Trusts, the exploitation of African gold, diamonds, ivory and rubber, outdoes in villainy the worst that has ever been imagined of the buccaneers of the Spanish Main. Captain Kidd would have marooned a modern Trust magnate for conduct unworthy of a gentleman of fortune. The law every day seizes on unsuccessful scoundrels of this type and punishes them with a cruelty worse than their own, with the result that they come out of the torture house more dangerous than they went in, and renew their evil doing (nobody will employ them at anything else) until they are again seized, again tormented, and again let loose, with the same result.

But the successful scoundrel is dealt with very differently, and very Christianly. He is not only forgiven: he is idolized, respected, made much of, all but worshipped. Society returns him good for evil in the most extravagant overmeasure. And with what result? He begins to idolize himself, to respect himself, to live up to the treatment he receives. He preaches sermons; he writes books of the most edifying advice to young men, and actually persuades himself that he got on by taking his own advice; he endows educational institutions; he supports charities; he dies finally in the odor of sanctity, leaving a will which is a monument of public spirit and bounty. And all this without any change in his character. The spots of the leopard and the stripes of the tiger are as brilliant as ever; but the conduct of the world towards him has changed; and his conduct has changed accordingly. You have only to reverse your attitude towards him—to lay hands on his property, revile him, assault him, and he will be a brigand again in a moment, as ready to crush you as you are to crush him, and quite as full of pretentious moral reasons for doing it.

In short, when Major Barbara says that there are no scoundrels, she is right: there are no absolute scoundrels, though there are impracticable people of whom I shall treat presently. Every reasonable man (and woman) is a potential scoundrel and a potential good citizen. What a man is depends on his character; but what he does, and what we think of what he does, depends on his circumstances. The characteristics that ruin a man in one class make him eminent in another. The characters that behave differently in different circumstances behave alike in similar circumstances. Take a common English character like that of Bill Walker. We meet Bill everywhere:

9. In Hugo's *Les Misérables* (1862), Jean Valjean, hardened by being imprisoned for stealing a loaf of bread, steals from a kindly bishop who gives him shelter. The novel describes Valjean's moral regeneration.

on the judicial bench, on the episcopal bench, in the Privy Council, at the War Office and Admiralty, as well as in the Old Bailey dock or in the ranks of casual unskilled labor.[1] And the morality of Bill's characteristics varies with these various circumstances. The faults of the burglar are the qualities of the financier: the manners and habits of a duke would cost a city clerk his situation. In short, though character is independent of circumstances, conduct is not; and our moral judgments of character are not: both are circumstantial. Take any condition of life in which the circumstances are for a mass of men practically alike: felony, the House of Lords, the factory, the stables, the gipsy encampment or where you please! In spite of diversity of character and temperament, the conduct and morals of the individuals in each group are as predictable and as alike in the main as if they were a flock of sheep, morals being mostly only social habits and circumstantial necessities. Strong people know this and count upon it. In nothing have the master-minds of the world been distinguished from the ordinary suburban season-ticket holder more than in their straightforward perception of the fact that mankind is practically a single species, and not a menagerie of gentlemen and bounders, villains and heroes, cowards and daredevils, peers and peasants, grocers and aristocrats, artisans and laborers, washerwomen and duchesses, in which all the grades of income and caste represent distinct animals who must not be introduced to one another or intermarry. Napoleon constructing a galaxy of generals and courtiers, and even of monarchs, out of his collection of social nobodies; Julius Caesar appointing as governor of Egypt the son of a freedman—one who but a short time before would have been legally disqualified for the post even of a private soldier in the Roman army; Louis XI making his barber his privy councillor: all these had in their different ways a firm hold of the scientific fact of human equality, expressed by Barbara in the Christian formula that all men are children of one father. A man who believes that men are naturally divided into upper and lower and middle classes morally is making exactly the same mistake as the man who believes that they are naturally divided in the same way socially. And just as our persistent attempts to found political institutions on a basis of social inequality have always produced long periods of destructive friction relieved from time to time by violent explosions of revolution; so the attempt—will Americans please note—to found moral institutions on a basis of moral inequality can lead to nothing but unnatural Reigns of the Saints relieved by licentious Restorations; to Americans who have made divorce a public institution turning the face of Europe into one huge sardonic smile by refusing to stay in the same hotel with a Russian man of genius who has changed wives without the sanction of South Dakota;[2] to grotesque hypocrisy, cruel persecution, and final utter confusion of conventions and compliances with benevolence and respectability. It is quite useless to declare that all men are born free if you deny that they are born good. Guarantee a man's goodness and his liberty will take care of itself. To guarantee his freedom on condition that you approve of his moral character is formally to abolish all freedom whatsoever, as every man's liberty is at the mercy of a moral indictment which any fool can trump up against everyone who violates custom, whether as a prophet or as a rascal. This is the lesson Democracy has to learn before it can become anything but the most oppressive of all the priesthoods.

1. The Privy Council consists of senior politicians, members of the judiciary and the Church; the Admiralty governs the affairs of the Royal Navy; the "Old Bailey" houses the Royal Courts of Justice in London.
2. The Russian writer Maxim Gorki came to the United States in 1905 accompanied by a woman who was not his wife; when this was discovered, he was evicted from his hotel, and Mark Twain, among others, refused to attend a banquet in his honor.

Let us now return to Bill Walker and his case of conscience against the Salvation Army. Major Barbara, not being a modern Tetzel,[3] or the treasurer of a hospital, refuses to sell absolution to Bill for a sovereign. Unfortunately, what the Army can afford to refuse in the case of Bill Walker, it cannot refuse in the case of Bodger. Bodger is master of the situation because he holds the purse strings. "Strive as you will," says Bodger, in effect: "me you cannot do without. You cannot save Bill Walker without my money." And the Army answers, quite rightly under the circumstances, "We will take money from the devil himself sooner than abandon the work of Salvation." So Bodger pays his conscience-money and gets the absolution that is refused to Bill. In real life Bill would perhaps never know this. But I, the dramatist whose business it is to shew the connexion between things that seem apart and unrelated in the haphazard order of events in real life, have contrived to make it known to Bill, with the result that the Salvation Army loses its hold of him at once.

But Bill may not be lost, for all that. He is still in the grip of the facts and of his own conscience, and may find his taste for blackguardism permanently spoiled. Still, I cannot guarantee that happy ending. Walk through the poorer quarters of our cities on Sunday when the men are not working, but resting and chewing the cud of their reflections. You will find one expression common to every mature face: the expression of cynicism. The discovery made by Bill Walker about the Salvation Army has been made by everyone there. They have found that every man has his price; and they have been foolishly or corruptly taught to mistrust and despise him for that necessary and salutary condition of social existence. When they learn that General Booth, too, has his price, they do not admire him because it is a high one, and admit the need of organizing society so that he shall get it in an honorable way: they conclude that his character is unsound and that all religious men are hypocrites and allies of their sweaters and oppressors. They know that the large subscriptions which help to support the Army are endowments, not of religion, but of the wicked doctrine of docility in poverty and humility under oppression; and they are rent by the most agonizing of all the doubts of the soul, the doubt whether their true salvation must not come from their most abhorrent passions, from murder, envy, greed, stubbornness, rage, and terrorism, rather than from public spirit, reasonableness, humanity, generosity, tenderness, delicacy, pity and kindness. The confirmation of that doubt, at which our newspapers have been working so hard for years past, is the morality of militarism; and the justification of militarism is that circumstances may at any time make it the true morality of the moment. It is by producing such moments that we produce violent and sanguinary revolutions, such as the one now in progress in Russia and the one which Capitalism in England and America is daily and diligently provoking.[4]

At such moments it becomes the duty of the Churches to evoke all the powers of destruction against the existing order. But if they do this, the existing order must forcibly suppress them. Churches are suffered to exist only on condition that they preach submission to the State as at present capitalistically organized. The Church of England itself is compelled to add to the thirty-six articles in which it formulates its

---

3. The German preacher Johann Tetzel's sale of papal indulgences caused Martin Luther (1483–1546) to nail his "Ninety-Five Theses" critical of the Roman Catholic Church to the door of Wittenberg Castle Church in Germany, sparking the Protestant Reformation in Europe.

4. The year (1905) was marked by a series of revolutionary disturbances in Russia; in response the Tsar promised to hold elections for a national parliament, which took place in 1906.

religious tenets,[5] three more in which it apologetically protests that the moment any of these articles comes in conflict with the State it is to be entirely renounced, abjured, violated, abrogated and abhorred, the policeman being a much more important person than any of the Persons of the Trinity. And this is why no tolerated Church nor Salvation Army can ever win the entire confidence of the poor. It must be on the side of the police and the military, no matter what it believes or disbelieves; and as the police and the military are the instruments by which the rich rob and oppress the poor (on legal and moral principles made for the purpose), it is not possible to be on the side of the poor and of the police at the same time. Indeed the religious bodies, as the almoners of the rich,[6] become a sort of auxiliary police, taking off the insurrectionary edge of poverty with coals and blankets, bread and treacle, and soothing and cheering the victims with hopes of immense and inexpensive happiness in another world when the process of working them to premature death in the service of the rich is complete in this.

CHRISTIANITY AND ANARCHISM

Such is the false position from which neither the Salvation Army nor the Church of England nor any other religious organization whatever can escape except through a reconstitution of society. Nor can they merely endure the State passively, washing their hands of its sins. The State is constantly forcing the consciences of men by violence and cruelty. Not content with exacting money from us for the maintenance of its soldiers and policemen, its gaolers and executioners, it forces us to take an active personal part in its proceedings on pain of becoming ourselves the victims of its violence. As I write these lines, a sensational example is given to the world. A royal marriage has been celebrated, first by sacrament in a cathedral, and then by a bullfight having for its main amusement the spectacle of horses gored and disembowelled by the bull, after which, when the bull is so exhausted as to be no longer dangerous, he is killed by a cautious matador. But the ironic contrast between the bullfight and the sacrament of marriage does not move anyone. Another contrast—that between the splendor, the happiness, the atmosphere of kindly admiration surrounding the young couple, and the price paid for it under our abominable social arrangements in the misery, squalor and degradation of millions of other young couples—is drawn at the same moment by a novelist, Mr Upton Sinclair, who chips a corner of the veneering from the huge meat packing industries of Chicago, and shews it to us as a sample of what is going on all over the world underneath the top layer of prosperous plutocracy. One man is sufficiently moved by that contrast to pay his own life as the price of one terrible blow at the responsible parties. His poverty has left him ignorant enough to be duped by the pretence that the innocent young bride and bridegroom, put forth and crowned by plutocracy as the heads of a State in which they have less personal power than any policeman, and less influence than any Chairman of a Trust, are responsible. At them accordingly he launches his sixpennorth of fulminate, missing his mark, but scattering the bowels of as many horses as any bull in the arena, and slaying twentythree persons, besides wounding ninetynine.[7] And of all these, the horses alone are innocent of the guilt he is avenging: had he blown all

5. The main doctrinal statement of the Church of England is its "Thirty-Nine Articles."
6. Distributors of charity (alms) on their behalf.
7. In May 1906 Princess Ena of Battenberg, a member of the British royal family, married King Alfonso of Spain; a bomb, disguised in a bouquet of flowers, was thrown at the royal coach; a student of 18 was arrested.

Madrid to atoms with every adult person in it, not one could have escaped the charge of being an accessory, before, at, and after the fact, to poverty and prostitution, to such wholesale massacre of infants as Herod never dreamt of, to plague, pestilence and famine, battle, murder and lingering death—perhaps not one who had not helped, through example, precept, connivance, and even clamor, to teach the dynamiter his well-learnt gospel of hatred and vengeance, by approving every day of sentences of years of imprisonment so infernal in their unnatural stupidity and panic-stricken cruelty, that their advocates can disavow neither the dagger nor the bomb without stripping the mask of justice and humanity from themselves also.

Be it noted that at this very moment there appears the biography of one of our dukes,[8] who, being a Scot, could argue about politics, and therefore stood out as a great brain among our aristocrats. And what, if you please, was his grace's favorite historical episode, which he declared he never read without intense satisfaction? Why, the young General Bonapart's pounding of the Paris mob to pieces in 1795, called in playful approval by our respectable classes "the whiff of grapeshot," though Napoleon, to do him justice, took a deeper view of it, and would fain have had it forgotten.[9] And since the Duke of Argyll was not a demon, but a man of like passions with ourselves, by no means rancorous or cruel as men go, who can doubt that all over the world proletarians of the ducal kidney are now revelling in "the whiff of dynamite" (the flavor of the joke seems to evaporate a little, does it not?) because it was aimed at the class they hate even as our argute[1] duke hated what he called the mob.

In such an atmosphere there can be only one sequel to the Madrid explosion. All Europe burns to emulate it. Vengeance! More blood! Tear "the Anarchist beast" to shreds. Drag him to the scaffold. Imprison him for life. Let all civilized States band together to drive his like off the face of the earth; and if any State refuses to join, make war on it. This time the leading London newspaper, anti-Liberal and therefore anti-Russian in politics, does not say "Serve you right" to the victims, as it did, in effect, when Bobrikoff, and De Plehve, and Grand Duke Sergius, were in the same manner unofficially fulminated into fragments.[2] No: fulminate our rivals in Asia by all means, ye brave Russian revolutionaries; but to aim at an English princess! monstrous! hideous! hound down the wretch to his doom; and observe, please, that we are a civilized and merciful people, and, however much we may regret it, must not treat him as Ravaillac and Damiens were treated.[3] And meanwhile, since we have not yet caught him, let us soothe our quivering nerves with the bullfight, and comment in a courtly way on the unfailing tact and good taste of the ladies of our royal houses, who, though presumably of full normal natural tenderness, have been so effectually broken in to fashionable routine that they can be taken to see the horses slaughtered as helplessly as they could no doubt be taken to a gladiator show, if that happened to be the mode just now.

Strangely enough, in the midst of this raging fire of malice, the one man who still has faith in the kindness and intelligence of human nature is the fulminator, now a hunted wretch, with nothing, apparently, to secure his triumph over all the prisons

---

8. The Duke of Argyle, prominent Scottish aristocrat, politician, and writer.
9. In late 1795, Napoleon put down a revolt in Paris on behalf of the revolutionary National Convention.
1. Shrewd.
2. Nikolay Bobrikov (1839–1904), Russian governor of Finland until his assassination; V. K. De Plehve (1846–1904), Russian interior minister until his assassination; according to the report in The Times (London), at

his trial the assassin of the Russian Grand Duke Serge (d. 1905) "refused to plead, declaring that he was not a criminal before his judges but a prisoner taken in civil war. He was sentenced to death."
3. François Ravaillac (1578–1610) assassinated Henry IV of France; Robert-François Damiens (1714–1757) was condemned to a horrible death following his attempt on the life of Louis XV of France.

and scaffolds of infuriate Europe except the revolver in his pocket and his readiness to discharge it at a moment's notice into his own or any other head. Think of him setting out to find a gentleman and a Christian in the multitude of human wolves howling for his blood. Think also of this: that at the very first essay he finds what he seeks, a veritable grandee of Spain, a noble, high-thinking, unterrified, malice-void soul, in the guise—of all masquerades in the world!—of a modern editor. The Anarchist wolf, flying from the wolves of plutocracy, throws himself on the honor of the man. The man, not being a wolf (nor a London editor), and therefore not having enough sympathy with his exploit to be made bloodthirsty by it, does not throw him back to the pursuing wolves—gives him, instead, what help he can to escape, and sends him off acquainted at last with a force that goes deeper than dynamite, though you cannot buy so much of it for sixpence. That righteous and honorable high human deed is not wasted on Europe, let us hope, though it benefits the fugitive wolf only for a moment. The plutocratic wolves presently smell him out. The fugitive shoots the unlucky wolf whose nose is nearest; shoots himself; and then convinces the world, by his photograph, that he was no monstrous freak of reversion to the tiger, but a good looking young man with nothing abnormal about him except his appalling courage and resolution (that is why the terrified shriek Coward at him): one to whom murdering a happy young couple on their wedding morning would have been an unthinkably unnatural abomination under rational and kindly human circumstances.

Then comes the climax of irony and blind stupidity. The wolves, balked of their meal of fellow-wolf, turn on the man, and proceed to torture him, after their manner, by imprisonment, for refusing to fasten his teeth in the throat of the dynamiter and hold him down until they came to finish him.

Thus, you see, a man may not be a gentleman nowadays even if he wishes to. As to being a Christian, he is allowed some latitude in that matter, because, I repeat, Christianity has two faces. Popular Christianity has for its emblem a gibbet, for its chief sensation a sanguinary execution after torture, for its central mystery an insane vengeance bought off by a trumpery expiation. But there is a nobler and profounder Christianity which affirms the sacred mystery of Equality, and forbids the glaring futility and folly of vengeance, often politely called punishment or justice. The gibbet part of Christianity is tolerated. The other is criminal felony. Connoisseurs in irony are well aware of the fact that the only editor in England who denounces punishment as radically wrong, also repudiates Christianity; calls his paper The Freethinker; and has been imprisoned for "bad taste" under the law against blasphemy.[4]

SANE CONCLUSIONS

And now I must ask the excited reader not to lose his head on one side or the other, but to draw a sane moral from these grim absurdities. It is not good sense to propose that laws against crime should apply to principals only and not to accessories whose consent, counsel, or silence may secure impunity to the principal. If you institute punishment as part of the law, you must punish people for refusing to punish. If you have a police, part of its duty must be to compel everybody to assist the police. No doubt if your laws are unjust, and your policemen agents of oppression, the result will be an unbearable violation of the private consciences of citizens. But that cannot be helped: the remedy is, not to license everybody to thwart the law if they please, but

---

4. The secularist journalist George William Foote was jailed for blasphemy in 1883.

to make laws that will command the public assent, and not to deal cruelly and stupidly with law-breakers. Everybody disapproves of burglars; but the modern burglar, when caught and overpowered by a householder, usually appeals, and often, let us hope, with success, to his captor not to deliver him over to the useless horrors of penal servitude. In other cases the law-breaker escapes because those who could give him up do not consider his breach of the law a guilty action. Sometimes, even, private tribunals are formed in opposition to the official tribunals; and these private tribunals employ assassins as executioners, as was done, for example, by Mahomet[5] before he had established his power officially, and by the Ribbon lodges of Ireland in their long struggle with the landlords.[6] Under such circumstances, the assassin goes free although everybody in the district knows who he is and what he has done. They do not betray him, partly because they justify him exactly as the regular Government justifies its official executioner, and partly because they would themselves be assassinated if they betrayed him: another method learnt from the official government. Given a tribunal, employing a slayer who has no personal quarrel with the slain; and there is clearly no moral difference between official and unofficial killing.

In short, all men are anarchists with regard to laws which are against their consciences, either in the preamble or in the penalty. In London our worst anarchists are the magistrates,[7] because many of them are so old and ignorant that when they are called upon to administer any law that is based on ideas or knowledge less than half a century old, they disagree with it, and being mere ordinary homebred private Englishmen without any respect for law in the abstract, naïvely set the example of violating it. In this instance the man lags behind the law; but when the law lags behind the man, he becomes equally an anarchist. When some huge change in social conditions, such as the industrial revolution of the eighteenth and nineteenth centuries, throws our legal and industrial institutions out of date, Anarchism becomes almost a religion. The whole force of the most energetic geniuses of the time in philosophy, economics, and art, concentrates itself on demonstrations and reminders that morality and law are only conventions, fallible and continually obsolescing. Tragedies in which the heroes are bandits, and comedies in which law-abiding and conventionally moral folk are compelled to satirize themselves by outraging the conscience of the spectators every time they do their duty, appear simultaneously with economic treatises entitled "What is Property? Theft!" and with histories of "The Conflict between Religion and Science."

Now this is not a healthy state of things. The advantages of living in society are proportionate, not to the freedom of the individual from a code, but to the complexity and subtlety of the code he is prepared not only to accept but to uphold as a matter of such vital importance that a lawbreaker at large is hardly to be tolerated on any plea. Such an attitude becomes impossible when the only men who can make themselves heard and remembered throughout the world spend all their energy in raising our gorge against current law, current morality, current respectability, and legal property. The ordinary man, uneducated in social theory even when he is schooled in Latin verse, cannot be set against all the laws of his country and yet persuaded to regard law in the abstract as vitally necessary to society. Once he is brought to repudiate the laws and institutions he knows, he will repudiate the very conception of

---

5. Muhammad, founder of Islam.
6. The 19th-century Ribbon Societies carried out acts of violence against landlords, priests, and others, in protest against high rents on land.
7. Officials conducting minor criminal cases and preliminary hearings.

law and the very groundwork of institutions, ridiculing human rights, extolling brainless methods as "historical," and tolerating nothing except pure empiricism in conduct, with dynamite as the basis of politics and vivisection as the basis of science. That is hideous; but what is to be done? Here am I, for instance, by class a respectable man, by common sense a hater of waste and disorder, by intellectual constitution legally minded to the verge of pedantry, and by temperament apprehensive and economically disposed to the limit of old-maidishness; yet I am, and have always been, and shall now always be, a revolutionary writer, because our laws make law impossible; our liberties destroy all freedom; our property is organized robbery; our morality is an impudent hypocrisy; our wisdom is administered by inexperienced or malexperienced dupes, our power wielded by cowards and weaklings, and our honor false in all its points. I am an enemy of the existing order for good reasons; but that does not make my attacks any less encouraging or helpful to people who are its enemies for bad reasons. The existing order may shriek that if I tell the truth about it, some foolish person may drive it to become still worse by trying to assassinate it. I cannot help that, even if I could see what worse it could do than it is already doing. And the disadvantage of that worst even from its own point of view is that society, with all its prisons and bayonets and whips and ostracisms and starvations, is powerless in the face of the Anarchist who is prepared to sacrifice his own life in the battle with it. Our natural safety from the cheap and devastating explosives which every Russian student can make, and every Russian grenadier has learnt to handle in Manchuria,[8] lies in the fact that brave and resolute men, when they are rascals, will not risk their skins for the good of humanity, and, when they are not, are sympathetic enough to care for humanity, abhorring murder, and never committing it until their consciences are outraged beyond endurance. The remedy is, then, simply not to outrage their consciences.

Do not be afraid that they will not make allowances. All men make very large allowances indeed before they stake their own lives in a war to the death with society. Nobody demands or expects the millennium. But there are two things that must be set right, or we shall perish, like Rome, of soul atrophy disguised as empire.

The first is, that the daily ceremony of dividing the wealth of the country among its inhabitants shall be so conducted that no crumb shall, save as a criminal's ration, go to any able-bodied adults who are not producing by their personal exertions not only a full equivalent for what they take, but a surplus sufficient to provide for their superannuation and pay back the debt due for their nurture.

The second is that the deliberate infliction of malicious injuries which now goes on under the name of punishment be abandoned; so that the thief, the ruffian, the gambler, and the beggar, may without inhumanity be handed over to the law, and made to understand that a State which is too humane to punish will also be too thrifty to waste the life of honest men in watching or restraining dishonest ones. That is why we do not imprison dogs. We even take our chance of their first bite. But if a dog delights to bark and bite, it goes to the lethal chamber. That seems to me sensible. To allow the dog to expiate his bite by a period of torment, and then let him loose in a much more savage condition (for the chain makes a dog savage) to bite again and expiate again, having meanwhile spent a great deal of human life and happiness in the task of chaining and feeding and tormenting him, seems to me idiotic

8. The Russo-Japanese war of 1904–1905 was fought over possession of the Chinese province of Manchuria.

and superstitious. Yet that is what we do to men who bark and bite and steal. It would be far more sensible to put up with their vices, as we put up with their illnesses, until they give more trouble than they are worth, at which point we should, with many apologies and expressions of sympathy, and some generosity in complying with their last wishes, place them in the lethal chamber and get rid of them. Under no circumstances should they be allowed to expiate their misdeeds by a manufactured penalty, to subscribe to a charity, or to compensate the victims. If there is to be no punishment there can be no forgiveness. We shall never have real moral responsibility until everyone knows that his deeds are irrevocable, and that his life depends on his usefulness. Hitherto, alas! humanity has never dared face these hard facts. We frantically scatter conscience money and invent systems of conscience banking, with expiatory penalties, atonements, redemptions, salvations, hospital subscription lists and what not, to enable us to contract-out of the moral code. Not content with the old scapegoat and sacrificial lamb, we deify human saviors, and pray to miraculous virgin intercessors. We attribute mercy to the inexorable; soothe our consciences after committing murder by throwing ourselves on the bosom of divine love; and shrink even from our own gallows because we are forced to admit that it, at least, is irrevocable—as if one hour of imprisonment were not as irrevocable as any execution!

If a man cannot look evil in the face without illusion, he will never know what it really is, or combat it effectually. The few men who have been able (relatively) to do this have been called cynics, and have sometimes had an abnormal share of evil in themselves, corresponding to the abnormal strength of their minds; but they have never done mischief unless they intended to do it. That is why great scoundrels have been beneficent rulers whilst amiable and privately harmless monarchs have ruined their countries by trusting to the hocus-pocus of innocence and guilt, reward and punishment, virtuous indignation and pardon, instead of standing up to the facts without either malice or mercy. Major Barbara stands up to Bill Walker in that way, with the result that the ruffian who cannot get hated, has to hate himself. To relieve this agony he tries to get punished; but the Salvationist whom he tries to provoke is as merciless as Barbara, and only prays for him. Then he tries to pay, but can get nobody to take his money. His doom is the doom of Cain, who, failing to find either a savior, a policeman, or an almoner to help him to pretend that his brother's blood no longer cried from the ground, had to live and die a murderer.[9] Cain took care not to commit another murder, unlike our railway shareholders (I am one) who kill and maim shunters by hundreds to save the cost of automatic couplings, and make atonement by annual subscriptions to deserving charities. Had Cain been allowed to pay off his score, he might possibly have killed Adam and Eve for the mere sake of a second luxurious reconciliation with God afterwards. Bodger, you may depend on it, will go on to the end of his life poisoning people with bad whisky, because he can always depend on the Salvation Army or the Church of England to negotiate a redemption for him in consideration of a trifling percentage of his profits.

There is a third condition too, which must be fulfilled before the great teachers of the world will cease to scoff at its religions. Creeds must become intellectually honest. At present there is not a single credible established religion in the world. That is perhaps the most stupendous fact in the whole world-situation. This play of mine, Major Barbara, is, I hope, both true and inspired; but whoever says that it all happened, and

---

9. In Genesis 4, Adam and Eve's son Cain kills his brother Abel out of jealousy and becomes a fugitive.

that faith in it and understanding of it consist in believing that it is a record of an actual occurrence, is, to speak according to Scripture, a fool and a liar, and is hereby solemnly denounced and cursed as such by me, the author, to all posterity.

London, June 1906

Major Barbara

ACT 1

It is after dinner in January 1906, in the library in Lady Britomart Undershaft's house in Wilton Crescent. A large and comfortable settee is in the middle of the room, upholstered in dark leather. A person sitting on it (it is vacant at present) would have, on his right, Lady Britomart's writing table, with the lady herself busy at it; a smaller writing table behind him on his left; the door behind him on Lady Britomart's side; and a window with a window seat directly on his left. Near the window is an armchair.

Lady Britomart is a woman of fifty or thereabouts, well dressed and yet careless of her dress, well bred and quite reckless of her breeding, well mannered and yet appallingly out-spoken and indifferent to the opinion of her interlocutors, amiable and yet peremptory, arbitrary, and high-tempered to the last bearable degree, and withal a very typical managing matron of the upper class, treated as a naughty child until she grew into a scolding mother, and finally settling down with plenty of practical ability and worldly experience, limited in the oddest way with domestic and class limitations, conceiving the universe exactly as if it were a large house in Wilton Crescent, though handling her corner of it very effectively on that assumption, and being quite enlightened and liberal as to the books in the library, the pictures on the walls, the music in the portfolios, and the articles in the papers.

Her son, Stephen, comes in. He is a gravely correct young man under 25, taking himself very seriously, but still in some awe of his mother, from childish habit and bachelor shyness rather than from any weakness of character.

STEPHEN Whats[1] the matter?

LADY BRITOMART Presently, Stephen.

[*Stephen submissively walks to the settee and sits down. He takes up a Liberal weekly called* The Speaker.]

LADY BRITOMART Dont begin to read, Stephen. I shall require all your attention.

STEPHEN It was only while I was waiting—

LADY BRITOMART Dont make excuses, Stephen. [*He puts down* The Speaker.] Now! [*She finishes her writing; rises; and comes to the settee.*] I have not kept you waiting very long, I think.

STEPHEN Not at all, mother.

LADY BRITOMART Bring me my cushion. [*He takes the cushion from the chair at the desk and arranges it for her as she sits down on the settee.*] Sit down. [*He sits down and fingers his tie nervously.*] Dont fiddle with your tie, Stephen: there is nothing the matter with it.

STEPHEN I beg your pardon. [*He fiddles with his watch chain instead.*]

LADY BRITOMART Now are you attending to me, Stephen?

STEPHEN Of course, mother.

---

1. Shaw favored simplifying English spelling; his contractions are written without apostrophes.

LADY BRITOMART No: it's not of course. I want something much more than your everyday matter-of-course attention. I am going to speak to you very seriously, Stephen. I wish you would let that chain alone.

STEPHEN [*hastily relinquishing the chain*] Have I done anything to annoy you, mother? If so, it was quite unintentional.

LADY BRITOMART [*astonished*] Nonsense! [*With some remorse.*] My poor boy, did you think I was angry with you?

STEPHEN What is it, then, mother? You are making me very uneasy.

LADY BRITOMART [*squaring herself at him rather aggressively*] Stephen: may I ask how soon you intend to realize that you are a grown-up man, and that I am only a woman?

STEPHEN [*amazed*] Only a—

LADY BRITOMART Dont repeat my words, please: it is a most aggravating habit. You must learn to face life seriously, Stephen. I really cannot bear the whole burden of our family affairs any longer. You must advise me: you must assume the responsibility.

STEPHEN I!

LADY BRITOMART Yes, you, of course. You were 24 last June. Youve been at Harrow[2] and Cambridge. Youve been to India and Japan. You must know a lot of things, now; unless you have wasted your time most scandalously. Well, advise me.

STEPHEN [*much perplexed*] You know I have never interfered in the household—

LADY BRITOMART No: I should think not. I dont want you to order the dinner.

STEPHEN I mean in our family affairs.

LADY BRITOMART Well, you must interfere now; for they are getting quite beyond me.

STEPHEN [*troubled*] I have thought sometimes that perhaps I ought; but really, mother, I know so little about them; and what I do know is so painful! it is so impossible to mention some things to you—[*He stops, ashamed.*]

LADY BRITOMART I suppose you mean your father.

STEPHEN [*almost inaudibly*] Yes.

LADY BRITOMART My dear: we cant go on all our lives not mentioning him. Of course you were quite right not to open the subject until I asked you to; but you are old enough now to be taken into my confidence, and to help me to deal with him about the girls.

STEPHEN But the girls are all right. They are engaged.

LADY BRITOMART [*complacently*] Yes: I have made a very good match for Sarah. Charles Lomax will be a millionaire at 35. But that is ten years ahead; and in the meantime his trustees cannot under the terms of his father's will allow him more than £800 a year.

STEPHEN But the will says also that if he increases his income by his own exertions, they may double the increase.

LADY BRITOMART Charles Lomax's exertions are much more likely to decrease his income than to increase it. Sarah will have to find at least another £800 a year for the next ten years; and even then they will be as poor as church mice. And what about Barbara? I thought Barbara was going to make the most brilliant career of all of you. And what does she do? Joins the Salvation Army; discharges her maid; lives on a pound a week; and walks in one evening with a professor of Greek

---

2. Harrow is a prestigious private boys' school, founded in 1571.

whom she has picked up in the street, and who pretends to be a Salvationist, and actually plays the big drum for her in public because he has fallen head over ears in love with her.

STEPHEN I was certainly rather taken aback when I heard they were engaged. Cusins is a very nice fellow, certainly: nobody would ever guess that he was born in Australia; but—

LADY BRITOMART Oh, Adolphus Cusins will make a very good husband. After all, nobody can say a word against Greek: it stamps a man at once as an educated gentleman. And my family, thank Heaven, is not a pig-headed Tory one. We are Whigs, and believe in liberty.[3] Let snobbish people say what they please: Barbara shall marry, not the man they like, but the man I like.

STEPHEN Of course I was thinking only of his income. However, he is not likely to be extravagant.

LADY BRITOMART Dont be too sure of that, Stephen. I know your quiet, simple, refined, poetic people like Adolphus: quite content with the best of everything! They cost more than your extravagant people, who are always as mean as they are second rate. No: Barbara will need at least £2000 a year. You see it means two additional households. Besides, my dear, you must marry soon. I dont approve of the present fashion of philandering bachelors and late marriages; and I am trying to arrange something for you.

STEPHEN It's very good of you, mother; but perhaps I had better arrange that for myself.

LADY BRITOMART Nonsense! you are much too young to begin matchmaking: you would be taken in by some pretty little nobody. Of course I dont mean that you are not to be consulted: you know that as well as I do. [Stephen closes his lips and is silent.] Now dont sulk, Stephen.

STEPHEN I am not sulking, mother. What has all this got to do with—with—with my father?

LADY BRITOMART My dear Stephen: where is the money to come from? It is easy enough for you and the other children to live on my income as long as we are in the same house; but I cant keep four families in four separate houses. You know how poor my father is: he has barely seven thousand a year now; and really, if he were not the Earl of Stevenage, he would have to give up society. He can do nothing for us. He says, naturally enough, that it is absurd that he should be asked to provide for the children of a man who is rolling in money. You see, Stephen, your father must be fabulously wealthy, because there is always a war going on somewhere.

STEPHEN You need not remind me of that, mother. I have hardly ever opened a newspaper in my life without seeing our name in it. The Undershaft torpedo! The Undershaft quick firers! The Undershaft ten inch! the Undershaft disappearing rampart gun! the Undershaft submarine! and now the Undershaft aerial battleship! At Harrow they called me the Woolwich Infant.[4] At Cambridge it was the same. A little brute at King's[5] who was always trying to get up revivals, spoilt my Bible—your first birthday present to me—by writing under my name, "Son and

---

3. The Whigs supported the rights of Parliament against the Crown in the late 17th century, became associated with the rise to political power of the middle classes in the 18th and early 19th centuries through reform, and were succeeded by the Liberal Party in the later 19th century.

4. An arsenal in Woolwich, a district of southeast London, was the main government site for the testing and manufacture of arms.
5. King's College at Cambridge University.

heir to Undershaft and Lazarus, Death and Destruction Dealers: address Christendom and Judea." But that was not so bad as the way I was kowtowed to everywhere because my father was making millions by selling cannons.

LADY BRITOMART It is not only the cannons, but the war loans that Lazarus arranges under cover of giving credit for the cannons. You know, Stephen, it's perfectly scandalous. Those two men, Andrew Undershaft and Lazarus, positively have Europe under their thumbs. That is why your father is able to behave as he does. He is above the law. Do you think Bismarck or Gladstone or Disraeli could have openly defied every social and moral obligation all their lives as your father has? They simply wouldnt have dared. I asked Gladstone to take it up. I asked The Times to take it up. I asked the Lord Chamberlain[6] to take it up. But it was just like asking them to declare war on the Sultan.[7] They wouldnt. They said they couldnt touch him. I believe they were afraid.

STEPHEN What could they do? He does not actually break the law.

LADY BRITOMART Not break the law! He is always breaking the law. He broke the law when he was born: his parents were not married.

STEPHEN Mother! Is that true?

LADY BRITOMART Of course it's true: that was why we separated.

STEPHEN He married without letting you know this!

LADY BRITOMART [rather taken aback by this inference] Oh no. To do Andrew justice, that was not the sort of thing he did. Besides, you know the Undershaft motto: Unashamed. Everybody knew.

STEPHEN But you said that was why you separated.

LADY BRITOMART Yes, because he was not content with being a foundling himself: he wanted to disinherit you for another foundling. That was what I couldnt stand.

STEPHEN [ashamed] Do you mean for—for—for—

LADY BRITOMART Dont stammer, Stephen. Speak distinctly.

STEPHEN But this is so frightful to me, mother. To have to speak to you about such things!

LADY BRITOMART It's not pleasant for me, either, especially if you are still so childish that you must make it worse by a display of embarrassment. It is only in the middle classes, Stephen, that people get into a state of dumb helpless horror when they find that there are wicked people in the world. In our class, we have to decide what is to be done with wicked people; and nothing should disturb our self-possession. Now ask your question properly.

STEPHEN Mother: have you no consideration for me? For Heaven's sake either treat me as a child, as you always do, and tell me nothing at all; or tell me everything and let me take it as best I can.

LADY BRITOMART Treat you as a child! What do you mean? It is most unkind and ungrateful of you to say such a thing. You know I have never treated any of you as children. I have always made you my companions and friends, and allowed you perfect freedom to do and say whatever you liked, so long as you liked what I could approve of.

STEPHEN [desperately] I daresay we have been the very imperfect children of a very perfect mother; but I do beg you to let me alone for once, and tell me about this horrible business of my father wanting to set me aside for another son.

---

6. The official in charge of the Royal Household; he also licensed plays for public performance.

7. The Sultan of Turkey and the Ottoman Empire.

LADY BRITOMART [*amazed*] Another son! I never said anything of the kind. I never dreamt of such a thing. This is what comes of interrupting me.

STEPHEN But you said—

LADY BRITOMART [*cutting him short*] Now be a good boy, Stephen, and listen to me patiently. The Undershafts are descended from a foundling in the parish of St Andrew Undershaft in the city. That was long ago, in the reign of James the First. Well, this foundling was adopted by an armorer and gun-maker. In the course of time the foundling succeeded to the business; and from some notion of gratitude, or some vow or something, he adopted another foundling, and left the business to him. And that foundling did the same. Ever since that, the cannon business has always been left to an adopted foundling named Andrew Undershaft.

STEPHEN But did they never marry? Were there no legitimate sons?

LADY BRITOMART Oh yes: they married just as your father did; and they were rich enough to buy land for their own children and leave them well provided for. But they always adopted and trained some foundling to succeed them in the business; and of course they always quarrelled with their wives furiously over it. Your father was adopted in that way; and he pretends to consider himself bound to keep up the tradition and adopt somebody to leave the business to. Of course I was not going to stand that. There may have been some reason for it when the Undershafts could only marry women in their own class, whose sons were not fit to govern great estates. But there could be no excuse for passing over my son.

STEPHEN [*dubiously*] I am afraid I should make a poor hand of managing a cannon foundry.

LADY BRITOMART Nonsense! you could easily get a manager and pay him a salary.

STEPHEN My father evidently had no great opinion of my capacity.

LADY BRITOMART Stuff, child! you were only a baby: it had nothing to do with your capacity. Andrew did it on principle, just as he did every perverse and wicked thing on principle. When my father remonstrated, Andrew actually told him to his face that history tells us of only two successful institutions: one the Undershaft firm, and the other the Roman Empire under the Antonines.[8] That was because the Antonine emperors all adopted their successors. Such rubbish! The Stevenages are as good as the Antonines, I hope; and you are a Stevenage. But that was Andrew all over. There you have the man! Always clever and unanswerable when he was defending nonsense and wickedness: always awkward and sullen when he had to behave sensibly and decently!

STEPHEN Then it was on my account that your home life was broken up, mother. I am sorry.

LADY BRITOMART Well, dear, there were other differences. I really cannot bear an immoral man. I am not a Pharisee, I hope; and I should not have minded his merely doing wrong things: we are none of us perfect. But your father didnt exactly do wrong things: he said them and thought them: that was what was so dreadful. He really had a sort of religion of wrongness. Just as one doesnt mind men practising immorality so long as they own that they are in the wrong by preaching morality; so I couldnt forgive Andrew for preaching immorality while he practised morality. You would all have grown up without principles, without any knowledge

8. Second-century Roman emperors, under whose rule the empire enjoyed a period of relative enlightenment and stability.

of right and wrong, if he had been in the house. You know, my dear, your father was a very attractive man in some ways. Children did not dislike him; and he took advantage of it to put the wickedest ideas into their heads, and make them quite unmanageable. I did not dislike him myself: very far from it; but nothing can bridge over moral disagreement.

STEPHEN All this simply bewilders me, mother. People may differ about matters of opinion, or even about religion; but how can they differ about right and wrong? Right is right; and wrong is wrong; and if a man cannot distinguish them properly, he is either a fool or a rascal: thats all.

LADY BRITOMART [touched] Thats my own boy! [She pats his cheek.] Your father never could answer that: he used to laugh and get out of it under cover of some affectionate nonsense. And now that you understand the situation, what do you advise me to do?

STEPHEN Well, what can you do?

LADY BRITOMART I must get the money somehow.

STEPHEN We cannot take money from him. I had rather go and live in some cheap place like Bedford Square or even Hampstead[9] than take a farthing of his money.

LADY BRITOMART But after all, Stephen, our present income comes from Andrew.

STEPHEN [shocked] I never knew that.

LADY BRITOMART Well, you surely didnt suppose your grandfather had anything to give me. The Stevenages could not do everything for you. We gave you social position. Andrew had to contribute something. He had a very good bargain, I think.

STEPHEN [bitterly] We are utterly dependent on him and his cannons, then?

LADY BRITOMART Certainly not: the money is settled. But he provided it. So you see it is not a question of taking money from him or not: it is simply a question of how much. I dont want any more for myself.

STEPHEN Nor do I.

LADY BRITOMART But Sarah does; and Barbara does. That is, Charles Lomax and Adolphus Cusins will cost them more. So I must put my pride in my pocket and ask for it, I suppose. That is your advice, Stephen, is it not?

STEPHEN No.

LADY BRITOMART [sharply] Stephen!

STEPHEN Of course if you are determined—

LADY BRITOMART I am not determined: I ask your advice; and I am waiting for it. I will not have all the responsibility thrown on my shoulders.

STEPHEN [obstinately] I would die sooner than ask him for another penny.

LADY BRITOMART [resignedly] You mean that I must ask him. Very well, Stephen: it shall be as you wish. You will be glad to know that your grandfather concurs. But he thinks I ought to ask Andrew to come here and see the girls. After all, he must have some natural affection for them.

STEPHEN Ask him here!!!

LADY BRITOMART Do not repeat my words, Stephen. Where else can I ask him?

STEPHEN I never expected you to ask him at all.

LADY BRITOMART Now dont tease, Stephen. Come! you see that it is necessary that he should pay us a visit, dont you?

STEPHEN [reluctantly] I suppose so, if the girls cannot do without his money.

9. Solidly upper-middle-class residential areas of London.

LADY BRITOMART Thank you, Stephen: I knew you would give me the right advice when it was properly explained to you. I have asked your father to come this evening. [*Stephen bounds from his seat.*] Dont jump, Stephen: it fidgets me.

STEPHEN [*in utter consternation*] Do you mean to say that my father is coming here tonight—that he may be here at any moment?

LADY BRITOMART [*looking at her watch*] I said nine. [*He gasps. She rises.*] Ring the bell, please. [*Stephen goes to the smaller writing table; presses a button on it; and sits at it with his elbows on the table and his head in his hands, outwitted and overwhelmed.*] It is ten minutes to nine yet; and I have to prepare the girls. I asked Charles Lomax and Adolphus to dinner on purpose that they might be here. Andrew had better see them in case he should cherish any delusions as to their being capable of supporting their wives. [*The butler enters: Lady Britomart goes behind the settee to speak to him.*] Morrison: go up to the drawing room and tell everybody to come down here at once. [*Morrison withdraws. Lady Britomart turns to Stephen.*] Now remember, Stephen: I shall need all your countenance and authority. [*He rises and tries to recover some vestige of these attributes.*] Give me a chair, dear. [*He pushes a chair forward from the wall to where she stands, near the smaller writing table. She sits down; and he goes to the armchair, into which he throws himself.*] I dont know how Barbara will take it. Ever since they made her a major in the Salvation Army she has developed a propensity to have her own way and order people about which quite cows me sometimes. It's not ladylike: I'm sure I dont know where she picked it up. Anyhow, Barbara shant bully me; but still it's just as well that your father should be here before she has time to refuse to meet him or make a fuss. Dont look nervous, Stephen: it will only encourage Barbara to make difficulties. *I* am nervous enough, goodness knows; but I dont shew it.

[*Sarah and Barbara come in with their respective young men, Charles Lomax and Adolphus Cusins. Sarah is slender, bored, and mundane. Barbara is robuster, jollier, much more energetic. Sarah is fashionably dressed: Barbara is in Salvation Army uniform. Lomax, a young man about town, is like many other young men about town. He is afflicted with a frivolous sense of humor which plunges him at the most inopportune moments into paroxysms of imperfectly suppressed laughter. Cusins is a spectacled student, slight, thin haired, and sweet voiced, with a more complex form of Lomax's complaint. His sense of humor is intellectual and subtle, and is complicated by an appalling temper. The lifelong struggle of a benevolent temperament and a high conscience against impulses of inhuman ridicule and fierce impatience has set up a chronic strain which has visibly wrecked his constitution. He is a most implacable, determined, tenacious, intolerant person who by mere force of character presents himself as—and indeed actually is—considerate, gentle, explanatory, even mild and apologetic, capable possibly of murder, but not of cruelty or coarseness. By the operation of some instinct which is not merciful enough to blind him with the illusions of love, he is obstinately bent on marrying Barbara. Lomax likes Sarah and thinks it will be rather a lark to marry her. Consequently he has not attempted to resist Lady Britomart's arrangements to that end.*

All four look as if they had been having a good deal of fun in the drawing room. The girls enter first, leaving the swains outside. Sarah comes to the settee. Barbara comes in after her and stops at the door.]

BARBARA Are Cholly and Dolly to come in?

LADY BRITOMART [*forcibly*] Barbara: I will not have Charles called Cholly: the vulgarity of it positively makes me ill.

BARBARA It's all right, mother: Cholly is quite correct nowadays. Are they to come in?

LADY BRITOMART Yes, if they will behave themselves.

BARBARA [*through the door*] Come in, Dolly; and behave yourself.

[*Barbara comes to her mother's writing table. Cusins enters smiling, and wanders towards Lady Britomart.*]

SARAH [*calling*] Come in, Cholly. [*Lomax enters, controlling his features very imperfectly, and places himself vaguely between Sarah and Barbara.*]

LADY BRITOMART [*peremptorily*] Sit down, all of you. [*They sit. Cusins crosses to the window and seats himself there. Lomax takes a chair. Barbara sits at the writing table and Sarah on the settee.*] I dont in the least know what you are laughing at, Adolphus. I am surprised at you, though I expected nothing better from Charles Lomax.

CUSINS [*in a remarkably gentle voice*] Barbara has been trying to teach me the West Ham[1] Salvation March.

LADY BRITOMART I see nothing to laugh at in that; nor should you if you are really converted.

CUSINS [*sweetly*] You were not present. It was really funny, I believe.

LOMAX Ripping.

LADY BRITOMART Be quiet, Charles. Now listen to me, children. Your father is coming here this evening.

[*General stupefaction. Lomax, Sarah, and Barbara rise: Sarah scared, and Barbara amused and expectant.*]

LOMAX [*remonstrating*] Oh I say!

LADY BRITOMART You are not called on to say anything, Charles.

SARAH Are you serious, mother?

LADY BRITOMART Of course I am serious. It is on your account, Sarah, and also on Charles's. [*Silence. Sarah sits, with a shrug. Charles looks painfully unworthy.*] I hope you are not going to object, Barbara.

BARBARA I! why should I? My father has a soul to be saved like anybody else. He's quite welcome as far as I am concerned. [*She sits on the table, and softly whistles "Onward, Christian Soldiers."*]

LOMAX [*still remonstrant*] But really, dont you know! Oh I say!

LADY BRITOMART [*frigidly*] What do you wish to convey, Charles?

LOMAX Well, you must admit that this is a bit thick.

LADY BRITOMART [*turning with ominous suavity to Cusins*] Adolphus: you are a professor of Greek. Can you translate Charles Lomax's remarks into reputable English for us?

CUSINS [*cautiously*] If I may say so, Lady Brit, I think Charles has rather happily expressed what we all feel. Homer, speaking of Autolycus,[2] uses the same phrase. πυκινὸν δόμον 'ελθεῖν means a bit thick.

LOMAX [*handsomely*] Not that I mind, you know, if Sarah dont. [*He sits.*]

LADY BRITOMART [*crushingly*] Thank you. Have I your permission, Adolphus, to invite my own husband to my own house?

CUSINS [*gallantly*] You have my unhesitating support in everything you do.

LADY BRITOMART Tush! Sarah: have you nothing to say?

---

1. A working-class area of East London.

2. In Homer's epics, Autolycus is Odysseus's shifty grandfather.

SARAH Do you mean that he is coming regularly to live here?

LADY BRITOMART Certainly not. The spare room is ready for him if he likes to stay for a day or two and see a little more of you; but there are limits.

SARAH Well, he cant eat us, I suppose. *I* dont mind.

LOMAX [*chuckling*] I wonder how the old man will take it.

LADY BRITOMART Much as the old woman will, no doubt, Charles.

LOMAX [*abashed*] I didnt mean—at least—

LADY BRITOMART You didnt think, Charles. You never do; and the result is, you never mean anything. And now please attend to me, children. Your father will be quite a stranger to us.

LOMAX I suppose he hasnt seen Sarah since she was a little kid.

LADY BRITOMART Not since she was a little kid, Charles, as you express it with that elegance of diction and refinement of thought that seem never to desert you. Accordingly—er—[*Impatiently.*] Now I have forgotten what I was going to say. That comes of your provoking me to be sarcastic, Charles. Adolphus: will you kindly tell me where I was.

CUSINS [*sweetly*] You were saying that as Mr Undershaft has not seen his children since they were babies, he will form his opinion of the way you have brought them up from their behavior tonight, and that therefore you wish us all to be particularly careful to conduct ourselves well, especially Charles.

LADY BRITOMART [*with emphatic approval*] Precisely.

LOMAX Look here, Dolly: Lady Brit didnt say that.

LADY BRITOMART [*vehemently*] I did, Charles. Adolphus's recollection is perfectly correct. It is most important that you should be good; and I do beg you for once not to pair off into opposite corners and giggle and whisper while I am speaking to your father.

BARBARA All right, mother. We'll do you credit. [*She comes off the table, and sits in her chair with ladylike elegance.*]

LADY BRITOMART Remember, Charles, that Sarah will want to feel proud of you instead of ashamed of you.

LOMAX Oh I say! theres nothing to be exactly proud of, dont you know.

LADY BRITOMART Well, try and look as if there was.

[*Morrison, pale and dismayed, breaks into the room in unconcealed disorder.*]

MORRISON Might I speak a word to you, my lady?

LADY BRITOMART Nonsense! Shew him up.

MORRISON Yes, my lady. [*He goes.*]

LOMAX Does Morrison know who it is?

LADY BRITOMART Of course. Morrison has always been with us.

LOMAX It must be a regular corker for him, dont you know.

LADY BRITOMART Is this a moment to get on my nerves, Charles, with your outrageous expressions?

LOMAX But this is something out of the ordinary, really—

MORRISON [*at the door*] The—er—Mr Undershaft. [*He retreats in confusion.*]

[*Andrew Undershaft comes in. All rise. Lady Britomart meets him in the middle of the room behind the settee.*

Andrew is, on the surface, a stoutish, easygoing elderly man, with kindly patient manners, and an engaging simplicity of character. But he has a watchful, deliberate, waiting, listening face, and formidable reserves of power, both bodily and mental, in his capacious chest and long head. His gentleness is partly that of a strong man who has learnt by experience that his natural grip hurts ordinary people unless he handles them very carefully, and partly the mellowness of age and success. He is also a little shy in his present very delicate situation.]

LADY BRITOMART Good evening, Andrew.

UNDERSHAFT How d'ye do, my dear.

LADY BRITOMART You look a good deal older.

UNDERSHAFT [*apologetically*] I am somewhat older. [*Taking her hand with a touch of courtship.*] Time has stood still with you.

LADY BRITOMART [*throwing away his hand*] Rubbish! This is your family.

UNDERSHAFT [*surprised*] Is it so large? I am sorry to say my memory is failing very badly in some things. [*He offers his hand with paternal kindness to Lomax.*]

LOMAX [*jerkily shaking his hand*] Ahdedoo.

UNDERSHAFT I can see you are my eldest. I am very glad to meet you again, my boy.

LOMAX [*remonstrating*] No, but look here dont you know—[*Overcome.*] Oh I say!

LADY BRITOMART [*recovering from momentary speechlessness*] Andrew: do you mean to say that you dont remember how many children you have?

UNDERSHAFT Well, I am afraid I—. They have grown so much—er. Am I making any ridiculous mistake? I may as well confess: I recollect only one son. But so many things have happened since, of course—er—

LADY BRITOMART [*decisively*] Andrew: you are talking nonsense. Of course you have only one son.

UNDERSHAFT Perhaps you will be good enough to introduce me, my dear.

LADY BRITOMART That is Charles Lomax, who is engaged to Sarah.

UNDERSHAFT My dear sir, I beg your pardon.

LOMAX Notatall. Delighted, I assure you.

LADY BRITOMART This is Stephen.

UNDERSHAFT [*bowing*] Happy to make your acquaintance, Mr Stephen. Then [*going to Cusins*] you must be my son. [*Taking Cusins' hands in his.*] How are you, my young friend? [*To Lady Britomart.*] He is very like you, my love.

CUSINS You flatter me, Mr Undershaft. My name is Cusins: engaged to Barbara. [*Very explicitly.*] That is Major Barbara Undershaft, of the Salvation Army. That is Sarah, your second daughter. This is Stephen Undershaft, your son.

UNDERSHAFT My dear Stephen, I beg your pardon.

STEPHEN Not at all.

UNDERSHAFT Mr Cusins: I am much indebted to you for explaining so precisely. [*Turning to Sarah.*] Barbara, my dear—

SARAH [*prompting him*] Sarah.

UNDERSHAFT Sarah, of course. [*They shake hands. He goes over to Barbara.*] Barbara—I am right this time, I hope?

BARBARA Quite right. [*They shake hands.*]

LADY BRITOMART [*resuming command*] Sit down, all of you. Sit down, Andrew. [*She comes forward and sits on the settee. Cusins also brings his chair forward on her left. Barbara and Stephen resume their seats. Lomax gives his chair to Sarah and goes for another.*]

UNDERSHAFT Thank you, my love.

LOMAX [*conversationally, as he brings a chair forward between the writing table and the settee, and offers it to Undershaft*] Takes you some time to find out exactly where you are, dont it?

UNDERSHAFT [*accepting the chair, but remaining standing*] That is not what embarrasses me, Mr Lomax. My difficulty is that if I play the part of a father, I shall produce the effect of an intrusive stranger; and if I play the part of a discreet stranger, I may appear a callous father.

LADY BRITOMART There is no need for you to play any part at all, Andrew. You had much better be sincere and natural.

UNDERSHAFT [*submissively*] Yes, my dear: I daresay that will be best. [*He sits down comfortably.*] Well, here I am. Now what can I do for you all?

LADY BRITOMART You need not do anything, Andrew. You are one of the family. You can sit with us and enjoy yourself.

[*A painfully conscious pause. Barbara makes a face at Lomax, whose too long suppressed mirth immediately explodes in agonized neighings.*]

LADY BRITOMART [*outraged*] Charles Lomax: if you can behave yourself, behave yourself. If not, leave the room.

LOMAX I'm awfully sorry, Lady Brit; but really you know, upon my soul! [*He sits on the settee between Lady Britomart and Undershaft, quite overcome.*]

BARBARA Why dont you laugh if you want to, Cholly? It's good for your inside.

LADY BRITOMART Barbara: you have had the education of a lady. Please let your father see that; and dont talk like a street girl.

UNDERSHAFT Never mind me, my dear. As you know, I am not a gentleman; and I was never educated.

LOMAX [*encouragingly*] Nobody'd know it, I assure you. You look all right, you know.

CUSINS Let me advise you to study Greek, Mr Undershaft. Greek scholars are privileged men. Few of them know Greek; and none of them know anything else; but their position is unchallengeable. Other languages are the qualifications of waiters and commercial travellers: Greek is to a man of position what the hallmark is to silver.

BARBARA Dolly: dont be insincere. Cholly: fetch your concertina and play something for us.

LOMAX [*jumps up eagerly, but checks himself to remark doubtfully to Undershaft*] Perhaps that sort of thing isnt in your line, eh?

UNDERSHAFT I am particularly fond of music.

LOMAX [*delighted*] Are you? Then I'll get it. [*He goes upstairs for the instrument.*]

UNDERSHAFT Do you play, Barbara?

BARBARA Only the tambourine. But Cholly's teaching me the concertina.

UNDERSHAFT Is Cholly also a member of the Salvation Army?

BARBARA No: he says it's bad form to be a dissenter.[3] But I dont despair of Cholly. I made him come yesterday to a meeting at the dock gates, and take the collection in his hat.

UNDERSHAFT [*looks whimsically at his wife*] !!

LADY BRITOMART It is not my doing, Andrew. Barbara is old enough to take her own way. She has no father to advise her.

BARBARA Oh yes she has. There are no orphans in the Salvation Army.

UNDERSHAFT Your father there has a great many children and plenty of experience, eh?

BARBARA [*looking at him with quick interest and nodding*] Just so. How did you come to understand that? [*Lomax is heard at the door trying the concertina.*]

LADY BRITOMART Come in, Charles. Play us something at once.

LOMAX Righto! [*He sits down in his former place, and preludes.*]

---

3. A member of a Protestant sect that refuses the authority of the Established Church.

UNDERSHAFT One moment, Mr Lomax. I am rather interested in the Salvation
   Army. Its motto might be my own: Blood and Fire.
LOMAX [shocked] But not your sort of blood and fire, you know.
UNDERSHAFT My sort of blood cleanses: my sort of fire purifies.
BARBARA So do ours. Come down tomorrow to my shelter—the West Ham shel-
   ter—and see what we're doing. We're going to march to a great meeting in the
   Assembly Hall at Mile End.[4] Come and see the shelter and then march with us: it
   will do you a lot of good. Can you play anything?
UNDERSHAFT In my youth I earned pennies, and even shillings occasionally, in
   the streets and in public house parlors by my natural talent for stepdancing. Later
   on, I became a member of the Undershaft orchestral society, and performed pass-
   ably on the tenor trombone.
LOMAX [scandalized—putting down the concertina] Oh I say!
BARBARA Many a sinner has played himself into heaven on the trombone, thanks
   to the Army.
LOMAX [to Barbara, still rather shocked] Yes; but what about the cannon business, dont
   you know? [To Undershaft.] Getting into heaven is not exactly in your line, is it?
LADY BRITOMART Charles!!!
LOMAX Well; but it stands to reason, dont it? The cannon business may be neces-
   sary and all that: we cant get on without cannons; but it isnt right, you know. On
   the other hand, there may be a certain amount of tosh about the Salvation
   Army—I belong to the Established Church myself—but still you cant deny that
   it's religion; and you cant go against religion, can you? At least unless youre downright immoral, dont you know.
UNDERSHAFT You hardly appreciate my position, Mr Lomax—
LOMAX [hastily] I'm not saying anything against you personally—
UNDERSHAFT Quite so, quite so. But consider for a moment. Here I am, a profiteer
   in mutilation and murder. I find myself in a specially amiable humor just now
   because, this morning, down at the foundry, we blew twenty-seven dummy soldiers into fragments with a gun which formerly destroyed only thirteen.
LOMAX [leniently] Well, the more destructive war becomes, the sooner it will be
   abolished, eh?
UNDERSHAFT Not at all. The more destructive war becomes the more fascinating
   we find it. No, Mr Lomax: I am obliged to you for making the usual excuse for my
   trade; but I am not ashamed of it. I am not one of those men who keep their
   morals and their business in watertight compartments. All the spare money my
   trade rivals spend on hospitals, cathedrals, and other receptacles for conscience
   money, I devote to experiments and researches in improved methods of destroying
   life and property. I have always done so; and I always shall. Therefore your Christmas card moralities of peace on earth and goodwill among men are of no use to
   me. Your Christianity, which enjoins you to resist not evil, and to turn the other
   cheek, would make me a bankrupt. My morality—my religion—must have a place
   for cannons and torpedoes in it.
STEPHEN [coldly—almost sullenly] You speak as if there were half a dozen moralities
   and religions to choose from, instead of one true morality and one true religion.
UNDERSHAFT For me there is only one true morality; but it might not fit you, as
   you do not manufacture aerial battleships. There is only one true morality for
   every man; but every man has not the same true morality.

---

4. A working-class area of East London.

LOMAX [overtaxed] Would you mind saying that again? I didnt quite follow it.

CUSINS It's quite simple. As Euripides says, one man's meat is another man's poison morally as well as physically.

UNDERSHAFT Precisely.

LOMAX Oh, that! Yes, yes, yes. True. True.

STEPHEN In other words, some men are honest and some are scoundrels.

BARBARA Bosh! There are no scoundrels.

UNDERSHAFT Indeed? Are there any good men?

BARBARA No. Not one. There are neither good men nor scoundrels: there are just children of one Father; and the sooner they stop calling one another names the better. You neednt talk to me: I know them. Ive had scores of them through my hands: scoundrels, criminals, infidels, philanthropists, missionaries, county councillors, all sorts. Theyre all just the same sort of sinner; and theres the same salvation ready for them all.

UNDERSHAFT May I ask have you ever saved a maker of cannons?

BARBARA No. Will you let me try?

UNDERSHAFT Well, I will make a bargain with you. If I go to see you tomorrow in your Salvation Shelter, will you come the day after to see me in my cannon works?

BARBARA Take care. It may end in your giving up the cannons for the sake of the Salvation Army.

UNDERSHAFT Are you sure it will not end in your giving up the Salvation Army for the sake of the cannons?

BARBARA I will take my chance of that.

UNDERSHAFT And I will take my chance of the other. [They shake hands on it.] Where is your shelter?

BARBARA In West Ham. At the sign of the cross. Ask anybody in Canning Town.[5] Where are your works?

UNDERSHAFT In Perivale St Andrews. At the sign of the sword. Ask anybody in Europe.

LOMAX Hadnt I better play something?

BARBARA Yes. Give us Onward, Christian Soldiers.

LOMAX Well, thats rather a strong order to begin with, dont you know. Suppose I sing Thourt passing hence, my brother. It's much the same tune.

BARBARA It's too melancholy. You get saved, Cholly; and youll pass hence, my brother, without making such a fuss about it.

LADY BRITOMART Really, Barbara, you go on as if religion were a pleasant subject. Do have some sense of propriety.

UNDERSHAFT I do not find it an unpleasant subject, my dear. It is the only one that capable people really care for.

LADY BRITOMART [looking at her watch] Well, if you are determined to have it, I insist on having it in a proper and respectable way. Charles: ring for prayers.

[General amazement. Stephen rises in dismay.]

LOMAX [rising] Oh I say!

UNDERSHAFT [rising] I am afraid I must be going.

LADY BRITOMART You cannot go now, Andrew: it would be most improper. Sit down. What will the servants think?

UNDERSHAFT My dear: I have conscientious scruples. May I suggest a compromise? If Barbara will conduct a little service in the drawing room, with Mr Lomax as organist, I will attend it willingly. I will even take part, if a trombone can be procured.

5. A district built to house laborers in the London docks.

LADY BRITOMART Dont mock, Andrew.

UNDERSHAFT [shocked—to Barbara] You dont think I am mocking, my love, I hope.

BARBARA No, of course not; and it wouldnt matter if you were: half the Army came to their first meeting for a lark. [Rising.] Come along. [She throws her arm round her father and sweeps him out, calling to the others from the threshold.] Come, Dolly. Come, Cholly.

    [Cusins rises.]

LADY BRITOMART I will not be disobeyed by everybody. Adolphus: sit down. [He does not.] Charles: you may go. You are not fit for prayers: you cannot keep your countenance.

LOMAX Oh I say! [He goes out.]

LADY BRITOMART [continuing] But you, Adolphus, can behave yourself if you choose to. I insist on your staying.

CUSINS My dear Lady Brit: there are things in the family prayer book that I couldnt bear to hear you say.

LADY BRITOMART What things, pray?

CUSINS Well, you would have to say before all the servants that we have done things we ought not to have done, and left undone things we ought to have done, and that there is no health in us. I cannot bear to hear you doing yourself such an injustice, and Barbara such an injustice. As for myself, I flatly deny it: I have done my best. I shouldnt dare to marry Barbara—I couldnt look you in the face—if it were true. So I must go to the drawing room.

LADY BRITOMART [offended] Well, go. [He starts for the door.] And remember this, Adolphus [he turns to listen]: I have a very strong suspicion that you went to the Salvation Army to worship Barbara and nothing else. And I quite appreciate the very clever way in which you systematically humbug me. I have found you out. Take care Barbara doesnt. Thats all.

CUSINS [with unruffled sweetness] Dont tell on me. [He steals out.]

LADY BRITOMART Sarah: if you want to go, go. Any thing's better than to sit there as if you wished you were a thousand miles away.

SARAH [languidly] Very well, mamma. [She goes.]

    [Lady Britomart, with a sudden flounce, gives way to a little gust of tears.]

STEPHEN [going to her] Mother: whats the matter?

LADY BRITOMART [swishing away her tears with her handkerchief] Nothing. Foolishness. You can go with him, too, if you like, and leave me with the servants.

STEPHEN Oh, you mustnt think that, mother. I—I dont like him.

LADY BRITOMART The others do. That is the injustice of a woman's lot. A woman has to bring up her children; and that means to restrain them, to deny them things they want, to set them tasks, to punish them when they do wrong, to do all the unpleasant things. And then the father, who has nothing to do but pet them and spoil them, comes in when all her work is done and steals their affection from her.

STEPHEN He has not stolen our affection from you. It is only curiosity.

LADY BRITOMART [violently] I wont be consoled, Stephen. There is nothing the matter with me. [She rises and goes towards the door.]

STEPHEN Where are you going, mother?

LADY BRITOMART To the drawing room, of course. [She goes out. Onward, Christian Soldiers, on the concertina, with tambourine accompaniment, is heard when the door opens.] Are you coming, Stephen?

STEPHEN No. Certainly not. [*She goes. He sits down on the settee, with compressed lips and an expression of strong dislike.*]

ACT 2

The yard of the West Ham shelter of the Salvation Army is a cold place on a January morning. The building itself, an old warehouse, is newly whitewashed. Its gabled end projects into the yard in the middle, with a door on the ground floor, and another in the loft above it without any balcony or ladder, but with a pulley rigged over it for hoisting sacks. Those who come from this central gable end into the yard have the gateway leading to the street on their left, with a stone horse-trough just beyond it, and, on the right, a penthouse shielding a table from the weather. There are forms at the table; and on them are seated a man and a woman, both much down on their luck, finishing a meal of bread (one thick slice each, with margarine and golden syrup) and diluted milk.

The man, a workman out of employment, is young, agile, a talker, a poser, sharp enough to be capable of anything in reason except honesty or altruistic considerations of any kind. The woman is a commonplace old bundle of poverty and hard-worn humanity. She looks sixty and probably is forty-five. If they were rich people, gloved and muffed and well wrapped up in furs and overcoats, they would be numbed and miserable; for it is a grindingly cold raw January day; and a glance at the background of grimy warehouses and leaden sky visible over the whitewashed walls of the yard would drive any idle rich person straight to the Mediterranean. But these two, being no more troubled with visions of the Mediterranean than of the moon, and being compelled to keep more of their clothes in the pawnshop, and less on their persons, in winter than in summer, are not depressed by the cold: rather are they stung into vivacity, to which their meal has just now given an almost jolly turn. The man takes a pull at his mug, and then gets up and moves about the yard with his hands deep in his pockets, occasionally breaking into a stepdance.

THE WOMAN Feel better arter your meal, sir?

THE MAN No. Call that a meal! Good enough for you, praps; but wot is it to me, an intelligent workin man.

THE WOMAN Workin man! Wot are you?

THE MAN Painter.

THE WOMAN [*sceptically*] Yus, I dessay.

THE MAN Yus, you dessay! I know. Every loafer that cant do nothink calls isself a painter. Well, I'm a real painter: grainer, finisher, thirty-eight bob[1] a week when I can get it.

THE WOMAN Then why dont you go and get it?

THE MAN I'll tell you why. Fust: I'm intelligent—fffff! it's rotten cold here [*he dances a step or two*]—yes: intelligent beyond the station o life into which it has pleased the capitalists to call me; and they dont like a man that sees through em. Second, an intelligent bein needs a doo share of appiness; so I drink somethink cruel when I get the chawnce. Third, I stand by my class and do as little as I can so's to leave arf the job for me fellow workers. Fourth, I'm fly[2] enough to know wots inside the law and wots outside it; and inside it I do as the capitalists do: pinch wot I can lay me ands on. In a proper state of society I am sober, industrious and honest: in Rome, so to speak, I do as the Romans do. Wots the consequence? When trade is bad—and it's rotten bad just now—and the employers az to sack arf their men, they generally start on me.

1. Shillings.   2. Clever.

THE WOMAN Whats your name?

THE MAN Price. Bronterre O'Brien Price. Usually called Snobby Price, for short.

THE WOMAN Snobby's a carpenter, ain't it? You said you was a painter.

PRICE Not that kind of snob, but the genteel sort. I'm too uppish, owing to my intelligence, and my father being a Chartist[3] and a reading, thinking man: a stationer, too. I'm none of your common hewers of wood and drawers of water; and dont you forget it. [He returns to his seat at the table, and takes up his mug.] Wots your name?

THE WOMAN Rummy Mitchens, sir.

PRICE [quaffing the remains of his milk to her] Your elth, Miss Mitchens.

RUMMY [correcting him] Missis Mitchens.

PRICE Wot! Oh Rummy, Rummy! Respectable married woman, Rummy, gittin rescued by the Salvation Army by pretendin to be a bad un. Same old game!

RUMMY What am I to do? I cant starve. Them Salvation lasses is dear good girls; but the better you are, the worse they likes to think you were before they rescued you. Why shouldnt they av a bit o credit, poor loves? theyre worn to rags by their work. And where would they get the money to rescue us if we was to let on we're no worse than other people? You know what ladies and gentlemen are.

PRICE Thievin swine! Wish I ad their job, Rummy, all the same. Wot does Rummy stand for? Pet name praps?

RUMMY Short for Romola.

PRICE For wot!?

RUMMY Romola. It was out of a new book.[4] Somebody me mother wanted me to grow up like.

PRICE We're companions in misfortune, Rummy. Both on us got names that nobody cawnt pronounce. Consequently I'm Snobby and youre Rummy because Bill and Sally wasnt good enough for our parents. Such is life!

RUMMY Who saved you, Mr Price? Was it Major Barbara?

PRICE No: I come here on my own. I'm going to be Bronterre O'Brien Price, the converted painter. I know wot they like. I'll tell em how I blasphemed and gambled and wopped my poor old mother—

RUMMY [shocked] Used you to beat your mother?

PRICE Not likely. She used to beat me. No matter: you come and listen to the converted painter, and youll hear how she was a pious woman that taught me me prayers at er knee, an how I used to come home drunk and drag her out o bed be er snow white airs, an lam into er with the poker.

RUMMY Thats whats so unfair to us women. Your confessions is just as big lies as ours: you dont tell what you really done no more than us; but you men can tell your lies right out at the meetins and be made much of for it; while the sort o confessions we az to make az to be wispered to one lady at a time. It aint right, spite of all their piety.

PRICE Right! Do you spose the Army'd be allowed if it went and did right? Not much. It combs our air and makes us good little blokes to be robbed and put upon. But I'll play the game as good as any of em. I'll see somebody struck by lightnin, or hear a voice sayin "Snobby Price: where will you spend eternity?" I'll av a time of it, I tell you.

---

3. A member of the Chartist workers' movement (1838–1848).

4. *Romola* (1863), a novel by George Eliot set in 15th- century Florence; Romola, the daughter of an old blind scholar, discovers her duty in self-sacrifice.

RUMMY You wont be let drink, though.

PRICE I'll take it out in gorspellin, then. I dont want to drink if I can get fun enough any other way.

[*Jenny Hill, a pale, overwrought, pretty Salvation lass of 18, comes in through the yard gate, leading Peter Shirley, a half hardened, half worn-out elderly man, weak with hunger.*]

JENNY [*supporting him*] Come! pluck up. I'll get you something to eat. Youll be all right then.

PRICE [*rising and hurrying officiously to take the old man off Jenny's hands*] Poor old man! Cheer up, brother: youll find rest and peace and appiness ere. Hurry up with the food, miss: e's fair done. [*Jenny hurries into the shelter.*] Ere, buck up, daddy! she's fetchin y'a thick slice o breadn treacle, an a mug o skyblue. [*He seats him at the corner of the table.*]

RUMMY [*gaily*] Keep up your old art! Never say die!

SHIRLEY I'm not an old man. I'm only 46. I'm as good as ever I was. The grey patch come in my hair before I was thirty. All it wants is three pennorth o hair dye: am I to be turned on the streets to starve for it? Holy God! I've worked ten to twelve hours a day since I was thirteen, and paid my way all through; and now am I to be thrown into the gutter and my job given to a young man that can do it no better than me because Ive black hair that goes white at the first change?

PRICE [*cheerfully*] No good jawrin about it. Youre ony a jumped-up, jerked-off, orspittle-turned-out incurable of an ole workin man: who cares about you? Eh? Make the thievin swine give you a meal: theyve stole many a one from you. Get a bit o your own back. [*Jenny returns with the usual meal.*] There you are, brother. Awsk a blessin an tuck that into you.

SHIRLEY [*looking at it ravenously but not touching it, and crying like a child*] I never took anything before.

JENNY [*petting him*] Come, come! the Lord sends it to you: he wasnt above taking bread from his friends; and why should you be? Besides, when we find you a job you can pay us for it if you like.

SHIRLEY [*eagerly*] Yes, yes: thats true. I can pay you back: it's only a loan. [*Shivering.*] Oh Lord! oh Lord! [*He turns to the table and attacks the meal ravenously.*]

JENNY Well, Rummy, are you more comfortable now?

RUMMY God bless you, lovey! youve fed my body and saved my soul, havnt you? [*Jenny, touched, kisses her.*] Sit down and rest a bit: you must be ready to drop.

JENNY Ive been going hard since morning. But theres more work than we can do. I mustnt stop.

RUMMY Try a prayer for just two minutes. Youll work all the better after.

JENNY [*her eyes lighting up*] Oh isnt it wonderful how a few minutes prayer revives you! I was quite lightheaded at twelve o'clock, I was so tired; but Major Barbara just sent me to pray for five minutes; and I was able to go on as if I had only just begun. [*To Price.*] Did you have a piece of bread?

PRICE [*with unction*] Yes, miss; but Ive got the piece that I value more; and thats the peace that passeth hall hannerstennin.

RUMMY [*fervently*] Glory Hallelujah!

[*Bill Walker, a rough customer of about 25, appears at the yard gate and looks malevolently at Jenny.*]

JENNY That makes me so happy. When you say that, I feel wicked for loitering here. I must get to work again.

[*She is hurrying to the shelter, when the new-comer moves quickly up to the door and intercepts her. His manner is so threatening that she retreats as he comes at her truculently, driving her down the yard.*]

BILL Aw knaow you. Youre the one that took awy maw girl. Youre the one that set er agen me. Well, I'm gowin to ev er aht. Not that Aw care a carse for er or you: see? Bat Aw'll let er knaow; and Aw'll let you knaow. Aw'm gowing to give her a doin thatll teach er to cat awy from me. Nah in wiv you and tell er to cam aht afore Aw cam in and kick er aht. Tell er Bill Walker wants er. She'll knaow wot thet means; and if she keeps me witin itll be worse. You stop to jawr beck at me, and Aw'll stawt on you: d'ye eah? Theres your wy. In you gow. [*He takes her by the arm and slings her towards the door of the shelter. She falls on her hand and knee. Rummy helps her up again.*]

PRICE [*rising, and venturing irresolutely towards Bill*] Easy there, mate. She aint doin you no arm.

BILL Oo are you callin mite? [*Standing over him threateningly.*] Youre gowin to stend ap for er, aw yer? Put ap your ends.

RUMMY [*running indignantly to him to scold him*] Oh, you great brute—[*He instantly swings his left hand back against her face. She screams and reels back to the trough, where she sits down, covering her bruised face with her hands and rocking herself and moaning with pain.*]

JENNY [*going to her*] Oh, God forgive you! How could you strike an old woman like that?

BILL [*seizing her by the hair so violently that she also screams, and tearing her away from the old woman*] You Gawd forgimme again an Aw'll Gawd forgive you one on the jawr thetll stop you pryin for a week. [*Holding her and turning fiercely on Price.*] Ev you ennything to sy agen it?

PRICE [*intimidated*] No, matey: she aint anything to do with me.

BILL Good job for you! Aw'd pat two meals into you and fawt you with one finger arter, you stawved cur. [*To Jenny.*] Nah are you gowin to fetch aht Mog Ebbijem; or em Aw to knock your fice off you and fetch her meself?

JENNY [*writhing in his grasp*] Oh please someone go in and tell Major Barbara—[*she screams again as he wrenches her head down; and Price and Rummy flee into the shelter.*]

BILL You want to gow in and tell your Mijor of me, do you?

JENNY Oh please dont drag my hair. Let me go.

BILL Do you or downt you? [*She stifles a scream.*] Yus or nao?

JENNY God give me strength—

BILL [*striking her with his fist in the face*] Gow an shaow her thet, and tell her if she wants one lawk it to cam and interfere with me. [*Jenny, crying with pain, goes into the shed. He goes to the form and addresses the old man.*] Eah: finish your mess; an git aht o maw wy.

SHIRLEY [*springing up and facing him fiercely, with the mug in his hand*] You take a liberty with me, and I'll smash you over the face with the mug and cut your eye out. Aint you satisfied—young whelps like you—with takin the bread out o the mouths of your elders that have brought you up and slaved for you, but you must come shovin and cheekin and bullyin in here, where the bread o charity is sickenin in our stummicks?

BILL [*contemptuously, but backing a little*] Wot good are you, you aold palsy mag? Wot good are you?

SHIRLEY As good as you and better. I'll do a day's work agen you or any fat young soaker of your age. Go and take my job at Horrockses, where I worked for ten year. They want young men there: they cant afford to keep men over forty-five. Theyre very sorry—give you a character and happy to help you to get anything suited to your years—sure a steady man wont be long out of a job. Well, let em try you. Theyll find the differ. What do you know? Not as much as how to beeyave yourself—layin your dirty fist across the mouth of a respectable woman!

BILL Downt provowk me to ly it acrost yours: d'ye eah?

SHIRLEY [with blighting contempt] Yes: you like an old man to hit, dont you, when youve finished with the women. I aint seen you hit a young one yet.

BILL [stung] You loy, you aold soupkitchener, you. There was a yang menn eah. Did Aw offer to itt him or did Aw not?

SHIRLEY Was he starvin or was he not? Was he a man or only a crosseyed thief an a loafer? Would you hit my son-in-law's brother?

BILL Oo's ee?

SHIRLEY Todger Fairmile o Balls Pond. Him that won £20 off the Japanese wrastler at the music hall by standin out 17 minutes 4 seconds agen him.

BILL [sullenly] Aw'm nao music awl wrastler. Ken he box?

SHIRLEY Yes: an you cant.

BILL Wot! Aw cawnt, cawnt Aw? Wots thet you sy [threatening him]?

SHIRLEY [not budging an inch] Will you box Todger Fairmile if I put him on to you? Say the word.

BILL [subsiding with a slouch] Aw'll stend ap to enny menn alawv, if he was ten Todger Fairmawls. But Aw dont set ap to be a perfeshnal.

SHIRLEY [looking down on him with unfathomable disdain] You box! Slap an old woman with the back o your hand! You hadnt even the sense to hit her where a magistrate couldnt see the mark of it, you silly young lump of conceit and ignorance. Hit a girl in the jaw and ony make her cry! If Todger Fairmile'd done it, she wouldnt a got up inside o ten minutes, no more than you would if he got on to you. Yah! I'd set about you myself if I had a week's feedin in me instead o two months' starvation. [He turns his back on him and sits down moodily at the table.]

BILL [following him and stooping over him to drive the taunt in] You loy! youve the bread and treacle in you that you cam eah to beg.

SHIRLEY [bursting into tears] Oh God! it's true: I'm only an old pauper on the scrap heap. [Furiously.] But youll come to it yourself; and then youll know. Youll come to it sooner than a teetotaller like me, fillin yourself with gin at this hour o the mornin!

BILL Aw'm nao gin drinker, you oald lawr; bat wen Aw want to give my girl a bloomin good awdin Aw lawk to ev a bit o devil in me: see? An eah Aw emm, talkin to a rotten aold blawter like you sted o givin her wot for. [Working himself into a rage.] Aw'm gowin in there to fetch her aht. [He makes vengefully for the shelter door.]

SHIRLEY Youre going to the station on a stretcher, more likely; and theyll take the gin and the devil out of you there when they get you inside. You mind what youre about: the major here is the Earl o Stevenage's granddaughter.

BILL [checked] Garn!

SHIRLEY Youll see.

BILL [his resolution oozing] Well, Aw aint dan nathin to er.

SHIRLEY Spose she said you did! who'd believe you?

BILL [*very uneasy, skulking back to the corner of the penthouse*] Gawd! theres no jastice in this cantry. To think wot them people can do! Aw'm as good as er.

SHIRLEY Tell her so. It's just what a fool like you would do.

[*Barbara, brisk and businesslike, comes from the shelter with a note book, and addresses herself to Shirley. Bill, cowed, sits down in the corner on a form, and turns his back on them.*]

BARBARA Good morning.

SHIRLEY [*standing up and taking off his hat*] Good morning, miss.

BARBARA Sit down: make yourself at home. [*He hesitates; but she puts a friendly hand on his shoulder and makes him obey.*] Now then! since youve made friends with us, we want to know all about you. Names and addresses and trades.

SHIRLEY Peter Shirley. Fitter. Chucked out two months ago because I was too old.

BARBARA [*not at all surprised*] Youd pass still. Why didnt you dye your hair?

SHIRLEY I did. Me age come out at a coroner's inquest on me daughter.[5]

BARBARA Steady?

SHIRLEY Teetotaller. Never out of a job before. Good worker. And sent to the knackers like an old horse!

BARBARA No matter: if you did your part God will do his.

SHIRLEY [*suddenly stubborn*] My religion's no concern of anybody but myself.

BARBARA [*guessing*] I know. Secularist?

SHIRLEY [*hotly*] Did I offer to deny it?

BARBARA Why should you? My own father's a Secularist, I think. Our Father— yours and mine—fulfils himself in many ways; and I daresay he knew what he was about when he made a Secularist of you. So buck up, Peter! we can always find a job for a steady man like you. [*Shirley, disarmed and a little bewildered, touches his hat. She turns from him to Bill.*] Whats your name?

BILL [*insolently*] Wots thet to you?

BARBARA [*calmly making a note*] Afraid to give his name. Any trade?

BILL Oo's afride to give is nime? [*Doggedly, with a sense of heroically defying the House of Lords in the person of Lord Stevenage.*] If you want to bring a chawge agen me, bring it. [*She waits, unruffled.*] Moy nime's Bill Walker.

BARBARA [*as if the name were familiar: trying to remember how*] Bill Walker? [*Recollecting*] Oh, I know: youre the man that Jenny Hill was praying for inside just now. [*She enters his name in her note book.*]

BILL Oo's Jenny Ill? And wot call as she to pry for me?

BARBARA I dont know. Perhaps it was you that cut her lip.

BILL [*defiantly*] Yus, it was me that cat her lip. Aw aint afride o you.

BARBARA How could you be, since youre not afraid of God? Youre a brave man, Mr Walker. It takes some pluck to do our work here; but none of us dare lift our hand against a girl like that, for fear of her father in heaven.

BILL [*sullenly*] I want nan o your kentin jawr. I spowse you think Aw cam eah to beg from you, like this demmiged lot eah. Not me. Aw downt want your bread and scripe and ketlep. Aw dont blieve in your Gawd, no more than you do yourself.

BARBARA [*sunnily apologetic and ladylike, as on a new footing with him*] Oh, I beg your pardon for putting your name down, Mr Walker. I didnt understand. I'll strike it out.

---

5. A coroner holds inquests on violent or accidental deaths.

BILL [*taking this as a slight, and deeply wounded by it*] Eah! you let maw nime alown. Aint it good enaff to be in your book?

BARBARA [*considering*] Well, you see, theres no use putting down your name unless I can do something for you, is there? Whats your trade?

BILL [*still smarting*] Thets nao concern o yours.

BARBARA Just so. [*Very businesslike.*] I'll put you down as [*writing*] the man who—struck—poor little Jenny Hill—in the mouth.

BILL [*rising threateningly*] See eah. Awve ed enaff o this.

BARBARA [*quite sunny and fearless*] What did you come to us for?

BILL Aw cam for maw gel, see? Aw cam to tike her aht o this and to brike er jawr for er.

BARBARA [*complacently*] You see I was right about your trade. [*Bill, on the point of retorting furiously, finds himself, to his great shame and terror, in danger of crying instead. He sits down again suddenly.*] Whats her name?

BILL [*dogged*] Er nime's Mog Ebbijem: thets wot her nime is.

BARBARA Mog Habbijam! Oh, she's gone to Canning Town, to our barracks there.

BILL [*fortified by his resentment of Mog's perfidy*] Is she? [*Vindictively.*] Then Aw'm gowin to Kennintahn arter her. [*He crosses to the gate; hesitates; finally comes back at Barbara.*] Are you loyin to me to git shat o me?

BARBARA I dont want to get shut of you. I want to keep you here and save your soul. Youd better stay: youre going to have a bad time today, Bill.

BILL Oo's gowin to give it to me? You, preps?

BARBARA Someone you dont believe in. But youll be glad afterwards.

BILL [*slinking off*] Aw'll gow to Kennintahn to be aht o reach o your tangue. [*Suddenly turning on her with intense malice.*] And if Aw downt fawnd Mog there, Aw'll cam beck and do two years for you, selp me Gawd if Aw downt!

BARBARA [*a shade kindlier, if possible*] It's no use, Bill. She's got another bloke.

BILL Wot!

BARBARA One of her own converts. He fell in love with her when he saw her with her soul saved, and her face clean, and her hair washed.

BILL [*surprised*] Wottud she wash it for, the carroty slat? It's red.

BARBARA It's quite lovely now, because she wears a new look in her eyes with it. It's a pity youre too late. The new bloke has put your nose out of joint, Bill.

BILL Aw'll put his nowse aht o joint for him. Not that Aw care a carse for er, mawnd thet. But Aw'll teach her to drop me as if Aw was dirt. And Aw'll teach him to meddle with maw judy. Wots iz bleedin nime?

BARBARA Sergeant Todger Fairmile.

SHIRLEY [*rising with grim joy*] I'll go with him, miss. I want to see them two meet. I'll take him to the infirmary when it's over.

BILL [*to Shirley, with undissembled misgiving*] Is thet im you was speakin on?

SHIRLEY Thats him.

BILL Im that wrastled in the music awl?

SHIRLEY The competitions at the National Sportin Club was worth nigh a hundred a year to him. He's gev em up now for religion; so he's a bit fresh for want of the exercise he was accustomed to. He'll be glad to see you. Come along.

BILL Wots is wight?

SHIRLEY Thirteen four.[6] [*Bill's last hope expires.*]

---

6. Almost 200 pounds.

BARBARA Go and talk to him, Bill. He'll convert you.

SHIRLEY He'll convert your head into a mashed potato.

BILL [sullenly] Aw aint afride of im. Aw aint afride of ennybody. Bat e can lick me. She's dan me. [He sits down moodily on the edge of the horse trough.]

SHIRLEY You aint going. I thought not. [He resumes his seat.]

BARBARA [calling] Jenny!

JENNY [appearing at the shelter door with a plaster on the corner of her mouth] Yes, Major.

BARBARA Send Rummy Mitchens out to clear away here.

JENNY I think she's afraid.

BARBARA [her resemblance to her mother flashing out for a moment] Nonsense! she must do as she's told.

JENNY [calling into the shelter] Rummy: the Major says you must come.
    [Jenny comes to Barbara, purposely keeping on the side next Bill, lest he should suppose that she shrank from him or bore malice.]

BARBARA Poor little Jenny! Are you tired? [Looking at the wounded cheek.] Does it hurt?

JENNY No: it's all right now. It was nothing.

BARBARA [critically] It was as hard as he could hit, I expect. Poor Bill! You dont feel angry with him, do you?

JENNY Oh no, no, no: indeed I dont, Major, bless his poor heart! [Barbara kisses her; and she runs away merrily into the shelter. Bill writhes with an agonizing return of his new and alarming symptoms, but says nothing. Rummy Mitchens comes from the shelter.]

BARBARA [going to meet Rummy] Now Rummy, bustle. Take in those mugs and plates to be washed; and throw the crumbs about for the birds.
    [Rummy takes the three plates and mugs; but Shirley takes back his mug from her, as there is still some milk left in it.]

RUMMY There aint any crumbs. This aint a time to waste good bread on birds.

PRICE [appearing at the shelter door] Gentleman come to see the shelter, Major. Says he's your father.

BARBARA All right. Coming. [Snobby goes back into the shelter, followed by Barbara.]

RUMMY [stealing across to Bill and addressing him in a subdued voice, but with intense conviction] I'd av the lor of you, you flat eared pignosed potwalloper, if she'd let me. Youre no gentleman, to hit a lady in the face. [Bill, with greater things moving in him, takes no notice.]

SHIRLEY [following her] Here! in with you and dont get yourself into more trouble by talking.

RUMMY [with hauteur] I aint ad the pleasure o being hintroduced to you, as I can remember. [She goes into the shelter with the plates.]

SHIRLEY Thats the—

BILL [savagely] Downt you talk to me, d'ye eah? You lea me alown, or Aw'll do you a mischief. Aw'm not dirt under your feet, ennywy.

SHIRLEY [calmly] Dont you be afeerd. You aint such prime company that you need expect to be sought after. [He is about to go into the shelter when Barbara comes out, with Undershaft on her right.]

BARBARA Oh, there you are, Mr Shirley! [Between them.] This is my father: I told you he was a Secularist, didn't I? Perhaps youll be able to comfort one another.

UNDERSHAFT [startled] A Secularist! Not the least in the world: on the contrary, a confirmed mystic.

BARBARA Sorry, I'm sure. By the way, papa, what is your religion? in case I have to introduce you again.

UNDERSHAFT My religion? Well, my dear, I am a Millionaire. That is my religion.

BARBARA Then I'm afraid you and Mr Shirley wont be able to comfort one another after all. Youre not a Millionaire, are you, Peter?

SHIRLEY No; and proud of it.

UNDERSHAFT [gravely] Poverty, my friend, is not a thing to be proud of.

SHIRLEY [angrily] Who made your millions for you? Me and my like. Whats kep us poor? Keepin you rich. I wouldnt have your conscience, not for all your income.

UNDERSHAFT I wouldnt have your income, not for all your conscience, Mr Shirley. [He goes to the penthouse and sits down on a form.]

BARBARA [stopping Shirley adroitly as he is about to retort] You wouldnt think he was my father, would you, Peter? Will you go into the shelter and lend the lasses a hand for a while: we're worked off our feet.

SHIRLEY [bitterly] Yes: I'm in their debt for a meal, aint I?

BARBARA Oh, not because youre in their debt, but for love of them, Peter, for love of them. [He cannot understand, and is rather scandalized.] There! dont stare at me. In with you; and give that conscience of yours a holiday. [Bustling him into the shelter.]

SHIRLEY [as he goes in] Ah! it's a pity you never was trained to use your reason, miss. Youd have been a very taking lecturer on Secularism.

[Barbara turns to her father.]

UNDERSHAFT Never mind me, my dear. Go about your work; and let me watch it for a while.

BARBARA All right.

UNDERSHAFT For instance, whats the matter with that outpatient over there?

BARBARA [looking at Bill, whose attitude has never changed, and whose expression of brooding wrath has deepened] Oh, we shall cure him in no time. Just watch. [She goes over to Bill and waits. He glances up at her and casts his eyes down again, uneasy, but grimmer than ever.] It would be nice to just stamp on Mog Habbijam's face, wouldnt it, Bill?

BILL [starting up from the trough in consternation] It's a loy: Aw never said so. [She shakes her head.] Oo taold you wot was in moy mawnd?

BARBARA Only your new friend.

BILL Wot new friend?

BARBARA The devil, Bill. When he gets round people they get miserable, just like you.

BILL [with a heartbreaking attempt at devil-may-care cheerfulness] Aw aint miserable. [He sits down again, and stretches his legs in an attempt to seem indifferent.]

BARBARA Well, if youre happy, why dont you look happy, as we do?

BILL [his legs curling back in spite of him] Aw'm eppy enaff, Aw tell you. Woy cawnt you lea me alown? Wot ev I dan to you? Aw aint smashed your fice, ev Aw?

BARBARA [softly: wooing his soul] It's not me thats getting at you, Bill.

BILL Oo else is it?

BARBARA Somebody that doesnt intend you to smash women's faces, I suppose. Somebody or something that wants to make a man of you.

BILL [blustering] Mike a menn o me! Aint Aw a menn? eh? Oo sez Aw'm not a menn?

BARBARA Theres a man in you somewhere, I suppose. But why did he let you hit poor little Jenny Hill? That wasnt very manly of him, was it?

BILL [tormented] Ev dan wiv it, Aw tell you. Chack it. Aw'm sick o your Jenny Ill and er silly little fice.

BARBARA Then why do you keep thinking about it? Why does it keep coming up against you in your mind? Youre not getting converted, are you?

BILL [*with conviction*] Not ME. Not lawkly.

BARBARA Thats right, Bill. Hold out against it. Put out your strength. Dont lets get you cheap. Todger Fairmile said he wrestled for three nights against his salvation harder than he ever wrestled with the Jap at the music hall. He gave in to the Jap when his arm was going to break. But he didnt give in to his salvation until his heart was going to break. Perhaps youll escape that. You havnt any heart, have you?

BILL Wot d'ye mean? Woy aint Aw got a awt the sime as ennybody else?

BARBARA A man with a heart wouldnt have bashed poor little Jenny's face, would he?

BILL [*almost crying*] Ow, will you lea me alown? Ev Aw ever offered to meddle with you, that you cam neggin and provowkin me lawk this? [*He writhes convulsively from his eyes to his toes.*]

BARBARA [*with a steady soothing hand on his arm and a gentle voice that never lets him go*] It's your soul thats hurting you, Bill, and not me. Weve been through it all ourselves. Come with us, Bill. [*He looks wildly round.*] To brave manhood on earth and eternal glory in heaven. [*He is on the point of breaking down.*] Come. [*A drum is heard in the shelter; and Bill, with a gasp, escapes from the spell as Barbara turns quickly. Adolphus enters from the shelter with a big drum.*] Oh! there you are, Dolly. Let me introduce a new friend of mine, Mr Bill Walker. This is my bloke, Bill: Mr Cusins. [*Cusins salutes with his drumstick.*]

BILL Gowin to merry im?

BARBARA Yes.

BILL [*fervently*] Gawd elp im! Gaw-aw-aw-awd elp im!

BARBARA Why? Do you think he wont be happy with me?

BILL Awve aony ed to stend it for a mawnin: e'll ev to stend it for a lawftawm.

CUSINS That is a frightful reflection, Mr Walker. But I cant tear myself away from her.

BILL Well, Aw ken. [*To Barbara.*] Eah! do you knaow where Aw'm gowin to, and wot Aw'm gowin to do?

BARBARA Yes: youre going to heaven; and youre coming back here before the week's out to tell me so.

BILL You loy. Aw'm gowin to Kennintahn, to spitin Todger Fairmawl's eye. Aw beshed Jenny Ill's fice; an nar Aw'll git me aown fice beshed and cam beck and shaow it to er. Ee'll itt me ardern Aw itt her. Thatll mike us square. [*To Adolphus.*] Is thet fair or is it not? Youre a genlmn: you oughter knaow.

BARBARA Two black eyes wont make one white one, Bill.

BILL Aw didnt awst you. Cawnt you never keep your mahth shat? Oy awst the genlmn.

CUSINS [*reflectively*] Yes: I think youre right, Mr Walker. Yes: I should do it. It's curious: it's exactly what an ancient Greek would have done.

BARBARA But what good will it do?

CUSINS Well, it will give Mr Fairmile some exercise; and it will satisfy Mr Walker's soul.

BILL Rot! there aint nao such a thing as a saoul. Ah kin you tell wevver Awve a saoul or not? You never seen it.

BARBARA Ive seen it hurting you when you went against it.

BILL [*with compressed aggravation*] If you was maw gel and took the word aht o me mahth lawk thet, Aw'd give you sathink youd feel urtin, Aw would. [*To Adolphus.*] You tike maw tip, mite. Stop er jawr; or youll doy afoah your tawm. [*With intense expression.*] Wore aht: thets wot youll be: wore aht. [*He goes away through the gate.*]

CUSINS [*looking after him*] I wonder!

BARBARA Dolly! [*Indignant, in her mother's manner.*]

CUSINS Yes, my dear, it's very wearing to be in love with you. If it lasts, I quite think I shall die young.

BARBARA Should you mind?

CUSINS Not at all. [*He is suddenly softened, and kisses her over the drum, evidently not for the first time, as people cannot kiss over a big drum without practice. Undershaft coughs.*]

BARBARA It's all right, papa, weve not forgotten you. Dolly: explain the place to papa: I havnt time. [*She goes busily into the shelter.*]

[*Undershaft and Adolphus now have the yard to themselves. Undershaft, seated on a form, and still keenly attentive, looks hard at Adolphus. Adolphus looks hard at him.*]

UNDERSHAFT I fancy you guess something of what is in my mind, Mr Cusins. [*Cusins flourishes his drumsticks as if in the act of beating a lively rataplan,[7] but makes no sound.*] Exactly so. But suppose Barbara finds you out!

CUSINS You know, I do not admit that I am imposing on Barbara. I am quite genuinely interested in the views of the Salvation Army. The fact is, I am a sort of collector of religions; and the curious thing is that I find I can believe them all. By the way, have you any religion?

UNDERSHAFT Yes.

CUSINS Anything out of the common?

UNDERSHAFT Only that there are two things necessary to Salvation.

CUSINS [*disappointed, but polite*] Ah, the Church Catechism. Charles Lomax also belongs to the Established Church.

UNDERSHAFT The two things are—

CUSINS Baptism and—

UNDERSHAFT No. Money and gunpowder.

CUSINS [*surprised, but interested*] That is the general opinion of our governing classes. The novelty is in hearing any man confess it.

UNDERSHAFT Just so.

CUSINS Excuse me: is there any place in your religion for honor, justice, truth, love, mercy and so forth?

UNDERSHAFT Yes: they are the graces and luxuries of a rich, strong, and safe life.

CUSINS Suppose one is forced to choose between them and money or gunpowder?

UNDERSHAFT Choose money and gunpowder; for without enough of both you cannot afford the others.

CUSINS That is your religion?

UNDERSHAFT Yes.

[*The cadence of this reply makes a full close in the conversation, Cusins twists his face dubiously and contemplates Undershaft. Undershaft contemplates him.*]

CUSINS Barbara wont stand that. You will have to choose between your religion and Barbara.

UNDERSHAFT So will you, my friend. She will find out that that drum of yours is hollow.

CUSINS Father Undershaft: you are mistaken: I am a sincere Salvationist. You do not understand the Salvation Army. It is the army of joy, of love, of courage: it has banished the fear and remorse and despair of the old hell-ridden evangelical sects: it marches to fight the devil with trumpet and drum, with music and dancing, with banner and palm, as becomes a sally from heaven by its happy garrison. It picks the waster out of the public house and makes a man of him: it finds a worm wriggling in a back kitchen, and lo! a woman! Men and women of rank too, sons and daughters

7. Drumming sound.

of the Highest. It takes the poor professor of Greek, the most artificial and self-suppressed of human creatures, from his meal of roots, and lets loose the rhapsodist in him; reveals the true worship of Dionysos to him; sends him down the public street drumming dithyrambs [*He plays a thundering flourish on the drum.*]

UNDERSHAFT You will alarm the shelter.

CUSINS Oh, they are accustomed to these sudden ecstasies. However, if the drum worries you—[*He pockets the drumsticks; unhooks the drum; and stands it on the ground opposite the gateway.*]

UNDERSHAFT Thank you.

CUSINS You remember what Euripides says about your money and gunpowder?

UNDERSHAFT No.

CUSINS [*declaiming*]

> One and another
> In money and guns may outpass his brother;[8]
> And men in their millions float and flow
> And seethe with a million hopes as leaven;
> And they win their will; or they miss their will;
> And their hopes are dead or are pined for still;
> But whoe'er can know
> As the long days go
> That to live is happy, has found his heaven.

My translation: what do you think of it?

UNDERSHAFT I think, my friend, that if you wish to know, as the long days go, that to live is happy, you must first acquire money enough for a decent life, and power enough to be your own master.

CUSINS You are damnably discouraging. [*He resumes his declamation.*]

> Is it so hard a thing to see
> That the spirit of God—whate'er it be—
> The law that abides and changes not, ages long,
> The Eternal and Nature-born: these things be strong?
> What else is Wisdom? What of Man's endeavor,
> Or God's high grace so lovely and so great?
> To stand from fear set free? to breathe and wait?
> To hold a hand uplifted over Fate?
> And shall not Barbara be loved for ever?[9]

UNDERSHAFT Euripides mentions Barbara, does he?

CUSINS It is a fair translation. The word means Loveliness.

UNDERSHAFT May I ask—as Barbara's father—how much a year she is to be loved for ever on?

CUSINS As for Barbara's father, that is more your affair than mine. I can feed her by teaching Greek: that is about all.

---

8. Cusins is quoting from the English scholar Gilbert Murray's translation of *The Bacchae* (1906) by Euripides; in Murray's version, this line reads "In gold and power may outpass his brother."

9. The final lines in Murray's translation read "To hold a hand uplifted over Hate; / And shall not loveliness be loved for ever?"

UNDERSHAFT Do you consider it a good match for her?

CUSINS [*with polite obstinacy*] Mr Undershaft: I am in many ways a weak, timid, ineffectual person; and my health is far from satisfactory. But whenever I feel that I must have anything, I get it, sooner or later. I feel that way about Barbara. I dont like marriage: I feel intensely afraid of it; and I dont know what I shall do with Barbara or what she will do with me. But I feel that I and nobody else must marry her. Please regard that as settled.—Not that I wish to be arbitrary; but why should I waste your time in discussing what is inevitable?

UNDERSHAFT You mean that you will stick at nothing: not even the conversion of the Salvation Army to the worship of Dionysos.

CUSINS The business of the Salvation Army is to save, not to wrangle about the name of the pathfinder. Dionysos or another: what does it matter?

UNDERSHAFT [*rising and approaching him*] Professor Cusins: you are a young man after my own heart.

CUSINS Mr Undershaft: you are, as far as I am able to gather, a most infernal old rascal; but you appeal very strongly to my sense of ironic humor.

[*Undershaft mutely offers his hand. They shake.*]

UNDERSHAFT [*suddenly concentrating himself*] And now to business.

CUSINS Pardon me. We are discussing religion. Why go back to such an uninteresting and unimportant subject as business?

UNDERSHAFT Religion is our business at present, because it is through religion alone that we can win Barbara.

CUSINS Have you, too, fallen in love with Barbara?

UNDERSHAFT Yes, with a father's love.

CUSINS A father's love for a grown-up daughter is the most dangerous of all infatuations. I apologize for mentioning my own pale, coy, mistrustful fancy in the same breath with it.

UNDERSHAFT Keep to the point. We have to win her; and we are neither of us Methodists.

CUSINS That doesnt matter. The power Barbara wields here—the power that wields Barbara herself—is not Calvinism, not Presbyterianism, not Methodism—

UNDERSHAFT Not Greek Paganism either, eh?

CUSINS I admit that. Barbara is quite original in her religion.

UNDERSHAFT [*triumphantly*] Aha! Barbara Undershaft would be. Her inspiration comes from within herself.

CUSINS How do you suppose it got there?

UNDERSHAFT [*in towering excitement*] It is the Undershaft inheritance. I shall hand on my torch to my daughter. She shall make my converts and preach my gospel—

CUSINS What! Money and gunpowder!

UNDERSHAFT Yes, money and gunpowder. Freedom and power. Command of life and command of death.

CUSINS [*urbanely: trying to bring him down to earth*] This is extremely interesting, Mr Undershaft. Of course you know that you are mad.

UNDERSHAFT [*with redoubled force*] And you?

CUSINS Oh, mad as a hatter. You are welcome to my secret since I have discovered yours. But I am astonished. Can a madman make cannons?

UNDERSHAFT Would anyone else than a madman make them? And now [*with surging energy*] question for question. Can a sane man translate Euripides?

CUSINS No.

UNDERSHAFT [*seizing him by the shoulder*] Can a sane woman make a man of a waster or a woman of a worm?

CUSINS [*reeling before the storm*] Father Colossus—Mammoth Millionaire—

UNDERSHAFT [*pressing him*] Are there two mad people or three in this Salvation shelter today?

CUSINS You mean Barbara is as mad as we are?

UNDERSHAFT [*pushing him lightly off and resuming his equanimity suddenly and completely*] Pooh, Professor! let us call things by their proper names. I am a millionaire; you are a poet; Barbara is a savior of souls. What have we three to do with the common mob of slaves and idolators? [*He sits down again with a shrug of contempt for the mob.*]

CUSINS Take care! Barbara is in love with the common people. So am I. Have you never felt the romance of that love?

UNDERSHAFT [*cold and sardonic*] Have you ever been in love with Poverty, like St Francis? Have you ever been in love with Dirt, like St Simeon![1] Have you ever been in love with disease and suffering, like our nurses and philanthropists? Such passions are not virtues, but the most unnatural of all the vices. This love of the common people may please an earl's granddaugther and a university professor; but I have been a common man and a poor man; and it has no romance for me. Leave it to the poor to pretend that poverty is a blessing: leave it to the coward to make a religion of his cowardice by preaching humility: we know better than that. We three must stand together above the common people: how else can we help their children to climb up beside us? Barbara must belong to us, not to the Salvation Army.

CUSINS Well, I can only say that if you think you will get her away from the Salvation Army by talking to her as you have been talking to me, you dont know Barbara.

UNDERSHAFT My friend: I never ask for what I can buy.

CUSINS [*in a white fury*] Do I understand you to imply that you can buy Barbara?

UNDERSHAFT No; but I can buy the Salvation Army.

CUSINS Quite impossible.

UNDERSHAFT You shall see. All religious organizations exist by selling themselves to the rich.

CUSINS Not the Army. That is the Church of the poor.

UNDERSHAFT All the more reason for buying it.

CUSINS I dont think you quite know what the Army does for the poor.

UNDERSHAFT Oh yes I do. It draws their teeth: that is enough for me as a man of business.

CUSINS Nonsense! It makes them sober—

UNDERSHAFT I prefer sober workmen. The profits are larger.

CUSINS —honest—

UNDERSHAFT Honest workmen are the most economical.

CUSINS —attached to their homes—

UNDERSHAFT So much the better: they will put up with anything sooner than change their shop.

---

1. St. Simeon Stylites, 5th-century Syrian hermit, lived for over 35 years on a small platform on top of a high pillar.

CUSINS —happy—

UNDERSHAFT An invaluable safeguard against revolution.

CUSINS —unselfish—

UNDERSHAFT Indifferent to their own interests, which suits me exactly.

CUSINS —with their thoughts on heavenly things—

UNDERSHAFT [rising] And not on Trade Unionism nor Socialism. Excellent.

CUSINS [revolted] You really are an infernal old rascal.

UNDERSHAFT [indicating Peter Shirley, who has just come from the shelter and strolled dejectedly down the yard between them] And this is an honest man!

SHIRLEY Yes; and what av I got by it? [He passes on bitterly and sits on the form, in the corner of the penthouse.]

    [Snobby Price, beaming sanctimoniously, and Jenny Hill, with a tambourine full of coppers, come from the shelter and go to the drum, on which Jenny begins to count the money.]

UNDERSHAFT [replying to Shirley] Oh, your employers must have got a good deal by it from first to last. [He sits on the table, with one foot on the side form. Cusins, overwhelmed, sits down on the same form nearer the shelter. Barbara comes from the shelter to the middle of the yard. She is excited and a little overwrought.]

BARBARA Weve just had a splendid experience meeting at the other gate in Cripps's Lane. Ive hardly ever seen them so much moved as they were by your confession, Mr Price.

PRICE I could almost be glad of my past wickedness if I could believe that it would elp to keep hathers stright.

BARBARA So it will, Snobby. How much, Jenny?

JENNY Four and tenpence, Major.

BARBARA Oh Snobby, if you had given your poor mother just one more kick, we should have got the whole five shillings!

PRICE If she heard you say that, miss, she'd be sorry I didnt. But I'm glad. Oh what a joy it will be to her when she hears I'm saved!

UNDERSHAFT Shall I contribute the odd twopence, Barbara? The millionaire's mite, eh? [He takes a couple of pennies from his pocket.]

BARBARA How did you make that twopence?

UNDERSHAFT As usual. By selling cannons, torpedoes, submarines, and my new patent Grand Duke hand grenade.

BARBARA Put it back in your pocket. You cant buy your salvation here for twopence: you must work it out.

UNDERSHAFT Is twopence not enough? I can afford a little more, if you press me.

BARBARA Two million millions would not be enough. There is bad blood on your hands; and nothing but good blood can cleanse them. Money is no use. Take it away [She turns to Cusins.] Dolly: you must write another letter for me to the papers. [He makes a wry face.] Yes: I know you dont like it; but it must be done. The starvation this winter is beating us: everybody is unemployed. The General says we must close this shelter if we cant get more money. I force the collections at the meetings until I am ashamed: dont I Snobby?

PRICE It's a fair treat to see you work it, miss. The way you got them up from three-and-six to four-and-ten with that hymn, penny by penny and verse by verse, was a caution. Not a Cheap Jack on Mile End Waste could touch you at it.

BARBARA Yes; but I wish we could do without it. I am getting at last to think more of the collection than of the people's souls. And what are those hatfuls of pence and halfpence? We want thousands! tens of thousands! hundreds of thousands! I want to convert people, not to be always begging for the Army in a way I'd die sooner than beg for myself.

UNDERSHAFT [in profound irony] Genuine unselfishness is capable of anything, my dear.

BARBARA [unsuspectingly, as she turns away to take the money from the drum and put it in a cash bag she carries] Yes, isnt it? [Undershaft looks sardonically at Cusins.]

CUSINS [aside to Undershaft] Mephistopheles! Machiavelli![2]

BARBARA [tears coming into her eyes as she ties the bag and pockets it] How are we to feed them? I cant talk religion to a man with bodily hunger in his eyes. [Almost breaking down.] It's frightful.

JENNY [running to her] Major, dear—

BARBARA [rebounding] No: dont comfort me. It will be all right. We shall get the money.

UNDERSHAFT How?

JENNY By praying for it, of course. Mrs Baines says she prayed for it last night; and she has never prayed for it in vain: never once. [She goes to the gate and looks out into the street.]

BARBARA [who has dried her eyes and regained her composure] By the way, dad, Mrs Baines has come to march with us to our big meeting this afternoon; and she is very anxious to meet you, for some reason or other. Perhaps she'll convert you.

UNDERSHAFT I shall be delighted, my dear.

JENNY [at the gate: excitedly] Major! Major! heres that man back again.

BARBARA What man?

JENNY The man that hit me. Oh, I hope he's coming back to join us.

[Bill Walker, with frost on his jacket, comes through the gate, his hands deep in his pockets and his chin sunk between his shoulders, like a cleaned-out gambler. He halts between Barbara and the drum.]

BARBARA Hullo, Bill! Back already!

BILL [nagging at her] Bin talkin ever sence, ev you?

BARBARA Pretty nearly. Well, has Todger paid you out for poor Jenny's jaw?

BILL Nao e aint.

BARBARA I thought your jacket looked a bit snowy.

BILL Sao it is snaowy. You want to knaow where the snaow cam from, downt you?

BARBARA Yes.

BILL Well, it cam from orf the grahnd in Pawkinses Corner in Kennintahn. It got rabbed orf be maw shaoulders: see?

BARBARA Pity you didnt rub some off with your knees, Bill! That would have done you a lot of good.

BILL [with sour mirthless humor] Aw was sivin another menn's knees at the tawm. E was kneelin on moy ed, e was.

JENNY Who was kneeling on your head?

BILL Todger was. E was pryin for me: pryin camfortable wiv me as a cawpet. Sow was Mog. Sao was the aol bloomin meetin. Mog she sez "Ow Lawd brike is stabborn sperrit; bat downt urt is dear art." Thet was wot she said. "Downt urt is dear art"! An er blowk—thirteen stun four!—kneelin wiv all is wight on me. Fanny, aint it?

---

2. Mephistopheles, a hellish spirit, often personifying the devil; Niccolo Machiavelli, Italian statesman and author; in his book The Prince (1532) he presents an amoral and calculating tyrant as the model of princely conduct.

JENNY Oh no. We're so sorry, Mr Walker.

BARBARA [*enjoying it frankly*] Nonsense! of course it's funny. Served you right, Bill! You must have done something to him first.

BILL [*doggedly*] Aw did wot Aw said Aw'd do. Aw spit in is eye. E looks ap at the skoy and sez, "Ow that Aw should be fahnd worthy to be spit upon for the gospel's sike!" e sez; an Mog sez "Glaory Allelloolier!"; an then e called me Braddher, an dahned me as if Aw was a kid and e was me mather worshin me a Setterda nawt. Aw ednt jast nao shaow wiv im at all. Arf the street pryed; an the tather arf larfed fit to split theirselves. [*To Barbara.*] There! are you settisfawd nah?

BARBARA [*her eyes dancing*] Wish I'd been there, Bill.

BILL Yus: youd a got in a hextra bit o talk on me, wouldnt you?

JENNY I'm so sorry, Mr Walker.

BILL [*fiercely*] Downt you gow bein sorry for me: youve no call. Listen eah. Aw browk your jawr.

JENNY No, it didnt hurt me: indeed it didnt, except for a moment. It was only that I was frightened.

BILL Aw downt want to be forgive be you, or be ennybody. Wot Aw did Aw'll py for. Aw trawd to gat me aown jawr browk to settisfaw you—

JENNY [*distressed*] Oh no—

BILL [*impatiently*] Tell y' Aw did: cawnt you listen to wots bein taold you? All Aw got be it was bein mide a sawt of in the pablic street for me pines. Well, if Aw cawnt settisfaw you one wy, Aw ken anather. Listen eah! Aw ed two quid³ sived agen the frost; an Awve a pahnd of it left. A mite o mawn last week ed words with the judy e's gowing to merry. E give er wot-for; an e's bin fawnd fifteen bob. E ed a rawt to itt er cause they was gowin to be merrid; but Aw ednt nao rawt to itt you; sao put anather fawv bob on an call it a pahnd's worth. [*He produces a sovereign.*] Eahs the manney. Tike it; and lets ev no more o your forgivin an prying and your Mijor jawrin me. Let wot Aw dan be dan an pide for; and let there be a end of it.

JENNY Oh, I couldnt take it, Mr Walker. But if you would give a shilling or two to poor Rummy Mitchens! you really did hurt her; and she's old.

BILL [*contemptuously*] Not lawkly. Aw'd give her anather as soon as look at er. Let her ev the lawr o me as she threatened! She aint forgiven me: not mach. Wot Aw dan to er is not on me mawnd—wot she [*indicating Barbara*] mawt call on me conscience—no more than stickin a pig. It's this Christian gime o yours that Aw wownt ev plyed agen me: this bloomin forgivin an neggin an jawrin that mikes a menn thet sore that iz lawf's a burdn to im. Aw wownt ev it, Aw tell you; sao tike your manney and stop thraowin your silly beshed fice hap agen me.

JENNY Major: may I take a little of it for the Army?

BARBARA No: the Army is not to be bought. We want your soul, Bill; and we'll take nothing less.

BILL [*bitterly*] Aw knaow. Me an maw few shillins is not good enaff for you. Youre a earl's grendorter, you are. Nathink less than a anderd pahnd for you.

UNDERSHAFT Come, Barbara! you could do a great deal of good with a hundred pounds. If you will set this gentleman's mind at ease by taking his pound, I will give the other ninety-nine.

[*Bill, dazed by such opulence, instinctively touches his cap.*]

---

3. Two pounds.

BARBARA Oh, youre too extravagant, papa. Bill offers twenty pieces of silver. All you need offer is the other ten. That will make the standard price to buy anybody who's for sale. I'm not; and the Army's not. [*To Bill.*] Youll never have another quiet moment, Bill, until you come round to us. You cant stand out against your salvation.

BILL [*sullenly*] Aw cawnt stend aht agen music awl wrastlers and awtful tangued women. Awve offered to py. Aw can do no more. Tike it or leave it. There it is. [*He throws the sovereign on the drum, and sits down on the horse-trough. The coin fascinates Snobby Price, who takes an early opportunity of dropping his cap on it.*]

[*Mrs Baines comes from the shelter. She is dressed as a Salvation Army Commissioner. She is an earnest looking woman of about 40 with a caressing, urgent voice, and an appealing manner.*]

BARBARA This is my father, Mrs Baines. [*Undershaft comes from the table, taking his hat off with marked civility.*] Try what you can do with him. He wont listen to me, because he remembers what a fool I was when I was a baby. [*She leaves them together and chats with Jenny.*]

MRS BAINES Have you been shewn over the shelter, Mr Undershaft? You know the work we're doing, of course.

UNDERSHAFT [*very civilly*] The whole nation knows it, Mrs Baines.

MRS BAINES No, sir: the whole nation does not know it, or we should not be crippled as we are for want of money to carry our work through the length and breadth of the land. Let me tell you that there would have been rioting this winter in London but for us.

UNDERSHAFT You really think so?

MRS BAINES I know it. I remember 1886, when you rich gentlemen hardened your hearts against the cry of the poor. They broke the windows of your clubs in Pall Mall.[4]

UNDERSHAFT [*gleaming with approval of their method*] And the Mansion House Fund went up next day from thirty thousand pounds to seventy-nine thousand![5] I remember quite well.

MRS BAINES Well, wont you help me to get at the people? They wont break windows then. Come here, Price. Let me shew you to this gentleman [*Price comes to be inspected.*] Do you remember the window breaking?

PRICE My ole father thought it was the revolution, maam.

MRS BAINES Would you break windows now?

PRICE Oh no, maam. The windows of eaven av bin opened to me. I know now that the rich man is a sinner like myself.

RUMMY [*appearing above at the loft door*] Snobby Price!

SNOBBY Wot is it?

RUMMY Your mother's askin for you at the other gate in Cripp's Lane. She's heard about your confession [*Price turns pale.*]

MRS BAINES Go, Mr Price; and pray with her.

JENNY You can go through the shelter, Snobby.

PRICE [*to Mrs Baines*] I couldnt face her now, maam, with all the weight of my sins fresh on me. Tell her she'll find her son at ome, waitin for her in prayer. [*He skulks off through the gate, incidentally stealing the sovereign on his way out by picking up his cap from the drum.*]

MRS BAINES [*with swimming eyes*] You see how we take the anger and the bitterness against you out of their hearts, Mr Undershaft.

---

4. A fashionable London thoroughfare; in February 1886 a large meeting in nearby Trafalgar Square turned violent, and the windows of clubs and shops were smashed.

5. The Mansion House (completed 1752) is the official residence of the Lord Mayor of London; the fund was for relief of the unemployed.

UNDERSHAFT It is certainly most convenient and gratifying to all large employers of labor, Mrs Baines.

MRS BAINES Barbara: Jenny: I have good news: most wonderful news. [*Jenny runs to her.*] My prayers have been answered. I told you they would, Jenny, didnt I?

JENNY Yes, yes.

BARBARA [*moving nearer to the drum*] Have we got money enough to keep the shelter open?

MRS BAINES I hope we shall have enough to keep all the shelters open. Lord Saxmundham has promised us five thousand pounds—

BARBARA Hooray!

JENNY Glory!

MRS BAINES —if—

BARBARA "If!" If what?

MRS BAINES —if five other gentlemen will give a thousand each to make it up to ten thousand.

BARBARA Who is Lord Saxmundham? I never heard of him.

UNDERSHAFT [*who has pricked up his ears at the peer's name, and is now watching Barbara curiously*] A new creation, my dear. You have heard of Sir Horace Bodger?

BARBARA Bodger! Do you mean the distiller? Bodger's whisky!

UNDERSHAFT That is the man. He is one of the greatest of our public benefactors. He restored the cathedral at Hakington. They made him a baronet for that. He gave half a million to the funds of his party: they made him a baron for that.

SHIRLEY What will they give him for the five thousand?

UNDERSHAFT There is nothing left to give him. So the five thousand, I should think, is to save his soul.

MRS BAINES Heaven grant it may! Oh Mr Undershaft, you have some very rich friends. Cant you help us towards the other five thousand? We are going to hold a great meeting this afternoon at the Assembly Hall in the Mile End Road. If I could only announce that one gentleman had come forward to support Lord Saxmundham, others would follow. Dont you know somebody? couldnt you? wouldnt you? [*her eyes fill with tears*] oh, think of those poor people, Mr Undershaft: think of how much it means to them, and how little to a great man like you.

UNDERSHAFT [*sardonically gallant*] Mrs Baines: you are irresistible. I cant disappoint you; and I cant deny myself the satisfaction of making Bodger pay up. You shall have your five thousand pounds.

MRS BAINES Thank God!

UNDERSHAFT You dont thank me?

MRS BAINES Oh sir, dont try to be cynical: dont be ashamed of being a good man. The Lord will bless you abundantly; and our prayers will be like a strong fortification round you all the days of your life. [*With a touch of caution.*] You will let me have the cheque to shew at the meeting, wont you? Jenny: go in and fetch a pen and ink. [*Jenny runs to the shelter door.*]

UNDERSHAFT Do not disturb Miss Hill: I have a fountain pen [*Jenny halts. He sits at the table and writes the cheque. Cusins rises to make room for him. They all watch him silently.*]

BILL [*cynically, aside to Barbara, his voice and accent horribly debased*] Wot prawce selvytion nah?

BARBARA Stop. [*Undershaft stops writing: they all turn to her in surprise.*] Mrs Baines: are you really going to take this money?

MRS BAINES [astonished] Why not, dear?

BARBARA Why not! Do you know what my father is? Have you forgotten that Lord Saxmundham is Bodger the whisky man? Do you remember how we implored the County Council to stop him from writing Bodger's Whisky in letters of fire against the sky; so that the poor drink-ruined creatures on the Embankment could not wake up from their snatches of sleep without being reminded of their deadly thirst by that wicked sky sign? Do you know that the worst thing I have had to fight here is not the devil, but Bodger, Bodger, Bodger, with his whisky, his distilleries, and his tied houses?[6] Are you going to make our shelter another tied house for him, and ask me to keep it?

BILL Rotten dranken whisky it is too.

MRS BAINES Dear Barbara: Lord Saxmundham has a soul to be saved like any of us. If heaven has found the way to make a good use of his money, are we to set ourselves up against the answer to our prayers?

BARBARA I know he has a soul to be saved. Let him come down here; and I'll do my best to help him to his salvation. But he wants to send his cheque down to buy us, and go on being as wicked as ever.

UNDERSHAFT [with a reasonableness which Cusins alone perceives to be ironical] My dear Barbara: alcohol is a very necessary article. It heals the sick—

BARBARA It does nothing of the sort.

UNDERSHAFT Well, it assists the doctor: that is perhaps a less questionable way of putting it. It makes life bearable to millions of people who could not endure their existence if they were quite sober. It enables Parliament to do things at eleven at night that no sane person would do at eleven in the morning. Is it Bodger's fault that this inestimable gift is deplorably abused by less than one per cent of the poor? [He turns again to the table; signs the cheque; and crosses it.]

MRS BAINES Barbara: will there be less drinking or more if all those poor souls we are saving come tomorrow and find the doors of our shelters shut in their faces? Lord Saxmundham gives us the money to stop drinking—to take his own business from him.

CUSINS [impishly] Pure self-sacrifice on Bodger's part, clearly! Bless dear Bodger! [Barbara almost breaks down as Adolphus, too, fails her.]

UNDERSHAFT [tearing out the cheque and pocketing the book as he rises and goes past Cusins to Mrs Baines] I also, Mrs Baines, may claim a little disinterestedness. Think of my business! think of the widows and orphans! the men and lads torn to pieces with shrapnel and poisoned with lyddite![7] [Mrs Baines shrinks; but he goes on remorselessly] the oceans of blood, not one drop of which is shed in a really just cause! the ravaged crops! the peaceful peasants forced, women and men, to till their fields under the fire of opposing armies on pain of starvation! the bad blood of the fierce little cowards at home who egg on others to fight for the gratification of their national vanity! All this makes money for me: I am never richer, never busier than when the papers are full of it. Well, it is your work to preach peace on earth and good will to men. [Mrs Baines's face lights up again.] Every convert you make is a vote against war. [Her lips move in prayer.] Yet I give you this money to help you to hasten my own commercial ruin. [He gives her the cheque.]

CUSINS [mounting the form in an ecstasy of mischief] The millennium will be inaugurated by the unselfishness of Undershaft and Bodger. Oh be joyful! [He takes the drum-sticks from his pocket and flourishes them.]

---

6. Pubs owned by a brewery or distillery.   7. A High explosive.

MRS BAINES [*taking the cheque*] The longer I live the more proof I see that there is an Infinite Goodness that turns everything to the work of salvation sooner or later. Who would have thought that any good could have come out of war and drink? And yet their profits are brought today to the feet of salvation to do its blessed work. [*She is affected to tears.*]

JENNY [*running to Mrs Baines and throwing her arms round her*] Oh dear! how blessed, how glorious it all is!

CUSINS [*in a convulsion of irony*] Let us seize this unspeakable moment. Let us march to the great meeting at once. Excuse me just an instant. [*He rushes into the shelter. Jenny takes her tambourine from the drum head.*]

MRS BAINES Mr Undershaft: have you ever seen a thousand people fall on their knees with one impulse and pray? Come with us to the meeting. Barbara shall tell them that the Army is saved, and saved through you.

CUSINS [*returning impetuously from the shelter with a flag and a trombone, and coming between Mrs Baines and Undershaft*] You shall carry the flag down the first street, Mrs Baines. [*He gives her the flag.*] Mr Undershaft is a gifted trombonist: he shall intone an Olympian diapason[8] to the West Ham Salvation March. [*Aside to Undershaft, as he forces the trombone on him.*] Blow, Machiavelli, blow.

UNDERSHAFT [*aside to him, as he takes the trombone*] The trumpet in Zion! [*Cusins rushes to the drum, which he takes up and puts on. Undershaft continues, aloud.*] I will do my best. I could vamp a bass if I knew the tune.

CUSINS It is a wedding chorus from one of Donizetti's operas; but we have converted it. We convert everything to good here, including Bodger. You remember the chorus. "For thee immense rejoicing—immenso giubilo—immenso giubilo." [*With drum obbligato.*] Rum tum ti tum tum, tum tum ti ta—

BARBARA Dolly: you are breaking my heart.

CUSINS What is a broken heart more or less here? Dionysos Undershaft has descended. I am possessed.

MRS BAINES Come, Barbara: I must have my dear Major to carry the flag with me.

JENNY Yes, yes, Major darling.

CUSINS [*Snatches the tambourine out of Jenny's hand and mutely offers it to Barbara.*]

BARBARA [*coming forward a little as she puts the offer behind her with a shudder, whilst Cusins recklessly tosses the tambourine back to Jenny and goes to the gate*] I cant come.

JENNY Not come!

MRS BAINES [*with tears in her eyes*] Barbara: do you think I am wrong to take the money?

BARBARA [*impulsively going to her and kissing her*] No, no: God help you, dear, you must: you are saving the Army. Go; and may you have a great meeting!

JENNY But arnt you coming?

BARBARA No. [*She begins taking off the silver S brooch from her collar.*]

MRS BAINES Barbara: what are you doing?

JENNY Why are you taking your badge off? You cant be going to leave us, Major.

BARBARA [*quietly*] Father: come here.

UNDERSHAFT [*coming to her*] My dear! [*Seeing that she is going to pin the badge on his collar, he retreats to the penthouse in some alarm.*]

BARBARA [*following him*] Dont be frightened. [*She pins the badge on and steps back towards the table, shewing him to the others.*] There! It's not much for £5000, is it?

MRS BAINES Barbara: if you wont come and pray with us, promise me you will pray for us.

BARBARA I cant pray now. Perhaps I shall never pray again.

---

8. A grand burst of sound; in Greek mythology, Mount Olympus was the home of the gods.

MRS BAINES Barbara!

JENNY Major!

BARBARA [almost delirious] I cant bear any more. Quick march!

CUSINS [calling to the procession in the street outside] Off we go. Play up, there! Immenso giubilo. [He gives the time with his drum; and the band strikes up the march, which rapidly becomes more distant as the procession moves briskly away.]

MRS BAINES I must go, dear. Youre overworked: you will be all right tomorrow. We'll never lose you. Now Jenny: step out with the old flag. Blood and Fire! [She marches out through the gate with her flag.]

JENNY Glory Hallelujah! [Flourishing her tambourine and marching.]

UNDERSHAFT [to Cusins, as he marches out past him easing the slide of his trombone] "My ducats and my daughter!"[9]

CUSINS [following him out] Money and gunpowder!

BARBARA Drunkenness and Murder! My God: why hast thou forsaken me?[1]
   [She sinks on the form with her face buried in her hands. The march passes away into silence. Bill Walker steals across to her.]

BILL [taunting] Wot prawce selvytion nah?

SHIRLEY Dont you hit her when she's down.

BILL She itt me wen aw wiz dahn. Waw shouldnt Aw git a bit o me aown beck?

BARBARA [raising her head] I didnt take your money, Bill. [She crosses the yard to the gate and turns her back on the two men to hide her face from them.]

BILL [sneering after her] Naow, it warnt enaff for you. [Turning to the drum, he misses the money.] Ellow! If you aint took it sammun else ez. Weres it gorn? Bly me if Jenny Ill didnt tike it arter all!

RUMMY [screaming at him from the loft] You lie, you dirty black-guard! Snobby Price pinched it off the drum when he took up his cap. I was up here all the time an see im do it.

BILL Wot! Stowl maw manney! Waw didnt you call thief on him, you silly aold macker you?

RUMMY To serve you aht for ittin me across the fice. It's cost y'pahnd, that az. [Raising a paean of squalid triumph.] I done you. I'm even with you. Uve ad it aht o y—
   [Bill snatches up Shirley's mug and hurls it at her. She slams the loft door and vanishes. The mug smashes against the door and falls in fragments.]

BILL [beginning to chuckle] Tell us, aol menn, wot o'clock this mawnin was it wen im as they call Snobby Prawce was sived?

BARBARA [turning to him more composedly, and with unspoiled sweetness] About half past twelve, Bill. And he pinched your pound at a quarter to two. I know. Well, you cant afford to lose it. I'll send it to you.

BILL [his voice and accent suddenly improving] Not if Aw wiz to stawve for it. Aw aint to be bought.

SHIRLEY Aint you? Youd sell yourself to the devil for a pint o beer; only there aint no devil to make the offer.

BILL [unashamed] Sao Aw would, mite, and often ev, cheerful. But she cawnt baw me. [Approaching Barbara.] You wanted maw saoul, did you? Well, you aint got it.

BARBARA I nearly got it, Bill. But weve sold it back to you for ten thousand pounds.

SHIRLEY And dear at the money!

---

9. In Shakespeare's play The Merchant of Venice, the Jewish money-lender Shylock lends money to a Christian merchant, which he subsequently loses along with his daughter when she elopes with a Christian.

1. Christ's last words on the Cross (Mark 15.34).

BARBARA No, Peter: it was worth more than money.

BILL [*salvationproof*] It's nao good: you cawnt get rahnd me nah. Aw downt blieve in it; and Awve seen tody that Aw was rawt. [*Going.*] Sao long, aol soupkitchener! Ta, ta, Mijor Earl's Grendorter! [*Turning at the gate.*] Wot prawce selvytion nah? Snobby Prawce! Ha! ha!

BARBARA [*offering her hand*] Goodbye, Bill.

BILL [*taken aback, half plucks his cap off; then shoves it on again defiantly*] Git aht. [*Barbara drops her hand, discouraged. He has a twinge of remorse.*] But thets aw rawt, you knaow. Nathink pasnl. Naow mellice. Sao long, Judy. [*He goes.*]

BARBARA No malice. So long, Bill.

SHIRLEY [*shaking his head*] You make too much of him, miss, in your innocence.

BARBARA [*going to him*] Peter: I'm like you now. Cleaned out, and lost my job.

SHIRLEY Youve youth an hope. Thats two better than me.

BARBARA I'll get you a job, Peter. Thats hope for you: the youth will have to be enough for me. [*She counts her money.*] I have just enough left for two teas at Lockharts, a Rowton doss for you,[2] and my tram and bus home. [*He frowns and rises with offended pride. She takes his arm.*] Dont be proud, Peter: it's sharing between friends. And promise me youll talk to me and not let me cry. [*She draws him towards the gate.*]

SHIRLEY Well, I'm not accustomed to talk to the like of you—

BARBARA [*urgently*] Yes, yes: you must talk to me. Tell me about Tom Paine's books and Bradlaugh's lectures. Come along.[3]

SHIRLEY Ah, if you would only read Tom Paine in the proper spirit, miss! [*They go out through the gate together.*]

ACT 3

Next day after lunch Lady Britomart is writing in the library in Wilton Crescent. Sarah is reading in the armchair near the window. Barbara, in ordinary fashionable dress, pale and brooding, is on the settee. Charles Lomax enters. He starts on seeing Barbara fashionably attired and in low spirits.

LOMAX Youve left off your uniform!

[*Barbara says nothing; but an expression of pain passes over her face.*]

LADY BRITOMART [*warning him in low tones to be careful*] Charles!

LOMAX [*much concerned, coming behind the settee and bending sympathetically over Barbara*] I'm awfully sorry, Barbara. You know I helped you all I could with the concertina and so forth. [*Momentously.*] Still, I have never shut my eyes to the fact that there is a certain amount of tosh about the Salvation Army. Now the claims of the Church of England—

LADY BRITOMART Thats enough, Charles. Speak of something suited to your mental capacity.

LOMAX But surely the Church of England is suited to all our capacities.

BARBARA [*pressing his hand*] Thank you for your sympathy, Cholly. Now go and spoon with Sarah.

LOMAX [*dragging a chair from the writing table and seating himself affectionately by Sarah's side*] How is my ownest today?

2. Lord Rowton set up a series of hostels for working men in the late 19th century; a "doss" is a cheap bed.
3. Thomas Paine (1737–1809), English-born radical and supporter of revolutionary causes; Charles Bradlaugh (1833–1891), an atheist and radical Member of Parliament.

SARAH I wish you wouldnt tell Cholly to do things, Barbara. He always comes straight and does them. Cholly: we're going to the works this afternoon.

LOMAX What works?

SARAH The cannon works.

LOMAX What? your governor's shop!

SARAH Yes.

LOMAX Oh I say!

[*Cusins enters in poor condition. He also starts visibly when he sees Barbara without her uniform.*]

BARBARA I expected you this morning, Dolly. Didnt you guess that?

CUSINS [*sitting down beside her*] I'm sorry. I have only just breakfasted.

SARAH But weve just finished lunch.

BARBARA Have you had one of your bad nights?

CUSINS No: I had rather a good night: in fact, one of the most remarkable nights I have ever passed.

BARBARA The meeting?

CUSINS No: after the meeting.

LADY BRITOMART You should have gone to bed after the meeting. What were you doing?

CUSINS Drinking.

LADY BRITOMART ⎫ ⎧Adolphus!
SARAH   ⎬ ⎨Dolly!
BARBARA   ⎪ ⎪Dolly!
LOMAX   ⎭ ⎩Oh I say!

LADY BRITOMART What were you drinking, may I ask?

CUSINS A most devilish kind of Spanish burgundy, warranted free from added alcohol: a Temperance burgundy in fact. Its richness in natural alcohol made any addition superfluous.

BARBARA Are you joking, Dolly?

CUSINS [*patiently*] No. I have been making a night of it with the nominal head of this household: that is all.

LADY BRITOMART Andrew made you drunk!

CUSINS No: he only provided the wine. I think it was Dionysos who made me drunk. [*To Barbara.*] I told you I was possessed.

LADY BRITOMART Youre not sober yet. Go home to bed at once.

CUSINS I have never before ventured to reproach you, Lady Brit; but how could you marry the Prince of Darkness?

LADY BRITOMART It was much more excusable to marry him than to get drunk with him. That is a new accomplishment of Andrew's, by the way. He usent to drink.

CUSINS He doesnt now. He only sat there and completed the wreck of my moral basis, the rout of my convictions, the purchase of my soul. He cares for you, Barbara. That is what makes him so dangerous to me.

BARBARA That has nothing to do with it, Dolly. There are larger loves and diviner dreams than the fireside ones. You know that, dont you?

CUSINS Yes: that is our understanding. I know it. I hold to it. Unless he can win me on that holier ground he may amuse me for a while; but he can get no deeper hold, strong as he is.

BARBARA Keep to that; and the end will be right. Now tell me what happened at the meeting?

CUSINS It was an amazing meeting. Mrs Baines almost died of emotion. Jenny Hill simply gibbered with hysteria. The Prince of Darkness played his trombone like a madman: its brazen roarings were like the laughter of the damned. 117 conversions took place then and there. They prayed with the most touching sincerity and gratitude for Bodger, and for the anonymous donor of the £5000. Your father would not let his name be given.

LOMAX That was rather fine of the old man, you know. Most chaps would have wanted the advertisement.

CUSINS He said all the charitable institutions would be down on him like kites on a battle-field if he gave his name.

LADY BRITOMART Thats Andrew all over. He never does a proper thing without giving an improper reason for it.

CUSINS He convinced me that I have all my life been doing improper things for proper reasons.

LADY BRITOMART Adolphus: now that Barbara has left the Salvation Army, you had better leave it too. I will not have you playing that drum in the streets.

CUSINS Your orders are already obeyed, Lady Brit.

BARBARA Dolly: were you ever really in earnest about it? Would you have joined if you had never seen me?

CUSINS [disingenuously] Well—er—well, possibly, as a collector of religions—

LOMAX [cunningly] Not as a drummer, though, you know. You are a very clearheaded brainy chap, Dolly; and it must have been apparent to you that there is a certain amount of tosh about—

LADY BRITOMART Charles: if you must drivel, drivel like a grown-up man and not like a schoolboy.

LOMAX [out of countenance] Well, drivel is drivel, dont you know, whatever a man's age.

LADY BRITOMART In good society in England, Charles, men drivel at all ages by repeating silly formulas with an air of wisdom. Schoolboys make their own formulas out of slang, like you. When they reach your age, and get political private secretaryships[1] and things of that sort, they drop slang and get their formulas out of the Spectator or The Times. You had better confine yourself to The Times. You will find that there is a certain amount of tosh about The Times; but at least its language is reputable.

LOMAX [overwhelmed] You are so awfully strong-minded, Lady Brit—

LADY BRITOMART Rubbish! [Morrison comes in.] What is it?

MORRISON If you please, my lady, Mr Undershaft has just drove up to the door.

LADY BRITOMART Well, let him in. [Morrison hesitates.] Whats the matter with you?

MORRISON Shall I announce him, my lady; or is he at home here, so to speak, my lady?

LADY BRITOMART Announce him.

MORRISON Thank you, my lady. You wont mind my asking, I hope. The occasion is in a manner of speaking new to me.

LADY BRITOMART Quite right. Go and let him in.

MORRISON Thank you, my lady. [He withdraws.]

LADY BRITOMART Children: go and get ready. [Sarah and Barbara go upstairs for their out-of-door wraps.] Charles: go and tell Stephen to come down here in five minutes: you will find him in the drawing room. [Charles goes.] Adolphus tell them to send round the carriage in about fifteen minutes. [Adolphus goes.]

---

1. A minor parliamentary appointment.

MORRISON [*at the door*] Mr Undershaft.

[*Undershaft comes in. Morrison goes out.*]

UNDERSHAFT Alone! How fortunate!

LADY BRITOMART [*rising*] Dont be sentimental, Andrew. Sit down. [*She sits on the settee: he sits beside her, on her left. She comes to the point before he has time to breathe.*] Sarah must have £800 a year until Charles Lomax comes into his property. Barbara will need more, and need it permanently, because Adolphus hasnt any property.

UNDERSHAFT [*resignedly*] Yes, my dear: I will see to it. Anything else? for yourself, for instance?

LADY BRITOMART I want to talk to you about Stephen.

UNDERSHAFT [*rather wearily*] Dont, my dear. Stephen doesnt interest me.

LADY BRITOMART He does interest me. He is our son.

UNDERSHAFT Do you really think so? He has induced us to bring him into the world; but he chose his parents very incongruously, I think. I see nothing of myself in him, and less of you.

LADY BRITOMART Andrew: Stephen is an excellent son, and a most steady, capable, highminded young man. You are simply trying to find an excuse for disinheriting him.

UNDERSHAFT My dear Biddy: the Undershaft tradition disinherits him. It would be dishonest of me to leave the cannon foundry to my son.

LADY BRITOMART It would be most unnatural and improper of you to leave it to anyone else, Andrew. Do you suppose this wicked and immoral tradition can be kept up for ever? Do you pretend that Stephen could not carry on the foundry just as well as all the other sons of the big business houses?

UNDERSHAFT Yes: he could learn the office routine without understanding the business, like all the other sons; and the firm would go on by its own momentum until the real Undershaft—probably an Italian or a German—would invent a new method and cut him out.

LADY BRITOMART There is nothing that any Italian or German could do that Stephen could not do. And Stephen at least has breeding.

UNDERSHAFT The son of a foundling! Nonsense!

LADY BRITOMART My son, Andrew! And even you may have good blood in your veins for all you know.

UNDERSHAFT True. Probably I have. That is another argument in favour of a foundling.

LADY BRITOMART Andrew: dont be aggravating. And dont be wicked. At present you are both.

UNDERSHAFT This conversation is part of the Undershaft tradition, Biddy. Every Undershaft's wife has treated him to it ever since the house was founded. It is mere waste of breath. If the tradition be ever broken it will be for an abler man than Stephen.

LADY BRITOMART [*pouting*] Then go away.

UNDERSHAFT [*deprecatory*] Go away!

LADY BRITOMART Yes: go away. If you will do nothing for Stephen, you are not wanted here. Go to your foundling, whoever he is; and look after him.

UNDERSHAFT The fact is, Biddy—

LADY BRITOMART Dont call me Biddy. I dont call you Andy.

UNDERSHAFT I will not call my wife Britomart: it is not good sense. Seriously, my love, the Undershaft tradition has landed me in a difficulty. I am getting on in years; and my partner Lazarus has at last made a stand and insisted that the succession must be settled one way or the other; and of course he is quite right. You see, I havent found a fit successor yet.

LADY BRITOMART [obstinately] There is Stephen.

UNDERSHAFT Thats just it: all the foundlings I can find are exactly like Stephen.

LADY BRITOMART Andrew!!

UNDERSHAFT I want a man with no relations and no schooling: that is, a man who would be out of the running altogether if he were not a strong man. And I cant find him. Every blessed foundling nowadays is snapped up in his infancy by Barnardo homes,[2] or School Board officers, or Boards of Guardians; and if he shews the least ability he is fastened on by schoolmasters; trained to win scholarships like a racehorse; crammed with secondhand ideas; drilled and disciplined in docility and what they call good taste; and lamed for life so that he is fit for nothing but teaching. If you want to keep the foundry in the family, you had better find an eligible foundling and marry him to Barbara.

LADY BRITOMART Ah! Barbara! Your pet! You would sacrifice Stephen to Barbara.

UNDERSHAFT Cheerfully. And you, my dear, would boil Barbara to make soup for Stephen.

LADY BRITOMART Andrew: this is not a question of our likings and dislikings: it is a question of duty. It is your duty to make Stephen your successor.

UNDERSHAFT Just as much as it is your duty to submit to your husband. Come, Biddy! these tricks of the governing class are of no use with me. I am one of the governing class myself; and it is waste of time giving tracts to a missionary. I have the power in this matter; and I am not to be humbugged into using it for your purposes.

LADY BRITOMART Andrew: you can talk my head off; but you cant change wrong into right. And your tie is all on one side. Put it straight.

UNDERSHAFT [disconcerted] It wont stay unless it's pinned [he fumbles at it with childish grimaces]—

[Stephen comes in.]

STEPHEN [at the door] I beg your pardon [About to retire.]

LADY BRITOMART No: come in, Stephen. [Stephen comes forward to his mother's writing table.]

UNDERSHAFT [not very cordially] Good afternoon.

STEPHEN [coldly] Good afternoon.

UNDERSHAFT [to Lady Britomart] He knows all about the tradition, I suppose?

LADY BRITOMART Yes. [To Stephen] It is what I told you last night, Stephen.

UNDERSHAFT [sulkily] I understand you want to come into the cannon business.

STEPHEN I go into trade! Certainly not.

UNDERSHAFT [opening his eyes, greatly eased in mind and manner] Oh! in that case—

LADY BRITOMART Cannons are not trade, Stephen. They are enterprise.

STEPHEN I have no intention of becoming a man of business in any sense. I have no capacity for business and no taste for it. I intend to devote myself to politics.

2. Thomas John Barnardo (1845–1905), the British pioneer of social work, set up many homes for destitute children.

UNDERSHAFT [rising] My dear boy: this is an immense relief to me. And I trust it may prove an equally good thing for the country. I was afraid you would consider yourself disparaged and slighted. [He moves towards Stephen as if to shake hands with him.]

LADY BRITOMART [rising and interposing] Stephen: I cannot allow you to throw away an enormous property like this.

STEPHEN [stiffly] Mother: there must be an end of treating me as a child, if you please. [Lady Britomart recoils, deeply wounded by his tone.] Until last night I did not take your attitude seriously, because I did not think you meant it seriously. But I find now that you left me in the dark as to matters which you should have explained to me years ago. I am extremely hurt and offended. Any further discussion of my intentions had better take place with my father, as between one man and another.

LADY BRITOMART Stephen! [She sits down again, her eyes filling with tears.]

UNDERSHAFT [with grave compassion] You see, my dear, it is only the big men who can be treated as children.

STEPHEN I am sorry, mother, that you have forced me—

UNDERSHAFT [stopping him] Yes, yes, yes, yes: thats all right, Stephen. She wont interfere with you any more: your independence is achieved: you have won your latchkey. Dont rub it in; and above all, dont apologize. [He resumes his seat.] Now what about your future, as between one man and another—I beg your pardon, Biddy: as between two men and a woman.

LADY BRITOMART [who has pulled herself together strongly] I quite understand, Stephen. By all means go your own way if you feel strong enough. [Stephen sits down magisterially in the chair at the writing table with an air of affirming his majority.]

UNDERSHAFT It is settled that you do not ask for the succession to the cannon business.

STEPHEN I hope it is settled that I repudiate the cannon business.

UNDERSHAFT Come, come! dont be so devilishly sulky: it's boyish. Freedom should be generous. Besides, I owe you a fair start in life in exchange for disinheriting you. You cant become prime minister all at once. Havent you a turn for something? What about literature, art, and so forth?

STEPHEN I have nothing of the artist about me, either in faculty or character, thank Heaven!

UNDERSHAFT A philosopher, perhaps? Eh?

STEPHEN I make no such ridiculous pretension.

UNDERSHAFT Just so. Well, there is the army, the navy, the Church, the Bar. The Bar requires some ability. What about the Bar?

STEPHEN I have not studied law. And I am afraid I have not the necessary push—I believe that is the name barristers give to their vulgarity—for success in pleading.

UNDERSHAFT Rather a difficult case, Stephen. Hardly anything left but the stage, is there? [Stephen makes an impatient movement.] Well, come! is there anything you know or care for?

STEPHEN [rising and looking at him steadily] I know the difference between right and wrong.

UNDERSHAFT [hugely tickled] You dont say so! What! no capacity for business, no knowledge of law, no sympathy with art, no pretension to philosophy; only a simple knowledge of the secret that has puzzled all the philosophers, baffled all the lawyers, muddled all the men of business, and ruined most of the artists: the secret of right and wrong. Why, man, youre a genius, a master of masters, a god! At twentyfour, too!

STEPHEN [*keeping his temper with difficulty*] You are pleased to be facetious. I pretend to nothing more than any honorable English gentleman claims as his birthright. [*He sits down angrily.*]

UNDERSHAFT Oh, thats everybody's birthright. Look at poor little Jenny Hill, the Salvation lassie! she would think you were laughing at her if you asked her to stand up in the street and teach grammar or geography or mathematics or even drawing room dancing; but it never occurs to her to doubt that she can teach morals and religion. You are all alike, you respectable people. You cant tell me the bursting strain of a ten-inch gun, which is a very simple matter; but you all think you can tell me the bursting strain of a man under temptation. You darent handle high explosives; but youre all ready to handle honesty and truth and justice and the whole duty of man, and kill one another at that game. What a country! What a world!

LADY BRITOMART [*uneasily*] What do you think he had better do, Andrew?

UNDERSHAFT Oh, just what he wants to do. He knows nothing and he thinks he knows everything. That points clearly to a political career. Get him a private secretaryship to someone who can get him an Under Secretaryship; and then leave him alone. He will find his natural and proper place in the end on the Treasury Bench.[3]

STEPHEN [*springing up again*] I am sorry, sir, that you force me to forget the respect due to you as my father. I am an Englishman and I will not hear the Government of my country insulted. [*He thrusts his hands in his pockets, and walks angrily across to the window.*]

UNDERSHAFT [*with a touch of brutality*] The government of your country! *I* am the government of your country: I, and Lazarus. Do you suppose that you and half a dozen amateurs like you, sitting in a row in that foolish gabble shop, can govern Undershaft and Lazarus? No, my friend: you will do what pays *us*. You will make war when it suits us, and keep peace when it doesnt. You will find out that trade requires certain measures when we have decided on those measures. When I want anything to keep my dividends up, you will discover that my want is a national need. When other people want something to keep my dividends down, you will call out the police and military. And in return you shall have the support and applause of my newspapers, and the delight of imagining that you are a great statesman. Government of your country! Be off with you, my boy, and play with your caucuses and leading articles and historic parties and great leaders and burning questions and the rest of your toys. *I* am going back to my counting-house to pay the piper and call the tune.

STEPHEN [*actually smiling, and putting his hand on his father's shoulder with indulgent patronage*] Really, my dear father, it is impossible to be angry with you. You dont know how absurd all this sounds to me. You are very properly proud of having been industrious enough to make money; and it is greatly to your credit that you have made so much of it. But it has kept you in circles where you are valued for your money and deferred to for it, instead of in the doubtless very old-fashioned and behind-the-times public school and university where I formed my habits of mind. It is natural for you to think that money governs England; but you must allow me to think I know better.

UNDERSHAFT And what does govern England, pray?

---

3. An under secretary is a junior minister; the Treasury Bench is the seat on which senior ministers of the governing party sit in parliament.

STEPHEN Character, father, character.

UNDERSHAFT Whose character? Yours or mine?

STEPHEN Neither yours nor mine, father, but the best elements in the English national character.

UNDERSHAFT Stephen: Ive found your profession for you. Youre a born journalist. I'll start you with a high-toned weekly review. There!

[Before Stephen can reply Sarah, Barbara, Lomax, and Cusins come in ready for walking. Barbara crosses the room to the window and looks out. Cusins drifts amiably to the armchair. Lomax remains near the door, whilst Sarah comes to her mother. Stephen goes to the smaller writing table and busies himself with his letters.]

SARAH Go and get ready, mamma: the carriage is waiting. [Lady Britomart leaves the room.]

UNDERSHAFT [to Sarah] Good day, my dear. Good afternoon, Mr Lomax.

LOMAX [vaguely] Ahdedoo.

UNDERSHAFT [to Cusins] Quite well after last night, Euripides, eh?

CUSINS As well as can be expected.

UNDERSHAFT Thats right. [To Barbara.] So you are coming to see my death and devastation factory, Barbara?

BARBARA [at the window] You came yesterday to see my salvation factory. I promised you a return visit.

LOMAX [coming forward between Sarah and Undershaft] Youll find it awfully interesting. Ive been through the Woolwich Arsenal; and it gives you a ripping feeling of security, you know, to think of the lot of beggars we could kill if it came to fighting. [To Undershaft, with sudden solemnity.] Still, it must be rather an awful reflection for you, from the religious point of view as it were. Youre getting on, you know, and all that.

SARAH You dont mind Cholly's imbecility, papa, do you?

LOMAX [much taken aback] Oh I say!

UNDERSHAFT Mr Lomax looks at the matter in a very proper spirit, my dear.

LOMAX Just so. Thats all I meant, I assure you.

SARAH Are you coming, Stephen?

STEPHEN Well, I am rather busy—er—[magnanimously] Oh well, yes: I'll come. That is, if there is room for me.

UNDERSHAFT I can take two with me in a little motor I am experimenting with for field use. You wont mind its being rather unfashionable. It's not painted yet; but it's bullet proof.

LOMAX [appalled at the prospect of confronting Wilton Crescent in an unpainted motor] Oh I say!

SARAH The carriage for me, thank you. Barbara doesnt mind what she's seen in.

LOMAX I say, Dolly, old chap: do you really mind the car being a guy? Because of course if you do I'll go in it. Still—

CUSINS I prefer it.

LOMAX Thanks awfully, old man. Come, my ownest. [He hurries out to secure his seat in the carriage. Sarah follows him.]

CUSINS [moodily walking across to Lady Britomart's writing table] Why are we two coming to this Works Department of Hell? that is what I ask myself.

BARBARA I have always thought of it as a sort of pit where lost creatures with blackened faces stirred up smoky fires and were driven and tormented by my father? Is it like that, dad?

UNDERSHAFT [*scandalized*] My dear! It is a spotlessly clean and beautiful hillside town.

CUSINS With a Methodist chapel? Oh do say theres a Methodist chapel.

UNDERSHAFT There are two: a Primitive one and a sophisticated one. There is even an Ethical Society; but it is not much patronized, as my men are all strongly religious. In the High Explosives Sheds they object to the presence of Agnostics as unsafe.

CUSINS And yet they dont object to you!

BARBARA Do they obey all your orders?

UNDERSHAFT I never give them any orders. When I speak to one of them it is "Well, Jones, is the baby doing well? and has Mrs Jones made a good recovery?" "Nicely, thank you, sir." And thats all.

CUSINS But Jones has to be kept in order. How do you maintain discipline among your men?

UNDERSHAFT I dont. They do. You see, the one thing Jones wont stand is any rebellion from the man under him, or any assertion of social equality between the wife of the man with 4 shillings a week less than himself, and Mrs Jones! Of course they all rebel against me, theoretically. Practically, every man of them keeps the man just below him in his place. I never meddle with them. I never bully them. I dont even bully Lazarus. I say that certain things are to be done; but I dont order anybody to do them. I dont say, mind you, that there is no ordering about and snubbing and even bullying. The men snub the boys and order them about; the carmen snub the sweepers; the artisans snub the unskilled laborers; the foremen drive and bully both the laborers and artisans; the assistant engineers find fault with the foremen; the chief engineers drop on the assistants; the departmental managers worry the chiefs; and the clerks have tall hats and hymnbooks and keep up the social tone by refusing to associate on equal terms with anybody. The result is a colossal profit, which comes to me.

CUSINS [*revolted*] You really are a—well, what I was saying yesterday.

BARBARA What was he saying yesterday?

UNDERSHAFT Never mind, my dear. He thinks I have made you unhappy. Have I?

BARBARA Do you think I can be happy in this vulgar silly dress? I! who have worn the uniform. Do you understand what you have done to me? Yesterday I had a man's soul in my hand. I set him in the way of life with his face to salvation. But when we took your money he turned back to drunkenness and derision. [*With intense conviction.*] I will never forgive you that. If I had a child, and you destroyed its body with your explosives—if you murdered Dolly with your horrible guns—I could forgive you if my forgiveness would open the gates of heaven to you. But to take a human soul from me, and turn it into the soul of a wolf! that is worse than any murder.

UNDERSHAFT Does my daughter despair so easily? Can you strike a man to the heart and leave no mark on him?

BARBARA [*her face lighting up*] Oh, you are right: he can never be lost now: where was my faith?

CUSINS Oh, clever clever devil!

BARBARA You may be a devil; but God speaks through you sometimes. [*She takes her father's hands and kisses them.*] You have given me back my happiness: I feel it deep down now, though my spirit is troubled.

UNDERSHAFT You have learnt something. That always feels at first as if you had lost something.

BARBARA Well, take me to the factory of death; and let me learn something more. There must be some truth or other behind all this frightful irony. Come, Dolly. [*She goes out.*]

CUSINS My guardian angel! [*To Undershaft.*] Avaunt! [*He follows Barbara.*]

STEPHEN [*quietly, at the writing table*] You must not mind Cusins, father. He is a very amiable good fellow; but he is a Greek scholar and naturally a little eccentric.

UNDERSHAFT Ah, quite so, Thank you, Stephen. Thank you. [*He goes out.*]

[*Stephen smiles patronizingly; buttons his coat responsibly; and crosses the room to the door. Lady Britomart, dressed for out-of-doors, opens it before he reaches it. She looks round for the others; looks at Stephen; and turns to go without a word.*]

STEPHEN [*embarrassed*] Mother—

LADY BRITOMART Dont be apologetic, Stephen. And dont forget that you have outgrown your mother. [*She goes out.*]

[*Perivale St Andrews lies between two Middlesex hills, half climbing the northern one. It is an almost smokeless town of white walls, roofs of narrow green slates or red tiles, tall trees, domes, campaniles, and slender chimney shafts, beautifully situated and beautiful in itself. The best view of it is obtained from the crest of a slope about half a mile to the east, where the high explosives are dealt with. The foundry lies hidden in the depths between, the tops of its chimneys sprouting like huge skittles into the middle distance. Across the crest runs an emplacement of concrete, with a firestep,[4] and a parapet which suggests a fortification, because there is a huge cannon of the obsolete Woolwich Infant pattern peering across it at the town. The cannon is mounted on an experimental gun carriage: possibly the original model of the Undershaft disappearing rampart gun alluded to by Stephen. The firestep, being a convenient place to sit, is furnished here and there with straw disc cushions; and at one place there is the additional luxury of a fur rug. Barbara is standing on the firestep, looking over the parapet towards the town. On her right is the cannon; on her left the end of a shed raised on piles, with a ladder of three or four steps up to the door, which opens outwards and has a little wooden landing at the threshold, with a fire bucket in the corner of the landing. Several dummy soldiers more or less mutilated, with straw protruding from their gashes, have been shoved out of the way under the landing. A few others are nearly upright against the shed; and one has fallen forward and lies, like a grotesque corpse, on the emplacement. The parapet stops short of the shed, leaving a gap which is the beginning of the path down the hill through the foundry to the town. The rug is on the firestep near this gap. Down on the emplacement behind the cannon is a trolley carrying a huge conical bombshell with a red band painted on it. Further to the right is the door of an office, which, like the shed, is of the lightest possible construction. Cusins arrives by the path from the town.*]

BARBARA Well?

CUSINS Not a ray of hope. Everything perfect! wonderful! real! It only needs a cathedral to be a heavenly city instead of a hellish one.

BARBARA Have you found out whether they have done anything for old Peter Shirley?

CUSINS They have found him a job as gatekeeper and time-keeper. He's frightfully miserable. He calls the time-keeping brainwork, and says he isnt used to it; and his gate lodge is so splendid that he's ashamed to use the rooms, and skulks in the scullery.

4. A platform from which firing takes place.

BARBARA Poor Peter!

[*Stephen arrives from the town. He carries a fieldglass.*]

STEPHEN [*enthusiastically*] Have you two seen the place? Why did you leave us?

CUSINS I wanted to see everything I was not intended to see; and Barbara wanted to make the men talk.

STEPHEN Have you found anything discreditable?

CUSINS No. They call him Dandy Andy and are proud of his being a cunning old rascal; but it's all horribly, frightfully, immorally, unanswerably perfect.

[*Sarah arrives.*]

SARAH Heavens! what a place! [*She crosses to the trolley.*] Did you see the nursing home!? [*She sits down on the shell.*]

STEPHEN Did you see the libraries and schools?

SARAH Did you see the ball room and the banqueting chamber in the Town Hall!?

STEPHEN Have you gone into the insurance fund, the pension fund, the building society, the various applications of cooperation!?

[*Undershaft comes from the office, with a sheaf of telegrams in his hand.*]

UNDERSHAFT Well, have you seen everything? I'm sorry I was called away. [*Indicating the telegrams.*] Good news from Manchuria.

STEPHEN Another Japanese victory?[5]

UNDERSHAFT Oh, I dont know. Which side wins does not concern us here. No: the good news is that the aerial battleship is a tremendous success. At the first trial it has wiped out a fort with three hundred soldiers in it.

CUSINS [*from the platform*] Dummy soldiers?

UNDERSHAFT [*striding across to Stephen and kicking the prostrate dummy brutally out of his way*] No: the real thing.

[*Cusins and Barbara exchange glances. Then Cusins sits on the step and buries his face in his hands. Barbara gravely lays her hand on his shoulder. He looks up at her in whimsical desperation.*]

UNDERSHAFT Well, Stephen, what do you think of the place?

STEPHEN Oh, magnificent. A perfect triumph of modern industry. Frankly, my dear father, I have been a fool: I had no idea of what it all meant: of the wonderful forethought, the power of organization, the administrative capacity, the financial genius, the colossal capital it represents. I have been repeating to myself as I came through your streets "Peace hath her victories no less renowned than War." I have only one misgiving about it all.

UNDERSHAFT Out with it.

STEPHEN Well, I cannot help thinking that all this provision for every want of your workmen may sap their independence and weaken their sense of responsibility. And greatly as we enjoyed our tea at that splendid restaurant—how they gave us all that luxury and cake and jam and cream for threepence I really cannot imagine!—still you must remember that restaurants break up home life. Look at the continent, for instance! Are you sure so much pampering is really good for the men's characters?

UNDERSHAFT Well you see, my dear boy, when you are organizing civilization you have to make up your mind whether trouble and anxiety are good things or not. If you decide that they are, then, I take it, you simply dont organize civilization; and

---

5. The Russo-Japanese War was fought between 1904 and 1905, with victory going to Japan.

there you are, with trouble and anxiety enough to make us all angels! But if you decide the other way, you may as well go through with it. However, Stephen, our characters are safe here. A sufficient dose of anxiety is always provided by the fact that we may be blown to smithereens at any moment.

SARAH By the way, papa, where do you make the explosives?

UNDERSHAFT In separate little sheds, like that one. When one of them blows up, it costs very little; and only the people quite close to it are killed.

[*Stephen, who is quite close to it, looks at it rather scaredly, and moves away quickly to the cannon. At the same moment the door of the shed is thrown abruptly open; and a foreman in overalls and list slippers*[6] *comes out on the little landing and holds the door for Lomax, who appears in the doorway.*]

LOMAX [*with studied coolness*] My good fellow: you neednt get into a state of nerves. Nothing's going to happen to you; and I suppose it wouldnt be the end of the world if anything did. A little bit of British pluck is what you want, old chap. [*He descends and strolls across to Sarah.*]

UNDERSHAFT [*to the foreman*] Anything wrong, Bilton?

BILTON [*with ironic calm*] Gentleman walked into the high explosives shed and lit a cigaret, sir: thats all.

UNDERSHAFT Ah, quite so. [*Going over to Lomax*] Do you happen to remember what you did with the match?

LOMAX Oh come! I'm not a fool. I took jolly good care to blow it out before I chucked it away.

BILTON The top of it was red hot inside, sir.

LOMAX Well, suppose it was! I didn't chuck it into any of your messes.

UNDERSHAFT Think no more of it, Mr Lomax. By the way, would you mind lending me your matches.

LOMAX [*offering his box*] Certainly.

UNDERSHAFT Thanks. [*He pockets the matches.*]

LOMAX [*lecturing to the company generally*] You know, these high explosives dont go off like gunpowder, except when theyre in a gun. When theyre spread loose, you can put a match to them without the least risk: they just burn quietly like a bit of paper. [*Warming to the scientific interest of the subject.*] Did you know that, Undershaft? Have you ever tried?

UNDERSHAFT Not on a large scale, Mr Lomax. Bilton will give you a sample of gun cotton when you are leaving if you ask him. You can experiment with it at home. [*Bilton looks puzzled.*]

SARAH Bilton will do nothing of the sort, papa. I suppose it's your business to blow up the Russians and Japs; but you might really stop short of blowing up poor Cholly. [*Bilton gives it up and retires into the shed.*]

LOMAX My ownest, there is no danger. [*He sits beside her on the shell.*]

[*Lady Britomart arrives from the town with a bouquet.*]

LADY BRITOMART [*impetuously*] Andrew: you shouldnt have let me see this place.

UNDERSHAFT Why, my dear?

LADY BRITOMART Never mind why: you shouldnt have: thats all. To think of all that [*indicating the town*] being yours! and that you have kept it to yourself all these years!

UNDERSHAFT It does not belong to me. I belong to it. It is the Undershaft inheritance.

---

6. Cloth overshoe worn to prevent friction that could cause sparks.

LADY BRITOMART It is not. Your ridiculous cannons and that noisy banging foundry may be the Undershaft inheritance; but all that plate and linen, all that furniture and those houses and orchards and gardens belong to us. They belong to me: they are not a man's business. I wont give them up. You must be out of your senses to throw them all away; and if you persist in such folly, I will call in a doctor.

UNDERSHAFT [stooping to smell the bouquet] Where did you get the flowers, my dear?

LADY BRITOMART Your men presented them to me in your William Morris Labor Church.

CUSINS Oh! It needed only that. A Labor Church! [He mounts the firestep distractedly, and leans with his elbows on the parapet, turning his back to them.]

LADY BRITOMART Yes, with Morris's words in mosaic letters ten feet high round the dome. NO MAN IS GOOD ENOUGH TO BE ANOTHER MAN'S MASTER. The cynicism of it!

UNDERSHAFT It shocked the men at first, I am afraid. But now they take no more notice of it than of the ten commandments in church.

LADY BRITOMART Andrew: you are trying to put me off the subject of the inheritance by profane jokes. Well, you shant. I dont ask it any longer for Stephen: he has inherited far too much of your perversity to be fit for it. But Barbara has rights as well as Stephen. Why should not Adolphus succeed to the inheritance? I could manage the town for him; and he can look after the cannons, if they are really necessary.

UNDERSHAFT I should ask nothing better if Adolphus were a foundling. He is exactly the sort of new blood that is wanted in English business. But he's not a foundling; and theres an end of it. [He makes for the office door.]

CUSINS [turning to them] Not quite. [They all turn and stare at him.]. I think—Mind! I am not committing myself in any way as to my future course—but I think the foundling difficulty can be got over. [He jumps down to the emplacement.]

UNDERSHAFT [coming back to him] What do you mean?

CUSINS Well, I have something to say which is in the nature of a confession.

SARAH
LADY BRITOMART
BARBARA } Confession!
STEPHEN } Oh I say!
LOMAX

CUSINS Yes, a confession. Listen, all. Until I met Barbara I thought myself in the main an honorable, truthful man, because I wanted the approval of my conscience more than I wanted anything else. But the moment I saw Barbara, I wanted her far more than the approval of my conscience.

LADY BRITOMART Adolphus!

CUSINS It is true. You accused me yourself, Lady Brit, of joining the Army to worship Barbara; and so I did. She bought my soul like a flower at a street corner; but she bought it for herself.

UNDERSHAFT What! Not for Dionysos or another?

CUSINS Dionysos and all the others are in herself. I adored what was divine in her, and was therefore a true worshipper. But I was romantic about her too. I thought she was a woman of the people, and that a marriage with a professor of Greek would be far beyond the wildest social ambitions of her rank.

LADY BRITOMART Adolphus!!

LOMAX Oh I say!!!

CUSINS When I learnt the horrible truth—

LADY BRITOMART What do you mean by the horrible truth, pray?

CUSINS That she was enormously rich; that her grandfather was an earl; that her father was the Prince of Darkness—

UNDERSHAFT Chut!

CUSINS —and that I was only an adventurer trying to catch a rich wife, then I stooped to deceive her about my birth.

BARBARA [rising] Dolly!

LADY BRITOMART Your birth! Now Adolphus, dont dare to make up a wicked story for the sake of these wretched cannons. Remember: I have seen photographs of your parents; and the Agent General for South Western Australia knows them personally and has assured me that they are most respectable married people.

CUSINS So they are in Australia; but here they are outcasts. Their marriage is legal in Australia, but not in England. My mother is my father's deceased wife's sister;[7] and in this island I am consequently a foundling. [Sensation.]

BARBARA Silly! [She climbs to the cannon, and leans, listening, in the angle it makes with the parapet.]

CUSINS Is the subterfuge good enough, Machiavelli?

UNDERSHAFT [thoughtfully] Biddy: this may be a way out of the difficulty.

LADY BRITOMART Stuff! A man cant make cannons any the better for being his own cousin instead of his proper self. [She sits down on the rug with a bounce that expresses her downright contempt for their casuistry.]

UNDERSHAFT [to Cusins] You are an educated man. That is against the tradition.

CUSINS Once in ten thousand times it happens that the schoolboy is a born master of what they try to teach him. Greek has not destroyed my mind: it has nourished it. Besides, I did not learn it at an English public school.

UNDERSHAFT Hm! Well, I cannot afford to be too particular: you have cornered the foundling market. Let it pass. You are eligible, Euripides: you are eligible.

BARBARA Dolly: yesterday morning, when Stephen told us all about the tradition, you became very silent; and you have been strange and excited ever since. Were you thinking of your birth then?

CUSINS When the finger of Destiny suddenly points at a man in the middle of his breakfast, it makes him thoughtful.

UNDERSHAFT Aha! You have had your eye on the business, my young friend, have you?

CUSINS Take care! There is an abyss of moral horror between me and your accursed aerial battleships.

UNDERSHAFT Never mind the abyss for the present. Let us settle the practical details and leave your final decision open. You know that you will have to change your name. Do you object to that?

CUSINS Would any man named Adolphus—any man called Dolly!—object to be called something else?

UNDERSHAFT Good. Now, as to money! I propose to treat you handsomely from the beginning. You shall start at a thousand a year.

CUSINS [with sudden heat, his spectacles twinkling with mischief] A thousand! You dare offer a miserable thousand to the son-in-law of a millionaire! No, by Heavens,

---

7. English law forbad such marriages until 1866.

Machiavelli! you shall not cheat me. You cannot do without me; and I can do without you. I must have two thousand five hundred a year for two years. At the end of that time, if I am a failure, I go. But if I am a success, and stay on, you must give me the other five thousand.

UNDERSHAFT What other five thousand?

CUSINS To make the two years up to five thousand a year. The two thousand five hundred is only half pay in case I should turn out a failure. The third year I must have ten per cent on the profits.

UNDERSHAFT [*taken aback*] Ten per cent! Why, man, do you know what my profits are?

CUSINS Enormous, I hope: otherwise I shall require twenty-five per cent.

UNDERSHAFT But, Mr Cusins, this is a serious matter of business. You are not bringing any capital into the concern.

CUSINS What! no capital! Is my mastery of Greek no capital? Is my access to the subtlest thought, the loftiest poetry yet attained by humanity, no capital? My character! my intellect! my life! my career! what Barbara calls my soul! are these no capital? Say another word; and I double my salary.

UNDERSHAFT Be reasonable—

CUSINS [*peremptorily*] Mr Undershaft: you have my terms. Take them or leave them.

UNDERSHAFT [*recovering himself*] Very well. I note your terms; and I offer you half.

CUSINS [*disgusted*] Half!

UNDERSHAFT [*firmly*] Half.

CUSINS You call yourself a gentleman; and you offer me half!!

UNDERSHAFT I do not call myself a gentleman; but I offer you half.

CUSINS This to your future partner! your successor! your son-in-law!

BARBARA You are selling your own soul, Dolly, not mine. Leave me out of the bargain, please.

UNDERSHAFT Come! I will go a step further for Barbara's sake. I will give you three fifths; but that is my last word.

CUSINS Done!

LOMAX Done in the eye! Why, *I* get only eight hundred, you know.

CUSINS By the way, Mac, I am a classical scholar, not an arithmetical one. Is three fifths more than half or less?

UNDERSHAFT More, of course.

CUSINS I would have taken two hundred and fifty. How you can succeed in business when you are willing to pay all that money to a University don[8] who is obviously not worth a junior clerk's wages!—well! What will Lazarus say?

UNDERSHAFT Lazarus is a gentle romantic Jew who cares for nothing but string quartets and stalls at fashionable theatres. He will be blamed for your rapacity in money matters, poor fellow! as he has hitherto been blamed for mine. You are a shark of the first order, Euripides. So much the better for the firm!

BARBARA Is the bargain closed, Dolly? Does your soul belong to him now?

CUSINS No: the price is settled: that is all. The real tug of war is still to come. What about the moral question?

LADY BRITOMART There is no moral question in the matter at all, Adolphus. You must simply sell cannons and weapons to people whose cause is right and just, and refuse them to foreigners and criminals.

8. Professor.

UNDERSHAFT [*determinedly*] No: none of that. You must keep the true faith of an Armorer, or you dont come in here.

CUSINS What on earth is the true faith of an Armorer?

UNDERSHAFT To give arms to all men who offer an honest price for them, without respect of persons or principles: to aristocrat and republican, to Nihilist and Tsar, to Capitalist and Socialist, to Protestant and Catholic, to burglar and policeman, to black man, white man and yellow man, to all sorts and conditions, all nationalities, all faiths, all follies, all causes and all crimes. The first Undershaft wrote up in his shop IF GOD GAVE THE HAND, LET NOT MAN WITHHOLD THE SWORD. The second wrote up ALL HAVE THE RIGHT TO FIGHT: NONE HAVE THE RIGHT TO JUDGE. The third wrote up TO MAN THE WEAPON: TO HEAVEN THE VICTORY. The fourth had no literary turn; so he did not write up anything; but he sold cannons to Napoleon under the nose of George the Third. The fifth wrote up PEACE SHALL NOT PREVAIL SAVE WITH A SWORD IN HER HAND. The sixth, my master, was the best of all. He wrote up NOTHING IS EVER DONE IN THIS WORLD UNTIL MEN ARE PREPARED TO KILL ONE ANOTHER IF IT IS NOT DONE. After that, there was nothing left for the seventh to say. So he wrote up, simply, UNASHAMED.

CUSINS My good Machiavelli, I shall certainly write something up on the wall; only, as I shall write it in Greek, you wont be able to read it. But as to your Armorer's faith, if I take my neck out of the noose of my own morality I am not going to put it into the noose of yours. I shall sell cannons to whom I please and refuse them to whom I please. So there!

UNDERSHAFT From the moment when you become Andrew Undershaft, you will never do as you please again. Dont come here lusting for power, young man.

CUSINS If power were my aim I should not come here for it. You have no power.

UNDERSHAFT None of my own, certainly.

CUSINS I have more power than you, more will. You do not drive this place: it drives you. And what drives the place?

UNDERSHAFT [*enigmatically*] A will of which I am a part.

BARBABA [*startled*] Father! Do you know what you are saying; or are you laying a snare for my soul?

CUSINS Dont listen to his metaphysics, Barbara. The place is driven by the most rascally part of society, the money hunters, the pleasure hunters, the military promotion hunters; and he is their slave.

UNDERSHAFT Not necessarily. Remember the Armorer's Faith. I will take an order from a good man as cheerfully as from a bad one. If you good people prefer preaching and shirking to buying my weapons and fighting the rascals, dont blame me. I can make cannons: I cannot make courage and conviction. Bah! you tire me, Euripides, with your morality mongering. Ask Barbara: she understands. [*He suddenly reaches up and takes Barbara's hands, looking powerfully into her eyes.*] Tell him, my love, what power really means.

BARBARA [*hypnotized*] Before I joined the Salvation Army, I was in my own power; and the consequence was that I never knew what to do with myself. When I joined it, I had not time enough for all the things I had to do.

UNDERSHAFT [*approvingly*] Just so. And why was that, do you suppose?

BARBARA Yesterday I should have said, because I was in the power of God. [*She resumes her self-possession, withdrawing her hands from his with a power equal to his own.*] But you came and shewed me that I was in the power of Bodger and Undershaft. Today I feel—oh! how can I put it into words? Sarah: do you remember the earthquake at Cannes, when we were little children?—how little the surprise of the first shock mattered compared to the dread and horror of waiting for the second? That is how I feel in this place today. I stood on the rock I thought eternal; and without a word of warning it reeled and crumbled under me. I was safe with an infinite wisdom watching me, an army marching to Salvation with me; and in a moment, at a stroke of your pen in a cheque book, I stood alone; and the heavens were empty. That was the first shock of the earthquake: I am waiting for the second.

UNDERSHAFT Come, come, my daughter! dont make too much of your little tinpot tragedy. What do we do here when we spend years of work and thought and thousands of pounds of solid cash on a new gun or an aerial battleship that turns out just a hairsbreadth wrong after all? Scrap it. Scrap it without wasting another hour or another pound on it. Well, you have made for yourself something that you call a morality or a religion or what not. It doesnt fit the facts. Well, scrap it. Scrap it and get one that does fit. That is what is wrong with the world at present. It scraps its obsolete steam engines and dynamos; but it wont scrap its old prejudices and its old moralities and its old religions and its old political constitutions. Whats the result? In machinery it does very well; but in morals and religion and politics it is working at a loss that brings it nearer bankruptcy every year. Dont persist in that folly. If your old religion broke down yesterday, get a newer and a better one for tomorrow.

BARBARA Oh how gladly I would take a better one to my soul! But you offer me a worse one. [Turning on him with sudden vehemence.] Justify yourself: shew me some light through the darkness of this dreadful place, with its beautifully clean workshops, and respectable workmen, and model homes.

UNDERSHAFT Cleanliness and respectability do not need justification, Barbara: they justify themselves. I see no darkness here, no dreadfulness. In your Salvation shelter I saw poverty, misery, cold and hunger. You gave them bread and treacle and dreams of heaven. I give from thirty shillings a week to twelve thousand a year. They find their own dreams; but I look after the drainage.

BARBARA And their souls?

UNDERSHAFT I save their souls just as I saved yours.

BARBARA [revolted] You saved my soul! What do you mean?

UNDERSHAFT I fed you and clothed you and housed you. I took care that you should have money enough to live handsomely—more than enough; so that you could be wasteful, careless, generous. That saved your soul from the seven deadly sins.

BARBARA [bewildered] The seven deadly sins!

UNDERSHAFT Yes, the deadly seven. [Counting on his fingers.] Food, clothing, firing, rent, taxes, respectability and children. Nothing can lift those seven millstones from Man's neck but money; and the spirit cannot soar until the mill stones are lifted. I lifted them from your spirit. I enabled Barbara to become Major Barbara; and I saved her from the crime of poverty.

CUSINS Do you call poverty a crime?

UNDERSHAFT The worst of crimes. All the other crimes are virtues beside it: all the other dishonors are chivalry itself by comparison. Poverty blights whole cities; spreads horrible pestilences; strikes dead the very souls of all who come within sight, sound, or smell of it. What you call crime is nothing: a murder here and a theft there, a blow now and a curse then: what do they matter? they are only the accidents and illnesses of life: there are not fifty genuine professional criminals in London. But there are millions of poor people, abject people, dirty people, ill fed, ill clothed people. They poison us morally and physically: they kill the happiness of society: they force us to do away with our own liberties and to organize unnatural cruelties for fear they should rise against us and drag us down into their abyss. Only fools fear crime: we all fear poverty. Pah! [turning on Barbara] you talk of your half-saved ruffian in West Ham: you accuse me of dragging his soul back to perdition. Well, bring him to me here; and I will drag his soul back again to salvation for you. Not by words and dreams; but by thirtyeight shillings a week, a sound house in a handsome street, and a permanent job. In three weeks he will have a fancy waistcoat; in three months a tall hat and a chapel sitting; before the end of the year he will shake hands with a duchess at a Primrose League meeting, and join the Conservative Party.[9]

BARBARA And will he be the better for that?

UNDERSHAFT You know he will. Dont be a hypocrite, Barbara. He will be better fed, better housed, better clothed, better behaved; and his children will be pounds heavier and bigger. That will be better than an American cloth mattress in a shelter, chopping firewood, eating bread and treacle, and being forced to kneel down from time to time to thank heaven for it: knee drill, I think you call it. It is cheap work converting starving men with a Bible in one hand and a slice of bread in the other. I will undertake to convert West Ham to Mahometanism on the same terms. Try your hand on my men: their souls are hungry because their bodies are full.

BARBARA And leave the east end to starve?

UNDERSHAFT [his energetic tone dropping into one of bitter and brooding remembrance] I was an east ender.[1] I moralized and starved until one day I swore that I would be a full-fed free man at all costs; that nothing should stop me except a bullet, neither reason nor morals nor the lives of other men. I said "Thou shalt starve ere I starve"; and with that word I became free and great. I was a dangerous man until I had my will: now I am a useful, beneficent, kindly person. That is the history of most self-made millionaires, I fancy. When it is the history of every Englishman we shall have an England worth living in.

LADY BRITOMART Stop making speeches, Andrew. This is not the place for them.

UNDERSHAFT [punctured] My dear: I have no other means of conveying my ideas.

LADY BRITOMART Your ideas are nonsense. You got on because you were selfish and unscrupulous.

UNDERSHAFT Not at all. I had the strongest scruples about poverty and starvation. Your moralists are quite unscrupulous about both: they make virtues of them. I had rather be a thief than a pauper. I had rather be a murderer than a slave. I dont want to be either; but if you force the alternative on me, then, by Heaven, I'll chose the braver and more moral one. I hate poverty and slavery worse than any other crimes whatsoever. And let me tell you this. Poverty and slavery have stood up for centuries to your sermons and leading articles: they will not stand up to my machine guns. Dont preach at them: dont reason with them. Kill them.

BARBARA Killing. Is that your remedy for everything?

UNDERSHAFT It is the final test of conviction, the only lever strong enough to overturn a social system, the only way of saying Must. Let six hundred and seventy fools loose in the streets; and three policemen can scatter them. But huddle

---

9. One of the two major British political parties, in power almost continuously between the late 1880s and 1906. The Primrose League, founded in 1883, was a political movement designed to build support for the Conservatives.

1. From the working-class East End of London.

them together in a certain house in Westminster; and let them go through certain ceremonies and call themselves certain names until at last they get the courage to kill; and your six hundred and seventy fools become a government.[2] Your pious mob fills up ballot papers and imagines it is governing its masters; but the ballot paper that really governs is the paper that has a bullet wrapped up in it.

CUSINS That is perhaps why, like most intelligent people, I never vote.

UNDERSHAFT Vote! Bah! When you vote, you only change the names of the cabinet. When you shoot, you pull down governments, inaugurate new epochs, abolish old orders and set up new. Is that historically true, Mr Learned Man, or is it not?

CUSINS It is historically true. I loathe having to admit it. I repudiate your sentiments. I abhor your nature. I defy you in every possible way. Still, it is true. But it ought not to be true.

UNDERSHAFT Ought! ought! ought! ought! ought! Are you going to spend your life saying ought, like the rest of our moralists? Turn your oughts into shalls, man. Come and make explosives with me. Whatever can blow men up can blow society up. The history of the world is the history of those who had courage enough to embrace this truth. Have you the courage to embrace it, Barbara?

LADY BRITOMART Barbara: I positively forbid you to listen to your father's abominable wickedness. And you, Adolphus, ought to know better than to go about saying that wrong things are true. What does it matter whether they are true if they are wrong?

UNDERSHAFT What does it matter whether they are wrong if they are true?

LADY BRITOMART [rising] Children: come home instantly. Andrew: I am exceedingly sorry I allowed you to call on us. You are wickeder than ever. Come at once.

BARBARA [shaking her head] It's no use running away from wicked people, mamma.

LADY BRITOMART It is every use. It shews your disapprobation of them.

BARBARA It does not save them.

LADY BRITOMART I can see that you are going to disobey me. Sarah: are you coming home or are you not?

SARAH I daresay it's very wicked of papa to make cannons; but I dont think I shall cut him on that account.

LOMAX [pouring oil on the troubled waters] The fact is, you know, there is a certain amount of tosh about this notion of wickedness. It doesnt work. You must look at facts. Not that I would say a word in favor of anything wrong; but then, you see, all sorts of chaps are always doing all sorts of things; and we have to fit them in somehow, dont you know. What I mean is that you cant go cutting everybody; and thats about what it comes to. [Their rapt attention to his eloquence makes him nervous.] Perhaps I dont make myself clear.

LADY BRITOMART You are lucidity itself, Charles. Because Andrew is successful and has plenty of money to give to Sarah, you will flatter him and encourage him in his wickedness.

LOMAX [unruffled] Well, where the carcase is, there will the eagles be gathered, dont you know. [To Undershaft.] Eh? What?

UNDERSHAFT Precisely. By the way, may I call you Charles?

LOMAX Delighted. Cholly is the usual ticket.

UNDERSHAFT [to Lady Britomart] Biddy—

LADY BRITOMART [violently] Dont dare call me Biddy. Charles Lomax: you are a

---

2. There are now 651 members of the House of Commons.

fool. Adolphus Cusins: you are a Jesuit.[3] Stephen: you are a prig. Barbara: you are a lunatic. Andrew: you are a vulgar tradesman. Now you all know my opinion; and my conscience is clear, at all events. [*She sits down with a vehemence that the rug fortunately softens.*]

UNDERSHAFT My dear: you are the incarnation of morality. [*She snorts.*] Your conscience is clear and your duty done when you have called everybody names. Come, Euripides! it is getting late; and we all want to go home. Make up your mind.

CUSINS Understand this, you old demon——

LADY BRITOMART Adolphus!

UNDERSHAFT Let him alone, Biddy. Proceed, Euripides.

CUSINS You have me in a horrible dilemma. I want Barbara.

UNDERSHAFT Like all young men, you greatly exaggerate the difference between one young woman and another.

BARBARA Quite true, Dolly.

CUSINS I also want to avoid being a rascal.

UNDERSHAFT [*with biting contempt*] You lust for personal righteousness, for self-approval, for what you call a good conscience, for what Barbara calls salvation, for what I call patronizing people who are not so lucky as yourself.

CUSINS I do not: all the poet in me recoils from being a good man. But there are things in me that I must reckon with. Pity——

UNDERSHAFT Pity! The scavenger of misery.

CUSINS Well, love.

UNDERSHAFT I know. You love the needy and the outcast: you love the oppressed races, the negro, the Indian ryot,[4] the underdog everywhere. Do you love the Japanese? Do you love the French? Do you love the English?

CUSINS No. Every true Englishman detests the English. We are the wickedest nation on earth; and our success is a moral horror.

UNDERSHAFT That is what comes of your gospel of love, is it?

CUSINS May I not love even my father-in-law?

UNDERSHAFT Who wants your love, man? By what right do you take the liberty of offering it to me? I will have your due heed and respect, or I will kill you. But your love! Damn your impertinence!

CUSINS [*grinning*] I may not be able to control my affections, Mac.

UNDERSHAFT You are fencing, Euripides. You are weakening: your grip is slipping. Come! try your last weapon. Pity and love have broken in your hand: forgiveness is still left.

CUSINS No: forgiveness is a beggar's refuge. I am with you there: we must pay our debts.

UNDERSHAFT Well said. Come! you will suit me. Remember the words of Plato.

CUSINS [*starting*] Plato! You dare quote Plato to me!

UNDERSHAFT Plato says, my friend, that society cannot be saved until either the Professors of Greek take to making gunpowder, or else the makers of gunpowder become Professors of Greek.

CUSINS Oh, tempter, cunning tempter!

UNDERSHAFT Come! choose, man, choose.

CUSINS But perhaps Barbara will not marry me if I make the wrong choice.

BARBARA Perhaps not.

CUSINS [*desperately perplexed*] You hear!

3. A priest of the Society of Jesus a Catholic religious order; in largely Protestant Britain, a byword for false, or casuistical, reasoning.
4. Peasant.

BARBARA Father: do you love nobody?

UNDERSHAFT I love my best friend.

LADY BRITOMART And who is that, pray?

UNDERSHAFT My bravest enemy. That is the man who keeps me up to the mark.

CUSINS You know, the creature is really a sort of poet in his way. Suppose he is a great man, after all!

UNDERSHAFT Suppose you stop talking and make up your mind, my young friend.

CUSINS But you are driving me against my nature. I hate war.

UNDERSHAFT Hatred is the coward's revenge for being intimidated. Dare you make war on war? Here are the means: my friend Mr Lomax is sitting on them.

LOMAX [springing up] Oh I say! You dont mean that this thing is loaded, do you? My ownest: come off it.

SARAH [sitting placidly on the shell] If I am to be blown up, the more thoroughly it is done the better. Dont fuss, Cholly.

LOMAX [to Undershaft, strongly remonstrant] Your own daughter, you know!

UNDERSHAFT So I see. [To Cusins.] Well, my friend, may we expect you here at six tomorrow morning?

CUSINS [firmly] Not on any account. I will see the whole establishment blown up with its own dynamite before I will get up at five. My hours are healthy, rational hours: eleven to five.

UNDERSHAFT Come when you please: before a week you will come at six and stay until I turn you out for the sake of your health. [Calling.] Bilton! [He turns to Lady Britomart, who rises.] My dear: let us leave these two young people to themselves for a moment. [Bilton comes from the shed.] I am going to take you through the gun cotton shed.

BILTON [barring the way] You cant take anything explosive in here, sir.

LADY BRITOMART What do you mean? Are you alluding to me?

BILTON [unmoved] No, maam. Mr Undershaft has the other gentleman's matches in his pocket.

LADY BRITOMART [abruptly] Oh! I beg your pardon. [She goes into the shed.]

UNDERSHAFT Quite right, Bilton, quite right: here you are. [He gives Bilton the box of matches.] Come, Stephen. Come, Charles. Bring Sarah. [He passes into the shed.]
    [Bilton opens the box and deliberately drops the matches into the fire-bucket.]

LOMAX Oh! I say [Bilton stolidly hands him the empty box.] Infernal nonsense! Pure scientific ignorance! [He goes in.]

SARAH Am I all right, Bilton?

BILTON Youll have to put on list slippers, miss: thats all. Weve got em inside. [She goes in.]

STEPHEN [very seriously to Cusins] Dolly, old fellow, think. Think before you decide. Do you feel that you are a sufficiently practical man? It is a huge undertaking, an enormous responsibility. All this mass of business will be Greek to you.

CUSINS Oh, I think it will be much less difficult than Greek.

STEPHEN Well, I just want to say this before I leave you to yourselves. Dont let anything I have said about right and wrong prejudice you against this great chance in life. I have satisfied myself that the business is one of the highest character and a credit to our country. [Emotionally.] I am very proud of my father. I—[Unable to proceed, he presses Cusins' hand and goes hastily into the shed, followed by Bilton.]
    [Barbara and Cusins, left alone together, look at one another silently.]

CUSINS Barbara: I am going to accept this offer.

BARBARA I thought you would.

CUSINS You understand, dont you, that I had to decide without consulting you. If I had thrown the burden of the choice on you, you would sooner or later have despised me for it.

BARBARA Yes: I did not want you to sell your soul for me any more than for this inheritance.

CUSINS It is not the sale of my soul that troubles me: I have sold it too often to care about that. I have sold it for a professorship. I have sold it for an income. I have sold it to escape being imprisoned for refusing to pay taxes for hangmen's ropes and unjust wars and things that I abhor. What is all human conduct but the daily and hourly sale of our souls for trifles? What I am now selling it for is neither money nor position nor comfort, but for reality and for power.

BARBARA You know that you will have no power, and that he has none.

CUSINS I know. It is not for myself alone. I want to make power for the world.

BARBARA I want to make power for the world too; but it must be spiritual power.

CUSINS I think all power is spiritual: these cannons will not go off by themselves. I have tried to make spiritual power by teaching Greek. But the world can never be really touched by a dead language and a dead civilization. The people must have power; and the people cannot have Greek. Now the power that is made here can be wielded by all men.

BARBARA Power to burn women's houses down and kill their sons and tear their husbands to pieces.

CUSINS You cannot have power for good without having power for evil too. Even mother's milk nourishes murderers as well as heroes. This power which only tears men's bodies to pieces has never been so horribly abused as the intellectual power, the imaginative power, the poetic, religious power that can enslave men's souls. As a teacher of Greek I gave the intellectual man weapons against the common man. I now want to give the common man weapons against the intellectual man. I love the common people. I want to arm them against the lawyers, the doctors, the priests, the literary men, the professors, the artists, and the politicians, who, once in authority, are more disastrous and tyrannical than all the fools, rascals, and impostors. I want a power simple enough for common men to use, yet strong enough to force the intellectual oligarchy to use its genius for the general good.

BARBARA Is there no higher power than that [pointing to the shell]?

CUSINS Yes; but that power can destroy the higher powers just as a tiger can destroy a man: therefore Man must master that power first. I admitted this when the Turks and Greeks were last at war.[5] My best pupil went out to fight for Hellas. My parting gift to him was not a copy of Plato's Republic, but a revolver and a hundred Undershaft cartridges. The blood of every Turk he shot—if he shot any—is on my head as well as on Undershaft's. That act committed me to this place for ever. Your father's challenge has beaten me. Dare I make war on war? I dare. I must. I will. And now, is it all over between us?

BARBARA [touched by his evident dread of her answer] Silly baby Dolly! How could it be!

CUSINS [overjoyed] Then you—you—you—Oh for my drum! [He flourishes imaginary drumsticks.]

BARBARA [angered by his levity] Take care, Dolly, take care. Oh, if only I could get away from you and from father and from it all! if I could have the wings of a dove and fly away to heaven!

---

5. Turkey declared war on Greece in 1897, following revolts against Turkish rule in Crete; Greece was rescued by the European powers.

CUSINS And leave me!

BARBARA Yes, you, and all the other naughty mischievous children of men. But I cant. I was happy in the Salvation Army for a moment. I escaped from the world into a paradise of enthusiasm and prayer and soul saving; but the moment our money ran short, it all came back to Bodger: it was he who saved our people: he, and the Prince of Darkness, my papa. Undershaft and Bodger: their hands stretch everywhere: when we feed a starving fellow creature, it is with their bread, because there is no other bread; when we tend the sick, it is in the hospitals they endow; if we turn from the churches they build, we must kneel on the stones of the streets they pave. As long as that lasts, there is no getting away from them. Turning our backs on Bodger and Undershaft is turning our backs on life.

CUSINS I thought you were determined to turn your back on the wicked side of life.

BARBARA There is no wicked side: life is all one. And I never wanted to shirk my share in whatever evil must be endured, whether it be sin or suffering. I wish I could cure you of middle-class ideas, Dolly.

CUSINS [gasping] Middle cl—! A snub! A social snub to me! from the daughter of a foundling!

BARBARA That is why I have no class, Dolly: I come straight out of the heart of the whole people. If I were middle-class I should turn my back on my father's business; and we should both live in an artistic drawing room, with you reading the reviews in one corner, and I in the other at the piano, playing Schumann: both very superior persons, and neither of us a bit of use. Sooner than that, I would sweep out the guncotton shed, or be one of Bodger's barmaids. Do you know what would have happened if you had refused papa's offer?

CUSINS I wonder!

BARBARA I should have given you up and married the man who accepted it. After all, my dear old mother has more sense than any of you. I felt like her when I saw this place—felt that I must have it—that never, never, never could I let it go; only she thought it was the houses and the kitchen ranges and the linen and china, when it was really all the human souls to be saved: not weak souls in starved bodies, sobbing with gratitude for a scrap of bread and treacle, but fullfed, quarrelsome, snobbish, uppish creatures, all standing on their little rights and dignities, and thinking that my father ought to be greatly obliged to them for making so much money for him—and so he ought. That is where salvation is really wanted. My father shall never throw it in my teeth again that my converts were bribed with bread. [She is transfigured.] I have got rid of the bribe of bread. I have got rid of the bribe of heaven. Let God's work be done for its own sake: the work he had to create us to do because it cannot be done except by living men and women. When I die, let him be in my debt, not I in his; and let me forgive him as becomes a woman of my rank.

CUSINS Then the way of life lies through the factory of death?

BARBARA Yes, through the raising of hell to heaven and of man to God, through the unveiling of an eternal light in the Valley of The Shadow. [Seizing him with both hands.] Oh, did you think my courage would never come back? did you believe that I was a deserter? that I, who have stood in the streets, and taken my people to my heart, and talked of the holiest and greatest things with them, could ever turn back and chatter foolishly to fashionable people about nothing in a drawing room? Never, never, never, never: Major Barbara will die with the colors. Oh! and I have my dear little Dolly boy still; and he has found me my place and my work. Glory Hallelujah! [She kisses him.]

CUSINS My dearest: consider my delicate health. I cannot stand as much happiness as you can.

BARBARA Yes: it is not easy work being in love with me, is it? But it's good for you. [*She runs to the shed, and calls, childlike.*] Mamma! Mamma! [*Bilton comes out of the shed, followed by Undershaft.*] I want Mamma.

UNDERSHAFT She is taking off her list slippers, dear. [*He passes on to Cusins.*] Well? What does she say?

CUSINS She has gone right up into the skies.

LADY BRITOMART [*coming from the shed and stopping on the steps, obstructing Sarah, who follows with Lomax. Barbara clutches like a baby at her mother's skirt.*] Barbara: when will you learn to be independent and to act and think for yourself? I know as well as possible what that cry of "Mamma, Mamma," means. Always running to me!

SARAH [*touching Lady Britomart's ribs with her finger tips and imitating a bicycle horn*] Pip! pip!

LADY BRITOMART [*highly indignant*] How dare you say Pip! pip! to me, Sarah? You are both very naughty children. What do you want, Barbara?

BARBARA I want a house in the village to live in with Dolly. [*Dragging at the skirt.*] Come and tell me which one to take.

UNDERSHAFT [*to Cusins*] Six o'clock tomorrow morning, Euripides.

THE END

COMPANION READING

Emmeline Pankhurst: Address[1]

Mrs. Hepburn, Ladies and Gentlemen: Many people come to Hartford to address meetings as advocates of some reform. Tonight it is not to advocate a reform that I address a meeting in Hartford. I do not come here as an advocate, because whatever position the suffrage movement may occupy in the United States of America, in England it has passed beyond the realm of advocacy and it has entered into the sphere of practical politics. It has become the subject of revolution and civil war, and so tonight I am not here to advocate woman suffrage. American suffragists can do that very well for themselves. I am here as a soldier who has temporarily left the field of battle in order to explain—it seems strange it should have to be explained—what civil war is like when civil war is waged by women. I am not only here as a soldier temporarily absent from the field of battle; I am here—and that, I think, is the strangest part of my coming—I am here as a person who, according to the law courts of my country, it has been decided, is of no value to the community at all; and I am adjudged because of my life to be a dangerous person, under sentence of penal servitude in a convict prison. So you see there is some special interest in hearing so unusu-

1. Emmeline Pankhurst (1858–1928) founded the Women's Social and Political Union (WSPU) in 1903, an organization devoted to the cause of female suffrage. From 1906 onward members of the organization, who were known as "suffragettes," began to engage in mildly militant tactics, such as the breaking up of political meetings and obstruction. In 1908 both Mrs. Pankhurst and her daughter Christabel were imprisoned for issuing a pamphlet inviting people to "rush the House of Commons." Following this episode, the Pankhursts' campaign steadily became more militant, and suffragette attacks on property increased; the Liberal government of the day responded by increasing penalties, and it was to escape these that Christabel fled to Paris in 1912 to direct the campaign from there. Her mother, though, was less fortunate and was sentenced to nine months in prison. She was released early following a hunger strike.

Such tactics established a pattern. Under the terms of the Prisoners (Temporary Discharge for Ill-Health) Act of 1913, popularly known as the "Cat and Mouse Act," female hunger-strikers would be released from prison only to be rearrested once they had regained their health. In these years Mrs. Pankhurst was under a constant threat of arrest and reimprisonment, a fact that she dwells on in this speech delivered on a lecture tour to America in 1913. With the outbreak of war, the WSPU called off its activities and the government released all prisoners; limited female suffrage was granted in 1918.

Leaders of the Actress Franchise League. One of the remarkable features of the suffragist movement in Britain was the spectacular manner it often adopted, from the carefully costumed and staged protest rallies of groups like the Actress Franchise League to the hunger strikes, and consequent forced feedings, later instigated by more militant feminists impatient with the pace of change. Women's Social and Political Union member Kitty Marion, for instance, recalled the dismay expressed by a Bishop who had enjoyed the "beautiful processions" of the early days of the movement. "Yes," Marion replied, "but our beautiful processions didn't get us the vote . . . and we want the vote!"

al a person address you. I dare say, in the minds of many of you—you will perhaps forgive me this personal touch—that I do not look either very like a soldier or very like a convict, and yet I am both.

Now, first of all I want to make you understand the inevitableness of revolution and civil war, even on the part of women, when you reach a certain stage in the development of a community's life. It is not at all difficult if revolutionaries come to you from Russia, if they come to you from China, or from any other part of the world, if they are men, to make you understand revolution in five minutes, every man and every woman to understand revolutionary methods when they are adopted by men. Many of you have expressed sympathy, probably even practical sympathy, with revolutionaries in Russia.[2] I dare say you have followed with considerable interest the story of how the Chinese revolutionary, Sun Yat Sen,[3] conducted the Chinese revolution from England. And yet I find in American newspapers there is a great deal of misunderstanding of the fact that one of the chief minds engaged in conducting the women's revolution is, for purposes of convenience, located in Paris. It is quite easy for you to understand—it would not be necessary for me to enter into explanations at all—the desirability of revolution if I were a man, in any of these countries, even in a part of the British Empire known to you as Ireland. If an Irish revolutionary had addressed this meeting, and many have addressed meetings all over the United States during the last twenty or thirty years, it would not be necessary for that revolutionary to explain the need of revolution beyond saying that the people of his country were

2. The Russian Revolution of 1905 forced many concessions from the government, including elections to a national parliament.

3. A leading figure in the 1911 revolution that overthrew the Manchu dynasty; the first president of the Chinese Republic.

denied—and by people, meaning men—were denied the right of self-government. That would explain the whole situation. If I were a man and I said to you: "I come from a country which professes to have representative institutions and yet denies me, a taxpayer, an inhabitant of the country, representative rights," you would at once understand that that human being, being a man, was justified in the adoption of revolutionary methods to get representative institutions. But since I am a woman it is necessary in the twentieth century to explain why women have adopted revolutionary methods in order to win the rights of citizenship.

You see, in spite of a good deal that we hear about revolutionary methods not being necessary for American women, because American women are so well off, most of the men of the United States quite calmly acquiesce in the fact that half of the community are deprived absolutely of citizen rights, and we women, in trying to make our case clear, always have to make as part of our argument, and urge upon men in our audience the fact—a very simple fact—that women are human beings. It is quite evident you do not all realize we are human beings or it would not be necessary to argue with you that women may, suffering from intolerable injustice, be driven to adopt revolutionary methods. We have, first of all to convince you we are human beings, and I hope to be able to do that in the course of the evening before I sit down, but before doing that, I want to put a few political arguments before you—not arguments for the suffrage, because I said when I opened, I didn't mean to do that,—but arguments for the adoption of militant methods in order to win political rights.

A great many of you have been led to believe, from the somewhat meagre accounts you get in the newspapers, that in England there is a strange manifestation taking place, a new form of hysteria being swept across part of the feminist population of those Isles, and this manifestation takes the shape of irresponsible breaking of windows, burning of letters, general inconvenience to respectable, honest business people who want to attend to their business. It is very irrational you say; even if these women had sufficient intelligence to understand what they were doing, and really did want the vote, they have adopted very irrational means for getting the vote. "How are they going to persuade people that they ought to have the vote by breaking their windows?" you say. Now, if you say that, it shows you do not understand the meaning of our revolution at all, and I want to show you that when damage is done to property it is not done in order to convert people to woman suffrage at all. It is a practical political means, the only means we consider open to voteless persons to bring about a political situation, which can only be solved by giving women the vote.

* * *

Men have done splendid things in this world; they have made great achievements in engineering; they have done splendid organization work; but they have failed, they have miserably failed, when it has come to dealing with the lives of human beings. They stand self-confessed failures, because the problems that perplex civilization are absolutely appalling today. Well, that is the function of women in life; it is our business to care for human beings, and we are determined that we must come without delay to the saving of the race. The race must be saved, and it can only be saved through the emancipation of women.

Well, ladies and gentlemen. I want to say that I am very thankful to you for listening to me here tonight: I am glad if I have been able even to a small extent to explain to you something of the English situation. I want to say that I am not here to apologize. I do not care very much even whether you really understand, because when you are in a fighting movement, a movement which every fibre of your being has forced you to enter, it is not the approval of other human beings that you want; you are so concentrated on your object that you mean to achieve that object even if the whole world was up in arms against you. So I am not here tonight to apologize or to win very much your approbation. People have said: "Why does Mrs. Pankhurst come to America; has she come to America to rouse American women to be militant?" No, I have not come to America to arouse American women to be militant. I believe that American women, as their earnestness increases, as they realize the need for the enfranchisement of their sex, will find out for themselves the best way to secure that object. Each nation must work out its own salvation, and so the American women will find their own way and use their own methods capably.

Other people have said: "What right has Mrs. Pankhurst to come to America and ask for American dollars?" Well, I think I have the right that all oppressed people have to ask for practical sympathy of others freer than themselves. Your right to send to France and ask for help was never questioned. You did it, and you got that help. Men of all nationalities have come to America, and they have not gone away empty-handed, because American sympathy has been extended to struggling peoples all over the world.

In England, if you could understand it, there is the most pathetic and the most courageous fight going on, because you find the people whom you have been accustomed to look upon as weak and reliant, the people you have always thought leaned upon other people for protection, have stood up and are fighting for themselves. Women have found a new kind of self-respect, a new kind of energy, a new kind of strength; and I think that of all oppressed peoples who might claim your sympathy and support, women who are fighting this fight unknown in the history of humanity before, fighting this fight in the twentieth century for greater powers of self-development, self-expression and self-government, might very well attract the sympathy and the practical help of American people.

There hasn't been a victory the women of America have won that we have not rejoiced in. I think as we have read month by month of the new States that have been added to the list of fully enfranchised States, perhaps we who know how hard the fight is, have rejoiced even more than American women themselves. I have heard cheers ring out in a meeting in London when the news of some new State being added to the list was given, cheers louder and more enthusiastic than I have ever heard for any victory in an American meeting. It is very true that those who are fighting a hard battle, those who are sacrificing greatly in order to win a victory, appreciate victories and are more enthusiastic when victories are won. We have rejoiced whole-heartedly in your victories. We feel that those victories have been easier perhaps because of the hard times that we were having, because out of our militant movement in the storm centre of the suffrage movement have gone waves that have helped to rouse women all over the world. You could only explain the strange phenomena in that way. Ten years ago there was hardly any woman suffrage movement at all. Now even in China and Japan, in India, in Turkey, everywhere, women are rising up and asking for these larger opportunities which modern conditions demand that women should have; and we women think that we have helped. Well, if we have helped at all, if, as has been said from the Chair tonight, we have even helped to rouse suffrage enthusiasm in Connecticut, can you blame me very much if I come and tell you of the desperate struggle we are having, of how the government is trying to break us down in every possible way, even by involving us in lawsuits, and trying to frighten our subscribers by threatening to prosecute even people who help us by subscribing money? Can you wonder I come over to America? Have you read about American dollars that have been given the Irish law-breakers? So here am I. I come in the intervals of prison appearance; I come after having been four times imprisoned under the Cat and Mouse Act, probably going back to be rearrested as soon as I set my foot on British soil. I come to ask you to help to win this fight. If we win it, this hardest of all fights, then, to be sure, in the future it is going to be made easier for women all over the world to win their fight when their time comes. So I make no apologies for coming, and I make no apologies, Mrs. Hepburn, for asking this audience, if any of them feel inclined, to help me to take back some money from America and put it with the money that I know our women are raising by desperate personal sacrifice at home, so that when we begin our next year's campaign, facing a general election, as probably we shall face next year, our anxieties on the money side will not be so heavy as they would have been if I had not found strength and health enough to come and carry out this somewhat arduous tour in the United States of America.

Shakes Versus Shav

Preface

This in all actuarial probability is my last play and the climax of my eminence, such as it is. I thought my career as a playwright was finished when Waldo Lanchester of the Malvern Marionette Theatre, our chief living puppet master, sent me figures of two puppets, Shakespear and myself, with a request that I should supply one of my famous dramas for them, not to last longer than ten minutes or thereabouts. I accomplished this feat, and was gratified by Mr Lanchester's immediate approval.[1]

I have learnt part of my craft as conductor of rehearsals (producer, they call it) from puppets. Their unvarying intensity of facial expression, impossible for living actors, keeps the imagination of the spectators continuously stimulated. When one of them is speaking or tumbling and the rest left aside, these, though in full view, are invisible, as they should be. Living actors have to learn that they too must be invisible while the protagonists are conversing, and therefore must not move a muscle nor change their expression, instead of, as beginners mostly do, playing to them and robbing them of the audience's undivided attention.

Puppets have also a fascination of their own, because there is nothing wonderful in a living actor moving and speaking, but that wooden headed dolls should do so is a marvel that never palls.

And they can survive treatment that would kill live actors. When I first saw them in my boyhood nothing delighted me more than when all the puppets went up in a balloon and presently dropped from the skies with an appalling crash on the floor.

Nowadays the development of stagecraft into filmcraft may destroy the idiosyncratic puppet charm. Televised puppets could enjoy the scenic backgrounds of the cinema. Sound recording could enable the puppet master to give all his attention to the strings he is manipulating, the dialogue being spoken by a company of first-rate speakers as in the theatre. The old puppet master spoke all the parts himself in accents which he differentiated by Punch-and-Judy squeaks and the like. I can imagine the puppets simulating living performers so perfectly that the spectators will be completely illuded. The result would be the death of puppetry; for it would lose its charm with its magic. So let reformers beware.

1. The play was first performed in 1949 by the Waldo Lanchester Marionette Theatre in Malvern, England.

Nothing can extinguish my interest in Shakespear. It began when I was a small boy, and extends to Stratford-upon-Avon, where I have attended so many bardic festivals that I have come to regard it almost as a supplementary birthplace of my own.

No year passes without the arrival of a batch of books contending that Shakespear was somebody else. The argument is always the same. Such early works as Venus and Adonis, Lucrece, and Love's Labour's Lost, could not possibly have been written by an illiterate clown and poacher who could hardly write his own name. This is unquestionably true. But the inference that Shakespear did not write them does not follow. What does follow is that Shakespear was not an illiterate clown but a well read grammar-schooled son in a family of good middle-class standing, cultured enough to be habitual playgoers and private entertainers of the players.

This, on investigation, proves to be exactly what Shakespear was. His father, John Shakespear, Gent, was an alderman who demanded a coat of arms which was finally granted. His mother was of equal rank and social pretension. John finally failed commercially, having no doubt let his artist turn get the better of his mercantile occupation, and leave him unable to afford a university education for William, had he ever wanted to make a professional scholar of him.

These circumstances interest me because they are just like my own. They were a considerable cut above those of Bunyan and Cobbett, both great masters of language, who nevertheless could not have written Venus and Adonis nor Love's Labour's Lost.[2] One does not forget Bunyan's "The Latin I Borrow." Shakespear's standing was nearer to Ruskin's, whose splendid style owes much more to his mother's insistence on his learning the Bible by heart than to his Oxford degree.[3]

So much for Bacon-Shakespear and all the other fables founded on that entirely fictitious figure Shaxper or Shasper the illiterate bumpkin.

Enough too for my feeling that the real Shakespear might have been myself, and for the shallow mistaking of it for mere professional jealousy.

Ayot Saint Lawrence, 1949

[*Shakes enters and salutes the audience with a flourish of his hat.*]

SHAKES Now is the winter of our discontent
    Made glorious summer by the Malvern sun.[4]
    I, William Shakes, was born in Stratford town,
    Where every year a festival is held
    To honour my renown not for an age
    But for all time.[5] Hither I raging come
    An infamous impostor to chastize,
    Who in an ecstasy of self-conceit
    Shortens my name to Shav, and dares pretend
    Here to reincarnate my very self,

---

2. John Bunyan, author of the religious allegory *The Pilgrim's Progress* (1678, 1684), attended only a village school; William Cobbett, author of the much admired sketches *Rural Rides* (1830), was self-educated.
3. In his autobiography *Praeterita*, John Ruskin describes the stern religion of his mother.

4. The play is made up of a tissue of quotations from Shakespeare's plays. Cf. here *Richard III* 1.1.1–2.
5. In his dedictory poem to the first collected edition of Shakespeare's plays (1623), the dramatist and poet Ben Jonson wrote, "He was not of an age, but for all time."

And in your stately playhouse to set up
A festival, and plant a mulberry
In most presumptuous mockery of mine.
Tell me, ye citizens of Malvern,
Where I may find this caitiff.° Face to face   coward
Set but this fiend of Ireland and myself;
And leave the rest to me. [*Shav enters.*] Who art thou,
That rearst a forehead almost rivalling mine?

SHAV Nay, who art thou, that knowest not these features
Pictured throughout the globe? Who should I be
But G. B. S.?

SHAKES   What! Stand, thou shameless fraud.
For one or both of us the hour is come.
Put up your hands.

SHAV Come on.

[*They spar. Shakes knocks Shav down with a straight left and begins counting him out, stooping over him and beating the seconds with his finger.*]

SHAKES Hackerty-backerty one, Hackerty-backerty two.
Hackerty-backerty three . . . Hackerty-backerty nine—

[*At the count of nine Shav springs up and knocks Shakes down with a right to the chin.*]

SHAV [*counting*] Hackerty-backerty one, . . . Hackerty-backerty ten. Out.

SHAKES Out! And by thee! Never. [*He rises.*] Younger you are
By full three hundred years, and therefore carry
A heavier punch than mine; but what of that?
Death will soon finish you; but as for me,
Not marble nor the gilded monuments
Of princes—

SHAV   —shall outlive your powerful rhymes.[6]
So you have told us: I have read your sonnets.

SHAKES Couldst write Macbeth?

SHAV   No need. He has been bettered
By Walter Scott's Rob Roy.[7] Behold, and blush.

[*Rob Roy and Macbeth appear, Rob in Highland tartan and kilt with claymore, Macbeth in kingly costume.*]

MACBETH Thus far into the bowels of the land
Have we marched on without impediment.
Shall I still call you Campbell?

ROB [*in a strong Scotch accent*] Caumill me no Caumills.
Ma fet is on ma native heath: ma name's Macgregor.

MACBETH I have no words. My voice is in my sword. Lay on, Rob Roy;
And damned be he that proves the smaller boy.

[*He draws and stands on guard. Rob draws; spins round several times like a man throwing a hammer; and finally cuts off Macbeth's head at one stroke.*]

ROB Whaur's your Wullie Shaxper the noo?

[*Bagpipe and drum music, to which Rob dances off.*]

6. Shakespeare's Sonnet 55 begins "Not marble nor the gilded monuments / Of princes shall outlive this pow'rful rhyme."

7. *Rob Roy* (1817), novel by Sir Walter Scott; it concerns the stirring deeds of Scottish clansman Rob Roy Macgregor.

MACBETH [*headless*] I will return to Stratford: the hotels
  Are cheaper there. [*He picks up his head, and goes off with it under his arm to the tune of British Grenadiers.*]
SHAKES Call you this cateran°   marauder
  Better than my Macbeth, one line from whom
  Is worth a thousand of your piffling plays?
SHAV Quote one. Just one. I challenge thee. One line.
SHAKES "The shardborne beetle with his drowsy hum."
SHAV Hast never heard of Adam Lindsay Gordon?[8]
SHAKES A name that sings. What of him?
SHAV   He eclipsed
  Thy shardborne beetle. Hear his mighty lines.
    [*Reciting*]
  "The beetle booms adown the glooms
  And bumps among the clumps."
SHAKES [*roaring with laughter*] Ha ha! Ho ho! My lungs like chanticleer
  Must crow their fill. This fellow hath an ear.
  How does it run? "The beetle booms—
SHAV Adown the glooms—
SHAKES And bumps—
SHAV Among the clumps." Well done, Australia!
    [*Shav laughs.*]
SHAKES Laughest thou at thyself? Pullst thou my leg?
SHAV There is more fun in heaven and earth, sweet William,
  Than is dreamt of in your philosophy.[9]
SHAKES Where is thy Hamlet? Couldst thou write King Lear?
SHAV Aye, with his daughters all complete. Couldst thou
  Have written Heartbreak House? Behold my Lear.[1]
    [*A transparency is suddenly lit up, shewing Captain Shotover seated, as in Millais' picture called North-West Passage, with a young woman of virginal beauty.*]
SHOTOVER [*raising his hand and intoning*]
  I built a house for my daughters and opened the doors thereof
  That men might come for their choosing, and their betters spring from their love;
  But one of them married a numskull: the other a liar wed;
  And now she must lie beside him even as she made her bed.
THE VIRGIN "Yes: this silly house, this strangely happy house, this agonizing house, this house without foundations. I shall call it Heartbreak House."
SHOTOVER Enough. Enough. Let the heart break in silence.
    [*The picture vanishes.*]
SHAKES You stole that word from me: did I not write
  "The heartache and the thousand natural woes
  That flesh is heir to"?[2]
SHAV   You were not the first
  To sing of broken hearts. I was the first

---

8. Australian poet, author of *Bush Ballads and Galloping Rhymes* (1870).
9. *Hamlet* 1.5.166–67: "There are more things in heaven and earth, Horatio, / Than are dreamt of in your philosophy."

1. Shaw's play *Heartbreak House* (1920) describes the impact of a young female guest on the household of 88-year-old Captain Shotover; the Virgin's speech that follows is a quotation from the play.
2. *Hamlet* 3.1.61–63.

That taught your faithless Timons how to mend them.[3]
SHAKES Taught what you could not know. Sing if you can
   My cloud capped towers, my gorgeous palaces,
   My solemn temples. The great globe itself,
   Yea, all which it inherit, shall dissolve—
SHAV —and like this foolish little show of ours
   Leave not a wrack behind.[4] So you have said.
   I say the world will long outlast our day.
   Tomorrow and tomorrow and tomorrow
   We puppets shall replay our scene.[5] Meanwhile,
   Immortal William dead and turned to clay
   May stop a hole to keep the wind away.
   Oh that that earth which kept the world in awe
   Should patch a wall t' expel the winter's flaw![6]
SHAKES These words are mine, not thine.
SHAV   Peace, jealous Bard:
   We both are mortal. For a moment suffer
   My glimmering light to shine.
   [*A light appears between them.*]
SHAKES   Out, out, brief candle![7] [*He puffs it out.*]
   [*Darkness. The play ends.*]

THE END

LETTERS
To Francis Collison[1]

Springburn. Strachur
20th August 1903

Now I ask you, Mr Collison, as a sensible man, what the devil you suppose I want with a canary. I am a vegetarian, and cant eat it; and it is not big enough to eat me. But you are not a sensible man: you are a "fancier"; and you believe that the height of earthly happiness is to be surrounded with pigeons & Persian cats & guinea pigs & rabbits, with a tub full of toads & newts under the counter. I once had a canary, a little green brute that flew in through the open window one day & would not go away. I hated it and it hated me. I bought it a cage—a thing I abhor—& gave it everything I could find at the seedsman's; but it was utterly miserable & did its best to make me miserable until some benevolent person stole it. I have been happy ever since until this day, when I have received from Woking the devastating news that you have inflicted another canary on me. Now if you had sent me a sea-gull or a nightjar (the nightjar is my favorite bird) I could have let it loose & watched it flying & stalked it with a camera—the only sort of sport I can endure—; but this unhappy little wretch would be killed if it flew about, and will do nothing but titivate itself in its absurd cage (I have telegraphed to the gardener's wife to buy the largest cage in Woking for

---

3. *Timon of Athens* describes a misanthrope.
4. *The Tempest* 4.1.151–56.
5. *Macbeth* 5.5.19–21.
6. Adapting *Hamlet* 5.1.236–39. Hamlet is speaking of "Imperious Caesar, dead and turned to clay."
7. *Macbeth* 5.5.23–25: "Out, out, brief candle! / Life's but

a walking shadow, a poor player / That struts and frets his hour upon the stage."
1. Shaw had loaned money to Francis Collison, a small shopkeeper, some years earlier. Collison chose to express his gratitude by sending a pet canary to Shaw; he also offered Shaw a kitten.

it) and make a confounded noise which will frighten all the thrushes & blackbirds away. And now, having taken advantage of my being away on my holiday to introduce this ornithological pest into my household, you want to send me a kitten as well. Why, man, the kitten will kill the canary when it grows up. Have you no common sense? Prince Sam indeed! Damn Prince Sam! I am a republican, and care nothing for your Princes. Do you suppose I want a noisome little beast to cover my house with its excrements, and bring all the cats in Woking to celebrate its debaucheries with nocturnal yowlings? You speak of it as "her"; so I conclude it is a female, which means that I shall have sixteen mongrels added to the menagerie every two months. Mrs Ricketts of Bishops Stortford ought to be ashamed of herself. What did I ever do to her or to you that you should heap these injuries on me? Did my books ever do you any harm? Did they disturb you with silly whistlings at your work, or bring forth litters of little books that you had to drown? In your letter of the 5th, you said you would forward the animals "when convenient to me and mine." I said to myself, "Thank God: he will wait until I ask him for the accursed things; and in the meantime he will be happy nursing the detestable kitten & trying to teach the bird tunes." But in the excess & exuberance of your destructive benevolence you were not content to wait. You sent the bird; and for all I know, the wretched kitten may now be on its way. My only hope is in the gardener's wife. She has one canary already; and perhaps, if I make her a present of the cage, she will consent to take the other if I offer her five shillings a week for the term of its natural life. I shall then hear it only when I walk in the garden; and at every trill I shall curse the name of F. Collison.

G. Bernard Shaw

To Eleanor Robson

10 Adelphi Terrace W C
13th April 1905

To the Gifted, Beautiful & Beloved—Greeting.
My dear Miss Eleanor

Fate has done its work. I have put you out of my mind and settled down hard to my business since you left England.[2] After weary months of mere commercial affairs & rehearsals, I have begun another play—half finished it, indeed; and lo! there you are in the middle of it. I said I would write a play for you; but I did not mean in the least to keep my promise. I swear I never thought of you until you came up a trap in the middle of the stage & got into my heroine's empty clothes and said Thank you: I am the mother of that play. Though I am not sure that you are not its father; for you simply danced in here & captivated me & then deserted me & left me with my unborn play to bring into existence. I simply dare not count the number of months. Anyhow the heroine is so like you that I see nobody in the wide world who can play her except you.

And the play is wildly impossible, of course. You are a major in the Salvation Army & you do wonderful & mystical things in the most natural & prosaic way. It would run for a week. But what a week that would be! When are you coming over?

yrs ever & ever
G. Bernard Shaw

2. Eleanor Robson (b. 1879), British actress, was at the time living in New York. Shaw had begun *Major Barbara* a month earlier.

To Louis Calvert[3]

Derry. Rosscarbery
23rd July 1905

Dear Calvert

Can you play the trombone? If not, I beg you to acquire a smattering of the art during your holidays. I am getting on with the new play scrap by scrap; and the part of the millionaire cannon founder is becoming more and more formidable. Broadbent and Keegan rolled into one, with Mephistopheles thrown in; that is what it is like. [Sydney Grundy's] Business is Business will be cheap melodrama in comparison. Irving and Tree will fade into third class when Calvert takes the stage as Andrew Undershaft.[4] It will be TREMENJOUS, simply. But there is a great scene at the end of the second act where he buys up the Salvation Army, and has to take part in a march to a big meeting. Barker will play the tamborine. You will have a trombone—or a bombardon if you prefer that instrument—and it would add greatly to the effect if you could play it prettily. Besides, if you took to music you could give up those confounded cigars and save your voice and your memory (both wrecks, like Mario's,[5] from thirty-seven cigars a day) for this immense part. It is very long, speeches longer than Keegan's, and dozens of them, and infinite nuances of execution. Undershaft is diabolically subtle, gentle, self-possessed, powerful, stupendous, as well as amusing and interesting. There are the makings of ten Hamlets and six Othellos in his mere leavings. Learning it will half kill you; but you can retire next day as pre-eminent and unapproachable. That penny-plain and tuppence-colored pirate Brassbound will be beneath your notice then. I have put him off for another year, as I cannot get the right Lady Cicely.[6] Vedrenne, unluckily, has read my plays at Margate and is now full of the most insane proposals—wants Brassbound instantly with you and Kate Rorke, for one thing.

But the trombone is the urgent matter of the moment. By the way, trombone players never get cholera nor consumption—never die, in fact, until extreme old age makes them incapable of working the slide.

G. Bernard Shaw

To Louis Calvert

10 Adelphi Terrace W C
29th November 1905

My dear Calvert

I see with disgust that the papers all say that your Undershaft was a magnificent piece of acting, and Major Barbara a rottenly undramatic play, instead of pointing out that Major B. is a masterpiece and you the most infamous amateur that ever disgraced the boards.

Do let me put Cremlin into it. A man who could let the seven deadly sins go for nothing could sit on a hat without making an audience laugh. I have taken a box for Friday and had a hundredweight of cabbages, dead cats, eggs, and gingerbeer bottles stacked in it. Every word you fluff, every speech you unact, I will shy something at you. Before you go on the stage I will insult you until your temper gets the better of your liver. You

---

3. The actor who was to play the role of Undershaft in the play's first production.
4. Sir Henry Irving (1838–1905) was a celebrated actor and theater manager. Sir Herbert Beerbohm Tree (1853–1917) was the most successful actor-manager of

the day; he was the brother of the satirist Max Beerbohm.
5. Giovanni Matteo Mario (1810–1883), celebrated Italian tenor.
6. Shaw's play Captain Brassbound's Conversion was first performed in 1900.

are an impostor, a sluggard, a blockhead, a shirk, a malingerer, and the worst actor that ever lived or ever will live. I will apologize to the public for engaging you: I will tell your mother of you. Barker played you off the stage; Cremlin dwarfed you; Bill annihilated you; Clare Greet took all eyes from you.[7] If you do not recover yourself next time, a thunderbolt will end you. If you are too lazy to study the lines, *I'll* coach you in them. That last act MUST be saved, or I'll withdraw the play and cut you off with a shilling.

yours

G.B.S.

To William Stead[8]

10 Adelphi Terrace W C
13th December 1905

Glad you liked it. But the cap & bells are necessary. Without them people settle down into a comfortable solemn feeling that they have done something good, and in fact dispose of the whole matter creditably & sufficiently, when they have assented to the play & enjoy it. It is just at that point that a laugh in their face disconcerts them & leaves them without the fatal impression that I have solved the problem for them.

G.B.S.

To *The Times*[9]

Sir,—This is a terrible moment in our national life. We are not often thoroughly frightened. When England trembles the world knows that a great peril overshadows our island. It is not the first time that we have faced dangers that have made even our gayest and bravest clench their teeth and hold their breath. We watched the Armada creeping slowly up the Channel.[1] We wiped our brow when chance revealed the treason of Guy Fawkes.[2] We are listening even now for the bugle of the German invader, and scanning the waves we rule for the periscope of the French submarine.[3] But until now we have faced our fate like men, with our Parliament unshaken in our midst, grandly calm as the Roman senators who sat like statues when Brennus and his barbarians charged blood-stained into their hall.[4] When Charles Bradlaugh,[5] the most muscular man in England, dashed into the House of Commons to claim a seat in that august Assembly the police carried him, titanically struggling, down the stairs, deposited him in the yard with a shattered fountain pen, and disdainfully set him free to do his worst. It was but the other day that a desperado arose in the Strangers' Gallery of the House of Commons and burst into disorderly eloquence. Without a moment's hesitation the dauntless attendants hurled themselves upon him, and extruded him from our Legislature. He was not haled before the magistrate; he was not imprisoned; no man deigned to ask securities for his good behaviour; the British lion scorned protection against so puny an antagonist.

But the strongest nerves give way at last. The warriors of Philip were, when all is said, only men. German soldiers, French bluejackets, Guy Fawkes, Bradlaugh, and the stranger

7. Fred Cremlin played Peter Shirley and Clare Greet played Rummy Mitchens.
8. William Stead (1849–1912), journalist, had questioned Shaw's use of farcical devices.
9. On 23 October 1906, ten women were arrested at the House of Commons, charged with "using threatening and abusive words." Among them was Anne Cobden-Sanderson, daughter of Richard Cobden, a prominent economist. Following reports of her harsh treatment in prison, Shaw published this letter in the London *Times* on 31 October 1906.

1. In 1588 Philip II of Spain sent a naval armada to invade England; it was defeated.
2. The best-known conspirator in the "Gunpowder Plot," which aimed to blow up James I and parliament in 1606.
3. From 1906 to 1914 there was growing tension between England and Germany, ultimately leading to war.
4. According to legend, Brennus was the leader of a band of Gauls who captured Rome in 390 B.C.
5. Radical politician, forbidden to take up his seat in Parliament from 1880–1885 due to his professed atheism.

in the gallery, bold and dangerous as they were, were no females. The peril to-day wears a darker, deadlier aspect. Ten women—ten petticoated, long-stockinged, corseted females have hurled themselves on the British Houses of Parliament. Desperate measures are necessary. I have a right to speak in this matter, because it was in my play *Man and Superman*[6] that my sex were first warned of woman's terrible strength and man's miserable weakness.

It is a striking confirmation of the correctness of my views that the measures which have always been deemed sufficient to protect the House of Commons against men are not to be trusted against women. Take, for example, the daughters of Richard Cobden, long known to everybody worth knowing in London as among the most charming and interesting women of our day. One of them—one only—and she the slightest and rosiest of the family—did what the herculean Charles Bradlaugh did. To the immortal glory of our Metropolitan Police they did not blench. They carried the lady out even as they carried Bradlaugh. But they did not dare to leave her at large as they left him. They held on to her like grim death until they had her safe under bolt and bar, until they had stripped her to see that she had no weapons concealed, until a temperate diet of bread and cocoa should have abated her perilous forces. She—and the rest of the terrible ten.

For the moment we have time to breathe. But has the Government considered the fact that owing to the imperfections of our law these ladies will be at large again before many weeks are passed? I ask, in the name of the public, whether proper precautions have been taken. It is not enough for Mr Herbert Gladstone, Mr Haldane, Mr Asquith, and Sir Henry Campbell-Bannerman[7] to sit there pale and determined, with drawn lips and folded arms, helplessly awaiting a renewal of the assault—an assault the consequences of which no man can foresee. It is their duty without a moment's delay to quadruple the police staff inside the Houses of Parliament. Westminster and Vauxhall bridges should be strongly held by the Guards. If necessary, special constables should be enrolled. I am no coward; but I do not want to see a repetition of the folly that found us unprepared in 1899.

I submit, however, that if these precautions are taken we might, perhaps, venture to let Mrs Cobden-Sanderson and her friends out. As a taxpayer, I object to having to pay for her bread and cocoa when her husband is, not only ready, but apparently even anxious to provide a more generous diet at home. After all, if Mr Cobden-Sanderson is not afraid, surely, the rest of us may pluck up a little. We owe something to Mr Cobden-Sanderson,[8] both as one of our most distinguished artist craftsmen and as a most munificent contributor in crises where public interests have been at stake. If Mrs Cobden-Sanderson must remain a prisoner whilst the Home Secretary is too paralysed with terror to make that stroke of the pen for which every sensible person in the three kingdoms is looking to him, why on earth cannot she be imprisoned in her own house? We should still look ridiculous, but at least the lady would not be a martyr. I suppose nobody in the world really wishes to see one of the nicest women in England suffering from the coarsest indignity and the most injurious form of ill-treatment that the law could inflict on a pickpocket. It gives us an air of having lost our tempers and made fools of ourselves, and of being incapable of acting generously now that we have had time to come to our senses. Surely, there can be no two opinions among sane people as to what we ought to do.

Will not the Home Secretary rescue us from a ridiculous, an intolerable, and incidentally a revoltingly spiteful and unmanly situation?

Yours, &c.,
G. Bernard Shaw

6. First performed in 1905.
7. Members of the Liberal government then in power.
8. Thomas James Cobden-Sanderson (1840–1922), book designer and friend of Shaw's.

The Great War: Confronting the Modern

The multiplying technological, artistic, and social changes at the turn of the twentieth century impressed that generation's artists as a rupture with the past. And no event so graphically suggested that human history had "changed, changed utterly," as World War I—"the Great War."

Great Britain, like its enemy Germany, entered the war with idealistic aims. Prime Minister H. H. Asquith put the justice of the British case this way in a speech to the House of Commons on 7 August 1914: "I do not think any nation ever entered into a great conflict—and this is one of the greatest that history will ever know—with a clearer conscience or stronger conviction that it is fighting not for aggression, not for the maintenance of its own selfish ends, but in defence of principles the maintenance of which is vital to the civilization of the world." But cynicism set in quickly—first among ground troops on the Western Front, dug into trenches and watching "progress" that could be measured in yards per day. Soon the British public became disillusioned with the war effort, partly as a result of technological advances in the news media. Daily papers in England carried photographs from the front, and while editorial policy generally supported the British government and printed heroic images of the fighting, this sanitized version of the war was largely offset by the long published lists of casualties; during the four years and three months that Britain was involved in the war, more than a million British troops—an average of fifteen hundred per day—were killed in action.

The war's lasting legacy was a sense of bitterly rebuffed idealism, bringing with it a suspicion of progress, technology, government, bureaucracy, nationalism, and conventional morality—themes probed in new ways by the period's writers. Just as the war had involved radically new strategies and new technologies, writers intensified their search for new forms and modes of expression as they and their compatriots found themselves in the midst of a conflict unlike anything previously known in the annals of history.

Blast

Wyndham Lewis (1884–1957), founder of the provocative arts magazine *Blast,* was often at odds with his sometime co-conspirator Ezra Pound: indeed both men were usually at odds with most of their friends. But they did agree on one thing: that the writers of Edwardian and Georgian England had failed to throw off the deadening literary mannerisms of the previous century. "As for the nineteenth century," Pound wrote, "with all respects to its achievements, I think we shall look back upon it as a rather blurry, messy sort of a period, a rather sentimentalistic, mannerish sort of a period."

Some violent corrective was needed. The name of Lewis's magazine was intended to suggest an explosive charge that would blow away tired literary and social conventions. It was a calculated assault on good taste, both in its contents and, more immediately, in its form: an oversized, bright pink cover with the single word *BLAST* splashed diagonally across it. Lewis carefully oversaw the details of typography; visually and rhetorically, *Blast* is indebted to the polemical style of the Italian artist F. T. Marinetti (1876–1944), the founder of Italian futurism. Marinetti's vivid manifestos for futurism celebrated a modern aesthetic of speed, technology, and power. Lewis in turn founded a movement he called Vorticism, and *Blast* bore the subtitle *The Review of the Great English Vortex.*

The definition of *vorticism* was left intentionally hazy; as canny an observer as the Vorticist painter William Roberts, one of the signatories of the manifesto, claimed that Vorticism was first and foremost "a slogan." In 1915 Lewis defined it this way: "By Vorticism we mean (a) ACTIVITY as opposed to the tasteful PASSIVITY of Picasso; (b) SIGNIFICANCE as opposed to the

Wyndham Lewis. *The Creditors* (design for *Timon of Athens*). 1912–1913.

dull or anecdotal character to which the Naturalist is condemned; (c) ESSENTIAL MOVEMENT and ACTIVITY (such as the energy of a mind) as opposed to the imitative cinematography, the fuss and hysterics of the Futurists."

In its disorienting layout of typography, the *Vorticist Manifesto* is as much a visual as a literary statement, reflecting the multiple and always skewed interest of its primary author, Lewis. Born on a yacht off the coast of Nova Scotia, he had moved to London with his mother when his parents separated in 1893. A precocious painter, he won a scholarship to the progressive Slade School of Art at age sixteen, but moved to Paris before completing his studies. He returned to London in 1909 and began a career as a painter and writer. During the War, he served both as an artillery officer and as a commissioned war artist. He also wrote an experimental novel, *Tarr* (1918), and went on to produce a range of works in the dozen years thereafter, including pro-fascist political theory in *The Art of Being Ruled* (1926) and more general cultural criticism in *Time and Western Man* (1927), in which he attacked the modern cult of subjectivity. During the thirties, he became increasingly unpopular in London, first as a result of a satirical novel, *The Apes of God*, which lampooned figures in the literary and art world and their patrons; following two libel actions against him, publishers became wary of taking on his works. Lewis and his wife spent the years of World War II living in poverty in America and Canada; after the war, he returned to England, where he became an art critic for the British Broadcasting Corporation. He continued to draw, paint, and write memoirs, satirical stories, and an allegorical fantasy in several volumes.

Along with the *Vorticist Manifesto*, the first issue of *Blast* included poetry by Pound, fiction by Ford Madox Ford and Rebecca West, a play by Lewis, and illustrations by Lewis and others. The timing of the first issue couldn't have been worse: after delays caused by typesetting difficulties, *Blast* went on sale in London on June 20, 1914; World War I began just a few weeks later. While Lewis and his confederates had declared war on conventional artistic and literary taste with their "puce monster"—an advertisement for the first issue announced the "END OF THE CHRISTIAN ERA"—they were usurped by a much more pressing conflict. As Lewis later wrote, "In 1914 I produced a huge review called *Blast,* which for the most part I wrote myself. That was my first public appearance. Immediately the War broke out and put an end to all that." Lewis brought out a second issue in July 1915, attempting to fend off charges of irrelevancy with a special "War Number" that included T. S. Eliot's "Preludes" and "Rhapsody on a Windy Night" and a manifesto from the sculptor Henri Gaudier-Brzeska, "written from the trenches," which concludes poignantly with an obituary for Gaudier, "Mort pour la Patrie" (died for the fatherland). But by this time, *Blast* itself was for all intents and purposes dead; its second issue was its last. Short-lived though it was, however, *Blast* was remarkably important in clearing the way for the new art of modernism.

VORTICIST MANIFESTO
LONG LIVE THE VORTEX!

Long live the great art vortex sprung up in the centre of this town!

We stand for the Reality of the Present—not for the sentimental Future, or the sacripant[1] Past.

We want to leave Nature and Men alone.

We do not want to make people wear Futurist Patches, or fuss men to take to pink and sky-blue trousers.

We are not their wives or tailors.

The only way Humanity can help artists is to remain independent and work unconsciously.

WE NEED THE UNCONSCIOUSNESS OF HUMANITY—their stupidity, animalism and dreams.

We believe in no perfectibility except our own.

Intrinsic beauty is in the Interpreter and Seer, not in the object or content.[2]

We do not want to change the appearance of the world, because we are not Naturalists, Impressionists or Futurists (the latest form of Impressionism), and do not depend on the appearance of the world for our art.

WE ONLY WANT THE WORLD TO LIVE, and to feel its crude energy flowing through us.

It may be said that great artists in England are always revolutionary, just as in France any really fine artist had a strong traditional vein.

Blast sets out to be an avenue for all those vivid and violent ideas that could reach the Public in no other way.

Blast will be popular, essentially. It will not appeal to any particular class, but to the fundamental and popular instincts in every class and description of people, **TO THE INDIVIDUAL.** The moment a man feels or realizes himself as an artist, he ceases to belong to any milieu or time. Blast is created for this timeless, fundamental Artist that exists in everybody.

1. Boasting of valor.
2. Although the Vorticists go on to differentiate themselves from the Impressionists, this statement is very close to the impressionism articulated by Walter Pater in *The Renaissance* (1873); see page 1759.

The Man in the Street and the Gentleman are equally ignored.

Popular art does not mean the art of the poor people, as it is usually supposed to. It means the art of the individuals.

Education (art education and general education) tends to destroy the creative instinct. Therefore it is in times when education has been non-existent that art chiefly flourished.

But it is nothing to do with "the People."

It is a mere accident that that is the most favourable time for the individual to appear.

To make the rich of the community shed their education skin, to destroy politeness, standardization and academic, that is civilized, vision, is the task we have set ourselves.

We want to make in England not a popular art, not a revival of lost folk art, or a romantic fostering of such unactual conditions, but to make individuals, wherever found.

We will convert the King if possible.

A VORTICIST KING! WHY NOT?

DO YOU THINK LLOYD GEORGE[3] HAS THE VORTEX IN HIM?

MAY WE HOPE FOR ART FROM LADY MOND?[4]

We are against the glorification of "the People," as we are against snobbery. It is not necessary to be an outcast bohemian, to be unkempt or poor, any more than it is necessary to be rich or handsome, to be an artist. Art is nothing to do with the coat you wear. A top-hat can well hold the Sixtine.[5] A cheap cap could hide the image of Kephren.

AUTOMOBILISM (Marinetteism) bores us. We don't want to go about making a hullo-bulloo about motor cars, anymore than about knives and forks, elephants or gas-pipes.

Elephants are **VERY BIG.** Motor cars go quickly.

Wilde gushed twenty years ago about the beauty of machinery. Gissing,[6] in his romantic delight with modern lodging houses was futurist in this sense.

The futurist is a sensational and sentimental mixture of the aesthete of 1890 and the realist of 1870.

The "Poor" are detestable animals! They are only picturesque and amusing for the sentimentalist or the romantic! The "Rich" are bores without a single exception, *en tant que riches* [so far as they are rich]!

We want those simple and great people found everywhere.

Blast presents an art of Individuals.

MANIFESTO.

1

BLAST First (from politeness) ENGLAND
CURSE ITS CLIMATE FOR ITS SINS AND INFECTIONS
DISMAL SYMBOL, set round our bodies,
of effeminate lout within.

---

3. David Lloyd George, British statesman, and Prime Minister 1916–1922.
4. A leader of fashionable London society.

5. The Sistine Chapel in the Vatican.
6. George Gissing (1857–1903), naturalist novelist.

VICTORIAN VAMPIRE, the LONDON cloud sucks
the TOWN'S heart.

A 1000 MILE LONG, 2 KILOMETER Deep

BODY OF WATER even, is pushed against us
from the Floridas, TO MAKE US MILD.
OFFICIOUS MOUNTAINS keep back DRASTIC WINDS

SO MUCH VAST MACHINERY TO PRODUCE

> THE CURATE of "Eltham"
> BRITANNIC AESTHETE
> WILD NATURE CRANK
> DOMESTICATED POLICEMAN
> LONDON COLISEUM
> SOCIALIST-PLAYWRIGHT
> DALY'S MUSICAL COMEDY
> GAIETY CHORUS GIRL
> TONKS[7]

CURSE

the flabby sky that can manufacture no snow, but can only drop the sea on us in a drizzle like a poem by Mr. Robert Bridges.[8]

CURSE

the lazy air that cannot stiffen the back of the **SERPENTINE**, or put Aquatic steel half way down the **MANCHESTER CANAL**.

_____

But ten years ago we saw distinctly both snow and ice here.
May some vulgarly inventive, but useful person, arise, and restore to us the necessary **BLIZZARDS**.

LET US ONCE MORE WEAR THE ERMINE
OF THE NORTH.

WE BELIEVE IN THE EXISTENCE OF THIS USEFUL LITTLE CHEMIST IN OUR MIDST!

7. Henry Tonks, a teacher at the Slade School of Art (where Lewis and other Vorticists studied) who resisted as "contamination" such modern innovations as Post-Impressionism and Cubism.
8. Poet Laureate from 1913 until his death in 1930, noted for his technical skill and high moral tone.

2
OH BLAST FRANCE

| pig plagiarism
| BELLY
| SLIPPERS
| POODLE TEMPER
| BAD MUSIC

SENTIMENTAL GALLIC GUSH
SENSATIONALISM
FUSSINESS.

PARISIAN PAROCHIALISM.

Complacent young man, so much respect for Papa and his son!—Oh!— Papa is wonderful: but all papas are!

BLAST

APERITIFS (Pernots, Amers picon)
Bad change
Naively seductive Houri salon-
    picture Cocottes
Slouching blue porters (can carry
    a pantechnicon)
Stupidly rapacious people at
    every step
Economy maniacs
Bouillon Kub (for being a bad pun)

PARIS.

Clap-trap Heaven of amative
    German professor.
Ubiquitous lines of silly little trees.
Arcs de Triomphe.
Imperturbable, endless prettiness.
Large empty cliques, higher up.
Bad air for the individual.

BLAST
MECCA OF THE AMERICAN

because it is not other side of Suez Canal, instead of an afternoon's ride from London.

3
CURSE
WITH EXPLETIVE OF WHIRLWIND
THE BRITANNIC AESTHETE

CREAM OF THE SNOBBISH EARTH
ROSE OF SHARON OF GOD-PRIG
   OF SIMIAN VANITY
SNEAK AND SWOT OF THE SCHOOL-ROOM
IMBERB (or Berbed when in Belsize)-PEDANT

PRACTICAL JOKER
DANDY
CURATE

BLAST all products of phlegmatic cold
Life of LOOKER-ON.
CURSE

SNOBBERY
(disease of feminity)
FEAR OF RIDICULE
(arch vice of inactive, sleepy)
PLAY
STYLISM
SINS AND PLAGUES
of this LYMPHATIC finished
(we admit in every sense
finished)
VEGETABLE HUMANITY.

4
BLAST

THE SPECIALIST
"PROFESSIONAL"
"GOOD WORKMAN"
"GROVE-MAN"
ONE ORGAN MAN

BLAST THE

AMATEUR
SCIOLAST
ART-PIMP
JOURNALIST
SELF MAN
NO-ORGAN MAN

5
BLAST HUMOUR

Quack ENGLISH drug for stupidity and sleepiness.
Arch enemy of REAL, conventionalizing like

> gunshot, freezing supple
> REAL in ferocious chemistry
> of laughter.

BLAST SPORT
HUMOUR'S FIRST COUSIN AND ACCOMPLICE.

> Impossibility for Englishman to be grave and
>   keep his end up, psychologically.
> Impossible for him to use Humour as well
>   and be <u>persistently</u> grave.
> Alas! necessity for big doll's show in front
>   of mouth.
> Visitation of Heaven on
>   English Miss
>   gums, canines of **FIXED GRIN**
>   Death's head symbol of Anti-Life.

CURSE those who will hang over this
Manifesto with SILLY CANINES exposed.

6
BLAST

years 1837 to 1900

Curse abysmal inexcusable middle-class (also Aristocracy and
Proletariat).

BLAST

pasty shadow cast by gigantic BOEHM[9]
(Imagined at introduction of BOURGEOIS VICTORIAN
VISTAS).
WRING THE NECK OF all sick inventions born in that pro-
gressive white wake.

9. Joseph Edgar Boehm (1834–1890), sculptor for Queen Victoria.

BLAST   their weeping whiskers—hirsute
RHETORIC of EUNUCH and STYLIST—
SENTIMENTAL HYGIENICS
ROUSSEAUISMS (wild Nature cranks)
FRATERNIZING WITH MONKEYS
DIABOLICS—raptures and roses
of the erotic bookshelves
culminating in
PURGATORY OF PUTNEY.[1]
CHAOS OF ENOCH ARDENS[2]

laughing Jennys[3]
Ladies with Pains
good-for-nothing Guineveres.

SNOBBISH BORROVIAN running after
GIPSY KINGS and ESPADAS[4]
bowing the knee to
wild Mother Nature,
her feminine contours,
Unimaginative insult to
MAN.

DAMN

all those to-day who have taken on that Rotten Menagerie, and still crack their whips and tumble in Piccadilly Circus, as though London were a provincial town.

WE WHISPER IN YOUR EAR A GREAT SECRET.

LONDON IS NOT A PROVINCIAL TOWN.

We will allow Wonder Zoos. But we do not want the
GLOOMY VICTORIAN CIRCUS in
Piccadilly Circus.

IT IS PICCADILLY'S CIRCUS!

NOT MEANT FOR MENAGERIES trundling
out of Sixties DICKENSIAN CLOWNS,
CORELLI[5] LADY RIDERS, TROUPS
OF PERFORMING GIPSIES (who
complain besides that 1/6 a night
does not pay fare back to Clapham).

---

1. A middle-class suburb of London.
2. *Enoch Arden* (1864), a sentimental narrative poem by Tennyson.
3. From Dante Gabriel Rossetti's popular poem *Jenny* (1870), again disliked for its sentimentality.

4. Refers to the contemporary popularity of the gypsy romances of George Borrow, such as *The Zincali* (1841).
5. Marie Corelli, pseud. of Mary Mackay (1855–1924), author of best-selling religious novels and romances.

BLAST[6]

The Post Office   Frank Brangwyn   Robertson Nicol
Rev. Pennyfeather   Galloway Kyle
(Bells)   (Cluster of Grapes)
Bishop of London and all his posterity
Galsworthy   Dean Inge   Croce   Matthews
Rev Meyer   Seymour Hicks
Lionel Cust   C. B. Fry   Bergson Abdul Bahai
Hawtrey   Edward Elgar   Sardlea
Filson Young   Marie Corelli   Geddes
Codliver Oil   St. Loe Strachey   Lyceum Club
Rhabindraneth Tagore   Lord Glenconner of Glen
Weiniger   Norman Angel   Ad. Mahon
Mr. and Mrs. Dearmer   Beecham   Ella
A. C. Benson   (Pills, Opera, Thomas)   Sydney Webb
British Academy   Messrs. Chapell
Countess of Warwick   George Edwards
Willie Ferraro   Captain Cook   R. J. Campbell
Clan Thesiger   Martin Harvey   William Archer
George Grossmith   R. H. Benson
Annie Besant   Chenil   Clan Meynell
Father Vaughan   Joseph Holbrooke   Clan Strachey

1

BLESS ENGLAND!

BLESS ENGLAND

FOR ITS SHIPS

which switchback on Blue, Green and
Red SEAS all around the PINK
EARTH-BALL,

BIG BETS ON EACH.

BLESS ALL SEAFARERS.

THEY exchange not one LAND for another, but one ELEMENT for
ANOTHER. The MORE against the LESS ABSTRACT.

---

6. The list of those blasted by the Vorticists falls, according to the critic William Wees, into seven categories: (1) members of the (literary and cultural) Establishment (e.g., William Archer, drama critic of the *Nation*); (2) people who represented popular or snobbish fads (e.g., Sir Abdul Baha Bahai, leader of the Bahai faith); (3) high-minded popular writers, (e.g., Marie Corelli); (4) mediocre but popular figures (e.g., the poet Ella Wheeler Wilcox); (5) fuzzy-minded reformers and idealists (e.g., Sidney Webb, a leader of the Fabian Socialist organization); (6) "popular figures whom the Vorticists just didn't like" (e.g., C. B. Fry, a cricket player); and (7) "blasting just for the fun of it . . . or blasting that grew from special circumstances and private reasons known only to insiders" (e.g., the Post Office and Cod Liver Oil). See William C. Wees, *Vorticism and the English Avant-Garde* (1972), pp. 217–227.

BLESS the vast planetary abstraction of the **OCEAN.**

BLESS THE ARABS OF THE **ATLANTIC.**
THIS ISLAND MUST BE CONTRASTED WITH THE BLEAK WAVES.

BLESS ALL PORTS.

PORTS, RESTLESS MACHINES of

> scooped out basins
> heavy insect dredgers
> monotonous cranes
> stations
> lighthouses, blazing
>   through the frosty
>   starlight, cutting the
>   storm like a cake
> beaks of infant boats,
>   side by side,
> heavy chaos of
>   wharves,
> steep walls of
>   factories
> womanly town

BLESS these **MACHINES** that work the little boats across
clean liquid space, in beelines.

BLESS the great **PORTS**

> HULL
> LIVERPOOL
> LONDON
> NEWCASTLE-ON-TYNE
> BRISTOL
> GLASGOW

BLESS ENGLAND,

Industrial Island machine, pyramidal workshop,
its apex at Shetland, discharging itself on the sea.

BLESS

> cold
> magnanimous
> delicate
> gauche
> fanciful
> stupid

ENGLISHMEN.

2

BLESS the HAIRDRESSER.

He attacks Mother Nature for a small fee.
Hourly he ploughs heads for sixpence,
Scours chins and lips for threepence.
He makes systematic mercenary war on this
WILDNESS.
He trims aimless and retrograde growths
   into CLEAN ARCHED SHAPES and
   ANGULAR PLOTS.

   BLESS this HESSIAN (or SILESIAN) **EXPERT**[7]
   correcting the grotesque anachronisms
      of our physique.

3

BLESS ENGLISH HUMOUR

It is the great barbarous weapon of
the genius among races.
The wild MOUNTAIN RAILWAY from IDEA
to IDEA, in the ancient Fair of LIFE.

BLESS **SWIFT**   for his solemn bleak
                  wisdom of laughter.

SHAKESPEARE   for his bitter Northern
                  Rhetoric of humour.

BLESS ALL ENGLISH EYES
   that grow crows-feet with their
   FANCY and ENERGY.

BLESS this hysterical WALL built round
   the EGO.

BLESS the solitude of LAUGHTER.

BLESS the separating, ungregarious
   BRITISH GRIN.

4

BLESS FRANCE

for its BUSHELS of VITALITY
to the square inch.

---

7. From German industrial regions.

HOME OF MANNERS (the Best, the WORST and interesting mixtures).
MASTERLY PORNOGRAPHY (great enemy of progress).
COMBATIVENESS
GREAT HUMAN SCEPTICS
DEPTHS OF ELEGANCE
FEMALE QUALITIES
FEMALES
BALLADS of its PREHISTORIC APACHE
Superb hardness and hardiesse of its
Voyou° type, rebellious adolescent.   raffish
Modesty and humanity of many there.
GREAT FLOOD OF LIFE pouring out
of wound of 1797.[8]
Also bitterer stream from 1870.[9]
STAYING POWER, like a cat.

BLESS[1]

Bridget   Berrwolf   Bearline   Cranmer Byng
Frieder Graham   The Pope   Maria de Tomaso
Captain Kemp   Munroe   Gaby   Jenkins
R. B. Cuningham Grahame   Barker
(not his brother)   (John and Granville)
Mrs. Wil Finnimore   Madame Strindberg   Carson
Salvation Army   Lord Howard de Walden
Capt. Craig   Charlotte Corday   Cromwell
Mrs. Duval   Mary Robertson   Lillie Lenton
Frank Rutter   Castor Oil   James Joyce
Leveridge   Lydia Yavorska   Preb. Carlyle   Jenny
Mon. le compte de Gabulis   Smithers   Dick Burge
33 Church Street   Sievier   Gertie Millar
Norman Wallis   Miss Fowler   Sir Joseph Lyons
Martin Wolff   Watt   Mrs. Hepburn
Alfree   Tommy   Captain Kendell   Young Ahearn
Wilfred Walter   Kate Lechmere   Henry Newbolt
Lady Aberconway   Frank Harris   Hamel
Gilbert Canaan   Sir James Mathew Barry
Mrs. Belloc Lowdnes   W. L. George   Rayner
George Robey   George Mozart   Harry Weldon

---

8. The rise of Napoleon Bonaparte.
9. Beginning of Franco-Prussian War and end of the Second Empire, led by Napoleon Bonaparte's nephew Napoleon III.
1. This list of the blessed falls, according to William Wees, into four categories: (1) "some of the blessings, like most of the blasts, seemed designed to affront repsectable public opinion" (e.g., the Pope and the Salvation Army); (2) "working class entertainments such as boxing and music halls"; (3) "a few selected representatives of the fine arts" (e.g., James Joyce); and (4) "friends of the Vorticists or of the avant-garde in general" (e.g., Frank Rutter and P. J. Konody, two sympathetic art critics).

Chaliapine   George Hirst   Graham White
Hucks   Salmet   Shirley Kellogg   Bandsman Rice
Petty Officer Curran   Applegarth   Konody
Colin Bell   Lewis Hind   LEFRANC
Hubert   Commercial Process Co.

MANIFESTO.

I.

1. Beyond Action and Reaction we would establish ourselves.
2. We start from opposite statements of a chosen world. Set up violent structure of adolescent clearness between two extremes.
3. We discharge ourselves on both sides.
4. We fight first on one side, then on the other, but always for the SAME cause, which is neither side or both sides and ours.
5. Mercenaries were always the best troops.
6. We are Primitive Mercenaries in the Modern World.
7. Our Cause is NO-MAN'S.
8. We set Humour at Humour's throat.
   Stir up Civil War among peaceful apes.
9. We only want Humour if it has fought like Tragedy.
10. We only want Tragedy if it can clench its side-muscles like hands on its belly, and bring to the surface a laugh like a bomb.

II.

1. We hear from America and the Continent all sorts of disagreeable things about England: "the unmusical, anti-artistic, unphilosophic country."
2. We quite agree.
3. Luxury, sport, the famous English "Humour," the thrilling ascendancy and idée fixe of Class, producing the most intense snobbery in the World; heavy stagnant pools of Saxon blood, incapable of anything but the song of a frog, in home-counties:——these phenomena give England a peculiar distinction in the wrong sense, among the nations.
4. This is why England produces such good artists from time to time.
5. This is also the reason why a movement towards art and imagination could burst up here, from this lump of compressed life, with more force than anywhere else.
6. To believe that it is necessary for or conducive to art, to "improve" life, for instance——make architecture, dress, ornament, in "better taste," is absurd.
7. The Art-instinct is permanently primitive.
8. In a chaos of imperfection, discord, etc., it finds the same stimulus as in Nature.
9. The artist of the modern movement is a savage (in no sense an "advanced," perfected, democratic, Futurist individual of Mr. Marinetti's limited imagination): this enormous, jangling, journalistic, fairy desert of modern life serves him as Nature did more technically primitive man.

[10] As the steppes and the rigours of the Russian winter, when the peasant has to lie for weeks in his hut, produces that extraordinary acuity of feeling and intelligence we associate with the Slav; so England is just now the most favourable country for the appearance of a great art.

III.

[1] We have made it quite clear that there is nothing Chauvinistic or picturesquely patriotic about our contentions.

[2] But there is violent boredom with that feeble Europeanism, abasement of the miserable "intellectual" before anything coming from Paris, Cosmopolitan sentimentality, which prevails in so many quarters.

[3] Just as we believe that an Art must be organic with its Time,
So we insist that what is actual and vital for the South, is ineffectual and unactual in the North.

[4] Fairies have disappeared from Ireland (despite foolish attempts to revive them)[2] and the bull-ring languishes in Spain.

[5] But mysticism on the one hand, gladiatorial instincts, blood and asceticism on the other, will be always actual, and springs of Creation for these two peoples.

[6] The English Character is based on the Sea.

[7] The particular qualities and characteristics that the sea always engenders in men are those that are, among the many diagnostics of our race, the most fundamentally English.

[8] That unexpected universality as well, found in the completest English artists, is due to this.

IV.

[1] We assert that the art for these climates, then, must be a northern flower.

[2] And we have implied what we believe should be the specific nature of the art destined to grow up in this country, and models of whose flue decorate the pages of this magazine.

[3] It is not a question of the characterless material climate around us.
Were that so the complication of the Jungle, dramatic Tropic growth, the vastness of American trees, would not be for us.

[4] But our industries, and the Will that determined, face to face with its needs, the direction of the modern world, has reared up steel trees where the green ones were lacking; has exploded in useful growths, and found wilder intricacies than those of Nature.

V.

[1] We bring clearly forward the following points, before further defining the character of this necessary native art.

2. The Celtic Revival was a nostalgic movement in Irish arts and letters.

[2] At the freest and most vigorous period of ENGLAND'S history, her literature, then chief Art, was in many ways identical with that of France.

[3] Chaucer was very much cousin of Villon[3] as an artist.

[4] Shakespeare and Montaigne[4] formed one literature.

[5] But Shakespeare reflected in his imagination a mysticism, madness and delicacy peculiar to the North, and brought equal quantities of Comic and Tragic together.

[6] Humour is a phenomenon caused by sudden pouring of culture into Barbary.[5]

[7] It is intelligence electrified by flood of Naivety.

[8] It is Chaos invading Concept and bursting it like nitrogen.

[9] It is the Individual masquerading as Humanity like a child in clothes too big for him.

[10] Tragic Humour is the birthright of the North.

[11] Any great Northern Art will partake of this insidious and volcanic chaos.

[12] No great ENGLISH Art need be ashamed to share some glory with France, tomorrow it may be with Germany, where the Elizabethans did before it.

[13] But it will never be French, any more than Shakespeare was, the most catholic and subtle Englishman.

VI.

[1] The Modern World is due almost entirely to Anglo-Saxon genius,—its appearance and its spirit.

[2] Machinery, trains, steam-ships, all that distinguishes externally our time, came far more from here than anywhere else.

[3] In dress, manners, mechanical inventions, LIFE, that is, ENGLAND, has influenced Europe in the same way that France has in Art.

[4] But busy with this LIFE-EFFORT, she has been the last to become conscious of the Art that is an organism of this new Order and Will of Man.

[5] Machinery is the greatest Earth-medium: incidentally it sweeps away the doctrines of a narrow and pedantic Realism at one stroke.

[6] By mechanical inventiveness, too, just as Englishmen have spread themselves all over the Earth, they have brought all the hemispheres about them in their original island.

[7] It cannot be said that the complication of the Jungle, dramatic tropic growths, the vastness of American trees, is not for us.

[8] For, in the forms of machinery, Factories, new and vaster buildings, bridges and works, we have all that, naturally, around us.

VII.

[1] Once this consciousness towards the new possibilities of expression in present life has come, however, it will be more the legitimate property of Englishmen than of any other people in Europe.

[2] It should also, as it is by origin theirs, inspire them more forcibly and directly.

---

3. François Villon (1431–1463?), French poet.
4. Michel de Montaigne (1533–1592), French essayist.

5. An old name for the western part of North Africa; possibly used here to mean "barbarity."

3 They are the inventors of this bareness and hardness, and should be the great enemies of Romance.

4 The Romance peoples will always be, at bottom, its defenders.

5 The Latins are at present, for instance, in their "discovery" of sport, their Futuristic gush over machines, aeroplanes, etc., the most romantic and sentimental "moderns" to be found.

6 It is only the second-rate people in France or Italy who are thorough revolutionaries.

7 In England, on the other hand, there Is no vulgarity in revolt.

8 Or, rather, there is no revolt, it is the normal state.

9 So often rebels of the North and the South are diametrically opposed species.

10 The nearest thing in England to a great traditional French artist, is a great revolutionary English one.

Signatures for Manifesto⁶

R. Aldington
Arbuthnot
L. Atkinson
Gaudier Brzeska
J. Dismorr
C. Hamilton
E. Pound
W. Roberts
H. Sanders
E. Wadsworth
Wyndham Lewis

Rebecca West: Indissoluble Matrimony

Rebecca West (1892–1983) is increasingly appreciated as a writer of fiction, literary criticism, political commentary, and biography, as well as one of the most important journalists of the century. Born Cicely Fairfield in Ireland, she was educated in Edinburgh after her father died when she was ten years old. She became an actress in London, taking the stage name "Rebecca West" from a heroine she had played in Ibsen's drama *Rosmersholm*. By the time she was twenty, she was becoming active in left-wing journalism and in agitation for women's rights. In 1914, when she wrote *Indissoluble Matrimony*, she was involved in a love affair with the free-thinking but married novelist H. G. Wells, with whom she had a son; at the same time, she was working on a critical biography of Henry James. She went on to write searching and sometimes critical essays on male modernists like Joyce, Eliot, and Lawrence, and perceptive essays on Virginia Woolf and Katherine Mansfield. Throughout her life, she wrote both novels and political journalism, notably a major study of Balkan politics and culture, *Black Lamb*

6. The signatories to the manifesto are Richard Aldington, English writer and man of letters; Malcolm Arbuthnot, professional photographer; Lawrence Atkinson, Vorticist artist; Henri Gaudier-Brzeska, Vorticist sculptor and contributor to *Blast* who was killed in the trenches in World War I and whose obituary was included in *Blast II*; Jessica Dismoor, artist whose illustrations were included in *Blast*; Cuthbert Hamilton, avant-garde artist; Ezra Pound; William Roberts, painter; Helen Saunders, Vorticist designer; Edward Wadsworth, Vorticist painter; and Wyndham Lewis.

and Grey Falcon (1942), and a series of brilliant reports on the Nuremberg trials of Nazi war criminals at the end of World War II, collected as *A Train of Powder* (1955). She was made Dame Commander of the British Empire in 1959. Like her political writing, her fiction is notable for its irreverent probing of modernity's fault lines. Though never an orthodox feminist, West demonstrated a keen insight into the psychology of women and men, and portrayed the straitened thinking that made feminism's ultimate victory anything but a foregone conclusion.

Indissoluble Matrimony

When George Silverton opened the front door he found that the house was not empty for all its darkness. The spitting noise of the striking of damp matches and mild, growling exclamations of annoyance told him that his wife was trying to light the dining-room gas. He went in and with some short, hostile sound of greeting lit a match and brought brightness into the little room. Then, irritated by his own folly in bringing private papers into his wife's presence, he stuffed the letters he had brought from the office deep into the pockets of his overcoat. He looked at her suspiciously, but she had not seen them, being busy in unwinding her orange motor-veil. His eyes remained on her face to brood a little sourly on her moving loveliness, which he had not been sure of finding: for she was one of those women who create an illusion alternately of extreme beauty and extreme ugliness. Under her curious dress, designed in some pitifully cheap and worthless stuff by a successful mood of her indiscreet taste—she had black blood in her—her long body seemed pulsing with some exaltation. The blood was coursing violently under her luminous yellow skin, and her lids, dusky with fatigue, drooped contentedly over her great humid black eyes. Perpetually she raised her hand to the mass of black hair that was coiled on her thick golden neck, and stroked it with secretive enjoyment, as a cat licks its fur. And her large mouth smiled frankly, but abstractedly, at some digested pleasure.

There was a time when George would have looked on this riot of excited loveliness with suspicion. But now he knew it was almost certainly caused by some trifle—a long walk through stinging weather, the report of a Socialist victory at a by-election, or the intoxication of a waltz refrain floating from the municipal band-stand across the flats of the local recreation ground. And even if it had been caused by some amorous interlude he would not have greatly cared. In the ten years since their marriage he had lost the quality which would have made him resentful. He now believed that quality to be purely physical. Unless one was in good condition and responsive to the messages sent out by the flesh Evadne could hardly concern one. He turned the bitter thought over in his heart and stung himself by deliberately gazing unmoved upon her beautiful joyful body.

"Let's have supper now!" she said rather greedily.

He looked at the table and saw she had set it before she went out. As usual she had been in an improvident hurry: it was carelessly done. Besides, what an absurd supper to set before a hungry solicitor's clerk! In the centre, obviously intended as the principal dish, was a bowl of plums, softly red, soaked with the sun, glowing like jewels in the downward stream of the incandescent light. Besides them was a great yellow melon, its sleek sides fluted with rich growth, and a honey-comb glistening on a willow-pattern dish. The only sensible food to be seen was a plate of tongue laid at his place.

"I can't sit down to supper without washing my hands!"

While he splashed in the bathroom upstairs he heard her pull in a chair to the table and sit down to her supper. It annoyed him. There was no ritual about it. While he was eating tongue she would be crushing honey on new bread, or stripping a plum of its purple skin and holding the golden globe up to the gas to see the light filter through. The meal would pass in silence. She would innocently take his dumbness for a sign of abstraction and forbear to babble. He would find the words choked on his lips by the weight of dullness that always oppressed him in her presence. Then, just about the time when he was beginning to feel able to formulate his obscure grievances against her, she would rise from the table without a word and run upstairs to her work, humming in that uncanny, negro way of hers.

And so it was. She ate with an appalling catholicity of taste, with a nice child's love of sweet foods, and occasionally she broke into that hoarse beautiful croon. Every now and then she looked at him with too obvious speculations as to whether his silence was due to weariness or uncertain temper. Timidly she cut him an enormous slice of the melon, which he did not want. Then she rose abruptly and flung herself into the rocking chair on the hearth. She clasped her hands behind her head and strained backwards so that the muslin stretched over her strong breasts. She sang softly to the ceiling.

There was something about the fantastic figure that made him feel as though they were not properly married.

"Evadne?"

"'S?"

"What have you been up to this evening?"

"I was at Milly Stafordale's."

He was silent again. That name brought up the memory of his courting days. It was under the benign eyes of blonde, plebeian Milly that he had wooed the distracting creature in the rocking chair.

Ten years before, when he was twenty-five, his firm had been reduced to hysteria over the estates of an extraordinarily stupid old woman, named Mrs. Mary Ellerker. Her stupidity, grappling with the complexity of the sources of the vast income which rushed in spate from the properties of four deceased husbands, demanded oceans of explanations even over her weekly rents. Silverton alone in the office, by reason of a certain natural incapacity for excitement, could deal calmly with this marvel of imbecility. He alone could endure to sit with patience in the black-panelled drawing-room amidst the jungle of shiny mahogany furniture and talk to a mass of darkness, who rested heavily in the window-seat and now and then made an idiotic remark in a bright, hearty voice. But it shook even him. Mrs. Mary Ellerker was obscene. Yet she was perfectly sane and, although of that remarkable plainness noticeable in most oft-married women, in good enough physical condition. She merely presented the loathsome spectacle of an ignorant mind, contorted by the artificial idiocy of coquetry, lack of responsibility, and hatred of discipline, stripped naked by old age. That was the real horror of her. One feared to think how many women were really like Mrs. Ellerker under their armour of physical perfection or social grace. For this reason he turned eyes of hate on Mrs. Ellerker's pretty little companion, Milly Stafordale, who smiled at him over her embroidery with wintry northern brightness. When she was old she too would be obscene.

This horror obsessed him. Never before had he feared anything. He had never lived more than half-an-hour from a police station, and, as he had by some chance missed the melancholy clairvoyance of adolescence, he had never conceived of any horror with which the police could not deal. This disgust of women revealed to him that the world is a place of subtle perils. He began to fear marriage as he feared death. The thought of intimacy with some lovely, desirable and necessary wife turned him sick as he sat at his lunch. The secret obscenity of women! He talked darkly of it to his friends. He wondered why the Church did not provide a service for the absolution of men after marriage. Wife desertion seemed to him a beautiful return of the tainted body to cleanliness.

On his fifth visit to Mrs. Ellerker he could not begin his business at once. One of Milly Stafordale's friends had come in to sing to the old lady. She stood by the piano against the light, so that he saw her washed with darkness. Amazed, of tropical fruit. And before he had time to apprehend the sleepy wonder of her beauty, she had begun to sing. Now he knew that her voice was a purely physical attribute, built in her as she lay in her mother's womb, and no index of her spiritual values. But then, as it welled up from the thick golden throat and clung to her lips, it seemed a sublime achievement of the soul. It was smouldering contralto such as only those of black blood can possess. As she sang her great black eyes lay on him with the innocent shamelessness of a young animal, and he remembered hopefully that he was good looking. Suddenly she stood in silence, playing with her heavy black plait. Mrs. Ellerker broke into silly thanks. The girl's mother, who had been playing the accompaniment, rose and stood rolling up her music. Silverton, sick with excitement, was introduced to them. He noticed that the mother was a little darker than the conventions permit. Their name was Hannan—Mrs. Arthur Hannan and Evadne. They moved lithely and quietly out of the room, the girl's eyes still lingering on his face.

The thought of her splendour and the rolling echoes of her voice disturbed him all night. Next day, going to his office, he travelled with her on the horse-car that bound his suburb to Petrick. One of the horses fell lame, and she had time to tell him that she was studying at a commercial college. He quivered with distress. All the time he had a dizzy illusion that she was nestling up against him. They parted shyly. During the next few days they met constantly. He began to go and see them in the evening at their home—a mean flat crowded with cheap glories of bead curtains and Oriental hangings that set off the women's alien beauty. Mrs. Hannan was a widow and they lived alone, in a wonderful silence. He talked more than he had ever done in his whole life before. He took a dislike to the widow, she was consumed with fiery subterranean passions, no fit guardian for the tender girl.

Now he could imagine with what silent rapture Evadne had watched his agitation. Almost from the first she had meant to marry him. He was physically attractive, though not strong. His intellect was gently stimulating like a mild white wine. And it was time she married. She was ripe for adult things. This was the real wound in his soul. He had tasted of a divine thing created in his time for dreams out of her rich beauty, her loneliness, her romantic poverty, her immaculate youth. He had known love. And Evadne had never known anything more than a magnificent physical adventure which she had secured at the right time as she would have engaged a cab to take her to the station in time for the cheapest excursion train. It was a quick way to light-hearted living. With loathing he remembered how in the days of their engagement she used to gaze purely into his blinking eyes and with her unashamed kisses incite him to extravagant embraces. Now he cursed her for having obtained his spiritual revolution on false pretences. Only for a little time had he had his illusion, for their marriage was hastened by Mrs. Hannan's sudden death. After three months of savage mourning Evadne flung herself into marriage, and her excited candour had enlightened him very soon.

That marriage had lasted ten years. And to Evadne their relationship was just the same as ever. Her vitality needed him as it needed the fruit on the table before him. He shook with wrath and a sense of outraged decency.

"O George!" She was yawning widely.

"What's the matter?" he said without interest.

"It's so beastly dull."

"I can't help that, can I?"

"No." She smiled placidly at him. "We're a couple of dull dogs, aren't we? I wish we had children."

After a minute she suggested, apparently as an alternative amusement, "Perhaps the post hasn't passed."

As she spoke there was a rat-tat and the slither of a letter under the door. Evadne picked herself up and ran out into the lobby. After a second or two, during which she made irritating inarticulate exclamations, she came in reading the letter and stroking her bust with a gesture of satisfaction.

"They want me to speak at Longton's meeting on the nineteenth," she purred.

"Longton? What's he up to?"

Stephen Longton was the owner of the biggest iron works in Petrick, a man whose refusal to adopt the livery of busy oafishness thought proper to commercial men aroused the gravest suspicions.

"He's standing as Socialist candidate for the town council."

". . . Socialist!" he muttered.

He set his jaw. That was a side of Evadne he considered as little as possible. He had never been able to assimilate the fact that Evadne had, two years after their marriage, passed through his own orthodox Radicalism[1] to a passionate Socialism, and that after reading enormously of economics she had begun to write for the Socialist press and to speak successfully at meetings. In the jaundiced recesses of his mind he took it for granted that her work would have the lax fibre of her character: that it would be infected with her Oriental crudities. Although once or twice he had been congratulated on her brilliance, he mistrusted this phase of her activity as a caper of the sensualist. His eyes blazed on her and found the depraved, over-sexed creature, looking milder than a gazelle, holding out a hand-bill to him.

"They've taken it for granted!"

He saw her name—his name—

MRS. EVADNE SILVERTON.[2]

It was at first the blaze of stout scarlet letters on the dazzling white ground that made him blink. Then he was convulsed with rage.

"Georgie dear!"

She stepped forward and caught his weak body to her bosom. He wrenched himself away. Spiritual nausea made him determined to be a better man than her.

"A pair of you! You and Longton—!" he snarled scornfully. Then, seeing her startled face, he controlled himself.

"I thought it would please you," said Evadne, a little waspishly.

"You mustn't have anything to do with Longton," he stormed.

A change passed over her. She became ugly. Her face was heavy with intellect, her lips coarse with power. He was at arms with a Socialist lead. Much he would have preferred the bland sensualist again.

---

1. An extreme form of Liberalism, still comfortably within the continuum of British democratic politics; Socialism, which Evadne has embraced, advocates the abolition of the current system and is thus too extreme for George's bourgeois attitudes.

2. Evadne would have been addressed in polite society as "Mrs. George Silverton"; George reads this breach of decorum as one more sign that his wife is out of control. Leopold Bloom, the protagonist of James Joyce's *Ulysses*, makes a similar observation when his wife Molly receives a letter from her lover addressed to "Mrs. Marion Bloom."

"Why?"

"Because—his lips stuck together like blotting-paper—he's not the sort of man my wife should—should—"

With movements which terrified him by their rough energy, she folded up the bills and put them back in the envelope.

"George. I suppose you mean that he's a bad man." He nodded.

"I know quite well that the girl who used to be his typist is his mistress." She spoke it sweetly, as if reasoning with an old fool. "But she's got consumption. She'll be dead in six months. In fact, I think it's rather nice of him. To look after her and all that."

"My God!" He leapt to his feet, extending a shaking forefinger. As she turned to him, the smile dying on her lips, his excited weakness wrapped him in a paramnesic illusion:[3] it seemed to him that he had been through all this before—a long, long time ago. "My God, you talk like a woman off the streets!"

Evadne's lips lifted over her strong teeth. With clever cruelty she fixed his eyes with hers, well knowing that he longed to fall forward and bury his head on the table in a transport of hysterical sobs. After a moment of this torture she turned away, herself distressed by a desire to cry.

"How can you say such dreadful, dreadful things!" she protested, chokingly.

He sat down again. His eyes looked little and red, but they blazed on her. "I wonder if you are," he said softly.

"Are what?" she asked petulantly, a tear rolling down her nose.

"You know," he answered, nodding.

"George, George, George!" she cried.

"You've always been keen on kissing and making love, haven't you, my precious? At first you startled me, you did! I didn't know women were like that." From that morass he suddenly stepped on to a high peak of terror. Amazed to find himself sincere, he cried—"I don't believe good women are!"

"Georgie, how can you be so silly!" exclaimed Evadne shrilly. "You know quite well I've been as true to you as any woman could be." She sought his eyes with a liquid glance of reproach. He averted his gaze, sickened at having put himself in the wrong. For even while he degraded his tongue his pure soul fainted with loathing of her fleshliness.

"I—I'm sorry."

Too wily to forgive him at once, she showed him a lowering profile with downcast lids. Of course, he knew it was a fraud: an imputation against her chastity was no more poignant than a reflection on the cleanliness of her nails—rude and spiteful, but that was all. But for a time they kept up the deception, while she cleared the table in a steely silence.

"Evadne, I'm sorry. I'm tired." His throat was dry. He could not bear the discord of a row added to the horror of their companionship. "Evadne, do forgive me—I don't know what I meant by—"

"That's all right, silly!" she said suddenly and bent over the table to kiss him. Her brow was smooth. It was evident from her splendid expression that she was preoccupied. Then she finished clearing up the dishes and took them into the kitchen. While she was out of the room he rose from his seat and sat down in the armchair by the fire, setting his bull-dog pipe alight. For a very short time he was free of her

---

3. A condition in which fact and fiction become confused.

voluptuous presence. But she ran back soon, having put the kettle on and changed her blouse for a loose dressing-jacket, and sat down on the arm of his chair. Once or twice she bent and kissed his brow, but for the most part she lay back with his head drawn to her bosom, rocking herself rhythmically. Silverton, a little disgusted by their contact, sat quite motionless and passed into a doze. He revolved in his mind the incidents of his day's routine and remembered a snub from a superior. So he opened his eyes and tried to think of something else. It was then that he became conscious that the rhythm of Evadne's movement was not regular. It was broken as though she rocked in time to music. Music? His sense of hearing crept up to hear if there was any sound of music in the breaths she was emitting rather heavily every now and then. At first he could hear nothing. Then it struck him that each breath was a muttered phrase. He stiffened, and hatred flamed through his veins. The words came clearly through her lips. . . . "The present system of wage-slavery. . . ."

"Evadne!" He sprang to his feet. "You're preparing your speech!"

She did not move. "I am," she said.

"Damn it, you shan't speak!"

"Damn it, I will!"

"Evadne, you shan't speak! If you do I swear to God above I'll turn you out into the streets—." She rose and came towards him. She looked black and dangerous. She trod softly like a cat with her head down. In spite of himself, his tongue licked his lips in fear and he cowered a moment before he picked up a knife from the table. For a space she looked down on him and the sharp blade.

"You idiot, can't you hear the kettle's boiling over?"

He shrank back, letting the knife fall on the floor. For three minutes he stood there controlling his breath and trying to still his heart. Then he followed her into the kitchen. She was making a noise with a basinful of dishes.

"Stop that row."

She turned round with a dripping dish-cloth in her hand and pondered whether to throw it at him. But she was tired and wanted peace: so that she could finish the rough draft of her speech. So she stood waiting.

"Did you understand what I said then? If you don't promise me here and now—"

She flung her arms upwards with a cry and dashed past him. He made to run after her upstairs, but stumbled on the threshold of the lobby and sat with his ankle twisted under him, shaking with rage. In a second she ran downstairs again, clothed in a big cloak with black bundle clutched to her breast. For the first time in their married life she was seized with a convulsion of sobs. She dashed out of the front door and banged it with such passion that a glass pane shivered to fragments behind her.

"What's this? What's this?" he cried stupidly, standing up. He perceived with an insane certainty that she was going out to meet some unknown lover. "I'll come and tell him what a slut you are!" he shouted after her and stumbled to the door. It was jammed now and he had to drag at it.

The night was flooded with the yellow moonshine of midsummer: it seemed to drip from the lacquered leaves of the shrubs in the front garden. In its soft clarity he could see her plainly, although she was now two hundred yards away. She was hastening to the north end of Sumatra Crescent, an end that curled up the hill like a silly kitten's tail and stopped abruptly in green fields. So he knew that she was going to the young man who had just bought the Georgian Manor, whose elm-trees crowned the hill. Oh, how he hated her! Yet he must follow her, or else she would cover up her adulteries so that he could not take his legal revenge. So he began to run—silently, for he wore his carpet slippers. He was only a hundred yards behind her when she slipped through a gap in the hedge to tread a field-path. She still walked with pride, for though she was town-bred, night in the open seemed not at all fearful to her. As he shuffled in pursuit his carpet slippers were engulfed in a shining pool of mud: he raised one with a squelch, the other was left. This seemed the last humiliation. He kicked the other one off his feet and padded on in his socks, snuffling in anticipation of a cold. Then physical pain sent him back to the puddle to pluck out the slippers; it was a dirty job. His heart battered his breast as he saw that Evadne had gained the furthest hedge and was crossing the stile into the lane that ran up to the Manor gates.

"Go on, you beast!" he muttered, "Go on, go on!" After a scamper he climbed the stile and thrust his lean neck beyond a mass of wilted hawthorn bloom that crumbled into vagrant petals at his touch.

The lane mounted yellow as cheese to where the moon lay on his iron tracery of the Manor gates. Evadne was not there. Hardly believing his eyes he hobbled over into the lane and looked in the other direction. There he saw her disappearing round the bend of the road. Gathering himself up to a run, he tried to think out his bearings. He had seldom passed this way, and like most people without strong primitive instincts he had no sense of orientation. With difficulty he remembered that after a mile's mazy wanderings between high hedges this lane sloped suddenly to the bowl of heather overhung by the moorlands, in which lay the Petrick reservoirs, two untamed lakes.

"Eh! she's going to meet him by the water!" he cursed to himself. He remembered the withered ash tree, seared by lightning to its root, that stood by the road at the bare frontier of the moor. "May God strike her like that," he prayed," "as she fouls the other man's lips with her kisses. O God! let me strangle her. Or bury a knife deep in her breast." Suddenly he broke into a lolloping run. "O my Lord, I'll be able to divorce her. I'll be free. Free to live alone. To do my day's work and sleep my night's sleep without her. I'll get a job somewhere else and forget her. I'll bring her to the dogs. No clean man or woman in Petrick will look at her now. They won't have her to speak at that meeting now!" His throat swelled with joy, he leapt high in the air.

"I'll lie about her. If I can prove that she's wrong with this man they'll believe me if I say she's a bad woman and drinks. I'll make her name a joke. And then—"

He flung wide his arms in ecstasy: the left struck against stone. More pain than he had thought his body could hold convulsed him, so that he sank on the ground hugging his aching arm. He looked backwards as he writhed and saw that the hedge had stopped; above him was the great stone wall of the county asylum. The question broke on him—was there any lunatic in its confines so slavered with madness as he himself? Nothing but madness could have accounted for the torrent of ugly words, the sea of uglier thoughts that was now a part of him. "O God, me to turn like this!" he cried, rolling over full-length on the grassy bank by the roadside. That the infidelity of his wife, a thing that should have brought out the stern manliness of his true nature, should have discovered him as lecherous-lipped as any pot-house[4] lounger, was the most infamous accident of his married life. The sense of sin descended on him so that his tears flowed hot and bitterly. "Have I gone to the Unitarian chapel every Sunday morning and to the Ethical Society every evening for nothing?" his

4. Tavern.

spirit asked itself in its travail. "All those Browning lectures for nothing. . . ."[5] He said the Lord's Prayer several times and lay for a minute quietly crying. The relaxation of his muscles brought him a sense of rest which seemed forgiveness falling from God. The tears dried on his cheeks. His calmer consciousness heard the sound of rushing waters mingled with the beating of blood in his ears. He got up and scrambled round the turn of the road that brought him to the withered ash-tree.

He walked forward on the parched heatherland to the mound whose scarred sides, heaped with boulders, tufted with mountain grasses, shone before him in the moonlight. He scrambled up to it hurriedly and hoisted himself from ledge to ledge till he fell on his knees with a squeal of pain. His ankle was caught in a crevice of the rock. Gulping down his agony at this final physical humiliation he heaved himself upright and raced on to the summit, and found himself before the Devil's Cauldron, filled to the brim with yellow moonshine and the fiery play of summer lightning. The rugged crags opposite him were a low barricade against the stars to which the mound where he stood shot forward like a bridge. To the left of this the long Lisbech pond lay like a trailing serpent; its silver scales glittered as the wind swept down from the vaster moorlands to the east. To the right under a steep drop of twenty feet was the Whimsey pond, more sinister, shaped in an unnatural oval, sheltered from the wind by the high ridge so that the undisturbed moonlight lay across it like a sharp-edged sword.

He looked about for some sign of Evadne. She could not be on the land by the margin of the lakes, for the light blazed so strongly that each reed could be clearly seen like a black dagger stabbing the silver. He looked down Lisbech and saw far east a knot of red and green and orange lights. Perhaps for some devilish purpose Evadne had sought Lisbech railway station. But his volcanic mind had preserved one grain of sense that assured him that, subtle as Evadne's villainy might be, it would not lead her to walk five miles out of her way to a terminus which she could have reached in fifteen minutes by taking a train from the station down the road. She must be under cover somewhere here. He went down the gentle slope that fell from the top of the ridge to Lisbech pond in a disorder of rough heather, unhappy patches of cultivated grass, and coppices of silver birch, fringed with flaming broom that seemed faintly tarnished in the moonlight. At the bottom was a roughly hewn path which he followed in hot aimless hurry. In a little he approached a riot of falling waters. There was a slice ten feet broad carved out of the ridge, and to this narrow channel of black shining rock the floods of Lisbech leapt some feet and raced through to Whimsey. The noise beat him back. The gap was spanned by a gaunt thing of paint-blistered iron, on which he stood dizzily and noticed how the wide step that ran on each side of the channel through to the other pond was smeared with sinister green slime. Now his physical distress reminded him of Evadne, whom he had almost forgotten in contemplation of these lonely waters. The idea of her had been present but obscured, as sometimes toothache may cease active torture. His blood lust set him on and he staggered forward with covered ears. Even as he went something caught his eye in a thicket high up on the slope near the crags. Against the slender pride of some silver birches stood a gnarled hawthorn tree, its branches flattened under the stern moorland winds so that it grew squat like an opened umbrella. In its dark shadows, faintly illumined by a few boughs of withered blossom, there moved a strange bluish light. Even while he did not know what it was it made his flesh stir.

5. George's activities—Unitarian church, Ethical Society, Browning Society—suggest that he participated in public exercises of a high moral nature without giving himself over to traditional religious faith, which he would have seen as "irrational" and "unmanly."

The light emerged. It was the moonlight reflected from Evadne's body. She was clad in a black bathing dress, and her arms and legs and the broad streak of flesh laid bare by a rent down the back shone brilliantly white, so that she seemed like a grotesquely patterned wild animal as she ran down to the lake. Whirling her arms above her head she trampled down into the water and struck out strongly. Her movements were full of brisk delight and she swam quickly. The moonlight made her the centre of a little feathery blur of black and silver, with a comet's tail trailing in her wake.

Nothing in all his married life had ever staggered Silverton so much as this. He had imagined his wife's adultery so strongly that it had come to be. It was now as real as their marriage; more real than their courtship. So this seemed to be the last crime of the adulteress. She had dragged him over those squelching fields and these rough moors and changed him from a man of irritations, but no passions, into a cold designer of murderous treacheries, so that he might witness a swimming exhibition! For a minute he was stunned. Then he sprang down to the rushy edge and ran along in the direction of her course, crying—"Evadne! Evadne!" She did not hear him. At last he achieved a chest note and shouted—"Evadne! come here!" The black and silver feather shivered in mid-water. She turned immediately and swam back to shore. He suspected sullenness in her slowness, but was glad of it, for after the shock of this extraordinary incident he wanted to go to sleep. Drowsiness lay on him like lead. He shook himself like a dog and wrenched off his linen collar, winking at the bright moon to keep himself awake. As she came quite near he was exasperated by the happy, snorting breaths she drew, and strolled a pace or two up the bank. To his enragement the face she lifted as she waded to dry land was placid, and she scrambled gaily up the bank to his side.

"O George, why did you come!" she exclaimed quite affectionately, laying a damp hand on his shoulder.

"O damn it, what does this mean!" he cried, committing a horrid tenor squeak. "What are you doing?"

"Why. George," she said," "I came here for a bathe."

He stared into her face and could make nothing of it. It was only sweet surfaces of flesh, soft radiances of eye and lip, a lovely lie of comeliness. He forgot this present grievance in a cold search for the source of her peculiar hatefulness. Under this sick gaze she pouted and turned away with a peevish gesture. He made no sign and stood silent, watching her saunter to that gaunt iron bridge. The roar of the little waterfall did not disturb her splendid nerves and she drooped sensuously over the hand-rail, sniffing up the sweet night smell; too evidently trying to abase him to another apology.

A mosquito whirred into his face. He killed it viciously and strode off towards his wife, who showed by a common little toss of the head that she was conscious of his coming.

"Look here, Evadne!" he panted. "What did you come here for? Tell me the truth and I promise I'll not—I'll not—"

"Not WHAT, George?"

"O please, please tell me the truth, do Evadne!" he cried pitifully.

"But, dear, what is there to carry on about so? You went on so queerly about my meeting that my head felt fit to split, and I thought the long walk and the dip would do me good." She broke off, amazed at the wave of horror that passed over his face.

His heart sank. From the loose-lipped hurry in the telling of her story, from the bigness of her eyes and the lack of subtlety in her voice, he knew that this was the truth. Here was no adulteress whom he could accuse in the law courts and condemn into the street, no resourceful sinner whose merry crimes he could discover. Here was merely his good wife, the faithful attendant of his hearth, relentless wrecker of his soul.

She came towards him as a cat approaches a displeased master, and hovered about him on the stone coping of the noisy sluice.

"Indeed!" he found himself saying sarcastically. "Indeed!"

"Yes, George Silverton, indeed!" she burst out, a little frightened. "And why shouldn't I? I used to come here often enough on summer nights with poor Mamma—"

"Yes!" he shouted. It was exactly the sort of thing that would appeal to that weird half-black woman from the back of beyond. "Mamma!" he cried tauntingly, "Mamma!"

There was a flash of silence between them before Evadne, clutching her breast and balancing herself dangerously on her heels on the stone coping, broke into gentle shrieks. "You dare talk of my Mamma, my poor Mamma, and she cold in her grave! I haven't been happy since she died and I married you, you silly little misery, you!" Then the rage was suddenly wiped off her brain by the perception of a crisis.

The trickle of silence overflowed into a lake, over which their spirits flew, looking at each other's reflection in the calm waters: in the hurry of their flight they had never before seen each other. They stood facing one another with dropped heads, quietly thinking.

The strong passion which filled them threatened to disintegrate their souls as a magnetic current decomposes the electrolyte, so they fought to organise their sensations. They tried to arrange themselves and their lives for comprehension, but beyond sudden lyric visions of old incidents of hatefulness—such as a smarting quarrel of six years ago as to whether Evadne had or had not cheated the railway company out of one and eightpence on an excursion ticket—the past was intangible. It trailed behind this intense event as the pale hair trails behind the burning comet. They were pre-occupied with the moment. Quite often George had found a mean pleasure in the thought that by never giving Evadne a child he had cheated her out of one form of experience, and now he paid the price for this unnatural pride of sterility. For now the spiritual offspring of their intercourse came to birth. A sublime loathing was between them. For a little time it was a huge perilous horror, but afterwards, like men aboard a ship whose masts seek the sky through steep waves, they found a drunken pride in the adventure. This was the very absolute of hatred. It cheapened the memory of the fantasias of irritation and ill-will they had performed in the less boring moments of their marriage, and they felt dazed, as amateurs who had found themselves creating a masterpiece. For the first time they were possessed by a supreme emotion and they felt a glad desire to strip away restraint and express it nakedly. It was ecstasy; they felt tall and full of blood.

Like people who, bewitched by Christ, see the whole earth as the breathing body of God, so they saw the universe as the substance and the symbol of their hatred. The stars trembled overhead with wrath. A wind from behind the angry crags set the moonlight on Lisbech quivering with rage, and the squat hawthorn-tree creaked slowly like the irritation of a dull little man. The dry moors, parched with harsh anger, waited thirstily and, sending out the murmur of rustling mountain grass and the cry of wakening fowl, seemed to huddle closer to the lake. But this sense of the earth's sympathy slipped away from them and they loathed all matter as the dull wrapping of their flame-like passion. At their wishing matter fell away and they saw sarcastic visions. He saw her as a toad squatting on the clean earth, obscuring the stars and pressing down its hot moist body on the cheerful fields. She felt his long boneless body coiled round the roots of the lovely tree of life. They shivered fastidiously. With an uplifting sense of responsibility they realised that they must kill each other.

A bird rose over their heads with a leaping flight that made it seem as though its black body was bouncing against the bright sky. The foolish noise and motion precipitated their thoughts. They were broken into a new conception of life. They perceived that God is war and his creatures are meant to fight. When dogs walk through the world cats must climb trees. The virgin must snare the wanton, the fine lover must put the prude to the sword. The gross man of action walks, spurred on the bloodless bodies of the men of thought, who lie quiet and cunningly do not tell him where his grossness leads him. The flesh must smother the spirit, the spirit must set the flesh on fire and watch it burn. And those who were gentle by nature and shrank from the ordained brutality were betrayers of their kind, surrendering the earth to the seed of their enemies. In this war there is no discharge. If they succumbed to peace now, the rest of their lives would be dishonourable, like the exile of a rebel who has begged his life as the reward of cowardice. It was their first experience of religious passion, and they abandoned themselves to it so that their immediate personal qualities fell away from them. Neither his weakness nor her prudence stood in the way of the event.

They measured each other with the eye. To her he was a spidery thing against the velvet blackness and hard silver surfaces of the pond. The light soaked her bathing dress so that she seemed, against the jagged shadows of the rock cutting, as though she were clad in a garment of dark polished mail. Her knees were bent so clearly, her toes gripped the coping so strongly. He understood very clearly that if he did not kill her instantly she would drop him easily into the deep riot of waters. Yet for a space he could not move, but stood expecting a degrading death. Indeed, he gave her time to kill him. But she was without power too, and struggled weakly with a hallucination. The quarrel in Sumatra Crescent with its suggestion of vast and unmentionable antagonisms; her swift race through the moon-drenched countryside, all crepitant with night noises: the swimming in the wine-like lake: their isolation on the moor, which was expressedly hostile to them, as nature always is to lonely man: and this stark contest face to face, with their resentments heaped between them like a pile of naked swords—these things were so strange that her civilised self shrank back appalled. There entered into her the primitive woman who is the curse of all women: a creature of the most utter femaleness, useless, save for childbirth, with no strong brain to make her physical weakness a light accident, abjectly and corruptingly afraid of man. A squaw, she dared not strike her lord.

The illusion passed like a moment of faintness and left her enraged at having forgotten her superiority even for an instant. In the material world she had a thousand times been defeated into making prudent reservations and practising unnatural docilities. But in the world of thought she had maintained unfalteringly her masterfulness in spite of the strong yearning of her temperament towards voluptuous surrenders. That was her virtue. Its violation whipped her to action and she would have killed him at once, had not his moment come a second before hers. Sweating horribly, he had dropped his head forward on his chest: his eyes fell on her feet and marked the plebeian moulding of her ankle, which rose thickly over a crease of flesh from the heel to the calf. The woman was coarse in grain and pattern.

He had no instinct for honourable attack, so he found himself striking her in the stomach. She reeled from pain, not because his strength overcame hers. For the first time her eyes looked into his candidly open, unveiled by languor or lust: their hard brightness told him how she despised him for that unwarlike blow. He cried out as he realised that this was another of her despicable victories and that the whole burden of the crime now lay on him, for he had begun it. But the rage was stopped on his lips as her arms, flung wildly out as she fell backwards, caught him about the waist with abominable justness of eye and evil intention. So they fell body to body into the quarrelling waters.

The feathery confusion had looked so soft, yet it seemed the solid rock they struck. The breath shot out of him and suffocation warmly stuffed his ears and nose. Then the rock cleft and he was swallowed by a brawling blackness in which whirled a vortex that flung him again and again on a sharp thing that burned his shoulder. All about him fought the waters, and they cut his flesh like knives. His pain was past belief. Though God might be war, he desired peace in his time, and he yearned for another God—a child's God, an immense arm coming down from the hills and lifting him to a kindly bosom. Soon his body would burst for breath, his agony would smash in his breast bone. So great was his pain that his consciousness was strained to apprehend it, as a too tightly stretched canvas splits and rips.

Suddenly the air was sweet on his mouth. The starlight seemed as hearty as a cheer. The world was still there, the world in which he had lived, so he must be safe. His own weakness and loveableness induced enjoyable tears, and there was a delicious moment of abandonment to comfortable whining before he realised that the water would not kindly buoy him up for long, and that even now a hostile current clasped his waist. He braced his flaccid body against the sucking blackness and flung his head back so that the water should not bubble so hungrily against the cords of his throat. Above him the slime of the rock was sticky with moonbeams, and the leprous light brought to his mind a newspaper paragraph, read years ago, which told him that the dawn had discovered floating in some oily Mersey dock, under walls as infected with wet growth as this, a corpse whose blood-encrusted finger-tips were deeply cleft. On the instant his own finger-tips seemed hot with blood and deeply cleft from clawing at the impregnable rock. He screamed gaspingly and beat his hands through the strangling flood. Action, which he had always loathed and dreaded, had broken the hard mould of his self-possession, and the dry dust of his character was blown hither and thither by fear. But one sharp fragment of intelligence which survived this detrition of his personality perceived that a certain gleam on the rock about a foot above the water was not the cold putrescence of the slime, but certainly the hard and merry light of a moon-ray striking on solid metal. His left hand clutched upwards at it, and he swung from a rounded projection. It was, his touch told him, a leaden ring hanging obliquely from the rock, to which his memory could visualise precisely in some past drier time when Lisbech sent no flood to Whimsey, a waterman mooring a boat strewn with pale-bellied perch. And behind the stooping waterman he remembered a flight of narrow steps that led up a buttress to a stone shelf that ran through the cutting. Unquestionably he was safe. He swung in a happy rhythm from the ring, his limp body trailing like a caterpillar through the stream to the foot of the steps, while he gasped in strength. A part of him was in agony, for his arm was nearly dragged out of its socket and a part of him was embarrassed because his hysteria shook him with a deep rumbling chuckle that sounded as though he meditated on some unseemly joke; the whole was pervaded by a twilight atmosphere of unenthusiastic gratitude for his rescue, like the quietly cheerful tone of a Sunday evening sacred concert. After a minute's deep breathing he hauled himself up by the other hand and prepared to swing himself on to the steps.

But first, to shake off the wet worsted rags, once his socks, that now stuck uncomfortably between his toes, he splashed his feet outwards to midstream. A certain porpoise-like surface met his left foot. Fear dappled his face with goose flesh. Without turning his head he knew what it was. It was Evadne's fat flesh rising on each side of her deep-furrowed spine through the rent in her bathing dress.

Once more hatred marched through his soul like a king: compelling service by his godhead and, like all gods, a little hated for his harsh lieu[6] on his worshipper. He saw his wife as the curtain of flesh between him and celibacy, and solitude and all those delicate abstentions from life which his soul desired. He saw her as the invisible worm destroying the rose of the world with her dark secret love.[7] Now he knelt on the lowest stone step watching her wet seal-smooth head bobbing nearer on the waters. As her strong arms, covered with little dark points where her thick hairs were clotted with moisture, stretched out towards safety he bent forward and laid his hands on her head. He held her face under water. Scornfully he noticed the bubbles that rose to the surface from her protesting mouth and nostrils, and the foam raised by her arms and her thick ankles. To the end the creature persisted in turmoil, in movement, in action. . . .

She dropped like a stone. His hands, with nothing to resist them, slapped the water foolishly and he nearly overbalanced forward into the stream. He rose to his feet very stiffly. "I must be a very strong man," he said, as he slowly climbed the steps. "I must be a very strong man," he repeated, a little louder, as with a hot and painful rigidity of the joints he stretched himself out at full length along the stone shelf. Weakness closed him in like a lead coffin. For a little time the wetness of his clothes persisted in being felt: then the sensation oozed out of him and his body fell out of knowledge. There was neither pain nor joy nor any other reckless ploughing of the brain by nerves. He knew unconsciousness, or rather the fullest consciousness he had ever known. For the world became nothingness, and nothingness which is free from the yeasty nuisance of matter and the ugliness of generation was the law of his being. He was absorbed into vacuity, the untamed substance of the universe, round which he conceived passion and thought to circle as straws caught up by the wind. He saw God and lived.

In Heaven a thousand years are a day. And this little corner of time in which he found happiness shrank to a nut-shell as he opened his eyes again. This peace was hardly printed on his heart, yet the brightness of the night was blurred by the dawn. With the grunting carefulness of a man drunk with fatigue, he crawled along the stone shelf to the iron bridge, where he stood with his back to the roaring sluice and rested. All things seemed different now and happier. Like most timid people he disliked the night, and the commonplace hand which the dawn laid on the scene seemed to him a sanctification. The dimmed moon sank to her setting behind the crags. The jewel lights of Lisbech railway station were weak, cheerful twinklings. A steaming bluish milk of morning mist had been spilt on the hard silver surface of the lake, and the reeds no longer stabbed it like little daggers, but seemed a feathery fringe, like the pampas grass in the front garden in Sumatra Crescent. The black crags became brownish, and the mist disguised the sternness of the moor. This weakening of effects was exactly what he had always thought the extinction of Evadne would bring the world. He smiled happily at the moon.

Yet he was moved to sudden angry speech. "If I had my time over again," he said, "I wouldn't touch her with the tongs." For the cold he had known all along he would catch had settled in his head, and his handkerchief was wet through.

---

6. Discipline.

7. A reference to William Blake's poem *The Sick Rose*; see page 122.

He leaned over the bridge and looked along Lisbech and thought of Evadne. For the first time for many years he saw her image without spirits, and wondered without indignation why she had so often looked like the cat about to steal the cream. What was the cream? And did she ever steal it? Now he would never know. He thought of her very generously and sighed over the perversity of fate in letting so much comeliness.

"If she had married a butcher or a veterinary surgeon she might have been happy," he said, and shook his head at the glassy black water that slid under the bridge to that boiling sluice.

A gust of ague[8] reminded him that wet clothes clung to his fevered body and that he ought to change as quickly as possible, or expect to be laid up for weeks. He turned along the path that led back across the moor to the withered ash tree, and was learning the torture of bare feet on gravel when he cried out to himself: "I shall be hanged for killing my wife." It did not come as a trumpet-call, for he was one of those people who never quite hear what is said to them, and this deafishness extended in him to emotional things. It stole on him clamly, like a fog closing on a city. When he first felt hemmed in by this certainty he looked over his shoulder to the crags, remembering tales of how Jacobite fugitives had hidden on the moors for many weeks. There lay at least another day of freedom. But he was the kind of man who always goes home. He stumbled on, not very unhappy, except for his feet. Like many people of weak temperament he did not fear death. Indeed, it had a peculiar appeal to him; for while it was important, exciting, it did not, like most important and exciting things try to create action. He allowed his imagination the vanity of painting pictures. He saw himself standing in their bedroom, plotting this last event, with the white sheet and the high lights of the mahongany wardrobe shining ghostly at him through the darkness. He saw himself raising a thin hand to the gas bracket and turning on the tap. He saw himself staggering to their bed while death crept in at his nostrils. He saw his corpse lying in full daylight, and for the first time knew himself certainly, unquestionably dignified.

He threw back his chest in pride: but at that moment the path stopped and he found himself staggering down the mound of heatherland and boulders with bleeding feet. Always he had suffered from sore feet, which had not exactly disgusted but, worse still, disappointed Evadne. A certain wistfulness she had always evinced when she found herself the superior animal had enraged and humiliated him many times. He felt that sting him now, and flung himself down the mound cursing. When he stumbled up to the withered ash tree he hated her so much that it seemed as though she were alive again, and a sharp wind blowing down from the moor terrified him like her touch.

He rested there. Leaning against the stripped grey trunk, he smiled up at the sky, which was now so touched to ineffectiveness by the dawn that it looked like a tent of faded silk. There was the peace of weakness in him, which he took to be spiritual, because it had no apparent physical justification: but he lost it as his dripping clothes chilled his tired flesh. His discomfort reminded him that the phantasmic night was passing from him. Daylight threatened him: the daylight in which for so many years he had worked in the solicitor's office and been snubbed and ignored. "'The garish day,'" he murmured disgustedly, quoting the blasphemy of some hymn writer. He wanted his death to happen in this phantasmic night.

8. Fever.

So he limped his way along the road. The birds had not yet begun to sing, but the rustling noises of the night had ceased. The silent highway was consecrated to his proud progress. He staggered happily like a tired child returning from a lovely birthday walk: his death in the little bedroom, which for the first time he would have to himself, was a culminating treat to be gloated over like the promise of a favourite pudding for supper. As he walked he brooded dozingly on large and swelling thoughts. Like all people of weak passions and enterprise he loved to think of Napoleon, and in the shadow of the great asylum wall he strutted a few steps of his advance from murder to suicide, with arms crossed on his breast and thin legs trying to strut massively. He was so happy. He wished that a military band went before him, and pretended that the high hedges were solemn lines of men, stricken in awe to silence as their king rode out to some nobly self-chosen doom. Vast he seemed to himself, and magnificent like music, and solemn like the Sphinx. He had saved the earth from corruption by killing Evadne, for whom he now felt the unremorseful pity a conqueror might bestow on a devastated empire. He might have grieved that his victory brought him death, but with immense pride he found that the occasion was exactly described by a text. "He saved others, Himself He could not save."[9] He had missed the stile in the field above Sumatra Crescent and had to go back and hunt for it in the hedge. So quickly had his satisfaction borne him home.

The field had the fantastic air that jerry-builders[1] give to land poised on the knife-edge of town and country, so that he walked in romance to his very door. The unmarred grass sloped to a stone-hedge of towers of loose brick, trenches and mounds of shining clay, and the fine intentful spires of the scaffolding round the last unfinished house. And he looked down on Petrick. Though to the actual eye it was but a confusion of dark distances through the twilight, a breaking of velvety perspectives, he saw more intensely than ever before its squalid walls and squalid homes where mean men and mean women enlaced their unwholesome lives. Yet he did not shrink from entering for his great experience: as Christ did not shrink from being born in a stable. He swaggered with humility over the trodden mud of the field and the new white flags of Sumatra Crescent. Down the road before him there passed a dim figure, who paused at each lamp post and raised a long wand to behead the yellow gas-flowers that were now wilting before the dawn: a ghostly herald preparing the world to be his deathbed. The Crescent curved in quiet darkness, save for one house, where blazed a gas-lit room with undrawn blinds. The brightness had the startling quality of a scream. He looked in almost anxiously as he passed, and met the blank eyes of a man in evening clothes who stood by the window shaking a medicine. His face was like a wax mask softened by heat: the features were blurred with the suffering which comes from the spectacle of suffering. His eyes lay unshiftingly on George's face as he went by and he went on shaking the bottle. It seemed as though he would never stop.

In the hour of his grandeur George was not forgetful of the griefs of the little human people, but interceded with God for the sake of this stranger. Everything was beautiful, beautiful, beautiful.

His own little house looked solemn as a temple. He leaned against the lamppost at the gate and stared at its empty windows and neat bricks. The disorder of the shattered pane of glass could be overlooked by considering a sign that this house was a holy place: like the Passover blood on the lintel. The propriety of the evenly drawn

9. These are the words of the priests and elders mocking   1. Low-wage, slipshod workers.
Jesus at his crucifixion; Matthew 27.42.

blind pleased him enormously. He had always known that this was how the great tragic things of the world had accomplished themselves: quietly. Evadne's raging activity belonged to trivial or annoying things like spring-cleaning or thunderstorms. Well, the house belonged to him now. He opened the gate and went up the asphalt path, sourly noticing that Evadne had as usual left out the lawn-mower, though it might very easily have rained, with the wind coming up as it was. A stray cat that had been sleeping in the tuft of pampas grass in the middle of the lawn was roused by his coming, and fled insolently close to his legs. He hated all wild homeless things, and bent for a stone to throw at it. But instead his fingers touched a slug, which reminded him of the feeling of Evadne's flesh through the slit in her bathing dress. And suddenly the garden was possessed by her presence: she seemed to amble there as she had so often done, sowing seeds unwisely and tormenting the last days of an ailing geranium by insane transplantation, exclaiming absurdly over such mere weeds as morning glory. He caught the very clucking of her voice.... The front door opened at his touch.

The little lobby with its closed doors seemed stuffed with expectant silence. He realised that he had come to the theatre of his great adventure. Then panic seized him. Because this was the home where he and she had lived together so horribly he doubted whether he could do this splendid momentous thing, for here he had always been a poor thing with the habit of failure. His heart beat in him more quickly than his raw feet could pad up the oil-clothed stairs. Behind the deal door at the end of the passage was death. Nothingness! It would escape him, even the idea of it would escape him if he did not go to it at once. When he burst at last into its presence he felt so victorious that he sank back against the door waiting for death to come to him without turning on the gas. He was so happy. His death was coming true.

But Evadne lay on his deathbed. She slept there soundly, with her head flung back on the pillows so that her eyes and brow seemed small in shadow, and her mouth and jaw huge above her thick throat in the light. Her wet hair straggled across the pillow on to a broken cane chair covered with her tumbled clothes. Her breast, silvered with sweat, shone in the ray of the street lamp that had always disturbed their nights. The counterpane rose enormously over her hips in rolls of glazed linen. Out of mere innocent sleep her sensuality was distilling a most drunken pleasure.

Not for one moment did he think this a phantasmic appearance. Evadne was not the sort of woman to have a ghost.

Still leaning against the door, he tried to think it all out: but his thoughts came brokenly, because the dawnlight flowing in at the window confused him by its pale glare and that lax figure on the bed held his attention. It must have been that when he laid his murderous hands on her head she had simply dropped below the surface and swum a few strokes under water as any expert swimmer can. Probably he had never even put her into danger, for she was a great lusty creature and the weir was a little place. He had imagined the wonder and peril of the battle as he had imagined his victory. He sneezed exhaustingly, and from his physical distress realised how absurd it was ever to have thought that he had killed her. Bodies like his do not kill bodies like hers.

Now his soul was naked and lonely as though the walls of his body had fallen in at death, and the grossness of Evadne's sleep made him suffer more unlovely a destitution than any old beggarwoman squatting by the roadside in the rain. He had thought he had had what every man most desires: one night of power over a woman for the business of murder or love. But it had been a lie. Nothing beautiful had ever happened to him. He would have wept, but the hatred he had learnt on the moors obstructed all tears in his throat. At least this night had given him passion enough to put an end to it all.

Quietly he went to the window and drew down the sash. There was no fireplace, so that sealed the room. Then he crept over to the gas bracket and raised his thin hand, as he had imagined in his hour of vain glory by the lake.

He had forgotten Evadne's thrifty habit of turning off the gas at the main to prevent leakage when she went to bed.

He was beaten. He undressed and got into bed: as he had done every night for ten years, and as he would do every night until he died. Still sleeping, Evadne caressed him with warm arms.

Ezra Pound: The New Cake of Soap *and* Salutation the Third

Ezra Loomis Pound (1885–1972) was one of the most important, and most controversial, poets of the twentieth century. Born in Idaho and raised outside of Philadelphia, he wrote poetry and studied literature and half a dozen languages in college and during two years of a Ph.D. program at the University of Pennsylvania. He left graduate school in 1907 to become a professor of Romance languages at Wabash Presbyterian College in Indiana. Pound's academic career lasted one semester, at which point he traveled to Spain and Italy before settling in London. He took on literary London in 1908 with a breathtaking amount of enthusiasm, energy, and old-fashioned American optimism; before long he had made influential friends like Yeats, the poet/philosopher T. E. Hulme, and the novelist Ford Madox Ford. He published three volumes of poetry in the two years 1909–1910, and began a series of posts editing poetry and arts magazines, becoming increasingly influential as an arbiter and theorist of experimental literature and art. He was one of the first to champion the writing of such young unknowns as D. H. Lawrence, T. S. Eliot, and James Joyce. In 1912–1914, he led the "Imagist" movement in poetry, which emphasized direct, spare language, in poems often based on moments of vision. His slogan "Make It New" became a rallying-cry for many writers of his time; so pervasive was his influence that the critic Hugh Kenner has labeled these years "The Pound Era."

In Pound's own work, the use of brief, imagistic lyrics coexisted with a tendency toward sprawling works of poetic, cultural, historical, and economic commentary, sometimes taking the form of books of cultural or economic theory, sometimes in radio broadcasts, and often in poetic form. His multi-year and multi-sectioned poem *The Cantos*, begun in 1915, ranging widely across European and world history and culture, was often written while Pound was involving himself in his own century's greatest conflicts. He developed an admiration for the Italian fascist leader Mussolini, and spent World War II in Rome, where he made hundreds of radio broadcasts denouncing the Allies and the Jewish bankers whom he believed were underwriting opposition to Fascism. Captured by American forces at the end of the war, he was imprisoned outside Pisa as a war criminal. There, he translated Confucius and wrote a notable section of the Cantos, *The Pisan Cantos*. He was then sent back to the United States, but was found mentally unfit for trial for treason; he was confined for twelve years in an insane asylum in Washington, D.C. Finally he was released in 1958; he returned to Italy, where he lived, largely in silence, until his death in 1972.

The New Cake of Soap

Lo, how it gleams and glistens in the sun
Like the cheek of a Chesterton[1]

Salutation the Third

Let us deride the smugness of "The Times":
    GUFFAW!
      So much the gagged reviewers,
It will pay them when the worms are wriggling in their vitals;
5   These were they who objected to newness,
    HERE are their TOMB-STONES.
      They supported the gag and the ring:
    A little black BOX contains them.
      SO shall you be also,
10   You slut-bellied obstructionist,
      You sworn foe to free speech and good letters,
You fungus, you continuous gangrene.

Come, let us on with the new deal,
    Let us be done with Jews and Jobbery,[1]
15   Let us SPIT upon those who fawn on the JEWS for their money,
Let us out to the pastures.

PERHAPS I will die at thirty,
Perhaps you will have the pleasure of defiling my pauper's grave,
I wish you JOY, I proffer you ALL my assistance.
20   It has been your HABIT for long to do away with true poets,
You either drive them mad,[2] or else you blink at their suicides,
Or else you condone their drugs, and talk of insanity and genius,
BUT I will not go mad to please you.
    I will not FLATTER you with an early death.
25   OH, NO! I will stick it out,
    I will feel your hates wriggling about my feet,
And I will laugh at you and mock you,
And I will offer you consolations in irony,
    O fools, detesters of Beauty.

30   I have seen many who go about with supplications,
    Afraid to say how they hate you.
HERE is the taste of my BOOT,
    CARESS it, lick off the BLACKING.

---

1. G. K. Chesterton (1874–1936), popular essayist and
fiction writer. Pound disliked him both for his popularity,
and because he was reported to have said "If a thing is
worth doing, it's worth doing badly."
1. Pound's anti-Semitism was deep-seated and lifelong;
some of his *Cantos* were censored on first publication
because of their ugly portrayals of the Jews, who Pound
believed to be responsible for international economic
instability. When he revised the poem for inclusion in
the 1926 edition of his collection *Personae*, Pound

changed these lines to read: "Let us be done with panders
and jobbery, / Let us spit upon those who pat the big-bel-
lies for profit." Jobbery: Corruption in the conduct of
public affairs.
2. Pound may intend a reference here to the savage
review of Keats's *Endymion* that appeared in the *Quarterly
Review* and was believed to have caused, or at least hastened, Keats's death; Shelley refers to this incident in
"Adonais."

Rupert Brooke
1887–1915

Rupert Brooke was the first of Britain's "war poets," and the last poem he completed during his short lifetime—*The Soldier*—is alone enough to guarantee his lasting place in modern poetry.

Brooke rose with extraordinary speed to the center of the British literary establishment. While an undergraduate, he worked with the *Cambridge Review* and came into contact with such influential writers as Henry James, W. B. Yeats, Virginia Woolf, and Lytton Strachey, and the editor and publisher Edward Marsh. In 1912, after the publication of his first volume of poetry, Brooke suffered a nervous breakdown; after a short recovery period, he spent most of the next three years traveling. World War I began shortly after he returned to England in the spring of 1914; Brooke enlisted immediately and was commissioned on a ship that sailed to Antwerp, Belgium, where Brooke saw no action through early 1915. During this lull, Brooke wrote the war sonnets for which he is best remembered today. While his ship was sailing to Gallipoli, Brooke died of blood poisoning, before seeing combat duty.

It is nearly impossible, even at this late date, to separate Brooke the myth from Brooke the poet; he was something of a national hero even before his death, thanks to the popular reception of his volume of war sonnets, *Nineteen Fourteen*. In Brooke's writings about the war, the irony of early poems like *Heaven* ("And in that Heaven of all their wish, / There shall be no more land, say fish") falls away. These patriotic poems—and most especially *The Soldier*, in which Brooke seemed to have foreseen his own death—meshed perfectly with the temperament of the British people as the nation entered into war. When *The Soldier* was read aloud at Saint Paul's Cathedral in London on Easter Sunday, 1915, Brooke the man—whom Yeats called "the handsomest man in England"—was permanently immortalized as the symbol of English pride.

The Soldier

> If I should die, think only this of me:
>   That there's some corner of a foreign field
> That is forever England. There shall be
>   In that rich earth a richer dust concealed;
> 5 A dust whom England bore, shaped, made aware,
>   Gave, once, her flowers to love, her ways to roam,
> A body of England's, breathing English air,
>   Washed by the rivers, blest by suns of home.
>
> And think, this heart, all evil shed away,
> 10   A pulse in the Eternal mind, no less
>   Gives somewhere back the thoughts by England given,
> Her sights and sounds; dreams happy as her day;
>   And laughter, learnt of friends; and gentleness,
>   In hearts at peace, under an English heaven.

T. E. Lawrence
1888–1935

T. E. Lawrence is without question the most heroic and romantic British figure to have emerged from World War I; he must also be one of the most complex. While Britain's involvement in the war was focused primarily on the Western Front in France, Lawrence's war activities in the Middle East are now legendary, as is his account of those activities in *The Seven Pillars of Wisdom* (1926).

Lawrence of Arabia, as he is best known, wrote an honors thesis on the architecture of crusader castles in France, Syria, and Palestine while an undergraduate at Oxford; his research led him to three years of field work in the Middle East. When World War I ignited in 1914, Lawrence's expertise in Middle East geography was invaluable, and by December 1914 he was a lieutenant posted in Cairo.

England's strategic goal in the Middle East was to weaken Turkey, Germany's ally, by supporting the Arabs in their revolt against the Turks. Lawrence convinced the British to supply the rebels with arms and money; and Lawrence himself masterminded the military strategy in the region and organized guerrilla activities against Turkey. Lawrence distinguished himself and was promoted to the rank of lieutenant colonel. By the time the conquering Arab troops reached Damascus, however, Lawrence was physically and emotionally exhausted; he returned to England just before the Armistice and, disillusioned, refused the Order of the Bath and the Distinguished Service Order that George V attempted to bestow upon him.

His heroic campaign in the Middle East over, Lawrence had a difficult time finding a venue for his gifts. He drifted between writing, academic work, and military service under a series of assumed names; in 1921 he was persuaded to return to the Middle East as an adviser to then-colonial minister Winston Churchill. None of these occupations seems to have brought him satisfaction. In the meantime, however, Lawrence had been busily drafting and revising his memoir of the Arabian campaign, *The Seven Pillars of Wisdom;* it was published in a limited edition in 1926, and in a trade edition in 1935. The book was immediately popular with the British public.

Lawrence spent his subsequent years in self-imposed anonymity; describing his sense of purposelessness to a friend, he wrote "there is something broken in the works . . . my will, I think." He died in a motorcycling accident in May 1935. In 1962 Lawrence's legend was vividly brought forth again to a subsequent generation in the lush David Lean film *Lawrence of Arabia.*

from The Seven Pillars of Wisdom
Chapter 32

Dawn found us crossing a steep short pass out of Wadi[1] Kitan into the main drainage valley of these succeeding hills. We turned aside into Wadi Reimi, a tributary, to get water. There was no proper well, only a seepage hole in the stony bed of the valley; and we found it partly by our noses: though the taste, while as foul, was curiously unlike the smell. We refilled our water-skins. Arslan baked bread, and we rested for two hours. Then we went on through Wadi Amk, an easy green valley which made comfortable marching for the camels.

When the Amk turned westward we crossed it, going up between piles of the warped grey granite (like cold toffee) which was common up-country in the Hejaz.[2] The defile culminated at the foot of a natural ramp and staircase: badly broken, twisting, and difficult for camels, but short. Afterwards we were in an open valley for an hour, with low hills to the right and mountains to the left. There were water pools in the crags, and Merawin[3] tents under the fine trees which studded the flat. The fertility of the slopes was great: on them grazed flocks of sheep and goats. We got milk from the Arabs: the first milk my Ageyl[4] had been given in the two years of drought.

---

1. River bed or gorge.
2. Western area of present-day Saudi Arabia. It contains the Muslim Holy Cities of Mecca and Medina and was the center of the Arab Revolt declared by Sherif Hussein, Emir of Mecca and then ruler of the Hejaz, against the Ottoman Turks during World War I. At the time this area, along with most of the Middle East, was part of the Ottoman Empire.
3. One of the many Beduin tribes encountered by Lawrence;

he will often refer to the local tribesmen as "the Arabs," as here, if the name of the tribe is not specifically mentioned.
4. In ch. 24 Lawrence comments of the "Ageyl Camel Corps": "These Ageyl were Nejd townsmen . . . who had contracted for service as regular camel corps for a term of years. They were young from sixteen to twenty-five, and nice fellows, large-eyed, cheery, a bit educated, catholic, intelligent, good companions on the road."

The track out of the valley when we reached its head was execrable, and the descent beyond into Wadi Marrakh almost dangerous; but the view from the crest compensated us. Wadi Marrakh, a broad, peaceful avenue, ran between two regular straight walls of hills to a circus four miles off where valleys from left, right and front seemed to meet. Artificial heaps of uncut stone were piled about the approach. As we entered it, we saw that the grey hill-walls swept back on each side in a half-circle. Before us, to the south, the curve was barred across by a straight wall or step of blue-black lava, standing over a little grove of thorn trees. We made for these and lay down in their thin shade, grateful in such sultry air for any pretence of coolness.

The day, now at its zenith, was very hot; and my weakness had so increased that my head hardly held up against it. The puffs of feverish wind pressed like scorching hands against our faces, burning our eyes. My pain made me breathe in gasps through the mouth; the wind cracked my lips and seared my throat till I was too dry to talk, and drinking became sore; yet I always needed to drink, as my thirst would not let me lie still and get the peace I longed for. The flies were a plague.

The bed of the valley was of fine quartz gravel and white sand. Its glitter thrust itself between our eyelids; and the level of the ground seemed to dance as the wind moved the white tips of stubble grass to and fro. The camels loved this grass, which grew in tufts, about sixteen inches high, on slate-green stalks. They gulped down great quantities of it until the men drove them in and couched them by me. At the moment I hated the beasts, for too much food made their breath stink; and they rum-blingly belched up a new mouthful from their stomachs each time they had chewed and swallowed the last, till a green slaver flooded out between their loose lips over the side teeth, and dripped down their sagging chins.

Lying angrily there, I threw a stone at the nearest, which got up and wavered about behind my head: finally it straddled its back legs and staled in wide, bitter jets; and I was so far gone with the heat and weakness and pain that I just lay there and cried about it unhelping. The men had gone to make a fire and cook a gazelle one of them had fortunately shot; and I realized that on another day this halt would have been pleasant to me; for the hills were very strange and their colours vivid. The base had the warm grey of old stored sunlight; while about their crests ran narrow veins of granite-coloured stone, generally in pairs, following the contour of the skyline like the rusted metals of an abandoned scenic railway. Arslan said the hills were combed like cocks, a sharper observation.

After the men had fed we re-mounted, and easily climbed the first wave of the lava flood. It was short, as was the second, on the top of which lay a broad terrace with an alluvial plot of sand and gravel in its midst. The lava was a nearly clean floor of iron-red rock-cinders, over which were scattered fields of loose stone. The third and other steps ascended to the south of us: but we turned east, up Wadi Gara.

Gara had, perhaps, been a granite valley down whose middle the lava had flowed, slowly filling it, and arching itself up in a central heap. On each side were deep troughs, between the lava and the hill-side. Rain water flooded these as often as storms burst in the hills. The lava flow, as it coagulated, had been twisted like a rope, cracked, and bent back irregularly upon itself. The surface was loose with fragments through which many generations of camel parties had worn an inadequate and painful track.

We struggled along for hours, going slowly, our camels wincing at every stride as the sharp edges slipped beneath their tender feet. The paths were only to be seen by the droppings along them, and by the slightly bluer surfaces of the rubbed stones. The

Arabs declared them impassable after dark, which was to be believed, for we risked laming our beasts each time our impatience made us urge them on. Just before five in the afternoon, however, the way got easier. We seemed to be near the head of the valley, which grew narrow. Before us on the right, an exact cone-crater, with tidy furrows scoring it from lip to foot, promised good going; for it was made of black ash, clean as though sifted, with here and there a bank of harder soil, and cinders. Beyond it was another lava-field, older perhaps than the valleys, for its stones were smoothed, and between them were straths of flat earth, rank with weeds. In among these open spaces were Beduin tents,[5] whose owners ran to us when they saw us coming; and, taking our head-stalls with hospitable force, led us in.

They proved to be Sheikh Fahad el Hansha and his men: old and garrulous warriors who had marched with us to Wejh, and had been with Garland on that great occasion when his first automatic mine had succeeded under a troop train near Toweira station.[6] Fahad would not hear of my resting quietly outside his tent, but with the reckless equality of the desert men urged me into an unfortunate place inside among his own vermin. There he plied me with bowl after bowl of diuretic camel-milk between questions about Europe, my home tribe, the English camel-pasturages, the war in the Hejaz and the wars elsewhere, Egypt and Damascus, how Feisal was, why did we seek Abdulla, and by what perversity did I remain Christian, when their hearts and hands waited to welcome me to the Faith?[7]

So passed long hours till ten at night, when the guest-sheep was carried in, dismembered royally over a huge pile of buttered rice. I ate as manners demanded, twisted myself up in my cloak, and slept; my bodily exhaustion, after those hours of the worst imaginable marching, proofing me against the onslaught of lice and fleas. The illness, however, had stimulated my ordinarily sluggish fancy, which ran riot this night in dreams of wandering naked for a dark eternity over interminable lava (like scrambled egg gone iron-blue, and very wrong), sharp as insect-bites underfoot; and with some horror, perhaps a dead Moor, always climbing after us.

In the morning we woke early and refreshed, with our clothes stinging-full of fiery points feeding on us. After one more bowl of milk proffered us by the eager Fahad, I was able to walk unaided to my camel and mount her actively. We rode up the last piece of Wadi Gara to the crest, among cones of black cinders from a crater to the south. Thence we turned to a branch valley, ending in a steep and rocky chimney, up which we pulled our camels.

5. The Beduin were nomads who lived in the desert, unlike the town dwellers of the Hejaz. In ch. 14, Lawrence comments on the fierce independence of the Beduin tribes: "The town might sigh for the cloying inactivity of Ottoman rule: the tribes were convinced that they had made a free and Arab Government, and that each of them was It."

6. Wejh, then a small, Turkish-held port on the Red Sea, had been the target of a 1917 Anglo-Arab campaign to force Turkish withdrawal from the area. As part of this campaign, Major Garland, a British army officer, was training the Arab forces under Emir Feisal, Sherif Hussein's son, to use explosives. In ch. 17 Lawrence writes that Garland "had his own devices for mining trains and felling telegraphs and cutting metals. . . . [he] would shovel a handful of detonators into his pocket, with a string of primers, fuse, and fusees, and jump gaily on his camel for a week's ride to the Hejaz Railway."

7. Following the capture of Wejh, Arab tactics were to continue harrying the Turkish forces at Medina; Lawrence's part in this was "to go off to Abdulla in Wadi Ais, to find out why he had done nothing for two months, and to persuade him, if the Turks came out, to go straight at them" (ch. 31). The present extract describes that journey; Abdulla (1882–1951), second son of Sherif Hussein of Mecca, later became king of the new territory of Trans-Jordan, which was created by the 1919 peace arrangements. Feisal (1883–1933) later became king of the new territory of Iraq, which was similarly carved out of former Ottoman territories by the peace treaties of 1919. In ch. 12 Lawrence comments of Feisal that "I felt at first glance that this was the man I had come to Arabia to seek—the leader who would bring the Arab Revolt to full glory."

Beyond we had an easy descent into Wadi Murrmiya, whose middle bristled with lava like galvanized iron, on each side of which there were smooth sandy beds, good going. After a while we came to a fault in the flow, which served as a track to the other side. By it we crossed over, finding the lava pocketed with soils apparently of extreme richness, for in them were leafy trees and lawns of real grass, starred with flowers, the best grazing of all our ride, looking the more wonderfully green because of the blue-black twisted crusts of rock about. The lava had changed its character. Here were no piles of loose stones, as big as a skull or a man's hand, rubbed and rounded together; but bunched and crystallized fronds of metallic rock, altogether impassable for bare feet.

Another watershed conducted us to an open place where the Jeheina[8] had ploughed some eight acres of the thin soil below a thicket of scrub. They said there were like it in the neighbourhood other fields, silent witnesses to the courage and persistence of the Arabs. It was called Wadi Chetf, and after it was another broken river of lava, the worst yet encountered. A shadowy path zigzagged across it. We lost one camel with a broken fore-leg, the result of a stumble in a pot-hole; and the many bones which lay about showed that we were not the only party to suffer misfortune in the passage. However, this ended our lava, according to the guides, and we went thence forward along easy valleys with finally a long run up a gentle slope till dusk. The going was so good and the cool of the day so freshened me that we did not halt at nightfall, after our habit, but pushed on for an hour across the basin of Murrmiya into the basin of Wadi Ais, and there, by Tleih, we stopped for our last camp in the open.

I rejoiced that we were so nearly in, for fever was heavy on me. I was afraid that perhaps I was going to be really ill, and the prospect of falling into the well-meaning hands of tribesmen in such a state was not pleasant. Their treatment of every sickness was to burn holes in the patient's body at some spot believed to be the complement of the part affected. It was a cure tolerable to such as had faith in it, but torture to the unbelieving: to incur it unwillingly would be silly, and yet certain; for the Arabs' good intentions, selfish as their good digestions, would never heed a sick man's protesting.

The morning was easy, over open valleys and gentle rides into Wadi Ais. We arrived at Abu Markha, its nearest watering-place, just a few minutes after Sherif Abdulla had dismounted there, and while he was ordering his tents to be pitched in an acacia glade beyond the well. He was leaving his old camp at Bir el Amri, lower down the valley, as he had left Murabba, his camp before, because the ground had been fouled by the careless multitude of his men and animals. I gave him the documents from Feisal, explaining the situation in Medina, and the need we had of haste to block the railway. I thought he took it coolly; but, without argument, went on to say that I was a little tired after my journey, and with his permission would lie down and sleep a while. He pitched me a tent next his great marquee, and I went into it and rested myself at last. It had been a struggle against faintness day-long in the saddle to get here at all: and now the strain was ended with the delivery of my message, I felt that another hour would have brought the breaking point.

Chapter 33

About ten days I lay in that tent, suffering a bodily weakness which made my animal self crawl away and hide till the shame was passed. As usual in such circumstances my mind cleared, my senses became more acute, and I began at last to think

8. Local beduin.

consecutively of the Arab Revolt, as an accustomed duty to rest upon against the pain. It should have been thought out long before, but at my first landing in Hejaz there had been a crying need for action, and we had done what seemed to instinct best, not probing into the why, nor formulating what we really wanted at the end of all. Instinct thus abused without a basis of past knowledge and reflection had grown intuitive, feminine, and was now bleaching my confidence; so in this forced inaction I looked for the equation between my book-reading and my movements, and spent the intervals of uneasy sleeps and dreams in plucking at the tangle of our present.

As I have shown, I was unfortunately as much in command of the campaign as I pleased, and was untrained. In military theory I was tolerably read, my Oxford curiosity having taken me past Napoleon to Clausewitz and his school, to Caemmerer and Moltke, and the recent Frenchmen.[9] They had all seemed to be one-sided; and after looking at Jomini and Willisen, I had found broader principles in Saxe and Guibert and the eighteenth century. However, Clausewitz was intellectually so much the master of them, and his book so logical and fascinating, that unconsciously I accepted his finality, until a comparison of Kuhne and Foch[1] disgusted me with soldiers, wearied me of their officious glory, making me critical of all their light. In any case, my interest had been abstract, concerned with the theory and philosophy of warfare especially from the metaphysical side.

Now, in the field everything had been concrete, particularly the tiresome problem of Medina; and to distract myself from that I began to recall suitable maxims on the conduct of modern, scientific war. But they would not fit, and it worried me. Hitherto, Medina had been an obsession for us all; but now that I was ill, its image was not clear, whether it was that we were near to it (one seldom liked the attainable), or whether it was that my eyes were misty with too constant staring at the butt. One afternoon I woke from a hot sleep, running with sweat and pricking with flies, and wondered what on earth was the good of Medina to us? Its harmfulness had been patent when we were at Yenbo and the Turks in it were going to Mecca: but we had changed all that by our march to Wejh. To-day we were blockading the railway, and they only defending it. The garrison of Medina, reduced to an inoffensive size, were sitting in trenches destroying their own power of movement by eating the transport they could no longer feed. We had taken away their power to harm us, and yet wanted to take away their town. It was not a base for us like Wejh, nor a threat like Wadi Ais. What on earth did we want it for?[2]

The camp was bestirring itself after the torpor of the midday hours; and noises from the world outside began to filter in to me past the yellow lining of the tent-canvas, whose every hole and tear was stabbed through by a long dagger of sunlight. I heard the stamping and snorting of the horses plagued with flies where they stood in the shadow of the trees, the complaint of camels, the ringing of coffee mortars, distant shots. To their burden I began to drum out the aim in war. The books gave it pat—the destruction of the armed forces of the enemy by the one process—battle. Victory could be purchased only by blood. This was a hard saying for us. As the Arabs had no organized forces, a Turkish Foch would have no aim. The Arabs would not

9. Carl von Clausewitz (1780–1831), Prussian military strategist; in his book *On War*, Clausewitz rejected the limited objectives of 18th-century warfare in favor of total war. Count von Moltke, Chief of Prussian and German Staff from 1858 to 1888, led victories over Denmark, Austria, and France.

1. The Frenchman Marshal Foch (1851–1929) was com-

mander of Allied forces during the closing months of World War I.

2. Medina in fact remained in Turkish hands until the end of the war. Yenbo, a Red Sea port, had been a principal Arab base before the successful campaign against Wejh.

endure casualties. How would our Clausewitz buy his victory? Von der Goltz[3] had seemed to go deeper, saying it was necessary not to annihilate the enemy, but to break his courage. Only we showed no prospect of ever breaking anybody's courage.

However, Goltz was a humbug, and these wise men must be talking metaphors; for we were indubitably winning our war; and as I pondered slowly, it dawned on me that we had won the Hejaz war. Out of every thousand square miles of Hejaz nine hundred and ninety-nine were now free. Did my provoked jape at Vickery,[4] that rebellion was more like peace than like war, hold as much truth as haste? Perhaps in war the absolute did rule, but for peace a majority was good enough. If we held the rest, the Turks were welcome to the tiny fraction on which they stood, till peace or Doomsday showed them the futility of clinging to our window-pane.

I brushed off the same flies once more from my face patiently, content to know that the Hejaz War was won and finished with: won from the day we took Wejh, if we had had wit to see it. Then I broke the thread of my argument again to listen. The distant shots had grown and tied themselves into long, ragged volleys. They ceased. I strained my ears for the other sounds which I knew would follow. Sure enough across the silence came a rustle like the dragging of a skirt over the flints, around the thin walls of my tent. A pause, while the camel-riders drew up: and then the soggy tapping of canes on the thick of the beasts' necks to make them kneel.

They knelt without noise: and I timed it in my memory: first the hesitation, as the camels, looking down, felt the soil with one foot for a soft place; then the muffled thud and the sudden loosening of breath as they dropped on their fore-legs, since this party had come far and were tired; then the shuffle as the hind legs were folded in, and the rocking as they tossed from side to side thrusting outward with their knees to bury them in the cooler subsoil below the burning flints, while the riders, with a quick soft patter of bare feet, like birds over the ground, were led off tacitly either to the coffee hearth or to Abdulla's tent, according to their business. The camels would rest there, uneasily switching their tails across the shingle till their masters were free and looked to their stabling.

I had made a comfortable beginning of doctrine, but was left still to find an alternative end and means of war. Ours seemed unlike the ritual of which Foch was priest; and I recalled him, to see a difference in kind between him and us. In his modern war—absolute war he called it—two nations professing incompatible philosophies put them to the test of force. Philosophically, it was idiotic, for while opinions were arguable, convictions needed shooting to be cured; and the struggle could end only when the supporters of the one immaterial principle had no more means of resistance against the supporters of the other. It sounded like a twentieth-century restatement of the wars of religion, whose logical end was utter destruction of one creed, and whose protagonists believed that God's judgement would prevail.[5] This might do for France and Germany, but would not represent the British attitude. Our Army was not intelligently maintaining a philosophic conception in Flanders or on the Canal.[6] Efforts to make our men hate the enemy usually made them hate the fighting. Indeed Foch had knocked out his own argument by saying that such war depended on levy in

3. Baron Colmar von der Goltz (1843–1916), Prussian officer responsible for reorganizing Turkish forces prior to World War I.
4. Major Charles Vickery (1881–1951), member of the British military mission to the Hejaz.
5. Germany, France, and the Netherlands experienced prolonged periods of warfare in the 16th century as the religious situation introduced at the Reformation was alternately enforced and resisted.
6. Flanders is the region of northern France and Belgium on which many of the battles of World War I were fought; the protection of the [Suez] Canal, which joins the Mediterranean with the Red Sea at Suez in Egypt, was a British objective in the war with Turkey.

mass,[7] and was impossible with professional armies; while the old army was still the British ideal, and its manner the ambition of our ranks and our files. To me the Foch war seemed only an exterminative variety, no more absolute than another. One could as explicably call it "murder war." Clausewitz enumerated all sorts of war . . . personal wars, joint-proxy duels, for dynastic reasons . . . expulsive wars, in party politics . . . commercial wars, for trade objects . . . two wars seemed seldom alike. Often the parties did not know their aim, and blundered till the march of events took control. Victory in general habit leaned to the clear-sighted, though fortune and superior intelligence could make a sad muddle of nature's "inexorable" law.

I wondered why Feisal wanted to fight the Turks, and why the Arabs helped him, and saw that their aim was geographical, to extrude the Turk from all Arabic-speaking lands in Asia. Their peace ideal of liberty could exercise itself only so. In pursuit of the ideal conditions we might kill Turks, because we disliked them very much; but the killing was a pure luxury. If they would go quietly the war would end. If not we would urge them, or try to drive them out. In the last resort, we should be compelled to the desperate course of blood and the maximum of "murder war," but as cheaply as could be for ourselves, since the Arabs fought for freedom, and that was a pleasure to be tasted only by a man alive. Posterity was a chilly thing to work for, no matter how much a man happened to love his own, or other people's already produced children.

At this point a slave slapped my tent-door, and asked if the Emir might call. So I struggled into more clothes, and crawled over to his great tent to sound the depth of motive in him. It was a comfortable place, luxuriously shaded and carpeted deep in strident rugs, the aniline-dyed spoils of Hussein Mabeirig's house in Rabegh.[8] Abdulla passed most of his day in it, laughing with his friends, and playing games with Mohammed Hassan, the court jester. I set the ball of conversation rolling between him and Shakir and the chance sheiks, among whom was the fire-hearted Ferhan el Aida, the son of Doughty's Motlog;[9] and I was rewarded, for Abdulla's words were definite. He contrasted his hearers' present independence with their past servitude to Turkey, and roundly said that talk of Turkish heresy, or the immoral doctrine of *Yeni-Turan*,[1] or the illegitimate Caliphate was beside the point. It was Arab country, and the Turks were in it: that was the one issue. My argument preened itself.

The next day a great complication of boils developed out, to conceal my lessened fever, and to chain me down yet longer in impotence upon my face in this stinking tent. When it grew too hot for dreamless dozing, I picked up my tangle again, and went on ravelling it out, considering now the whole house of war in its structural aspect, which was strategy, in its arrangements, which were tactics, and in the sentiment of its inhabitants, which was psychology; for my personal duty was command, and the commander, like the master architect, was responsible for all.

7. Mass mobilization.
8. Coastal town, approximately halfway between Medina and Mecca; Hussein Mabeirig, leader of the local population, was a Turkish sympathizer who had fled in the face of a rebel Arab advance.
9. Charles Montagu Doughty was the author of the widely read *Travels in Arabia Deserta* (1888).
1. A slogan of the "Young Turks," a modernization movement in Turkey that was hostile to much that the old Ottoman Empire represented, including clerical influence in state affairs; it achieved a major victory in 1908 by deposing the Sultan, Abdülhamid II. Lawrence trans-

lates the slogan in ch. 4: "Turkey made Turkish for the Turks—*Yeni-Turan*—became the cry." The Ottoman Sultan's self-ascribed title of "Caliph," or spiritual leader of all Muslims, was used in support of Turkish war aims; according to Lawrence (ch. 5), when Feisal rebelled against Turkish authority and "raised the Arab flag, the pan-Islamic supra-national state, for which [Sultan] Abdul Hamid had massacred and worked and died, and the German hope of the co-operation of Islam in the world-plans of the Kaiser, passed into the realm of dreams."

The first confusion was the false antithesis between strategy, the aim in war, the synoptic regard seeing each part relative to the whole, and tactics, the means towards a strategic end, the particular steps of its staircase. They seemed only points of view from which to ponder the elements of war, the Algebraical element of things, a Biological element of lives, and the Psychological element of ideas.

The Algebraical element looked to me a pure science, subject to mathematical law, inhuman. It dealt with known variables, fixed conditions, space and time, inorganic things like hills and climates and railways, with mankind in type-masses too great for individual variety, with all artificial aids and the extensions given our faculties by mechanical invention. It was essentially formulable.

Here was a pompous, professional beginning. My wits, hostile to the abstract, took refuge in Arabia again. Translated into Arabic, the algebraic factor would first take practical account of the area we wished to deliver, and I began idly to calculate how many square miles: sixty: eighty: one hundred: perhaps one hundred and forty thousand square miles. And how would the Turks defend all that? No doubt by a trench line across the bottom, if we came like an army with banners; but suppose we were (as we might be) an influence, an idea, a thing intangible, invulnerable, without front or back, drifting about like a gas? Armies were like plants, immobile, firm-rooted, nourished through long stems to the head. We might be a vapour, blowing where we listed. Our kingdoms lay in each man's mind; and as we wanted nothing material to live on, so we might offer nothing material to the killing. It seemed a regular soldier might be helpless without a target, owning only what he sat on, and subjugating only what, by order, he could poke his rifle at.

Then I figured out how many men they would need to sit on all this ground, to save it from our attack-in-depth, sedition putting up her head in every unoccupied one of those hundred thousand square miles. I knew the Turkish Army exactly, and even allowing for their recent extension of faculty by aeroplanes and guns and armoured trains (which made the earth a smaller battlefield) still it seemed they would have need of a fortified post every four square miles, and a post could not be less than twenty men. If so, they would need six hundred thousand men to meet the illwills of all the Arab peoples, combined with the active hostility of a few zealots.

How many zealots could we have? At present we had nearly fifty thousand: sufficient for the day. It seemed the assets in this element of war were ours. If we realized our raw materials and were apt with them, then climate, railway, desert, and technical weapons could also be attached to our interests. The Turks were stupid; the Germans behind them dogmatical. They would believe that rebellion was absolute like war, and deal with it on the analogy of war. Analogy in human things was fudge, anyhow; and war upon rebellion was messy and slow, like eating soup with a knife.

This was enough of the concrete; so I sheered off ἐπιστήμη [understanding], the mathematical element, and plunged into the nature of the biological factor in command. Its crisis seemed to be the breaking point, life and death, or less finally, wear and tear. The war-philosophers had properly made an art of it, and had elevated one item, "effusion of blood," to the height of an essential, which became humanity in battle, an act touching every side of our corporal being, and very warm. A line of variability. Man, persisted like leaven through its estimates, making them irregular. The components were sensitive and illogical, and generals guarded themselves by the device of a reserve, the significant medium of their art. Goltz had said that if you knew the enemy's strength, and he was fully deployed, then you could dispense with a reserve: but this was never. The possibility of accident, of some flaw in materials was always in the general's mind, and the reserve unconsciously held to meet it.

The "felt" element in troops, not expressible in figures, had to be guessed at by the equivalent of Plato's δόξα [judgment], and the greatest commander of men was he whose intuitions most nearly happened. Nine-tenths of tactics were certain enough to be teachable in schools; but the irrational tenth was like the kingfisher flashing across the pool, and in it lay the test of generals. It could be ensued only by instinct (sharpened by thought practising the stroke) until at the crisis it came naturally, a reflex. There had been men whose δόξα so nearly approached perfection that by its road they reached the certainty of 'επιστήμη. The Greeks might have called such genius for command νόησις [understanding] had they bothered to rationalize revolt.

My mind see-sawed back to apply this to ourselves, and at once knew that it was not bounded by mankind, that it applied also to materials. In Turkey things were scarce and precious, men less esteemed than equipment. Our cue was to destroy, not the Turk's army, but his minerals. The death of a Turkish bridge or rail, machine or gun or charge of high explosive, was more profitable to us than the death of a Turk. In the Arab Army at the moment we were chary both of materials and of men. Governments saw men only in mass; but our men, being irregulars, were not formations, but individuals. An individual death, like a pebble dropped in water, might make but a brief hole; yet rings of sorrow widened out therefrom. We could not afford casualties.

Materials were easier to replace. It was our obvious policy to be superior in some one tangible branch; gun-cotton or machine-guns or whatever could be made decisive. Orthodoxy had laid down the maxim, applied to men, of being superior at the critical point and moment of attack. We might be superior in equipment in one dominant moment or respect; and for both things and men we might give the doctrine a twisted negative side, for cheapness' sake, and be weaker than the enemy everywhere except in that one point or matter. The decision of what was critical would always be ours. Most wars were wars of contact, both forces striving into touch to avoid tactical surprise. Ours should be a war of detachment. We were to contain the enemy by the silent threat of a vast unknown desert, not disclosing ourselves till we attacked. The attack might be nominal, directed not against him, but against his stuff; so it would not seek either his strength or his weakness, but his most accessible material. In railway-cutting it would be usually an empty stretch of rail; and the more empty, the greater the tactical success. We might turn our average into a rule (not a law, since war was antinomian) and develop a habit of never engaging the enemy. This would chime with the numerical plea for never affording a target. Many Turks on our front had no chance all the war to fire on us, and we were never on the defensive except by accident and in error.

The corollary of such a rule was perfect "intelligence," so that we could plan in certainty. The chief agent must be the general's head; and his understanding must be faultless, leaving no room for chance. Morale, if built on knowledge, was broken by ignorance. When we knew all about the enemy we should be comfortable. We must take more pains in the service of news than any regular staff.

I was getting through my subject. The algebraical factor had been translated into terms of Arabia, and fitted like a glove. It promised victory. The biological factor had dictated to us a development of the tactical line most in accord with the genius of our tribesmen. There remained the psychological element to build up an apt shape. I went to Xenophon[2] and stole, to name it, his word *diathetics*,[3] which had been the art of Cyrus before he struck.

Of this our "propaganda" was the stained and ignoble offspring. It was the pathic, almost the ethical, in war. Some of it concerned the crowd, an adjustment of its spirit to the point where it became useful to exploit in action, and the pre-direction of this changing spirit to a certain end. Some of it concerned the individual, and then it became a rare art of human kindness, transcending, by purposed emotion, the gradual logical sequence of the mind. It was more subtle than tactics, and better worth doing, because it dealt with uncontrollables, with subjects incapable of direct command. It considered the capacity for mood of our men, their complexities and mutability, and the cultivation of whatever in them promised to profit our intention. We had to arrange their minds in order of battle just as carefully and as formally as other officers would arrange their bodies. And not only our own men's minds, though naturally they came first. We must also arrange the minds of the enemy, so far as we could reach them; then those other minds of the nation supporting us behind the firing line, since more than half the battle passed there in the back; then the minds of the enemy nation waiting the verdict; and of the neutrals looking on; circle beyond circle.

There were many humiliating material limits, but no moral impossibilities; so that the scope of our diathetical activities was unbounded. On it we should mainly depend for the means of victory on the Arab front: and the novelty of it was our advantage. The printing press, and each newly-discovered method of communication favoured the intellectual above the physical, civilization paying the mind always from the body's funds. We kindergarten soldiers were beginning our art of war in the atmosphere of the twentieth century, receiving our weapons without prejudice. To the regular officer, with the tradition of forty generations of service behind him, the antique arms were the most honoured. As we had seldom to concern ourselves with what our men did, but always with what they thought, the diathetic for us would be more than half the command. In Europe it was set a little aside, and entrusted to men outside the General Staff. In Asia the regular elements were so weak that irregulars could not let the metaphysical weapon rust unused.

Battles in Arabia were a mistake, since we profited in them only by the ammunition the enemy fired off. Napoleon had said it was rare to find generals willing to fight battles; but the curse of this war was that so few would do anything else. Saxe had told us that irrational battles were the refuges of fools: rather they seemed to me impositions on the side which believed itself weaker, hazards made unavoidable either by lack of land room or by the need to defend a material property dearer than the lives of soldiers. We had nothing material to lose, so our best line was to defend nothing and to shoot nothing. Our cards were speed and time, not hitting power. The invention of bully beef had profited us more than the invention of gunpowder, but gave us strategical, rather than tactical strength, since in Arabia range was more than force, space greater than the power of armies.

I had now been eight days lying in this remote tent, keeping my ideas general, till my brain, sick of unsupported thinking, had to be dragged to its work by an effort of will, and went off into a doze whenever that effort was relaxed. The fever passed:

2. Ancient Greek soldier and historian (431–350 B.C.), author of the *Anabasis*, a work describing the expedition into modern Anatolia (ancient Achaemenia) of a group of Greek mercenaries in support of Cyrus, son of King Darius II, who was attempting to seize the Achaemenian throne.

3. Translates approximately as "propaganda."

my dysentery ceased; and with restored strength the present again became actual to me. Facts concrete and pertinent thrust themselves into my reveries; and my inconstant wit bore aside towards all these roads of escape. So I hurried into line my shadowy principles, to have them once precise before my power to evoke them faded.

It seemed to me proven that our rebellion had an unassailable base, guarded not only from attack, but from the fear of attack. It had a sophisticated alien enemy, disposed as an army of occupation in an area greater than could be dominated effectively from fortified posts. It had a friendly population, of which some two in the hundred were active, and the rest quietly sympathetic to the point of not betraying the movements of the minority. The active rebels had the virtues of secrecy and self-control, and the qualities of speed, endurance and independence of arteries of supply. They had technical equipment enough to paralyse the enemy's communications. A province would be won when we had taught the civilians in it to die for our ideal of freedom. The presence of the enemy was secondary. Final victory seemed certain, if the war lasted long enough for us to work it out.

Chapter 122

By morning, after the sudden fashion of troubles, they were ended and our ship sailing under a clear sky. The armoured cars came in, and the pleasure of our men's sedate faces heartened me. Pisani[4] arrived, and made me laugh, so bewildered was the good soldier by the political hubbub. He gripped his military duty as a rudder to steer him through. Damascus was normal, the shops open, street merchants trading, the electric tramcars restored, grain and vegetables and fruits coming in well.[5]

The streets were being watered to lay the terrible dust of three war-years' lorry traffic. The crowds were slow and happy, and numbers of British troops were wandering in the town, unarmed. The telegraph was restored with Palestine, and with Beyrout, which the Arabs had occupied in the night. As long ago as Wejh I had warned them, when they took Damascus to leave Lebanon for sop to the French and take Tripoli instead; since as a port it outweighed Beyrout, and England would have played the honest broker for it on their behalf in the Peace Settlement. So I was grieved by their mistake, yet glad they felt grown-up enough to reject me.[6]

Even the hospital was better. I had urged Chauvel[7] to take it over, but he would not. At the time I thought he meant to overstrain us, to justify his taking away our government of the town. However, since, I have come to feel that the trouble between us was a delusion of the ragged nerves which were jangling me to distraction these days. Certainly Chauvel won the last round, and made me feel mean, for when he heard that I was leaving he drove round with Godwin[8] and thanked me outright

4. Commander of a small contingent of French soldiers in the region.
5. This extract recounts the triumphant occupation by Arab forces of the Syrian city of Damascus. This marked the de facto defeat of Turkey in the war.
6. Under the terms of the secret 1915 Anglo-French "Sykes-Picot" agreement (named after the negotiators on each side), the postwar Arab Middle East was to be divided up into British and French "spheres of influence"; the French were to decide the affairs of the north and west (present-day Syria and the Lebanon), the British the south and east (present-day Palestine, Iraq, and Jordan). Lawrence apparently thought at this stage that French ambitions in the area could be satisfied by "leaving them" the Lebanon; if so, he was to be bitterly disappointed by

the outcome of the postwar negotiations, where the Sykes-Picot agreement was made the basis for the postwar order. Feisal was forced out of Syria, which became a French "mandate" under the peace treaties. In the introductory chapter to the Seven Pillars Lawrence writes of the Conference: "we stammered that we had worked for a new heaven and a new earth, and they thanked us kindly and made their peace . . . The [British] Cabinet raised the Arabs to fight for us by definite promises of self-government afterwards. . . . I was continually and bitterly ashamed."
7. Sir Henry Chauvel was in charge of the Australian forces in Palestine, which initially occupied Damascus.
8. Australian chief of staff.

for my help in his difficulties. Still, the hospital was improving of itself. Fifty prisoners had cleaned the courtyard, burning the lousy rubbish. A second gang had dug another great grave-pit in the garden, and were zealously filling it as opportunity offered. Others had gone through the wards, washing every patient, putting them into cleaner shirts, and reversing their mattresses to have a tolerably decent side up. We had found food suitable for all but critical cases, and each ward had some Turkish-spoken orderly within hearing, if a sick man called. One room we had cleared, brushed out and disinfected, meaning to transfer into it the less ill cases, and do their room in turn.

At this rate three days would have seen things very fit, and I was proudly contemplating other benefits when a medical major strode up and asked me shortly if I spoke English. With a brow of disgust for my skirts and sandals he said "You're in charge?" Modestly I smirked that in a way I was, and then he burst out, "Scandalous, disgraceful, outrageous, ought to be shot . . ." At this onslaught I cackled out like a chicken, with the wild laughter of strain; it did feel extraordinarily funny to be so cursed just as I had been pluming myself on having bettered the apparently hopeless.

The major had not entered the charnel house of yesterday, nor smelt it, nor seen us burying those bodies of ultimate degradation, whose memory had started me up in bed, sweating and trembling, a few hours since.[9] He glared at me, muttering "Bloody brute." I hooted out again, and he smacked me over the face and stalked off, leaving me more ashamed than angry, for in my heart I felt he was right, and that anyone who pushed through to success a rebellion of the weak against their masters must come out of it so stained in estimation that afterward nothing in the world would make him feel clean. However, it was nearly over.

When I got back to the hotel crowds were besetting it, and at the door stood a grey Rolls-Royce, which I knew for Allenby's. I ran in and found him there with Clayton and Cornwallis and other noble people.[1] In ten words he gave his approval to my having impertinently imposed Arab Governments, here and at Deraa, upon the chaos of victory.[2] He confirmed the appointment of Ali Riza Rikabi as his Military Governor, under the orders of Feisal, his Army Commander, and regulated the Arab sphere and Chauvel's.

He agreed to take over my hospital and the working of the railway. In ten minutes all the maddening difficulties had slipped away. Mistily I realized that the harsh days of my solitary battling had passed. The lone hand had won against the world's odds, and I might let my limbs relax in this dreamlike confidence and decision and kindness which were Allenby.

Then we were told that Feisal's special train had just arrived from Deraa. A message was hurriedly sent him by Young's mouth,[3] and we waited till he came, upon a tide of cheering which beat up against our windows. It was fitting the two chiefs should meet for the first time in the heart of their victory; with myself still acting as the interpreter between them.

9. In the disorder attendant upon Turkish evacuation of the city and the Allied entrance into it, conditions at the Turkish military hospital were allowed to deteriorate. Lawrence describes the appalling conditions in ch. 121.
1. Sir Gilbert Clayton (1875–1929), principal British intelligence officer; Kinahan Cornwallis (1883–1959), British intelligence officer; Field Marshal Lord Allenby

(1861–1936), director of British military operations in Palestine.
2. In ch. 120 Lawrence describes his appointment of new Arab governors in the wake of Turkish defeat; though apparently accepted by Allenby, these arrangements were not upheld at Versailles.
3. Hubert Young (1885–1950), British officer serving (like Lawrence) as Anglo-Arab liaison.

Allenby gave me a telegram from the Foreign Office, recognizing to the Arabs the status of belligerents;[4] and told me to translate it to the Emir: but none of us knew what it meant in English, let alone in Arabic: and Feisal, smiling through the tears which the welcome of his people had forced from him, put it aside to thank the Commander-in-Chief for the trust which had made him and his movement. They were a strange contrast: Feisal, large-eyed, colourless and worn, like a fine dagger; Allenby, gigantic and red and merry, fit representative of the Power which had thrown a girdle of humour and strong dealing round the world.

When Feisal had gone, I made to Allenby the last (and also I think the first) request I ever made him for myself—leave to go away. For a while he would not have it; but I reasoned, reminding him of his year-old promise, and pointing out how much easier the New Law would be if my spur were absent from the people. In the end he agreed; and then at once I knew how much I was sorry.

[AFTERWORD]

Damascus had not seemed a sheath for my sword, when I landed in Arabia: but its capture disclosed the exhaustion of my main springs of action. The strongest motive throughout had been a personal one, not mentioned here, but present to me, I think, every hour of these two years. Active pains and joys might fling up, like towers, among my days: but, refluent as air, this hidden urge re-formed, to be the persisting element of life, till near the end. It was dead, before we reached Damascus.

Next in force had been a pugnacious wish to win the war: yoked to the conviction that without Arab help England could not pay the price of winning its Turkish sector. When Damascus fell, the Eastern war—probably the whole war—drew to an end.

Then I was moved by curiosity. "Super flumina Babylonis,"[5] read as a boy, had left me longing to feel myself the node of a national movement. We took Damascus, and I feared. More than three arbitrary days would have quickened in me a root of authority.

There remained historical ambition, insubstantial as a motive by itself. I had dreamed, at the City School in Oxford, of hustling into form, while I lived, the new Asia which time was inexorably bringing upon us. Mecca was to lead to Damascus; Damascus to Anatolia, and afterwards to Bagdad;

and then there was Yemen. Fantasies,
these will seem, to such as are able to call
my beginning an ordinary effort.

Siegfried Sassoon
1886–1967

It is tempting to describe a poet like Siegfried Sassoon by emphasizing his differences from the hugely popular Rupert Brooke. Sassoon was born to a wealthy Jewish family, who made

---

4. The official recognition of the Arabs as "belligerents" in the conflict was important since it would allow them representation at the peace conference to come.
5. "By the rivers of Babylon" (Latin), Psalm 137. (The Israelites bewail their exile in Babylon; the verse continues "there we sat down, yea, we wept, when we remembered Zion.")

their fortune in India; he lived a life of ease before the war, writing slight Georgian poetry and hunting foxes. World War I suddenly and unequivocally changed all that. Sassoon served with the Royal Welsh Fusiliers, and before the end of 1915 saw action in France; he helped a wounded soldier to safety during heavy fire, for which he was awarded a Military Cross. After being wounded himself, Sassoon refused to return to battle; from his hospital bed, he wrote an open letter to the war department suggesting that the war was being unnecessarily prolonged, and as a result, he narrowly avoided a court-martial. Owing to the intervention of his fellow soldier the poet Robert Graves, he was instead committed to a hospital and treated for "shell-shock." He returned to the front in 1919, and was wounded a second time.

Where the war poetry of Brooke is patriotic to the point of sentimentality, Sassoon's verse is characterized by an unrelentingly realistic portrayal of the horrors of modern warfare. And where Brooke's poetry was eagerly welcomed by an anxious public, Sassoon's was largely reject-ed as either unpatriotic or unnecessarily grotesque. After the war, he lived in seclusion in the country, writing memoirs and poetry—though rarely with the shock value of his early war poems.

Glory of Women

You love us when we're heroes, home on leave,
Or wounded in a mentionable place.
You worship decorations; you believe
That chivalry redeems the war's disgrace.
5   You make us shells. You listen with delight,
By tales of dirt and danger fondly thrilled.
You crown our distant ardours while we fight,
And mourn our laurelled memories when we're killed.
You can't believe that British troops "retire"
10   When hell's last horror breaks them, and they run,
Trampling the terrible corpses—blind with blood.
    O German mother dreaming by the fire,
While you are knitting socks to send your son
His face is trodden deeper in the mud.

Craiglockhart,[1] 1917

Everyone Sang

Everyone suddenly burst out singing;
And I was filled with such delight
As prisoned birds must find in freedom,
Winging wildly across the white
5   Orchards and dark-green fields; on—on—and out of sight.
Everyone's voice was suddenly lifted;
And beauty came like the setting sun:
My heart was shaken with tears; and horror
Drifted away . . . O, but Everyone
10   Was a bird; and the song was wordless; the singing will never be done.

April 1919

---

1. A hospital near Edinburgh, Scotland, where Sassoon (along with Wilfred Owen) was treated for shell shock.

Wilfred Owen
1893–1918

The poet C. Day Lewis wrote that Owen's poems were "certainly the finest written by any English poet of the First War." In his small body of poems Owen manages to combine his friend Siegfried Sassoon's outrage at the horror of the war with a formal and technical skill reminiscent of his idols Keats and Shelley. Sassoon himself characterized their differences as poets this way: "My trench-sketches were like rockets, sent up to illuminate the darkness. . . . It was Owen who revealed how, out of realistic horror and scorn, poetry might be made."

Owen grew up on the Welsh border in Shropshire, the landscape A. E. Housman was to celebrate in his poetry. After finishing technical school, Owen spent two years in training with an evangelical Church of England vicar, trying to decide whether to pursue formal training as a clergyman. As a result of his experiences, Owen became dissatisfied with the institutional church's response to the poverty and suffering of England's least privileged citizens. In October 1915 he enlisted with the Artists' Rifles, and on 29 December 1916, he left for France as a lieutenant with the Lancashire Fusiliers.

Owen quickly became disillusioned with the war; as a result of almost unimaginable privations, which included being blown into the air while he slept in a foxhole, Owen suffered a breakdown, and was sent to the Craiglockhart War Hospital in Edinburgh. Owen composed nearly all of his poetry in the fourteen months of his rehabilitation, between August 1917 and September 1918; though hard to imagine, it is quite possible that if he had not been sent back to Great Britain to recover from his "shell shock," we might now know nothing of his poetry. While at Craiglockhart he met Sassoon and found his true voice and mode; he published his first poems on war themes anonymously in the hospital's magazine, which he edited. In September 1918 Owen returned to the battlefields of France; he was killed in action at Sambre Canal on November 4, 1918, one week before the Armistice. Dylan Thomas called Owen "one of the four most profound influences upon the poets who came after him"—the others being Hopkins, Yeats, and Eliot.

Anthem for Doomed Youth

What passing-bells for these who die as cattle?
   Only the monstrous anger of the guns.
   Only the stuttering rifles' rapid rattle
Can patter out their hasty orisons.°   *prayers*
5   No mockeries now for them; no prayers nor bells,
   Nor any voice of mourning save the choirs,—
The shrill, demented choirs of wailing shells;
   And bugles calling for them from sad shires.

What candles may be held to speed them all?
10   Not in the hands of boys, but in their eyes
Shall shine the holy glimmers of good-byes.
   The pallor of girls' brows shall be their pall;[1]
Their flowers the tenderness of patient minds,
And each slow dusk a drawing-down of blinds.

1. The cloth draped over a coffin.

Strange Meeting

It seemed that out of battle I escaped
Down some profound dull tunnel, long since scooped
Through granites which titanic wars had groined.°   *joined together*
Yet also there encumbered sleepers groaned,
5   Too fast in thought or death to be bestirred.
Then, as I probed them, one sprang up, and stared
With piteous recognition in fixed eyes,
Lifting distressful hands as if to bless.
And by his smile, I knew that sullen hall,
10   By his dead smile I knew we stood in Hell.
With a thousand pains that vision's face was grained;
Yet no blood reached there from the upper ground,
And no guns thumped, or down the flues made moan.
"Strange friend," I said, "here is no cause to mourn."
15   "None," said that other, "save the undone years,
The hopelessness. Whatever hope is yours,
Was my life also; I went hunting wild
After the wildest beauty in the world,
Which lies not calm in eyes, or braided hair,
20   But mocks the steady running of the hour,
And if it grieves, grieves richlier than here.
For of my glee might many men have laughed,
And of my weeping something had been left,
Which must die now. I mean the truth untold,
25   The pity of war, the pity war distilled.
Now men will go content with what we spoiled,
Or, discontent, boil bloody, and be spilled.
They will be swift with swiftness of the tigress.
None will break ranks, though nations trek from progress.
30   Courage was mine, and I had mystery,
Wisdom was mine, and I had mastery:
To miss the march of this retreating world
Into vain citadels that are not walled.
Then, when much blood had clogged their chariot-wheels,
35   I would go up and wash them from sweet wells,
Even with truths that lie too deep for taint.
I would have poured my spirit without stint
But not through wounds; not on the cess of war.
Foreheads of men have bled where no wounds were.
40   I am the enemy you killed, my friend.
I knew you in this dark: for so you frowned
Yesterday through me as you jabbed and killed.
I parried; but my hands were loath and cold.
Let us sleep now. . . ."

Dulce Et Decorum Est[1]

Bent double, like old beggars under sacks,
Knock-kneed, coughing like hags, we cursed through sludge,

---

1. From the *Odes* of the Roman satirist Horace (65–8 B.C.): Dulce et decorum est pro patria mori [sweet and fitting it is to die for your fatherland].

Till on the haunting flares we turned our backs
And towards our distant rest began to trudge.
5   Men marched asleep. Many had lost their boots
But limped on, blood-shod. All went lame; all blind;
Drunk with fatigue; deaf even to the hoots
Of tired, outstripped Five-Nines[2] that dropped behind.

Gas! Gas! Quick, boys!—An ecstasy of fumbling,
10   Fitting the clumsy helmets just in time;
But someone still was yelling out and stumbling
And flound'ring like a man in fire or lime[3] . . .
Dim, through the misty panes and thick green light,
As under a green sea, I saw him drowning.

15   In all my dreams, before my helpless sight,
He plunges at me, guttering, choking, drowning.

If in some smothering dreams you too could pace
Behind the wagon that we flung him in,
And watch the white eyes writhing in his face,
20   His hanging face, like a devil's sick of sin;
If you could hear, at every jolt, the blood
Come gargling from the froth-corrupted lungs,
Obscene as cancer, bitter as the cud
Of vile, incurable sores on innocent tongues,—
25   My friend, you would not tell with such high zest
To children ardent for some desperate glory,
The old Lie: Dulce et decorum est
Pro patria mori.

Isaac Rosenberg
1890–1918

World War I was the spur that goaded some poets, like Wilfred Owen, into the writing of poetry; for Isaac Rosenberg the war was simply the catalyst for a more vivid and powerful verse. Rosenberg began writing poetry on Jewish themes when he was just fifteen; he had published two volumes of poems and a verse play, *Moses*, by the time he joined the army in 1916. Rosenberg's experience of the war was, in important ways, different from the other poets represented here. To begin with, he was the son of Lithuanian Jewish immigrants who had settled in the East End, London's Jewish ghetto. As a child, Rosenberg lived with severe poverty; he was forced to leave school at fourteen to help support his family. He went to war not as an officer, but as a private; as the critic Irving Howe writes, "No glamorous fatality hangs over Rosenberg's head: he was just a clumsy, stuttering Jewish doughboy." He was killed while on patrol outside the trenches—a private's dangerous assignment.

His experiences on the Western Front seem to have provided him with the perfect canvas for his essentially religious art. Siegfried Sassoon, alluding to Rosenberg's training as an artist at the Slade School, later described his poems as "scriptural and sculptural": "His experiments were a strenuous effort for impassioned expression; his imagination had a sinewy and muscular aliveness; often he saw things in terms of sculpture, but he did not carve or chisel; he *modeled*

---

2. Artillery shells used by the Germans.

3. Calcium oxide, a powerfully caustic alkali used, among other purposes, for cleaning the flesh off the bones of corpses.

words with fierce energy and aspiration." His less-than-genteel background also made Rosenberg impatient with the patriotic sentiments of a poet like Rupert Brooke, for whose "begloried sonnets" he had nothing but contempt. In the poetry of Rosenberg, by contrast—according to Sassoon—"words and images obey him, instead of leading him into over-elaboration." Interest in Rosenberg's poetry has recently been revived by critics interested in his use of Jewish themes; the critic Harold Bloom, for instance, calls Rosenberg "an English poet with a Jewish difference," and suggests that he is "the best Jewish poet writing in English that our century has given us."

Break of Day in the Trenches

The darkness crumbles away—
It is the same old druid[1] Time as ever.
Only a live thing leaps my hand—
A queer sardonic rat—
5   As I pull the parapet's poppy
To stick behind my ear.
Droll rat, they would shoot you if they knew
Your cosmopolitan sympathies.
Now you have touched this English hand
10 You will do the same to a German—
Soon, no doubt, if it be your pleasure
To cross the sleeping green between.
It seems you inwardly grin as you pass
Strong eyes, fine limbs, haughty athletes
15 Less chanced than you for life,
Bonds to the whims of murder,
Sprawled in the bowels of the earth,
The torn fields of France.
What do you see in our eyes
20 At the shrieking iron and flame
Hurled through still heavens?
What quaver—what heart aghast?
Poppies whose roots are in man's veins
Drop, and are ever dropping;
25 But mine in my ear is safe,
Just a little white with the dust.

1916   1922

David Jones
1895–1974

David Jones's long narrative poem *In Parenthesis* is arguably the great literary text of World War I. While other poets have more vividly recreated the horrors of the war, and prose chroniclers like Robert Graves have analyzed more precisely the futility and banality of trench warfare, Jones's "writing"—the only generic label he was willing to assign *In Parenthesis*—combines the resources of both poetry and prose, and brings to bear a historical, religious, and

---

1. Member of an ancient Celtic religion.

mythical framework through which to understand the war. In Jones's text the Great War is revealed to be just the most recent battle in the great war that is human history.

Jones was born near London to an English mother and Welsh father; his father impressed upon him the richness of his Welsh heritage. After leaving grammar school, Jones enrolled in art school; when war broke out, however, he was quick to enlist, and joined the Royal Welch Fusiliers as an infantryman in January 1915. He served on the Western Front until March 1918, having been wounded at the battle of the Somme in June 1916; he remarked later that the war "had a permanent effect upon me and has affected my work in all sorts of ways." After the war, Jones went to Ditchling Common, a Catholic artists' guild run by the writer and sculptor Eric Gill. Jones was attracted to Gill's regimen of work and prayer; he converted to Roman Catholicism in 1921 and soon joined the guild, where he lived and worked until 1933.

Jones did not begin to write *In Parenthesis* until 1928. The poem tells the story of Private John Ball, from his embarkation from England in December 1915 to the battle of the Somme. The text modulates from straightforward narrative to a kind of prose poetry to stretches of pure poetry, incorporating echoes and allusions of texts, from the Welsh epic *The Mabinogion* to the medieval battle epic *Y Gododdin* to Malory's *Morte d'Arthur* to Shakespeare's history plays to Eliot's *The Waste Land*—as well as drawing from "subliterary" sources such as soldier's slang. *In Parenthesis* is difficult and allusive, as are many other monumental works of modernist literature, like Joyce's *Ulysses* and *Finnegans Wake*, Pound's *Cantos*, and Eliot's *The Waste Land*. While this difficulty has sometimes kept away the readers Jones deserves, the critic Thomas Dilworth calls *In Parenthesis* "the only authentic and successful epic poem in the language since *Paradise Lost*."

In Parenthesis differs from other war poetry in argument as well as form; the poem is not simply a protest against the war but rather an attempt to place the war into a world-historical context. As the critic Samuel Rees writes, it "is not a poem either to provoke or to end a war . . . except as it adds to the accumulation of testimony to the stupidities and brutality of history that each age must learn from or, more likely, ignore." In the writing he produced after *In Parenthesis* Jones continued to be concerned with contemporary society's loss of interest in the past, and with the depersonalizing effects of technology; his other great poem, *The Anathemata*, was judged by W. H. Auden to be "probably the finest long poem in English in this century."

from In Parenthesis[1]
Part 1. The Many Men So Beautiful[2]

'49 Wyatt, 01549 Wyatt.
Coming sergeant.
Pick 'em up, pick 'em up—I'll stalk within yer chamber.
Private Leg . . . sick.
Private Ball . . . absent.
'01 Ball, '01 Ball, Ball of No. 1.
Where's Ball, 2501 Ball—you corporal,
Ball of your section.
Movement round and about the Commanding Officer.
Bugler, will you sound "Orderly Sergeants."

---

1. In his preface, Jones writes: "This writing is called 'In Parenthesis' because I have written it in a kind of space between—I don't know between quite what—but as you turn aside to do something; and because for us amateur soldiers (and especially for the writer, who was not only an amateur, but grotesquely incompetent, a knocker-over of piles, a parade's despair) the war itself was a parenthe-

sis—how glad we thought we were to step outside its brackets at the end of '18—and also because our curious type of existence here is altogether in parenthesis."
2. Coleridge, *Ancient Mariner*, part iv, verse 4 [Jones's note]. "The many men, so beautiful! / And they all dead did lie: / And a thousand thousand slimy things / Lived on; and so did I."

David Jones. Etching of World War I soldier (frontispiece to *In Parenthesis*). 1937.

A hurrying of feet from three companies converging on the little group apart where on horses sit the central command. But from "B" Company there is no such darting out. The Orderly Sergeant of "B" is licking the stub end of his lead pencil; it divides a little his fairish moist moustache.

Heavily jolting and sideway jostling, the noise of liquid shaken in a small vessel by a regular jogging movement, a certain clinking ending in a shuffling of the feet sidelong—all clear and distinct in that silence peculiar to parade grounds and to refectories. The silence of a high order, full of peril in the breaking of it, like the coming on parade of John Ball.

He settles between numbers 4 and 5 of the rear rank. It is as ineffectual as the ostrich in her sand. Captain Gwynn does not turn or move or give any sign.

Have that man's name taken if you please, Mr. Jenkins.

Take that man's name, Sergeant Snell.

Take his name, corporal.

Take his name take his number—charge him—late on parade—the Battalion being paraded for overseas—warn him for Company Office.

Have you got his name Corporal Quilter.

Temporary unpaid Lance-Corporal Aneirin Merddyn Lewis had somewhere in his Welsh depths a remembrance of the nature of man, of how a lance-corporal's stripe is but held vicariously and from on high, is of one texture with an eternal economy. He brings in a manner, baptism, and metaphysical order to the bankruptcy of the occasion.

'01 Ball is it—there was a man in Bethesda late for the last bloody judgment.

Corporal Quilter on the other hand knew nothing of these things.

Private Ball's pack, ill adjusted and without form, hangs more heavily on his shoulder blades, a sense of ill-usage pervades him. He withdraws within himself to soothe himself—the inequity of those in high places is forgotten. From where he stood heavily, irksomely at ease, he could see, half-left between 7 and 8 of the front rank, the profile of Mr. Jenkins and the elegant cut of his war-time rig and his flax head held front; like San Romano's[3] foreground squire, unhelmeted; but we don't have lances now nor banners nor trumpets. It pains the lips to think of bugles—and did they blow Defaulters[4] on the Uccello horns.

He put his right hand behind him to ease his pack, his cold knuckles find something metallic and colder.

No mess-tin cover.

Shining sanded mess-tin giving back the cold early light. *Improperly dressed, the Battalion being paraded for overseas.* His imaginings as to the precise relationship of this general indictment from the book to his own naked mess-tin were with suddenness and most imperatively impinged upon, as when an animal hunted, stopping in some ill-chosen covert to consider the wickedness of man, is started into fresh effort by the cry and breath of dogs dangerously and newly near. For the chief huntsman is winding his horn, the officer commanding is calling his Battalion by name—whose own the sheep are.

55th Battalion!

Fifty-fifth Bat-tal-i-on

'talion!!

From "D" to "A" his eyes knew that parade. He detected no movement. They were properly at ease.

Reverberation of that sudden command broke hollowly upon the emptied huts behind "D" Company's rear platoons. They had only in them the rolled mattresses, the neatly piled bed-boards and the empty tea-buckets of the orderly-men, emptied of their last gun-fire.[5]

Stirrups taut and pressing upward in the midst of his saddle he continues the ritual words by virtue of which a regiment is moved in column of route:

. . . the Battalion will move in column of fours to the right—"A" Company—"A" Company leading.

Words lost, yet given continuity by that thinner command from in front of No. 1. Itself to be wholly swallowed up by the concerted movement of arms in which the spoken word effected what it signified.

"A" Company came to the slope, their files of four turn right. The complex of command and heel-iron turned confuse the morning air. The rigid structure of their lines knows a swift mobility, patterns differently for those sharp successive cries.

---

3. Cf. painting, "Rout of San Romano." Paolo Uccello (Nat. Gal.) [Jones's note].
4. Soldiers convicted by a court-martial.

5. Tea served to troops before first parade. Rouse parade [Jones's note].

Mr. P. D. I. Jenkins who is twenty years old has now to do his business:
No. 7 Platoon—number seven.
number seven—right—by the right.
How they sway in the swing round for all this multiplicity of gear.
Keept'y'r dressing.
Sergeant Snell did his bit.
Corporal Quilter intones:
Dress to the right—no—other right.
Keep those slopes.
Keep those sections of four.
Pick those knees up.
Throw those chests out.
Hold those heads up.
Stop that talking.
Keep those chins in.
Left left lef'—lef' righ' lef'—you Private Ball it's you I'v got me glad-eye on.

So they came outside the camp. The liturgy of a regiment departing has been sung. Empty wet parade ground. A campwarden, some unfit men and other details loiter, dribble away, shuffle off like men whose ship has sailed.
    The long hutment lines stand. Not a soul. It rains harder: torn felt lifts to the wind above Hut 10, Headquarter Company; urinal concrete echoes for a solitary whistler. Corrugated iron empty—no one. Chill gust slams the vacant canteen door.

Miss Veronica Best who runs the hut for the bun-wallahs[6] stretches on her palliasse,[7] she's sleepy, she can hear the band: We've got too many buns—and all those wads[8]—you knew they were going—why did you order them—they won't be in after rouse-parade even—they've gone.
    Know they've gone—shut up—Jocks from Bardown move in Monday. Violet turns to sleep again.

Horses' tails are rather good—and the way this one springs from her groomed flanks.
    He turns slightly in his saddle.
    You may march at ease.
    No one said march easy Private Ball, you're bleedin' quick at some things ain't yer.

The Squire from the Rout of San Romano smokes Melachrino No. 9.
    The men may march easy and smoke, Sergeant Snell.

Some like tight belts and some like loose belts—trussed-up pockets—cigarettes in ammunition pouches—rifle-bolts, webbing, buckles and rain—gotta light mate—give us a match chum. How cold the morning is and blue, and how mysterious in cupped hands glow the match-lights of a concourse of men, moving so early in the morning.
    The body of the high figure in front of the head of the column seemed to change his position however so slightly. It rains on the transparent talc of his map-case.

---

6. Person pertaining to: e.g. staff-wallah; person addicted to: e.g. bun-wallah [Jones's note].

7. Straw mattress.
8. Canteen sandwiches [Jones's note].

The Major's horse rubs noses with the horse of the superior officer. Their docked manes brush each, as two friends would meet. The dark horse snorts a little for the pulling at her bridle rein.

In "D" Company round the bend of the road in the half-light is movement, like a train shunting, when the forward coaches buffer the rear coaches back. The halt was unexpected. How heavy and how top-heavy is all this martial panoply and how the ground seems to press upward to afflict the feet.

The bastard's lost his way already.

Various messages are passed.

Some lean on their rifles as aged men do on sticks in stage-plays. Some lean back with the muzzle of the rifle supporting the pack in the position of gentlewomen at field sports, but not with so great assurance.

It's cold when you stop marching with all this weight and icy down the back.

Battalion cyclists pass the length of the column. There is fresh stir in "A" Company.

Keep your column distance.

The regular rhythm of the march has re-established itself.

The rain increases with the light and the weight increases with the rain. In all that long column in brand-new overseas boots weeping blisters stick to the hard wool of grey government socks.

I'm bleedin' cripple already Corporal, confides a limping child.

Kipt' that step there.

Keep that proper distance.

Keept' y'r siction o' four—can't fall out me little darlin'.

Corporal Quilter subsides, he too retreats within himself, he has his private thoughts also.

It's a proper massacre of the innocents in a manner of speaking, no so-called seven ages o' man only this bastard military age.

Keep that step there.

Keep that section distance.

Hand us thet gas-pipe young Saunders—let's see you shape—you too, little Benjamin—hang him about like a goddam Chris'us tree—use his ample shoulders for an armoury-rack—it is his part to succour the lambs of the flock.

With some slackening of the rain the band had wiped their instruments. Broken catches on the wind-gust came shrilly back:

Of Hector and Lysander and such great names as these—the march proper to them.[9]

So they went most of that day and it rained with increasing vigour until night-fall. In the middle afternoon the outer parts of the town of embarkation were reached. They halted for a brief while; adjusted puttees,[1] straightened caps, fastened undone buttons, tightened rifle-slings and attended each one to his own bedraggled and irregular condition. The band recommenced playing; and at the attention and in excellent step they passed through the suburbs, the town's centre, and so towards the docks. The people of that town did not acclaim them, nor stop about their business—for it was late in the second year.[2]

---

9. *The British Grenadiers* is the ceremonial march of all Grenadier and Fusilier Regiments [Jones's note].

1. Leggings.
2. That is to say in December 1915 [Jones's note].

By some effort of a corporate will the soldierly bearing of the text books maintained itself through the town, but with a realisation of the considerable distance yet to be covered through miles of dock, their frailty reasserted itself—which slackening called for fresh effort from the Quilters and the Snells, but at this stage with a more persuasive intonation, with almost motherly concern.

Out of step and with a depressing raggedness of movement and rankling of tempers they covered another mile between dismal sheds, high and tarred. Here funnels and mastheads could be seen. Here the influence of the sea and of the tackle and ways of its people fell upon them. They revived somewhat, and for a while. Yet still these interminable ways between—these incessant halts at junctions. Once they about-turned. Embarkation officers, staff people of all kinds and people who looked as though they were in the Navy but who were not, consulted with the Battalion Commander. A few more halts, more passing of messages,—a further intensifying of their fatigue. The platoons of the leading company unexpectedly wheel. The spacious shed is open at either end, windy and comfortless. Multifarious accoutrements, metal and cloth and leather sink with the perspiring bodies to the concrete floor.

Certain less fortunate men were detailed for guard, John Ball amongst them. The others lay, where they first sank down, wet with rain and sweat. They smoked; they got very cold. They were given tins of bully beef and ration biscuits for the first time, and felt like real expeditionary soldiers. Sometime between midnight and 2 a.m. they were paraded. Slowly, and with every sort of hitch, platoon upon platoon formed single file and moved toward an invisible gangway. Each separate man found his own feet stepping in the darkness on an inclined plane, the smell and taste of salt and machinery, the texture of rope, and the glimmer of shielded light about him.

So without sound of farewell or acclamation, shrouded in a dense windy darkness, they set toward France. They stood close on deck and beneath deck, each man upholstered in his life-belt. From time to time a seaman would push between them about some duty belonging to his trade.

Under a high-slung arc-light whose cold clarity well displayed all their sea weariness, their long cramped-upness and fatigue, they stumblingly and one by one trickled from the ship on to French land. German prisoners in green tunics, made greener by the light, heavily unloading timber at a line of trucks—it still rained, and a bitter wind in from the sea.

A young man, comfortable in a short fleece jacket, stood smoking, immediately beneath the centre of the arc—he gave orders in a pleasant voice, that measured the leisure of his circumstances and of his class. Men move to left and right within the orbit of the light, and away into the half darkness, undefined, beyond it.

"B" Company were conducted by a guide, through back ways between high shuttered buildings, to horse-stalls, where they slept. In the morning, they were given Field Service postcards—and sitting in the straw they crossed out what did not apply, and sent them to their mothers, to their sweethearts.

Toward evening on the same day they entrained in cattle trucks; and on the third day, which was a Sunday, sunny and cold, and French women in deep black were hurrying across flat land—they descended from their grimy, littered, limb restricting, slatted vehicles, and stretched and shivered at a siding. You feel exposed and apprehensive in this new world.

from *Part 4. King Pellam's Launde*[3]

Lance-Corporal Lewis looked about him and on all this liquid action.

It may be remembered Seithenin and the desolated cantrefs, the sixteen fortified places, the great cry of the sea, above the sigh of Gwyddno when his entrenchments stove in.[4] Anyway he kept the joke to himself for there was none to share it in that company, for although Watcyn knew everything about the Neath fifteen, and could sing *Sospan Fach*[5] to make the traverse ring, he might have been an Englishman when it came to matters near to Aneirin's heart. For Watcyn was innocent of his descent from Aeneas, was unaware of Geoffrey Arthur and his cooked histories,[6] or Twm Shon Catti[7] for the matter of that—which pained his lance-corporal friend, for whom Troy still burned, and sleeping kings return, and wild men might yet stir from Mawddwy secrecies.[8] And he who will not come again from his reconnaissance— they've searched his breeches well, they've given him an ivy crown—ein llyw olaf— whose wounds they do bleed by day and by night in December wood.[9]

Lance-Corporal Lewis fed on these things.

Corporal Quilter made investigation round and about the lean-to. No human being was visible in the trench or on the open track. A man, seemingly native to the place, a little thick man, swathed with sacking, a limp, saturated bandolier thrown over one shoulder and with no other accoutrements, gorgeted in woollen Balaclava,[1] groped out from between two tottering corrugated uprights, his great moustaches beaded with condensation under his nose. Thickly greaved with mud so that his boots and puttees and sandbag tie-ons were become one whole of trickling ochre. His minute pipe had its smoking bowl turned inversely. He spoke slowly. He told the corporal that this was where shovels were usually drawn for any fatigue in the supports.[2] He slipped back quickly, with a certain animal caution, into his hole; to almost

---

3. Cf. Malory, book ii, ch. 16 [Jones's note]. In that chapter of Malory's *Morte D'Arthur*, King Pellam rides out through his land and "found the people dead, slain on every side."
4. Refers to tradition of the inundation of Cantref Gwaelod ruled over by Gwyddno, whose drunken dyke-warden, Seithenin, failed to attend to his duties [Jones's note].
5. Cf. song, Sospan Fach, associated with Rugby Football matches; often heard among Welsh troops in France. The refrain runs:

> Sospan fach yn berwi ar y tan,
> Sospan fawr yn berwi ar y llawr.
> a'r gath wedi crafu Joni bach,

which implies, I think, that the little saucepan is boiling on the fire, the big saucepan on the floor, and pussy-cat has scratched of calamitous happenings, Mary Ann has hurt her finger, the scullion is not too well, the baby cries in its cradle—it also talks of Dai who goes for a soldier. There is an English version that introduced the words "Old Fritz took away our only fry-pan"—which lends it more recent association [Jones's note].
6. See the story in Geoffrey of Monmouth (Geoffrey Arthur), of how Aeneas, after the fall of Troy, journeyed to Italy (as in the *Aeneid*), how his grandson Brute eventually came to this island and founded the British Kingdom, with the New Troy, London, as its chief city, and how he is regarded as the father of the British race [Jones's note].
7. The story of Twm Shon Catti is a local version of that general theme: audacious-robber-become-able-magistrate-married-to-beautiful-heiress. He is associated with the Tregaron-Llandovery district. A very broad-sheet type of hero [Jones's note].
8. "The Red-haired Bandits of Mawddwy" are notorious in local tradition. Historically a band of outlaws who troubled the authorities in mid-Wales in the 16th century, about whom legend has accumulated. Perhaps they have become identified with that idea of a mysterious (red?) race lurking in fastnesses which I seem to have heard about elsewhere [Jones's note].
9. "Our last ruler," the last Llywelyn. Killed on December 10th–11th, 1282 near Cefn-y-Bedd in the woods of Buelt; decapitated, his head crowned with ivy. A relic of the Cross was found "in his breeches pocket." The greatest English poet of our time has written: "And sang within the bloody wood / When Agamemnon cried aloud." If the song of birds accompanied Llywelyn's death cry, with that chorus-end, ended the last vestiges of what remained of that order of things which arose out of the Roman eclipse in this Island. "Ein llyw olaf" is an appellation charged with much significance, if we care at all to consider ancient things come at last to their term. He belonged, already, before they pierced him, to the dead of Camlann. We venerate him, dead, between the winter oaks. His contemporary Gruffyddap yr Ynad Côch sang of his death: "The voice of Lamentation is heard in every place . . . the course of nature is changed . . . the trees of the forest furiously rush against each other" [Jones's note]. The poet Jones refers to is T. S. Eliot; he quotes from *Sweeney Among the Nightingales*.
1. A wool helmet with a flap covering the neck
2. Area of second line of trenches in front system, usually a few hundred yeards to rear of front line [Jones's note].

immediately poke out his wool-work head, to ask if anyone had the time of day or could spare him some dark shag or a picture-paper. Further, should they meet a white dog in the trench her name was Belle, and he would like to catch any bastard giving this Belle the boot.

John Ball told him the time of day.

No one had any dark shag.

No one had a picture-paper.

They certainly would be kind to the bitch, Belle. They'd give her half their iron rations—Jesus—they'd let her bite their backsides without a murmur.

He draws-to the sacking curtain over his lair.

Corporal Quilter beckoned his men to where a series of disused fire-bays led from the main trench.

Picks, shovels, dredging-ladles, carriers, containers, gas-rattles,[3] two of Mrs. Thingumajig's patent gas-dispersing flappers,[4] emptied S.A.A.[5] boxes, grenade boxes, two bales of revetting-wire, pine stakes; rusted-to-bright-orange barbed wire of curious design—three coils of it; fine good new dark efficient corkscrew staples, splayed-out all ways; three drums of whale oil, the splintered stock of a Mauser rifle, two unexploded yellow-ochre toffee-apples,[6] their strong rods unrusted; three left-leg gum-boots; a Scotch officer's fine bright bonnet; some type of broken pump, its rubber slack punctured, coiled like a dead slime-beast, reared its brass nozzle out from under rum-jar and picket-maul.[7]

This trove piled haphazardly, half-submerged. You must have a lumber room where you have habitation.

Corporal Quilter calls the leading man. He indicates with a jerk of the head the job of work.

One and one, from one pair of hands to another equally reluctant, they pass the shovels the length of the file.

Corporal Quilter stands watching.

There wanted one shovel to the number of the party. Private Saunders devised that he should be the unprovided man, by the expedient of busying himself with his left puttee, conveniently come down.

Corporal Quilter spits from time to time on the duck-board. He hands to Private Saunders a dredging-ladle and the heavier pick, the other he takes himself. He gives the word of command to move on.

The warden of stores withdraws again his curtain; his shiny thread-bare hind-parts first thrust out—now his whole hair-suit torso, now his aboriginal mask.

N.C.O.[8] in charge of party—you corporal.

Corporal Quilter signatures the chit.[9]

12 shovels

2 picks

1 ladle.

See yer bring 'em again—all the so-called complement.

---

3. Wooden clappers used to give gas alarm [Jones's note].
4. Properly called "The Ayrton Fan." Designed to disperse gas hanging in dugouts or trenches Any simple invention appearing among the troops was attributed to female ingenuity [Jones's note].
5. Small Arms Ammunition. Ball-cartridge [Jones's note].
6. English trench-mortar projectile, the shape of which

suggested that name—also, if I remember rightly, yellow paint was used on some part of them—which would add to the similarity [Jones's note].
7. Heavy mallet for driving home stakes used in wire entanglements [Jones's note].
8. Noncommissioned officer.
9. Bill.

They watched him vanish, mandrill fashion, into his enclosure. They wondered how long a time it took to become so knit with the texture of this country-side, so germane to the stuff about, so moulded by, made proper to, the special environment dictated by a stationary war.

Another ten minutes brought them to a double forking of earthworks. Here they recrossed the road, sharp right; a single barricade of sandbags rose direct from the stone sets to afford some meagre shield. There was no parados,[1] and as they filed over, each man turned his head toward the left, toward north west, a toward-home glancing, back down the broken avenue.

Extending fields spread flatly, far to either side, uninterrupted to the sight, not any longer barriered nor revetted in. It was a great goodness in their eyes, this expanse, they drank in this visual freedom gladly, and were disposed to linger before dropping one by one down, where Sandbag Alley meets the road on the north-east side. With that descending this gate to their prison-house of earth closed-to, which had momentarily stood ajar, tantalisingly upon the western escape, where the way led back by the forward batteries—to Hen's Post where you roost in comparative shelter, to Curzon Post where the support platoon take off their boots by day and sleep like rajahs on a palliasse, if things pan out reasonably. To the reserves, to billets,[2] to buildings two stories high, yet roofed intact—and further still to steadings[3] where the mules fidget in their lines and make their palaeolithic cries against the distant flares. To where rosy orderlies smooth the coats of mares they grown as leisurely as boys in Barsetshire. To the very marches of the forward zone, to where mess-caterers write their bogus chits. Where once a day, perhaps, the pickled pilchards jostle the Gentleman's Relish on the top shelf, with the vibration. Where Frenchmen's children are at play about the steep weed-grown incline of a '14 Johnson hole,[4] and each other casement shows its grubby paste-board:

BIÈRE
EGG CHIP 3 FRANC
CAFÉ AU LAIT
ENGLISH SPOKE HEER

And Corporal Bardolph stays and stays.

And beyond again—recedes green kilometre; flat, neat, Hobbema-scape[5]—but the contours and the pressure vary when you reach
Ste. Marie Cappel.
It's healthy O it's pleasant to be, in
Clairmarais.

After which are places known only by report.
To here they come by day from Whitehall, and sky-blue foederati[6] from The Province, starred, gold-faced, wreathed with silver bay—talk through interpreters. And gorget-patches blaze in their variety, but
O christ the blanco,
O the visitations O—so they say.

---

1. A mound of earth at the back of a trench, designed to protect against attack from the rear.
2. Barracks.
3. The outbuildings around a farmhouse.
4. Large shell-hole, called after Jack Johnson. It is a term associated more with the earlier period of the war; later on one seldom heard it used [Jones's note].
5. Meindert Hobbema (1638–1709) was a Dutch landscape artist.
6. Allies; possibly a play on the word *fodder*, i.e. canon fodder.

They drift up with these Songs of Arcady from time to time.

The zones aren't really water-tight you know.

Sometimes in quiet areas when the morning's aired, they do appear—immaculate, bright-greaved ambassadors, to the spirits in prison; who sip their starry nectar from nickel flasks at noon.

They knock their briars[7] out on their bright *talaria*.[8] They grace the trench like wall-flowers, for an hour; as spirits lightly come from many mansions, and the avenues, where they sit below the pseudo-Fragonards[9] cross-legged, slacked, or lie at night under a Baroque cupidon,[1] guiding the campaign.

After that there is only the Big Ship.[2]

To all this then the road led back, without deviation from Sandbag Alley; which does excuse their dawdling feet.

The same stenches, remembered from the darkness, impuried the heavy air, in and around these deep decaying ramparts. Bobby Saunders felt his last-night sickness wretchedly return, an added misery to his melting bowels. His pick and long ladle tangle with his rifle slung. They let him drop to the rear to find a tumbled, antique, wattled-bay to be alone in.

He was back again, fallen in at the tail of the file. Sallow as Christmas clown, pink lidded, a skimpy woodbine[3] stuck to his bleached under-lip, irregularly burned, its glow as ruby sequin-shine—worn wryly on goosey flesh on thrashed circus-child.

No party wanted here corporal.

The sapper, workmanly, and with deliberate care, scrapes quite bright his turned shovel-blade.

Just packing up, corporal, bin getting this bit clear since stand-down, better see the gaffer—a bit along be the piss-house next the Gas-post—most like.

They sagged on their digging gear. The freshly-spread chloride threw upward pallid light as Jack Frost would, and unexpected facets tell. This searching unfamiliar influence cast new pallor, and when they looked from each to each they seemed to each a very ghastly crew.

Corporal Quilter comes again. He spits on the slats. He lights a cigarette.

Wash out—'bout turn, lead on back.
Move on, the leading man
lead on in front,
lead on out.

The storeman found the complement correct. In half an hour they were back in the fire-trench traverses.

Corporal Quilter gave them no formal dismissal, nor did he enquire further what duties his party might next perform. Each one of them disposed himself in some part of their few yards of trench, and for an hour or more were left quite undisturbed, to each his own business. To talk together of the morning's affairs; to fall easily to sleep;

---

7. Pipes.
8. Winged sandals, like those worn by Mercury.
9. Jean Honoré Fragonard (1732–1806) painted scenes of idealized love.
1. A beautiful young person; Cupid-like.
2. (1) Generic term for any cross-channel boat, conveying troops from France back to England. (2) Leave-boat.

(3) That mythological, desired ship, which would, at the termination of hostilities, bring all expeditionary men, maimed or whole, home again. Here, these town-bred Tommies would seem to have the seed of a very potent mythological theme [Jones's note].
3. Cigarette.

to search for some personally possessed thing, wedged tightly between articles drawn from the Quartermaster; to re-read yet again the last arrived letter; to see if the insistent water were penetrated within the stout valise canvas, sufficiently to make useless the very thing you could do with; to look at illustrations in last week's limp and soiled *Graphic*, of Christmas preparations with the Fleet, and full-page portraits of the High Command; to be assured that the spirit of the troops is excellent, that the nation proceeds confidently in its knowledge of victory, that Miss Ashwell would perform before all ranks, that land-girls stamp like girls in Luna.

The two Joneses were in argument.

Private Ball groped in his pack to find his book. The Indian paper was abominably adhered, especially for split finger-tips—and one anthology is as bad as a library and there is no new thing under the sun.[4]

> *Takis, on the motheris breast sowkand,*
> *The babe full of benignitie:—*
>   · · ·
> *He takis the campion in the stour,*
>   · · ·
> *He has tane Rowll of Aberdene,*
> *And gentill Rowll of Corstorphine;*
> *Two better fallowis did no man see:—*[5]

He closed the book—he would eat some chocolate.

Aneirin Lewis sat motionless in the far corner of the bay. The man from Rotherhithe looked to the well-being of his mouth-organ.[6] Private Watcyn was trying to read the scores on the reverse side of Private Thomas's *Western Mail*—as do men in railway carriages. Bobby Saunders slept.

The midday quietness was quite unbroken. They changed sentries at five minutes to the hour, and even this was done without a word for the "relief" or the "relieved," regardless of proper usage. A faulty detonated 4.2 deranged the picketed wire outside the trench as the new sentry took over, making him hug closer the parapet, in expectation; but the capricious gunners let be at that, for their ways are inscrutable.

The day wore on without any happening. The sun unseen reached his low meridian. They ate what bread remained from breakfast and opened tins of beef, and more successfully made some tea. The feebleness of before-noon abated, gave place to an after-lunch content. With the passing hours the wind veered from south to southeast to east. Men sneezed, it grew noticeably colder. The sentry at the Gas Post put up the Alert notice. They were almost eager when required to fill sandbags to repair a freshly destroyed defence. They warmed to their work, and found some interest in this remaking. They strengthened their hands like the builders at the water-gate, and everyone wore his harness and so builded other than the watcher at the fire-step,[7] who saw mirrored a new influence break the topmost headers of his parapets; and creep down that dun hostile wall and bathe the rusted tangle of his outer belt—now sweep all the waste with horizontal beam.

---

4. This is the oft-repeated wisdom of the Preacher in Ecclesiastes.
5. Private Ball reads from "Lament for the Makaris" by William Dunbar (?1456–?1513), Scottish poet and priest. The poem is an elegy for the transitoriness of created things, including friends of the poet; it includes the refrain "Timor mortis conturbat me" ("Fear of death disturbs me").
6. Harmonica.
7. Cf. Nehemiah iii and iv [Jones's note]. These chapters describe the rebuilding of the walls of Jerusalem.

Hidden since the dawn he shines at his departing: fretted like captive-fire at boundary-mound. Each interstice burned between lath and common rafter—each cranny bright, where four walls yet held precariously, purlin and principal, far away over, beyond the parados, in the west.

Tomorrow, before daybreak, a ranging heavy will find the foundations and leave the kitchen flooring pounded like red-pepper, with Cecile's school satchel still hanging at its peg; and the Papal Blessing punctured in its gimcrack frame, poking from the midden. Ober-Leutnant Müller will be blamed for failing to locate a British battery.

The watcher at the fire-step began to hope that his friends would so make an end of their work as to spread their tea-napery of news-sheets, to make the dixie[8] boil to synchronise with his relief.

The last direct radiance gave out, his wire and rising glacis[9] went cold and unillumined, yet clearly defined, in an evenly distributed after-visibility. The cratered earth, of all growing things bereaved, bore that uncreaturely impressiveness of telescope-observed bodies—where even pterodactyl would feel the place unfriendly.

His mates came from the building-up, and work of restoration; the watched dixie almost boiled. Watcyn had already opened the *Dairymaid* canned butter, it was just light enough to know the green and gilt of the enamelled tin. It was an extremely good brand. The light from their gusty culinary flame began to tell warmly on the nearer surfaces. The walls with the skeleton roof stood quite black now against an even clearness, and showed for the last time what remained of that unity intended of their builders. The sky overhead looked crisp as eggshell, wide-domed of porcelain, that suddenly would fracture to innumerable stars. The thin mud on the fire-steps slats glistened, sharpened into rime. The up-to-ankle water became intolerably cold. Two men hasten from the communication trench. They deposit grenade-boxes in a recess used for that purpose and quickly go away. A young man in a British warm, his fleecy muffler cosy to his ears, enquired if anyone had seen the Liaison Officer from Corps, as one who asks of the Tube-lift man at Westminster the whereabouts of the Third Sea Lord. Vacant faces turned to him. He was advised to try Mr. Jenkins in the sap.[1] He turned again, the way he came. Sergeant Snell hurried along the trench carrying a Véry-light pistol; he detailed four men for company rations as he passed. The man with the loose tea and sugar shook some part of it from the sack into the boiling water; and as he poured he heard unmistakable words, nearing, traverse by traverse from the right.

Mr. Jenkins was back from the sap:

Drink that stuff quickly and stand-to.

He is away again with no other word.

No-man's-land[2] whitened rigid: all its contours silver filigreed, as damascened.[3] With the coming dark, ground-mist creeps back to regain the hollow places; across the rare atmosphere you could hear foreign men cough, and stamp with foreign feet. Things seen precisely just now lost exactness. Biez wood became only a darker shape uncertainly expressed. Your eyes begin to strain after escaping definitions. Whether that picket-iron moved toward or some other fell away, or after all is it an animate thing just there by the sap-head or only the slight frosted-sway of suspended wire.

---

8. Kettle.
9. A bank of earth in front of the fortification.
1. Trench.

2. The uncontrolled area between two opposing armies.
3. Decorated with wavy lines.

A long way off a machine-gunner seemed as one tuning an instrument, who strikes the same note quickly, several times, and now a lower one, singly; while scene-shifters thud and scrape behind expectant curtaining; and impatient shuffling of the feet—in the stalls they take out watches with a nervous hand, they can hardly bear it.

Now the fixed-riflemen take notice: it is almost time for ration-parties to perambulate the road.

The first star tremored: her fragile ray as borne on quivering exsultet-reed. From Gretchen Trench lights begin to rise, the first to splutter out, ill discharged.

Have you seen grinning boys fumble with points of flame who blame the taper's damp. At last, one adequately fused, soars competently up in hurrying challenge, to stand against that admirable bright, as crystal cut, lit singly to herald the immediateness of night.

In a quarter of an hour it was quite dark.

You are told to stand-down.

Night-sentries are posted in twos.

Men detailed are to report at once.

Messages drift from bay to bay.

Pass it along—Mr. Prys-Picton's patrol will go out at 8.30 from Pope's Nose and will return by the Sally-Port. Sentries will not fire in this area. The countersign is "Harlequin."

The Lewis-team by the road are experimenting through their newly enlarged loop-hole.

Fans of orange light broke in dancing sequence beyond his lines.

Bursts in groups of four jarred the frosted air with ringing sound.

Brittle discord waft back from the neighbourhood of the Richebourg truckway.

Guns of swift response opened on his back areas. In turn his howitzers coalboxed the Supports.

So gathered with uneven pulse the night-antiphonal: mortared-canisters careened oblique descent with meteor trail; and men were dumb and held their breath for this, as for no thing other.

In the next sector the continued vibrating developed greater weight.

High signal-flares shot up to agitate the starred serenity: red and green and white.[4]

The N.C.O. at the Gas Post looked to his apparatus, and placed in a convenient sequence his ready rocket-gear.

But it peters out; and with the lull they speak to each other.

The sentries stand more erect.

They whistle, softly.

Solitary star-shells toss as the dark deepens.

Mr. Prys-Picton's patrol came in, well before midnight.

from *Part 6. Pavilions and Captains of Hundreds*[5]

John Ball heard the noise of the carpenters where he squatted to clean his rifle. Which hammering brought him disquiet more than the foreboding gun-fire which gathered intensity with each half-hour. He wished they'd stop that hollow tap-tapping. He'd take a walk. He'd go and find his friend with the Lewis guns. And perhaps Olivier would be there. No orders were out yet, and tea would not yet be up.

---

4. Coloured rockets used as a gas S.O.S. [Jones's note].
5. Malory, and Hist. Bks. of O.T. [Jones's note]. The term "pavillions" in Malory refers to the large tents erected for long-term sieges; "captains of hundreds" refers to military leaders throughout the Old Testament books of Numbers, Deuteronomy, and Chronicles.

These three seldom met except for very brief periods out of the line—at Brigade rest perhaps—or if some accident of billeting threw them near together. These three loved each other, but the routine of their lives made chances of foregathering rare. These two with linked arms walked together in a sequestered place above the company lines and found a grassy slope to sit down on. And Signaller Olivier came soon and sat with them. And you feel a bit less windy.

They talked of ordinary things. Of each one's friends at home; those friends unknown to either of the other two. Of the possible duration of the war. Of how they would meet and in what good places afterwards. Of the dissimilar merits of Welsh-men and Cockneys. Of the diverse virtues of Regular and Temporary Officers. Of if you'd ever read the books of Mr. Wells.[6] Of the poetry of Rupert Brooke. Of how you really couldn't very well carry more than one book at a time in your pack. Of the losses of the Battalion since they'd come to France. Of the hateful discomfort of having no greatcoats with fighting-order, of how bad this was. Of how everybody ought rightly to have Burberry's,[7] like officers. Of how German knee boots were more proper to trench war than puttees. Of how privileged Olivier was because he could manage to secrete a few personal belongings along with the signaller's impedimenta. Of how he was known to be a favourite with the Regimental and how he'd feel the draught if he were back with his platoon. Of whether they three would be together for the Duration, and how you hoped so very much indeed. Of captains of thousands and of hundreds, of corporals, of many things. Of the Lloyd George administration, of the Greek, Venizelos, who Olivier said was important, of whom John Ball had never previously heard. Of the neutrality of Spain. Of whether the French nation was nice or nasty. Of whether anyone would ever get leave and what it would be like if you did. Of how stripes, stars, chevrons, specialisations, jobs away from the battalion, and all distinguishing marks were better resisted for as long as possible. Of how it were best to take no particular notice, to let the stuff go over you, how it were wise to lie doggo[8] and to wait the end.

And watched the concentration in the valley.

Where the road switch-backed the nearer slope, tilted, piled-to-overloading limbers, their checking brakes jammed down, and pack-beasts splayed their nervous fore-legs—stiffened to the incline. And where it cut the further hill a mechanised ambulance climbed up and over, and another came toward.

Every few minutes thinned-out smoke wreaths spread up from beyond, to signify the norm of his withdrawing range and the reluctant ebb of his fire. But now and then a more presuming burst would seem to overreach its mark and plunge up white rubble this side; for although the tide be most certainly outbound, yet will some local flow, swell in with make-believe recovery, to flood again the drying shingle and mock with saucy spray the accuracy of their tide-charts; make brats too venturesome flop back with belly-full and guardian nurse girls squeal.

> Amelia's second-best parasol
> sails the raging main;
> her fine fancy's properly split
> she wont see that ever

they cut it a bit too fine

---

6. H. G. Wells, writer of novels and short fiction.   8. Hidden.
7. High-quality raincoats.

and there was scattering from that maiming all over the shop, and the wind right up, and two or three lay sidelong on that hill, and Ginger O'Hara the padre's[9] bloke and O the white bodies in the trouble. And a great untidiness breaching the neat line of bivvies;[1] and unpiled arms by great violence with rove-off piling swivels.

> The Quarter's knocked-off[2] S.R.D.[3]
> > is blown to buggery,
> diluted and far from home[4]
> > what won't half get him shirty.

Mules broke amuck across the open ground, where it said no traffic by daylight, just where his last salvo made dark corona for the hill.

Echoes that make you sit up and take notice tumbled to and fro the hollow in emptied hard collapse, quite other than the sustained, boomed-out

> boom-oom, boom-oom

and the felt recoil,
shocked up from the trained muzzles which sway their sylvan masquerade with each discharge.

John Ball and his friends were watching from their grassy knoll.

A certain liveliness.

He's not half so disposed to turn the other cheek as yesterday.

The signaller was rather in the know or anyway his trade gave him ear to the gossip at H.Q.

He's got snug in his new positions and brought up more heavies our people reckoned on that the Second-in-Command on the wire with Brigade and I gathered our strafe hadn't really begun not till two one four o hours I fancy O we shan't do anything for twenty-four hours of course but of course they may change all that—tamper with the menu every five minutes—in fact orderly room has assumed a real Change Alley atmosphere and talk about tenterhooks and all on thorns and how you really don't know from one minute to the next it's a proper shemozzle. You'd hardly credit it—who do you suppose would not first sit down and think if he be able with a half-brigade—and the Reg'mental looks the Major up and down and takes him for a damned Derbyite—Reg'mental's superb but he can't get over the second Boer War.

The Lewis gunner pulled up bits of daisy.

Waiting for the Esses Essses Bubble to go up—is—abitofa sstrain—I reckon.

New dilapidations on the further hill made the other two attend.

He's got the road this time.

Proper crumps.

I wonder if we'll shift him really.

What's the odds.

What bit of line do you fancy for the winter vacation, when this show's petered gently out.

It's now or never they reckon—they all agree to that you know.

This year next year some time then hold Court of Enquiry as to the probable causes contributing to the loss of the War by Land.

---

9. Priest's.

1. Bivouacs, or temporary encampments.

2. Pinched, stolen [Jones's note].

3. These initials were stamped on every ration rum-jar, and were interpreted by the troops: "Service Rum Dilut-ed" [Jones's note].

4. Refers to statement frequently made by exasperated soldiers: "Fed up, ——d up and far from ——ing home" [Jones's note].

Do you suppose.
that rows of Field-Marshals
Don Ac Ac Gees,
G Esses 0, 1, 2 and 3 and
Ac Ac Q Emma Gees will
fall on their dress-swords[5]

Our young men shall see visions.[6] 25201 Ball has clicked for the gift of bloody prophecy, what a wheeze—*hara-kiri* [suicide] parade by Whitehall Gate—with Royal Mary in her ermine stole and all the king's horses, and the Chaplain General.

He wormed about a bit on his stomach to get quite comfortable and looked intently into the eye of a buttercup.

The Chaplain General will explain how it's a Christian act after all. Give 'em burial in Paul's, there will be letters to *The Times* saying it should have been the Abbey, of course always the Abbey—of course—failing the long mound over the water.

By the way, the C.S.M. of "D" has laid a wager with the Reg'mental over this show—stands to snaffle a hundred francs if the cavalry get going.

Safe as the Waacs dearie, might as well count on the White Knight or the Great Twin Brothers.

Why not?—I'm all for victory: how—good—it—would—be.

Castorneck on Pollux in harness on the right—boot to boot to Aunty Bembridge with her Mafeking V.C.[7]—all in their battle-bowlers—more preferably with plumes—when we go over—this Conchy[8] propaganda's no bon for the troops—hope Jerry puts one on Mecklenburg Square—instead of fussing patriotic Croydon. He'd have to gas the whole district, and Golders Green as well, to be efficacious and—half the B.E.F.[9]—I shouldn't wonder.

And the Lewis gunner uprooting idly with stretched out arm still lying on his stomach turned his left cheek to the wiry downland grass and screwed up his right eye.

Why not join the At-trocities Commission sstraight away—toot sweet—mutilate Little Willie—garrotte Mr. Bertrand-bloody-Russell[1] with the Union Flag—detail Fr. Vaughan[2] O.C. Sergeant Instructors—to pr-reach a course of sermons on the Bull Ring[3] to further foster the offensive spirit.

Tea's up "B" Company.

Roll up—roll up for yer char.

Roll up me lucky lads.

So long—come again soon, don't get nabbed tapping the Gen'ral's wire—I'd hate to see you shot at dawn.

---

5. South sea Bubble, Deputy Assistant Adjutant General, General Staff Officer 1st, 2nd and 3rd grades, Acting Assistant Quartermaster General, in Signaller's Alphabet [Jones's note]. The South Sea Bubble was an 18th-century investment disaster, in which British speculators invested money in the South Sea Company, founded to trade slaves with Spanish America.

6. Cf. Joel 2.28: "And afterward, / I will pour out my Spirit on all people. / Your sons and daughters will prophesy, / your old men will dream dreams, / your young men will see visions."

7. A Victoria's Cross medal, awarded for acts of conspicuous bravery in the presence of the enemy; Mafeking, South Africa, was the site in 1899–1900 of a protracted

battle in the Boer War.

8. Slang for conscientious objector.

9. British Expeditionary Force.

1. Bertrand Russell (1872–1970), British philosopher and mathematician, was jailed for his opposition to World War I.

2. Eminent R. C. preacher; reputed to have urged greater zeal in the destruction of enemy personnel [Jones's note].

3. The large training ground at Rouen, associated with intensive exercises of all kinds, particularly "assault drill." A paradise for Staff Instructors; detested by all frontfighters. The nature of the Ring is perhaps best described in the staff jargon elucidating the object of its curriculum, "to foster the offensive spirit" [Jones's note].

"B" Company were making a queue about the field kitchen and each returning to his group of friends between the bivouac lines with their steaming mess-tins.

And after tea it was a summer evening, simply heavenly if it wasn't for the midges and it was odd not having Fatigues or anything much of course you couldn't get far & you couldn't get a wet anyhow and the whole up and down of the valley like proletarian holiday. But engines positioned for the assault and the paraphernalia of the gunners and all that belongs to the preparation toward a general action and corrugated tin shelters and hastily contrived arbours and a place of tabernacles and of no long continuing nor abidingness, yet not by no means haphazard nor prejudicial to good-order.

Well you couldn't go far afield because of the stand-by but blokes came across from "A" and the other companies to see their friends and people talked a good bit about what the Show was going to be like and were all agog but no one seemed to know anything much as to anything and you got the same served up again garnished with a different twist and emphasis maybe and some would say such and such and others would say the matter stood quite otherwise and there would be a division among them and lily-livered blokes looked awfully unhappy, people you never would expect it of and same the other way the oddest types seemed itching for a set-to quite genuine it would appear but after all who can read or search out the secret places you get a real eye-opener now and then and any subsequent revealing seldom conforms and you misconstrue his apparent noble bearing and grope about in continued misapprehension or can it by any manner of means be that everyone is interiorly in as great misery and unstably set as you are and is the essential unity of mankind chiefly monstrated in this faint-heartness and breeze-right-up aptitude.

Joe Donkin, that never had spoken to anyone since he joined the Battalion at Divisional Rest[4] in April except to pass the time of day a grave and solitary man whose civvy occupation no one seemed to know about but old Craddock his most near associate—they always managed to get on the same Fatigue and used to sit silent together in the boozer—this Craddock said he knew but wouldn't divulge but said it was a job no decent man need be ashamed on anyway. Joe looked more set up than ever previous and said outright and before them all that this is what he had 'listed for and how he would most certainly avenge his five brethren from the same womb as himself on these miscreant bastard square-heads and sons of bitches who in a '15 show in these parts so he declared had shamefully done four of them to death in some Jock reg'ment it seemed and the youngest of all six was at this same hour when he Joe Donkin sat and spoke with them going near skelington in Jerry concentration camp back there. Private Float joking and unadvised and because of his inherent inability to get the hang of this man's sensitivity said it serves 'em right for 'listing in a crush like that and how the kilties always got it in the neck if they didn't beat it soon enough which they more generally did and got his arse kicked by this Joe who was in no jocund mood but singly resolved and fore-arming himself in the inward man to be the better and more wholly addressed toward this enterprise of making expiation life for life if by any means he might for the gassing before Fricourt on the same day of the four brothers Donkin all good men of their hands. He said as how blood was thicker nor water three times and went off with Private Craddock and no other word to his bothy[5] at the furthest end of the lines.

---

4. A period when the entire Division was withdrawn from the line to reorganise and recuperate. It was attended by an access of discipline and physical training and the arrival of new dragts. To some temperaments "Div. Rest" was not welcome [Jones's note].

5. Hut.

The other slope was still sun-lighted, but it was getting almost cool on this east-facing hill, and the creeping down and so across so gradually, gathered to itself, minute by minute, the lesser cast-shadows, the little glints and smallnesses, garnered all these accidents of light within a large lengthened calm. Very soon the high ridge-line alone caught cast lateral ray. But for long after that, his shrapnel bursts, away beyond, were gauffered at their spreading edges with reflected gold. Across the evening, homing birds, birds of the air with nests cawed on high above them waiting, and the preparation there. Oddly stirred winds gusted coolish to your face, that might have borne things webbed and blind, or the grey owl suddenly. And some people began settling down for the night or at least to get a snooze before this talked-of bombardment loosed off to make it difficult. Some of them were already fallen to sleep, but the more solicitous disposed themselves in groups and stood about on that hill, and rather tended to speak in undertones as though to not hasten or not disturb, to not activate too soon the immense potential empoweredness—and talk about impending dooms—it fair gets you in the guts.

Let 'em kip on now and take their rest.

But they roused them now and platoon commanders came—and orderly sergeants with orders and orderly corporals with some final detail and runners countermanding last minute memoranda. And bivvies all go down and unlacing of ground-sheets and each one very concerned with his own affairs and spreading out things on the earth, and rolling up tightly and making last adjustments and—what bastard's knocked-off me trenching-tool-blade-carrier.

They eat whatever cannot conveniently be taken.

They ate John Ball's seed-cake.

Standing together already trussed-up in battle-order with two extra bandoliers slung, and rifles in their hands—in haste they ate it.

And crumbs go down between your webbing—but better carry it in belly than leave it.

He managed to get the tin of sardines into his tunic's left bottom pocket, along with the two grenades.

Just like them—they issued four apiece just when you gathered you'd everything neatly arranged.

In fumbling and haste they did these things.

It was the beginning of the darkness and they moved toward the further ridge.

Now they moved, all the four companies, each platoon at fifty yards' interval. On either side their line of march the waiting batteries.

No. 7 had begun to feel the pull of the incline and No. 6 were coping with the steepest bit, and the leading files of "A" Company's most advanced platoon already had such sight as the July half-light would allow, of the place beyond—whose bodies knew already the relaxation of the further descent. It was exactly 9.39 by John Ball's luminous wrist-watch when it happened.

It was not so much that the noise surprised you—although you had to spit in a bloke's ear to make any impression.

They spent some hours of that night failing to get contact with the unit to be relieved, but before day broke, No. 7 occupied a shallow trench, freshly digged. They put out wire. It commenced to rain.

Hour on hour the gunfire did not relax nor lessen, in fact took on a more tremendous depth.

Rain clouds thickened to wintry dark across the summer night, broke a soaker over them, more confused them where some sought with inutile trenching tools to deepen against his retaliatory fire. Or some just curled up and chanced it.

No one seemed to know the dispositions of the place but Sergeant Quilter was of the opinion that his platoon occupied a bit of the new advanced line. In this he felt some satisfaction. Mr. Jenkins seemed not to be existent. But soon he re-appears—he says that no one has the foggiest notion who is where.

He urges an improvement for their meagre cover.

He digs himself.

When daylight fully came they were withdrawn across the open, which seemed silly, and he obviously saw them and put across Woolly-Bears[6] low over them scampering like disturbed game.

And now you seemed to be in some foreign awfully well made place engineered deep in the gleaming chalk. And the sun stood burning straight above the lie of this trench when the rain stopped and you felt faint for the noisomeness sweated up from the white walls, and all the odds and ends lying about were so newfangle and by the hands of strange men and how is a man to know the habits of their God, whether He smites suddenly or withholds, if you mishandle the things set apart, the objects of His people He is jealous of. You sit with circumspection and you rise with care. And black script inscription at different junctions pointed. And all the arrangements of the place like somebody else's house. The late occupants seem respectable enough by their appointments and certainly one up on the kind of life you've had any experience of for some while. Everything well done and convenient electric light fittings. Cosy, too, and nothing gimcrack and everything of the best. You hope they haven't left any infernal and exactly-timed machines for you before they legged it.

God knows what it was all about, but they moved you back again that evening to another field of bivouac.

And you saw the whole depth of the advance and gauged the nature of the contest yard by yard, and made some estimate of the expenditure and how they'd bargained for each hundred feet with Shylock batteries. You marked how meshed intricacies of wire and cunning nest had played sharp tricks on green and eager plaintiffs. They lay heaped for this bloody suing.

Back past the broken village on the hill—gleamed white inner—plaster where the apse[7] bared in cross section its engineered masonry, which great shearing away and deeps displaying only more made shine out from victim stone the intellection of the builders. For here were blasted bare the opportune thrust, the lively interior contriving, the bright bones of the thing. And the grave-yard huddled—silver black and filigree Mary-Helps and the funerary glass shivered where they ask of your charity. And the civvy dead who died in the Lord with *Libera nos* and full observance, churned and shockt from rest all out-harrowed and higgledy-piggledly along with those other— wood white with heavy script for mortuary monument, for these shovelled just into surface soil like dog—with perhaps an *Our Father* said if it was extra quiet.

---

6. Very heavy German shrapnel, the burst of which gave off a dense blackish smoke, that sprawled the air in a thick rolling compact cloud [Jones's note].
7. Vaulted end of a church.

But all the old women in Bavaria are busy with their novenas, you bet your life, and don't sleep lest the watch should fail, nor weave for the wire might trip his darling feet and the dead Karl might not come home.

Nor spill the pitcher at the well—he told Josef how slippery it was out there.[8]
O clemens, O pia and
turn all out of alignment the English guns amen.[9]

And mules died: their tough clipt hides that have a homely texture flayed horridly to make you weep, sunk in their servility of chain and leather. There had been only time to shove them just out of the road.

They lay with little sleep one more night in bivouac and went again next day to that bewilderment of white-worked fosse and gallery, artful traverse, and well-planned shelter, that had been his Front System.

And in the afternoon rain, saw, for the first time, infantry go forward to assault.

No. 7 were disposed in high overlooking ground. So that John Ball & the rest could comfortably, and in cover, because of the run of their trench, observe, as cockaded men of privilege were used to do, who pointed with their batons where the low smoke went before the forming squadrons on a plain. They wondered for each long stretched line going so leisurely down the slope and up again, strained eyes to catch last glimpses where the creeping smoke-screen gathered each orderly deployment within itself. They wondered for the fate of each tenuous assumption—settled back to their immediate duties in the trench. As sea-board men, who watch some perilous outgoing dip to a shrouded speck; who come down from the white sea-wall, turn eyes from the white in-swell and get down to some job of work.

Some time during the night they were moved by a guide into their own assembly positions.

from *Part 7. The Five Unmistakable Marks*[1]

At the gate of the wood you try a last adjustment, but slung so, it's an impediment, it's of detriment to your hopes, you had best be rid of it—the sagging webbing and all and what's left of your two fifty—but it were wise to hold on to your mask.

You're clumsy in your feebleness, you implicate your tin-hat rim with the slack sling of it.

Let it lie for the dews to rust it, or ought you to decently cover the working parts.

Its dark barrel, where you leave it under the oak, reflects the solemn star that rises urgently from Cliff Trench.

It's a beautiful doll for us
it's the Last Reputable Arm.

But leave it—under the oak.

---

8. Cf. *Golden Bough*, under "sympathetic magic" [Jones's note]. Sir James Frazer's 12-volume study of world myth was enormously suggestive to modernist writers like Jones and T. S. Eliot. "Sympathetic magic" is the notion that one thing or event can affect another at some distance, because of a "sympathetic" connection between them. In this regard, Frazer discusses the sympathetic connection between a king and his nation.
9. Cf. terminating lines of the *Salve Regina* [Jones's note]. The "Salve Regina" ("Hail Queen") is the best known of

the four Breviary anthems of the Blessed Virgin Mary, in the Catholic liturgy.
1. Printed here is the conclusion to the chapter, which closes *In Parenthesis*. The chapter's title comes from Lewis Carroll's narrative poem *The Hunting of the Snark*, which concerns a voyage in search of the Snark; "warranted, genuine Snarks" can be identified by "five unmistakable marks." The poem ends with the death of the explorer who discovers the Snark.

leave it for a Cook's tourist to the Devastated Areas[2] and crawl as far as you can and wait for the bearers.

Mrs. Willy Hartington has learned to draw sheets and so has Miss Melpomené;[3] and on the south lawns,
men walk in red white and blue
under the cedars
and by every green tree
and beside comfortable waters.
But why dont the bastards come—
Bearers!—stret-cher bear-errs!
or do they divide the spoils at the Aid-Post.[4]
    But how many men do you suppose could bear away a third of us: drag just a little further—he yet may counter-attack.

Lie still under the oak
next to the Jerry
and Sergeant Jerry Coke.
    The feet of the reserves going up tread level with your forehead; and no word for you; they whisper one with another; pass on, inward;
these latest succours:
green Kimmerii[5] to bear up the war.

Oeth and Annoeth's hosts they were
who in that night grew
younger men
younger striplings.[6]

The geste says this and the man who was on the field . . . and who wrote the book . . . the man who does not know this has not understood anything.[7]

━━━ ═◆═ ━━━

Katherine Mansfield
1888–1923

Katherine Mansfield was one of the twentieth century's most gifted writers of short fiction. As Elizabeth Bowen has written, Mansfield realized that "the short story . . . is not intended to be the medium either for exploration or long-term development of character. Character cannot

---

2. This may appear to be an anachronism, but I remember in 1917 discussing with a friend the possibilities of tourist activity if peace ever came. I remember we went into details and wondered if the inexploded projectile lying near us would go up under a holiday-maker, and how people would stand to be photographed on our parapets. I recall feeling very angry about this, as you do if you think of strangers ever occupying a house you live in, and which has, for you, particular associations [Jones's note].
3. Greek muse of tragedy.
4. The R.A.M.C. was suspected by disgruntled men of the fighting units of purloining articles from the kit of the wounded and the dead. Their regimental initials were commonly interpreted: "Rob All My Comrades" [Jones's note].
5. In Homer, the Kimmerioi were a race who lived in

eternal darkness, "on whom the sun never looks."
6. Cf. Englyn 30 of the *Englynion y Beddeu*, "The Stanzas of the Graves." See Rhys, *Origin of the Englyn, Y Cymmrodor*, vol. xviii. Oeth and Annoeth's hosts occur in Welsh tradition as a mysterious body of troops that seem to have some affinity with the Legions. They were said to "fight as well in the covert as in the open." Cf. *The Iolo MSS* [Jones's note].
7. Cf. Chanson de Roland, lines 2095–8:

    Co dit la geste e cil qui el camp fut,
    [Li ber Gilie por qui Deus fait vertuz]
    E fist la chartre [el muster de Loum].
    Ki tant ne set, ne l'ad prod entendut.

I have used Mr. Rene Hague's translation [Jones's note].

be more than *shown*. . . ." Mansfield thus turned the short story away from contrived plot conventions, and toward the illumination of small events as they reveal the fabric of a life, making of short fiction an almost dramatic form.

Mansfield was born in Wellington, New Zealand. She moved to England more or less permanently before her twentieth birthday, but many of her most successful stories return to her childhood and her homeland for their subject. The path to this mature fiction was complicated, however; when she arrived in London in 1908, Mansfield was pregnant. She quickly married and the same day left her husband, who was not the child's father; she went to a German spa, where she miscarried. This tumultuous background is reflected in the bitter stories of her first volume, *In a German Pension*. In 1911 Mansfield met John Middleton Murray, editor and man of letters, with whom she remained until the end of her life.

Paradoxically, the horrors of World War I (in which her brother Leslie was killed) had an uplifting effect on Mansfield's writing. The result of the war, she wrote, is that "Now we know ourselves for what we are. In a way its a tragic knowledge. Its as though, even while we live again we face death. But *through Life*: thats the point. We see death in life as we see death in a flower that is fresh unfolded. Our hymn is to the flower's beauty—we would make that beauty immortal because we *know*."

One important element of Mansfield's "tragic knowledge" was the awareness that she was dying; she suffered her first tubercular hemorrhage in 1918, and never regained her health. She remained dedicated to her art until the very end, however, producing nineteen major stories during the last nineteen months of her life; Virginia Woolf, who admired and even envied Mansfield's talent, wrote that "No one felt more seriously the importance of writing than she did." The story included here, *Daughters of the Late Colonel*, diagnoses with both tenderness and horror the spiritual death that Mansfield saw around her. It invokes a theme that has been important in twentieth-century literature from Henry James's *The Beast in the Jungle* to Samuel Beckett's *Waiting for Godot*, and beyond: that, as John Lennon put it, "Life is what happens to you / While you're busy making other plans."

The Daughters of the Late Colonel

1

The week after was one of the busiest weeks of their lives. Even when they went to bed it was only their bodies that lay down and rested; their minds went on, thinking things out, talking things over, wondering, deciding, trying to remember where . . .

Constantia lay like a statue, her hands by her sides, her feet just overlapping each other, the sheet up to her chin. She stared at the ceiling.

"Do you think father would mind if we gave his top-hat to the porter?"

"The porter?" snapped Josephine. "Why ever the porter? What a very extraordinary idea!"

"Because," said Constantia slowly, "he must often have to go to funerals. And I noticed at—at the cemetery that he only had a bowler." She paused. "I thought then how very much he'd appreciate a top-hat. We ought to give him a present, too. He was always very nice to father."

"But," cried Josephine, flouncing on her pillow and staring across the dark at Constantia, "father's head!" And suddenly, for one awful moment, she nearly giggled. Not, of course, that she felt in the least like giggling. It must have been habit. Years ago, when they had stayed awake at night talking, their beds had simply heaved. And now the porter's head, disappearing, popped out, like a candle, under father's hat. . . . The giggle mounted, mounted; she clenched her hands; she fought it down; she frowned fiercely at the dark and said "Remember" terribly sternly.

"We can decide to-morrow," she sighed.

Constantia had noticed nothing; she sighed.

"Do you think we ought to have our dressing-gowns dyed as well?"

"Black?" almost shrieked Josephine.

"Well, what else?" said Constantia. "I was thinking—it doesn't seem quite sincere, in a way, to wear black out of doors and when we're fully dressed, and then when we're at home—"

"But nobody sees us," said Josephine. She gave the bedclothes such a twitch that both her feet became uncovered, and she had to creep up the pillows to get them well under again.

"Kate does," said Constantia. "And the postman very well might."

Josephine thought of her dark-red slippers, which matched her dressing-gown, and of Constantia's favourite indefinite green ones which went with hers. Black! Two black dressing-gowns and two pairs of black woolly slippers, creeping off to the bathroom like black cats.

"I don't think it's absolutely necessary," said she.

Silence. Then Constantia said, "We shall have to post the papers with the notice in them to-morrow to catch the Ceylon mail. . . . How many letters have we had up till now?"

"Twenty-three."

Josephine had replied to them all, and twenty-three times when she came to "We miss our dear father so much" she had broken down and had to use her handkerchief, and on some of them even to soak up a very light-blue tear with an edge of blotting-paper. Strange! She couldn't have put it on—but twenty-three times. Even now, though, when she said over to herself sadly. "We miss our dear father so much" she could have cried if she'd wanted to.

"Have you got enough stamps?" came from Constantia.

"Oh, how can I tell?" said Josephine crossly. "What's the good of asking me that now?"

"I was just wondering," said Constantia mildly.

Silence again. There came a little rustle, a scurry, a hop.

"A mouse," said Constantia.

"It can't be a mouse because there aren't any crumbs," said Josephine.

"But it doesn't know there aren't," said Constantia.

A spasm of pity squeezed her heart. Poor little thing! She wished she'd left a tiny piece of biscuit on the dressing-table. It was awful to think of it not finding anything. What would it do?

"I can't think how they manage to live at all," she said slowly.

"Who?" demanded Josephine.

And Constantia said more loudly than she meant to, "Mice."

Josephine was furious. "Oh, what nonsense, Con!" she said. "What have mice got to do with it? You're asleep."

"I don't think I am," said Constantia. She shut her eyes to make sure. She was.

Josephine arched her spine, pulled up her knees, folded her arms so that her fists came under her ears, and pressed her cheek hard against the pillow.

2

Another thing which complicated matters was they had Nurse Andrews staying on with them that week. It was their own fault; they had asked her. It was Josephine's idea. On the morning—well, on the last morning, when the doctor had gone, Josephine had said to Constantia, "Don't you think it would be rather nice if we asked Nurse Andrews to stay on for a week as our guest?"

"Very nice," said Constantia.

"I thought," went on Josephine quickly, "I should just say this afternoon, after I've paid her, 'My sister and I would be very pleased, after all you've done for us, Nurse Andrews, if you would stay on for a week as our guest.' I'd have to put that in about being our guest in case—"

"Oh, but she could hardly expect to be paid!" cried Constantia.

"One never knows," said Josephine sagely.

Nurse Andrews had, of course, jumped at the idea. But it was a bother. It meant they had to have regular sit-down meals at the proper times, whereas if they'd been alone they could just have asked Kate if she wouldn't have minded bringing them a tray wherever they were. And meal-times now that the strain was over were rather a trial.

Nurse Andrews was simply fearful about butter. Really they couldn't help feeling that about butter, at least, she took advantage of their kindness. And she had that maddening habit of asking for just an inch more bread to finish what she had on her plate, and then, at the last mouthful, absent-mindedly—of course it wasn't absent-mindedly—taking another helping. Josephine got very red when this happened, and she fastened her small, beadlike eyes on the tablecloth as if she saw a minute strange insect creeping through the web of it. But Constantia's long, pale face lengthened and set, and she gazed away—away—far over the desert, to where that line of camels unwound like a thread of wool. . . .

"When I was with Lady Tukes," said Nurse Andrews, "she had such a dainty little contrayvance for the buttah. It was a silvah Cupid balanced on the—on the bordah of a glass dish, holding a tayny fork. And when you wanted some buttah you simply pressed his foot and he bent down and speared you a piece. It was quite a gayme."

Josephine could hardly bear that. But "I think those things are very extravagant" was all she said.

"But whey?" asked Nurse Andrews, beaming through her eye-glasses. "No one, surely, would take more buttah than one wanted—would one?"

"Ring, Con," cried Josephine. She couldn't trust herself to reply.

And proud young Kate, the enchanted princess, came in to see what the old tabbies wanted now. She snatched away their plates of mock something or other and slapped down a white, terrified blancmange.

"Jam, please, Kate," said Josephine kindly.

Kate knelt and burst open the sideboard, lifted the lid of the jam-pot, saw it was empty, put it on the table, and stalked off.

"I'm afraid," said Nurse Andrews a moment later, "there isn't any."

"Oh, what a bother!" said Josephine. She bit her lip. "What had we better do?"

Constantia looked dubious. "We can't disturb Kate again," she said softly.

Nurse Andrews waited, smiling at them both. Her eyes wandered, spying at everything behind her eye-glasses. Constantia in despair went back to her camels. Josephine frowned heavily—concentrated. If it hadn't been for this idiotic woman she and Con would, of course, have eaten their blancmange without. Suddenly the idea came.

"I know," she said. "Marmalade. There's some marmalade in the sideboard. Get it, Con."

"I hope," laughed Nurse Andrews, and her laugh was like a spoon tinkling against a medicine-glass—"I hope it's not very bittah marmalayde."

3

But, after all, it was not long now, and then she'd be gone for good. And there was no getting over the fact that she had been very kind to father. She had nursed him day and night at the end. Indeed, both Constantia and Josephine felt privately she had rather overdone the not leaving him at the very last. For when they had gone in to say good-bye Nurse Andrews had sat beside his bed the whole time, holding his wrist and pretending to look at her watch. It couldn't have been necessary. It was so tactless, too. Supposing father had wanted to say something—something private to them. Not that he had. Oh, far from it! He lay there, purple, a dark, angry purple in the face, and never even looked at them when they came in. Then, as they were standing there, wondering what to do, he had suddenly opened one eye. Oh, what a difference it would have made, what a difference to their memory of him, how much easier to tell people about it, if he had only opened both! But no—one eye only. It glared at them a moment and then . . . went out.

4

It had made it very awkward for them when Mr Farolles, of St John's, called the same afternoon.

"The end was quite peaceful, I trust?" were the first words he said as he glided towards them through the dark drawing-room.

"Quite," said Josephine faintly. They both hung their heads. Both of them felt certain that eye wasn't at all a peaceful eye.

"Won't you sit down?" said Josephine.

"Thank you, Miss Pinner," said Mr Farolles gratefully. He folded his coat-tails and began to lower himself into father's armchair, but just as he touched it he almost sprang up and slid into the next chair instead.

He coughed. Josephine clasped her hands; Constantia looked vague.

"I want you to feel, Miss Pinner," said Mr Farolles, "and you, Miss Constantia, that I'm trying to be helpful. I want to be helpful to you both, if you will let me. These are the times," said Mr Farolles, very simply and earnestly, "when God means us to be helpful to one another."

"Thank you very much, Mr Farolles," said Josephine and Constantia.

"Not at all," said Mr Farolles gently. He drew his kid gloves through his fingers and leaned forward. "And if either of you would like a little Communion, either or both of you, here *and* now, you have only to tell me. A little Communion is often very help—a great comfort," he added tenderly.

But the idea of a little Communion terrified them. What! In the drawing-room by themselves—with no—no altar or anything! The piano would be much too high, thought Constantia, and Mr Farolles could not possibly lean over it with the chalice. And Kate would be sure to come bursting in and interrupt them, thought Josephine. And supposing the bell rang in the middle? It might be somebody important—about their mourning. Would they get up reverently and go out, or would they have to wait . . . in torture?

"Perhaps you will send round a note by your good Kate if you would care for it later," said Mr Farolles.

"Oh yes, thank you very much!" they both said.

Mr Farolles got up and took his black straw hat from the round table.

"And about the funeral," he said softly. "I may arrange that—as your dear father's old friend and yours, Miss Pinner—and Miss Constantia?"

Josephine and Constantia got up too.

"I should like it to be quite simple," said Josephine firmly, "and not too expensive. At the same time, I should like—"

"A good one that will last," thought dreamy Constantia, as if Josephine were buying a nightgown. But of course Josephine didn't say that. "One suitable to our father's position." She was very nervous.

"I'll run round to our good friend Mr Knight," said Mr Farolles soothingly. "I will ask him to come and see you. I am sure you will find him very helpful indeed."

5

Well, at any rate, all that part of it was over, though neither of them could possibly believe that father was never coming back. Josephine had had a moment of absolute terror at the cemetery, while the coffin was lowered, to think that she and Constantia had done this thing without asking his permission. What would father say when he found out? For he was bound to find out sooner or later. He always did. "Buried. You two girls had me *buried!*" She heard his stick thumping. Oh, what would they say? What possible excuse could they make? It sounded such an appalling heartless thing to do. Such a wicked advantage to take of a person because he happened to be helpless at the moment. The other people seemed to treat it all as a matter of course. They were strangers; they couldn't be expected to understand that father was the very last person for such a thing to happen to. No, the entire blame for it all would fall on her and Constantia. And the expense, she thought, stepping into the tight-buttoned cab. When she had to show him the bills. What would he say then?

She heard him absolutely roaring, "And do you expect me to pay for this gimcrack excursion of yours?"

"Oh," groaned poor Josephine aloud, "we shouldn't have done it, Con!"

And Constantia, pale as a lemon in all that blackness, said in a frightened whisper, "Done what, Jug?"

"Let them bu-bury father like that," said Josephine, breaking down and crying into her new, queer-smelling mourning handkerchief.

"But what else could we have done?" asked Constantia wonderingly. "We couldn't have kept him, Jug—we couldn't have kept him unburied. At any rate, not in a flat that size."

Josephine blew her nose; the cab was dreadfully stuffy.

"I don't know," she said forlornly. "It is all so dreadful. I feel we ought to have tried to, just for a time at least. To make perfectly sure. One thing's certain"—and her tears sprang out again—"father will never forgive us for this—never!"

6

Father would never forgive them. That was what they felt more than ever when, two mornings later, they went into his room to go through his things. They had discussed it quite calmly. It was even down on Josephine's list of things to be done. *Go through father's things and settle about them.* But that was a very different matter from saying after breakfast:

"Well, are you ready, Con?"

"Yes, Jug—when you are."

"Then I think we'd better get it over."

It was dark in the hall. It had been a rule for years never to disturb father in the morning, whatever happened. And now they were going to open the door without knocking even. . . . Constantia's eyes were enormous at the idea; Josephine felt weak in the knees.

"You—you go first," she gasped, pushing Constantia.

But Constantia said, as she always had said on those occasions, "No, Jug, that's not fair. You're eldest."

Josephine was just going to say—what at other times she wouldn't have owned to for the world—what she kept for her very last weapon, "But you're tallest," when they noticed that the kitchen door was open, and there stood Kate. . . .

"Very stiff," said Josephine, grasping the door-handle and doing her best to turn it. As if anything ever deceived Kate!

It couldn't be helped. That girl was . . . Then the door was shut behind them, but—but they weren't in father's room at all. They might have suddenly walked through the wall by mistake into a different flat altogether. Was the door just behind them? They were too frightened to look. Josephine knew that if it was it was holding itself tight shut; Constantia felt that, like the doors in dreams, it hadn't any handle at all. It was the coldness which made it so awful. Or the whiteness—which? Everything was covered. The blinds were down, a cloth hung over the mirror, a sheet hid the bed; a huge fan of white paper filled the fireplace. Constantia timidly put out her hand; she almost expected a snowflake to fall. Josephine felt a queer tingling in her nose, as if her nose was freezing. Then a cab klop-klopped over the cobbles below, and the quiet seemed to shake into little pieces.

"I had better pull up a blind," said Josephine bravely.

"Yes, it might be a good idea," whispered Constantia.

They only gave the blind a touch, but it flew up and the cord flew after, rolling round the blindstick, and the little tassel tapped as if trying to get free. That was too much for Constantia.

"Don't you think—don't you think we might put it off for another day?" she whispered.

"Why?" snapped Josephine, feeling, as usual, much better now that she knew for certain that Constantia was terrified. "It's got to be done. But I do wish you wouldn't whisper, Con."

"I didn't know I was whispering," whispered Constantia.

"And why do you keep on staring at the bed?" said Josephine, raising her voice almost defiantly. "There's nothing *on* the bed."

"Oh, Jug, don't say so!" said poor Connie. "At any rate, not so loudly."

Josephine felt herself that she had gone too far. She took a wide swerve over to the chest of drawers, put out her hand, but quickly drew it back again.

"Connie!" she gasped, and she wheeled round and leaned with her back against the chest of drawers.

"Oh, Jug—what?"

Josephine could only glare. She had the most extraordinary feeling that she had just escaped something simply awful. But how could she explain to Constantia that father was in the chest of drawers? He was in the top drawer with his handkerchiefs and neckties, or in the next with his shirts and pyjamas, or in the lowest of all with his suits. He was watching there, hidden away—just behind the door-handle—ready to spring.

She pulled a funny old-fashioned face at Constantia, just as she used to in the old days when she was going to cry.

"I can't open," she nearly wailed.

"No, don't, Jug," whispered Constantia earnestly. "It's much better not to. Don't let's open anything. At any rate, not for a long time."

"But—but it seems so weak," said Josephine, breaking down.

"But why not be weak for once, Jug?" argued Constantia, whispering quite fiercely. "If it is weak." And her pale stare flew from the locked writing-table—so safe—to the huge glittering wardrobe, and she began to breathe in a queer, panting way. "Why shouldn't we be weak for once in our lives, Jug? It's quite excusable. Let's be weak—be weak, Jug. It's much nicer to be weak than to be strong."

And then she did one of those amazingly bold things that she'd done about twice before in their lives; she marched over to the wardrobe, turned the key, and took it out of the lock. Took it out of the lock and held it up to Josephine, showing Josephine by her extraordinary smile that she knew what she'd done, she'd risked deliberately father being in there among his overcoats.

If the huge wardrobe had lurched forward, had crashed down on Constantia, Josephine wouldn't have been surprised. On the contrary, she would have thought it the only suitable thing to happen. But nothing happened. Only the room seemed quieter than ever, and bigger flakes of cold air fell on Josephine's shoulders and knees. She began to shiver.

"Come, Jug," said Constantia, still with that awful callous smile, and Josephine followed just as she had that last time, when Constantia had pushed Benny into the round pond.

7

But the strain told on them when they were back in the dining-room. They sat down, very shaky, and looked at each other.

"I don't feel I can settle to anything," said Josephine, "until I've had something. Do you think we could ask Kate for two cups of hot water?"

"I really don't see why we shouldn't," said Constantia carefully. She was quite normal again. "I won't ring. I'll go to the kitchen door and ask her."

"Yes, do," said Josephine, sinking down into a chair. "Tell her, just two cups, Con, nothing else—on a tray."

"She needn't even put the jug on, need she?" said Constantia, as though Kate might very well complain if the jug had been there.

"Oh, certainly not! The jug's not at all necessary. She can pour it direct out of the kettle," cried Josephine, feeling that would be a labour-saving indeed.

Their cold lips quivered at the greenish brims. Josephine curved her small red hands round the cup; Constantia sat up and blew on the wavy stream, making it flutter from one side to the other.

"Speaking of Benny," said Josephine.

And though Benny hadn't been mentioned Constantia immediately looked as though he had.

"He'll expect us to send him something of father's, of course. But it's so difficult to know what to send to Ceylon."

"You mean things get unstuck so on the voyage," murmured Constantia.

"No, lost," said Josephine sharply. "You know there's no post. Only runners."

Both paused to watch a black man in white linen drawers running through the pale fields for dear life, with a large brown-paper parcel in his hands. Josephine's black man was tiny; he scurried along glistening like an ant. But there was something blind and tireless about Constantia's tall, thin fellow, which made him, she decided, a very unpleasant person indeed. . . . On the veranda, dressed all in white and wearing a cork helmet, stood Benny. His right hand shook up and down, as father's did when he was impatient. And behind him, not in the least interested, sat Hilda, the unknown sister-in-law. She swung in a cane rocker and flicked over the leaves of the *Tatler*.

"I think his watch would be the most suitable present," said Josephine.

Constantia looked up; she seemed surprised.

"Oh, would you trust a gold watch to a native?"

"But of course I'd disguise it," said Josephine. "No one would know it was a watch." She liked the idea of having to make a parcel such a curious shape that no one could possibly guess what it was. She even thought for a moment of hiding the watch in a narrow cardboard corset-box that she'd kept by her for a long time, waiting for it to come in for something. It was such beautiful firm cardboard. But, no, it wouldn't be appropriate for this occasion. It had lettering on it: *Medium Women's 28. Extra Firm Busks*. It would be almost too much of a surprise for Benny to open that and find father's watch inside.

"And of course it isn't as though it would be going—ticking, I mean," said Constantia, who was still thinking of the native love of jewellery. "At least," she added, "it would be very strange if after all that time it was."

8

Josephine made no reply. She had flown off on one of her tangents. She had suddenly thought of Cyril. Wasn't it more usual for the only grandson to have the watch? And then dear Cyril was so appreciative, and a gold watch meant so much to a young man. Benny, in all probability, had quite got out of the habit of watches; men so seldom wore waistcoats in those hot climates. Whereas Cyril in London wore them from year's end to year's end. And it would be so nice for her and Constantia, when he came to tea, to know it was there. "I see you've got on grandfather's watch, Cyril." It would be somehow so satisfactory.

Dear boy! What a blow his sweet, sympathetic little note had been! Of course they quite understood; but it was most unfortunate.

"It would have been such a point, having him," said Josephine.

"And he would have enjoyed it so," said Constantia, not thinking what she was saying.

However, as soon as he got back he was coming to tea with his aunties. Cyril to tea was one of their rare treats.

"Now, Cyril, you mustn't be frightened of our cakes. Your Auntie Con and I bought them at Buszard's this morning. We know what a man's appetite is. So don't be ashamed of making a good tea."

Josephine cut recklessly into the rich dark cake that stood for her winter gloves or the soling and heeling of Constantia's only respectable shoes. But Cyril was most unmanlike in appetite.

"I say, Aunt Josephine, I simply can't. I've only just had lunch, you know."

"Oh, Cyril, that can't be true! It's after four," cried Josephine. Constantia sat with her knife poised over the chocolate-roll.

"It is, all the same," said Cyril. "I had to meet a man at Victoria, and he kept me hanging about till . . . there was only time to get lunch and to come on here. And he gave me—phew"—Cyril put his hand to his forehead—"a terrific blow-out," he said.

It was disappointing—to-day of all days. But still he couldn't be expected to know.

"But you'll have a meringue, won't you, Cyril?" said Aunt Josephine. "These meringues were bought specially for you. Your dear father was so fond of them. We were sure you are, too."

"I *am*, Aunt Josephine," cried Cyril ardently. "Do you mind if I take half to begin with?"

"Not at all, dear boy; but we mustn't let you off with that."

"Is your dear father still so fond of meringues?" asked Auntie Con gently. She winced faintly as she broke through the shell of hers.

"Well, I don't quite know, Auntie Con," said Cyril breezily. At that they both looked up.

"Don't know?" almost snapped Josephine. "Don't know a thing like that about your own father, Cyril?"

"Surely," said Auntie Con softly.

Cyril tried to laugh it off. "Oh, well," he said, "it's such a long time since—" He faltered. He stopped. Their faces were too much for him.

"Even *so*," said Josephine.

And Auntie Con looked.

Cyril put down his teacup. "Wait a bit," he cried. "Wait a bit, Aunt Josephine. What am I thinking of?"

He looked up. They were beginning to brighten. Cyril slapped his knee.

"Of course," he said, "it was meringues. How could I have forgotten? Yes, Aunt Josephine, you're perfectly right. Father's most frightfully keen on meringues."

They didn't only beam. Aunt Josephine went scarlet with pleasure; Auntie Con gave a deep, deep sigh.

"And now, Cyril, you must come and see father," said Josephine. "He knows you were coming to-day."

"Right," said Cyril, very firmly and heartily. He got up from his chair; suddenly he glanced at the clock.

"I say, Auntie Con, isn't your clock a bit slow? I've got to meet a man at—at Paddington just after five. I'm afraid I shan't be able to stay very long with grandfather."

"Oh, he won't expect you to stay *very* long!" said Aunt Josephine.

Constantia was still gazing at the clock. She couldn't make up her mind if it was fast or slow. It was one or the other, she felt almost certain of that. At any rate, it had been.

Cyril still lingered. "Aren't you coming along, Auntie Con?"

"Of course," said Josephine, "we shall all go. Come on, Con."

9

They knocked at the door, and Cyril followed his aunts into grandfather's hot, sweet-ish room.

"Come on," said Grandfather Pinner. "Don't hang about. What is it? What've you been up to?"

He was sitting in front of a roaring fire, clasping his stick. He had a thick rug over his knees. On his lap there lay a beautiful pale yellow silk handkerchief.

"It's Cyril, father," said Josephine shyly. And she took Cyril's hand and led him forward.

"Good afternoon, grandfather," said Cyril, trying to take his hand out of Aunt Josephine's. Grandfather Pinner shot his eyes at Cyril in the way he was famous for. Where was Auntie Con? She stood on the other side of Aunt Josephine; her long arms hung down in front of her; her hands were clasped. She never took her eyes off grandfather.

"Well," said Grandfather Pinner, beginning to thump, "what have you got to tell me?"

What had he, what had he got to tell him? Cyril felt himself smiling like a perfect imbecile. The room was stifling, too.

But Aunt Josephine came to his rescue. She cried brightly, "Cyril says his father is still very fond of meringues, father dear."

"Eh?" said Grandfather Pinner, curving his hand like a purple meringue-shell over one ear.

Josephine repeated, "Cyril says his father is still very fond of meringues."

"Can't hear," said old Colonel Pinner. And he waved Josephine away with his stick, then pointed with his stick to Cyril. "Tell me what she's trying to say," he said.

(My God!) "Must I?" said Cyril, blushing and staring at Aunt Josephine.

"Do, dear," she smiled. "It will please him so much."

"Come on, out with it!" cried Colonel Pinner testily, beginning to thump again.

And Cyril leaned forward and yelled, "Father's still very fond of meringues."

At that Grandfather Pinner jumped as though he had been shot.

"Don't shout!" he cried. "What's the matter with the boy? *Meringues!* What about 'em?"

"Oh, Aunt Josephine, must we go on?" groaned Cyril desperately.

"It's quite all right, dear boy," said Aunt Josephine, as though he and she were at the dentist's together. "He'll understand in a minute." And she whispered to Cyril, "He's getting a bit deaf, you know." Then she leaned forward and really bawled at Grandfather Pinner, "Cyril only wanted to tell you, father dear, that *his* father is still very fond of meringues."

Colonel Pinner heard that time, heard and brooded, looking Cyril up and down.

"What an esstrordinary thing!" said old Grandfather Pinner. "What an esstrordinary thing to come all this way here to tell me!"

And Cyril felt it *was.*

"Yes, I shall send Cyril the watch," said Josephine.

"That would be very nice," said Constantia. "I seem to remember last time he came there was some little trouble about the time."

10

They were interrupted by Kate bursting through the door in her usual fashion, as though she had discovered some secret panel in the wall.

"Fried or boiled?" asked the bold voice.

Fried or boiled? Josephine and Constantia were quite bewildered for the moment. They could hardly take it in.

"Fried or boiled what, Kate?" asked Josephine, trying to begin to concentrate.

Kate gave a loud sniff. "Fish."

"Well, why didn't you say so immediately?" Josephine reproached her gently. "How could you expect us to understand, Kate? There are a great many things in this world, you know, which are fried or boiled." And after such a display of courage she said quite brightly to Constantia, "Which do you prefer, Con?"

"I think it might be nice to have it fried," said Constantia. "On the other hand, of course boiled fish is very nice. I think I prefer both equally well . . . Unless you . . . In that case—"

"I shall fry it," said Kate, and she bounced back, leaving their door open and slamming the door of her kitchen.

Josephine gazed at Constantia; she raised her pale eyebrows until they rippled away into her pale hair. She got up. She said in a very lofty, imposing way, "Do you mind following me into the drawing-room, Constantia? I've something of great importance to discuss with you."

For it was always to the drawing-room they retired when they wanted to talk over Kate.

Josephine closed the door meaningly. "Sit down, Constantia," she said, still very grand. She might have been receiving Constantia for the first time. And Con looked round vaguely for a chair, as though she felt indeed quite a stranger.

"Now the question is," said Josephine, bending forward, "whether we shall keep her or not."

"That is the question," agreed Constantia.

"And this time," said Josephine firmly, "we must come to a definite decision."

Constantia looked for a moment as though she might begin going over all the other times, but she pulled herself together and said, "Yes, Jug."

"You see, Con," explained Josephine, "everything is so changed now." Constantia looked up quickly. "I mean," went on Josephine, "we're not dependent on Kate as we were." And she blushed faintly. "There's not father to cook for."

"That is perfectly true," agreed Constantia. "Father certainly doesn't want any cooking now, whatever else—"

Josephine broke in sharply. "You're not sleepy, are you, Con?"

"Sleepy, Jug?" Constantia was wide-eyed.

"Well, concentrate more," said Josephine sharply, and she returned to the subject. "What it comes to is, if we did"—and this she barely breathed, glancing at the door—"give Kate notice"—she raised her voice again—"we could manage our own food."

"Why not?" cried Constantia. She couldn't help smiling. The idea was so exciting. She clasped her hands. What should we live on, Jug?"

"Oh, eggs in various forms!" said Jug, lofty again. "And, besides, there are all the cooked foods."

"But I've always heard," said Constantia, "they are considered so very expensive."

"Not if one buys them in moderation," said Josephine. But she tore herself away from this fascinating bypath and dragged Constantia after her.

"What we've got to decide now, however, is whether we really do trust Kate or not."

Constantia leaned back. Her flat little laugh flew from her lips.

"Isn't it curious, Jug," said she, "that just on this one subject I've never been able to quite make up my mind?"

11

She never had. The whole difficulty was to prove anything. How did one prove things, how could one? Suppose Kate had stood in front of her and deliberately made a face. Mightn't she very well have been in pain? Wasn't it impossible, at any rate, to ask Kate if she was making a face at her? If Kate answered "No"—and of course she would say "No"—what a position! How undignified! Then again Constantia suspected, she was almost certain that Kate went to her chest of drawers when she and Josephine were out, not to take things but to spy. Many times she had come back to find her amethyst cross in the most unlikely places, under her lace ties or on top of her evening Bertha. More than once she had laid a trap for Kate. She had arranged things in a special order and then called Josephine to witness.

"You see, Jug?"

"Quite, Con."

"Now we shall be able to tell."

But, oh dear, when she did go to look, she was as far off from a proof as ever! If anything was displaced, it might so very well have happened as she closed the drawer; a jolt might have done it so easily.

"You come, Jug, and decide. I really can't. It's too difficult."

But after a pause and a long glare Josephine would sigh, "Now you've put the doubt into my mind, Con, I'm sure I can't tell myself."

"Well, we can't postpone it again," said Josephine. "If we postpone it this time—"

12

But at that moment in the street below a barrel-organ struck up. Josephine and Constantia sprang to their feet together.

"Run, Con," said Josephine. "Run quickly. There's sixpence on the—"

Then they remembered. It didn't matter. They would never have to stop the organ-grinder again. Never again would she and Constantia be told to make that monkey take his noise somewhere else. Never would sound that loud, strange bellow when father thought they were not hurrying enough. The organ-grinder might play there all day and the stick would not thump.

> It never will thump again,
> It never will thump again,

played the barrel-organ.

What was Constantia thinking? She had such a strange smile; she looked different. She couldn't be going to cry.

"Jug, Jug," said Constantia softly, pressing her hands together. "Do you know what day it is? It's Saturday. It's a week to-day, a whole week."

> A week since father died,
> A week since father died,

cried the barrel-organ. And Josephine, too, forgot to be practical and sensible; she smiled faintly, strangely. On the Indian carpet there fell a square of sunlight, pale red; it came and went and came—and stayed, deepened—until it shone almost golden.

"The sun's out," said Josephine, as though it really mattered.

A perfect fountain of bubbling notes shook from the barrel-organ, round, bright notes, carelessly scattered.

Constantia lifted her big, cold hands as if to catch them, and then her hands fell again. She walked over to the mantelpiece to her favourite Buddha. And the stone and gilt image, whose smile always gave her such a queer feeling, almost a pain and yet a pleasant pain, seemed to-day to be more than smiling. He knew something; he had a secret. "I know something that you don't know," said her Buddha. Oh, what was it, what could it be? And yet she had always felt there was . . . something.

The sunlight pressed through the windows, thieved its way in, flashed its light over the furniture and the photographs. Josephine watched it. When it came to mother's photograph, the enlargement over the piano, it lingered as though puzzled to find so little remained of mother, except the earrings shaped like tiny pagodas and a black feather boa. Why did the photographs of dead people always fade so? wondered Josephine. As soon as a person was dead their photograph died too. But, of course, this one of mother was very old. It was thirty-five years old. Josephine remembered standing on a chair and pointing out that feather boa to Constantia and telling her that it was a snake that had killed their mother in Ceylon. . . . Would everything have been different if mother hadn't died? She didn't see why. Aunt Florence had lived with them until they had left school, and they had moved three times and had their yearly holiday and . . . and there'd been changes of servants, of course.

Some little sparrows, young sparrows they sounded, chirped on the window-ledge. *Yeep-eyeep-yeep.* But Josephine felt they were not sparrows, not on the window-ledge. It was inside her, that queer little crying noise. *Yeep-eyeep-yeep.* Ah, what was it crying, so weak and forlorn?

If mother had lived, might they have married? But there had been nobody for them to marry. There had been father's Anglo-Indian friends before he quarreled with them. But after that she and Constantia never met a single man except clergymen. How did one meet men? Or even if they'd met them, how could they have got to know men well enough to be more than strangers? One read of people having adventures, being followed, and so on. But nobody had ever followed Constantia and her. Oh yes, there had been one year at Eastbourne a mysterious man at their boarding-house who had put a note on the jug of hot water outside their bedroom door! But by the time Connie had found it the steam had made the writing too faint to read; they couldn't even make out to which of them it was addressed. And he had left next day. And that was all. The rest had been looking after father, and at the same time keeping out of father's way. But now? But now? The thieving sun touched Josephine gently. She lifted her face. She was drawn over to the window by gentle beams. . . .

Until the barrel-organ stopped playing Constantia stayed before the Buddha, wondering, but not as usual, not vaguely. This time her wonder was like longing. She remembered the times she had come in here, crept out of bed in her nightgown when the moon was full, and lain on the floor with her arms outstretched, as though she was crucified. Why? The big, pale moon had made her do it. The horrible dancing figures on the carved screen had leered at her and she hadn't minded. She remembered too how, whenever they were at the seaside, she had gone off by herself and got as close to the sea as she could, and sung something, something she had made up, while she gazed all over that restless water. There had been this other life, running out, bringing things home in bags, getting things on approval, discussing them with

Jug, and taking them back to get more things on approval, and arranging father's trays and trying not to annoy father. But it all seemed to have happened in a kind of tunnel. It wasn't real. It was only when she came out of the tunnel into the moonlight or by the sea or into a thunderstorm that she really felt herself. What did it mean? What was it she was always wanting? What did it all lead to? Now? Now?

She turned away from the Buddha with one of her vague gestures. She went over to where Josephine was standing. She wanted to say something to Josephine, something frightfully important, about—about the future and what . . .

"Don't you think perhaps—" she began.

But Josephine interrupted her. "I was wondering if now—" she murmured. They stopped; they waited for each other.

"Go on, Con," said Josephine.

"No, no, Jug; after you," said Constantia.

"No, say what you were going to say. You began," said Josephine.

"I . . . I'd rather hear what you were going to say first," said Constantia.

"Don't be absurd, Con."

"Really, Jug."

"Connie!"

"Oh, *Jug!*"

A pause. Then Constantia said faintly, "I can't say what I was going to say, Jug, because I've forgotten what it was . . . that I was going to say."

Josephine was silent for a moment. She stared at a big cloud where the sun had been. Then she replied shortly, "I've forgotten too."

—◆—

Robert Graves
1895–1985

Goodbye to All That, Robert Graves's autobiography through the year 1929, contains some of the most immediate and closely observed writing about World War I. The sense of immediacy conveyed in this prose derives in part from Graves's close brush with death at the battle of the Somme. Graves was unconscious for twenty-four hours with severe chest wounds and, as he relates below, his commanding officer wrote to his mother to break the news of his death; "I *was* dead, an hour or more," Graves later wrote in the poem *Escape*. But in this instance, at least, the grave was not strong enough to contain Graves, and he was able to write his mother about a week later, on his twenty-first birthday, that he was alive and recovering.

Graves went on to a long and productive career, publishing approximately 140 books and 800 shorter works, writing both poetry and fiction until his fortieth birthday, then concentrating on his poetry and mythopoetic literary theory for the next forty years, before effectively retiring in 1975. The best known of the novels is the Roman historical novel *I, Claudius*, which along with *Claudius the God and His Wife Messalina* was brilliantly adapted for television by the BBC in the 1970s. The poetry and poetics of the second half of his life revolve around his concept of the "White Goddess," which Graves details in his best-known critical work, *The White Goddess: A Historical Grammar of Poetic Myth* (1948). Graves, working closely with the American poet Laura Riding, came to believe that the vocation of the poet was to become a devotee of a muselike goddess who on the one hand inspires but, on the other hand ultimately destroys her disciples; "the main theme of all poetry," Graves wrote, "is, properly, the relations of man and woman." This pose put him at odds with most of the modernist literary establishment, and the criticism of his later years was dedicated to tilting at the false gods of the modernist literary pantheon. He spent his later years living in relative seclusion on the Mediterranean island of Majorca.

from Goodbye to All That
Chapter 17

I was one of about thirty instructors at the Havre[1] "Bull Ring," where newly-arrived drafts were sent for technical instruction before going up the line. Most of my colleagues were specialists in musketry, machine-gun, gas, or bombs. I had no specialist training, only general experience. I was put on instructional work in trench relief and trench discipline in a model set of trenches. My principal other business was arms-drill. One day it rained, and the commandant of the Bull Ring suddenly ordered me to lecture in the big concert hall. "There are three thousand men there waiting for you, and you're the only available officer with a loud enough voice to make himself heard." They were Canadians, so instead of giving my usual semi-facetious lecture on "How to be happy though in the trenches," I paid them the compliment of telling them the story of Loos,[2] and what a balls-up it was, and why it was a balls-up. It was the only audience that I ever held for an hour with real attention. I expected the commandant to be furious with me because the principal object of the Bull Ring was to inculcate the offensive spirit, but he took it well and I had several more concert-hall lectures put on me after this.

In the instructors' mess the chief subjects of conversation besides local and technical talk were *morale,* the reliability of various divisions in battle, the value of different training methods, and war-morality, with particular reference to atrocities. We talked more freely there than would have been possible either in England or in the trenches. We decided that about a third of the troops in the British Expeditionary Force were dependable on all occasions; these were the divisions that were always called on for the most important tasks. About a third were variable, that is, where a division contained one or two bad battalions, but could be more or less trusted. The remainder were more or less untrustworthy; being put in positions of comparative safety they had about a quarter of the casualties that the best divisions had. It was a matter of pride to belong to one of the recognized best divisions—the Seventh, the Twenty-ninth, Guards', First Canadian, for instance. They were not pampered when in reserve as the German storm-troops were, but promotion, leave, and the chance of a wound came quicker in them. The mess agreed that the most dependable British troops were the Midland county regiments, industrial Yorkshire and Lancashire troops, and the Londoners. The Ulsterman, Lowland Scots and Northern English were pretty good. The Catholic Irish and the Highland Scots were not considered so good—they took unnecessary risks in trenches and had unnecessary casualties, and in battle, though they usually made their objective, they too often lost it in the counter-attack; without officers they were no good. English southern county regiments varied from good to very bad. All overseas troops were good. The dependability of divisions also varied with their seniority in date of promotion. The latest formed regular divisions and the second-line territorial divisions, whatever their recruiting area, were usually inferior. Their senior officers and warrant-officers were not good enough.

We once discussed which were the cleanest troops in trenches, taken in nationalities. We agreed on a list like this, in descending order: English and German Protestants; Northern Irish, Welsh and Canadians; Irish and German Catholics; Scottish;

---

1. Le Havre, a seaport in northern France.   2. The scene of an early setback for the Allies.

Mohammedan Indians; Algerians; Portuguese; Belgians; French. The Belgians and French were put there for spite; they were not really dirtier than the Algerians or Portuguese.

Atrocities. Propaganda reports of atrocities were, we agreed, ridiculous. Atrocities against civilians were surely few. We remembered that while the Germans were in a position to commit atrocities against enemy civilians, Germany itself, except for the early Russian cavalry raid, had never had the enemy on her soil. We no longer believed accounts of unjustified German atrocities in Belgium; knowing the Belgians now at first-hand. By atrocities we meant, specifically, rape, mutilation and torture, not summary shootings of suspected spies, harbourers of spies, *francs-tireurs* [sharpshooters], or disobedient local officials. If the atrocity list was to include the accidental-on-purpose bombing or machine-gunning of civilians from the air, the Allies[3] were now committing as many atrocities as the Germans. French and Belgian civilians had often tried to win our sympathy and presents by exhibiting mutilations of children—stumps of hands and feet, for instance—representing them as deliberate, fiendish atrocities when they were merely the result of shell-fire, British or French shell-fire as likely as not. We did not believe that rape was any more common on the German side of the line than on the Allied side. It was unnecessary. Of course, a bully-beef diet, fear of death, and absence of wives made ample provision of women necessary in the occupied areas. No doubt the German army authorities provided brothels in the principal French towns behind the line, as did the French on the Allied side. But the voluntary system would suffice. We did not believe stories of forcible enlistment of women.

As for atrocities against soldiers. The difficulty was to say where to draw the line. For instance, the British soldier at first regarded as atrocious the use of bowie-knives by German patrols. After a time he learned to use them himself; they were cleaner killing weapons than revolvers or bombs. The Germans regarded as atrocious the British Mark VII rifle bullet, which was more apt to turn on striking than the German bullet. For true atrocities, that is, personal rather than military violations of the code of war, there were few opportunities. The most obvious opportunity was in the interval between surrender of prisoners and their arrival (or non-arrival) at headquarters. And it was an opportunity of which advantage was only too often taken. Nearly every instructor in the mess knew of specific cases when prisoners had been murdered on the way back. The commonest motives were, it seems, revenge for the death of friends or relations, jealousy of the prisoner's pleasant trip to a comfortable prison camp in England, military enthusiasm, fear of being suddenly overpowered by the prisoners or, more simply, not wanting to be bothered with the escorting job. In any of these cases the conductors would report on arrival at headquarters that a German shell had killed the prisoners; no questions would be asked. We had every reason to believe that the same thing happened on the German side, where prisoners, as useless mouths to feed in a country already on short rations, were even less welcome. We had none of us heard of prisoners being more than threatened at headquarters to get military information from them; the sort of information that trench-prisoners could give was not of sufficient importance to make torture worth while; in any case it was found that when treated kindly prisoners were anxious, in gratitude, to tell as much as they knew.

3. The nations of the Triple Entente (Great Britain, France, Russia) and their allies (Belgium, Serbia, Japan, Italy)—including, loosely, the United States—which united to oppose the Central Powers (Germany, Austria-Hungary, Turkey, and Bulgaria) in World War I.

The troops that had the worst reputation for acts of violence against prisoners were the Canadians (and later the Australians). With the Canadians the motive was said to be revenge for a Canadian found crucified with bayonets through his hands and feet in a German trench; this atrocity was never substantiated, nor did we believe the story freely circulated that the Canadians crucified a German officer in revenge shortly afterwards. (Of the Australians the only thing to be said was that they were only two generations removed from the days of Ralph Rashleigh and Marcus Clarke.[4]) How far this reputation for atrocities was deserved, and how far it was due to the overseas habit of bragging and leg-pulling, we could not decide. We only knew that to have committed atrocities against prisoners was, among the overseas men, and even among some British troops, a boast, not a confession.

I heard two first-hand accounts later in the war.

A Canadian-Scot: "I was sent back with three bloody prisoners, you see, and one was limping and groaning, so I had to keep on kicking the sod down the trench. He was an officer. It was getting dark and I was getting fed up, so I thought: 'I'll have a bit of a game.' I had them covered with the officer's revolver and I made 'em open their pockets. Then I dropped a Mills' bomb[5] in each, with the pin out, and ducked behind a traverse. Bang, bang, bang! No more bloody prisoners. No good Fritzes[6] but dead 'uns."

An Australian: "Well, the biggest lark I had was at Morlancourt when we took it the first time. There were a lot of Jerries[7] in a cellar and I said to 'em: 'Come out, you Camarades.' So out they came, a dozen of 'em, with their hands up. 'Turn out your pockets,' I told 'em. They turned 'em out. Watches and gold and stuff, all dinkum.[8] Then I said: 'Now back into your cellar, you sons of bitches.' For I couldn't be bothered with 'em. When they were all down I threw half a dozen Mills' bombs in after 'em. I'd got the stuff all right, and we weren't taking prisoners that day."

The only first-hand account I heard of large-scale atrocities was from an old woman at Cardonette on the Somme, with whom I was billeted in July 1916. It was at Cardonette that a battalion of French Turcos[9] overtook the rear guard of a German division retreating from the Marne in September 1914. The Turcos surprised the dead-weary Germans while they were still marching in column. The old woman went, with gestures, through a pantomime of slaughter, ending: "Et enfin ces animaux leur ont arraché les oreilles et les ont mis à la poche."[1] The presence of coloured troops in Europe was, from the German point of view, we knew, one of the chief Allied atrocities. We sympathized. Recently, at Flixécourt, one of the instructors told us, the cook of a corps headquarter-mess used to be visited at the château every morning by a Turco; he was orderly to a French liaison officer. The Turco used to say: "Tommy,[2] give Johnny pozzy," and a tin of plum and apple jam used to be given him. One afternoon the corps was due to shift, so that morning the cook said to the Turco, giving him his farewell tin: "Oh, la, la, Johnny, napoo pozzy to-morrow." The Turco would not believe it. "Yes, Tommy, mate," he said, "pozzy for Johnny to-morrow, to-morrow, to-morrow." To get rid of him the cook said: "Fetch me the head of a Fritz, Johnny, to-night. I'll ask the general to give you pozzy to-morrow, to-morrow, to-morrow." "All right, mate," said the Turco, "me get Fritz head to-night, general give me pozzy to-morrow." That evening the mess cook of the new corps that

---

4. Novelists of criminal life in 19th-century Australia, where British convicts were often sent.
5. A high-explosive grenade.
6. Germans.
7. German soldiers.

8. Authentic [Australian slang].
9. Native Algerians who served in the French infantry.
1. "And finally these animals tore off their ears and put them in their pockets."
2. A British soldier.

had taken over the château was surprised to find a Turco asking for him and swinging a bloody head in a sandbag. "Here's Fritz head, mate," said the Turco, "general give me pozzy to-morrow, to-morrow, to-morrow." As Flixécourt was twenty miles or more behind the line . . . He did not need to end the story, but swore it was true, because he had seen the head.

We discussed the continuity of regimental *morale*. A captain in a line battalion of one of the Surrey regiments said: "It all depends on the reserve battalion at home." He had had a year's service when the war broke out; the battalion, which had been good, had never recovered from the first battle of Ypres. He said: "What's wrong with us is that we have a rotten depot. The drafts are bad and so we get a constant re-infection." He told me one night in our sleeping hut: "In both the last two attacks that we made I had to shoot a man of my company to get the rest out of the trench. It was so bloody awful that I couldn't stand it. It's the reason why I applied to be sent down here." This was not the usual loose talk that one heard at the base. He was a good fellow and he was speaking the truth. I was sorrier for Phillips—that was not his name—than for any other man I met in France. He deserved a better regiment. There was never any trouble with the Royal Welch like that. The boast of every good battalion in France was that it had never lost a trench; both our battalions made it. This boast had to be understood broadly; it meant never having been forced out of a trench by an enemy attack without recapturing it before the action ended. Capturing a German trench and being unable to hold it for lack of reinforcements did not count, nor did retirement from a trench by order or when the battalion of the left or right had broken and left a flank in the air. And in the final stages of the war trenches could be honourably abandoned as being entirely obliterated by bombardment, or because not really trenches at all, but a line of selected shell-craters.

We all agreed on the value of arms-drill as a factor in *morale*. "Arms-drill as it should be done," someone said, "is beautiful, especially when the company feels itself as a single being and each movement is not a movement of every man together, but a single movement of one large creature." I used to have big bunches of Canadians to drill four or five hundred at a time. Spokesmen came forward once and asked what sense there was in sloping and ordering arms and fixing and unfixing bayonets. They said they had come to France to fight and not to guard Buckingham Palace. I told them that in every division of the four in which I had served there had been three different kinds of troops. Those that had guts but were no good at drill; those that were good at drill but had no guts; and those that had guts and were good at drill. These last fellows were, for some reason or other, much the best men in a show. I didn't know why and I didn't care. I told them that when they were better at fighting than the Guards' Division they could perhaps afford to neglect their arms-drill.

We often theorized in the mess about drill. We knew that the best drill never came from being bawled at by a sergeant-major, that there must be perfect respect between the man who gives the order and the men that carry it through. The test of drill came, I said, when the officer gave an incorrect word of command. If the company could carry through the order intended without hesitation, or, suppose the order happened to be impossible, could stand absolutely still or continue marching without any disorder in the ranks, that was good drill. The corporate spirit that came from drilling together was regarded by some instructors as leading to loss of initiative in the men drilled. Others denied this and said it acted just the other way round. "Suppose there is a section of men with rifles, and they are isolated from the rest of the company and have no N.C.O.[3] in charge and meet a machine-gun. Under the stress of danger that section will have that all-one-body feeling of drill and will obey an imaginary word of command. There will be no communication between its members, but there will be a drill movement. Two men will quite naturally open fire on the machine-gun while the remainder will work round, part on the left flank and part on the right, and the final rush will be simultaneous. Leadership is supposed to be the perfection for which drill has been instituted. That is wrong. Leadership is only the first stage. Perfection of drill is communal action. Drill may seem to be antiquated parade-ground stuff, but it is the foundation of tactics and musketry. It was parade-ground musketry that won all the battles in our regimental histories; this war will be won by parade-ground tactics. The simple drill tactics of small units fighting in limited spaces—fighting in noise and confusion so great that leadership is quite impossible." In spite of variance on this point we all agreed that regimental pride was the greatest moral force that kept a battalion going as an effective fighting unit, contrasting it particularly with patriotism and religion.

Patriotism. There was no patriotism in the trenches. It was too remote a sentiment, and rejected as fit only for civilians. A new arrival who talked patriotism would soon be told to cut it out. As Blighty,[4] Great Britain was a quiet, easy place to get back to out of the present foreign misery, but as a nation it was nothing. The nation included not only the trench-soldiers themselves and those who had gone home wounded, but the staff, Army Service Corps, lines of communication troops, base units, home-service units, and then civilians down to the detested grades of journalists, profiteers, "starred" men exempted from enlistment, conscientious objectors, members of the Government. The trench-soldier, with this carefully graded caste-system of honour, did not consider that the German trench-soldier might have exactly the same system himself. He thought of Germany as a nation in arms, a unified nation inspired with the sort of patriotism that he despised himself. He believed most newspaper reports of conditions and sentiments in Germany, though believing little or nothing of what he read about conditions and sentiments in England. His cynicism, in fact, was not confined to his own country. But he never underrated the German as a soldier. Newspaper libels on Fritz's courage and efficiency were resented by all trench-soldiers of experience.

Religion. It was said that not one soldier in a hundred was inspired by religious feeling of even the crudest kind. It would have been difficult to remain religious in the trenches though one had survived the irreligion of the training battalion at home. A regular sergeant at Montagne, a Second Battalion man, had recently told me that he did not hold with religion in time of war. He said that the niggers (meaning the Indians) were right in officially relaxing their religious rules when they were fighting. "And all this damn nonsense, sir—excuse me, sir—that we read in the papers, sir, about how miraculous it is that the wayside crucifixes are always getting shot at but the figure of our Lord Jesus somehow don't get hurt, it fairly makes me sick, sir." This was to explain why in giving practice fire-orders from the hilltop he had shouted out: "Seven hundred, half left, bloke on cross, five rounds consecrate, Fire!" His platoon, even the two men whose letters home always had the same formal beginning: "Dear Sister in Christ," or "Dear Brother in Christ," blazed away.

The troops, while ready to believe in the Kaiser as a comic personal devil, were aware that the German soldier was, on the whole, more devout than himself in the worship of God. In the instructors' mess we spoke freely of God and Gott as opposed

3. Noncommissioned officer.   4. England.

tribal deities. For the regimental chaplains as a body we had no respect. If the regimental chaplains had shown one tenth the courage, endurance, and other human qualities that the regimental doctors showed, we agreed, the British Expeditionary Force might well have started a religious revival. But they had not. The fact is that they were under orders not to get mixed up with the fighting, to stay behind with the transport and not to risk their lives. No soldier could have any respect for a chaplain who obeyed these orders, and yet there was not in our experience one chaplain in fifty who was not glad to obey them. Occasionally on a quiet day in a quiet sector the chaplain would make a daring afternoon visit to the support line and distribute a few cigarettes, and that was all. But he was always in evidence back in rest-billets. Sometimes the colonel would summon him to come up with the rations and bury the day's dead, and he would arrive, speak his lines, and hastily retire. The position was made difficult by the respect that most of the commanding officers had for the cloth, but it was a respect that they soon outwore. The colonel in one battalion I served with got rid of four new chaplains in as many months. Finally he applied for a Roman Catholic chaplain, alleging a change of faith in the men under his command. For, as I should have said before, the Roman Catholics were not only permitted in posts of danger, but definitely enjoined to be wherever fighting was so that they could give extreme unction to the dying. And we had never heard of an R.C. chaplain who was unwilling to do all that was expected of him and more. It was recalled that Father Gleeson of the Munsters, when all the officers were put out of action at the first battle of Ypres, stripped off his black badges and, taking command of the survivors, held the line.

Anglican chaplains were remarkably out of touch with their troops. I told how the Second Battalion chaplain just before the Loos fighting had preached a violent sermon on the battle against sin, and how one old soldier behind me had grumbled: "Christ, as if one bloody push wasn't enough to worry about at a time." The Catholic padre, on the other hand, had given his men his blessing and told them that if they died fighting for the good cause they would go straight to Heaven, or at any rate would be excused a great many years in Purgatory. Someone told us of the chaplain of his battalion when he was in Mesopotamia, how on the eve of a big battle he had preached a sermon on the commutation of tithes. This was much more sensible than the battle against sin, he said; it was quite up in the air, and took the men's minds off the fighting.

I was feeling a bit better after a few weeks at the base, though the knowledge that this was only temporary relief was with me all the time. One day I walked out of the mess to begin the afternoon's work on the drill ground. I had to pass by the place where bombing instruction was given. A group of men was standing around the table where the various types of bombs were set out for demonstration. There was a sudden crash. An instructor of the Royal Irish Rifles had been giving a little unofficial instruction before the proper instructor arrived. He had picked up a No. 1 percussion grenade and said: "Now, lads, you've got to be careful with this chap. Remember that if you touch anything while you're swinging it, it will go off." To illustrate the point he rapped it against the edge of the table. It killed him and another man and wounded twelve others more or less severely.

Chapter 20

Four days after the raid we heard that we were due for the Somme. We marched through Béthune, which had been much knocked about and was nearly deserted, to Fouquières, and there entrained for the Somme. The Somme railhead was near

Amiens and we marched by easy stages through Cardonette, Daours, and Buire, until we came to the original front line, close to the place where David Thomas[5] had been killed. The fighting had moved two miles on. This was on the afternoon of 14th July. At 4 a.m. on the 15th July we moved up the Méaulte-Fricourt-Bazentin road which wound through "Happy Valley" and found ourselves in the more recent battle area. Wounded men and prisoners came streaming past us. What struck me most was the number of dead horses and mules lying about; human corpses I was accustomed to, but it seemed wrong for animals to be dragged into the war like this. We marched by platoons, at fifty yards distance. Just beyond Fricourt we found a German shell-barrage across the road. So we left it and moved over thickly shell-pitted ground until 8 a.m., when we found ourselves on the fringe of Mametz Wood, among the dead of our new-army battalions that had been attacking Mametz Wood. We halted in thick mist. The Germans had been using lachrymatory shell[6] and the mist held the fumes; we coughed and swore. We tried to smoke, but the gas had got into the cigarettes, so we threw them away. Later we wished we had not, because it was not the cigarettes that had been affected so much as our own throats. The colonel called up the officers and we pulled out our maps. We were expecting orders for an attack. When the mist cleared we saw a German gun with "First Battalion Royal Welch Fusiliers" chalked on it. It was evidently a trophy. I wondered what had happened to Siegfried[7] and my friends of A Company. We found the battalion quite close in bivouacs; Siegfried was still alive, as were Edmund Dadd and two other A Company officers. The battalion had been in heavy fighting. In their first attack at Fricourt they had overrun our opposite number in the German army, the Twenty-third Infantry Regiment, who were undergoing a special disciplinary spell in the trenches because an inspecting staff-officer, coming round, had found that all the officers were back in Mametz village in a deep dug-out instead of up in the trenches with their men. (It was said that throughout that bad time in March in the German trenches opposite to us there had been no officer of higher rank than corporal.) Their next objective had been The Quadrangle, a small copse this side of Mametz Wood. I was told that Siegfried had then distinguished himself by taking single-handed a battalion frontage that the Royal Irish Regiment had failed to take the day before. He had gone over with bombs in daylight, under covering fire from a couple of rifles, and scared the occupants out. It was a pointless feat; instead of reporting or signalling for reinforcements he sat down in the German trench and began dozing over a book of poems which he had brought with him. When he finally went back he did not report. The colonel was furious. The attack on Mametz Wood had been delayed for two hours because it was reported that British patrols were still out. "British patrols" were Siegfried and his book of poems. "It would have got you a D.S.O.[8] if you'd only had more sense," stormed the colonel. Siegfried had been doing heroic things ever since I had left the battalion. His nickname in the Seventh Division was "Mad Jack." He was given a Military Cross for bringing in a wounded lance-corporal from a mine-crater close to the German lines, under heavy fire. He was one of the rare exceptions to the rule against the decoration of Third Battalion officers. I did not see Siegfried this time; he was down with the transport having a rest. So I sent him a rhymed letter, by one of our own transport men, about the times that we were going to have together when the war ended; how,

5. A British officer and close friend of Graves's, who was killed in March 1916; his death nearly caused Graves a nervous collapse. Thomas is represented in Siegfried Sassoon's autobiographical *Memoirs of a Fox-Hunting Man* (1928) in the character of Dick Tiltwood.

6. Tear gas.

7. Siegfried Sassoon.

8. Distinguished Service Order.

after a rest at Harlech, we were going for a visit to the Caucasus and Persia and China; and what good poetry we would write. It was in answer to one he had written to me from the army school at Flixécourt a few weeks previously (which appears in *The Old Huntsman*).

I went for a stroll with Edmund Dadd, who was now commanding A Company. Edmund was cursing: "It's not fair, Robert. You remember A Company under Richardson was always the best company. Well, it's kept up its reputation, and the C.O.[9] shoves us in as the leading company of every show, and we get our objectives and hold them, and so we've got to do the same again the next time. And he says that I'm indispensable in the company, so he makes me go over every time instead of giving me a rest and letting my second-in-command take his turn. I've had five shows in just over a fortnight and I can't go on being lucky every time. The colonel's about due for his C.B.[1] Apparently A Company is making sure of it for him."

For the next two days we were in bivouacs outside the wood. We were in fighting kit and the nights were wet and cold. I went into the wood to find German overcoats to use as blankets. Mametz Wood was full of dead of the Prussian Guards Reserve, big men, and of Royal Welch and South Wales Borderers of the new-army battalions, little men. There was not a single tree in the wood unbroken. I got my greatcoats and came away as quickly as I could, climbing over the wreckage of green branches. Going and coming, by the only possible route, I had to pass by the corpse of a German with his back propped against a tree. He had a green face, spectacles, close shaven hair; black blood was dripping from the nose and beard. He had been there for some days and was bloated and stinking. There had been bayonet fighting in the wood. There was a man of the South Wales Borderers and one of the Lehr regiment who had succeeded in bayoneting each other simultaneously. A survivor of the fighting told me later that he had seen a young soldier of the Fourteenth Royal Welch bayoneting a German in parade-ground style, automatically exclaiming as he had been taught: "In, out, on guard." He said that it was the oddest thing he had heard in France.

I found myself still superstitious about looting or collecting souvenirs. The greatcoats were only a loan, I told myself. Almost the only souvenir I had allowed myself to keep was a trench periscope, a little rod-shaped metal one sent me from home; when I poked it up above the parapet it offered only an inch-square target to the German snipers. Yet a sniper at Cuinchy, in May, drilled it through, exactly central, at four hundred yards range. I sent it home, but had no time to write a note of explanation. My mother, misunderstanding, and practical as usual, took it back to the makers and made them change it for a new one.

Our brigade, the Nineteenth, was the reserve brigade of the Thirty-third Division; the other brigades, the Ninety-ninth and Hundredth, had attacked Martinpuich two days previously and had been stopped with heavy losses as soon as they started. Since then we had had nothing to do but sit about in shell-holes and watch the artillery duel going on. We had never seen artillery so thick. On the 18th we moved up to a position just to the north of Bazentin le Petit to relieve the Tyneside Irish. I was with D Company. The guide who was taking us up was hysterical and had forgotten the way; we put him under arrest and found it ourselves. As we went up through the ruins of the village we were shelled. We were accustomed to that, but

---

9. Commanding officer.

1. Companion of the Bath, a British military honor.

they were gas shells.[2] The standing order with regard to gas shells was not to put on one's respirator but hurry on. Up to that week there had been no gas shells except lachrymatory ones; these were the first of the real kind, so we lost about half a dozen men. When at last we arrived at the trenches, which were scooped at a roadside and only about three feet deep, the company we were relieving hurried out without any of the usual formalities; they had been badly shaken. I asked their officer where the Germans were. He said he didn't know, but pointed vaguely towards Martinpuich, a mile to our front. Then I asked him where and what were the troops on our left. He didn't know. I cursed him and he went off. We got into touch with C Company behind us on the right and with the Fourth Suffolks not far off on the left. We began deepening the trenches and locating the Germans; they were in a trench-system about five hundred yards away but keeping fairly quiet.

The next day there was very heavy shelling at noon; shells were bracketing along our trench about five yards short and five yards over, but never quite getting it. We were having dinner and three times running my cup of tea was spilt by the concussion and filled with dirt. I was in a cheerful mood and only laughed. I had just had a parcel of kippers[3] from home; they were far more important than the bombardment—I recalled with appreciation one of my mother's sayings: "Children, remember this when you eat your kippers; kippers cost little, yet if they cost a hundred guineas a pair they would still find buyers among the millionaires." Before the shelling had started a tame magpie had come into the trench; it had apparently belonged to the Germans who had been driven out of the village by the Gordon Highlanders a day or two before. It was looking very draggled. "That's one for sorrow," I said. The men swore that it spoke something in German as it came in, but I did not hear it. I was feeling tired and was off duty, so without waiting for the bombardment to stop I went to sleep in the trench. I decided that I would just as soon be killed asleep as awake. There were no dug-outs, of course. I always found it easy now to sleep through bombardments. I was conscious of the noise in my sleep, but I let it go by. Yet if anybody came to wake me for my watch or shouted "Stand-to!" I was alert in a second. I had learned to go to sleep sitting down, standing up, marching, lying on a stone floor, or in any other position, at a moment's notice at any time of day or night. But now I had a dreadful nightmare; it was as though somebody was handling me secretly, choosing the place to drive a knife into me. Finally, he gripped me in the small of the back. I woke up with a start, shouting, and punched the small of my back where the hand was. I found that I had killed a mouse that had been frightened by the bombardment and run down my neck.

That afternoon the company got an order through from the brigade to build two cruciform strong-points at such-and-such a map reference. Moodie, the company commander, and I looked at our map and laughed. Moodie sent back a message that he would be glad to do so, but would require an artillery bombardment and strong reinforcements because the points selected, half way to Martinpuich, were occupied in force by the enemy. The colonel came up and verified this. He said that we should build the strong-point about three hundred yards forward and two hundred yards apart. So one platoon stayed behind in the trench and the other went out and started digging. A cruciform strong-point consisted of two trenches, each some thirty yards long, crossing at right angles to each other; it was wired all round, so that it looked, in diagram, like a hot-cross bun. The defenders could bring fire to bear against an

---

2. Either chlorine or mustard gas, used by the Germans in World War I, causing blistering of the skin and lungs, blindness, and even death.

3. Smoked herring.

attack from any direction. We were to hold each of these points with a Lewis gun[4] and a platoon of men.

It was a bright moonlight night. My way to the strong-point on the right took me along the Bazentin-High Wood road. A German sergeant-major, wearing a pack and full equipment, was lying on his back in the middle of the road, his arms stretched out wide. He was a short, powerful man with a full black beard. He looked sinister in the moonlight; I needed a charm to get myself past him. The simplest way, I found, was to cross myself. Evidently a brigade of the Seventh Division had captured the road and the Germans had been shelling it heavily. It was a sunken road and the defenders had begun to scrape fire-positions in the north bank, facing the Germans. The work had apparently been interrupted by a counter-attack. They had done no more than scrape hollows in the lower part of the bank. To a number of these little hollows wounded men had crawled, put their heads and shoulders inside and died there. They looked as if they had tried to hide from the black beard. They were Gordon Highlanders.

I was visiting the strong-point on the right. The trench had now been dug two or three feet down and a party of Engineers had arrived with coils of barbed wire for the entanglement. I found that work had stopped. The whisper went round: "Get your rifles ready. Here comes Fritz." I lay down flat to see better, and about seventy yards away in the moonlight I could make out massed figures. I immediately sent a man back to the company to find Moodie and ask him for a Lewis gun and a flare-pistol. I restrained the men, who were itching to fire, telling them to wait until they came closer. I said: "They probably don't know we're here and we'll get more of them if we let them come right up close. They may even surrender." The Germans were wandering about irresolutely and we wondered what the game was. There had been a number of German surrenders at night recently, and this might be one on a big scale. Then Moodie came running with a Lewis gun, the flare-pistol, and a few more men with rifle-grenades. He decided to give the enemy a chance. He sent up a flare and fired a Lewis gun over their heads. A tall officer came running towards us with his hands up in surrender. He was surprised to find that we were not Germans. He said that he belonged to the Public Schools Battalion in our own brigade. Moodie asked him what the hell he was doing. He said that he was in command of a patrol. He was sent back for a few more of his men, to make sure it was not a trick. The patrol was half a company of men wandering about aimlessly between the lines, their rifles slung over their shoulders, and, it seemed, without the faintest idea where they were or what information they were supposed to bring back. This Public Schools Battalion was one of four or five others which had been formed some time in 1914. Their training had been continually interrupted by large numbers of men being withdrawn as officers for other regiments. The only men left, in fact, seemed to be those who were unfitted to hold commissions; yet unfitted by their education to make good soldiers in the ranks. The other battalions had been left behind in England as training battalions; only this one had been sent out. It was a constant embarrassment to the brigade.

I picked up a souvenir that night. A German gun-team had been shelled as it was galloping out of Bazentin towards Martinpuich. The horses and the driver had been killed. At the back of the limber[5] were the gunners' treasures. Among them was a large lump of chalk wrapped up in a piece of cloth; it had been carved and decorated in colours with military mottos, the flags of the Central Powers, and the names of the various battles in which the gunner had served. I sent it as a present to Dr. Dunn. I

---

4. A lightweight machine gun.   5. A horse-drawn vehicle carrying a field-gun.

am glad to say that both he and it survived the war; he is in practice at Glasgow, and the lump of chalk is under a glass case in his consulting room. The evening of the next day, July 19th, we were relieved. We were told that we would be attacking High Wood, which we could see a thousand yards away to the right at the top of a slope. High Wood was on the main German battle-line, which ran along the ridge, with Delville Wood not far off on the German left. Two British brigades had already attempted it; in both cases the counter-attack had driven them out. Our battalion had had a large number of casualties and was now only about four hundred strong.

I have kept a battalion order issued at midnight:

To O.C.B Co.   2nd R.W.F.   20.7.16.

Companies	will	move	as	under
to	same	positions	in	S14b
as	were	to	have	been
taken	over	from	Cameronians	aaa
	A Coy.	12.30 a.m.		
	B Coy.	12.45 a.m.		
	C Coy.	1 a.m.		
	D Coy.	1.15 a.m.	aaa	
	At	2 a.m.	Company	Commanders
will	meet	C.O.	at	X
Roads	S14b 99.	aaa		
Men	will	lie	down	and
get	under	cover	but	equipment
will	not	be	taken	off aaa

S14b 99 was a map reference for Bazentin churchyard. We lay here on the reverse slope of a slight ridge about half a mile from the wood. I attended the meeting of company commanders; the colonel told us the plan. He said: "Look here, you fellows, we're in reserve for this attack. The Cameronians are going up to the wood first, then the Fifth Scottish Rifles; that's at five a.m. The Public Schools Battalion are in support if anything goes wrong. I don't know if we shall be called on; if we are, it will mean that the Jocks have legged it.[6] As usual," he added. This was an appeal to prejudice. "The Public Schools Battalion is, well, what we know, so if we are called for, that means it will be the end of us." He said this with a laugh and we all laughed. We were sitting on the ground protected by the road-bank; a battery of French 75's was firing rapid over our heads about twenty yards away. There was a very great concentration of guns in Happy Valley now. We could hardly hear what he was saying. He told us that if we did get orders to reinforce, we were to shake out in artillery formation; once in the wood we were to hang on like death. Then he said good-bye and good luck and we rejoined our companies.

At this juncture the usual inappropriate message came through from Division. Division could always be trusted to send through a warning about verdigris on vermorel-sprayers,[7] or the keeping of pets in trenches, or being polite to our allies, or some other triviality, when an attack was in progress. This time it was an order for a private in C Company to report immediately to the assistant provost-marshal back at Albert,

---

6. Scottish soldiers have run away.   7. Equipment used to spray water to absorb poisonous gases.

under escort of a lance-corporal. He was for a court-martial. A sergeant of the company was also ordered to report as a witness in the case. The private was charged with the murder of a French civilian in an *estaminet* [tavern] at Béthune about a month previously. Apparently there had been a good deal of brandy going and the French civilian, who had a grudge against the British (it was about his wife), started to tease the private. He was reported, somewhat improbably, as having said: "English no bon, Allmand très bon. War fineesh, napoo the English.[8] Allmand win." The private had immediately drawn his bayonet and run the man through. At the court-martial the private was exculpated; the French civil representative commended him for having "energetically repressed local defeatism." So he and the two N.C.O.'s missed the battle.

What the battle that they missed was like I pieced together afterwards. The Jocks did get into the wood and the Royal Welch were not called on to reinforce until eleven o'clock in the morning. The Germans put down a barrage along the ridge where we were lying, and we lost about a third of the battalion before our show started. I was one of the casualties.

It was heavy stuff, six and eight inch. There was so much of it that we decided to move back fifty yards; it was when I was running that an eight-inch shell burst about three paces behind me. I was able to work that out afterwards by the line of my wounds. I heard the explosion and felt as though I had been punched rather hard between the shoulder-blades, but had no sensation of pain. I thought that the punch was merely the shock of the explosion; then blood started trickling into my eye and I felt faint and called to Moodie: "I've been hit." Then I fell down. A minute or two before I had had two very small wounds on my left hand; they were in exactly the same position as the two, on my right hand, that I had got during the preliminary bombardment at Loos. This I had taken as a sign that I would come through all right. For further security I had repeated to myself a line of Nietzsche's, whose poems, in French, I had with me:

> Non, tu ne peus pas me tuer.[9]

It was the poem about a man on the scaffold with the red-bearded executioner standing over him. (This copy of Nietzsche, by the way, had contributed to the suspicions about me as a spy. Nietzsche was execrated in the papers as the philosopher of German militarism; he was more popularly interpreted as a William le Queux[1] mystery-man—the sinister figure behind the Kaiser.)

One piece of shell went through my left thigh, high up near the groin; I must have been at the full stretch of my stride to have escaped emasculation. The wound over the eye was nothing; it was a little chip of marble, possibly from one of the Bazentin cemetery headstones. This and a finger wound, which split the bone, probably came from another shell that burst in front of me. The main wound was made by a piece of shell that went in two inches below the point of my right shoulder and came out through my chest two inches above my right nipple, in a line between it and the base of my neck.

My memory of what happened then is vague. Apparently Doctor Dunn came up through the barrage with a stretcher-party, dressed my wound, and got me down to the old German dressing-station at the north end of Mametz Wood. I just remember being put on the stretcher and winking at the stretcher-bearer sergeant who was looking at me and saying: "Old Gravy's got it, all right." The dressing-station was overworked that day; I was laid in a corner on a stretcher and remained unconscious for more than twenty-four hours.

8. "English no good, German very good."
9. No, you cannot kill me.
1. Author of the popular novel *The Invasion of 1910* (1906), in which "the greatest of all wars" begins with the invasion of England.

It was about ten o'clock on the 20th that I was hit. Late that night the colonel came to the dressing-station; he saw me lying in the corner and was told that I was done for. The next morning, the 21st, when they were clearing away the dead, I was found to be still breathing; so they put me on an ambulance for Heilly, the nearest field-hospital. The pain of being jolted down the Happy Valley, with a shell-hole at every three or four yards of the roads, woke me for awhile. I remember screaming. But once back on the better roads I became unconscious again. That morning the colonel wrote the usual formal letters of condolence to the next-of-kin of the six or seven officers who had been killed. This was his letter to my mother:

22/7/16

DEAR MRS. GRAVES,
I very much regret to have to write and tell you your son has died of wounds. He was very gallant, and was doing so well and is a great loss.
He was hit by a shell and very badly wounded, and died on the way down to the base I believe. He was not in bad pain, and our doctor managed to get across and attend him at once.
We have had a very hard time, and our casualties have been large. Believe me you have all our sympathy in your loss, and we have lost a very gallant soldier.
Please write to me if I can tell you or do anything.

Yours sincerely,
***

Later he made out the official casualty list and reported me died of wounds. It was a long casualty list, because only eighty men were left in the battalion.

Heilly was on the railway; close to the station was the hospital—marquee tents with the red cross painted prominently on the roofs to discourage air-bombing. It was fine July weather and the tents were insufferably hot. I was semi-conscious now, and realized my lung-wound by the shortness of breath. I was amused to watch the little bubbles of blood, like red soap-bubbles, that my breath made when it escaped through the hole of the wound. The doctor came over to me. I felt sorry for him; he looked as though he had not had any sleep for days. I asked him for a drink. He said: "Would you like some tea?" I whispered: "Not with condensed milk in it." He said: "I'm afraid there's no fresh milk." Tears came to my eyes; I expected better of a hospital behind the lines. He said: "Will you have some water?" I said: "Not if it's boiled." He said: "It is boiled. And I'm afraid I can't give you anything with alcohol in it in your present condition." I said: "Give me some fruit then." He said: "I have seen no fruit for days." But a few minutes later he came back with two rather unripe greengages. I felt so grateful that I promised him a whole orchard when I recovered.

The nights of the 22nd and 23rd were very bad. Early on the morning of the 24th, when the doctor came to see how I was, I said: "You must send me away from here. The heat will kill me." It was beating through the canvas on my head. He said: "Stick it out. It's your best chance to lie here and not to be moved. You'd not reach the base alive." I said: "I'd like to risk the move. I'll be all right, you'll see." Half an hour later he came back. "Well, you're having it your way. I've just got orders to evacuate every case in the hospital. Apparently the Guards have been in it up at Delville Wood and we'll have them all coming in to-night." I had no fears now about dying. I was content to be wounded and on the way home.

I had been given news of the battalion from a brigade-major, wounded in the leg, who was in the next bed to me. He looked at my label and said: "I see you're in the

Second Royal Welch Fusiliers. Well, I saw your High Wood show through field-glass-es. The way your battalion shook out into artillery formation, company by company—with each section of four or five men in file at fifty yards interval and distance—going down into the hollow and up the slope through the barrage, was the most beautiful bit of parade-ground drill I've ever seen. Your company officers must have been superb." I happened to know that one company at least had started without a single officer. I asked him whether they had held the wood. He said: "They hung on at the near end. I believe what happened was that the Public Schools Battalion came away as soon as it got dark; and so did the Scotsmen. Your chaps were left there alone for some time. They steadied themselves by singing. Later, the chaplain—R.C. of course—Father McCabe, brought the Scotsmen back. They were Glasgow Catholics and would follow a priest where they wouldn't follow an officer. The middle of the wood was impossible for either the Germans or your fellows to hold. There was a terrific concentration of artillery on it. The trees were splintered to matchwood. Late that night the survivors were relieved by a brigade of the Seventh Division; your First Battalion was in it."

That evening I was put in the hospital train. They could not lift me from the stretch-er to put me on a bunk, for fear of starting haemorrhage in the lung; so they laid the stretcher on top of it, with the handles resting on the head-rail and foot-rail. I had been on the same stretcher since I was wounded. I remember the journey only as a nightmare.

My back was sagging, and I could not raise my knees to relieve the cramp because the bunk above me was only a few inches away. A German officer on the other side of the carriage groaned and wept unceasingly. He had been in an aeroplane crash and had a compound fracture of the leg. The other wounded men were cursing him and telling him to stow it and be a man, but he went on, keeping every one awake. He was not delirious, only frightened and in great pain. An orderly gave me a pencil and paper and I wrote home to say that I was wounded but all right. This was July 24th, my twenty-first birthday, and it was on this day, when I arrived at Rouen, that my death officially occurred. My parents got my letter two days after the letter from the colonel; mine was dated July 23rd, because I had lost count of days when I was unconscious; his was dated the 22nd. They could not decide whether my letter had been written just before I died and misdated, or whether I had died just after writing it. "Died of wounds" was, however, so much more circumstantial than "killed" that they gave me up. I was in No. 8 Hospital at Rouen; an exchâteau[2] high above the town. The day after I arrived a Cooper aunt of mine, who had married a Frenchman, came up to the hospital to visit a nephew in the South Wales Borderers who had just had a leg ampu-tated. She happened to see my name in a list on the door of the ward, so she wrote to my mother to reassure her. On the 30th I had a letter from the colonel:

30/7/16

DEAR VON RUNICKE,

I cannot tell you how pleased I am you are alive. I was told your number was up for certain, and a letter was supposed to have come in from Field Ambulance saying you had gone under.

Well, it's good work. We had a rotten time, and after succeeding in doing practi-cally the impossible we collected that rotten crowd and put them in their places, but directly dark came they legged it. It was too sad.

We lost heavily. It is not fair putting brave men like ours alongside that crowd. I also wish to thank you for your good work and bravery, and only wish you could have

2. Commandeered castle.

been with them. I have read of bravery but I have never seen such magnificent and wonderful disregard for death as I saw that day. It was almost uncanny—it was so great. I once heard an old officer in the Royal Welch say the men would follow you to Hell; but these chaps would bring you back and put you in a dugout in Heaven.

Good luck and a quick recovery. I shall drink your health to-night.

***

I had little pain all this time, but much discomfort; the chief pain came from my finger, which had turned septic because nobody had taken the trouble to dress it, and was throbbing. And from the thigh, where the sticky medical plaster, used to hold down the dressing, pulled up the hair painfully when it was taken off each time the wound was dressed. My breath was very short still. I contrasted the pain and discomfort favourably with that of the operation on my nose of two months back; for this I had won no sympathy at all from anyone, because it was not an injury contracted in war. I was weak and petulant and muddled. The R.A.M.C.[3] bugling outraged me. The "Rob All My Comrades," I complained, had taken everything I had except a few papers in my tunic-pocket and a ring which was too tight on my finger to be pulled off; and now they mis-blew the Last Post flat and windily, and with the pauses in the wrong places, just to annoy me. I remember that I told an orderly to put the bugler under arrest and jump to it or I'd report him to the senior medical officer.

Next to me was a Welsh boy, named O.M. Roberts, who had joined us only a few days before he was hit. He told me about High Wood; he had reached the edge of the wood when he was wounded in the groin. He had fallen into a shell-hole. Some time in the afternoon he had recovered consciousness and seen a German officer working round the edge of the wood, killing off the wounded with an automatic pistol. Some of our lightly-wounded were, apparently, not behaving as wounded men should; they were sniping. The German worked nearer. He saw Roberts move and came towards him, fired and hit him in the arm. Roberts was very weak and tugged at his Webley.[4] He had great difficulty in getting it out of the holster. The German fired again and missed. Roberts rested the Webley against the lip of the shell-hole and tried to pull the trigger; he was not strong enough. The German was quite close now and was going to make certain of him this time. Roberts said that he just managed to pull the trigger with the fingers of both hands when the German was only about five yards away. The shot took the top of his head off. Roberts fainted.

The doctors had been anxiously watching my lung, which was gradually filling with blood and pressing my heart too far away to the left of my body; the railway journey had restarted the haemorrhage. They marked the gradual progress of my heart with an indelible pencil on my skin and said that when it reached a certain point they would have to aspirate me. This sounded a serious operation, but it only consisted of putting a hollow needle into my lung through the back and drawing the blood off into a vacuum flask through it. I had a local anæsthetic; it hurt no more than a vaccination, and I was reading the Gazette de Rouen as the blood hissed into the flask. It did not look much, perhaps half a pint. That evening I heard a sudden burst of lovely singing in the courtyard where the ambulances pulled up. I recognized the quality of the voices. I said to Roberts: "The First Battalion have been in it again," and asked a nurse to verify it; I was right. It was their Delville Wood show, I think, but I am uncertain now of the date.

A day or two later I was taken back to England by hospital ship.

[END OF PERSPECTIVES: THE GREAT WAR]

---

3. Royal Army Medical Corps.   4. Revolver.

❦❧❦

Speeches on Irish Independence

Through the eight centuries of British rule in Ireland, Irish nationalist sentiment remained strong, though it was often forced underground. Ireland had gained a hundred members in the British Parliament when the United Kingdom was formed in 1801, yet on crucial issues they were regularly outvoted by the English majority. As Ireland gradually recovered from the effects of the famine of the 1840s, nationalist agitation increased, only inflamed by English attempts at repression. In 1870 the Home Rule League was formed, to press for legislative independence. In 1877 the League elected as its parliamentary leader a bold young nationalist named Charles Stewart Parnell (1846–1891), who came to dominate the movement for the ensuing dozen years; his tragic fall from power in 1889 shocked both his supporters and his detractors. For Yeats and Joyce especially, Parnell was proof of their suspicion that, as Joyce's character Stephen Dedalus was to put it, Ireland is "the old sow that eats her farrow."

Parnell assembled a powerful coalition in Parliament, bringing other business to a halt until Irish issues were considered. After years of negotiation, the Liberal prime minister Gladstone agreed to introduce a Home Rule bill in 1886. The bill was defeated, but passage was believed to be just a matter of time. Parnell's fortunes were quickly to turn, however. On Christmas Eve, 1889, Captain William O'Shea, a moderate Home Rule member, brought a divorce action against his wife Katherine ("Kitty"), and named Parnell as respondent. Parnell had been conducting an affair with Kitty O'Shea since 1880; some suggest that Captain O'Shea had long known this, and brought the action at this point for political gain. As a result of the divorce, the Irish parliamentary party removed Parnell from the leadership, and the Catholic hierarchy in Ireland turned against him, declaring him unfit for public office; a large portion of the Irish people abandoned him as well. Others, especially in Dublin, remained fiercely loyal to Parnell; but he was a broken man, and died just a few months after his marriage to Kitty O'Shea in June 1891.

The ensuing years were marked by token reforms and by division in Ireland, between ardent nationalists, moderate reformers, and Protestants who opposed weakened ties to England. The Irish republic can be dated from the Easter Rising in 1916 which, though unsuccessful, started the movement toward Irish independence which resulted six years later in the founding of the Irish Free State. After the failure of a third Home Rule bill in 1914, the Irish Republican Brotherhood stepped up their activities and began planning for a large-scale revolutionary uprising. In the spring of 1916 the Irish statesman Sir Roger Casement traveled to Germany to raise support for the planned uprising, but he managed only to obtain some obsolete firearms and was arrested on his return to Ireland. Three days later, on Easter Monday, April 24, a small force of about a thousand rebels seized the General Post Office and other city buildings, and declared a provisional Republican government, in a stirring proclamation read on the Post Office steps by Padriac Pearce, the planned president. W. B. Yeats vividly evokes that historical moment, and its transformation into nationalist mythology, in his poem *Easter, 1916*. Street fighting continued for about a week, until Pearse and other leaders were forced to surrender. The execution of these leaders helped to rally support for the Republican cause among the Irish people and contributed to the founding of the Irish Republican Army (IRA) in 1919. Guided by the brilliant tactician Michael Collins, the IRA harrassed British troops and kept them from crushing the nationalist resistance.

As a result of this ongoing state of virtual civil war, the British government was ultimately forced to pass the Government of Ireland Act in 1920, dividing Ireland into two self-governing areas, Northern Ireland and Southern Ireland. Historically, the south has been primarily Catholic (currently more than 90 percent), and the north Protestant (about 65 percent); all twentieth-century political divisions of Ireland have been made with the awareness of these religious and cultural differences. At the close of 1921, the Anglo-Irish Treaty laid the groundwork for Ireland's twenty-six southern counties to establish an Irish Free State, the Republic of

Ireland; the six counties of Northern Ireland would retain their status as a member of the United Kingdom. Michael Collins, who negotiated the 1921 treaty, was ambushed and killed in 1922 by opponents of Irish partition. This division of the island remains in effect today, although recurrent terrorist violence of the IRA has been directed at winning independence as well for Northern Ireland. Thus while Ireland and England are still somewhat uneasy neighbors, 1922 marks the incomplete realization of a 750-year-old dream—in the words of a popular ballad, the dream that Ireland might be "a nation once again."

Charles Stewart Parnell
At Limerick

I firmly believe that, bad as are the prospects of this country, out of that we will obtain good for Ireland. * * * It is the duty of the Irish tenant farmers to combine amongst themselves and ask for a reduction of rent, and if they get no reduction where a reduction is necessary, then I say that it is the duty of the tenant to pay no rent until he gets it. And if they combined in that way, if they stood together, and if being refused a reasonable and just reduction, they kept a firm grip of their homesteads, I can tell them that no power on earth could prevail against the hundreds of thousands of the tenant farmers of this country. Do not fear. You are not to be exterminated as you were in 1847,[1] and take my word for it it will not be attempted. You should ask for concessions that are just. Ask for them in a proper manner, and good landlords will give these conditions. But for the men who had always shown themselves regardless of right and justice in their dealings with these questions, I say it is necessary for you to maintain a firm and determined attitude. If you maintain that attitude victory must be yours. If when a farm was tenantless, owing to any cause, you refuse to take it, and the present most foolish competition amongst farmers came to an end, as undoubtedly it now must, these men who are forgetful of reason and of common sense must come to reconsider their position. I believe that the land of a country ought to be owned by the people of the country. And I think we should centre our exertions upon attaining that end. * * * When we have the people of this country prosperous, self-reliant, and confident of the future, we will have an Irish nation which will be able to hold its own amongst the nations of the world. We will have a country which will be able to speak with the enemy in the gate—we will have a people who will understand their rights, and, knowing those rights, will be resolved to maintain them. We must all have this without injustice to any individual.

Before the House of Commons[1]

* * * I can assure the House that it is not my belief that anything I can say, or wish to say at this time, will have the slightest effect on the public opinion of the House, or upon the public opinion of this country. I have been accustomed during my political life to rely upon the public opinion of those whom I have desired to help, and with whose aid I have worked for the cause of prosperity and freedom in Ireland: and the utmost that I desire to do in the very few words which I shall address to this House, is

---

1. After the failure of the potato crops in 1845 and 1846, and English refusal to suspend rent payments of Irish tenant farmers, 1847 was perhaps the year of most extreme suffering and starvation. During the years of the Potato Famine, the Irish population plummeted, through starvation, disease, and emigration, from about 8.5 million in

1845 to 6.6 million in 1851. This national tragedy forms the backdrop for Parnell's remarks (31 August 1879) to the tenant farmers of Limerick, who seemed to be facing an agricultural crisis of similar magnitude.
1. Delivered 23 February 1883.

to make my position clear to the Irish people at home and abroad from the unjust aspersions which have been cast upon me by a man[2] who ought to be ashamed to devote his high ability to the task of traducing[3] them. I don't wish to reply to the questions of the right hon. gentleman. I consider he has no right to question me, standing as he does in a position very little better than an informer with regard to the secrets of the men with whom he was associated, and he has not even the pretext of that remarkable informer whose proceedings we have lately heard of.[4] He had not even the pretext of that miserable man that he was attempting to save his own life. No, sir: other motives of less importance seem to have weighed with the right hon. gentleman in the extraordinary course which he has adopted on the present occasion of going out of his way to collect together a series of extracts, perhaps nine or ten in number, out of a number of speeches—many hundreds and thousands—delivered during the Land League movement[5] by other people and not by me, upon which to found an accusation against me for what has been said and done by others. * * * The right hon. gentleman has asked me to defend myself. Sir, I have nothing to defend myself for. The right hon. gentleman has confessed that he attempted to obtain a declaration or public promise from me which would have the effect of discrediting me with the Irish people. He has admitted that he failed in that attempt, and failing in that attempt, he lost his own reputation. He boasted last night that he had deposed me from some imaginary position which he was pleased to assign to me; but, at least, I have this consolation—that he also deposed himself. * * * I have taken very little part in Irish politics since my release from Kilmainham.[6] I expressed my reason for that upon the passing of the Crimes Act.[7] I said that, in my judgment, the Crimes Act would result in such a state of affairs that between the Government and secret societies it would be impossible for constitutional agitation to exist in Ireland. I believe so still. * * * It would have been far better if you were going to pass an Act of this kind and to administer an Act of this kind as you are going to administer it, and as you are obliged to administer it—up to the hilt—that it should be done by the seasoned politician who is now in disgrace. Call him back to his post! Send him to help Lord Spencer[8] in his congenial work of the gallows in Ireland! Send him to look after the Secret Inquisitions of Dublin Castle! Send him to superintend the payment of blood money! Send him to distribute the taxes which an unfortunate and starving peasantry have to pay for crimes not committed by them! All this would be congenial work. We invite you to man your ranks, and send your ablest and best men. Push forward the task of misgoverning Ireland! For my part I am confident as to the future of Ireland. Although her horizon may appear at this moment clouded, I believe that our people will survive the present oppression as we have survived many and worse ones. And although our progress may be slow it will be sure, and the time will come when this House and the people of this country will admit once again that they have been mistaken; that they have been deceived by those who ought to be ashamed of deceiving them; that they have been led astray as to the method of governing a noble, a

2. William Edward Forster, chief secretary for Ireland, had attacked Parnell at the beginning of the 1883 session.
3. Slandering.
4. James Carey (1845–1883), one of the Invincibles (an Irish nationalist group who killed the Irish chief secretary and undersecretary in Dublin's Phoenix Park in May 1882). After his arrest, he turned informer but was killed by another of the Invincibles while the British government attempted to transport him to safety in South Africa.
5. A division of the Home Rule Confederation, founded in 1879 by Michael Davitt and led by Parnell, that fought for the tenant farmers' security of tenure, fair rents on property, and their freedom to sell their property.
6. A jail in Dublin where Parnell was held between October 1881 and May 1882, after a series of popular speeches to the Irish people couched in violent language.
7. A coercion act against Irish agitation passed in 1881.
8. John Poyntz, fifth Earl of Spencer; Lord Lieutenant of Ireland for a second term (1882–1885).

generous, and an impulsive people; that they will reject their present leaders who are conducting them into the terrible course, which, I am sorry to say, the Government appears to be determined to enter; that they will reject these guides and leaders with just as much determination as they rejected the services of the right hon. gentleman the member of Bradford.[9]

At Portsmouth, After the Defeat of Mr. Gladstone's Home Rule Bill[1]

It is, I believe, about the first time I have had the honour of addressing a mainly English audience. And I have been induced to do so now because I rely greatly upon the spirit of fair play among the English masses, and because the issues for my country are so great and so vital at the present moment—the issues which underlie this present struggle—that the Irishman who remains silent when it might be possible to do something to help his country would be more unworthy than tongue could describe. * * * I have, in my career as a member of Parliament, never wittingly injured the cause of the English working man. I have done something to show my sympathy for the masses of the people of this country. * * * Some years ago it was my privilege to strike with English members a successful blow in favour of the abolition of flogging in the army and navy. We were met then by the very same arguments as we are met with today, and from the same class of persons. It was said by the late Lord Beaconsfield[2] that the integrity of the British Empire would be endangered if flogging were abolished, and he called a great meeting at one of the Ministerial offices in London, a great meeting of his supporters both in the Lords and Commons, for the purpose of exhorting them to stand shoulder to shoulder in defence of the British Empire against the abolition of flogging in the army. * * * I have shown you that in some respects the Irish settlement proposed by Mr Gladstone does not give a Parliament, a Legislature with the powers possessed by Grattan's Parliament;[3] but I have shown you on the other hand that as regards our own exclusively domestic business it gives larger powers, more important powers, more valuable powers for Ireland itself than was possessed by Grattan's, and therefore we think that this settlement proposed by Mr Gladstone will prove a more durable settlement than the restitution of the Grattan Parliament or the Repeal of the Union would prove. * * * Imperial unity does not require or necessitate unity of Parliaments. Will you carry that away with you and remember it, because it is the keystone of our whole proceedings. * * * I should say that Ireland would justly deserve to lose her privilege if she passed laws oppressive of the minority. * * * So far as coercion was concerned it has not brought you any nearer to the end of the Irish question. * * * One great fault in English coercion has been that no matter what your intentions have been when you have commenced coercion, you have never discriminated between political agitators and breakers of the law. * * * Lord Carnarvon[4] will not deny that he was as strong a Home Ruler as I was last August, and that when he went over to Ireland he became stronger and stronger every day he lived in that country. There is another thing he has not denied: he has not denied that he sought an interview with me in order to speak to me and consult with me about a Constitution for Ireland.[5] * * * Untold is the guilt of that man who,

9. I.e., William Edward Forster.
1. The first Home Rule bill, which would have given Ireland a "wide measure of autonomy"; Parnell gave this speech (25 June 1886), shortly after the bill's defeat.
2. Benjamin Disraeli, Prime Minister of England in 1868, and from 1874 to 1880.

3. Henry Grattan was leader of the movement that gave Ireland legislative independence in 1782.
4. Lord lieutenant of Ireland from 1885 to 1886 and member of the British Parliament.
5. Parnell and Carnarvon met on 1 August 1885, and discussed Irish Home Rule and an Irish Constitution.

for party purposes, does not take advantage of the spirit which is abroad amongst the English to put the hand of the Irish into that of the English to close the strife of centuries—a strife that has been of no advantage to the people of either country; a strife that has only been for the benefit of the money-grabbing landlords; a strife that has impeded popular progress in England as well as in Ireland, and that must continue to impede it; a strife which is fanned for the purpose of cheating you out of your rights, and to divert the energies of the newly enfranchised masses of Great Britain from the redress of their grievances to the odious task of oppressing and keeping down the small sister country.

Speech Delivered in Committee Room No. 15[1]

The men whose ability is now so conspicuously exercised as that of Mr. Healy and Mr. Sexton, will have to bear their responsibility for this. * * * Why did you encourage me to come forward and maintain my leadership in the face of the world if you were not going to stand by me? * * * I want to ask you before you vote my deposition to be sure you are getting value for it. * * * I know what Mr. Gladstone will do for you; I know what Mr. Morley[2] will do for you; and I know there is not a single one of the lot to be trusted unless you trust yourselves. Be to your own selves true and hence it follows, as the day the night, thou can'st not be false to any man.[3] * * * If I am to leave you tonight I should like to leave you in security. I should like, and it is not an unfair thing for me to ask, that I should come within sight of the Promised Land; that I should come with you, having come so far, if not to the end of this course, that I should at least come with you as far as you will allow and permit me to come with you, at least until it is absolutely sure that Ireland and I can go no further.

Proclamation of the Irish Republic
Poblacht na h Eireann[1]
THE PROVISIONAL GOVERNMENT OF THE IRISH REPUBLIC
TO
THE PEOPLE OF IRELAND

Irishmen and Irishwomen:

In the name of God and of the dead generations from which she receives her old tradition of nationhood, Ireland, through us, summons her children to her flag and strikes for her freedom.

Having organised and trained her manhood through her secret revolutionary organisation, the Irish Republican Brotherhood, and through her open miltary organisations, the Irish Volunteers and the Irish Citizen Army, having patiently perfected her discipline, having resolutely waited for the right moment to reveal itself, she now seizes that moment, and, supported by her exiled children in America and by gallant allies in Europe, but relying in the first on her own strength, she strikes in full confidence of victory.

---

1. Office of Parnell's party in Dublin. Parnell spoke to the party leadership on 6 December 1890 following a motion by Timothy Healy and Thomas Sexton to depose him as their leader in Parliament. Healy had been a Member of Parliament allied with Parnell's legislative agenda; Sexton had also supported Parnell in Parliament. In the wake of Parnell's involvement with the O'Shea divorce case, however, both abandoned Parnell and withdrew their support for his policies—an act of treachery which inspired James Joyce's first literary production, at age 8, a poem titled "Et Tu, Healy?"
2. John Morley (1838–1923), twice Chief Secretary for Ireland.
3. A paraphrase of lines from Polonius's speech in *Hamlet*, 1.3.78–80.
1. *Irish Republic*, in the Irish language.

We declare the right of the people of Ireland to the ownership of Ireland, and to the unfettered control of Irish destinies, to be sovereign and indefeasible. The long usurpation of that right by a foreign people and government has not extinguished the right, nor can it ever be extinguished except by the destruction of the Irish people. In every generation the Irish have asserted their right to National freedom and sovereignty; six times during the past three hundred years they have asserted it in arms. Standing on that fundamental right and again asserting it in arms in the face of the world, we hereby proclaim the Irish Republic as a Sovereign Independent State, and we pledge our lives and the lives of our comrades-in-arms to the cause of its freedom, of its welfare, and of its exaltation among the nations.

The Irish Republic is entitled to, and hereby claims, the allegiance of every Irishman and Irishwoman. The Republic guarantees religious and civil liberty, equal rights and equal opportunities to all its citizens, and declares its resolve to pursue the happiness and prosperity of the whole nation and of all its parts, cherishing all the children of the nation equally, and oblivious of the differences carefully fostered by an alien government, which have divided a minority from the majority in the past.

Until our arms have brought the opportune moment for the establishment of a permanent National Government, representative of the whole people of Ireland and elected by the suffrages of all her men and women,[2] the Provisional Government, hereby constituted, will administer the civil and military affairs of the Republic in trust for the people.

We place the cause of the Irish Republic under the protection of the Most High God, Whose blessing we invoke upon our arms, and we pray that no one who serves that cause will dishonor it by cowardice, inhumanity, or rapine. In this supreme hour the Irish nation must, by its valour and discipline and by the readiness of its children to sacrifice themselves for the common good, prove itself worthy of the august destiny to which it is called.

Signed on Behalf of the Provisional Government,
THOMAS J. CLARKE,
SEAN MACDIARMADA,
THOMAS MACDONAGH,
P. H. PEARSE,
EAMONN CEANNT,
JAMES CONNOLLY,
JOSEPH PLUNKETT.

Easter 1916

Padraic Pearse
Kilmainham Prison[1]

The following is the substance of what I said when asked today by the President of the Court-Martial at Richmond Barracks whether I had anything to say in my defence:

I desire, in the first place, to repeat what I have already said in letters to General Maxwell and Brigadier General Lowe.[2] My object in agreeing to an uncondi-

---

2. This call for women's suffrage in the Irish Republic predates full British women's suffrage by 12 years, and American women's suffrage by four years.
1. 2 May 1916. Pearse had been arrested on 29 April 1916,

ending the street fighting that had begun when he read the Proclamation of the Irish Republic on April 16. Pearse was executed at the conclusion of this military trial.
2. Leaders of the British troops during the Easter Rising.

tional surrender was to prevent the further slaughter of the civil population of Dublin and to save the lives of our gallant fellows, who, having made for six days a stand unparalleled in military history, were now surrounded, and in the case of those under the immediate command of H.Q., without food. I fully understand now, as then, that my own life is forfeit to British law, and I shall die very cheerfully if I can think that the British Government, as it has already shown itself strong, will now show itself magnanimous enough to accept my single life in forfeiture and to give a general amnesty to the brave men and boys who have fought at my bidding.[3]

In the second place, I wish it to be understood that any admissions I make here are to be taken as involving myself alone. They do not involve and must not be used against anyone who acted with me, not even those who may have set their names to documents with me. (The Court assented to this.)

I admit that I was Commandant-General Commanding-in-Chief of the forces of the Irish Republic which have been acting against you for the past week, and that I was President of the Provisional Government. I stand over all my acts and words done or spoken, in these capacities. When I was a child of ten I went on my bare knees by my bedside one night and promised God that I should devote my life to an effort to free my country. I have kept the promise. I have helped to organize, to arm, to train, and to discipline my fellow-countrymen to the sole end that, when the time came, they might fight for Irish freedom. The time, as it seemed to me, did come, and we went into the fight. I am glad we did, we seem to have lost, but we have not lost. To refuse to fight would have been to lose, to fight is to win; we have kept faith with the past, and handed on a tradition to the future. I repudiate the assertion of the prosecutor that I sought to aid and abet England's enemy. Germany is no more to me than England is. I asked and accepted German aid in the shape of arms and an expeditionary force, we neither asked for nor accepted German gold, nor had any traffic with Germany but what I state. My object was to win Irish freedom. We struck the first blow ourselves, but I should have been glad of an ally's aid.

I assume that I am speaking to Englishmen who value their freedom and who profess to be fighting for the freedom of Belgium and Serbia;[4] believe that we too love freedom and desire it. To us it is more desirable than anything in the world. If you strike us down now we shall rise again and renew the fight, you cannot conquer Ireland, you cannot extinguish the Irish passion for freedom; if our deed has not been sufficient to win freedom then our children will win it by a better deed.

Michael Collins
The Substance of Freedom[1]

* * * We gather here today to uphold and to expound the Treaty. It was not our intention to hold any meetings until the issue was definitely before the electorate. But as a campaign has been begun in the country by Mr. de Valera and his followers we cannot afford to wait longer.

---

3. This was not to be the case; in addition to Pearse, several other conspirators were executed by the British.
4. In World War I.
1. The text is compiled from reports of audience members for Collins's speech at a public meeting on 5 March 1922. The "treaty" in question is the Anglo-Irish Treaty establishing 26 of Ireland's 32 counties as the Irish Free State and set-

ting up a parliamentary government in Ireland. The treaty was opposed by Eamon de Valera, a surviving leader of the Easter Rising and leader of Sinn Féin, the Irish Republican organization whose Irish name means "Ourselves Alone." Though he was imprisoned by the newly formed Free State for his refusal to sign the treaty, he later went on to serve as both Prime Minister and President of Ireland.

Mr de Valera's campaign is spoken of as a campaign against the Treaty. It is not really that.

The Irish people have already ratified the Treaty through their elected representatives. And the people of Ireland will stand by that ratification. The weekly paper of our opponents, which they call *The Republic of Ireland*, admits that ratification. Document No. 2[2] lapsed with the approval by the Dáil of the Treaty, they said in a leading article in the issue of February 21st; and in the issue of February 28th it is said "alternative documents are no longer in question."

No, it is not a campaign against the Treaty.

Nothing would disconcert Mr. de Valera and his followers more than the wrecking of the Treaty, than the loss of what has been secured by the Treaty.

It is a campaign, not against the Treaty, but against the Free State. And not only against the Free State, but still more against those who stand for the Free State. "Please God we will win," said Mr. de Valera last Sunday at Ennis, "and then there will be an end to the Free State." And if there were an end to the Free State, what then? What is the object of our opponents? I will tell you what it is.

In the same leading article of February 28th (in *The Republic of Ireland*) they say: "The Republican position is clear," and "We stand against the Treaty for the maintenance of the Republic."

The maintenance of the Republic [exclaimed Mr. Collins]. That is very curious. Because in the previous week's issue we were told by a member of the Dáil Cabinet that before the Truce of July last[3] it had become plain that it was physically impossible to secure Ireland's ideal of a completely isolated Republic in the immediate future, otherwise than by driving the overwhelmingly superior British forces out of the country. * * *

I will tell you what has happened since.

The Treaty has been brought back. It has brought and is bringing such freedom to Ireland in the transference to us of all governmental powers, but, above all, in the departure of the British armed forces, that it has become safe, and simple, and easy, and courageous to stand now for what was surrendered in July, because the British armed forces were still here.

We could not beat the British out by force, so the Republican ideal was surrendered. But when we have beaten them out by the Treaty the Republican ideal, which was surrendered in July, is restored.

The object of Mr de Valera and his party emerges. They are stealing our clothes.

We have beaten out the British by means of the Treaty. While damning the Treaty, and us with it, they are taking advantage of the evacuation which the Treaty secures.

After the surrender of the Republican ideal in July we were sent over to make a Treaty with England.

Some of us were sent very much against our wishes. That is well-known to our opponents. Everyone knew then, and it is idle and dishonest to deny now, that in the event of a settlement some postponement of the realisation of our full national sentiment would have to be agreed to.

---

2. A document proposing an alternative arrangement, put forward by a private session of the Dáil Éireann (Irish Parliament) in December 1921.

3. A 1921 truce that led to negotiations and the Anglo-Irish Treaty.

We were not strong enough to realise the full Republican ideal. In addition, we must remember that there is a strong minority in our country up in the North-East that does not yet share our national views, but has to be reckoned with. In view of these things I claim that we brought back the fullest measure of freedom obtainable—the solid substance of independence.

We signed the Treaty believing it gave us such freedom. Our opponents make use of the advantage of the Treaty while they vilify it and us. The position gained by the Treaty provides them with a jumping off ground. After dropping the Republic while the British were still here, they shout bravely for it now from the safe foothold provided for them by means of the Treaty.

It is a mean campaign.

We were left with the Herculean labour and the heavy responsibility of taking over a Government. This would be a colossal task for the most experienced men of any nation. And we are young and not experienced. While we are thus engaged our former comrades go about the country talking. They tell the people to think of their own strength and the weakness of the enemy. Yes! and what is it that has made us strong and the enemy weak in the last few months? Yes, the enemy becomes weaker every day as his numbers grow less. And as they grow less, louder and louder do our opponents shout for the Republic which they surrendered in July last.

What has made the enemy weaker? The enemy that was then too strong for us? Is it the division in our ranks, which is Mr. de Valera's achievement, and which is already threatening a suspension of the evacuation? Or is it the Treaty which is our achievement?

Mr de Valera, in Limerick last Sunday, compared Ireland to a party that had set out to cross a desert, and they had come to a green spot, he said, and there were some who came along to tell them to lie down and stay there, and be satisfied and not go on.

Yes, we had come by means of the Treaty to a green oasis, the last in the long weary desert over which the Irish nation has been travelling. Oases are the resting-places of the desert, and unless the traveller finds them and refreshes himself he never reaches his destination.

Ireland has been brought to the last one, beyond which there is but a little and an easy stretch to go. The nation has earned the right to rest for a little while we renew our strength, and restore somewhat our earlier vigour.

But there are some amongst us who, while they take full advantage of the oasis—only a fool or a madman would fail to do that—complain of those who have led them to it. They find fault with it. They do nothing to help. They are poisoning the wells, wanting now to hurry on, seeing the road ahead short and straight, wanting the glory for themselves of leading the Irish nation over it, while unwilling to fill and shoulder the pack.

We are getting the British armed forces out of Ireland. Because of that evacuation our opponents are strong enough and brave enough now to say: "They are traitors who got you this. We are men of principle. We stand for the Republic"—that Republic which it was physically impossible to secure until the traitors had betrayed you.

Have we betrayed you? * * *

The arrangement in regard to North-East Ulster is not ideal. But then the position in North-East Ulster is not ideal.

If the Free State is established, however, union is certain. Forces of persuasion and pressure are embodied in the Treaty which will bring the North-East into a united Ireland. If they join us they can have control in their own area. If they stay outside Ireland, then they can only have their own corner, and cannot, and will not, have the counties and areas which belong to Ireland and to the Irish people, according to the wishes of the inhabitants.

Then upon the area remaining outside will fall the burdens and restrictions of the 1920 Partition Act.[4] These disabilities cannot be removed without our consent. If the North-East does not come in, then they are deciding upon bankruptcy for themselves and, remember, this is not our wish but their own.

We must not, however, take a gloomy view of this situation, for, with the British gone, the incentive to partition is gone; but the evacuation is held up by our own disunion—if the Free State is threatened, as long as there is any hope of seeing it destroyed, the North-East will remain apart. Partition will remain.

Destroy the Free State, and you perpetuate Partition. You destroy all hopes of union.

It is best to speak out plainly.

Destroy the Free State now and you destroy more even than the hope, the certainty of union. You destroy our hopes of national freedom, all realisation in our generation of the democratic right of the people of Ireland to rule themselves without interference from any outside power. * * *

But the aim of all of us can be for unity and independence. In public matters it must be realised that we cannot get all each one wants. We have to agree to get what is essential.

We have to agree to sink individual differences or only to work for them on legitimate lines which do not undermine and destroy the basis on which all rests and which alone makes it possible for us all, as Irishmen and women, to pursue our own aims freely in Ireland, namely, the union and independence of the nation as a whole.

We must be Irish first and last, and must be Republicans or Document Two-ites, or Free Staters, only within the limits which leave Ireland strong, united and free.

Would any other form of freedom which was obtainable now, which would have been acquiesced in by so large a body of our countrymen, have fulfilled the objects of Sinn Féin better, have put us in such a strong position to secure any that are yet unfulfilled?

We claim that the solid substance of freedom has been won, and that full powers are in the hands of the nation to mould its own life, quite as full for that purpose as if we had already our freedom in the Republican form.

Any difficulties will not be of our own making. There is no enemy nor any foreign Government here any longer to hinder us. Will we not take the fruits of victory, or do we mean to let them decay in our hands, while we wrangle as to whether they are ripe or whether they have exactly the bloom and shape we dreamed of before they had ripened?

No freedom when realised has quite the glory dreamed of by the captive.

[END OF SPEECHES ON IRISH INDEPENDENCE]

---

4. The act that divided Ireland politically into Northern Ireland (Ulster) and the Republic of Ireland.

William Butler Yeats
1865–1939

Beginning his career as a poet during the languid 1880s and 1890s, Yeats fought, as Ezra Pound said of T. S. Eliot, to modernize himself on his own. At a time when Irish poetry seemed to be in danger of ossifying into a sentimental, self-indulgent luxury, Yeats instead forged a verse that would serve as an exacting instrument of introspection and national inquiry. As a conse-quence, all modern Irish writing—most clearly poetry, but prose, drama, and literary nonfic-tion as well—is directly in his debt.

Yeats was born in the Dublin suburb of Sandymount, but his spiritual home, the land of his mother Susan Pollexfen and her people, was the countryside of County Sligo. His father, John Butler Yeats, was an amateur philosopher, an insolvent painter, and a refugee from the legal profession; his grandfather and great-grandfather were both clergymen of the Church of Ireland. Through his mother's family, Yeats traced a close connection with the countryside of Ireland, and the myths and legends of the Irish people. Both parents belonged to the Anglo-Irish Protestant ascendancy, a heritage Yeats remained fiercely proud of all his life; but the suc-cess of his poetry, in part, lay in his ability to reconcile the British literary tradition with the native materials of the Irish Catholic tradition.

As he tells it in his autobiography, Yeats's childhood was not a happy one; in 1915 he wrote: "I remember little of childhood but its pain." His father, though a talented painter, lacked the ability to turn his gifts to profit; he would linger over a single portrait for months and sometimes years, revising ceaselessly. When Yeats was three, his father moved his family to London in order to put himself to school as a painter; their existence, though intellectually and artistically rich and stimulating, was quite straitened financially. The young Yeats found Lon-don sterile and joyless; fortunately for his imagination, and his future poetry, portions of each year were spent in the Sligo countryside, where Yeats spent time gathering the local folklore and taking long, wide-ranging walks and pony rides. The family remained in London until 1875, and had four more children (though one brother died in childhood). All his surviving sib-lings were to remain important to Yeats in his artistic life: his brother Jack B. Yeats became an important Irish painter, and his sisters Lily and Lolly together founded the Dun Emer Press, lat-er called the Cuala Press, which published limited-edition volumes of some of Yeats's poetry.

In 1880 the family returned permanently to Ireland, settling first in Howth, in Dublin Bay; the city of Dublin, with its largely unsung history and tradition, fueled Yeats's imagina-tion in a way that London never had. When the time for college came, Yeats was judged unlikely to pass Trinity College's entrance exams, and he was sent instead to the Metropolitan School of Art, apparently in preparation to follow in his father's footsteps. His true gift, it soon appeared, was not for drawing and painting but for poetry. He steeped himself in the Romantic poets, especially Shelley and Keats, as well as the English poet of Irish residence Edmund Spenser. His first poems were published in the *Dublin University Review* in March 1885.

Yeats's early work is self-evidently apprentice work; it draws heavily on the late-Roman-tic, pre-Raphaelite ambience so important in the painting of his father and his father's col-leagues. He also began to take an active interest in the various mystical movements that were then finding a foothold in Dublin and London, and with friends formed a Hermetic Society in Dublin as an antidote to the humanist rationalism to which his father was so passionately attached. At the same time—almost as a self-administered antidote to the teachings of mystics like the Brahmin teacher Mohini Chatterji—Yeats began to attend the meetings of several Dublin political and debating societies, and became increasingly interested in the nationalist artistic revival that would become known as the Irish Renaissance or Celtic Revival. Unlike most of his debating society comrades, Yeats imagined this political and cultural renaissance as resulting from a marriage of Blakean opposites: "I had noticed that Irish Catholics among whom had been born so many political martyrs had not the good taste, the household courtesy and decency of the Protestant Ireland I had known, yet Protestant Ireland seemed to think of nothing but getting on in the world. I thought we might bring the halves together if we had a national literature that made Ireland beautiful in the memory, and yet had been freed from provincialism by an exacting criticism, a European pose."

The Yeats family moved back to London in 1887; finances were difficult as ever, and Yeats contributed to the family's upkeep by editing two anthologies, *Poems and Ballads of Young Ireland* (1888) and *Fairy and Folk Tales of the Irish Peasantry* (1888). His own first collection of poems, *The Wanderings of Oisin and Other Poems*, was published in the following year; the poems are resolutely romantic, Yeats himself describing his manner at the time as "in all things Pre-Raphaelite." The poems were well received, but the praise of one reader in particular caught Yeats's attention. The statuesque beauty Maud Gonne appeared at Yeats's door with an introduction from the Irish revolutionary John O'Leary, and declared that the title poem had brought her to tears. It was a fateful meeting; throughout five decades Yeats continued to write to Gonne, for Gonne—the critic M. L. Rosenthal has suggested that "virtually every poem celebrating a woman's beauty or addressing a beloved woman has to do with her." Rosenthal might have added, every poem decrying the sacrifice of life to politics, including *No Second Troy, Easter 1916, A Prayer for My Daughter,* and others, all of which lament Gonne's increasing political fanaticism. This fanaticism, which Gonne considered simply patriotism, made impossible the spiritual and emotional consummation that Yeats so fervently desired. He proposed marriage, but she declined, marrying instead an Irish soldier who would later be executed for his role in the Easter Rising of 1916. Yeats is, among his other distinctions, a great poet of unrequited love.

The 1890s in London were heady times for a young poet. Yeats became even more active in his studies of the occult, studying with the charismatic Theosophist Madame Blavatsky and attending meetings of the Order of the Golden Dawn, a Christian cabalist society. The practical upshot of these activities for his later poetry was a confirmed belief in a storehouse of all human experience and knowledge, which he called variously the *Spiritus Mundi* and *Anima Mundi*, invoked in later poems like *The Second Coming* (1920). In 1891 Yeats, together with Ernest Rhys, founded the Rhymers' Club, which brought him into almost nightly contact with such important literary figures as Lionel Johnson, Ernest Dowson, Arthur Symons, and Oscar Wilde; during this same period, he established the Irish Literary Society in London, and the National Literary Society in Dublin. Clearly, something of a program for modern Irish poetry was beginning to emerge, even if Yeats himself wasn't yet quite ready to write it. Yeats also spent the years from 1887 to 1891 studying the writings of that most mystic of English poets, William Blake; working with his father's friend Edwin Ellis, he produced an edition of and extended commentary on Blake's prophetic writings. Summing up the lesson of Blake's writings, Yeats wrote: "I had learned from Blake to hate all abstractions."

Romantic abstraction was easier to abjure in principle than in practice; Yeats's poetry of the 1890s still hankers after what one of his dramatis personae would later call "the loveliness that has long faded from the world." As one critic has written, "Early Yeats was the best poetry in English in late Victorian times; but they were bad times." Yeats began the process of throwing off the false manners of his pre-Raphaelite upbringing with his play *The Countess Cathleen,* first performed by the Abbey Theatre, funded by subscriptions collected by his good friend Lady Augusta Gregory. Yeats's play, like Synge's *Playboy of the Western World* years later on that same stage, offended Irish sensibilities; in it, Cathleen sells her soul in order to protect Irish peasants from starvation. Yeats's volume *The Wind Among the Reeds* (1899) closes out the 1890s quite conveniently; it is ethereal, beautiful, and mannered. With this volume, Yeats's early phase comes to a close.

The early years of the twentieth century found Yeats concentrating his energies on the writing of poetic dramas, including, *The Pot of Broth* (1902) and *On Baile's Strand* (1904), for his fledgling Irish National Theatre. In 1903, the small Dun Emer Press published his volume of poems *In the Seven Woods*. These poems, including *Adam's Curse*, show Yeats working in a more spare idiom, the cadences and rhythms closer to those of actual speech—a consequence, some have argued, of his years writing for the stage. New poems published in *The Green Helmet and Other Poems* (1910) display Yeats as an increasingly mature and confident poet; his treatment of Maud Gonne in *No Second Troy*, for instance, shows a tragic acceptance of the fact that he will never have her, nor master her indomitable spirit. In *A Coat*, the poem that closes the 1914 collection *Responsibilities*, Yeats writes of the embroidered cloak he had fashioned for himself in his early poems, whose vanity is now brought home to him by the gaudiness of his imitators. He resolves, in the volume's closing lines, to set his cloak aside, "For there's more enterprise / In walking naked." This sense was strengthened by his close work, during the winter of 1912–1913, with Ezra Pound, in a cottage in rural Sussex. Both studied the stripped-down Japanese Noh drama and the Orientalist Ernest Fennollosa's work on the Chinese ideogram, and both men no doubt reinforced one another's increasing desire for a poetry that would be, in Pound's phrase, "closer to the bone."

The Easter Rising of 1916 took Yeats by surprise; he was in England at the time and complained of not having been informed in advance. A number of the rebel leaders were personal friends; he writes their names into Irish literature in *Easter 1916*, an excruciatingly honest, and ambivalent, exploration of the nature of heroism and nationalism. Yeats's mixed feelings about the revolution derived in part from a concern that some of his early writings, like the nationalist *The Countess Cathleen*, might have contributed to the slaughter that followed in the wake of Easter 1916; as he wrote many years later, he couldn't help but wonder, "Did that play of mine send out / Certain men the English shot?"

The intricacies of Yeats's emotional and romantic life would require an essay of their own. His first marriage proposal to Maud Gonne in 1891, politely refused, set a pattern that was to remain in place for many years; though a number of poems try to reason through the affair, Yeats remained tragically attracted to this woman who did not return his affection, and multiple proposals were turned down as routinely as the first. He would have done as well, he was to write years later, to profess his love "to a statue in a museum." In the summer of 1917 things reached such a pass that Yeats proposed to Maud Gonne's adopted daughter Iseult; here, again, he was refused. Then, hastily, in October 1917 he married a longtime friend Georgiana ("George") Hyde-Lees. For all the tragicomedy leading up to the marriage, Yeats could not have chosen better; George was intelligent and sympathetic, and she brought the additional gift of an interest in mysticism and a facility in automatic writing that Yeats was soon to take full advantage of. Since early childhood, Yeats had heard voices speaking to him, and when he was twenty-one a voice commanded him "Hammer your thoughts into unity"; this charge had weighed on his mind for years, and his various experiments in mysticism and esoteric religions were intended to discover the system wherein his thoughts might be made to cohere.

With George, Yeats finally created that system on his own; its fullest exposition is found in *A Vision* (1928), though elements of it turn up in his poems beginning as early as *No Second Troy*. The system is complicated enough to fill out over 300 pages in the revised (1937) edition; at the heart of the system, though, is a simple diagram of two interpenetrating cones, oriented horizontally, such that the tip of each cone establishes the center of the base of the opposite cone. These two cones describe the paths of two turning gyres, or spirals, representing two alternating antithetical ages which make up human history. Yeats saw history as composed of cycles of approximately 2,000 years; his apocalyptic poem *The Second Coming*, for instance, describes the anxiety caused by the recognition that the 2,000 years of Christian (in Yeats's terms, "primary") values were about to be succeeded by an antithetical age—the "rough beast" of a time characterized by values and beliefs in every way hostile to those of the Christian era. For Yeats, however, as for William Blake, this vacillation and tension between contraries was not to be regretted; Blake taught that "without Contraries is no progression," and Yeats, that "all the gains of man come from conflict with the opposite of his true being."

Yeats's greatest phase begins with the poems of *Michael Robartes and the Dancer* (1921). His mytho-historical system informs a number of the poems written in the 1920s and after; it explains, for instance, why Yeats saw the brutal rape of Leda by Zeus in the form of a swan as a precursor of the traditional Christian iconography of the Virgin Mary "visited" by God the Father in the form of a dove. A logical corollary of Yeats's belief in historical recurrence was the philosophy, articulated best in his late poem *Lapis Lazuli*, of tragic joy: "All things fall and are built again, / And those that build them again are gay." In a letter inspired by the gift of lapis lazuli that the poem celebrates, Yeats wrote to a friend: "To me the supreme aim is an act of faith or reason to make one rejoice in the midst of tragedy." The influence of the writing of Nietzsche, whom Yeats had been reading, is apparent in these formulations.

While continuing to push at the boundaries of modern literature and modern poetry, Yeats also enjoyed the role of statesman. In the fall of 1922, Yeats was made a senator of the new Irish Free State; in 1923 he was awarded the Nobel Prize for literature, the first Irish writer ever to receive the award. The 1930s also saw Yeats flirt briefly with fascism, as did other writers like Pound and Wyndham Lewis. Yeats's belief in the importance of an aristocracy, and his disappointment over the excesses of revolutionary zeal demonstrated in the Irish civil war, for a time during the 1930s made the fascist program of the Irish Blueshirt movement look attractive. He composed *Three Songs to the Same Tune* as rallying songs for the Blueshirts, but the poems were too recherché for any such use. He soon became disillusioned with the party.

Yeats continued to write major poetry almost until his death; his growing ill health seems only to have made his poetry stronger and more defiant, as evidenced in such sinuous and clearsighted poems as *Lapis Lazuli* and the bawdy Crazy Jane poems. In the work published as *Last Poems* (1939), Yeats most satisfactorily put into practice what he had much earlier discovered in theory: that he must, as he wrote in *The Circus Animals' Desertion*, return for his poetry to "the foul rag-and-bone shop of the heart." After a long period of heart trouble, Yeats died on 28 January 1939; he was buried in Roquebrune, France, where he and George had been spending the winter. In 1948 he was reinterred, as he had wished, in Drumcliff churchyard near Sligo, where his grandfather and great-grandfather had served as rectors. Again according to his wishes, his epitaph is that which he wrote for himself in *Under Ben Bulben*:

> Cast a cold eye
> On life, on death.
> Horseman, pass by!

The Lake Isle of Innisfree[1]

I will arise and go now, and go to Innisfree,
And a small cabin build there, of clay and wattles° made: woven twigs
Nine bean-rows will I have there, a hive for the honey-bee,
And live alone in the bee-loud glade.

5   And I shall have some peace there, for peace comes dropping slow,
Dropping from the veils of the morning to where the cricket sings;
There midnight's all a glimmer, and noon a purple glow,
And evening full of the linnet's° wings.   song bird

I will arise and go now, for always night and day
10   I hear lake water lapping with low sounds by the shore;

---

1. A small island in Lough Gill outside the town of Sligo, near the border with Northern Ireland.

While I stand on the roadway, or on the pavements grey,
I hear it in the deep heart's core.

1890   1890

Who Goes with Fergus?[1]

Who will go drive with Fergus now,
And pierce the deep wood's woven shade,
And dance upon the level shore?
Young man, lift up your russet brow,
5   And lift your tender eyelids, maid,
And brood on hopes and fear no more.
And no more turn aside and brood
Upon love's bitter mystery;
For Fergus rules the brazen° cars,   brass
10   And rules the shadows of the wood,
And the white breast of the dim sea
And all dishevelled wandering stars.

1893

No Second Troy[1]

Why should I blame her that she filled my days
With misery, or that she would of late
Have taught to ignorant men most violent ways,
Or hurled the little streets upon the great,
5   Had they but courage equal to desire?
What could have made her peaceful with a mind
That nobleness made simple as a fire,
With beauty like a tightened bow, a kind
That is not natural in an age like this,
10   Being high and solitary and most stern?
Why, what could she have done, being what she is?
Was there another Troy for her to burn?

1908   1910

The Fascination of What's Difficult

The fascination of what's difficult
Has dried the sap out of my veins, and rent
Spontaneous joy and natural content
Out of my heart. There's something ails our colt
5   That must, as if it had not holy blood
Nor on Olympus leaped from cloud to cloud,
Shiver under the lash, strain, sweat and jolt
As though it dragged road metal. My curse on plays
That have to be set up in fifty ways,
10   On the day's war with every knave and dolt,

---

1. The poem is a lyric from the second scene of Yeats's play *The Countess Cathleen*. Fergus was an ancient Irish king who gave up his throne to feast, fight, and hunt.

1. Yeats here compares Maud Gonne to Helen of Troy; the Trojan War began from two kings' rivalry over Helen.

Theatre business, management of men.
I swear before the dawn comes round again
I'll find the stable and pull out the bolt.

1910   1910

The Wild Swans at Coole[1]

The trees are in their autumn beauty,
The woodland paths are dry,
Under the October twilight the water
Mirrors a still sky;
5   Upon the brimming water among the stones
Are nine-and-fifty swans.

The nineteenth autumn has come upon me
Since I first made my count;
I saw, before I had well finished,
10   All suddenly mount
And scatter wheeling in great broken rings
Upon their clamorous wings.

I have looked upon those brilliant creatures,
And now my heart is sore.
15   All's changed since I, hearing at twilight,
The first time on this shore,
The bell-beat of their wings above my head,
Trod with a lighter tread.

Unwearied still, lover by lover,
20   They paddle in the cold
Companionable streams or climb the air;
Their hearts have not grown old;
Passion or conquest, wander where they will,
Attend upon them still.

25   But now they drift on the still water,
Mysterious, beautiful;
Among what rushes will they build,
By what lake's edge or pool
Delight men's eyes when I awake some day
30   To find they have flown away?

1916   1917

Easter 1916[1]

I have met them at close of day
Coming with vivid faces
From counter or desk among grey
Eighteenth-century houses.
5   I have passed with a nod of the head

---

1. Coole Park was the name of the estate of Yeats's patron
Lady Gregory in Galway.

1. The Irish Republic was declared on Easter Monday
1916.

Or polite meaningless words,
Or have lingered awhile and said
Polite meaningless words,
And thought before I had done
10 Of a mocking tale or a gibe°   *taunt*
To please a companion
Around the fire at the club,
Being certain that they and I
But lived where motley° is worn: *jester's outfit*
15 All changed, changed utterly:
A terrible beauty is born.

That woman's days were spent
In ignorant good-will,
Her nights in argument
20 Until her voice grew shrill.[2]
What voice more sweet than hers
When, young and beautiful,
She rode to harriers?°   *hunting dogs*
This man[3] had kept a school
25 And rode our wingèd horse;
This other[4] his helper and friend
Was coming into his force;
He might have won fame in the end,
So sensitive his nature seemed,
30 So daring and sweet his thought.
This other man[5] I had dreamed
A drunken, vainglorious lout.
He had done most bitter wrong
To some who are near my heart,
35 Yet I number him in the song;
He, too, has resigned his part
In the casual comedy;
He, too, has been changed in his turn,
Transformed utterly:
40 A terrible beauty is born.

Hearts with one purpose alone
Through summer and winter seem
Enchanted to a stone
To trouble the living stream.
45 The horse that comes from the road,
The rider, the birds that range
From cloud to tumbling cloud,
Minute by minute they change;
A shadow of cloud on the stream
50 Changes minute by minute;

2. Countess Markiewicz, née Constance Gore-Booth, played a prominent part in the Easter Rising and was sentenced to be executed; her sentence was later reduced to imprisonment.
3. Padraic Pearse.
4. Thomas MacDonagh, poet executed for his role in the rebellion.
5. Major John MacBride, briefly married to Maud Gonne, was also executed.

A horse-hoof slides on the brim,
And a horse plashes within it;
The long-legged moor-hens dive,
And hens to moor-cocks call;
55   Minute by minute they live:
The stone's in the midst of all.

Too long a sacrifice
Can make a stone of the heart.
O when may it suffice?
60   That is Heaven's part, our part
To murmur name upon name,
As a mother names her child
When sleep at last has come
On limbs that had run wild.
65   What is it but nightfall?
No, no, not night but death;
Was it needless death after all?
For England may keep faith
For all that is done and said.
70   We know their dream; enough
To know they dreamed and are dead;
And what if excess of love
Bewildered them till they died?
I write it out in a verse—
75   MacDonagh and MacBride
And Connolly[6] and Pearse
Now and in time to be,
Wherever green is worn,
Are changed, changed utterly:
80   A terrible beauty is born.
1916   1916

The Second Coming[1]

Turning and turning in the widening gyre°   *circle or spiral*
The falcon cannot hear the falconer;
Things fall apart; the centre cannot hold;
Mere anarchy is loosed upon the world,
5   The blood-dimmed tide is loosed, and everywhere
The ceremony of innocence is drowned;
The best lack all conviction, while the worst
Are full of passionate intensity.

Surely some revelation is at hand;
10   Surely the Second Coming is at hand.
The Second Coming! Hardly are those words out
When a vast image out of *Spiritus Mundi*[2]

---

6. James Connolly, Marxist commander-in-chief of the
Easter rebels; also executed.
1. Traditionally, the return of Christ to earth on Judgment Day.

2. A storehouse of images and symbols common to all
humankind; similar to Carl Jung's notion of the collective unconscious.

Troubles my sight: somewhere in sands of the desert
A shape with lion body and the head of a man,
15 A gaze blank and pitiless as the sun,
Is moving its slow thighs, while all about it
Reel shadows of the indignant desert birds.
The darkness drops again; but now I know
That twenty centuries of stony sleep
20 Were vexed to nightmare by a rocking cradle,
And what rough beast, its hour come round at last,
Slouches towards Bethlehem to be born?

1919   1921

A Prayer for My Daughter

Once more the storm is howling, and half hid
Under this cradle-hood and coverlid
My child sleeps on. There is no obstacle
But Gregory's wood and one bare hill
5 Whereby the haystack- and roof-levelling wind,
Bred on the Atlantic, can be stayed;
And for an hour I have walked and prayed
Because of the great gloom that is in my mind.

I have walked and prayed for this young child an hour
10 And heard the sea-wind scream upon the tower,
And under the arches of the bridge, and scream
In the elms above the flooded stream;
Imagining in excited reverie
That the future years had come,
15 Dancing to a frenzied drum,
Out of the murderous innocence of the sea.

May she be granted beauty and yet not
Beauty to make a stranger's eye distraught,
Or hers before a looking-glass, for such,
20 Being made beautiful overmuch,
Consider beauty a sufficient end,
Lose natural kindness and maybe
The heart-revealing intimacy
That chooses right, and never find a friend.

25 Helen[1] being chosen found life flat and dull
And later had much trouble from a fool,
While that great Queen,[2] that rose out of the spray,
Being fatherless could have her way
Yet chose a bandy-leggèd smith[3] for man.
30 It's certain that fine women eat
A crazy salad with their meat
Whereby the Horn of Plenty is undone.

1. Helen of Troy, who left her husband Menelaus for Paris.
2. Aphrodite, Greek goddess of love, born from the sea.
3. Aphrodite's husband Hephaestus, the god of fire, was lame.

In courtesy I'd have her chiefly learned;
Hearts are not had as a gift but hearts are earned
35   By those that are not entirely beautiful;
Yet many, that have played the fool
For beauty's very self, has charm made wise,
And many a poor man that has roved,
Loved and thought himself beloved,
40   From a glad kindness cannot take his eyes.

May she become a flourishing hidden tree
That all her thoughts may like the linnet° be,   song bird
And have no business but dispensing round
Their magnanimities of sound,
45   Nor but in merriment begin a chase,
Nor but in merriment a quarrel.
O may she live like some green laurel
Rooted in one dear perpetual place.

My mind, because the minds that I have loved,
50   The sort of beauty that I have approved,
Prosper but little, has dried up of late,
Yet knows that to be choked with hate
May well be of all evil chances chief.
If there's no hatred in a mind
55   Assault and battery of the wind
Can never tear the linnet from the leaf.

An intellectual hatred is the worst,
So let her think opinions are accursed.
Have I not seen the loveliest woman born
60   Out of the mouth of Plenty's horn,
Because of her opinionated mind
Barter that horn and every good
By quiet natures understood
For an old bellows full of angry wind?

65   Considering that, all hatred driven hence,
The soul recovers radical innocence
And learns at last that it is self-delighting,
Self-appeasing, self-affrighting,
And that its own sweet will is Heaven's will;
70   She can, though every face should scowl
And every windy quarter howl
Or every bellows burst, be happy still.

And may her bridegroom bring her to a house
Where all's accustomed, ceremonious;
75   For arrogance and hatred are the wares
Peddled in the thoroughfares.
How but in custom and in ceremony
Are innocence and beauty born?
Ceremony's a name for the rich horn,
80   And custom for the spreading laurel tree.

June 1919   1919

Sailing to Byzantium[1]

1

That is no country for old men. The young
In one another's arms, birds in the trees,
—Those dying generations—at their song,
The salmon-falls, the mackerel-crowded seas,
5   Fish, flesh, or fowl, commend all summer long
Whatever is begotten, born, and dies.
Caught in that sensual music all neglect
Monuments of unageing intellect.

2

An aged man is but a paltry thing,
10   A tattered coat upon a stick, unless
Soul clap its hands and sing, and louder sing
For every tatter in its mortal dress,
Nor is there singing school but studying
Monuments of its own magnificence;
15   And therefore I have sailed the seas and come
To the holy city of Byzantium.

3

O sages standing in God's holy fire
As in the gold mosaic of a wall,
Come from the holy fire, perne° in a gyre,   *spin*
20   And be the singing-masters of my soul.
Consume my heart away; sick with desire
And fastened to a dying animal
It knows not what it is; and gather me
Into the artifice of eternity.

4

25   Once out of nature I shall never take
My bodily form from any natural thing,
But such a form as Grecian goldsmiths make
Of hammered gold and gold enamelling
To keep a drowsy Emperor awake;—
30   Or set upon a golden bough to sing
To lords and ladies of Byzantium
Of what is past, or passing, or to come.

1926   1927

Meditations in Time of Civil War

1. Ancestral Houses

Surely among a rich man's flowering lawns,
Amid the rustle of his planted hills,
Life overflows without ambitious pains;
And rains down life until the basin spills,
5   And mounts more dizzy high the more it rains
As though to choose whatever shape it wills

---

1. Constantinople, now called Istanbul, capital of the Byzantine Empire and the holy city of Eastern Christianity.

And never stoop to a mechanical
Or servile shape, at others' beck and call.

Mere dreams, mere dreams! Yet Homer had not sung
10   Had he not found it certain beyond dreams
That out of life's own self-delight had sprung
The abounding glittering jet; though now it seems
As if some marvellous empty sea-shell flung
Out of the obscure dark of the rich streams,
15   And not a fountain, were the symbol which
Shadows the inherited glory of the rich.

Some violent bitter man, some powerful man
Called architect and artist in, that they,
Bitter and violent men, might rear in stone
20   The sweetness that all longed for night and day,
The gentleness none there had ever known;
But when the master's buried mice can play,
And maybe the great-grandson of that house,
For all its bronze and marble, 's but a mouse.

25   O what if gardens where the peacock strays
With delicate feet upon old terraces,
Or else all Juno¹ from an urn displays
Before the indifferent garden deities;
O what if levelled lawns and gravelled ways
30   Where slippered Contemplation finds his ease
And Childhood a delight for every sense,
But take our greatness with our violence?
What if the glory of escutcheoned° doors,   *shield-shaped*
And buildings that a haughtier age designed,
35   The pacing to and fro on polished floors
Amid great chambers and long galleries, lined
With famous portraits of our ancestors;
What if those things the greatest of mankind
Consider most to magnify, or to bless,
40   But take our greatness with our bitterness?

2. My House

An ancient bridge, and a more ancient tower,
A farmhouse that is sheltered by its wall,
An acre of stony ground,
Where the symbolic rose can break in flower,
5   Old ragged elms, old thorns innumerable,
The sound of the rain or sound
Of every wind that blows;
The stilted water-hen
Crossing stream again
10   Scared by the splashing of a dozen cows;

---

1. Roman Goddess of marriage and patroness of women; the peacock was sacred to her as a symbol of immortality.

A winding stair, a chamber arched with stone,
A grey stone fireplace with an open hearth,
A candle and written page.
Il Penseroso's Platonist[2] toiled on

15   In some like chamber, shadowing forth
How the daemonic rage
Imagined everything.
Benighted travellers
From markets and from fairs

20   Have seen his midnight candle glimmering.

Two men have founded here. A man-at-arms
Gathered a score of horse and spent his days
In this tumultuous spot,
Where through long wars and sudden night alarms

25   His dwindling score and he seemed castaways
Forgetting and forgot;
And I, that after me
My bodily heirs may find,
To exalt a lonely mind,

30   Befitting emblems of adversity.

3. My Table

Two heavy trestles, and a board
Where Sato's[3] gift, a changeless sword,
By pen and paper lies,
That it may moralise

5   My days out of their aimlessness.
A bit of an embroidered dress
Covers its wooden sheath.
Chaucer had not drawn breath
When it was forged. In Sato's house,

10   Curved like new moon, moon-luminous,
It lay five hundred years.
Yet if no change appears
No moon; only an aching heart
Conceives a changeless work of art.

15   Our learned men have urged
That when and where 'twas forged
A marvellous accomplishment,
In painting or in pottery, went
From father unto son

20   And through the centuries ran
And seemed unchanging like the sword.
Soul's beauty being most adored,
Men and their business took
The soul's unchanging look;

25   For the most rich inheritor,

---

2. Follower of the idealist philosophy of Plato, in Milton's
poem *Il Penseroso* ("The Contemplative").

3. Junzo Sato, Japanese consul who presented Yeats with
an ancestral ceremonial sword.

Knowing that none could pass Heaven's door
That loved inferior art,
Had such an aching heart
That he, although a country's talk
30   For silken clothes and stately walk,
Had waking wits; it seemed
Juno's peacock screamed.

4. My Descendants

Having inherited a vigorous mind
From my old fathers, I must nourish dreams
And leave a woman and a man behind
As vigorous of mind, and yet it seems
5   Life scarce can cast a fragrance on the wind,
Scarce spread a glory to the morning beams,
But the torn petals strew the garden plot;
And there's but common greenness after that.

And what if my descendants lose the flower
10   Through natural declension of the soul,
Through too much business with the passing hour,
Through too much play, or marriage with a fool?
May this laborious stair and this stark tower
Become a roofless ruin that the owl
15   May build in the cracked masonry and cry
Her desolation to the desolate sky.

The Primum Mobile[4] that fashioned us
Has made the very owls in circles move;
And I, that count myself most prosperous,
20   Seeing that love and friendship are enough,
For an old neighbour's friendship chose the house
And decked and altered it for a girl's love,
And know whatever flourish and decline
These stones remain their monument and mine.

5. The Road at My Door

An affable Irregular,[5]
A heavily-built Falstaffian[6] man,
Comes cracking jokes of civil war
As though to die by gunshot were
5   The finest play under the sun.

A brown Lieutenant and his men,
Half dressed in national uniform,
Stand at my door, and I complain

---

4. Prime mover (Latin); part of the Ptolemaic system that
described the revolution of the heavens around the earth.
5. A member of the Irish Republican Army (IRA), which
opposed any cooperation with British power and started

the civil war.
6. Robust, bawdy, witty; after Sir John Falstaff, comic
character in Shakespeare's *The Merry Wives of Windsor*
and *Henry IV*.

Of the foul weather, hail and rain,
10   A pear tree broken by the storm.

I count those feathered balls of soot
The moor-hen guides upon the stream,
To silence the envy in my thought;
And turn towards my chamber, caught
15   In the cold snows of a dream.

6. The Stare's Nest by My Window

The bees build in the crevices
Of loosening masonry, and there
The mother birds bring grubs and flies.
My wall is loosening; honey-bees,
5   Come build in the empty house of the stare.°   starling

We are closed in, and the key is turned
On our uncertainty; somewhere
A man is killed, or a house burned,
Yet no clear fact to be discerned:
10   Come build in the empty house of the stare.

A barricade of stone or of wood;
Some fourteen days of civil war;
Last night they trundled down the road
That dead young soldier in his blood:
15   Come build in the empty house of the stare.

We had fed the heart on fantasies,
The heart's grown brutal from the fare;
More substance in our enmities
Than in our love; O honey-bees,
20   Come build in the empty house of the stare.

7. I See Phantoms of Hatred and of the Heart's Fullness and of the Coming Emptiness

I climb to the tower-top and lean upon broken stone,
A mist that is like blown snow is sweeping over all,
Valley, river, and elms, under the light of a moon
That seems unlike itself, that seems unchangeable,
5   A glittering sword out of the east. A puff of wind
And those white glimmering fragments of the mist sweep by.
Frenzies bewilder, reveries perturb the mind;
Monstrous familiar images swim to the mind's eye.

"Vengeance upon the murderers," the cry goes up,
10   "Vengeance for Jacques Molay."[7] In cloud-pale rags, or in lace,

---

7. Jacques de Molay, Grand Master of the Knights Templar who was burned as a witch in 1314.

The rage-driven, rage-tormented, and rage-hungry troop,
Trooper belabouring trooper, biting at arm or at face,
Plunges towards nothing, arms and fingers spreading wide
For the embrace of nothing; and I, my wits astray

15 Because of all that senseless tumult, all but cried
For vengeance on the murderers of Jacques Molay.

Their legs long, delicate and slender, aquamarine their eyes,
Magical unicorns bear ladies on their backs.
The ladies close their musing eyes. No prophecies,

20 Remembered out of Babylonian almanacs,
Have closed the ladies' eyes, their minds are but a pool
Where even longing drowns under its own excess;
Nothing but stillness can remain when hearts are full
Of their own sweetness, bodies of their loveliness.

25 The cloud-pale unicorns, the eyes of aquamarine,
The quivering half-closed eyelids, the rags of cloud or of lace,
Or eyes that rage has brightened, arms it has made lean,
Give place to an indifferent multitude, give place
To brazen hawks. Nor self-delighting reverie,

30 Nor hate of what's to come, nor pity for what's gone,
Nothing but grip of claw, and the eye's complacency,
The innumerable clanging wings that have put out the moon.

I turn away and shut the door, and on the stair
Wonder how many times I could have proved my worth

35 In something that all others understand or share;
But O! ambitious heart, had such a proof drawn forth
A company of friends, a conscience set at ease,
It had but made us pine the more. The abstract joy,
The half-read wisdom of daemonic images,

40 Suffice the ageing man as once the growing boy.
1921   1928

Nineteen Hundred and Nineteen

Many ingenious lovely things are gone
That seemed sheer miracle to the multitude,
Protected from the circle of the moon
That pitches common things about. There stood

5 Amid the ornamental bronze and stone
An ancient image made of olive wood—
And gone are Phidias'[1] famous ivories
And all the golden grasshoppers and bees.

We too had many pretty toys when young;

10 A law indifferent to blame or praise,
To bribe or threat; habits that made old wrong
Melt down, as it were wax in the sun's rays;
Public opinion ripening for so long

1. A 5th-century B.C. Greek sculptor.

We thought it would outlive all future days.
15   O what fine thought we had because we thought
That the worst rogues and rascals had died out.

All teeth were drawn, all ancient tricks unlearned,
And a great army but a showy thing;
What matter that no cannon had been turned
20   Into a ploughshare? Parliament and king
Thought that unless a little powder burned
The trumpeters might burst with trumpeting
And yet it lack all glory; and perchance
The guardsmen's drowsy chargers would not prance.

25   Now days are dragon-ridden, the nightmare
Rides upon sleep: a drunken soldiery
Can leave the mother, murdered at her door,
To crawl in her own blood, and go scot-free;
The night can sweat with terror as before
30   We pieced our thoughts into philosophy,
And planned to bring the world under a rule,
Who are but weasels fighting in a hole.

He who can read the signs nor sink unmanned
Into the half-deceit of some intoxicant
35   From shallow wits; who knows no work can stand,
Whether health, wealth or peace of mind were spent
On master-work of intellect or hand,
No honour leave its mighty monument,
Has but one comfort left: all triumph would
40   But break upon his ghostly solitude.

But is there any comfort to be found?
Man is in love and loves what vanishes,
What more is there to say? That country round
None dared admit, if such a thought were his,
45   Incendiary or bigot could be found
To burn that stump on the Acropolis,
Or break in bits the famous ivories
Or traffic in the grasshoppers or bees.

2

When Loie Fuller's[2] Chinese dancers enwound
50   A shining web, a floating ribbon of cloth,
It seemed that a dragon of air
Had fallen among dancers, had whirled them round
Or hurried them off on its own furious path;
So the Platonic Year
55   Whirls out new right and wrong,
Whirls in the old instead;
All men are dancers and their tread
Goes to the barbarous clangour of a gong.

2. American dancer (1862–1928).

3

Some moralist or mythological poet[3]
60   Compares the solitary soul to a swan;
I am satisfied with that,
Satisfied if a troubled mirror show it,
Before that brief gleam of its life be gone,
An image of its state;
65   The wings half spread for flight,
The breast thrust out in pride
Whether to play, or to ride
Those winds that clamour of approaching night.

A man in his own secret mediation
70   Is lost amid the labyrinth that he has made
In art or politics;
Some Platonist affirms that in the station
Where we should cast off body and trade
The ancient habit sticks,
75   And that if our works could
But vanish with our breath
That were a lucky death,
For triumph can but mar our solitude.

The swan has leaped into the desolate heaven:
80   That image can bring wildness, bring a rage
To end all things, to end
What my laborious life imagined, even
The half-imagined, the half-written page;
O but we dreamed to mend
85   Whatever mischief seemed
To afflict mankind, but now
That winds of winter blow
Learn that we were crack-pated when we dreamed.

4

We, who seven years ago
90   Talked of honour and of truth,
Shriek with pleasure if we show
The weasel's twist, the weasel's tooth.

5

Come let us mock at the great
That had such burdens on the mind
95   And toiled so hard and late
To leave some monument behind,
Nor thought of the levelling wind.

Come let us mock at the wise;
With all those calendars whereon
100   They fixed old aching eyes,
They never saw how seasons run,
And now but gape at the sun.

3. Possibly Shelley in *Prometheus Unbound*, 2.5.72–74.

Come let us mock at the good
That fancied goodness might be gay,
105 And sick of solitude
Might proclaim a holiday:
Wind shrieked—and where are they?

Mock mockers after that
That would not lift a hand maybe
110 To help good, wise or great
To bar that foul storm out, for we
Traffic in mockery.

6

Violence upon the roads: violence of horses;
Some few have handsome riders, are garlanded
115 On delicate sensitive ear or tossing mane,
But wearied running round and round in their courses
All break and vanish, and evil gathers head:

Herodias' daughters have returned again,[4]
A sudden blast of dusty wind and after
120 Thunder of feet, tumult of images,
Their purpose in the labyrinth of the wind;
And should some crazy hand dare touch a daughter
All turn with amorous cries, or angry cries,
According to the wind, for all are blind.
125 But now wind drops, dust settles; thereupon
There lurches past, his great eyes without thought
Under the shadow of stupid straw-pale locks,
That insolent fiend Robert Artisson[5]
To whom the love-lorn Lady Kyteler brought
130 Bronzed peacock feathers, red combs of her cocks.

1919

Leda and the Swan[1]

A sudden blow: the great wings beating still
Above the staggering girl, her thighs caressed
By the dark webs, her nape caught in his bill,
He holds her helpless breast upon his breast.

5 How can those terrified vague fingers push
The feathered glory from her loosening thighs?
And how can body, laid in that white rush,
But feel the strange heart beating where it lies?

A shudder in the loins engenders there
10 The broken wall, the burning roof and tower

4. Herodias told her daughter Salome to ask Herod for the head of John the Baptist on a platter (Matthew 14.8).
5. An evil spirit much run after in Kilkenny at the start of the fourteenth century [Yeats's note]. He was said to have seduced Dame Alice Kyteler, who poisoned her husbands and was accused of sacrificing cocks and peacocks to him.
1. In Greek mythology, Zeus came to Leda in the form of a swan and raped her; Helen of Troy and Clytemnestra were their offspring.

And Agamemnon[2] dead.
                    Being so caught up,
So mastered by the brute blood of the air,
Did she put on his knowledge with his power
Before the indifferent beak could let her drop?

1923   1924

Among School Children

1

I walk through the long schoolroom questioning;
A kind old nun in a white hood replies;
The children learn to cipher and to sing,
To study reading-books and history,
To cut and sew, be neat in everything
In the best modern way—the children's eyes
In momentary wonder stare upon
A sixty-year-old smiling public man.

2

I dream of a Ledaean[1] body, bent
Above a sinking fire, a tale that she
Told of a harsh reproof, or trivial event
That changed some childish day to tragedy—
Told, and it seemed that our two natures blent
Into a sphere from youthful sympathy,
Or else, to alter Plato's parable,
Into the yolk and white of the one shell.[2]

3

And thinking of that fit of grief or rage
I look upon one child or t'other there
And wonder if she stood so at that age—
For even daughters of the swan can share
Something of every paddler's heritage—
And had that colour upon cheek or hair,
And thereupon my heart is driven wild:
She stands before me as a living child.

4

Her present image floats into the mind—
Did Quattrocento[3] finger fashion it
Hollow of cheek as though it drank the wind
And took a mess of shadows for its meat?
And I though never of Ledaean kind
Had pretty plumage once—enough of that,
Better to smile on all that smile, and show
There is a comfortable kind of old scarecrow.

---

2. Brother of Menelaus, husband of Helen. When she was abducted by Paris, Agamemnon fought to rescue her. He was murdered by his wife Clytemnestra on his return home.
1. Of Leda, the mother of Helen of Troy.

2. According to Plato's parable in the *Symposium*, male and female were once the two halves of a single body; it was subsequently cut in half like a hard-boiled egg.
3. Fifteenth-century artists of Italy's Renaissance.

5

What youthful mother, a shape upon her lap
Honey of generation had betrayed,
35   And that must sleep, shriek, struggle to escape
As recollection or the drug decide,
Would think her son, did she but see that shape
With sixty or more winters on its head,
A compensation for the pang of his birth,
40   Or the uncertainty of his setting forth?

6

Plato thought nature but a spume° that plays   *froth*
Upon a ghostly paradigm of things;
Solider Aristotle played the taws[4]
Upon the bottom of a king of kings;
45   World-famous golden-thighed Pythagoras[5]
Fingered upon a fiddle-stick or strings
What a star sang and careless Muses heard:
Old clothes upon old sticks to scare a bird.

7

Both nuns and mothers worship images,
50   But those the candles light are not as those
That animate a mother's reveries,
But keep a marble or a bronze repose.
And yet they too break hearts—O Presences
That passion, piety or affection knows,
55   And that all heavenly glory symbolise—
O self-born mockers of man's enterprise;

8

Labour is blossoming or dancing where
The body is not bruised to pleasure soul,
Nor beauty born out of its own despair,
60   Nor blear-eyed wisdom out of midnight oil.
O chestnut tree, great rooted blossomer,
Are you the leaf, the blossom or the bole?
O body swayed to music, O brightening glance,
How can we know the dancer from the dance?

1926   1927

Byzantium

The unpurged images of day recede;
The Emperor's drunken soldiery are abed;
Night resonance recedes, night-walkers' song
After great cathedral gong;
5   A starlit or a moonlit dome disdains
All that man is,
All mere complexities,
The fury and the mire of human veins.

4. A leather strap, used to spin a top.
5. A 6th-century B.C. Greek philosopher who developed a mathematical basis for the universe and music.

Before me floats an image, man or shade,
Shade more than man, more image than a shade;
For Hades' bobbin° bound in mummy-cloth   *spool*
May unwind the winding path;
A mouth that has no moisture and no breath
Breathless mouths may summon;
I hail the superhuman;
I call it death-in-life and life-in-death.

Miracle, bird or golden handiwork,
More miracle than bird or handiwork,
Planted on the starlit golden bough,
Can like the cocks of Hades crow,
Or, by the moon embittered, scorn aloud
In glory of changeless metal
Common bird or petal
And all complexities of mire or blood.

At midnight on the Emperor's pavement flit
Flames that no faggot° feeds, nor steel has lit,   *bundle of sticks*
Nor storm disturbs, flames begotten of flame,
Where blood-begotten spirits come
And all complexities of fury leave,
Dying into a dance,
An agony of trance,
An agony of flame that cannot singe a sleeve.

Astraddle on the dolphin's mire and blood,
Spirit after spirit! The smithies break the flood,
The golden smithies of the Emperor!
Marbles of the dancing floor
Break bitter furies of complexity,
Those images that yet
Fresh images beget,
That dolphin-torn, that gong-tormented sea.
1930   1932

10
15
20
25
30
35
40

Crazy Jane Talks with the Bishop

I met the Bishop on the road
And much said he and I.
"Those breasts are flat and fallen now
Those veins must soon be dry;
Live in a heavenly mansion,
Not in some foul sty."

"Fair and foul are near of kin,
And fair needs foul," I cried.
"My friends are gone, but that's a truth
Nor grave nor bed denied,
Learned in bodily lowliness
And in the heart's pride.

5
10

"A woman can be proud and stiff
When on love intent;
15   But Love has pitched his mansion in
The place of excrement;
For nothing can be sole or whole
That has not been rent."

1931   1932

Lapis Lazuli[1]

(For Harry Clifton[2])

I have heard that hysterical women say
They are sick of the palette and fiddle-bow,
Of poets that are always gay,
For everybody knows or else should know
5   That if nothing drastic is done
Aeroplane and Zeppelin will come out,
Pitch like King Billy bomb-balls[3] in
Until the town lie beaten flat.

All perform their tragic play,
10   There struts Hamlet, there is Lear,
That's Ophelia, that Cordelia;[4]
Yet they, should the last scene be there,
The great stage curtain about to drop,
If worthy their prominent part in the play,
15   Do not break up their lines to weep.
They know that Hamlet and Lear are gay;
Gaiety transfiguring all that dread.
All men have aimed at, found and lost;
Black out; Heaven blazing into the head:
20   Tragedy wrought to its uttermost.
Though Hamlet rambles and Lear rages,
And all the drop scenes drop at once
Upon a hundred thousand stages,
It cannot grow by an inch or an ounce.

25   On their own feet they came, or on shipboard,
Camel-back, horse-back, ass-back, mule-back,
Old civilisations put to the sword.
Then they and their wisdom went to rack:
No handiwork of Callimachus[5]
30   Who handled marble as if it were bronze,
Made draperies that seemed to rise
When sea-wind swept the corner, stands;
His long lamp chimney shaped like the stem
Of a slender palm, stood but a day;

1. A rich blue mineral producing the pigment ultramarine; used by the ancients for decoration.
2. A friend who gave Yeats a carving in lapis lazuli on his birthday.
3. German bombs; "King Billy" is a nickname for Kaiser Wilhelm II.
4. Characters from *Hamlet* and *King Lear*.
5. Greek poet, grammarian, critic, and sculptor (c. 310–c. 240 B.C.).

35 All things fall and are built again
    And those that build them again are gay.

    Two Chinamen, behind them a third,
    Are carved in Lapis Lazuli,
    Over them flies a long-legged bird
40 A symbol of longevity;
    The third, doubtless a serving-man,
    Carries a musical instrument.

    Every discolouration of the stone,
    Every accidental crack or dent
45 Seems a water-course or an avalanche,
    Or lofty slope where it still snows
    Though doubtless plum or cherry-branch
    Sweetens the little half-way house
    Those Chinamen climb towards, and I
50 Delight to imagine them seated there;
    There, on the mountain and the sky,
    On all the tragic scene they stare.
    One asks for mournful melodies;
    Accomplished fingers begin to play.
55 Their eyes mid many wrinkles, their eyes,
    Their ancient, glittering eyes, are gay.

1936   1938

The Circus Animals' Desertion

1

    I sought a theme and sought for it in vain,
    I sought it daily for six weeks or so.
    Maybe at last being but a broken man
    I must be satisfied with my heart, although
5   Winter and summer till old age began
    My circus animals were all on show,
    Those stilted boys, that burnished chariot,
    Lion and woman and the Lord knows what.

2

    What can I but enumerate old themes,
10 First that sea-rider Oisin[1] led by the nose
    Through three enchanted islands, allegorical dreams,
    Vain gaiety, vain battle, vain repose,
    Themes of the embittered heart, or so it seems,
    That might adorn old songs or courtly shows;
15 But what cared I that set him on to ride,
    I, starved for the bosom of his fairy bride.

    And then a counter-truth filled out its play,
    "The Countess Cathleen"[2] was the name I gave it,

---

1. Mythical Irish poet-warrior, son of the great Finn, who crossed the sea on an enchanted horse; hero of Yeats's early narrative poem The Wanderings of Oisin.

2. Yeats's play The Countess Cathleen (1899) tells the traditional story of Kathleen ni Houlihan, allegorical symbol of Ireland.

She, pity-crazed, had given her soul away
20   But masterful Heaven had intervened to save it.
I thought my dear must her own soul destroy
So did fanaticism and hate enslave it,
And this brought forth a dream and soon enough
This dream itself had all my thought and love.

25   And when the Fool and Blind Man stole the bread
Cuchulain[3] fought the ungovernable sea;
Heart mysteries there, and yet when all is said
It was the dream itself enchanted me:
Character isolated by a deed
30   To engross the present and dominate memory.
Players and painted stage took all my love
And not those things that they were emblems of.

3

Those masterful images because complete
Grew in pure mind but out of what began?
35   A mound of refuse or the sweepings of a street,
Old kettles, old bottles, and a broken can,
Old iron, old bones, old rags, that raving slut
Who keeps the till. Now that my ladder's gone
I must lie down where all the ladders start
40   In the foul rag and bone shop of the heart.

1939

Under Ben Bulben[1]

1

Swear by what the Sages spoke
Round the Mareotic Lake[2]
That the Witch of Atlas[3] knew,
Spoke and set the cocks a-crow.

5   Swear by those horsemen, by those women
Complexion and form prove superhuman,
That pale, long-visaged company
That airs an immortality
Completeness of their passions won;
10   Now they ride the wintry dawn
Where Ben Bulben sets the scene.

Here's the gist of what they mean.

2

Many times man lives and dies
Between his two eternities,
15   That of race and that of soul,

---

3. Hero of the medieval Irish epic *The Tain*, who single-
handedly defended Ulster.
1. A mountain in County Sligo.
2. An ancient region south of Alexandria, Egypt, known
as a center of Neoplatonism.
3. *The Witch of Atlas* is the title of a poem by Percy Shelley.

And ancient Ireland knew it all.
Whether man dies in his bed
Or the rifle knocks him dead,
A brief parting from those dear
20   Is the worst man has to fear.
Though grave-diggers' toil is long,
Sharp their spades, their muscle strong,
They but thrust their buried men
Back in the human mind again.

3

25   You that Mitchel's prayer have heard,
"Send war in our time, O Lord!"[4]
Know that when all words are said
And a man is fighting mad,
Something drops from eyes long blind,
30   He completes his partial mind,
For an instant stands at ease,
Laughs aloud, his heart at peace.
Even the wisest man grows tense
With some sort of violence
35   Before he can accomplish fate,
Know his work or choose his mate.

4

Poet and sculptor do the work,
Nor let the modish painter shirk
What his great forefathers did,
40   Bring the soul of man to God,
Make him fill the cradles right.

Measurement began our might:
Forms a stark Egyptian[5] thought,
Forms that gentler Phidias wrought.
45   Michael Angelo left a proof
On the Sistine Chapel roof,
Where but half-awakened Adam
Can disturb globe-trotting Madam
Till her bowels are in heat,
50   Proof that there's a purpose set
Before the secret working mind:
Profane perfection of mankind.

Quattrocento[6] put in paint
On backgrounds for a God or Saint
55   Gardens where a soul's at ease;
Where everything that meets the eye,

---

4. John Mitchel, revolutionary patriot, wrote "Give us war in our time, O Lord!" while in prison.
5. Plotinus, 3rd-century A.D. Egyptian-born philosopher, founder of Neoplatonism.
6. Fifteenth-century artists of Italy's Renaissance.

Flowers and grass and cloudless sky
Resemble forms that are, or seem
When sleepers wake and yet still dream,
60   And when it's vanished still declare,
With only bed and bedstead there,
That Heavens had opened.
                                    Gyres run on;
When that greater dream had gone
Calvert and Wilson, Blake and Claude,[7]
65   Prepared a rest for the people of God,
Palmer's phrase,[8] but after that
Confusion fell upon our thought.

5

Irish poets learn your trade,
Sing whatever is well made,
70   Scorn the sort now growing up
All out of shape from toe to top,
Their unremembering hearts and heads
Base-born products of base beds.
Sing the peasantry, and then
75   Hard-riding country gentlemen,
The holiness of monks, and after
Porter-drinkers' randy° laughter;   lusty
Sing the lords and ladies gay
That were beaten into the clay
80   Through seven heroic centuries;[9]
Cast your mind on other days
That we in coming days may be
Still the indomitable Irishry.

6

Under bare Ben Bulben's head
85   In Drumcliff[1] churchyard Yeats is laid.
An ancestor was rector there
Long years ago; a church stands near,
By the road an ancient cross.
No marble, no conventional phrase,
90   On limestone quarried near the spot
By his command these words are cut:

        Cast a cold eye
        On life, on death.
        Horseman, pass by!

1938   1939

---

7. Edward Calvert (1799–1883), English painter and engraver, disciple of Blake; Richard Wilson (1714–1782), British landscape painter; Claude Lorrain (1600–1682), French landscape painter.

8. Samuel Palmer (1805–1881), English painter of vision-

ary landscapes and admirer of Blake.

9. I.e., the seven centuries since the conquest of Ireland by Henry II.

1. A village lying on the slopes of Ben Bulben, where Yeats was buried.

James Joyce
1882–1941

James Joyce was one of the great innovators who brought the novel into the modern era. As T. S. Eliot put it, Joyce made "the modern world possible for art." The poet Edith Sitwell wrote that by the turn of the century, "language had become, not so much an abused medium, as a dead and outworn thing, in which there was no living muscular system. Then came the rebirth of the medium, and this was effected, as far as actual vocabularies were concerned, very largely by such prose writers as Mr. James Joyce and Miss Gertrude Stein." Joyce objected to this flaccidity, citing examples in the work of George Moore, the most important Irish novelist of the first decade of the twentieth; Moore's novel *The Untilled Field*, Joyce complained to his brother Stanislaus, was "damned stupid," "dull and flat" and "ill written." In a comment that would have pleased Joyce, one critic writing in 1929 declared that Joyce had by that date "conclusively reduced all the pretensions of the realistic novel to absurdity."

James Augustus Aloysius Joyce was born in Rathgar, a middle-class suburb of Dublin; though he was to leave Ireland more or less permanently at age twenty-two, Ireland generally, and "Dear Dirty Dublin" specifically, were never far from his mind and writing. He was the eldest surviving son in a large family consisting, according to his father, of "sixteen or seventeen children." His father, John Stanislaus Joyce, born and raised in Cork, was a tax collector and sometime Parnellite political employee; his mother was Mary Jane Joyce, née Murray. There is no better imaginative guide to the twists and turns of Joyce's family fortunes, and their effect on the young writer, than his first novel, *A Portrait of the Artist as a Young Man*; the life of Joyce's autobiographical hero Stephen Dedalus closely follows Joyce's own. The novel brings young Stephen from his earliest memories, through his Catholic schooling at Clongowes Wood College and Belvedere College, up to his graduation from University College, Dublin, and departure for Paris. Like Stephen, Joyce in these years first considered entering the priesthood, then began regarding Catholicism with increasing skepticism and irony, coming to view religion, family, and nation as three kinds of net or trap. One of the most important events of the early part of Joyce's life was the betrayal and subsequent death of "the uncrowned king of Ireland," Charles Stewart Parnell, the political leader who was working hard to make Home Rule for Ireland a reality; his demise, after his adulterous affair with Kitty O'Shea was discovered, was remembered by Joyce in his first poem, *Et Tu, Healy*—which he wrote at the age of eight—and in a haunting story, *Ivy Day in the Committee Room*. Joyce moved to Paris after graduation in 1902 and began medical studies, but he soon had to return to Dublin, as his mother was dying. Joyce gave up the idea of a medical career, which his father could not afford to finance in any event; he briefly tried teaching school, and sought to define himself as a writer.

Like Dedalus, the young Joyce first concentrated on writing poetry. The majority of his early poems were collected in the volume *Chamber Music* (1907); both the strength and weakness of the poems is suggested by the praise of Arthur Symons, who in his review in the *Nation* described the lyrics as "tiny, evanescent things." Poetry was ultimately to prove a dead end for Joyce; though he brought out one more volume of thirteen poems during his lifetime (*Pomes Penyeach*, 1927), and wrote one forgettable play (*Exiles*, 1918), prose fiction is the primary area in which Joyce's influence continues to be felt.

The year 1904 proved to be an absolute watershed in Joyce's development as a writer. In January 1904—indeed, perhaps in the single day 7 January 1904—Joyce wrote an impressionistic prose sketch which would ultimately serve as the manifesto for his first novel. From this beginning, Joyce shaped his novel, which was to have been called *Stephen Hero*; and though he worked on it steadily for more than three years, and the manuscript grew to almost a thousand pages, the novel was not coming together in quite the way Joyce had hoped. Hence in the fall of 1907, he began cutting and radically reshaping the material into what would become *A Portrait of the Artist as a Young Man*, one of the finest examples of the *Künstlerroman* (novel of artistic growth) in English; H. G. Wells called it "by far the most living and convincing picture that exists of an Irish Catholic upbringing."

June 16, 1904, in particular is a crucial day in the Joycean calendar, for it is "Bloomsday"—the day on which the events narrated in *Ulysses* take place—and according to legend, it is the day that Nora Barnacle first agreed to go out walking with Joyce. Joyce's father thought Nora's maiden name a good omen, suggesting that she would "stick to him," and indeed she did; without the benefit of marriage, she agreed to accompany him four months later on his artistic exile to the Continent, and though they were not legally married until 1931, she proved a faithful and devoted partner, a small spot of stability amidst the chaos of Joyce's life. They settled for several years in Trieste, Italy, where Joyce taught English at a Berlitz school and where their two children, Giorgio and Lucia, were born. Joyce returned briefly to Ireland in 1909, seeking unsuccessfully to get work published and to start a movie theater; after another brief visit in 1912, he never returned. He spent most of World War I in Zurich, then moved to Paris, where he eked out an existence with the help of several benefactors as his reputation began to grow.

He had begun his first book in June or July 1904, invited by the Irish man of letters "A.E." (George Russell) to submit a short story to his paper *The Irish Homestead*. Joyce began writing the series of fifteen stories that would be published in 1914 as *Dubliners*. In letters to London publisher Grant Richards about his conception for the short stories, Joyce wrote that he planned the volume to be a chapter of Ireland's "moral history" and that in writing it he had "taken the first step towards the spiritual liberation of my country." Richards, however, objected to the stark realism—or sordidness—of several scenes, and pressed Joyce to eliminate vulgarisms; Joyce refused. Finally, desperate to have the book published, Joyce wrote to Richards: "I seriously believe that you will retard the course of civilisation in Ireland by preventing the Irish people from having one good look at themselves in my nicely polished looking-glass."

During this period, Joyce also experimented with a form of short prose sketch that he called the "epiphany." An epiphany, as it is defined in *Stephen Hero*, is "a sudden spiritual manifestation, whether in the vulgarity of speech or of gesture or in a memorable phase of the mind itself." It consequently falls to the artist to "record these epiphanies with extreme care, seeing that they themselves are the most delicate and evanescent of moments." One benefit of Joyce's experimentation with prose epiphanies is that the searching realism and psychological richness of the stories in *Dubliners* are conveyed with a lucid economy of phrasing—what Joyce called "a style of scrupulous meanness"—and by a similar penchant for understatement on the level of plot. The stories often seem to "stop," rather than end; time and again, Joyce withholds the tidy conclusion that conventional fiction had trained readers to expect. In story after story, characters betray what Joyce termed their "paralysis"—a paralysis of the will that prevents them from breaking out of deadening habit. The final story of the collection, *The Dead*—written after the volume had ostensibly been completed, and comprising a broader scope and larger cast of characters than the other stories—is Joyce's finest work of short fiction, and justly praised as one of the great stories of our time; it was filmed, quite sensitively and beautifully, by director John Huston, the last film project before his death.

A second decisive year for Joyce was 1914. Having completed *Dubliners*, Joyce seems never to have thought seriously about writing short fiction again; and throughout the period he was writing his stories, he continued to work on *A Portrait*. As was the case with *Dubliners*, negotiations for the publication of *A Portrait* were extremely difficult; despite its dazzling language, few editors could get beyond the opening pages, with their references to bedwetting and their use of crude slang. Even though the novel had been published serially in *The Egoist* beginning in 1914, and was praised by influential writers like W. B. Yeats, H. G. Wells, and Ezra Pound, the book was rejected by every publisher in London to whom Joyce offered it, before finally being accepted by B. W. Huebsch in New York, and published in December 1916.

With both his stories and his first novel between hard covers, Joyce was finally able to concentrate his energies on the one novel for which, more than any other, he will be remembered—*Ulysses*; that work, too, had begun in 1914. The novel is structured, loosely, on eighteen episodes from Homer's *Odyssey*; Leopold Bloom, advertising salesman, is a modern-day Ulysses, the streets of Dublin his Aegean Sea, and Molly Bloom his (unfaithful) Penelope. Stephen Dedalus, stuck teaching school and estranged from his real father, is an unwitting Telemachus (Ulysses' son) in search of a father. Critics have disagreed over the years as to how seriously readers should take these Homeric parallels; Eliot understood them to be of the utmost importance—"a way of controlling, of ordering, of giving a shape and a significance to the immense panorama of futility and anarchy which is contemporary history"—while the equally supportive Pound suggested that the parallel structure was merely "the remains of a medieval allegorical culture; it matters little, it is a question of cooking, which does not restrict the action, nor inconvenience it, nor harm the realism, nor the contemporaneity of the action."

Concomitant with the Homeric structure, Joyce sought to give each of his eighteen chapters its own style. Chapter 12, focusing on Bloom's encounter with Dublin's Cyclops, called "the Citizen," is written in a style of "gigantism"—full of mock-epic epithets and catalogues, playfully suggestive of the style of ancient Celtic myth and legend. Chapter 13, which parallels Odysseus's encounter with Nausicäa, is written in the exaggerated style of Victorian women's magazines and sentimental fiction, a style which Joyce characterized as "a namby-pamby jammy marmalady drawersy (alto-là!) style with effects of incense, mariolatry, masturbation, stewed cockles, painter's palette, chitchat, circumlocutions, etc etc." While realist writers sought constantly to flush artifice from their writing, to arrive finally at a style which would be value-neutral, Joyce takes the English language on a voyage in the opposite direction; each chapter, as he wrote to his patron Harriet Shaw Weaver, left behind it "a burnt-up field." It would be difficult to overestimate the influence that *Ulysses* has had on modern writing; Eliot's candid response to the novel, reported in a letter to Joyce, was "I have nothing but admiration; in fact, I wish, for my own sake, that I had not read it."

Other people wanted to make sure that no one else would read it. *Ulysses* was promptly banned as obscene, in Ireland, England, and many other countries. Copies were smuggled into the United States, where a pirated edition was published, paying Joyce no royalties. Finally in 1933, in a landmark decision, a federal judge found that the book's frank language and sexual discussions were fully justified artistically—though he allowed that "*Ulysses* is a rather strong draught to ask some sensitive, though normal, persons to take."

In 1923, with *Ulysses* published, Joyce suddenly reinvented himself and his writing once again, and turned his attention to the writing of the novel that would occupy him almost until his death—*Finnegans Wake*. If *Ulysses* attacks the novel form at the level of style, *Finnegans Wake* targets the very structures of the English language. The story, in its broad outlines, is adapted from a vaudeville music-hall number, "Finnegan's Wake"; the novel's "protagonist," called by myriad names most of which bear the initials H.C.E. (Humphrey Chimpden Earwicker, Here Comes Everybody), has fallen in a drunken stupor, and the content of his dream is, apparently, the novel we read. But since the book is a night book, so Joyce felt that the language must be a night language, a meeting-place of dream and desire, rather than the straightforward language of the day. The novel's language is a neologismic amalgam of more than a dozen modern and ancient languages—a hybrid that devotees call "Wakese"; when questioned as to the wisdom of such a strategy, Joyce replied that *Ulysses* had proved English to be inadequate. "I'd like a language," he told his friend Stefan Zweig, "which is above all languages, a language to which all will do service. I cannot express myself in English without enclosing myself in a tradition." Though *Finnegans Wake* is of a complexity to frustrate even some of Joyce's most ardent admirers, interest in the novel has, if anything, increased in the wake of poststructuralist criticism, and shows no signs of letting up soon.

On 13 January 1941, Joyce died of a perforated ulcer; his illness and death almost certainly owed something to an adult life of rather heavy drinking. Though his oeuvre consists largely of one volume of short stories and three novels, his importance for students of modern literature is extraordinary. As Richard Ellmann writes at the opening of his magisterial biography, "We are still learning to be James Joyce's contemporaries, to understand our interpreter."

from DUBLINERS
Eveline

She sat at the window watching the evening invade the avenue. Her head was leaned against the window curtains and in her nostrils was the odour of dusty cretonne.[1] She was tired.

Few people passed. The man out of the last house passed on his way home; she heard his footsteps clacking along the concrete pavement and afterwards crunching on the cinder path before the new red houses. One time there used to be a field there in which they used to play every evening with other people's children. Then a man from Belfast bought the field and built houses in it—not like their little brown houses but bright brick houses with shining roofs. The children of the avenue used to play together in that field—the Devines, the Waters, the Dunns, little Keogh the cripple, she and her brothers and sisters. Ernest, however, never played: he was too grown up. Her father used often to hunt them in out of the field with his blackthorn stick; but usually little Keogh used to keep *nix*[2] and call out when he saw her father coming. Still they seemed to have been rather happy then. Her father was not so bad then; and besides, her mother was alive. That was a long time ago; she and her brothers and sisters were all grown up; her mother was dead. Tizzie Dunn was dead, too, and the Waters had gone back to England. Everything changes. Now she was going to go away like the others, to leave her home.

Home! She looked round the room, reviewing all its familiar objects which she had dusted once a week for so many years, wondering where on earth all the dust came from. Perhaps she would never see again those familiar objects from which she had never dreamed of being divided. And yet during all those years she had never found out the name of the priest whose yellowing photograph hung on the wall above the broken harmonium[3] beside the coloured print of the promises made to Blessed Margaret Mary Alacoque.[4] He had been a school friend of her father. Whenever he showed the photograph to a visitor her father used to pass it with a casual word:

—He is in Melbourne now.

She had consented to go away, to leave her home. Was that wise? She tried to weigh each side of the question. In her home anyway she had shelter and food; she had those whom she had known all her life about her. Of course she had to work hard both in the house and at business. What would they say of her in the Stores when they found out that she had run away with a fellow? Say she was a fool, perhaps; and her place would be filled up by advertisement. Miss Gavan would be glad. She had always had an edge on her, especially whenever there were people listening.

—Miss Hill, don't you see these ladies are waiting?

—Look lively, Miss Hill, please.

1. Heavy cotton fabric.
2. To serve as a lookout.
3. A small reed organ.
4. Catholic saint who took a vow of chastity at age four and carved the name "Jesus" into her chest with a knife as an adolescent. In 1673 she experienced a series of revelations; these resulted in the founding of the Devotion to the Sacred Heart of Jesus.

She would not cry many tears at leaving the Stores.

But in her new home, in a distant unknown country, it would not be like that. Then she would be married—she, Eveline. People would treat her with respect then. She would not be treated as her mother had been. Even now, though she was over nineteen, she sometimes felt herself in danger of her father's violence. She knew it was that that had given her the palpitations. When they were growing up he had never gone for her, like he used to go for Harry and Ernest, because she was a girl; but latterly he had begun to threaten her and say what he would do to her only for her dead mother's sake. And now she had nobody to protect her. Ernest was dead and Harry, who was in the church decorating business, was nearly always down somewhere in the country. Besides, the invariable squabble for money on Saturday nights had begun to weary her unspeakably. She always gave her entire wages—seven shillings—and Harry always sent up what he could but the trouble was to get any money from her father. He said she used to squander the money, that she had no head, that he wasn't going to give her his hard-earned money to throw about the streets, and much more, for he was usually fairly bad of a Saturday night. In the end he would give her the money and ask her had she any intention of buying Sunday's dinner. Then she had to rush out as quickly as she could and do her marketing, holding her black leather purse tightly in her hand as she elbowed her way through the crowds and returning home late under her load of provisions. She had hard work to keep the house together and to see that the two young children who had been left to her charge went to school regularly and got their meals regularly. It was hard work—a hard life—but now that she was about to leave it she did not find it a wholly undesirable life.

She was about to explore another life with Frank. Frank was very kind, manly, open-hearted. She was to go away with him by the night-boat to be his wife and to live with him in Buenos Ayres where he had a home waiting for her. How well she remembered the first time she had seen him; he was lodging in a house on the main road where she used to visit. It seemed a few weeks ago. He was standing at the gate, his peaked cap pushed back on his head and his hair tumbled forward over a face of bronze. Then they had come to know each other. He used to meet her outside the Stores every evening and see her home. He took her to see *The Bohemian Girl*[5] and she felt elated as she sat in an unaccustomed part of the theatre with him. He was awfully fond of music and sang a little. People knew that they were courting and, when he sang about the lass that loves a sailor, she always felt pleasantly confused. He used to call her Poppens out of fun. First of all it had been an excitement for her to have a fellow and then she had begun to like him. He had tales of distant countries. He had started as a deck boy at a pound a month on a ship of the Allan Line going out to Canada. He told her the names of the ships he had been on and the names of the different services. He had sailed through the Straits of Magellan and he told her stories of the terrible Patagonians.[6] He had fallen on his feet in Buenos Ayres, he said, and had come over to the old country just for a holiday. Of course, her father had found out the affair and had forbidden her to have anything to say to him.

—I know these sailor chaps, he said.

One day he had quarrelled with Frank and after that she had to meet her lover secretly.

---

5. An opera (1843) by Irish composer Michael William Balfe, based on a tale by Cervantes about a rich girl kid-napped by gypsies and an exiled nobleman.
6. Native peoples of Southern Argentina.

The evening deepened in the avenue. The white of two letters in her lap grew indistinct. One was to Harry; the other was to her father. Ernest had been her favorite but she liked Harry too. Her father was becoming old lately, she noticed; he would miss her. Sometimes he could be very nice. Not long before, when she had been laid up for a day, he had read her out a ghost story and made toast for her at the fire. Another day, when their mother was alive, they had all gone for a picnic to the Hill of Howth.[7] She remembered her father putting on her mother's bonnet to make the children laugh.

Her time was running out but she continued to sit by the window, leaning her head against the window curtain, inhaling the odour of dusty cretonne. Down far in the avenue she could hear a street organ playing. She knew the air.[8] Strange that it should come that very night to remind her of the promise to her mother, her promise to keep the home together as long as she could. She remembered the last night of her mother's illness; she was again in the close dark room at the other side of the hall and outside she heard a melancholy air of Italy. The organ-player had been ordered to go away and given sixpence. She remembered her father strutting back into the sick-room saying:

—Damned Italians! coming over here!

As she mused the pitiful vision of her mother's life laid its spell on the very quick of her being—that life of commonplace sacrifices closing in final craziness. She trembled as she heard again her mother's voice saying constantly with foolish insistence:

—Derevaun Seraun! Derevaun Seraun![9]

She stood up in a sudden impulse of terror. Escape! She must escape! Frank would save her. He would give her life, perhaps love, too. But she wanted to live. Why should she be unhappy? She had a right to happiness. Frank would take her in his arms, fold her in his arms. He would save her.

She stood among the swaying crowd in the station at the North Wall.[1] He held her hand and she knew that he was speaking to her, saying something about the passage over and over again. The station was full of soldiers with brown baggages. Through the wide doors of the sheds she caught a glimpse of the black mass of the boat, lying in beside the quay wall, with illumined portholes. She answered nothing. She felt her cheek pale and cold and, out of a maze of distress, she prayed to God to direct her, to show her what was her duty. The boat blew a long mournful whistle into the mist. If she went, to-morrow she would be on the sea with Frank, steaming toward Buenos Ayres. Their passage had been booked. Could she still draw back after all he had done for her? Her distress awoke a nausea in her body and she kept moving her lips in silent fervent prayer.

A bell clanged upon her heart. She felt him seize her hand:

—Come!

All the seas of the world tumbled about her heart. He was drawing her into them: he would drown her. She gripped with both hands at the iron railing.

—Come!

No! No! No! It was impossible. Her hands clutched the iron in frenzy. Amid the seas she sent a cry of anguish!

7. Northeast of Dublin, the hill dominates Dublin Bay.
8. Tune.
9. Though some commentators have suggested the phrase is Irish, it seems more likely to be incoherent nonsense.

1. A point of embarkation in Dublin for passenger ships—but those, as critic Hugh Kenner points out, heading for Liverpool, not Buenos Aires.

—Eveline! Evvy!

He rushed beyond the barrier and called to her to follow. He was shouted at to go on but he still called to her. She set her white face to him, passive, like a helpless animal. Her eyes gave him no sign of love or farewell or recognition.

Clay

The matron had given her leave to go out as soon as the women's tea was over and Maria looked forward to her evening out. The kitchen was spick and span: the cook said you could see yourself in the big copper boilers. The fire was nice and bright and on one of the side-tables were four very big barmbracks.[1] These barmbracks seemed uncut; but if you went closer you would see that they had been cut into long thick even slices and were ready to be handed round at tea. Maria had cut them herself.

Maria was a very, very small person indeed but she had a very long nose and a very long chin. She talked a little through her nose, always soothingly: Yes, my dear, and No, my dear. She was always sent for when the women quarrelled over their tubs and always succeeded in making peace. One day the matron had said to her:

—Maria, you are a veritable peace-maker!

And the sub-matron and two of the Board ladies[2] had heard the compliment. And Ginger Mooney was always saying what she wouldn't do to the dummy[3] who had charge of the irons if it wasn't for Maria. Everyone was so fond of Maria.

The women would have their tea at six o'clock and she would be able to get away before seven. From Ballsbridge to the Pillar, twenty minutes; from the Pillar to Drumcondra, twenty minutes; and twenty minutes to buy the things. She would be there before eight. She took out her purse with the silver clasps and read again the words A Present from Belfast. She was very fond of that purse because Joe had brought it to her five years before when he and Alphy had gone to Belfast on a Whit-Monday[4] trip. In the purse were two half-crowns and some coppers. She would have five shillings clear after paying tram fare. What a nice evening they would have, all the children singing! Only she hoped that Joe wouldn't come in drunk. He was so different when he took any drink.

Often he had wanted her to go and live with them; but she would have felt herself in the way (though Joe's wife was ever so nice with her) and she had become accustomed to the life of the laundry. Joe was a good fellow. She had nursed him and Alphy too; and Joe used often say:

—Mamma is mamma but Maria is my proper mother.

After the break-up at home the boys had got her that position in the Dublin by Lamplight laundry,[5] and she liked it. She used to have such a bad opinion of Protestants but now she thought they were very nice people, a little quiet and serious, but still very nice people to live with. Then she had her plants in the conservatory and she liked looking after them. She had lovely ferns and wax-plants and, whenever anyone came to visit her, she always gave the visitor one or two slips from her conservatory. There was one thing she didn't like and that was the tracts[6] on the walls; but the matron was such a nice person to deal with, so genteel.

---

1. Speckled cakes or currant buns.
2. Members of the governing board of the Dublin by Lamplight Laundry.
3. Slang for a mute person.
4. Holiday following Whitsunday, the seventh Sunday after Easter.

5. Joyce's invented benevolent society, run by Protestant women, "saves" Dublin's prostitutes from a life on the streets by giving them honest work in a laundry. Maria works for the laundry but appears not to be a reformed prostitute herself.
6. Evangelical religious texts.

When the cook told her everything was ready she went into the women's room and began to pull the big bell. In a few minutes the women began to come in by twos and threes, wiping their steaming hands in their petticoats and pulling down the sleeves of their blouses over their red steaming arms. They settled down before their huge mugs which the cook and the dummy filled up with hot tea, already mixed with milk and sugar in huge tin cans. Maria superintended the distribution of the barm-brack and saw that every woman got her four slices. There was a great deal of laugh-ing and joking during the meal. Lizzie Fleming said Maria was sure to get the ring and, though Fleming had said that for so many Hallow Eves, Maria had to laugh and say she didn't want any ring or man either; and when she laughed her grey-green eyes sparkled with disappointed shyness and the tip of her nose nearly met the tip of her chin. Then Ginger Mooney lifted up her mug of tea and proposed Maria's health while all the other women clattered with their mugs on the table, and said she was sorry she hadn't a sup of porter[7] to drink it in. And Maria laughed again till the tip of her nose nearly met the tip of her chin and till her minute body nearly shook itself asunder because she knew that Mooney meant well though, of course, she had the notions of a common woman.

But wasn't Maria glad when the women had finished their tea and the cook and the dummy had begun to clear away the tea-things! She went into her little bedroom and, remembering that the next morning was a mass morning, changed the hand of the alarm from seven to six. Then she took off her working skirt and her house-boots and laid her best skirt out on the bed and her tiny dress-boots beside the foot of the bed. She changed her blouse too and, as she stood before the mirror, she thought of how she used to dress for mass on Sunday morning when she was a young girl; and she looked with quaint affection at the diminutive body which she had so often adorned. In spite of its years she found it a nice tidy little body.

When she got outside the streets were shining with rain and she was glad of her old brown raincloak. The tram was full and she had to sit on the little stool at the end of the car, facing all the people, with her toes barely touching the floor. She arranged in her mind all she was going to do and thought how much better it was to be independent and to have your own money in your pocket. She hoped they would have a nice evening. She was sure they would but she could not help thinking what a pity it was Alphy and Joe were not speaking. They were always falling out now but when they were boys together they used to be the best of friends: but such was life.

She got out of her tram at the Pillar and ferreted her way quickly among the crowds. She went into Downes's cakeshop but the shop was so full of people that it was a long time before she could get herself attended to. She bought a dozen of mixed penny cakes, and at last came out of the shop laden with a big bag. Then she thought what else would she buy: she wanted to buy something really nice. They would be sure to have plenty of apples and nuts. It was hard to know what to buy and all she could think of was cake. She decided to buy some plumcake but Downes's plumcake had not enough almond icing on top of it so she went over to a shop in Henry Street. Here she was a long time in suiting herself and the stylish young lady behind the counter, who was evidently a little annoyed by her, asked her was it wedding-cake she wanted to buy. That made Maria blush and smile at the young lady; but the young lady took it all very seriously and finally cut a thick slice of plumcake, par-celled it up and said:

7. A heavy, dark brown ale.

—Two-and-four, please.

She thought she would have to stand in the Drumcondra tram because none of the young men seemed to notice her but an elderly gentleman made room for her. He was a stout gentleman and he wore a brown hard hat; he had a square red face and a greyish moustache. Maria thought he was a colonel-looking gentleman and she reflected how much more polite he was than the young men who simply stared straight before them. The gentleman began to chat with her about Hallow Eve and the rainy weather. He supposed the bag was full of good things for the little ones and said it was only right that the youngsters should enjoy themselves while they were young. Maria agreed with him and favoured him with demure nods and hems. He was very nice with her, and when she was getting out at the Canal Bridge she thanked him and bowed, and he bowed to her and raised his hat and smiled agreeably; and while she was going up along the terrace, bending her tiny head under the rain, she thought how easy it was to know a gentleman even when he has a drop taken.

Everybody said: O, here's Maria! when she came to Joe's house. Joe was there, having come home from business, and all the children had their Sunday dresses on. There were two big girls in from next door and games were going on. Maria gave the bag of cakes to the eldest boy, Alphy, to divide and Mrs Donnelly said it was too good of her to bring such a big bag of cakes and made all the children say:

—Thanks, Maria.

But Maria said she had brought something special for papa and mamma, something they would be sure to like, and she began to look for her plumcake. She tried in Downes's bag and then in the pockets of her raincloak and then on the hallstand but nowhere could she find it. Then she asked all the children had any of them eaten it—by mistake, of course—but the children all said no and looked as if they did not like to eat cakes if they were to be accused of stealing. Everybody had a solution for the mystery and Mrs Donnelly said it was plain that Maria had left it behind her in the tram. Maria, remembering how confused the gentleman with the greyish moustache had made her, coloured with shame and vexation and disappointment. At the thought of the failure of her little surprise and of the two and fourpence she had thrown away for nothing she nearly cried outright.

But Joe said it didn't matter and made her sit down by the fire. He was very nice with her. He told her all that went on in his office, repeating for her a smart answer which he had made to the manager. Maria did not understand why Joe laughed so much over the answer he had made but she said that the manager must have been a very overbearing person to deal with. Joe said he wasn't so bad when you knew how to take him, that he was a decent sort so long as you didn't rub him the wrong way. Mrs Donnelly played the piano for the children and they danced and sang. Then the two next-door girls handed round the nuts. Nobody could find the nutcrackers and Joe was nearly getting cross over it and asked how did they expect Maria to crack nuts without a nutcracker. But Maria said she didn't like nuts and that they weren't to bother about her. Then Joe asked would she take a bottle of stout[8] and Mrs Donnelly said there was port wine too in the house if she would prefer that. Maria said she would rather they didn't ask her to take anything: but Joe insisted.

So Maria let him have his way and they sat by the fire talking over old times and Maria thought she would put in a good word for Alphy. But Joe cried that God might strike him stone dead if ever he spoke a word to his brother again and Maria said she

---

8. An extra-strength ale.

was sorry she had mentioned the matter. Mrs Donnelly told her husband it was a great shame for him to speak that way of his own flesh and blood but Joe said that Alphy was no brother of his and there was nearly being a row[9] on the head of it. But Joe said he would not lose his temper on account of the night it was and asked his wife to open some more stout. The two next-door girls had arranged some Hallow Eve games[1] and soon everything was merry again. Maria was delighted to see the children so merry and Joe and his wife in such good spirits. The next-door girls put some saucers on the table and then led the children up to the table, blindfold. One got the prayer-book and the other three got the water; and when one of the next-door girls got the ring Mrs Donnelly shook her finger at the blushing girl as much as to say: O, I know all about it! They insisted then on blindfolding Maria and leading her up to the table to see what she would get; and, while they were putting on the bandage, Maria laughed and laughed again till the tip of her nose nearly met the tip of her chin.

They led her up to the table amid laughing and joking and she put her hand out in the air as she was told to do. She moved her hand about here and there in the air and descended on one of the saucers. She felt a soft wet substance with her fingers and was surprised that nobody spoke or took off her bandage. There was a pause for a few seconds; and then a great deal of scuffling and whispering. Somebody said something about the garden, and at last Mrs Donnelly said something very cross to one of the next-door girls and told her to throw it out at once: that was no play. Maria understood that it was wrong that time and so she had to do it over again: and this time she got the prayer-book.

After that Mrs Donnelly played Miss McCloud's Reel for the children and Joe made Maria take a glass of wine. Soon they were all quite merry again and Mrs Donnelly said Maria would enter a convent before the year was out because she had got the prayer-book. Maria had never seen Joe so nice to her as he was that night, so full of pleasant talk and reminiscences. She said they were all very good to her.

At last the children grew tired and sleepy and Joe asked Maria would she not sing some little song before she went, one of the old songs. Mrs Donnelly said Do, please, Maria! and so Maria had to get up and stand beside the piano. Mrs Donnelly bade the children be quiet and listen to Maria's song. Then she played the prelude and said Now, Maria! and Maria, blushing very much, began to sing in a tiny quavering voice. She sang I Dreamt that I Dwelt,[2] and when she came to the second verse she sang again:

> I dreamt that I dwelt in marble halls
>> With vassals and serfs at my side
> And of all who assembled within those walls
>> That I was the hope and the pride.
> I had riches too great to count, could boast
>> Of a high ancestral name,
> But I also dreamt, which pleased me most,
>> That you loved me still the same.

9. Argument.
1. The primary game that Maria and the girls play is a traditional Irish Halloween game. In its original version, a blindfolded girl would be led to three plates, and would choose one. Choosing the plate with a ring meant that she would soon marry; water meant she would emigrate

(probably to America); and soil, or clay, meant she would soon die. In modern times, a prayer book was substituted for this unsavory third option, suggesting that the girl would enter a convent.
2. Aria from Act 2 of The Bohemian Girl.

But no one tried to show her her mistake;[3] and when she had ended her song Joe was very much moved. He said that there was no time like the long ago and no music for him like poor old Balfe, whatever other people might say; and his eyes filled up so much with tears that he could not find what he was looking for and in the end he had to ask his wife to tell him where the corkscrew was.

Ivy Day in the Committee Room[1]

Old Jack raked the cinders together with a piece of cardboard and spread them judiciously over the whitening dome of coals. When the dome was thinly covered his face lapsed into darkness but, as he set himself to fan the fire again, his crouching shadow ascended the opposite wall and his face slowly re-emerged into light. It was an old man's face, very bony and hairy. The moist blue eyes blinked at the fire and the moist mouth fell open at times, munching once or twice mechanically when it closed. When the cinders had caught he laid the piece of cardboard against the wall, sighed and said:

—That's better now, Mr O'Connor.

Mr O'Connor, a grey-haired young man, whose face was disfigured by many blotches and pimples, had just brought the tobacco for a cigarette into a shapely cylinder but when spoken to he undid his handiwork meditatively. Then he began to roll the tobacco again meditatively and after a moment's thought decided to lick the paper.

—Did Mr Tierney say when he'd be back? he asked in a husky falsetto.

—He didn't say.

Mr O'Connor put his cigarette into his mouth and began to search his pockets. He took out a pack of thin paste-board cards.

—I'll get you a match, said the old man.

—Never mind, this'll do, said Mr O'Connor.

He selected one of the cards and read what was printed on it:

Municipal Elections

ROYAL EXCHANGE WARD[2]

Mr Richard J. Tierney, P.L.G.,[3] respectfully
solicits the favour of your vote
and influence at the coming election
in the Royal Exchange Ward

Mr O'Connor had been engaged by Mr Tierney's agent to canvass one part of the ward but, as the weather was inclement and his boots let in the wet, he spent a great part of the day sitting by the fire in the Committee Room in Wicklow Street with Jack, the old caretaker. They had been sitting thus since the short day had grown dark. It was the sixth of October, dismal and cold out of doors.

---

3. Maria repeats the first verse rather than singing the second.

1. On October 6—the anniversary of Parnell's death—it was customary among his followers to wear a sprig of ivy in his honor; Committee Room No. 15 was the scene of Parnell's emotional final speech as leader of the Irish par-

liamentary party (see page 2299). Parnell's betrayal and demise form the backdrop of the story; the other personages are fictional.

2. A political ward near the center of Dublin.

3. Poor Law Guardian, elected to oversee the local relief rolls.

Mr O'Connor tore a strip off the card and, lighting it, lit his cigarette. As he did so the flame lit up a leaf of dark glossy ivy in the lapel of his coat. The old man watched him attentively and then, taking up the piece of cardboard again, began to fan the fire slowly while his companion smoked.

—Ah, yes, he said, continuing, it's hard to know what way to bring up children. Now who'd think he'd turn out like that! I sent him to the Christian Brothers[4] and I done what I could for him, and there he goes boosing about. I tried to make him someway decent.

He replaced the cardboard wearily.

—Only I'm an old man now I'd change his tune for him. I'd take the stick to his back and beat him while I could stand over him—as I done many a time before. The mother, you know, she cocks him up with this and that. . . .

—That's what ruins children, said Mr O'Connor.

—To be sure it is, said the old man. And little thanks you get for it, only impudence. He takes th'upper hand of me whenever he sees I've a sup taken. What's the world coming to when sons speaks that way of their father?

—What age is he? said Mr O'Connor.

—Nineteen, said the old man.

—Why don't you put him to something?[5]

—Sure, amn't I never done at the drunken bowsy ever since he left school? *I won't keep you,* I says. *You must get a job for yourself.* But, sure, it's worse whenever he gets a job; he drinks it all.

Mr O'Connor shook his head in sympathy, and the old man fell silent, gazing into the fire. Someone opened the door of the room and called out:

—Hello! Is this a Freemason's[6] meeting?

—Who's that? said the old man.

—What are you doing in the dark? asked a voice.

—Is that you, Hynes? asked Mr O'Connor.

—Yes. What are you doing in the dark? said Mr Hynes, advancing into the light of the fire.

He was a tall slender young man with a light brown moustache. Imminent little drops of rain hung at the brim of his hat and the collar of his jacket-coat was turned up.

—Well, Mat, he said to Mr O'Connor, how goes it?

Mr O'Connor shook his head. The old man left the hearth and, after stumbling about the room returned with two candlesticks which he thrust one after the other into the fire and carried to the table. A denuded room came into view and the fire lost all its cheerful colour. The walls of the room were bare except for a copy of an election address. In the middle of the room was a small table on which papers were heaped.

Mr Hynes leaned against the mantelpiece and asked:

—Has he paid you yet?

—Not yet, said Mr O'Connor. I hope to God he'll not leave us in the lurch to-night.

Mr Hynes laughed.

—O, he'll pay you. Never fear, he said.

—I hope he'll look smart about it if he means business, said Mr O'Connor.

---

4. The Irish Christian Brothers, a conservative Catholic order, operate a number of day schools throughout Ireland.

5. I.e., get him a job.

6. A worldwide secret, fraternal order.

—What do you think, Jack? said Mr Hynes satirically to the old man.

The old man returned to his seat by the fire, saying:

—It isn't but he has it, anyway. Not like the other tinker.[7]

—What other tinker? said Mr Hynes.

—Colgan, said the old man scornfully.

—Is it because Colgan's a working-man you say that? What's the difference between a good honest bricklayer and a publican[8]—eh? Hasn't the working-man as good a right to be in the Corporation[9] as anyone else—ay, and a better right than those shoneens[1] that are always hat in hand before any fellow with a handle to his name? Isn't that so, Mat? said Mr. Hynes, addressing Mr O'Connor.

—I think you're right, said Mr O'Connor.

—One man is a plain honest man with no hunker-sliding[2] about him. He goes in to represent the labour classes. This fellow you're working for only wants to get some job or other.

—Of course, the working-classes should be represented, said the old man.

—The working-man, said Mr Hynes, gets all kicks and no halfpence. But it's labour produces everything. The working-man is not looking for fat jobs for his sons and nephews and cousins. The working-man is not going to drag the honour of Dublin in the mud to please a German monarch.[3]

—How's that? said the old man.

—Don't you know they want to present an address of welcome to Edward Rex if he comes here next year? What do we want kowtowing to a foreign king?

—Our man won't vote for the address, said Mr O'Connor. He goes in on the Nationalist ticket.

—Won't he? said Mr Hynes. Wait till you see whether he will or not. I know him. Is it Tricky Dicky Tierney?

—By God! perhaps you're right, Joe, said Mr O'Connor. Anyway, I wish he'd turn up with the spondulics.[4]

The three men fell silent. The old man began to rake more cinders together. Mr Hynes took off his hat, shook it and then turned down the collar of his coat, displaying, as he did so, an ivy leaf in the lapel.

—If this man was alive, he said, pointing to the leaf, we'd have no talk of an address of welcome.

—That's true, said Mr O'Connor.

—Musha, God be with them times! said the old man. There was some life in it then.

The room was silent again. Then a bustling little man with a snuffling nose and very cold ears pushed in the door. He walked over quickly to the fire, rubbing his hands as if he intended to produce a spark from them.

—No money, boys, he said.

—Sit down here, Mr Henchy, said the old man, offering him his chair.

—O, don't stir, Jack, don't stir, said Mr Henchy.

He nodded curtly to Mr Hynes and sat down on the chair which the old man vacated.

—Did you serve Aungier Street? he asked Mr O'Connor.

---

7. A gypsy or beggar; a general term of abuse.
8. Bar keeper.
9. The Dublin civil service.
1. Good-for-nothings.
2. Laziness.

3. In July 1903, Edward VII of England, who was related to the German monarch, visited Dublin; the Dublin Corporation refused to make an address of welcome.
4. Money.

—Yes, said Mr O'Connor, beginning to search his pockets for memoranda.

—Did you call on Grimes?

—I did.

—Well? How does he stand?

—He wouldn't promise. He said: *I won't tell anyone what way I'm going to vote.* But I think he'll be all right.

—Why so?

—He asked me who the nominators were; and I told him. I mentioned Father Burke's name. I think it'll be all right.

Mr Henchy began to snuffle and to rub his hands over the fire at a terrific speed. Then he said:

—For the love of God, Jack, bring us a bit of coal. There must be some left.

The old man went out of the room.

—It's no go, said Mr Henchy, shaking his head. I asked the little shoeboy, but he said: *O, now, Mr Henchy, when I see the work going on properly I won't forget you, you may be sure.* Mean little tinker! 'Usha, how could he be anything else?

—What did I tell you, Mat? said Mr Hynes. Tricky Dicky Tierney.

—O, he's as tricky as they make 'em, said Mr Henchy. He hasn't got those little pigs' eyes for nothing. Blast his soul! Couldn't he pay up like a man instead of: *O, now, Mr Henchy, I must speak to Mr Fanning. . . . I've spent a lot of money?* Mean little shoeboy of hell! I suppose he forgets the time his little old father kept the hand-me-down shop in Mary's Lane.

—But is that a fact? asked Mr O'Connor.

—God, yes, said Mr Henchy. Did you never hear that? And the men used to go in on Sunday morning before the houses were open to buy a waistcoat or a trousers—moya! But Tricky Dicky's little old father always had a tricky little black bottle up in a corner. Do you mind now? That's that. That's where he first saw the light.

The old man returned with a few lumps of coal which he placed here and there on the fire.

—That's a nice how-do-you-do, said Mr O'Connor. How does he expect us to work for him if he won't stump up?

—I can't help it, said Mr Henchy. I expect to find the bailiffs in the hall when I go home.

Mr Hynes laughed and, shoving himself away from the mantelpiece with the aid of his shoulders, made ready to leave.

—It'll be all right when King Eddie comes, he said. Well, boys, I'm off for the present. See you later. 'Bye, 'bye.

He went out of the room slowly. Neither Mr Henchy nor the old man said anything but, just as the door was closing, Mr O'Connor who had been staring moodily into the fire, called out suddenly:

—'Bye, Joe.

Mr Henchy waited a few moments and then nodded in the direction of the door.

—Tell me, he said across the fire, what brings our friend in here? What does he want?

—'Usha, poor Joe! said Mr O'Connor, throwing the end of his cigarette into the fire, he's hard up like the rest of us.

Mr Henchy snuffled vigorously and spat so copiously that he nearly put out the fire which uttered a hissing protest.

—To tell you my private and candid opinion, he said, I think he's a man from the other camp. He's a spy of Colgan's if you ask me. *Just go round and try and find out how they're getting on. They won't suspect you.* Do you twig?[5]

—Ah, poor Joe is a decent skin, said Mr O'Connor.

—His father was a decent respectable man, Mr Henchy admitted: Poor old Larry Hynes! Many a good turn he did in his day! But I'm greatly afraid our friend is not nineteen carat. Damn it, I can understand a fellow being hard up but what I can't understand is a fellow sponging. Couldn't he have some spark of manhood about him?

—He doesn't get a warm welcome from me when he comes, said the old man. Let him work for his own side and not come spying around here.

—I don't know, said Mr O'Connor dubiously, as he took out cigarette-papers and tobacco. I think Joe Hynes is a straight man. He's a clever chap, too, with the pen. Do you remember that thing he wrote . . . ?

—Some of these hillsiders and fenians[6] are a bit too clever if you ask me, said Mr Henchy. Do you know what my private and candid opinion is about some of those little jokers? I believe half of them are in the pay of the Castle.[7]

—There's no knowing, said the old man.

—O, but I know it for a fact, said Mr Henchy. They're Castle hacks. . . . I don't say Hynes. . . . No, damn it, I think he's a stroke above that. . . . But there's a certain little nobleman with a cock-eye—you know the patriot I'm alluding to?

Mr O'Connor nodded.

—There's a lineal descendant of Major Sirr[8] for you if you like! O, the heart's blood of a patriot! That's a fellow now that'd sell his country for fourpence—ay—and go down on his bended knees and thank the Almighty Christ he had a country to sell.

There was a knock at the door.

—Come in! said Mr Henchy.

A person resembling a poor clergyman or a poor actor appeared in the doorway. His black clothes were tightly buttoned on his short body and it was impossible to say whether he wore a clergyman's collar or a layman's because the collar of his shabby frock-coat, the uncovered buttons of which reflected the candlelight, was turned up about his neck. He wore a round hat of hard black felt. His face, shining with rain-drops, had the appearance of damp yellow cheese save where two rosy spots indicated the cheekbones. He opened his very long mouth suddenly to express disappointment and at the same time opened wide his very bright blue eyes to express pleasure and surprise.

—O, Father Keon! said Mr Henchy, jumping up from his chair. Is that you? Come in!

—O, no, no, no! said Father Keon quickly, pursing his lips as if he were addressing a child.

—Won't you come in and sit down?

—No, no, no! said Father Keon, speaking in a discreet indulgent velvety voice. Don't let me disturb you now! I'm just looking for Mr Fanning. . . .

—He's round at the *Black Eagle*, said Mr Henchy. But won't you come in and sit down a minute?

---

5. Do you get it?
6. The Fenians, also known as Hillside men, were a secret organization trying to overthrow English government in Ireland.

7. Dublin Castle, headquarters of the English government in Dublin.
8. Henry Charles Sirr, chief of Dublin police who worked with the English in putting down the rebellion of 1798.

—No, no, thank you. It was just a little business matter, said Father Keon. Thank you, indeed.

He retreated from the doorway and Mr Henchy, seizing one of the candlesticks, went to the door to light him downstairs.

—O, don't trouble, I beg!

—No, but the stairs is so dark.

—No, no, I can see.... Thank you, indeed.

—Are you right now?

—All right, thanks.... Thanks.

Mr Henchy returned with the candlestick and put it on the table. He sat down again at the fire. There was silence for a few moments.

—Tell me, John, said Mr O'Connor, lighting his cigarette with another paste-board card.

—Hm?

—What is he exactly?

—Ask me an easier one, said Mr Henchy.

—Fanning and himself seem to me very thick. They're often in Kavanagh's together. Is he a priest at all?

—'Mmmyes, I believe so.... I think he's what you call a black sheep. We haven't many of them, thank God! but we have a few.... He's an unfortunate man of some kind....

—And how does he knock it out?[9] asked Mr O'Connor.

—That's another mystery.

—Is he attached to any chapel or church or institution or—

—No, said Mr Henchy. I think he's travelling on his own account.... God forgive me, he added, I thought he was the dozen of stout.

—Is there any chance of a drink itself? asked Mr O'Connor.

—I'm dry too, said the old man.

—I asked that little shoeboy three times, said Mr Henchy, would he send up a dozen of stout. I asked him again now but he was leaning on the counter in his shirt-sleeves having a deep goster[1] with Alderman Cowley.

—Why didn't you remind him? said Mr O'Connor.

—Well, I couldn't go over while he was talking to Alderman Cowley. I just waited till I caught his eye, and said: *About that little matter I was speaking to you about....* *That'll be all right, Mr H.,* he said. Yerra, sure the little hop-o'-my-thumb has forgotten all about it.

—There's some deal on in that quarter, said Mr O'Connor thoughtfully. I saw the three of them hard at it yesterday at Suffolk Street corner.

—I think I know the little game they're at, said Mr Henchy. You must owe the City Fathers money nowadays if you want to be made Lord Mayor. Then they'll make you Lord Mayor. By God! I'm thinking seriously of becoming a City Father myself. What do you think? Would I do for the job?

Mr O'Connor laughed.

—So far as owing money goes....

—Driving out of the Mansion House, said Mr Henchy, in all my vermin,[2] with Jack here standing up behind me in a powdered wig—eh?

9. How does he make a living?
1. Gossip session.

2. A pun on the *ermine* trimming the robes of the Lord Mayor.

—And make me your private secretary, John.

—Yes. And I'll make Father Keon my private chaplain. We'll have a family party.

—Faith, Mr Henchy, said the old man, you'd keep up better style than some of them. I was talking one day to old Keegan, the porter. *And how do you like your new master, Pat?* says I to him. *You haven't much entertaining now,* says I. *Entertaining!* says he. *He'd live on the smell of an oil-rag.* And do you know what he told me? Now, I declare to God, I didn't believe him.

—What? said Mr Henchy and Mr O'Connor.

—He told me: *What do you think of a Lord Mayor of Dublin sending out for a pound of chops for his dinner? How's that for high living?* says he. *Wisha! wisha,* says I. *A pound of chops,* says he, *coming into the Mansion House. Wisha!* says I, *what kind of people is going at all now?*

At this point there was a knock at the door, and a boy put in his head.

—What is it? said the old man.

—From the *Black Eagle,* said the boy, walking in sideways and depositing a basket on the floor with a noise of shaken bottles.

The old man helped the boy to transfer the bottles from the basket to the table and counted the full tally. After the transfer the boy put his basket on his arm and asked:

—Any bottles?

—What bottles? said the old man.

—Won't you let us drink them first? said Mr Henchy.

—I was told to ask for bottles.

—Come back to-morrow, said the old man.

—Here, boy! said Mr Henchy, will you run over to O'Farrell's and ask him to lend us a corkscrew—for Mr Henchy, say. Tell him we won't keep it a minute. Leave the basket there.

The boy went out and Mr Henchy began to rub his hands cheerfully, saying:

—Ah, well, he's not so bad after all. He's as good as his word, anyhow.

—There's no tumblers, said the old man.

—O, don't let that trouble you, Jack, said Mr Henchy. Many's the good man before now drank out of the bottle.

—Anyway, it's better than nothing, said Mr O'Connor.

—He's not a bad sort, said Mr Henchy, only Fanning has such a loan of him. He means well, you know, in his own tinpot[3] way.

The boy came back with the corkscrew. The old man opened three bottles and was handing back the corkscrew when Mr Henchy said to the boy:

—Would you like a drink, boy?

—If you please, sir, said the boy.

The old man opened another bottle grudgingly, and handed it to the boy.

—What age are you? he asked.

—Seventeen, said the boy.

As the old man said nothing further the boy took the bottle, said: *Here's my best respects, sir* to Mr Henchy, drank the contents, put the bottle back on the table and wiped his mouth with his sleeve. Then he took up the corkscrew and went out of the door sideways, muttering some form of salutation.

—That's the way it begins, said the old man.

3. Cheapskate.

—The thin edge of the wedge, said Mr Henchy.

The old man distributed the three bottles which he had opened and the men drank from them simultaneously. After having drunk each placed his bottle on the mantel-piece within hand's reach and drew in a long breath of satisfaction.

—Well, I did a good day's work to-day, said Mr Henchy, after a pause.

—That so, John?

—Yes. I got him one or two sure things in Dawson Street, Crofton and myself. Between ourselves, you know, Crofton (he's a decent chap, of course), but he's not worth a damn as a canvasser. He hasn't a word to throw to a dog. He stands and looks at the people while I do the talking.

Here two men entered the room. One of them was a very fat man, whose blue serge clothes seemed to be in danger of falling from his sloping figure. He had a big face which resembled a young ox's face in expression, staring blue eyes and a grizzled moustache. The other man, who was much younger and frailer, had a thin clean-shaven face. He wore a very high double collar and a wide-brimmed bowler hat.

—Hello, Crofton! said Mr Henchy to the fat man. Talk of the devil. . . .

—Where did the boose come from? asked the young man. Did the cow calve?

—O, of course, Lyons spots the drink first thing! said Mr O'Connor, laughing.

—Is that the way you chaps canvass, said Mr Lyons, and Crofton and I out in the cold and rain looking for votes?

—Why, blast your soul, said Mr Henchy, I'd get more votes in five minutes than you two'd get in a week.

—Open two bottles of stout, Jack, said Mr O'Connor.

—How can I? said the old man, when there's no corkscrew?

—Wait now, wait now! said Mr Henchy, getting up quickly. Did you ever see this little trick?

He took two bottles from the table and, carrying them to the fire, put them on the hob.[4] Then he sat down again by the fire and took another drink from his bottle. Mr Lyons sat on the edge of the table, pushed his hat towards the nape of his neck and began to swing his legs.

—Which is my bottle? he asked.

—This lad, said Mr Henchy.

Mr Crofton sat down on a box and looked fixedly at the other bottle on the hob. He was silent for two reasons. The first reason, sufficient in itself, was that he had nothing to say; the second reason was that he considered his companions beneath him. He had been a canvasser for Wilkins, the Conservative,[5] but when the Conservatives had withdrawn their man and, choosing the lesser of two evils, given their support to the Nationalist candidate, he had been engaged to work for Mr Tierney.

In a few minutes an apologetic *Pok!* was heard as the cork flew out of Mr Lyons' bottle. Mr Lyons jumped off the table, went to the fire, took his bottle and carried it back to the table.

—I was just telling them, Crofton, said Mr Henchy, that we got a good few votes to-day.

—Who did you get? asked Mr Lyons.

4. Ledge at the back of a fireplace.
5. In this context, a Conservative candidate is one who

supports English rule in Ireland, a Nationalist one who opposes it.

—Well, I got Parkes for one, and I got Atkinson for two, and I got Ward of Dawson Street. Fine old chap he is, too—regular old toff,[6] old Conservative! *But isn't your candidate a Nationalist?* said he. He's a respectable man, said I. *He's in favour of whatever will benefit this country. He's a big ratepayer,*[7] I said. *He has extensive house property in the city and three places of business and isn't it to his own advantage to keep down the rates? He's a prominent and respected citizen,* said I, *and a Poor Law Guardian, and he doesn't belong to any party, good, bad, or indifferent.* That's the way to talk to 'em.

—And what about the address to the King? said Mr Lyons, after drinking and smacking his lips.

—Listen to me, said Mr Henchy. What we want in this country, as I said to old Ward, is capital. The King's coming here will mean an influx of money into this country. The citizens of Dublin will benefit by it. Look at all the factories down by the quays there, idle! Look at all the money there is in the country if we only worked the old industries, the mills, the shipbuilding yards and factories. It's capital we want.

—But look here, John, said Mr O'Connor. Why should we welcome the King of England? Didn't Parnell himself . . .

—Parnell, said Mr Henchy, is dead. Now, here's the way I look at it. Here's this chap come to the throne after his old mother keeping him out of it till the man was grey. He's a man of the world, and he means well by us. He's a jolly fine decent fellow, if you ask me, and no damn nonsense about him. He just says to himself: *The old one never went to see these wild Irish. By Christ, I'll go myself and see what they're like.* And are we going to insult the man when he comes over here on a friendly visit? Eh? Isn't that right, Crofton?

Mr Crofton nodded his head.

—But after all now, said Mr Lyons argumentatively, King Edward's life, you know, is not the very . . .[8]

—Let bygones be bygones, said Mr Henchy. I admire the man personally. He's just an ordinary knockabout like you and me. He's fond of his glass of grog and he's a bit of a rake, perhaps, and he's a good sportsman. Damn it, can't we Irish play fair?

—That's all very fine, said Mr Lyons. But look at the case of Parnell now.

—In the name of God, said Mr Henchy, where's the analogy between the two cases?

—What I mean, said Mr Lyons, is we have our ideals. Why, now, would we welcome a man like that? Do you think now after what he did Parnell was a fit man to lead us? And why, then, would we do it for Edward the Seventh?

—This is Parnell's anniversary, said Mr O'Connor, and don't let us stir up any bad blood. We all respect him now that he's dead and gone—even the Conservatives, he added, turning to Mr Crofton.

Pok! The tardy cork flew out of Mr Crofton's bottle. Mr Crofton got up from his box and went to the fire. As he returned with his capture he said in a deep voice:

—Our side of the house respects him because he was a gentleman.

—Right you are, Crofton! said Mr Henchy fiercely. He was the only man that could keep that bag of cats in order. *Down, ye dogs! Lie down, ye curs!* That's the way he treated them. Come in, Joe! Come in! he called out, catching sight of Mr Hynes in the doorway.

Mr Hynes came in slowly.

—Open another bottle of stout, Jack, said Mr Henchy. O, I forgot there's no corkscrew! Here, show me one here and I'll put it at the fire.

---

6. Gentleman.
7. Taxpayer.

8. Edward VII's behavior had been somewhat notorious before he became king.

The old man handed him another bottle and he placed it on the hob.

—Sit down, Joe, said Mr O'Connor, we're just talking about the Chief.

—Ay, ay! said Mr Henchy.

Mr Hynes sat on the side of the table near Mr Lyons but said nothing.

—There's one of them, anyhow, said Mr Henchy, that didn't renege him. By God, I'll say for you, Joe! No, by God, you stuck to him like a man!

—O, Joe, said Mr O'Connor suddenly. Give us that thing you wrote—do you remember? Have you got it on you?

—O, ay! said Mr Henchy. Give us that. Did you ever hear that, Crofton? Listen to this now: splendid thing.

—Go on, said Mr O'Connor. Fire away, Joe.

Mr Hynes did not seem to remember at once the piece to which they were alluding but, after reflecting a while, he said:

—O, that thing is it. . . . Sure, that's old now.

—Out with it, man! said Mr O'Connor.

—'Sh, 'sh, said Mr Henchy. Now, Joe!

Mr Hynes hesitated a little longer. Then amid the silence he took off his hat, laid it on the table and stood up. He seemed to be rehearsing the piece in his mind. After a rather long pause he announced:

The Death of Parnell
6TH OCTOBER 1891

He cleared his throat once or twice and then began to recite:

> He is dead. Our Uncrowned King is dead.
>   O, Erin,[9] mourn with grief and woe
> For he lies dead whom the fell gang
>   Of modern hypocrites laid low.
>
> He lies slain by the coward hounds
>   He raised to glory from the mire;
> And Erin's hopes and Erin's dreams
>   Perish upon her monarch's pyre.
>
> In palace, cabin or in cot
>   The Irish heart where'er it be
> Is bowed with woe—for he is gone
>   Who would have wrought her destiny.
>
> He would have had his Erin famed,
>   The green flag gloriously unfurled,
> Her statesmen, bards and warriors raised
>   Before the nations of the World.
>
> He dreamed (alas, 'twas but a dream!)
>   Of Liberty: but as he strove
> To clutch that idol, treachery
>   Sundered him from the thing he loved.
>
> Shame on the coward caitiff[1] hands
>   That smote their Lord or with a kiss

9. A poetic name for Ireland.   1. Despicable.

Betrayed him to the rabble-rout
*   Of fawning priests—no friends of his.*

May everlasting shame consume
*   The memory of those who tried*
To befoul and smear th' exalted name
*   Of one who spurned them in his pride.*

He fell as fall the mighty ones,
*   Nobly undaunted to the last,*
And death has now united him
*   With Erin's heroes of the past.*

No sound of strife disturb his sleep!
*   Calmly he rests: no human pain*
Or high ambition spurs him now
*   The peaks of glory to attain.*

They had their way: they laid him low.
*   But Erin, list, his spirit may*
Rise, like the Phoenix from the flames,
*   When breaks the dawning of the day,*

The day that brings us Freedom's reign.
*   And on that day may Erin well*
Pledge in the cup she lifts to Joy
*   One grief—the memory of Parnell.*

Mr Hynes sat down again on the table. When he had finished his recitation there was a silence and then a burst of clapping: even Mr Lyons clapped. The applause continued for a little time. When it had ceased all the auditors drank from their bottles in silence.

Pok! The cork flew out of Mr Hynes' bottle, but Mr Hynes remained sitting, flushed and bareheaded on the table. He did not seem to have heard the invitation.

—Good man, Joe! said Mr O'Connor, taking out his cigarette papers and pouch the better to hide his emotion.

—What do you think of that, Crofton? cried Mr Henchy. Isn't that fine? What? Mr Crofton said that it was a very fine piece of writing.

The Dead

Lily, the caretaker's daughter, was literally run off her feet. Hardly had she brought one gentleman into the little pantry behind the office on the ground floor and helped him off with his overcoat than the wheezy hall-door bell clanged again and she had to scamper along the bare hallway to let in another guest. It was well for her she had not to attend to the ladies also. But Miss Kate and Miss Julia had thought of that and had converted the bathroom upstairs into a ladies' dressing-room. Miss Kate and Miss Julia were there, gossiping and laughing and fussing, walking after each other to the head of the stairs, peering down over the banisters and calling down to Lily to ask her who had come.

It was always a great affair, the Misses Morkan's annual dance. Everybody who knew them came to it, members of the family, old friends of the family, the members of Julia's choir, any of Kate's pupils that were grown up enough and even some of

Mary Jane's pupils too. Never once had it fallen flat. For years and years it had gone off in splendid style as long as anyone could remember; ever since Kate and Julia, after the death of their brother Pat, had left the house in Stoney Batter[1] and taken Mary Jane, their only niece, to live with them in the dark gaunt house on Usher's Island,[2] the upper part of which they had rented from Mr Fulham, the cornfactor on the ground floor. That was a good thirty years ago if it was a day. Mary Jane, who was then a little girl in short clothes, was now the main prop of the household for she had the organ in Haddington Road.[3] She had been through the Academy[4] and gave a pupils' concert every year in the upper room of the Antient Concert Rooms. Many of her pupils belonged to better-class families on the Kingstown and Dalkey line.[5] Old as they were, her aunts also did their share. Julia, though she was quite grey, was still the leading soprano in Adam and Eve's,[6] and Kate, being too feeble to go about much, gave music lessons to beginners on the old square piano in the back room. Lily, the caretaker's daughter, did housemaid's work for them. Though their life was modest they believed in eating well; the best of everything: diamond-bone sirloins, three-shilling tea and the best bottled stout.[7] But Lily seldom made a mistake in the orders so that she got on well with her three mistresses. They were fussy, that was all. But the only thing they would not stand was back answers.

Of course they had good reason to be fussy on such a night. And then it was long after ten o'clock and yet there was no sign of Gabriel and his wife. Besides they were dreadfully afraid that Freddy Malins might turn up screwed.[8] They would not wish for worlds that any of Mary Jane's pupils should see him under the influence; and when he was like that it was sometimes very hard to manage him. Freddy Malins always came late but they wondered what could be keeping Gabriel: and that was what brought them every two minutes to the banisters to ask Lily had Gabriel or Freddy come.

—O, Mr Conroy, said Lily to Gabriel when she opened the door for him, Miss Kate and Miss Julia thought you were never coming. Good-night, Mrs Conroy.

—I'll engage[9] they did, said Gabriel, but they forget that my wife here takes three mortal hours to dress herself.

He stood on the mat, scraping the snow from his goloshes, while Lily led his wife to the foot of the stairs and called out:

—Miss Kate, here's Mrs Conroy.

Kate and Julia came toddling down the dark stairs at once. Both of them kissed Gabriel's wife, said she must be perished alive and asked was Gabriel with her.

—Here I am as right as the mail, Aunt Kate! Go on up. I'll follow, called out Gabriel from the dark.

He continued scraping his feet vigorously while the three women went upstairs, laughing, to the ladies' dressing-room. A light fringe of snow lay like a cape on the shoulders of his overcoat and like toecaps on the toes of his goloshes; and, as the buttons of his overcoat slipped with a squeaking noise through the snow-stiffened frieze, a cold fragrant air from out-of-doors escaped from crevices and folds.

—Is it snowing again, Mr Conroy? asked Lily.

1. A district in northwest Dublin.
2. Two adjoining quays on the south side of the River Liffey.
3. Played the organ in a church on the Haddington Road.
4. Royal Academy of Music.
5. The train line connecting Dublin to the affluent suburbs south of the city.
6. A Dublin church.
7. An extra-strength ale.
8. Drunk.
9. Wager.

She had preceded him into the pantry to help him off with his overcoat. Gabriel smiled at the three syllables she had given his surname and glanced at her. She was a slim, growing girl, pale in complexion and with hay-coloured hair. The gas in the pantry made her look still paler. Gabriel had known her when she was a child and used to sit on the lowest step nursing a rag doll.

—Yes, Lily, he answered, and I think we're in for a night of it.

He looked up at the pantry ceiling, which was shaking with the stamping and shuffling of feet on the floor above, listened for a moment to the piano and then glanced at the girl, who was folding his overcoat carefully at the end of a shelf.

—Tell me, Lily, he said in a friendly tone, do you still go to school?

—O no, sir, she answered. I'm done schooling this year and more.

—O, then, said Gabriel gaily, I suppose we'll be going to your wedding one of these fine days with your young man, eh?

The girl glanced back at him over her shoulder and said with great bitterness:

—The men that is now is only all palaver[1] and what they can get out of you.

Gabriel coloured as if he felt he had made a mistake and, without looking at her, kicked off his goloshes and flicked actively with his muffler at his patent-leather shoes.

He was a stout tallish young man. The high colour of his cheeks pushed upwards even to his forehead where it scattered itself in a few formless patches of pale red; and on his hairless face there scintillated restlessly the polished lenses and the bright gilt rims of the glasses which screened his delicate and restless eyes. His glossy black hair was parted in the middle and brushed in a long curve behind his ears where it curled slightly beneath the groove left by his hat.

When he had flicked lustre into his shoes he stood up and pulled his waistcoat down more tightly on his plump body. Then he took a coin rapidly from his pocket.

—O Lily, he said, thrusting it into her hands, it's Christmas-time, isn't it? Just . . . here's a little. . . .

He walked rapidly towards the door.

—O no, sir! cried the girl, following him. Really, sir, I wouldn't take it.

—Christmas-time! Christmas-time! said Gabriel, almost trotting to the stairs and waving his hand to her in deprecation.

The girl, seeing that he had gained the stairs, called out after him:

—Well, thank you, sir.

He waited outside the drawing-room door until the waltz should finish, listening to the skirts that swept against it and to the shuffling of feet. He was still discomposed by the girl's bitter and sudden retort. It had cast a gloom over him which he tried to dispel by arranging his cuffs and the bows of his tie. Then he took from his waistcoat pocket a little paper and glanced at the headings he had made for his speech. He was undecided about the lines from Robert Browning for he feared they would be above the heads of his hearers. Some quotation that they could recognise from Shakespeare or from the Melodies[2] would be better. The indelicate clacking of the men's heels and the shuffling of their soles reminded him that their grade of culture differed from his. He would only make himself ridiculous by quoting poetry to them which they could not understand. They would think that he was airing his superior education. He would fail with them just as he had failed with the girl in the pantry. He had taken up a wrong tone. His whole speech was a mistake from first to last, an utter failure.

---

1. Empty talk.

2. Thomas Moore's *Irish Melodies*, a perennial favorite volume of poetry.

Just then his aunts and his wife came out of the ladies' dressing-room. His aunts were two small plainly dressed old women. Aunt Julia was an inch or so taller. Her hair, drawn low over the tops of her ears, was grey; and grey also, with darker shadows, was her large flaccid face. Though she was stout in build and stood erect her slow eyes and parted lips gave her the appearance of a woman who did not know where she was or where she was going. Aunt Kate was more vivacious. Her face, healthier than her sister's, was all puckers and creases, like a shrivelled red apple, and her hair, braided in the same old-fashioned way, had not lost its ripe nut colour.

They both kissed Gabriel frankly. He was their favourite nephew, the son of their dead elder sister, Ellen, who had married T.J. Conroy of the Port and Docks.

—Gretta tells me you're not going to take a cab back to Monkstown[3] to-night, Gabriel, said Aunt Kate.

—No, said Gabriel, turning to his wife, we had quite enough of that last year, hadn't we. Don't you remember, Aunt Kate, what a cold Gretta got out of it? Cab windows rattling all the way, and the east wind blowing in after we passed Merrion. Very jolly it was. Gretta caught a dreadful cold.

Aunt Kate frowned severely and nodded her head at every word.

—Quite right, Gabriel, quite right, she said. You can't be too careful.

—But as for Gretta there, said Gabriel, she'd walk home in the snow if she were let. Mrs Conroy laughed.

—Don't mind him, Aunt Kate, she said. He's really an awful bother, what with green shades for Tom's eyes at night and making him do the dumb-bells, and forcing Eva to eat the stirabout.[4] The poor child! And she simply hates the sight of it! . . . O, but you'll never guess what he makes me wear now!

She broke out into a peal of laughter and glanced at her husband, whose admiring and happy eyes had been wandering from her dress to her face and hair. The two aunts laughed heartily too, for Gabriel's solicitude was a standing joke with them.

—Goloshes! said Mrs Conroy. That's the latest. Whenever it's wet underfoot I must put on my goloshes. Tonight even he wanted me to put them on, but I wouldn't. The next thing he'll buy me will be a diving suit.

Gabriel laughed nervously and patted his tie reassuringly while Aunt Kate nearly doubled herself, so heartily did she enjoy the joke. The smile soon faded from Aunt Julia's face and her mirthless eyes were directed towards her nephew's face. After a pause she asked:

—And what are goloshes, Gabriel?

—Goloshes, Julia! exclaimed her sister. Goodness me, don't you know what goloshes are? You wear them over your . . . over your boots, Gretta, isn't it?

—Yes, said Mrs Conroy. Guttapercha[5] things. We both have a pair now. Gabriel says everyone wears them on the continent.

—O, on the continent, murmured Aunt Julia, nodding her head slowly.

Gabriel knitted his brows and said, as if he were slightly angered:

—It's nothing very wonderful but Gretta thinks it very funny because she says the word reminds her of Christy Minstrels.[6]

—But tell me, Gabriel, said Aunt Kate, with brisk tact. Of course, you've seen about the room. Gretta was saying . . .

—O, the room is all right, replied Gabriel. I've taken one in the Gresham.[7]

---

3. An elegant suburb south of Dublin.
4. Porridge.
5. Rubberized fabric.

6. A 19th-century minstrel show.
7. The most elegant hotel in Dublin.

—To be sure, said Aunt Kate, by far the best thing to do. And the children, Gretta, you're not anxious about them?

—O, for one night, said Mrs Conroy. Besides, Bessie will look after them.

—To be sure, said Aunt Kate again. What a comfort it is to have a girl like that, one you can depend on! There's that Lily, I'm sure I don't know what has come over her lately. She's not the girl she was at all.

Gabriel was about to ask his aunt some questions on this point but she broke off suddenly to gaze after her sister who had wandered down the stairs and was craning her neck over the banisters.

—Now, I ask you, she said, almost testily, where is Julia going? Julia! Julia! Where are you going?

Julia, who had gone halfway down one flight, came back and announced blandly:

—Here's Freddy.

At the same moment a clapping of hands and a final flourish of the pianist told that the waltz had ended. The drawing-room door was opened from within and some couples came out. Aunt Kate drew Gabriel aside hurriedly and whispered into his ear:

—Slip down, Gabriel, like a good fellow and see if he's all right, and don't let him up if he's screwed. I'm sure he's screwed. I'm sure he is.

Gabriel went to the stairs and listened over the banisters. He could hear two persons talking in the pantry. Then he recognised Freddy Malins' laugh. He went down the stairs noisily.

—It's such a relief, said Aunt Kate to Mrs Conroy, that Gabriel is here. I always feel easier in my mind when he's here. . . . Julia, there's Miss Daly and Miss Power will take some refreshment. Thanks for your beautiful waltz, Miss Daly. It made lovely time.

A tall wizen-faced man, with a stiff grizzled moustache and swarthy skin, who was passing out with his partner said:

—And may we have some refreshment, too, Miss Morkan?

—Julia, said Aunt Kate summarily, and here's Mr Browne and Miss Furlong. Take them in, Julia, with Miss Daly and Miss Power.

—I'm the man for the ladies, said Mr Browne, pursing his lips until his moustache bristled and smiling in all his wrinkles. You know, Miss Morkan, the reason they are so fond of me is—

He did not finish his sentence, but, seeing that Aunt Kate was out of earshot, at once led the three young ladies into the back room. The middle of the room was occupied by two square tables placed end to end, and on these Aunt Julia and the caretaker were straightening and smoothing a large cloth. On the sideboard were arrayed dishes and plates, and glasses and bundles of knives and forks and spoons. The top of the closed square piano served also as a sideboard for viands[8] and sweets. At a smaller sideboard in one corner two young men were standing, drinking hop-bitters.[9]

Mr Browne led his charges thither and invited them all, in jest, to some ladies' punch, hot, strong and sweet. As they said they never took anything strong he opened three bottles of lemonade for them. Then he asked one of the young men to move aside, and, taking hold of the decanter, filled out for himself a goodly measure of whisky. The young men eyed him respectfully while he took a trial sip.

—God help me, he said, smiling, it's the doctor's orders.

His wizened face broke into a broader smile, and the three young ladies laughed in musical echo to his pleasantry, swaying their bodies to and fro, with nervous jerks of their shoulders. The boldest said:

---

8. Meats.

9. Dry ale.

—O, now, Mr Browne, I'm sure the doctor never ordered anything of the kind.

Mr Browne took another sip of his whisky and said, with sidling mimicry:

—Well, you see, I'm like the famous Mrs Cassidy, who is reported to have said: *Now, Mary Grimes, if I don't take it, make me take it, for I feel I want it.*

His hot face had leaned forward a little too confidentially and he had assumed a very low Dublin accent so that the young ladies, with one instinct, received his speech in silence. Miss Furlong, who was one of Mary Jane's pupils, asked Miss Daly what was the name of the pretty waltz she had played; and Mr Browne, seeing that he was ignored, turned promptly to the two young men who were more appreciative.

A red-faced young woman, dressed in pansy, came into the room, excitedly clapping her hands and crying:

—Quadrilles![1] Quadrilles!

Close on her heels came Aunt Kate, crying:

—Two gentlemen and three ladies, Mary Jane!

—O, here's Mr Bergin and Mr Kerrigan, said Mary Jane. Mr Kerrigan, will you take Miss Power? Miss Furlong, may I get you a partner, Mr Bergin. O, that'll just do now.

—Three ladies, Mary Jane, said Aunt Kate.

The two young gentlemen asked the ladies if they might have the pleasure, and Mary Jane turned to Miss Daly.

—O, Miss Daly, you're really awfully good, after playing for the last two dances, but really we're so short of ladies to-night.

—I don't mind in the least, Miss Morkan.

—But I've a nice partner for you, Mr Bartell D'Arcy, the tenor. I'll get him to sing later on. All Dublin is raving about him.

—Lovely voice, lovely voice! said Aunt Kate.

As the piano had twice begun the prelude to the first figure Mary Jane led her recruits quickly from the room. They had hardly gone when Aunt Julia wandered slowly into the room, looking behind her at something.

—What is the matter, Julia? asked Aunt Kate anxiously. Who is it?

Julia, who was carrying in a column of table-napkins, turned to her sister and said, simply, as if the question had surprised her:

—It's only Freddy, Kate, and Gabriel with him.

In fact right behind her Gabriel could be seen piloting Freddy Malins across the landing. The latter, a young man of about forty, was of Gabriel's size and build, with very round shoulders. His face was fleshy and pallid, touched with colour only at the thick hanging lobes of his ears and at the wide wings of his nose. He had coarse features, a blunt nose, a convex and receding brow, tumid and protruded lips. His heavy-lidded eyes and the disorder of his scanty hair made him look sleepy. He was laughing heartily in a high key at a story which he had been telling Gabriel on the stairs and at the same time rubbing the knuckles of his left fist backwards and forwards into his left eye.

—Good-evening, Freddy, said Aunt Julia.

Freddy Malins bade the Misses Morkan good-evening in what seemed an off-hand fashion by reason of the habitual catch in his voice and then, seeing that Mr Browne was grinning at him from the sideboard, crossed the room on rather shaky legs and began to repeat in an undertone the story he had just told to Gabriel.

—He's not so bad, is he? said Aunt Kate to Gabriel.

Gabriel's brows were dark but he raised them quickly and answered:

—O no, hardly noticeable.

1. A French square dance.

—Now, isn't he a terrible fellow! she said. And his poor mother made him take the pledge on New Year's Eve. But come on, Gabriel, into the drawing-room.

Before leaving the room with Gabriel she signalled to Mr Browne by frowning and shaking her forefinger in warning to and fro. Mr Browne nodded in answer and, when she had gone, said to Freddy Malins:

—Now, then, Teddy, I'm going to fill you out a good glass of lemonade just to buck you up.

Freddy Malins, who was nearing the climax of his story, waved the offer aside impatiently but Mr Browne, having first called Freddy Malins' attention to a disarray in his dress, filled out and handed him a full glass of lemonade. Freddy Malins' left hand accepted the glass mechanically, his right hand being engaged in the mechanical readjustment of his dress. Mr Browne, whose face was once more wrinkling with mirth, poured out for himself a glass of whisky while Freddy Malins exploded, before he had well reached the climax of his story, in a kink of high-pitched bronchitic laughter and, setting down his untasted and overflowing glass, began to rub the knuckles of his left fist backwards and forwards into his left eye, repeating words of his last phrase as well as his fit of laughter would allow him.

Gabriel could not listen while Mary Jane was playing her Academy piece, full of runs and difficult passages, to the hushed drawing-room. He liked music but the piece she was playing had no melody for him and he doubted whether it had any melody for the other listeners, though they had begged Mary Jane to play something. Four young men, who had come from the refreshment-room to stand in the door-way at the sound of the piano, had gone away quietly in couples after a few minutes. The only persons who seemed to follow the music were Mary Jane herself, her hands racing along the key-board or lifted from it at the pauses like those of a priestess in momentary imprecation, and Aunt Kate standing at her elbow to turn the page.

Gabriel's eyes, irritated by the floor, which glittered with beeswax under the heavy chandelier, wandered to the wall above the piano. A picture of the balcony scene in *Romeo and Juliet* hung there and beside it was a picture of the two murdered princes[2] in the Tower which Aunt Julia had worked in red, blue and brown wools when she was a girl. Probably in the school they had gone to as girls that kind of work had been taught, for one year his mother had worked for him as a birthday present a waistcoat of purple tabinet,[3] with little foxes' heads upon it, lined with brown satin and having round mulberry buttons. It was strange that his mother had had no musical talent though Aunt Kate used to call her the brains carrier of the Morkan family. Both she and Julia had always seemed a little proud of their serious and matronly sister. Her photograph stood before the pierglass.[4] She held an open book on her knees and was pointing out something in it to Constantine who, dressed in a man-o'-war suit, lay at her feet. It was she who had chosen the names for her sons for she was very sensible of the dignity of family life. Thanks to her, Constantine was now senior curate in Balbriggan[5] and, thanks to her, Gabriel himself had taken his degree in the Royal University.[6] A shadow passed over his face as he remembered her sullen opposition to his marriage. Some slighting phrases she had used still rankled in his memory; she had once spoken of Gretta as being country cute and that was not true of Gretta at all. It was Gretta who had nursed her during all her last long illness in their house at Monkstown.

---

2. The young sons of Edward IV, murdered in the Tower of London by order of their uncle, Edward III.
3. Silk and wool fabric.
4. A large high mirror.
5. Seaport 19 miles southeast of Dublin.
6. The Royal University of Ireland, established in 1882.

He knew that Mary Jane must be near the end of her piece for she was playing again the opening melody with runs of scales after every bar and while he waited for the end the resentment died down in his heart. The piece ended with a trill of octaves in the treble and a final deep octave in the bass. Great applause greeted Mary Jane as, blushing and rolling up her music nervously, she escaped from the room. The most vigorous clapping came from the four young men in the doorway who had gone away to the refreshment-room at the beginning of the piece but had come back when the piano had stopped.

Lancers[7] were arranged. Gabriel found himself partnered with Miss Ivors. She was a frank-mannered talkative young lady, with a freckled face and prominent brown eyes. She did not wear a low-cut bodice and the large brooch which was fixed in the front of her collar bore on it an Irish device.

When they had taken their places she said abruptly:

—I have a crow to pluck with you.

—With me? said Gabriel.

She nodded her head gravely.

—What is it? asked Gabriel, smiling at her solemn manner.

—Who is G. C.? answered Miss Ivors, turning her eyes upon him.

Gabriel coloured and was about to knit his brows, as if he did not understand, when she said bluntly:

—O, innocent Amy! I have found out that you write for The Daily Express.[8] Now, aren't you ashamed of yourself?

—Why should I be ashamed of myself? asked Gabriel, blinking his eyes and trying to smile.

—Well, I'm ashamed of you, said Miss Ivors frankly. To say you'd write for a rag like that. I didn't think you were a West Briton.[9]

A look of perplexity appeared on Gabriel's face. It was true that he wrote a literary column every Wednesday in The Daily Express, for which he was paid fifteen shillings. But that did not make him a West Briton surely. The books he received for review were almost more welcome than the paltry cheque. He loved to feel the covers and turn over the pages of newly printed books. Nearly every day when his teaching in the college was ended he used to wander down the quays to the second-hand booksellers, to Hickey's on Bachelor's Walk, to Webb's or Massey's on Aston's Quay, or to O'Clohissey's in the by-street. He did not know how to meet her charge. He wanted to say that literature was above politics. But they were friends of many years' standing and their careers had been parallel, first at the University and then as teachers: he could not risk a grandiose phrase with her. He continued blinking his eyes and trying to smile and murmured lamely that he saw nothing political in writing reviews of books.

When their turn to cross had come he was still perplexed and inattentive. Miss Ivors promptly took his hand in a warm grasp and said in a soft friendly tone:

—Of course, I was only joking. Come, we cross now.

When they were together again she spoke of the University question[1] and Gabriel felt more at ease. A friend of hers had shown her his review of Browning's poems. That was how she had found out the secret: but she liked the review immensely. Then she said suddenly:

---

7. A type of quadrille for 8 or 16 people.
8. A conservative paper opposed to the struggle for Irish independence.
9. Disparaging term for people wishing to identify Ireland as British.

1. Ireland's oldest most and prestigious university, Trinity College, was open only to Protestants; the "University question" involved, in part, the provision of quality university education to Catholics.

—O, Mr Conroy, will you come for an excursion to the Aran Isles[2] this summer? We're going to stay there a whole month. It will be splendid out in the Atlantic. You ought to come. Mr Clancy is coming, and Mr Kilkelly and Kathleen Kearney. It would be splendid for Gretta too if she'd come. She's from Connacht,[3] isn't she?

—Her people are, said Gabriel shortly.

—But you will come, won't you? said Miss Ivors, laying her warm hand eagerly on his arm.

—The fact is, said Gabriel, I have already arranged to go—

—Go where? asked Miss Ivors.

—Well, you know, every year I go for a cycling tour with some fellows and so—

—But where? asked Miss Ivors.

—Well, we usually go to France or Belgium or perhaps Germany, said Gabriel awkwardly.

—And why do you go to France and Belgium, said Miss Ivors, instead of visiting your own land?

—Well, said Gabriel, it's partly to keep in touch with the languages and partly for a change.

—And haven't you your own language to keep in touch with—Irish? asked Miss Ivors.

—Well, said Gabriel, if it comes to that, you know, Irish is not my language.

Their neighbours had turned to listen to the cross-examination. Gabriel glanced right and left nervously and tried to keep his good humour under the ordeal which was making a blush invade his forehead.

—And haven't you your own land to visit, continued Miss Ivors, that you know nothing of, your own people, and your own country?

—O, to tell you the truth, retorted Gabriel suddenly, I'm sick of my own country, sick of it!

—Why? asked Miss Ivors.

Gabriel did not answer for his retort had heated him.

—Why? repeated Miss Ivors.

They had to go visiting together and, as he had not answered her, Miss Ivors said warmly:

—Of course, you've no answer.

Gabriel tried to cover his agitation by taking part in the dance with great energy. He avoided her eyes for he had seen a sour expression on her face. But when they met in the long chain he was surprised to feel his hand firmly pressed. She looked at him from under her brows for a moment quizzically until he smiled. Then, just as the chain was about to start again, she stood on tiptoe and whispered into his ear:

—West Briton!

When the lancers were over Gabriel went away to a remote corner of the room where Freddy Malins' mother was sitting. She was a stout feeble old woman with white hair. Her voice had a catch in it like her son's and she stuttered slightly. She had been told that Freddy had come and that he was nearly all right. Gabriel asked her whether she had had a good crossing. She lived with her married daughter in Glasgow and came to Dublin on a visit once a year. She answered placidly that she had had a beautiful crossing and that the captain had been most attentive to her. She

2. Islands off the west coast of Ireland where the people   3. A province on the west coast of Ireland.
still retained their traditional culture and spoke Irish.

spoke also of the beautiful house her daughter kept in Glasgow, and of all the nice friends they had there. While her tongue rambled on Gabriel tried to banish from his mind all memory of the unpleasant incident with Miss Ivors. Of course the girl or woman, or whatever she was, was an enthusiast but there was a time for all things. Perhaps he ought not to have answered her like that. But she had no right to call him a West Briton before people, even in joke. She had tried to make him ridiculous before people, heckling him and staring at him with her rabbit's eyes.

He saw his wife making her way towards him through the waltzing couples. When she reached him she said into his ear:

—Gabriel, Aunt Kate wants to know won't you carve the goose as usual. Miss Daly will carve the ham and I'll do the pudding.

—All right, said Gabriel.

—She's sending in the younger ones first as soon as this waltz is over so that we'll have the table to ourselves.

—Were you dancing? asked Gabriel.

—Of course I was. Didn't you see me? What words had you with Molly Ivors?

—No words. Why? Did she say so?

—Something like that. I'm trying to get that Mr D'Arcy to sing. He's full of conceit, I think.

—There were no words, said Gabriel moodily, only she wanted me to go for a trip to the west of Ireland and I said I wouldn't.

His wife clasped her hands excitedly and gave a little jump.

—O, do go, Gabriel, she cried. I'd love to see Galway again.

—You can go if you like, said Gabriel coldly.

She looked at him for a moment, then turned to Mrs Malins and said:

—There's a nice husband for you, Mrs Malins.

While she was threading her way back across the room Mrs Malins, without adverting to the interruption, went on to tell Gabriel what beautiful places there were in Scotland and beautiful scenery. Her son-in-law brought them every year to the lakes and they used to go fishing. Her son-in-law was a splendid fisher. One day he caught a fish, a beautiful big big fish, and the man in the hotel boiled it for their dinner.

Gabriel hardly heard what she said. Now that supper was coming near he began to think again about his speech and about the quotation. When he saw Freddy Malins coming across the room to visit his mother Gabriel left the chair free for him and retired into the embrasure of the window. The room had already cleared and from the back room came the clatter of plates and knives. Those who still remained in the drawing-room seemed tired of dancing and were conversing quietly in little groups. Gabriel's warm trembling fingers tapped the cold pane of the window. How cool it must be outside! How pleasant it would be to walk out alone, first along by the river and then through the park! The snow would be lying on the branches of the trees and forming a bright cap on the top of the Wellington Monument.[4] How much more pleasant it would be there than at the supper-table!

He ran over the headings of his speech: Irish hospitality, sad memories, the Three Graces, Paris, the quotation from Browning. He repeated to himself a phrase he had written in his review: *One feels that one is listening to a thought-tormented music*. Miss Ivors had praised the review. Was she sincere? Had she really any life of her own

---

4. A monument to the Duke of Wellington, an Irish-born English military hero, located in Phoenix Park, Dublin's major public park.

behind all her propagandism? There had never been any ill-feeling between them until that night. It unnerved him to think that she would be at the supper-table, looking up at him while he spoke with her critical quizzing eyes. Perhaps she would not be sorry to see him fail in his speech. An idea came into his mind and gave him courage. He would say, alluding to Aunt Kate and Aunt Julia: *Ladies and Gentlemen, the generation which is now on the wane among us may have had its faults but for my part I think it had certain qualities of hospitality, of humour, of humanity, which the new and very serious and hypereducated generation that is growing up around us seems to me to lack.* Very good: that was one for Miss Ivors. What did he care that his aunts were only two ignorant old women?

A murmur in the room attracted his attention. Mr Browne was advancing from the door, gallantly escorting Aunt Julia, who leaned upon his arm, smiling and hanging her head. An irregular musketry of applause escorted her also as far as the piano and then, as Mary Jane seated herself on the stool, and Aunt Julia, no longer smiling, half turned so as to pitch her voice fairly into the room, gradually ceased. Gabriel recognised the prelude. It was that of an old song of Aunt Julia's—*Arrayed for the Bridal.*[5] Her voice, strong and clear in tone, attacked with great spirit the runs which embellish the air and though she sang very rapidly she did not miss even the smallest of the grace notes. To follow the voice, without looking at the singer's face, was to feel and share the excitement of swift and secure flight. Gabriel applauded loudly with all the others at the close of the song and loud applause was borne in from the invisible supper-table. It sounded so genuine that a little colour struggled into Aunt Julia's face as she bent to replace in the music-stand the old leather-bound song-book that had her initials on the cover. Freddy Malins, who had listened with his head perched sideways to hear her better, was still applauding when everyone else had ceased and talking animatedly to his mother who nodded her head gravely and slowly in acquiescence. At last, when he could clap no more, he stood up suddenly and hurried across the room to Aunt Julia whose hand he seized and held in both his hands, shaking it when words failed him or the catch in his voice proved too much for him.

—I was just telling my mother, he said, I never heard you sing so well, never. No, I never heard your voice so good as it is to-night. Now! Would you believe that now? That's the truth. Upon my word and honour that's the truth. I never heard your voice sound so fresh and so . . . so clear and fresh, never.

Aunt Julia smiled broadly and murmured something about compliments as she released her hand from his grasp. Mr Browne extended his open hand towards her and said to those who were near him in the manner of a showman introducing a prodigy to an audience:

—Miss Julia Morkan, my latest discovery!

He was laughing very heartily at this himself when Freddy Malins turned to him and said:

—Well, Browne, if you're serious you might make a worse discovery. All I can say is I never heard her sing half so well as long as I am coming here. And that's the honest truth.

—Neither did I, said Mr. Browne. I think her voice has greatly improved.

Aunt Julia shrugged her shoulders and said with meek pride:

—Thirty years ago I hadn't a bad voice as voices go.

---

5. A popular but challenging song set to music from Bellini's opera *I Puritani* (1835).

—I often told Julia, said Aunt Kate emphatically, that she was simply thrown away in that choir. But she never would be said by me.

She turned as if to appeal to the good sense of the others against a refractory child while Aunt Julia gazed in front of her, a vague smile of reminiscence playing on her face.

—No, continued Aunt Kate, she wouldn't be said or led by anyone, slaving there in that choir night and day, night and day. Six o'clock on Christmas morning! And all for what?

—Well, isn't it for the honour of God, Aunt Kate? asked Mary Jane, twisting round on the piano-stool and smiling.

Aunt Kate turned fiercely on her niece and said:

—I know all about the honour of God, Mary Jane, but I think it's not at all honourable for the pope to turn out the women out of the choirs that have slaved there all their lives and put little whipper-snappers of boys over their heads. I suppose it is for the good of the Church if the pope does it. But it's not just, Mary Jane, and it's not right.

She had worked herself into a passion and would have continued in defence of her sister for it was a sore subject with her but Mary Jane, seeing that all the dancers had come back, intervened pacifically:

—Now, Aunt Kate, you're giving scandal to Mr Browne who is of the other persuasion.

Aunt Kate turned to Mr Browne, who was grinning at this allusion to his religion, and said hastily:

—O, I don't question the pope's being right. I'm only a stupid old woman and I wouldn't presume to do such a thing. But there's such a thing as common everyday politeness and gratitude. And if I were in Julia's place I'd tell that Father Healy straight up to his face . . .

—And besides, Aunt Kate, said Mary Jane, we really are all hungry and when we are hungry we are all very quarrelsome.

—And when we are thirsty we are also quarrelsome, added Mr Browne.

—So that we had better go to supper, said Mary Jane, and finish the discussion afterwards.

On the landing outside the drawing-room Gabriel found his wife and Mary Jane trying to persuade Miss Ivors to stay for supper. But Miss Ivors, who had put on her hat and was buttoning her cloak, would not stay. She did not feel in the least hungry and she had already overstayed her time.

—But only for ten minutes, Molly, said Mrs Conroy. That won't delay you.

—To take a pick itself, said Mary Jane, after all your dancing.

—I really couldn't, said Miss Ivors.

—I am afraid you didn't enjoy yourself at all, said Mary Jane hopelessly.

—Ever so much, I assure you, said Miss Ivors, but you really must let me run off now.

—But how can you get home? asked Mrs Conroy.

—O, it's only two steps up the quay.

Gabriel hesitated a moment and said:

—If you will allow me, Miss Ivors, I'll see you home if you really are obliged to go.

But Miss Ivors broke away from them.

—I won't hear of it, she cried. For goodness sake go in to your suppers and don't mind me. I'm quite well able to take care of myself.

—Well, you're the comical girl, Molly, said Mrs Conroy frankly.

—*Beannacht libh*,[6] cried Miss Ivors, with a laugh, as she ran down the staircase.

Mary Jane gazed after her, a moody puzzled expression on her face, while Mrs Conroy leaned over the banisters to listen for the hall-door. Gabriel asked himself was he the cause of her abrupt departure. But she did not seem to be in ill humour: she had gone away laughing. He stared blankly down the staircase.

At that moment Aunt Kate came toddling out of the supper-room, almost wringing her hands in despair.

—Where is Gabriel? she cried. Where on earth is Gabriel? There's everyone waiting in there, stage to let, and nobody to carve the goose!

—Here I am, Aunt Kate! cried Gabriel, with sudden animation, ready to carve a flock of geese, if necessary.

A fat brown goose lay at one end of the table and at the other end, on a bed of creased paper strewn with sprigs of parsley, lay a great ham, stripped of its outer skin and peppered over with crust crumbs, a neat paper frill round its shin and beside this was a round of spiced beef. Between these rival ends ran parallel lines of side-dishes: two little minsters of jelly, red and yellow; a shallow dish full of blocks of blancmange and red jam, a large green leaf-shaped dish with a stalk-shaped handle, on which lay bunches of purple raisins and peeled almonds, a companion dish on which lay a solid rectangle of Smyrna figs, a dish of custard topped with grated nutmeg, a small bowl full of chocolates and sweets wrapped in gold and silver papers and a glass vase in which stood some tall celery stalks. In the centre of the table there stood, as sentries to a fruit-stand which upheld a pyramid of oranges and American apples, two squat old-fashioned decanters of cut glass, one containing port and the other dark sherry. On the closed square piano a pudding in a huge yellow dish lay in waiting and behind it were three squads of bottles of stout and ale and minerals, drawn up according to the colours of their uniforms, the first two black, with brown and red labels, the third and smallest squad white, with transverse green sashes.

Gabriel took his seat boldly at the head of the table and, having looked to the edge of the carver, plunged his fork firmly into the goose. He felt quite at ease now for he was an expert carver and liked nothing better than to find himself at the head of a well-laden table.

—Miss Furlong, what shall I send you? he asked. A wing or a slice of the breast?

—Just a small slice of the breast.

—Miss Higgins, what for you?

—O, anything at all, Mr Conroy.

While Gabriel and Miss Daly exchanged plates of goose and plates of ham and spiced beef Lily went from guest to guest with a dish of hot floury potatoes wrapped in a white napkin. This was Mary Jane's idea and she had also suggested apple sauce for the goose but Aunt Kate had said that plain roast goose without apple sauce had always been good enough for her and she hoped she might never eat worse. Mary Jane waited on her pupils and saw that they got the best slices and Aunt Kate and Aunt Julia opened and carried across from the piano bottles of stout and ale for the gentlemen and bottles of minerals for the ladies. There was a great deal of confusion and laughter and noise, the noise of orders and counter-orders, of knives and forks, of corks and glass-stoppers. Gabriel began to carve second helpings as soon as he had finished the first round without serving himself. Everyone protested loudly so that he

---

6. Farewell (Irish).

compromised by taking a long draught of stout for he had found the carving hot work. Mary Jane settled down quietly to her supper but Aunt Kate and Aunt Julia were still toddling round the table, walking on each other's heels, getting in each other's way and giving each other unheeded orders. Mr Browne begged of them to sit down and eat their suppers and so did Gabriel but they said there was time enough so that, at last, Freddy Malins stood up and, capturing Aunt Kate, plumped her down on her chair amid general laughter.

When everyone had been well served Gabriel said, smiling:

—Now, if anyone wants a little more of what vulgar people call stuffing let him or her speak.

A chorus of voices invited him to begin his own supper and Lily came forward with three potatoes which she had reserved for him.

—Very well, said Gabriel amiably, as he took another preparatory draught, kindly forget my existence, ladies and gentlemen, for a few minutes.

He set to his supper and took no part in the conversation with which the table covered Lily's removal of the plates. The subject of talk was the opera company which was then at the Theatre Royal. Mr Bartell D'Arcy, the tenor, a dark-complexioned young man with a smart moustache, praised very highly the leading contralto of the company but Miss Furlong thought she had a rather vulgar style of production. Freddy Malins said there was a negro chieftain singing in the second part of the Gaiety pantomime who had one of the finest tenor voices he had ever heard.

—Have you heard him? he asked Mr Bartell D'Arcy across the table.

—No, answered Mr Bartell D'Arcy carelessly.

—Because, Freddy Malins explained, now I'd be curious to hear your opinion of him. I think he has a grand voice.

—It takes Teddy to find out the really good things, said Mr Browne familiarly to the table.

—And why couldn't he have a voice too? asked Freddy Malins sharply. Is it because he's only a black?

Nobody answered this question and Mary Jane led the table back to the legitimate opera. One of her pupils had given her a pass for *Mignon.* Of course it was very fine, she said, but it made her think of poor Georgina Burns. Mr Browne could go back farther still, to the old Italian companies that used to come to Dublin—Tietjens, Ilma de Murzka, Campanini, the great Trebelli, Giuglini, Ravelli, Aramburo.[7] Those were the days, he said, when there was something like singing to be heard in Dublin. He told too of how the top gallery of the old Royal used to be packed night after night, of how one night an Italian tenor had sung five encores to *Let Me Like a Soldier Fall,* introducing a high C every time, and of how the gallery boys would sometimes in their enthusiasm unyoke the horses from the carriage of some great *prima donna* and pull her themselves through the streets to her hotel. Why did they never play the grand old operas now, he asked, *Dinorah, Lucrezia Borgia?* Because they could not get the voices to sing them: that was why.

—O, well, said Mr Bartell D'Arcy, I presume there are as good singers to-day as there were then.

—Where are they? asked Mr Browne defiantly.

—In London, Paris, Milan, said Mr Bartell D'Arcy warmly. I suppose Caruso,[8] for example, is quite as good, if not better than any of the men you have mentioned.

7. Famous 19th-century operatic singers.
8. Enrico Caruso (1874–1921), a famous tenor.

—Maybe so, said Mr Browne. But I may tell you I doubt it strongly.

—O, I'd give anything to hear Caruso sing, said Mary Jane.

—For me, said Aunt Kate, who had been picking a bone, there was only one tenor. To please me, I mean. But I suppose none of you ever heard of him.

—Who was he, Miss Morkan? asked Mr Bartell D'Arcy politely.

—His name, said Aunt Kate, was Parkinson. I heard him when he was in his prime and I think he had then the purest tenor voice that was ever put into a man's throat.

—Strange, said Mr Bartell D'Arcy. I never even heard of him.

—Yes, yes, Miss Morkan is right, said Mr Browne. I remember hearing of old Parkinson but he's too far back for me.

—A beautiful pure sweet mellow English tenor, said Aunt Kate with enthusiasm.

Gabriel having finished, the huge pudding was transferred to the table. The clatter of forks and spoons began again. Gabriel's wife served out spoonfuls of the pudding and passed the plates down the table. Midway down they were held up by Mary Jane, who replenished them with raspberry or orange jelly or with blancmange and jam. The pudding was of Aunt Julia's making and she received praises for it from all quarters. She herself said that it was not quite brown enough.

—Well, I hope, Miss Morkan, said Mr Browne, that I'm brown enough for you because, you know, I'm all brown.

All the gentlemen, except Gabriel, ate some of the pudding out of compliment to Aunt Julia. As Gabriel never ate sweets the celery had been left for him. Freddy Malins also took a stalk of celery and ate it with his pudding. He had been told that celery was a capital thing for the blood and he was just then under doctor's care. Mrs Malins, who had been silent all through the supper, said that her son was going down to Mount Melleray[9] in a week or so. The table then spoke to Mount Melleray, how bracing the air was down there, how hospitable the monks were and how they never asked for a penny-piece from their guests.

—And do you mean to say, asked Mr Browne incredulously, that a chap can go down there and put up there as if it were a hotel and live on the fat of the land and then come away without paying a farthing?

—O, most people give some donation to the monastery when they leave, said Mary Jane.

—I wish we had an institution like that in our Church, said Mr Browne candidly.

He was astonished to hear that the monks never spoke, got up at two in the morning and slept in their coffins. He asked what they did it for.

—That's the rule of the order, said Aunt Kate firmly.

—Yes, but why? asked Mr Browne.

Aunt Kate repeated that it was the rule, that was all. Mr Browne still seemed not to understand. Freddy Malins explained to him, as best he could, that the monks were trying to make up for the sins committed by all the sinners in the outside world. The explanation was not very clear for Mr Browne grinned and said:

—I like that idea very much but wouldn't a comfortable spring bed do them as well as a coffin?

—The coffin, said Mary Jane, is to remind them of their last end.

As the subject had grown lugubrious it was buried in a silence of the table during which Mrs Malins could be heard saying to her neighbour in an indistinct undertone:

—They are very good men, the monks, very pious men.

---

9. Site of a Trappist monastery in the south of Ireland.

The raisins and almonds and figs and apples and oranges and chocolates and sweets were now passed about the table and Aunt Julia invited all the guests to have either port or sherry. At first Mr Bartell D'Arcy refused to take either but one of his neighbours nudged him and whispered something to him upon which he allowed his glass to be filled. Gradually as the last glasses were being filled the conversation ceased. A pause followed, broken only by the noise of the wine and by unsettlings of chairs. The Misses Morkan, all three, looked down at the tablecloth. Someone coughed once or twice and then a few gentlemen patted the table gently as a signal for silence. The silence came and Gabriel pushed back his chair and stood up.

The patting at once grew louder in encouragement and then ceased altogether. Gabriel leaned his ten trembling fingers on the tablecloth and smiled nervously at the company. Meeting a row of upturned faces he raised his eyes to the chandelier. The piano was playing a waltz tune and he could hear the skirts sweeping against the drawing-room door. People, perhaps, were standing in the snow on the quay outside, gazing up at the lighted windows and listening to the waltz music. The air was pure there. In the distance lay the park where the trees were weighted with snow. The Wellington Monument wore a gleaming cap of snow that flashed westward over the white field of Fifteen Acres.[1]

He began:

—Ladies and Gentlemen.

—It has fallen to my lot this evening, as in years past, to perform a very pleasing task but a task for which I am afraid my poor powers as a speaker are all too inadequate.

—No, no! said Mr Browne.

—But, however that may be, I can only ask you tonight to take the will for the deed and to lend me your attention for a few moments while I endeavour to express to you in words what my feelings are on this occasion.

—Ladies and Gentlemen. It is not the first time that we have gathered together under this hospitable roof, around this hospitable board. It is not the first time that we have been the recipients—or perhaps, I had better say, the victims—of the hospitality of certain good ladies.

He made a circle in the air with his arm and paused. Everyone laughed or smiled at Aunt Kate and Aunt Julia and Mary Jane who all turned crimson with pleasure. Gabriel went on more boldly:

—I feel more strongly with every recurring year that our country has no tradition which does it so much honour and which it should guard so jealously as that of its hospitality. It is a tradition that is unique as far as my experience goes (and I have visited not a few places abroad) among the modern nations. Some would say, per-haps, that with us it is rather a failing than anything to be boasted of. But granted even that, it is, to my mind, a princely failing, and one that I trust will long be culti-vated among us. Of one thing, at least, I am sure. As long as this one roof shelters the good ladies aforesaid—and I wish from my heart it may do so for many and many a long year to come—the tradition of genuine warm-hearted courteous Irish hospitali-ty, which our forefathers have handed down to us and which we in turn must hand down to our descendants, is still alive among us.

A hearty murmur of assent ran round the table. It shot through Gabriel's mind that Miss Ivors was not there and that she had gone away discourteously: and he said with confidence in himself:

---

1. A section of Phoenix Park.

—Ladies and Gentlemen.

—A new generation is growing up in our midst, a generation actuated by new ideas and new principles. It is serious and enthusiastic for these new ideas and its enthusiasm, even when it is misdirected, is, I believe, in the main sincere. But we are living in a sceptical and, if I may use the phrase, a thought-tormented age: and sometimes I fear that this new generation, educated or hypereducated as it is, will lack those qualities of humanity, of hospitality, of kindly humour which belonged to an older day. Listening to-night to the names of all those great singers of the past it seemed to me, I must confess, that we were living in a less spacious age. Those days might, without exaggeration, be called spacious days: and if they are gone beyond recall let us hope, at least, that in gatherings such as this we shall still speak of them with pride and affection, still cherish in our hearts the memory of those dead and gone great ones whose fame the world will not willingly let die.

—Hear, hear! said Mr Browne loudly.

—But yet, continued Gabriel, his voice falling into a softer inflection, there are always in gatherings such as this sadder thoughts that will recur to our minds: thoughts of the past, of youth, of changes, of absent faces that we miss here to-night. Our path through life is strewn with many such sad memories: and were we to brood upon them always we could not find the heart to go on bravely with our work among the living. We have all of us living duties and living affections which claim, and rightly claim, our strenuous endeavours.

—Therefore, I will not linger on the past. I will not let any gloomy moralising intrude upon us here to-night. Here we are gathered together for a brief moment from the bustle and rush of our everyday routine. We are met here as friends, in the spirit of good-fellowship, as colleagues, also to a certain extent, in the true spirit of *camaraderie*, and as the guests of—what shall I call them?—the Three Graces[2] of the Dublin musical world.

The table burst into applause and laughter at this sally. Aunt Julia vainly asked each of her neighbors in turn to tell her what Gabriel had said.

—He says we are the Three Graces, Aunt Julia, said Mary Jane.

Aunt Julia did not understand but she looked up, smiling, at Gabriel, who continued in the same vein:

—Ladies and Gentlemen.

—I will not attempt to play to-night the part that Paris[3] played on another occasion. I will not attempt to choose between them. The task would be an invidious one and one beyond my poor powers. For when I view them in turn, whether it be our chief hostess herself, whose good heart, whose too good heart, has become a byword with all who know her, or her sister, who seems to be gifted with perennial youth and whose singing must have been a surprise and a revelation to us all to-night, or, last but not least, when I consider our youngest hostess, talented, cheerful, hard-working and the best of nieces, I confess, Ladies and Gentlemen, that I do not know to which of them I should award the prize.

Gabriel glanced down at his aunts and, seeing the large smile on Aunt Julia's face and the tears which had risen to Aunt Kate's eyes, hastened to his close. He raised his glass of port gallantly, while every member of the company fingered a glass expectantly, and said loudly:

---

2. Companions to the Muses in Greek mythology.
3. Paris was the judge of a divine beauty contest in which

Hera, Athena, and Aphrodite competed; his selection of Aphrodite was, indirectly, the cause of the Trojan war.

—Let us toast them all three together. Let us drink to their health, wealth, long life, happiness and prosperity and may they long continue to hold the proud and self-won position which they hold in their profession and the position of honour and affection which they hold in our hearts.

All the guests stood up, glass in hand, and, turning towards the three seated ladies, sang in unison, with Mr Browne as leader:

> *For they are jolly gay fellows,*
> *For they are jolly gay fellows,*
> *For they are jolly gay fellows,*
> *Which nobody can deny.*

Aunt Kate was making frank use of her handkerchief and even Aunt Julia seemed moved. Freddy Malins beat time with his pudding-fork and the singers turned towards one another, as if in melodious conference, while they sang, with emphasis:

> *Unless he tells a lie,*
> *Unless he tells a lie,*

Then, turning once more towards their hostesses, they sang:

> *For they are jolly gay fellows,*
> *For they are jolly gay fellows,*
> *For they are jolly gay fellows,*
> *Which nobody can deny.*

The acclamation which followed was taken up beyond the door of the supper-room by many of the other guests and renewed time after time, Freddy Malins acting as officer with his fork on high.

The piercing morning air came into the hall where they were standing so that Aunt Kate said:

—Close the door, somebody. Mrs Malins will get her death of cold.

—Browne is out there, Aunt Kate, said Mary Jane.

—Browne is everywhere, said Aunt Kate, lowering her voice.

Mary Jane laughed at her tone.

—Really, she said archly, he is very attentive.

—He has been laid on here like the gas, said Aunt Kate in the same tone, all during the Christmas.

She laughed herself this time good-humouredly and then added quickly:

—But tell him to come in, Mary Jane, and close the door. I hope to goodness he didn't hear me.

At that moment the hall-door was opened and Mr Browne came in from the doorstep, laughing as if his heart would break. He was dressed in a long green over-coat with mock astrakhan cuffs and collar and wore on his head an oval fur cap. He pointed down the snow-covered quay from where the sound of shrill prolonged whistling was borne in.

—Teddy will have all the cabs in Dublin out, he said.

Gabriel advanced from the little pantry behind the office, struggling into his overcoat and looking round the hall, said:

—Gretta not down yet?

—She's getting on her things, Gabriel, said Aunt Kate.

—Who's playing up there? asked Gabriel.

—Nobody. They're all gone.

—O no, Aunt Kate, said Mary Jane. Bartell D'Arcy and Miss O'Callaghan aren't gone yet.

—Someone is strumming at the piano, anyhow, said Gabriel.

Mary Jane glanced at Gabriel and Mr Browne and said with a shiver:

—It makes me feel cold to look at you two gentlemen muffled up like that. I wouldn't like to face your journey home at this hour.

—I'd like nothing better this minute, said Mr Browne stoutly, than a rattling fine walk in the country or a fast drive with a good spanking goer between the shafts.

—We used to have a very good horse and trap at home, said Aunt Julia sadly.

—The never-to-be-forgotten Johnny, said Mary Jane, laughing.

Aunt Kate and Gabriel laughed too.

—Why, what was wonderful about Johnny? asked Mr Browne.

—The late lamented Patrick Morkan, our grandfather, that is, explained Gabriel, commonly known in his later years as the old gentleman, was a glue-boiler.

—O, now, Gabriel, said Aunt Kate, laughing, he had a starch mill.

—Well, glue or starch, said Gabriel, the old gentleman had a horse by the name of Johnny. And Johnny used to work in the old gentleman's mill, walking round and round in order to drive the mill. That was all very well; but now comes the tragic part about Johnny. One fine day the old gentleman thought he'd like to drive out with the quality to a military review in the park.

—The Lord have mercy on his soul, said Aunt Kate compassionately.

—Amen, said Gabriel. So the old gentleman, as I said, harnessed Johnny and put on his very best tall hat and his very best stock collar and drove out in grand style from his ancestral mansion somewhere near Back Lane, I think.

Everyone laughed, even Mrs Malins, at Gabriel's manner and Aunt Kate said:

—O now, Gabriel, he didn't live in Back Lane, really. Only the mill was there.

—Out from the mansion of his forefathers, continued Gabriel, he drove with Johnny. And everything went on beautifully until Johnny came in sight of King Billy's statue:[4] and whether he fell in love with the horse King Billy sits on or whether he thought he was back again in the mill, anyhow he began to walk round the statue.

Gabriel paced in a circle round the hall in his goloshes amid the laughter of the others.

—Round and round he went, said Gabriel, and the old gentleman, who was a very pompous old gentleman, was highly indignant. *Go on, sir! What do you mean, sir! Johnny! Johnny! Most extraordinary conduct! Can't understand the horse!*

The peals of laughter which followed Gabriel's imitation of the incident were interrupted by a resounding knock at the hall-door. Mary Jane ran to open it and let in Freddy Malins. Freddy Malins, with his hat well back on his head and his shoulders humped with cold, was puffing and steaming after his exertions.

—I could only get one cab, he said.

—O, we'll find another along the quay, said Gabriel.

—Yes, said Aunt Kate. Better not keep Mrs Malins standing in the draught.

Mrs Malins was helped down the front steps by her son and Mr Browne and, after many manoeuvres, hoisted into the cab. Freddy Malins clambered in after her and spent a long time settling her on the seat, Mr Browne helping him with advice.

---

4. Statue of William of Orange, who defeated the Irish Catholic forces in the Battle of the Boyne in 1690, which stood in College Green in front of Trinity College in the heart of Dublin. It was seen as a symbol of British imperial oppression.

At last she was settled comfortably and Freddy Malins invited Mr Browne into the cab. There was a good deal of confused talk, and then Mr Browne got into the cab. The cabman settled his rug over his knees, and bent down for the address. The confusion grew greater and the cabman was directed differently by Freddy Malins and Mr Browne, each of whom had his head out through a window of the cab. The difficulty was to know where to drop Mr Browne along the route and Aunt Kate, Aunt Julia and Mary Jane helped the discussion from the doorstep with cross-directions and contradictions and abundance of laughter. As for Freddy Malins he was speechless with laughter. He popped his head in and out of the window every moment, to the great danger of his hat, and told his mother how the discussion was progressing till at last Mr Browne shouted to the bewildered cabman above the din of everybody's laughter:

—Do you know Trinity College?

—Yes, sir, said the cabman.

—Well, drive bang up against Trinity College gates, said Mr Browne, and then we'll tell you where to go. You understand now?

—Yes, sir, said the cabman.

—Make like a bird for Trinity College.

—Right, sir, cried the cabman.

The horse was whipped up and the cab rattled off along the quay amid a chorus of laughter and adieus.

Gabriel had not gone to the door with the others. He was in a dark part of the hall gazing up the staircase, a woman was standing near the top of the first flight, in the shadow also. He could not see her face but he could see the terracotta and salmonpink panels of her skirt which the shadow made appear black and white. It was his wife. She was leaning on the banisters, listening to something. Gabriel was surprised at her stillness and strained his ear to listen also. But he could hear little save the noise of laughter and dispute on the front steps, a few chords struck on the piano and a few notes of a man's voice singing.

He stood still in the gloom of the hall, trying to catch the air that the voice was singing and gazing up at his wife. There was grace and mystery in her attitude as if she were a symbol of something. He asked himself what is a woman standing on the stairs in the shadow, listening to distant music, a symbol of. If he were a painter he would paint her in that attitude. Her blue felt hat would show off the bronze of her hair against the darkness and the dark panels of her skirt would show off the light ones. *Distant Music* he would call the picture if he were a painter.

The hall-door was closed; and Aunt Kate, Aunt Julia and Mary Jane came down the hall, still laughing.

—Well, isn't Freddy terrible? said Mary Jane. He's really terrible.

Gabriel said nothing but pointed up the stairs towards where his wife was standing. Now that the hall-door was closed the voice and the piano could be heard more clearly. Gabriel held up his hand for them to be silent. The song seemed to be in the old Irish tonality and the singer seemed uncertain both of his words and of his voice. The voice, made plaintive by distance and by the singer's hoarseness, faintly illuminated the cadence of the air with words expressing grief:

> O, the rain falls on my heavy locks
> And the dew wets my skin,
> My babe lies cold . . .

—O, exclaimed Mary Jane. It's Bartell D'Arcy singing and he wouldn't sing all the night. O, I'll get him to sing a song before he goes.

—O do, Mary Jane, said Aunt Kate.

Mary Jane brushed past the others and ran to the staircase but before she reached it the singing stopped and the piano was closed abruptly.

—O, what a pity! she cried. Is he coming down, Gretta?

Gabriel heard his wife answer yes and saw her come down towards them. A few steps behind her were Mr Bartell D'Arcy and Miss O'Callaghan.

—O, Mr D'Arcy, cried Mary Jane, it's downright mean of you to break off like that when we were all in raptures listening to you.

—I have been at him all the evening, said Miss O'Callaghan, and Mrs Conroy too and he told us he had a dreadful cold and couldn't sing.

—O, Mr D'Arcy, said Aunt Kate, now that was a great fib to tell.

—Can't you see that I'm as hoarse as a crow? said Mr D'Arcy roughly.

He went into the pantry hastily and put on his overcoat. The others, taken aback by his rude speech, could find nothing to say. Aunt Kate wrinkled her brows and made signs to the others to drop the subject. Mr D'Arcy stood swathing his neck carefully and frowning.

—It's the weather, said Aunt Julia, after a pause.

—Yes, everybody has colds, said Aunt Kate readily, everybody.

—They say, said Mary Jane, we haven't had snow like it for thirty years; and I read this morning in the newspapers that the snow is general all over Ireland.

—I love the look of snow, said Aunt Julia sadly.

—So do I, said Miss O'Callaghan. I think Christmas is never really Christmas unless we have the snow on the ground.

—But poor Mr D'Arcy doesn't like the snow, said Aunt Kate, smiling.

Mr D'Arcy came from the pantry, full swathed and buttoned, and in a repentant tone told them the history of his cold. Everyone gave him advice and said it was a great pity and urged him to be very careful of his throat in the night air. Gabriel watched his wife who did not join in the conversation. She was standing right under the dusty fanlight and the flame of the gas lit up the rich bronze of her hair which he had seen her drying at the fire a few days before. She was in the same attitude and seemed unaware of the talk about her. At last she turned towards them and Gabriel saw that there was colour on her cheeks and that her eyes were shining. A sudden tide of joy went leaping out of his heart.

—Mr D'Arcy, she said, what is the name of that song you were singing?

—It's called *The Lass of Aughrim*, said Mr D'Arcy, but I couldn't remember it properly. Why? Do you know it?

—*The Lass of Aughrim*, she repeated. I couldn't think of the name.

—It's a very nice air, said Mary Jane. I'm sorry you were not in voice to-night.

—Now, Mary Jane, said Aunt Kate, don't annoy Mr D'Arcy. I won't have him annoyed.

Seeing that all were ready to start she shepherded them to the door where good-night was said:

—Well, good-night, Aunt Kate, and thanks for the pleasant evening.

—Good-night, Gabriel. Good-night, Gretta!

—Good-night, Aunt Kate, and thanks ever so much. Good-night, Aunt Julia.

—O, good-night, Gretta, I didn't see you.

—Good-night, Mr D'Arcy. Good-night, Miss O'Callaghan.

—Good-night, Miss Morkan.

—Good-night, again.

—Good-night, all. Safe home.

—Good-night. Good-night.

The morning was still dark. A dull yellow light brooded over the houses and the river; and the sky seemed to be descending. It was slushy underfoot; and only streaks and patches of snow lay on the roofs, on the parapets of the quay and on the area railings. The lamps were still burning redly in the murky air and, across the river, the palace of the Four Courts[5] stood out menacingly against the heavy sky.

She was walking on before him with Mr Bartell D'Arcy, her shoes in a brown parcel tucked under one arm and her hands holding her skirt up from the slush. She had no longer any grace of attitude but Gabriel's eyes were still bright with happiness. The blood went bounding along his veins; and the thoughts went rioting through his brain, proud, joyful, tender, valorous.

She was walking on before him so lightly and so erect that he longed to run after her noiselessly, catch her by the shoulders and say something foolish and affectionate into her ear. She seemed to him so frail that he longed to defend her against something and then to be alone with her. Moments of their secret life together burst like stars upon his memory. A heliotrope envelope was lying beside his breakfast-cup and he was caressing it with his hand. Birds were twittering in the ivy and the sunny web of the curtain was shimmering along the floor: he could not eat for happiness. They were standing on the crowded platform and he was placing a ticket inside the warm palm of her glove. He was standing with her in the cold, looking in through a grated window at a man making bottles in a roaring furnace. It was very cold. Her face, fragrant in the cold air, was quite close to his; and suddenly she called out to the man at the furnace:

—Is the fire hot, sir?

But the man could not hear her with the noise of the furnace. It was just as well. He might have answered rudely.

A wave of yet more tender joy escaped from his heart and went coursing in warm flood along his arteries. Like the tender fires of stars moments of their life together, that no one knew of or would ever know of, broke upon and illumined his memory. He longed to recall to her those moments, to make her forget the years of their dull existence together and remember only their moments of ecstasy. For the years, he felt, had not quenched his soul or hers. Their children, his writing, her household cares had not quenched all their souls' tender fire. In one letter that he had written to her then he had said: *Why is it that words like these seem to me so dull and cold? Is it because there is no word tender enough to be your name?*

Like distant music these words that he had written years before were borne towards him from the past. He longed to be alone with her. When the others had gone away, when he and she were in their room in the hotel, then they would be alone together. He would call her softly:

—Gretta!

Perhaps she would not hear at once: she would be undressing. Then something in his voice would strike her. She would turn and look at him. . . .

At the corner of Winetavern Street they met a cab. He was glad of its rattling noise as it saved him from conversation. She was looking out of the window and seemed tired. The others spoke only a few words, pointing out some building or

5. The Irish law courts.

street. The horse galloped along wearily under the murky morning sky, dragging his old rattling box after his heels, and Gabriel was again in a cab with her, galloping to catch the boat, galloping to their honeymoon.

As the cab drove across O'Connell Bridge Miss O'Callaghan said:

—They say you never cross O'Connell Bridge without seeing a white horse.

—I see a white man this time, said Gabriel.

—Where? asked Mr Bartell D'Arcy.

Gabriel pointed to the statue, on which lay patches of snow. Then he nodded familiarly to it and waved his hand.

—Good-night, Dan,[6] he said gaily.

When the cab drew up before the hotel Gabriel jumped out and, in spite of Mr Bartell D'Arcy's protest, paid the driver. He gave the man a shilling over his fare. The man saluted and said:

—A prosperous New Year to you, sir.

—The same to you, said Gabriel cordially.

She leaned for a moment on his arm in getting out of the cab and while standing at the curbstone, bidding the others good-night. She leaned lightly on his arm, as lightly as when she had danced with him a few hours before. He had felt proud and happy then, happy that she was his, proud of her grace and wifely carriage. But now, after the kindling again of so many memories, the first touch of her body, musical and strange and perfumed, sent through him a keen pang of lust. Under cover of her silence he pressed her arm closely to his side; and, as they stood at the hotel door, he felt that they had escaped from their lives and duties, escaped from home and friends and run away together with wild and radiant hearts to a new adventure.

An old man was dozing in a great hooded chair in the hall. He lit a candle in the office and went before them to the stairs. They followed him in silence, their feet falling in soft thuds on the thickly carpeted stairs. She mounted the stairs behind the porter, her head bowed in the ascent, her frail shoulders curved as with a burden, her skirt girt tightly about her. He could have flung his arms about her hips and held her still for his arms were trembling with desire to seize her and only the stress of his nails against the palms of his hands held the wild impulse of his body in check. The porter halted on the stairs to settle his guttering candle. They halted too on the steps below him. In the silence Gabriel could hear the falling of the molten wax into the tray and the thumping of his own heart against his ribs.

The porter led them along a corridor and opened a door. Then he set his unstable candle down on a toilet-table and asked at what hour they were to be called in the morning.

—Eight, said Gabriel.

The porter pointed to the tap of the electric-light and began a muttered apology but Gabriel cut him short.

—We don't want any light. We have light enough from the street. And I say, he added, pointing to the candle, you might remove that handsome article, like a good man.

The porter took up his candle again, but slowly for he was surprised by such a novel idea. Then he mumbled good-night and went out. Gabriel shot the lock to.

---

6. A statue of Daniel O'Connell, 19th-century nationalist leader, stands at the south end of Sackville Street (now called O'Connell Street).

A ghostly light from the street lamp lay in a long shaft from one window to the door. Gabriel threw his overcoat and hat on a couch and crossed the room towards the window. He looked down into the street in order that his emotion might calm a little. Then he turned and leaned against a chest of drawers with his back to the light. She had taken off her hat and cloak and was standing before a large swinging mirror, unhooking her waist. Gabriel paused for a few moments, watching her, and then said:

—Gretta!

She turned away from the mirror slowly and walked along the shaft of light towards him. Her face looked so serious and weary that the words would not pass Gabriel's lips. No, it was not the moment yet.

—You looked tired, he said.

—I am a little, she answered.

—You don't feel ill or weak?

—No, tired: that's all.

She went on to the window and stood there, looking out. Gabriel waited again and then, fearing that diffidence was about to conquer him, he said abruptly:

—By the way, Gretta!

—What is it?

—You know that poor fellow Malins? he said quickly.

—Yes. What about him?

—Well, poor fellow, he's a decent sort of chap after all, continued Gabriel in a false voice. He gave me back that sovereign I lent him and I didn't expect it really. It's a pity he wouldn't keep away from that Browne, because he's not a bad fellow at heart.

He was trembling now with annoyance. Why did she seem so abstracted? He did not know how he could begin. Was she annoyed, too, about something? If she would only turn to him or come to him of her own accord! To take her as she was would be brutal. No, he must see some ardour in her eyes first. He longed to be master of her strange mood.

—When did you lend him the pound? she asked, after a pause.

Gabriel strove to restrain himself from breaking out into brutal language about the sottish Malins and his pound. He longed to cry to her from his soul, to crush her body against his, to overmaster her. But he said:

—O, at Christmas, when he opened that little Christmas-card shop in Henry Street.

He was in such a fever of rage and desire that he did not hear her come from the window. She stood before him for an instant, looking at him strangely. Then, suddenly raising herself on tiptoe and resting her hands lightly on his shoulders, she kissed him.

—You are a very generous person, Gabriel, she said.

Gabriel, trembling with delight at her sudden kiss and at the quaintness of her phrase, put his hands on her hair and began smoothing it back, scarcely touching it with his fingers. The washing had made it fine and brilliant. His heart was brimming over with happiness. Just when he was wishing for it she had come to him of her own accord. Perhaps her thoughts had been running with his. Perhaps she had felt the impetuous desire that was in him and then the yielding mood had come upon her. Now that she had fallen to him so easily he wondered why he had been so diffident.

He stood, holding her head between his hands. Then, slipping one arm swiftly about her body and drawing her towards him, he said softly:

—Gretta dear, what are you thinking about?

She did not answer nor yield wholly to his arm. He said again, softly:

—Tell me what it is, Gretta. I think I know what is the matter. Do I know?

She did not answer at once. Then she said in an outburst of tears:

—O, I am thinking about that song, *The Lass of Aughrim*.

She broke loose from him and ran to the bed and, throwing her arms across the bed-rail, hid her face. Gabriel stood stock-still for a moment in astonishment and then followed her. As he passed in the way of the cheval-glass he caught sight of himself in full length, his broad, well-filled shirt-front, the face whose expression always puzzled him when he saw it in a mirror and his glimmering gilt-rimmed eyeglasses. He halted a few paces from her and said:

—What about the song? Why does that make you cry?

She raised her head from her arms and dried her eyes with the back of her hand like a child. A kinder note than he had intended went into his voice.

—Why, Gretta? he asked.

—I am thinking about a person long ago who used to sing that song.

—And who was the person long ago? asked Gabriel, smiling.

—It was a person I used to know in Galway when I was living with my grandmother, she said.

The smile passed away from Gabriel's face. A dull anger began to gather again at the back of his mind and the dull fires of his lust began to glow angrily in his veins.

—Someone you were in love with? he asked ironically.

—It was a young boy I used to know, she answered, named Michael Furey. He used to sing that song, *The Lass of Aughrim*. He was very delicate.

Gabriel was silent. He did not wish her to think that he was interested in this delicate boy.

—I can see him so plainly, she said after a moment. Such eyes as he had: big dark eyes! And such an expression in them—an expression!

—O then, you were in love with him? said Gabriel.

—I used to go out walking with him, she said, when I was in Galway.

A thought flew across Gabriel's mind.

—Perhaps that was why you wanted to go to Galway with that Ivors girl? he said coldly.

She looked at him and asked in surprise:

—What for?

Her eyes made Gabriel feel awkward. He shrugged his shoulders and said:

—How do I know? To see him perhaps.

She looked away from him along the shaft of light towards the window in silence.

—He is dead, she said at length. He died when he was only seventeen. Isn't it a terrible thing to die so young as that?

—What was he? asked Gabriel, still ironically.

—He was in the gasworks, she said.

Gabriel felt humiliated by the failure of his irony and by the evocation of this figure from the dead, a boy in the gasworks. While he had been full of memories of their secret life together, full of tenderness and joy and desire, she had been comparing him in her mind with another. A shameful consciousness of his own person assailed him. He saw himself as a ludicrous figure, acting as a pennyboy[7] for his aunts,

7. Errand boy.

a nervous well-meaning sentimentalist, orating to vulgarians and idealising his own clownish lusts, the pitiable fatuous fellow he had caught a glimpse of in the mirror. Instinctively he turned his back more to the light lest she might see the shame that burned upon his forehead.

He tried to keep up his tone of cold interrogation but his voice when he spoke was humble and indifferent.

—I suppose you were in love with this Michael Furey, Gretta, he said.

—I was great with him at that time, she said.

Her voice was veiled and sad. Gabriel, feeling now how vain it would be to try to lead her whither he had purposed, caressed one of her hands and said, also sadly:

—And what did he die of so young, Gretta? Consumption, was it?

—I think he died for me, she answered.[8]

A vague terror seized Gabriel at this answer as if, at that hour when he had hoped to triumph, some impalpable and vindictive being was coming against him, gathering forces against him in its vague world. But he shook himself free of it with an effort of reason and continued to caress her hand. He did not question her again for he felt that she would tell him of herself. Her hand was warm and moist: it did not respond to his touch but he continued to caress it just as he had caressed her first letter to him that spring morning.

—It was in the winter, she said, about the beginning of the winter when I was going to leave my grandmother's and come up here to the convent. And he was ill at the time in his lodgings in Galway and wouldn't be let out and his people in Oughterard[9] were written to. He was in decline, they said, or something like that. I never knew rightly.

She paused for a moment and sighed.

—Poor fellow, she said. He was very fond of me and he was such a gentle boy. We used to go out together, walking, you know, Gabriel, like the way they do in the country. He was going to study singing only for his health. He had a very good voice, poor Michael Furey.

—Well; and then? asked Gabriel.

—And then when it came to the time for me to leave Galway and come up to the convent he was much worse and I wouldn't be let see him so I wrote a letter saying I was going up to Dublin and would be back in the summer and hoping he would be better then.

She paused for a moment to get her voice under control and then went on:

—Then the night before I left I was in my grandmother's house in Nuns' Island, packing up, and I heard gravel thrown up against the window. The window was so wet I couldn't see so I ran downstairs as I was and slipped out the back into the garden and there was the poor fellow at the end of the garden, shivering.

—And did you not tell him to go back? asked Gabriel.

—I implored him to go home at once and told him he would get his death in the rain. But he said he did not want to live. I can see his eyes as well as well! He was standing at the end of the wall where there was a tree.

—And did he go home? asked Gabriel.

8. Gretta here echoes the words of Yeats's Cathleen ni Houlihan: "Singing I am about a man I knew one time, yellow-haired Donough that was hanged in Galway. . . . He died for love of me: many a man has died for love of me." The play was first performed in Dublin on 2 April 1902.

9. A small village in Western Ireland.

—Yes, he went home. And when I was only a week in the convent he died and he was buried in Oughterard where his people came from. O, the day I heard that, that he was dead!

She stopped, choking with sobs, and, overcome by emotion, flung herself face downward on the bed, sobbing in the quilt. Gabriel held her hand for a moment longer, irresolutely, and then, shy of intruding on her grief, let it fall gently and walked quietly to the window.

She was fast asleep.

Gabriel, leaning on his elbow, looked for a few moments unresentfully on her tangled hair and half-open mouth, listening to her deep-drawn breath. So she had had that romance in her life: a man had died for her sake. It hardly pained him now to think how poor a part he, her husband, had played in her life. He watched her while she slept as though he and she had never lived together as man and wife. His curious eyes rested long upon her face and on her hair: and, as he thought of what she must have been then, in that time of her first girlish beauty, a strange friendly pity for her entered his soul. He did not like to say even to himself that her face was no longer beautiful but he knew that it was no longer the face for which Michael Furey had braved death.

Perhaps she had not told him all the story. His eyes moved to the chair over which she had thrown some of her clothes. A petticoat string dangled to the floor. One boot stood upright, its limp upper fallen down: the fellow of it lay upon its side. He wondered at his riot of emotions of an hour before. From what had it proceeded? From his aunt's supper, from his own foolish speech, from the wine and dancing, the merry-making when saying good-night in the hall, the pleasure of the walk along the river in the snow. Poor Aunt Julia! She, too, would soon be a shade with the shade of Patrick Morkan and his horse. He had caught that haggard look upon her face for a moment when she was singing *Arrayed for the Bridal*. Soon, perhaps, he would be sitting in that same drawing-room, dressed in black, his silk hat on his knees. The blinds would be drawn down and Aunt Kate would be sitting beside him, crying and blowing her nose and telling him how Julia had died. He would cast about in his mind for some words that might console her, and would find only lame and useless ones. Yes, yes: that would happen very soon.

The air of the room chilled his shoulders. He stretched himself cautiously along under the sheets and lay down beside his wife. One by one they were all becoming shades. Better pass boldly into that other world, in the full glory of some passion, than fade and wither dismally with age. He thought of how she who lay beside him had locked in her heart for so many years that image of her lover's eyes when he had told her that he did not wish to live.

Generous tears filled Gabriel's eyes. He had never felt like that himself towards any woman but he knew that such a feeling must be love. The tears gathered more thickly in his eyes and in the partial darkness he imagined he saw the form of a young man standing under a dripping tree. Other forms were near. His soul had approached that region where dwell the vast hosts of the dead. He was conscious of, but could not apprehend, their wayward and flickering existence. His own identity was fading out into a grey impalpable world: the solid world itself which these dead had one time reared and lived in was dissolving and dwindling.

A few light taps upon the pane made him turn to the window. It had begun to snow again. He watched sleepily the flakes, silver and dark, falling obliquely against the lamplight. The time had come for him to set out on his journey westward. Yes, the newspapers were right: snow was general all over Ireland. It was falling on every part of the dark central plain, on the treeless hills, falling softly upon the Bog of Allen and, farther westward, softly falling into the dark mutinous Shannon waves.[1] It was falling, too, upon every part of the lonely churchyard on the hill where Michael Furey lay buried. It lay thickly drifted on the crooked crosses and headstones, on the spears of the little gate, on the barren thorns. His soul swooned slowly as he heard the snow falling faintly through the universe and faintly falling, like the descent of their last end, upon all the living and the dead.

Ulysses

Ulysses boldly announced that modern literature had set itself new tasks and devised new means to "make it new." In his review of the novel, T. S. Eliot wrote that Joyce had discovered "a way of controlling, of ordering, of giving a shape and a significance to the panorama of futility and anarchy which is contemporary history. . . . It is, I seriously believe, a step toward making the modern world possible for art . . . ." The technique with which Joyce shaped his materials Eliot called (at Joyce's suggestion) the mythical method—using ancient myth to suggest "a continuous parallel between contemporaneity and antiquity." Joyce's purposes in using myth—in the case of *Ulysses*, a series of parallels to Homer's *Odyssey*—are open to debate; but he was quite frank about the fact that each of the novel's eighteen chapters was modeled, however loosely, on one of Odysseus's adventures. Thus Leopold Bloom, the novel's advertising-salesman protagonist, is in some sense a modern-day Odysseus; rather than finding his way back from Troy and the Trojan Wars, he simply navigates his way through a very full day in Dublin on June 16, 1904. This day, however, has its perils. Bloom, a Jew, is set upon by anti-Semites, threatened with violence, and driven from the pub where he drinks; much later, in Dublin's red-light district, he rescues a very drunk young poet, Stephen Dedalus, from arrest, and takes him back to his home for a cup of cocoa and conversation. Foremost among Bloom's tests on this particular day, however, is his knowledge that his wife Molly will consummate an affair with the brash, egotistical tenor Blazes Boylan—an affair which, owing to his own shortcomings as a husband, Bloom is unwilling to stop.

The chapter given here is the pivotal seventh chapter, in which the realism of the earlier chapters begins to be invaded by other modes of observation and narration. Set in the offices of the *Freeman's Journal* where Bloom works, the chapter takes on a parodoxically reportorial perspective, complete with headlines. Chapter 7 is usually called the "Aeolus" chapter, after its parallel episode in the *Odyssey*. In Book 10, having escaped the Cyclops, Odysseus reaches an island ruled by Aeolus, lord of the winds. Aeolus offers to help Odysseus by trapping all ill winds in a bag which Odysseus then takes with him on his ship; when they are within sight of home, however, Odysseus falls asleep and his crew, curious and jealous about what their captain might have stowed in the bag, open it, releasing the winds and driving the crew back to Aeolia. Joyce builds into his chapter myraid references to wind and air in many forms—from arias to belches, and from conversational shooting the breeze to rhetorical hot air. As Bloom tries to do his job, forget about Molly's plans, and find acceptance among co-workers who will always see him as an outsider, he narrowly misses meeting up with Stephen Dedalus. Stephen has come to the newspaper to deliver a letter on hoof and mouth disease, written by the headmaster of the school where he is teaching. This far from exalted errand only increases Stephen's unease as he negotiates the provincial literary and journalistic world of Dublin, looking for ways to free himself, and capture Dublin, in his art.

---

1. Where Ireland's longest river, the Shannon, empties into the sea.

Photo of Sackville Street (now O'Connell Street), Dublin, with view of Nelson's Pillar.

from **Ulysses**

[CHAPTER 7. AEOLUS]

IN THE HEART OF THE HIBERNIAN METROPOLIS

Before Nelson's pillar trams slowed, shunted, changed trolley, started for Blackrock, Kingstown and Dalkey, Clonskea, Rathgar and Terenure, Palmerston Park and upper Rathmines, Sandymount Green, Rathmines, Ringsend, and Sandymount Tower, Harold's Cross.[1] The hoarse Dublin United Tramway Company's timekeeper bawled them off:

—Rathgar and Terenure!

—Come on, Sandymount Green!

Right and left parallel clanging ringing a doubledecker and a singledeck moved from their railheads, swerved to the down line, glided parallel.

—Start, Palmerston Park!

THE WEARER OF THE CROWN

Under the porch of the general post office shoeblacks called and polished. Parked in North Prince's street His Majesty's vermilion mailcars, bearing on their sides the royal initials, E. R.,[2] received loudly flung sacks of letters, postcards, lettercards, parcels, insured and paid, for local, provincial, British and overseas delivery.

1. The names of various tramlines going out from Nelson's Pillar in central Dublin.

2. Edward Rex (Edward VII of England).

GENTLEMEN OF THE PRESS

Grossbooted draymen rolled barrels dullthudding out of Prince's stores and bumped them up on the brewery float. On the brewery float bumped dullthudding barrels rolled by grossbooted draymen out of Prince's stores.

—There it is, Red Murray said. Alexander Keyes.

—Just cut it out, will you? Mr Bloom said, and I'll take it round to the *Telegraph* office.

The door of Ruttledge's office creaked again. Davy Stephens, minute in a large capecoat, a small felt hat crowning his ringlets, passed out with a roll of papers under his cape, a king's courier.

Red Murray's long shears sliced out the advertisement from the newspaper in four clean strokes. Scissors and paste.

—I'll go through the printingworks, Mr Bloom said, taking the cut square.

—Of course, if he wants a par,[3] Red Murray said earnestly, a pen behind his ear, we can do him one.

—Right, Mr Bloom said with a nod. I'll rub that in.

We.

WILLIAM BRAYDEN, ESQUIRE, OF OAKLANDS, SANDYMOUNT

Red Murray touched Mr Bloom's arm with the shears and whispered:

—Brayden.[4]

Mr Bloom turned and saw the liveried porter raise his lettered cap as a stately figure entered between the newsboards of the *Weekly Freeman and National Press* and the *Freeman's Journal and National Press*. Dullthudding Guinness's barrels. It passed stately up the staircase steered by an umbrella, a solemn beardframed face. The broadcloth back ascended each step: back. All his brains are in the nape of his neck, Simon Dedalus says. Welts of flesh behind on him. Fat folds of neck, fat, neck, fat, neck.

—Don't you think his face is like Our Saviour? Red Murray whispered.

The door of Ruttledge's office whispered: ee: cree. They always build one door opposite another for the wind to. Way in. Way out.

Our Saviour: beardframed oval face: talking in the dusk. Mary, Martha. Steered by an umbrella sword to the footlights: Mario the tenor.[5]

—Or like Mario, Mr Bloom said.

—Yes, Red Murray agreed. But Mario was said to be the picture of Our Saviour. Jesus Mario with rougy cheeks, doublet and spindle legs. Hand on his heart. In *Martha*.[6]

> *Co-ome thou lost one,*
> *Co-ome thou dear one*

THE CROZIER[7] AND THE PEN

—His grace phoned down twice this morning, Red Murray said gravely.

They watched the knees, legs, boots vanish. Neck.

3. A paragraph.
4. Irish barrister (1865–1933) and editor of the *Freeman's Journal*.
5. Giovanni Matteo (1810–1883), known onstage as "Mario."
6. Light opera (1847) by Friedrich von Flotow.
7. Bishop's staff.

A telegram boy stepped in nimbly, threw an envelope on the counter and stepped off posthaste with a word:

—Freeman!

Mr Bloom said slowly:

—Well, he is one of our saviours also.

A meek smile accompanied him as he lifted the counterflap, as he passed in through a sidedoor and along the warm dark stairs and passage, along the now reverberating boards. But will he save the circulation? Thumping, thumping.

He pushed in the glass swingdoor and entered, stepping over strewn packing paper. Through a lane of clanking drums he made his way towards Nannetti's reading closet.[8]

Hynes here too: account of the funeral probably. Thumping thump.

WITH UNFEIGNED REGRET IT IS WE ANNOUNCE THE DISSOLUTION OF A MOST RESPECTED DUBLIN BURGESS

This morning the remains of the late Mr Patrick Dignam. Machines. Smash a man to atoms if they got him caught. Rule the world today. His machineries are pegging away too. Like these, got out of hand: fermenting. Working away, tearing away. And that old grey rat tearing to get in.

HOW A GREAT DAILY ORGAN IS TURNED OUT

Mr Bloom halted behind the foreman's spare body, admiring a glossy crown.

Strange he never saw his real country. Ireland my country. Member for College green. He boomed that workaday worker tack for all it was worth. It's the ads and side features sell a weekly not the stale news in the official gazette. Queen Anne is dead. Published by authority in the year one thousand and. Demesne situate in the townland of Rosenallis, barony of Tinnahinch. To all whom it may concern schedule pursuant to statute showing return of number of mules and jennets exported from Ballina. Nature notes. Cartoons. Phil Blake's weekly Pat and Bull story. Uncle Toby's page for tiny tots. Country bumpkin's queries. Dear Mr Editor, what is a good cure for flatulence? I'd like that part. Learn a lot teaching others. The personal note. M. A. P.[9] Mainly all pictures. Shapely bathers on golden strand. World's biggest balloon. Double marriage of sisters celebrated. Two bridegrooms laughing heartily at each other. Cuprani too, printer. More Irish than the Irish.

The machines clanked in threefour time. Thump, thump, thump. Now if he got paralysed there and no one knew how to stop them they'd clank on and on the same, print it over and over and up and back. Monkeydoodle the whole thing. Want a cool head.

—Well, get it into the evening edition, councillor, Hynes said.

Soon be calling him my lord mayor. Long John is backing him, they say.

The foreman, without answering, scribbled press on a corner of the sheet and made a sign to a typesetter. He handed the sheet silently over the dirty glass screen.

—Right: thanks, Hynes said moving off.

Mr Bloom stood in his way.

---

8. Joseph Patrick Nannetti (1851–1915), Irish-Italian printer and politician, a Dublin Member of Parliament.

9. Mainly About People, a weekly paper.

—If you want to draw the cashier is just going to lunch, he said, pointing backward with his thumb.

—Did you? Hynes asked.

—Mm, Mr Bloom said. Look sharp and you'll catch him.

—Thanks, old man, Hynes said. I'll tap him too.

He hurried on eagerly towards the *Freeman's Journal*.

Three bob I lent him in Meagher's. Three weeks. Third hint.

WE SEE THE CANVASSER AT WORK

Mr Bloom laid his cutting on Mr Nannetti's desk.

—Excuse me, councillor, he said. This ad, you see. Keyes, you remember.

Mr Nannetti considered the cutting a while and nodded.

—He wants it in for July, Mr Bloom said.

The foreman moved his pencil towards it.

—But wait, Mr Bloom said. He wants it changed. Keyes, you see. He wants two keys at the top.

Hell of a racket they make. He doesn't hear it. Nannan. Iron nerves. Maybe he understands what I.

The foreman turned round to hear patiently and, lifting an elbow, began to scratch slowly in the armpit of his alpaca jacket.

—Like that, Mr Bloom said, crossing his forefingers at the top.

Let him take that in first.

Mr Bloom, glancing sideways up from the cross he had made, saw the foreman's sallow face, think he has a touch of jaundice, and beyond the obedient reels feeding in huge webs of paper. Clank it. Clank it. Miles of it unreeled. What becomes of it after? O, wrap up meat, parcels: various uses, thousand and one things.

Slipping his words deftly into the pauses of the clanking he drew swiftly on the scarred woodwork.

HOUSE OF KEY(E)S

—Like that, see. Two crossed keys here. A circle. Then here the name Alexander Keyes, tea, wine and spirit merchant. So on.

Better not teach him his own business.

—You know yourself, councillor, just what he wants. Then round the top in leaded: the house of keys. You see? Do you think that's a good idea?

The foreman moved his scratching hand to his lower ribs and scratched there quietly.

—The idea, Mr Bloom said, is the house of keys. You know, councillor, the Manx parliament. Innuendo of home rule.[1] Tourists, you know, from the isle of Man. Catches the eye, you see. Can you do that?

I could ask him perhaps about how to pronounce that *voglio*.[2] But then if he didn't know only make it awkward for him. Better not.

---

1. The House of Keyes is the lower house of the Isle of Man Parliament. The Isle of Man enjoyed Home Rule, which Parnell was trying to win for Ireland.

2. In Mozart's opera *Don Giovanni*, Don Giovanni tries to seduce a peasant girl, Zerlina, on her wedding day. Tempted, Zerlina sings *"voglio e non vorrei"* ("I want to

and I wouldn't like to"). Bloom's wife Molly is rehearsing this song; Bloom worries both that Molly may be mispronouncing the word (the g of *voglio* is silent) and, more importantly, that the line may accurately represent her willingness to enter into an affair with her eager suitor Blazes Boylan.

—We can do that, the foreman said. Have you the design?

—I can get it, Mr Bloom said. It was in a Kilkenny paper. He has a house there too. I'll just run out and ask him. Well, you can do that and just a little par calling attention. You know the usual. Highclass licensed premises. Longfelt want. So on.

The foreman thought for an instant.

—We can do that, he said. Let him give us a three months' renewal.

A typesetter brought him a limp galleypage. He began to check it silently. Mr Bloom stood by, hearing the loud throbs of cranks, watching the silent typesetters at their cases.

ORTHOGRAPHICAL

Want to be sure of his spelling. Proof fever. Martin Cunningham forgot to give us his spellingbee conundrum this morning. It is amusing to view the unpar one ar alleled embarra two ars is it? double ess ment of a harassed pedlar while gauging au the symmetry with a y of a peeled pear under a cemetery wall. Silly, isn't it? Cemetery put in of course on account of the symmetry.

I could have said when he clapped on his topper. Thank you. I ought to have said something about an old hat or something. No, I could have said. Looks as good as new now. See his phiz[3] then.

Sllt. The nethermost deck of the first machine jogged forward its flyboard with sllt the first batch of quirefolded papers. Sllt. Almost human the way it sllt to call attention. Doing its level best to speak. That door too sllt creaking, asking to be shut. Everything speaks in its own way. Sllt.

NOTED CHURCHMAN AN OCCASIONAL CONTRIBUTOR

The foreman handed back the galleypage suddenly, saying:

—Wait. Where's the archbishop's letter? It's to be repeated in the *Telegraph*. Where's what's his name?

He looked about him round his loud unanswering machines.

—Monks, sir? a voice asked from the castingbox.

—Ay. Where's Monks?

—Monks!

Mr Bloom took up his cutting. Time to get out.

—Then I'll get the design, Mr Nannetti, he said, and you'll give it a good place I know.

—Monks!

—Yes, sir.

Three months' renewal. Want to get some wind off my chest first. Try it anyhow. Rub in August: good idea: horseshow month. Ballsbridge. Tourists over for the show.[4]

A DAYFATHER

He walked on through the caseroom, passing an old man, bowed, spectacled, aproned. Old Monks, the dayfather. Queer lot of stuff he must have put through his hands in his time: obituary notices, pubs' ads, speeches, divorce suits, found drowned.

---

3. Physiognomy; face.
4. An important horse show is held every August in the Royal Dublin Society's showgrounds in the suburb of Ballsbridge.

Nearing the end of his tether now. Sober serious man with a bit in the savingsbank I'd say. Wife a good cook and washer. Daughter working the machine in the parlour. Plain Jane, no damn nonsense.

AND IT WAS THE FEAST OF THE PASSOVER

He stayed in his walk to watch a typesetter neatly distributing type. Reads it backwards first. Quickly he does it. Must require some practice that. mangiD kcirtaP. Poor papa with his hagadah book, reading backwards with his finger to me. Pessach.[5] Next year in Jerusalem. Dear, O dear! All that long business about that brought us out of the land of Egypt and into the house of bondage *alleluia*.[6] *Shema Israel Adonai Elohenu*. No, that's the other.[7] Then the twelve brothers, Jacob's sons. And then the lamb and the cat and the dog and the stick and the water and the butcher and then the angel of death kills the butcher and he kills the ox and the dog kills the cat.[8] Sounds a bit silly till you come to look into it well. Justice it means but it's everybody eating everyone else. That's what life is after all. How quickly he does that job. Practice makes perfect. Seems to see with his fingers.

Mr Bloom passed on out of the clanking noises through the gallery on to the landing. Now am I going to tram it out all the way and then catch him out perhaps. Better phone him up first. Number? Same as Citron's house. Twentyeight. Twentyeight double four.

ONLY ONCE MORE THAT SOAP[9]

He went down the house staircase. Who the deuce scrawled all over those walls with matches? Looks as if they did it for a bet. Heavy greasy smell there always is in those works. Lukewarm glue in Thom's next door when I was there.

He took out his handkerchief to dab his nose. Citronlemon? Ah, the soap I put there. Lose it out of that pocket. Putting back his handkerchief he took out the soap and stowed it away, buttoned, into the hip pocket of his trousers.

What perfume does your wife use? I could go home still: tram: something I forgot. Just to see before dressing. No. Here. No.[1]

A sudden screech of laughter came from the *Evening Telegraph* office. Know who that is. What's up? Pop in a minute to phone. Ned Lambert it is.

He entered softly.

ERIN, GREEN GEM OF THE SILVER SEA

—The ghost walks, professor MacHugh murmured softly, biscuitfully to the dusty windowpane.

Mr Dedalus, staring from the empty fireplace at Ned Lambert's quizzing face, asked of it sourly:

---

5. Passover; "Next year in Jerusalem" is the final phrase in the Passover night home ceremony when families read the *haggadah* ("story") of the exodus of the Israelites from Egypt (Exodus 12).

6. The Bible actually says "out of Egypt, *from* the house of bondage" (Exodus 13.14).

7. "Hear, O Israel, the Lord our God" (Deuteronomy 6.4)—a daily prayer, not part of the Passover ceremony.

8. Recalling the "Chad Gadya" (One Lamb), a Passover song.

9. Bloom purchased a lemon-scented cake of soap in the "Lotus Eaters" episode (ch. 5); it fits awkwardly in his trousers pocket, and thus intrudes into the narrative from time to time.

1. Bloom considers rushing home and heading off the imminent affair between Molly and Blazes Boylan; his own postal "affair" with Martha Clifford (the sentence "What perfume does your wife use?" is remembered from one of her letters) puts the idea in his head.

—Agonising Christ, wouldn't it give you a heartburn on your arse?

Ned Lambert, seated on the table, read on:

—*Or again, note the meanderings of some purling rill as it babbles on its way, fanned by gentlest zephyrs tho' quarrelling with the stony obstacles, to the tumbling waters of Neptune's blue domain, mid mossy banks, played on by the glorious sunlight or 'neath the shadows cast o'er its pensive bosom by the overarching leafage of the giants of the forest.* What about that, Simon? he asked over the fringe of his newspaper. How's that for high?

—Changing his drink, Mr Dedalus said.

Ned Lambert, laughing, struck the newspaper on his knees, repeating:

—*The pensive bosom and the overarsing leafage.* O boys! O, boys!

—And Xenophon looked upon Marathon, Mr Dedalus said, looking again on the fireplace and to the window, and Marathon looked on the sea.[2]

—That will do, professor MacHugh cried from the window. I don't want to hear any more of the stuff.

He ate off the crescent of water biscuit he had been nibbling and, hungered, made ready to nibble the biscuit in his other hand.

High falutin stuff. Bladderbags. Ned Lambert is taking a day off I see. Rather upsets a man's day a funeral does. He has influence they say. Old Chatterton, the vicechancellor is his granduncle or his greatgranduncle. Close on ninety they say. Subleader for his death written this long time perhaps. Living to spite them. Might go first himself. Johnny, make room for your uncle. The right honourable Hedges Eyre Chatterton. Daresay he writes him an odd shaky cheque or two on gale days. Windfall when he kicks out. Alleluia.

—Just another spasm, Ned Lambert said.

—What is it? Mr Bloom asked.

—A recently discovered fragment of Cicero's[3] Professor MacHugh answered with pomp of tone. *Our lovely land.*

SHORT BUT TO THE POINT

—Whose land? Mr Bloom said simply.

—Most pertinent question, the professor said between his chews. With an accent on the whose.

—Dan Dawson's land, Mr Dedalus said.

—Is it his speech last night? Mr Bloom asked.

Ned Lambert nodded.

—But listen to this, he said.

The doorknob hit Mr Bloom in the small of the back as the door was pushed in.

—Excuse me, J. J. O'Molloy said, entering.

Mr Bloom moved nimbly aside.

—I beg yours, he said.

—Good day, Jack.

—Come in. Come in.

—Good day.

—How are you, Dedalus?

---

2. Quoting "The Isles of Greece," a poem by Byron included in *Don Juan*, Canto III.   3. Roman rhetorician and statesman (106–43 B.C.).

—Well. And yourself?

J. J. O'Molloy shook his head.

SAD

Cleverest fellow at the junior bar he used to be. Decline poor chap. That hectic flush spells finis for a man. Touch and go with him. What's in the wind, I wonder. Money worry.

—*Or again if we but climb the serried mountain peaks.*

—You're looking extra.

—Is the editor to be seen? J. J. O'Molloy asked, looking towards the inner door.

—Very much so, professor MacHugh said. To be seen and heard. He's in his sanctum with Lenehan.

J. J. O'Molloy strolled to the sloping desk and began to turn back the pink pages of the file.

Practice dwindling. A mighthavebeen. Losing heart. Gambling. Debts of honour. Reaping the whirlwind. Used to get good retainers from D. and T. Fitzgerald. Their wigs to show the grey matter. Brains on their sleeve like the statue in Glasnevin.[4] Believe he does some literary work for the *Express* with Gabriel Conroy.[5] Wellread fellow. Myles Crawford began on the *Independent*. Funny the way those newspaper men veer about when they get wind of a new opening. Weathercocks. Hot and cold in the same breath. Wouldn't know which to believe. One story good till you hear the next. Go for one another baldheaded in the papers and then all blows over. Hailfellow well met the next moment.

—Ah, listen to this for God' sake, Ned Lambert pleaded. *Or again if we but climb the serried mountain peaks . . .*

—Bombast! the professor broke in testily. Enough of the inflated windbag!

—*Peaks*, Ned Lambert went on, *towering high on high, to bathe our souls, as it were . . .*

—Bathe his lips, Mr Dedalus said. Blessed and eternal God! Yes? Is he taking anything for it?

—*As 'twere, in the peerless panorama of Ireland's portfolio, unmatched, despite their wellpraised prototypes in other vaunted prize regions for very beauty, of bosky grove and undulating plain and luscious pastureland of vernal green, steeped in the transcendent translucent glow of our mild mysterious Irish twilight . . .*

—The moon, professor MacHugh said. He forgot Hamlet.

HIS NATIVE DORIC[6]

—*That mantles the vista far and wide and wait till the glowing orb of the moon shine forth to irradiate her silver effulgence . . .*

—O! Mr Dedalus cried, giving vent to a hopeless groan, shite and onions! That'll do, Ned. Life is too short.

He took off his silk hat and, blowing out impatiently his bushy moustache, welshcombed his hair with raking fingers.

---

4. Site of the large Catholic cemetery in Dublin, where much of the "Hades" episode (ch. 6) takes place.
5. Character in Joyce's story *The Dead*.

6. Rustic dialect, named after the early, simple Doric style in Greece.

Ned Lambert tossed the newspaper aside, chuckling with delight. An instant after a hoarse bark of laughter burst over professor MacHugh's unshaven blackspectacled face.

—Doughy Daw! he cried.

WHAT WETHERUP SAID

All very fine to jeer at it now in cold print but it goes down like hot cake that stuff. He was in the bakery line too wasn't he? Why they call him Doughy Daw. Feathered his nest well anyhow. Daughter engaged to that chap in the inland revenue office with the motor. Hooked that nicely. Entertainments. Open house. Big blow out. Wetherup always said that. Get a grip of them by the stomach.

The inner door was opened violently and a scarlet beaked face, crested by a comb of feathery hair, thrust itself in. The bold blue eyes stared about them and the harsh voice asked:

—What is it?

—And here comes the sham squire himself,[7] professor MacHugh said grandly.

—Getououthat, you bloody old pedagogue! the editor said in recognition.

—Come, Ned, Mr Dedalus said, putting on his hat. I must get a drink after that.

—Drink! the editor cried. No drinks served before mass.

—Quite right too, Mr Dedalus said, going out. Come on, Ned.

Ned Lambert sidled down from the table. The editor's blue eyes roved towards Mr Bloom's face, shadowed by a smile.

—Will you join us, Myles? Ned Lambert asked.

MEMORABLE BATTLES RECALLED

—North Cork militia! the editor cried, striding to the mantelpiece. We won every time! North Cork and Spanish officers![8]

—Where was that, Myles? Ned Lambert asked with a reflective glance at his toecaps.

—In Ohio! the editor shouted.

—So it was, begad, Ned Lambert agreed.

Passing out he whispered to J. J. O'Molloy:

—Incipient jigs.[9] Sad case.

—Ohio! the editor crowed in high treble from his uplifted scarlet face. My Ohio!

—A perfect cretic![1] the professor said. Long, short and long.

O, HARP EOLIAN![2]

He took a reel of dental floss from his waistcoat pocket and, breaking off a piece, twanged it smartly between two and two of his resonant unwashed teeth.

—Bingbang, bangbang.

Mr Bloom, seeing the coast clear, made for the inner door.

---

7. Pretending to identify the editor with a disreputable predecessor, Francis Higgins (1746–1802), who had seduced a woman by pretending to be a country squire.
8. This nonsensical piece of rhetoric invokes the North Cork Militia, which was involved in the failed Rebellion of 1798 and lost every battle it was involved in.
9. Probably the tremors caused by abrupt withdrawal from heavy alcohol use.

1. A poetic foot, made up of one short syllable between two long syllables.
2. The aeolian harp, popular as a symbol among the Romantic poets, is strung so as to allow the passing winds to "play" it. The harp is the national emblem of Ireland.

—Just a moment, Mr Crawford, he said. I just want to phone about an ad.

He went in.

—What about that leader this evening? professor MacHugh asked, coming to the editor and laying a firm hand on his shoulder.

—That'll be all right, Myles Crawford said more calmly. Never you fret. Hello, Jack. That's all right.

—Good day, Myles, J. J. O'Molloy said, letting the pages he held slip limply back on the file. Is that Canada swindle case on today?

The telephone whirred inside.

—Twentyeight . . . No, twenty . . . Double four . . . Yes.

SPOT THE WINNER

Lenehan came out of the inner office with *Sport's* tissues.

—Who wants a dead cert for the Gold cup? he asked. Sceptre with O. Madden up.[3]

He tossed the tissues on to the table.

Screams of newsboys barefoot in the hall rushed near and the door was flung open.

—Hush, Lenehan said. I hear feetstoops.

Professor MacHugh strode across the room and seized the cringing urchin by the collar as the others scampered out of the hall and down the steps. The tissues rustled up in the draught, floated softly in the air blue scrawls and under the table came to earth.

—It wasn't me, sir. It was the big fellow shoved me, sir.

—Throw him out and shut the door, the editor said. There's a hurricane blowing.

Lenehan began to paw the tissues up from the floor, grunting as he stooped twice.

—Waiting for the racing special, sir, the newsboy said. It was Pat Farrell shoved me, sir.

He pointed to two faces peering in round the doorframe.

—Him, sir.

—Out of this with you, professor MacHugh said gruffly.

He hustled the boy out and banged the door to.

J. J. O'Molloy turned the files crackingly over, murmuring, seeking:

—Continued on page six, column four.

—Yes . . . *Evening Telegraph* here, Mr Bloom phoned from the inner office. Is the boss . . . ? Yes, *Telegraph* . . . To where? . . . Aha! Which auction rooms? . . . Aha! I see . . . Right. I'll catch him.

A COLLISION ENSUES

The bell whirred again as he rang off. He came in quickly and bumped against Lenehan who was struggling up with the second tissue.

—*Pardon, monsieur*, Lenehan said, clutching him for an instant and making a grimace.

—My fault, Mr Bloom said, suffering his grip. Are you hurt? I'm in a hurry.

—Knee, Lenehan said.

3. A complicated subplot throughout the novel: Lenehan, looking up horse racing information, asks Bloom (in ch. 6) if he can have a look at Bloom's newspaper. Bloom tells him to take it, for he was just about to "throw it away." Since there's a longshot running in the Gold Cup race at Ascot called Throwaway, Lenehan thinks Bloom is trying to pass him insider information, and wagers a large sum on the horse, who does not win.

He made a comic face and whined, rubbing his knee:

—The accumulation of the *anno Domini*.

—Sorry, Mr Bloom said.

He went to the door and, holding it ajar, paused. J. J. O'Molloy slapped the heavy pages over. The noise of two shrill voices, a mouthorgan, echoed in the bare hallway from the newsboys squatted on the doorsteps:

> We are the boys of Wexford
> Who fought with heart and hand.[4]

EXIT BLOOM

—I'm just running round to Bachelor's walk, Mr Bloom said, about this ad of Keyes's. Want to fix it up. They tell me he's round there in Dillon's.

He looked indecisively for a moment at their faces. The editor who, leaning against the mantelshelf, had propped his head on his hand, suddenly stretched forth an arm amply.

—Begone! he said. The world is before you.[5]

—Back in no time, Mr Bloom said, hurrying out.

J. J. O'Molloy took the tissues from Lenehan's hand and read them, blowing them apart gently, without comment.

—He'll get that advertisement, the professor said, staring through his black-rimmed spectacles over the crossblind. Look at the young scamps after him.

—Show. Where? Lenehan cried, running to the window.

A STREET CORTEGE

Both smiled over the crossblind at the file of capering newsboys in Mr Bloom's wake, the last zigzagging white on the breeze a mocking kite, a tail of white bowknots.

—Look at the young guttersnipe behind him hue and cry, Lenehan said, and you'll kick. O, my rib risible! Taking off his flat spaugs and the walk.[6] Small nines. Steal upon larks.

He began to mazurka[7] in swift caricature across the floor on sliding feet past the fireplace to J. J. O'Molloy who placed the tissues in his receiving hands.

—What's that? Myles Crawford said with a start. Where are the other two gone?

—Who? the professor said, turning. They're gone round to the Oval for a drink. Paddy Hooper is there with Jack Hall. Came over last night.

—Come on then, Myles Crawford said. Where's my hat?

He walked jerkily into the office behind, parting the vent of his jacket, jingling his keys in his back pocket. They jingled then in the air and against the wood as he locked his desk drawer.

—He's pretty well on, professor MacHugh said in a low voice.

—Seems to be, J. J. O'Molloy said, taking out a cigarette case in murmuring meditation, but it is not always as it seems. Who has the most matches?

---

4. From a ballad, *The Boys of Wexford*, by R. Dwyer Joyce (1830–1883) about the rebellion of 1798—whose heroes turned to drink in later years.
5. The editor here echoes the close of Milton's *Paradise Lost*, as Adam and Eve leave Eden (12.846).
6. I.e., imitating Bloom's big feet and manner of walking.
7. A lively Polish dance.

THE CALUMET OF PEACE[8]

He offered a cigarette to the professor and took one himself. Lenehan promptly struck a match for them and lit their cigarettes in turn. J. J. O'Molloy opened his case again and offered it.

—*Thanky vous*, Lenehan said, helping himself.

The editor came from the inner office, a straw hat awry on his brow. He declaimed in song, pointing sternly at professor MacHugh:

> *'Twas rank and fame that tempted thee,*
> *'Twas empire charmed thy heart.*[9]

The professor grinned, locking his long lips.

—Eh? You bloody old Roman empire? Myles Crawford said.

He took a cigarette from the open case. Lenehan, lighting it for him with quick grace, said:

—Silence for my brandnew riddle!

—*Imperium romanum*, J. J. O'Molloy said gently. It sounds nobler than British or Brixton. The word reminds one somehow of fat in the fire.

Myles Crawford blew his first puff violently towards the ceiling.

—That's it, he said. We are the fat. You and I are the fat in the fire. We haven't got the chance of a snowball in hell.

THE GRANDEUR THAT WAS ROME

—Wait a moment, professor MacHugh said, raising two quiet claws. We mustn't be led away by words, by sounds of words. We think of Rome, imperial, imperious, imperative.

He extended elocutionary arms from frayed stained shirtcuffs, pausing:

—What was their civilisation? Vast, I allow: but vile. *Cloacae*: sewers. The jews in the wilderness and on the mountaintop said: *It is meet to be here. Let us build an altar to Jehovah.* The Roman, like the Englishman who follows in his footsteps, brought to every new shore on which he set his foot (on our shore he never set it) only his cloacal obsession. He gazed about him in his toga and he said: *It is meet to be here. Let us construct a watercloset.*[1]

—Which they accordingly did do, Lenehan said. Our old ancient ancestors, as we read in the first chapter of Guinness's,[2] were partial to the running stream.

—They were nature's gentlemen, J. J. O'Molloy murmured. But we have also Roman law.

—And Pontius Pilate is its prophet, professor MacHugh responded.

—Do you know that story about chief baron Palles? J. J. O'Molloy asked. It was at the royal university dinner. Everything was going swimmingly . . .

—First my riddle, Lenehan said. Are you ready?

Mr O'Madden Burke, tall in copious grey of Donegal tweed, came in from the hallway. Stephen Dedalus, behind him, uncovered as he entered.

---

8. The "peace pipe" of Native Americans.
9. Aria from the opera *The Rose of Castille* (1857), by Irish composer Michael William Balfe.
1. Toilet. The claim of an English "cloacal obsession" ironically reverses a charge made against Joyce himself by the English writer H. G. Wells, who had reviewed *A Portrait of the Artist* in 1917, in the (aptly titled) magazine

Nation. Wells wrote, "Mr. Joyce has a cloacal obsession. He would bring back into the general picture of life aspects which modern drainage and modern decorum have taken out of ordinary intercourse and conversation."
2. A pun on Genesis, the first book of the Bible, and Guinness, producers of stout and lager in Dublin.

—*Entrez, mes enfants!*[3] Lenehan cried.

—I escort a suppliant, Mr O'Madden Burke said melodiously. Youth led by Experience visits Notoriety.

—How do you do? the editor said, holding out a hand. Come in. Your governor is just gone.

? ? ?

Lenehan said to all:

—Silence! What opera resembles a railway line? Reflect, ponder, excogitate, reply.

Stephen handed over the typed sheets, pointing to the title and signature.

—Who? the editor asked.

Bit torn off.

—Mr Garrett Deasy, Stephen said.

—That old pelters, the editor said. Who tore it? Was he short taken?[4]

> On swift sail flaming
> From storm and south
> He comes, pale vampire,
> Mouth to my mouth.

—Good day, Stephen, the professor said, coming to peer over their shoulders. Foot and mouth? Are you turned . . . ?

Bullockbefriending bard.[5]

SHINDY IN WELLKNOWN RESTAURANT

—Good day, sir, Stephen answered, blushing. The letter is not mine. Mr Garrett Deasy asked me to . . .

—O, I know him, Myles Crawford said, and knew his wife too. The bloodiest old tartar God ever made. By Jesus, she had the foot and mouth disease and no mistake! The night she threw the soup in the waiter's face in the Star and Garter. Oho!

A woman brought sin into the world. For Helen, the runaway wife of Menelaus, ten years the Greeks. O'Rourke, prince of Breffni.

—Is he a widower? Stephen asked.

—Ay, a grass one,[6] Myles Crawford said, his eye running down the typescript. Emperor's horses. Habsburg. An Irishman saved his life on the ramparts of Vienna. Don't you forget! Maximilian Karl O'Donnell, graf von Tirconnel in Ireland. Sent his heir over to make the king an Austrian fieldmarshal now. Going to be trouble there one day. Wild geese.[7] O yes, every time. Don't you forget that!

—The moot point is did he forget it, J. J. O'Molloy said quietly, turning a horseshoe paperweight. Saving princes is a thank you job.

---

3. Enter, my children!

4. Stephen had agreed to take a letter to the editor from his employer, a schoolmaster named Garrett Deasy, and to try to place it with one of the Dublin newspapers. A piece is missing because Stephen later had an idea for a poem while walking on the beach but had nothing to write on; the editor playfully suggests that a small bit has been torn off for use as toilet tissue. The italicized lines are the poetry Stephen composed on the torn-off paper, an adaptation of a Gaelic poem translated by the nation-

alist poet Douglas Hyde in *Love Songs of Connacht* (1893): "He came from the South; / His breast to my bosom, / His mouth to my mouth."

5. The mock-Homeric epithet suggests that in helping Deasy place his letter about cattle disease, Stephen has become a poet ("bard") who has befriended the cattle ("bullocks").

6. A grass widower is a man separated from his wife.

7. Irish expatriates.

Professor MacHugh turned on him.

—And if not? he said.

—I'll tell you how it was, Myles Crawford began. A Hungarian it was one day . . .

LOST CAUSES
NOBLE MARQUESS MENTIONED

—We were always loyal to lost causes, the professor said. Success for us is the death of the intellect and of the imagination. We were never loyal to the successful. We serve them. I teach the blatant Latin language. I speak the tongue of a race the acme of whose mentality is the maxim: time is money. Material domination. *Dominus!* Lord! Where is the spirituality? Lord Jesus! Lord Salisbury. A sofa in a westend club. But the Greek!

KYRIE ELEISON![8]

A smile of light brightened his darkrimmed eyes, lengthened his long lips.

—The Greek! he said again. *Kyrios!* Shining word! The vowels the Semite and the Saxon know not. *Kyrie!* The radiance of the intellect. I ought to profess Greek, the language of the mind. *Kyrie eleison!* The closetmaker and the cloacamaker will never be lords of our spirit. We are liege subjects of the catholic chivalry of Europe that foundered at Trafalgar and of the empire of the spirit, not an *imperium*, that went under with the Athenian fleets at Aegospotami. Yes, yes. They went under. Pyrrhus, misled by an oracle, made a last attempt to retrieve the fortunes of Greece.[9] Loyal to a lost cause.

He strode away from them towards the window.

—They went forth to battle, Mr O'Madden Burke said greyly, but they always fell.

—Boohoo! Lenehan wept with a little noise. Owing to a brick received in the latter half of the *matinée*. Poor, poor, poor Pyrrhus!

He whispered then near Stephen's ear:

LENEHAN'S LIMERICK

> *There's a ponderous pundit MacHugh*
> *Who wears goggles of ebony hue.*
> *As he mostly sees double*
> *To wear them why trouble?*
> *I can't see the Joe Miller. Can you?*

In mourning for Sallust,[1] Mulligan says. Whose mother is beastly dead.

Myles Crawford crammed the sheets into a sidepocket.

—That'll be all right, he said. I'll read the rest after. That'll be all right.

Lenehan extended his hands in protest.

—But my riddle! he said. What opera is like a railway line?

—Opera? Mr O'Madden Burke's sphinx face reriddled.

---

8. Lord have mercy [upon us] (Greek). A formal part of the Mass.

9. The Greek general Pyrrhus (318–272 B.C.) was led to believe, in a dream, that he would triumph over the Spartans, but he was defeated.

1. Roman historian and senator (86–34 B.C.), known for political corruption. The idea of mourning reminds Stephen of a remark made by his friend Malachi ("Buck") Mulligan, about which the two had argued that morning: when Stephen had visited Mulligan at his aunt's house Mulligan had described Stephen as "Dedalus, whose mother is beastly dead."

Lenehan announced gladly:

—*The Rose of Castille*. See the wheeze? Rows of cast steel. Gee!

He poked Mr O'Madden Burke mildly in the spleen. Mr O'Madden Burke fell back with grace on his umbrella, feigning a gasp.

—Help! he sighed. I feel a strong weakness.

Lenehan, rising to tiptoe, fanned his face rapidly with the rustling tissues.

The professor, returning by way of the files, swept his hand across Stephen's and Mr O'Madden Burke's loose ties.

—Paris, past and present, he said. You look like communards.[2]

—Like fellows who had blown up the Bastile, J. J. O'Molloy said in quiet mockery. Or was it you shot the lord lieutenant of Finland between you? You look as though you had done the deed. General Bobrikoff.

—We were only thinking about it, Stephen said.

OMNIUM GATHERUM[3]

—All the talents, Myles Crawford said. Law, the classics . . .

—The turf, Lenehan put in.

—Literature, the press.

—If Bloom were here, the professor said. The gentle art of advertisement.

—And Madam Bloom, Mr O'Madden Burke added. The vocal muse. Dublin's prime favorite.

Lenehan gave a loud cough.

—Ahem! he said very softly. O, for a fresh of breath air! I caught a cold in the park. The gate was open.

"YOU CAN DO IT!"

The editor laid a nervous hand on Stephen's shoulder.

—I want you to write something for me, he said. Something with a bite in it. You can do it. I see it in your face. *In the lexicon of youth* . . .

See it in your face. See it in your eye. Lazy idle little schemer.[4]

—Foot and mouth disease! the editor cried in scornful invective. Great nationalist meeting in Borris-in-Ossory. All balls! Bulldosing the public! Give them something with a bite in it. Put us all into it, damn its soul. Father, Son and Holy Ghost and Jakes M'Carthy.

—We can all supply mental pabulum, Mr O'Madden Burke said.

Stephen raised his eyes to the bold unheeding stare.

—He wants you for the pressgang, J. J. O'Molloy said.

THE GREAT GALLAHER

—You can do it, Myles Crawford repeated, clenching his hand in emphasis. Wait a minute. We'll paralyse Europe as Ignatius Gallaher used to say when he was on the shaughraun,[5] doing billiardmarking in the Clarence. Gallaher, that was a pressman

---

2. Members of the left-wing Commune of Paris, who controlled Paris for three months in 1871.

3. Mock-Latin for hodgepodge.

4. Professor MacHugh's innocent remark, "I see it in your face," unfortunately reminds Stephen of the language of one of the priests at his parochial school, who accused Stephen of breaking his glasses intentionally in order to get out of work. (*A Portrait of the Artist*, I.iv.)

5. Wandering (Gaelic).

for you. That was a pen. You know how he made his mark? I'll tell you. That was the smartest piece of journalism ever known. That was in eightyone, sixth of May, time of the invincibles, murder in the Phoenix park, before you were born, I suppose. I'll show you.

He pushed past them to the files.

—Look at here, he said turning. The *New York World* cabled for a special. Remember that time?

Professor MacHugh nodded.

—*New York World*, the editor said, excitedly pushing back his straw hat. Where it took place. Tim Kelly, or Kavanagh I mean, Joe Brady and the rest of them. Where Skin-the-Goat drove the car. Whole route, see?

—Skin-the-Goat, Mr O'Madden Burke said. Fitzharris. He has that cabman's shelter, they say, down there at Butt bridge. Holohan told me. You know Holohan?

—Hop and carry one, is it? Myles Crawford said.

—And poor Gumley is down there too, so he told me, minding stones for the corporation. A night watchman.

Stephen turned in surprise.

—Gumley? he said. You don't say so? A friend of my father's, is he?

—Never mind Gumley, Myles Crawford cried angrily. Let Gumley mind the stones, see they don't run away. Look at here. What did Ignatius Gallaher do? I'll tell you. Inspiration of genius. Cabled right away. Have you *Weekly Freeman* of 17 March? Right. Have you got that?

He flung back pages of the files and stuck his finger on a point.

—Take page four, advertisement for Bransome's coffee, let us say. Have you got that? Right.

The telephone whirred.

A DISTANT VOICE

—I'll answer it, the professor said going.

—B is parkgate. Good.

His finger leaped and struck point after point, vibrating.

—T is viceregal lodge. C is where murder took place. K is Knockmaroon gate.

The loose flesh of his neck shook like a cock's wattles. An illstarched dicky jutted up and with a rude gesture he thrust it back into his waistcoat.

—Hello? *Evening Telegraph* here . . . Hello? . . . Who's there? . . . Yes . . . Yes . . . Yes . . .

—F to P is the route Skin-the-Goat drove the car for an alibi. Inchicore, Roundtown, Windy Arbour, Palmerston Park, Ranelagh. F. A. B. P. Got that? X is Davy's publichouse in upper Leeson street.

The professor came to the inner door.

—Bloom is at the telephone, he said.

—Tell him go to hell, the editor said promptly. X is Burke's publichouse, see?

CLEVER, VERY

—Clever, Lenehan said. Very.

—Gave it to them on a hot plate, Myles Crawford said, the whole bloody history.

Nightmare from which you will never awake.[6]

—I saw it, the editor said proudly. I was present, Dick Adams, the besthearted bloody Corkman the Lord ever put the breath of life in, and myself.

Lenehan bowed to a shape of air, announcing:

—Madam, I'm Adam. And Able was I ere I saw Elba.

—History! Myles Crawford cried. The Old Woman of Prince's street was there first. There was weeping and gnashing of teeth over that. Out of an advertisement. Gregor Grey made the design for it. That gave him the leg up. Then Paddy Hooper worked Tay Pay who took him on to the *Star*. Now he's got in with Blumenfeld. That's press. That's talent. Pyatt! He was all their daddies!

—The father of scare journalism, Lenehan confirmed, and the brother-in-law of Chris Callinan.

—Hello? . . . Are you there? . . . Yes, he's here still. Come across yourself.

—Where do you find a pressman like that now, eh? the editor cried.

He flung the pages down.

—Clamn dever, Lenehan said to Mr O'Madden Burke.

—Very smart, Mr O'Madden Burke said.

Professor MacHugh came from the inner office.

—Talking about the invincibles, he said, did you see that some hawkers were up before the recorder . . .

—O yes, J. J. O'Molloy said eagerly. Lady Dudley was walking home through the park to see all the trees that were blown down by that cyclone last year and thought she'd buy a view of Dublin. And it turned out to be a commemoration postcard of Joe Brady or Number One or Skin-the-Goat. Right outside the viceregal lodge, imagine!

—They're only in the hook and eye department, Myles Crawford said. Psha! Press and the bar! Where have you a man now at the bar like those fellows, like Whiteside, like Isaac Butt, like silvertongued O'Hagan?[7] Eh? Ah, bloody nonsense! Only in the halfpenny place.

His mouth continued to twitch unspeaking in nervous curls of disdain.

Would anyone wish that mouth for her kiss? How do you know? Why did you write it then?

RHYMES AND REASONS

Mouth, south. Is the mouth south someway? Or the south a mouth? Must be some. South, pout, out, shout, drouth. Rhymes: two men dressed the same, looking the same, two by two.

> . . . . *la tua pace*
> . . . . *che parlar ti piace*
> *mentre che il vento, come fa, si tace.*[8]

6. In the course of a tortured discussion with Mr. Deasy about British and Irish politics and history in chapter 2, Stephen had exclaimed, "History is a nightmare from which I am trying to awake."

7. James Whiteside (1804–1876), Isaac Butt (1813–1879), and Thomas O'Hagan (1812–1885) were Irish barristers and orators.

8. From Canto 5 of Dante's *Inferno*; the speakers are adulterous lovers, Francesca and Paolo, who tell Dante: "Were the world's King our friend . . . we would entreat Him for thy peace, . . . and speak as thou shalt please, While the winds cease to howl, as now they cease" (lines 92, 94, 96).

He saw them three by three, approaching girls, in green, in rose, in russet, entwining, *per l'aer perso*[9] in mauve, in purple, *quella pacifica oriafiamma*,[1] in gold of oriflamme, *di rimirar fè più ardenti*.[2] But I old men, penitent, leadenfooted, underdarkneath the night: mouth south: tomb womb.

—Speak up for yourself, Mr O'Madden Burke said.

SUFFICIENT FOR THE DAY . . .

J. J. O'Molloy, smiling palely, took up the gage.

—My dear Myles, he said, flinging his cigarette aside, you put a false construction on my words. I hold no brief, as at present advised, for the third profession *qua* profession but your Cork legs are running away with you. Why not bring in Henry Grattan and Flood and Demosthenes and Edmund Burke?[3] Ignatius Gallaher we all know and his Chapelizod boss, Harmsworth of the farthing press, and his American cousin of the Bowery gutter sheet not to mention *Paddy Kelly's Budget, Pue's Occurrences* and our watchful friend *The Skibbereen Eagle*. Why bring in a master of forensic eloquence like Whiteside? Sufficient for the day is the newspaper thereof.[4]

LINKS WITH BYGONE DAYS OF YORE

—Grattan and Flood wrote for this very paper, the editor cried in his face. Irish volunteers. Where are you now? Established 1763. Dr Lucas. Who have you now like John Philpot Curran? Psha!

—Well, J. J. O'Molloy said, Bushe K. C., for example.

—Bushe? the editor said. Well, yes. Bushe, yes. He has a strain of it in his blood. Kendal Bushe or I mean Seymour Bushe.

—He would have been on the bench long ago, the professor said, only for . . . But no matter.

J. J. O'Molloy turned to Stephen and said quietly and slowly:

—One of the most polished periods I think I ever listened to in my life fell from the lips of Seymour Bushe. It was in that case of fratricide, the Childs murder case. Bushe defended him.

> *And in the porches of mine ear did pour.*[5]

By the way how did he find that out? He died in his sleep. Or the other story, beast with two backs?[6]

—What was that? the professor asked.

ITALIA, MAGISTRA ARTIUM

—He spoke on the law of evidence, J. J. O'Molloy said, of Roman justice as contrasted with the earlier Mosaic code, the *lex talionis*. And he cited the Moses of Michelangelo in the Vatican.

---

9. Through the black air.
1. That peaceful gold flame.
2. More ardent to look again. From Dante's *Inferno* and *Paradiso*.
3. Irish statesmen Henry Grattan (1746–1820) and Henry Flood (1732–1791), as well as the Irish-born Edmund Burke (1729–1797), were among the greatest orators of their day. Demosthenes (c. 384–322 B.C.) is traditionally

considered the greatest of Greek orators.
4. Revising Jesus's saying, "Sufficient for the day is the evil thereof" (Matthew 6.34).
5. This is Hamlet's father's description of his poisoning by his brother Claudius, in *Hamlet* (1.5.62–63). "And in the porches of my ears did pour / The leperous distillment."
6. Again from Shakespeare—this time, *Othello*; the phrase means sexual intercourse.

—Ha.

—A few wellchosen words, Lenehan prefaced. Silence!

Pause. J. J. O'Molloy took out his cigarettecase.

False lull. Something quite ordinary.

Messenger took out his match box thoughtfully and lit his cigar.

I have often thought since on looking back over that strange time that it was that small act, trivial in itself, that striking of that match, that determined the whole aftercourse of both our lives.

A POLISHED PERIOD

J. J. O'Molloy resumed, moulding his words:

—He said of it: *that stony effigy in frozen music, horned and terrible, of the human form divine, that eternal symbol of wisdom and of prophecy which, if aught that the imagination or the hand of sculptor has wrought in marble of soultransfigured and of soultransfiguring deserves to live, deserves to live.*

His slim hand with a wave graced echo and fall.

—Fine! Myles Crawford said at once.

—The divine afflatus, Mr O'Madden Burke said.

—You like it? J. J. O'Molloy asked Stephen.

Stephen, his blood wooed by grace of language and gesture, blushed. He took a cigarette from the case. J. J. O'Molloy offered his case to Myles Crawford. Lenehan lit their cigarettes as before and took his trophy, saying:

—Muchibus thankibus.

A MAN OF HIGH MORALE

—Professor Magennis was speaking to me about you, J. J. O'Molloy said to Stephen. What do you think really of that hermetic crowd, the opal hush poets: A. E. the master mystic? That Blavatsky woman started it.[7] She was a nice old bag of tricks. A. E. has been telling some yankee interviewer that you came to him in the small hours of the morning to ask him about planes of consciousness. Magennis thinks you must have been pulling A. E.'s leg. He is a man of the very highest morale, Magennis.

Speaking about me. What did he say? What did he say? What did he say about me? Don't ask.

—No, thanks, professor MacHugh said, waving the cigarette case aside. Wait a moment. Let me say one thing. The finest display of oratory I ever heard was a speech made by John F. Taylor[8] at the college historical society. Mr Justice Fitzgibbon, the present lord justice of appeal, had spoken and the paper under debate was an essay (new for those days), advocating the revival of the Irish tongue.

He turned towards Myles Crawford and said:

—You know Gerald Fitzgibbon. Then you can imagine the style of his discourse.

—He is sitting with Tim Healy, J. J. O'Molloy said, rumour has it, on the Trinity college estates commission.

—He is sitting with a sweet thing in a child's frock, Myles Crawford said. Go on. Well?

---

7. Refers generally to the interest in mysticism, and specifically the Theosophy of Madame Blavatsky (1831–1891), who stressed the fellowship of all humanity and the transmigration of souls. Her disciple A.E. (pseud.

of George Russell, 1867–1935) was a minor Irish poet and mystic, and friend of W. B. Yeats.

8. John F. Taylor (c. 1850–1902), Irish barrister and journalist. Taylor did make this speech on 24 October 1901.

—It was the speech, mark you, the professor said, of a finished orator, full of courteous haughtiness and pouring in chastened diction I will not say the vials of his wrath but pouring the proud man's contumely upon the new movement. It was then a new movement. We were weak, therefore worthless.

He closed his long thin lips an instant but, eager to be on, raised an outspanned hand to his spectacles and, with trembling thumb and ringfinger touching lightly the black rims, steadied them to a new focus.

IMPROMPTU

In ferial tone he addressed J. J. O'Molloy:

—Taylor had come there, you must know, from a sickbed. That he had prepared his speech I do not believe for there was not even one shorthandwriter in the hall. His dark lean face had a growth of shaggy beard round it. He wore a loose white silk neckcloth and altogether he looked (though he was not) a dying man.

His gaze turned at once but slowly from J. J. O'Molloy's towards Stephen's face and then bent at once to the ground, seeking. His unglazed linen collar appeared behind his bent head, soiled by his withering hair. Still seeking, he said:

—When Fitzgibbon's speech had ended John F. Taylor rose to reply. Briefly, as well as I can bring them to mind, his words were these.

He raised his head firmly. His eyes bethought themselves once more. Witless shellfish swam in the gross lenses to and fro, seeking outlet.

He began:

—Mr chairman, ladies and gentlemen: Great was my admiration in listening to the remarks addressed to the youth of Ireland a moment since by my learned friend. It seemed to me that I had been transported into a country far away from this country, into an age remote from this age, that I stood in ancient Egypt and that I was listening to the speech of some highpriest of that land addressed to the youthful Moses.

His listeners held their cigarettes poised to hear, their smokes ascending in frail stalks that flowered with his speech. And let our crooked smokes. Noble words coming. Look out. Could you try your hand at it yourself?

—And it seemed to me that I heard the voice of that Egyptian highpriest raised in a tone of like haughtiness and like pride. I heard his words and their meaning was revealed to me.

FROM THE FATHERS

It was revealed to me that those things are good which yet are corrupted which neither if they were supremely good nor unless they were good, could be corrupted. Ah, curse you! That's saint Augustine.

—Why will you jews not accept our culture, our religion and our language? You are a tribe of nomad herdsmen: we are a mighty people. You have no cities nor no wealth: our cities are hives of humanity and our galleys, trireme and quadrireme, laden with all manner merchandise furrow the waters of the known globe. You have but emerged from primitive conditions: we have a literature, a priesthood, an agelong history and a polity.

Nile.

Child, man, effigy.

By the Nilebank the babemaries kneel, cradle of bulrushes: a man supple in combat: stonehorned, stonebearded, heart of stone.

—*You pray to a local and obscure idol: our temples, majestic and mysterious, are the abodes of Isis and Osiris, of Horus and Ammon Ra. Yours serfdom, awe and humbleness: ours thunder and the seas. Israel is weak and few are her children: Egypt is an host and terrible are her arms. Vagrants and daylabourers are you called: the world trembles at our name.*

A dumb belch of hunger cleft his speech. He lifted his voice above it boldly:

—*But, ladies and gentlemen, had the youthful Moses listened to and accepted that view of life, had he bowed his head and bowed his will and bowed his spirit before that arrogant admonition he would never have brought the chosen people out of their house of bondage nor followed the pillar of the cloud by day. He would never have spoken with the Eternal amid lightnings on Sinai's mountaintop nor ever have come down with the light of inspiration shining in his countenance and bearing in his arms the tables of the law, graven in the language of the outlaw.*

He ceased and looked at them, enjoying a silence.

OMINOUS—FOR HIM!

J. J. O'Molloy said not without regret:

—And yet he died without having entered the land of promise.

—A sudden–at–the–moment–though–from–lingering–illness–often–previously–expectorated–demise, Lenehan added. And with a great future behind him.

The troop of bare feet was heard rushing along the hallway and pattering up the staircase.

—That is oratory, the professor said uncontradicted.

Gone with the wind. Hosts at Mullaghmast and Tara of the kings. Miles of ears of porches. The tribune's words howled and scattered to the four winds. A people sheltered within his voice. Dead noise. Akasic records of all that ever anywhere wherever was.[9] Love and laud him: me no more.

I have money.

—Gentlemen, Stephen said. As the next motion on the agenda paper may I suggest that the house do now adjourn?

—You take my breath away. It is not perchance a French compliment? Mr O'Madden Burke asked. 'Tis the hour, methinks, when the winejug, metaphorically speaking, is most grateful in Ye ancient hostelry.

—That it be and hereby is resolutely resolved. All who are in favour say ay, Lenehan announced. The contrary no. I declare it carried. To which particular boosingshed . . . ? My casting vote is: Mooney's!

He led the way, admonishing:

—We will sternly refuse to partake of strong waters, will we not? Yes, we will not. By no manner of means.

Mr O'Madden Burke, following close, said with an ally's lunge of his umbrella:

—Lay on, Macduff![1]

—Chip of the old block! the editor cried, slapping Stephen on the shoulder. Let us go. Where are those blasted keys?

He fumbled in his pocket pulling out the crushed typesheets.

---

9. Parody of the language of Theosophy.

1. These are Macbeth's words when he discovers that Macduff is to be his executioner (*Macbeth*, 5.8.33).

—Foot and mouth. I know. That'll be all right. That'll go in. Where are they? That's all right.

He thrust the sheets back and went into the inner office.

LET US HOPE

J. J. O'Molloy, about to follow him in, said quietly to Stephen:

—I hope you will live to see it published. Myles, one moment.

He went into the inner office, closing the door behind him.

—Come along, Stephen, the professor said. That is fine, isn't it? It has the prophetic vision. *Fuit Ilium!*[2] The sack of windy Troy. Kingdoms of this world. The masters of the Mediterranean are fellaheen today.

The first newsboy came pattering down the stairs at their heels and rushed out into the street, yelling:

—Racing special!

Dublin. I have much, much to learn.

They turned to the left along Abbey street.

—I have a vision too, Stephen said.

—Yes? the professor said, skipping to get into step. Crawford will follow.

Another newsboy shot past them, yelling as he ran:

—Racing special!

DEAR DIRTY DUBLIN

Dubliners.

—Two Dublin vestals, Stephen said, elderly and pious, have lived fifty and fiftythree years in Fumbally's lane.

—Where is that? the professor asked.

—Off Blackpitts, Stephen said.

Damp night reeking of hungry dough. Against the wall. Face glistering tallow under her fustian shawl. Frantic hearts. Akasic records. Quicker, darlint!

On now. Dare it. Let there be life.

—They want to see the views of Dublin from the top of Nelson's pillar. They save up three and tenpence in a red tin letterbox moneybox. They shake out the threepenny bits and sixpences and coax out the pennies with the blade of a knife. Two and three in silver and one and seven in coppers. They put on their bonnets and best clothes and take their umbrellas for fear it may come on to rain.

—Wise virgins, professor MacHugh said.[3]

LIFE ON THE RAW

—They buy one and fourpenceworth of brawn[4] and four slices of panloaf at the north city diningrooms in Marlborough street from Miss Kate Collins, proprietress. . . . They purchase four and twenty ripe plums from a girl at the foot of Nelson's pillar to take off the thirst of the brawn. They give two threepenny bits to the gentleman at

2. Troy is no more; from Virgil's *Aeneid* 3.325.
3. In Matthew 25.1–13, Jesus tells the parable of the wise

and foolish virgins.
4. Cold, jellied meatloaf.

the turnstile and begin to waddle slowly up the winding staircase, grunting, encouraging each other, afraid of the dark, panting, one asking the other have you the brawn, praising God and the Blessed Virgin, threatening to come down, peeping at the airslits. Glory be to God. They had no idea it was that high.

Their names are Anne Kearns and Florence MacCabe. Anne Kearns has the lumbago for which she rubs on Lourdes water given her by a lady who got a bottleful from a passionist father. Florence MacCabe takes a crubeen and a bottle of double X[5] for supper every Saturday.

—Antithesis, the professor said nodding twice. Vestal virgins. I can see them. What's keeping our friend?

He turned.

A bevy of scampering newsboys rushed down the steps, scampering in all directions, yelling, their white papers fluttering. Hard after them Myles Crawford appeared on the steps, his hat aureoling his scarlet face, talking with J. J. O'Molloy.

—Come along, the professor cried, waving his arm.

He set off again to walk by Stephen's side.

—Yes, he said. I see them.

RETURN OF BLOOM

Mr Bloom, breathless, caught in a whirl of wild newsboys near the offices of the *Irish Catholic* and *Dublin Penny Journal*, called:

—Mr Crawford! A moment!

—*Telegraph!* Racing special!

—What is it? Myles Crawford said, falling back a pace.

A newsboy cried in Mr Bloom's face:

—Terrible tragedy in Rathmines! A child bit by a bellows!

INTERVIEW WITH THE EDITOR

—Just this ad, Mr Bloom said, pushing through towards the steps, puffing, and taking the cutting from his pocket. I spoke with Mr Keyes just now. He'll give a renewal for two months, he says. After he'll see. But he wants a par to call attention in the *Telegraph* too, the Saturday pink. And he wants it copied if it's not too late I told councillor Nannetti from the *Kilkenny People*. I can have access to it in the national library. House of keys, don't you see? His name is Keyes. It's a play on the name. But he practically promised he'd give the renewal. But he wants just a little puff. What will I tell him, Mr Crawford?

K. M. A.

—Will you tell him he can kiss my arse? Myles Crawford said throwing out his arm for emphasis. Tell him that straight from the stable.

A bit nervy. Look out for squalls. All off for a drink. Arm in arm. Lenehan's yachting cap on the cadge beyond. Usual blarney. Wonder is that young Dedalus the moving spirit. Has a good pair of boots on him today. Last time I saw him he had his heels on view. Been walking in muck somewhere. Careless chap. What was he doing in Irishtown?[6]

5. A pig's foot and a bottle of beer.
6. During the funeral procession, Bloom and the other members of the funeral party saw Stephen walking along the beach at Sandymount, near Irishtown.

—Well, Mr Bloom said, his eyes returning, if I can get the design I suppose it's worth a short par. He'd give the ad I think. I'll tell him . . .

K. M. R. I. A

—He can kiss my royal Irish arse, Myles Crawford cried loudly over his shoulder. Any time he likes, tell him.

While Mr Bloom stood weighing the point and about to smile he strode on jerkily.

RAISING THE WIND

—*Nulla bona,*[7] Jack, he said, raising his hand to his chin. I'm up to here. I've been through the hoop myself. I was looking for a fellow to back a bill for me no later than last week. You must take the will for the deed. Sorry, Jack. With a heart and a half if I could raise the wind anyhow.

J. J. O'Molloy pulled a long face and walked on silently. They caught up on the others and walked abreast.

—When they have eaten the brawn and the bread and wiped their twenty fingers in the paper the bread was wrapped in, they go nearer to the railings.

—Something for you, the professor explained to Myles Crawford. Two old Dublin women on the top of Nelson's pillar.

SOME COLUMN!—THAT'S WHAT WADDLER ONE SAID

—That's new, Myles Crawford said. That's copy. Out for the waxies' Dargle. Two old trickies, what?

—But they are afraid the pillar will fall, Stephen went on. They see the roofs and argue about where the different churches are: Rathmines' blue dome, Adam and Eve's, saint Laurence O'Toole's. But it makes them giddy to look so they pull up their skirts . . .

THOSE SLIGHTLY RAMBUNCTIOUS FEMALES

—Easy all, Myles Crawford said. No poetic licence. We're in the archdiocese here.

—And settle down on their striped petticoats, peering up at the statue of the onehandled adulterer.[8]

—Onehandled adulterer! the professor cried. I like that. I see the idea. I see what you mean.

DAMES DONATE DUBLIN'S CITS
SPEEDPILLS VELOCITOUS AEROLITHS, BELIEF

—It gives them a crick in their necks, Stephen said, and they are too tired to look up or down or to speak. They put the bag of plums between them and eat the plums out of it, one after another, wiping off with their handkerchiefs the plumjuice that dribbles out of their mouths and spitting the plumstones slowly out between the railings.

He gave a sudden loud young laugh as a close. Lenehan and Mr O'Madden Burke, hearing, turned, beckoned and led on across towards Mooney's.

—Finished? Myles Crawford said. So long as they do no worse.

---

7. "No goods": i.e., no money to lend.
8. Admiral Lord Nelson (1758–1805) was one-armed after a battlefield injury and was involved in a widely publicized extramarital affair.

SOPHIST WALLOPS HAUGHTY HELEN SQUARE ON PROBOSCIS.
SPARTANS GNASH MOLARS.
ITHACANS VOW PEN IS CHAMP.

—You remind me of Antisthenes, the professor said, a disciple of Gorgias, the sophist. It is said of him that none could tell if he were bitterer against others or against himself. He was the son of a noble and a bondwoman. And he wrote a book in which he took away the palm of beauty from Argive Helen and handed it to poor Penelope.

Poor Penelope. Penelope Rich.[9]

They made ready to cross O'Connell street.

HELLO THERE, CENTRAL!

At various points along the eight lines tramcars with motionless trolleys stood in their tracks, bound for or from Rathmines, Rathfarnham, Kingstown, Blackrock and Dalkey, Sandymount Green, Ringsend and Sandymount Tower, Donnybrook, Palmerston Park and Upper Rathmines, all still, becalmed in short circuit. Hackney cars, cabs, delivery waggons, mailvans, private broughams, aerated mineral water floats with rattling crates of bottles, rattled, rolled, horsedrawn, rapidly.

WHAT?—AND LIKEWISE—WHERE?

—But what do you call it? Myles Crawford asked. Where did they get the plums?

VIRGILIAN, SAYS PEDAGOGUE.
SOPHOMORE PLUMPS FOR OLD MAN MOSES.

—Call it, wait, the professor said, opening his long lips wide to reflect. Call it, let me see. Call it: *Deus nobis haec otia fecit.*[1]

—No, Stephen said, I call it *A Pisgah Sight of Palestine or The Parable of The Plums.*[2]

—I see, the professor said.

He laughed richly.

—I see, he said again with new pleasure. Moses and the promised land. We gave him that idea, he added to J. J. O'Molloy.

HORATIO IS CYNOSURE[3] THIS FAIR JUNE DAY

J. J. O'Molloy sent a weary sidelong glance towards the statue and held his peace.

—I see, the professor said.

He halted on sir John Gray's pavement island and peered aloft at Nelson through the meshes of his wry smile.

DIMINISHED DIGITS PROVE TOO TITILLATING
FOR FRISKY FRUMPS. ANNE WIMBLES, FLO
WANGLES-YET CAN YOU BLAME THEM?

—Onehandled adulterer, he said smiling grimly. That tickles me I must say.

—Tickled the old ones too, Myles Crawford said, if the God Almighty's truth was known.

---

9. Adulterous noblewoman (1562–1607), the lovely "Stella" of Sir Philip Sidney's *Astrophel and Stella* (1591).
1. God has made this peace for us (Latin; from Virgil, *Eclogues* 1:6).

2. Moses was granted a view of Israel from the top of Mount Pisgah, without being allowed to enter in before his death; see Deuteronomy 34.1–5.
3. The center of attention.

Finnegans Wake

Among twentieth-century texts—indeed, among all texts—*Finnegans Wake* is *sui generis*, the only one of its kind. Having completed the complex and multifaceted critique of language, narrative, consciousness, sexuality, and politics of *Ulysses*—an in-depth exploration of one day in the life of a Dublin Everyman—Joyce set out in *Finnegans Wake* to write a book of the night: "One great part of every human existence is passed in a state which cannot be rendered sensible by the use of wideawake language, cutanddry grammar and goahead plot," Joyce wrote to his patron Harriet Shaw Weaver. Thus while *Ulysses* seeks to exploit the resources of the English language and English prose styles, *Finnegans Wake* instead attempts to create a new language, by synthesizing elements of many languages (at least sixty-five modern and ancient languages) and utilizing allusions to and structures from many mythological and religious systems.

The basic plot of *Finnegans Wake* is quite simple. The protagonist H.C.E.—while his initials remain constant, his name shifts among various possibilities like Humphrey Chimpden Earwicker, Howth Castle and Environs, Here Comes Everybody, and Hush! Caution! Echoland!—lies unconscious or asleep as the book opens. Like Tim Finnegan in the vaudeville song "Finnegan's Wake," who rises from the dead when splashed with whiskey by mourners at his wake, H.C.E. keeps coming to life in new forms. The thoughts and events recounted by the book may take place within his unconscious/dreaming mind. Those thoughts and events cluster around the relationships in the Earwicker family—H.C.E.'s wife A.L.P. (most often Anna Livia Plurabelle, from the Latin name for the River Liffey which runs through Dublin), their twin sons Shem ("the Penman") and Shaun ("the Post"), and their daughter Isobel ("Issy"). H.C.E.'s fall is symbolic of the biblical Fall; the book is filled with rumor and gossip regarding some kind of sexual indiscretion perpetrated by H.C.E. in Dublin's Phoenix Park. And the symbol of the phoenix, which rises from its own ashes, is poetically appropriate to the figure of H.C.E./Tim Finnegan/Finn Macool (legendary Irish hero), who will fall but must always rise again. Joyce underscores this cyclical view of human life and human history in *Finnegans Wake* by employing a mythological framework derived from the *New Science* (1725) of Italian philosopher Giambattista Vico; the occurence in the text of hundred-letter "thunderclaps" signals the shift from one historical period to the next.

Asked the book's meaning, Joyce once replied, "It's meant to make you laugh." All the same, an entire scholarly industry has grown up—as Joyce hoped—to elucidate the book's thousands of outrageous puns and recondite allusions. Yet the book is best encountered, particularly on a first reading, as a rich prose poetry, and Joyce meant seriously the advice he gave to first-time readers: "It is all so simple. If anyone doesn't understand a passage, all he need do is read it aloud." The prose achieved its formidable complexity by a process of accretion. Starting with a comparatively straightforward first draft of a chapter, Joyce reworked it as many as nine times, each time adding—and rarely subtracting—jokes, asides, levels and layers of meaning. The ultimate result is marked both by universality and confusion—a "chaosmos," in the book's own term.

In order to show the process, and to give aid in reading the final version, the selected passages given here are accompanied by Joyce's marked-up early drafts, as edited by David Hayman in *A First-Draft Version of Finnegans Wake*; these run at the bottom of each page, below the corresponding final text. Simple additions to the first draft are shown in italics; deleted words are crossed out, followed by their replacements in boldface. Further levels of addition and substitution are shown in brackets and in bold italics. A careful reading of all this will go far to clarify the final version, and will also show how steadily Joyce built up both the humor and the poetry of his material.

To give a flavor of what a word-for-word explanation would look like, the opening paragraph is annotated, rather than being accompanied by the first draft version. These annotations are Joyce's own, taken from a letter to Harriet Shaw Weaver. The first selection is the opening, which tells of Finnegan's fall. It tells as well of the riotous party around his body as the mourners get drunk at his funeral wake—from which Finnegan will be reborn as H.C.E.

from **Finnegans Wake**
[THE FALL]

riverrun, past Eve and Adam's, from swerve of shore to bend of bay, brings us by a commodius vicus of recirculation back to Howth[1] Castle and Environs.

Sir Tristram,[2] violer[3] d'amores, fr'over the short sea, had passencore[4] rearrived[5] from North Armorica on this side the scraggy isthmus[6] of Europe Minor to wielderfight[7] his penisolate war: nor had topsawyer's rocks by the stream Oconee exaggerated[8] themselse[9] to Laurens County's gorgios while they went doublin[1] their mumper all the time: nor avoice from afire[2] bellowsed[3] mishe mishe[4] to tauftauf[5] thuartpeatrick[6]: not yet, though venissoon after, had a kidscad buttended a bland old isaac[7]: not yet, though all's fair in vanessy, were sosie[8] sesthers wroth with twone nathandjoe. Rot a peck of pa's malt[9] had Jhem or Shen brewed by arclight[1] and rory end to the regginbrow[2] was to be seen ringsome[3] on the aquaface.[4]

The fall (bababadalgharaghtakamminarronnkonnbronntonnerronntuonnthunntro-varrhounawnskawntoohoohoordenenthurnuk!) of a once wallstrait oldparr is retaled early in bed and later on life down through all christian minstrelsy. The great fall of the offwall entailed at such short notice the pftjschute of Finnegan, erse solid man, that the humptyhillhead of humself promptly sends an unquiring one well to the west in quest of his tumptytumtoes: and their upturnpikepointandplace is at the knock out in the park where oranges have been laid to rust upon the green since devlinsfirst loved livvy.

The ~~story~~ **tale** of the fall is retailed early in bed and later in life throughout most christian minstrelsy. The *great* fall of the wall ~~at once~~ entailed **at such short notice** the fall of Finnigan, *the solid man,* ~~and~~ that the humpty ~~hill~~ **hillhead** himself ~~promptly~~ **promptly** sends an ~~inquiring~~ **unquiring** one well to the west in quest of his tumptytumtoes. ~~Two facts have come down to us~~ ~~Their resting~~ **The upturnpikepoint** *for place* is at the knock out in the park where there have ~~always~~ been oranges ~~on~~ **laid on** the green ~~always~~ **ever & ~~ever~~ evermore** since the ~~Devlin~~ **Devlins** first loved ~~liffey~~ **livy**. What ~~cha~~*

---

1. Howth (pron Hoaeth) = Dan Hoved {head}. Howth = an island for old geographers.
2. Sir Amory Tristram 1st earl of Howth changed his name to Saint Lawrence, b in Brittany (North Armorica). Tristan et Iseult, passim.
3. Viola in all moods and senses.
4. Passencore = pas encore and *ricorsi storici* of Vico.
5. Rearrived = idem.
6. Isthmus of Sutton a neck of land between Howth head and the plain.
7. Wielderfight = wiederfechten = refight.
8. Exaggerare = to mound up.
9. Themselse = another dublin 5000 inhabitants.
1. Dublin, Laurens Co, Georgia, founded by a Dubliner, Peter Sawyer, on r. Oconee. Its motto: Doubling all the time.
2. The flame of Christianity kindled by S. Patrick on Holy Saturday in defiance of royal orders.
3. Bellowed = the response of the peatfire of faith to the windy words of the apostle.

4. Mishe = I am (Irish) i.e. Christian.
5. Tauf = baptise (German).
6. Thou art Peter and upon this rock etc (a pun in the original aramaic). Lat: Tu es Petrus et super hanc petram.
7. Parnell ousted Isaac Butt from leadership. The venison purveyor Jacob got the blessing meant for Esau.
8. Miss Vanhomrigh and Miss Johnson [Jonathan Swift's correspondents "Stella" and "Vanessa"] had the same christian name. Sosie = double.
9. Willy brewed a peck of maut. Noah planted the vine and was drunk.
1. John Jameson is the greatest Dublin distiller. Arthur Guinness is the greatest Dublin brewer.
2. Rory = Irish = red. rory = Latin, roridus = dewy. At the rainbow's end are dew and the colour red: bloody end to the lie in Anglo-Irish = no lie. regginbrow = German regenbogen + rainbow.
3. Ringsome = German ringsum, around.
4. When all vegetation is covered by the flood there are no eyebrows on the face of the Waterworld.

What clashes here of wills gen wonts, oystrygods gaggin fishy-gods! Brékkek Kékkek Kékkek Kékkek! Kóax Kóax Kóax! Ualu Ualu Ualu! Quaouauh! Where the Baddelaries partisans are still out to mathmaster Malachus Micgranes and the Verdons catapelting the camibalistics out of the Whyteboyce of Hoodie Head. Assiegates and boomeringstroms. Sod's brood, be me fear! Sanglorians, save! Arms apeal with larms, appalling. Killykillkilly: a toll, a toll. What chance cuddleys, what cashels aired and ventilated! What bidimetoloves sinduced by what tegotetabsolvers! What true feeling for their's hayair with what strawng voice of false jiccup! O here here how hoth sprowled met the duskt the father of fornicationists but, (O my shining stars and body!) how hath fanespanned most high heaven the skysign of soft advertisement! But was iz? Iseut? Ere were sewers? The oaks of ald now they lie in peat yet elms leap where askes lay. Phall if you but will, rise you must: and none so soon either shall the pharce for the nunce come to a setdown secular phoenish.

Bygmester Finnegan, of the Stuttering Hand, freemen's maurer, lived in the broadest way immarginable in his rushlit toofarback for messuages before joshuan judges had given us numbers or Helviticus committed deuteronomy (one yeastyday he sternely struxk his tete in a tub for to watsch the future of his fates but ere he swiftly stook it out again, by the might of moses, the very water was eviparated and all the guennesses had met their exodus so that ought to show you what a pentschanjeuchy chap he was!) and during mighty odd years this man of hod, cement and edifices in Toper's Thorp piled buildung supra buildung pon the banks for the livers by the Soangso. He addle liddle phifie Annie ugged the little craythur. Wither hayre in honds tuck up your part inher. Oftwhile balbulous, mithre ahead, with goodly trowel in grasp and ivoroiled overalls which he habitacularly fondseed, like Haroun Childeric Eggeberth he would caligulate by multiplicables the alltitude and malltitude until he seesaw by neatlight of the liquor wheretwin 'twas born, his roundhead staple of other days to rise in undress maisonry upstanded (joygrantit!), a waalworth of a skyerscape of most eyeful hoyth entowerly, erigenating from next to nothing and celescalating the himals and all, hierarchitectitiptitoploftical, with a burning bush abob off its baubletop and with larrons o'toolers clittering up and tombles a'buckets clottering down.

---

clashes of wills & wits were not here and there abouts! What chance cuddleys, what castles aired & ventilated, what biddymetolives sinduced by what ~~egosetabsolvers~~ **tegotetabsolvers,** what true feeling for *hay* hair with false voice of ~~hayeup ja~~ **jiccup,** what ~~rorycrucians~~* **rosycrucians** ~~byelected by rival~~ **contested of simily** emilies! ~~But~~ **And** O here how has sprawled upon the dust the father of ~~fornications fornicationers~~ **fornicationists** but O, my *shining* stars and body, how has finespanned in high heaven the skysign of soft advertisement. ~~Was~~ **Wasis?** Isot! Ere ~~we~~ were sure? The oaks of old *maythey* ~~rest~~ **rust** in peat. Elms leap where ashes lay. Till never-never may our pharce be phoenished!

Bygmister Finnegan *of the Stuttering Hand,* builder, lived ~~on~~ in the broadest way *imaginable* ~~imaginoble unm~~* **imarginable** *in his* [rushlit] *toofarback for messuages and* during mighty odd years this man of Hod *Cement &* ~~made~~ **piled** buildung ~~upon~~ **super** buildung ~~on~~ **pon** the banks ~~of~~ **for** the livers by the ~~Soandso~~ **Soangso.** He addle iddle ~~wife~~ **wyfie** ~~and he annie~~ **Annie** hugged the liddle crathur ~~wither~~ **Wither** ~~tear tare in hares~~ **hayre in honds** tuck up your ~~pardner~~ **part-in-her.** ~~though~~ **Though** *oftwhile balbulous* [He would see by the light of the liquor his roundup tower to rise on itslef [(~~joy grant it~~ **joygrantit!**)], *with a skierscape of an eyeful hoyth entirely and larrons* ~~of toolers~~ *o' toolers clittering up on it & tumblers a' buckets clottering down.]*

Of the first was he to bare arms and a name: Wassaily Booslaeugh of Riesenge-
borg. His crest of huroldry, in vert with ancillars, troublant, argent, a hegoak, pour-
suivant, horrid, horned. His scutschum fessed, with archers strung, helio, of the second. Hootch is for husbandman handling his hoe. Hohohoho, Mister Finn, you're
going to be Mister Finnagain! Comeday morm and, O, you're vine! Sendday's eve
and, ah, you're vinegar! Hahahaha, Mister Funn, you're going to be fined again!

What then agentlike brought about that tragoady thundersday this municipal sin
business? Our cubehouse still rocks as earwitness to the thunder of his arafatas but we
hear also through successive ages that shebby choruysh of unkalified muzzlenimiissile-
hims that would blackguardise the whitestone ever hurtleturtled out of heaven. Stay us
wherefore in our search for tighteousness, O Sustainer, what time we rise and when we
take up to toothmick and before we lump down upown our leatherbed and in the night
and at the fading of the stars! For a nod to the nabir is better than wink to the wabsanti.
Otherways wesways like that provost scoffing bedoueen the jebel and the jpysian sea.
Cropherb the crunchbracken shall decide. Then we'll know if the feast is a flyday. She
has a gift of seek on site and she allcasually ansars helpers, the dreamydeary. Heed!
Heed! It may half been a missfired brick, as some say, or it mought have been due to a
collupsus of his back promises, as others looked at it. (There extand by now one thousand and one stories, all told, of the same). But so sore did abe ite ivvy's holired abbles,
(what with the wallhall's horrors of rollsrights, carhacks, stonengens, kisstvanes,
tramtrees, fargobawlers, autokinotons, hippohobbilies, streetfleets, tournintaxes,
megaphoggs, circuses and wardsmoats and basilikerks and aeropagods and the hoyse and
the jollybrool and the peeler in the coat and the mecklenburk bitch bite at his ear and
the merlinburrow burrocks and his fore old porecourts, the bore the more, and his blight-
black workingstacks at twelvepins a dozen and the noobibusses sleighding along Safety-
first Street and the derryjellybies snooping around Tell-No-Tailors' Corner and the
fumes and the hopes and the strupithump of his ville's indigenous romekeepers, home-
sweepers, domecreepers, thurum and thurum in fancymud murumd and all the uproor
from all the aufroofs, a roof for may and a reef for hugh butt under his bridge suits tony)
wan warning Phill filt tippling full. His howd feeled heavy, his hoddit did shake. (There
was a wall of course in erection) Dimb! He stottered from the latter. Damb! he was dud.
Dumb! Mastabatoom, mastabadtomm, when a mon merries his lute is all long. For
whole the world to see.

---

*The first was he to bare arms and the name. His creast [in vert with ancillars:] a
hegoat, horrid, horned. His shield, fessed, helio [with archers strung,] of the second.* Haitch
is for Husbandman ~~planting~~ handling his hoe. Hohohoho Mister Finn you're going
to be ~~Mr~~ Mister Finn again. Comeday ~~morning~~ morm ~~when and your you're feelin
ho~~ oh, you're Vine! senday ~~end evening~~ eve ~~you're foulin~~*, and, ah,* Vinegar. Hahahaha Mister ~~Finn Fine~~ Funn you're going to be fined again.

And, as sure as ~~Eve~~ Abe ~~ate little~~ bit Ivvy's red apples, wan warning Finn felt
tippling full. His ~~howth~~ howd filled heavy, his ~~hodd~~ hoddit did shake. *There was a
wall in course of erection.* He ~~fell~~ stottered from the latter. Damb! He was ~~dead~~ dudd.
~~Dump~~ Dumb! *For all the world to see.*

Shize? I should shee! Macool, Macool, orra whyi deed ye diie? of a trying thirstay mournin? Sobs they sighdid at Fillagain's chrissormiss wake, all the hoolivans of the nation, prostrated in their consternation and their duodisimally profusive plethora of ululation. There was plumbs and grumes and cheriffs and citherers and raiders and cinemen too. And the all gianed in with the shoutmost shoviality. Agog and magog and the round of them agrog. To the continuation of that celebration until Hanand-hunigan's extermination! Some in kinkin corass, more, kankan keening. Belling him up and filling him down. He's stiff but he's steady is Priam Olim ! 'Twas he was the dacent gaylabouring youth. Sharpen his pillowscone, tap up his bier! E'erawhere in this whorl would ye hear sich a din again? With their deepbrow fundigs and the dusty fidelios. They laid him brawdawn alanglast bed. With a bockalips of finisky fore his feet. And a barrowload of guenesis hoer his head. Tee the tootal of the fluid hang the twoddle of the fuddled, O !

[SHEM THE PENMAN]

[*This passage tells the story of Shem, one of H.C.E.'s sons. He's a writer and, like all writers, something of a plagiarist; Shem, it should be noted, is the Irish form of James, Joyce's Christian name. For a finale, Shem distills an ink from his own excrement, and writes his life's story over the surface of his own body.*]

One cannot even begin to post figure out a statuesquo ante as to how slow in reality the excommunicated Drumcondriac, nate Hamis, really was. Who can say how many pseudostylic shamiana, how few or how many of the most venerated public impostures, how very many piously forged palimpsests slipped in the first place by this morbid process from his pelagiarist pen?

Be that as it may, but for that light phantastic of his gnose's glow as it slid lucifericiously within an inch of its page (he would touch at its from time to other, the red eye of his fear in saddishness, to ensign the colours by the beerlitz in his mathness and his educandees to outhue to themselves in the cries of girlglee: gember!

Size! I should say! ~~MacCool~~, **Macool,** macool, why did ye die! Sore They sighed at ~~Finn~~ **Funnigan's** ~~wake chrismiss~~ **chrissormiss** ~~cake~~ <wake>. There was plumbs and ~~grooms~~ **grumes** and sheriffs and ~~zitherers~~ **citherers** & raiders and cittamen too. And ~~they~~ all chimed in with the shoutmost shoviality. 'Twas he was the cacent gaylabour-ing youth! ~~His A scone as for his pillow~~ Sharphen his pillowscone tap up his bier. Arrah where in this world would you hear such a din again ~~it*~~ ~~say*~~? The ~~owl~~ **whole** hangsigns & the ~~thirsty thirstey~~ **therstey** fidelios! They laid him ~~low~~ **lax** ~~along his last~~ **broadon** his bed. With ~~abuckalyps~~ **abucketlips** of finisky at his feet & a bar-rowload of ~~guinesis guenesis~~ **guennesis** at his head. ~~To~~ **Tee** the ~~total~~ **tootal** of the fulid & the twaddle of the fuddled, O.

[SHEM THE PENMAN]

One cannot even begin to imagine how really low such a creature really was. Who knows how many unsigned first copies of original masterpieces, how many pseudosty-lous shamiana, how few of the most venerated public impostures, how very many palimpsests slipped from that plagiarist pen?

inkware! chonchambre! cinsero! zinnzabar! tincture and gin!) Nibs never would have quilled a seriph to sheepskin. By that rosy lampoon's effluvious burning and with help of the simulchronic flush in his pann (a ghinee a ghirk he ghets there!) he scrabbled and scratched and scriobbled and skrevened nameless shamelessness about everybody ever he met, even sharing a precipitation under the idlish tarriers' umbrella of a showerproof wall, while all over up and down the four margins of this rancid Shem stuff the evilsmeller (who was devoted to Uldfadar Sardanapalus) used to stipple endlessly inartistic portraits of himself in the act of reciting old Nichiabelli's monolook interyerear Hanno, o Nonanno, acce'l brubblemm'as, ser Autore, q.e.d., a heartbreakingly handsome young paolo with love lyrics for the goyls in his eyols, a plaintiff's tanner vuice, a jucal inkome of one hundred and thirtytwo dranchmas per yard from Broken Hill stranded estate, Camebreech mannings, cutting a great dash in a brandnew two guinea dress suit and a burled hogsford hired for a Fursday evenin merry pawty, anna loavely long pair of inky Italian moostarshes glistering with boric vaseline and frangipani. Puh! How unwhisperably so!

The house O'Shea or O'Shame, Quivapieno, known as the Haunted Inkbottle, no number Brimstone Walk, Asia in Ireland, as it was infested with the raps, with his penname SHUT sepiascraped on the doorplate and a blind of black sailcloth over its wan phwinshogue, in which the soulcontracted son of the secret cell groped through life at the expense of the taxpayers, dejected into day and night with jesuit bark and bitter bite, calicohydrants of zolfor and scoppialamina by full and forty Queasisanos, every day in everyone's way more exceeding in violent abuse of self and others, was the worst, it is hoped, even in our western playboyish world for pure mousefarm filth. You brag of your brass castle or your tyled house in ballyfermont? Niggs, niggs and niggs again. For this was a stinksome inkenstink, quite puzzonal to the wrottel. Smatterafact, Angles aftanon browsing there thought not Edam reeked more rare. My wud! The warped flooring of the lair and soundconducting walls thereof, to say nothing of the uprights and imposts, were persianly literatured with burst loveletters, telltale stories, stickyback snaps, doubtful eggshells, bouchers, flints, borers, puffers,

---

Be that as it may, But for his nose's glow as it slid so close to the parchment he would never have penned a word to paper. By that rosy lamp's effluvious burning he scribbled & scratched nameless shamelessness about everybody ever he met, even sheltering for 5 minutes from a *spring* shower under the dogs' mbrella of a public wall, *while* all over *& up & down* the *two* margins of his foul text ~~he~~ the evilsmeller used to draw ~~endless~~ **endlessly** *inartistic* portraits of himself as a strikingly handsome yound man with love lyrics in his eyes *a tiptop tenor voice,* ~~an~~ *a [ducal] income of £20,000 a year [derived] from landed property, Oxford manners, morals and* , *a brandnew 3 guinea evening suit for a party,* & a lovely pair of inky ~~Italian~~ **Italian's** moustaches. How unwhisperably low!

The house of ~~Shem~~ **Shame,** *infested with the raps* & known as the haunted inkbottle, in which he groped through life at the expense of the taxpayers, *injected* into day & night by 40 quacks ~~grown~~ day by day ~~increasing~~ **exceeding** in violent abuse of self & others, was the worst, it is *practically* believed *even* in our *playboyish* western world for pure filth. The *warped* ~~floor~~ **flooring** *of his lair* was persianly ~~carpeted~~ **literatured** with burst ~~letters~~ **loveletters** *citizens'* throwaways, [*telltale stories,*] stick-

amygdaloid almonds, rindless raisins, alphybettyformed verbage, vivlical viasses, ompiter dictas, visus umbique, ahems and ahahs, imeffible tries at speech unasyllabled, you owe mes, eyoldhyms, fluefoul smut, fallen lucifers, vestas which had served, showered ornaments, borrowed brogues, reversibles jackets, blackeye lenses, family jars, falsehair shirts, Godforsaken scapulars, neverworn breeches, cutthroat ties, counterfeit franks, best intentions, curried notes, upset latten tintacks, unused mill and stumpling stones, twisted quills, painful digests, magnifying wineglasses, solid objects cast at goblins, once current puns, quashed quotatoes, messes of mottage, unquestionable issue papers, seedy ejaculations, limerick damns, crocodile tears, spilt ink, blasphematory spits, stale shestnuts, schoolgirl's, young ladies, milkmaids', washerwomen's, shopkeepers' wives, merry widows', ex nuns', vice abbess's, pro virgins', super whores', silent sisters', Charleys' aunts', grand-mothers', mothers'-in-laws, fostermothers', godmothers' garters, tress clippings from right, lift and cintrum, worms of snot, toothsome pickings, cans of Swiss condensed bilk, highbrow lotions, kisses from the antipodes, presents from pickpockets, borrowed plumes, relaxable handgrips, princess promises, lees of whine, deoxodised carbons, convertible collars, diviliouker doffers, broken wafers, unloosed shoe latchets, crooked strait waistcoats, fresh horrors from Hades, globules of mercury, undeleted glete, glass eyes for an eye, gloss teeth for a tooth, war moans, special sighs, longsufferings of longstanding, ahs ohs ouis sis jas jos gias neys thaws sos, yeses and yeses and yeses, to which, if one has the stomach to add the breakages, upheavals distortions, inversions of all this chambermade music one stands, given a grain of goodwill, a fair chance of actually seeing the whirling dervish, Tumult, son of Thunder, self exiled in upon his ego, a nightlong a shaking betwixtween white or reddr hawrors, noondayterrorised to skin and bone by an ineluctable phantom (may the Shaper have mercery on him!) writing the mystery of himsel in furniture.

---

yback snapshots, ~~cockroaches~~ **bullcockroaches,** ~~dated post-dated~~ **doubtful** eggshells, you owe mes, ~~fluefallen~~ **fluefoul** smut, fallen lucifers, vestas ~~which had served~~, *borrowed brogues, cutthroat ties, reversible jackets, blackeyed glasses, neverworn breeches, Godforsaken scapulars, falsehair shirts,* twisted ~~goose~~ quills, ~~ejaculated~~ **seedy ejaculations,** crocodiles' tears, spilt ink, blasphematory spits, stale chestnuts, ~~girls~~ **schoolgirls** *young* ladies' *peasant* maidens' ~~city~~ *married* wives' *merry* widows' *3* nuns' ~~womens'~~ **workwomens'** *fat* abbess's *prudent* virgins' *wedable* **impudent** whores' *silent* sisters' *Charleys* aunts' grandmothers' mothers-in-laws' fostermothers' godmothers' garters, ~~snotworms~~ **worms of snot,** *counterfeit francs* ~~good~~ **best** intentions, *new quotatoes, limerick damns,* ~~stale~~ **once** *current puns,* [*unquestionable issue papers, messes of mottage,*] princess promises, *lees of wine,* broken wafers, *showered ornaments,* unloosed shoe latchets, deoxidised carbons, crushed straight waistcoats, globules of mercury, undeleted glete, toothsome pickings, ~~dam~~ *fireproof fireworks,* ohs ouis sees gras jas neys thaws ahs yeses and yeses and yeses, *tress clippings.* To which [*if one has the stomach*] add [*the*] *breakages, upheavals, inversions, distortions, of* [*all*] *this chambermade music & one* [*stands a fair chance of*] *actually* ~~sees~~ **seeing** *the whirling dervish, exiled in upon his ego,* [*noonday terrorized by an ineluctable shadow,*] *writing the history of himself in furniture.* Of course ~~the~~ **our** low ~~creature~~ **hero** was *& had to be a selfvaleter so he got up* ~~what~~ **whatever** *is meant by a kitchenette & fowlhouse for the sake of eggs in what was meant for a closet.* Naturally he never needed such an ~~alcove~~ **alcohove** for his

Of course our low hero was a self valeter by choice of need so up he got up whatever is meant by a stourbridge clay kitchenette and lithargogalenu fowlhouse for the sake of akes (the umpple does not fall very far from the dumpertree) which the moromelodious jigsmith, in defiance of the Uncontrollable Birth Preservativation (Game and Poultry) Act, playing lallaryrook cookerynook, by the dodginess of his lentern, brooled and cocked and potched in an athanor, whites and yolks and yilks and whotes to the frulling fredonnance of Mas blanca que la blanca hermana and Amarilla, muy bien, with cinnamon and locusts and wild beeswax and liquorice and Carrageen moss and blaster of Barry's and Asther's mess and Huster's micture and Yellownan's embrocation and Pinkingtone's patty and stardust and sinner's tears, acuredent to Sharadan's Art of Panning, chanting, for all regale to the like of the legs he left behind with Litty fun Letty fan Leven, his cantraps of fermented words, abracadabra calubra culorum, (his oewfs à la Madame Gabrielle de l'Eglise, his avgs à la Mistress B. de B. Meinfelde, his eiers Usquadmala à la pomme de ciel, his uoves, oves and uves à la Sulphate de Soude, his ochiuri sowtay sowmmonay a la Monseigneur, his soufflosion of oogs with somekat on toyast à la Mère Puard, his Poggadovies alla Fenella, his Frideggs à la Tricarême) in what was meant for a closet (Ah ho! If only he had listened better to the four masters that infanted him Father Mathew and Le Père Noble and Pastor Lucas and Padre Aguilar—not forgetting Layteacher Baudwin! Ah ho!) His costive Satan's antimonian manganese limolitmious nature never needed such an alcove so, when Robber and Mumsell, the pulpic dictators, on the nudgment of their legal advisers, Messrs Codex and Podex, and under his own benefiction of their pastor Father Flammeus Falconer, boycotted him of all muttonsuet candles and romeruled stationery for any purpose, he winged away on a wildgoup's chase across the kathartic ocean and made synthetic ink and sensitive paper for his own end out of his wit's waste. You ask, in Sam Hill, how? Let manner and matter of this for these our sporting times be cloaked up in the language of blushfed porporates that an Anglican ordinal, not reading his own rude dunsky tunga, may ever behold the brand of scarlet on the brow of her of Babylon and feel not the pink one in his own damned cheek.

Primum opifex, altus prosator, ad terram viviparam et cunctipotentem sine ullo pudore nec venia, suscepto pluviali atque discinctis perizomatis, natibus nudis uti nati fuissent, sese adpropinquans, flens et gemens, in manum suam evacuavit (highly prosy, crap in his hand, sorry!), postea, animale nigro exoneratus, classicum pulsans, stercus proprium, quod appellavit deiectiones suas, in vas olim honorabile tristitiae

---

purpose and when George W Robber, the ~~paper stat~~ paper king, boycotted him of all stationery & muttonsuet candles for any purpose he went away & made synthetic ink ~~for~~ & unruled ~~foolscap~~ parchment for ~~it~~ himself ~~with~~ out of his wits' ends. How? Let [the manner & the matter of] it [for these [our] sporting times] be ~~veiled~~ cloaked up in the language of ~~blushing~~ blushfed cardinals ~~lest~~ that [the] Anglican ~~cardinals~~ cardinal, [not] reading his own ~~words~~ rude speech, [may always] behold the scarlet [brand] on the brown of ~~the~~ her of Babylon yet feel not the pink one in his [own damned] cheek

[Following "his own damned cheek," the first-draft version also describes Shem's next actions in Latin, with interjections in English. A translation of the final version would be:] First the creator, lofty proser, toward the fecund and all-potent earth, with

posuit, eodem sub invocatione fratrorum geminorum Medardi et Godardi laete ac melliflue minxit, psalmum qui incipit: Lingua mea calamus scribae velociter scriben-tis: magna voce cantitans (did a piss, says he was dejected, asks to be exonerated), demum ex stercore turpi cum divi Orionis iucunditate mixto, cocto, frigorique expos-ito, encaustum sibi fecit indelibile (faked O'Ryan's, the indelible ink).

Then, pious Eneas, conformant to thc fulminant firman which enjoins on the tremylose terrian that, when the call comes, he shall produce nichthemerically from his unheavenly body a no uncertain quantity of obscene matter not protected by copriright in the United Stars of Ourania or bedeed and bedood and bedang and bedung to him, with this double dye, brought to blood heat, gallic acid on iron ore, through the bowels of his misery, flashly, faithly, nastily, appropriately, this Esuan Menschavik and the first till last alshemist wrote over every square inch of the only foolscap available, his own body, till by its corrosive sublimation one continuous present tense integument slowly unfolded all marryvoising moodmoulded cyclewheeling history (thereby, he said, reflecting from his own individual person life unlivable, transaccidentated through the slow fires of consciousness into a dividual chaos, perilous, potent, common to allflesh, human only, mortal) but with each word that would not pass away the squidself which he had squirtscreened from the crystalline world waned chagreenold and doriangrayer in its dudhud. This exists that isits after having been said we know. And dabal take dab-nal! And the dal dabal dab aldanabal! So perhaps, agglaggagglomeratively asaspenking, after all and arklast fore arklyst on his last public misappearance, circling the square, for the deathfête of Saint Ignaceous Poisonivy, of the Fickle Crowd (hopon the sexth day of Hogsober, killim our king, layum low!) and brandishing his bellbearing stylo, the shining keyman of the wilds of change, if what is sauce for the zassy is souse for the zazi-mas, the blond cop who thought it was ink was out of his depth but bright in the main.

---

neither shame nor modesty, a little weepily loosened his belt; with his buttocks naked as the day he was born, reaching up to himself, moaning and groaning, he evacuated in his hand (highly prosy, crap in his hand, sorry!); then, having unloaded this living blackness, blowing on a trumpet, he took his own dung, which he called his "dejections," and put this gloominess in a formerly honorable container, into which, invoking the twin brothers Medard and Godard, he joyfully and mellifluously urinated, loudly singing the psalm that begins: My tongue is the reed of a swiftly-writ-ing scribe (did a piss, says he was dejected, asks to be exonerated), then finally, hav-ing mixed in the foul dung, with the joy of the divine Orion he cooked it and set it out to cool, making his own indelible encaustic (faked O'Ryan's, the indelible ink).

With the *double* eye he wrote minutely, appropriately over every part of the only foolscap available, his own body, till *one* integument slowly unfolded universal history *the [varied **progressive**] reflection from his [individual] person of lived life **unlivable** transaccidentated in the slow fire of consciousness into a dividual chaos, perilous, potent, common to all flesh, mortal only,* & that self which he hid from the world grew darker* & darker in *its* outlook. So perhaps when he last at his last *public* disappearance the blond cop, who thought it was ink, was out.

[Anna Livia Plurabelle]

[*This is the close of the most beautiful chapter in the novel—the chapter that Joyce was willing to stake his reputation upon. Anna Livia Plurabelle is in part a personification of the River Liffey which flows through the center of Dublin; consequently, Joyce incorporated the names of over 500 rivers to make the chapter "flow." In this passage, two washerwomen on opposite sides of the river have an increasingly difficult time hearing one another, as the river widens as it approaches the sea and the noise of the river itself increases; night is falling, as well, making it increasingly difficult for them to see one another.*]

Well, you know or don't you kennet or haven't I told you every telling has a taling and that's the he and the she of it. Look, look, the dusk is growing! My branches lofty are taking root. And my cold cher's gone ashley. Fieluhr? Filou! What age is at? It saon is late. 'Tis endless now senne eye or erewone last saw Waterhouse's clogh. They took it asunder, I hurd thum sigh. When will they reassemble it? O, my back, my back, my bach! I'd want to go to Achesles-Pains. Pingpong! There's the Belle for Sexaloitez! And Concepta de Send-us-pray! Pang! Wring out the clothes! Wring in the dew! Godavari, vert the showers! And grant thaya grace! Aman. Will we spread them here now? Ay, we will. Flip! Spread on your bank and I'll spread mine on mine. Flep! It's what I'm doing. Spread! It's churning chill. Der went is rising. I'll lay a few stones on the hostel sheets. A man and his bride embraced between them. Else I'd have sprinkled and folded them only. And I'll tie my butcher's apron here. It's suety yet. The strollers will pass it by. Six shifts, ten kerchiefs, nine to hold to the fire and this for the code, the convent napkins, twelve, one baby's shawl. Good mother Jossiph knows, she said. Whose head? Mutter snores? Deataceas! Wharnow are alle her childer, say? In kingdome gone or power to come or gloria be to them farther? Allalivial, allalluvial! Some here, more no more, more again lost alla stranger. I've heard tell that same brooch of the Shannons was married into a family in Spain. And all the Dunders de Dunnes in Markland's Vineland beyond Brendan's herring pool takes number nine in yangsee's hats. And one of Biddy's beads went bobbing till she rounded up lost histereve with a marigold and a cobbler's candle in a side strain of a

---

Well you know & don't you know but every story has an end look, look ~~it's growing~~ the dusk is growing. *What time is it? It must be late. It's ages now since I* ~~last~~ *or anyone saw Waterhouse's clock. They took it asunder I heard them say. When will they reassemble it?* Wring out the clothes. Wring in the dusk. Will we spread them here? *Yes, we will.* Spread on your side and I'll spread mine on mine. Where are all her childer now? Some here, more ~~gone~~ **no more,** more again gone to the stranger. I've heard tell that same brooch of the Shannons was married into a family beyond the ocean. And all the Dunnes takes eights in hats. But all that's left now to the last of the Meaghers I'm told it's a kneebuckle & two buttons in the front. Do you tell me that now? I do, in troth. Is that the Dunboyne *on his* statue behind you there riding his high horse? That! Throw the cobwebs from your eyes, woman, & spread your linen proper. What is ~~at all~~ but a blackberry growth or ~~a~~ **the** *grey mare ass them four old*

main drain of a manzinahurries off Bachelor's Walk. But all that's left to the last of the Meaghers in the loup of the years prefixed and between is one kneebuckle and two hooks in the front. Do you tell me that now? I do in troth. Orara por Orbe and poor Las Animas! Ussa, Ulla, we're umbas all! Mezha, didn't you hear it a deluge of times, ufer and ufer, respund to spond? You deed, you deed! I need, I need! It's that irrawaddyng I've stoke in my aars. It all but husheth the lethest zswound. Oronoko! What's your trouble? Is that the great Finnleader himself in his joakimono on his statue riding the high hone there forehengist? Father of Otters, it is himself! Yonne there! Isset that? On Fallareen Common? You're thinking of Astley's Amphitheayter where the bobby restrained you making sugarstuck pouts to the ghostwhite horse of the Peppers. Throw the cobwebs from your eyes, woman, and spread your washing proper! It's well I know your sort of slop. Flap! Ireland sober is Ireland stiff Lord help you, Maria, full of grease, the load is with me! Your prayers. I sonht zo! Madammangut! Were you lifting your elbow, tell us, glazy cheeks, in Conway's Carrigacurra canteen? Was I what, hobbledyhips? Flop! Your rere gait's creakorheuman bitts your butts disagrees. Amn't I up since the damp tawn, marthared mary allacook, with Corrigan's pulse and varicoarse veins, my pramaxle smashed, Alice Jane in decline and my oneeyed mongrel twice run over, soaking and bleaching boiler rags, and sweating cold, a widow like me, for to deck my tennis champion son, the laundryman with the lavandier flannels? You won your limpopo limp fron the husky hussars when Collars and Cuffs was heir to the town and your slur gave the stink to Carlow. Holy Scamander, I sar it again! Near the golden falls. Icis on us! Seints of light! Zezere! Subdue your noise, you hamble creature! What is it but a blackburry growth or the dwyergray ass them four old codgers owns. Are you meanam Tarpey and Lyons and Gregory? I meyne now, thank all, the four of them, and the roar of them, that draves that stray in the mist and old Johnny MacDougal along with them. Is that the Poolbeg flasher beyant, pharphar, or a fireboat coasting nyar the Kishtna or a glow I behold within a hedge or my Garry come back from the Indes? Wait till the honeying of the lune, love! Die eve, little eve, die! We see that wonder in your eye. We'll meet again, we'll part once more. The spot I'll seek if the hour you'll find. My chart shines high where the blue milk's upset. Forgivemequick, I'm going! Bubye! And you, pluck your watch, forgetmenot. Your evenlode. So save to jurna's end! My sights are swimming thicker on me by the shadows to this place. I sow home slowly now by own way, moyvalley way. Towy I too, rathmine.

Ah, but she was the queer old skeowsha anyhow, Anna Livia, trinkettoes! And sure he was the quare old buntz too, Dear Dirty Dumpling, foostherfather of fingalls and dotthergills. Gammer and gaffer we're all their gangsters. Hadn't he seven

---

~~fellows~~ **codgers** own. *Do you mean Tarpey & Lyons & Gregory? I do the four codgers themselves and old Johnny MacDougal along with them.* My sight is getting thick now with shadows about me. I'll go home slowly my way. So will I too by mine.

But She was the queer old ~~one~~ **skeowska** anyhow, Anna Livia *twinkletoes*. And sure he was a queer old ~~hunks~~ **buntz** too ~~Furry Humphrey~~ *dear* **Dirty Dumpling,** *father of [each &] all of us.* Hadn't he the seven wives. He had paps too, ~~big &~~ **large**

dams to wive him? And every dam had her seven crutches. And every crutch had its seven hues. And each hue had a differing cry. Sudds for me and supper for you and the doctor's bill for Joe John. Befor! Bifur! He married his markets, cheap by foul, I know, like any Etrurian Catholic Heathen, in their pinky limony creamy birnies and their turkiss indienne mauves. But at milkidmass who was the spouse? Then all that was was fair. Tys Elvenland! Teems of times and happy returns. The seim anew. Ordovico or viricordo. Anna was, Livia is, Plurabelle's to be. Northmen's thing made southfolk's place but howmulty plurators made eachone in person? Latin me that, my trinity scholard, out of eure sanscreed into oure eryan! Hircus Civis Eblanensis! He had buckgoat paps on him, soft ones for orphans. Ho, Lord! Twins of his bosom. Lord save us! And ho! Hey? What all men. Hot? His tittering daughters of. Whawk?

Can't hear with the waters of. The chittering waters of. Flittering bats, fieldmice bawk talk. Ho! Are you not gone ahome? What Thom Malone? Can't hear with bawk of bats, all thim liffeying waters of. Ho, talk save us! My foos won't moos. I feel as old as yonder elm. A tale told of Shaun or Shem? All Livia's daughtersons. Dark hawks hear us. Night! Night! My ho head halls. I feel as heavy as yonder stone. Tell me of John or Shaun? Who were Shem and Shaun the living sons or daughters of? Night now! Tell me, tell me, tell me, elm! Night night! Telmetale of stem or stone. Beside the rivering waters of, hitherandthithering waters of. Night!

---

soft ones. ~~The Lord save us and bless us! and The O~~ **Ho** Lard. Twins of his chest. ~~The O~~ **Ho** Lord save us! And what all men ~~have~~. *His tittering* Daughters* of ~~him~~. ~~Amen~~. **Bawk.**

~~I can't~~ **Can't** hear with the waters of. ~~The~~ **Them** chittering water of. Flittering bats and mice all ~~bawking~~ **bawk** *talk*. Are you not ~~gone home~~ **goneahome**? ~~Is that That Mrs. Malone~~ **What wrong Malone**? Can't hear the bawk of bats, all the liffeying waters of. Old talk save us! *My feet won't move*. I feel as old as yonder elm. A tale told of Shaun ~~and~~ **or** Shem? *All* Livia's daughtersons. Dark hawks hear us. Night night. My *old* head falls. I feel as heavy as *yonder* stone. Tell me of John or Shaun? Who were Shem ~~or~~ **and** Shaun the living sons or daughters of? Night now? Tell me, *tell me*, elm. Nighty night! Tell me a tale of stone. Beside the rivering waters of hither & thither water of. Night!

T. S. Eliot

1888–1965

T. S. Eliot was one of the dominant forces in English-language poetry of the twentieth century. When the entire body of Eliot's writing and influence is taken into account—not only his relatively modest poetic and dramatic production, but his literary criticism, his religious and cultural criticism, his editorial work at the British publishing house Faber and Faber, his influence on younger poets coming up in his wake, and quite simply his *presence* as a literary and cultural icon—no one looms larger. As one of those younger poets, Karl Shapiro, has written: "Eliot is untouchable; he is Modern Literature incarnate and an institution unto himself." Eliot's obituary in *Life* magazine declared that "Our age beyond any doubt has been, and will continue to be, the Age of Eliot."

Thomas Stearns Eliot was born in Saint Louis, Missouri. The roots of Eliot's family tree go deep into American, and specifically New England, soil. His ancestor Andrew Eliot was one of the original settlers of the Massachusetts Bay Colony, emigrating from East Coker, in Somerset, England, in the mid-seventeenth century; he later became one of the jurors who tried the Salem "witches." The Eliots became a distinguished New England family; the Eliot family tree includes a president of Harvard University and three U.S. Presidents (John Adams, John Quincy Adams, and Rutherford B. Hayes). In 1834 the Reverend William Greenleaf Eliot, the poet's grandfather, graduated from Harvard and moved to Saint Louis, where he established the city's first Unitarian church; he went on to found Washington University, and became its chancellor in 1872. It was into this family environment—redolent of New England, New England religion (Unitarianism), and New England educational tradition (Harvard)—that Eliot was born in 1888. And yet in a 1960 essay, Eliot wrote "My urban imagery was that of Saint Louis, upon which that of Paris and London had been superimposed." The sights and sounds of Saint Louis impressed themselves deeply on Eliot's young imagination, especially the looming figure of the Mississippi River (which he was to call "a strong brown god" in *The Dry Salvages*).

From age ten Eliot attended Smith Academy in Saint Louis—also founded by his grandfather—and spent his last year of secondary school at the Milton Academy in Milton, Massachusetts, in preparation for his entrance into Harvard in 1906. Eliot went on to take his A.B. (1909) and M.A. (1910) degrees from Harvard and largely completed a Ph.D. in philosophy from Harvard, first spending a relatively unstructured year in Paris, attending lectures at the Sorbonne and hearing Henri Bergson lecture at the Collège de France. He wrote a doctoral dissertation on the neo-idealist philosopher F. H. Bradley in 1916, which was accepted by the philosophy department at Harvard, but he never returned to Cambridge to defend the dissertation and take the degree. Eliot's year in Paris was crucial in many ways; in addition to breathing in the vital Parisian intellectual and artistic scene, he soaked up the writing of late-nineteenth-century French poets like Jules Laforgue, Tristan Corbière, and Charles Baudelaire.

Eliot's poems are deeply indebted both to French and to British poets. The poem with which Eliot broke onto the modern poetry scene was *The Love Song of J. Alfred Prufrock*, composed between 1910 and 1911. In a strikingly new and jarring idiom, the poem builds on the dramatic monologues of Robert Browning, breaking up the unified voice at the center of Browning's experiments with startling juxtapositions and transitions, and adding the violent and disturbing imagery of the French symbolist poets. The resulting poem is a heavily ironic "love song" in which neither lover nor beloved exists with any solidity outside the straitjacket of "a formulated phrase"; Prufrock, like modern European humanity whom he represents, is unable to penetrate the thick husk of habit, custom, and cliché to arrive at something substantial.

2418   T. S. Eliot

Eliot, and the poem, came to the notice of modern literature impresario Ezra Pound; in 1915 Pound saw to it that *Prufrock* was published in Harriet Monroe's influential *Poetry* magazine, as well as in his own *Catholic Anthology*, which brought Eliot to the notice of the (largely hostile) British literary establishment in the person of reviewers like the *Quarterly Review's* Arthur Waugh. Eliot wrote three other great poems in this early period, *Portrait of a Lady*, *Preludes*, and *Rhapsody on a Windy Night*. Like *Prufrock*, the poems deal unflinchingly with loneliness, alienation, isolation; while isolation is hardly a new theme for poetry, Eliot suggests in a particularly modernist form in these poems that our isolation from others derives from, and tragically mirrors, our isolation from ourselves. This internalized alienation was also one of the themes of Eliot's early and influential review essay *The Metaphysical Poets* (1921); in that piece, he suggested that English poetry had suffered through a long drought, dating from about the time of Milton, caused by what Eliot termed a "dissociation of sensibility." At the time of the metaphysical poets (in the seventeenth century), a poet, or any sensitive thinker, was a unified whole; "A thought to Donne," Eliot writes, "was an experience; it modified his sensibility. . . . the ordinary man's experience is chaotic, irregular, fragmentary." That chaotic consciousness seemed to Eliot especially pronounced in the early decades of the twentieth century; though not sanguine of easy solutions, he did believe that modern poets, writing a poetry that would synthesize the seemingly unrelated sensations and experiences of modern men and women, might show a way out of "the immense panorama of futility and anarchy which is contemporary history," as he wrote in 1923 in a review of Joyce's *Ulysses*.

A collection of Eliot's early poems was published in 1917 as *Prufrock and Other Observations* by the Egoist Press, through the offices of Pound. For the remainder of the decade, however, Eliot's poetic output was small; feeling himself at a creative cul de sac, he wrote a few poems in French in 1917, including *Dans le Restaurant* which later appeared, trimmed and translated, as a part of *The Waste Land*. On Pound's suggestion, Eliot set himself, as a formal exercise, to write several poems modeled on the quatrains of Théophile Gautier. Arguably the most significant and influential of Eliot's early writings, however, were his many critical essays and book reviews; between 1916 and 1921 he wrote nearly a hundred essays and reviews, many of which were published in 1920 as *The Sacred Wood*. Critics still disagree as to whether Eliot's poetry or critical prose has been the more influential; the most important of Eliot's critical precepts, such as the "impersonality" of poetry and the inherent difficulty of modern writing, have entered wholesale into the way that modern literature is studied and taught. Eliot's critical principles, complemented and extended by academics such as I. A. Richards, make up the foundation of what came to be known as the New Criticism, a major mode of reading that emphasizes close attention to verbal textures and to poetic ironies, paradoxes, and tensions between disparate elements—all prominent features of Eliot's own poetry.

Eliot lived in modest circumstances for several years, working as a schoolteacher and then a bank clerk between 1916 and 1922. He then edited an increasingly influential quarterly, *The Criterion* (1922–1939), and became an editor at Faber and Faber, a post he retained until his death. His reputation as a poet was confirmed in 1922 with *The Waste Land*, the epochal work that remains Eliot's best-known and most influential poem; Pound called it "about enough . . . to make the rest of us shut up shop." More than any other text of the century, *The Waste Land* forcibly changed the idiom that contemporary poetry must adopt if it were to remain contemporary. Perhaps the poem's most impressive formal achievement, created in no small part through Ezra Pound's judicious editorial work, is its careful balance between structure and chaos, unity and fragmentation; this poise is created in the poem in equal parts by the mythical structures Eliot used to undergird the contemporary action and the pedantic footnotes he added to the poem, after its periodical publication in the *Dial*, to call the reader's attention to those structures. *The Waste Land*— like *Ulysses*, *Finnegans Wake*, Pound's *Cantos*, and a number of other important texts—looks unified largely because we readers look for it to be unified. Such a style of reading is one of the great triumphs of modernism, and one Eliot was instrumental in teaching to readers and teachers alike.

The Waste Land is justly celebrated for giving voice to the nearly universal pessimism and alienation of the early decades of the twentieth century Europe—though Eliot maintained to the end that he was not a spokesperson for his generation or for anything else, and that the poem was "only the relief of a personal and wholly insignificant grouse against life; it is just a piece of rhythmical grumbling." Owing to the development of recording technology, to "give voice" in this case is not merely a metaphor, for Eliot's recording of *The Waste Land*, in what Virginia Woolf called Eliot's "sepulchral voice," has been tremendously influential on two generations of poets and students. Eliot's critical principle of "impersonality," however, has sometimes served to obscure how very personal, on one level, the poem is. The poem was completed during Eliot's convalescence at a sanatorium in Margate, England ("On Margate Sands. / I can connect / Nothing with nothing," the speaker despairs in section 3, "The Fire Sermon") and in Lausanne, Switzerland; the speaker, like the poet, is reduced to shoring the fragments of a disappearing civilization against his ruin. The poem also bears painful testimony to the increasingly desperate state of Eliot's wife Vivien Haigh-Wood, whom he had married in 1915; she suffered terribly from what was at the time called "nervousness," and had finally to be institutionalized in 1938. Whole stretches of one-sided "dialogue" from the "A Game of Chess" section would seem to have been taken verbatim from the couple's private conversations: "My nerves are very bad to-night. Yes, bad. Stay with me. / Speak to me. Why do you never speak? Speak." On the draft of the poem, Pound wrote "photography" alongside this passage. *The Waste Land* remains one of the century's most incisive and insightful texts regarding the breakdown of social, communal, cultural, and personal relationships.

In 1930 Eliot's next important poem, the introspective and confessional *Ash Wednesday*, was published; in the time since the publication of *The Waste Land*, however, Eliot's personal belief system had undergone a sea change. In June 1927 he was baptized into the Anglican church; five months later, he was naturalized as a British citizen. In his 1928 monograph *For Lancelot Andrewes*, Eliot declared himself to be "classicist in literature, royalist in politics, and Anglo-Catholic in religion." His poem *Journey of the Magi*, published as a pamphlet a month after his baptism, addresses the journey Eliot himself had made through death to a rebirth—precisely the rebirth which, in the opening lines of *The Waste Land*, seems an impossibility.

The 1930s also saw Eliot's entry into the theater, with three poetic dramas: *The Rock* (1934), *Murder in the Cathedral* (1935), and *The Family Reunion* (1939). In his later years, these highbrow dramas were complemented with a handful of more popular social dramas, *The Cocktail Party* (1950), *The Confidential Clerk* (1954), and *The Elder Statesman* (1959). Though celebrated by critics at the time for their innovative use of verse and their willingness to wrestle with both modern problems and universal themes, the plays have slipped in popularity in recent years. Nevertheless, as fate would have it, Eliot is the posthumous librettist of one of the most successful musicals in the history of British and American theater: his playful children's book *Old Possum's Book of Practical Cats* (1939), light verse written for the enjoyment of his godchildren, was transformed by Andrew Lloyd Webber in 1980 into the smash-hit musical *Cats*.

Eliot's final poetic achievement—and, for many, his greatest—is the set of four poems published together in 1943 as *Four Quartets*. Eliot believed them to be the best of his writing; "The *Four Quartets*: I rest on those," he told an interviewer in 1959. Structurally—though the analogy is a loose one—Eliot modeled the *Quartets* on the late string quartets of Beethoven, especially the last, the A Minor Quartet; as early as 1931 he had written the poet Stephen Spender, "I have the A Minor Quartet on the gramophone, and I find it quite inexhaustible to study. There is a sort of heavenly or at least more than human gaiety about some of his later things which one imagines might come to oneself as the fruit of reconcilliation and relief after immense suffering; I should like to get something of that into verse before I die."

Eliot's last years were brightened by increasing public accolades, including the Nobel Prize for literature in 1948; he became a very popular speaker on the public lecture circuit, attracting an audience of 15,000, for instance, at a lecture at the University of Minnesota in

1956, later published as *The Frontiers of Criticism*. These public appearances largely took the place of creative writing after 1960. In January 1947 Vivien Eliot died in an institution; a decade later, he married Esme Valery Fletcher, and enjoyed a fulfilling companionate marriage until his death in January 1965. Like Hardy and Yeats, Eliot expressed his wish to be buried in his ancestors' parish church, in his case at East Coker, the home of his ancestor Andrew Eliot; thus, in his death and burial, the opening of his poem *East Coker* is literalized: "In my beginning is my end."

The Love Song of J. Alfred Prufrock

> S'io credessi che mia risposta fosse
> a persona che mai tornasse al mondo,
> questa fiamma staria senza più scosse.
> Ma per ciò che giammai di questo fondo
> non tornò vivo alcun, s'i'odo il vero,
> senza tema d'infamia ti rispondo.[1]

Let us go then, you and I,
When the evening is spread out against the sky
Like a patient etherised upon a table;
Let us go, through certain half-deserted streets,
5 The muttering retreats
Of restless nights in one-night cheap hotels
And sawdust restaurants with oyster-shells:
Streets that follow like a tedious argument
Of insidious intent
10 To lead you to an overwhelming question . . .
Oh, do not ask, "What is it?"
Let us go and make our visit.

In the room the women come and go
Talking of Michelangelo.

15 The yellow fog that rubs its back upon the window-panes,
The yellow smoke that rubs its muzzle on the window-panes,
Licked its tongue into the corners of the evening,
Lingered upon the pools that stand in drains,
Let fall upon its back the soot that falls from chimneys,
20 Slipped by the terrace, made a sudden leap,
And seeing that it was a soft October night,
Curled once about the house, and fell asleep.

And indeed there will be time
For the yellow smoke that slides along the street
25 Rubbing its back upon the window-panes;
There will be time, there will be time
To prepare a face to meet the faces that you meet;
There will be time to murder and create,
And time for all the works and days of hands

---

1. From Dante's *Inferno* (27.61–66). Dante asks one of the damned souls for its name, and it replies: "If I thought my answer were for one who could return to the world, I would not reply, but as none ever did return alive from this depth, without fear of infamy I answer thee."

30   That lift and drop a question on your plate;
     Time for you and time for me,
     And time yet for a hundred indecisions,
     And for a hundred visions and revisions,
     Before the taking of a toast and tea.

35   In the room the women come and go
     Talking of Michelangelo.

     And indeed there will be time
     To wonder, "Do I dare?" and, "Do I dare?"
     Time to turn back and descend the stair,
40   With a bald spot in the middle of my hair—
     (They will say: "How his hair is growing thin!")
     My morning coat, my collar mounting firmly to the chin,
     My necktie rich and modest, but asserted by a simple pin—
     (They will say: "But how his arms and legs are thin!")
45   Do I dare
     Disturb the universe?
     In a minute there is time
     For decisions and revisions which a minute will reverse.

     For I have known them all already, known them all—
50   Have known the evenings, mornings, afternoons,
     I have measured out my life with coffee spoons;
     I know the voices dying with a dying fall
     Beneath the music from a farther room.
         So how should I presume?

55   And I have known the eyes already, known them all—
     The eyes that fix you in a formulated phrase,
     And when I am formulated, sprawling on a pin,
     When I am pinned and wriggling on the wall,
     Then how should I begin
60   To spit out all the butt-ends of my days and ways?
         And how should I presume?

     And I have known the arms already, known them all—
     Arms that are braceleted and white and bare
     (But in the lamplight, downed with light brown hair!)
65   Is it perfume from a dress
     That makes me so digress?
     Arms that lie along a table, or wrap about a shawl.
         And should I then presume?
         And how should I begin?

         . . .

70   Shall I say, I have gone at dusk through narrow streets
     And watched the smoke that rises from the pipes
     Of lonely men in shirt-sleeves, leaning out of windows? . . .

     I should have been a pair of ragged claws
     Scuttling across the floors of silent seas.

         . . .

75 And the afternoon, the evening, sleeps so peacefully!
Smoothed by long fingers,
Asleep . . . tired . . . or it malingers,
Stretched on the floor, here beside you and me.
Should I, after tea and cakes and ices,
80 Have the strength to force the moment to its crisis?
But though I have wept and fasted, wept and prayed,
Though I have seen my head (grown slightly bald) brought
in upon a platter,[2]
I am no prophet—and here's no great matter;
I have seen the moment of my greatness flicker,
85 And I have seen the eternal Footman hold my coat, and snicker,
And in short, I was afraid.

And would it have been worth it, after all,
After the cups, the marmalade, the tea,
Among the porcelain, among some talk of you and me,
90 Would it have been worth while,
To have bitten off the matter with a smile,
To have squeezed the universe into a ball
To roll it towards some overwhelming question,
To say: "I am Lazarus, come from the dead,
95 Come back to tell you all, I shall tell you all"[3]—
If one, settling a pillow by her head,
        Should say: "That is not what I meant at all.
        That is not it, at all."

And would it have been worth it, after all,
100 Would it have been worth while,
After the sunsets and the dooryards and the sprinkled streets,
After the novels, after the teacups, after the skirts that trail
along the floor—
And this, and so much more?—
It is impossible to say just what I mean!
105 But as if a magic lantern[4] threw the nerves in patterns on a
screen:
Would it have been worth while
If one, settling a pillow or throwing off a shawl,
And turning toward the window, should say:
        "That is not it at all,
110   That is not what I meant, at all."

No! I am not Prince Hamlet, nor was meant to be;
Am an attendant lord, one that will do
To swell a progress, start a scene or two,
Advise the prince; no doubt, an easy tool,
115 Deferential, glad to be of use,
Politic, cautious, and meticulous;

2. Cf. Matthew 14. John the Baptist was beheaded by Herod and his head was brought to his wife, Herodias, on a platter.
3. Cf. John 11. Jesus raised Lazarus from the grave after he had been dead four days.
4. A device that employs a candle to project images, rather like a slide projector.

Full of high sentence, but a bit obtuse;
At times, indeed, almost ridiculous—
Almost, at times, the Fool.

120   I grow old . . . I grow old . . .
I shall wear the bottoms of my trousers rolled.

Shall I part my hair behind? Do I dare to eat a peach?
I shall wear white flannel trousers, and walk upon the beach.
I have heard the mermaids singing, each to each.

125   I do not think that they will sing to me.

I have seen them riding seaward on the waves
Combing the white hair of the waves blown back
When the wind blows the water white and black.

We have lingered in the chambers of the sea
130   By sea-girls wreathed with seaweed red and brown
Till human voices wake us, and we drown.

COMPANION READINGS

Arthur Waugh:[1] [Cleverness and the New Poetry]

Cleverness is, indeed, the pitfall of the New Poetry. There is no question about the ingenuity with which its varying moods are exploited, its elaborate symbolism evolved, and its sudden, disconcerting effect exploded upon the imagination. Swift, brilliant images break into the field of vision, scatter like rockets, and leave a trail of flying fire behind. But the general impression is momentary; there are moods and emotions, but no steady current of ideas behind them. Further, in their determination to surprise and even to puzzle at all costs these young poets are continually forgetting that the first essence of poetry is beauty; and that, however much you may have observed the world around you, it is impossible to translate your observation into poetry, without the intervention of the spirit of beauty, controlling the vision, and reanimating the idea.

The temptations of cleverness may be insistent, but its risks are equally great: how great indeed will, perhaps, be best indicated by the example of the "Catholic Anthology," which apparently represents the very newest of all the new poetic movements of the day. This strange little volume bears upon its cover a geometrical device, suggesting that the material within holds the same relation to the art of poetry as the work of the Cubist school hold to the art of painting and design. The product of the volume is mainly American in origin, only one or two of the contributors being of indisputably English birth. But it appears here under the auspices of a house associated with some of the best poetry of the younger generation, and is prefaced by a short lyric by Mr W. B. Yeats, in which that honoured representative of a very different school of inspiration makes bitter fun of scholars and critics, who

Edit and annotate the lines
That young men, tossing on their beds,
Rhymed out in love's despair
To flatter beauty's ignorant ear.

1. Influential publisher, editor and critic (1866–1943); father of novelist Evelyn Waugh. The *Catholic Anthology* (1914), which Waugh attacks in this review from the *Quarterly Review* (London), was edited by Ezra Pound and included Eliot's *The Love Song of J. Alfred Prufrock* and printed W. B. Yeats's *The Scholars* as a preface.

The reader will not have penetrated far beyond this warning notice before he finds himself in the very stronghold of literary rebellion, if not of anarchy. Mr Orrick Johns may be allowed to speak for his colleagues, as well as for himself:

> This is the song of youth,
> This is the cause of myself;
> I knew my father well and he was a fool,
> Therefore will I have my own foot in the path before I take a step;
> I will go only into new lands,
> And I will walk on no plank-walks.
> The horses of my family are wind-broken,
> And the dogs are old,
> And the guns rust;
> I will make me a new bow from an ash-tree,
> And cut up the homestead into arrows.

And Mr Ezra Pound takes up the parable in turn, in the same wooden prose, cut into battens:

> Come, my songs, let us express our baser passions.
> Let us express our envy for the man with a steady job and no worry about the future.
> You are very idle, my songs,
> I fear you will come to a bad end.
> You stand about the streets. You loiter at the corners and bus-stops,
> You do next to nothing at all.
> You do not even express our inner nobility,
> You will come to a very bad end.
> And I? I have gone half cracked.[2]

It is not for his audience to contradict the poet, who for once may be allowed to pronounce his own literary epitaph. But this, it is to be noted, is the "poetry" that was to say nothing that might not be said "actually in life—under emotion,"[3] the sort of emotion that settles down into the banality of a premature decrepitude:

> I grow old. . . . I grow old . . .
> I shall wear the bottoms of my trousers rolled.
> Shall I part my hair behind? Do I dare to eat a peach?
> I shall wear white flannel trousers, and walk upon the beach.
> I have heard the mermaids singing, each to each.
> I do not think that they will sing to me.

Here, surely, is the reduction to absurdity of that school of literary license which, beginning with the declaration "I knew my father well and he was a fool" naturally proceeds to the convenient assumption that everything which seemed wise and true to the father must inevitably be false and foolish to the son. Yet if the fruits of emancipation are to be recognised in the unmetrical, incoherent banalities of these literary "Cubists," the state of Poetry is indeed threatened with anarchy which will end in something worse even than "red ruin and the breaking up of laws." From such a catastrophe the humour, commonsense, and artistic judgment of the best of the new "Georgians" will assuredly save their generation; nevertheless, a hint of warning may

---

2. From Pound's *Further Instructions*.

3. Waugh here paraphrases Wordsworth's prescription in the Preface to *Lyrical Ballads*.

not be altogether out of place. It was a classic custom in the family hall, when the feast was at its height, to display a drunken slave among the sons of the household, to the end that they, being ashamed at the ignominious folly of his gesticulations, might determine never to be tempted into such a pitiable condition themselves. The custom had its advantages; for the wisdom of the younger generation was found to be fostered more surely by a single example than by a world of homily and precept.

Ezra Pound: Drunken Helots and Mr. Eliot[1]

Genius has I know not what peculiar property, its manifestations are various, but however diverse and dissimilar they may be, they have at least one property in common. It makes no difference in what art, in what mode, whether the most conservative, or the most ribald-revolutionary, or the most diffident; if in any land, or upon any floating deck over the ocean, or upon some newly contrapted craft in the aether, genius manifests itself, at once some elderly gentleman has a flux of bile from his liver; at once from the throne or the easy Cowperian[2] sofa, or from the gutter, or from the oeconomical press room there bursts a torrent of elderly words, splenetic, irrelevant, they form themselves instinctively into large phrases denouncing the inordinate product.

This peculiar kind of *rabbia* [madness] might almost be taken as the test of a work of art, mere talent seems incapable of exciting it. "You can't fool me, sir, you're a scoundrel," bawls the testy old gentleman.

Fortunately the days when "that very fiery particle" could be crushed out by the "Quarterly" are over, but it interests me, as an archaeologist, to note that the firm which no longer produces Byron, but rather memoirs, letters of the late Queen, etc., is still running a review, and that this review is still where it was in 1812, or whatever the year was; and that, not having an uneducated Keats to condemn, a certain Mr. Waugh is scolding about Mr. Eliot.[3]

All I can find out, by asking questions concerning Mr. Waugh, is that he is "a very old chap," "a reviewer." From internal evidence we deduce that he is, like the rest of his generation of English *gens-de-lettres* [men of letters], ignorant of Laforgue; of De Régnier's "Odelettes," of his French contemporaries generally, of De Gourmont's "Litanies," of Tristan Corbière, Laurent Tailhade.[4] This is by no means surprising. We are used to it from his "b'ilin'."[5]

However, he outdoes himself, he calls Mr. Eliot a "drunken helot." So called they Anacreon[6] in the days of his predecessors, but from the context in the "Quarterly" article I judge that Mr. Waugh does not intend the phrase as a compliment, he is trying to be abusive, and moreover, he in his limited way has succeeded.

Let us sample the works of the last "Drunken Helot." I shall call my next anthology "Drunken Helots" if I can find a dozen poems written half so well as the following:

---

1. Pound replied to Waugh's review in the *Egoist*, June 1917. A "helot" is a serf or slave.
2. After 18th-century poet William Cowper.
3. As in *Salutation the Third* (page 2225), Pound invokes the savage review of Keats that appeared in the *Quarterly Review* and was believed by his friends to have hastened Keats's death.
4. A series of French writers and texts that Pound admired. Jules Laforgue (1860–1887) was a French poet who helped develop free verse; he was an important influence on Eliot's early poetry. Henri de Régnier (1864–1936) was a French symbolist poet; Remy de Gourmont (1858–1915) was an influential French poet, novelist, essayist, publisher, and literary critic; Tristan Corbière, pseudonym for Édouard Joachim Corbière (1854–1919), was a French poet who worked with common speech and slang; and Laurent Tailhade (1854–1919) was a satiric French poet.
5. Byline, identifying the author of a newspaper article.
6. Greek writer of love poems and drinking songs.

[Quotes *Conversation Galante*]

Our helot has a marvellous neatness. There is a comparable finesse in Laforgue's "Votre âme est affaire d'oculiste," but hardly in English verse.

Let us reconsider this drunkenness:

[Quotes *La Figlia Che Piange*]

And since when have helots taken to reading Dante and Marlowe? Since when have helots made a new music, a new refinement, a new method of turning old phrases into new by their aptness? However the "Quarterly," the century old, the venerable, the praeclarus,[7] the voice of Gehova[8] and Co., Sinai and 51A Albemarle Street, London, W. 1, has pronounced this author a helot. They are all for an aristocracy made up of, possibly, Tennyson, Southey and Wordsworth, the flunkey, the dull and the duller. Let us sup with the helots. Or perhaps the good Waugh is a wag,[9] perhaps he hears with the haspirate[1] and wishes to pun on Mr. Heliot's name: a bright bit of syzygy.[2]

I confess his type of mind puzzles me, there is no telling what he is up to.

I do not wish to misjudge him, this theory may be the correct one. You never can tell when old gentlemen grow facetious. He does not mention Mr. Eliot's name; he merely takes his lines and abuses them. The artful dodger,[3] he didn't (*sotto voce*[4]) "he didn't want 'people' to know that Mr. Eliot was a poet".

The poem he chooses for malediction is the title poem, "Prufrock." It is too long to quote entire.

[Quotes portion of *Prufrock*]

Let us leave the silly old Waugh. Mr. Eliot has made an advance on Browning. He has also made his dramatis personae contemporary and convincing. He has been an individual in his poems. I have read the contents of this book over and over, and with continued joy in the freshness, the humanity, the deep quiet culture. "I have tried to write of a few things that really have moved me" is so far as I know, the sum of Mr. Eliot's "poetic theory." His practice has been a distinctive cadence, a personal modus of arrangement, remote origins in Elizabethan English and in the modern French masters, neither origin being sufficiently apparent to affect the personal quality. It is writing without pretence. Mr. Eliot at once takes rank with the five or six living poets whose English one can read with enjoyment.

The "Egoist" has published the best prose writer of my generation. It follows its publication of Joyce by the publication of a "new" poet who is at least unsurpassed by any of his contemporaries, either of his own age or his elders.

It is perhaps "unenglish" to praise a poet whom one can read with enjoyment. Carlyle's generation wanted "improving" literature, Smile's "Self-Help"[5] and the rest of it. Mr. Waugh dates back to that generation, the virus is in his blood, he can't

---

7. Preeminent.
8. Jehovah.
9. Joker.
1. To aspirate is to add the "h" sound to the begining of a word: thus Eliot becomes "Hel[i]ot."
2. Any two related things (either similar or opposite).

3. The Artful Dodger is the name of Fagan's favorite pickpocket in Dickens's *Oliver Twist*.
4. In a low voice.
5. Samuel Smiles's *Self-Help* (1859) preached the Victorian gospel of self-improvement.

help it. The exactitude of the younger generation gets on his nerves, and so on and so on. He will "fall into line in time" like the rest of the bread-and-butter reviewers. Intelligent people will read "J. Alfred Prufrock"; they will wait with some eagerness for Mr. Eliot's further inspirations. It is 7.30 p.m. I have had nothing alcoholic today, nor yet yesterday. I said the same sort of thing about James Joyce's prose over two years ago. I am now basking in the echoes. Only a half-caste rag for the propagation of garden suburbs, and a local gazette in Rochester, N.Y., U.S.A., are left whining in opposition. * * *

However, let us leave these bickerings, this stench of the printing-press, weekly and quarterly, let us return to the gardens of the Muses,

> Till human voices wake us and we drown,

as Eliot has written in conclusion to the poem which the "Quarterly" calls the *reductio ad absurdum*:[6]

> I have seen them riding seaward on the waves
> Combing the white hair of the waves blown back
> When the wind blows the water white and black.
>
> We have lingered in the chambers of the sea
> By sea-girls wreathed with seaweed red and brown
> Till human voices wake us, and we drown.

The poetic mind leaps the gulf from the exterior world, the trivialities of Mr. Prufrock, diffident, ridiculous, in the drawing-room, Mr. Apollinax's laughter "submarine and profound" transports him from the desiccated new-statesmanly atmosphere of Professor Canning-Cheetah's. Mr. Eliot's melody rushes out like the thought of Fragilion "among the birch-trees."[7] Mr. Waugh is my bitten macaroon at this festival.

Gerontion[1]

*Thou hast nor youth nor age
But as it were an after dinner sleep
Dreaming of both.*[2]

Here I am, an old man in a dry month,
Being read to by a boy, waiting for rain.
I was neither at the hot gates
Nor fought in the warm rain
5   Nor knee deep in the salt marsh, heaving a cutlass,
Bitten by flies, fought.
My house is a decayed house,
And the Jew squats on the window sill, the owner,
Spawned in some estaminet° of Antwerp,   *café*
10   Blistered in Brussels, patched and peeled in London.

---

6. Reduction to absurdity (Latin), the rhetorical technique of pushing the consequences of an idea to the point where it looks ridiculous.

7. The names and images in this sentence not taken from *Prufrock* are from another of Eliot's early poems, *Mr. Apollinax*. The poem ends with the lines, "Of dowager Mrs. Phlaccus, and Professor and Mrs. Cheetah / I remember a slice of lemon, and a bitten macaroon."

1. From the Greek word meaning "old man." While still working on what was to become *The Waste Land*, Eliot had considered printing *Gerontion* as a kind of prelude; Pound disapproved of the idea, and it was dropped.

2. Loosely quoted from Shakespeare's *Measure for Measure* (3.1.32–34).

The goat coughs at night in the field overhead;
Rocks, moss, stonecrop, iron, merds.°   *droppings, shit*
The woman keeps the kitchen, makes tea,
Sneezes at evening, poking the peevish gutter.
15   I an old man,
A dull head among windy spaces.

Signs are taken for wonders. "We would see a sign!"[3]
The word within a word, unable to speak a word,
Swaddled with darkness. In the juvescence° of the year   *youth*
20   Came Christ the tiger

In depraved May, dogwood and chestnut, flowering judas,[4]
To be eaten, to be divided, to be drunk
Among whispers; by Mr. Silvero
With caressing hands, at Limoges[5]
25   Who walked all night in the next room;
By Hakagawa, bowing among the Titians;[6]
By Madame de Tornquist, in the dark room
Shifting the candles; Fräulein von Kulp
Who turned in the hall, one hand on the door.
30   Vacant shuttles
Weave the wind. I have no ghosts,
An old man in a draughty house
Under a windy knob.

After such knowledge, what forgiveness? Think now
35   History has many cunning passages, contrived corridors
And issues, deceives with whispering ambitions,
Guides us by vanities. Think now
She gives when our attention is distracted
And what she gives, gives with such supple confusions
40   That the giving famishes the craving. Gives too late
What's not believed in, or is still believed,
In memory only, reconsidered passion. Gives too soon
Into weak hands, what's thought can be dispensed with
Till the refusal propagates a fear. Think
45   Neither fear nor courage saves us. Unnatural vices
Are fathered by our heroism. Virtues
Are forced upon us by our impudent crimes.
These tears are shaken from the wrath-bearing tree.

The tiger springs in the new year. Us he devours. Think at last
50   We have not reached conclusion, when I
Stiffen in a rented house. Think at last
I have not made this show purposelessly
And it is not by any concitation°   *stirring up*
Of the backward devils.

3. Eliot here echoes the sermon by Anglican theologican Lancelot Andrewes (1555–1626) on Matthew: "An evil and adulterous generation seeketh after a sign; and there shall no sign be given to it, but the sign of the prophet Jonas." (Matthew 12.39).
4. A flowering shrub-tree, named after Judas Iscariot; according to legend, Judas hanged himself on this type of tree after betraying Jesus.
5. City in France; home of fine china of the same name.
6. Painter of the Italian Renaissance (1477–1576) known for his female nudes.

55 I would meet you upon this honestly.
    I that was near your heart was removed therefrom
    To lose beauty in terror, terror in inquisition.
    I have lost my passion: why should I need to keep it
    Since what is kept must be adulterated?
60 I have lost my sight, smell, hearing, taste and touch:
    How should I use them for your closer contact?

    These with a thousand small deliberations
    Protract the profit of their chilled delirium,
    Excite the membrane, when the sense has cooled,
65 With pungent sauces, multiply variety
    In a wilderness of mirrors. What will the spider do,
    Suspend its operations, will the weevil
    Delay? De Bailhache, Fresca, Mrs. Cammel, whirled
    Beyond the circuit of the shuddering Bear[7]
70 In fractured atoms. Gull against the wind, in the windy straits
    Of Belle Isle,[8] or running on the Horn.[9]
    White feathers in the snow, the Gulf claims,
    And an old man driven by the Trades[1]
    To a sleepy corner.

75   Tenants of the house,
    Thoughts of a dry brain in a dry season.

The Waste Land

Like Conrad's *Heart of Darkness*—from which Eliot had originally planned to take his epigraph, "The horror! the horror!"—*The Waste Land* has become part of the symbolic landscape of twentieth-century Western culture; the text, like Conrad's, has been appropriated by commentators high and low, left and right, as an especially apt description of the psychosocial and interpersonal malaise of modern Europeans. Late in 1921 Eliot, who was suffering under a number of pressures both personal and artistic, took three months' leave from his job at Lloyd's Bank and went for a "rest cure" at a clinic in Lausanne, Switzerland. On his way he passed through Paris and showed the manuscript of the poem—really manuscripts of a number of fragments, whose interrelationship Eliot was trying to work out—to Ezra Pound; Pound and Eliot went through the poem again as Eliot returned to London in January 1922. Pound's editorial work was considerable, as the facsimile edition of the draft reveals; Pound said that he performed the poem's "caesarian operation," and Eliot dedicated *The Waste Land* to Pound—*il miglior fabbro* ("the better craftsman," a phrase from Dante).

The most obvious feature of *The Waste Land* is its difficulty. Eliot was perhaps the first poet and literary critic to argue that such "difficulty" was not just a necessary evil but in fact a constitutive element of poetry that would come to terms with the modern world. In his review of a volume of metaphysical poetry, Eliot implicitly links the complex poetry of Donne and Marvell with the task of the modern poet: "We can only say that it appears likely that poets in our civilization, as it exists at present, must be *difficult*. Our civilization comprehends great variety and complexity, and this variety and complexity, playing upon a refined sensibility, must produce various and complex results." In the case of *The Waste Land*, the difficulty lies primarily in the poem's dense tissue of quotations from and allusions to other texts; as Eliot's

7. The constellation Ursa Major, also called the Great Bear or Big Dipper.
8. The passage between Newfoundland and southern

Labrador.
9. Cape Horn, the southernmost point of South America.
1. The trade winds, nearly constant tropical winds.

own footnotes to the poem demonstrate, the poem draws its strength, and achieves a kind of universality, by making implicit and explicit reference to texts as widely different as Ovid's *Metamorphoses* and a World War I Australian marching song.

Beyond the density of the poem's quotations and allusions, Eliot hoped to suggest the possibilty of an order beneath the chaos. In his review of Joyce's *Ulysses* (published in November 1923) Eliot was to describe the "mythical method," deploying allusions to classical mythology to suggest an implicit (and recurring) order beneath contemporary history; and while his use of myth was not so methodical as Joyce's, his use of vegetation myth and romance structures points outside the world of the poem to "another world," where the brokenness of the waste land might be healed. At the time of writing the poem, however, Eliot could not see clearly where that healing might come from.

The Waste Land[1]

"Nam Sibyllam quidem Cumis ego ipse oculis meis vidi in ampulla pendere, et cum illi pueri dicerent: Σίβυλλα τί θέλεις; respondebat illa: ἀποθανεῖν θέλω."[2]

FOR EZRA POUND
il miglior fabbro.

I. THE BURIAL OF THE DEAD

April is the cruellest month, breeding
Lilacs out of the dead land, mixing
Memory and desire, stirring
Dull roots with spring rain.
5 Winter kept us warm, covering
Earth in forgetful snow, feeding
A little life with dried tubers.
Summer surprised us, coming over the Starnbergersee[3]
With a shower of rain; we stopped in the colonnade,
10 And went on in sunlight, into the Hofgarten[4],
And drank coffee, and talked for an hour.
Bin gar keine Russin, stamm' aus Litauen, echt deutsch.[5]
And when we were children, staying at the arch-duke's,
My cousin's, he took me out on a sled,
15 And I was frightened. He said, Marie,
Marie, hold on tight. And down we went.

1. Not only the title, but the plan and a good deal of the incidental symbolism of the poem were suggested by Miss Jessie L. Weston's book on the Grail legend: *From Ritual to Romance* (Cambridge). Indeed, so deeply am I indebted, Miss Weston's book will elucidate the difficulties of the poem much better than my notes can do; and I recommend it (apart from the great interest of the book itself) to any who think such elucidation of the poem worth the trouble. To another work of anthropology I am indebted in general, one which has influenced our generation profoundly; I mean *The Golden Bough*; I have used especially the two volumes *Adonis, Attis, Osiris*. Anyone who is acquainted with these works will immediately recognize in the poem certain references to vegetation ceremonies [Eliot's note]. Sir James Frazer (1854–1941)

brought out the twelve volumes of *The Golden Bough*, a vast work of anthropology and comparative mythology and religion, between 1890 and 1915, with a supplement published in 1936.
2. From the *Satyricon* of Petronius (first century A.D.). "For once I myself saw with my own eyes the Sybil at Cumae hanging in a cage, and when the boys said to her, 'Sybil, what do you want?' she replied, 'I want to die.'" The Sybil was granted anything she wished by Apollo, if only she would be his; she made the mistake of asking for everlasting life, without asking for eternal youth.
3. A lake near Munich.
4. A public park in Munich, with a zoo and cafés.
5. "I'm not a Russian at all; I come from Lithuania, a true German."

In the mountains, there you feel free.
I read, much of the night, and go south in the winter.

What are the roots that clutch, what branches grow
20 Out of this stony rubbish? Son of man,[6]
You cannot say, or guess, for you know only
A heap of broken images, where the sun beats,
And the dead tree gives no shelter, the cricket no relief,[7]
And the dry stone no sound of water. Only
25 There is shadow under this red rock,
(Come in under the shadow of this red rock),
And I will show you something different from either
Your shadow at morning striding behind you
Or your shadow at evening rising to meet you;
30 I will show you fear in a handful of dust.
            Frisch weht der Wind
            Der Heimat zu
            Mein Irisch Kind,
            Wo weilest du?[8]
35 "You gave me hyacinths first a year ago;
They called me the hyacinth girl."
—Yet when we came back, late, from the hyacinth garden,
Your arms full, and your hair wet, I could not
Speak, and my eyes failed, I was neither
40 Living nor dead, and I knew nothing,
Looking into the heart of light, the silence.
Oed' und leer das Meer.[9]

Madame Sosostris, famous clairvoyante,
Had a bad cold, nevertheless
45 Is known to be the wisest woman in Europe,
With a wicked pack of cards.[1] Here, said she,
Is your card, the drowned Phoenician Sailor,
(Those are pearls that were his eyes.[2] Look!)
Here is Belladonna, the Lady of the Rocks,
50 The lady of situations.
Here is the man with three staves, and here the Wheel,

6. Cf. Ezekiel 2.7 [Eliot's note]. Ezekiel 2.8 reads: "But thou, son of man, hear what I say unto thee; Be not thou rebellious like that rebellious house: open thy mouth, and eat that I give thee."

7. Cf. Ecclesiastes 12.5 [Eliot's note]. "They shall be afraid of that which is high, and fears shall be in the way, and the almond tree shall flourish, and the grasshopper shall be a burden, and desire shall fail."

8. V. *Tristan and Isolde*, i, verses 5–8 [Eliot's note]. In Wagner's opera, Tristan sings this about Isolde, the woman he is leaving behind as he sails for home: "Fresh blows the wind to the homeland; my Irish child, where are you waiting?"

9. Id. iii, verse 24 [Eliot's note]. Tristan is dying and waiting for Isolde to come to him, but a shepherd, whom Tristan has hired to keep watch for her ship, reports only "Desolate and empty the sea."

1. I am not familiar with the exact constitution of the Tarot pack of cards, from which I have obviously departed to suit my own convenience. The Hanged Man, a member of the traditional pack, fits my purpose in two ways: because he is associated in my mind with the Hanged God of Frazer, and because I associated him with the hooded figure in the passage of the disciples to Emmaus in Part V. The Phoenician Sailor and the Merchant appear later; also the "crowds of people," and Death by Water is executed in Part IV. The Man with Three Staves (an authentic member of the Tarot pack) I associate, quite arbitrarily, with the Fisher King Himself [Eliot's note].

2. From Ariel's song, in Shakespeare's *The Tempest*: "Full fathom five thy father lies; / Of his bones are coral made; / Those are pearls that were his eyes: / Nothing of him that doth fade, / But doth suffer a sea-change" (1.2.399–403).

And here is the one-eyed merchant, and this card,
Which is blank, is something he carries on his back,
Which I am forbidden to see. I do not find
55   The Hanged Man.[3] Fear death by water.
I see crowds of people, walking round in a ring.
Thank you. If you see dear Mrs. Equitone,
Tell her I bring the horoscope myself:
One must be so careful these days.

60   Unreal City,[4]
Under the brown fog of a winter dawn,
A crowd flowed over London Bridge, so many,
I had not thought death had undone so many.[5]
Sighs, short and infrequent, were exhaled,[6]
65   And each man fixed his eyes before his feet.
Flowed up the hill and down King William Street,
To where Saint Mary Woolnoth kept the hours
With a dead sound on the final stroke of nine.[7]
There I saw one I knew, and stopped him, crying: "Stetson!
70   You who were with me in the ships at Mylae![8]
That corpse you planted last year in your garden,
Has it begun to sprout? Will it bloom this year?
Or has the sudden frost disturbed its bed?
O keep the Dog far hence, that's friend to men,[9]
75   Or with his nails he'll dig it up again!
You! hypocrite lecteur!—mon semblable,—mon frère!"[1]

II. A GAME OF CHESS[2]

The Chair she sat in, like a burnished throne,[3]
Glowed on the marble, where the glass
Held up by standards wrought with fruited vines
80   From which a golden Cupidon peeped out
(Another hid his eyes behind his wing)
Doubled the flames of sevenbranched candelabra
Reflecting light upon the table as
The glitter of her jewels rose to meet it,
85   From satin cases poured in rich profusion.
In vials of ivory and coloured glass
Unstoppered, lurked her strange synthetic perfumes,

---

3. The tarot card that depicts a man hanging by one foot from a cross.
4. Cf. Baudelaire: "Fourmillante cité, cité pleine de rêves, / Où le spectre en plein jour raccroche le passant" [Eliot's note].
5. Cf. *Inferno*, iii.55–7: "si lunga tratta / di gente, ch'io non avrei mai creduto / che morte tanta n'avesse disfatta" [Eliot's note]. "Such an endless train, / Of people, it never would have entered in my head / There were so many men whom death had slain."
6. Cf. *Inferno*, iv. 25–7: "Ouivi, secondo che per ascoltare, / non avea pianto, ma' che di sospiri, / che l'aura eterna facevan tremare" [Eliot's note]. "We heard no

loud complaint, no crying there, / No sound of grief except the sound of sighing / Quivering forever through the eternal air."
7. A phenomenon which I have often noticed [Eliot's note].
8. The Battle of Mylae (260 B.C.) in the First Punic War.
9. Cf. the Dirge in Webster's *White Devil* [Eliot's note].
1. V. Baudelaire, Preface to *Fleurs du Mal* [Eliot's note]. "Hypocrite reader—my double—my brother!"
2. Cf. Thomas Middleton's drama *A Game at Chess* (1625), a political satire.
3. Cf. *Antony and Cleopatra*, II. ii. 190 [Eliot's note].

Unguent, powdered, or liquid—troubled, confused
And drowned the sense in odours; stirred by the air
90   That freshened from the window, these ascended
In fattening the prolonged candle-flames,
Flung their smoke into the laquearia,[4]
Stirring the pattern on the coffered ceiling.
Huge sea-wood fed with copper
95   Burned green and orange, framed by the coloured stone,
In which sad light a carvèd dolphin swam.
Above the antique mantel was displayed
As though a window gave upon the sylvan scene[5]
The change of Philomel, by the barbarous king[6]
100   So rudely forced; yet there the nightingale[7]
Filled all the desert with inviolable voice
And still she cried, and still the world pursues,
"Jug Jug" to dirty ears.
And other withered stumps of time
105   Were told upon the walls; staring forms
Leaned out, leaning, hushing the room enclosed.
Footsteps shuffled on the stair.
Under the firelight, under the brush, her hair
Spread out in fiery points
110   Glowed into words, then would be savagely still.

"My nerves are bad to-night. Yes, bad. Stay with me.
Speak to me. Why do you never speak. Speak.
        What are you thinking of? What thinking? What?
I never know what you are thinking. Think."

115   I think we are in rats' alley[8]
Where the dead men lost their bones.

"What is that noise?"
                                    The wind under the door.[9]
"What is that noise now? What is the wind doing?"
120   Nothing again nothing.

                                                          "Do
"You know nothing? Do you see nothing? Do you remember
Nothing?"
I remember
125   Those are pearls that were his eyes.

---

4. "Laquearia. V. *Aeneid*, I.726: "dependent lychni laque-
aribus aureis / incensi, et noctem flammis funalia vin-
cunt." [Eliot's note]. "Burning lamps hang from the gold-
panelled ceiling / And torches dispel the night with their
flames"; a *laquearia* is a panelled ceiling. The passage from
Virgil's *Aeneid* describes the banquet given by Dido for
her lover Aeneas.
5. "Sylvan scene. V. Milton, *Paradise Lost*, iv. 140 [Eliot's
note]. "And over head up grew / Insuperable height of
loftiest shade, / Cedar, and Pine, and Fir, and branching
Palm, / A Silvan Scene, and as the ranks ascend / Shade
above shade, a woody Theatre / Of stateliest view" The

passage describes the Garden of Eden, as seen through
Satan's eyes.
6. V. Ovid, *Metamorphoses*, vi, Philomela [Eliot's note].
Philomela was raped by King Tereus, her sister's husband,
and was then changed into a nightingale.
7. Cf. Part III, l. 204 [Eliot's note].
8. Cf. Part III, l. 195 [Eliot's note].
9. Cf. Webster: "Is the wind in that door still?" [Eliot's
note]. From John Webster's *The Devil's Law Case*,
3.2.162. The doctor asks this question when he discovers
that a "murder victim" is still breathing.

"Are you alive, or not? Is there nothing in your head?"[1]
                                                    But

O O O O that Shakespeherian Rag—[2]
It's so elegant
130 So intelligent
"What shall I do now? What shall I do?"
"I shall rush out as I am, and walk the street
With my hair down, so. What shall we do tomorrow?
What shall we ever do?"
135   The hot water at ten.
     And if it rains, a closed car at four.
     And we shall play a game of chess,
     Pressing lidless eyes and waiting for a knock upon the
          door.[3]
     When Lil's husband got demobbed,° I said—   *demobilized*
140 I didn't mince my words, I said to her myself,
     HURRY UP PLEASE ITS TIME[4]
     Now Albert's coming back, make yourself a bit smart.
     He'll want to know what you done with that money he gave you
     To get yourself some teeth. He did, I was there.
145 You have them all out, Lil, and get a nice set,
     He said, I swear, I can't bear to look at you.
     And no more can't I, I said, and think of poor Albert,
     He's been in the army four years, he wants a good time,
     And if you don't give it him, there's others will, I said.
150 Oh is there, she said. Something o' that, I said.
     Then I'll know who to thank, she said, and give me a straight look.
     HURRY UP PLEASE ITS TIME
     If you don't like it you can get on with it, I said.
     Others can pick and choose if you can't.
155 But if Albert makes off, it won't be for lack of telling.
     You ought to be ashamed, I said, to look so antique.
     (And her only thirty-one.)
     I can't help it, she said, pulling a long face,
     It's them pills I took, to bring it off, she said.
160 (She's had five already, and nearly died of young George.)
     The chemist[5] said it would be all right, but I've never been the same.
     You *are* a proper fool, I said.
     Well, if Albert won't leave you alone, there it is, I said,
     What you get married for if you don't want children?
165 HURRY UP PLEASE ITS TIME
     Well, that Sunday Albert was home, they had a hot gammon,°   *ham*
     And they asked me in to dinner, to get the beauty of it hot—
     HURRY UP PLEASE ITS TIME
     HURRY UP PLEASE ITS TIME

---

1. Cf. Part I, l. 37, 48 [Eliot's note].
2. Quoting an American ragtime song featured in Zieg-
field's Follies of 1912.
3. Cf. the game of chess in Middleton's *Women beware*

Women [Eliot's note].
4. A British pub-keeper's call for a last round before closing.
5. Pharmacist.

170   Goonight Bill. Goonight Lou. Goonight May. Goonight.
            Ta ta. Goonight. Goonight.
            Good night, ladies, good night, sweet ladies, good night, good night.[6]

III. The Fire Sermon

            The river's tent is broken; the last fingers of leaf
            Clutch and sink into the wet bank. The wind
175   Crosses the brown land, unheard. The nymphs are departed.
            Sweet Thames, run softly, till I end my song.[7]
            The river bears no empty bottles, sandwich papers,
            Silk handkerchiefs, cardboard boxes, cigarette ends
            Or other testimony of summer nights. The nymphs are departed.
180   And their friends, the loitering heirs of City directors;
            Departed, have left no addresses.
            By the waters of Leman[8] I sat down and wept . . .
            Sweet Thames, run softly till I end my song,
            Sweet Thames, run softly, for I speak not loud or long.
185   But at my back in a cold blast I hear
            The rattle of the bones, and chuckle spread from ear to ear.

            A rat crept softly through the vegetation
            Dragging its slimy belly on the bank
            While I was fishing in the dull canal
190   On a winter evening round behind the gashouse
            Musing upon the king my brother's wreck
            And on the king my father's death before him.[9]
            White bodies naked on the low damp ground
            And bones cast in a little low dry garret,
195   Rattled by the rat's foot only, year to year.
            But at my back from time to time I hear[1]
            The sound of horns and motors, which shall bring[2]
            Sweeney to Mrs. Porter in the spring.
            O the moon shone bright on Mrs. Porter[3]
200   And on her daughter
            They wash their feet in soda water
            Et O ces voix d'enfants, chantant dans la coupole![4]

            Twit twit twit
            Jug jug jug jug jug jug

---

6. Ophelia speaks these words in Shakespeare's *Hamlet,* and they are understood by the King as certain evidence of her insanity: "Good night ladies, good night. Sweet ladies, good night, good night" (4.5.72–73).

7. V. Spenser, *Prothalamion* [Eliot's note]; Spenser's poem (1596) celebrates the double marriage of Lady Elizabeth and Lady Katherine Somerset.

8. Lake Geneva. The line echoes Psalm 137, in which, exiled in Babylon, the Hebrew poets are too full of grief to sing.

9. Cf. *The Tempest,* I. ii [Eliot's note].

1. Cf. Marvell, *To His Coy Mistress* [Eliot's note]. "But at my back I always hear / Time's wingéd chariot hurrying near."

2. Cf. Day, *Parliament of Bees:* "When of the sudden, listening, you shall hear, / A noise of horns and hunting, which shall bring / Actaeon to Diana in the spring, / Where all shall see her naked skin . . ." [Eliot's note].

3. I do not know the origin of the ballad from which these are taken: it was reported to me from Sydney, Australia [Eliot's note]. Sung by Australian soldiers in World War I; "O the moon shone bright on Mrs. Porter / And on the daughter / Of Mrs. Porter / They wash their feet in soda water / And so they oughter / To keep them clean."

4. V. Verlaine, *Parsifal* [Eliot's note]. "And O those children's voices singing in the dome." Paul Verlaine's sonnet describes Parsifal, who keeps himself pure in hopes of seeing the holy grail, and has his feet washed before entering the castle.

205   So rudely forc'd.
        Tereu

        Unreal City
        Under the brown fog of a winter noon
        Mr. Eugenides, the Smyrna[5] merchant
210   Unshaven, with a pocket full of currants
        C.i.f.[6] London: documents at sight,
        Asked me in demotic° French   *vulgar*
        To luncheon at the Cannon Street Hotel[7]
        Followed by a weekend at the Metropole.[8]

215   At the violet hour, when the eyes and back
        Turn upward from the desk, when the human engine waits
        Like a taxi throbbing waiting,
        I Tiresias,[9] though blind, throbbing between two lives,
        Old man with wrinkled female breasts, can see
220   At the violet hour, the evening hour that strives
        Homeward, and brings the sailor home from sea,[1]
        The typist home at teatime, clears her breakfast, lights
        Her stove, and lays out food in tins.
        Out of the window perilously spread
225   Her drying combinations touched by the sun's last rays,
        On the divan are piled (at night her bed)
        Stockings, slippers, camisoles, and stays.
        I Tiresias, old man with wrinkled dugs
        Perceived the scene, and foretold the rest—
230   I too awaited the expected guest.

---

5. Seaport in western Turkey.
6. The currants were quoted at a price "carriage and insurance free to London"; and the Bill of Lading, etc., were to be handed to the buyer upon payment of the sight draft [Eliot's note].
7. A Hotel in London near the train station used for travel to and from continental Europe.
8. An upscale seaside resort hotel in Brighton.
9. Tiresias, although a mere spectator and not indeed a "character," is yet the most important personage in the poem, uniting all the rest. Just as the one-eyed merchant, seller of currants, melts into the Phoenician Sailor, and the latter is not wholly distinct from Ferdinand Prince of Naples, so all the women are one woman, and the two sexes meet in Tiresias. What Tiresias *sees*, in fact, is the substance of the poem. The whole passage from Ovid is of great anthropological interest: ". . . Cum Iunone iocos et 'maior vestra profecto est / Quam, quae contingit maribus,' dixisse, 'voluptas.' / Illa negat; placuit quae sit sententia docti / Quaerere Tiresiae: venus huic erat utraque nota. / Nam duo magnorum viridi coeuntia silva / Corpora serpentum baculi violaverat ictu / Deque viro factus, mirabile, femina septem / Egerat autumnos; octavo rursus eosdem / Vidit et 'est vestrae si tanta potentia plagae,' / Dixit 'ut auctoris sortem in contraria mutet, / Nunc quoque vos feriam!' percussis anguibus isdem / Forma prior redit genetivaque venit imago. / Arbiter hic igitur sumptus de lite iocosa / Dicta Iovis firmat; gravius Saturnia iusto / Nec pro materia fertur doluisse suique / Iudicis aeterna damnavit lumina nocte, / At pater omnipotens (neque enim licet inrita cuiquam / Facta dei fecisse deo) pro lumine adempto / Scire futura dedit poenamque levavit honore" [Eliot's note]. This passage from Ovid's *Metamorphosis* describes Tiresias's sex change: "[The story goes that once Jove, having drunk a great deal,] jested with Juno. He said, 'Your pleasure in love is really greater than that enjoyed by men.' She denied it; so they decided to seek the opinion of the wise Tiresias, for he knew both aspects of love. For once, with a blow of his staff, he had committed violence on two huge snakes as they copulated in the green forest; and—wonderful to tell—was turned from a man into a woman and thus spent seven years. In the eighth year he saw the same snakes again and said: 'If a blow struck at you is so powerful that it changes the sex of the giver, I will now strike at you again.' With these words he struck the snakes, and his former shape was restored to him and he became as he had been born. So he was appointed arbitrator in the playful quarrel, and supported Jove's statement. It is said that Saturnia [i.e., Juno] was quite disproportionately upset, and condemned the arbitrator to perpetual blindness. But the almighty father (for no god may undo what has been done by another god), in return for the sight that was taken away, gave him the power to know the future and so lightened the penalty paid by the honor."
1. This may not appear as exact as Sappho's lines but I had in mind the "longshore" or "dory" fisherman, who returns at nightfall [Eliot's note]. "Hesperus, thou bringst home all things bright morning scattered: thou bringst the sheep, the goat, the child to the mother."

He, the young man carbuncular,° arrives,   *pimply*
A small house agent's clerk, with one bold stare,
One of the low on whom assurance sits
As a silk hat on a Bradford[2] millionaire.
235   The time is now propitious, as he guesses,
The meal is ended, she is bored and tired,
Endeavours to engage her in caresses
Which still are unreproved, if undesired.
Flushed and decided, he assaults at once;
240   Exploring hands encounter no defence;
His vanity requires no response,
And makes a welcome of indifference.
(And I Tiresias have foresuffered all
Enacted on this same divan or bed;
245   I who have sat by Thebes below the wall
And walked among the lowest of the dead.)
Bestows one final patronising kiss,
And gropes his way, finding the stairs unlit . . .

She turns and looks a moment in the glass,
250   Hardly aware of her departed lover;
Her brain allows one half-formed thought to pass:
"Well now that's done: and I'm glad it's over."
When lovely woman stoops to folly and[3]
Paces about her room again, alone,
255   She smoothes her hair with automatic hand,
And puts a record on the gramophone.

"This music crept by me upon the waters"[4]
And along the Strand, up Queen Victoria Street.
O City city, I can sometimes hear
260   Beside a public bar in Lower Thames Street,
The pleasant whining of a mandoline
And a clatter and a chatter from within
Where fishmen lounge at noon: where the walls
Of Magnus Martyr[5] hold
265   Inexplicable splendour of Ionian white and gold.

The river sweats[6]
Oil and tar
The barges drift
With the turning tide

---

2. An industrial town in Yorkshire; many of its residents became wealthy during World War I.
3. V. Goldsmith, the song in *The Vicar of Wakefield* [Eliot's note]. Oliver Goldsmith's character Olivia, on returning to the place where she was seduced, sings, "When lovely woman stoops to folly / And finds too late that men betray / What charm can soothe her melancholy, / What art can wash her guilt away? / The only art her guilt to cover, / To hide her shame from every eye, / To give repentance to her lover / And wring his bosom— is to die."

4. V. *The Tempest,* as above [Eliot's note].
5. The interior of St. Magnus Martyr is to my mind one of the finest among Wren's interiors. See *The Proposed Demolition of Nineteen City Churches* (P.S. King & Son, Ltd.) [Eliot's note].
6. The Song of the (three) Thames-daughters begins here. From line 292 to 306 inclusive they speak in turn. V. *Gotterdammerung,* III.I: the Rhine-daughters [Eliot's note]. In Richard Wagner's opera, *Twilight of the Gods,* the Rhine maidens, when their gold is stolen, lament that the beauty of the river is gone.

270   Red sails
       Wide
       To leeward, swing on the heavy spar.
       The barges wash
       Drifting logs
275   Down Greenwich reach
       Past the Isle of Dogs.[7]
                  Weialala leia
                  Wallala leialala

       Elizabeth and Leicester[8]
280   Beating oars
       The stern was formed
       A gilded shell
       Red and gold
       The brisk swell
285   Rippled both shores
       Southwest wind
       Carried down stream
       The peal of bells
       White towers
290   Weialala leia
                  Wallala leialala

       "Trams and dusty trees.
       Highbury bore me. Richmond and Kew[9]
       Undid me. By Richmond I raised my knees
295   Supine on the floor of a narrow canoe."

       "My feet are at Moorgate,[1] and my heart
       Under my feet. After the event
       He wept. He promised 'a new start.'
       I made no comment. What should I resent?"

300   "On Margate Sands.[2]
       I can connect
       Nothing with nothing.
       The broken fingernails of dirty hands.
       My people humble people who expect
305   Nothing."
                  la la

7. Greenwich is a borough on the south bank of the River Thames; the Isle of Dogs is a peninsula in East London formed by a sharp bend in the Thames called Greenwich Reach.

8. V. Froude, *Elizabeth*, vol. I, Ch. iv, letter of De Quadra to Philip of Spain: "In the afternoon we were in a barge, watching the games on the river. (The Queen) was alone with Lord Robert and myself on the poop, when they began to talk nonsense, and went so far that Lord Robert at last said, as I was on the spot there was no reason why they should not be married if the queen pleased" [Eliot's note].

9. "Cf. *Purgatorio*, V. 133: "Ricorditi di me, che son la Pia; / Siena mi fe', disfecemi Maremma." [Eliot's note]. "Remember me, that I am called Piety; / Sienna made me and Maremma undid me." Highbury, Richmond, and Kew are suburbs of London near the Thames.

1. A slum in East London.

2. A seaside resort in the Thames estuary.

To Carthage then I came[3]

Burning burning burning burning[4]
O Lord Thou pluckest me out[5]
310   O Lord Thou pluckest

burning

IV. DEATH BY WATER

Phlebas the Phoenician, a fortnight dead,
Forgot the cry of gulls, and the deep sea swell
And the profit and loss.
315   A current under sea
Picked his bones in whispers. As he rose and fell
He passed the stages of his age and youth
Entering the whirlpool.
                              Gentile or Jew
320   O you who turn the wheel and look to windward,
Consider Phlebas, who was once handsome and tall as you.

V. WHAT THE THUNDER SAID[6]

After the torchlight red on sweaty faces
After the frosty silence in the gardens
After the agony in stony places
325   The shouting and the crying
Prison and palace and reverberation
Of thunder of spring over distant mountains
He who was living is now dead
We who were living are now dying
330   With a little patience

Here is no water but only rock
Rock and no water and the sandy road
The road winding above among the mountains
Which are mountains of rock without water
335   If there were water we should stop and drink
Amongst the rock one cannot stop or think
Sweat is dry and feet are in the sand
If there were only water amongst the rock
Dead mountain mouth of carious° teeth that cannot spit   *rotting*
340   Here one can neither stand nor lie nor sit

---

3. V. St. Augustine's *Confessions*: "to Carthage then I came, where a cauldron of unholy loves sang all about mine ears" [Eliot's note].

4. The complete text of the Buddha's Fire Sermon (which corresponds in importance to the Sermon on the Mount) from which these words are taken, will be found translated in the late Henry Clarke Warren's *Buddhism in Translation* (Harvard Oriental Series). Mr. Warren was one of the great pioneers of Buddhist studies in the Occident [Eliot's note].

5. From St. Augustine's *Confessions* again. The collocation of these two representatives of eastern and western asceticism, as the culmination of this part of the poem, is not an accident [Eliot's note]. Augustine writes: "I entangle my steps with these outward beauties, but thou pluckest me out, O Lord, Thou pluckest me out."

6. In the first part of Part V three themes are employed: the journey to Emmaus, the approach to the Chapel Perilous (see Miss Weston's book), and the present decay of eastern Europe [Eliot's note].

There is not even silence in the mountains
But dry sterile thunder without rain
There is not even solitude in the mountains
But red sullen faces sneer and snarl
345   From doors of mudcracked houses
                                  If there were water
   And no rock
   If there were rock
   And also water
350   And water
   A spring
   A pool among the rock
   If there were the sound of water only
   Not the cicada
355   And dry grass singing
   But sound of water over a rock
   Where the hermit-thrush sings in the pine trees
   Drip drop drip drop drop drop drop[7]
   But there is no water

360   Who is the third who walks always beside you?
   When I count, there are only you and I together[8]
   But when I look ahead up the white road
   There is always another one walking beside you
   Gliding wrapt in a brown mantle, hooded
365   I do not know whether a man or a woman
   —But who is that on the other side of you?

   What is that sound high in the air[9]
   Murmur of maternal lamentation
   Who are those hooded hordes swarming
370   Over endless plains, stumbling in cracked earth
   Ringed by the flat horizon only
   What is the city over the mountains
   Cracks and reforms and bursts in the violet air
   Falling towers
375   Jerusalem Athens Alexandria

---

7. This is *Turdus aonalaschkae pallasii,* the hermit-thrush which I have heard in Quebec County. Chapman says (*Handbook of Birds of Eastern North America*) "it is most at home in secluded woodland and thickety retreats. . . . Its notes are not remarkable for variety or volume, but in purity and sweetness of tone and exquisite modulation they are unequalled." Its "water-dripping song" is justly celebrated [Eliot's note].

8. The following lines were stimulated by the account of one of the Antarctic expeditions (I forget which, but I think one of Shackleton's): it was related that the party of explorers, at the extremity of their strength, had the constant delusion that there was one more member than could actually be counted [Eliot's note]. There seems also to be an echo of the account of Jesus meeting his disciples on the road to Emmaus: "Jesus himself drew near, and

went with them. But their eyes were holden that they should not know him" (Luke 24.13–16).

9. Cf. Hermann Hesse, *Blick ins Chaos:* "Schon ist halb Europa, schon ist zumindest der halbe Osten Europas auf dem Wege zum Chaos, fährt betrunken im heiligen Wahn am Abgrund entlang und singt dazu, singt betrunken und hymnisch wie Dmitri Karamasoff sang. Ueber diese Lieder lacht der Bürger beleidigt, der Heilige und Seher hört sie mit Tränen" [Eliot's note]. "Already half of Europe, already at least half of Eastern Europe, on the way to chaos, drives drunk in sacred infatuation along the edge of the precipice, singing drunkenly, as though singing hymns, as Dmitri Karamazov sang. The offended bourgeois laughs at the songs; the saint and the seer hear them with tears."

Vienna London
Unreal

A woman drew her long black hair out tight
And fiddled whisper music on those strings
380 And bats with baby faces in the violet light
Whistled, and beat their wings
And crawled head downward down a blackened wall
And upside down in air were towers
Tolling reminiscent bells, that kept the hours
385 And voices singing out of empty cisterns and exhausted wells

In this decayed hole among the mountains
In the faint moonlight, the grass is singing
Over the tumbled graves, about the chapel
There is the empty chapel, only the wind's home.
390 It has no windows, and the door swings,
Dry bones can harm no one.
Only a cock stood on the rooftree
Co co rico co co rico
In a flash of lightning. Then a damp gust
395 Bringing rain

Ganga[1] was sunken, and the limp leaves
Waited for rain, while the black clouds
Gathered far distant, over Himavant.[2]
The jungle crouched, humped in silence.
400 Then spoke the thunder
DA
Datta: what have we given?[3]
My friend, blood shaking my heart
The awful daring of a moment's surrender
405 Which an age of prudence can never retract
By this, and this only, we have existed
Which is not to be found in our obituaries
Or in memories draped by the beneficent spider[4]
Or under seals broken by the lean solicitor
410 In our empty rooms
DA
Dayadhvam: I have heard the key[5]
Turn in the door once and turn once only

---

1. The river Ganges.
2. The Himalayas.
3. "Datta, dayadhvam, damyata" (Give, sympathize, control). The fable of the meaning of the Thunder is found in the *Brihadaranyaka—Upanishad*, 5, 1. A translation is found in Deussen's *Sechzig Upanishads des Veda*, p. 489 [Eliot's note]. "That very thing is repented even today by the heavenly voice, in the form of thunder, in the form of thunder as 'Da,' 'Da,' 'Da,'. . . . Therefore one should practice these three things: self-control, alms-giving, and compassion."
4. Cf. Webster, *The White Devil*, v. vi: ". . . they'll remarry / Ere the worm pierce your winding-sheet, ere the spider / make a thin curtain for your epitaphs" [Eliot's note].

5. Cf. *Inferno*, xxxiii. 46: "ed io sentii chiavar l'uscio di sotto / all'orrible torre." Also F. H. Bradley, *Appearance and Reality*, p. 346: "My external sensations are no less private to myself than are my thoughts or my feelings. In either case my experience falls within my own circle, a circle closed on the outside; and, with all its elements alike, every sphere is opaque to the others which surround it. . . . In brief, regarded as an existence which appears in a soul, the whole world for each is peculiar and private to that soul." [Eliot's note]. In the passage from the *Inferno*, Ugolino tells Dante of his imprisonment and starvation until he became so desperate that he ate his children: "And I heard below me the door of the horrible tower being locked."

We think of the key, each in his prison
415   Thinking of the key, each confirms a prison
Only at nightfall, aethereal rumours
Revive for a moment a broken Coriolanus[6]
DA
Damyata: The boat responded
420   Gaily, to the hand expert with sail and oar
The sea was calm, your heart would have responded
Gaily, when invited, beating obedient
To controlling hands

I sat upon the shore
425   Fishing, with the arid plain behind me[7]
Shall I at least set my lands in order?
London Bridge is falling down falling down falling down
Poi s'ascose nel foco che gli affina[8]
Quando fiam uti chelidon—O swallow swallow[9]
430   *Le Prince d'Aquitaine à la tour abolie*[1]
These fragments I have shored against my ruins
Why then Ile fit you. Hieronymo's mad againe.[2]
Datta. Dayadhvam. Damyata.
Shantih   shantih   shantih[3]

Journey of the Magi[1]

"A cold coming we had of it,
Just the worst time of the year
For a journey, and such a long journey:
The ways deep and the weather sharp,
5   The very dead of winter."
And the camels galled, sore-footed, refractory,
Lying down in the melting snow.
There were times we regretted
The summer palaces on slopes, the terraces,
10   And the silken girls bringing sherbet.
Then the camel men cursing and grumbling
And running away, and wanting their liquor and women,
And the night-fires going out, and the lack of shelters,
And the cities hostile and the towns unfriendly

6. In Shakespeare's play of the same name, Coriolanus is a Roman general who is exiled and later leads the enemy in an attack against the Romans.

7. V. Weston, *From Ritual to Romance*; chapter on the Fisher King [Eliot's note].

8. V. *Purgatorio*, xxvi.148: "Ara vos prec per aquella valor / que vos condus al som de l'escalina, / sovegna vos a temps de ma dolor." / Poi s'ascose nel foco che gli affina" [Eliot's note]. In this passage, the poet Arnaut Daniel speaks to Dante: "Now I pray you, by the goodness that guides you to the top of this staircase, be mindful in time of my suffering."

9. V. *Pervigilium Veneris*. Cf. Philomela in Parts II and III [Eliot's note]. Philomel asks, "When shall I be a swallow?"

1. V. Gerard de Nerval, Sonnet *El Desdichado* [Eliot's note]. "The Prince of Aquitane in the ruined tower."

2. V. Kyd's *Spanish Tragedy* [Eliot's note]. The subtitle of Kyd's play is, "Hieronymo's Mad Againe." His son having been murdered, Hieronymo is asked to compose a court play, to which he responds "Why then Ile fit you"; his son's murder is revenged in the course of the play.

3. Shantih. Repeated as here, a formal ending to an Upanishad. "The Peace which passeth understanding" is a feeble translation of the content of this word [Eliot's note]. The Upanishads are poetic commentaries on the Hindu Scriptures.

1. The narrative of the poem is based upon the tradition of the three wise men who journeyed to Bethlehem to worship the infant Christ; cf. Matthew 2.1–12.

15 And the villages dirty and charging high prices:
A hard time we had of it.
At the end we preferred to travel all night,
Sleeping in snatches,
With the voices singing in our ears, saying
20 That this was all folly.

Then at dawn we came down to a temperate valley,
Wet, below the snow line, smelling of vegetation,
With a running stream and a water-mill beating the darkness
And three trees on the low sky.
25 And an old white horse galloped away in the meadow.
Then we came to a tavern with vine-leaves over the lintel,
Six hands at an open door dicing for pieces of silver,
And feet kicking the empty wine-skins.
But there was no information, and so we continued
30 And arrived at evening, not a moment too soon
Finding the place; it was (you may say) satisfactory.

All this was a long time ago, I remember,
And I would do it again, but set down
This set down
35 This: were we led all that way for
Birth or Death? There was a Birth, certainly,
We had evidence and no doubt. I had seen birth and death,
But had thought they were different; this Birth was
Hard and bitter agony for us, like Death, our death.
40 We returned to our places, these Kingdoms,
But no longer at ease here, in the old dispensation,
With an alien people clutching their gods.
I should be glad of another death.

1927

FROM FOUR QUARTETS
Burnt Norton[1]

τοῦ λόγου δ᾽ ἐόντος ξυνοῦ ζώουσιν οἱ πολλοὶ ὡς ἰδίαν
ἔχοντες φρόνησιν.[2]

I. p. 77. Fr. 2

ὁδὸς ἄνω κάτω μία καὶ ὡυτή.[3]

I. p. 89. Fr. 60

Diels: Die Fragmente der Vorsokratiker (Herakleitos).

1

Time present and time past
Are both perhaps present in time future,

---

1. A large country house in Gloucestershire, England, named for an earlier house on the site that had burned down in the 17th century.
2. Although the Word governs all things, most people live as though they had wisdom of their own. (From the Greek philosopher Heraclitus, c. 500 B.C.)
3. The way up and the way down are the same.

And time future contained in time past.
If all time is eternally present
5   All time is unredeemable.
What might have been is an abstraction
Remaining a perpetual possibility
Only in a world of speculation.
What might have been and what has been
10   Point to one end, which is always present.
Footfalls echo in the memory
Down the passage which we did not take
Towards the door we never opened
Into the rose-garden. My words echo
15   Thus, in your mind.
                          But to what purpose
Disturbing the dust on a bowl of rose-leaves
I do not know.
                    Other echoes
Inhabit the garden. Shall we follow?
Quick, said the bird, find them, find them,
20   Round the corner. Through the first gate,
Into our first world, shall we follow
The deception of the thrush? Into our first world.
There they were, dignified, invisible,
Moving without pressure, over the dead leaves,
25   In the autumn heat, through the vibrant air,
And the bird called, in response to
The unheard music hidden in the shrubbery,
And the unseen eyebeam crossed, for the roses
Had the look of flowers that are looked at.
30   There they were as our guests, accepted and accepting.
So we moved, and they, in a formal pattern,
Along the empty alley, into the box circle,
To look down into the drained pool.
Dry the pool, dry concrete, brown edged,
35   And the pool was filled with water out of sunlight,
And the lotos rose, quietly, quietly,
The surface glittered out of heart of light,
And they were behind us, reflected in the pool.
Then a cloud passed, and the pool was empty.
40   Go, said the bird, for the leaves were full of children,
Hidden excitedly, containing laughter.
Go, go, go, said the bird: human kind
Cannot bear very much reality.
Time past and time future
45   What might have been and what has been
Point to one end, which is always present.

                           2

Garlic and sapphires in the mud
Clot the bedded axle-tree.
The trilling wire in the blood
50   Sings below inveterate scars

Appeasing long forgotten wars.
The dance along the artery
The circulation of the lymph
Are figured in the drift of stars

55   Ascend to summer in the tree
We move above the moving tree
In light upon the figured leaf
And hear upon the sodden floor
Below, the boarhound and the boar

60   Pursue their pattern as before
But reconciled among the stars.

At the still point of the turning world. Neither flesh nor fleshless;
Neither from nor towards; at the still point, there the dance is,
But neither arrest nor movement. And do not call it fixity,

65   Where past and future are gathered. Neither movement
          from nor towards,
Neither ascent nor decline. Except for the point, the still point,
There would be no dance, and there is only the dance.
I can only say, *there* we have been: but I cannot say where.
And I cannot say, how long, for that is to place it in time.

70   The inner freedom from the practical desire,
The release from action and suffering, release from the inner
And the outer compulsion, yet surrounded
By a grace of sense, a white light still and moving,
Erhebung[4] without motion, concentration

75   Without elimination, both a new world
And the old made explicit, understood
In the completion of its partial ecstasy,
The resolution of its partial horror.
Yet the enchainment of past and future

80   Woven in the weakness of the changing body,
Protects mankind from heaven and damnation[5]
Which flesh cannot endure.
                              Time past and time future
Allow but a little consciousness.
To be conscious is not to be in time

85   But only in time can the moment in the rose-garden,
The moment in the arbour where the rain beat,
The moment in the draughty church at smokefall
Be remembered; involved with past and future.
Only through time time is conquered.

                              3
90   Here is a place of disaffection
Time before and time after
In a dim light: neither daylight
Investing form with lucid stillness
Turning shadow into transient beauty

---

4. Lifting up; the German philosopher Hegel's term for a new stage in understanding.

95   With slow rotation suggesting permanence
        Nor darkness to purify the soul
        Emptying the sensual with deprivation
        Cleansing affection from the temporal.
        Neither plenitude nor vacancy. Only a flicker
100   Over the strained time-ridden faces
        Distracted from distraction by distraction

        Filled with fancies and empty of meaning
        Tumid apathy with no concentration
        Men and bits of paper, whirled by the cold wind
105   That blows before and after time,
        Wind in and out of unwholesome lungs
        Time before and time after.
        Eructation° of unhealthy souls   *belching*
        Into the faded air, the torpid
110   Driven on the wind that sweeps the gloomy hills of London,
        Hampstead and Clerkenwell, Campden and Putney,
        Highgate, Primrose and Ludgate. Not here
        Not here the darkness, in this twittering world.

        Descend lower, descend only
115   Into the world of perpetual solitude,
        World not world, but that which is not world,
        Internal darkness, deprivation
        And destitution of all property,
        Desiccation of the world of sense,
120   Evacuation of the world of fancy,
        Inoperancy of the world of spirit;
        This is the one way, and the other
        Is the same, not in movement
        But abstention from movement; while the world moves
125   In appetency,° on its metalled ways   *desire*
        Of time past and time future.

                               4
        Time and the bell have buried the day,
        The black cloud carries the sun away.
        Will the sunflower turn to us, will the clematis
130   Stray down, bend to us; tendril and spray
        Clutch and cling?
        Chill
        Fingers of yew be curled
        Down on us? After the kingfisher's wing
135   Has answered light to light, and is silent, the light is still
        At the still point of the turning world.

                               5
        Words move, music moves
        Only in time; but that which is only living
        Can only die. Words, after speech, reach
140   Into the silence. Only by the form, the pattern,
        Can words or music reach
        The stillness, as a Chinese jar still

Moves perpetually in its stillness.
Not the stillness of the violin, while the note lasts,
145   Not that only, but the co-existence,
Or say that the end precedes the beginning,
And the end and the beginning were always there
Before the beginning and after the end.
And all is always now. Words strain,
150   Crack and sometimes break, under the burden,
Under the tension, slip, slide, perish,
Decay with imprecision, will not stay in place,
Will not stay still. Shrieking voices
Scolding, mocking, or merely chattering,
155   Always assail them. The Word in the desert
Is most attacked by voices of temptation,
The crying shadow in the funeral dance,
The loud lament of the disconsolate chimera.

The detail of the pattern is movement,
160   As in the figure of the ten stairs.[5]
Desire itself is movement
Not in itself desirable;
Love is itself unmoving,
Only the cause and end of movement,
165   Timeless, and undesiring
Except in the aspect of time
Caught in the form of limitation
Between un-being and being.
Sudden in a shaft of sunlight
170   Even while the dust moves
There rises the hidden laughter
Of children in the foliage
Quick now, here, now, always—
Ridiculous the waste sad time
175   Stretching before and after.
1935   1935, 1943

Tradition and the Individual Talent

1

In English writing we seldom speak of tradition, though we occasionally apply its name
in deploring its absence. We cannot refer to "the tradition" or to "a tradition"; at most,
we employ the adjective in saying that the poetry of So-and-so is "traditional" or even
"too traditional." Seldom, perhaps, does the word appear except in a phrase of censure. If
otherwise, it is vaguely approbative,[1] with the implication, as to the work approved, of
some pleasing archaeological reconstruction. You can hardly make the word agreeable to
English ears without this comfortable reference to the reassuring science of archaeology.

   Certainly the word is not likely to appear in our appreciations of living or dead
writers. Every nation, every race, has not only its own creative, but its own critical
turn of mind; and is even more oblivious of the shortcomings and limitations of its

---

5. St. John of the Cross used this figure to describe the   1. Approving.
way to achieve mystical union with God.

critical habits than of those of its creative genius. We know, or think we know, from the enormous mass of critical writing that has appeared in the French language the critical method or habit of the French; we only conclude (we are such unconscious people) that the French are "more critical" than we, and sometimes even plume ourselves a little with the fact, as if the French were the less spontaneous. Perhaps they are; but we might remind ourselves that criticism is as inevitable as breathing, and that we should be none the worse for articulating what passes in our minds when we read a book and feel an emotion about it, for criticizing our own minds in their work of criticism. One of the facts that might come to light in this process is our tendency to insist, when we praise a poet, upon those aspects of his work in which he least resembles any one else. In these aspects or parts of his work we pretend to find what is individual, what is the peculiar essence of the man. We dwell with satisfaction upon the poet's difference from his predecessors, especially his immediate predecessors; we endeavour to find something that can be isolated in order to be enjoyed. Whereas if we approach a poet without this prejudice we shall often find that not only the best, but the most individual parts of his work may be those in which the dead poets, his ancestors, assert their immortality most vigorously. And I do not mean the impressionable period of adolescence, but the period of full maturity.

Yet if the only form of tradition, of handing down, consisted in following the ways of the immediate generation before us in a blind or timid adherence to its successes, "tradition" should positively be discouraged. We have seen many such simple currents soon lost in the sand; and novelty is better than repetition. Tradition is a matter of much wider significance. It cannot be inherited, and if you want it you must obtain it by great labour. It involves, in the first place, the historical sense, which we may call nearly indispensable to any one who would continue to be a poet beyond his twenty-fifth year; and the historical sense involves a perception, not only of the pastness of the past, but of its presence; the historical sense compels a man to write not merely with his own generation in his bones, but with a feeling that the whole of the literature of Europe from Homer and within it the whole of the literature of his own country has a simultaneous existence and composes a simultaneous order. This historical sense, which is a sense of the timeless as well as of the temporal and of the timeless and of the temporal together, is what makes a writer traditional. And it is at the same time what makes a writer most acutely conscious of his place in time, of his own contemporaneity.

No poet, no artist of any art, has his complete meaning alone. His significance, his appreciation is the appreciation of his relation to the dead poets and artists. You cannot value him alone; you must set him, for contrast and comparison, among the dead. I mean this as a principle of aesthetic, not merely historical, criticism. The necessity that he shall conform, that he shall cohere, is not onesided; what happens when a new work of art is created is something that happens simultaneously to all the works of art which preceded it. The existing monuments form an ideal order among themselves, which is modified by the introduction of the new (the really new) work of art among them. The existing order is complete before the new work arrives; for order to persist after the supervention[2] of novelty, the whole existing order must be, if ever so slightly, altered; and so the relations, proportions, values of each work of art toward the whole are readjusted; and this is conformity between the old and the new. Whoever has approved this idea of order, of the form of European, of English litera-

2. The appearance of something additional.

ture will not find it preposterous that the past should be altered by the present as much as the present is directed by the past. And the poet who is aware of this will be aware of great difficulties and responsibilities.

In a peculiar sense he will be aware also that he must inevitably be judged by the standards of the past. I say judged, not amputated, by them; not judged to be as good as, or worse or better than, the dead; and certainly not judged by the canons of dead critics. It is a judgment, a comparison, in which two things are measured by each other. To conform merely would be for the new work not really to conform at all; it would not be new, and would therefore not be a work of art. And we do not quite say that the new is more valuable because it fits in; but its fitting in is a test of its value— a test, it is true, which can only be slowly and cautiously applied, for we are none of us infallible judges of conformity. We say: it appears to conform, and is perhaps individual, or it appears individual, and may conform; but we are hardly likely to find that it is one and not the other.

To proceed to a more intelligible exposition of the relation of the poet to the past: he can neither take the past as a lump, an indiscriminate bolus,[3] nor can he form himself wholly on one or two private admirations, nor can he form himself wholly upon one preferred period. The first course is inadmissible, the second is an important experience of youth, and the third is a pleasant and highly desirable supplement. The poet must be very conscious of the main current, which does not at all flow invariably through the most distinguished reputations. He must be quite aware of the obvious fact that art never improves, but that the material of art is never quite the same. He must be aware that the mind of Europe—the mind of his own country—a mind which he learns in time to be much more important than his own private mind—is a mind which changes, and that this change is a development which abandons nothing en route, which does not superannuate either Shakespeare, or Homer, or the rock drawing of the Magdalenian draughtsmen.[4] That this development, refinement perhaps, complication certainly, is not, from the point of view of the artist, any improvement. Perhaps not even an improvement from the point of view of the psychologist or not to the extent which we imagine; perhaps only in the end based upon a complication in economics and machinery. But the difference between the present and the past is that the conscious present is an awareness of the past in a way and to an extent which the past's awareness of itself cannot show.

Some one said: "The dead writers are remote from us because we know so much more than they did." Precisely, and they are that which we know.

I am alive to a usual objection to what is clearly part of my programme for the métier of poetry. The objection is that the doctrine requires a ridiculous amount of erudition (pedantry), a claim which can be rejected by appeal to the lives of poets in any pantheon. It will even be affirmed that much learning deadens or perverts poetic sensibility. While, however, we persist in believing that a poet ought to know as much as will not encroach upon his necessary receptivity and necessary laziness, it is not desirable to confine knowledge to whatever can be put into a useful shape for examinations, drawing-rooms, or the still more pretentious modes of publicity. Some can absorb knowledge, the more tardy must sweat for it. Shakespeare acquired more essential history from Plutarch than most men could from the whole British Museum. What is to be

---

3. A lump; a mass of chewed food.

4. Drawings of hunting scenes, rendered in caves in France and Spain, c. 13,000–10,000 B.C.

insisted upon is that the poet must develop or procure the consciousness of the past and that he should continue to develop this consciousness throughout his career.

What happens is a continual surrender of himself as he is at the moment to something which is more valuable. The progress of an artist is a continual self-sacrifice, a continual extinction of personality.

There remains to define this process of depersonalization and its relation to the sense of tradition. It is in this depersonalization that art may be said to approach the condition of science. I, therefore, invite you to consider, as a suggestive analogy, the action which takes place when a bit of finely filiated[5] platinum is introduced into a chamber containing oxygen and sulphur dioxide.

2

Honest criticism and sensitive appreciation are directed not upon the poet but upon the poetry. If we attend to the confused cries of the newspaper critics and the *susurrus* [buzzing] of popular repetition that follows, we shall hear the names of poets in great numbers; if we seek not Blue-book[6] knowledge but the enjoyment of poetry, and ask for a poem, we shall seldom find it. I have tried to point out the importance of the relation of the poem to other poems by other authors, and suggested the conception of poetry as a living whole of all the poetry that has ever been written. The other aspect of this Impersonal theory of poetry is the relation of the poem to its author. And I hinted, by an analogy, that the mind of the mature poet differs from that of the immature one not precisely in any valuation of "personality," not being necessarily more interesting, or having "more to say," but rather by being a more finely perfected medium in which special, or very varied, feelings are at liberty to enter into new combinations.

The analogy was that of the catalyst. When the two gases previously mentioned are mixed in the presence of a filament of platinum, they form sulphurous acid. This combination takes place only if the platinum is present; nevertheless the newly formed acid contains no trace of platinum, and the platinum itself is apparently unaffected; has remained inert, neutral, and unchanged. The mind of the poet is the shred of platinum. It may partly or exclusively operate upon the experience of the man himself; but, the more perfect the artist, the more completely separate in him will be the man who suffers and the mind which creates; the more perfectly will the mind digest and transmute the passions which are its material.

The experience, you will notice, the elements which enter the presence of the transforming catalyst, are of two kinds: emotions and feelings. The effect of a work of art upon the person who enjoys it is an experience different in kind from any experience not of art. It may be formed out of one emotion, or may be a combination of several; and various feelings, inhering for the writer in particular words or phrases or images, may be added to compose the final result. Or great poetry may be made without the direct use of any emotion whatever: composed out of feelings solely. Canto XV of the *Inferno* (Brunetto Latini) is a working up of the emotion evident in the situation; but the effect, though single as that of any work of art, is obtained by considerable complexity of detail. The last quatrain gives an image, a feeling attaching to an image, which "came," which did not develop simply out of what precedes, but which was probably in suspension in the poet's mind until the proper combination arrived for it to add itself to.[7] The poet's mind is in fact a receptacle for seizing and

---

5. Eliot apparently means "made into filaments."
6. Official government publication.
7. He [Brunetto Latini] turned then, and he seemed, / across that plain, like one of those who run / for the green cloth at Verona; and of those, / more like the one who wins, than those who lose (*Inferno*, 15.119–122).

storing up numberless feelings, phrases, images, which remain there until all the particles which can unite to form a new compound are present together.

If you compare several representative passages of the greatest poetry you see how great is the variety of types of combination, and also how completely any semi-ethical criterion of "sublimity" misses the mark. For it is not the "greatness," the intensity, of the emotions, the components, but the intensity of the artistic process, the pressure, so to speak, under which the fusion takes place, that counts. The episode of Paolo and Francesca employs a definite emotion, but the intensity of the poetry is something quite different from whatever intensity in the supposed experience it may give the impression of. It is no more intense, furthermore, than Canto XXVI, the voyage of Ulysses, which has not the direct dependence upon an emotion.[8] Great variety is possible in the process of transmutation of emotion: the murder of Agamemnon,[9] or the agony of Othello, gives an artistic effect apparently closer to a possible original than the scenes from Dante. In the Agamemnon, the artistic emotion approximates to the emotion of an actual spectator; in Othello to the emotion of the protagonist himself. But the difference between art and the event is always absolute; the combination which is the murder of Agamemnon is probably as complex as that which is the voyage of Ulysses. In either case there has been a fusion of elements. The ode of Keats contains a number of feelings which have nothing particular to do with the nightingale, but which the nightingale, partly, perhaps, because of its attractive name, and partly because of its reputation, served to bring together.

The point of view which I am struggling to attack is perhaps related to the metaphysical theory of the substantial unity of the soul: for my meaning is, that the poet has, not a "personality" to express, but a particular medium, which is only a medium and not a personality, in which impressions and experiences combine in peculiar and unexpected ways. Impressions and experiences which are important for the man may take no place in the poetry, and those which become important in the poetry may play quite a negligible part in the man, the personality.

I will quote a passage which is unfamiliar enough to be regarded with fresh attention in the light—or darkness—of these observations:

> And now methinks I could e'en chide myself
> For doating on her beauty, though her death
> Shall be revenged after no common action.
> Does the silkworm expend her yellow labours
> For thee? For thee does she undo herself?
> Are lordships sold to maintain ladyships
> For the poor benefit of a bewildering minute?
> Why does yon fellow falsify highways,
> And put his life between the judge's lips,
> To refine such a thing—keeps horse and men
> To beat their valours for her? . . . [1]

In this passage (as is evident if it is taken in its context) there is a combination of positive and negative emotions: an intensely strong attraction toward beauty and an equal-

---

8. Dante's *Inferno*, Canto 5, tells the story of the lovers Paolo and Francesca; Canto 26 tells of the suffering of Ulysses in hell.

9. In Aeschylus's drama *Agamemnon*, Clytemnestra kills her husband Agamemnon for having sacrificed her daughter, Iphigenia, to the goddess Artemis.

1. From Cyril Tourneur's *The Revenger's Tragedy* (1607), 3.4; the speaker is addressing the skull of his former beloved, murdered after she refused to respond to an evil duke's advances. The revenger will make up the skull to look alive, putting poison on its lips; the evil Duke then dies when he kisses this supposed maiden in a dusky garden.

ly intense fascination by the ugliness which is contrasted with it and which destroys it. This balance of contrasted emotion is in the dramatic situation to which the speech is pertinent, but that situation alone is inadequate to it. This is, so to speak, the structural emotion, provided by the drama. But the whole effect, the dominant tone, is due to the fact that a number of floating feelings, having an affinity to this emotion by no means superficially evident, have combined with it to give us a new art emotion.

It is not in his personal emotions, the emotions provoked by particular events in his life, that the poet is in any way remarkable or interesting. His particular emotions may be simple, or crude, or flat. The emotion in his poetry will be a very complex thing, but not with the complexity of the emotions of people who have very complex or unusual emotions in life. One error, in fact, of eccentricity in poetry is to seek for new human emotions to express; and in this search for novelty in the wrong place it discovers the perverse. The business of the poet is not to find new emotions, but to use the ordinary ones and, in working them up into poetry, to express feelings which are not in actual emotions at all. And emotions which he has never experienced will serve his turn as well as those familiar to him. Consequently, we must believe that "emotion recollected in tranquillity"[2] is an inexact formula. For it is neither emotion, nor recollection, nor, without distortion of meaning, tranquillity. It is a concentration, and a new thing resulting from the concentration, of a very great number of experiences which to the practical and active person would not seem to be experiences at all; it is a concentration which does not happen consciously or of deliberation. These experiences are not "recollected," and they finally unite in an atmosphere which is "tranquil" only in that it is a passive attending upon the event. Of course this is not quite the whole story. There is a great deal, in the writing of poetry, which must be conscious and deliberate. In fact, the bad poet is usually unconscious where he ought to be conscious, and conscious where he ought to be unconscious. Both errors tend to make him "personal." Poetry is not a turning loose of emotion, but an escape from emotion; it is not the expression of personality, but an escape from personality. But, of course, only those who have personality and emotions know what it means to want to escape from these things.

3

ὁ δὲ νοῦς ἴσως θειότερον τι καὶ ἀπαθές ἐστιν.[3]

This essay proposes to halt at the frontier of metaphysics or mysticism, and confine itself to such practical conclusions as can be applied by the responsible person interested in poetry. To divert interest from the poet to the poetry is a laudable aim: for it would conduce to a juster estimation of actual poetry, good and bad. There are many people who appreciate the expression of sincere emotion in verse, and there is a smaller number of people who can appreciate technical excellence. But very few know when there is an expression of *significant* emotion, emotion which has its life in the poem and not in the history of the poet. The emotion of art is impersonal. And the poet cannot reach this impersonality without surrendering himself wholly to the work to be done. And he is not likely to know what is to be done unless he lives in what is not merely the present, but the present moment of the past, unless he is conscious, not of what is dead, but of what is already living.

---

2. This is Wordsworth's famous description of poetry in the Preface to *Lyrical Ballads*; see page 336.

3. The mind is doubtless something more divine and unimpressionable (From Aristotle's *De Anima* [*On the Soul*]).

Virginia Woolf
1882–1941

Virginia Woolf is the foremost woman writer of the twentieth century, writing in any language; within British literature, Woolf is in the company of James Joyce, T. S. Eliot, William Butler Yeats and few others as a major author, of whatever gender. To take account of the transformations in modern English literature—in language, in style, and in substance—requires reckoning with Virginia Woolf, one of the chief architects of literary modernism. By 1962 Edward Albee could sardonically title a play *Who's Afraid of Virginia Woolf?*, knowing that her name would signify the greatness of modern literature. Woolf wrote luminous and intricate novels, two pivotal books on sexual politics, society, and war, several volumes of short stories and collected essays, reviews and pamphlets, and thirty volumes of a remarkable diary. Woolf was a woman of letters in an almost old-fashioned sense, one of the century's subtlest observers of social and psychic life, and a hauntingly beautiful prose writer.

Woolf's writing career began in childhood but was officially launched in 1915 with the publication of her first novel, *The Voyage Out*, when she was thirty-three. *The Voyage Out* was an emblematic beginning for her public career as a novelist, with its title suggesting the need to venture forth, to make a voyage into the world and out of the imprisonments of life and language. This novel paid special homage to *Heart of Darkness*, Joseph Conrad's story of a voyage through Africa that uncovers the heart of Europe's imperial encounter with the African continent and its exploited people. The theme resonated for Woolf throughout her books, because she too concentrated on the costs—both social and personal—of attempting to gain freedom. With the exception of *Orlando* (1928), a playful and flamboyant novel with a few scenes set in Turkey and Russia, Woolf was never again to set a novel outside the geographical confines of England. Voyaging out had become a matter of voyaging within. Woolf does not turn away from the larger world; she sets that larger world and its history squarely in England.

Woolf's own roots went deep in Victorian literary culture. She was born in 1882 into a privileged and illustrious British professional family with connections to the world of letters on both sides. She was the third child of the marriage of Leslie Stephen and Julia Duckworth, both of whom had been widowed; Leslie Stephen had married a daughter of the novelist William Thackeray, and Julia had been the wife of a publisher, and was connected to a long line of judges, teachers, and magistrates. Woolf's father, eventually to become Sir Leslie, was a prominent editor and a striving philosopher, who was appointed president of the London Library. His fame was to come not from his philosophical work but from his massive *Dictionary of National Biography*, a book that placed, and ranked, the leading figures of British national life for many centuries. Woolf's *Orlando*, with its subtitle: *A Biography*, spoofed the entire enterprise of the biography of great men by having *her* great man, Orlando, unexpectedly turn into a woman halfway through the novel.

Woolf grew up as an intensely literary child, surrounded by her father's project of arbitrating the greatness of the (mostly) men of letters she nonetheless sought to emulate. Her mother Julia was a famed beauty, whose magical grace was captured in the photographs of her equally famous relative, the photographer Julia Margaret Cameron. Woolf was to provide a haunting portrait of both her mother and father in her novel *To the Lighthouse* (1927), where the beautiful and consummately maternal Mrs. Ramsay ministers to her irascible and intellectually tormented philosopher husband, Mr. Ramsay, until her sudden death deprives the family and its circle of friends of their ballast in life. Julia Stephen's premature death in 1895 had cast just such a pall over her own family, especially over thirteen-year-old Virginia, who had a mental breakdown. Breakdowns would recur at intervals throughout her life.

The death-haunted life characteristic of the Victorian family was Virginia Woolf's own experience. Two years after Julia died, Woolf's beloved half-sister and mother substitute, Stel-

Virginia Woolf and T. S. Eliot.

la Duckworth, died in childbirth at the age of twenty-seven. Woolf was also to lose her difficult but immensely loved father in 1904 (not so coincidentally, the same year Virginia was to publish her first essay and review), and her brother Thoby died of typhoid contracted on a trip to Greece with her in 1906. The novel *Jacob's Room* (1922) deals with a young man named Jacob and his college room, as perceived by his sister after his death in World War I. The items in Jacob's room are cloaked in memory and live in the consciousness of the sister as far more than precious objects—memory infuses them with shared life. The dead return again and again in Woolf's imagination and in her imaginative work; her development of the "moment of consciousness" in her writing, her novels' concentration on the binding powers of memory, and her invocation of the spreading, intertwining branches of human relations persisting even after death, may be the effect of her painful tutelage in loss.

As an upper-class woman, Woolf and her sisters were not given a formal education, while Thoby and Adrian both went to fine schools and ultimately to university. The sense of having been deliberately shut out of education by virtue of her sex, was to inflect all of Woolf's writing and thinking. Education is a pervasive issue in her novels, and an enormous issue in her essays on social and political life, *A Room of One's Own* (1929) and *Three Guineas* (1938). Woolf became an autodidact, steeping herself in English literature, history, political theory, and art history, but she never lost the keen anguish nor the self-doubt occasioned by the closed doors of the academy to women. Education became for Woolf perhaps the key to transforming the role and the perception of women in society, and writing became her own mode of entry into the public world.

In 1912, Virginia Stephens married Leonard Woolf, like herself a member of the Bloomsbury group, but unlike her in being a Jew and coming from a commercial and far less illustrious family. Leonard Woolf was an "outsider" in anti-Semitic Britain no less than Virginia, who as a great woman writer was equally outside the norm. An accomplished writer in his own right, a political theorist and an activist in socialist issues and in anti-imperialist causes, Leonard Woolf devoted himself to Virginia and to her writing career. They established and ran the Hogarth Press together, an imprint that was to publish all of Virginia's books, as well as many important works of poetry, prose, and criticism from others. Virginia Woolf's erotic and emotional ties to women, and, in particular, her romance with Vita Sackville-West, while not necessarily explicit sexual—no one seems to know for a certainty—were indubitably of the greatest importance to her life. Despite this, she placed Leonard Woolf and their marriage at the center of her being, and their rich and complex partnership weathered Virginia's numerous mental breakdowns. When she felt another episode of depression overtaking her in 1941, it was partly her reluctance to subject Leonard to what she saw as the burden of her madness which tragically led her to drown herself in the river near their home and their beloved press.

Woolf's themes and techniques are all seen in the two stories included here. *Mrs Dalloway in Bond Street* (1923) is a story that became the germ of Woolf's great novel *Mrs Dalloway* (1925). For this story she returned to a character she had created in *The Voyage Out*, where Clarissa Dalloway appeared as the wife of Richard Dalloway, a diplomat. In recounting Clarissa Dalloway's excursion to fashionable Bond Street for a pair of gloves, Woolf uses a "stream of consciousness" technique that places the reader inside Clarissa's mind, showing how the modulations of thoughts can turn the simplest events into occasions for reflection on a host of themes: the changes wrought by the passage of time; the persisting effects of the First World War; the complex relations between men and women, middle-class people and servants, modern literature and its predecessors. This story is followed by *The Lady in the Looking-Glass: A Reflection* (1929), whose major characters are the lady of the title—and her drawing-room. "Examine for a moment an ordinary mind on an ordinary day," Woolf wrote in an essay on *Modern Fiction* in 1925:

> The mind receives a myriad impressions—trivial, fantastic, evanescent, or engraved with the sharpness of steel. From all sides they come, an incessant shower of innumerable atoms; and, as they fall, as they shape themselves into the life of Monday or Tuesday, the accent falls differently from of old; the moment of importance came not here but there; so that, if a writer were a free man and not a slave, if he could write what he chose, not what he must, if he could base his work upon his own feeling and not upon convention, there would be no plot, no comedy, no tragedy, no love interest or catastrophe in the accepted style, and perhaps not a single button sewn on as the Bond Street tailors would have it.

Woolf's stories are written out of her own painfully won freedom of observation; the passages that follow from *A Room of One's Own* and *Three Guineas* meditate on the ways in which society and even human character would have to change in order for such freedom to spread.

Mrs Dalloway in Bond Street

Mrs Dalloway said she would buy the gloves herself. Big Ben was striking as she stepped out into the street. It was eleven o'clock and the unused hour was fresh as if issued to children on a beach. But there was something solemn in the deliberate swing of the repeated strokes; something stirring in the murmur of wheels and the shuffle of footsteps.

No doubt they were not all bound on errands of happiness. There is much more to be said about us than that we walk the streets of Westminster.[1] Big Ben too is nothing but steel rods consumed by rust were it not for the care of H.M's Office of Works. Only for Mrs Dalloway the moment was complete; for Mrs Dalloway June was fresh. A happy childhood—and it was not to his daughters only that Justin Parry had seemed a fine fellow (weak of course on the Bench); flowers at evening, smoke rising; the caw of rooks falling from ever so high, down down through the October air— there is nothing to take the place of childhood. A leaf of mint brings it back: or a cup with a blue ring.

Poor little wretches, she sighed, and pressed forward. Oh, right under the horses' noses, you little demon! and there she was left on the kerb stretching her hand out, while Jimmy Dawes grinned on the further side.

A charming woman, posed, eager, strangely white-haired for her pink cheeks, so Scope Purvis, C.B., saw her as he hurried to his office. She stiffened a little, waiting for Durtnall's van to pass. Big Ben struck the tenth; struck the eleventh stroke. The leaden circles dissolved in the air. Pride held her erect, inheriting, handing on, acquainted with discipline and with suffering. How people suffered, how they suffered, she thought, thinking of Mrs Foxcroft at the Embassy last night decked with jewels, eating her heart out, because that nice boy was dead, and now the old Manor House (Durtnall's van passed) must go to a cousin.

"Good morning to you," said Hugh Whitbread raising his hat rather extravagantly by the china shop, for they had known each other as children. "Where are you off to?"

"I love walking in London," said Mrs Dalloway. "Really it's better than walking in the country!"

"We've just come up," said Hugh Whitbread. "Unfortunately to see doctors."

"Milly?" said Mrs Dalloway, instantly compassionate.

"Out of sorts," said Hugh Whitbread. "That sort of thing. Dick all right?"

"First rate!" said Clarissa.

Of course, she thought, walking on, Milly is about my age—fifty—fifty-two. So it is probably *that*. Hugh's manner had said so, said it perfectly—dear old Hugh, thought Mrs Dalloway, remembering with amusement, with gratitude, with emotion, how shy, like a brother—one would rather die than speak to one's brother—Hugh had always been, when he was at Oxford, and came over, and perhaps one of them (drat the thing!) couldn't ride. How then could women sit in Parliament? How could they do things with men? For there is this extraordinarily deep instinct, something inside one; you can't get over it; it's no use trying; and men like Hugh respect it without our saying it, which is what one loves, thought Clarissa, in dear old Hugh.

She had passed through the Admiralty Arch and saw at the end of the empty road with its thin trees Victoria's white mound, Victoria's billowing motherliness, amplitude and homeliness, always ridiculous, yet how sublime thought Mrs Dalloway, remembering Kensington Gardens and the old lady in horn spectacles and being told by Nanny to stop dead still and bow to the Queen. The flag flew above the Palace. The King and Queen were back then. Dick had met her at lunch the other day—a thoroughly nice woman. It matters so much to the poor, thought Clarissa, and to the soldiers. A man in bronze stood heroically on a pedestal with a gun on her

---

1. District of central London, including the Houses of Parliament (with their famous clock tower "Big Ben"); it is also a fashionable residential area.

View of Regent Street, London, 1927.

left hand side—the South African war. It matters, thought Mrs Dalloway walking towards Buckingham Palace. There it stood four-square, in the broad sunshine, uncompromising, plain. But it was character she thought; something inborn in the race; what Indians respected. The Queen went to hospitals, opened bazaars—the Queen of England, thought Clarissa, looking at the Palace. Already at this hour a motor car passed out at the gates; soldiers saluted; the gates were shut. And Clarissa, crossing the road, entered the Park, holding herself upright.

June had drawn out every leaf on the trees. The mothers of Westminster with mottled breasts gave suck to their young. Quite respectable girls lay stretched on the grass. An elderly man, stooping very stiffly, picked up a crumpled paper, spread it out flat and flung it away. How horrible! Last night at the Embassy Sir Dighton had said, "If I want a fellow to hold my horse, I have only to put up my hand." But the religious question is far more serious than the economic, Sir Dighton had said, which she thought extraordinarily interesting, from a man like Sir Dighton. "Oh, the country will never know what it has lost," he had said, talking, of his own accord, about dear Jack Stewart.

She mounted the little hill lightly. The air stirred with energy. Messages were passing from the Fleet to the Admiralty. Piccadilly and Arlington Street and the Mall seemed to chafe the very air in the Park and lift its leaves hotly, brilliantly, upon waves of that divine vitality which Clarissa loved. To ride; to dance; she had adored all that. Or going on long walks in the country, talking, about books, what to do with one's life, for young people were amazingly priggish—oh, the things one had said! But one had conviction. Middle age is the devil. People like Jack'll never know that, she thought; for he never once thought of death, never, they said, knew he was dying. And now can never mourn—how did it go?—a head grown grey. . . . From the contagion of the world's slow stain. . . . Have drunk their cup a round or two before. . . . From the contagion of the world's slow stain![2] She held herself upright.

But how Jack would have shouted! Quoting Shelley, in Piccadilly! "You want a pin," he would have said. He hated frumps. "My God Clarissa! My God Clarissa!"— she could hear him now at the Devonshire House party, about poor Sylvia Hunt in her amber necklace and that dowdy old silk. Clarissa held herself upright for she had spoken aloud and now she was in Piccadilly, passing the house with the slender green columns, and the balconies; passing club windows full of newspapers; passing old Lady Burdett Coutt's house where the glazed white parrot used to hang; and Devonshire House, without its gilt leopards; and Claridge's, where she must remember Dick wanted her to leave a card on Mrs Jepson or she would be gone. Rich Americans can be very charming. There was St James's Palace; like a child's game with bricks; and now—she had passed Bond Street—she was by Hatchard's book shop. The stream was endless—endless—endless. Lords, Ascot, Hurlingham[3]—what was it? What a duck, she thought, looking at the frontispiece of some book of memoirs spread wide in the bow window, Sir Joshua perhaps or Romney; arch, bright, demure; the sort of girl—like her own Elizabeth—the only *real* sort of girl. And there was that absurd book, *Soapy Sponge*, which Jum used to quote by the yard; and Shakespeare's Sonnets. She knew them by heart. Phil and she had argued all day about the Dark Lady, and Dick had said straight out at dinner that night that he had never heard of her. Really, she had married him for that! He had never read Shakespeare! There must be some little cheap book she could buy for Milly—*Cranford*[4] of course! Was there ever anything so enchanting as the cow in petticoats? If only people had that sort of humour, that sort of self-respect now, thought Clarissa, for she remembered the broad pages; the sentences ending; the characters—how one talked about them as if they were real. For all the great things one must go to the past, she thought. From the contagion of the world's slow stain. . . . Fear no more the heat o' the sun. . . . And now can never mourn, can never mourn, she repeated, her eyes straying over the window; for it ran in her head; the test of great poetry; the moderns had never written anything one wanted to read about death, she thought; and turned.

Omnibuses joined motor cars; motor cars vans; vans taxicabs; taxicabs motor cars—here was an open motor car with a girl, alone. Up till four, her feet tingling, I know, thought Clarissa, for the girl looked washed out, half asleep, in the corner of the car after the dance. And another car came; and another. No! No! No! Clarissa smiled good-naturedly. The fat lady had taken every sort of trouble, but diamonds! orchids! at this hour of the morning! No! No! No! The excellent policeman would, when the time came, hold up his hand. Another motor car passed. How utterly unattractive! Why should a girl of that age paint black round her eyes? And a young man with a girl, at this hour, when the country—The admirable policeman raised his hand and Clarissa acknowledging his sway, taking her time, crossed, walked towards Bond Street; saw the narrow crooked street, the yellow banners; the thick notched telegraph wires stretched across the sky.

---

2. From *Adonais* (stanza 40), Percy Shelley's elegy on the early death of Keats; see page 687.
3. Locations of fashionable sporting events (cricket, horse racing, and polo).
4. Popular novel by Elizabeth Gaskell (1810–1865); see page 1453.

A hundred years ago her great-great-grandfather, Seymour Parry, who ran away with Conway's daughter, had walked down Bond Street. Down Bond Street the Parrys had walked for a hundred years, and might have met the Dalloways (Leighs on the mother's side) going up. Her father got his clothes from Hill's. There was a roll of cloth in the window, and here just one jar on a black table, incredibly expensive; like the thick pink salmon on the ice block at the fishmonger's. The jewels were exquisite—pink and orange stars, paste, Spanish, she thought, and chains of old gold; starry buckles, little brooches which had been worn on sea-green satin by ladies with high head-dresses. But no looking! One must economise. She must go on past the picture dealer's where one of the odd French pictures hung, as if people had thrown confetti—pink and blue—for a joke. If you had lived with pictures (and it's the same with books and music) thought Clarissa, passing the Aeolian Hall, you can't be taken in by a joke.

The river of Bond Street was clogged. There, like a queen at a tournament, raised, regal, was Lady Bexborough. She sat in her carriage, upright, alone, looking through her glasses. The white glove was loose at her wrist. She was in black, quite shabby, yet, thought Clarissa, how extraordinarily it tells, breeding, self-respect, never saying a word too much or letting people gossip; an astonishing friend; no one can pick a hole in her after all these years, and now, there she is, thought Clarissa, passing the Countess who waited powdered, perfectly still, and Clarissa would have given anything to be like that, the mistress of Clarefield, talking politics, like a man. But she never goes anywhere, thought Clarissa, and it's quite useless to ask her, and the carriage went on and Lady Bexborough was borne past like a queen at a tournament, though she had nothing to live for and the old man is failing and they say she is sick of it all, thought Clarissa and the tears actually rose to her eyes as she entered the shop.

"Good morning," said Clarissa in her charming voice. "Gloves," she said with her exquisite friendliness and putting her bag on the counter began, very slowly, to undo the buttons. "White gloves," she said. "Above the elbow," and she looked straight into the shopwoman's face—but this was not the girl she remembered? She looked quite old. "These really don't fit," said Clarissa. The shop-girl looked at them. "Madame wears bracelets?" Clarissa spread out her fingers. "Perhaps it's my rings." And the girl took the grey gloves with her to the end of the counter.

Yes, thought Clarissa, it's the girl I remember, she's twenty years older. . . . There was only one other customer, sitting sideways at the counter, her elbow poised, her bare hand drooping vacant; like a figure on a Japanese fan, thought Clarissa, too vacant perhaps, yet some men would adore her. The lady shook her head sadly. Again the gloves were too large. She turned round the glass. "Above the wrist," she reproached the grey-headed woman, who looked and agreed.

They waited; a clock ticked; Bond Street hummed, dulled, distant; the woman went away holding gloves. "Above the wrist," said the lady, mournfully, raising her voice. And she would have to order chairs, ices, flowers, and cloak-room tickets, thought Clarissa. The people she didn't want would come; the others wouldn't. She would stand by the door. They sold stockings—silk stockings. A lady is known by her gloves and her shoes, old Uncle William used to say. And through the hanging silk stockings, quivering silver she looked at the lady, sloping shouldered, her hand drooping, her bag slipping, her eyes vacantly on the floor. It would be intolerable if dowdy women came to her party! Would one have liked Keats if he had worn red socks? Oh, at last—she drew into the counter and it flashed into her mind:

"Do you remember before the war you had gloves with pearl buttons?"

"French gloves, Madame?"

"Yes, they were French," said Clarissa. The other lady rose very sadly and took her bag, and looked at the gloves on the counter. But they were all too large—always too large at the wrist.

"With pearl buttons," said the shop-girl, who looked ever so much older. She split the lengths of tissue paper apart on the counter. With pearl buttons, thought Clarissa, perfectly simple—how French!

"Madame's hands are so slender," said the shop-girl, drawing the glove firmly, smoothly, down over her rings. And Clarissa looked at her arm in the looking-glass. The glove hardly came to the elbow. Were there others half an inch longer? Still it seemed tiresome to bother her—perhaps the one day in the month, thought Clarissa, when it's an agony to stand. "Oh, don't bother," she said. But the gloves were brought.

"Don't you get fearfully tired," she said in her charming voice, "standing? When d'you get your holiday?"

"In September, Madame, when we're not so busy."

When we're in the country thought Clarissa. Or shooting. She has a fortnight at Brighton. In some stuffy lodging. The landlady takes the sugar. Nothing would be easier than to send her to Mrs Lumley's right in the country (and it was on the tip of her tongue). But then she remembered how on their honeymoon Dick had shown her the folly of giving impulsively. It was much more important, he said, to get trade with China. Of course he was right. And she could feel the girl wouldn't like to be given things. There she was in her place. So was Dick. Selling gloves was her job. She had her own sorrows quite separate, "and now can never mourn, can never mourn," the words ran in her head, "From the contagion of the world's slow stain," thought Clarissa holding her arm stiff, for there are moments when it seems utterly futile (the glove was drawn off leaving her arm flecked with powder)—simply one doesn't believe, thought Clarissa, any more in God.

The traffic suddenly roared; the silk stockings brightened. A customer came in.

"White gloves," she said, with some ring in her voice that Clarissa remembered.

It used, thought Clarissa, to be so simple. Down, down through the air came the caw of the rooks. When Sylvia died, hundreds of years ago, the yew hedges looked so lovely with the diamond webs in the mist before early church. But if Dick were to die to-morrow? As for believing in God—no, she would let the children choose, but for herself, like Lady Bexborough, who opened the bazaar, they say, with the telegram in her hand—Roden, her favourite, killed—she would go on. But why, if one doesn't believe? For the sake of others, she thought taking the glove in her hand. The girl would be much more unhappy if she didn't believe.

"Thirty shillings," said the shop-woman. "No, pardon me Madame, thirty-five. The French gloves are more."

For one doesn't live for oneself, thought Clarissa.

And then the other customer took a glove, tugged it, and it split.

"There!" she exclaimed.

"A fault of the skin," said the grey-headed woman hurriedly. "Sometimes a drop of acid in tanning. Try this pair, Madame."

"But it's an awful swindle to ask two pound ten!"

Clarissa looked at the lady; the lady looked at Clarissa.

"Gloves have never been quite so reliable since the war," said the shop-girl, apologising, to Clarissa.

But where had she seen the other lady?—elderly, with a frill under her chin; wearing a black ribbon for gold eyeglasses; sensual, clever, like a Sargent drawing. How one can tell from a voice when people are in the habit, thought Clarissa, of making other people—"It's a shade too tight," she said—obey. The shop-woman went off again. Clarissa was left waiting. Fear no more she repeated, playing her finger on the counter. Fear no more the heat o' the sun. Fear no more she repeated. There were little brown spots on her arm. And the girl crawled like a snail. Thou thy wordly task hast done. Thousands of young men had died that things might go on. At last! Half an inch above the elbow; pearl buttons; five and a quarter. My dear slow-coach, thought Clarissa, do you think I can sit here the whole morning? Now you'll take twenty-five minutes to bring me my change!

There was a violent explosion in the street outside. The shop-women cowered behind the counters. But Clarissa, sitting very upright, smiled at the other lady. "Miss Anstruther!" she exclaimed.

The Lady in the Looking-Glass: A Reflection[1]

People should not leave looking-glasses hanging in their rooms any more than they should leave open cheque books or letters confessing some hideous crime. One could not help looking, that summer afternoon, in the long glass that hung outside in the hall. Chance had so arranged it. From the depths of the sofa in the drawing-room one could see reflected in the Italian glass not only the marble-topped table opposite, but a stretch of the garden beyond. One could see a long grass path leading between banks of tall flowers until, slicing off an angle, the gold rim cut it off.

The house was empty, and one felt, since one was the only person in the drawing-room, like one of those naturalists who, covered with grass and leaves, lie watching the shyest animals—badgers, otters, kingfishers—moving about freely, themselves unseen. The room that afternoon was full of such shy creatures, lights and shadows, curtains blowing, petals falling—things that never happen, so it seems, if someone is looking. The quiet old country room with its rugs and stone chimney pieces, its sunken book-cases and red and gold lacquer cabinets, was full of such nocturnal creatures. They came pirouetting across the floor, stepping delicately with high-lifted feet and spread tails and pecking allusive beaks as if they had been cranes or flocks of elegant flamingoes whose pink was faded, or peacocks whose trains were veined with silver. And there were obscure flushes and darkenings too, as if a cuttlefish had suddenly suffused the air with purple; and the room had its passions and rages and envies and sorrows coming over it and clouding it, like a human being. Nothing stayed the same for two seconds together.

But, outside, the looking-glass reflected the hall table, the sunflowers, the garden path so accurately and so fixedly that they seemed held there in their reality unescapably. It was a strange contrast—all changing here, all stillness there. One could not help looking from one to the other. Meanwhile, since all the doors and windows were open in the heat, there was a perpetual sighing and ceasing sound, the voice of the transient and the perishing, it seemed, coming and going like human breath, while in the looking-glass things had ceased to breathe and lay still in the trance of immortality.

Half an hour ago the mistress of the house, Isabella Tyson, had gone down the grass path in her thin summer dress, carrying a basket, and had vanished, sliced off by

1. Published in *Harper's Magazine*, December 1929.

the gilt rim of the looking-glass. She had gone presumably into the lower garden to pick flowers; or as it seemed more natural to suppose, to pick something light and fantastic and leafy and trailing, traveller's joy, or one of those elegant sprays of convolvulus that twine round ugly walls and burst here and there into white and violet blossoms. She suggested the fantastic and the tremulous convolvulus rather than the upright aster, the starched zinnia, or her own burning roses alight like lamps on the straight posts of their rose trees. The comparison showed how very little, after all these years, one knew about her; for it is impossible that any woman of flesh and blood of fifty-five or sixty should be really a wreath or a tendril. Such comparisons are worse than idle and superficial—they are cruel even, for they come like the convolvulus itself trembling between one's eyes and the truth. There must be truth; there must be a wall. Yet it was strange that after knowing her all these years one could not say what the truth about Isabella was; one still made up phrases like this about convolvulus and traveller's joy. As for facts, it was a fact that she was a spinster; that she was rich; that she had bought this house and collected with her own hands—often in the most obscure corners of the world and at great risk from poisonous stings and Oriental diseases—the rugs, the chairs, the cabinets which now lived their nocturnal life before one's eyes. Sometimes it seemed as if they knew more about her than we, who sat on them, wrote at them, and trod on them so carefully, were allowed to know. In each of these cabinets were many little drawers, and each almost certainly held letters, tied with bows of ribbon, sprinkled with sticks of lavender or rose leaves. For it was another fact—if facts were what one wanted—that Isabella had known many people, had had many friends; and thus if one had the audacity to open a drawer and read her letters, one would find the traces of many agitations, of appointments to meet, of upbraidings for not having met, long letters of intimacy and affection, violent letters of jealousy and reproach, terrible final words of parting—for all those interviews and assignations had led to nothing—that is, she had never married, and yet, judging from the mask-like indifference of her face, she had gone through twenty times more of passion and experience than those whose loves are trumpeted forth for all the world to hear. Under the stress of thinking about Isabella, her room became more shadowy and symbolic; the corners seemed darker, the legs of chairs and tables more spindly and hieroglyphic.

Suddenly these reflections were ended violently and yet without a sound. A large black form loomed into the looking-glass; blotted out everything, strewed the table with a packet of marble tablets veined with pink and grey, and was gone. But the picture was entirely altered. For the moment it was unrecognisable and irrational and entirely out of focus. One could not relate these tablets to any human purpose. And then by degrees some logical process set to work on them and began ordering and arranging them and bringing them into the fold of common experience. One realised at last that they were merely letters. The man had brought the post.

There they lay on the marble-topped table, all dripping with light and colour at first and crude and unabsorbed. And then it was strange to see how they were drawn in and arranged and composed and made part of the picture and granted that stillness and immortality which the looking-glass conferred. They lay there invested with a new reality and significance and with a greater heaviness, too, as if it would have needed a chisel to dislodge them from the table. And, whether it was fancy or not, they seemed to have become not merely a handful of casual letters but to be tablets graven with eternal truth—if one could read them, one would know everything there was to be known about Isabella, yes, and about life, too. The pages inside those marble-looking envelopes must be cut deep and scored thick with meaning. Isabella would come in, and take them, one by one, very slowly, and open them, and read them carefully word by word, and then with a profound sigh of comprehension, as if she had seen to the bottom of everything, she would tear the envelopes to little bits and tie the letters together and lock the cabinet drawer in her determination to conceal what she did not wish to be known.

The thought served as a challenge. Isabella did not wish to be known—but she should no longer escape. It was absurd, it was monstrous. If she concealed so much and knew so much one must prize her open with the first tool that came to hand—the imagination. One must fix one's mind upon her at that very moment. One must fasten her down there. One must refuse to be put off any longer with sayings and doings such as the moment brought forth—with dinners and visits and polite conversations. One must put oneself in her shoes. If one took the phrase literally, it was easy to see the shoes in which she stood, down in the lower garden, at this moment. They were very narrow and long and fashionable—they were made of the softest and most flexible leather. Like everything she wore, they were exquisite. And she would be standing under the high hedge in the lower part of the garden, raising the scissors that were tied to her waist to cut some dead flower, some overgrown branch. The sun would beat down on her face, into her eyes; but no, at the critical moment a veil of cloud covered the sun, making the expression of her eyes doubtful—was it mocking or tender, brilliant or dull? One could only see the indeterminate outline of her rather faded, fine face looking at the sky. She was thinking, perhaps, that she must order a new net for the strawberries; that she must send flowers to Johnson's widow; that it was time she drove over to see the Hippesleys in their new house. Those were the things she talked about at dinner certainly. But one was tired of the things that she talked about at dinner. It was her profounder state of being that one wanted to catch and turn to words, the state that is to the mind what breathing is to the body, what one calls happiness or unhappiness. At the mention of those words it became obvious, surely, that she must be happy. She was rich; she was distinguished; she had many friends; she travelled—she bought rugs in Turkey and blue pots in Persia. Avenues of pleasure radiated this way and that from where she stood with her scissors raised to cut the trembling branches while the lacy clouds veiled her face.

Here with a quick movement of her scissors she snipped the spray of traveller's joy and it fell to the ground. As it fell, surely some light came in too, surely one could penetrate a little farther into her being. Her mind then was filled with tenderness and regret. . . . To cut an overgrown branch saddened her because it had once lived, and life was dear to her. Yes, and at the same time the fall of the branch would suggest to her how she must die herself and all the futility and evanescence of things. And then again quickly catching this thought up, with her instant good sense, she thought life had treated her well; even if fall she must, it was to lie on the earth and moulder sweetly into the roots of violets. So she stood thinking. Without making any thought precise—for she was one of those reticent people whose minds hold their thoughts enmeshed in clouds of silence—she was filled with thoughts. Her mind was like her room, in which lights advanced and retreated, came pirouetting and stepping delicately, spread their tails, pecked their way; and then her whole being was suffused, like the room again, with a cloud of some profound knowledge, some unspoken regret, and then she was full of locked drawers, stuffed with letters, like her cabinets. To talk of "prizing her open" as if she were an oyster, to use any but the finest and subtlest and most pliable tools upon her was impious and absurd. One must imagine—here was she in the looking-glass. It made one start.

She was so far off at first that one could not see her clearly. She came lingering and pausing, here straightening a rose, there lifting a pink to smell it, but she never stopped; and all the time she became larger and larger in the looking-glass, more and more completely the person into whose mind one had been trying to penetrate. One verified her by degrees—fitted the qualities one had discovered into this visible body. There were her grey-green dress, and her long shoes, her basket, and something sparkling at her throat. She came so gradually that she did not seem to derange the pattern in the glass, but only to bring in some new element which gently moved and altered the other objects as if asking them, courteously, to make room for her. And the letters and the table and the grass walk and the sunflowers which had been waiting in the looking-glass separated and opened out so that she might be received among them. At last there she was, in the hall. She stopped dead. She stood by the table. She stood perfectly still. At once the looking-glass began to pour over her a light that seemed to fix her; that seemed like some acid to bite off the unessential and superficial and to leave only the truth. It was an enthralling spectacle. Everything dropped from her—clouds, dress, basket, diamond—all that one had called the creeper and convolvulus. Here was the hard wall beneath. Here was the woman herself. She stood naked in that pitiless light. And, there was nothing. Isabella was perfectly empty. She had no thoughts. She had no friends. She cared for nobody. As for her letters, they were all bills. Look, as she stood there, old and angular, veined and lined, with her high nose and her wrinkled neck, she did not even trouble to open them.

People should not leave looking-glasses hanging in their rooms.

A Room of One's Own

A Room of One's Own is difficult to categorize—it is a long essay, a non-fiction novella, a political pamphlet, and a philosophical discourse all in one. Its effects have not been so difficult to categorize—Virginia Woolf's idiosyncratic text has been recognized as a classic from the time of its publication in 1929. The book was a departure from Woolf's output until then; she was a major literary figure, having already published such key novels as *Jacob's Room, Mrs Dalloway, To the Lighthouse*, and *Orlando*, and she was an established essayist with a formidable reputation as an arbiter of the literary tradition. One way of characterizing this book is to see that it represents Woolf's scrutiny of her own position as a woman writer, a self-examination of her public position that inevitably became a political document. The focus is not on Woolf's life or her work per se, but rather on the social and psychological conditions that would make such a life generally possible. The book creates a microcosm of such possibility in the "room" of its title; the book itself is a room within which its author contemplates and analyzes the dimensions of social space for women. Woolf recognizes that seemingly neutral social space, the room of cultural agency just as the room of writing, is in truth a gendered space. She directs her political inquiry toward the making and remaking of such rooms.

A Room of One's Own comes from established traditions of writing as well. It draws on the conversational tone and novelistic insight of the literary essay as perfected in the nineteenth century by such writers as Charles Lamb—whose *Oxford in the Vacation* (see page 966) was certainly in Woolf's mind when she wrote the opening chapter of her essay. At the same time, Woolf's book joins a lineage of feminist political philosophy, whose most eloquent exponent prior to Woolf herself was Mary Wollstonecraft, who joined the rhetorical ranks of Rousseau and John Stuart Mill with the publication of *A Vindication of the Rights of Woman*, her passionately reasoned exhortation for the equal and universal human rights of women. (Selections from Wollstonecraft's *Vindication* can be found on page 208.) The century and a half since Wollstonecraft had produced a rich history of feminist agitation and feminist thought. Virginia Woolf draws on this less-known tradition, invoking nineteenth-century figures from the women's movement like

Emily Davies, Josephine Butler, and Octavia Hill. She also places her deliberations in the context of the suffragist movement and its fraught history in Britain. Virginia Woolf was strongly engaged in the debates of the suffrage movement, and its divisions over radical action or more conciliatory political approaches. Much of Woolf's long essay is devoted to demonstrating the subversive quality of occupying the blank page, and wielding the printed word.

As politically motivated as A Room of One's Own is, it is equally a literary text. Woolf draws on all the intricacies of literary tropes and figures to mount her argument for women's education, women's equality, women's social presence. Not the least of her strategies is her manipulation of the rhetoric of address—in other words, the audience implied by the language of a text. Woolf creates an ironic space, or room, in which she is a playfully ambiguous speaker addressing an uncertain audience: women at the colleges where she has been invited to speak, but also men and women alike who will read her printed text. By doing so, she keeps an ironic tension in play, holding at bay her anger at being censored or silenced by male readers by creating a sense of privacy and secrecy among women. This underscores Woolf's primary argument, the need for autonomy and self-determination. Her modest proposal, although faintly ironic, is also eminently pragmatic—the room of one's own that is her metaphor for the college classroom or the blank canvas or the book's page is at the same time the actual room, paid for and unintruded upon by domestic worries or social codes, whose possession permits a woman to find out who she may be.

from A Room of One's Own
Chapter 1

But, you may say, we asked you to speak about women and fiction—what has that got to do with a room of one's own?[1] I will try to explain. When you asked me to speak about women and fiction I sat down on the banks of a river and began to wonder what the words meant. They might mean simply a few remarks about Fanny Burney; a few more about Jane Austen; a tribute to the Brontës and a sketch of Haworth Parsonage under snow; some witticisms if possible about Miss Mitford; a respectful allusion to George Eliot; a reference to Mrs Gaskell and one would have done.[2] But at second sight the words seemed not so simple. The title women and fiction might mean, and you may have meant it to mean, women and what they are like; or it might mean women and the fiction that they write; or it might mean women and the fiction that is written about them; or it might mean that somehow all three are inextricably mixed together and you want me to consider them in that light. But when I began to consider the subject in this last way, which seemed the most interesting, I soon saw that it had one fatal drawback. I should never be able to come to a conclusion. I should never be able to fulfil what is, I understand, the first duty of a lecturer—to hand you after an hour's discourse a nugget of pure truth to wrap up between the pages of your notebooks and keep on the mantelpiece for ever. All I could do was to offer you an opinion upon one minor point—a woman must have money and a room of her own if she is to write fiction; and that, as you will see, leaves the great problem of the true nature of woman and the true nature of fiction unsolved. I have shirked the duty of coming to a conclusion upon these two questions—women and fiction remain, so far as I am concerned, unsolved problems. But in order to make some amends I am going to do what I can to show you how I arrived at this opinion about the room and the money. I am going to develop in your presence as fully and

---

1. Woolf delivered her essay in a shorter version to meetings first at two women's colleges, Newnham and Girton   College, Cambridge University, in October 1928.
2. Important 19th-century novelists.

freely as I can the train of thought which led me to think this. Perhaps if I lay bare the ideas, the prejudices, that lie behind this statement you will find that they have some bearing upon women and some upon fiction. At any rate, when a subject is highly controversial—and any question about sex is that—one cannot hope to tell the truth. One can only show how one came to hold whatever opinion one does hold. One can only give one's audience the chance of drawing their own conclusions as they observe the limitations, the prejudices, the idiosyncrasies of the speaker. Fiction here is likely to contain more truth than fact. Therefore I propose, making use of all the liberties and licences of a novelist, to tell you the story of the two days that preceded my coming here—how, bowed down by the weight of the subject which you have laid upon my shoulders, I pondered it, and made it work in and out of my daily life. I need not say that what I am about to describe has no existence; Oxbridge is an invention; so is Fernham;[3] "I" is only a convenient term for somebody who has no real being. Lies will flow from my lips, but there may perhaps be some truth mixed up with them; it is for you to seek out this truth and to decide whether any part of it is worth keeping. If not, you will of course throw the whole of it into the wastepaper basket and forget all about it.

Here then was I (call me Mary Beton, Mary Seton, Mary Carmichael[4] or by any name you please—it is not a matter of any importance) sitting on the banks of a river a week or two ago in fine October weather, lost in thought. That collar I have spoken of, women and fiction, the need of coming to some conclusion on a subject that raises all sorts of prejudices and passions, bowed my head to the ground. To the right and left bushes of some sort, golden and crimson, glowed with the colour, even it seemed burnt with the heat, of fire. On the further bank the willows wept in perpetual lamentation, their hair about their shoulders. The river reflected whatever it chose of sky and bridge and burning tree, and when the undergraduate had oared his boat through the reflections they closed again, completely, as if he had never been. There one might have sat the clock round lost in thought. Thought—to call it by a prouder name than it deserved—had let its line down into the stream. It swayed, minute after minute, hither and thither among the reflections and the weeds, letting the water lift it and sink it, until—you know the little tug—the sudden conglomeration of an idea at the end of one's line: and then the cautious hauling of it in, and the careful laying of it out? Alas, laid on the grass how small, how insignificant this thought of mine looked; the sort of fish that a good fisherman puts back into the water so that it may grow fatter and be one day worth cooking and eating. I will not trouble you with that thought now, though if you look carefully you may find it for yourselves in the course of what I am going to say.

But however small it was, it had, nevertheless, the mysterious property of its kind—put back into the mind, it became at once very exciting, and important; and as it darted and sank, and flashed hither and thither, set up such a wash and tumult of ideas that it was impossible to sit still. It was thus that I found myself walking with extreme rapidity across a grass plot. Instantly a man's figure rose to intercept me. Nor did I at first understand that the gesticulations of a curious-looking object, in a cutaway coat and evening shirt, were aimed at me. His face expressed horror and indig-

---

3. "Oxbridge" was in fact the common slang term for Oxford and Cambridge universities. "Fernham" suggests Newnham College.
4. Three of the four Marys who by tradition were atten-

dants to Mary, Queen of Scots (executed in 1567), and who figure in many Scottish ballads; the fourth was Mary Hamilton.

nation. Instinct rather than reason came to my help; he was a Beadle; I was a woman. This was the turf; there was the path. Only the Fellows and Scholars are allowed here; the gravel is the place for me.[5] Such thoughts were the work of a moment. As I regained the path the arms of the Beadle sank, his face assumed its usual repose, and though turf is better walking than gravel, no very great harm was done. The only charge I could bring against the Fellows and Scholars of whatever the college might happen to be was that in protection of their turf, which has been rolled for 300 years in succession, they had sent my little fish into hiding.

What idea it had been that had sent me so audaciously trespassing I could not now remember. The spirit of peace descended like a cloud from heaven, for if the spirit of peace dwells anywhere, it is in the courts and quadrangles of Oxbridge on a fine October morning. Strolling through those colleges past those ancient halls the roughness of the present seemed smoothed away; the body seemed contained in a miraculous glass cabinet through which no sound could penetrate, and the mind, freed from any contact with facts (unless one trespassed on the turf again), was at liberty to settle down upon whatever meditation was in harmony with the moment. As chance would have it, some stray memory of some old essay about revisiting Oxbridge in the long vacation brought Charles Lamb to mind—Saint Charles, said Thackeray,[6] putting a letter of Lamb's to his forehead. Indeed, among all the dead (I give you my thoughts as they came to me), Lamb is one of the most congenial; one to whom one would have liked to say, Tell me then how you wrote your essays? For his essays are superior even to Max Beerbohm's, I thought, with all their perfection, because of that wild flash of imagination, that lightning crack of genius in the middle of them which leaves them flawed and imperfect, but starred with poetry. Lamb then came to Oxbridge perhaps a hundred years ago. Certainly he wrote an essay—the name escapes me—about the manuscript of one of Milton's poems which he saw here.[7] It was *Lycidas* perhaps, and Lamb wrote how it shocked him to think it possible that any word in *Lycidas* could have been different from what it is. To think of Milton changing the words in that poem seemed to him a sort of sacrilege. This led me to remember what I could of *Lycidas* and to amuse myself with guessing which word it could have been that Milton had altered, and why. It then occurred to me that the very manuscript itself which Lamb had looked at was only a few hundred yards away, so that one could follow Lamb's footsteps across the quadrangle to that famous library where the treasure is kept. Moreover, I recollected, as I put this plan into execution, it is in this famous library that the manuscript of Thackeray's *Esmond* is also preserved. The critics often say that *Esmond* is Thackeray's most perfect novel. But the affectation of the style, with its imitation of the eighteenth century, hampers one, so far as I remember; unless indeed the eighteenth-century style was natural to Thackeray—a fact that one might prove by looking at the manuscript and seeing whether the alterations were for the benefit of the style or of the sense. But then one would have to decide what is style and what is meaning, a question which—but here I was actually at the door which leads into the library itself. I must have opened it, for instantly there issued, like a guardian angel barring the way with a flutter of black gown

5. A beadle is a disciplinary officer. The fellows of Oxbridge colleges typically tutor the undergraduates, who are divided into scholars and commoners. The commoners form the majority of the student body.
6. William Makepeace Thackeray (1811–1863), novelist and journalist, Woolf's father's first father-in-law.

7. Lamb's *Oxford in the Vacation*—describing the locales Lamb himself was too poor to attend in term time. The manuscript of Milton's elegy *Lycidas* (1638) is in the Wren Library of Trinity College, Cambridge, together with that of Thackeray's novel *The History of Henry Esmond* (1852).

instead of white wings, a deprecating, silvery, kindly gentleman, who regretted in a low voice as he waved me back that ladies are only admitted to the library if accompanied by a Fellow of the College or furnished with a letter of introduction.

That a famous library has been cursed by a woman is a matter of complete indifference to a famous library. Venerable and calm, with all its treasures safe locked within its breast, it sleeps complacently and will, so far as I am concerned, so sleep for ever. Never will I wake those echoes, never will I ask for that hospitality again, I vowed as I descended the steps in anger. Still an hour remained before luncheon, and what was one to do? Stroll on the meadows? sit by the river? Certainly it was a lovely autumn morning; the leaves were fluttering red to the ground; there was no great hardship in doing either. But the sound of music reached my ear. Some service or celebration was going forward. The organ complained magnificently as I passed the chapel door. Even the sorrow of Christianity sounded in that serene air more like the recollection of sorrow than sorrow itself; even the groanings of the ancient organ seemed lapped in peace. I had no wish to enter had I the right, and this time the verger might have stopped me, demanding perhaps my baptismal certificate, or a letter of introduction from the Dean. But the outside of these magnificent buildings is often as beautiful as the inside. Moreover, it was amusing enough to watch the congregation assembling, coming in and going out again, busying themselves at the door of the chapel like bees at the mouth of a hive. Many were in cap and gown; some had tufts of fur on their shoulders; others were wheeled in bath-chairs; others, though not past middle age, seemed creased and crushed into shapes so singular that one was reminded of those giant crabs and crayfish who heave with difficulty across the sand of an aquarium. As I leant against the wall the University indeed seemed a sanctuary in which are preserved rare types which would soon be obsolete if left to fight for existence on the pavement of the Strand.[8] Old stories of old deans and old dons came back to mind, but before I had summoned up courage to whistle—it used to be said that at the sound of a whistle old Professor ———— instantly broke into a gallop—the venerable congregation had gone inside. The outside of the chapel remained. As you know, its high domes and pinnacles can be seen, like a sailing-ship always voyaging never arriving, lit up at night and visible for miles, far away across the hills. Once, presumably, this quadrangle with its smooth lawns, its massive buildings, and the chapel itself was marsh too, where the grasses waved and the swine rootled. Teams of horses and oxen, I thought, must have hauled the stone in wagons from far countries, and then with infinite labour the grey blocks in whose shade I was now standing were poised in order one on top of another, and then the painters brought their glass for the windows, and the masons were busy for centuries up on that roof with putty and cement, spade and trowel. Every Saturday somebody must have poured gold and silver out of a leathern purse into their ancient fists, for they had their beer and skittles presumably of an evening. An unending stream of gold and silver, I thought, must have flowed into this court perpetually to keep the stones coming and the masons working; to level, to ditch, to dig and to drain. But it was then the age of faith, and money was poured liberally to set these stones on a deep foundation, and when the stones were raised, still more money was poured in from the coffers of kings and queens and great nobles to ensure that hymns should be sung here and scholars taught. Lands were granted; tithes were paid. And when the age of faith was over and the age of reason had come, still the same flow of gold and silver went on; fellowships

8. A thoroughfare in central London.

were founded; lectureships endowed; only the gold and silver flowed now, not from the coffers of the king, but from the chests of merchants and manufacturers, from the purses of men who had made, say, a fortune from industry, and returned, in their wills, a bounteous share of it to endow more chairs, more lectureships, more fellowships in the university where they had learnt their craft. Hence the libraries and laboratories; the observatories; the splendid equipment of costly and delicate instruments which now stands on glass shelves, where centuries ago the grasses waved and the swine rooted. Certainly, as I strolled round the court, the foundation of gold and silver seemed deep enough; the pavement laid solidly over the wild grasses. Men with trays on their heads went busily from staircase to staircase. Gaudy blossoms flowered in window-boxes. The strains of the gramophone blared out from the rooms within. It was impossible not to reflect—the reflection whatever it may have been was cut short. The clock struck. It was time to find one's way to luncheon.

It is a curious fact that novelists have a way of making us believe that luncheon parties are invariably memorable for something very witty that was said, or for something very wise that was done. But they seldom spare a word for what was eaten. It is part of the novelist's convention not to mention soup and salmon and ducklings, as if soup and salmon and ducklings were of no importance whatsoever, as if nobody ever smoked a cigar or drank a glass of wine. Here, however, I shall take the liberty to defy that convention and to tell you that the lunch on this occasion began with soles, sunk in a deep dish, over which the college cook had spread a counterpane of the whitest cream, save that it was branded here and there with brown spots like the spots on the flanks of a doe. After that came the partridges, but if this suggests a couple of bald, brown birds on a plate you are mistaken. The partridges, many and various, came with all their retinue of sauces and salads, the sharp and the sweet, each in its order; their potatoes, thin as coins but not so hard; their sprouts, foliated as rosebuds but more succulent. And no sooner had the roast and its retinue been done with than the silent serving-man, the Beadle himself perhaps in a milder manifestation, set before us, wreathed in napkins, a confection which rose all sugar from the waves. To call it pudding and so relate it to rice and tapioca would be an insult. Meanwhile the wineglasses had flushed yellow and flushed crimson; had been emptied; had been filled. And thus by degrees was lit, halfway down the spine, which is the seat of the soul, not that hard little electric light which we call brilliance, as it pops in and out upon our lips, but the more profound, subtle and subterranean glow, which is the rich yellow flame of rational intercourse. No need to hurry. No need to sparkle. No need to be anybody but oneself. We are all going to heaven and Vandyck[9] is of the company—in other words, how good life seemed, how sweet its rewards, how trivial this grudge or that grievance, how admirable friendship and the society of one's kind, as, lighting a good cigarette, one sunk among the cushions in the window-seat.

If by good luck there had been an ash-tray handy, if one had not knocked the ash out of the window in default, if things had been a little different from what they were, one would not have seen, presumably, a cat without a tail. The sight of that abrupt and truncated animal padding softly across the quadrangle changed by some fluke of the subconscious intelligence the emotional light for me. It was as if some one had let fall a shade. Perhaps the excellent hock was relinquishing its hold. Certainly, as I watched the Manx cat pause in the middle of the lawn as if it too questioned the universe, something seemed lacking, something seemed different. But what was lacking,

9. Sir Anthony Van Dyck, prominent 17-century society painter.

what was different, I asked myself, listening to the talk. And to answer that question I had to think myself out of the room, back into the past, before the war indeed,[1] and to set before my eyes the model of another luncheon party held in rooms not very far distant from these; but different. Everything was different. Meanwhile the talk went on among the guests, who were many and young, some of this sex, some of that; it went on swimmingly, it went on agreeably, freely, amusingly. And as it went on I set it against the background of that other talk, and as I matched the two together I had no doubt that one was the descendant, the legitimate heir of the other. Nothing was changed; nothing was different save only—here I listened with all my ears not entirely to what was being said, but to the murmur or current behind it. Yes, that was it—the change was there. Before the war at a luncheon party like this people would have said precisely the same things but they would have sounded different, because in those days they were accompanied by a sort of humming noise, not articulate, but musical, exciting, which changed the value of the words themselves. Could one set that humming noise to words? Perhaps with the help of the poets one could. A book lay beside me and, opening it, I turned casually enough to Tennyson. And here I found Tennyson was singing:

> There has fallen a splendid tear
>> From the passion-flower at the gate.
> She is coming, my dove, my dear;
>> She is coming, my life, my fate;
> The red rose cries, "She is near, she is near";
>> And the white rose weeps, "She is late";
> The larkspur listens, "I hear, I hear";
>> And the lily whispers, "I wait."[2]

Was that what men hummed at luncheon parties before the war? And the women?

> My heart is like a singing bird
>> Whose nest is in a water'd shoot;
> My heart is like an apple tree
>> Whose boughs are bent with thick-set fruit;
> My heart is like a rainbow shell
>> That paddles in a halcyon sea;
> My heart is gladder than all these
>> Because my love is come to me.[3]

Was that what women hummed at luncheon parties before the war?

There was something so ludicrous in thinking of people humming such things even under their breath at luncheon parties before the war that I burst out laughing, and had to explain my laughter by pointing at the Manx cat, who did look a little absurd, poor beast, without a tail, in the middle of the lawn. Was he really born so, or had he lost his tail in an accident? The tailless cat, though some are said to exist in the Isle of Man, is rarer than one thinks. It is a queer animal, quaint rather than beautiful. It is strange what a difference a tail makes—you know the sort of things one says as a lunch party breaks up and people are finding their coats and hats.

This one, thanks to the hospitality of the host, had lasted far into the afternoon. The beautiful October day was fading and the leaves were falling from the trees in the avenue as I walked through it. Gate after gate seemed to close with gentle finali-

---

1. World War I.
2. From Tennyson's Maud (1855), lines 908–915.

3. The first stanza of Christina Rossetti's poem A Birthday (1857); see page 1710.

ty behind me. Innumerable beadles were fitting innumerable keys into well-oiled locks; the treasure-house was being made secure for another night. After the avenue one comes out upon a road—I forget its name—which leads you, if you take the right turning, along to Fernham.[4] But there was plenty of time. Dinner was not till half-past seven. One could almost do without dinner after such a luncheon. It is strange how a scrap of poetry works in the mind and makes the legs move in time to it along the road. Those words—

> There has fallen a splendid tear
>   From the passion-flower at the gate.
> She is coming, my dove, my dear—

sang in my blood as I stepped quickly along towards Headingley. And then, switching off into the other measure, I sang, where the waters are churned up by the weir:

> My heart is like a singing bird
>   Whose nest is in a water'd shoot;
> My heart is like an apple tree—

What poets, I cried aloud, as one does in the dusk, what poets they were!

In a sort of jealousy, I suppose, for our own age, silly and absurd though these comparisons are, I went on to wonder if honestly one could name two living poets now as great as Tennyson and Christina Rossetti were then. Obviously it is impossible, I thought, looking into those foaming waters, to compare them. The very reason why the poetry excites one to such abandonment, such rapture, is that it celebrates some feeling that one used to have (at luncheon parties before the war perhaps), so that one responds easily, familiarly, without troubling to check the feeling, or to compare it with any that one has now. But the living poets express a feeling that is actually being made and torn out of us at the moment. One does not recognize it in the first place; often for some reason one fears it; one watches it with keenness and compares it jealously and suspiciously with the old feeling that one knew. Hence the difficulty of modern poetry; and it is because of this difficulty that one cannot remember more than two consecutive lines of any good modern poet. For this reason—that my memory failed me—the argument flagged for want of material. But why, I continued, moving on towards Headingley, have we stopped humming under our breath at luncheon parties? Why has Alfred ceased to sing

> She is coming, my dove, my dear?

Why has Christina ceased to respond

> My heart is gladder than all these
> Because my love is come to me?

Shall we lay the blame on the war? When the guns fired in August 1914, did the faces of men and women show so plain in each other's eyes that romance was killed? Certainly it was a shock (to women in particular with their illusions about education, and so on) to see the faces of our rulers in the light of the shell-fire. So ugly they looked—German, English, French—so stupid. But lay the blame where one will, on whom one will, the illusion which inspired Tennyson and Christina Rossetti to sing so passionately about the coming of their loves is far rarer now than then. One has

---

4. Both Girton and Newnham Colleges, established only in the late 19th century, are outside the old university area of Cambridge.

only to read, to look, to listen, to remember. But why say "blame"? Why, if it was an illusion, not praise the catastrophe, whatever it was, that destroyed illusion and put truth in its place? For truth . . . those dots mark the spot where, in search of truth, I missed the turning up to Fernham. Yes indeed, which was truth and which was illusion, I asked myself. What was the truth about these houses, for example, dim and festive now with their red windows in the dusk, but raw and red and squalid, with their sweets and their boot-laces, at nine o'clock in the morning? And the willows and the river and the gardens that run down to the river, vague now with the mist stealing over them, but gold and red in the sunlight—which was the truth, which was the illusion about them? I spare you the twists and turns of my cogitations, for no conclusion was found on the road to Headingley, and I ask you to suppose that I soon found out my mistake about the turning and retraced my steps to Fernham.

As I have said already that it was an October day, I dare not forfeit your respect and imperil the fair name of fiction by changing the season and describing lilacs hanging over garden walls, crocuses, tulips and other flowers of spring. Fiction must stick to facts, and the truer the facts the better the fiction—so we are told. Therefore it was still autumn and the leaves were still yellow and falling, if anything, a little faster than before, because it was now evening (seven twenty-three to be precise) and a breeze (from the south-west to be exact) had risen. But for all that there was something odd at work:

> My heart is like a singing bird
> Whose nest is in a water'd shoot;
> My heart is like an apple tree
> Whose boughs are bent with thick-set fruit—

perhaps the words of Christina Rossetti were partly responsible for the folly of the fancy—it was nothing of course but a fancy—that the lilac was shaking its flowers over the garden walls, and the brimstone butterflies were scudding hither and thither, and the dust of the pollen was in the air. A wind blew, from what quarter I know not, but it lifted the half-grown leaves so that there was a flash of silver grey in the air. It was the time between the lights when colours undergo their intensification and purples and golds burn in window-panes like the beat of an excitable heart; when for some reason the beauty of the world revealed and yet soon to perish (here I pushed into the garden, for, unwisely, the door was left open and no beadles seemed about), the beauty of the world which is so soon to perish, has two edges, one of laughter, one of anguish, cutting the heart asunder. The gardens of Fernham lay before me in the spring twilight, wild and open, and in the long grass, sprinkled and carelessly flung, were daffodils and bluebells, not orderly perhaps at the best of times, and now wind-blown and waving as they tugged at their roots. The windows of the building, curved like ships' windows among generous waves of red brick, changed from lemon to silver under the flight of the quick spring clouds. Somebody was in a hammock, somebody, but in this light they were phantoms only, half guessed, half seen, raced across the grass—would no one stop her?—and then on the terrace, as if popping out to breathe the air, to glance at the garden, came a bent figure, formidable yet humble, with her great forehead and her shabby dress—could it be the famous scholar, could it be J—— H—— herself?[5] All was dim, yet intense too, as if the scarf which the dusk had flung over the garden were torn asunder by star or sword—the flash of some terrible reality leaping, as its way is, out of the heart of the spring. For youth——

---

5. Jane Harrison, a famous classical scholar.

Here was my soup. Dinner was being served in the great dining-hall. Far from being spring it was in fact an evening in October. Everybody was assembled in the big dining-room. Dinner was ready. Here was the soup. It was a plain gravy soup. There was nothing to stir the fancy in that. One could have seen through the transparent liquid any pattern that there might have been on the plate itself. But there was no pattern. The plate was plain. Next came beef with its attendant greens and potatoes—a homely trinity, suggesting the rumps of cattle in a muddy market, and sprouts curled and yellowed at the edge, and bargaining and cheapening, and women with string bags on Monday morning. There was no reason to complain of human nature's daily food, seeing that the supply was sufficient and coal-miners doubtless were sitting down to less. Prunes and custard followed. And if any one complains that prunes, even when mitigated by custard, are an uncharitable vegetable (fruit they are not), stringy as a miser's heart and exuding a fluid such as might run in misers' veins who have denied themselves wine and warmth for eighty years and yet not given to the poor, he should reflect that there are people whose charity embraces even the prune. Biscuits and cheese came next, and here the water-jug was liberally passed round, for it is the nature of biscuits to be dry, and these were biscuits to the core. That was all. The meal was over. Everybody scraped their chairs back; the swing-doors swung violently to and fro; soon the hall was emptied of every sign of food and made ready no doubt for breakfast next morning. Down corridors and up staircases the youth of England went banging and singing. And was it for a guest, a stranger (for I had no more right here in Fernham than in Trinity or Somerville or Girton or Newnham or Christchurch),[6] to say, "The dinner was not good," or to say (we were now, Mary Seton and I, in her sitting-room), "Could we not have dined up here alone?" for if I had said anything of the kind I should have been prying and searching into the secret economies of a house which to the stranger wears so fine a front of gaiety and courage. No, one could say nothing of the sort. Indeed, conversation for a moment flagged. The human frame being what it is, heart, body and brain all mixed together, and not contained in separate compartments as they will be no doubt in another million years, a good dinner is of great importance to good talk. One cannot think well, love well, sleep well, if one has not dined well. The lamp in the spine does not light on beef and prunes. We are all *probably* going to heaven, and Vandyck is, we *hope*, to meet us round the next corner—that is the dubious and qualifying state of mind that beef and prunes at the end of the day's work breed between them. Happily my friend, who taught science, had a cupboard where there was a squat bottle and little glasses—(but there should have been sole and partridge to begin with)—so that we were able to draw up to the fire and repair some of the damages of the day's living. In a minute or so we were slipping freely in and out among all those objects of curiosity and interest which form in the mind in the absence of a particular person, and are naturally to be discussed on coming together again—how somebody has married, another has not; one thinks this, another that; one has improved out of all knowledge, the other most amazingly gone to the bad—with all those speculations upon human nature and the character of the amazing world we live in which spring naturally from such beginnings. While these things were being said, however, I became shamefacedly aware of a current setting in of its own accord and carrying everything forward to an end of its own. One might be talking of Spain or Portugal, of book or racehorse, but

6. Trinity, Girton, and Newnham are colleges of Cambridge University; Somerville and Christchurch are at Oxford.

the real interest of whatever was said was none of those things, but a scene of masons on a high roof some five centuries ago. Kings and nobles brought treasure in huge sacks and poured it under the earth. This scene was for ever coming alive in my mind and placing itself by another of lean cows and a muddy market and withered greens and the stringy hearts of old men—these two pictures, disjointed and disconnected and nonsensical as they were, were for ever coming together and combating each other and had me entirely at their mercy. The best course, unless the whole talk was to be distorted, was to expose what was in my mind to the air, when with good luck it would fade and crumble like the head of the dead king when they opened the coffin at Windsor. Briefly, then, I told Miss Seton about the masons who had been all those years on the roof of the chapel, and about the kings and queens and nobles bearing sacks of gold and silver on their shoulders, which they shovelled into the earth; and then how the great financial magnates of our own time came and laid cheques and bonds, I suppose, where the others had laid ingots and rough lumps of gold. All that lies beneath the colleges down there, I said; but this college, where we are now sitting, what lies beneath its gallant red brick and the wild unkempt grasses of the garden? What force is behind the plain china off which we dined, and (here it popped out of my mouth before I could stop it) the beef, the custard and the prunes?

Well, said Mary Seton, about the year 1860—Oh, but you know the story, she said, bored, I suppose, by the recital. And she told me—rooms were hired. Committees met. Envelopes were addressed. Circulars were drawn up. Meetings were held; letters were read out; so-and-so has promised so much; on the contrary, Mr ——— won't give a penny. The *Saturday Review* has been very rude. How can we raise a fund to pay for offices? Shall we hold a bazaar? Can't we find a pretty girl to sit in the front row? Let us look up what John Stuart Mill said on the subject.[7] Can any one persuade the editor of the ——— to print a letter? Can we get Lady ——— to sign it? Lady ——— is out of town. That was the way it was done, presumably, sixty years ago, and it was a prodigious effort, and a great deal of time was spent on it. And it was only after a long struggle and with the utmost difficulty that they got thirty thousand pounds together.[8] So obviously we cannot have wine and partridges and servants carrying tin dishes on their heads, she said. We cannot have sofas and separate rooms. "The amenities," she said, quoting from some book or other, "will have to wait."[9]

At the thought of all those women working year after year and finding it hard to get two thousand pounds together, and as much as they could do to get thirty thousand pounds, we burst out in scorn at the reprehensible poverty of our sex. What had our mothers been doing then that they had no wealth to leave us? Powdering their noses? Looking in at shop windows? Flaunting in the sun at Monte Carlo? There were some photographs on the mantel-piece. Mary's mother—if that was her picture—may have been a wastrel in her spare time (she had thirteen children by a minister of the church), but if so her gay and dissipated life had left too few traces of its pleasures on her face. She was a homely body; an old lady in a plaid shawl which was fastened

---

7. In 1869 Mill published his essay *The Subjection of Women*, which argued forcefully for women's suffrage and their right to equality with men.

8. "We are told that we ought to ask for £30,000 at least ... It is not a large sum, considering that there is to be but one college of this sort for Great Britain, Ireland and the Colonies, and considering how easy it is to raise immense sums for boys' schools. But considering how few people really wish women to be educated, it is a good deal."—Lady Stephen, *Life of Miss Emily Davies* [Woolf's note].

9. Every penny which could be scraped together was set aside for building, and the amenities had to be postponed.—R. Strachey, *The Cause* [Woolf's note].

by a large cameo; and she sat in a basket-chair, encouraging a spaniel to look at the camera, with the amused, yet strained expression of one who is sure that the dog will move directly the bulb is pressed. Now if she had gone into business; had become a manufacturer of artificial silk or a magnate on the Stock Exchange; if she had left two or three hundred thousand pounds to Fernham, we could have been sitting at our ease tonight and the subject of our talk might have been archaeology, botany, anthropology, physics, the nature of the atom, mathematics, astronomy, relativity, geography. If only Mrs Seton and her mother and her mother before her had learnt the great art of making money and had left their money, like their fathers and their grandfathers before them, to found fellowships and lectureships and prizes and scholarships appropriated to the use of their own sex, we might have dined very tolerably up here alone off a bird and a bottle of wine; we might have looked forward without undue confidence to a pleasant and honourable lifetime spent in the shelter of one of the liberally endowed professions. We might have been exploring or writing; mooning about the venerable places of the earth; sitting contemplative on the steps of the Parthenon, or going at ten to an office and coming home comfortably at half-past four to write a little poetry. Only, if Mrs Seton and her like had gone into business at the age of fifteen, there would have been—that was the snag in the argument—no Mary. What, I asked, did Mary think of that? There between the curtains was the October night, calm and lovely, with a star or two caught in the yellowing trees. Was she ready to resign her share of it and her memories (for they had been a happy family, though a large one) of games and quarrels up in Scotland, which she is never tired of praising for the fineness of its air and the quality of its cakes, in order that Fernham might have been endowed with fifty thousand pounds or so by a stroke of the pen? For, to endow a college would necessitate the suppression of families altogether. Making a fortune and bearing thirteen children—no human being could stand it. Consider the facts, we said. First there are nine months before the baby is born. Then the baby is born. Then there are three or four months spent in feeding the baby. After the baby is fed there are certainly five years spent in playing with the baby. You cannot, it seems, let children run about the streets. People who have seen them running wild in Russia say that the sight is not a pleasant one. People say, too, that human nature takes its shape in the years between one and five. If Mrs Seton, I said, had been making money, what sort of memories would you have had of games and quarrels? What would you have known of Scotland, and its fine air and cakes and all the rest of it? But it is useless to ask these questions, because you would never have come into existence at all. Moreover, it is equally useless to ask what might have happened if Mrs Seton and her mother and her mother before her had amassed great wealth and laid it under the foundations of college and library, because, in the first place, to earn money was impossible for them, and in the second, had it been possible, the law denied them the right to possess what money they earned. It is only for the last forty-eight years that Mrs Seton has had a penny of her own. For all the centuries before that it would have been her husband's property—a thought which, perhaps, may have had its share in keeping Mrs Seton and her mothers off the Stock Exchange.[1] Every penny I earn, they may have said, will be taken from me and disposed of

1. The late 19th century saw the passage of legislation designed to improve the legal status of women. In 1870 the Married Women's Property Act allowed women to retain £200 of their own earnings (which previously had automatically become the property of her husband); in 1884 a further act gave married women the same rights over property as unmarried women, and allowed them to carry on trades or businesses using their property.

according to my husband's wisdom—perhaps to found a scholarship or to endow a fellowship in Balliol or Kings,[2] so that to earn money, even if I could earn money, is not a matter that interests me very greatly. I had better leave it to my husband.

At any rate, whether or not the blame rested on the old lady who was looking at the spaniel, there could be no doubt that for some reason or other our mothers had mismanaged their affairs very gravely. Not a penny could be spared for "amenities"; for partridges and wine, beadles and turf, books and cigars, libraries and leisure. To raise bare walls out of the bare earth was the utmost they could do.

So we talked standing at the window and looking, as so many thousands look every night, down on the domes and towers of the famous city beneath us. It was very beautiful, very mysterious in the autumn moonlight. The old stone looked very white and venerable. One thought of all the books that were assembled down there; of the pictures of old prelates and worthies hanging in the panelled rooms; of the painted windows that would be throwing strange globes and crescents on the pavement; of the tablets and memorials and inscriptions; of the fountains and the grass; of the quiet rooms looking across the quiet quadrangles. And (pardon me the thought) I thought, too, of the admirable smoke and drink and the deep armchairs and the pleasant carpets: of the urbanity, the geniality, the dignity which are the offspring of luxury and privacy and space. Certainly our mothers had not provided us with anything comparable to all this—our mothers who found it difficult to scrape together thirty thousand pounds, our mothers who bore thirteen children to ministers of religion at St Andrews.

So I went back to my inn, and as I walked through the dark streets I pondered this and that, as one does at the end of the day's work. I pondered why it was that Mrs Seton had no money to leave us; and what effect poverty has on the mind; and what effect wealth has on the mind; and I thought of the queer old gentlemen I had seen that morning with tufts of fur upon their shoulders; and I remembered how if one whistled one of them ran; and I thought of the organ booming in the chapel and of the shut doors of the library; and I thought how unpleasant it is to be locked out; and I thought how it is worse perhaps to be locked in; and, thinking of the safety and prosperity of the one sex and of the poverty and insecurity of the other and of the effect of tradition and of the lack of tradition upon the mind of a writer, I thought at last that it was time to roll up the crumpled skin of the day, with its arguments and its impressions and its anger and its laughter, and cast it into the hedge. A thousand stars were flashing across the blue wastes of the sky. One seemed alone with an inscrutable society. All human beings were laid asleep—prone, horizontal, dumb. Nobody seemed stirring in the streets of Oxbridge. Even the door of the hotel sprang open at the touch of an invisible hand—not a boots was sitting up to light me to bed, it was so late.

from *Chapter 3*

It would have been impossible, completely and entirely, for any woman to have written the plays of Shakespeare in the age of Shakespeare. Let me imagine, since facts are so hard to come by, what would have happened had Shakespeare had a wonderfully gifted sister, called Judith, let us say. Shakespeare himself went, very probably—his mother was an heiress—to the grammar school, where he may have learnt

2. Balliol is a college of Oxford University; King's is at Cambridge.

Latin—Ovid, Virgil, and Horace—and the elements of grammar and logic. He was, it is well known, a wild boy who poached rabbits, perhaps shot a deer, and had, rather sooner than he should have done, to marry a woman in the neighbourhood, who bore him a child rather quicker than was right. That escapade sent him to seek his fortune in London. He had, it seemed, a taste for the theatre; he began by holding horses at the stage door. Very soon he got work in the theatre, became a successful actor, and lived at the hub of the universe, meeting everybody, knowing everybody, practising his art on the boards, exercising his wits in the streets, and even getting access to the palace of the queen. Meanwhile his extraordinarily gifted sister, let us suppose, remained at home. She was as adventurous, as imaginative, as agog to see the world as he was. But she was not sent to school. She had no chance of learning grammar and logic, let alone of reading Horace and Virgil. She picked up a book now and then, one of her brother's perhaps, and read a few pages. But then her parents came in and told her to mend the stockings or mind the stew and not moon about with books and papers. They would have spoken sharply but kindly, for they were substantial people who knew the conditions of life for a woman and loved their daughter—indeed, more likely than not she was the apple of her father's eye. Perhaps she scribbled some pages up in an apple loft on the sly, but was careful to hide them or set fire to them. Soon, however, before she was out of her teens, she was to be betrothed to the son of a neighbouring wool-stapler. She cried out that marriage was hateful to her, and for that she was severely beaten by her father. Then he ceased to scold her. He begged her instead not to hurt him, not to shame him in this matter of her marriage. He would give her a chain of beads or a fine petticoat, he said; and there were tears in his eyes. How could she disobey him? How could she break his heart? The force of her own gift alone drove her to it. She made up a small parcel of her belongings, let herself down by a rope one summer's night and took the road to London. She was not seventeen. The birds that sang in the hedge were not more musical than she was. She had the quickest fancy, a gift like her brother's, for the tune of words. Like him, she had a taste for the theatre. She stood at the stage door; she wanted to act, she said. Men laughed in her face. The manager—a fat, loose-lipped man—guffawed. He bellowed something about poodles dancing and women acting—no woman, he said, could possibly be an actress. He hinted—you can imagine what. She could get no training in her craft. Could she even seek her dinner in a tavern or roam the streets at midnight? Yet her genius was for fiction and lusted to feed abundantly upon the lives of men and women and the study of their ways. At last—for she was very young, oddly like Shakespeare the poet in her face, with the same grey eyes and rounded brows—at last Nick Greene the actor-manager took pity on her; she found herself with child by that gentleman and so—who shall measure the heat and violence of the poet's heart when caught and tangled in a woman's body?—killed herself one winter's night and lies buried at some cross-roads where the omnibuses now stop outside the Elephant and Castle.[3]

That, more or less, is how the story would run, I think, if a woman in Shakespeare's day had had Shakespeare's genius. But for my part, I agree with the deceased bishop, if such he was—it is unthinkable that any woman in Shakespeare's day should have had Shakespeare's genius. For genius like Shakespeare's is not born among labouring, uneducated, servile people. It was not born in England among the Saxons and the Britons. It is not born today among the working classes. How, then,

---

3. A tavern on the outskirts of South London.

could it have been born among women whose work began, according to Professor Trevelyan,[4] almost before they were out of the nursery, who were forced to it by their parents and held to it by all the power of law and custom? Yet genius of a sort must have existed among women as it must have existed among the working classes. Now and again an Emily Brontë or a Robert Burns blazes out and proves its presence. But certainly it never got itself on to paper. When, however, one reads of a witch being ducked, of a woman possessed by devils, of a wise woman selling herbs, or even of a very remarkable man who had a mother, then I think we are on the track of a lost novelist, a suppressed poet, of some mute and inglorious Jane Austen, some Emily Brontë who dashed her brains out on the moor or mopped and mowed about the highways crazed with the torture that her gift had put her to. Indeed, I would venture to guess that Anon, who wrote so many poems without signing them, was often a woman. It was a woman Edward Fitzgerald,[5] I think, suggested who made the ballads and the folk-songs, crooning them to her children, beguiling her spinning with them, or the length of the winter's night.

This may be true or it may be false—who can say?—but what is true in it, so it seemed to me, reviewing the story of Shakespeare's sister as I had made it, is that any woman born with a great gift in the sixteenth century would certainly have gone crazed, shot herself, or ended her days in some lonely cottage outside the village, half witch, half wizard, feared and mocked at. For it needs little skill in psychology to be sure that a highly gifted girl who had tried to use her gift for poetry would have been so thwarted and hindered by other people, so tortured and pulled asunder by her own contrary instincts, that she must have lost her health and sanity to a certainty. No girl could have walked to London and stood at a stage door and forced her way into the presence of actor-managers without doing herself a violence and suffering an anguish which may have been irrational—for chastity may be a fetish invented by certain societies for unknown reasons—but were none the less inevitable. Chastity had then, it has even now, a religious importance in a woman's life, and has so wrapped itself round with nerves and instincts that to cut it free and bring it to the light of day demands courage of the rarest. To have lived a free life in London in the sixteenth century would have meant for a woman who was poet and playwright a nervous stress and dilemma which might well have killed her. Had she survived, whatever she had written would have been twisted and deformed, issuing from a strained and morbid imagination. And undoubtedly, I thought, looking at the shelf where there are no plays by women, her work would have gone unsigned. That refuge she would have sought certainly. It was the relic of the sense of chastity that dictated anonymity to women even so late as the nineteenth century. Currer Bell, George Eliot, George Sand,[6] all the victims of inner strife as their writings prove, sought ineffectively to veil themselves by using the name of a man. Thus they did homage to the convention, which if not implanted by the other sex was liberally encouraged by them (the chief glory of a woman is not to be talked of, said Pericles, himself a much-talked-of man), that publicity in women is detestable.[7] Anonymity runs in their blood. The desire to be veiled still possesses them. They are not even now as concerned about the health of their fame as men are, and, speaking generally, will pass a

4. George Trevelyan (1876–1962), historian.
5. Poet and translator (1809–1883).
6. Currer Bell, pen name of Charlotte Brontë; George Eliot, pen name of Mary Ann Evans; George Sand, pen name of Amandine Aurore Lucille Dupin (1804–1876).

7. The Athenian statesman Pericles was reported by the historian Thucydides to have said, "That woman is most praiseworthy whose name is least bandied about on men's lips, whether for praise or dispraise."

tombstone or a signpost without feeling an irresistible desire to cut their names on it, as Alf, Bert or Chas. must do in obedience to their instinct, which murmurs if it sees a fine woman go by, or even a dog, Ce chien est à moi [that dog is mine]. And, of course, it may not be a dog, I thought, remembering Parliament Square, the Sieges Allee[8] and other avenues; it may be a piece of land or a man with curly black hair. It is one of the great advantages of being a woman that one can pass even a very fine negress without wishing to make an Englishwoman of her.

That woman, then, who was born with a gift of poetry in the sixteenth century, was an unhappy woman, a woman at strife against herself. All the conditions of her life, all her own instincts, were hostile to the state of mind which is needed to set free whatever is in the brain. But what is the state of mind that is most propitious to the act of creation, I asked. Can one come by any notion of the state that furthers and makes possible that strange activity? Here I opened the volume containing the Tragedies of Shakespeare. What was Shakespeare's state of mind, for instance, when he wrote *Lear* and *Antony and Cleopatra*? It was certainly the state of mind most favourable to poetry that there has ever existed. But Shakespeare himself said nothing about it. We only know casually and by chance that he "never blotted a line." Nothing indeed was ever said by the artist himself about his state of mind until the eighteenth century perhaps. Rousseau perhaps began it.[9] At any rate, by the nineteenth century self-consciousness had developed so far that it was the habit for men of letters to describe their minds in confessions and autobiographies. Their lives also were written, and their letters were printed after their deaths. Thus, though we do not know what Shakespeare went through when he wrote *Lear*, we do know what Carlyle went through when he wrote the *French Revolution*; what Flaubert went through when he wrote *Madame Bovary*; what Keats was going through when he tried to write poetry against the coming of death and the indifference of the world.

And one gathers from this enormous modern literature of confession and self-analysis that to write a work of genius is almost always a feat of prodigious difficulty. Everything is against the likelihood that it will come from the writer's mind whole and entire. Generally material circumstances are against it. Dogs will bark; people will interrupt; money must be made; health will break down. Further, accentuating all these difficulties and making them harder to bear is the world's notorious indifference. It does not ask people to write poems and novels and histories; it does not need them. It does not care whether Flaubert finds the right word or whether Carlyle scrupulously verifies this or that fact. Naturally, it will not pay for what it does not want. And so the writer, Keats, Flaubert, Carlyle, suffers, especially in the creative years of youth, every form of distraction and discouragement. A curse, a cry of agony, rises from those books of analysis and confession. "Mighty poets in their misery dead"—that is the burden of their song. If anything comes through in spite of all this, it is a miracle, and probably no book is born entire and uncrippled as it was conceived.

But for women, I thought, looking at the empty shelves, these difficulties were infinitely more formidable. In the first place, to have a room of her own, let alone a quiet room or a sound-proof room, was out of the question, unless her parents were exceptionally rich or very noble, even up to the beginning of the nineteenth century. Since her pin money, which depended on the good will of her father, was only enough to keep her clothed, she was debarred from such alleviations as came even to

8. Victory Road, a thoroughfare in Berlin.
9. Jean-Jacques Rousseau, 18th-century political philoso-

pher and novelist, author of a famous memoir, *Confessions*.

Keats or Tennyson or Carlyle, all poor men, from a walking tour, a little journey to France, from the separate lodging which, even if it were miserable enough, sheltered them from the claims and tyrannies of their families. Such material difficulties were formidable; but much worse were the immaterial. The indifference of the world which Keats and Flaubert and other men of genius have found so hard to bear was in her case not indifference but hostility. The world did not say to her as it said to them, Write if you choose; it makes no difference to me. The world said with a guffaw, Write? What's the good of your writing? Here the psychologists of Newnham and Girton might come to our help, I thought, looking again at the blank spaces on the shelves. For surely it is time that the effect of discouragement upon the mind of the artist should be measured, as I have seen a dairy company measure the effect of ordinary milk and Grade A milk upon the body of the rat. They set two rats in cages side by side, and of the two one was furtive, timid and small, and the other was glossy, bold and big. Now what food do we feed women as artists upon? I asked, remembering, I suppose, that dinner of prunes and custard. To answer that question I had only to open the evening paper and to read that Lord Birkenhead is of opinion—but really I am not going to trouble to copy out Lord Birkenhead's opinion upon the writing of women. What Dean Inge says I will leave in peace.[1] The Harley Street specialist may be allowed to rouse the echoes of Harley Street with his vociferations without raising a hair on my head. I will quote, however, Mr Oscar Browning,[2] because Mr Oscar Browning was a great figure in Cambridge at one time, and used to examine the students at Girton and Newnham. Mr Oscar Browning was wont to declare "that the impression left on his mind, after looking over any set of examination papers, was that, irrespective of the marks he might give, the best woman was intellectually the inferior of the worst man." After saying that Mr Browning went back to his rooms— and it is this sequel that endears him and makes him a human figure of some bulk and majesty—he went back to his rooms and found a stable-boy lying on the sofa—"a mere skeleton, his cheeks were cavernous and sallow, his teeth were black, and he did not appear to have the full use of his limbs. . . . 'That's Arthur' [said Mr Browning]. 'He's a dear boy really and most high-minded.'" The two pictures always seem to me to complete each other. And happily in this age of biography the two pictures often do complete each other, so that we are able to interpret the opinions of great men not only by what they say, but by what they do.

But though this is possible now, such opinions coming from the lips of important people must have been formidable enough even fifty years ago. Let us suppose that a father from the highest motives did not wish his daughter to leave home and become writer, painter or scholar. "See what Mr Oscar Browning says," he would say; and there was not only Mr Oscar Browning; there was the Saturday Review; there was Mr Greg[3]—the "essentials of a woman's being," said Mr Greg emphatically, "are that *they are supported by, and they minister to, men*"—there was an enormous body of masculine opinion to the effect that nothing could be expected of women intellectually. Even if her father did not read out loud these opinions, any girl could read them for herself; and the reading, even in the nineteenth century, must have lowered her vitality, and told profoundly upon her work. There would always have been that assertion—you cannot do this, you are incapable of doing that—to protest against, to overcome.

1. F. E. Smith, Lord Birkenhead (1872–1930), British statesman; William Ralph Inge (1860–1954), Dean of St. Paul's Cathedral in London.

2. Cambridge historian (1837–1923).
3. Sir Walter Greg (1879–1959), scholar and bibliographer.

Probably for a novelist this germ is no longer of much effect; for there have been women novelists of merit. But for painters it must still have some sting in it; and for musicians, I imagine, is even now active and poisonous in the extreme. The woman composer stands where the actress stood in the time of Shakespeare. Nick Greene, I thought, remembering the story I had made about Shakespeare's sister, said that a woman acting put him in mind of a dog dancing. Johnson repeated the phrase two hundred years later of women preaching.[4] And here, I said, opening a book about music, we have the very words used again in this year of grace, 1928, of women who try to write music. "Of Mlle. Germaine Tailleferre one can only repeat Dr. Johnson's dictum concerning a woman preacher, transposed into terms of music. 'Sir, a woman's composing is like a dog's walking on his hind legs. It is not done well, but you are surprised to find it done at all.'"[5] So accurately does history repeat itself.

Thus, I concluded, shutting Mr Oscar Browning's life and pushing away the rest, it is fairly evident that even in the nineteenth century a woman was not encouraged to be an artist. On the contrary, she was snubbed, slapped, lectured and exhorted. Her mind must have been strained and her vitality lowered by the need of opposing this, of disproving that. For here again we come within range of that very interesting and obscure masculine complex which has had so much influence upon the woman's movement; that deep-seated desire, not so much that *she* shall be inferior as that *he* shall be superior, which plants him wherever one looks, not only in front of the arts, but barring the way to politics too, even when the risk to himself seems infinitesimal and the suppliant humble and devoted. Even Lady Bessborough, I remembered, with all her passion for politics, must humbly bow herself and write to Lord Granville Leveson-Gower:[6] ". . . notwithstanding all my violence in politics and talking so much on that subject, I perfectly agree with you that no woman has any business to meddle with that or any other serious business, farther than giving her opinion (if she is ask'd)." And so she goes on to spend her enthusiasm where it meets with no obstacle whatsoever upon that immensely important subject, Lord Granville's maiden speech in the House of Commons. The spectacle is certainly a strange one, I thought. The history of men's opposition to women's emancipation is more interesting perhaps than the story of that emancipation itself. An amusing book might be made of it if some young student at Girton or Newnham would collect examples and deduce a theory—but she would need thick gloves on her hands, and bars to protect her of solid gold.

But what is amusing now, I recollected, shutting Lady Bessborough, had to be taken in desperate earnest once. Opinions that one now pastes in a book labelled cock-a-doodle-dum and keeps for reading to select audiences on summer nights once drew tears, I can assure you. Among your grandmothers and great-grandmothers there were many that wept their eyes out. Florence Nightingale shrieked aloud in her agony.[7] Moreover, it is all very well for you, who have got yourselves to college and enjoy sitting-rooms—or is it only bed-sitting-rooms?—of your own to say that genius should disregard such opinions; that genius should be above caring what is said of it. Unfortunately, it is precisely the men or women of genius who mind most what is said of them. Remember Keats. Remember the words he had cut on his tombstone.

---

4. Samuel Johnson (1709–1784), poet and man of letters.
5. *A Survey of Contemporary Music*, Cecil Gray, p. 246 [Woolf's note].
6. Lady Bessborough (1761–1821), correspondent of the

British statesman Lord Granville.
7. See *Cassandra*, by Florence Nightingale, printed in *The Cause*, by R. Strachey [Woolf's note]; see page 1583.

Think of Tennyson; think—but I need hardly multiply instances of the undeniable, if very unfortunate, fact that it is the nature of the artist to mind excessively what is said about him. Literature is strewn with the wreckage of men who have minded beyond reason the opinions of others.

And this susceptibility of theirs is doubly unfortunate, I thought, returning again to my original enquiry into what state of mind is most propitious for creative work, because the mind of an artist, in order to achieve the prodigious effort of freeing whole and entire the work that is in him, must be incandescent, like Shakespeare's mind, I conjectured, looking at the book which lay open at *Antony and Cleopatra*. There must be no obstacle in it, no foreign matter unconsumed.

For though we say that we know nothing about Shakespeare's state of mind, even as we say that, we are saying something about Shakespeare's state of mind. The reason perhaps why we know so little of Shakespeare—compared with Donne or Ben Jonson or Milton—is that his grudges and spites and antipathies are hidden from us. We are not held up by some "revelation" which reminds us of the writer. All desire to protest, to preach, to proclaim an injury, to pay off a score, to make the world the witness of some hardship or grievance was fired out of him and consumed. Therefore his poetry flows from him free and unimpeded. If ever a human being got his work expressed completely, it was Shakespeare. If ever a mind was incandescent, unimpeded, I thought, turning again to the bookcase, it was Shakespeare's mind.

from *Chapter 4*

The extreme activity of mind which showed itself in the later eighteenth century among women—the talking, and the meeting, the writing of essays on Shakespeare, the translating of the classics—was founded on the solid fact that women could make money by writing. Money dignifies what is frivolous if unpaid for. It might still be well to sneer at "blue stockings with an itch for scribbling," but it could not be denied that they could put money in their purses. Thus, towards the end of the eighteenth century a change came about which, if I were rewriting history, I should describe more fully and think of greater importance than the Crusades or the Wars of the Roses. The middle-class woman began to write. For if *Pride and Prejudice* matters, and *Middlemarch* and *Villette* and *Wuthering Heights* matter,[8] then it matters far more than I can prove in an hour's discourse that women generally, and not merely the lonely aristocrat shut up in her country house among her folios and her flatterers, took to writing. Without those forerunners, Jane Austen and the Brontës and George Eliot could no more have written than Shakespeare could have written without Marlowe, or Marlowe without Chaucer, or Chaucer without those forgotten poets who paved the ways and tamed the natural savagery of the tongue. For masterpieces are not single and solitary births; they are the outcome of many years of thinking in common, of thinking by the body of the people, so that the experience of the mass is behind the single voice. Jane Austen should have laid a wreath upon the grave of Fanny Burney, and George Eliot done homage to the robust shade of Eliza Carter—the valiant old woman who tied a bell to her bedstead in order that she might wake early and learn Greek. All women together ought to let flowers fall upon the tomb of Aphra Behn[9]

8. *Pride and Prejudice* (1813), a novel by Jane Austen; *Middlemarch* (1871–1872) by George Eliot; *Villette* (1853) by Charlotte Brontë; *Wuthering Heights* (1847) by Emily Brontë.
9. A dramatist and the first English woman to earn a living by writing (1640–1689). Westminster Abbey, in central London, is the burial place of many of the English kings and queens, as well as of famous poets and statesmen.

which is, most scandalously but rather appropriately, in Westminster Abbey, for it was she who earned them the right to speak their minds. It is she—shady and amorous as she was—who makes it not quite fantastic for me to say to you tonight: Earn five hundred a year by your wits.

Here, then, one had reached the early nineteenth century. And here, for the first time, I found several shelves given up entirely to the works of women. But why, I could not help asking, as I ran my eyes over them, were they, with very few exceptions, all novels? The original impulse was to poetry. The "supreme head of song" was a poetess. Both in France and in England the women poets precede the women novelists. Moreover, I thought, looking at the four famous names, what had George Eliot in common with Emily Brontë? Did not Charlotte Brontë fail entirely to understand Jane Austen? Save for the possibly relevant fact that not one of them had a child, four more incongruous characters could not have met together in a room—so much so that it is tempting to invent a meeting and a dialogue between them. Yet by some strange force they were all compelled, when they wrote, to write novels. Had it something to do with being born of the middle class, I asked; and with the fact, which Miss Emily Davies a little later was so strikingly to demonstrate,[1] that the middle-class family in the early nineteenth century was possessed only of a single sitting-room between them? If a woman wrote, she would have to write in the common sitting-room. And, as Miss Nightingale was so vehemently to complain,—"women never have an half hour . . . that they can call their own"—she was always interrupted. Still it would be easier to write prose and fiction there than to write poetry or a play. Less concentration is required. Jane Austen wrote like that to the end of her days. "How she was able to effect all this," her nephew writes in his Memoir, "is surprising, for she had no separate study to repair to, and most of the work must have been done in the general sitting-room, subject to all kinds of casual interruptions. She was careful that her occupation should not be suspected by servants or visitors or any persons beyond her own family party."[2] Jane Austen hid her manuscripts or covered them with a piece of blotting-paper. Then, again, all the literary training that a woman had in the early nineteenth century was training in the observation of character, in the analysis of emotion. Her sensibility had been educated for centuries by the influences of the common sitting-room. People's feelings were impressed on her; personal relations were always before her eyes. Therefore, when the middle-class woman took to writing, she naturally wrote novels, even though, as seems evident enough, two of the four famous women here named were not by nature novelists. Emily Brontë should have written poetic plays; the overflow of George Eliot's capacious mind should have spread itself when the creative impulse was spent upon history or biography. They wrote novels, however; one may even go further, I said, taking Pride and Prejudice from the shelf, and say that they wrote good novels. Without boasting or giving pain to the opposite sex, one may say that Pride and Prejudice is a good book. At any rate, one would not have been ashamed to have been caught in the act of writing Pride and Prejudice. Yet Jane Austen was glad that a hinge creaked, so that she might hide her manuscript before any one came in. To Jane Austen there was something discreditable in writing Pride and Prejudice. And, I wondered, would Pride and Prejudice have been a better novel if Jane Austen had not thought it necessary to hide her manuscript from visitors? I read a page or two to see; but I could not

1. (Sarah) Emily Davies was prominent in the movement to secure university education for women in the 19th century and was chief founder of Girton College, Cambridge (1873).

2. Memoir of Jane Austen, by her nephew, James Edward Austen-Leigh [Woolf's note].

find any signs that her circumstances had harmed her work in the slightest. That, perhaps, was the chief miracle about it. Here was a woman about the year 1800 writing without hate, without bitterness, without fear, without protest, without preaching. That was how Shakespeare wrote, I thought, looking at *Antony and Cleopatra*; and when people compare Shakespeare and Jane Austen, they may mean that the minds of both had consumed all impediments; and for that reason we do not know Jane Austen and we do not know Shakespeare, and for that reason Jane Austen pervades every word that she wrote, and so does Shakespeare. If Jane Austen suffered in any way from her circumstances it was in the narrowness of life that was imposed upon her. It was impossible for a woman to go about alone. She never travelled; she never drove through London in an omnibus or had luncheon in a shop by herself. But perhaps it was the nature of Jane Austen not to want what she had not. Her gift and her circumstances matched each other completely. But I doubt whether that was true of Charlotte Brontë, I said, opening *Jane Eyre* and laying it beside *Pride and Prejudice*.[3]

I opened it at chapter twelve and my eye was caught by the phrase, "Anybody may blame me who likes." What were they blaming Charlotte Brontë for, I wondered? And I read how Jane Eyre used to go up on to the roof when Mrs Fairfax was making jellies and looked over the fields at the distant view. And then she longed—and it was for this that they blamed her—that "then I longed for a power of vision which might overpass that limit; which might reach the busy world, towns, regions full of life I had heard of but never seen: that then I desired more of practical experience than I possessed; more of intercourse with my kind, of acquaintance with variety of character than was here within my reach. I valued what was good in Mrs Fairfax, and what was good in Adèle; but I believed in the existence of other and more vivid kinds of goodness, and what I believed in I wished to behold.

"Who blames me? Many, no doubt, and I shall be called discontented. I could not help it: the restlessness was in my nature; it agitated me to pain sometimes. . . .

"It is vain to say human beings ought to be satisfied with tranquillity: they must have action; and they will make it if they cannot find it. Millions are condemned to a stiller doom than mine, and millions are in silent revolt against their lot. Nobody knows how many rebellions ferment in the masses of life which people earth. Women are supposed to be very calm generally: but women feel just as men feel; they need exercise for their faculties and a field for their efforts as much as their brothers do; they suffer from too rigid a restraint, too absolute a stagnation, precisely as men would suffer; and it is narrow-minded in their more privileged fellow-creatures to say that they ought to confine themselves to making puddings and knitting stockings, to playing on the piano and embroidering bags. It is thoughtless to condemn them, or laugh at them, if they seek to do more or learn more than custom has pronounced necessary for their sex.

"When thus alone I not unfrequently heard Grace Poole's laugh. . . ."

That is an awkward break, I thought. It is upsetting to come upon Grace Poole all of a sudden. The continuity is disturbed. One might say, I continued, laying the book down beside *Pride and Prejudice*, that the woman who wrote those pages had

---

3. Woolf goes on to describe parts of the plot of *Jane Eyre*; Jane Eyre, a penniless orphan, having suffered greatly during her schooling, takes up the post of governess to Adele, the daughter of Mr. Rochester, a man of strange moods. Rochester falls in love with Jane, who agrees to marry him; however this is prevented by Rochester's mad wife—whom Rochester has locked in the attic, concealing her existence from Jane—who tears Jane's wedding veil on the eve of the marriage. Rochester at first tells Jane that Grace Poole, a servant, had been responsible for this and other strange events, including the uncanny laughter occasionally heard in the house.

more genius in her than Jane Austen; but if one reads them over and marks that jerk in them, that indignation, one sees that she will never get her genius expressed whole and entire. Her books will be deformed and twisted. She will write in a rage where she should write calmly. She will write foolishly where she should write wisely. She will write of herself where she should write of her characters. She is at war with her lot. How could she help but die young, cramped and thwarted?

One could not but play for a moment with the thought of what might have happened if Charlotte Brontë had possessed say three hundred a year—but the foolish woman sold the copyright of her novels outright for fifteen hundred pounds; had somehow possessed more knowledge of the busy world, and towns and regions full of life; more practical experience, and intercourse with her kind and acquaintance with a variety of character. In those words she puts her finger exactly not only upon her own defects as a novelist but upon those of her sex at that time. She knew, no one better, how enormously her genius would have profited if it had not spent itself in solitary visions over distant fields; if experience and intercourse and travel had been granted her. But they were not granted; they were withheld; and we must accept the fact that all those good novels, *Villette, Emma, Wuthering Heights, Middlemarch*, were written by women without more experience of life than could enter the house of a respectable clergyman; written too in the common sitting-room of that respectable house and by women so poor that they could not afford to buy more than a few quires of paper at a time upon which to write *Wuthering Heights* or *Jane Eyre*. One of them, it is true, George Eliot, escaped after much tribulation, but only to a secluded villa in St John's Wood. And there she settled down in the shadow of the world's disapproval.[4] "I wish it to be understood," she wrote, "that I should never invite any one to come and see me who did not ask for the invitation"; for was she not living in sin with a married man and might not the sight of her damage the chastity of Mrs Smith or whoever it might be that chanced to call? One must submit to the social convention, and be "cut off from what is called the world." At the same time, on the other side of Europe, there was a young man living freely with this gipsy or with that great lady; going to the wars; picking up unhindered and uncensored all that varied experience of human life which served him so splendidly later when he came to write his books. Had Tolstoi lived at the Priory in seclusion with a married lady "cut off from what is called the world," however edifying the moral lesson, he could scarcely, I thought, have written *War and Peace*.

But one could perhaps go a little deeper into the question of novel-writing and the effect of sex upon the novelist. If one shuts one's eyes and thinks of the novel as a whole, it would seem to be a creation owning a certain looking-glass likeness to life, though of course with simplifications and distortions innumerable. At any rate, it is a structure leaving a shape on the mind's eye, built now in squares, now pagoda shaped, now throwing out wings and arcades, now solidly compact and domed like the Cathedral of Saint Sofia at Constantinople.[5] This shape, I thought, thinking back over certain famous novels, starts in one the kind of emotion that is appropriate to it. But that emotion at once blends itself with others, for the "shape" is not made by the relation of stone to stone, but by the relation of human being to human being. Thus

---

4. Following a strictly religious childhood, the novelist George Eliot lost her faith and eloped with G. H. Lewes, a married man, with whom she lived for the rest of his life; her family never forgave her.

5. The Hagia Sophia, a domed basilica completed in A.D. 537, named for the female personification of Wisdom in the Bible.

a novel starts in us all sorts of antagonistic and opposed emotions. Life conflicts with something that is not life. Hence the difficulty of coming to any agreement about novels, and the immense sway that our private prejudices have upon us. On the one hand, we feel, You—John the hero—must live, or I shall be in the depths of despair. On the other, we feel, Alas, John, you must die, because the shape of the book requires it. Life conflicts with something that is not life. Then since life it is in part, we judge it as life. James is the sort of man I most detest, one says. Or, This is a farrago of absurdity. I could never feel anything of the sort myself. The whole structure, it is obvious, thinking back on any famous novel, is one of infinite complexity, because it is thus made up of so many different judgments, of so many different kinds of emotion. The wonder is that any book so composed holds together for more than a year or two, or can possibly mean to the English reader what it means for the Russian or the Chinese. But they do hold together occasionally very remarkably. And what holds them together in these rare instances of survival (I was thinking of *War and Peace*) is something that one calls integrity, though it has nothing to do with paying one's bills or behaving honourably in an emergency. What one means by integrity, in the case of the novelist, is the conviction that he gives one that this is the truth. Yes, one feels, I should never have thought that this could be so; I have never known people behaving like that. But you have convinced me that so it is, so it happens. One holds every phrase, every scene to the light as one reads—for Nature seems, very oddly, to have provided us with an inner light by which to judge of the novelist's integrity or disintegrity. Or perhaps it is rather that Nature, in her most irrational mood, has traced in invisible ink on the walls of the mind a premonition which these great artists confirm; a sketch which only needs to be held to the fire of genius to become visible. When one so exposes it and sees it come to life one exclaims in rapture, But this is what I have always felt and known and desired! And one boils over with excitement, and, shutting the book even with a kind of reverence as if it were something very precious, a stand-by to return to as long as one lives, one puts it back on the shelf, I said, taking *War and Peace* and putting it back in its place. If, on the other hand, these poor sentences that one takes and tests rouse first a quick and eager response with their bright colouring and their dashing gestures but there they stop: something seems to check them in their development: or if they bring to light only a faint scribble in that corner and a blot over there, and nothing appears whole and entire, then one heaves a sigh of disappointment and says, Another failure. This novel has come to grief somewhere.

And for the most part, of course, novels do come to grief somewhere. The imagination falters under the enormous strain. The insight is confused; it can no longer distinguish between the true and the false; it has no longer the strength to go on with the vast labour that calls at every moment for the use of so many different faculties. But how would all this be affected by the sex of the novelist, I wondered, looking at *Jane Eyre* and the others. Would the fact of her sex in any way interfere with the integrity of a woman novelist—that integrity which I take to be the backbone of the writer? Now, in the passages I have quoted from *Jane Eyre*, it is clear that anger was tampering with the integrity of Charlotte Brontë the novelist. She left her story, to which her entire devotion was due, to attend to some personal grievance. She remembered that she had been starved of her proper due of experience—she had been made to stagnate in a parsonage mending stockings when she wanted to wander free over the world. Her imagination swerved from indignation and we feel it swerve. But there were many more influences than anger tugging at her imagination and deflecting it from its path. Ignorance, for instance. The portrait of Rochester is drawn in the dark. We feel the influence of fear in it; just as we constantly feel an acidity which is the result of oppression, a buried suffering smouldering beneath her passion, a rancour which contracts those books, splendid as they are, with a spasm of pain.

And since a novel has this correspondence to real life, its values are to some extent those of real life. But it is obvious that the values of women differ very often from the values which have been made by the other sex; naturally, this is so. Yet it is the masculine values that prevail. Speaking crudely, football and sport are "important"; the worship of fashion, the buying of clothes "trivial." And these values are inevitably transferred from life to fiction. This is an important book, the critic assumes, because it deals with war. This is an insignificant book because it deals with the feelings of women in a drawing-room. A scene in a battlefield is more important than a scene in a shop—everywhere and much more subtly the difference of value persists. The whole structure, therefore, of the early nineteenth-century novel was raised, if one was a woman, by a mind which was slightly pulled from the straight, and made to alter its clear vision in deference to external authority. One has only to skim those old forgotten novels and listen to the tone of voice in which they are written to divine that the writer was meeting criticism; she was saying this by way of aggression, or that by way of conciliation. She was admitting that she was "only a woman," or protesting that she was "as good as a man." She met that criticism as her temperament dictated, with docility and diffidence, or with anger and emphasis. It does not matter which it was; she was thinking of something other than the thing itself. Down comes her book upon our heads. There was a flaw in the centre of it. And I thought of all the women's novels that lie scattered, like small pock-marked apples in an orchard, about the secondhand book shops of London. It was the flaw in the centre that had rotted them. She had altered her values in deference to the opinion of others.

But how impossible it must have been for them not to budge either to the right or to the left. What genius, what integrity it must have required in face of all that criticism, in the midst of that purely patriarchal society, to hold fast to the thing as they saw it without shrinking. Only Jane Austen did it and Emily Brontë. It is another feather, perhaps the finest, in their caps. They wrote as women write, not as men write. Of all the thousand women who wrote novels then, they alone entirely ignored the perpetual admonitions of the eternal pedagogue—write this, think that. They alone were deaf to that persistent voice, now grumbling, now patronising, now domineering, now grieved, now shocked, now angry, now avuncular, that voice which cannot let women alone, but must be at them, like some too conscientious governess, adjuring them, like Sir Egerton Brydges,[6] to be refined; dragging even into the criticism of poetry criticism of sex; admonishing them, if they would be good and win, as I suppose, some shiny prize, to keep within certain limits which the gentleman in question thinks suitable:[7] ". . . female novelists should only aspire to excellence by courageously acknowledging the limitations of their sex."[8] That puts the matter in a

6. Scholar and editor (1762–1837), Brydges had criticized the writings of Margaret Cavendish, Duchess of Newcastle (1623–1674), for what he considered to be their coarse language.
7. "[She] has a metaphysical purpose, and that is a dangerous obsession, especially with a woman, for women rarely possess men's healthy love of rhetoric. It is a strange lack in the sex which is in other things more primitive and more materialistic."—New Criterion, June 1928 [Woolf's note].
8. "If, like the reporter, you believe that female novelists should only aspire to excellence by courageously acknowledging the limitations of their sex (Jane Austen [has] demonstrated how gracefully this gesture can be accomplished). . . ." —Life and Letters, August 1928 [Woolf's note].

nutshell, and when I tell you, rather to your surprise, that this sentence was written not in August 1828 but in August 1928, you will agree, I think, that however delightful it is to us now, it represents a vast body of opinion—I am not going to stir those old pools, I take only what chance has floated to my feet—that was far more vigorous and far more vocal a century ago. It would have needed a very stalwart young woman in 1828 to disregard all those snubs and chidings and promises of prizes. One must have been something of a firebrand to say to oneself, Oh, but they can't buy literature too. Literature is open to everybody. I refuse to allow you, Beadle though you are, to turn me off the grass. Lock up your libraries if you like; but there is no gate, no lock, no bolt that you can set upon the freedom of my mind.

But whatever effect discouragement and criticism had upon their writing—and I believe that they had a very great effect—that was unimportant compared with the other difficulty which faced them (I was still considering those early nineteenth-century novelists) when they came to set their thoughts on paper—that is that they had no tradition behind them, or one so short and partial that it was of little help. For we think back through our mothers if we are women. It is useless to go to the great men writers for help, however much one may go to them for pleasure. Lamb, Browne, Thackeray, Newman, Sterne, Dickens, De Quincey—whoever it may be—never helped a woman yet, though she may have learnt a few tricks of them and adapted them to her use. The weight, the pace, the stride of a man's mind are too unlike her own for her to lift anything substantial from him successfully. The ape is too distant to be sedulous. Perhaps the first thing she would find, setting pen to paper, was that there was no common sentence ready for her use. All the great novelists like Thackeray and Dickens and Balzac have written a natural prose, swift but not slovenly, expressive but not precious, taking their own tint without ceasing to be common property. They have based it on the sentence that was current at the time. The sentence that was current at the beginning of the nineteenth century ran something like this perhaps: "The grandeur of their works was an argument with them, not to stop short, but to proceed. They could have no higher excitement or satisfaction than in the exercise of their art and endless generations of truth and beauty. Success prompts to exertion; and habit facilitates success." That is a man's sentence; behind it one can see Johnson, Gibbon[9] and the rest. It was a sentence that was unsuited for a woman's use. Charlotte Brontë, with all her splendid gift for prose, stumbled and fell with that clumsy weapon in her hands. George Eliot committed atrocities with it that beggar description. Jane Austen looked at it and laughed at it and devised a perfectly natural, shapely sentence proper for her own use and never departed from it. Thus, with less genius for writing than Charlotte Brontë, she got infinitely more said. Indeed, since freedom and fullness of expression are of the essence of the art, such a lack of tradition, such a scarcity and inadequacy of tools, must have told enormously upon the writing of women. Moreover, a book is not made of sentences laid end to end, but of sentences built, if an image helps, into arcades or domes. And this shape too has been made by men out of their own needs for their own uses. There is no reason to think that the form of the epic or of the poetic plays suits a woman any more than the sentence suits her. But all the older forms of literature were hardened and set by the time she became a writer. The novel alone was young enough to be soft in her hands—another reason, perhaps, why she wrote novels. Yet who shall say that even now "the novel" (I give it inverted commas to mark my sense of the words' inadequacy), who shall say that even this most pliable of all forms is rightly shaped for her use?

9. Edward Gibbon, author of *The History of the Decline and Fall of the Roman Empire* (1776–1788).

No doubt we shall find her knocking that into shape for herself when she has the free use of her limbs; and providing some new vehicle, not necessarily in verse, for the poetry in her. For it is the poetry that is still denied outlet. And I went on to ponder how a woman nowadays would write a poetic tragedy in five acts—would she use verse—would she not use prose rather?

But these are difficult questions which lie in the twilight of the future. I must leave them, if only because they stimulate me to wander from my subject into trackless forests where I shall be lost and, very likely, devoured by wild beasts. I do not want, and I am sure that you do not want me, to broach that very dismal subject, the future of fiction, so that I will only pause here one moment to draw your attention to the great part which must be played in that future so far as women are concerned by physical conditions. The book has somehow to be adapted to the body, and at a venture one would say that women's books should be shorter, more concentrated, than those of men, and framed so that they do not need long hours of steady and uninterrupted work. For interruptions there will always be. Again, the nerves that feed the brain would seem to differ in men and women, and if you are going to make them work their best and hardest, you must find out what treatment suits them—whether these hours of lectures, for instance, which the monks devised, presumably, hundreds of years ago, suit them—what alternations of work and rest they need, interpreting rest not as doing nothing but as doing something but something that is different; and what should that difference be? All this should be discussed and discovered; all this is part of the question of women and fiction. And yet, I continued, approaching the bookcase again, where shall I find that elaborate study of the psychology of women by a woman? If through their incapacity to play football women are not going to be allowed to practise medicine——

Happily my thoughts were now given another turn.

Chapter 6

Next day the light of the October morning was falling in dusty shafts through the uncurtained windows, and the hum of traffic rose from the street. London then was winding itself up again; the factory was astir; the machines were beginning. It was tempting, after all this reading, to look out of the window and see what London was doing on the morning of the twenty-sixth of October 1928. And what was London doing? Nobody, it seemed, was reading *Antony and Cleopatra*. London was wholly indifferent, it appeared, to Shakespeare's plays. Nobody cared a straw—and I do not blame them—for the future of fiction, the death of poetry or the development by the average woman of a prose style completely expressive of her mind. If opinions upon any of these matters had been chalked on the pavement, nobody would have stooped to read them. The nonchalance of the hurrying feet would have rubbed them out in half an hour. Here came an errand-boy; here a woman with a dog on a lead. The fascination of the London street is that no two people are ever alike; each seems bound on some private affair of his own. There were the business-like, with their little bags; there were the drifters rattling sticks upon area railings; there were affable characters to whom the streets serve for clubroom, hailing men in carts and giving information without being asked for it. Also there were funerals to which men, thus suddenly reminded of the passing of their own bodies, lifted their hats. And then a very distinguished gentleman came slowly down a doorstep and paused to avoid collision with a bustling lady who had, by some means or other, acquired a splendid fur coat and a bunch of Parma violets. They all seemed separate, self-absorbed, on business of their own.

At this moment, as so often happens in London, there was a complete lull and suspension of traffic. Nothing came down the street; nobody passed. A single leaf detached itself from the plane tree at the end of the street, and in that pause and suspension fell. Somehow it was like a signal falling, a signal pointing to a force in things which one had overlooked. It seemed to point to a river, which flowed past, invisibly, round the corner, down the street, and took people and eddied them along, as the stream at Oxbridge had taken the undergraduate in his boat and the dead leaves. Now it was bringing from one side of the street to the other diagonally a girl in patent leather boots, and then a young man in a maroon overcoat; it was also bringing a taxi-cab; and it brought all three together at a point directly beneath my window; where the taxi stopped; and the girl and the young man stopped; and they got into the taxi; and then the cab glided off as if it were swept on by the current elsewhere.

The sight was ordinary enough; what was strange was the rhythmical order with which my imagination had invested it; and the fact that the ordinary sight of two people getting into a cab had the power to communicate something of their own seeming satisfaction. The sight of two people coming down the street and meeting at the corner seems to ease the mind of some strain, I thought, watching the taxi turn and make off. Perhaps to think, as I had been thinking these two days, of one sex as distinct from the other is an effort. It interferes with the unity of the mind. Now that effort had ceased and that unity had been restored by seeing two people come together and get into a taxi-cab. The mind is certainly a very mysterious organ, I reflected, drawing my head in from the window, about which nothing whatever is known, though we depend upon it so completely. Why do I feel that there are severances and oppositions in the mind, as there are strains from obvious causes on the body? What does one mean by "the unity of the mind," I pondered, for clearly the mind has so great a power of concentrating at any point at any moment that it seems to have no single state of being. It can separate itself from the people in the street, for example, and think of itself as apart from them, at an upper window looking down on them. Or it can think with other people spontaneously, as, for instance, in a crowd waiting to hear some piece of news read out. It can think back through its fathers or through its mothers, as I have said that a woman writing thinks back through her mothers. Again if one is a woman one is often surprised by a sudden splitting off of consciousness, say in walking down Whitehall,[1] when from being the natural inheritor of that civilisation, she becomes, on the contrary, outside of it, alien and critical. Clearly the mind is always altering its focus, and bringing the world into different perspectives. But some of these states of mind seem, even if adopted spontaneously, to be less comfortable than others. In order to keep oneself continuing in them one is unconsciously holding something back, and gradually the repression becomes an effort. But there may be some state of mind in which one could continue without effort because nothing is required to be held back. And this perhaps, I thought, coming in from the window, is one of them. For certainly when I saw the couple get into the taxi-cab the mind felt as if, after being divided, it had come together again in a natural fusion. The obvious reason would be that it is natural for the sexes to co-operate. One has a profound, if irrational, instinct in favour of the theory that the union of man and woman makes for the greatest satisfaction, the most complete happiness. But the sight of the two people getting into the taxi and the satisfaction it gave me made me also ask whether there are two sexes in the mind corresponding to the two sexes in

---

1. A main thoroughfare in central London and site of government offices.

the body, and whether they also require to be united in order to get complete satisfaction and happiness. And I went on amateurishly to sketch a plan of the soul so that in each of us two powers preside, one male, one female; and in the man's brain, the man predominates over the woman, and in the woman's brain, the woman predominates over the man. The normal and comfortable state of being is that when the two live in harmony together, spiritually co-operating. If one is a man, still the woman part of the brain must have effect; and a woman also must have intercourse with the man in her. Coleridge perhaps meant this when he said that a great mind is androgynous.[2] It is when this fusion takes place that the mind is fully fertilised and uses all its faculties. Perhaps a mind that is purely masculine cannot create, any more than a mind that is purely feminine, I thought. But it would be well to test what one meant by man-womanly, and conversely by woman-manly, by pausing and looking at a book or two.

Coleridge certainly did not mean, when he said that a great mind is androgynous, that it is a mind that has any special sympathy with women; a mind that takes up their cause or devotes itself to their interpretation. Perhaps the androgynous mind is less apt to make these distinctions than the single-sexed mind. He meant, perhaps, that the androgynous mind is resonant and porous; that it transmits emotion without impediment; that it is naturally creative, incandescent and undivided. In fact one goes back to Shakespeare's mind as the type of the androgynous, of the man-womanly mind, though it would be impossible to say what Shakespeare thought of women. And if it be true that it is one of the tokens of the fully developed mind that it does not think specially or separately of sex, how much harder it is to attain that condition now than ever before. Here I came to the books by living writers, and there paused and wondered if this fact were not at the root of something that had long puzzled me. No age can ever have been as stridently sex-conscious as our own; those innumerable books by men about women in the British Museum are a proof of it. The Suffrage campaign was no doubt to blame.[3] It must have roused in men an extraordinary desire for self-assertion; it must have made them lay an emphasis upon their own sex and its characteristics which they would not have troubled to think about had they not been challenged. And when one is challenged, even by a few women in black bonnets, one retaliates, if one has never been challenged before, rather excessively. That perhaps accounts for some of the characteristics that I remember to have found here, I thought, taking down a new novel by Mr A, who is in the prime of life and very well thought of, apparently, by the reviewers. I opened it. Indeed, it was delightful to read a man's writing again. It was so direct, so straightforward after the writing of women. It indicated such freedom of mind, such liberty of person, such confidence in himself. One had a sense of physical well-being in the presence of this well-nourished, well-educated, free mind, which had never been thwarted or opposed, but had had full liberty from birth to stretch itself in whatever way it liked. All this was admirable. But after reading a chapter or two a shadow seemed to lie across the page. It was a straight dark bar, a shadow shaped something like the letter "I." One began dodging this way and that to catch a glimpse of the landscape behind it. Whether that was indeed a tree or a woman walking I was not quite sure. Back one was always hailed to the letter "I." One began to be tired of "I." Not but what this "I"

2. The poet Samuel Taylor Coleridge made the remark in September 1832—"a great mind must be androgynous"—and it was duly recorded in his *Table Talk*.
3. The campaign for women's suffrage, which had been steadily gaining support during the 19th century, resorted to unconstitutional methods following the founding of the Women's Social and Political Union in 1903. See Emmeline Pankhurst's *Address* on page 2178.

was a most respectable "I"; honest and logical; as hard as a nut, and polished for centuries by good teaching and good feeding. I respect and admire that "I" from the bottom of my heart. But—here I turned a page or two, looking for something or other—the worst of it is that in the shadow of the letter "I" all is shapeless as mist. Is that a tree? No, it is a woman. But . . . she has not a bone in her body, I thought, watching Phoebe, for that was her name, coming across the beach. Then Alan got up and the shadow of Alan at once obliterated Phoebe. For Alan had views and Phoebe was quenched in the flood of his views. And then Alan, I thought, has passions; and here I turned page after page very fast, feeling that the crisis was approaching, and so it was. It took place on the beach under the sun. It was done very openly. It was done very vigorously. Nothing could have been more indecent. But . . . I had said "but" too often. One cannot go on saying "but." One must finish the sentence somehow, I rebuked myself. Shall I finish it, "But . . . I am bored!" But why was I bored? Partly because of the dominance of the letter "I" and the aridity, which, like the giant beech tree, it casts within its shade. Nothing will grow there. And partly for some more obscure reason. There seemed to be some obstacle, some impediment of Mr A's mind which blocked the fountain of creative energy and shored it within narrow limits. And remembering the lunch party at Oxbridge, and the cigarette ash and the Manx cat and Tennyson and Christina Rossetti all in a bunch, it seemed possible that the impediment lay there. As he no longer hums under his breath, "There has fallen a splendid tear from the passion-flower at the gate," when Phoebe crosses the beach, and she no longer replies, "My heart is like a singing bird whose nest is in a water'd shoot," when Alan approaches what can he do? Being honest as the day and logical as the sun, there is only one thing he can do. And that he does, to do him justice, over and over (I said, turning the pages) and over again. And that, I added, aware of the awful nature of the confession, seems somehow dull. Shakespeare's indecency uproots a thousand other things in one's mind, and is far from being dull. But Shakespeare does it for pleasure; Mr A, as the nurses say, does it on purpose. He does it in protest. He is protesting against the equality of the other sex by asserting his own superiority. He is therefore impeded and inhibited and self-conscious as Shakespeare might have been if he too had known Miss Clough[4] and Miss Davies. Doubtless Elizabethan literature would have been very different from what it is if the woman's movement had begun in the sixteenth century and not in the nineteenth.

What, then, it amounts to, if this theory of the two sides of the mind holds good, is that virility has now become self-conscious—men, that is to say, are now writing only with the male side of their brains. It is a mistake for a woman to read them, for she will inevitably look for something that she will not find. It is the power of suggestion that one most misses, I thought, taking Mr B the critic in my hand and reading, very carefully and very dutifully, his remarks upon the art of poetry. Very able they were, acute and full of learning; but the trouble was, that his feelings no longer communicated; his mind seemed separated into different chambers; not a sound carried from one to the other. Thus, when one takes a sentence of Mr B into the mind it falls plump to the ground—dead; but when one takes a sentence of Coleridge into the mind, it explodes and gives birth to all kinds of other ideas, and that is the only sort of writing of which one can say that it has the secret of perpetual life.

---

4. Anne Jemima Clough (1820–1892), feminist and first Principal of Newnham College, Cambridge.

But whatever the reason may be, it is a fact that one must deplore. For it means—here I had come to rows of books by Mr Galsworthy and Mr Kipling—that some of the finest works of our greatest living writers fall upon deaf ears. Do what she will a woman cannot find in them that fountain of perpetual life which the critics assure her is there. It is not only that they celebrate male virtues, enforce male values and describe the world of men; it is that the emotion with which these books are permeated is to a woman incomprehensible. It is coming, it is gathering, it is about to burst on one's head, one begins saying long before the end. That picture will fall on old Jolyon's head;[5] he will die of the shock; the old clerk will speak over him two or three obituary words; and all the swans on the Thames will simultaneously burst out singing. But one will rush away before that happens and hide in the gooseberry bushes, for the emotion which is so deep, so subtle, so symbolical to a man moves a woman to wonder. So with Mr Kipling's officers who turn their backs; and his Sowers who sow the Seed; and his Men who are alone with their Work; and the Flag—one blushes at all these capital letters as if one had been caught eavesdropping at some purely masculine orgy. The fact is that neither Mr Galsworthy nor Mr Kipling has a spark of the woman in him. Thus all their qualities seem to a woman, if one may generalise, crude and immature. They lack suggestive power. And when a book lacks suggestive power, however hard it hits the surface of the mind it cannot penetrate within.

And in that restless mood in which one takes books out and puts them back again without looking at them I began to envisage an age to come of pure, of self-assertive virility, such as the letters of professors (take Sir Walter Raleigh's letters, for instance) seem to forebode, and the rulers of Italy have already brought into being.[6] For one can hardly fail to be impressed in Rome by the sense of unmitigated masculinity; and whatever the value of unmitigated masculinity upon the state, one may question the effect of it upon the art of poetry. At any rate, according to the newspapers, there is a certain anxiety about fiction in Italy. There has been a meeting of academicians whose object it is "to develop the Italian novel." "Men famous by birth, or in finance, industry or the Fascist corporations" came together the other day and discussed the matter, and a telegram was sent to the Duce expressing the hope "that the Fascist era would soon give birth to a poet worthy of it." We may all join in that pious hope, but it is doubtful whether poetry can come out of an incubator. Poetry ought to have a mother as well as a father. The Fascist poem, one may fear, will be a horrid little abortion such as one sees in a glass jar in the museum of some county town. Such monsters never live long, it is said; one has never seen a prodigy of that sort cropping grass in a field. Two heads on one body do not make for length of life.

However, the blame for all this, if one is anxious to lay blame, rests no more upon one sex than upon the other. All seducers and reformers are responsible, Lady Bessborough when she lied to Lord Granville; Miss Davies when she told the truth to Mr Greg. All who have brought about a state of sex-consciousness are to blame, and it is they who drive me, when I want to stretch my faculties on a book, to seek it in that happy age, before Miss Davies and Miss Clough were born, when the writer used both sides of his mind equally. One must turn back to Shakespeare then, for Shakespeare was androgynous; and so was Keats and Sterne and Cowper and Lamb and Coleridge. Shelley perhaps was sexless. Milton and Ben Jonson had a dash too much

---

5. A climactic moment in John Galsworthy's novel sequence *The Forsyte Saga* (1906–1929).
6. Sir Walter Raleigh was Professor of English Literature at Oxford; his *Letters* were published in 1926. Woolf refers to the nascent Italian Fascist state.

of the male in them. So had Wordsworth and Tolstoi. In our time Proust was wholly androgynous, if not perhaps a little too much of a woman. But that failing is too rare for one to complain of it, since without some mixture of the kind the intellect seems to predominate and the other faculties of the mind harden and become barren. However, I consoled myself with the reflection that this is perhaps a passing phase; much of what I have said in obedience to my promise to give you the course of my thoughts will seem out of date; much of what flames in my eyes will seem dubious to you who have not yet come of age.

Even so, the very first sentence that I would write here, I said, crossing over to the writing-table and taking up the page headed Women and Fiction, is that it is fatal for any one who writes to think of their sex. It is fatal to be a man or woman pure and simple; one must be woman-manly or man-womanly. It is fatal for a woman to lay the least stress on any grievance; to plead even with justice any cause; in any way to speak consciously as a woman. And fatal is no figure of speech; for anything written with that conscious bias is doomed to death. It ceases to be fertilised. Brilliant and effective, powerful and masterly, as it may appear for a day or two, it must wither at nightfall; it cannot grow in the minds of others. Some collaboration has to take place in the mind between the woman and the man before the act of creation can be accomplished. Some marriage of opposites has to be consummated. The whole of the mind must lie wide open if we are to get the sense that the writer is communicating his experience with perfect fullness. There must be freedom and there must be peace. Not a wheel must grate, not a light glimmer. The curtains must be close drawn. The writer, I thought, once his experience is over, must lie back and let his mind celebrate its nuptials in darkness. He must not look or question what is being done. Rather, he must pluck the petals from a rose or watch the swans float calmly down the river. And I saw again the current which took the boat and the undergraduate and the dead leaves; and the taxi took the man and the woman, I thought, seeing them come together across the street, and the current swept them away, I thought, hearing far off the roar of London's traffic, into that tremendous stream.

Here, then, Mary Beton ceases to speak. She has told you how she reached the conclusion—the prosaic conclusion—that it is necessary to have five hundred a year and a room with a lock on the door if you are to write fiction or poetry. She has tried to lay bare the thoughts and impressions that led her to think this. She has asked you to follow her flying into the arms of a Beadle, lunching here, dining there, drawing pictures in the British Museum, taking books from the shelf, looking out of the window. While she has been doing all these things, you no doubt have been observing her failings and foibles and deciding what effect they have had on her opinions. You have been contradicting her and making whatever additions and deductions seem good to you. That is all as it should be, for in a question like this truth is only to be had by laying together many varieties of error. And I will end now in my own person by anticipating two criticisms, so obvious that you can hardly fail to make them.

No opinion has been expressed, you may say, upon the comparative merits of the sexes even as writers. That was done purposely, because, even if the time had come for such a valuation—and it is far more important at the moment to know how much money women had and how many rooms than to theorise about their capacities—even if the time had come I do not believe that gifts, whether of mind or character, can be weighed like sugar and butter, not even in Cambridge, where they are so adept at putting people into classes and fixing caps on their heads and letters after their names. I do not believe that even the Table of Precedency which you will find in Whitaker's *Almanac*[7] represents a final order of values, or that there is any sound reason to suppose that a Commander of the Bath will ultimately walk in to dinner behind a Master in Lunacy. All this pitting of sex against sex, of quality against quality; all this claiming of superiority and imputing of inferiority, belong to the private-school stage of human existence where there are "sides," and it is necessary for one side to beat another side, and of the utmost importance to walk up to a platform and receive from the hands of the Headmaster himself a highly ornamental pot. As people mature they cease to believe in sides or in Headmasters or in highly ornamental pots. At any rate, where books are concerned, it is notoriously difficult to fix labels of merit in such a way that they do not come off. Are not reviews of current literature a perpetual illustration of the difficulty of judgment? "This great book," "this worthless book," the same book is called by both names. Praise and blame alike mean nothing. No, delightful as the pastime of measuring may be, it is the most futile of all occupations, and to submit to the decrees of the measurers the most servile of attitudes. So long as you write what you wish to write, that is all that matters; and whether it matters for ages or only for hours, nobody can say. But to sacrifice a hair of the head of your vision, a shade of its colour, in deference to some Headmaster with a silver pot in his hand or to some professor with a measuring-rod up his sleeve, is the most abject treachery, and the sacrifice of wealth and chastity which used to be said to be the greatest of human disasters, a mere flea-bite in comparison.

Next I think that you may object that in all this I have made too much of the importance of material things. Even allowing a generous margin for symbolism, that five hundred a year stands for the power to contemplate, that a lock on the door means the power to think for oneself, still you may say that the mind should rise above such things; and that great poets have often been poor men. Let me then quote to you the words of your own Professor of Literature, who knows better than I do what goes to the making of a poet. Sir Arthur Quiller-Couch writes:[8]

"What are the great poetical names of the last hundred years or so? Coleridge, Wordsworth, Byron, Shelly, Landor, Keats, Tennyson, Browning, Arnold, Morris, Rossetti, Swinburne . . . we may stop there. Of these, all but Keats, Browning, Rossetti were University men; and of these three, Keats, who died young, cut off in his prime, was the only one not fairly well to do. It may seem a brutal thing to say, and it is a sad thing to say: but, as a matter of hard fact, the theory that poetical genius bloweth where it listeth, and equally in poor and rich, holds little truth. As a matter of hard fact, nine out of those twelve were University men: which means that somehow or other they procured the means to get the best education England can give. As a matter of hard fact, of the remaining three you know that Browning was well to do, and I challenge you that, if he had not been well to do, he would no more have attained to write *Saul* or *The Ring and the Book* than Ruskin would have attained to writing *Modern Painters* if his father had not dealt prosperously in business. Rossetti had a small private income; and, moreover, he painted. There remains but Keats; whom Atropos[9] slew young, as she slew John Clare in a mad-house, and James Thomson by the laudanum he took to drug disappointment. These are dreadful facts, but let us face them. It is—however dishonouring to us as a nation—certain that, by some fault in our commonwealth, the poor poet has not in these days, nor has had for

---

7. A compendium of general information first published in 1868.
8. *The Art of Writing*, by Sir Arthur Quiller-Couch

[Woolf's note]. Quiller-Couch was then Professor of English Literature at Cambridge University.
9. One of the three Fates in Greek mythology.

two hundred years, a dog's chance. Believe me—and I have spent a great part of ten years in watching some three hundred and twenty elementary schools—we may prate of democracy, but actually, a poor child in England has little more hope than had the son of an Athenian slave to be emancipated into that intellectual freedom of which great writings are born."

Nobody could put the point more plainly. "The poor poet has not in these days, nor has had for two hundred years, a dog's chance . . . a poor child in England has little more hope than had the son of an Athenian slave to be emancipated into that intellectual freedom of which great writings are born." That is it. Intellectual freedom depends upon material things. Poetry depends upon intellectual freedom. And women have always been poor, not for two hundred years merely, but from the beginning of time. Women have had less intellectual freedom than the sons of Athenian slaves. Women, then, have not had a dog's chance of writing poetry. That is why I have laid so much stress on money and a room of one's own. However, thanks to the toils of those obscure women in the past, of whom I wish we knew more, thanks, curiously enough, to two wars, the Crimean which let Florence Nightingale out of her drawing-room, and the European War which opened the doors to the average woman some sixty years later, these evils are in the way to be bettered. Otherwise you would not be here tonight, and your chance of earning five hundred pounds a year, precarious as I am afraid that it still is, would be minute in the extreme.

Still, you may object, why do you attach so much importance to this writing of books by women when, according to you, it requires so much effort, leads perhaps to the murder of one's aunts, will make one almost certainly late for luncheon, and may bring one into very grave disputes with certain very good fellows? My motives, let me admit, are partly selfish. Like most uneducated Englishwomen, I like reading—I like reading books in the bulk. Lately my diet has become a trifle monotonous; history is too much about wars; biography too much about great men; poetry has shown, I think, a tendency to sterility, and fiction—but I have sufficiently exposed my disabilities as a critic of modern fiction and will say no more about it. Therefore I would ask you to write all kinds of books, hesitating at no subject however trivial or however vast. By hook or by crook, I hope that you will possess yourselves of money enough to travel and to idle, to contemplate the future or the past of the world, to dream over books and loiter at street corners and let the line of thought dip deep into the stream. For I am by no means confining you to fiction. If you would please me—and there are thousands like me—you would write books of travel and adventure, and research and scholarship, and history and biography, and criticism and philosophy and science. By so doing you will certainly profit the art of fiction. For books have a way of influencing each other. Fiction will be much the better for standing cheek by jowl with poetry and philosophy. Moreover, if you consider any great figure of the past, like Sappho, like the Lady Murasaki,[1] like Emily Brontë, you will find that she is an inheritor as well as an originator, and has come into existence because women have come to have the habit of writing naturally; so that even as a prelude to poetry such activity on your part would be invaluable.

But when I look back through these notes and criticise my own train of thought as I made them, I find that my motives were not altogether selfish. There runs through these comments and discursions the conviction—or is it the instinct?—that

1. Sappho (c. mid-7th century B.C.), Greek woman poet; Shikibu Murasaki (978–1014) wrote *The Tale of Genji*, a major early work of Japanese literature.

good books are desirable and that good writers, even if they show every variety of human depravity, are still good human beings. Thus when I ask you to write more books I am urging you to do what will be for your good and for the good of the world at large. How to justify this instinct or belief I do not know, for philosophic words, if one has not been educated at a university, are apt to play one false. What is meant by "reality"? It would seem to be something very erratic, very undependable—now to be found in a dusty road, now in a scrap of newspaper in the street, now in a daffodil in the sun. It lights up a group in a room and stamps some casual saying. It overwhelms one walking home beneath the stars and makes the silent world more real than the world of speech—and then there it is again in an omnibus in the uproar of Piccadilly.[2] Sometimes, too, it seems to dwell in shapes too far away for us to discern what their nature is. But whatever it touches, it fixes and makes permanent. That is what remains over when the skin of the day has been cast into the hedge; that is what is left of past time and of our loves and hates. Now the writer, as I think, has the chance to live more than other people in the presence of this reality. It is his business to find it and collect it and communicate it to the rest of us. So at least I infer from reading *Lear* or *Emma* or *La Recherche du Temps Perdu.* For the reading of these books seems to perform a curious couching operation on the senses; one sees more intensely afterwards; the world seems bared of its covering and given an intenser life. Those are the enviable people who live at enmity with unreality; and those are the pitiable who are knocked on the head by the thing done without knowing or caring. So that when I ask you to earn money and have a room of your own, I am asking you to live in the presence of reality, an invigorating life, it would appear, whether one can impart it or not.

Here I would stop, but the pressure of convention decrees that every speech must end with a peroration. And a peroration addressed to women should have something, you will agree, particularly exalting and ennobling about it. I should implore you to remember your responsibilities, to be higher, more spiritual; I should remind you how much depends upon you, and what an influence you can exert upon the future. But those exhortations can safely, I think, be left to the other sex, who will put them, and indeed have put them, with far greater eloquence than I can compass. When I rummage in my own mind I find no noble sentiments about being companions and equals and influencing the world to higher ends. I find myself saying briefly and prosaically that it is much more important to be oneself than anything else. Do not dream of influencing other people, I would say, if I knew how to make it sound exalted. Think of things in themselves.

And again I am reminded by dipping into newspapers and novels and biographies that when a woman speaks to women she should have something very unpleasant up her sleeve. Women are hard on women. Women dislike women. Women . . . but are you not sick to death of the word? I can assure you that I am. Let us agree, then, that a paper read by a woman to women should end with something particularly disagreeable.

But how does it go? What can I think of? The truth is, I often like women. I like their unconventionality. I like their subtlety. I like their anonymity. I like—but I must not run on in this way. That cupboard there,—you say it holds clean table-napkins only; but what if Sir Archibald Bodkin were concealed among them?[3] Let me

2. A district of London.
3. Sir Archibald Bodkin was then Director of Public Prosecutions; his office had been responsible for the 1928 prosecution of Radclyffe Hall's novel *The Well of Loneli*- ness on a charge of obscenity. It was subsequently banned. Woolf had wanted to give evidence in the book's defense at the trial, but expert witnesses were not allowed by the presiding magistrate.

then adopt a sterner tone. Have I, in the preceding words, conveyed to you sufficiently the warnings and reprobation of mankind? I have told you the very low opinion in which you were held by Mr Oscar Browning. I have indicated what Napoleon
once thought of you and what Mussolini thinks now. Then, in case any of you aspire
to fiction, I have copied out for your benefit the advice of the critic about courageously acknowledging the limitations of your sex. I have referred to Professor X and
given prominence to his statement that women are intellectually, morally and physically inferior to men. I have handed on all that has come my way without going in
search of it, and here is a final warning—from Mr John Langdon Davies.[4] Mr John
Langdon Davies warns women "that when children cease to be altogether desirable,
women cease to be altogether necessary." I hope you will make a note of it.

How can I further encourage you to go about the business of life? Young women,
I would say, and please attend, for the peroration is beginning, you are, in my opinion, disgracefully ignorant. You have never made a discovery of any sort of importance. You have never shaken an empire or led an army into battle. The plays of
Shakespeare are not by you, and you have never introduced a barbarous race to the
blessings of civilisation. What is your excuse? It is all very well for you to say, pointing to the streets and squares and forests of the globe swarming with black and white
and coffee-coloured inhabitants, all busily engaged in traffic and enterprise and love-
making, we have had other work on our hands. Without our doing, those seas would
be unsailed and those fertile lands a desert. We have borne and bred and washed and
taught, perhaps to the age of six or seven years, the one thousand six hundred and
twenty-three million human beings who are, according to statistics, at present in
existence, and that, allowing that some had help, takes time.

There is truth in what you say—I will not deny it. But at the same time may I
remind you that there have been at least two colleges for women in existence in England since the year 1866; that after the year 1880 a married woman was allowed by
law to possess her own property; and that in 1919—which is a whole nine years
ago—she was given a vote? May I also remind you that the most of the professions
have been open to you for close on ten years now? When you reflect upon these
immense privileges and the length of time time during which they have been
enjoyed, and the fact that there must be at this moment some two thousand women
capable of earning over five hundred a year in one way or another, you will agree that
the excuse of lack of opportunity, training, encouragement, leisure and money no
longer holds good. Moreover, the economists are telling us that Mrs Seton has had
too many children. You must, of course, go on bearing children, but, so they say, in
twos and threes, not in tens and twelves.

Thus, with some time on your hands and with some book learning in your
brains—you have had enough of the other kind, and are sent to college partly, I suspect, to be uneducated—surely you should embark upon another stage of your very
long, very laborious and highly obscure career. A thousand pens are ready to suggest
what you should do and what effect you will have. My own suggestion is a little fantastic, I admit; I prefer, therefore, to put it in the form of fiction.

I told you in the course of this paper that Shakespeare had a sister; but do not
look for her in Sir Sidney Lee's life of the poet. She died young—alas, she never
wrote a word. She lies buried where the omnibuses now stop, opposite the Elephant
and Castle. Now my belief is that this poet who never wrote a word and was buried at

---

4. *A Short History of Women*, by John Langford Davies [Woolf's note].

the crossroads still lives. She lives in you and in me, and in many other women who are not here tonight, for they are washing up the dishes and putting the children to bed. But she lives; for great poets do not die; they are continuing presences; they need only the opportunity to walk among us in the flesh. This opportunity, as I think, it is now coming within your power to give her. For my belief is that if we live another century or so—I am talking of the common life which is the real life and not of the little separate lives which we live as individuals—and have five hundred a year each of us and rooms of our own; if we have the habit of freedom and the courage to write exactly what we think; if we escape a little from the common sitting-room and see human beings not always in their relation to each other but in relation to reality; and the sky, too, and the trees or whatever it may be in themselves; if we look past Milton's bogey, for no human being should shut out the view; if we face the fact, for it is a fact, that there is no arm to cling to, but that we go alone and that our relation is to the world of reality and not only to the world of men and women, then the opportunity will come and the dead poet who was Shakespeare's sister will put on the body which she has so often laid down. Drawing her life from the lives of the unknown who were her forerunners, as her brother did before her, she will be born. As for her coming without that preparation, without that effort on our part, without that determination that when she is born again she shall find it possible to live and write her poetry, that we cannot expect, for that would be impossible. But I maintain that she would come if we worked for her, and that so to work, even in poverty and obscurity, is worth while.

Three Guineas

Three Guineas marked Virginia Woolf's return to the genre she had employed in *A Room of One's Own*: the extended political and literary essay with a feminist theme. Like the earlier essay, this text is cast as a response to a request—in this case, a letter from an unnamed man asking her opinions on the prevention of war. Woolf wrote *Three Guineas* in 1938, against the backdrop of impending world war. Her analysis of gender inequality, and the social construction of those conditions of inequality, is intensified in the later work because of the urgency of the imminent war. Woolf uses her critique of sexism to investigate the perpetuation of violence in human history and to argue that the same dominances that bring about female inequality are responsible for the evils of war.

Woolf's argument is anything but simple, and her text anything but a straightforward polemic. Her rhetoric is laced with irony and an almost savage playfulness, in light of the seriousness of the historical moment. The primary metaphor of this work—as of her novel *Orlando* (1928)—is that of costume and dress. Hardly a retreat to a frivolous subject, the emphasis on clothing cloaks Woolf's understanding of the invented nature of social power. In other words, she does not attribute male dominance to biological superiority on the part of men; instead, she investigates the degree to which human hierarchies of gender, of class, and of race are made by human culture and are thus "conventional," just as fashion is. While there is something grotesque about comparing Nazi uniforms to the vestments and robes of the clergy, as Woolf does in the essay, her purpose is to scandalously unveil this truth of culture, and thereby to suggest that dominance can be reversed or transformed.

Woolf uses the lens of sexism to investigate the nature of authority—which is generally male authority in the institutions of modern society. Woolf is not reductive in doing this—she never implies that women are "better" in ethical or other ways, nor that authority is less vile when abused by women, as it occasionally is. She is eager to find the skeleton key to unlock the mystery of brute authority, and to warn against the militarism she saw as a permanent feature of British as well as German society. Woolf does not exempt any national culture or any group from susceptibility to power and its corrupting effects. In this essay, which shocked its audience in a way the more playful *A Room of One's Own* did not, she offers a comparative survey of the institutions of authority, or civil society. The vestments of power, Woolf shows, can be adopted by groups and by entire nations and even civilizations. *Three Guineas* is a clarion call to arms, to the weapons of thought and education as alternatives to the unthinkable horrors of a second world war. Virginia Woolf saw her prophecy of war come true shortly after its publication, and that fatal fact, as much as her own mental illness, was a push toward the suicide that claimed her life in 1941.

from Three Guineas[1]

Three years is a long time to leave a letter unanswered, and your letter has been lying without an answer even longer than that. I had hoped that it would answer itself, or that other people would answer it for me. But there it is with its question—How in your opinion are we to prevent war?—still unanswered.

It is true that many answers have suggested themselves, but none that would not need explanation, and explanations take time. In this case, too, there are reasons why it is particularly difficult to avoid misunderstanding. A whole page could be filled with excuses and apologies; declarations of unfitness, incompetence, lack of knowledge, and experience: and they would be true. But even when they were said there would still remain some difficulties so fundamental that it may well prove impossible for you to understand or for us to explain. But one does not like to leave so remarkable a letter as yours—a letter perhaps unique in the history of human correspondence, since when before has an educated man asked a woman how in her opinion war can be prevented?—unanswered. Therefore let us make the attempt; even if it is doomed to failure.

In the first place let us draw what all letter-writers instinctively draw, a sketch of the person to whom the letter is addressed. Without someone warm and breathing on the other side of the page, letters are worthless. You, then, who ask the question, are a little grey on the temples; the hair is no longer thick on the top of your head. You have reached the middle years of life not without effort, at the Bar;[2] but on the whole your journey has been prosperous. There is nothing parched, mean or dissatisfied in your expression. And without wishing to flatter you, your prosperity—wife, children, house—has been deserved. You have never sunk into the contented apathy of middle life, for, as your letter from an office in the heart of London shows, instead of turning on your pillow and prodding your pigs, pruning your pear trees—you have a few acres in Norfolk—you are writing letters, attending meetings, presiding over this and that, asking questions, with the sound of the guns in your ears. For the rest, you began your education at one of the great public schools and finished it at the university.

It is now that the first difficulty of communication between us appears. Let us rapidly indicate the reason. We both come of what, in this hybrid age when, though birth is mixed, classes still remain fixed, it is convenient to call the educated class. When we meet in the flesh we speak with the same accent; use knives and forks in the same way; expect maids to cook dinner and wash up after dinner; and can talk during dinner without much difficulty about politics and people; war and peace; barbarism and civilization—all the questions indeed suggested by your letter. Moreover,

1. A guinea had been a gold coin worth one pound and one shilling (21 shillings); although no longer in circulation, guineas were used in determining professional fees and luxury items.
2. In Britain, "the Bar" refers collectively to lawyers; to be called to the Bar means to enter the profession.

we both earn our livings. But . . . those three dots mark a precipice, a gulf so deeply cut between us that for three years and more I have been sitting on my side of it wondering whether it is any use to try to speak across it. Let us then ask someone else—it is Mary Kingsley—to speak for us.[3] "I don't know if I ever revealed to you the fact that being allowed to learn German was *all* the paid-for education I ever had. Two thousand pounds was spent on my brother's, I still hope not in vain."[4] Mary Kingsley is not speaking for herself alone; she is speaking, still, for many of the daughters of educated men. And she is not merely speaking for them; she is also pointing to a very important fact about them, a fact that must profoundly influence all that follows: the fact of Arthur's Education Fund. You, who have read *Pendennis*,[5] will remember how the mysterious letters A.E.F. figured in the household ledgers. Ever since the thirteenth century English families have been paying money into that account. From the Pastons[6] to the Pendennises, all educated families from the thirteenth century to the present moment have paid money into that account. It is a voracious receptacle. Where there were many sons to educate it required a great effort on the part of the family to keep it full. For your education was not merely in book-learning; games educated your body; friends taught you more than books or games. Talk with them broadened your outlook and enriched your mind. In the holidays you travelled; acquired a taste for art; a knowledge of foreign politics; and then, before you could earn your own living, your father made you an allowance upon which it was possible for you to live while you learnt the profession which now entitles you to add the letters K.C.[7] to your name. All this came out of Arthur's Education Fund. And to this your sisters, as Mary Kingsley indicates, made their contribution. Not only did their own education, save for such small sums as paid the German teacher, go into it; but many of those luxuries and trimmings which are, after all, an essential part of education—travel, society, solitude, a lodging apart from the family house—they were paid into it too. It was a voracious receptacle, a solid fact—Arthur's Education Fund—a fact so solid indeed that it cast a shadow over the entire landscape. And the result is that though we look at the same things, we see them differently. What is that congregation of buildings there, with a semi-monastic look, with chapels and halls and green playing-fields? To you it is your old school, Eton or Harrow;[8] your old university, Oxford or Cambridge; the source of memories and of traditions innumerable. But to us, who see it through the shadow of Arthur's Education Fund, it is a schoolroom table; an omnibus going to a class; a little woman with a red nose who is not well

3. Mary Kingsley traveled extensively in West Africa in the final decade of the 19th century, publishing an account of her expeditions in 1897; see page 1846.
4. *The Life of Mary Kingsley*, by Stephen Gwynn, p. 15. It is difficult to get exact figures of the sums spent on the education of educated men's daughters. About £20 or £30 presumably covered the entire cost of Mary Kingsley's education (b. 1862; d. 1900). A sum of £100 may be taken as about the average in the 19th century and even later. The women thus educated often felt the lack of education very keenly. "I always feel the defects of my education most painfully when I go out," wrote Anne J. Clough, the first Principal of Newnham (*Life of Anne J. Clough*, by B. A Clough, p. 60) . . .
But the educated man's daughter in the 19th century was even more ignorant of life than of books. One reason for that ignorance is suggested by the following quotation: "It was supposed that most men were not 'virtuous', that is, that nearly all would be capable of accosting and annoying—or worse—any unaccompanied young woman whom they met." ("Society and the Season," by Mary, Countess of Lovelace, in *Fifty Years*, 1882–1932, p. 37.) She was therefore confined to a very narrow circle; and her "ignorance and indifference" to anything outside it was excusable. The connection between that ignorance and the 19th-century conception of manhood, which—witness the Victorian hero—made "virtue" and virility incompatible is obvious. In a well-known passage, Thackeray complains of the limitations which virtue and virility between them impose upon his art [Woolf's note].
5. *The History of Pendennis* (1848–1850), a novel by William Makepeace Thackeray.
6. *The Paston Letters* (c. 1420–1504) are a record of the domestic conditions of a well-to-do medieval family.
7. King's Counsel; the title for senior barristers.
8. Prestigious boys' schools.

educated herself but has an invalid mother to support; an allowance of £50 a year with which to buy clothes, give presents and take journeys on coming to maturity. Such is the effect that Arthur's Education Fund has had upon us. So magically does it change the landscape that the noble courts and quadrangles of Oxford and Cambridge often appear to educated men's daughters[9] like petticoats with holes in them, cold legs of mutton, and the boat train starting for abroad while the guard slams the door in their faces.

* * *

Here then is your own letter. In that, as we have seen, after asking for an opinion as to how to prevent war, you go on to suggest certain practical measures by which we can help you to prevent it. These are it appears that we should sign a manifesto, pledging ourselves "to protect culture and intellectual liberty";[1] that we should join a certain society, devoted to certain measures whose aim is to preserve peace; and, finally, that we should subscribe to that society which like the others is in need of funds.

First, then, let us consider how we can help you to prevent war by protecting culture and intellectual liberty, since you assure us that there is a connection between those rather abstract words and these very positive photographs—the photographs of dead bodies and ruined houses.

But if it was surprising to be asked for an opinion how to prevent war, it is still more surprising to be asked to help you in the rather abstract terms of your manifesto to protect culture and intellectual liberty. Consider, Sir, in the light of the facts given above, what this request of yours means. It means that in the year 1938 the sons of educated men are asking the daughters to help them to protect culture and intellectual liberty. And why, you may ask, is that so surprising? Suppose that the Duke of Devonshire, in his star and garter,[2] stepped down into the kitchen and said to the maid who was peeling potatoes with a smudge on her cheek: "Stop your potato peel-

9. Our ideology is still so inveterately anthropocentric that it has been necessary to coin this clumsy term—educated man's daughter—to describe the class whose fathers have been educated at public schools and universities. Obviously, if the term "bourgeois" fits her brother, it is grossly incorrect to use it of one who differs so profoundly in the two prime characteristics of the bourgeoisie—capital and environment [Woolf's note].

1. It is to be hoped that some methodical person has made a collection of the various manifestoes and questionnaires issued broadcast during the years 1936–7. Private people of no political training were invited to sign appeals asking their own and foreign governments to change their policy; artists were asked to fill up forms stating the proper relation of the artist to the State, to religion, to morality; pledges were required that the writer should use English grammatically and avoid vulgar expressions; and dreamers were invited to analyse their dreams. By way of inducement it was generally proposed to publish the results in the daily or weekly Press. What effect this inquisition has had upon governments it is for the politician to say. Upon literature, since the output of books is unstaunched, and grammar would seem to be neither better nor worse, the effect is problematical. But the inquisition . . . points, indirectly, to the death of the Siren, that much ridiculed and often upper-class lady who by keeping open house for the aristocracy, plutocracy, intelligentsia, ignorantsia, etc., tried to provide all classes with a talking-ground or scratching-post where they could rub up minds, manners and morals more pri-

vately, and perhaps as usefully. The part that the Siren played in promoting culture and intellectual liberty in the 18th century is held by historians to be of some importance. Even in our own day she had her uses. Witness W. B. Yeats—"How often have I wished that he [Synge] might live long enough to enjoy that communion with idle, charming cultivated women which Balzac in one of his dedications calls 'the chief consolation of genius'!" (*Dramatis Personae*, W. B. Yeats, p. 127.) Lady St. Helier who, as Lady Jeune, preserved the 18th-century tradition, informs us, however, that "Plovers' eggs at 2s 6d. apiece, forced strawberries, early asparagus, *petits poussins* . . . are now considered almost a necessity by anyone aspiring to give a good dinner" (1909); and her remark that the reception day was "very fatiguing . . . how exhausted I felt when half-past seven came, and how gladly at eight o' clock I sat down to a peaceful *tête-à-tête* dinner with my husband!" (*Memories of Fifty Years*, by Lady St. Helier, pp. 3, 5, 182) may explain why such houses are shut, why such hostesses are dead, and why therefore the intelligentsia, the ignorantsia, the aristocracy, the bureaucracy, the bourgeoisie, etc., are driven (unless somebody will revive that society on an economic basis) to do their talking in public. But in view of the multitude of manifestoes and questionnaires now in circulation it would be foolish to suggest another into the minds and motives of the Inquisitors [Woolf's note].

2. Badges of the Order of the Garter, the highest English Order of Knighthood.

ing, Mary, and help me to construe this rather difficult passage in Pindar,"[3] would not Mary be surprised and run screaming to Louisa the cook, "Lawks, Louie, Master must be mad!" That, or something like it, is the cry that rises to our lips when the sons of educated men ask us, their sisters, to protect intellectual liberty and culture. But let us try to translate the kitchenmaid's cry into the language of educated people.

Once more we must beg you, Sir, to look from our angle, from our point of view, at Arthur's Education Fund. Try once more, difficult though it is to twist your head in that direction, to understand what it has meant to us to keep that receptacle filled all these centuries so that some 10,000 of our brothers may be educated every year at Oxford and Cambridge. It has meant that we have already contributed to the cause of culture and intellectual liberty more than any other class in the community. For have not the daughters of educated men paid into Arthur's Education Fund from the year 1262 to the year 1870 all the money that was needed to educate themselves, bating such miserable sums as went to pay the governess, the German teacher, and the dancing master? Have they not paid with their own education for Eton and Harrow, Oxford and Cambridge, and all the great schools and universities on the continent—the Sorbonne and Heidelberg, Salamanca and Padua and Rome? Have they not paid so generously and lavishly if so indirectly, that when at last, in the nineteenth century, they won the right to some paid-for education for themselves, there was not a single woman who had received enough paid-for education to be able to teach them?[4] And now, out of the blue, just as they were hoping that they might filch not only a little of that same university education for themselves but some of the trimmings—travel, pleasure, liberty—for themselves, here is your letter informing them that the whole of that vast, that fabulous sum—for whether counted directly in cash, or indirectly in things done without, the sum that filled Arthur's Education Fund is vast—has been wasted or wrongly applied. With what other purpose were the universities of Oxford and Cambridge founded, save to protect culture and intellectual liberty? For what other object did your sisters go without teaching or travel or luxuries themselves except that with the money so saved their brothers should go to schools and universities and there learn to protect culture and intellectual liberty? But now since you proclaim them in danger and ask us to add our voice to yours, and our sixpence to your guinea, we must assume that the money so spent was wasted and that those societies have failed. Yet, the reflection must intrude, if the public schools and universities with their elaborate machinery for mind-training and body-training have failed, what reason is there to think that your society, sponsored though it is by distinguished names, is going to succeed, or that your manifesto, signed though it is by still more distinguished names, is going to convert? Ought you not, before you lease an office, hire a secretary, elect a committee and appeal for funds, to consider why those schools and universities have failed?

That, however, is a question for you to answer. The question which concerns us is what possible help we can give you in protecting culture and intellectual liberty—we who have been shut out from the universities so repeatedly, and are only now admitted so restrictedly; we who have received no paid-for education whatsoever, or so little that we can only read our own tongue and write our own language, we who

3. Greek poet (c. 522–443 B.C.), famous for his poems celebrating the victors at the ancient Olympic Games.
4. "He did begin however on May 13th (1844) to lecture weekly at Queen's College which Maurice and other professors at King's had established a year before, primarily for the examination and training of governesses. Kingsley was ready to share in this unpopular task because he believed in the higher education of women." (*Charles Kingsley,* by Margaret Farrand Thorp, p. 65) [Woolf's note].

are, in fact, members not of the intelligentsia but of the ignorantsia? To confirm us in our modest estimate of our own culture and to prove that you in fact share it there is Whitaker with his facts. Not a single educated man's daughter, Whitaker says, is thought capable of teaching the literature of her own language at either university. Nor is her opinion worth asking, Whitaker informs us, when it comes to buying a picture for the National Gallery, a portrait for the Portrait Gallery, or a mummy for the British Museum. How then can it be worth your while to ask us to protect culture and intellectual liberty when, as Whitaker proves with his cold facts, you have no belief that our advice is worth having when it comes to spending the money, to which we have contributed, in buying culture and intellectual liberty for the State? Do you wonder that the unexpected compliment takes us by surprise? Still, there is your letter. There are facts in that letter, too. In it you say that war is imminent; and you go on to say, in more languages than one—here is the French version: *Seule la culture désintéressée peut garder le monde de sa ruine*[5]—you go on to say that by protecting intellectual liberty and our inheritance of culture we can help you to prevent war. And since the first statement at least is indisputable and any kitchenmaid even if her French is defective can read and understand the meaning of "Air Raid Precautions" when written in large letters upon a blank wall, we cannot ignore your request on the plea of ignorance or remain silent on the plea of modesty. Just as any kitchenmaid would attempt to construe a passage in Pindar if told that her life depended on it, so the daughters of educated men, however little their training qualifies them, must consider what they can do to protect culture and intellectual liberty if by so doing they can help you to prevent war. So let us by all means in our power examine this further method of helping you, and see, before we consider your request that we should join your society, whether we can sign this manifesto in favour of culture and intellectual liberty with some intention of keeping our word.

*   *   *

Thus, Sir, it becomes clear that we must make our appeal only to those daughters of educated men who have enough to live upon. To them we might address ourselves in this wise: "Daughters of educated men who have enough to live upon . . ." But again the voice falters: again the prayer peters out into separate dots. For how many of them are there? Dare we assume in the face of Whitaker, of the laws of property, of the wills in the newspapers, of facts in short, that 1,000, 500, or even 250 will answer when thus addressed? However that may be, let the plural stand and continue: "Daughters of educated men who have enough to live upon, and read and write your own language for your own pleasure, may we very humbly entreat you to sign this gentleman's manifesto with some intention of putting your promise into practice?"

Here, if indeed they consent to listen, they might very reasonably ask us to be more explicit—not indeed to define culture and intellectual liberty, for they have books and leisure and can define the words for themselves. But what, they may well ask, is meant by this gentleman's "disinterested" culture, and how are we to protect that and intellectual liberty in practice? Now as they are daughters, not sons, we may begin by reminding them of a compliment once paid them by a great historian. "Mary's conduct," says Macaulay, "was really a signal instance of that perfect disinter-

5. "Only disinterested culture can save the world from ruin." The French, as the above quotation shows, are as active as the English in issuing manifestoes. That the French, who refuse to allow the women of France to vote, and still inflict upon them laws whose almost medieval severity can be studied in *The Position of Women in Contemporary France*, by Frances Clark, should appeal to English women to help them to protect liberty and culture must cause surprise [Woolf's note].

estedness and self-devotion of which man seems to be incapable, but which is some-times found in women."[6] Compliments, when you are asking a favour, never come amiss. Next let us refer them to the tradition which has long been honoured in the private house—the tradition of chastity. "Just as for many centuries, Madam," we might plead, "it was thought vile for a woman to sell her body without love, but right to give it to the husband whom she loved, so it is wrong, you will agree, to sell your mind without love, but right to give it to the art which you love." "But what," she may ask, "is meant by 'selling your mind without love'?" "Briefly," we might reply, "to write at the command of another person what you do not want to write for the sake of money. But to sell a brain is worse than to sell a body, for when the body seller has sold her momentary pleasure she takes good care that the matter shall end there. But when a brain seller has sold her brain, its anaemic, vicious and diseased progeny are let loose upon the world to infect and corrupt and sow the seeds of disease in others. Thus we are asking you, Madam, to pledge yourself not to commit adultery of the brain because it is a much more serious offence than the other." "Adultery of the brain," she may reply, "means writing what I do not want to write for the sake of money. Therefore you ask me to refuse all publishers, editors, lecture agents and so on who bribe me to write or to speak what I do not want to write or to speak for the sake of money?" "That is so, Madam; and we further ask that if you should receive proposals for such sales you will resent them and expose them as you would resent and expose such proposals for selling your body, for your own sake and for the sake of others. But we would have you observe that the verb 'to adulterate' means, according to the dictionary, 'to falsify by admixture of baser ingredients.' Money is not the only baser ingredient. Advertisement and publicity are also adulterers. Thus, culture mixed with personal charm, or culture mixed with advertisement and publicity, are also adulterated forms of culture. We must ask you to abjure them; not to appear on public platforms; not to lecture; not to allow your private face to be published, or details of your private life; not to avail yourself, in short, of any of the forms of brain prostitution which are so insidiously suggested by the pimps and panders of the brain-selling trade; or to accept any of those baubles and labels by which brain merit is advertised and certified—medals, honours, degrees—we must ask you to refuse them absolutely, since they are all tokens that culture has been prostituted and intellectual liberty sold into captivity."

Upon hearing this definition, mild and imperfect as it is, of what it means, not merely to sign your manifesto in favour of culture and intellectual liberty, but to put that opinion into practice, even those daughters of educated men who have enough to live upon may object that the terms are too hard for them to keep. For they would mean loss of money which is desirable, loss of fame which is universally held to be agreeable, and censure and ridicule which are by no means negligible. Each would be the butt of all who have an interest to serve or money to make from the sale of brains. And for what reward? Only, in the rather abstract terms of your manifesto, that they would thus "protect culture and intellectual liberty," not by their opinion but by their practice.

Since the terms are so hard, and there is no body in existence whose ruling they need respect or obey, let us consider what other method of persuasion is left to us. Only, it would seem, to point to the photographs—the photographs of dead bodies and ruined houses. Can we bring out the connection between them and prostituted culture and intellectual slavery and make it so clear that the one implies the other,

---

6. Macaulay's *History of England*, Vol III, p. 278 (standard edition) [Woolf's note].

that the daughters of educated men will prefer to refuse money and fame, and to be the objects of scorn and ridicule rather than suffer themselves, or allow others to suffer, the penalties there made visible? It is difficult in the short time at our disposal, and with the weak weapons in our possession, to make that connection clear, but if what you, Sir, say is true, and there is a connection and a very real one between them, we must try to prove it.

* * *

Now that we have tried to see how we can help you to prevent war by attempting to define what is meant by protecting culture and intellectual liberty let us consider your next and inevitable request: that we should subscribe to the funds of your society. For you, too, are an honorary treasurer, and like the other honorary treasurers in need of money. Since you, too, are asking for money it might be possible to ask you, also, to define your aims, and to bargain and to impose terms as with the other honorary treasurers. What then are the aims of your society? To prevent war, of course. And by what means? Broadly speaking, by protecting the rights of the individual; by opposing dictatorship; by ensuring the democratic ideals of equal opportunity for all. Those are the chief means by which as you say, "the lasting peace of the world can be assured." Then, Sir, there is no need to bargain or to haggle. If those are your aims, and if, as it is impossible to doubt, you mean to do all in your power to achieve them, the guinea is yours—would that it were a million! The guinea is yours; and the guinea is a free gift, given freely.

But the word "free" is used so often, and has come, like used words, to mean so little, that it may be well to explain exactly, even pedantically, what the word "free" means in this context. It means here that no right or privilege is asked in return. The giver is not asking you to admit her to the priesthood of the Church of England; or to the Stock Exchange; or to the Diplomatic Service. The giver has no wish to be "English" on the same terms that you yourself are "English." The giver does not claim in return for the gift admission to any profession; any honour, title, or medal; any professorship or lectureship; any seat upon any society, committee or board. The gift is free from all such conditions because the one right of paramount importance to all human beings is already won. You cannot take away her right to earn a living. Now then for the first time in English history an educated man's daughter can give her brother one guinea of her own making at his request for the purpose specified above without asking for anything in return. It is a free gift, given without fear, without flattery, and without conditions. That, Sir, is so momentous an occasion in the history of civilization that some celebration seems called for. But let us have done with the old ceremonies—the Lord Mayor, with turtles and sheriffs in attendance, tapping nine times with his mace upon a stone while the Archbishop of Canterbury in full canonicals invokes a blessing.[7] Let us invent a new ceremony for this new occasion. What more fitting than to destroy an old word, a vicious and corrupt word that has done much harm in its day and is now obsolete? The word "feminist" is the word indicated. That word, according to the dictionary, means "one who champions the rights of women." Since the only right, the right to earn a living, has been won, the word no longer has a meaning. And a word without a meaning is a dead word, a corrupt word. Let us therefore celebrate this occasion by cremating the corpse. Let us write that word in large black letters on a sheet of foolscap; then solemnly apply a match to the paper. Look, how it burns! What a light dances over the world! Now let us bray the ashes in a mortar with a goosefeather pen, and declare in unison singing together

7. The Lord Mayor of London is a largely ceremonial figure; the Archbishop of Canterbury is the senior bishop of the Church of England.

that anyone who uses that word in future is a ring-the-bell-and-run-away-man,[8] a mischief maker, a groper among old bones, the proof of whose defilement is written in a smudge of dirty water upon his face. The smoke has died down; the word is destroyed. Observe, Sir, what has happened as the result of our celebration. The word "feminist" is destroyed; the air is cleared; and in that clearer air what do we see? Men and women working together for the same cause. The cloud has lifted from the past too. What were they working for in the nineteenth century—those queer dead women in their poke bonnets and shawls? The very same cause for which we are working now. "Our claim was no claim of women's rights only;"—it is Josephine Butler[9] who speaks—"it was larger and deeper; it was a claim for the rights of all—all men and women—to the respect in their persons of the great principles of Justice and Equality and Liberty." The words are the same as yours; the claim is the same as yours. The daughters of educated men who were called, to their resentment, "feminists" were in fact the advance guard of your own movement. They were fighting the same enemy that you are fighting and for the same reasons. They were fighting the tyranny of the patriarchal state as you are fighting the tyranny of the Fascist state. Thus we are merely carrying on the same fight that our mothers and grandmothers fought; their words prove it; your words prove it. But now with your letter before us we have your assurance that you are fighting with us, not against us. That fact is so inspiring that another celebration seems called for. What could be more fitting than to write more dead words, more corrupt words, upon more sheets of paper and burn them—the words, Tyrant, Dictator, for example? But, alas, those words are not yet obsolete. We can still shake out eggs from newspapers; still smell a peculiar and unmistakable odour in the region of Whitehall and Westminster. And abroad the monster has come more openly to the surface. There is no mistaking him there. He has widened his scope. He is interfering now with your liberty; he is dictating how you shall live; he is making distinctions not merely between the sexes, but between the races. You are feeling in your own persons what your mothers felt when they were shut out, when they were shut up, because they were women. Now you are being shut out, you are being shut up, because you are Jews, because you are democrats, because of race, because of religion. It is not a photograph that you look upon any longer; there you go, trapesing along in the procession yourselves. And that makes a difference. The whole iniquity of dictatorship, whether in Oxford or Cambridge, in Whitehall or Downing Street, against Jews or against women, in England, or in Germany, in Italy or in Spain is now apparent to you. But now we are fighting together. The daughters and sons of educated men are fighting side by side. That fact is so inspiring, even if no celebration is yet possible, that if this one guinea could be multiplied a million times all those guineas should be at your service without any other conditions than those that you have imposed upon yourself. Take this one guinea then and use it to assert "the rights of all—all men and women—to the respect in their persons of the great principles of Justice and Equality and Liberty." Put this penny candle in the window of your new society, and may we live to see the day when in the blaze of our common freedom the words tyrant and dictator shall be burnt to ashes, because the words tyrant and dictator shall be obsolete.

---

8. This word has been coined in order to define those who make use of words with the desire to hurt but at the same time to escape detection. In a transitional age when many qualities are changing their value, new words to express new values are much to be desired. Vanity, for example, which would seem to lead to severe complica-
tions of cruelty and tyranny, judging from evidence supplied abroad, is still masked by a name with trivial associations. A supplement to the *Oxford English Dictionary* is indicated [Woolf's note].
9. Feminist involved in the movement for educational reform (1828–1906).

That request then for a guinea answered, and the cheque signed, only one further request of yours remains to be considered—it is that we should fill up a form and become members of your society. On the face of it that seems a simple request, easily granted. For what can be simpler than to join the society to which this guinea has just been contributed? On the face of it, how easy, how simple; but in the depths, how difficult, how complicated. . . . What possible doubts, what possible hesitations can those dots stand for? What reason or what emotion can make us hesitate to become members of a society whose aims we approve, to whose funds we have contributed? It may be neither reason nor emotion, but something more profound and fundamental than either. It may be difference. Different we are, as facts have proved, both in sex and in education. And it is from that difference, as we have already said, that our help can come, if help we can, to protect liberty, to prevent war. But if we sign this form which implies a promise to become active members of your society, it would seem that we must lose that difference and therefore sacrifice that help. ✻ ✻ ✻

✻ ✻ ✻ Thus, Sir, while we respect you as a private person and prove it by giving you a guinea to spend as you choose, we believe that we can help you most effectively by refusing to join your society; by working for our common ends—justice and equality and liberty for all men and women—outside your society, not within.

But this, you will say, if it means anything, can only mean that you, the daughters of educated men, who have promised us your positive help, refuse to join our society in order that you may make another of your own. And what sort of society do you propose to found outside ours, but in co-operation with it, so that we may both work together for our common ends? That is a question which you have every right to ask, and which we must try to answer in order to justify our refusal to sign the form you send. Let us then draw rapidly in outline the kind of society which the daughters of educated men found and join outside your society but in co-operation with its ends. In the first place, this new society, you will be relieved to learn, would have no honorary treasurer, for it would need no funds. It would have no office, no committee, no secretary; it would call no meetings; it would hold no conferences. If name it must have, it could be called the Outsiders' Society. That is not a resonant name, but it has the advantage that it squares with facts—the facts of history, of law, of biography; even, it may be, with the still hidden facts of our still unknown psychology. It would consist of educated men's daughters working in their own class—how indeed can they work in any other?[1]—and by their own methods for liberty, equality and peace. Their first duty, to which they would bind themselves not by oath, for oaths and ceremonies have no part in a society which must be anonymous and elastic

---

1. In the 19th century much valuable work was done for the working class by educated men's daughters in the only way that was then open to them. But now that some of them at least have received an expensive education, it is arguable that they can work much more effectively by remaining in their own class and using the methods of that class to improve a class which stands much in need of improvement. If on the other hand the educated (as so often happens) renounce the very qualities which education should have brought—reason, tolerance, knowledge—and play at belonging to the working class and adopting its cause, they merely expose that cause to the ridicule of the educated class and do nothing to improve their own. But the number of books written by the educated about the working class would seem to show that the glamour of the working class and the emotional relief afforded by adopting its cause, are today as irresistible to the middle class as the glamour of the aristocracy was 20 years ago (see *A la Recherche du Temps Perdu*). Meanwhile it would be interesting to know what the true-born working man or woman thinks of the playboys and playgirls of the educated class who adopt the working-class cause without sacrificing middle-class capital, or sharing working-class experience. "The average housewife," according to Mrs Murphy, Home Service Director of the British Commercial Gas Association, "washed an acre of dirty dishes, a mile of glass and three miles of clothes and scrubbed five miles of floor yearly." (*Daily Telegraph*, September 29th, 1937.) For a more detailed account of working-class life, see *Life as We Have Known It* by Co-operative working women, edited by Margaret Llewelyn Davies. *The Life of Joseph Wright* also gives a remarkable account of working-class life at first hand and not through pro-proletarian spectacles [Woolf's note].

before everything, would be not to fight with arms. This is easy for them to observe, for in fact, as the papers inform us, "the Army Council have no intention of opening recruiting for any women's corps.[2]" The country ensures it. Next they would refuse in the event of war to make munitions or nurse the wounded. Since in the last war both these activities were mainly discharged by the daughters of working men, the pressure upon them here too would be slight, though probably disagreeable. On the other hand the next duty to which they would pledge themselves is one of considerable difficulty, and calls not only for courage and initiative, but for the special knowledge of the educated man's daughter. It is, briefly, not to incite their brothers to fight, or to dissuade them, but to maintain an attitude of complete indifference. But the attitude expressed by the word "indifference" is so complex and of such importance that it needs even here further definition. Indifference in the first place must be given a firm footing upon fact. As it is a fact that she cannot understand what instinct compels him, what glory, what interest, what manly satisfaction fighting provides for him— "without war there would be no outlet for the manly qualities which fighting develops"—as fighting thus is a sex characteristic which she cannot share, the counterpart some claim of the maternal instinct which he cannot share, so is it an instinct which she cannot judge. The outsider therefore must leave him free to deal with this instinct by himself, because liberty of opinion must be respected, especially when it is based upon an instinct which is as foreign to her as centuries of tradition and education can make it.[3] This is a fundamental and instinctive distinction upon which indifference may be based. But the outsider will make it her duty not merely to base her indifference upon instinct, but upon reason. When he says, as history proves that he has said, and may say again, "I am fighting to protect our country" and thus seeks to rouse her patriotic emotion, she will ask herself, "What does 'our country' mean to me an outsider?" To decide this she will analyse the meaning of patriotism in her own case. She will inform herself of the position of her sex and her class in the past. She will inform herself of the amount of land, wealth and property in the possession of her own sex and class in the present—how much of "England" in fact belongs to her. From the same sources she will inform herself of the legal protection which the law has given her in the past and now gives her. And if he adds that he is fighting to protect her body, she will reflect upon the degree of physical protection that she now enjoys when the words "Air Raid Precaution" are written on blank walls. And if he says that he is fighting to protect England from foreign rule, she will reflect that for her there are no "foreigners," since by law she becomes a foreigner if she marries a foreigner. And she will do her best to make this a fact, not by forced fraternity, but by human sympathy. All these facts will convince her reason (to put it in a nutshell) that her sex and class has very little to thank England for in the past; not much to thank England for in the present; while the security of her person in the future is highly dubious. But probably she will have imbibed, even from the governess, some

2. "It was stated yesterday at the War Office that the Army Council have no intention of opening recruiting for any women's corps." (The Times, October 22nd, 1937.) This marks a prime distinction between the sexes. Pacifism is enforced upon women. Men are still allowed liberty of choice [Woolf's note].

3. The following quotation shows, however, that if sanctioned the fighting instinct easily develops. "The eyes deeply sunk into the sockets, the features acute, the amazon keeps herself very straight on the stirrups at the head of her squadron . . . Five English parliamentaries look at this woman with the respectful and a bit restless admiration one feels for a 'fauve' of an unknown species . . . The amazon Amalia rides in fact a magnificent dapple-grey horse, with glossy hair, which flatters like a parade horse . . . This woman who has killed five men—but who feels not sure about the sixth—was for the envoys of the House of Commons an excellent introducer to the Spanish War." (The Matyrdom of Madrid, Inedited Witnesses, by Louis Delaprée, pp. 34, 5, 6. Madrid, 1937) [Woolf's note].

romantic notion that Englishmen, those fathers and grandfathers whom she sees marching in the picture of history, are "superior" to the men of other countries. This she will consider it her duty to check by comparing French historians with English; German with French; the testimony of the ruled—the Indians or the Irish, say—with the claims made by their rulers. Still some "patriotic" emotion, some ingrained belief in the intellectual superiority of her own country over other countries may remain. Then she will compare English painting with French painting; English music with German music; English literature with Greek literature, for translations abound. When all these comparisons have been faithfully made by the use of reason, the outsider will find herself in possession of very good reasons for her indifference. She will find that she has no good reason to ask her brother to fight on her behalf to protect "our" country. "'Our country,'" she will say, "throughout the greater part of its history has treated me as a slave; it has denied me education or any share in its possessions. 'Our' country still ceases to be mine if I marry a foreigner. 'Our' country denies me the means of protecting myself, forces me to pay others a very large sum annually to protect me, and is so little able, even so, to protect me that Air Raid precautions are written on the wall. Therefore if you insist upon fighting to protect me, or 'our' country, let it be understood, soberly and rationally between us, that you are fighting to gratify a sex instinct which I cannot share; to procure benefits which I have not shared and probably will not share; but not to gratify my instincts, or to protect myself or my country. For," the outsider will say, "in fact, as a woman, I have no country. As a woman I want no country. As a woman my country is the whole world." And if, when reason has said its say, still some obstinate emotion remains, some love of England dropped into a child's ears by the cawing of rooks in an elm tree, by the splash of waves on a beach, or by English voices murmuring nursery rhymes, this drop of pure, if irrational, emotion she will make serve her to give to England first what she desires of peace and freedom for the whole world.

Such then will be the nature of her "indifference" and from this indifference certain actions must follow. She will bind herself to take no share in patriotic demonstrations; to assent to no form of national self-praise; to make no part of any claque or audience that encourages war; to absent herself from military displays, tournaments, tattoos, prize-givings and all such ceremonies as encourage the desire to impose "our" civilization or "our" dominion upon other people. The psychology of private life, moreover, warrants the belief that this use of indifference by the daughters of educated men would help materially to prevent war. For psychology would seem to show that it is far harder for human beings to take action when other people are indifferent and allow them complete freedom of action, than when their actions are made the centre of excited emotion. The small boy struts and trumpets outside the window: implore him to stop; he goes on; say nothing; he stops. That the daughters of educated men then should give their brothers neither the white feather of cowardice nor the red feather of courage, but no feather at all;[4] that they should shut the bright eyes that rain influence, or let those eyes look elsewhere when war is discussed—that is the duty to which outsiders will train themselves in peace before the threat of death inevitably makes reason powerless.

---

4. During the First World War in Britain patriotic women would hand a white feather to men who seemed to have evaded military service.

Such then are some of the methods by which the society, the anonymous and secret Society of Outsiders would help you, Sir, to prevent war and to ensure freedom. * * *

It would be easy to define in greater number and more exactly the duties of those who belong to the Society of Outsiders, but not profitable. Elasticity is essential; and some degree of secrecy, as will be shown later, is at present even more essential. But the description thus loosely and imperfectly given is enough to show you, Sir, that the Society of Outsiders has the same ends as your society—freedom, equality, peace; but that it seeks to achieve them by the means that a different sex, a different tradition, a different education, and the different values which result from those differences have placed within our reach. Broadly speaking, the main distinction between us who are outside society and you who are inside society must be that whereas you will make use of the means provided by your position—leagues, conferences, campaigns, great names, and all such public measures as your wealth and political influence place within your reach—we, remaining outside, will experiment not with public means in public but with private means in private. Those experiments will not be merely critical but creative. To take two obvious instances:—the outsiders will dispense with pageantry not from any puritanical dislike of beauty. On the contrary, it will be one of their aims to increase private beauty; the beauty of spring, summer, autumn; the beauty of flowers, silks, clothes; the beauty which brims not only every field and wood but every barrow in Oxford Street;[5] the scattered beauty which needs only to be combined by artists in order to become visible to all. But they will dispense with the dictated, regimented, official pageantry, in which only one sex takes an active part—those ceremonies, for example, which depend upon the deaths of kings, or their coronations to inspire them. Again, they will dispense with personal distinctions—medals, ribbons, badges, hoods, gowns—not from any dislike of personal adornment, but because of the obvious effect of such distinctions to constrict, to stereotype and to destroy. Here, as so often, the example of the Fascist States is at hand to instruct us—for if we have no example of what we wish to be, we have, what is perhaps equally valuable, a daily and illuminating example of what we do not wish to be. With the example then, that they give us of the power of medals, symbols, orders and even, it would seem, of decorated ink-pots[6] to hypnotize the human mind it must be our aim not to submit ourselves to such hypnotism. We must extinguish the coarse glare of advertisement and publicity, not merely because the limelight is apt to be held in incompetent hands, but because of the psychological effect of such illumination upon those who receive it. Consider next time you drive along a country road the attitude of a rabbit caught in the glare of a head-lamp—its glazed eyes, its rigid paws. Is there not good reason to think without going outside our own country, that the "attitudes," the false and unreal positions taken by the human form in England as well as in Germany, are due to the limelight which paralyses the free action of the human faculties and inhibits the human power to change and create new wholes much as a strong head-lamp paralyses the little creatures who run out of the darkness into its beams? It is a guess; guessing is dangerous; yet we have some reason to guide us in the guess that ease and freedom, the power to change and the power to grow,

5. Busy commercial street in central London.
6. To speak accurately, "a large silver plaque in the form of the Reich eagle . . . was created by President Hindenburg for scientists and other distinguished civilians . . . It may not be worn. It is usually placed on the writing-desk of the recipient." (Daily paper, April 21st, 1936) [Woolf's note].

can only be preserved by obscurity; and that if we wish to help the human mind to create, and to prevent it from scoring the same rut repeatedly, we must do what we can to shroud it in darkness.

* * *

It seems, Sir, as we listen to the voices of the past, as if we were looking at the photograph again, at the picture of dead bodies and ruined houses that the Spanish Government sends us almost weekly.[7] Things repeat themselves it seems. Pictures and voices are the same today as they were 2,000 years ago.

Such then is the conclusion to which our enquiry into the nature of fear has brought us—the fear which forbids freedom in the private house. That fear, small, insignificant and private as it is, is connected with the other fear, the public fear, which is neither small nor insignificant, the fear which has led you to ask us to help you to prevent war. Otherwise we should not be looking at the picture again. But it is not the same picture that caused us at the beginning of this letter to feel the same emotions—you called them "horror and disgust"; we called them horror and disgust. For as this letter has gone on, adding fact to fact, another picture has imposed itself upon the foreground. It is the figure of a man; some say, others deny, that he is Man himself,[8] the quintessence of virility, the perfect type of which all the others are imperfect adumbrations. He is a man certainly. His eyes are glazed; his eyes glare. His body, which is braced in an unnatural position, is tightly cased in a uniform. Upon the breast of that uniform are sewn several medals and other mystic symbols. His hand is upon a sword. He is called in German and Italian Führer or Duce; in our own language Tyrant or Dictator. And behind him lie ruined houses and dead bodies—men, women and children. But we have not laid that picture before you in order to excite once more the sterile emotion of hate. On the contrary it is in order to release other emotions such as the human figure, even thus crudely in a coloured photograph, arouses in us who are human beings. For it suggests a connection and for us a very important connection. It suggests that the public and the private worlds are inseparably connected; that the tyrannies and servilities of the one are the tyrannies and servilities of the other. But the human figure even in a photograph suggests other and more complex emotions. It suggests that we cannot dissociate ourselves from that figure but are ourselves that figure. It suggests that we are not passive spectators doomed to unresisting obedience but by our thoughts and actions can ourselves change that figure. A common interest unites us; it is one world, one life. How essential it is that we should realise that unity the dead bodies, the ruined houses prove. For such will be our ruin if you in the immensity of your public abstractions forget the private figure, or if we in the intensity of our private emotions forget the public world. Both houses will be ruined, the public and the private, the material and the spiritual, for they are inseparably connected. But with your letter before us we have reason to hope. For by asking our help you recognise that connection; and by reading

7. The Republican Government in Spain was then engaged in a war against Fascist forces intent on seizing power; by 1939 the Fascists had gained control of the country.
8. The nature of manhood and the nature of womanhood are frequently defined by both Italian and German dictators. Both repeatedly insist that it is the nature of man and indeed the essence of manhood to fight . . . It is possible that the Fascist States by revealing to the younger generation at least the need for emancipation from the old conception of virility are doing for the male sex what the Crimean and the European wars did for their sisters. Professor Huxley, however, warns us that "any considerable alteration of the hereditary constitution is an affair of millennia, not of decades." On the other hand, as science also assures us that our life on earth is "an affair of millennia, not of decades," some alteration in the hereditary constitution may be worth attempting [Woolf's note].

your words we are reminded of other connections that lie far deeper than the facts on the surface. Even here, even now your letter tempts us to shut our ears to these little facts, these trivial details, to listen not to the bark of the guns and the bray of the gramophones but to the voices of the poets, answering each other, assuring us of a unity that rubs out divisions as if they were chalk marks only; to discuss with you the capacity of the human spirit to overflow boundaries and make unity out of multiplicity. But that would be to dream—to dream the recurring dream that has haunted the human mind since the beginning of time; the dream of peace, the dream of freedom. But, with the sound of the guns in your ears you have not asked us to dream. You have not asked us what peace is; you have asked us how to prevent war. Let us then leave it to the poets to tell us what the dream is; and fix our eyes upon the photograph again: the fact.

Whatever the verdict of others may be upon the man in uniform—and opinions differ—there is your letter to prove that to you the picture is the picture of evil. And though we look upon that picture from different angles our conclusion is the same as yours—it is evil. We are both determined to do what we can to destroy the evil which that picture represents, you by your methods, we by ours. And since we are different, our help must be different. What ours can be we have tried to show—how imperfectly, how superficially there is no need to say.[9] But as a result the answer to your question must be that we can best help you to prevent war not by repeating your words and following your methods but by finding new words and creating new methods. We can best help you to prevent war not by joining your society but by remaining outside your society but in co-operation with its aim. That aim is the same for us both. It is to assert "the rights of all—all men and women—to the respect in their persons of the great principles of Justice and Equality and Liberty." To elaborate further is unnecessary, for we have every confidence that you interpret those words as we do. And excuses are unnecessary, for we can trust you to make allowances for those deficiencies which we foretold and which this letter has abundantly displayed.

To return then to the form that you have sent and ask us to fill up: for the reasons given we will leave it unsigned. But in order to prove as substantially as possible that our aims are the same as yours, here is the guinea, a free gift, given freely, without any other conditions than you choose to impose upon yourself. It is the third of three guineas; but the three guineas, you will observe, though given to three different treasurers are all given to the same cause, for the causes are the same and inseparable.

Now, since you are pressed for time, let me make an end; apologising three times over to the three of you, first for the length of this letter, second for the smallness of the contribution, and thirdly for writing at all. The blame for that however rests upon you, for this letter would never have been written had you not asked for an answer to your own.

9. Coleridge however expresses the views and aims of the outsiders with some accuracy in the following passage: "Man must be *free* or to what purpose was he made a Spirit of Reason, and not a Machine of Instinct? Man must *obey*; or wherefore has he a conscience? The powers, which create this difficulty, contain its solution likewise, for *their* service is perfect freedom." . . . To which may be added a quotation from Walt Whitman: "Of Equality—as if it harm'd me, giving others the same chances and rights as myself—as if it were not indispensable to my own rights that others possess the same." And finally the words of a half-forgotten novelist, George Sand, are worth considering: "All lives are bound up with each other, and any human being who would describe his or her selfhood in isolation, without linking it to that of his or her fellows, would only offer a mystery to be untangled . . . That kind of individuality has by itself neither meaning nor importance. It only takes on any kind of meaning by becoming a part of the general life, by grounding itself together with the individuality of each of my fellows, and through that gesture it becomes a part of history." (*Histoire de ma Vie* [The Story of My Life], by George Sand, pp. 240–1) [Woolf's note, quoting Sand in French].

from **The Diaries**

Friday 1 January [1915]

To start this diary rightly, it should begin on the last day of the old year, when, at breakfast, I received a letter from Mrs Hallett. She said that she had had to dismiss Lily[1] at a moments notice, owing to her misbehaviour. We naturally supposed that a certain kind of misbehaviour was meant; a married gardener, I hazarded. Our speculations made us both uncomfortable all day. Now this morning I hear from Lily herself. She writes, very calmly, that she left because Mrs Hallett was "insulting" to her; having been given a day & nights holiday, she came back at 8.30 A.M. "not early enough." What is the truth? This, I guess: Mrs H. is an old angry woman, meticulous, indeed as we knew tyrannical, about her servants; & Lily honestly meant no wrong. But I have written for particulars—another lady wanting a character at once. Then I had to write to Mrs Waterlow about the chimney sweeping charges foisted on us, such a letter as comes naturally to the strong character, but not to the weak. And then we tramped to the Co-ops.[2] in rain & cold to protest against their bookkeeping. Manager a bored languid young man, repeating rather than defending himself. Half way home we heard "British warship . . . British warship" & found that the Formidable has been sunk in the channel.[3] We were kept awake last night by New Year Bells. At first I thought they were ringing for a victory.

Saturday 2 January [1915]

This is the kind of day which if it were possible to choose an altogether average sample of our life, I should select. We breakfast; I interview Mrs Le Grys. She complains of the huge Belgian appetites, & their preference for food fried in butter. "They never *give* one anything" she remarked. The Count, taking Xmas dinner with them, insisted, after Pork & Turkey, that he wanted a third meat. Therefore Mrs Le G. hopes that the war will soon be over. If they eat thus in their exile, how must they eat at home, she wonders?[4] After this, L[eonard]. & I both settle down to our scribbling. He finishes his Folk Story review, & I do about 4 pages of poor Effie's story;[5] we lunch; & read the papers, agree that there is no news. I read Guy Mannering upstairs for 20 minutes;[6] & then we take Max [a dog] for a walk. Halfway up to the Bridge, we found ourselves cut off by the river, which rose visibly, with a little ebb & flow, like the pulse of a heart. Indeed, the road we had come along was crossed, after 5 minutes, by a stream several inches deep. One of the queer things about the suburbs is that the vilest little red villas are always let, & that not one of them has an open window, or an uncurtained window. I expect that people take a pride in their curtains, & there is great rivalry among neighbours. One house had curtains of yellow silk, striped with lace insertion. The rooms inside must be in semi-darkness; & I suppose rank with the smell of meat & human beings. I believe that being curtained is a mark of respectability—Sophie[7] used to insist upon it. And then I did my marketing. Saturday night is the great buying night; & some counters are besieged by three rows of

1. A maid.
2. A British retail chain.
3. The H.M.S. *Formidable* was torpedoed by a German submarine.
4. Belgian refugees were housed in English homes follow-ing the German invasion of Belgium.
5. Later published as *Night and Day* (1919).
6. *Guy Mannering* (1815), a novel by Sir Walter Scott.
7. A former family cook.

women. I always choose the empty shops, where I suppose, one pays ½ a lb. more. And then we had tea, & honey & cream; & now L. is typewriting his article; & we shall read all the evening & go to bed.

Thursday 11 October [1917]

The dinner last night went off: the delicate things were discussed. We could both wish that ones first impression of K.M.[8] was not that she stinks like a—well civet cat that had taken to street walking. In truth, I'm a little shocked by her commonness at first sight; lines so hard & cheap. However, when this diminishes, she is so intelligent & inscrutable that she repays friendship. My saying—Chaste & the Unchaste—was exaggerated by Murry for reasons of his own; reasons that make him wish all of a sudden to break with Garsington.[9] We discussed Henry James, & K.M. was illuminating I thought. A munition worker called Leslie Moor came to fetch her—another of these females on the border land of propriety, & naturally inhabiting the underworld—rather vivacious, sallow skinned, without any attachment to one place rather than another. Today poor L. had to go the round of Drs & committees, with a visit to Squire thrown in. His certifications are repeated. He weighs only 9.6. I bought my winter store of gloves, got a reference in the London Library, & met L. at Spikings for tea. Heaven blessed us by sending a quick train, & we came home, very glad to be home, over our fire, though we had to light it, & cook up our dinner, owing to the servants off day.

Thursday 6 December [1917]

When I wrote that we were only at the beginning of our days work, last night, I spoke more truly than I knew. Nothing was further from our minds than air raids; a bitter night, no moon up till eleven. At 5 however, I was wakened by L. to a most instant sense of guns: as if one's faculties jumped up fully dressed. We took clothes, quilts, a watch & a torch; the guns sounding nearer as we went down stairs to sit with the servants on the ancient black horse hair chest wrapped in quilts in the kitchen passage. Lottie having said she felt bad, passed on to a general rattle of jokes & comments which almost silenced the guns. They fired very quickly, apparently towards Barnes. Slowly the sounds got more distant, & finally ceased; we unwrapped ourselves & went back to bed. In ten minutes there could be no question of staying there: guns apparently at Kew. Up we jumped, more hastily this time, since I remember leaving my watch, & trailing cloak & stockings behind me. Servants apparently calm & even jocose. In fact one talks through the noise, rather bored by having to talk at 5 A.M. than anything else. Guns at one point so loud that the whistle of the shell going up followed the explosion. One window did, I think, rattle. Then silence. Cocoa was brewed for us, & off we went again. Having trained one's ears to listen one can't get them not to for a time; & as it was after 6, carts were rolling out of stables, motor cars throbbing, & then prolonged ghostly whistlings which meant, I suppose, Belgian work people recalled to the munitions factory. At last in the distance I heard bugles; L. was by this time asleep, but the dutiful boy scouts came down our road & wakened him carefully; it struck me how sentimental the suggestion of the sound was, & how thousands of old ladies were offering up their thanksgivings at the sound,

8. The writer Katherine Mansfield; see page 2265.
9. John Middleton Murray (1889–1957), critic and journalist, married Katherine Mansfield in 1918. Garsington
Manor was the home of Lady Ottoline Morrell.

& connecting him (a boy scout with small angel wings) with some joyful vision—
And then I went to sleep, but the servants sat up with their heads out of the window
in the bitter cold—frost white on the roofs—until the bugle sounded, when they
went back to the kitchen and sat there till breakfast. The logic of the proceeding
escapes me.

Today we have printed, & discussed the raid, which, according to the Star I
bought was the work of 25 Gothas, attacking in 5 squadrons & 2 were brought down.
A perfectly still & fine winter's day, so about 5.30-tomorrow morning perhaps—

Monday 21 January [1918]

Here I was interrupted on the verge of a description of London at the meeting of
sun set & moon rise. I drove on top of a Bus from Oxford St. to Victoria station, &
observed how the passengers were watching the spectacle: the same sense of interest
& mute attention shown as in the dress circle before some pageant. A Spring night;
blue sky with a smoke mist over the houses. The shops were still lit; but not the
lamps, so that there were bars of light all down the streets; & in Bond Street I was at
a loss to account for a great chandelier of light at the end of the street; but it proved
to be several shop windows jutting out into the road, with lights on different tiers.
Then at Hyde Park Corner the search light rays out, across the blue; part of a pageant
on a stage where all has been wonderfully muted down. The gentleness of the scene
was what impressed me; a twilight view of London. Houses very large & looking
stately. Now & then someone, as the moon came into view, remarked upon the
chance for an air raid. We escaped though, a cloud rising towards night.

Friday 8 August [1918]

In the absence of human interest, which makes us peaceful & content, one may
as well go on with Byron. Having indicated that I am ready, after a century, to fall in
love with him, I suppose my judgment of Don Juan[1] may be partial. It is the most
readable poem of its length ever written, I suppose; a quality which it owes in part to
the springy random haphazard galloping nature of its method. This method is a discovery by itself. Its what one has looked for in vain—a[n] elastic shape which will
hold whatever you choose to put into it. Thus he could write out his mood as it came
to him; he could say whatever came into his head. He wasn't committed to be poetical; & thus escaped his evil genius of the false romantic & imaginative. When he is
serious he is sincere; & he can impinge upon any subject he likes. He writes 16 canto's without once flogging his flanks. He had, evidently, the able witty mind of what
my father Sir Leslie would have called a thoroughly masculine nature. I maintain
that these illicit kind of books are far more interesting than the proper books which
respect illusions devoutly all the time. Still, it doesn't seem an easy example to follow; & indeed like all free & easy things, only the skilled & mature really bring them
off successfully. But Byron was full of ideas—a quality that gives his verse a toughness, & drives me to little excursions over the surrounding landscape or room in the
middle of my reading. And tonight I shall have the pleasure of finishing him—
though why, considering that I've enjoyed almost every stanza, this should be a pleasure I really dont know. But so it always is, whether the books a good book or a bad

---

1. Byron's satirical epic poem *Don Juan* (1819–1824); see page 569.

book. Maynard Keynes admitted in the same way that he always cuts off the advertisements at the end with one hand while he's reading, so as to know exactly how much he has to get through. * * *

Sunday (Easter) 20 April [1919]

* * * In the idleness which succeeds any long article, & Defoe is the 2nd leader this month, I got out this diary, & read as one always does read one's own writing, with a kind of guilty intensity. I confess that the rough & random style of it, often so ungrammatical, & crying for a word altered, afflicted me somewhat. I am trying to tell whichever self it is that reads this hereafter that I can write very much better; & take no time over this; & forbid her to let the eye of man behold it. And now I may add my little compliment to the effect that it has a slapdash & vigour, & sometimes hits an unexpected bulls eye. But what is more to the point is my belief that the habit of writing thus for my own eye only is good practise. It loosens the ligaments. Never mind the misses & the stumbles. Going at such a pace as I do I must make the most direct & instant shots at my object, & thus have to lay hands on words, choose them, & shoot them with no more pause than is needed to put my pen in the ink. I believe that during the past year I can trace some increase of ease in my professional writing which I attribute to my casual half hours after tea. Moreover there looms ahead of me the shadow of some kind of form which a diary might attain to. I might in the course of time learn what it is that one can make of this loose, drifting material of life; finding another use for it than the use I put it to, so much more consciously & scrupulously, in fiction. What sort of diary should I like mine to be? Something loose knit, & yet not slovenly, so elastic that it will embrace any thing, solemn, slight or beautiful that comes into my mind. I should like it to resemble some deep old desk, or capacious hold-all, in which one flings a mass of odds & ends without looking them through. I should like to come back, after a year or two, & find that the collection had sorted itself & refined itself & coalesced, as such deposits so mysteriously do, into a mould, transparent enough to reflect the light of our life, & yet steady, tranquil composed with the aloofness of a work of art. The main requisite, I think on re-reading my old volumes, is not to play the part of censor, but to write as the mood comes or of anything whatever; since I was curious to find how I went for things put in haphazard, & found the significance to lie where I never saw it at the time. But looseness quickly becomes slovenly. A little effort is needed to face a character or an incident which needs to be recorded. * * *

Wednesday 7 January [1920]

To begin the year on the last pages of my old book—the few I've not torn off for letter writing—is all upside-down of course; but of a part with the character of the work.

This is our last evening. We sit over the fire waiting for post—the cream of the day, I think. Yet every part of the day here has its merits—even the breakfast without toast. That—however it begins—ends with Pippins; most mornings the sun comes in; we finish in good temper; & I go off to the romantic chamber over grass rough with frost & ground hard as brick. Then Mrs Dedman comes to receive orders—to give them, really, for she has planned our meals to suit her days cooking before she comes. We share her oven. The result is always savoury—stews & mashes & deep many coloured dishes swimming in gravy thick with carrots & onions. Elsie, aged 18, can be spoken to as though she had a head on her shoulders. The house is empty by half past eleven; empty now at five o'clock; we tend our fire, cook coffee, read, I find, luxuriously, peacefully, at length.

But I should not spend my time on an indoor chronicle; unless I lazily shirked the describing of winter down & meadow—the recording of what takes my breath away at every turn. Heres the sun out for example & all the upper twigs of the trees as if dipped in fire; the trunks emerald green; even bark bright tinted, & variable as the skin of a lizard. Then theres Asheham hill smoke misted; the windows of the long train spots of sun; the smoke lying back on the carriages like a rabbits lop ears. The chalk quarry glows pink; & my water meadows lush as June, until you see that the grass is short, & rough as a dogfishes back. But I could go on counting what I've noticed page after page. Every day or nearly I've walked towards a different point & come back with a string of these matchings & marvels. Five minutes from the house one is out in the open, a great pull over Asheham; &, as I say, every direction bears fruit. Once we went over the cornfield & up onto the down—a dim Sunday afternoon—muddy on the road, but dry up above. The long down grass pale, & as we pushed through it, up got a hawk at our feet, seeming to trail near the ground, as if weighted down—attached to something. It let the burden fall, & rose high as we came up. We found the wings of a partridge attached to [a] bleeding stump, for the Hawk had almost done his meal. We saw him go back to find it. Further down the hill side a great white owl "wavy" (for that describes his way of weaving a web round a tree—the plumy soft look of him in the dusk adding truth to the word) "wavy in the dusk," flew behind the hedge as we came past. Village girls were returning, & calling out to friends in doors. So we cross the field & churchyard, find our coke burnt through to red, toast the bread—& the evening comes.

L. has spent most of his time pruning the apple trees, & tying plums to the wall. To do this he wears two jackets, 2 pairs of socks, two pairs of gloves; even so the cold bites through. These last days have been like frozen water, ruffled by the wind into atoms of ice against the cheek; then, in the shelter, forming round you in a still pool.

* * *

Wednesday 16 August [1922]

I should be reading Ulysses, & fabricating my case for & against. I have read 200 pages so far—not a third; & have been amused, stimulated, charmed interested by the first 2 or 3 chapters—to the end of the Cemetery scene; & then puzzled, bored, irritated, & disillusioned as by a queasy undergraduate scratching his pimples. And Tom,[2] great Tom, thinks this on a par with War & Peace! An illiterate, underbred book it seems to me: the book of a self taught working man, & we all know how distressing they are, how egotistic, insistent, raw, striking, & ultimately nauseating. When one can have the cooked flesh, why have the raw? But I think if you are anaemic, as Tom is, there is a glory in blood. Being fairly normal myself I am soon ready for the classics again. I may revise this later. I do not compromise my critical sagacity. I plant a stick in the ground to mark page 200.

2. T. S. Eliot.

For my own part I am laboriously dredging my mind for Mrs Dalloway & bringing up light buckets. I don't like the feeling I'm writing too quickly. I must press it together. I wrote 4 thousand words of reading in record time, 10 days; but then it was merely a quick sketch of Pastons, supplied by books. Now I break off, according to my quick change theory, to write Mrs D. (who ushers in a host of others, I begin to perceive) then I do Chaucer; & finish the first chapter early in September. By the time, I have my Greek beginning perhaps, in my head;[3] & so the future is all pegged out; & when Jacob is rejected in America & ignored in England,[4] I shall be philosophically driving my plough fields away. They are cutting the corn all over the country, which supplies that metaphor, & perhaps excuses it. But I need no excuses, since I am not writing for the Lit Sup. Shall I ever write for them again? * * *

Wednesday 6 September [1922]

* * * I finished Ulysses, & think it a mis-fire. Genius it has I think; but of the inferior water. The book is diffuse. It is brackish. It is pretentious. It is underbred, not only in the obvious sense, but in the literary sense. A first rate writer, I mean, respects writing too much to be tricky; startling; doing stunts. I'm reminded all the time of some callow board school boy, say like Henry Lamb, full of wits & powers, but so self-conscious & egotistical that he loses his head, becomes extravagant, mannered, uproarious, ill at ease, makes kindly people feel sorry for him, & stern ones merely annoyed; & one hopes he'll grow out of it; but as Joyce is 40 this scarcely seems likely. I have not read it carefully; & only once; & it is very obscure; so no doubt I have scamped the virtue of it more than is fair. I feel that myriads of tiny bullets pepper one & spatter one; but one does not get one deadly wound straight in the face—as from Tolstoy, for instance; but it is entirely absurd to compare him with Tolstoy.

Tuesday 19 June [1923]

I took up this book with a kind of idea that I might say something about my writing—which was prompted by glancing at what K.M. said about *her* writing in the Dove's Nest.[5] But I only glanced. She said a good deal about feeling things deeply: also about being pure, which I wont criticise, though of course I very well could. But now what do I feel about *my* writing?—this book, that is, The Hours,[6] if thats its name? One must write from deep feeling, said Dostoevsky. And do I? Or do I fabricate with words, loving them as I do? No I think not. In this book I have almost too many ideas. I want to give life & death, sanity & insanity; I want to criticise the social system, & to show it at work, at its most intense—But here I may be posing. I heard from Ka [Arnold-Forster] this morning that she doesn't like In the Orchard.[7] At once I feel refreshed. I become anonymous, a person who writes for the love of it. She takes away the motive of praise, & lets me feel that without any praise, I should be content to go on. This is what Duncan [Grant] said of his painting the other night. I feel as if I slipped off all my ball dresses & stood naked—which as I remember was a very pleasant thing to do. But to go on. Am I writing The Hours from deep emotion? Of course the mad part tries me so much, makes my mind squint so badly

3. Woolf refers to her book of critical essays *The Common Reader* (1925), which begins with the essays *The Pastons and Chaucer* and *On Not Knowing Greek*.
4. Woolf's novel *Jacob's Room* (1923).
5. J. M. Murray wrote an introduction to Mansfield's *The Dove's Nest and Other Stories* (1923), which quotes extracts from her journal.
6. "The Hours" was an early title for *Mrs. Dalloway* (1925).
7. *In the Orchard* (1923), an essay by Woolf.

that I can hardly face spending the next weeks at it. Its a question though of these characters. People, like Arnold Bennett, say I cant create, or didn't in J[acob]'s R[oom], characters that survive. My answer is—but I leave that to the Nation:[8] its only the old argument that character is dissipated into shreds now: the old post-Dostoevsky argument. I daresay its true, however, that I haven't that "reality" gift. I insubstantise, wilfully to some extent, distrusting reality—its cheapness. But to get further. Have I the power of conveying the true reality? Or do I write essays about myself? Answer these questions as I may, in the uncomplimentary sense, & still there remains this excitement. To get to the bones, now I'm writing fiction again I feel my force flow straight from me at its fullest. After a dose of criticism I feel that I'm writing sideways, using only an angle of my mind. This is justification; for free use of the faculties means happiness. I'm better company, more of a human being. Nevertheless, I think it most important in this book to go for the central things, even though they dont submit, as they should however, to beautification in language. No, I don't nail my crest to the Murrys, who work in my flesh after the manner of the jigger insect. Its annoying, indeed degrading, to have these bitternesses. Still, think of the 18th Century. But then they were overt, not covert, as now.

I foresee, to return to The Hours, that this is going to be the devil of a struggle. The design is so queer & so masterful. I'm always having to wrench my substance to fit it. The design is certainly original, & interests me hugely. I should like to write away & away at it, very quick and fierce. Needless to say, I cant. In three weeks from today I shall be dried up. * * *

Monday 5 May [1924]

* * * London is enchanting. I step out upon a tawny coloured magic carpet, it seems, & get carried into beauty without raising a finger. The nights are amazing, with all the white porticoes & broad silent avenues. And people pop in & out, lightly, divertingly like rabbits; & I look down Southampton Row, wet as a seal's back or red & yellow with sunshine, & watch the omnibus going & coming, & hear the old crazy organs. One of these days I will write about London, & how it takes up the private life & carries it on, without any effort. Faces passing lift up my mind; prevent it from settling, as it does in the stillness at Rodmell. * * *

Friday 17 October [1924]

It is disgraceful. I did run up stairs thinking I'd make time to enter that astounding fact—the last words of the last page of Mrs Dalloway; but was interrupted. Anyhow I did them a week ago yesterday. "For there she was." & I felt glad to be quit of it, for it has been a strain the last weeks, yet fresher in the head; with less I mean of the usual feeling that I've shaved through, & just kept my feet on the tight rope. I feel indeed rather more fully relieved of my meaning than usual—whether this will stand when I re-read is doubtful. But in some ways this book is a feat; finished without break from illness, wh. is an exception; & written really, in one year; & finally, written from the end of March to the 8th of October without more than a few days break for writ-

---

8. In a 1923 review of *Jacob's Room*, the novelist Arnold Bennett had written that "I have seldom read a cleverer book than Virginia Woolf's *Jacob's Room* . . . But the characters do not vitally survive in the mind because the author has been obsessed by details of originality and cleverness." Woolf's reply, *Mr. Bennett and Mrs. Brown*, mocking Bennett's realist fiction as "thin gruel," appeared in the *Nation and Athenaeum* in December 1923.

ing journalism. So it may differ from the others. Anyhow, I feel that I have exorcised the spell wh. Murry & others said I had laid myself under after Jacob's Room. The only difficulty is to hold myself back from writing others. My cul-de-sac, as they called it, stretches so far, & shows such vistas. I see already The Old Man. * * *

Thursday 18 June [1925]

No, Lytton does not like Mrs Dalloway, &, what is odd, I like him all the better for saying so, & don't much mind. What he says is that there is a discordancy between the ornament (extremely beautiful) & what happens (rather ordinary—or unimportant). This is caused he thinks by some discrepancy in Clarissa herself; he thinks she is disagreeable & limited, but that I alternately laugh at her, & cover her, very remarkably, with myself. So that I think as a whole, the book does not ring solid; yet, he says, it is a whole; & he says sometimes the writing is of extreme beauty. What can one call it but genius? he said! Coming when, one never can tell. Fuller of genius, he said than anything I had done. Perhaps, he said, you have not yet mastered your method. You should take something wilder & more fantastic, a frame work that admits of anything, like Tristram Shandy.[9] But then I should lose touch with emotions, I said. Yes, he agreed, there must be reality for you to start from. Heaven knows how you're to do it. But he thought me at the beginning, not at the end. And he said C[ommon].R[eader]. was divine, a classic; Mrs D. being, I fear, a flawed stone. This is very personal, he said & old fashioned perhaps; yet I think there is some truth in it. For I remember the night at Rodmell when I decided to give it up, because I found Clarissa in some way tinselly. Then I invented her memories. But I think some distaste for her persisted. Yet, again, that was true to my feeling for Kitty,[1] & one must dislike people in art without its mattering, unless indeed it is true that certain characters detract from the importance of what happens to them. None of this hurts me, or depresses me. Its odd that when Clive & others (several of them) say it is a masterpiece, I am not much exalted; when Lytton picks holes, I get back into my working fighting mood, which is natural to me. I don't see myself a success. I like the sense of effort better. The sales collapsed completely for 3 days; now a little dribble begins again. I shall be more than pleased if we sell 1500. Its now 1250.

July 20th. Have sold about 1550

Monday 21 December [1925]

But no Vita! But Vita for 3 days at Long Barn,[2] from which L[eonard]. & I returned yesterday. These Sapphists *love* women; friendship is never untinged with amorosity. In short, my fears & refrainings, my "impertinence" my usual self-consciousness in intercourse with people who mayn't want me & so on—were all, as L. said, sheer fudge; &, partly thanks to him (he made me write) I wound up this wounded & stricken year in great style. I like her & being with her, & the splendour—she shines in the grocers shop in Sevenoaks with a candle lit radiance, stalking on legs like beech trees, pink glowing, grape clustered, pearl hung. That is the secret of her glamour, I suppose. Anyhow she found me incredibly dowdy, no woman

9. *Tristram Shandy* (1759–1767), an open-ended, episodic novel by Laurence Sterne.
1. Katherine Maxse (1867–1922), a prominent hostess in

Woolf's youth, was a model for Clarissa Dalloway.
2. Country home of Vita Sackville-West and her husband Harold Nicolson.

cared less for personal appearance—no one put on things in the way I did. Yet so beautiful, &c. What is the effect of all this on me? Very mixed. There is her maturity & full breastedness: her being so much in full sail on the high tides, where I am coasting down backwaters; her capacity I mean to take the floor in any company, to represent her country, to visit Chatsworth, to control silver, servants, chow dogs; her motherhood (but she is a little cold & offhand with her boys) her being in short (what I have never been) a real woman. Then there is some voluptuousness about her; the grapes are ripe; & not reflective. No. In brain & insight she is not as highly organised as I am. But then she is aware of this, & so lavishes on me the maternal protection which, for some reason, is what I have always most wished from everyone. What L. gives me, & Nessa [Vanessa Bell] gives me, & Vita, in her more clumsy external way, tries to give me. For of course, mingled with all this glamour, grape clusters & pearl necklaces, there is something loose fitting. How much, for example, shall I really miss her when she is motoring across the desert? I will make a note on that next year. Anyhow, I am very glad that she is coming to tea today, & I shall ask her, whether she minds my dressing so badly? I think she does. I read her poem; which is more compact, better seen & felt than anything yet of hers. * * *

[Saturday 31 July 1926]

My own Brain

Here is a whole nervous breakdown in miniature. We came on Tuesday. Sank into a chair, could scarcely rise; everything insipid; tasteless, colourless. Enormous desire for rest. Wednesday—only wish to be alone in the open air. Air delicious—avoided speech; could not read. Thought of my own power of writing with veneration, as of something incredible, belonging to someone else; never again to be enjoyed by me. Mind a blank. Slept in my chair. Thursday. No pleasure in life whatsoever; but felt perhaps more attuned to existence. Character & idiosyncracy as Virginia Woolf completely sunk out. Humble & modest. Difficulty in thinking what to say. Read automatically, like a cow chewing cud. Slept in chair. Friday. Sense of physical tiredness; but slight activity of the brain. Beginning to take notice. Making one or two plans. No power of phrase making. Difficulty in writing to Lady Colefax. Saturday (today) much clearer & lighter. Thought I could write, but resisted, or found it impossible. A desire to read poetry set in on Friday. This brings back a sense of my own individuality. Read some Dante & Bridges, without troubling to understand, but got pleasure from them. Now I begin to wish to write notes, but not yet novel. But today senses quickening. No "making up" power yet; no desire to cast scenes in my book. Curiosity about literature returning: want to read Dante, Havelock Ellis, & Berlioz autobiography; also to make a looking glass with shell frame. These processes have sometimes been spread over several weeks. * * *

Wednesday 15 September [1926]

A State of Mind

Woke up perhaps at 3. Oh its beginning its coming—the horror—physically like a painful wave swelling about the heart—tossing me up. I'm unhappy unhappy! Down—God, I wish I were dead. Pause. But why am I feeling this? Let me watch the wave rise. I watch. Vanessa. Children. Failure. Yes; I detect that. Failure failure. (The wave rises). Oh they laughed at my taste in green paint! Wave crashes. I wish I were dead! I've only a few years to live I hope. I cant face this horror any more—(this is the wave spreading out over me).

This goes on; several times, with varieties of horror. Then, at the crisis, instead of the pain remaining intense, it becomes rather vague. I doze. I wake with a start. The wave again! The irrational pain: the sense of failure; generally some specific incident, as for example my taste in green paint, or buying a new dress, or asking Dadie for the week end, tacked on.

At last I say, watching as dispassionately as I can, Now take a pull of yourself. No more of this. I reason. I take a census of happy people & unhappy. I brace myself to shove to throw to batter down. I begin to march blindly forward. I feel obstacles go down. I say it doesn't matter. Nothing matters. I become rigid & straight, & sleep again, & half wake & feel the wave beginning & watch the light whitening & wonder how, this time, breakfast & daylight will overcome it; & then hear L. in the passage & simulate, for myself as well as for him, great cheerfulness; & generally am cheerful, by the time breakfast is over. Does everyone go through this state? Why have I so little control? It is not creditable, nor lovable. It is the cause of much waste & pain in my life.

Saturday 27 October [1928]

Thank God, my long toil at the women's lecture[3] is this moment ended. I am back from speaking at Girton, in floods of rain. Starved but valiant young women—that's my impression. Intelligent eager, poor; & destined to become schoolmistresses in shoals. I blandly told them to drink wine & have a room of their own. Why should all the splendour, all the luxury of life be lavished on the Julians & the Francises, & none on the Phares & the Thomases?[4] There's Julian not much relishing it, perhaps. I fancy sometimes the world changes. I think I see reason spreading. But I should have liked a closer & thicker knowledge of life. I should have liked to deal with real things sometimes. I get such a sense of tingling & vitality from an evenings talk like that; one's angularities & obscurities are smoothed & lit. How little one counts, I think: how little anyone counts; how fast & furious & masterly life is; & how all these thousands are swimming for dear life. I felt elderly & mature. And nobody respected me. They were very eager, egotistical, or rather not much impressed by age & repute. Very little reverence or that sort of thing about. The corridors of Girton are like vaults in some horrid high church cathedral—on & on they go, cold & shiny—with a light burning. High gothic rooms; acres of bright brown wood; here & there a photograph. * * *

Wednesday 23 October [1929]

As it is true—I write only for an hour—then sink back feeling I cannot keep my brain on that spin any more—then typewrite, & am done by 12—I will here sum up my impressions before publishing a Room of One's Own. It is a little ominous that Morgan wont review it.[5] It makes me suspect that there is a shrill feminine tone in it which my intimate friends will dislike. I forecast, then, that I shall get no criticism, except of the evasive jocular kind, from Lytton, Roger & Morgan; that the press will be kind & talk of its charm, & sprightiness; also I shall be attacked for a feminist & hinted at for a sapphist; Sibyl will ask me to luncheon; I shall get a good many letters from young women. I am afraid it will not be taken seriously. Mrs Woolf is so accom-

3. The lecture that became A Room of One's Own.
4. Elsie Phare was a student at Newnham College, Cambridge; Margaret Thomas was a student at Girton College. Their invitations had brought Woolf to Cambridge. Julian

Bell, Woolf's nephew, was a student at King's College.
5. He [E. M. Forster] wrote yesterday 3rd Dec. & said he very much liked it [Woolf's note].

plished a writer that all she says makes easy reading . . . this very feminine logic . . . a book to be put in the hands of girls. I doubt that I mind very much. The Moths; but I think it is to be waves, is trudging along;[6] & I have that to refer to, if I am damped by the other. It is a trifle, I shall say; so it is, but I wrote it with ardour & conviction.

* * *

Friday 20 May [1938]

Time & again I have meant to write down my expectations, dreads, & so on, waiting the publication on—I think June 2nd—of 3 G[uinea]s—but haven't, because what with living in the solid world of Roger, & then (again this morning) in the airy world of Poyntz Hall I feel extremely little.[7] And dont want to rouse feeling. What I'm afraid of is the taunt Charm & emptiness. The book I wrote with such violent feelings to relieve that immense pressure will not dimple the surface. That is my fear. Also I'm uneasy at taking this role in the public eye—afraid of autobiography in public. But the fears are entirely outbalanced (this is honest) by the immense relief & peace I have gained, & enjoy this moment. Now I am quit of that poison & excitement. Nor is that all. For having spat it out, my mind is made up. I need never recur or repeat. I am an outsider. I can take my way: experiment with my own imagination in my own way. The pack may howl, but it shall never catch me. And even if the pack—reviewers, friends, enemies—pays me no attention or sneers, still I'm free. This is the actual result of that spiritual conversion (I cant bother to get the right words) in the autumn of 1933—or 4—when I rushed through London, buying, I remember, a great magnifying glass, from sheer ecstasy, near Blackfriars: when I gave the man who played the harp half a crown for talking to me about his life in the Tube station. The omens are mixed: L. is less excited than I hoped; Nessa highly ambiguous; Miss Hepworth & Mrs Nicholls say "Women owe a great deal to Mrs Woolf" & I have promised Pippa to supply books. Now for R.'s letters & Monks H—at the moment windy & cold.

Wednesday 14 September [1938]

Things worse today. Rioting in Prague. Sudeten ultimatum. It looks as if Hitler meant to slide sideways into war. Raises riots: will say cant be stopped.[8] This came on the 9.30 wireless last night. This morning more marking time. No one knows. Headachy, partly screw of Roger partly this gloom. So I'm stopping Roger;[9] as we go up to lunch with Bella tomorrow. And whats the private position? So black I cant gather together. Work I suppose. If it is war, then every country joins in: chaos. To oppose this with Roger my only private position. Well thats an absurd little match to strike. But its a hopeless war this—when we know winning means nothing. So we're committed, for the rest of our lives, to public misery. This will be slashed with private too. * * *

6. "The Moths" was an early title for The Waves (1931).
7. "Poyntz Hall" later became Between the Acts (1941).
8. The German Chancellor Adolf Hitler had been putting pressure on the Czechoslovak government to allow the incorporation of that country's German minority into Germany, even though this would mean the disintegration of Czechoslovakia. A speech Hitler made at Nuremberg had given the signal for the German minority (the "Sudeten Germans") in Czechoslovakia to riot; the Czech government imposed martial law, the immediate

revocation of which was then demanded by the German government in Berlin. British Prime Minister Neville Chamberlain flew to meet Hitler, and, fearful of war and in the face of German threats to invade Czechoslovakia, informed the Czechs that Britain and France would not support them against German demands. The Germans soon took over Czechoslovakia.
9. Woolf was working on a biography of her friend, Roger Fry, published in 1940 as Roger Fry: A Biography.

[*Saturday 1 October* 1938]

A violent storm—purple ink clouds—dissolving like blots of ink in water—strong enough to drive us in here in the middle of our game. L. is storing apples—finest harvest for perhaps some years. No longer a matter of concern. We were to live on apples honey & cabbage. Postman delivered an oration—"just my own thoughts" on War & Dictators. How all will worship C[hamberlai]n. now: but in 5 years time we may be saying we ought to have put him, Hitler, down now. These dictators & their lust for power—they cant stop. He'll get stronger & stronger. Then . . . But now we cant help being glad of peace. Its human nature. We're made that way. A solid clear spoken if repetitive private thinker who kept our letters waiting 10 minutes. Only the N. Statesman &c. Soon looked through & tossed aside. Peace when they went to Press hung on a straw. Now grown (we suppose) to a rope—unless this storm is symbolical; its odd how susceptible the mind becomes to weather symbols—roping everything in—in crises like this is, or was. Of course there's bound to be a turn against relief—but I'm watching the storm—as in violent illness. One turns peevish & has a sense of emptiness. I should fill this now either by letter writing or sketching R. wh last as the least burdensome, I will do.

Sunday 29 January [1939]

Yes, Barcelona has fallen: Hitler speaks tomorrow; the next dress rehearsal begins: I have seen Marie Stopes, Princesse de Polignac, Philip & Pippin, & Dr Freud in the last 3 days,[1] also had Tom to dinner & to the Stephens' party.

Dr Freud gave me a narcissus. Was sitting in a great library with little statues at a large scrupulously tidy shiny table. We like patients on chairs. A screwed up shrunk very old man: with a monkeys light eyes, paralysed spasmodic movements, inarticulate: but alert. On Hitler. Generation before the poison will be worked out. About his books. Fame? I was infamous rather than famous, didnt make £50 by his first book. Difficult talk. An interview. Daughter & Martin helped. Immense potential, I mean an old fire now flickering. When we left he took up the stand What are *you* going to do? The English—war.

Wednesday 6 September [1939]

Our first air raid warning at 8.30 this morning. A warbling that gradually insinuates itself as I lay in bed. So dressed & walked on the terrace with L. Sky clear. All cottages shut. Breakfast. All clear. During the interval a raid on Southwark. No news. The Hepworths came on Monday. Rather like a sea voyage. Forced conversation. Boredom. All meaning has run out of everything. Scarcely worth reading papers. The BBC gives any news the day before. Emptiness. Inefficiency. I may as well record these things. My plan is to force my brain to work on Roger. But Lord this is the worst of all my life's experiences. I note that force is the dullest of experiences. It means feeling only bodily feelings: one gets cold & torpid. Endless interruptions. We have done the curtains. We have carried coals &c into the cottage for the 8 Battersea women & children. The expectant mothers are all quarrelling. Some went back yesterday. We took the car to be hooded, met Nessa, were driven to tea at

---

1. Sigmund Freud, mortally ill with cancer of the jaw, had fled the Nazis and settled in Hampstead with his daughter Anna.

Charleston. Yes, its an empty meaningless world now. Am I a coward? Physically I expect I am. Going to London tomorrow I expect frightens me. At a pinch eno' adrenalin is secreted to keep one calm. But my brain stops. I took up my watch this morning & then put it down. Lost. That kind of thing annoys me. No doubt one can conquer this. But my mind seems to curl up & become undecided. To cure this one had better read a solid book like Tawney, an exercise of the muscles. The Hepworths are travelling books in Brighton. Shall I walk? Yes. Its the gnats & flies that settle on noncombatants. This war has begun in cold blood. One merely feels that the killing machine has to be set in action. So far, The Athena has been sunk. It seems entirely meaningless—a perfunctory slaughter, like taking a jar in one hand, a hammer in the other. Why must this be smashed? Nobody knows. This feeling is different from any before. And all the blood has been let out of common life. No movies or theatres allowed. No letters, except strays from America. "Reviewing"[2] rejected by Atlantic. No friends write or ring up. Yes, a long sea voyage, with strangers making conversation, & lots of small bothers & arrangements seems the closest I can get. Of course all creative power is cut off. * * *

Monday 13 May [1940]

I admit to some content, some closing of a chapter, & peace that comes with it, from posting my proofs today: I admit—because we're in the 3rd day of "the greatest battle in history." It began (here) with the 8 oclock wireless announcing, as I lay half asleep, the invasion of Holland & Belgium. The third day of the Battle of Waterloo. Apple blossom snowing the garden. A bowl lost in the pond. Churchill exhorting all men to stand together. "I have nothing to offer but blood & tears & sweat."[3] These vast formless shapes further circulate. They aren't substances; but they make everything else minute. Duncan saw an air battle over Charleston—a silver pencil & a puff of smoke. Percy has seen the wounded arriving in their boots. So my little moment of peace comes in a yawning hollow. But though L. says he has petrol in the garage for suicide shd. Hitler win, we go on. Its the vastness, & the smallness, that make this possible. So intense are my feelings (about Roger): yet the circumference (the war) seems to make a hoop round them. No, I cant get the odd incongruity of feeling intensely & at the same time knowing that there's no importance in that feeling. Or is there, as I sometimes think, more importance than ever? * * *

Sunday 22 December [1940]

How beautiful they were, those old people—I mean father & mother—how simple, how clear, how untroubled. I have been dipping into old letters & fathers memoirs. He loved her—oh & was so candid & reasonable & transparent—& had such a fastidious delicate mind, educated, & transparent. How serene & gay even their life reads to me: no mud; no whirlpools. And so human—with the children & the little hum & song of the nursery. But if I read as a contemporary I shall lose my childs vision & so must stop. Nothing turbulent; nothing involved: no introspection.

2. An essay on book reviewing.
3. Germany invaded Holland, Belgium, and Luxembourg on 10 May; on the same day Neville Chamberlain resigned as prime minister, and Winston Churchill took office at the head of a coalition government. In seeking support for his administration, Churchill said "I have nothing to offer but blood, toil, tears and sweat"; see page 2680 for this speech.

Bloomsbury and Modernism

Bloomsbury is the name of a neighborhood in London, an area of small park squares bordered by serene rows of townhouses, in close proximity to the British Museum and its famous Reading Room, to the ancient hive of legal offices Lincoln Inn Fields, and to busy thoroughfares like Tottenham Court Row for commerce and shopping. "Bloomsbury" names more than a neighborhood in modern British culture, however: It has also come to designate the group of enormously influential British artists and thinkers who began living there in the early years of the twentieth century, whose private friendships and alliances became a public vision of a modern way of life, a personal understanding of ethics, and a set of criteria for modernity in everything from painting to economic analysis to literature to sexual behavior—of which there was a lot—which in turn fashioned a movement in modern British society. This movement, which had no official policy and no doctrines or dogmas, was directed toward freedom in the widest sense—creative freedom, sexual freedom, intellectual freedom, and freedom especially from the strictures of Victorian and Edwardian norms.

The beginnings of Bloomsbury as a cultural movement were almost accidental. A group of friends and former roommates from Trinity College, Cambridge University, formed its nucleus, including among them Lytton Strachey, Roger Fry, John Maynard Keynes, Clive Bell, Walter Lamb, Duncan Grant, Saxon Sydney-Turner, Leonard Woolf, and Thoby Stephen, brother of the future Virginia Woolf. These postgraduates either took houses or rooms in the vicinity of Thoby's apartments in Bloomsbury, or became frequent visitors, as did Thoby's sisters Virginia and Vanessa. At first the loose association of friends essentially replicated their college days, devoting long and late hours to conversation and excited critiques of one another's work; what already marked the group as different was their inclusion of women in these conversations, which were freewheeling and uncensored. The then-shocking freedom of this Bloomsbury life pleased Virginia and especially Vanessa, who married Clive Bell and had love affairs with several other members of the group. More importantly, she became a painter, and her house in Bloomsbury and, later, the country estate Charleston she shared with Clive Bell, was the feminine staging ground for many of the Bloomsbury experiments in art and culture. Bloomsbury brought about a sea change in British culture in terms of sexual mores, and a new freedom to recreate the domestic world and the place of men and women in it.

What had started as one long dinner party at the turn of the century was recognized, by 1910, as a phenomenon; people beyond the circle of friends themselves started to speak of "Bloomsbury" as a catchphrase for what was newest and most daring in artistic, social, and political thought, and of the "Bloomsberries" themselves, if a little enviously, as a vanguard for public and private experiments in freedom. Several members of the group had studied with the eminent philosopher G. E. Moore at Cambridge, and were influenced by his philosophy of ethics, which made ethical behavior a matter of personal decision, of what is right for the individual, and not a matter of social norms. The individual Bloomsberries made powerful creative achievements in art and art criticism, in economics and philosophy, in literature, in history and biography, in stage and theater design, and in political thought and practice. To these achievements they added unconventional experiments in living: sexual involvements before and outside of marriage, an openly practiced homosexuality, female independence and equality, and the equally daring belief in social equality and anti-imperialism.

By 1925 many of the Bloomsbury group had attained the height of their professional or creative fields: Virginia Woolf was one of the leading modern novelists in Britain, John Maynard Keynes had transformed economic theory and policy, Roger Fry had changed the evaluation of modern art, Lytton Strachey had altered the understanding of Victorian culture, Vanessa Bell had created a new artistic palette of color and form. By then "Bloomsbury" had

The garden-room at Charleston, Vanessa and Clive Bell's country estate.

geographically broken up, in that its members had left the neighborhood for other areas of England, had married or divorced or formed new partnerships; yet the Bloomsberries remained loyal to each other throughout their lives, and their work, whatever its nature, was always done with the original audience of Bloomsbury friends in mind. Bloomsbury had become synonymous with ethical and intellectual freedom—Bloomsbury itself had become a state of mind.

✦ ≡✦≡ ✦

Lytton Strachey
1880–1932

A founding member of the Bloomsbury group, Lytton Strachey revolutionized the art of biography. Strachey was an essayist, a poet, a dramatist and drama critic, a writer of fiction and a literary critic. He fused these disparate talents in his biographical masterpiece, *Eminent Victorians* (1918), and in two subsequent major biographies, *Queen Victoria* (1921) and *Elizabeth and Essex* (1928). Strachey brought to these studies a dramatic intensity and an analytic sense of historical context. In *Eminent Victorians*, Strachey painted brilliant portraits of Florence Nightingale and of three other leading figures: the educator Thomas Arnold, the churchman Cardinal Manning, and General Charles Gordon. These four portraits were as subtle in psychological motivation as they were powerful in contesting the ideological influence of these Victorians, whose "eminence" he wished to question and resist in the twentieth century.

Son of an Indian administrator, (Giles) Lytton Strachey attended Trinity College, Cambridge, with his lifelong friends Thoby Stephen, Clive Bell, John Maynard Keynes, and Leonard Woolf, making him part of the original nucleus of the Bloomsbury group. Strachey's iconoclasm began early; he was rejected for an academic career at Cambridge because of a controversial paper he had submitted on a British statesman. He then made his living as a freelance drama critic and a literary essayist. He was immersed in French literature and culture, and his writing about it formed part of the broadening influence of Bloomsbury on British culture in general, making it less parochial and more open to modernity and modernist art. Strachey's flamboyance and his openly homosexual lifestyle also had an impact on British culture and its tolerance for alternative sexualities and domestic arrangements. Strachey's many lovers included several of the male members of Bloomsbury, while he lived platonically with the female painter Dora Carrington.

Strachey's ironic attitudes toward both political and gender roles come together in his incisive portrait of Florence Nightingale and her world. With unsparing wit, Strachey details the British military and political establishment's desperate attempts to resist Nightingale's agitation for major reform in military health and hygiene. Strachey views Nightingale with a lively but unsentimental sympathy, showing her as both a proto-feminist and a tyrannical manipulator of the bumbling bureaucrats who tried to carry on military business as usual, affording enlisted men such minimal sanitation and such primitive medical treatment that thousands of soldiers died from conditions in their own camps. Strachey's novelistic blending of psychological portraiture and social criticism had an electric effect on his contemporaries, and a lasting influence on historical writing: the fully rounded people who emerge in biographies of the modern period are traceable to Strachey's pioneering work.

from Eminent Victorians
Preface

The history of the Victorian Age will never be written: we know too much about it. For ignorance is the first requisite of the historian—ignorance, which simplifies and clarifies, which selects and omits, with a placid perfection unattainable by the highest art. Concerning the Age which has just passed, our fathers and our grandfathers have poured forth and accumulated so vast a quantity of information that the industry of a Ranke would be submerged by it, and the perspicacity of a Gibbon would quail before it.[1] It is not by the direct method of a scrupulous narration that the explorer of the past can hope to depict that singular epoch. If he is wise, he will adopt a subtler strategy. He will attack his subject in unexpected places; he will fall upon the flank, or the rear; he will shoot a sudden, revealing searchlight into obscure recesses, hitherto undivined. He will row out over that great ocean of material, and lower down into it, here and there, a little bucket, which will bring up to the light of day some characteristic specimen, from those far depths, to be examined with a careful curiosity. Guided by these considerations, I have written the ensuing studies. I have attempted, through the medium of biography, to present some Victorian visions to the modern eye. They are, in one sense, haphazard visions—that is to say, my choice of subjects has been determined by no desire to construct a system or to prove a theory, but by simple motives of convenience and of art. It has been my purpose to illustrate rather than to explain. It would have been futile to hope to tell even a *précis* [summary] of the truth about the Victorian age, for the shortest *précis* must fill innumerable volumes. But, in the lives of an ecclesiastic, an educational authority, a woman of action, and a man of adventure, I have sought to examine and elucidate certain fragments of the truth which took my fancy and lay to my hand.

I hope, however, that the following pages may prove to be of interest from the strictly biographical no less than from the historical point of view. Human beings are too important to be treated as mere symptoms of the past. They have a value which is

---

1. Leopold von Ranke (1795–1886), German historian, widely credited with having introduced scholarly method into the writing of history; Edward Gibbon, author of the monumental *History of the Decline and Fall of the Roman Empire* (1776–1788).

independent of any temporal processes—which is eternal, and must be felt for its own sake. The art of biography seems to have fallen on evil times in England. We have had, it is true, a few masterpieces, but we have never had, like the French, a great biographical tradition; we have had no Fontenelles and Condorcets[2], with their incomparable *éloges* [eulogies], compressing into a few shining pages the manifold existences of men. With us, the most delicate and humane of all the branches of the art of writing has been relegated to the journeymen of letters; we do not reflect that it is perhaps as difficult to write a good life as to live one. Those two fat volumes, with which it is our custom to commemorate the dead—who does not know them, with their ill-digested masses of material, their slipshod style, their tone of tedious pane-gyric, their lamentable lack of selection, of detachment, of design?[3] They are as familiar as the *cortège* of the undertaker, and wear the same air of slow, funereal bar-barism. One is tempted to suppose, of some of them, that they were composed by that functionary, as the final item of his job. The studies in this book are indebted, in more ways than one, to such works—works which certainly deserve the name of Standard Biographies. For they have provided me not only with much indispensable information, but with something even more precious—an example. How many lessons are to be learnt from them! But it is hardly necessary to particularise. To pre-serve, for instance, a becoming brevity—a brevity which excludes everything that is redundant and nothing that is significant—that, surely, is the first duty of the biogra-pher. The second, no less surely, is to maintain his own freedom of spirit. It is not his business to be complimentary; it is his business to lay bare the facts of the case, as he understands them. That is what I have aimed at in this book—to lay bare the facts of some cases, as I understand them, dispassionately, impartially, and without ulterior intentions. To quote the words of a Master—"Je n'impose rien; je ne propose rien: j'expose."[4]

L. S.

A list of the principal sources from which I have drawn is appended to each Biography. I would indicate, as an honourable exception to the current commodity, Sir Edward Cook's excellent "Life of Florence Nightingale,"[5] without which my own study, though composed on a very different scale and from a decidedly different angle, could not have been written.

from *Florence Nightingale*

I

Everyone knows the popular conception of Florence Nightingale.[1] The saintly, self-sacrificing woman, the delicate maiden of high degree who threw aside the pleasures of a life of ease to succour the afflicted, the Lady with the Lamp, gliding through the horrors of the hospital at Scutari,[2] and consecrating with the radiance of her good-ness the dying soldier's couch—the vision is familiar to all. But the truth was differ-

---

2. Bernard Le Bovier Fontenelle (1657–1757), French scientist and man of letters; Marie-Jean-Antoine-Nicolas de Caritat, Marquis de Condorcet (1743–1794), French philosopher.
3. The Victorian preference for heavy two-volume "stan-dard" biographies was legendary; Strachey's series of sketches was a conscious repudiation of it.

4. "I impose nothing; I suggest nothing; I expose" (French).
5. Cook published his (two-volume) biography of Nightingale in 1913.
1. For more about Nightingale, see her principal listing on page 1583.
2. The site of English military hospitals in Turkey during the Crimean War.

ent. The Miss Nightingale of fact was not as facile fancy painted her. She worked in another fashion, and towards another end; she moved under the stress of an impetus which finds no place in the popular imagination. A Demon possessed her. Now demons, whatever else they may be, are full of interest. And so it happens that in the real Miss Nightingale there was more that was interesting than in the legendary one; there was also less that was agreeable.

Her family was extremely well-to-do, and connected by marriage with a spreading circle of other well-to-do families. There was a large country house in Derbyshire; there was another in the New Forest; there were Mayfair rooms for the London season and all its finest parties; there were tours on the Continent with even more than the usual number of Italian operas and of glimpses at the celebrities of Paris. Brought up among such advantages, it was only natural to suppose that Florence would show a proper appreciation of them by doing her duty in that state of life unto which it had pleased God to call her—in other words, by marrying, after a fitting number of dances and dinner-parties, an eligible gentleman, and living happily ever afterwards. Her sister, her cousins, all the young ladies of her acquaintance, were either getting ready to do this or had already done it. It was inconceivable that Florence should dream of anything else; yet dream she did. Ah! To do her duty in that state of life unto which it had pleased God to call her! Assuredly she would not be behindhand in doing her duty; but unto what state of life *had* it pleased God to call her? That was the question. God's calls are many, and they are strange. Unto what state of life had it pleased Him to call Charlotte Corday, or Elizabeth of Hungary?[3] What was that secret voice in her ear, if it was not a call? Why had she felt, from her earliest years, those mysterious promptings towards . . . she hardly knew what but certainly towards something very different from anything around her? Why, as a child in the nursery, when her sister had shown a healthy pleasure in tearing her dolls to pieces, had *she* shown an almost morbid one in sewing them up again? Why was she driven now to minister to the poor in their cottages, to watch by sick-beds, to put her dog's wounded paw into elaborate splints as if it was a human being? Why was her head filled with queer imaginations of the country house at Embley turned, by some enchantment, into a hospital, with herself as matron moving about among the beds? Why was even her vision of heaven itself filled with suffering patients to whom she was being useful? So she dreamed and wondered, and, taking out her diary, she poured into it the agitations of her soul. And then the bell rang, and it was time to go and dress for dinner.

As the years passed, a restlessness began to grow upon her. She was unhappy, and at last she knew it. Mrs Nightingale, too, began to notice that there was something wrong. It was very odd; what could be the matter with dear Flo? Mr Nightingale suggested that a husband might be advisable; but the curious thing was that she seemed to take no interest in husbands. And with her attractions, and her accomplishments, too! There was nothing in the world to prevent her making a really brilliant match. But no! She would think of nothing but how to satisfy that singular craving of hers to be *doing* something. As if there was not plenty to do in any case, in the ordinary way, at home. There was the china to look after, and there was her father to be read to after dinner. Mrs Nightingale could not understand it; and then one day her perplexity was changed to consternation and alarm. Florence announced an extreme desire to go to

---

3. Charlotte Corday assassinated the French revolutionary Jean-Paul Marat in 1793; Saint Elizabeth of Hungary was a 13th-century princess famed for her devotion to the poor.

Salisbury Hospital for several months as a nurse; and she confessed to some visionary plan of eventually setting up in a house of her own in a neighbouring village, and there founding "something like a Protestant Sisterhood, without vows, for women of educated feelings." The whole scheme was summarily brushed aside as preposterous; and Mrs Nightingale, after the first shock of terror, was able to settle down again more or less comfortably to her embroidery. But Florence, who was now twenty-five and felt that the dream of her life had been shattered, came near to desperation.

And, indeed, the difficulties in her path were great. For not only was it an almost unimaginable thing in those days for a woman of means to make her own way in the world and to live in independence, but the particular profession for which Florence was clearly marked out both by her instincts and her capacities was at that time a peculiarly disreputable one. A "nurse" meant then a coarse old woman, always ignorant, usually dirty, often brutal, a Mrs Gamp,[4] in bunched-up sordid garments, tippling at the brandy-bottle or indulging in worse irregularities. The nurses in the hospitals were especially notorious for immoral conduct; sobriety almost unknown among them; and they could hardly be trusted to carry out the simplest medical duties. Certainly, things have changed since those days; and that they *have* changed is due, far more than to any other human being, to Miss Nightingale herself. It is not to be wondered at that her parents should have shuddered at the notion of their daughter devoting her life to such an occupation. "It was as if," she herself said afterwards, "I had wanted to be a kitchen-maid." Yet the want, absurd, impracticable as it was, not only remained fixed immovably in her heart, but grew in intensity day by day. Her wretchedness deepened into a morbid melancholy. Everything about her was vile, and she herself, it was clear, to have deserved such misery, was even viler than her surroundings. Yes, she had sinned—"standing before God's judgment seat." "No one," she declared, "has so grieved the Holy Spirit"; of that she was quite certain. It was in vain that she prayed to be delivered from vanity and hypocrisy, and she could not bear to smile or to be gay, "because she hated God to hear her laugh, as if she had not repented of her sin."

A weaker spirit would have been overwhelmed by the load of such distresses—would have yielded or snapped. But this extraordinary young woman held firm, and fought her way to victory. With an amazing persistency, during the eight years that followed her rebuff over Salisbury Hospital, she struggled and worked and planned. While superficially she was carrying on the life of a brilliant girl in high society, while internally she was a prey to the tortures of regret and of remorse, she yet possessed the energy to collect the knowledge and to undergo the experience which alone could enable her to do what she had determined she would do in the end. In secret she devoured the reports of medical commissions, the pamphlets of sanitary authorities, the histories of hospitals and homes. She spent the intervals of the London season in ragged schools and workhouses. When she went abroad with her family, she used her spare time so well that there was hardly a great hospital in Europe with which she was not acquainted, hardly a great city whose slums she had not passed through. She managed to spend some days in a convent school in Rome, and some weeks as a "Soeur de Charité" [sister of Charity] in Paris. Then, while her mother and sister were taking the waters at Carlsbad,[5] she succeeded in slipping off to a nursing institution at Kaiserwerth, where she remained for more than three

---

4. A disreputable midwife, nurse, and "layer out" of the dead in Dickens's *Martin Chuzzlewit* (1844).   5. A spa town, today in the Czech Republic.

months. This was the critical event of her life. The experience which she gained as a nurse at Kaiserwerth formed the foundation of all her future action and finally fixed her in her career.

But one other trial awaited her. The allurements of the world she had brushed aside with disdain and loathing; she had resisted the subtler temptation which, in her weariness, had sometimes come upon her, of devoting her baffled energies to art or literature; the last ordeal appeared in the shape of a desirable young man. Hitherto, her lovers had been nothing to her but an added burden and a mockery; but now—. For a moment, she wavered. A new feeling swept over her—a feeling which she had never known before, which she was never to know again. The most powerful and the profoundest of all the instincts of humanity laid claim upon her. But it rose before her, that instinct, arrayed—how could it be otherwise?—in the inevitable habiliments of a Victorian marriage; and she had the strength to stamp it underfoot.

> I have an intellectual nature which requires satisfaction [she noted], and that would find it in him. I have a passional nature which requires satisfaction, and that would find it in him. I have a moral, an active nature which requires satisfaction, and that would not find it in his life. Sometimes I think that I will satisfy my passional nature at all events. . . .

But no, she knew in her heart that it could not be. "To be nailed to a continuation and exaggeration of my present life . . . to put it out of my power ever to be able to seize the chance of forming for myself a true and rich life"—that would be a suicide. She made her choice, and refused what was at least a certain happiness for a visionary good which might never come to her at all. And so she returned to her old life of waiting and bitterness.

> The thoughts and feelings that I have now [she wrote] I can remember since I was six years old. A profession, a trade, a necessary occupation, something to fill and employ all my faculties, I have always felt essential to me, I have always longed for. The first thought I can remember, and the last, was nursing work; and in the absence of this, education work, but more the education of the bad than of the young. . . . Everything has been tried, foreign travel, kind friends, everything. My God! What is to become of me?

A desirable young man? Dust and ashes! What was there desirable in such a thing as that? "In my thirty-first year," she noted in her diary, "I see nothing desirable but death."

Three more years passed, and then at last the pressure of time told; her family seemed to realise that she was old enough and strong enough to have her way; and she became the superintendent of a charitable nursing home in Harley Street.[6] She had gained her independence, though it was in a meagre sphere enough; and her mother was still not quite resigned: surely Florence might at least spend the summer in the country. At times, indeed, among her intimates, Mrs Nightingale almost wept. "We are ducks," she said with tears in her eyes, "who have hatched a wild swan." But the poor lady was wrong; it was not a swan that they had hatched; it was an eagle.

II

Miss Nightingale had been a year in her nursing–home in Harley Street, when Fate knocked at the door. The Crimean War broke out; the battle of the Alma was fought; and the terrible condition of our military hospitals at Scutari began to be known in

---

6. Nightingale was appointed superintendent of the Institution for the Care of Sick Gentlewomen in London in 1853, having completed her training as a nurse.

England. It sometimes happens that the plans of Providence are a little difficult to follow, but on this occasion all was plain; there was a perfect co-ordination of events. For
years Miss Nightingale had been getting ready; at last she was prepared—experienced,
free, mature, yet still young—she was thirty-four—desirous to serve, accustomed to
command: at that precise moment the desperate need of a great nation came, and she
was there to satisfy it. If the war had fallen a few years earlier, she would have lacked
the knowledge, perhaps even the power, for such a work; a few years later and she
would, no doubt, have been fixed in the routine of some absorbing task, and moreover,
she would have been growing old. Nor was it only the coincidence of Time that was
remarkable. It so fell out that Sidney Herbert[7] was at the War Office and in the Cabinet; and Sidney Herbert was an intimate friend of Miss Nightingale's, convinced, from
personal experience in charitable work, of her supreme capacity. After such premises, it
seems hardly more than a matter of course that her letter, in which she offered her services for the East, and Sidney Herbert's letter, in which he asked for them, should actually have crossed in the post. Thus it all happened, without a hitch. The appointment
was made, and even Mrs Nightingale, overawed by the magnitude of the venture, could
only approve. A pair of faithful friends offered themselves as personal attendants; thirty-eight nurses were collected; and within a week of the crossing of the letters Miss
Nightingale, amid a great burst of popular enthusiasm, left for Constantinople.[8]

Among the numerous letters which she received on her departure was one from
Dr Manning,[9] who at that time was working in comparative obscurity as a Catholic
priest in Bayswater. "God will keep you," he wrote, "and my prayer for you will be
that your one object of Worship, Pattern of Imitation, and source of consolation and
strength may be the Sacred Heart of our Divine Lord."

To what extent Dr Manning's prayer was answered must remain a matter of
doubt; but this much is certain, that, if ever a prayer was needed, it was needed then
for Florence Nightingale. For dark as had been the picture of the state of affairs at
Scutari, revealed to the English public in the despatches of the *Times* correspondent[1]
and in a multitude of private letters, yet the reality turned out to be darker still. What
had occurred was, in brief, the complete break-down of our medical arrangements at
the seat of war. The origins of this awful failure were complex and manifold; they
stretched back through long years of peace and carelessness in England; they could be
traced through endless ramifications of administrative incapacity—from the inherent
faults of confused systems to the petty bunglings of minor officials, from the
inevitable ignorance of Cabinet Ministers to the fatal exactitudes of narrow routine.
In the inquiries which followed it was clearly shown that the evil was in reality that
worst of all evils—one which has been caused by nothing in particular and for which
no one in particular is to blame. The whole organisation of the war machine was
incompetent and out of date. The old Duke had sat for a generation at the Horse
Guards repressing innovations with an iron hand.[2] There was an extraordinary over-

7. Secretary of State for War in the British government.
8. Today's Istanbul, Turkey.
9. Henry Manning was a leading member of the Oxford Movement, which from the 1840s argued against Protestant tendencies in the Church of England; his conversion to Roman Catholicism in 1851 sent shock waves through the Church. In 1865 he was made Roman Catholic Archbishop of Westminster and in 1871 Cardinal.
1. The (London) *Times*'s war correspondent, William Howard Russell, published a series of reports on the poor medical care given the British army in Turkey; these alerted the public, which enthusiastically supported Nightingale's mission.
2. Arthur Wellesley, first Duke of Wellington, commanded the British forces at the battle of Waterloo (1815), which finally ended Napoleon's ambitions; in later life he acted as Tory prime minister, and became known for his conservatism. He was made Commander-in-Chief of the army for life in 1842. Horse Guards Parade is in Whitehall in central London, the site of many government offices.

lapping of authorities, an almost incredible shifting of responsibilities to and fro. As for such a notion as the creation and the maintenance of a really adequate medical service for the army—in that atmosphere of aged chaos, how could it have entered anybody's head? Before the war, the easy-going officials at Westminster[3] were naturally persuaded that all was well—or at least as well as could be expected; when someone, for instance, actually had the temerity to suggest the formation of a corps of army nurses, he was at once laughed out of court. When the war had begun, the gallant British officers in control of affairs had other things to think about than the petty details of medical organisation. Who had bothered with such trifles in the Peninsula?[4] And surely, on that occasion, we had done pretty well. Thus the most obvious precautions were neglected, the most necessary preparations put off from day to day. The principal medical officer of the army, Dr Hall, was summoned from India at a moment's notice, and was unable to visit England before taking up his duties at the front. And it was not until after the battle of the Alma, when we had been at war for many months, that we acquired hospital accommodation at Scutari for more than a thousand men. Errors, follies, and vices on the part of individuals there doubtless were; but, in the general reckoning, they were of small account—insignificant symptoms of the deep disease of the body politic—the enormous calamity of administrative collapse.

Miss Nightingale arrived at Scutari—a suburb of Constantinople, on the Asiatic side of the Bosphorus—on November 4th, 1854; it was ten days after the battle of Balaclava, and the day before the battle of Inkerman.[5] The organisation of the hospitals, which had already given way under the stress of the battle of the Alma, was now to be subjected to the further pressure which these two desperate and bloody engagements implied. Great detachments of wounded were already beginning to pour in. The men, after receiving such summary treatment as could be given them at the smaller hospitals in the Crimea itself, were forthwith shipped in batches of two hundred across the Black Sea to Scutari. This voyage was in normal times one of four days and a half; but the times were no longer normal, and now the transit often lasted for a fortnight or three weeks. It received, not without reason, the name of "the middle passage." Between, and sometimes on the decks, the wounded, the sick, and the dying were crowded—men who had just undergone the amputation of limbs, men in the clutches of fever or of frostbite, men in the last stages of dysentery and cholera—without beds, sometimes without blankets, often hardly clothed. The one or two surgeons on board did what they could; but medical stores were lacking, and the only form of nursing available was that provided by a handful of invalid soldiers, who were usually themselves prostrate by the end of the voyage. There was no other food beside the ordinary salt rations of ship diet; and even the water was sometimes so stored that it was out of reach of the weak. For many months, the average of deaths during these voyages was seventy-four in the thousand; the corpses were shot out into the waters; and who shall say that they were the most unfortunate? At Scutari, the landing-stage, constructed with all the perverseness of Oriental ingenuity, could only be approached with great difficulty, and, in rough weather, not at all. When it was reached, what remained of the men in the ships had first to be disembarked, and then conveyed up a steep slope of a quarter of a mile to the nearest of the hospitals. The most serious cases might be put upon

---

3. In Parliament.
4. The Peninsular War (1808–1814) was that part of the Napoleonic Wars fought in the Iberian peninsula (Spain).

5. The battle of Balaclava took place in October 1854, Inkerman in November.

stretchers—for there were far too few for all; the rest were carried or dragged up the hill by such convalescent soldiers as could be got together, who were not too obviously infirm for the work. At last the journey was accomplished; slowly, one by one, living or dying, the wounded were carried up into the hospital. And in the hospital what did they find?

Lasciate ogni speranza, voi ch'entrate:[6] the delusive doors bore no such inscription; and yet behind them Hell yawned. Want, neglect, confusion, misery—in every shape and in every degree of intensity—filled the endless corridors and the vast apartments of the gigantic barrack-house, which, without forethought or preparation, had been hurriedly set aside as the chief shelter for the victims of the war. The very building itself was radically defective. Huge sewers underlay it, and cess-pools loaded with filth wafted their poison into the upper rooms. The floors were in so rotten a condition that many of them could not be scrubbed; the walls were thick with dirt; incredible multitudes of vermin swarmed everywhere. And, enormous as the building was, it was yet too small. It contained four miles of beds, crushed together so close that there was but just room to pass between them. Under such conditions, the most elaborate system of ventilation might well have been at fault; but here there was no ventilation. The stench was indescribable. "I have been well acquainted," said Miss Nightingale, "with the dwellings of the worst parts of most of the great cities in Europe, but have never been in any atmosphere which I could compare with that of the Barrack Hospital at night." The structural defects were equalled by the deficiencies in the commonest objects of hospital use. There were not enough bedsteads; the sheets were of canvas, and so coarse that the wounded men recoiled from them, begging to be left in their blankets; there was no bedroom furniture of any kind, and empty beer-bottles were used for candlesticks. There were no basins, no towels, no soap, no brooms, no mops, no trays, no plates; there were neither slippers nor scissors, neither shoebrushes nor blacking; there were no knives or forks or spoons. The supply of fuel was constantly deficient. The cooking arrangements were preposterously inadequate, and the laundry was a farce. As for purely medical materials, the tale was no better. Stretchers, splints, bandages—all were lacking; and so were the most ordinary drugs.

To replace such wants, to struggle against such difficulties, there was a handful of men overburdened by the strain of ceaseless work, bound down by the traditions of official routine, and enfeebled either by old age or inexperience or sheer incompetence. They had proved utterly unequal to their task. The principal doctor was lost in the imbecilities of a senile optimism. The wretched official whose business it was to provide for the wants of the hospital was tied fast hand and foot by red tape. A few of the younger doctors struggled valiantly, but what could they do? Unprepared, disorganised, with such help only as they could find among the miserable band of convalescent soldiers drafted off to tend their sick comrades, they were faced with disease, mutilation, and death in all their most appalling forms, crowded multitudinously about them in an ever increasing mass. They were like men in a shipwreck, fighting, not for safety, but for the next moment's bare existence—to gain, by yet another frenzied effort, some brief respite from the waters of destruction.

In these surroundings, those who had been long inured to scenes of human suffering—surgeons with a world-wide knowledge of agonies, soldiers familiar with fields of carnage, missionaries with remembrances of famine and of plague—yet

---

6. "Abandon all hope, you who enter here": the inscription over the entrance to Hell in Dante's *Inferno*, Canto 3.9.

found a depth of horror which they had never known before. There were moments, there were places, in the Barrack Hospital at Scutari, where the strongest hand was struck with trembling, and the boldest eye would turn away its gaze.

Miss Nightingale came, and she, at any rate, in that Inferno, did not abandon hope. For one thing, she brought material succour. Before she left London she had consulted Dr Andrew Smith, the head of the Army Medical Board, as to whether it would be useful to take out stores of any kind to Scutari; and Dr Andrew Smith had told her that "nothing was needed." Even Sidney Herbert had given her similar assurances; possibly, owing to an oversight, there might have been some delay in the delivery of the medical stores, which, he said, had been sent out from England "in profusion," but "four days would have remedied this." She preferred to trust her own instincts, and at Marseilles purchased a large quantity of miscellaneous provisions, which were of the utmost use at Scutari. She came, too, amply provided with money—in all, during her stay in the East, about £7000 reached her from private sources; and, in addition, she was able to avail herself of another valuable means of help. At the same time as herself, Mr Macdonald, of the *Times*, had arrived at Scutari, charged with the duty of administering the large sums of money collected through the agency of that newspaper in aid of the sick and wounded; and Mr Macdonald had the sense to see that the best use he could make of the *Times* Fund was to put it at the disposal of Miss Nightingale.

I cannot conceive [wrote an eye-witness], as I now calmly look back on the first three weeks after the arrival of the wounded from Inkerman, how it could have been possible to have avoided a state of things too disastrous to contemplate, had not Miss Nightingale been there, with the means placed at her disposal by Mr Macdonald.

But the official view was different. What! Was the public service to admit, by accepting outside charity, that it was unable to discharge its own duties without the assistance of private and irregular benevolence? Never! And accordingly when Lord Stratford de Redcliffe, our Ambassador at Constantinople, was asked by Mr Macdonald to indicate how the *Times* Fund could best be employed, he answered that there was indeed one object to which it might very well be devoted—the building of an English Protestant Church at Pera.[7]

Mr Macdonald did not waste further time with Lord Stratford, and immediately joined forces with Miss Nightingale. But, with such a frame of mind in the highest quarters, it is easy to imagine the kind of disgust and alarm with which the sudden intrusion of a band of amateurs and females must have filled the minds of the ordinary officer and the ordinary military surgeon. They could not understand it; what had women to do with war? Honest Colonels relieved their spleen by the cracking of heavy jokes about "the Bird"; while poor Dr Hall, a rough terrier of a man, who had worried his way to the top of his profession, was struck speechless with astonishment, and at last observed that Miss Nightingale's appointment was extremely droll.

Her position was, indeed, an official one, but it was hardly the easier for that. In the hospitals it was her duty to provide the services of herself and her nurses when they were asked for by the doctors, and not until then. At first some of the surgeons would have nothing to say to her, and, though she was welcomed by others, the majority were hostile and suspicious. But gradually she gained ground. Her good will could not be denied, and her capacity could not be disregarded. With consummate

---

7. A district of Istanbul.

tact, with all the gentleness of supreme strength, she managed at last to impose her personality upon the susceptible, overwrought, discouraged, and helpless group of men in authority who surrounded her. She stood firm; she was a rock in the angry ocean; with her alone was safety, comfort, life. And so it was that hope dawned at Scutari. The reign of chaos and old night began to dwindle; order came upon the scene, and common sense, and forethought, and decision, radiating out from the little room off the great gallery in the Barrack Hospital where day and night, the Lady Superintendent was at her task. Progress might be slow, but it was sure. The first sign of a great change came with the appearance of some of those necessary objects with which the hospitals had been unprovided for months. The sick men began to enjoy the use of towels and soap, knives and forks, combs and tooth-brushes. Dr Hall might snort when he heard of it, asking, with a growl, what a soldier wanted with a tooth-brush; but the good work went on. Eventually the whole business of purveying to the hospitals was, in effect, carried out by Miss Nightingale. She alone, it seemed, whatever the contingency, knew where to lay her hands on what was wanted; she alone could dispense her stores with readiness; above all she alone possessed the art of circumventing the pernicious influences of official etiquette. This was her greatest enemy, and sometimes even she was baffled by it. On one occasion 27,000 shirts sent out at her instance by the Home Government, arrived, were landed, and were only waiting to be unpacked. But the official "Purveyor" intervened; "he could not unpack them," he said, "without a Board." Miss Nightingale pleaded in vain; the sick and wounded lay half-naked shivering for want of clothing; and three weeks elapsed before the Board released the shirts. A little later, however, on a similar occasion, Miss Nightingale felt that she could assert her own authority. She ordered a Government consignment to be forcibly opened, while the miserable "Purveyor" stood by, wringing his hands in departmental agony.

Vast quantities of valuable stores sent from England lay, she found, engulfed in the bottomless abyss of the Turkish Customs House. Other ship-loads, buried beneath munitions of war destined for Balaclava, passed Scutari without a sign, and thus hospital materials were sometimes carried to and fro three times over the Black Sea, before they reached their destination. The whole system was clearly at fault, and Miss Nightingale suggested to the home authorities that a Government Store House should be instituted at Scutari for the reception and distribution of the consignments. Six months after her arrival this was done.

In the meantime she had reorganised the kitchens and the laundries in the hospitals. The ill-cooked hunks of meat, vilely served at irregular intervals, which had hitherto been the only diet for the sick men were replaced by punctual meals, well-prepared and appetising, while strengthening extra foods—soups and wines, and jellies ("preposterous luxuries," snarled Dr Hall)—were distributed to those who needed them. One thing, however, she could not effect. The separation of the bones from the meat was no part of official cookery: the rule was that the food must be divided into equal portions, and if some of the portions were all bone—well, every man must take his chance. The rule, perhaps, was not a very good one; but there it was. "It would require a new Regulation of the Service," she was told, "to bone the meat." As for the washing arrangements, they were revolutionised. Up to the time of Miss Nightingale's arrival the number of shirts which the authorities had succeeded in washing was seven. The hospital bedding, she found, was "washed" in cold water. She took a Turkish house, had boilers installed, and employed soldiers' wives to do the laundry work. The expenses were defrayed from her own funds and that of the *Times;* and henceforward the sick and wounded had the comfort of clean linen.

Then she turned her attention to their clothing. Owing to military exigencies the greater number of the men had abandoned their kit; their knapsacks were lost for ever; they possessed nothing but what was on their persons, and that was usually only fit for speedy destruction. The "Purveyor," of course, pointed out that, according to the regulations, all soldiers should bring with them into hospital an adequate supply of clothing, and he declared that it was no business of his to make good their deficiencies. Apparently, it was the business of Miss Nightingale. She procured socks, boots, and shirts in enormous quantities; she had trousers made, she rigged up dressing-gowns. "The fact is," she told Sidney Herbert, "I am now clothing the British Army."

All at once, word came from the Crimea that a great new contingent of sick and wounded might shortly be expected. Where were they to go? Every available inch in the wards was occupied; the affair was serious and pressing, and the authorities stood aghast. There were some dilapidated rooms in the Barrack Hospital, unfit for human habitation, but Miss Nightingale believed that if measures were promptly taken they might be made capable of accommodating several hundred beds. One of the doctors agreed with her; the rest of the officials were irresolute: it would be a very expensive job, they said; it would involve building; and who could take the responsibility? The proper course was that a representation should be made to the Director-General of the Army Medical Department in London; then the Director-General would apply to the Horse Guards, the Horse Guards would move the Ordnance, the Ordnance would lay the matter before the Treasury, and, if the Treasury gave its consent, the work might be correctly carried through, several months after the necessity for it had disappeared. Miss Nightingale, however, had made up her mind, and she persuaded Lord Stratford—or thought she had persuaded him—to give his sanction to the required expenditure. A hundred and twenty-five workmen were immediately engaged, and the work was begun. The workmen struck; whereupon Lord Stratford washed his hands of the whole business. Miss Nightingale engaged two hundred other workmen on her own authority, and paid the bill out of her own resources. The wards were ready by the required date; five hundred sick men were received in them; and all the utensils, including knives, forks, spoons, cans and towels, were supplied by Miss Nightingale.

This remarkable woman was in truth performing the function of an administrative chief. How had this come about? Was she not in reality merely a nurse? Was it not her duty simply to tend to the sick? And indeed, was it not as a ministering angel, a gentle "lady with a lamp" that she actually impressed the minds of her contemporaries? No doubt that was so; and yet it is no less certain that, as she herself said, the specific business of nursing was "the least important of the functions into which she had been forced." It was clear that in the state of disorganisation into which the hospitals at Scutari had fallen the most pressing, the really vital, need was for something more than nursing; it was for the necessary elements of civilised life—the commonest material objects, the most ordinary cleanliness, the rudimentary habits of order and authority. "Oh, dear Miss Nightingale," said one of her party as they were approaching Constantinople, "when we land, let there be no delays, let us get straight to nursing the poor fellows!" "The strongest will be wanted at the wash-tub," was Miss Nightingale's answer. And it was upon the wash-tub, and all that the wash-tub stood for, that she expended her greatest energies. Yet to say that is perhaps to say too much. For to those who watched her at work among the sick, moving day and night from bed to bed, with that unflinching courage, with that indefatigable vigilance, it seemed as if the concentrated force of an undivided and unparalleled devotion could hardly suffice for that portion of her task alone. Wherever, in those vast wards, suffering was at its worst and the need for help was greatest, there, as if by magic, was Miss Nightingale. Her superhuman equanimity would, at the moment of some ghastly operation, nerve the victim to endure and almost to hope. Her sympathy would assuage the pangs of dying and bring back to those still living something of the forgotten charm of life. Over and over again her untiring efforts rescued those whom the surgeons had abandoned as beyond the possibility of cure. Her mere presence brought with it a strange influence. A passionate idolatry spread among the men: they kissed her shadow as it passed. They did more. "Before she came," said a soldier, "there was cussin' and swearin', but after that it was as 'oly as a church." The most cherished privilege of the fighting man was abandoned for the sake of Miss Nightingale. In those "lowest sinks of human misery," as she herself put it, she never heard the use of one expression "which could distress a gentlewoman."

She was heroic; and these were the humble tributes paid by those of grosser mould to that high quality. Certainly, she was heroic. Yet her heroism was not of that simple sort so dear to the readers of novels and the compilers of hagiologies—the romantic sentimental heroism with which mankind loves to invest its chosen darlings: it was made of sterner stuff. To the wounded soldier on his couch of agony she might well appear in the guise of a gracious angel of mercy; but the military surgeons, and the orderlies, and her own nurses, and the "Purveyor," and Dr Hall, and even Lord Stratford himself could tell a different story. It was not by gentle sweetness and womanly self-abnegation that she had brought order out of chaos in the Scutari Hospitals, that, from her own resources, she had clothed the British Army, that she had spread her dominion over the serried and reluctant powers of the official world; it was by strict method, by stern discipline, by rigid attention to detail, by ceaseless labour, by the fixed determination of an indomitable will. Beneath her cool and calm demeanour lurked fierce and passionate fires. As she passed through the wards in her plain dress, so quiet, so unassuming, she struck the casual observer simply as the pattern of a perfect lady; but the keener eye perceived something more than that—the serenity of high deliberation in the scope of the capacious brow, the sign of power in the dominating curve of the thin nose, and the traces of a harsh and dangerous temper—something peevish, something mocking, and yet something precise—in the small and delicate mouth. There was humour in the face; but the curious watcher might wonder whether it was humour of a very pleasant kind; might ask himself, even as he heard the laughter and marked the jokes with which she cheered the spirits of her patients, what sort of sardonic merriment this same lady might not give vent to, in the privacy of her chamber. As for her voice, it was true of it, even more than of her countenance, that it "had that in it one must fain call master." Those clear tones were in no need of emphasis: "I never heard her raise her voice," said one of her companions. Only, when she had spoken, it seemed as if nothing could follow but obedience. Once, when she had given some direction, a doctor ventured to remark that the thing could not be done. "But it must be done," said Miss Nightingale. A chance bystander, who heard the words, never forgot through all his life the irresistible authority of them. And they were spoken quietly—very quietly indeed.

Late at night, when the long miles of beds lay wrapped in darkness, Miss Nightingale would sit at work in her little room, over her correspondence. It was one of the most formidable of all her duties. There were hundreds of letters to be written to the friends and relations of soldiers; there was the enormous mass of official documents to be dealt with; there were her own private letters to be answered; and, most important of all, there was the composition of her long and confidential reports to Sidney Herbert. These were by no means official communications. Her soul, pent up all day in the restraint and reserve of a vast responsibility, now at last poured itself out in these letters with all its natural vehemence, like a swollen torrent through an open sluice. Here, at least, she did not mince matters. Here she painted in her darkest colours the hideous scenes which surrounded her; here she tore away remorselessly the last veils still shrouding the abominable truth. Then she would fill pages with recommendations and suggestions, with criticisms of the minutest details of organisation, with elaborate calculations of contingencies, with exhaustive analyses and statistical statements piled up in breathless eagerness one on the top of the other. And then her pen, in the virulence of its volubility, would rush on to the discussion of individuals, to the denunciation of an incompetent surgeon or the ridicule of a self-sufficient nurse. Her sarcasm searched the ranks of the officials with the deadly and unsparing precision of a machine-gun. Her nicknames were terrible. She respected no one: Lord Stratford, Lord Raglan, Lady Stratford, Dr Andrew Smith, Dr Hall, the Commissary-General, the Purveyor—she fulminated against them all. The intolerable futility of mankind obsessed her like a nightmare, and she gnashed her teeth against it. "I do well to be angry," was the burden of her cry. How many just men were there at Scutari? How many who cared at all for the sick, or had done anything for their relief? Were there ten? Were there five? Was there even one? She could not be sure.

At one time, during several weeks, her vituperations descended upon the head of Sidney Herbert himself. He had misinterpreted her wishes, he had traversed her positive instructions, and it was not until he had admitted his error and apologised in abject terms that he was allowed again into favour. While this misunderstanding was at its height an aristocratic young gentleman arrived at Scutari with a recommendation from the Minister. He had come out from England filled with a romantic desire to render homage to the angelic heroine of his dreams. He had, he said, cast aside his life of ease and luxury; he would devote his days and nights to the service of that gentle lady; he would perform the most menial offices, he would "fag" for her,[8] he would be her footman—and feel requited by a single smile. A single smile, indeed, he had, but it was of an unexpected kind. Miss Nightingale at first refused to see him, and then, when she consented, believing that he was an emissary sent by Sidney Herbert to put her in the wrong over their dispute, she took notes of her conversation with him, and insisted on his signing them at the end of it. The young gentleman returned to England by the next ship.

This quarrel with Sidney Herbert was, however, an exceptional incident. Alike by him, and by Lord Panmure, his successor at the War Office, she was firmly supported; and the fact that during the whole of her stay at Scutari she had the Home Government at her back, was her trump card in her dealings with the hospital authorities. Nor was it only the Government that was behind her: public opinion in England early recognised the high importance of her mission, and its enthusiastic appreciation of her work soon reached an extraordinary height. The Queen herself was deeply moved. She made repeated inquiries as to the welfare of Miss Nightingale; she asked to see her accounts of the wounded, and made her the intermediary between the throne and the troops.

Let Mrs Herbert know [she wrote to the War Minister] that I wish Miss Nightingale and the ladies would tell these poor noble, wounded, and sick men that *no one* takes a warmer interest or feels *more* for their sufferings or admires their courage and heroism *more* than their Queen. Day and night she thinks of her beloved troops. So does the Prince. Beg Mrs Herbert to communicate these my words to those ladies, as I know that *our* sympathy is much valued by these noble fellows.

8. Perform menial labors on her behalf.

The letter was read aloud in the wards by the Chaplain. "It is a very feeling letter," said the men.

And so the months passed, and that fell winter which had begun with Inkerman and had dragged itself out through the long agony of the investment of Sebastopol, at last was over. In May, 1855, after six months of labour, Miss Nightingale could look with something like satisfaction at the condition of the Scutari hospitals. Had they done nothing more than survive the terrible strain which had been put upon them, it would have been a matter for congratulation; but they had done much more than that; they had marvellously improved. The confusion and the pressure in the wards had come to an end; order reigned in them, and cleanliness; the supplies were bountiful and prompt; important sanitary works had been carried out. One simple comparison of figures was enough to reveal the extraordinary change: the rate of mortality among the cases treated had fallen from 42 per cent. to 22 per thousand. But still the indefatigable lady was not satisfied. The main problem had been solved—the physical needs of the men had been provided for; their mental and spiritual needs remained. She set up and furnished reading-rooms and recreation-rooms. She started classes and lectures. Officers were amazed to see her treating their men as if they were human beings, and assured her that she would only end by "spoiling the brutes." But that was not Miss Nightingale's opinion, and she was justified. The private soldier began to drink less, and even—though that seemed impossible—to save his pay. Miss Nightingale became a banker for the army, receiving and sending home large sums of money every month. At last, reluctantly, the Government followed suit, and established machinery of its own for the remission of money. Lord Panmure, however, remained sceptical; "it will do no good," he pronounced; "the British soldier is not a remitting animal." But, in fact, during the next six months, £71,000 was sent home.

Amid all these activities, Miss Nightingale took up the further task of inspecting the hospitals in the Crimea itself. The labour was extreme, and the conditions of life were almost intolerable. She spent whole days in the saddle, or was driven over those bleak and rocky heights in a baggage cart. Sometimes she stood for hours in the heavily falling snow, and would only reach her hut at dead of night after walking for miles through perilous ravines. Her powers of resistance seemed incredible, but at last they were exhausted. She was attacked by fever, and for a moment came very near to death. Yet she worked on; if she could not move, she could at least write; and write she did until her mind had left her; and after it had left her, in what seemed the delirious trance of death itself, she still wrote. When, after many weeks, she was strong enough to travel, she was to return to England, but she utterly refused. She would not go back, she said, before the last of the soldiers had left Scutari.

This happy moment had almost arrived, when suddenly the smouldering hostilities of the medical authorities burst out into a flame. Dr Hall's labours had been rewarded by a K.C.B.[9]—letters which, as Miss Nightingale told Sidney Herbert, she could only suppose to mean "Knight of the Crimean Burial-grounds"—and the honour had turned his head. He was Sir John, and he would be thwarted no longer. Disputes had lately arisen between Miss Nightingale and some of the nurses in the Crimean hospitals. The situation had been embittered by rumours of religious dissensions, for, while the Crimean nurses were Roman Catholics, many of those at Scutari were suspected of a regrettable propensity towards the tenets of Dr Pusey.[1] Miss Nightingale was by no means disturbed by these sectarian differences, but any sugges-

9. Knight Commander of the Bath, a British order of knighthood.

1. Edward Pusey (1800–1882), one of the leaders of the Oxford Movement.

tion that her supreme authority over all the nurses with the Army was in doubt was enough to rouse her to fury; and it appeared that Mrs Bridgeman, the Reverend Mother in the Crimea, had ventured to call that authority in question. Sir John Hall thought that his opportunity had come, and strongly supported Mrs Bridgeman—or, as Miss Nightingale preferred to call her, the "Reverend Brickbat." There was a violent struggle; Miss Nightingale's rage was terrible. Dr Hall, she declared, was doing his best to "root her out of the Crimea." She would bear it no longer; the War Office was playing her false; there was only one thing to be done—Sidney Herbert must move for the production of papers in the House of Commons, so that the public might be able to judge between her and her enemies. Sidney Herbert with great difficulty calmed her down. Orders were immediately dispatched putting her supremacy beyond doubt, and the Reverend Brickbat withdrew from the scene. Sir John, however, was more tenacious. A few weeks later, Miss Nightingale and her nurses visited the Crimea for the last time, and the brilliant idea occurred to him that he could crush her by a very simple expedient—he would starve her into submission; and he actually ordered that no rations of any kind should be supplied to her. He had already tried this plan with great effect upon an unfortunate medical man whose presence in the Crimea he had considered an intrusion; but he was now to learn that such tricks were thrown away upon Miss Nightingale. With extraordinary foresight, she had brought with her a great supply of food; she succeeded in obtaining more at her own expense and by her own exertions; and thus for ten days, in that inhospitable country, she was able to feed herself and twenty-four nurses. Eventually the military authorities intervened in her favour, and Sir John had to confess that he was beaten.

It was not until July, 1856—four months after the Declaration of Peace—that Miss Nightingale left Scutari for England. Her reputation was now enormous, and the enthusiasm of the public was unbounded. The Royal approbation was expressed by the gift of a brooch, accompanied by a private letter.

> You are, I know, well aware [wrote Her Majesty] of the high sense I entertain of the Christian devotion which you have displayed during this great and bloody war, and I need hardly repeat to you how warm my admiration is for your services, which are fully equal to those of my dear and brave soldiers, whose sufferings you have had the *privilege* of alleviating in so merciful a manner. I am, however, anxious of marking my feelings in a manner which I trust will be agreeable to you, and therefore send you with this letter a brooch, the form and emblems of which commemorate your great and blessed work, and which I hope you will wear as a mark of the high approbation of your Sovereign!

"It will be a very great satisfaction to me," Her Majesty added, "to make the acquaintance of one who has set so bright an example to our sex."

The brooch, which was designed by the Prince Consort, bore a St George's cross in red enamel, and the Royal cypher surmounted by diamonds. The whole was encircled by the inscription, "Blessed are the Merciful."

⊷⊶

E. M. Forster
1879–1970

Edward Morgan Forster, fondly referred to by friends as Morgan or "Bunny," had an enormous effect on modern British literature and letters over the course of his long life. Born in 1879, Forster died at 91 in 1970, having traversed the course of British culture from its Victorian and imperial peak to the postimperial world of the Beatles and the waning of the British novel. His prolific output of novels, short stories, literary criticism, travel writing, and political essays had also waned by the time of his death, partly because the subject he most wished to write about—male homosexual love—was the final taboo of British literature he did not live to see broken. His autobiographical novel *Maurice*, describing an upper-class Englshman's finding of true love with a working-class man employed on a friend's estate, was published only in 1971, after Forster's death. The novels of Forster's youth and middle age remain classics of modern British literature—and the basis for several films in recent years. *Howards End* (1910) explores the fault lines between classes in British society, while *A Passage to India* (1924) defines the processes that would lead inexorably to the loss of Britain's empire.

Forster had a privileged upbringing, and a private education that led him to King's College, Cambridge, and degrees in classics and history. His family wealth allowed him to live in Greece, Italy, and Egypt after graduation in 1901; he spent part of World War I as a Red Cross volunteer in Alexandria, Egypt. He first traveled to India in 1912–1913, and later served as private secretary to the Maharajah of Dewas in 1921. Observing the tensions of empire first-hand, he became a journalist for the Labor Party's *Daily Herald*, later a radio broadcaster in the cause of Indian independence and a reviewer for the *New Statesman* and *Nation*. After Indian independence was achieved in 1947, he was brought to India in public tribute for his actions on behalf of the political solution to independence.

Forster had ties to the artists and writers of Bloomsbury, but he was always skeptical of the group as a clique or privileged "coterie." Despite this wariness, he was close to Virginia Woolf as friend and as literary influence: Woolf's *Mrs Dalloway* (1925) is modeled in part on *A Passage to India*, in that it takes one of its central characters from London to India and back. Like Woolf's novel, *A Passage to India* is notable for its use of multiple perspectives; Forster employed the shifting viewpoints of an elderly British woman, a Muslim Indian physician, and a male British educator and civil servant of empire, writing his story across the lines of difference of race, religion, gender, and culture. The essays he collected in *Adrift in India*, conversely, give Forster's own, skeptical, ironic observations of the interplay of tradition and modernity when he visited India in the waning years of British rule in India. One of Forster's most famous lines is from an essay on literary form: "Only connect," he wrote, and that call to make connection, whether in narrative form, or between classes, races, sexes, and countries, is the hallmark of his fiction and essays alike.

FROM ADRIFT IN INDIA
The Nine Gems of Ujjain

"There is the old building," said he, and pointed to a new building.

"But I want the ruins of which the stationmaster spoke; the palace that King Vikramaditya built, and adorned with Kalidas and the other eight.[1] Where is it? Where are they?"

"Old building," he repeated more doubtfully, and checked the horse. Far out to the left, behind a grove of trees, a white and fantastic mass cut into the dusty horizon. Otherwise India prevailed. Presently I said, "I think you are driving me wrong," and, since now nothing happened at all, added, "Very well, drive me in that direction." The horse then left the road and proceeded with a hesitating step across the fields.

Ujjain is famous in legend and fact, and as sacred as Benares,[2] and surely there should have been steps, and temples, and the holy river Sipra. Where were they? Since leaving the station we had seen nothing but crops and people, and birds, and

---

1. Kalidasa, the greatest Sanskrit poet and dramatist, was probably a 5th-century court poet at Ujjain in central India. He is best known for his play *Shakuntala* and for his narrative poem the *Meghaduta*, or "Cloud Messenger,"

which gives an erotically charged overview of the landscape of India.
2. A city in northern India sacred to Hindus.

horses as feeble as our own. The track we were following wavered and blurred, and offered alternatives; it had no earnestness of purpose like the tracks of England. And the crops were haphazard too—flung this way and that on the enormous earth, with patches of brown between them. There was no place for anything, and nothing was in its place. There was no time either. All the small change of the north rang false, and nothing remained certain but the dome of the sky and the disc of the sun.

Where the track frayed out into chaos the horse stopped, but the driver repeated "Old, very old," and pointed to the new building. We left the horse to dream. I ordered him to rejoin it. He said that he would, but looking back I found that he, too, was dreaming, sitting upon his heels, in the shadow of the castor-oil plants. I ordered him again, and this time he moved, but not in the direction of the horse. "Take care; we shall all lose one another," I shouted. But disintegration had begun, and my expedition was fraying out, like the track, like the fields.

Uncharioted, unattended, I reached the trees, and found under them, as everywhere, a few men. The plain lacks the romance of solitude. Desolate at the first glance, it conceals numberless groups of a few men. The grasses and the high crops sway, the distant path undulates, and is barred with brown bodies or heightened with saffron and crimson. In the evening the villages stand out and call to one another across emptiness with drums and fires. This clump of trees was apparently a village, for near the few men was a sort of enclosure surrounding a kind of street, and gods multiplied. The ground was littered with huts and rubbish for a few yards, and then the plain resumed; to continue in its gentle confusion as far as the eye could see.

But all unobserved, the plain was producing a hill, from the summit of which were visible ruins—the ruins. The scene amazed. They lay on the other side of a swift river, which had cut a deep channel in the soil, and flowed with a violence incredible in that drowsy land. There were waterfalls, chattering shallows, pools, and to the right a deep crack, where the whole stream gathered together and forced itself between jaws of stone. The river gave nothing to the land; no meadows or water weeds edged it. It flowed, like the Ganges of legend,[3] precipitate out of heaven across earth on its way to plunge under the sea and purify hell.

On the opposite bank rose the big modern building, which now quaintly resembled some castle on the Loire.[4] The ruins lay close to the stream—a keep of grey stone with a water-gate and steps. Some of the stones had fallen, some were carved, and, crossing the shallows, I climbed them. Beyond them appeared more ruins and another river.

This second river had been civilized. It came from the first and returned to it through murmurous curtains and weirs, and in its brief course had been built a water palace. It flowed through tanks of carved stone, and mirrored pavilions and broken causeways, whence a few men were bathing, and lovingly caressed their bodies and whispered that holiness may be gracious and life not all an illusion, and no plain interminable. It sang of certainties nearer than the sky, and having sung was reabsorbed into the first. As I gazed at it I realized that it was no river, but part of the ruined palace, and that men had carved it, as they had carved the stones.

Going back, I missed the shallows and had to wade. The pools, too shallow for alligators, suggested leeches, but all was well, and in the plain beyond a tonga[5] wandered aimlessly. It was mine, and my driver was not surprised that we had all met

3. A sacred river in northern India.
4. The Loire valley in France was a favored site for castles.

5. An animal-drawn conveyance.

again. Safe on the high road, I realized that I had not given one thought to the past. Was that really Vikramaditya's palace? Had Kalidas and the other eight ever prayed in those radiant waters? Kalidas describes Ujjain. In his poem of *The Cloud Messenger*—a poem as ill-planned and charming as my own expedition—he praises the beloved city. He feigns that a demi-god, exiled from his lady, employs a cloud to take her a message from him. An English cloud would go, but this is Hindu. The poem is occupied by an account of the places it might pass if it went far enough out of its course, and of those places the most out-of-the-way is Ujjain. Were the cloud to stray thither, it would enter the city with Sipra, the sacred stream, and would hear the old country people singing songs of mirth in the streets. While maidens clapped their hands, and peacocks their wings, it might enter perfumed balconies as a shower, or as a sunset radiance might cling round the arm of Shiva. In the evening, when women steal to their lovers "through darkness that a needle might divide," the cloud might show them the way by noiseless lightning-flash, and weary of their happiness and its own might repose itself among sleeping doves till dawn. Such was Kalidas' account of his home, and the other eight—was not one of them a lexicographer?—may have sported there with him. The groves near must have suggested to him the magic grove in *Sakuntala*, where the wood nymphs pushed wedding garments through the leaves. "Whence came these ornaments?" one of the characters inquires. "Has the holy hermit created them by an effort of his mind?" The conclusion, though natural, is wrong. "Not quite," answers another. "The sweet trees bore them unaided. While we gathered blossoms, fairy hands were stretched out." Cries a third, "We are only poor girls. How shall we know how such ornaments are put on? Still, we have seen pictures. We can imitate them." They adorn the bride. . . .

But it is only in books that the past can glow, and Kalidas faded as soon as I felt the waters of the Sipra round my ankle. I thought not of Sakuntala's ornaments, but of my own, now spread on the splashboard, and I wondered whether they would dry before we reached the railway station. One confusion enveloped Ujjain and all things. Why differentiate? I asked the driver what kind of trees those were, and he answered "Trees"; what was the name of that bird, and he said "Bird"; and the plain, interminable, murmured, "Old buildings are buildings, ruins are ruins."

Advance, India!

The house of the rationalistic family (Mohammedans[1]) lay close below that of my friends (English). We could see its red walls and corrugated iron roof through the deodars,[2] and its mass cut into the middle distances though without disturbing the line of the snows. It was a large house, but they were not, I believe, prominent in their community, and only flashed into notoriety on the occasion of this marriage, which was the first of its kind that the province had seen. We did not know them, but had received an invitation, together with the rest of the station, and as the sun was declining we clambered down and joined the crowd in their garden.

A public wedding! It would actually take place here. In the centre of the lawn was a dais on which stood a sofa, an armchair, and a table, edged with torn fringe, and round this dais a couple of hundred guests were grouped. The richer sat on chairs, the poorer on a long carpet against the wall. They were of various religions and races—Mohammedans, Hindus, Sikhs, Eurasians, English—and of various social

---

1. Muslims.   2. Shade trees.

standings, though mainly subordinate Government clerks; and they had come from various motives, friendship, curiosity, hostility—the ceremony nearly ended in a tumult, but we did not know this until the next day. The snows were seventy miles off in front, the house behind; the less rationalistic part of the family remained in purdah[3] there and watched the marriage through the blinds. Such was the setting.

After long delay the personages mounted. The Moulvi[4] took the armchair—a handsome, elderly man robed in black velvet and gold. He was joined by the bridegroom, who looked self-possessed, and by the unveiled bride. They sat side by side on the sofa, while guests murmured: "This is totally contrary to the Islamic law," and a child placed vasefuls of congested flowers. Then the bridegroom's brother arrived, and had a long conversation with the Moulvi. They grew more and more excited—gesticulated, struck their breasts, whispered and sighed at one another vehemently. There was some difficulty, but what it was no one could say. At last an agreement was reached, for the brother turned to the audience and announced in English that the marriage ceremony would begin with verses from the Koran. These were read, and "the next item," said the brother, "is a poem upon Conscience. An eminent poet will recite on Conscience in Urdu, but his words will be translated." The poet and his interpreter then joined the group on the dais, and spoke alternately, but not very clearly, for the poet himself knew English, and would correct the interpreter, and snatch at the manuscript. Arid verities rose into the evening air, the more depressing for the rags of Orientalism that clothed them. Conscience was this and that, and whatsoever the simile, there was no escaping her. "The sun illumines the world with light. Blessed be the sun and moon and stars, without which our eyes, that seem like stars, could not see. But there is another light, that of conscience—" and then conscience became a garden where the bulbul[5] of eloquence ever sang and the dews of oratory dropped, and those who ignored her would "roll among thorns." When she had had her fling the pair were made man and wife. Guest murmured, "Moulvi is omitting such-and-such an exhortation: most improper." Turning to the company, and more particularly to those upon the carpet, he said that it was not important how one was married, but how one behaved after marriage. This was his main point, and while he was making it we were handed refreshments, and the ceremony was more or less over.

It was depressing, almost heartrending, and opened the problem of India's future. How could this jumble end? Before the Moulvi finished a gramophone began, and before that was silent a memorable act took place. The sun was setting, and the orthodox withdrew from us to perform their evening prayer. They gathered on the terrace behind, to the number of twenty, and prostrated themselves towards Mecca.[6] Here was dignity and unity; here was a great tradition untainted by private judgment; they had not retained so much and rejected so much; they had accepted Islam unquestioningly, and the reward of such an acceptance is beauty. There was once a wedding in England where a talented lady, advanced, but not too advanced, rewrote her daughter's marriage service. Bad there, the effect was worse in India, where the opportunities for disaster are larger. Crash into the devotions of the orthodox birred the gramophone—

I'd sooner be busy with my little Lizzie,

---

3. Women's seclusion.
4. A religious personage.
5. Nightingale.

6. One of the holy cities of Islam (in present-day Saudi Arabia), birthplace of the Prophet Mohammed; Muslims turn toward Mecca in prayer.

and by a diabolic chance reached the end of its song as they ended the prayer. They rejoined us without self-consciousness, but the sun and the snows were theirs, not ours; they had obeyed; we had entered the unlovely chaos that lies between obedience and freedom—and that seems, alas! the immediate future of India. Guests discussed in nagging tones whether the rationalistic family had gone too far or might not have gone further. The bride might, at all events, have been veiled; she might, at all events, have worn English clothes. Eurasian children flew twittering through the twilight like bats, cups clinked, the gramophone was restarted, this time with an Indian record, and during the opening notes of a nautch [dance] we fled.

Next morning a friend (Sikh) came to breakfast, and told us that some of the guests had meant to protest against the innovations, and that the Moulvi had insisted in justifying himself to them; that was why he had argued on the dais and spoken afterwards. There was now great trouble among the Mohammedans in the station, and many said there had been no marriage at all. Our friend was followed by the bridegroom's brother, who thanked us for coming, said there had been no trouble in the community, and showed us the marriage lines. He said—"Some old-fashioned gentlemen did not understand at first—the idea was new. Then we explained, and they understood at once. The lady is advanced; very advanced . . . ." It appeared that she had advanced further than her husband, and the brother seemed thankful all was over without a scandal. "It was difficult," he cried. "We Moslems are not as advanced as the Hindus, and up here it is not like Bombay side, where such marriages are commoner. But we have done what we ought, and are consequently content." High sentiments fell from his lips, conscience shone and flowered and sang and banged, yet somehow he became a more dignified person. It hadn't at all events been an easy thing for two bourgeois families to jerk out of their rut, and it is actions like theirs, rather than the thoughts of a philosopher or the examples of kings, that advance a society. India had started—one had that feeling while this rather servile little clerk was speaking. For good or evil she had left the changeless snows and was descending into a valley whose further side is still invisible.

"Please write about this" were his parting words. "Please publish some account of it in English newspapers. It is a great step forward against superstition, and we want all to know."

Jodhpur[1]

There must be some mistake! It was surely impossible that a dragon, flapping a tail of stone, should crouch in the middle of houses; that, having reached an incredible height, his flanks should turn to masonry; that he should be ridged with a parapet and bristle with guns; and that upward again a palace should rise, crowning the dragon, and, like him, coloured pearl. This was in the dawn, when a belt of mist cut off the mountain from the lower earth. Later in the day there were contrasts between sun and shade. After the sun set the vision was one colour again—olive-black, merging into night—and the dragon's crown rested among stars.

It was a vision of which the English community, stationed three miles off on the plain, had never lost sight. They had none of the indifference to their surroundings that is considered good form elsewhere. They loved the city and the people living in

---

1. One of a group of princely states in northwest India.

it, and an outsider's enthusiasm, instead of boring them, appeared to give pleasure. Men and women, they shared the same club as the Indians, and under its gracious roof the "racial question" had been solved—not by reformers, who only accent the evils they define, but by the genius of the city, which gave everyone something to work for and think about. I had heard of this loyalty at the other end of the peninsula—it was avowedly rare. But no one had described the majesty that inspired it—the air blowing in from the desert, the sand and the purple stones, the hills with quarries and tanks beneath, and the palace-fortress on the highest hill, an amazement for ever, a dragon's crown. "I love these Rajpoots,"[2] an English official cried. "They have their faults, and one takes steps accordingly, but I love and respect them, and always shall." It was as if each race had made concessions. Ours seemed more sensitive than usual, the Indian more solid. A common ground for friendship had been contrived, "but if we were all somewhere else," he said, "I don't expect it would be the same."

Next morning I went to the fort. My companion was a landscape gardener from Bombay, who had been commissioned by the Ruler to contrive a park out of some of the low ground. He shook his head and remarked, "A place like this doesn't want a park." We had to make a wide circuit, since only a path approached the mountain on the city side. The citadel joined on to a wild country, covered for miles with walls that followed the tops of the hills. Below it were many smaller forts, one wider than the pedestal that bore it, and half-way up lay a green tarn[3] and the marble tomb of a prince. The fortress seemed part of the mountain—the distinction between Nature and Art, never strong in India, had here become negligible. The first gateway—there were five or six lines of defence—lay between cliffs of masonry, in whose sides had been hollowed caves for the guard. Each turn of the ascent was commanded by a window, and there were ambushes innumerable. At Daulatabad, in the Deccan, the defences must have been even stronger, for there the enemy had to climb a tunnel cut in the living rock and closed at the upper end by a bonfire. But Daulatabad is not crowned by romance, like this city. Presently the quality of the stone grew finer, and we walked beneath precipices whose upper ranges had been carved. "We must be getting up in between the palace somehow," said my companion. "I've been all these years, and didn't know there was such a place in India, or indeed in the world. What next?" Transepts like honeycomb answered him, and, cramped but splendid, the courtyard of the palace came into view.

We were met by the Keeper of the State Jewels, which were, as so often, stupid and ugly. No lady wears her predecessor's ornaments, and the gems had been recut and reset according to Regent Street. One necklace of emeralds—loot from the Mohammedans—had escaped emasculation. After the Treasury, we saw some other rooms, and admired the painted ceiling of the Durbar hall[4] and its mirrored sides. But the best was to come.

The passage continued by walls of increased elaboration—they concealed the zenana,[5] and how they smelt!—and emerged on to a platform of several acres, windswept and baked by the sun. The sense of space returned. On one side, far below, were vultures, on the other, still farther, lay the world of men. We could peer into their secrets with princely arrogance—a wedding procession, a family asleep, policemen drilling in a closed churchyard, camels, two women quarrelling on a house-top. The plans of the temples became clear: we could see their size and symmetry and

---

2. Or *Rajputs* (princes).
3. A mountain lake.

4. Assembly hall.
5. A secluded area for women.

their relation to the tanks. Then, tired of detail, we could glance at the grey-green bush, or overleaping civilization, rest on the encircling desert, and the ruins of forts ours had destroyed. A Rajpoot army idled on the platform. It was young and insolent, and played among the guns. These were of great age, some Dutch, others Indian, and cast in the shapes of fish, alligators, and dragons. The more reliable were fired in official salutes, and bursting occasionally would throw back the soldiers dead into the fort. Plenty were left, both of guns and Rajpoots, so no change was contemplated, though some day reform may come along with an electric button and a Babu.[6] Beyond the soldiers, on the downward slope, stood a shrine to a goddess. She had some usual name—Chamundi—but she lives here and not elsewhere, and is the daughter of the rock, if not the rock. Beyond Chamundi's appeared the Western city, with the dragon's tail flapping across it, and dividing it into wards, and hidden in the creases of the tail were deep pools of water, where Brahmans[7] scattered flowers or fed the fish.

This is the land of heroism, where deeds which would have been brutal elsewhere have been touched with glory. In Europe heroism has become joyless or slunk to museums: it exists as a living spell here. The civilization of Jodhpur, though limited, has never ceased to grow. It has not spread far or excelled in the arts, but it is as surely alive as the civilization of Agra is dead. Not as a poignant memory does it touch the heart of the son or the stranger. And when it does die, may it find a death complete and unbroken; may it never survive archaeologically, or hear, like Delhi, the trumpets of an official resurrection. One would wish for the sand to close in on the city, and the purple stones to show more frequently than they do through the soil; for the desert to resume the life it gave, and unobserved by men take back the dragon's crown. The wish may be granted. The kindred State of Jaisalmer struggles up to its throat against such a death, and "will only be saved by a railway." Railways can create. They cannot save, and for my own part I would leave heroes to heroic graves, and concentrate the blessings of progress upon the new Canal Colonies in the Punjab.

Midday. A loud and unscientific explosion. Everyone remains alive. The soldiers run laughing into the cool of the passage, and fall asleep there.

The Suppliant

Our friend—I will call him Obaidulla and give the account, which, greatly agitated, he poured forth to us on the roof of his house—our friend and his brother had been sitting in the verandah unpacking some books, when an old man approached. His appearance was ruffianly. "Good evening, gentlemen," he said. "Will you please subscribe to my son's railway journey, in order that he may reach Calcutta?" and he produced a forged subscription list. But he was a suppliant, a Moslem, and old. "I am a poor man myself," said our friend. "However, if your son will accept two rupees"[1]— and he gave them.

"I think you have come here to practise as a barrister," remarked the old man, as he sat down.

Obaidulla replied that he was correct; he had but recently arrived from England.

"I think you need a clerk."

6. A title of respect.
7. Members of the Hindu priestly caste.
1. The Indian monetary unit; equivalent to about 30

cents. There were 16 annas in one rupee and 12 pies (or paisa) in one anna.

"No, I do not need a clerk. I have as yet no connection in the city, and can do such work as I get unaided. We live very simply, as you see."

"You need a clerk. I will be your clerk."

"You are most kind, but at present I do not need a clerk."

"When's dinner?"

The theory that a suppliant leaves after a meal proved correct, and the brothers spent the evening arranging books with the help of their hall-porter, a dictatorial child of ten. They had acted courteously and felt happy. But towards midnight a ghari [carriage] rolled up piled with luggage. A dirty white turban stuck out of its window. "I am your clerk," said the old man. "Where is my room?" and he left them to pay the driver.

"But what could I do?" Obaidulla protested in answer to our cries. "What else could I do? One cannot be inhospitable, and he is old. He kept my servants up all night cleaning his hookah [pipe], and today he complains of them." He sighed, then said, laughing, "Alas! poor India! What next?"

We walked up and down, now scolding him, now joining in the lament. The roof seemed an exquisite place. It rose above the dust of the city into a world of green. The mangoes and toddy-palms and bel-trees pushed out of a hundred little gardens and courtyards, and expanded at our level into a city for the birds. The sun had set, an amazing purple bloomed in the orange of the western sky. Yet not even on the roof were we free. If we walked on its left side, we overlooked our next-door neighbour, a fat Hindu tradesman, and he would call up in English, "Gentlemen! Gentlemen! Go further away, please! These are lady-women quarters." And if we walked on the right we came in sight of other lady-women, less supervised or super-visible, who ran about on the top of their roof and waved long scarves. "A two-storey house is dangerous for a beginner," said Obaidulla elliptically, so we walked midway, while out of his own courtyard rose the growls of the suppliant—he corpulent mercifully and the staircase narrow.

We left depressed—partly because our friend did not urge us to stop to tea. Tea there was always delicious—peas done in butter were served with it, as were tangerines, as were guavas, sliced and peppered, and sometimes his married friends had sent sweets. But he could not well press us—the suppliant's table manners were too awful—nor could he come to tea with us, not liking to leave his brother alone, nor could they both come, fearing to leave the house. Our depression increased when we caught sight of the old man himself. A thousand insults (I was told) were implied in his salaam [greeting]. And from inquiries in the bazaar we had news that he really was a bad lot. Nothing could be done, for Obaidulla, though humorous and gentle, allowed no interference with his hospitality. We could only wonder for how long he would sacrifice his friends, his liberty, and his career, and reflect on the disadvantages of keeping house in the mediaeval style.

Next morning the suppliant called on us. We repelled him before he could speak, and soon afterwards Obaidulla tumbled up on his bicycle, radiant with joy. "A most fortunate thing has happened," he cried. "He has stolen one rupee four annas six pies from my servant's clothes and gone."

We congratulated him, and asked for details.

"Ah, ah! at last we are happy again. Now I can tell you. When the little boy caught him I did not know what to do. One cannot be impolite. I said: 'There seems to have been some misunderstanding,' and I waited. Very luckily he grew warm. He said: 'I never stop in a house where I am not trusted.' I answered: 'I am sorry to hear you say such a thing, and I have never said I do not trust you.'—'No, but your servants. Enough! Enough! I am your clerk no longer. I go.' I told him I was sorry to hear his decision, but perhaps he was wise. So he came straight round to you, having got all he could out of us! Oh, the old villain! The monster! It is a disgrace to India that such men exist! However, it cannot be helped, I suppose."

"And the money?"

"Oh, he took it, of course; of course. But I might have had to replace as much as fifty rupees. Well, that is all over, and today will you both come to tea?"

He was really too silly, and we gave him a good British talking to. He listened in silence, his eyes on the ground. When we had finished he raised them to mine and said:

"It is natural you should laugh at me. You are English, and have other customs. I should not have behaved like this in England myself. No doubt it all seems jolly funny." Then turning to his other critic, who was Indian, he added in sterner tones: "But you—I am ashamed of you. You ought to have understood. As long as we have money and food and houses we must share them, when asked, with the poor and the old. Shocking! Your heart has cooled. You have forgotten our traditions of hospitality. You have forgotten the East. I am very much ashamed of you indeed."

Roger Fry
1866–1934

Roger Eliot Fry was the most influential art critic in Britain from 1910 until his death in 1934. The year 1910 was pivotal because late that year Fry organized the first of two post-Impressionist painting exhibits that brought the work of Cézanne, van Gogh, Gauguin, Matisse, and Picasso to London's Grafton Galleries. By curating these shows, and by writing the art criticism that educated the public about these revolutionary painters, Roger Fry almost single-handedly changed the understanding of modern art in Britain. Virginia Woolf—who later wrote a biography of Fry—was probably alluding to this exhibition when she famously remarked that "On or about December 1910, human nature changed."

Educated at Cambridge University, Fry went on to study in Paris and Italy, painting landscapes and writing art criticism. After joining the Bloomsbury circle in 1911, he became part of the British artistic avant-garde as a designer, a painter, and most notably a potter. In 1913 he started the Omega Workshops, a modernist design studio that updated William Morris's idea of the creative workshop, contributing ceramics and textiles to its offerings. Fry's books include *Vision and Design* (1920) and *Art and Socialism* (1912), monographs on Giotto, Seurat, and Cézanne, and his published lectures, especially *Last Lectures* (1939), which demonstrates his interest in art beyond Western Europe. Through his doctrine of the importance of form over subject matter, Fry enabled a broad audience to understand the nature of modern abstraction and to perceive what he called the "significant form" of line, color, and shape as these replaced figural realism in modern art. His art criticism is of lasting value for its supple intelligence, wit, and clarity, and its eye for the beauty hidden in the shock of the new.

Culture and Snobbism[1]

It is a nice point, and one on which I have never yet been able to make up my mind, whether culture is more inimical to art than barbarism, or *vice versâ*. Culture, no doubt, tends to keep a tradition in existence, but just when the tradition thus careful-

1. Fry included this review essay, on Sir Claude Phillips' 1925 book *Emotion in Art*, in his collection *Transformations* (1927).

ly tended through some winter of neglect begins to show signs of life by putting out new shoots and blossoms, culture must needs do its best to destroy them. As the guardian and worshipper of the dead trunk, it tries to wipe off such impertinent excrescences, unable as it is to recognise in them the signs of life.

The late Sir Claude Phillips, for instance, pays tribute throughout his book, "Emotion in Art," to the greatest achievements of the art of the past; he exalted and kept alive the memory of Titian and Giorgione, but when he comes to talk of his contemporaries he makes us wonder what he found to admire in the old masters by speaking in almost the same glowing terms of Böcklin and Fritz von Uhde; he alludes to Monet, but he is silent about Seurat and Sisley and Cézanne,[2] not to mention those more modern artists whom also he had every opportunity to appraise.

For this book of reprinted articles makes it quite clear that Sir Claude was a very distinguished High Priest of Culture. The unction of his style was as oil to feed the undying flame in the Temple, and the savour of his epithets rose like incense before its altars. Like many great ecclesiastics, he was also an accomplished man of the world, neither an ascetic nor a prude; like them he enjoyed polished society, good wine, good food, and good stories. He was a charming and witty companion, whose good things were drawn from the vast store of learning and experience which his wonderful memory retained. But like other ecclesiastics, when he entered the Temple indued with his priestly garments, his whole manner changed. His language took on the peculiar unction of almost all devotional writing, and he bowed perpetually before the great gods of his Temple and rarely alluded to one of them without some time-honoured and sanctifying epithet. The very quality of his phrases changed; they took on the liturgical resonance which relegates sense to a subsidiary position. Perhaps Ruskin had showed the way, but it was Phillips more than any one else who framed and consolidated the ritual and liturgical use of the great Temple of Culture. He borrowed, no doubt, from other religions, but he adapted with extraordinary tact and skill. Thus it was that he came week after week to intone in the columns of the *Daily Telegraph* those reverential, decorous, and richly adorned services, some of which are reprinted here. Throughout these pages we hear "the blessed mutter of the Mass"—a Mass in which the names of all the deities and saints and all their great works are brought up in succession. It hardly matters whether Sir Claude Phillips says anything about their works or not; the main purpose is served if one after another their glorious names are brought to the worshipper's mind, in order to arouse his reverent awe and conduce to his edification. As we read these pages we are conscious of the presence of the Thrones, Dominations, Principalities, and Powers of the realm of art; we share humbly and at a distance in that new communion of the Saints. Almost infallibly Sir Claude strikes the right devotional attitude and finds the edifying epithet.

One of the well-known signs of this attitude is the reference to holy beings by some allusive translocution. A well-trained ecclesiastic having once named Elijah could hardly fail afterwards to refer to him as the "indomitable Tishbite." The effect of this is admirable, it assumes that reverent familiarity on the worshipper's part which is so desirable. Thus, Sir Claude has his repertory of allusions, "the gentle Urbinate," "the bee of Urbino," "the divine Sanzio," "the faultless Andrea," "the Frate," "the poet-painter of Valenciennes," "the great Cadorine," by which we are, as it were, made free of the mysteries. Still more significant is the fact that not even the

---

2. In other words, Phillips preferred contemporary mediocrities to advanced, post-Impressionist artists like Seurat, whom Frye sees as worthy successors to the great Renaissance painters Titian and Giorgione.

objects that have to do with the cult may be left without their appropriate adjective. I quote a passage in which he speaks of dancing in art: "Akin to these, but perhaps more vigorous still, and with less of cosmic suavity, are the child-angels who in joyous procession pass dancing along the front and sides of Donatello's 'Cantoria,' once in the Cathedral of Santa Maria del Fiori at Florence, but now in the little museum at the back of that mighty church." Here the information given in the last phrase is, of course, quite irrelevant to the argument, but it seems to bring up vague memories of holy things, and, what reveals the attitude, even this little scrap of topography helps to elevate us by reason of the insertion of the word "mighty." The true emotional touch is shown by this almost unconscious gesture. But let me quote another passage where the fervour of Sir Claude's Apostolate has more scope:

"And Mantegna,[3] harsh and tender, severe with a more than Roman severity, and yet of a mysticism in devotion as intense as that of any contemporary master, maintains the beholder in realms where the spirit droops and can hardly follow. The sublimity of Michelangelo himself is equalled in a 'Sybil and Prophet' of very moderate dimensions, formerly in the collection of the Duke of Buccleugh; the 'Infant Christ, as Ruler of the World,' of the Mond collection, stands apart in the quiet intensity with which it expresses worship on the one hand, and, on the other, the irradiation of the Universe by Divine Love. The 'Madonnas' of the Poldi-Pezzoli at Milan and the Gallery at Bergamo, express, as by hardly any other master they have been expressed, the sublime devotion, the tragic apprehension, of maternal love that is all human and yet in its immensity Divine. Face to face with his 'Adoration of the Magi' (formerly in the Ashburton collection), we experience the feeling of religious awe, almost of terror, that possessed the Wise Men of the East when, though royal still in splendour and in gravity, they knelt subdued and prostrate in worship at the feet of the Divine Babe."

There surely is the full organ roll of the Anglican liturgy at its best; see how the very names of Italian towns and of ducal collectors help to swell the diapason, and urge the worshipper to fresh ecstasies of acquiescence.

Decidedly Sir Claude Phillips was a great High Priest in that religion of culture which is so well adapted to the emotional needs of polite societies, and let me add that he had to the full the sense of his sacerdoce. He was the first to denounce any act of vandalism, he was the most scrupulous in avoiding any hint of simony, the most punctilious in the assertion of the claims of his religion, and the most conscientious in their observance.

There remains, of course, the question with which I started, what relation, if any, has this religion of culture to art? Some connection it surely has. It would be impossible for any one to have written these glowing pages unless he had looked long and with some genuine emotion at the innumerable masterpieces whose images he recalls and whose glories he recounts. But so far as I can find, there is no single piece of strictly esthetic appreciation in the whole of this book. Not once does Sir Claude come into contact with the actual vision of the artist. So far, indeed, does his habit of day-dreaming about pictures instead of looking at them go, that in an essay on "What the Brush cannot Paint," he actually says that, "The word-painting of the poet gives as definite a vision as that which arises from the brush-work of the painters." The word "definite" here is, of course, the exact opposite of the truth—the essence, and to a great extent the value, of the poet's image lying precisely in its indefiniteness.

---

3. Andrea Mantegna (1431–1506), Italian painter.

But Sir Claude did not accept definite images from pictures. He allowed the vision to set up in his mind an emotional state in which the vision itself was lost in the vague overtones of associated ideas and feelings. He shows his method when he says: "Not Millais in his 'Chill October,' not even Theodore Rousseau or Diaz, painting the festering herbage on some dark pool of the forest, walled in by the trees from which the last sere leaves drop in the silence, one by one." It matters little how poor the quality of the painting is (and how poor are these he cites!), when this agreeable day-dream with its soothing verbal accompaniment replaces so rapidly the painter's vision.

It is to this that we must look for the explanation of the strange paradox of this fervent hierodule of Raphael, Titian, and Poussin giving his priestly blessing to Böcklin and Fritz von Uhde, and turning aside from the more sincere efforts of modern art to write long rhapsodies over sentimental war-pictures which have already passed into Time's rubbish heap.

No doubt, then, Sir Claude derived a very genuine enjoyment from works of art, but I think that enjoyment was obtained without any direct communion with the artists' sensibility; what he saw and felt was the dramatic interpretation of the scene and its decorative setting, but most of all he felt the status of the work in question in the hierarchy of art, its cultural value, the exact degree of reverence which it might rightly claim from the devout. Reverence is, indeed, the key to all such religious attitudes, and reverence is, of course, as inimical to true esthetic experience as it is to the apprehension of truth. Reverence, and that goodwill which belongs to edification, may be, perhaps, of use to help the beginner to overcome the first difficulties of approach to what is finest in art, but if he is to get any real esthetic experience, he must learn to eschew reverence and to distrust his goodwill.

This is, indeed, the greatest difficulty of criticism, for past esthetic experiences always tend to stereotype themselves in our minds and set up within us the religious attitude. Sir Claude Phillips not only did not understand this, but would have looked upon such an attempt to react purely and freely in each case as a blasphemy against the whole religion of culture.

I still find I must leave the question open. Picture galleries and museums are Temples of Culture, not of Art. The artist and the esthete use them, no doubt: indeed, they depend on them; they would, none the less, never have had the social prestige, nor, perhaps, the energy, to have created them. The artist's debt to culture in that respect is immense, but he pays it in full when he discovers that the same social prestige of culture will turn upon him the moment he tries to create along the lines of the tradition which culture has preserved. To the cultured man the unpardonable sin is the creation of just those works which will become the ark of the covenant to some succeeding generation of cultured men.

This question of the part played by culture in a civilisation prompts the similar question of the rôle of snobbism. This useful word, the interest which we have received on lending the word "snob" to the French, describes a well-known class of experiences. Snobbery, from which it comes, describes the uncritical and enthusiastic acceptance of certain social values or pretensions, and snobbism should, I think, be kept for the distinct phenomenon of the equally blind acceptance of certain spiritual values or pretensions, whether intellectual or esthetic.

Can we distinguish between culture and snobbism? In both a certain religious attitude of worship is evident, and they are concerned largely with the same values. In both, too, communion with fellow worshippers is a matter of supreme importance, so that it is not always an easy matter to say of a particular act of devotion or article of faith to which Church it belongs. It may, indeed, partake of both, since these are not mutually exclusive doctrines.

There is, however, I think, a difference of mental attitude which the words enable us to distinguish. The snobbist, by his pilgrimage to the "right" picture gallery at the "right" moment, and his display there of the "right" enthusiasm before the "right" works of art is really upheld by the consciousness that those acts bring him into close communion with a certain group of people, and it is not altogether remote from his consciousness, although, perhaps, kept below its surface, that those people are socially influential. His acts tend to make certain that he will be "in the swim." It is this subtle connection between a certain esthetic creed and its social adherents that is, perhaps, too frankly revealed by the word "snobbism." The man of culture, on the other hand, lives in a world more detached from these considerations. His communion is not only with the living. By his acts of devotion he unites himself to a long line of historical precedents. He upholds the tradition which sensitive and contemplative spirits have handed on from generation to generation. And, since the verdicts of esthetic sensibility have a tendency to violent fluctuations, this traditional esthetic doctrine has called to its aid the steadying influence of learning and scholarship. So that the devotees of culture often acquire more merit by what they know about the history of a work of art than by what they feel in front of it. To them an artist does not become a serious artist until a learned monograph has been consecrated to his life work. Thus the cultured, linked to the past by a long line of predecessors and filled with a sense of responsibility for the future, tend to adopt a conservative attitude to contemporary art. Their imprimatur must not be lightly given. They yield in the end, and become the guardians of what they resisted, judging, perhaps rightly, that only its irresistibility justifies this consecration. The snobbist, on the other hand, whilst always respectful of learning, is too anxious to know the latest word to await its judgment. He tends, therefore, to march in step with the vanguard of any esthetic movement as soon as its victory is no longer in doubt. Until victory is fairly in view the movements of the true snobbist afford a fascinating spectacle, he— or perhaps she, for, thanks to the quicker social sense of women, they form the greatest and most devout part of the communion—shows the greatest anxiety and trepidation. A too overt adherence to the new doctrine at such a moment would precipitate him along a social blind alley and leave him in a position from which recovery is difficult and sometimes slightly ridiculous. On the other hand, to be left behind on the right track, though a fault more easily repaired, is to miss a supreme opportunity.

In thus describing some of the familiar experiences of modern life which affect the production of works of art, I have, I confess, a little over simplified for the sake of clearness. The situation is never so definite as I have suggested. To represent the true facts we must allow for the admixture in infinitely varying doses according to temperament and character of genuine esthetic feeling. Since social facts are of supreme importance to people's lives the social sense is likely to be more alert and potent than the esthetic, but it not unfrequently happens, especially with the young, that, impelled at first merely by a vague, and in itself respectable, instinct to share in the most vivid life of the day, not to be too much "out of it," they do acquire a genuine appreciation of works of art and pass through snobbism into the ranks of that small group of amateurs—in the proper sense of the word—whose influence is most profound in the creation and survival of works of art.

What is most to be admired in culture is its love of the contemplative attitude and its passion for exact scholarship. Its besetting sin is an over-cautious timidity, its desire for security above everything, its fear of life. Snobbism, at least, has the merit of trusting to the life of the moment with a certain recklessness. The roads of culture have been long laid down and are well patrolled, the snobbist follows into newly opened territory, and however anxiously he watches events, is bound to miss a genius or back a dud now and again.

Primarily, however, we are not concerned here with the psychology of the cultured or snobbist, but with the effect on art of their varying influence. And this can hardly be exaggerated, since the emergence and survival of any particular work of art are, I believe, as strictly conditioned by its ambience as is the emergence and survival of a type of animal or plant.

The artist, in whose breast the divine flame is kindled, finds himself confronted, then, with these two religions of culture and snobbism. But he is also aware of the presence of a vast inert mass, the great body of Philistines. These are the esthetic atheists who own no obedience to any doctrine, whose only allegiance is to their untutored and wayward satisfaction. These he regards from the first as enemies; but they are his frank and loyal enemies. Mr Podsnap's view of the arts he knows. It is clear, concise and perfectly intelligible. Dickens has explained it once for all in the following terms:

"Mr Podsnap's notions of the Arts in their integrity might have been stated thus. Literature; large print, respectively descriptive of getting up at eight, shaving close at a quarter-past, breakfasting at nine, going to the City at ten, coming home at half-past four, and dining at seven. Painting and sculpture; models and portraits representing Professors of getting up at eight, etc. Music; a respectable performance (without variations) on stringed and wind instruments, sedately expressive of getting up at 8, etc. Nothing else to be permitted to those same vagrants the Arts, on pain of excommunication. Nothing else To Be—anywhere!"—("Our Mutual Friend.")

The artist knows, then, exactly where he stands with the Philistine. With culture, too, his position is ascertainable. He finds himself, indeed, inspired and consoled by the great tradition which culture guards and proclaims. Through culture he is made free of the great art of the past and is encouraged to emulate its glories. It is only when he proceeds to do so that culture turns on him a sterner aspect. In imitating the attitude of the great masters he cannot possibly repeat their results, and thereupon the Grand Inquisitors of Culture scent heresy and make ready the *Auto da Fé*.[4]

In this quandary snobbism alone appears to hold out a succouring hand. To express anything at all is a crime with the Philistine, to express anything vital is a crime with culture, among the snobbists alone novelty may, under certain circumstances, be a positive virtue. It must be a novelty that is not altogether unprepared for, it must go further along a track to which snobbism has recently become habituated. Then, and then only, the snobbist will help with unstinting generosity.

The artist, then, is likely to find in snobbism his most potent ally, but, as happens in other alliances, he is likely at times to feel more kindly towards his open antagonist the Philistine than he does towards an ally whose activities are capricious and uncertain. He will find snobbism always pressing forward to catch the last word, far too eager to see any point in subtle or unobtrusive work. He will find it continually the victim of charlatanism and advertisement, or even where, as may well happen,

4. Ceremony for burning heretics at the stake.

it has accepted genuine talent, doing so with so undiscriminating an enthusiasm that only the strongest and purest natures can resist its dangerous seduction. His indignation will be the greater in that in its light-hearted way snobbism distorts the values and confuses the issues in just those things that he most cherishes, until he may come to regard it as the abomination of desolation desecrating his holiest places.

What I have elsewhere defined as the "Opificer"[5] is backed by considerable funds, both from the patronage of the State and other public bodies, and from the private patronage of the Philistine. But the pure artist finds that, apart from the support of those few individuals who not only have cultivated by careful study a natural love of art but possess the means to gratify their passion, almost the only fund on which he can rely depends on the favour of snobbism. At rather rare intervals in modern life this favour has been actively exercised, and when such a situation arises, as it has notoriously of late years in Paris, the enthusiasm of the snobbist has stirred to activity a crowd of speculative buyers who hope by spotting the winner in the field of aspiring talent to reap fabulous profits.

The artist, too, in so complex a world must be upheld by a religious conviction, an unwavering faith by which to steer his course among the devious currents of modern civilisation. Since he is in a small minority his creed will always tend to have a protestant tinge. He is a protestant against the materialism of Mr Podsnap, against the pontifical authority of the high priests of Culture, and against the capricious interferences of Snobbism. His religion, too, is a very intimate personal affair, it compels him to the assertion, often with fanatical vehemence, of his private values. He is a member of no wide communion—may, indeed, shun all communion whatever, though more probably he links himself in a close alliance with the few who share his convictions.

It is to Paris of the mid-nineteenth century, from 1830 to 1870, that we must turn to study the heroic period of this religion, the epoch of its great saints and martyrs. There we see to what a pitch of ecstasy and devotion this faith could raise its votaries. It was the age when Daumier[6] produced almost day by day, for some infinitesimal sum, masterpieces of tragic irony which made ministers tremble with rage and hate, and landed him in prison: it was the age when the Odéon [theater] was run by a director madly in love with poetry, who, backed by a troupe of famished but heroic actors, produced romantic plays one after another in the face of the outraged bourgeoisie and the frenzied enthusiasm of the Bohemians: it was the age when the fervour touched even the cafetiers and restaurant keepers, and a Mère Cadet would extend credit year after year, without a hint or a frown, to her penniless clients: it was the age when through the thousand accidents of open-air life in the streets and gardens of Paris the faithful, whether poets, actors, painters or musicians, discovered one another by almost invisible signs, and cemented life-long friendships on the strength of a chance word.

It was an age when snobbism scarcely existed or had not as yet tendered its munificence to the genuine artist. He, indeed, had to rely entirely on the far slenderer aid which disinterested but passionate amateurs could afford him—and these, it must be remembered, are always, the decisive factor in the highest kinds of artistic creation—and on the unstinting generosity with which the faithful helped one another out of their own poverty.

---

5. "Workman" or artistic hack.

6. Honoré Daumier (1808–1879), prolific French caricaturist, painter and sculptor.

And here we touch on a curious economic accident the importance of which as a determining condition of art production has never been properly emphasised. In modern life great works of art have generally been, and, I suspect, almost must be, produced in defiance of the tastes and predilections of society at large. The artist, therefore, except in those cases where he possesses inherited means, must be able to live and function on an extremely small sum. He must exist almost as sparrows do, by picking up the crumbs that fall from the rich man's table. That is to say, that Bohemian life, a life deprived of all superfluous and unnecessary elements, must not be too degrading, and must leave those who follow it some amenities, especially the possibility of meeting and exchanging their impressions and convictions. These conditions are fulfilled only where the standard of life in general is not too exacting. At first sight it may appear to make no difference whether the rule of life is, as in the United States, that salaries are high and prices and profits are also high, or, as in France, that salaries and prices are both low. But, in point of fact, one condition, the American, is fatal to the existence of a true Bohemia, and the other is propitious. In the case of America the sum necessary to support life is a large one, and though it can be earned with proportionate ease it can only be earned by some work the value of which society can recognise at once. In the case of France it is, or certainly was in the nineteenth century, so small that it might be picked up by part-time work at any one of the smaller crafts of industrial design for which France is conspicuous.

The highly organised production on a grand scale of America, with its large wages and high profits, leaves far fewer of those interstices in the social system into which the artist can insert himself, than does a society based on a multiplicity of small and individual producers. Here, indeed, we touch on one of those small accidental factors in social life which may exercise a decisive influence on artistic production. What wonder, then, that periods of artistic creation and impotence are as hard to predict or account for as the weather itself! Hitherto we have not made anything like as strenuous an effort at estimating and calculating these forces and conditions, doubtless because societies always tend to regard their spiritual products as superfluities. And yet there is a certain irony in the fact that every civilisation is ultimately judged by what of spiritual value it has contributed to the human patrimony. It is only at each present moment that this appears to be of so little consequence as to be negligible by the governing class.

＊＊＊

Virginia Woolf
Letter to Vanessa Bell[1]

Monday [16 August 1909]

Beloved,

＊ ＊ ＊ writing seems to me a queer thing. It does make a difference. I should never talk to you like this. For one thing, I dont know what mood you are in, and then— but the subtleties are infinite. The truth is, I am always trying to get behind words; and they flop down upon me suddenly. When I write to Ottoline [Morrell][2] or Lytton

---

1. Woolf was a prolific and revealing letter writer. She used letters both to reflect on her experiences and to try out ideas and images that she would later use in fiction.

Periodically, as in this letter to her sister, she writes about the act of writing itself.
2. Prominent hostess and patron of the arts (1873–1938).

[Strachey], I honour all the conventions, and love them. And then, you are much simpler than I am. I thought about that at the opera last night. How do you manage to see only one thing at a time? Without any of those reflections that distract me so much, and make people call me bad names. I suppose you are, as Lytton once said, the most complete human being of us all; and your simplicity is really that you take in much more than I do, who intensify atoms. * * *

Yr. B.

The Apes kiss you. * * *

Letter to Gerald Brenan[3]

Christmas Day 1922

Dear Gerald,

* * * I have been thinking a great deal about what you say of writing novels. One must renounce, you say. I can do better than write novels, you say. I don't altogether understand. I don't see how to write a book without people in it. Perhaps you mean that one ought not to attempt a "view of life"?—one ought to limit oneself to one's own sensations—at a quartet for instance; one ought to be lyrical, descriptive: but not set people in motion, and attempt to enter them, and give them impact and volume? Ah, but I'm doomed! As a matter of fact, I think that we all are. It is not possible now, and never will be, to say I renounce. Nor would it be a good thing for literature were it possible. This generation must break its neck in order that the next may have smooth going. For I agree with you that nothing is going to be achieved by us. Fragments—paragraphs—a page perhaps: but no more. Joyce to me seems strewn with disaster. I can't even see, as you see, his triumphs. A gallant approach, that is all that is obvious to me: then the usual smash and splinters (I have only read him, partly, once). The human soul, it seems to me, orientates itself afresh every now and then. It is doing so now. No one can see it whole, therefore. The best of us catch a glimpse of a nose, a shoulder, something turning away, always in movement. Still, it seems better to me to catch this glimpse, than to sit down with Hugh Walpole, Wells,[4] etc. etc. and make large oil paintings of fabulous fleshy monsters complete from top to toe. Of course, being under 30, this does not apply to you. To you, something more complete may be vouchsafed. If so, it will be partly because I, and some others, have made our attempts first. I have wandered from the point. Never mind. I am only scribbling, more to amuse myself than you, who may never read, or understand: for I am doubtful whether people, the best disposed towards each other, are capable of more than an intermittent signal as they forge past—a sentimental metaphor, leading obviously to ships, and night and storm and reefs and rocks, and the obscured, uncompassionate moon. I wish I had your letter for I could then go ahead; without so many jerks.

You said you were very wretched, didn't you? You described your liver rotting, and how you read all night, about the early fathers; and then walked, and saw the dawn. But were wretched, and tore up all you wrote, and felt you could never, never write—and compared this state of yours with mine, which you imagine to be secure, rooted, benevolent, industrious—you did not say dull—but somehow unattainable,

---

3. Novelist and critic.
4. Sir Hugh Walpole (1884–1941), novelist and critic;

H. G. Wells (1866–1946), novelist, journalist, sociologist, historian.

and I daresay, unreal. But you must reflect that I am 40: further, every 10 years, at 20, again at 30, such agony of different sorts possessed me that not content with rambling and reading I did most emphatically attempt to end it all; and should have been often thankful, if by stepping on one flagstone rather than another I could have been annihilated where I stood. I say this partly in vanity that you may not think me insipid; partly as a token (one of those flying signals out of the night and so on) that so we live, all of us who feel and reflect, with recurring cataclysms of horror: starting up in the night in agony: Every ten years brings, I suppose, one of those private orientations which match the vast one which is, to my mind, general now in the race. I mean, life has to be sloughed: has to be faced: to be rejected; then accepted on new terms with rapture. And so on, and so on; till you are 40, when the only problem is how to grasp it tighter and tighter to you, so quick it seems to slip, and so infinitely desirable is it.

As for writing, at 30 I was still writing, reading; tearing up industriously. I had not published a word (save reviews). I despaired. Perhaps at that age one is really most a writer. Then one cannot write, not for lack of skill, but because the object is too near, too vast. I think perhaps it must recede before one can take a pen to it. At any rate, at 20, 30, 40, and I've no doubt 50, 60, and 70, that to me is the task; not particularly noble or heroic, as I see it in my own case, for all my inclinations are to write; but the object of adoration to me, when there comes along someone capable of achieving—if only the page or paragraph; for there are no teachers, saints, prophets, good people, but the artists—as you said—But the last sentence is hopelessly unintelligible. Indeed, I am getting to the end of my letter writing capacity. I have many more things to say; but they cower under their coverlets, and nothing remains but to stare at the fire, and finger some book till the ideas freshen within me, or they once more become impartible.

I think, too, there is a great deal of excitement and fun and pure pleasure and brilliance in one's fellow creatures. I'm not sure that you shouldn't desert your mountain, take your chance, and adventure with your human faculties—friendships, conversations, relations, the mere daily intercourse. Why do young men hold books up before their eyes so long? French literature falls like a blue tint over the landscape.

But I am not saying what I mean, and had better stop. Only you must write to me again—anything that occurs to you—And what about something for the Hogarth Press?[5]

Leonard adds his wishes to mine for the future.

Yours

Virginia Woolf

P.S.

I add a postscript, which is intended to explain why I say that one must not renounce. I think I mean that beauty, which you say I sometimes achieve, is only got by the failure to get it; by grinding all the flints together; by facing what must be humiliation—the things one can't do—To aim at beauty deliberately, without this apparently insensate struggle, would result, I think, in little daisies and forget-me-nots—simpering sweetnesses—true love knots—But I agree that one must (we, in

---

5. A publishing concern owned by Virginia Woolf and her husband Leonard; it began operations in 1917 and went on to publish all of Woolf's work.

our generation must) renounce finally the achievement of the greater beauty: the beauty which comes from completeness, in such books as War and Peace, and Stendhal I suppose, and some of Jane Austen; and Sterne; and I rather suspect in Proust, of whom I have only read one volume. Only now that I have written this, I doubt its truth. Are we not always hoping? and though we fail every time, surely we do not fail so completely as we should have failed if we were not in the beginning, prepared to attack the whole. One must renounce, when the book is finished; but not before it is begun. Excuse me for boring on: you may have said nothing of the kind. I was wondering to myself why it is that though I try sometimes to limit myself to the thing I do well, I am always drawn on and on, by human beings, I think, out of the little circle of safety, on and on, to the whirlpools; when I go under.

Letter to Vita Sackville-West[6]

52 Tavistock Sqre. [W.C.1]

9th Oct. [1927]

    *** Yesterday morning I was in despair: You know that bloody book which Dadie and Leonard extort, drop by drop, from my breast? Fiction, or some title to that effect.[7] I couldn't screw a word from me; and at last dropped my head in my hands: dipped my pen in the ink, and wrote these words, as if automatically, on a clean sheet: Orlando: A Biography. No sooner had I done this than my body was flooded with rapture and my brain with ideas. I wrote rapidly till 12. Then I did an hour to Romance. So every morning I am going to write fiction (my own fiction) till 12; and Romance till 1. But listen; suppose Orlando turns out to be Vita; and its all about you and the lusts of your flesh and the lure of your mind (heart you have none, who go gallivanting down the lanes with Campbell)—suppose there's the kind of shimmer of reality which sometimes attaches to my people, as the lustre on an oyster shell (and that recalls another Mary [Hutchinson]) suppose, I say, that Sibyl [Colefax] next October says "Theres Virginia gone and written a book about Vita" and Ozzie [Dickinson] chaws with his great chaps and Byard [of Heinemann] guffaws, Shall you mind? Say yes, or No: Your excellence as a subject arises largely from your noble birth. (But whats 400 years of nobility, all the same?) and the opportunity thus given for florid descriptive passages in great abundance. Also, I admit, I should like to untwine and twist again some very odd, incongruous strands in you: going at length into the question of Campbell; and also, as I told you, it sprung upon me how I could revolutionise biography in a night: and so if agreeable to you I would like to toss this up in the air and see what happens. ***

    I am reading Knole and The Sackvilles.[8] Dear me; you know a lot: you have a rich dusky attic of a mind. O yes, I want very much to see you.

Yr V.W. (thats because of Campbell)

[END OF PERSPECTIVES: BLOOMSBURY AND MODERNISM]

---

6. The novelist and poet Vita Sackville-West, one of Woolf's closest friends; she served as a model for the androgynous hero/heroine of Woolf's Orlando (1928).
7. Phases of Fiction, a historical account of fiction writing, was published by the Bookman (New York) in 1929.

8. Vita Sackville-West was a member of an aristocratic family that traced its ancestors back to the 16th century. Knole was the name of the family estate; Vita published her book on the house and her family in 1922.

—•— ▰◆▰ —•—

D. H. Lawrence
1885–1930

D. H. Lawrence's meteoric literary life ended in Venice, Italy, in 1930, where he died at the age of forty-five, far from his birthplace in Nottinghamshire, the coal-mining heart of England. If Lawrence was something of a comet in British literature, arcing across its skies with vibrant energy and controversy while he lived, he was equally visible after his death in the excitement and danger that persisted like a halo around his texts. A formidable poet, an exceptional essayist and literary critic, and a major novelist, Lawrence created works that were pioneering in their defiant eroticism, their outspoken treatment of class politics, and their insistence on seeing British literature as part of world literature in a time of global crisis. Many of his writings were censored and unavailable in England until long after his death, or published in expurgated versions or in private printings. Their frank concentration on sexuality, and on female as well as male desire, continues to make Lawrence's novels provocative and even controversial today.

David Herbert Lawrence was the son of a coal miner. As a primarily self-educated writer who studied and taught at Nottingham University College, instead of Oxford or Cambridge, he was unlike many of his literary peers in being lower-class and outside the privileged literary and social circles they moved in. He essentially invented himself, drawing on the support and encouragement of his mother, and nurturing a clear-eyed and furious analysis of British class structure that pervades many of his novels. The sexual frankness of his work is accompanied by its economic frankness, its willingness to point out all the ways that culture and taste are fashioned by income as much as by ideas. The sense of being an outsider to the gentlemanly world of letters fed Lawrence's need to live and work outside Britain, and he traveled restlessly to Europe and America, to Australia and Mexico. Lawrence is deeply associated with many of the countries and places he lived in; with Italy, above all, in the power of his writing about Italian culture and landscape; with the United States, in classic analysis of American literature, and in works set in New Mexico and San Francisco; with France, Germany, and Switzerland as backdrops for his literary works and their cultural theorizing; with Australia for his commentary on this distant British colony and its indigenous peoples, in novels like *Kangaroo*; with Mexico and the primitivism and exoticism he explored in *The Plumed Serpent* and *Aaron's Rod*.

As peripatetic and as open to experience as Lawrence was, his great writing begins with novels and stories set in England. Some of his early and most exceptional works are, in fact, modernist versions of a central nineteenth-century literary genre, the *bildungsroman*, or the story of a personal education. Lawrence's *Sons and Lovers* (1912) has the autobiographical overtones that often accompany a coming-of-age narrative. Written after the death of his devoted mother Lydia Lawrence in 1910, the book delineates the experience of a young man who was as socially and economically disadvantaged as Lawrence himself, and the almost incestuous love between mother and son that allows him to break free from the crushing life in the mines that might have been his only option, and to follow his deep need for love, imagination, and poetry into the writing of literature. His later novel *The Rainbow* (published in an expurgated version in 1915) is also a *bildungsroman*, but featuring as its protagonist a female character and specifically feminine issues of education and freedom. In a preface to the novel, Lawrence wrote that he insisted on portraying characters that were not the old-fashioned character portraits of the past, relying on "the old stable ego." For Lawrence, people were internally fragmented, not completely self-aware, and above all governed by sexual currents that exceeded their conscious knowledge and control. In this Lawrence was profoundly influenced by Freud's discovery of the prominence and power of the unconscious. All of Lawrence's writing engages with the invisible and largely silent realm of the unconscious, whose wishes and impulses are a kind of dynamic dance running under the surface of the conscious sense of self.

To this dance of the unconscious rhythms of life Lawrence added an abiding fascination with myth. He joined most modernist writers in his interest in showing the persistence of myth in modern culture: Joyce, Woolf, Eliot and Faulkner all structured work around mythic parallels or mythic figures. For Lawrence, myth loomed importantly because it allowed for the discussion of hidden patterns and cycles in human action and human relationships, patterns that are much larger than the individual human being. Our personalities are illusions, Lawrence's fiction claims, because they mask deeper mythic forms. In *The Rainbow*, Lawrence draws his mythic structure from the Bible, and the cycles of birth, death, and rebirth in the story of Noah and the flood, with the rainbow of God's promise starting the cycle of rebirth over and over again.

One of Lawrence's greatest novels is *Women in Love*, a story of two sisters confronting modern life as they move out of their country's orbit and take on independence, sexual freedom, and careers in the world. He began writing it in 1916, during World War I. The war was as shattering to Lawrence as it was to every other British writer; for Lawrence, it was the apotheosis and the logical conclusion of the machine culture he hated for having spoiled England even before the war wreaked its devastation. Lawrence sharply criticized industrial capitalism, but not from the vantage point of an aristocratic worldview that regretted the loss of the landed estates. He thought and wrote as the son of a worker whose life was maimed by industrial toil in the mines, and as a school teacher of the impoverished children of miners and laborers who had lost their self-sufficient way of life on the land. Lawrence did not dream of a return to a golden feudal age, but he did dissect the ravages of industry and the connections between world war, capital, and modernization. *Women in Love* embraces these themes and more, as it turns to Europe and its classical culture to try to find a way out of the cultural impasse and sterility Lawrence saw around him. However, in this novel and others Lawrence writes of a death instinct visible for him in European culture, including its philosophy and art. At times, Lawrence's intense hatred of modernity led him to flirt with fascism, which occasionally seemed to him to promise a way out of the dead end of modern society and its hideous conflagrations in war. In order to rescue the life-affirming capacities of human society Lawrence sought out exotic and foreign cultures, and what he termed "primitive" cultures around the world—ostensibly unspoiled agricultural societies still predicated on myth rather than machine. These exotic alternatives, as Lawrence saw, were hardly utopian either, and most such societies were contaminated by colonization and Western influences. Lawrence did seek a less rationalized and less materialistic perspective in the "primitive" or archaic worlds he explored, and found that these cultures were more open to the life-giving force of sexuality. At once intense and engaging, his travel writing gives a sense of immediacy mingled with deep reflection.

Sexuality is the force in human life that most clearly derives from unconscious fantasies and desires, and on that basis it is at the heart of Lawrence's writing. Lawrence's work was thought shocking because it takes for granted the erotic elements hidden in the family—what Freud had called the "family romance." The alliances and the divisions between family members have an erotic component for Lawrence; in addition, relations to friends and to all others one encounters are sexualized in mysterious ways, often involving a powerful homoerotic current. Much of Lawrence's fiction seems to idealize a sexual state beyond words and beyond conscious understanding, and to depict this Lawrence draws on a beautiful incantatory style, filled with a highly musical repetition and rhythm.

Lawrence's own erotic career is as famous as his writing. The passion and frustrations of his marriage to the formidable Frieda Weekely (born Frieda von Richthofen) remained a hidden presence in all his writing after their marriage in 1914. When they met, Frieda was a married woman with an impressive erotic career behind her; she became a close partner in his political and cultural essay writing, and in his restless travels. They lived in Germany, Italy, and in Taos, New Mexico, among other locales. After his death in Italy, she and her then lover transported Lawrence's ashes back to Taos, and the two built a kind of shrine to Lawrence on the grounds of what had been his home with Frieda. It was in this region that they had explored Hispanic and Indian cultures under the sponsorship of a patron of the avant-garde, Mabel Dodge Luhan. Up until the mid-1980s it was possible to pay a dollar to the manager of the Taos Hotel and be admitted into his office, where numerous paintings by D. H. Lawrence were on display. Lawrence was a fascinating, if not a major, painter; the exhibits of his paintings in England were subject to the same censorship and public outrage as his novels. A viewer of the paintings could read them as an allegory for many of the disquieting themes of his literary work: the majority of them depict a couple, usually male and female, locked in an embrace that is as urgent as it is suffocating; around the edges of these couplings Lawrence painted menacing wolves and dogs, often with teeth bared or fangs dripping with blood, emblematic of the intensity and even the destructiveness of erotic relationships.

In his 1923 essay *Surgery for the Novel—or a Bomb*, Lawrence expresses his impatience with the endlessly refined analyses of modernists like Proust and Joyce. "What is the underlying impulse in us," he asks, "that will provide the motive power for a new state of things, when this democratic-industrial-lovey-dovey-darling-take-me-to-mama state of things is bust? *What next?*" His own efforts to forge a new mythic realism can be seen in his novella *The Fox*, also from 1923, which explores the interpenetration of human and animal, nature and social constraint, masculinity and feminity, sexual desire and deep aggression. The story's rural setting becomes a place at once of poverty and of beauty, in which Lawrence can counterpoint pursuits and entrapments on several levels, giving symbolic resonance to sharply observed naturalistic detail.

Lawrence's poetry explores related concerns. Like Thomas Hardy before him, Lawrence was equally gifted in both literary endeavors. Lawrence's poetry emanates from the same image-suffused, musically rhythmic, and tautly modern space as his prose works. Like Lawrence himself, his art desires to move *beyond*—beyond the old stable fictions of the ego in his prose, and beyond the old stable fiction of the lyric voice. In his poetry he accomplishes this by a preternatural immediacy, an intensity of "thereness" that includes what might in the past have seemed to be incoherent elements or fragmentary perspectives. What has been silent, veiled, or unconscious, in personal and in public life, rears up and announces itself in Lawrence's writing, appears on the page and defies silencing.

Piano

Softly, in the dusk, a woman is singing to me;
Taking me back down the vista of years, till I see
A child sitting under the piano, in the boom of the tingling strings
And pressing the small, poised feet of a mother who smiles as she sings.

5   In spite of myself, the insidious mastery of song
Betrays me back, till the heart of me weeps to belong
To the old Sunday evenings at home, with winter outside
And hymns in the cosy parlour, the tinkling piano our guide.

So now it is vain for the singer to burst into clamour
10   With the great black piano appassionato. The glamour
Of childish days is upon me, my manhood is cast
Down in the flood of remembrance, I weep like a child for the past.

1908   1913

Song of a Man Who Has Come Through

Not I, not I, but the wind that blows through me!
A fine wind is blowing the new direction of Time.

If only I let it bear me, carry me, if only it carry me!
If only I am sensitive, subtle, oh, delicate, a winged gift!
5   If only, most lovely of all, I yield myself and am borrowed
By the fine, fine wind that takes its course through the chaos of the world
Like a fine, an exquisite chisel, a wedge-blade inserted;
If only I am keen and hard like the sheer tip of a wedge
Driven by invisible blows,
10   The rock will split, we shall come at the wonder, we shall find the Hesperides.[1]

Oh, for the wonder that bubbles into my soul,
I would be a good fountain, a good well-head,
Would blur no whisper, spoil no expression.

What is the knocking?
15   What is the knocking at the door in the night?
It is somebody wants to do us harm.

No, no, it is the three strange angels.[2]
Admit them, admit them.

                                                    1917

Tortoise Shout

I thought he was dumb,
I said he was dumb,
Yet I've heard him cry.
First faint scream,
5   Out of life's unfathomable dawn,
Far off, so far, like a madness, under the horizon's dawning rim,
Far, far off, far scream.

Tortoise *in extremis*.

Why were we crucified into sex?
10   Why were we not left rounded off, and finished in ourselves,
As we began,
As he certainly began, so perfectly alone?

A far, was-it-audible scream,
Or did it sound on the plasm direct?

15   Worse than the cry of the new-born,
A scream,
A yell,
A shout,
A paean,
20   A death-agony,
A birth-cry,
A submission,
All tiny, tiny, far away, reptile under the first dawn.

---

1. Three sisters who guard a tree with golden apples at the end of the world; Hercules (Heracles) steals the apples as the eleventh of his twelve labors.

2. Probably the three angels who appeared to Abraham in Genesis 18, prior to the destruction of the cities of Sodom and Gomorrah.

War-cry, triumph, acute-delight, death-scream reptilian,
25 Why was the veil torn?
The silken shriek of the soul's torn membrane?
The male soul's membrane
Torn with a shriek half music, half horror.

Crucifixion.
30 Male tortoise, cleaving behind the hovel-wall of that dense female,
Mounted and tense, spread-eagle, out-reaching out of the shell
In tortoise-nakedness,
Long neck, and long vulnerable limbs extruded, spread-eagle over her
      house-roof,
And the deep, secret, all-penetrating tail curved beneath her walls,
35 Reaching and gripping tense, more reaching anguish in uttermost tension
Till suddenly, in the spasm of coition, tupping like a jerking leap, and oh!
Opening its clenched face from his outstretched neck
And giving that fragile yell, that scream,
Super-audible,
40 From his pink, cleft, old-man's mouth,
Giving up the ghost,
Or screaming in Pentecost,[1] receiving the ghost.

His scream, and his moment's subsidence,
The moment of eternal silence,
45 Yet unreleased, and after the moment, the sudden, startling jerk of coition,
      and at once
The inexpressible faint yell—
And so on, till the last plasm of my body was melted back
To the primeval rudiments of life, and the secret.

So he tups, and screams
50 Time after time that frail, torn scream
After each jerk, the longish interval,
The tortoise eternity,
Age-long, reptilian persistence,
Heart-throb, slow heart-throb, persistent for the next spasm.

55 I remember, when I was a boy,
I heard the scream of a frog, which was caught with his foot in the mouth
      of an up-starting snake;
I remember when I first heard bull-frogs break into sound in the spring;
I remember hearing a wild goose out of the throat of night
Cry loudly, beyond the lake of waters;
60 I remember the first time, out of a bush in the darkness, a nightingale's
      piercing cries and gurgles startled the depths of my soul;
I remember the scream of a rabbit as I went through a wood at midnight;
I remember the heifer in her heat, blorting and blorting through the hours,
      persistent and irrepressible;
I remember my first terror hearing the howl of weird, amorous cats;
I remember the scream of a terrified, injured horse, the sheet-lightning,

1. The day the Holy Spirit descended on Christ's disciples, which marked the beginning of the Christian church's mission
to the world.

65   And running away from the sound of a woman in labour, something like an
      owl whooing,
    And listening inwardly to the first bleat of a lamb,
    The first wail of an infant,
    And my mother singing to herself,
    And the first tenor singing of the passionate throat of a young collier,[2] who
      has long since drunk himself to death,
70   The first elements of foreign speech
    On wild dark lips.

    And more than all these,
    And less than all these,
    This last,
75   Strange, faint coition yell
    Of the male tortoise at extremity,
    Tiny from under the very edge of the farthest far-off horizon of life.

    The cross,
    The wheel on which our silence first is broken,
80   Sex, which breaks up our integrity, our single inviolability, our deep
      silence,
    Tearing a cry from us.

    Sex, which breaks us into voice, sets us calling across the deeps, calling,
      calling for the complement,
    Singing, and calling, and singing again, being answered, having found.
    Torn, to become whole again, after long seeking for what is lost,
85   The same cry from the tortoise as from Christ, the Osiris-cry of
      abandonment,[3]
    That which is whole, torn asunder,
    That which is in part, finding its whole again throughout the universe.

                    1921

Snake[1]

    A snake came to my water-trough
    On a hot, hot day, and I in pyjamas for the heat,
    To drink there.

    In the deep, strange-scented shade of the great dark carob tree
5   I came down the steps with my pitcher
    And must wait, must stand and wait, for there he was at the trough before me.

    He reached down from a fissure in the earth-wall in the gloom
    And trailed his yellow-brown slackness soft-bellied down, over the edge of
      the stone trough
    And rested his throat upon the stone bottom,
10   And where the water had dripped from the tap, in a small clearness,
    He sipped with his straight mouth,

2. A coal miner.
3. Osiris was a major god of ancient Egypt; he was slain and fragments of his corpse scattered; these were found and buried, and Osiris became ruler of the underworld.

1. Lawrence had an encounter with a snake drinking from a water trough while living in Taormina, Sicily, in July 1912.

Softly drank through his straight gums, into his slack long body,
Silently.

Someone was before me at my water-trough,
15   And I, like a second comer, waiting.

He lifted his head from his drinking, as cattle do,
And looked at me vaguely, as drinking cattle do,
And flickered his two-forked tongue from his lips, and mused a moment,
And stooped and drank a little more,
20   Being earth-brown, earth-golden from the burning bowels of the earth
On the day of Sicilian July, with Etna smoking.

The voice of my education said to me
He must be killed,
For in Sicily the black, black snakes are innocent, the gold are venomous.

25   And voices in me said, If you were a man
You would take a stick and break him now, and finish him off.

But must I confess how I liked him,
How glad I was he had come like a guest in quiet, to drink at my water-trough
And depart peaceful, pacified, and thankless,
30   Into the burning bowels of this earth?

Was it cowardice, that I dared not kill him?
Was it perversity, that I longed to talk to him?
Was it humility, to feel so honoured?
I felt so honoured.

35   And yet those voices:
If you were not afraid, you would kill him!

And truly I was afraid, I was most afraid,
But even so, honoured still more
That he should seek my hospitality
40   From out the dark door of the secret earth.

He drank enough
And lifted his head, dreamily, as one who has drunken,
And flickered his tongue like a forked night on the air, so black,
Seeming to lick his lips,
45   And looked around like a god, unseeing, into the air,
And slowly turned his head,
And slowly, very slowly, as if thrice adream,
Proceeded to draw his slow length curving round
And climb again the broken bank of my wall-face.

50   And as he put his head into that dreadful hole,
And as he slowly drew up, snake-easing his shoulders, and entered farther,
A sort of horror, a sort of protest against his withdrawing into that horrid
    black hole,
Deliberately going into the blackness, and slowly drawing himself after,
Overcame me now his back was turned.

55 I looked round, I put down my pitcher,
    I picked up a clumsy log
    And threw it at the water-trough with a clatter.

    I think it did not hit him,
    But suddenly that part of him that was left behind convulsed in
        undignified haste,
60 Writhed like lightning, and was gone
    Into the black hole, the earth-lipped fissure in the wall front,
    At which, in the intense still noon, I stared with fascination.

    And immediately I regretted it.
    I thought how paltry, how vulgar, what a mean act!
65 I despised myself and the voices of my accursed human education.

    And I thought of the albatross,
    And I wished he would come back, my snake.

    For he seemed to me again like a king,
    Like a king in exile, uncrowned in the underworld,
70 Now due to be crowned again.

    And so, I missed my chance with one of the lords
    Of life.
    And I have something to expiate;
    A pettiness.

                                                        1923

Bavarian Gentians

    Not every man has gentians in his house
    in soft September, at slow, sad Michaelmas.[1]

    Bavarian gentians, big and dark, only dark
    darkening the day-time, torch-like with the smoking blueness of Pluto's gloom,
5   ribbed and torch-like, with their blaze of darkness spread blue
    down flattening into points, flattened under the sweep of white day
    torch-flower of the blue-smoking darkness, Pluto's dark-blue daze,[2]
    black lamps from the halls of Dis, burning dark blue,
    giving off darkness, blue darkness, as Demeter's pale lamps give off light,
10 lead me then, lead the way.

    Reach me a gentian, give me a torch!
    let me guide myself with the blue, forked torch of this flower
    down the darker and darker stairs, where blue is darkened on blueness
    even where Persephone goes, just now, from the frosted September
15 to the sightless realm where darkness is awake upon the dark
    and Persephone herself is but a voice
    or a darkness invisible enfolded in the deeper dark

> of the arms Plutonic, and pierced with the passion of dense gloom,
>   among the splendour of torches of darkness, shedding darkness on the lost
>   bride and her groom.
> 1923, 1929   1932

The Fox

The two girls were usually known by their surnames, Banford and March. They had taken the farm together, intending to work it all by themselves: that is, they were going to rear chickens, make a living by poultry, and add to this by keeping a cow, and raising one or two young beasts. Unfortunately, things did not turn out well.

Banford was a small, thin, delicate thing with spectacles. She, however, was the principal investor, for March had little or no money. Banford's father, who was a tradesman in Islington,[1] gave his daughter the start, for her health's sake, and because he loved her, and because it did not look as if she would marry. March was more robust. She had learned carpentry and joinery at the evening classes in Islington. She would be the man about the place. They had, moreover, Banford's old grandfather living with them at the start. He had been a farmer. But unfortunately the old man died after he had been at Bailey Farm for a year. Then the two girls were left alone.

They were neither of them young: that is, they were near thirty. But they certainly were not old. They set out quite gallantly with their enterprise. They had numbers of chickens, black Leghorns and white Leghorns, Plymouths and Wyandottes; also some ducks; also two heifers in the fields. One heifer, unfortunately, refused absolutely to stay in the Bailey Farm closes. No matter how March made up the fences, the heifer was out, wild in the woods, or trespassing on the neighbouring pasture, and March and Banford were away, flying after her, with more haste than success. So this heifer they sold in despair. Then, just before the other beast was expecting her first calf, the old man died, and the girls, afraid of the coming event, sold her in a panic, and limited their attentions to fowls and ducks.

In spite of a little chagrin, it was a relief to have no more cattle on hand. Life was not made merely to be slaved away. Both girls agreed in this. The fowls were quite enough trouble. March had set up her carpenter's bench at the end of the open shed. Here she worked, making coops and doors and other appurtenances. The fowls were housed in the bigger building, which had served as barn and cow-shed in old days. They had a beautiful home, and should have been perfectly content. Indeed, they looked well enough. But the girls were disgusted at their tendency to strange illnesses, at their exacting way of life, and at their refusal, obstinate refusal to lay eggs.

March did most of the outdoor work. When she was out and about, in her puttees and breeches, her belted coat and her loose cap, she looked almost like some graceful, loose-balanced young man, for her shoulders were straight, and her movements easy and confident, even tinged with a little indifference or irony. But her face was not a man's face, ever. The wisps of her crisp dark hair blew about her as she stooped, her eyes were big and wide and dark, when she looked up again, strange, startled, shy and sardonic at once. Her mouth, too, was almost pinched as if in pain and irony. There was something odd and unexplained about her. She would stand balanced on one hip, looking at the fowls pattering about in the obnoxious fine mud

---

1. A district of London. The story is set in a rural region in Oxfordshire, sixty miles west of London.

of the sloping yard, and calling to her favourite white hen, which came in answer to her name. But there was an almost satirical flicker in March's big, dark eyes as she looked at her three-toed flock pottering about under her gaze, and the same slight dangerous satire in her voice as she spoke to the favoured Patty, who pecked at March's boot by way of friendly demonstration.

Fowls did not flourish at Bailey Farm, in spite of all that March did for them. When she provided hot food for them in the morning, according to rule, she noticed that it made them heavy and dozy for hours. She expected to see them lean against the pillars of the shed in their languid processes of digestion. And she knew quite well that they ought to be busily scratching and foraging about, if they were to come to any good. So she decided to give them their hot food at night, and let them sleep on it. Which she did. But it made no difference.

War conditions, again, were very unfavourable to poultry-keeping. Food was scarce and bad. And when the Daylight Saving Bill was passed, the fowls obstinately refused to go to bed as usual, about nine o'clock in the summer-time. That was late enough, indeed, for there was no peace till they were shut up and asleep. Now they cheerfully walked around, without so much as glancing at the barn, until ten o'clock or later. Both Banford and March disbelieved in living for work alone. They wanted to read or take a cycle-ride in the evening, or perhaps March wished to paint curvilinear swans on porcelain, with green background, or else make a marvellous fire-screen by processes of elaborate cabinet work. For she was a creature of odd whims and unsatisfied tendencies. But from all these things she was prevented by the stupid fowls.

One evil there was greater than any other. Bailey Farm was a little homestead, with ancient wooden barn and low-gabled farm-house, lying just one field removed from the edge of the wood. Since the war the fox was a demon. He carried off the hens under the very noses of March and Banford. Banford would start and stare through her big spectacles with all her eyes, as another squawk and flutter took place at her heels. Too late! Another white Leghorn gone. It was disheartening.

They did what they could to remedy it. When it became permitted to shoot foxes, they stood sentinel with their guns, the two of them, at the favoured hours. But it was no good. The fox was too quick for them. So another year passed, and another, and they were living on their losses, as Banford said. They let their farm-house one summer, and retired to live in a railway-carriage that was deposited as a sort of out-house in a corner of the field. This amused them, and helped their finances. None the less, things looked dark.

Although they were usually the best of friends, because Banford, though nervous and delicate, was a warm, generous soul, and March, though so odd and absent in herself, had a strange magnanimity, yet, in the long solitude, they were apt to become a little irritable with one another, tired of one another. March had four-fifths of the work to do, and though she did not mind, there seemed no relief, and it made her eyes flash curiously sometimes. Then Banford, feeling more nerve-worn than ever, would become despondent, and March would speak sharply to her. They seemed to be losing ground, somehow, losing hope as the months went by. There alone in the fields by the wood, with the wide country stretching hollow and dim to the round hills of the White Horse, in the far distance, they seemed to have to live too much off themselves. There was nothing to keep them up—and no hope.

The fox really exasperated them both. As soon as they had let the fowls out, in the early summer mornings, they had to take their guns and keep guard: and then again as soon as evening began to mellow, they must go once more. And he was so sly. He slid along in the deep grass; he was difficult as a serpent to see. And he seemed to circumvent the girls deliberately. Once or twice March had caught sight of the white tip of his brush, or the ruddy shadow of him in the deep grass, and she had let fire at him. But he made no account of this.

One evening March was standing with her back to the sunset, her gun under her arm, her hair pushed under her cap. She was half watching, half musing. It was her constant state. Her eyes were keen and observant, but her inner mind took no notice of what she saw. She was always lapsing into this odd, rapt state, her mouth rather screwed up. It was a question whether she was there, actually consciously present, or not.

The trees on the wood-edge were a darkish, brownish green in the full light—for it was the end of August. Beyond, the naked, copper-like shafts and limbs of the pine trees shone in the air. Nearer the rough grass, with its long, brownish stalks all agleam, was full of light. The fowls were round about—the ducks were still swimming on the pond under the pine trees. March looked at it all, saw it all, and did not see it. She heard Banford speaking to the fowls in the distance—and she did not hear. What was she thinking about? Heaven knows. Her consciousness was, as it were, held back.

She lowered her eyes, and suddenly saw the fox. He was looking up at her. His chin was pressed down, and his eyes were looking up. They met her eyes. And he knew her. She was spellbound—she knew he knew her. So he looked into her eyes, and her soul failed her. He knew her, he was not daunted.

She struggled, confusedly she came to herself, and saw him making off, with slow leaps over some fallen boughs, slow, impudent jumps. Then he glanced over his shoulder, and ran smoothly away. She saw his brush held smooth like a feather, she saw his white buttocks twinkle. And he was gone, softly, soft as the wind.

She put her gun to her shoulder, but even then pursed her mouth, knowing it was nonsense to pretend to fire. So she began to walk slowly after him, in the direction he had gone, slowly, pertinaciously. She expected to find him. In her heart she was determined to find him. What she would do when she saw him again she did not consider. But she was determined to find him. So she walked abstractedly about on the edge of the wood, with wide, vivid dark eyes, and a faint flush in her cheeks. She did not think. In strange mindlessness she walked hither and thither.

At last she became aware that Banford was calling her. She made an effort of attention, turned, and gave some sort of screaming call in answer. Then again she was striding off towards the homestead. The red sun was setting, the fowls were retiring towards their roost. She watched them, white creatures, black creatures, gathering to the barn. She watched them spellbound, without seeing them. But her automatic intelligence told her when it was time to shut the door.

She went indoors to supper, which Banford had set on the table. Banford chatted easily. March seemed to listen, in her distant, manly way. She answered a brief word now and then. But all the time she was as if spellbound. And as soon as supper was over, she rose again to go out, without saying why.

She took her gun again and went to look for the fox. For he had lifted his eyes upon her, and his knowing look seemed to have entered her brain. She did not so much think of him: she was possessed by him. She saw his dark, shrewd, unabashed eye looking into her, knowing her. She felt him invisibly master her spirit. She knew the way he lowered his chin as he looked up, she knew his muzzle, the golden brown, and the greyish white. And again she saw him glance over his shoulder at her, half inviting, half contemptuous and cunning. So she went, with her great startled eyes glowing, her gun under her arm, along the wood edge. Meanwhile the night fell, and a great moon rose above the pine trees. And again Banford was calling.

So she went indoors. She was silent and busy. She examined her gun, and cleaned it, musing abstractedly by the lamplight. Then she went out again, under the great moon, to see if everything was right. When she saw the dark crests of the pine trees against the blood-red sky, again her heart beat to the fox, the fox. She wanted to follow him, with her gun.

It was some days before she mentioned the affair to Banford. Then suddenly one evening she said:

"The fox was right at my feet on Saturday night."

"Where?" said Banford, her eyes opening behind her spectacles.

"When I stood just above the pond."

"Did you fire?" cried Banford.

"No, I didn't."

"Why not?"

"Why, I was too much surprised, I suppose."

It was the same old, slow, laconic way of speech March always had. Banford stared at her friend for a few moments.

"You saw him?" she cried.

"Oh yes! He was looking up at me, cool as anything."

"I tell you," cried Banford—"the cheek! They're not afraid of us, Nellie."

"Oh no," said March.

"Pity you didn't get a shot at him," said Banford.

"Isn't it a pity! I've been looking for him ever since. But I don't suppose he'll come so near again."

"I don't suppose he will," said Banford.

And she proceeded to forget about it, except that she was more indignant than ever at the impudence of the beggar. March also was not conscious that she thought of the fox. But whenever she fell into her half-musing, when she was half rapt and half intelligently aware of what passed under her vision, then it was the fox which somehow dominated her unconsciousness, possessed the blank half of her musing. And so it was for weeks, and months. No matter whether she had been climbing the trees for the apples, or beating down the last of the damsons, or whether she had been digging out the ditch from the duck-pond, or clearing out the barn, when she had finished, or when she straightened herself, and pushed the wisps of hair away again from her forehead, and pursed up her mouth again in an odd, screwed fashion, much too old for her years, there was sure to come over her mind the old spell of the fox, as it came when he was looking at her. It was as if she could smell him at these times. And it always recurred, at unexpected moments, just as she was going to sleep at night, or just as she was pouring the water into the tea-pot to make tea—it was the fox, it came over her like a spell.

So the months passed. She still looked for him unconsciously when she went towards the wood. He had become a settled effect in her spirit, a state permanently established, not continuous, but always recurring. She did not know what she felt or thought: only the state came over her, as when he looked at her.

The months passed, the dark evenings came, heavy, dark November, when March went about in high boots, ankle deep in mud, when the night began to fall at four o'clock, and the day never properly dawned. Both girls dreaded these times.

They dreaded the almost continuous darkness that enveloped them on their desolate little farm near the wood. Banford was physically afraid. She was afraid of tramps, afraid lest someone should come prowling around. March was not so much afraid as uncomfortable, and disturbed. She felt discomfort and gloom in all her physique.

Usually the two girls had tea in the sitting-room. March lighted a fire at dusk, and put on the wood she had chopped and sawed during the day. Then the long evening was in front, dark, sodden, black outside, lonely and rather oppressive inside, a little dismal. March was content not to talk, but Banford could not keep still. Merely listening to the wind in the pines outside, or the drip of water, was too much for her.

One evening the girls had washed up the tea-cups in the kitchen, and March had put on her house-shoes, and taken up a roll of crochet-work, which she worked at slowly from time to time. So she lapsed into silence. Banford stared at the red fire, which, being of wood, needed constant attention. She was afraid to begin to read too early, because her eyes would not bear any strain. So she sat staring at the fire, listening to the distant sounds, sound of cattle lowing, of a dull, heavy moist wind, of the rattle of the evening train on the little railway not far off. She was almost fascinated by the red glow of the fire.

Suddenly both girls started, and lifted their heads. They heard a footstep—distinctly a footstep. Banford recoiled in fear. March stood listening. Then rapidly she approached the door that led into the kitchen. At the same time they heard the footsteps approach the back door. They waited a second. The back door opened softly. Banford gave a loud cry. A man's voice said softly:

"Hello!"

March recoiled, and took a gun from a corner.

"What do you want?" she cried, in a sharp voice.

Again the soft, softly-vibrating man's voice said:

"Hello! What's wrong?"

"I shall shoot!" cried March. "What do you want?"

"Why, what's wrong? What's wrong?" came the soft, wondering, rather scared voice: and a young soldier, with his heavy kit on his back, advanced into the dim light.

"Why," he said, "who lives here then?"

"We live here," said March. "What do you want?"

"Oh!" came the long, melodious, wonder-note from the young soldier. "Doesn't William Grenfel live here then?"

"No—you know he doesn't."

"Do I? Do I? I don't, you see. He *did* live here, because he was my grandfather, and I lived here myself five years ago. What's become of him then?"

The young man—or youth, for he would not be more than twenty—now advanced and stood in the inner doorway. March, already under the influence of his strange, soft, modulated voice, stared at him spellbound. He had a ruddy, roundish face, with fairish hair, rather long, flattened to his forehead with sweat. His eyes were blue, and very bright and sharp. On his cheeks, on the fresh ruddy skin were fine, fair hairs, like a down, but sharper. It gave him a slightly glistening look. Having his heavy sack on his shoulders, he stooped, thrusting his head forward. His hat was loose in one hand. He stared brightly, very keenly from girl to girl, particularly at March, who stood pale, with great dilated eyes, in her belted coat and puttees, her hair knotted in a big crisp knot behind. She still had the gun in her hand. Behind her, Banford, clinging to the sofa-arm, was shrinking away, with half-averted head.

"I thought my grandfather still lived here? I wonder if he's dead."

"We've been here for three years," said Banford, who was beginning to recover her wits, seeing something boyish in the round head with its rather long, sweaty hair.

"Three years! You don't say so! And you don't know who was here before you?"

"I know it was an old man, who lived by himself."

"Ay! Yes, that's him! And what became of him then?"

"He died. I know he died."

"Ay! He's dead then!"

The youth stared at them without changing colour or expression. If he had any expression, besides a slight baffled look of wonder, it was one of sharp curiosity concerning the two girls; sharp, impersonal curiosity, the curiosity of that round young head.

But to March he was the fox. Whether it was the thrusting forward of his head, or the glisten of fine whitish hairs on the ruddy cheek-bones, or the bright, keen eyes, that can never be said: but the boy was to her the fox, and she could not see him otherwise.

"How is it you didn't know if your grandfather was alive or dead?" asked Banford, recovering her natural sharpness.

"Ay, that's it," replied the softly-breathing youth. "You see, I joined up in Canada, and I hadn't heard for three or four years. I ran away to Canada."

"And now have you just come from France?"

"Well—from Salonika really."

There was a pause, nobody knowing quite what to say.

"So you've nowhere to go now?" said Banford rather lamely.

"Oh, I know some people in the village. Anyhow, I can go to the 'Swan.'"

"You came on the train, I suppose. Would you like to sit down a bit?"

"Well—I don't mind."

He gave an odd little groan as he swung off his kit. Banford looked at March.

"Put the gun down," she said. "We'll make a cup of tea."

"Ay," said the youth. "We've seen enough of rifles."

He sat down rather tired on the sofa, leaning forward.

March recovered her presence of mind, and went into the kitchen. There she heard the soft young voice musing:

"Well, to think I should come back and find it like this!" He did not seem sad, not at all—only rather interestedly surprised.

"And what a difference in the place, eh?" he continued, looking round the room.

"You see a difference, do you?" said Banford.

"Yes—don't I."

His eyes were unnaturally clear and bright, though it was the brightness of abundant health.

March was busy in the kitchen preparing another meal. It was about seven o'clock. All the time, while she was active, she was attending to the youth in the sitting-room, not so much listening to what he said as feeling the soft run of his voice. She primmed up her mouth tighter and tighter, puckering it as if it were sewed, in her effort to keep her will uppermost. Yet her large eyes dilated and glowed in spite of her; she lost herself. Rapidly and carelessly she prepared the meal, cutting large chunks of bread and margarine—for there was no butter. She racked her brain to think of something else to put on the tray—she had only bread, margarine, and jam, and the larder was bare. Unable to conjure anything up, she went into the sitting-room with her tray.

She did not want to be noticed. Above all, she did not want him to look at her. But when she came in, and was busy setting the table just behind him, he pulled himself up from his sprawling, and turned and looked over his shoulder. She became pale and wan.

The youth watched her as she bent over the table, looked at her slim, well-shapen legs, at the belted coat dropping around her thighs, at the knot of dark hair, and his curiosity, vivid and widely alert, was again arrested by her.

The lamp was shaded with a dark-green shade, so that the light was thrown downwards and the upper half of the room was dim. His face moved bright under the light, but March loomed shadowy in the distance.

She turned round, but kept her eyes sideways, dropping and lifting her dark lashes. Her mouth unpuckered as she said to Banford:

"Will you pour out?"

Then she went into the kitchen again.

"Have your tea where you are, will you?" said Banford to the youth—"unless you'd rather come to the table."

"Well," said he, "I'm nice and comfortable here, aren't I? I will have it here, if you don't mind."

"There's nothing but bread and jam," she said. And she put his plate on a stool by him. She was very happy now, waiting on him. For she loved company. And now she was no more afraid of him than if he were her own younger brother. He was such a boy.

"Nellie," she called. "I've poured you a cup out."

March appeared in the doorway, took her cup, and sat down in a corner, as far from the light as possible. She was very sensitive in her knees. Having no skirts to cover them, and being forced to sit with them boldly exposed, she suffered. She shrank and shrank, trying not to be seen. And the youth, sprawling low on the couch, glanced up at her, with long, steady, penetrating looks, till she was almost ready to disappear. Yet she held her cup balanced, she drank her tea, screwed up her mouth and held her head averted. Her desire to be invisible was so strong that it quite baffled the youth. He felt he could not see her distinctly. She seemed like a shadow within the shadow. And ever his eyes came back to her, searching, unremitting, with unconscious fixed attention.

Meanwhile he was talking softly and smoothly to Banford, who loved nothing so much as gossip, and who was full of perky interest, like a bird. Also he ate largely and quickly and voraciously, so that March had to cut more chunks of bread and margarine, for the roughness of which Banford apologised.

"Oh, well," said March, suddenly speaking, "if there's no butter to put on it, it's no good trying to make dainty pieces."

Again the youth watched her, and he laughed, with a sudden, quick laugh, showing his teeth and wrinkling his nose.

"It isn't, is it," he answered in his soft, near voice.

It appeared he was Cornish by birth and upbringing. When he was twelve years old he had come to Bailey Farm with his grandfather, with whom he had never agreed very well. So he had run away to Canada, and worked far away in the West. Now he was here—and that was the end of it.

He was very curious about the girls, to find out exactly what they were doing. His questions were those of a farm youth; acute, practical, a little mocking. He was very much amused by their attitude to their losses: for they were amusing on the score of heifers and fowls.

"Oh, well," broke in March, "we don't believe in living for nothing but work."

"Don't you?" he answered. And again the quick young laugh came over his face. He kept his eyes steadily on the obscure woman in the corner.

"But what will you do when you've used up all your capital?" he said.

"Oh, I don't know," answered March laconically. "Hire ourselves out for land-workers, I suppose."

"Yes, but there won't be any demand for women land-workers now the war's over," said the youth.

"Oh, we'll see. We shall hold on a bit longer yet," said March, with a plangent, half-sad, half-ironical indifference.

"There wants a man about the place," said the youth softly.

Banford burst out laughing.

"Take care what you say," she interrupted. "We consider ourselves quite efficient."

"Oh," came March's slow plangent voice, "it isn't a case of efficiency, I'm afraid. If you're going to do farming you must be at it from morning till night, and you might as well be a beast yourself."

"Yes, that's it," said the youth. "You aren't willing to put yourselves into it."

"We aren't," said March, "and we know it."

"We want some of our time for ourselves," said Banford.

The youth threw himself back on the sofa, his face tight with laughter, and laughed silently but thoroughly. The calm scorn of the girls tickled him tremendously.

"Yes," he said, "but why did you begin then?"

"Oh," said March, "we had a better opinion of the nature of fowls then than we have now."

"Of Nature altogether, I'm afraid," said Banford. "Don't talk to me about Nature."

Again the face of the youth tightened with delighted laughter.

"You haven't a very high opinion of fowls and cattle, have you?" he said.

"Oh no—quite a low one," said March.

He laughed out.

"Neither fowls nor heifers," said Banford, "nor goats nor the weather."

The youth broke into a sharp yap of laughter, delighted. The girls began to laugh too, March turning aside her face and wrinkling her mouth in amusement.

"Oh, well," said Banford, "we don't mind, do we, Nellie?"

"No," said March, "we don't mind."

The youth was very pleased. He had eaten and drunk his fill. Banford began to question him. His name was Henry Grenfel—no, he was not called Harry, always Henry. He continued to answer with courteous simplicity, grave and charming. March, who was not included, cast long, slow glances at him from her recess, as he sat there on the sofa, his hands clasping his knees, his face under the lamp bright and alert, turned to Banford. She became almost peaceful at last. He was identified with the fox—and he was here in full presence. She need not go after him any more. There in the shadow of her corner she gave herself up to a warm, relaxed peace, almost like sleep, accepting the spell that was on her. But she wished to remain hidden. She was only fully at peace whilst he forgot her, talking to Banford. Hidden in the shadow of the corner, she need not any more be divided in herself, trying to keep up two planes of consciousness. She could at last lapse into the odour of the fox.

For the youth, sitting before the fire in his uniform, sent a faint but distinct odour into the room, indefinable, but something like a wild creature. March no longer tried to reserve herself from it. She was still and soft in her corner like a passive creature in its cave.

At last the talk dwindled. The youth relaxed his clasp of his knees, pulled himself together a little, and looked round. Again he became aware of the silent, half-invisible woman in the corner.

"Well," he said unwillingly, "I suppose I'd better be going, or they'll be in bed at the 'Swan.'"

"I'm afraid they're in bed, anyhow," said Banford. "They've all got this influenza."

"Have they!" he exclaimed. And he pondered. "Well," he continued, "I shall find a place somewhere."

"I'd say you could stay here, only———" Banford began.

He turned and watched her, holding his head forward.

"What?" he asked.

"Oh, well," she said, "propriety, I suppose." She was rather confused.

"It wouldn't be improper, would it?" he said, gently surprised.

"Not as far as we're concerned," said Banford.

"And not as far as *I'm* concerned," he said, with grave naiveté. "After all, it's my own home, in a way."

Banford smiled at this.

"It's what the village will have to say," she said.

There was a moment's blank pause.

"What do you say, Nellie?" asked Banford.

"I don't mind," said March, in her distinct tone. "The village doesn't matter to me, anyhow."

"No," said the youth, quick and soft. "Why should it? I mean, what should they say?"

"Oh, well," came March's plangent, laconic voice, "they'll easily find something to say. But it makes no difference what they say. We can look after ourselves."

"Of course you can," said the youth.

"Well then, stop if you like," said Banford. "The spare room is quite ready."

His face shone with pleasure.

"If you're quite sure it isn't troubling you too much," he said, with that soft courtesy which distinguished him.

"Oh, it's no trouble," they both said.

He looked, smiling with delight, from one to another.

"It's awfully nice not to have to turn out again, isn't it?" he said gratefully.

"I suppose it is," said Banford.

March disappeared to attend to the room. Banford was as pleased and thoughtful as if she had her own young brother home from France. It gave her just the same kind of gratification to attend on him, to get out the bath for him, and everything. Her natural warmth and kindliness had now an outlet. And the youth luxuriated in her sisterly attention. But it puzzled him slightly to know that March was silently working for him too. She was so curiously silent and obliterated. It seemed to him he had not really seen her. He felt he should not know her if he met her in the road.

That night March dreamed vividly. She dreamed she heard a singing outside which she could not understand, a singing that roamed round the house, in the fields, and in the darkness. It moved her so that she felt she must weep. She went out, and suddenly she knew it was the fox singing. He was very yellow and bright, like corn. She went nearer to him, but he ran away and ceased singing. He seemed near, and she wanted to touch him. She stretched out her hand, but suddenly he bit her wrist, and at the same instant, as she drew back, the fox, turning round to bound away, whisked his brush across her face, and it seemed his brush was on fire, for it seared and burned her mouth with a great pain. She awoke with the pain of it, and lay trembling as if she were really seared.

In the morning, however, she only remembered it as a distant memory. She arose and was busy preparing the house and attending to the fowls. Banford flew into the village on her bicycle to try and buy food. She was a hospitable soul. But alas, in the year 1918 there was not much food to buy. The youth came downstairs in his shirtsleeves. He was young and fresh, but he walked with his head thrust forward, so that his shoulders seemed raised and rounded, as if he had a slight curvature of the spine. It must have been only a manner of bearing himself, for he was young and vigorous. He washed himself and went outside, whilst the women were preparing breakfast.

He saw everything, and examined everything. His curiosity was quick and insatiable. He compared the state of things with that which he remembered before, and cast over in his mind the effect of the changes. He watched the fowls and the ducks, to see their condition; he noticed the flight of wood-pigeons overhead: they were very numerous; he saw the few apples high up, which March had not been able to reach; he remarked that they had borrowed a draw-pump, presumably to empty the big soft-water cistern which was on the north side of the house.

"It's a funny, dilapidated old place," he said to the girls, as he sat at breakfast.

His eyes were wise and childish, with thinking about things. He did not say much, but ate largely. March kept her face averted. She, too, in the early morning could not be aware of him, though something about the glint of his khaki reminded her of the brilliance of her dream-fox.

During the day the girls went about their business. In the morning he attended to the guns, shot a rabbit and a wild duck that was flying high towards the wood. That was a great addition to the empty larder. The girls felt that already he had earned his keep. He said nothing about leaving, however. In the afternoon he went to the village. He came back at tea-time. He had the same alert, forward-reaching look on his roundish face. He hung his hat on a peg with a little swinging gesture. He was thinking about something.

"Well," he said to the girls, as he sat at table. "What am I going to do?"

"How do you mean—what are you going to do?" said Banford.

"Where am I going to find a place in the village to stay?" he said.

"I don't know," said Banford. "Where do you think of staying?"

"Well"—he hesitated—"at the 'Swan' they've got this 'flu, and at the 'Plough and Harrow' they've got the soldiers who are collecting the hay for the army: besides, in the private houses, there's ten men and a corporal altogether billeted in the village, they tell me. I'm not sure where I could get a bed."

He left the matter to them. He was rather calm about it. March sat with her elbows on the table, her two hands supporting her chin, looking at him unconsciously. Suddenly he lifted his clouded blue eyes, and unthinking looked straight into March's eyes. He was startled as well as she. He, too, recoiled a little. March felt the same sly, taunting, knowing spark leap out of his eyes, as he turned his head aside, and fall into her soul, as had fallen from the dark eyes of the fox. She pursed her mouth as if in pain, as if asleep too.

"Well, I don't know," Banford was saying. She seemed reluctant, as if she were afraid of being imposed upon. She looked at March. But, with her weak, troubled sight, she only saw the usual semi-abstraction on her friend's face. "Why don't you speak, Nellie?" she said.

But March was wide-eyed and silent, and the youth, as if fascinated, was watching her without moving his eyes.

"Go on—answer something," said Banford. And March turned her head slightly aside, as if coming to consciousness, or trying to come to consciousness.

"What do you expect me to say?" she asked automatically.

"Say what you think," said Banford.

"It's all the same to me," said March.

And again there was silence. A pointed light seemed to be on the boy's eyes, penetrating like a needle.

"So it is to me," said Banford. "You can stop on here if you like."

A smile like a cunning little flame came over his face, suddenly and involuntarily. He dropped his head quickly to hide it, and remained with his head dropped, his face hidden.

"You can stop on here if you like. You can please yourself, Henry," Banford concluded.

Still he did not reply, but remained with his head dropped. Then he lifted his face. It was bright with a curious light, as if exultant, and his eyes were strangely clear as he watched March. She turned her face aside, her mouth suffering as if wounded, and her consciousness dim.

Banford became a little puzzled. She watched the steady, pellucid gaze of the youth's eyes as he looked at March, with the invisible smile gleaming on his face. She did not know how he was smiling, for no feature moved. It seemed only in the gleam, almost the glitter of the fine hairs on his cheeks. Then he looked with quite a changed look at Banford.

"I'm sure," he said in his soft, courteous voice, "you're awfully good. You're too good. You don't want to be bothered with me, I'm sure."

"Cut a bit of bread, Nellie," said Banford uneasily, adding: "It's no bother, if you like to stay. It's like having my own brother here for a few days. He's a boy like you are."

"That's awfully kind of you," the lad repeated. "I should like to stay ever so much, if you're sure I'm not a trouble to you."

"No, of course you're no trouble. I tell you, it's a pleasure to have somebody in the house besides ourselves," said warm-hearted Banford.

"But Miss March?" he said in his soft voice, looking at her.

"Oh, it's quite all right as far as I'm concerned," said March vaguely.

His face beamed, and he almost rubbed his hands with pleasure.

"Well then," he said, "I should love it, if you'd let me pay my board and help with the work."

"You've no need to talk about board," said Banford.

One or two days went by, and the youth stayed on at the farm. Banford was quite charmed by him. He was so soft and courteous in speech, not wanting to say much himself, preferring to hear what she had to say, and to laugh in his quick, half-mocking way. He helped readily with the work—but not too much. He loved to be out alone with the gun in his hands, to watch, to see. For his sharp-eyed, impersonal curiosity was insatiable, and he was most free when he was quite alone, half-hidden, watching.

Particularly he watched March. She was a strange character to him. Her figure, like a graceful young man's, piqued him. Her dark eyes made something rise in his soul, with a curious elate excitement, when he looked into them, an excitement he was afraid to let be seen, it was so keen and secret. And then her odd, shrewd speech made him laugh outright. He felt he must go further, he was inevitably impelled. But he put away the thought of her and went off towards the wood's edge with the gun.

The dusk was falling as he came home, and with the dusk, a fine, late November rain. He saw the fire-light leaping in the window of the sitting-room, a leaping light in the little cluster of the dark buildings. And he thought to himself it would be a good thing to have this place for his own. And then the thought entered him shrewdly: Why not marry March? He stood still in the middle of the field for some moments, the dead rabbit hanging still in his hand, arrested by this thought. His mind waited in amazement—it seemed to calculate—and then he smiled curiously to himself in acquiescence. Why not? Why not indeed? It was a good idea. What if it was rather ridiculous? What did it matter? What if she was older than he? It didn't matter. When he thought of her dark, startled, vulnerable eyes he smiled subtly to himself. He was older than she, really. He was master of her.

He scarcely admitted his intention even to himself. He kept it as a secret even from himself. It was all too uncertain as yet. He would have to see how things went. Yes, he would have to see how things went. If he wasn't careful, she would just simply mock at the idea. He knew, sly and subtle as he was, that if he went to her plainly and said: "Miss March, I love you and want you to marry me," her inevitable answer would be: "Get out. I don't want any of that tomfoolery." This was her attitude to men and their 'tomfoolery'. If he was not careful, she would turn round on him with her savage, sardonic ridicule, and dismiss him from the farm and from her own mind for ever. He would have to go gently. He would have to catch her as you catch a deer or a woodcock when you go out shooting. It's no good walking out into the forest and saying to the deer: "Please fall to my gun." No, it is a slow, subtle battle. When you really go out to get a deer, you gather yourself together, you coil yourself inside your- self, and you advance secretly, before dawn, into the mountains. It is not so much what you do, when you go out hunting, as how you feel. You have to be subtle and cunning and absolutely fatally ready. It becomes like a fate. Your own fate overtakes and determines the fate of the deer you are hunting. First of all, even before you come in sight of your quarry, there is a strange battle, like mesmerism. Your own soul, as a hunter, has gone out to fasten on the soul of the deer, even before you see any deer. And the soul of the deer fights to escape. Even before the deer has any wind of you, it is so. It is a subtle, profound battle of wills which takes place in the invisible. And it is a battle never finished till your bullet goes home. When you are *really* worked up to the true pitch, and you come at last into range, you don't then aim as you do when you are firing at a bottle. It is your own *will* which carries the bullet into the heart of your quarry. The bullet's flight home is a sheer projection of your own fate into the fate of the deer. It happens like a supreme wish, a supreme act of volition, not as a dodge of cleverness.

He was a huntsman in spirit, not a farmer, and not a soldier stuck in a regiment. And it was as a young hunter that he wanted to bring down March as his quarry, to make her his wife. So he gathered himself subtly together, seemed to withdraw into a kind of invisibility. He was not quite sure how he would go on. And March was sus- picious as a hare. So he remained in appearance just the nice, odd stranger-youth, staying for a fortnight on the place.

He had been sawing logs for the fire in the afternoon. Darkness came very early. It was still a cold, raw mist. It was getting almost too dark to see. A pile of short sawed logs lay beside the trestle. March came to carry them indoors, or into the shed, as he was busy sawing the last log. He was working in his shirt-sleeves, and did not notice her approach; she came unwillingly, as if shy. He saw her stooping to the bright-ended logs, and he stopped sawing. A fire like lightning flew down his legs in the nerves.

"March?" he said in his quiet, young voice.

She looked up from the logs she was piling.

"Yes!" she said.

He looked down on her in the dusk. He could see her not too distinctly.

"I wanted to ask you something," he said.

"Did you? What was it?" she said. Already the fright was in her voice. But she was too much mistress of herself.

"Why"—his voice seemed to draw out soft and subtle, it penetrated her nerves—"why, what do you think it is?"

She stood up, placed her hands on her hips, and stood looking at him transfixed, without answering. Again he burned with a sudden power.

"Well," he said, and his voice was so soft it seemed rather like a subtle touch, like the merest touch of a cat's paw, a feeling rather than a sound. "Well—I wanted to ask you to marry me."

March felt rather than heard him. She was trying in vain to turn aside her face. A great relaxation seemed to have come over her. She stood silent, her head slightly on one side. He seemed to be bending towards her, invisibly smiling. It seemed to her fine sparks came out of him.

Then very suddenly she said:

"Don't try any of your tomfoolery on me."

A quiver went over his nerves. He had missed. He waited a moment to collect himself again. Then he said, putting all the strange softness into his voice, as if he were imperceptibly stroking her:

"Why, it's not tomfoolery. It's not tomfoolery. I mean it. I mean it. What makes you disbelieve me?"

He sounded hurt. And his voice had such a curious power over her; making her feel loose and relaxed. She struggled somewhere for her own power. She felt for a moment that she was lost—lost—lost. The word seemed to rock in her as if she were dying. Suddenly again she spoke.

"You don't know what you are talking about," she said, in a brief and transient stroke of scorn. "What nonsense! I'm old enough to be your mother."

"Yes, I do know what I'm talking about. Yes, I do," he persisted softly, as if he were producing his voice in her blood. "I know quite well what I'm talking about. You're not old enough to be my mother. That isn't true. And what does it matter even if it was? You can marry me whatever age we are. What is age to me? And what is age to you! Age is nothing."

A swoon went over her as he concluded. He spoke rapidly—in the rapid Cornish fashion—and his voice seemed to sound in her somewhere where she was helpless against it. "Age is nothing!" The soft, heavy insistence of it made her sway dimly out there in the darkness. She could not answer.

A great exultance leaped like fire over his limbs. He felt he had won.

"I want to marry you, you see. Why shouldn't I?" he proceeded, soft and rapid. He waited for her to answer. In the dusk he saw her almost phosphorescent. Her eyelids were dropped, her face half-averted and unconscious. She seemed to be in his power. But he waited, watchful. He dared not yet touch her.

"Say then," he said, "say then you'll marry me. Say—say!" He was softly insistent.

"What?" she asked, faint, from a distance, like one in pain. His voice was now unthinkably near and soft. He drew very near to her.

"Say yes."

"Oh, I can't," she wailed helplessly, half-articulate, as if semi-conscious, and as if in pain, like one who dies. "How can I?"

"You can," he said softly, laying his hand gently on her shoulder as she stood with her head averted and dropped, dazed. "You can. Yes, you can. What makes you say you can't? You can. You can." And with awful softness he bent forward and just touched her neck with his mouth and his chin.

"Don't!" she cried, with a faint mad cry like hysteria, starting away and facing round on him. "What do you mean?" But she had no breath to speak with. It was as if she was killed.

"I mean what I say," he persisted softly and cruelly. "I want you to marry me. I want you to marry me. You know that, now, don't you? You know that, now? Don't you? Don't you?"

"What?" she said.

"Know," he replied.

"Yes," she said. "I know you say so."

"And you know I mean it, don't you?"

"I know you say so."

"You believe me?" he said.

She was silent for some time. Then she pursed her lips.

"I don't know what I believe," she said.

"Are you out there?" came Banford's voice, calling from the house.

"Yes, we're bringing in the logs," he answered.

"I thought you'd gone lost," said Banford disconsolately. "Hurry up, do, and come and let's have tea. The kettle's boiling."

He stooped at once to take an armful of little logs and carry them into the kitchen, where they were piled in a corner. March also helped, filling her arms and carrying the logs on her breast as if they were some heavy child. The night had fallen cold.

When the logs were all in, the two cleaned their boots noisily on the scraper outside, then rubbed them on the mat. March shut the door and took off her old felt hat—her farm-girl hat. Her thick, crisp, black hair was loose, her face was pale and strained. She pushed back her hair vaguely and washed her hands. Banford came hurrying into the dimly-lighted kitchen, to take from the oven the scones she was keeping hot.

"Whatever have you been doing all this time?" she asked fretfully. "I thought you were never coming in. And it's ages since you stopped sawing. What were you doing out there?"

"Well," said Henry, "we had to stop that hole in the barn to keep the rats out."

"Why, I could see you standing there in the shed. I could see your shirt-sleeves," challenged Banford.

"Yes, I was just putting the saw away."

They went in to tea. March was quite mute. Her face was pale and strained and vague. The youth, who always had the same ruddy, self-contained look on his face, as though he were keeping himself to himself, had come to tea in his shirt-sleeves as if he were at home. He bent over his plate as he ate his food.

"Aren't you cold?" said Banford spitefully. "In your shirt-sleeves."

He looked up at her, with his chin near his plate, and his eyes very clear, pellucid, and unwavering as he watched her.

"No, I'm not cold," he said with his usual soft courtesy. "It's much warmer in here than it is outside, you see."

"I hope it is," said Banford, feeling nettled by him. He had a strange, suave assurance and a wide-eyed bright look that got on her nerves this evening.

"But perhaps," he said softly and courteously, "you don't like me coming to tea without my coat. I forgot that."

"Oh, I don't mind," said Banford: although she *did*.

"I'll go and get it, shall I?" he said.

March's dark eyes turned slowly down to him.

"No, don't you bother," she said in her queer, twanging tone. "If you feel all right as you are, stop as you are." She spoke with a crude authority.

"Yes," said he, "I *feel* all right, if I'm not rude."

"It's usually considered rude," said Banford. "But we don't mind."

"Go along, 'considered rude,'" ejaculated March. "Who considers it rude?"

"Why, you do, Nellie—in anybody else," said Banford, bridling a little behind her spectacles, and feeling her food stick in her throat.

But March had again gone vague and unheeding, chewing her food as if she did not know she was eating at all. And the youth looked from one to another, with bright, watching eyes.

Banford was offended. For all his suave courtesy and soft voice, the youth seemed to her impudent. She did not like to look at him. She did not like to meet his clear, watchful eyes, she did not like to see the strange glow in his face, his cheeks with their delicate fine hair, and his ruddy skin that was quite dull and yet which seemed to burn with a curious heat of life. It made her feel a little ill to look at him: the quality of his physical presence was too penetrating, too hot.

After tea the evening was very quiet. The youth rarely went into the village. As a rule, he read: he was a great reader, in his own hours. That is, when he did begin, he read absorbedly. But he was not very eager to begin. Often he walked about the fields and along the hedges alone in the dark at night, prowling with a queer instinct for the night, and listening to the wild sounds.

To-night, however, he took a Captain Mayne Reid[2] book from Banford's shelf and sat down with knees wide apart and immersed himself in his story. His brownish fair hair was long, and lay on his head like a thick cap, combed sideways. He was still in his shirt-sleeves, and bending forward under the lamp-light, with his knees stuck wide apart and the book in his hand and his whole figure absorbed in the rather strenuous business of reading, he gave Banford's sitting-room the look of a lumber-camp. She resented this. For on her sitting-room floor she had a red Turkey rug and dark stain round, the fire-place had fashionable green tiles, the piano stood open with the latest dance music: she played quite well: and on the walls were March's hand-painted swans and water-lilies. Moreover, with the logs nicely, tremulously burning in the grate, the thick curtains drawn, the doors all shut, and the pine trees hissing and shuddering in the wind outside, it was cosy, it was refined and nice. She resented the big, raw, long-legged youth sticking his khaki knees out and sitting there with his soldier's shirt-cuffs buttoned on his thick red wrists. From time to time he turned a page, and from time to time he gave a sharp look at the fire, settling the logs. Then he immersed himself again in the intense and isolated business of reading.

2. Thomas Mayne Reid (1818–1883), writer of adventure stories.

March, on the far side of the table, was spasmodically crochetting. Her mouth was pursed in an odd way, as when she had dreamed the fox's brush burned it, her beautiful, crisp black hair strayed in wisps. But her whole figure was absorbed in its bearing, as if she herself was miles away. In a sort of semi-dream she seemed to be hearing the fox singing round the house in the wind, singing wildly and sweetly and like a madness. With red but well-shaped hands she slowly crochetted the white cotton, very slowly, awkwardly.

Banford was also trying to read, sitting in her low chair. But between those two she felt fidgety. She kept moving and looking round and listening to the wind, and glancing secretly from one to the other of her companions. March, seated on a straight chair, with her knees in their close breeches crossed, and slowly, laboriously crochetting, was also a trial.

"Oh dear!" said Banford. "My eyes are bad to-night." And she pressed her fingers on her eyes.

The youth looked up at her with his clear, bright look, but did not speak.

"Are they, Jill?" said March absently.

Then the youth began to read again, and Banford perforce returned to her book. But she could not keep still. After a while she looked up at March, and a queer, almost malignant little smile was on her thin face.

"A penny for them, Nell," she said suddenly.

March looked round with big, startled black eyes, and went pale as if with terror. She had been listening to the fox singing so tenderly, so tenderly, as he wandered round the house.

"What?" she said vaguely.

"A penny for them," said Banford sarcastically. "Or two-pence, if they're as deep as all that."

The youth was watching with bright, clear eyes from beneath the lamp.

"Why," came March's vague voice, "what do you want to waste your money for?"

"I thought it would be well spent," said Banford.

"I wasn't thinking of anything except the way the wind was blowing," said March.

"Oh dear," replied Banford, "I could have had as original thoughts as that myself. I'm afraid I *have* wasted my money this time."

"Well, you needn't pay," said March.

The youth suddenly laughed. Both women looked at him: March rather surprised-looking, as if she had hardly known he was there.

"Why, do you ever pay up on these occasions?" he asked.

"Oh yes," said Banford. "We always do. I've sometimes had to pass a shilling a week to Nellie, in the winter-time. It costs much less in summer."

"What, paying for each other's thoughts?" he laughed.

"Yes, when we've absolutely come to the end of everything else."

He laughed quickly, wrinkling his nose sharply like a puppy and laughing with quick pleasure, his eyes shining.

"It's the first time I ever heard of that," he said.

"I guess you'd hear of it often enough if you stayed a winter on Bailey Farm," said Banford lamentably.

"Do you get so tired, then?" he asked.

"So bored," said Banford.

"Oh!" he said gravely. "But why should you be bored?"

"Who wouldn't be bored?" said Banford.

"I'm sorry to hear that," he said gravely.

"You must be, if you were hoping to have a lively time here," said Banford. He looked at her long and gravely.

"Well," he said, with his odd, young seriousness, "it's quite lively enough for me."

"I'm glad to hear it," said Banford.

And she returned to her book. In her thin, frail hair were already many threads of grey, though she was not yet thirty. The boy did not look down, but turned his eyes to March, who was sitting with pursed mouth laboriously crochetting, her eyes wide and absent. She had a warm, pale, fine skin and a delicate nose. Her pursed mouth looked shrewish. But the shrewish look was contradicted by the curious lifted arch of her dark brows, and the wideness of her eyes; a look of startled wonder and vagueness. She was listening again for the fox, who seemed to have wandered farther off into the night.

From under the edge of the lamp-light the boy sat with his face looking up, watching her silently, his eyes round and very clear and intent. Banford, biting her fingers irritably, was glancing at him under her hair. He sat there perfectly still, his ruddy face tilted up from the low level under the light, on the edge of the dimness, and watching with perfect abstract intentness. March suddenly lifted her great, dark eyes from her crochetting and saw him. She started, giving a little exclamation.

"There he is!" she cried involuntarily, as if terribly startled.

Banford looked around in amazement, sitting up straight.

"Whatever has got you, Nellie?" she cried.

But March, her face flushed a delicate rose colour, was looking away to the door.

"Nothing! Nothing!" she said crossly. "Can't one speak?"

"Yes, if you speak sensibly," said Banford. "Whatever did you mean?"

"I don't know what I meant," cried March testily.

"Oh, Nellie, I hope you aren't going jumpy and nervy. I feel I can't stand another thing! Whoever did you mean? Did you mean Henry?" cried poor, frightened Banford.

"Yes. I suppose so," said March laconically. She would never confess to the fox.

"Oh dear, my nerves are all gone for to-night," wailed Banford.

At nine o'clock March brought in a tray with bread and cheese and tea—Henry had confessed that he liked a cup of tea. Banford drank a glass of milk and ate a little bread. And soon she said:

"I'm going to bed, Nellie. I'm all nerves to-night. Are you coming?"

"Yes, I'm coming the minute I've taken the tray away," said March.

"Don't be long then," said Banford fretfully. "Goodnight, Henry. You'll see the fire is safe, if you come up last, won't you?"

"Yes, Miss Banford, I'll see it's safe," he replied in his reassuring way.

March was lighting the candle to go to the kitchen. Banford took her candle and went upstairs. When March came back to the fire, she said to him:

"I suppose we can trust you to put out the fire and everything?" She stood there with her hand on her hip, and one knee loose, her head averted shyly, as if she could not look at him. He had his face lifted, watching her.

"Come and sit down a minute," he said softly.

"No, I'll be going. Jill will be waiting, and she'll get upset, if I don't come."

"What made you jump like that this evening?" he asked.

"When did I jump?" she retorted, looking at him.

"Why, just now you did," he said. "When you cried out."

"Oh!" she said. "Then!—Why, I thought you were the fox!" And her face screwed into a queer smile, half-ironic.

"The fox! Why the fox?" he asked softly.

"Why, one evening last summer when I was out with the gun I saw the fox in the grass nearly at my feet, looking straight up at me. I don't know—I suppose he made an impression on me." She turned aside her head again and let one foot stray loose, self-consciously.

"And did you shoot him?" asked the boy.

"No, he gave me such a start, staring straight at me as he did, and then stopping to look back at me over his shoulder with a laugh on his face."

"A laugh on his face!" repeated Henry, also laughing. "He frightened you, did he?"

"No, he didn't frighten me. He made an impression on me, that's all."

"And you thought I was the fox, did you?" he laughed, with the same queer, quick little laugh, like a puppy wrinkling his nose.

"Yes, I did, for the moment," she said. "Perhaps he'd been in my mind without my knowing."

"Perhaps you think I've come to steal your chickens or something," he said, with the same young laugh.

But she only looked at him with a wide, dark, vacant eye.

"It's the first time," he said, "that I've ever been taken for a fox. Won't you sit down for a minute?" His voice was very soft and cajoling.

"No," she said. "Jill will be waiting." But still she did not go, but stood with one foot loose and her face turned aside, just outside the circle of light.

"But won't you answer my question?" he said, lowering his voice still more.

"I don't know what question you mean."

"Yes, you do. Of course you do. I mean the question of you marrying me."

"No, I shan't answer that question," she said flatly.

"Won't you?" The queer, young laugh came on his nose again. "Is it because I'm like the fox? Is that why?" And still he laughed.

She turned and looked at him with a long, slow look.

"I wouldn't let that put you against me," he said. "Let me turn the lamp low, and come and sit down a minute."

He put his red hand under the glow of the lamp and suddenly made the light very dim. March stood there in the dimness quite shadowy, but unmoving. He rose silently to his feet, on his long legs. And now his voice was extraordinarily soft and suggestive, hardly audible.

"You'll stay a moment," he said. "Just a moment." And he put his hand on her shoulder. She turned her face from him. "I'm sure you don't really think I'm like the fox," he said, with the same softness and with a suggestion of laughter in his tone, a subtle mockery. "Do you now?" And he drew her gently towards him and kissed her neck, softly. She winced and trembled and hung away. But his strong, young arm held her, and he kissed her softly again, still on the neck, for her face was averted.

"Won't you answer my question? Won't you now?" came his soft, lingering voice. He was trying to draw her near to kiss her face. And he kissed her cheek softly, near the ear.

At that moment Banford's voice was heard calling fretfully, crossly from upstairs.

"There's Jill!" cried March, starting and drawing erect.

And as she did so, quick as lightning he kissed her on the mouth, with a quick, brushing kiss. It seemed to burn through her every fibre. She gave a queer little cry.

"You will, won't you? You will?" he insisted softly.

"Nellie! *Nellie!* Whatever are you so long for?" came Banford's faint cry from the outer darkness.

But he held her fast, and was murmuring with that intolerable softness and insistency:

"You will, won't you? Say yes! Say yes!"

March, who felt as if the fire had gone through her and scathed her, and as if she could do no more, murmured:

"Yes! Yes! Anything you like! Only let me go! Only let me go! Jill's calling."

"You know you've promised," he said insidiously.

"Yes! Yes! I do!" Her voice suddenly rose into a shrill cry. "All right, Jill, I'm coming."

Startled, he let her go, and she went straight upstairs.

In the morning at breakfast, after he had looked round the place and attended to the stock and thought to himself that one could live easily enough here, he said to Banford:

"Do you know what, Miss Banford?"

"Well, what?" said the good-natured, nervy Banford.

He looked at March, who was spreading jam on her bread.

"Shall I tell?" he said to her.

She looked up at him, and a deep pink colour flushed over her face.

"Yes, if you mean Jill," she said. "I hope you won't go talking all over the village, that's all." And she swallowed her dry bread with difficulty.

"Whatever's coming?" said Banford, looking up with wide, tired, slightly reddened eyes. She was a thin, frail little thing, and her hair, which was delicate and thin, was bobbed, so it hung softly by her worn face in its faded brown and grey.

"Why, what do you think?" he said, smiling like one who has a secret.

"How do I know!" said Banford.

"Can't you guess?" he said, making bright eyes and smiling, pleased with himself.

"I'm sure I can't. What's more, I'm not going to try."

"Nellie and I are going to be married."

Banford put down her knife out of her thin, delicate fingers, as if she would never take it up to eat any more. She stared with blank, reddened eyes.

"You what?" she exclaimed.

"We're going to get married. Aren't we, Nellie?" and he turned to March.

"You say so, anyway," said March, laconically. But again she flushed with an agonised flush. She, too, could swallow no more.

Banford looked at her like a bird that has been shot: a poor, little sick bird. She gazed at her with all her wounded soul in her face, at the deep-flushed March.

"Never!" she exclaimed, helpless.

"It's quite right," said the bright and gloating youth.

Banford turned aside her face, as if the sight of the food on the table made her sick. She sat like this for some moments, as if she were sick. Then, with one hand on the edge of the table, she rose to her feet.

"I'll *never* believe it, Nellie," she cried. "It's absolutely impossible!"

Her plaintive, fretful voice had a thread of hot anger and despair.

"Why? Why shouldn't you believe it?" asked the youth with all his soft, velvety impertinence in his voice.

Banford looked at him from her wide, vague eyes, as if he were some creature in a museum.

"Oh," she said languidly, "because she can never be such a fool. She can't lose her self-respect to such an extent." Her voice was cold and plaintive, drifting.

"In what way will she lose her self-respect?" asked the boy.

Banford looked at him with vague fixity from behind her spectacles.

"If she hasn't lost it already," she said.

He became very red, vermilion, under the slow, vague stare from behind the spectacles.

"I don't see it at all," he said.

"Probably you don't. I shouldn't expect you would," said Banford, with that straying mild tone of remoteness which made her words even more insulting.

He sat stiff in his chair, staring with hot, blue eyes from his scarlet face. An ugly look had come on his brow.

"My word, she doesn't know what she's letting herself in for," said Banford, in her plaintive, drifting, insulting voice.

"What has it got to do with you, anyway?" said the youth, in a temper.

"More than it has to do with you, probably," she replied, plaintive and venomous.

"Oh, has it! I don't see that at all," he jerked out.

"No, you wouldn't," she answered, drifting.

"Anyhow," said March, pushing back her hair and rising uncouthly. "It's no good arguing about it." And she seized the bread and the tea-pot and strode away to the kitchen.

Banford let her fingers stray across her brow and along her hair, like one bemused. Then she turned and went away upstairs.

Henry sat stiff and sulky in his chair, with his face and his eyes on fire. March came and went, clearing the table. But Henry sat on, stiff with temper. He took no notice of her. She had regained her composure and her soft, even, creamy complexion. But her mouth was pursed up. She glanced at him each time as she came to take things from the table, glanced from her large, curious eyes, more in curiosity than anything. Such a long, red-faced, sulky boy! That was all he was. He seemed as remote from her as if his red face were a red chimney-pot on a cottage across the fields, and she looked at him just as objectively, as remotely.

At length he got up and stalked out into the fields with the gun. He came in only at dinner-time, with the devil still in his face, but his manners quite polite. Nobody said anything particular; they sat each one at the sharp corner of a triangle, in obstinate remoteness. In the afternoon he went out again at once with the gun. He came in at nightfall with a rabbit and a pigeon. He stayed in all the evening, but hardly opened his mouth. He was in the devil of a temper, feeling he had been insulted.

Banford's eyes were red, she had evidently been crying. But her manner was more remote and supercilious than ever; the way she turned her head if he spoke at all, as if he were some tramp or inferior intruder of that sort, made his blue eyes go almost black with rage. His face looked sulkier. But he never forgot his polite intonation, if he opened his mouth to speak.

March seemed to flourish in this atmosphere. She seemed to sit between the two antagonists with a little wicked smile on her face, enjoying herself. There was even a sort of complacency in the way she laboriously crochetted this evening.

When he was in bed, the youth could hear the two women talking and arguing in their room. He sat up in bed and strained his ears to hear what they said. But he could hear nothing, it was too far off. Yet he could hear the soft, plaintive drip of Banford's voice, and March's deeper note.

The night was quiet, frosty. Big stars were snapping outside, beyond the ridge-tops of the pine trees. He listened and listened. In the distance he heard a fox yelping: and the dogs from the farms barking in answer. But it was not that he wanted to hear. It was what the two women were saying.

He got stealthily out of bed and stood by his door. He could hear no more than before. Very, very carefully he began to lift the door latch. After quite a time he had his door open. Then he stepped stealthily out into the passage. The old oak planks were cold under his feet, and they creaked preposterously. He crept very, very gently up the one step, and along by the wall, till he stood outside their door. And there he held his breath and listened. Banford's voice:

"No, I simply couldn't stand it. I should be dead in a month. Which is just what he would be aiming at, of course. That would just be his game, to see me in the churchyard. No, Nellie, if you were to do such a thing as to marry him, you could never stop here. I couldn't, I couldn't live in the same house with him. Oh!—oh! I feel quite sick with the smell of his clothes. And his red face simply turns me over. I can't eat my food when he's at the table. What a fool I was ever to let him stop. One ought *never* to try to do a kind action. It always flies back in your face like a boomerang."

"Well, he's only got two more days," said March.

"Yes, thank heaven. And when he's gone he'll never come in this house again. I feel so bad while he's here. And I know, I know he's only counting what he can get out of you. I *know* that's all it is. He's just a good-for-nothing, who doesn't want to work, and who thinks he'll live on us. But he won't live on me. If you're such a fool, then it's your own lookout. Mrs Burgess knew him all the time he was here. And the old man could never get him to do any steady work. He was off with the gun on every occasion, just as he is now. Nothing but the gun! Oh, I do hate it. You don't know what you're doing, Nellie, you don't. If you marry him he'll just make a fool of you. He'll go off and leave you stranded. I know he will, if he can't get Bailey Farm out of us—and he's not going to, while I live. While I live he's never going to set foot here. I know what it would be. He'd soon think he was master of both of us, as he thinks he's master of you already."

"But he isn't," said Nellie.

"He thinks he is, anyway. And that's what he wants: to come and be master here. Yes, imagine it! That's what we've got the place together for, is it, to be bossed and bullied by a hateful, red-faced boy, a beastly labourer. Oh, we *did* make a mistake when we let him stop. We ought never to have lowered ourselves. And I've had such a fight with all the people here, not to be pulled down to their level. No, he's not coming here. And then you see—if he can't have the place, he'll run off to Canada or somewhere again, as if he'd never known you. And here you'll be, absolutely ruined and made a fool of. I know I shall never have any peace of mind again."

"We'll tell him he can't come here. We'll tell him that," said March.

"Oh, don't you bother; I'm going to tell him that, and other things as well, before he goes. He's not going to have all his own way while I've got the strength left to speak. Oh, Nellie, he'll despise you, he'll despise you, like the awful little beast he is, if you give way to him. I'd no more trust him than I'd trust a cat not to steal. He's deep, he's deep, and he's bossy, and he's selfish through and through, as cold as ice. All he wants is to make use of you. And when you're no more use to him, then I pity you."

"I don't think he's as bad as all that," said March.

"No, because he's been playing up to you. But you'll find out, if you see much of him. Oh, Nellie, I can't bear to think of it."

"Well, it won't hurt you, Jill, darling."

"Won't it! Won't it! I shall never know a moment's peace again while I live, nor a moment's happiness. No, Nellie————" and Banford began to weep bitterly.

The boy outside could hear the stifled sound of the woman's sobbing, and could hear March's soft, deep, tender voice comforting, with wonderful gentleness and tenderness, the weeping woman.

His eyes were so round and wide that he seemed to see the whole night, and his ears were almost jumping off his head. He was frozen stiff. He crept back to bed, but felt as if the top of his head were coming off. He could not sleep. He could not keep still. He rose, quietly dressed himself, and crept out on to the landing once more. The women were silent. He went softly downstairs and out to the kitchen.

Then he put on his boots and his overcoat and took the gun. He did not think to go away from the farm. No, he only took the gun. As softly as possible he unfastened the door and went out into the frosty December night. The air was still, the stars bright, the pine trees seemed to bristle audibly in the sky. He went stealthily away down a fenceside, looking for something to shoot. At the same time he remembered that he ought not to shoot and frighten the women.

So he prowled round the edge of the gorse cover, and through the grove of tall old hollies, to the woodside. There he skirted the fence, peering through the darkness with dilated eyes that seemed to be able to grow black and full of sight in the dark, like a cat's. An owl was slowly and mournfully whooing round a great oak tree. He stepped stealthily with his gun, listening, listening, watching.

As he stood under the oaks of the wood-edge he heard the dogs from the neighbouring cottage up the hill yelling suddenly and startlingly, and the wakened dogs from the farms around barking answer. And suddenly it seemed to him England was little and tight, he felt the landscape was constricted even in the dark, and that there were too many dogs in the night, making a noise like a fence of sound, like the network of English hedges netting the view. He felt the fox didn't have a chance. For it must be the fox that had started all this hullabaloo.

Why not watch for him, anyhow! He would, no doubt, be coming sniffing round. The lad walked downhill to where the farmstead with its few pine trees crouched blackly. In the angle of the long shed, in the black dark, he crouched down. He knew the fox would be coming. It seemed to him it would be the last of the foxes in this loudly-barking, thick-voiced England, tight with innumerable little houses.

He sat a long time with his eyes fixed unchanging upon the open gateway, where a little light seemed to fall from the stars or from the horizon, who knows. He was sitting on a log in a dark corner with the gun across his knees. The pine trees snapped. Once a chicken fell off its perch in the barn with a loud crawk and cackle and commotion that startled him, and he stood up, watching with all his eyes, thinking it might be a rat. But he *felt* it was nothing. So he sat down again with the gun on his knees and his hands tucked in to keep them warm, and his eyes fixed unblinking on the pale reach of the open gateway. He felt he could smell the hot, sickly, rich smell of live chickens on the cold air.

And then—a shadow. A sliding shadow in the gateway. He gathered all his vision into a concentrated spark, and saw the shadow of the fox, the fox creeping on his belly through the gate. There he went, on his belly like a snake. The boy smiled to himself and brought the gun to his shoulder. He knew quite well what would happen. He knew the fox would go to where the fowl door was boarded up and sniff there. He knew he would lie there for a minute, sniffing the fowls within. And then he would start again prowling under the edge of the old barn, waiting to get in.

The fowl door was at the top of a slight incline. Soft, soft as a shadow the fox slid up this incline, and crouched with his nose to the boards. And at the same moment there was the awful crash of a gun reverberating between the old buildings, as if all the night had gone smash. But the boy watched keenly. He saw even the white belly of the fox as the beast beat his paws in death. So he went forward.

There was a commotion everywhere. The fowls were scuffling and crawking, the ducks were quark-quarking, the pony had stamped wildly to his feet. But the fox was on his side, struggling in his last tremors. The boy bent over him and smelt his foxy smell.

There was a sound of a window opening upstairs, then March's voice calling:

"Who is it?"

"It's me," said Henry; "I've shot the fox."

"Oh, goodness! You nearly frightened us to death."

"Did I? I'm awfully sorry."

"Whatever made you get up?"

"I heard him about."

"And have you shot him?"

"Yes, he's here," and the boy stood in the yard holding up the warm, dead brute. "You can't see, can you? Wait a minute." And he took his flash-light from his pocket and flashed it on to the dead animal. He was holding it by the brush. March saw, in the middle of the darkness, just the reddish fleece and the white belly and the white underneath of the pointed chin, and the queer, dangling paws. She did not know what to say.

"He's a beauty," he said. "He will make you a lovely fur."

"You don't catch me wearing a fox fur," she replied.

"Oh!" he said. And he switched off the light.

"Well, I should think you'll come in and go to bed again now," she said.

"Probably I shall. What time is it?"

"What time is it, Jill?" called March's voice. It was a quarter to one.

That night March had another dream. She dreamed that Banford was dead, and that she, March, was sobbing her heart out. Then she had to put Banford into her coffin. And the coffin was the rough wood-box in which the bits of chopped wood were kept in the kitchen, by the fire. This was the coffin, and there was no other, and March was in agony and dazed bewilderment, looking for something to line the box with, something to make it soft with, something to cover up the poor, dead darling. Because she couldn't lay her in there just in her white, thin night-dress, in the horrible wood-box. So she hunted and hunted, and picked up thing after thing, and threw it aside in the agony of dream-frustration. And in her dream-despair all she could find that would do was a fox-skin. She knew that it wasn't right, that this was not what she should have. But it was all she could find. And so she folded the brush of the fox, and laid her darling Jill's head on this, and she brought round the skin of the fox and laid it on the top of the body, so that it seemed to make a whole ruddy, fiery coverlet, and she cried and cried, and woke to find the tears streaming down her face.

The first thing that both she and Banford did in the morning was to go out to see the fox. Henry had hung it up by the heels in the shed, with its poor brush falling backwards. It was a lovely dog-fox in its prime, with a handsome, thick, winter coat: a lovely golden-red colour, and a great full brush with a delicate black and grey and pure white tip.

"Poor brute!" said Banford. "If it wasn't such a thieving wretch, you'd feel sorry for it."

March said nothing, but stood with her foot trailing aside, one hip out; her face was pale and her eyes big and black, watching the dead animal that was suspended upside down. White and soft as snow his belly: white and soft as snow. She passed her hand softly down it. And his wonderful black-glinted brush was full and frictional, wonderful. She passed her hand down this also, and quivered. Time after time she took the full fur of that thick tail between her fingers, and passed her hand slowly downwards. Wonderful, sharp, thick, splendour of a tail. And he was dead! She pursed her lips, and her eyes went black and vacant. Then she took the head in her hand.

Henry was sauntering up, so Banford walked rather pointedly away. March stood there bemused, with the head of the fox in her hand. She was wondering, wondering, wondering over his long, fine muzzle. For some reason it reminded her of a spoon or a spatula. She felt she could not understand it. The beast was a strange beast to her, incomprehensible, out of her range. Wonderful silver whiskers he had, like ice-threads. And pricked ears with hair inside. But that long, long, slender spoon of a nose!—and the marvellous white teeth beneath! It was to thrust forward and bite with, deep, deep, deep into the living prey, to bite and bite the blood.

"He's a beauty, isn't he?" said Henry, standing by.

"Oh yes, he's a fine big fox. I wonder how many chickens he's responsible for," she replied.

"A good many. Do you think he's the same one you saw in the summer?"

"I should think very likely he is," she replied.

He watched her, but he could make nothing of her. Partly she was so shy and virgin, and partly she was so grim, matter-of-fact, shrewish. What she said seemed to him so different from the look of her big, queer, dark eyes.

"Are you going to skin him?" she asked.

"Yes, when I've had breakfast, and got a board to peg him on."

"My word, what a strong smell he's got! Pooo! It'll take some washing off one's hands. I don't know why I was so silly as to handle him." And she looked at her right hand, that had passed down his belly and along his tail, and had even got a tiny streak of blood from one dark place in his fur.

"Have you seen the chickens when they smell him, how frightened they are?" he said.

"Yes, aren't they!"

"You must mind you don't get some of his fleas."

"Oh, fleas!" she replied, nonchalant.

Later in the day she saw the fox's skin nailed flat on a board, as if crucified. It gave her an uneasy feeling.

The boy was angry. He went about with his mouth shut, as if he had swallowed part of his chin. But in behaviour he was polite and affable. He did not say anything about his intention. And he left March alone.

That evening they sat in the dining-room. Banford wouldn't have him in her sitting-room any more. There was a very big log on the fire. And everybody was busy. Banford had letters to write, March was sewing a dress, and he was mending some little contrivance.

Banford stopped her letter-writing from time to time to look round and rest her eyes. The boy had his head down, his face hidden over his job.

"Let's see," said Banford. "What train do you go by, Henry?"

He looked up straight at her.

"The morning train. In the morning," he said.

"What, the eight-ten or the eleven-twenty?"

"The eleven-twenty, I suppose," he said.

"That is the day after to-morrow?" said Banford.

"Yes, the day after to-morrow."

"Mm!" murmured Banford, and she returned to her writing. But as she was licking her envelope, she asked:

"And what plans have you made for the future, if I may ask?"

"Plans?" he said, his face very bright and angry.

"I mean about you and Nellie, if you are going on with this business. When do you expect the wedding to come off?" She spoke in a jeering tone.

"Oh, the wedding!" he replied. "I don't know."

"Don't you know anything?" said Banford. "Are you going to clear out on Friday and leave things no more settled than they are?"

"Well, why shouldn't I? We can always write letters."

"Yes, of course you can. But I wanted to know because of this place. If Nellie is going to get married all of a sudden, I shall have to be looking round for a new partner."

"Couldn't she stay on here if she were married?" he said. He knew quite well what was coming.

"Oh," said Banford, "this is no place for a married couple. There's not enough work to keep a man going, for one thing. And there's no money to be made. It's quite useless your thinking of staying on here if you marry. Absolutely!"

"Yes, but I wasn't thinking of staying on here," he said.

"Well, that's what I want to know. And what about Nellie, then? How long is *she* going to be here with me, in that case?"

The two antagonists looked at one another.

"That I can't say," he answered.

"Oh, go along," she cried petulantly. "You must have some idea what you are going to do, if you ask a woman to marry you. Unless it's all a hoax."

"Why should it be a hoax? I am going back to Canada."

"And taking her with you?"

"Yes, certainly."

"You hear that, Nellie?" said Banford.

March, who had had her head bent over her sewing, now looked up with a sharp, pink blush on her face, and a queer, sardonic laugh in her eyes and on her twisted mouth.

"That's the first time I've heard that I was going to Canada," she said.

"Well, you have to hear it for the first time, haven't you?" said the boy.

"Yes, I suppose I have," she said nonchalantly. And she went back to her sewing.

"You're quite ready, are you, to go to Canada? Are you, Nellie?" asked Banford.

March looked up again. She let her shoulders go slack, and let her hand that held the needle lie loose in her lap.

"It depends on *how* I'm going," she said. "I don't think I want to go jammed up in the steerage, as a soldier's wife. I'm afraid I'm not used to that way."

The boy watched her with bright eyes.

"Would you rather stay over here while I go first?" he asked.

"I would, if that's the only alternative," she replied.

"That's much the wisest. Don't make it any fixed engagement," said Banford. "Leave yourself free to go or not after he's got back and found you a place, Nellie. Anything else is madness, madness."

"Don't you think," said the youth, "we ought to get married before I go—and then go together, or separate, according to how it happens?"

"I think it's a terrible idea," cried Banford.

But the boy was watching March.

"What do you think?" he asked her.

She let her eyes stray vaguely into space.

"Well, I don't know," she said. "I shall have to think about it."

"Why?" he asked pertinently.

"Why?" She repeated his question in a mocking way and looked at him laughing, though her face was pink again. "I should think there's plenty of reasons why."

He watched her in silence. She seemed to have escaped him. She had got into league with Banford against him. There was again the queer, sardonic look about her; she would mock stoically at everything he said or which life offered.

"Of course," he said, "I don't want to press you to do anything you don't wish to do."

"I should think not, indeed," cried Banford indignantly.

At bed-time Banford said plaintively to March:

"You take my hot bottle up for me, Nellie, will you?"

"Yes, I'll do it," said March, with the kind of willing unwillingness she so often showed towards her beloved but uncertain Jill.

The two women went upstairs. After a time March called from the top of the stairs: "Good-night, Henry. I shan't be coming down. You'll see to the lamp and the fire, won't you?"

The next day Henry went about with the cloud on his brow and his young cub's face shut up tight. He was cogitating all the time. He had wanted March to marry him and go back to Canada with him. And he had been sure she would do it. Why he wanted her he didn't know. But he did want her. He had set his mind on her. And he was convulsed with a youth's fury at being thwarted. To be thwarted, to be thwarted! It made him so furious inside that he did not know what to do with himself. But he kept himself in hand. Because even now things might turn out differently. She might come over to him. Of course she might. It was her business to do so.

Things drew to a tension again towards evening. He and Banford had avoided each other all day. In fact, Banford went in to the little town by the 11.20 train. It was market day. She arrived back on the 4.25. Just as the night was falling Henry saw her little figure in a dark-blue coat and a dark-blue tam-o'-shanter hat crossing the first meadow from the station. He stood under one of the wild pear trees, with the old dead leaves round his feet. And he watched the little blue figure advancing persistently over the rough winter-ragged meadow. She had her arms full of parcels, and advanced slowly, frail thing she was, but with that devilish little certainty which he so detested in her. He stood invisible under the pear tree, watching her every step. And if looks could have affected her, she would have felt a log of iron on each of her ankles as she made her way forward. "You're a nasty little thing, you are," he was saying softly, across the distance. "You're a nasty little thing. I hope you'll be paid back for all the harm you've done me for nothing. I hope you will—you nasty little thing. I hope you'll have to pay for it. You will, if wishes are anything. You nasty little creature that you are."

She was toiling slowly up the slope. But if she had been slipping back at every step towards the Bottomless Pit, he would not have gone to help her with her parcels. Aha, there went March, striding with her long, land stride in her breeches and her short tunic! Striding downhill at a great pace, and even running a few steps now and then, in her great solicitude and desire to come to the rescue of the little Banford. The boy watched her with rage in his heart. See her leap a ditch, and run, run as if a house was on fire, just to get to that creeping, dark little object down there! So, the Banford just stood still and waited. And March strode up and took *all* the parcels except a bunch of yellow chrysanthemums. These the Banford still carried—yellow chrysanthemums!

"Yes, you look well, don't you?" he said softly into the dusk air. "You look well, pottering up there with a bunch of flowers, you do. I'd make you eat them for your tea if you hug them so tight. And I'd give them you for breakfast again, I would. I'd give you flowers. Nothing but flowers."

He watched the progress of the two women. He could hear their voices: March always outspoken and rather scolding in her tenderness, Banford murmuring rather vaguely. They were evidently good friends. He could not hear what they said till they came to the fence of the home meadow, which they must climb. Then he saw March manfully climbing over the bars with all her packages in her arms, and on the still air he heard Banford's fretful:

"Why don't you let me help you with the parcels?" She had a queer, plaintive hitch in her voice. Then came March's robust and reckless:

"Oh, I can manage. Don't you bother about me. You've all you can do to get yourself over."

"Yes, that's all very well," said Banford fretfully. "You say, *Don't you bother about me,* and then all the while you feel injured because nobody thinks of you."

"When do I feel injured?" said March.

"Always. You always feel injured. Now you're feeling injured because I won't have that boy to come and live on the farm."

"I'm not feeling injured at all," said March.

"I know you are. When he's gone you'll sulk over it. I know you will."

"Shall I?" said March. "We'll see."

"Yes, we *shall* see, unfortunately. I can't think how you can make yourself so cheap. I can't *imagine* how you can lower yourself like it."

"I haven't lowered myself," said March.

"I don't know what you call it, then. Letting a boy like that come so cheeky and impudent and make a mug of you. I don't know what you think of yourself. How much respect do you think he's going to have for you afterwards? My word, I wouldn't be in your shoes, if you married him."

"Of course you wouldn't. My boots are a good bit too big for you, and not half dainty enough," said March, with rather a misfire sarcasm.

"I thought you had too much pride, really I did. A woman's got to hold herself high, especially with a youth like that. Why, he's impudent. Even the way he forced himself on us at the start."

"We asked him to stay," said March.

"Not till he'd almost forced us to. And then he's so cocky and self-assured. My word, he puts my back up. I simply can't imagine how you can let him treat you so cheaply."

"I don't let him treat me cheaply," said March. "Don't you worry yourself, nobody's going to treat me cheaply. And even you aren't, either." She had a tender defiance and a certain fire in her voice.

"Yes, it's sure to come back to me," said Banford bitterly. "That's always the end of it. I believe you only do it to spite me."

They went now in silence up the steep, grassy slope and over the brow, through the gorse bushes. On the other side of the hedge the boy followed in the dusk, at some little distance. Now and then, through the huge ancient hedge of hawthorn, risen into trees, he saw the two dark figures creeping up the hill. As he came to the top of the slope he saw the homestead dark in the twilight, with a huge old pear tree leaning from the near gable, and a little yellow light twinkling in the small side windows of the kitchen. He heard the clink of the latch and saw the kitchen door open into light as the two women went indoors. So they were at home.

And so!—this was what they thought of him. It was rather in his nature to be a listener, so he was not at all surprised whatever he heard. The things people said about him always missed him personally. He was only rather surprised at the women's way with one another. And he disliked the Banford with an acid dislike. And he felt drawn to the March again. He felt again irresistibly drawn to her. He felt there was a secret bond, a secret thread between him and her, something very exclusive, which shut out everybody else and made him and her possess each other in secret.

He hoped again that she would have him. He hoped with his blood suddenly firing up that she would agree to marry him quite quickly: at Christmas, very likely. Christmas was not far off. He wanted, whatever else happened, to snatch her into a hasty marriage and a consummation with him. Then for the future, they could arrange later. But he hoped it would happen as he wanted it. He hoped that to-night she would stay a little while with him, after Banford had gone upstairs. He hoped he could touch her soft, creamy cheek, her strange, frightened face. He hoped he could look into her dilated, frightened dark eyes, quite near. He hoped he might even put his hand on her bosom and feel her soft breasts under her tunic. His heart beat deep and powerful as he thought of that. He wanted very much to do so. He wanted to make sure of her soft woman's breasts under her tunic. She always kept the brown linen coat buttoned so close up to her throat. It seemed to him like some perilous secret, that her soft woman's breasts must be buttoned up in that uniform. It seemed to him, moreover, that they were so much softer, tenderer, more lovely and lovable, shut up in that tunic, than were the Banford's breasts, under her soft blouses and chiffon dresses. The Banford would have little iron breasts, he said to himself. For all her frailty and fretfulness and delicacy, she would have tiny iron breasts. But March, under her crude, fast, workman's tunic, would have soft, white breasts, white and unseen. So he told himself, and his blood burned.

When he went in to tea, he had a surprise. He appeared at the inner door, his face very ruddy and vivid and his blue eyes shining, dropping his head forward as he came in, in his usual way, and hesitating in the doorway to watch the inside of the room, keenly and cautiously, before he entered. He was wearing a long-sleeved waistcoat. His face seemed extraordinarily like a piece of the out-of-doors come indoors: as holly-berries do. In his second of pause in the doorway he took in the two women sitting at table, at opposite ends, saw them sharply. And to his amazement March was dressed in a dress of dull, green silk crape. His mouth came open in surprise. If she had suddenly grown a moustache he could not have been more surprised.

"Why," he said, "do you wear a dress, then?"

She looked up, flushing a deep rose colour, and twisting her mouth with a smile, said:

"Of course I do. What else do you expect me to wear but a dress?"

"A land girl's uniform, of course," said he.

"Oh," she cried, nonchalant, "that's only for this dirty, mucky work about here."

"Isn't it your proper dress, then?" he said.

"No, not indoors it isn't," she said. But she was blushing all the time as she poured out his tea. He sat down in his chair at table, unable to take his eyes off her. Her dress was a perfectly simple slip of bluey-green crape, with a line of gold stitching round the top and round the sleeves, which came to the elbow. It was cut just plain and round at the top, and showed her white, soft throat. Her arms he knew, strong and firm muscled, for he had often seen her with her sleeves rolled up. But he looked her up and down, up and down.

Banford, at the other end of the table, said not a word, but piggled with the sardine on her plate. He had forgotten her existence. He just simply stared at March while he ate his bread and margarine in huge mouthfuls, forgetting even his tea.

"Well, I never knew anything make such a difference!" he murmured, across his mouthfuls.

"Oh, goodness!" cried March, blushing still more. "I might be a pink monkey!"

And she rose quickly to her feet and took the tea-pot to the fire, to the kettle. And as she crouched on the hearth with her green slip about her, the boy stared more wide-eyed than ever. Through the crape her woman's form seemed soft and womanly. And when she stood up and walked he saw her legs move soft within her modernly short skirt. She had on black silk stockings, and small patent shoes with little gold buckles.

No, she was another being. She was something quite different. Seeing her always in the hard-cloth breeches, wide on the hips, buttoned on the knee, strong as armour, and in the brown puttees and thick boots, it had never occurred to him that she had a woman's legs and feet. Now it came upon him. She had a woman's soft, skirted legs, and she was accessible. He blushed to the roots of his hair, shoved his nose in his tea-cup and drank his tea with a little noise that made Banford simply squirm: and strangely, suddenly he felt a man, no longer a youth. He felt a man, with all a man's grave weight of responsibility. A curious quietness and gravity came over his soul. He felt a man, quiet, with a little of the heaviness of male destiny upon him.

She was soft and accessible in her dress. The thought went home in him like an everlasting responsibility.

"Oh, for goodness' sake, say something, somebody," cried Banford fretfully. "It might be a funeral." The boy looked at her, and she could not bear his face.

"A funeral!" said March, with a twisted smile. "Why, that breaks my dream."

Suddenly she had thought of Banford in the wood-box for a coffin.

"What, have you been dreaming of a wedding?" said Banford sarcastically.

"Must have been," said March.

"Whose wedding?" asked the boy.

"I can't remember," said March.

She was shy and rather awkward that evening, in spite of the fact that, wearing a dress, her bearing was much more subdued than in her uniform. She felt unpeeled and rather exposed. She felt almost improper.

They talked desultorily about Henry's departure next morning, and made the trivial arrangement. But of the matter on their minds, none of them spoke. They were rather quiet and friendly this evening; Banford had practically nothing to say. But inside herself she seemed still, perhaps kindly.

At nine o'clock March brought in the tray with the everlasting tea and a little cold meat which Banford had managed to procure. It was the last supper, so Banford did not want to be disagreeable. She felt a bit sorry for the boy, and felt she must be as nice as she could.

He wanted her to go to bed. She was usually the first. But she sat on in her chair under the lamp, glancing at her book now and then, and staring into the fire. A deep silence had come into the room. It was broken by March asking, in a rather small tone:

"What time is it, Jill?"

"Five past ten," said Banford, looking at her wrist.

And then not a sound. The boy had looked up from the book he was holding between his knees. His rather wide, cat-shaped face had its obstinate look, his eyes were watchful.

"What about bed?" said March at last.

"I'm ready when you are," said Banford.

"Oh, very well," said March. "I'll fill your bottle."

She was as good as her word. When the hot-water bottle was ready, she lit a candle and went upstairs with it. Banford remained in her chair, listening acutely. March came downstairs again.

"There you are, then," she said. "Are you going up?"

"Yes, in a minute," said Banford. But the minute passed, and she sat on in her chair under the lamp.

Henry, whose eyes were shining like a cat's as he watched from under his brows, and whose face seemed wider, more chubbed and cat-like with unalterable obstinacy, now rose to his feet to try his throw.

"I think I'll go and look if I can see the she-fox," he said. "She may be creeping round. Won't you come as well for a minute, Nellie, and see if we see anything?"

"Me!" cried March, looking up with her startled, wondering face.

"Yes. Come on," he said. It was wonderful how soft and warm and coaxing his voice could be, how near. The very sound of it made Banford's blood boil. "Come on for a minute," he said, looking down into her uplifted, unsure face.

And she rose to her feet as if drawn up by his young, ruddy face that was looking down on her.

"I should think you're never going out at this time of night, Nellie!" cried Banford.

"Yes, just for a minute," said the boy, looking round on her, and speaking with an odd, sharp yelp in his voice.

March looked from one to the other, as if confused, vague. Banford rose to her feet for battle.

"Why, it's ridiculous. It's bitter cold. You'll catch your death in that thin frock. And in those slippers. You're not going to do any such thing."

There was a moment's pause. Banford turtled up like a little fighting cock, facing March and the boy.

"Oh, I don't think you need worry yourself," he replied. "A moment under the stars won't do anybody any damage. I'll get the rug off the sofa in the dining-room. You're coming, Nellie."

His voice had so much anger and contempt and fury in it as he spoke to Banford: and so much tenderness and proud authority as he spoke to March, that the latter answered:

"Yes, I'm coming."

And she turned with him to the door.

Banford, standing there in the middle of the room, suddenly burst into a long wail and a spasm of sobs. She covered her face with her poor, thin hands, and her thin shoulders shook in an agony of weeping. March looked back from the door.

"Jill!" she cried in a frantic tone, like someone just coming awake. And she seemed to start towards her darling.

But the boy had March's arm in his grip, and she could not move. She did not know why she could not move. It was as in a dream when the heart strains and the body cannot stir.

"Never mind," said the boy softly. "Let her cry. Let her cry. She will have to cry sooner or later. And the tears will relieve her feelings. They will do her good."

So he drew March slowly through the doorway. But her last look was back to the poor little figure which stood in the middle of the room with covered face and thin shoulders shaken with bitter weeping.

In the dining-room he picked up the rug and said:

"Wrap yourself up in this."

She obeyed—and they reached the kitchen door, he holding her soft and firm by the arm, though she did not know it. When she saw the night outside she started back.

"I must go back to Jill," she said. "I *must*! Oh yes, I must."

Her tone sounded final. The boy let go of her and she turned indoors. But he seized her again and arrested her.

"Wait a minute," he said. "Wait a minute. Even if you go, you're not going yet."

"Leave go! Leave go!" she cried. "My place is at Jill's side. Poor little thing, she's sobbing her heart out."

"Yes," said the boy bitterly. "And your heart too, and mine as well."

"Your heart?" said March. He still gripped her and detained her.

"Isn't it as good as her heart?" he said. "Or do you think it's not?"

"Your heart?" she said again, incredulous.

"Yes, mine! Mine! Do you think I haven't *got* a heart?" And with his hot grasp he took her hand and pressed it under his left breast. "There's my heart," he said, "if you don't believe in it."

It was wonder which made her attend. And then she felt the deep, heavy, powerful stroke of his heart, terrible, like something from beyond. It was like something from beyond, something awful from outside, signalling to her. And the signal paralysed her. It beat upon her very soul, and made her helpless. She forgot Jill. She could not think of Jill any more. She could not think of her. That terrible signalling from outside!

The boy put his arm round her waist.

"Come with me," he said gently. "Come and let us say what we've got to say."

And he drew her outside, closed the door. And she went with him darkly down the garden path. That he should have a beating heart! And that he should have his arm round her, outside the blanket! She was too confused to think who he was or what he was.

He took her to a dark corner of the shed, where there was a tool-box with a lid, long and low.

"We'll sit here a minute," he said.

And obediently she sat down by his side.

"Give me your hand," he said.

She gave him both her hands, and he held them between his own. He was young, and it made him tremble.

"You'll marry me before I go back, won't you?" he pleaded.

"Why, aren't we both a pair of fools?" she said.

He had put her in the corner, so that she should not look out and see the lighted window of the house across the dark garden. He tried to keep her all there inside the shed with him.

"In what way a pair of fools?" he said. "If you go back to Canada with me, I've got a job and a good wage waiting for me, and it's a nice place, near the mountains. Why shouldn't you marry me? Why shouldn't we marry? I should like to have you there with me. I should like to feel I'd got somebody there, at the back of me, all my life."

"You'd easily find somebody else who'd suit you better," she said.

"Yes, I might easily find another girl. I know I could. But not one I really wanted. I've never met one I really wanted for good. You see, I'm thinking of all my life. If I marry, I want to feel it's for all my life. Other girls: well, they're just girls, nice enough to go a walk with now and then. Nice enough for a bit of play. But when I think of my life, then I should be very sorry to have to marry one of them, I should indeed."

"You mean they wouldn't make you a good wife."

"Yes, I mean that. But I don't mean they wouldn't do their duty by me. I mean—I don't know what I mean. Only when I think of my life, and of you, then the two things go together."

"And what if they didn't?" she said, with her odd, sardonic touch.

"Well, I think they would."

They sat for some time silent. He held her hands in his, but he did not make love to her. Since he had realised that she was a woman, and vulnerable, accessible, a certain heaviness had possessed his soul. He did not want to make love to her. He shrank from any such performance, almost with fear. She was a woman, and vulnerable, accessible to him finally, and he held back from that which was ahead, almost with dread. It was a kind of darkness he knew he would enter finally, but of which he did not want as yet even to think. She was the woman, and he was responsible for the strange vulnerability he had suddenly realised in her.

"No," she said at last, "I'm a fool. I know I'm a fool."

"What for?" he asked.

"To go on with this business."

"Do you mean me?" he asked.

"No, I mean myself. I'm making a fool of myself, and a big one."

"Why, because you don't want to marry me, really?"

"Oh, I don't know whether I'm against it, as a matter of fact. That's just it. I don't know."

He looked at her in the darkness, puzzled. He did not in the least know what she meant.

"And don't you know whether you like to sit here with me this minute or not?" he asked.

"No, I don't really. I don't know whether I wish I was somewhere else, or whether I like being here. I don't know, really."

"Do you wish you were with Miss Banford? Do you wish you'd gone to bed with her?" he asked, as a challenge.

She waited a long time before she answered.

"No," she said at last. "I don't wish that."

"And do you think you would spend all your life with her—when your hair goes white, and you are old?" he said.

"No," she said, without much hesitation. "I don't see Jill and me two old women together."

"And don't you think, when I'm an old man and you're an old woman, we might be together still, as we are now?" he said.

"Well, not as we are now," she replied. "But I could imagine—no, I can't. I can't imagine you an old man. Besides, it's dreadful!"

"What, to be an old man?"

"Yes, of course."

"Not when the time comes," he said. "But it hasn't come. Only it will. And when it does, I should like to think you'd be there as well."

"Sort of old age pensions," she said dryly.

Her kind of witless humour always startled him. He never knew what she meant. Probably she didn't quite know herself.

"No," he said, hurt.

"I don't know why you harp on old age," she said. "I'm not ninety."

"Did anybody ever say you were?" he asked, offended.

They were silent for some time, pulling different ways in the silence.

"I don't want you to make fun of me," he said.

"Don't you?" she replied, enigmatic.

"No, because just this minute I'm serious. And when I'm serious, I believe in not making fun of it."

"You mean nobody else must make fun of you," she replied.

"Yes, I mean that. And I mean I don't believe in making fun of it myself. When it comes over me so that I'm serious, then—there it is, I don't want it to be laughed at."

She was silent for some time. Then she said, in a vague, almost pained voice: "No, I'm not laughing at you."

A hot wave rose in his heart.

"You believe me, do you?" he asked.

"Yes, I believe you," she replied, with a twang of her old, tired nonchalance, as if she gave in because she was tired. But he didn't care. His heart was hot and clamorous.

"So you agree to marry me before I go?—perhaps at Christmas?"

"Yes, I agree."

"There!" he exclaimed. "That's settled it."

And he sat silent, unconscious, with all the blood burning in all his veins, like fire in all the branches and twigs of him. He only pressed her two hands to his chest, without knowing. When the curious passion began to die down, he seemed to come awake to the world.

"We'll go in, shall we?" he said: as if he realised it was cold.

She rose without answering.

"Kiss me before we go, now you've said it," he said.

And he kissed her gently on the mouth, with a young, frightened kiss. It made her feel so young, too, and frightened, and wondering: and tired, tired, as if she were going to sleep.

They went indoors. And in the sitting-room, there, crouched by the fire like a queer little witch, was Banford. She looked round with reddened eyes as they entered, but did not rise. He thought she looked frightening, unnatural, crouching there and looking round at them. Evil he thought her look was, and he crossed his fingers.

Banford saw the ruddy, elate face on the youth: he seemed strangely tall and bright and looming. And March had a delicate look on her face; she wanted to hide her face, to screen it, to let it not be seen.

"You've come at last," said Banford uglily.

"Yes, we've come," said he.

"You've been long enough for anything," she said.

"Yes, we have. We've settled it. We shall marry as soon as possible," he replied.

"Oh, you've settled it, have you! Well, I hope you won't live to repent it," said Banford.

"I hope so too," he replied.

"Are you going to bed *now*, Nellie?" said Banford.

"Yes, I'm going now."

"Then for goodness' sake come along."

March looked at the boy. He was glancing with his very bright eyes at her and at Banford. March looked at him wistfully. She wished she could stay with him. She wished she had married him already, and it was all over. For oh, she felt suddenly so safe with him. She felt so strangely safe and peaceful in his presence. If only she could sleep in his shelter, and not with Jill. She felt afraid of Jill. In her dim, tender state, it was agony to have to go with Jill and sleep with her. She wanted the boy to save her. She looked again at him.

And he, watching with bright eyes, divined something of what she felt. It puzzled and distressed him that she must go with Jill.

"I shan't forget what you've promised," he said, looking clear into her eyes, right into her eyes, so that he seemed to occupy all herself with his queer, bright look.

She smiled to him faintly, gently. She felt safe again—safe with him.

But in spite of all the boy's precautions, he had a setback. The morning he was leaving the farm he got March to accompany him to the market-town, about six miles away, where they went to the registrar and had their names stuck up as two people who were going to marry. He was to come at Christmas, and the wedding was to take place then. He hoped in the spring to be able to take March back to Canada with him, now the war was really over. Though he was so young, he had saved some money.

"You never have to be without *some* money at the back of you, if you can help it," he said.

So she saw him off in the train that was going West: his camp was on Salisbury Plain. And with big, dark eyes she watched him go, and it seemed as if everything real in life was retreating as the train retreated with his queer, chubby, ruddy face, that seemed so broad across the cheeks, and which never seemed to change its expression, save when a cloud of sulky anger hung on the brow, or the bright eyes fixed themselves in their stare. This was what happened now. He leaned there out of the carriage window as the train drew off, saying goodbye and staring back at her, but his face quite unchanged. There was no emotion on his face. Only his eyes tightened and became fixed and intent in their watching like a cat's when suddenly she sees something and stares. So the boy's eyes stared fixedly as the train drew away, and she was left feeling intensely forlorn. Failing his physical presence, she seemed to have nothing of him. And she had nothing of anything. Only his face was fixed in her mind: the full, ruddy, unchanging cheeks, and the straight snout of a nose and the two eyes staring above. All she could remember was how he suddenly wrinkled his nose when he laughed, as a puppy does when he is playfully growling. But him, himself, and what he was—she knew nothing, she had nothing of him when he left her.

On the ninth day after he had left her he received this letter.

Dear Henry,

I have been over it all again in my mind, this business of me and you, and it seems to me impossible. When you aren't there I see what a fool I am. When you are there you seem to blind me to things as they actually are. You make me see things all unreal, and I don't know what. Then when I am alone again with Jill I seem to come to my own senses and realise what a fool I am making of myself, and how I am treating you unfairly. Because it must be unfair to you for me to go on with this affair when I can't feel in my heart that I really love you. I know people talk a lot of stuff and nonsense about love, and I don't want to do that. I want to keep to plain facts and act in a sensible way. And that seems to me what I'm not doing. I don't see on what grounds I am going to marry you. I know I am not head over heels in love with you, as I have fancied myself to be with fellows when I was a young fool of a girl. You are an absolute stranger to me, and it seems to me you will always be one. So on what grounds am I going to marry you? When I think of Jill, she is ten times more real to me. I know her and I'm awfully fond of her, and I hate myself for a beast if I ever hurt her little finger. We have a life together. And even if it can't last for ever, it is a life while it does last. And it might last as long as either of us lives. Who knows how long we've got to live? She is a delicate little thing, perhaps nobody but me knows how delicate. And as for me, I feel I might fall down the well any day. What I don't seem to see at all is you. When I think of what I've been and what I've done with you, I'm afraid I am a few screws loose. I should be sorry to think that softening of the brain is setting in so soon, but that is what it seems like. You are such an absolute stranger, and so different from what I'm used to, and we don't seem to have a thing in common. As for love, the very word seems impossible. I know what love means even in Jill's case, and I know that in this affair with you it's an absolute impossibility. And then going to Canada. I'm sure I must have been clean off my chump when I promised such a thing. It makes me feel fairly frightened of myself. I feel I might do something really silly that I wasn't responsible for—and end my days in a lunatic asylum. You may think that's all I'm fit for after the way I've gone on, but it isn't a very nice thought for me. Thank goodness Jill is here, and her being here makes me feel sane again, else I don't know what I might do; I might have an accident with the gun one evening. I love Jill, and she makes me feel safe and sane, with her loving anger against me for being such a fool. Well, what I want to say is, won't you let us cry the whole thing off? I can't marry you, and really, I won't do such a thing if it seems to me wrong. It is all a great mistake. I've made a complete fool of myself, and all I can do is to apologise to you and ask you please to forget it, and please to take no further notice of me. Your fox-skin is nearly ready, and seems all right. I will post it to you if you will let me know if this address is still right, and if you will accept my apology for the awful and lunatic way I have behaved with you, and then let the matter rest.

Jill sends her kindest regards. Her mother and father are staying with us over Christmas.

Yours very sincerely,
ELLEN MARCH

The boy read this letter in camp as he was cleaning his kit. He set his teeth, and for a moment went almost pale, yellow round the eyes with fury. He said nothing and saw nothing and felt nothing but a livid rage that was quite unreasoning. Balked! Balked again! Balked! He wanted the woman, he had fixed like doom upon having her. He felt that was his doom, his destiny, and his reward, to have this woman. She was his heaven and hell on earth, and he would have none elsewhere. Sightless with rage and thwarted madness he got through the morning. Save that in his mind he was lurking and scheming towards an issue, he would have committed some insane act. Deep in himself he felt like roaring and howling and gnashing his teeth and breaking things. But he was too intelligent. He knew society was on top of him, and he must scheme. So with his teeth bitten together, and his nose curiously slightly lifted, like some creature that is vicious, and his eyes fixed and staring, he went through the morning's affairs drunk with anger and suppression. In his mind was one thing—Banford. He took no heed of all March's outpouring: none. One thorn rankled, stuck in his mind. Banford. In his mind, in his soul, in his whole being, one thorn rankling to insanity. And he would have to get it out. He would have to get the thorn of Banford out of his life, if he died for it.

With this one fixed idea in his mind, he went to ask for twenty-four hours' leave of absence. He knew it was not due to him. His consciousness was supernaturally keen. He knew where he must go—he must go to the captain. But how could he get at the captain? In that great camp of wooden huts and tents he had no idea where his captain was.

But he went to the officers' canteen. There was his captain standing talking with three other officers. Henry stood in the doorway at attention.

"May I speak to Captain Berryman?" The captain was Cornish like himself.

"What do you want?" called the captain.

"May I speak to you, Captain?"

"What do you want?" replied the captain, not stirring from among his group of fellow officers.

Henry watched his superior for a minute without speaking.

"You won't refuse me, sir, will you?" he asked gravely.

"It depends what it is."

"Can I have twenty-four hours' leave?"

"No, you've no business to ask."

"I know I haven't. But I must ask you."

"You've had your answer."

"Don't send me away, Captain."

There was something strange about the boy as he stood there so everlasting in the doorway. The Cornish captain felt the strangeness at once, and eyed him shrewdly.

"Why, what's afoot?" he said, curious.

"I'm in trouble about something. I must go to Blewbury," said the boy.

"Blewbury, eh? After the girls?"

"Yes, it is a woman, Captain." And the boy, as he stood there with his head reaching forward a little, went suddenly terribly pale, or yellow, and his lips seemed to give off pain. The captain saw and paled a little also. He turned aside.

"Go on, then," he said. "But for God's sake don't cause any trouble of any sort."

"I won't, Captain, thank you."

He was gone. The captain, upset, took a gin and bitters. Henry managed to hire a bicycle. It was twelve o'clock when he left the camp. He had sixty miles of wet and muddy crossroads to ride. But he was in the saddle and down the road without a thought of food.

At the farm, March was busy with a work she had had some time in hand. A bunch of Scotch fir trees stood at the end of the open shed, on a little bank where ran the fence between two of the gorse-shaggy meadows. The farthest of these trees was dead—it had died in the summer, and stood with all its needles brown and sere in the air. It was not a very big tree. And it was absolutely dead. So March determined to have it, although they were not allowed to cut any of the timber. But it would make such splendid firing, in these days of scarce fuel.

She had been giving a few stealthy chops at the trunk for a week or more, every now and then hacking away for five minutes, low down, near the ground, so no one should notice. She had not tried the saw, it was such hard work, alone. Now the tree stood with a great yawning gap in his base, perched, as it were, on one sinew, and ready to fall. But he did not fall.

It was late in the damp December afternoon, with cold mists creeping out of the woods and up the hollows, and darkness waiting to sink in from above. There was a bit of yellowness where the sun was fading away beyond the low woods of the distance. March took her axe and went to the tree. The small thud-thud of her blows resounded rather ineffectual about the wintry homestead. Banford came out wearing her thick coat, but with no hat on her head, so that her thin, bobbed hair blew on the uneasy wind that sounded in the pines and in the wood.

"What I'm afraid of," said Banford, "is that it will fall on the shed and we sh'll have another job repairing that."

"Oh, I don't think so," said March, straightening herself and wiping her arm over her hot brow. She was flushed red, her eyes were very wide open and queer, her upper lip lifted away from her two white, front teeth with a curious, almost rabbit look.

A little stout man in a black overcoat and a bowler hat came pottering across the yard. He had a pink face and a white beard and smallish, pale-blue eyes. He was not very old, but nervy, and he walked with little short steps.

"What do you think, father?" said Banford. "Don't you think it might hit the shed in falling?"

"Shed, no!" said the old man. "Can't hit the shed. Might as well say the fence."

"The fence doesn't matter," said March, in her high voice.

"Wrong as usual, am I!" said Banford, wiping her straying hair from her eyes.

The tree stood as it were on one spelch of itself, leaning, and creaking in the wind. It grew on the bank of a little dry ditch between the two meadows. On the top of the bank straggled one fence, running to the bushes up-hill. Several trees clustered there in the corner of the field near the shed and near the gate which led into the yard. Towards this gate, horizontal across the weary meadows, came the grassy, rutted approach from the high road. There trailed another rickety fence, long split poles joining the short, thick, wide-apart uprights. The three people stood at the back of the tree, in the corner of the shed meadow, just above the yard gate. The house, with its two gables and its porch, stood tidy in a little grassed garden across the yard. A little, stout, rosy-faced woman in a little red woollen shoulder shawl had come and taken her stand in the porch.

"Isn't it down yet?" she cried, in a high little voice.

"Just thinking about it," called her husband. His tone towards the two girls was always rather mocking and satirical. March did not want to go on with her hitting while he was there. As for him, he wouldn't lift a stick from the ground if he could help it, complaining, like his daughter, of rheumatics in his shoulder. So the three stood there a moment silent in the cold afternoon, in the bottom corner near the yard.

They heard the far-off taps of a gate, and craned to look. Away across, on the green horizontal approach, a figure was just swinging on to a bicycle again, and lurching up and down over the grass, approaching.

"Why, it's one of our boys—it's Jack," said the old man.

"Can't be," said Banford.

March craned her head to look. She alone recognised the khaki figure. She flushed, but said nothing.

"No, it isn't Jack, I don't think," said the old man, staring with little round blue eyes under his white lashes.

In another moment the bicycle lurched into sight, and the rider dropped off at the gate. It was Henry, his face wet and red and spotted with mud. He was altogether a muddy sight.

"Oh!" cried Banford, as if afraid. "Why, it's Henry!"

"What!" muttered the old man. He had a thick, rapid, muttering way of speaking, and was slightly deaf. "What? What? Who is it? Who is it, do you say? That young fellow? That young fellow of Nellie's? Oh! Oh!" And the satiric smile came on his pink face and white eyelashes.

Henry, pushing the wet hair off his steaming brow, had caught sight of them and heard what the old man said. His hot, young face seemed to flame in the cold light.

"Oh, are you all there!" he said, giving his sudden, puppy's little laugh. He was so hot and dazed with cycling he hardly knew where he was. He leaned the bicycle against the fence and climbed over into the corner on to the bank, without going into the yard.

"Well, I must say, we weren't expecting you," said Banford laconically.

"No, I suppose not," said he, looking at March.

She stood aside, slack, with one knee drooped and the axe resting its head loosely on the ground. Her eyes were wide and vacant, and her upper lip lifted from her teeth in that helpless, fascinated rabbit look. The moment she saw his glowing, red face it was all over with her. She was as helpless as if she had been bound. The moment she saw the way his head seemed to reach forward.

"Well, who is it? Who is it, anyway?" asked the smiling, satiric old man in his muttering voice.

"Why, Mr Grenfel, whom you've heard us tell about, father," said Banford coldly.

"Heard you tell about, I should think so. Heard of nothing else practically," muttered the elderly man, with his queer little jeering smile on his face. "How do you do," he added, suddenly reaching out his hand to Henry.

The boy shook hands just as startled. Then the two men fell apart.

"Cycled over from Salisbury Plain, have you?" asked the old man.

"Yes."

"Hm! Longish ride. How long d'it take you, eh? Some time, eh? Several hours, I suppose."

"About four."

"Eh? Four! Yes, I should have thought so. When are you going back, then?"

"I've got till to-morrow evening."

"Till to-morrow evening, eh? Yes. Hm! Girls weren't expecting you, were they?"

And the old man turned his pale-blue, round little eyes under their white lashes mockingly towards the girls. Henry also looked round. He had become a little awkward. He looked at March, who was still staring away into the distance as if to see where the cattle were. Her hand was on the pommel of the axe, whose head rested loosely on the ground.

"What were you doing there?" he asked in his soft, courteous voice. "Cutting a tree down?"

March seemed not to hear, as if in a trance.

"Yes," said Banford. "We've been at it for over a week."

"Oh! And have you done it all by yourselves then?"

"Nellie's done it all, I've done nothing," said Banford.

"Really! You must have worked quite hard," he said, addressing himself in a curious gentle tone direct to March. She did not answer, but remained half averted staring away towards the woods above as if in a trance.

"Nellie!" cried Banford sharply. "Can't you answer?"

"What—me?" cried March, starting round and looking from one to the other. "Did anyone speak to me?"

"Dreaming!" muttered the old man, turning aside to smile. "Must be in love, eh, dreaming in the day-time!"

"Did you say anything to me?" said March, looking at the boy as from a strange distance, her eyes wide and doubtful, her face delicately flushed.

"I said you must have worked hard at the tree," he replied courteously.

"Oh, that! Bit by bit. I thought it would have come down by now."

"I'm thankful it hasn't come down in the night, to frighten us to death," said Banford.

"Let me just finish it for you, shall I?" said the boy.

March slanted the axe-shaft in his direction.

"Would you like to?" she said.

"Yes, if you wish it," he said.

"Oh, I'm thankful when the thing's down, that's all," she replied, nonchalant.

"Which way is it going to fall?" said Banford. "Will it hit the shed?"

"No, it won't hit the shed," he said. "I should think it will fall there—quite clear. Though it might give a twist and catch the fence."

"Catch the fence!" cried the old man. "What, catch the fence! When it's leaning at that angle? Why, it's farther off than the shed. It won't catch the fence."

"No," said Henry, "I don't suppose it will. It has plenty of room to fall quite clear, and I suppose it will fall clear."

"Won't tumble backwards on top of us, will it?" asked the old man, sarcastic.

"No, it won't do that," said Henry, taking off his short overcoat and his tunic. "Ducks! Ducks! Go back!"

A line of four brown-speckled ducks led by a brown-and-green drake were stemming away downhill from the upper meadow, coming like boats running on a ruffled sea, cockling their way top speed downwards towards the fence and towards the little group of people, and cackling as excitedly as if they brought news of the Spanish Armada.

"Silly things! Silly things!" cried Banford, going forward to turn them off. But they came eagerly towards her, opening their yellow-green beaks and quacking as if they were so excited to say something.

"There's no food. There's nothing here. You must wait a bit," said Banford to them. "Go away. Go away. Go round to the yard."

They didn't go, so she climbed the fence to swerve them round under the gate and into the yard. So off they waggled in an excited string once more, wagging their rumps like the stems of little gondolas, ducking under the bar of the gate. Banford stood on the top of the bank, just over the fence, looking down on the other three.

Henry looked up at her, and met her queer, round-pupilled, weak eyes staring behind her spectacles. He was perfectly still. He looked away, up at the weak, leaning tree. And as he looked into the sky, like a huntsman who is watching a flying bird, he thought to himself: "If the tree falls in just such a way, and spins just so much as it falls, then the branch there will strike her exactly as she stands on top of that bank."

He looked at her again. She was wiping the hair from her brow again, with that perpetual gesture. In his heart he had decided her death. A terrible still force seemed in him, and a power that was just his. If he turned even a hair's breadth in the wrong direction, he would lose the power.

"Mind yourself, Miss Banford," he said. And his heart held perfectly still, in the terrible pure will that she should not move.

"Who, me, mind myself?" she cried, her father's jeering tone in her voice. "Why, do you think you might hit me with the axe?"

"No, it's just possible the tree might, though," he answered soberly. But the tone of his voice seemed to her to imply that he was only being falsely solicitous, and trying to make her move because it was his will to move her.

"Absolutely impossible," she said.

He heard her. But he held himself icy still, lest he should lose his power.

"No, it's just possible. You'd better come down this way."

"Oh, all right. Let us see some crack Canadian tree-felling," she retorted.

"Ready, then," he said, taking the axe, looking round to see he was clear.

There was a moment of pure, motionless suspense, when the world seemed to stand still. Then suddenly his form seemed to flash up enormously tall and fearful, he gave two swift, flashing blows, in immediate succession, the tree was severed, turning slowly, spinning strangely in the air and coming down like a sudden darkness on the earth. No one saw what was happening except himself. No one heard the strange little cry which Banford gave as the dark end of the bough swooped down, down on her. No one saw her crouch a little and receive the blow on the back of the neck. No one saw her flung outwards and laid, a little twitching heap, at the foot of the fence. No one except the boy. And he watched with intense bright eyes, as he would watch a wild goose he had shot. Was it winged or dead? Dead!

Immediately he gave a loud cry. Immediately March gave a wild shriek that went far, far down the afternoon. And the father started a strange bellowing sound.

The boy leapt the fence and ran to the fringe. The back of the neck and head was a mass of blood, of horror. He turned it over. The body was quivering with little convulsions. But she was dead really. He knew it, that it was so. He knew it in his soul and his blood. The inner necessity of his life was fulfilling itself, it was he who was to live. The thorn was drawn out of his bowels. So he put her down gently. She was dead.

He stood up. March was standing there petrified and absolutely motionless. Her face was dead white, her eyes big black pools. The old man was scrambling horribly over the fence.

"I'm afraid it's killed her," said the boy.

The old man was making curious, blubbering noises as he huddled over the fence. "What!" cried March, starting electric.

"Yes, I'm afraid," repeated the boy.

March was coming forward. The boy was over the fence before she reached it.

"What do you say, killed her?" she asked in a sharp voice.

"I'm afraid so," he answered softly.

She went still whiter, fearful. The two stood facing one another. Her black eyes gazed on him with the last look of resistance. And then in a last agonised failure she began to grizzle, to cry in a shivery little fashion of a child that doesn't want to cry, but which is beaten from within, and gives that little first shudder of sobbing which is not yet weeping, dry and fearful.

He had won. She stood there absolutely helpless, shuddering her dry sobs and her mouth trembling rapidly. And then, as in a child, with a little crash came the tears and the blind agony of sightless weeping. She sank down on the grass, and sat there with her hands on her breast and her face lifted in sightless, convulsed weeping. He stood above her, looking down on her, mute, pale, and everlasting seeming. He never moved, but looked down on her. And among all the torture of the scene, the torture of his own heart and bowels, he was glad, he had won.

After a long time he stooped to her and took her hands.

"Don't cry," he said softly. "Don't cry."

She looked up at him with tears running from her eyes, a senseless look of help-lessness and submission. So she gazed on him as if sightless, yet looking up to him. She would never leave him again. He had won her. And he knew it and was glad, because he wanted her for his life. His life must have her. And now he had won her. It was what his life must have.

But if he had won her, he had not yet got her. They were married at Christmas as he had planned, and he got again ten days' leave. They went to Cornwall, to his own village, on the sea. He realised that it was awful for her to be at the farm any more.

But though she belonged to him, though she lived in his shadow, as if she could not be away from him, she was not happy. She did not want to leave him: and yet she did not feel free with him. Everything round her seemed to watch her, seemed to press on her. He had won her, he had her with him, she was his wife. And she—she belonged to him, she knew it. But she was not glad. And he was still foiled. He realised that though he was married to her and possessed her in every possible way, apparently, and though she *wanted* him to possess her, she wanted it, she wanted nothing else, now, still he did not quite succeed.

Something was missing. Instead of her soul swaying with new life, it seemed to droop, to bleed, as if it were wounded. She would sit for a long time with her hand in his, looking away at the sea. And in her dark, vacant eyes was a sort of wound, and her face looked a little peaked. If he spoke to her, she would turn to him with a faint new smile, the strange, quivering little smile of a woman who has died in the old way of love, and can't quite rise to the new way. She still felt she ought to *do* something, to strain herself in some direction. And there was nothing to do, and no direction in which to strain herself. And she could not quite accept the submergence which his new love put upon her. If she was in love, she ought to *exert* herself, in some way, lov-ing. She felt the weary need of our day to *exert* herself in love. But she knew that in fact she must no more exert herself in love. He would not have the love which exert-ed itself towards him. It made his brow go black. No, he wouldn't let her exert her love towards him. No, she had to be passive, to acquiesce, and to be submerged under the surface of love. She had to be like the seaweeds she saw as she peered down from the boat, swaying forever delicately under water, with all their delicate fibrils put ten-derly out upon the flood, sensitive, utterly sensitive and receptive within the shad-owy sea, and never, never rising and looking forth above water while they lived. Never. Never looking forth from the water until they died, only then washing, corpses, upon the surface. But while they lived, always submerged, always beneath the wave. Beneath the wave they might have powerful roots, stronger than iron; they might be tenacious and dangerous in their soft waving within the flood. Beneath the water they might be stronger, more indestructible than resistant oak trees are on land. But it was always under-water, always under-water. And she, being a woman, must be like that.

And she had been so used to the very opposite. She had had to take all the thought for love and for life, and all the responsibility. Day after day she had been responsible for the coming day, for the coming year: for her dear Jill's health and happiness and well-being. Verily, in her own small way, she had felt herself responsible for the well-being of the world. And this had been her great stimulant, this grand feeling that, in her own small sphere, she was responsible for the well-being of the world.

And she had failed. She knew that, even in her small way, she had failed. She had failed to satisfy her own feeling of responsibility. It was so difficult. It seemed so grand and easy at first. And the more you tried, the more difficult it became. It had seemed so easy to make one beloved creature happy. And the more you tried, the worse the failure. It was terrible. She had been all her life reaching, reaching, and what she reached for seemed so near, until she had stretched to her utmost limit. And then it was always beyond her.

Always beyond her, vaguely, unrealisably beyond her, and she was left with nothingness at last. The life she reached for, the happiness she reached for, the well-being she reached for all slipped back, became unreal, the farther she stretched her hand. She wanted some goal, some finality—and there was none. Always this ghastly reaching, reaching, striving for something that might be just beyond. Even to make Jill happy. She was glad Jill was dead. For she had realised that she could never make her happy. Jill would always be fretting herself thinner and thinner, weaker and weaker. Her pains grew worse instead of less. It would be so for ever. She was glad she was dead.

And if Jill had married a man it would have been just the same. The woman striving, striving to make the man happy, striving within her own limits for the well-being of her world. And always achieving failure. Little, foolish successes in money or in ambition. But at the very point where she most wanted success, in the anguished effort to make some one beloved human being happy and perfect, there the failure was almost catastrophic. You wanted to make your beloved happy, and his happiness seemed always achievable. If only you did just this, that and the other. And you did this, that, and the other, in all good faith, and every time the failure became a little more ghastly. You could love yourself to ribbons and strive and strain yourself to the bone, and things would go from bad to worse, bad to worse, as far as happiness went. The awful mistake of happiness.

Poor March, in her good-will and her responsibility, she had strained herself till it seemed to her that the whole of life and everything was only a horrible abyss of nothingness. The more you reach after the fatal flower of happiness, which trembles so blue and lovely in a crevice just beyond your grasp, the more fearfully you become aware of the ghastly and awful gulf of the precipice below you, into which you will inevitably plunge, as into the bottomless pit, if you reach any farther. You pluck flower after flower—it is never *the* flower. The flower itself—its calyx is a horrible gulf, it is the bottomless pit.

That is the whole history of the search for happiness, whether it be your own or somebody else's that you want to win. It ends, and it always ends, in the ghastly sense of the bottomless nothingness into which you will inevitably fall if you strain any farther.

And women?—what goal can any woman conceive, except happiness? Just happiness for herself and the whole world. That, and nothing else. And so, she assumes the responsibility and sets off towards her goal. She can see it there, at the foot of the rainbow. Or she can see it a little way beyond, in the blue distance. Not far, not far.

But the end of the rainbow is a bottomless gulf down which you can fall forever without arriving, and the blue distance is a void pit which can swallow you and all your efforts into its emptiness, and still be no emptier. You and all your efforts. So, the illusion of attainable happiness!

Poor March, she had set off so wonderfully towards the blue goal. And the farther and farther she had gone, the more fearful had become the realisation of emptiness. An agony, an insanity at last.

She was glad it was over. She was glad to sit on the shore and look westwards over the sea, and know the great strain had ended. She would never strain for love and happiness any more. And Jill was safely dead. Poor Jill, poor Jill. It must be sweet to be dead.

For her own part, death was not her destiny. She would have to leave her destiny to the boy. But then, the boy. He wanted more than that. He wanted her to give herself without defences, to sink and become submerged in him. And she—she wanted to sit still, like a woman on the last milestone, and watch. She wanted to see, to know, to understand. She wanted to be alone: with him at her side.

And he! He did not want her to watch any more, to see any more, to understand any more. He wanted to veil her woman's spirit, as Orientals veil the woman's face. He wanted her to commit herself to him, and to put her independent spirit to sleep. He wanted to take away from her all her effort, all that seemed her very *raison d'être*. He wanted to make her submit, yield, blindly pass away out of all her strenuous consciousness. He wanted to take away her consciousness, and make her just his woman. Just his woman.

And she was so tired, so tired, like a child that wants to go to sleep, but which fights against sleep as if sleep were death. She seemed to stretch her eyes wider in the obstinate effort and tension of keeping awake. She *would* keep awake. She *would* know. She *would* consider and judge and decide. She *would* have the reins of her own life between her own hands. She *would* be an independent woman to the last. But she was so tired, so tired of everything. And sleep seemed near. And there was such rest in the boy.

Yet there, sitting in a niche of the high, wild cliffs of West Cornwall, looking over the westward sea, she stretched her eyes wider and wider. Away to the West, Canada, America. She *would* know and she *would* see what was ahead. And the boy, sitting beside her, staring down at the gulls, had a cloud between his brows and the strain of discontent in his eyes. He wanted her asleep, at peace in him. He wanted her at peace, asleep in him. And *there* she was, dying with the strain of her own wakefulness. Yet she would not sleep: no, never. Sometimes he thought bitterly that he ought to have left her. He ought never to have killed Banford. He should have left Banford and March to kill one another.

But that was only impatience: and he knew it. He was waiting, waiting to go West. He was aching almost in torment to leave England, to go West, to take March away. To leave this shore! He believed that as they crossed the seas, as they left this England which he so hated, because in some way it seemed to have stung him with poison, she would go to sleep. She would close her eyes at last and give in to him.

And then he would have her, and he would have his own life at last. He chafed, feeling he hadn't got his own life. He would never have it till she yielded and slept in him. Then he would have all his own life as a young man and a male, and she would have all her own life as a woman and a female. There would be no more of this awful straining. She would not be a man any more, an independent woman with a man's responsibility. Nay, even the responsibility for her own soul she would have to commit to him. He knew it was so, and obstinately held out against her, waiting for the surrender.

"You'll feel better when once we get over the seas to Canada over there," he said to her as they sat among the rocks on the cliff.

She looked away to the sea's horizon, as if it were not real. Then she looked round at him, with the strained, strange look of a child that is struggling against sleep.

"Shall I ?" She said.

"Yes," he answered quietly.

And her eyelids dropped with the slow motion, sleep weighing them unconscious. But she pulled them open again to say:

"Yes, I may. I can't tell. I can't tell what it will be like over there."

"If only we could go soon!" he said, with pain in his voice.

Surgery for the Novel—or a Bomb

You talk about the future of the baby, little cherub, when he's in the cradle cooing; and it's a romantic, glamorous subject. You also talk, with the parson, about the future of the wicked old grandfather who is at last lying on his death-bed. And there again you have a subject for much vague emotion, chiefly of fear this time.

How do we feel about the novel? Do we bounce with joy thinking of the wonderful novelistic days ahead? Or do we grimly shake our heads and hope the wicked creature will be spared a little longer? Is the novel on his death-bed, old sinner? Or is he just toddling round his cradle, sweet little thing? Let us have another look at him before we decide this rather serious case.

There he is, the monster with many faces, many branches to him, like a tree: the modern novel. And he is almost dual, like Siamese twins. On the one hand, the pale-faced, high-browed, earnest novel, which you have to take seriously; on the other, that smirking, rather plausible hussy, the popular novel.

Let us just for the moment feel the pulses of *Ulysses* and of Miss Dorothy Richardson and M. Marcel Proust, on the earnest side of Briareus;[1] on the other, the throb of *The Sheik* and Mr Zane Grey, and, if you will, Mr Robert Chambers and the rest.[2] Is *Ulysses* in his cradle? Oh, dear! What a grey face! And *Pointed Roofs*, are they a gay little toy for nice little girls? And M. Proust? Alas! You can hear the death-rattle in their throats. They can hear it themselves. They are listening to it with acute interest, trying to discover whether the intervals are minor thirds or major fourths. Which is rather infantile, really.

So there you have the "serious" novel, dying in a very long-drawn-out fourteen-volume death-agony, and absorbedly, childishly interested in the phenomenon. "Did I feel a twinge in my little toe, or didn't I?" asks every character of Mr Joyce or of Miss Richardson or M. Proust. Is my aura a blend of frankincense and orange pekoe and boot-blacking, or is it myrrh and bacon-fat and Shetland tweed? The audience round the death-bed gapes for the answer. And when, in a sepulchral tone, the answer comes at length, after hundreds of pages: "It is none of these, it is abysmal chloro-coryambasis,"[3] the audience quivers all over, and murmurs: "That's just how I feel myself."

---

1. Briareus aided Zeus in fighting the Titans, here represented by the epic modernist novels of Joyce, Proust, and Dorothy Richardson (author of a 12-volume sequence of novels, *Pilgrimage* (1915–1938), of which *Pointed Roofs* was the first).

2. *The Sheik* (1919) was a lurid best-seller by Edith Maude Hull; Zane Grey (1875–1939), popular American writer of westerns; Robert Chalmers (1865–1933), prolific American novelist.

3. A word of Lawrence's invention.

Which is the dismal, long-drawn-out comedy of the death-bed of the serious novel. It is self-consciousness picked into such fine bits that the bits are most of them invisible, and you have to go by smell. Through thousands and thousands of pages Mr Joyce and Miss Richardson tear themselves to pieces, strip their smallest emotions to the finest threads, till you feel you are sewed inside a wool mattress that is being slowly shaken up, and you are turning to wool along with the rest of the woolliness.

It's awful. And it's childish. It really is childish, after a certain age, to be absorbedly self-conscious. One has to be self-conscious at seventeen: still a little self-conscious at twenty-seven; but if we are going it strong at thirty-seven, then it is a sign of arrested development, nothing else. And if it is still continuing at forty-seven, it is obvious senile precocity.

And there's the serious novel: senile-precocious. Absorbedly, childishly concerned with *what I am*. "I am this, I am that, I am the other. My reactions are such, and such, and such. And, oh, Lord, if I liked to watch myself closely enough, if I liked to analyse my feelings minutely, as I unbutton my gloves, instead of saying crudely I unbuttoned them, then I could go on to a million pages instead of a thousand. In fact, the more I come to think of it, it is gross, it is uncivilized bluntly to say: I unbuttoned my gloves. After all, the absorbing adventure of it! Which button did I begin with?" etc.

The people in the serious novels are so absorbedly concerned with themselves and what they feel and don't feel, and how they react to every mortal button; and their audience as frenziedly absorbed in the application of the author's discoveries to their own reactions: "That's me! That's exactly it! I'm just finding myself in this book!" Why, this is more than death-bed, it is almost post-mortem behaviour.

Some convulsion or cataclysm will have to get this serious novel out of its self-consciousness. The last great war made it worse. What's to be done? Because, poor thing, it's really young yet. The novel has never become fully adult. It has never quite grown to years of discretion. It has always youthfully hoped for the best, and felt rather sorry for itself on the last page. Which is just childish. The childishness has become very long-drawn-out. So very many adolescents who drag their adolescence on into their forties and their fifties and their sixties! There needs some sort of surgical operation, somewhere.

Then the popular novels—the *Sheiks* and *Babbitts* and Zane Grey novels. They are just as self-conscious, only they do have more illusions about themselves. The heroines do think they are lovelier, and more fascinating, and purer. The heroes do see themselves more heroic, braver, more chivalrous, more fetching. The mass of the populace "find themselves" in the popular novels. But nowadays it's a funny sort of self they find. A Sheik with a whip up his sleeve, and a heroine with weals on her back, but adored in the end, adored, the whip out of sight, but the weals still faintly visible.

It's a funny sort of self they discover in the popular novels. And the essential moral of *If Winter Comes*, for example, is so shaky. "The gooder you are, the worse it is for you, poor you, oh, poor you. Don't you be so blimey good, it's not good enough." Or *Babbitt*:[4] "Go on, you make your pile, and then pretend you're too good for it. Put it over the rest of the grabbers that way. They're only pleased with themselves when they've made their pile. You go one better."

Always the same sort of baking-powder gas to make you rise: the soda counteracting the cream of tartar, and the tartar counteracted by the soda. Sheik heroines, duly whipped, wildly adored. Babbitts with solid fortunes, weeping from self-pity.

---

4. *If Winter Comes* (1915), a novel by American author A. S. M. Hutchinson; *Babbitt* (1922) by American author Sinclair Lewis.

Winter-Comes heroes as good as pie, hauled off to jail. *Moral:* Don't be too good, because you'll go to jail for it. *Moral:* Don't feel sorry for yourself till you've made your pile and don't need to feel sorry for yourself. *Moral:* Don't let him adore you till he's whipped you into it. Then you'll be partners in mild crime as well as in holy matrimony.

Which again is childish. Adolescence which *can't* grow up. Got into the self-conscious rut and going crazy, quite crazy in it. Carrying on their adolescence into middle age and old age, like the looney Cleopatra in *Dombey and Son*,[5] murmuring "Rose-coloured curtains" with her dying breath.

The future of the novel? Poor old novel, it's in a rather dirty, messy tight corner. And it's either got to get over the wall or knock a hole through it. In other words, it's got to grow up. Put away childish things like: "Do I love the girl, or don't I?"—"Am I pure and sweet, or am I not?"—"Do I unbutton my right glove first, or my left?"—"Did my mother ruin my life by refusing to drink the cocoa which my bride had boiled for her?" These questions and their answers don't really interest me any more, though the world still goes sawing them over. I simply don't care for any of these things now, though I used to. The purely emotional and self-analytical stunts are played out in me. I'm finished. I'm deaf to the whole band. But I'm neither *blasé* nor cynical, for all that. I'm just interested in something else.

Supposing a bomb were put under the whole scheme of things, what would we be after? What feelings do we want to carry through into the next epoch? What feelings will carry us through? What is the underlying impulse in us that will provide the motive power for a new state of things, when this democratic-industrial-lovey-dovey-darling-take-me-to-mamma state of things is bust?

What next? That's what interests me. "What now?" is no fun any more.

If you wish to look into the past for what-next books, you can go back to the Greek philosophers. Plato's Dialogues are queer little novels. It seems to me it was the greatest pity in the world, when philosophy and fiction got split. They used to be one, right from the days of myth. Then they went and parted, like a nagging married couple, with Aristotle and Thomas Aquinas and that beastly Kant.[6] So the novel went sloppy, and philosophy went abstract-dry. The two should come together again—in the novel.

You've got to find a new impulse for new things in mankind, and it's really fatal to find it through abstraction. No, no; philosophy and religion, they've both gone too far on the algebraical tack: Let X stand for sheep and Y for goats: then X minus Y equals Heaven, and X plus Y equals Earth, and Y minus X equals Hell. Thank you! But what coloured shirt does X have on?

The novel has a future. It's got to have the courage to tackle new propositions without using abstractions; it's got to present us with new, really new feelings, a whole line of new emotion, which will get us out of the emotional rut. Instead of snivelling about what is and has been, or inventing new sensations in the old line, it's got to break a way through, like a hole in the wall. And the public will scream and say it is sacrilege: because, of course, when you've been jammed for a long time in a tight corner, and you get really used to its stuffiness and its tightness, till you find it suffocatingly cozy; then, of course, you're horri-

---

5. In Dickens's novel *Dombey and Son* (1847–1948), the second wife of Mr. Dombey is known as "Cleopatra."
6. All systematic philosophers who wrote syllogistically; in a letter of 1928, Lawrence included Immanuel Kant in a list of "grand perverts."

fied when you see a new glaring hole in what was your cosy wall. You're horrified.
You back away from the cold stream of fresh air as if it were killing you. But gradually, first one and then another of the sheep filters through the gap, and finds a
new world outside.

from **Etruscan Places**

from The Painted Tombs of Tarquinia[1]

1

We arranged for the guide to take us to the painted tombs, which are the real fame of
Tarquinia. After lunch we set out, climbing to the top of the town, and passing
through the southwest gate, on the level hill-crest. Looking back, the wall of the
town, mediaeval, with a bit of more ancient black wall lower down, stands blank. Just
outside the gate are one or two forlorn new houses, then ahead, the long, running
tableland of the hill, with the white highway dipping and going on to Viterbo, inland.
   "All this hill in front," said the guide, "is tombs! All tombs! The city of the dead."
   So! Then this hill is the necropolis hill! The Etruscans never buried their dead
within the city walls. And the modern cemetery and the first Etruscan tombs lie
almost close up to the present city gate. Therefore, if the ancient city of Tarquinia
lay on this hill, it can have occupied no more space, hardly, than the present little
town of a few thousand people. Which seems impossible. Far more probably, the city
itself lay on that opposite hill there, which lies splendid and unsullied, running parallel to us.
   We walk across the wild bit of hilltop, where the stones crop out, and the first
rock-rose flutters, and the asphodels stick up. This is the necropolis. Once it had
many a tumulus, and streets of tombs. Now there is no sign of any tombs: no tumulus,
nothing but the rough bare hill-crest, with stones and short grass and flowers, the sea
gleaming away to the right, under the sun, and the soft land inland glowing very
green and pure.
   But we see a little bit of wall, built perhaps to cover a water-trough. Our guide
goes straight towards it. He is a fat, good-natured young man, who doesn't look as if
he would be interested in tombs. We are mistaken, however. He knows a good deal,
and has a quick, sensitive interest, absolutely unobtrusive, and turns out to be as
pleasant a companion for such a visit as one could wish to have.
   The bit of wall we see is a little hood of masonry with an iron gate, covering a little flight of steps leading down into the ground. One comes upon it all at once, in the
rough nothingness of the hillside. The guide kneels down to light his acetylene lamp,
and his old terrier lies down resignedly in the sun, in the breeze which rushes persistently from the southwest, over these long, exposed hilltops.
   The lamp begins to shine and smell, then to shine without smelling: the guide
opens the iron gate, and we descend the steep steps down into the tomb. It seems a
dark little hole underground: a dark little hole, after the sun of the upper world! But
the guide's lamp begins to flare up, and we find ourselves in a little chamber in the

1. The Etruscans were the most important people of early Italy. By the 4th century B.C. the Romans had driven them
into northern Italy (modern Tuscany), and gradually their cities, which included Tarquinia, fell to Rome. Little is
known about them or their language; Etruscan tombs in or near Tarquinia include the Tomba delle Leonesse (c.
530–20 B.C.), the Tomba del Citaredo (c. 500–490 B.C.), the Tomba del Leopardi (c. 480–70 B.C.) and the Tomba
del Triclinio (c. 470 B.C.), all of which contain wall paintings portraying scenes of music making, feasting, and
dancing.

rock, just a small, bare little cell of a room that some anchorite might have lived in. It is so small and bare and familiar, quite unlike the rather splendid spacious tombs at Cerveteri.

But the lamp flares bright, we get used to the change of light, and see the paintings on the little walls. It is the Tomb of Hunting and Fishing, so called from the pictures on the walls, and it is supposed to date from the sixth century B.C. It is very badly damaged, pieces of the wall have fallen away, damp has eaten into the colours, nothing seems to be left. Yet in the dimness we perceive flights of birds flying through the haze, with the draught of life still in their wings. And as we take heart and look closer we see the little room is frescoed all round with hazy sky and sea, with birds flying and fishes leaping, and little men hunting, fishing, rowing in boats. The lower part of the wall is all a blue-green sea with a silhouette surface that ripples all round the room. From the sea rises a tall rock, off which a naked man, shadowy but still distinct, is beautifully and cleanly diving into the sea, while a companion climbs up the rock after him, and on the water a boat waits with rested oars in it, three men watching the diver, the middle man standing up naked, holding out his arms. Meanwhile a great dolphin leaps behind the boat, a flight of birds soars upwards to pass the rock, in the clear air. Above all, from the bands of colour that border the wall at the top hang the regular loops of garlands, garlands of flowers and leaves and buds and berries, garlands which belong to maidens and to women, and which represent the flowery circle of the female life and sex. The top border of the wall is formed of horizontal stripes or ribands of colour that go all round the room, red and black and dull gold and blue and primrose, and these are the colours that occur invariably. Men are nearly always painted a darkish red, which is the colour of many Italians when they go naked in the sun, as the Etruscans went. Women are coloured paler, because women did not go naked in the sun.

At the end of the room, where there is a recess in the wall, is painted another rock rising from the sea, and on it a man with a sling is taking aim at the birds which rise scattering this way and that. A boat with a big paddle oar is holding off from the rock, a naked man amidships is giving a queer salute to the slinger, a man kneels over the bows with his back to the others, and is letting down a net. The prow of the boat has a beautifully painted eye, so the vessel shall see where it is going. In Syracuse you will see many a two-eyed boat to-day come swimming in to quay. One dolphin is diving down into the sea, one is leaping out. The birds fly, and the garlands hang from the border.

It is all small and gay and quick with life, spontaneous as only young life can be. If only it were not so much damaged, one would be happy, because here is the real Etruscan liveliness and naturalness. It is not impressive or grand. But if you are content with just a sense of the quick ripple of life, then here it is.

The little tomb is empty, save for its shadowy paintings. It has no bed of rock around it: only a deep niche for holding vases, perhaps vases of precious things. The sarcophagus stood on the floor, perhaps under the slinger on the end wall. And it stood alone, for this is an individual tomb, for one person only, as is usual in the older tombs of this necropolis.

In the gable triangle of the end wall, above the slinger and the boat, the space is filled in with one of the frequent Etruscan banqueting scenes of the dead. The dead man, sadly obliterated, reclines upon his banqueting couch with his flat wine-dish in his hand, resting on his elbow, and beside him, also half risen, reclines a handsome and jewelled lady in fine robes, apparently resting her left hand upon the naked breast of the man, and in her right holding up to him the garland—the garland of the female festive offering. Behind the man stands a naked slave-boy, perhaps with music, while another naked slave is just filling a wine-jug from a handsome amphora or wine-jar at the side. On the woman's side stands a maiden, apparently playing the flute: for a woman was supposed to play the flute at classic funerals; and beyond sit two maidens with garlands, one turning round to watch the banqueting pair, the other with her back to it all. Beyond the maidens in the corner are more garlands, and two birds, perhaps doves. On the wall behind the head of the banqueting lady is a problematic object, perhaps a bird-cage.

The scene is natural as life, and yet it has a heavy archaic fullness of meaning. It is the death-banquet; and at the same time it is the dead man banqueting in the underworld; for the underworld of the Etruscans was a gay place. While the living feasted out of doors, at the tomb of the dead, the dead himself feasted in like manner, with a lady to offer him garlands and slaves to bring him wine, away in the underworld. For the life on earth was so good, the life below could but be a continuance of it.

This profound belief in life, acceptance of life, seems characteristic of the Etruscans. It is still vivid in the painted tombs. There is a certain dance and glamour in all the movements, even in those of the naked slave-men. They are by no means downtrodden menials, let later Romans say what they will. The slaves in the tombs are surging with full life.

We come up the steps into the upper world, the sea-breeze and the sun. The old dog shambles to his feet, the guide blows out his lamp and locks the gate, we set off again, the dog trundling apathetic at his master's heels, the master speaking to him with that soft Italian familiarity which seems so very different from the spirit of Rome, the strong-willed Latin.

The guide steers across the hilltop, in the clear afternoon sun, towards another little hood of masonry. And one notices there is quite a number of these little gateways, built by the Government to cover the steps that lead down to the separate small tombs. It is utterly unlike Cerveteri, though the two places are not forty miles apart. Here there is no stately tumulus city, with its highroad between the tombs, and inside, rather noble, many-roomed houses of the dead. Here the little one-room tombs seem scattered at random on the hilltop, here and there: though probably, if excavations were fully carried out, here also we should find a regular city of the dead, with its streets and crossways. And probably each tomb had its little tumulus of piled earth, so that even above-ground there were streets of mounds with tomb entrances. But even so, it would be different from Cerveteri, from Caere; the mounds would be so small, the streets surely irregular. Anyhow, to-day there are scattered little one-room tombs, and we dive down into them just like rabbits popping down a hole. The place is a warren.

It is interesting to find it so different from Cerveteri. The Etruscans carried out perfectly what seems to be the Italian instinct: to have single, independent cities, with a certain surrounding territory, each district speaking its own dialect and feeling at home in its own little capital, yet the whole confederacy of city-states loosely linked together by a common religion and a more-or-less common interest. Even to-day Lucca is very different from Ferrara, and the language is hardly the same. In ancient Etruria this isolation of cities developing according to their own idiosyncrasy, within the loose union of a so-called nation, must have been complete. The contact between the plebs, the mass of the people, of Caere and Tarquinii must have been almost null. They were, no doubt, foreigners to one another. Only the Lucumones, the ruling sacred magistrates of noble family, the priests and the other nobles, and the merchants, must have kept up an intercommunion, speaking "correct" Etruscan, while the people, no doubt, spoke dialects varying so widely as to be different languages. To get any idea of the pre-Roman past we must break up the conception of oneness and uniformity, and see an endless confusion of differences.

We are diving down into another tomb, called, says the guide, the Tomb of the Leopards. Every tomb has been given a name, to distinguish it from its neighbours. The Tomb of the Leopards has two spotted leopards in the triangle of the end wall, between the roof-slopes. Hence its name.

The Tomb of the Leopards is a charming, cosy little room, and the paintings on the walls have not been so very much damaged. All the tombs are ruined to some degree by weather and vulgar vandalism, having been left and neglected like common holes, when they had been broken open again and rifled to the last gasp.

But still the paintings are fresh and alive: the ochre-reds and blacks and blues and blue-greens are curiously alive and harmonious on the creamy yellow walls. Most of the tomb walls have had a thin coat of stucco, but it is of the same paste as the living rock, which is fine and yellow, and weathers to a lovely creamy gold, a beautiful colour for a background.

The walls of this little tomb are a dance of real delight. The room seems inhabited still by Etruscans of the sixth century before Christ, a vivid, life-accepting people, who must have lived with real fullness. On come the dancers and the music-players, moving in a broad frieze towards the front wall of the tomb, the wall facing us as we enter from the dark stairs, and where the banquet is going on in all its glory. Above the banquet, in the gable angle, are the two spotted leopards, heraldically facing each other across a little tree. And the ceiling of rock has chequered slopes of red and black and yellow and blue squares, with a roof-beam painted with coloured circles, dark red and blue and yellow. So that all is colour, and we do not seem to be underground at all, but in some gay chamber of the past.

The dancers on the right wall move with a strange, powerful alertness onwards. The men are dressed only in a loose coloured scarf, or in the gay handsome chlamys[2] draped as a mantle. The *subulo* [leather worker] plays the double flute the Etruscans loved so much, touching the stops with big, exaggerated hands, the man behind him touches the seven-stringed lyre, the man in front turns round and signals with his left hand, holding a big wine-bowl in his right. And so they move on, on their long, sandalled feet, past the little berried olive trees, swiftly going with their limbs full of life, full of life to the tips.

This sense of vigorous, strong-bodied liveliness is characteristic of the Etruscans, and is somehow beyond art. You cannot think of art, but only of life itself, as if this were the very life of the Etruscans, dancing in their coloured wraps with massive yet exuberant naked limbs, ruddy from the air and the sea-light, dancing and fluting along through the little olive trees, out in the fresh day.

The end wall has a splendid banqueting scene. The feasters recline upon a checked or tartan couch-cover, on the banqueting couch, and in the open air, for they have little trees behind them. The six feasters are bold and full of life like the dancers, but they are strong, they keep their life so beautifully and richly inside them-

2. A cloak.

selves, they are not loose, they don't lose themselves even in their wild moments. They lie in pairs, man and woman, reclining equally on the couch, curiously friendly. The two end women are called *hetaerae*, courtesans; chiefly because they have yellow hair, which seems to have been a favourite feature in a woman of pleasure. The men are dark and ruddy, and naked to the waist. The women, sketched in on the creamy rock, are fair, and wear thin gowns, with rich mantles round their hips. They have a certain free bold look, and perhaps really are courtesans.

The man at the end is holding up, between thumb and forefinger, an egg, showing it to the yellow-haired woman who reclines next to him, she who is putting out her left hand as if to touch his breast. He, in his right hand, holds a large wine-dish, for the revel.

The next couple, man and fair-haired woman, are looking round and making the salute with the right hand curved over, in the usual Etruscan gesture. It seems as if they too are saluting the mysterious egg held up by the man at the end; who is, no doubt, the man who has died, and whose feast is being celebrated. But in front of the second couple a naked slave with a chaplet on his head is brandishing an empty wine-jug, as if to say he is fetching more wine. Another slave farther down is holding out a curious thing like a little axe, or fan. The last two feasters are rather damaged. One of them is holding up a garland to the other, but not putting it over his head, as they still put a garland over your head, in India, to honour you.

Above the banqueters, in the gable angle, the two great spotted male leopards hang out their tongues and face each other heraldically, lifting a paw, on either side of a little tree. They are the leopards or panthers of the underworld Bacchus,[3] guarding the exits and the entrances of the passion of life.

There is a mystery and a portentousness in the simple scenes which go deeper than commonplace life. It seems all so gay and light. Yet there is a certain weight, or depth of significance that goes beyond aesthetic beauty.

If one starts looking, there is much to see. But if one glances merely, there is nothing but a pathetic little room with unimposing, half-obliterated, scratchy little paintings in tempera.

There are many tombs. When we have seen one, up we go, a little bewildered, into the afternoon sun, across a tract of rough, tormented hill, and down again to the underground, like rabbits in a warren. The hilltop is really a warren of tombs. And gradually the underworld of the Etruscans becomes more real than the above day of the afternoon. One begins to live with the painted dancers and feasters and mourners, and to look eagerly for them. * * *

So we go on, seeing tomb after tomb, dimness after dimness, divided between the pleasure of finding so much and the disappointment that so little remains. One tomb after another, and nearly everything faded or eaten away, or corroded with alkali, or broken wilfully. Fragments of people at banquets, limbs that dance without dancers, birds that fly in nowhere, lions whose devouring heads are devoured away! Once it was all bright and dancing: the delight of the underworld; honouring the dead with wine, and flutes playing for a dance, and limbs whirling and pressing. And it was deep and sincere honour rendered to the dead and to the mysteries. It is contrary to our ideas; but the ancients had their own philosophy for it. * * *

The upper air is wide and pale, and somehow void. We cannot see either world any more, the Etruscan underworld nor the common day. Silently, tired, we walk

---

3. Roman name for Dionysus, Greek god of wine and excess.

back in the wind to the town, the old dog padding stoically behind. And the guide promises to take us to the other tombs to-morrow.

There is a haunting quality in the Etruscan representations. Those leopards with their long tongues hanging out: those flowing hippocampi; those cringing spotted deer, struck in flank and neck; they get into the imagination, and will not go out. And we see the wavy edge of the sea, the dolphins curving over, the diver going down clean, the little man climbing up the rock after him so eagerly. Then the men with beards who recline on the banqueting beds: how they hold up the mysterious egg! And the women with the conical head-dress, how strangely they lean forward, with caresses we no longer know! The naked slaves joyfully stoop to the wine-jars. Their nakedness is its own clothing, more easy than drapery. The curves of their limbs show pure pleasure in life, a pleasure that goes deeper still in the limbs of the dancers, in the big, long hands thrown out and dancing to the very ends of the fingers, a dance that surges from within, like a current in the sea. It is as if the current of some strong different life swept through them, different from our shallow current to-day: as if they drew their vitality from different depths that we are denied.

Yet in a few centuries they lost their vitality. The Romans took the life out of them. It seems as if the power of resistance to life, self-assertion and overbearing, such as the Romans knew: a power which must needs be moral, or carry morality with it, as a cloak for its inner ugliness: would always succeed in destroying the natural flowering of life. And yet there still are a few wild flowers and creatures.

The natural flowering of life! It is not so easy for human beings as it sounds. Behind all the Etruscan liveliness was a religion of life, which the chief men were seriously responsible for. Behind all the dancing was a vision, and even a science of life, a conception of the universe and man's place in the universe which made men live to the depth of their capacity.

To the Etruscan all was alive; the whole universe lived; and the business of man was himself to live amid it all. He had to draw life into himself, out of the wandering huge vitalities of the world. The cosmos was alive, like a vast creature. The whole thing breathed and stirred. Evaporation went up like breath from the nostrils of a whale, steaming up. The sky received it in its blue bosom, breathed it in and pondered on it and transmuted it, before breathing it out again. Inside the earth were fires like the heat in the hot red liver of a beast. Out of the fissures of the earth came breaths of other breathing, vapours direct from the living physical under-earth, exhalations carrying inspiration. The whole thing was alive, and had a great soul, or *anima*: and in spite of one great soul, there were myriad roving, lesser souls: every man, every creature and tree and lake and mountain and stream, was animate, had its own peculiar consciousness. And has it to-day.

The cosmos was one, and its *anima* was one; but it was made up of creatures. And the greatest creature was earth, with its soul of inner fire. The sun was only a reflection, or off-throw, or brilliant handful, of the great inner fire. But in juxtaposition to earth lay the sea, the waters that moved and pondered and held a deep soul of their own. Earth and waters lay side by side, together, and utterly different.

So it was. The universe, which was a single aliveness with a single soul, instantly changed, the moment you thought of it, and became a dual creature with two souls, fiery and watery, for ever mingling and rushing apart, and held by the great aliveness of the universe in an ultimate equilibrium. But they rushed together and they rushed apart, and immediately they became myriad: volcanoes and seas, then streams and mountains, trees, creatures, men. And everything was dual, or contained its own duality, for ever mingling and rushing apart. * * *

The people are not initiated into the cosmic ideas, nor into the awakened throb of more vivid consciousness. Try as you may, you can never make the mass of men throb with full awakenedness. They *cannot* be more than a little aware. So you must give them symbols, ritual and gesture, which will fill their bodies with life up to their own full measure. Any more is fatal. And so the actual knowledge must be guarded from them, lest knowing the formulae, without undergoing at all the experience that corresponds, they may become insolent and impious, thinking they have the all, when they have only an empty monkey-chatter. The esoteric knowledge will always be esoteric, since knowledge is an experience, not a formula. But it is foolish to hand out the formulae. A little knowledge is indeed a dangerous thing. No age proves it more than ours. Monkey-chatter is at last the most disastrous of all things.

The clue to the Etruscan life was the Lucumo, the religious prince. Beyond him were the priests and warriors. Then came the people and the slaves. People and warriors and slaves did not think about religion. There would soon have been no religion left. They felt the symbols and danced the sacred dances. For they were always kept *in touch*, physically, with the mysteries. The "touch" went from the Lucumo down to the merest slave. The blood-stream was unbroken. But "knowing" belonged to the high-born, the pure-bred.

So, in the tombs we find only the simple, uninitiated vision of the people. There is none of the priest-work of Egypt. The symbols are to the artist just wonder-forms, pregnant with emotion and good for decoration. It is so all the way through Etruscan art. The artists evidently were of the people, artisans. Presumably they were of the old Italic stock, and understood nothing of the religion in its intricate form, as it had come in from the East: though doubtless the crude principles of the official religion were the same as those of the primitive religion of the aborigines. The same crude principles ran through the religions of all the barbaric world of that time, Druid or Teutonic or Celtic.[4] But the newcomers in Etruria held secret the science and philosophy of their religion, and gave the people the symbols and the ritual, leaving the artists free to use the symbols as they would; which shows that there was no priest-rule.

Later, when scepticism came over all the civilised world, as it did after Socrates, the Etruscan religion began to die, Greeks and Greek rationalism flooded in, and Greek stories more or less took the place of the old Etruscan symbolic thought. Then again the Etruscan artists, uneducated, used the Greek stories as they had used the Etruscan symbols, quite freely, making them over again just to please themselves.

But one radical thing the Etruscan people never forgot, because it was in their blood as well as in the blood of their masters: and that was the mystery of the journey out of life, and into death; the death-journey, and the sojourn in the after-life. The wonder of their soul continued to play round the mystery of this journey and this sojourn.

In the tombs we see it, throes of wonder and vivid feeling throbbing over death. Man moves naked and glowing through the universe. Then comes death: he dives into the sea, he departs into the underworld. * * *

---

4. The Druids were religious leaders of the Celtic peoples who settled throughout Europe in pre-Roman times; the Teutons were Germanic peoples of northern Europe.

Birds fly portentously on the walls of the tombs. The artist must often have seen these priests, the augurs, with their crooked, bird-headed staffs in their hand, out on a high place watching the flight of larks or pigeons across the quarters of the sky. They were reading the signs and portents, looking for an indication, how they should direct the course of some serious affair. To us it may seem foolish. To them, hot-blooded birds flew through the living universe as feelings and premonitions fly through the breast of a man, or as thoughts fly through the mind. In their flight the suddenly roused birds, or the steady, far-coming birds, moved wrapped in a deeper consciousness, in the complex destiny of all things. And since all things corresponded in the ancient world, and man's bosom mirrored itself in the bosom of the sky, or *vice versa*, the birds were flying to a portentous goal, in the man's breast who watched, as well as flying their own way in the bosom of the sky. If the augur could see the birds flying *in his heart*, then he would know which way destiny too was flying for him.

The science of augury certainly was no exact science. But it was as exact as our sciences of psychology or political economy. And the augurs were as clever as our politicians, who also must practice divination, if ever they are to do anything worth the name. There is no other way when you are dealing with life. And if you live by the cosmos, you look in the cosmos for your clue. If you live by a personal god, you pray to him. If you are rational, you think things over. But it all amounts to the same thing in the end. Prayer, or thought or studying the stars, or watching the flight of birds, or studying the entrails of the sacrifice, it is all the same process, ultimately: of divination. All it depends on is the amount of *true*, sincere, religious concentration you can bring to bear on your object. An act of pure attention, if you are capable of it, will bring its own answer. And you choose that object to concentrate upon which will best focus your consciousness. Every real discovery made, every serious and significant decision ever reached, was reached and made by divination. The soul stirs, and makes an act of pure attention, and that is a discovery.

The science of the augur and the haruspex was not so foolish as our modern science of political economy.[5] If the hot liver of the victim cleared the soul of the haruspex, and made him capable of that ultimate inward attention which alone tells us the last thing we need to know, then why quarrel with the haruspex? To him, the universe was alive, and in quivering *rapport*. To him, the blood was conscious: he thought with his heart. To him, the blood was the red and shining stream of consciousness itself. Hence, to him, the liver, that great organ where the blood struggles and "overcomes death," was an object of profound mystery and significance. It stirred his soul and purified his consciousness; for it was also his victim. So he gazed into the hot liver, that was mapped out in fields and regions like the sky of stars, but these fields and regions were those of the red, shining consciousness that runs through the whole animal creation. And therefore it must contain the answer to his own blood's question. * * *

Turning from birds to animals, we find in the tombs the continual repetition of lion against deer. As soon as the world was created, according to the ancient idea, it took on duality. All things became dual, not only in the duality of sex, but in the

5. The augurs were official Roman diviners, who looked for signs in nature to determine whether the gods approved a proposed action; a haruspex was a diviner imported from Etruria.

polarity of action. This is the "impious pagan duality." It did not, however, contain the later pious duality of good and evil.

The leopard and the deer, the lion and the bull, the cat and the dove, or the partridge, these are part of the great duality, or polarity of the animal kingdom. But they do not represent good action and evil action. On the contrary, they represent the polarised activity of the divine cosmos, in its animal creation.

The treasure of treasures is the soul, which, in every creature, in every tree or pool, means that mysterious conscious point of balance or equilibrium between the two halves of the duality, the fiery and the watery. This mysterious point clothes itself in vividness after vividness from the right hand, and vividness after vividness from the left. And in death it does not disappear, but is stored in the egg, or in the jar, or even in the tree which brings it forth again.

But the soul itself, the conscious spark of every creature, is not dual; and being the immortal, it is also the altar on which our immortality and our duality is at last sacrificed.

So as the key-picture in the tombs, we have over and over again the heraldic beasts facing one another across the altar, or the tree, or the vase; and the lion is smiting the deer in the hip and throat. The deer is spotted, for day and night, the lion is dark and light the same.

The deer or lamb or goat or cow is the gentle creature with udder of overflowing milk and fertility; or it is the stag or ram or bull, the great father of the herd, with horns of power set obvious on the brow, and indicating the dangerous aspect of the beasts of fertility. These are the creatures of prolific, boundless procreation, the beasts of peace and increase. So even Jesus is the lamb.[6] And the endless, endless gendering of these creatures will fill all the earth with cattle till herds rub flanks all over the world, and hardly a tree can rise between.

But this must not be so, since they are only half, even of the animal creation. Balance must be kept. And this is the altar we are all sacrificed upon: it is even death; just as it is our soul and purest treasure.

So, on the other hand from the deer, we have lionesses and leopards. These, too, are male and female. These, too, have udders of milk and nourish young; as the wolf nourished the first Romans:[7] prophetically, as the destroyers of many deer, including the Etruscan. So these fierce ones guard the treasure and the gateway, which the prolific ones would squander or close up with too much gendering. They bite the deer in neck and haunch, where the great blood-streams run.

So the symbolism goes all through the Etruscan tombs. It is very much the symbolism of all the ancient world. But here it is not exact and scientific, as in Egypt. It is simple and rudimentary, and the artist plays with it as a child with fairy stories. Nevertheless, it is the symbolic element which rouses the deeper emotion, and gives the peculiarly satisfying quality to the dancing figures and the creatures. A painter like Sargent,[8] for example, is so clever. But in the end he is utterly uninteresting, a bore. He never has an inkling of his own triviality and silliness. One Etruscan leopard, even one little quail, is worth all the miles of him.

---

6. At the sight of Jesus, St. John the Baptist exclaimed, "Behold the Lamb of God, which taketh away the sins of the world" (John 1.29).

7. According to legend, Romulus and Remus, orphan founders of Rome, were suckled by a she-wolf.

8. John Singer Sargent (1856–1923), American painter.

———— ❧❦❧ ————

Evelyn Waugh
(1903–1966)

Few writers have demonstrated Evelyn Waugh's keen eye for the foibles and pretensions of the British aristocracy, while at the same time creating a gallery of vivid and memorable characters. He made a name for himself with his first novel *Decline and Fall* (1928), which is a thinly veiled autobiographical novel detailing Waugh's experiences at Oxford (which he left after three years without graduating) and as a schoolteacher (Waugh was fired from three schools in two years). The novel reveals a considerable gift as a social critic and satirist; all of the important writing Waugh would do for the next three and a half decades works in a similar vein.

Evelyn Waugh was born the son of Arthur Waugh, an influential late-Victorian literary critic and publisher (whose savage review of Eliot's *The Love Song of J. Alfred Prufrock* is reprinted on page 2423); reading and writing were central to Evelyn's childhood experience, as was an Anglican religious training. For a time, Waugh attempted to renounce both his religious faith and writing vocation; the publication of *Decline and Fall*, however, and his conversion to Catholicism (following the breakup of his brief first marriage) in 1930, confirmed both aspects of his calling. He went on to write a long string of critically and popularly successful novels, including *Vile Bodies* (1930), *Black Mischief* (1932), *A Handful of Dust* (1934), and *Put Out More Flags* (1942). His most enduringly popular novel (owing in part to its serialization by the BBC in 1980), is *Brideshead Revisited* (1945); a good deal of its interest lies in Waugh's vivid picture of the effete, aestheticist, homoerotic atmosphere of Oxford during his time there. His story *Cruise* (1936) is classic Waugh: biliously funny and sharply observant.

Cruise
Letters from a Young Lady of Leisure

S.S. *Glory of Greece*

Darling,

Well I said I would write and so I would have only goodness it was rough so didnt. Now everything is a bit more alright so I will tell you. Well as you know the cruise started at Monte Carlo[1] and when papa and all of us went to Victoria[2] we found that the tickets didnt include the journey there so Goodness how furious he was and said he wouldnt go but Mum said of course we must go and we said that too only papa had changed all his money into Liri or Franks on account of foreigners being so dishonest but he kept a shilling for the porter at Dover being methodical so then he had to change it back again and that set him wrong all the way to Monte Carlo and he wouldnt get me and Bertie a sleeper and wouldnt sleep himself in his through being so angry Goodness how Sad.

Then everything was much more alright the purser called him Colonel and he likes his cabin so he took Bertie to the casino and he lost and Bertie won and I think Bertie got a bit plastered at least he made a noise going to bed he's in the next cabin as if he were being sick and that was before we sailed. Bertie has got some books on Baroque art on account of his being at Oxford.

---

1. Gambling resort in southeast France.   2. London train station.

Well the first day it was rough and I got up and felt odd in the bath and the soap wouldnt work on account of salt water you see and came into breakfast and there was a list of so many things including steak and onions and there was a corking young man who said we are the only ones down may I sit here and it was going beautifully and he had steak and onions but it was no good I had to go back to bed just when he was saying there was nothing he admired so much about a girl as her being a good sailor goodness how sad.

The thing is not to have a bath and to be very slow in all movements. So next day it was Naples and we saw some Bertie churches and then that bit that got blown up in an earthquake and a poor dog killed they have a plaster cast of him goodness how sad.[3] Papa and Bertie saw some pictures we weren't allowed to see and Bill drew them for me afterwards and Miss P. tried to look too. I havent told you about Bill and Miss P. have I? Well Bill is rather old but clean looking and I dont suppose hes very old not really I mean and he's had a very disillusionary life on account of his wife who he says I wont say a word against but she gave him the raspberry with a foreigner and that makes him hate foreigners. Miss P. is called Miss Phillips and is lousy[4] she wears a yachting cap and is a bitch. And the way she makes up to the second officer is no ones business and its clear to the meanest intelligence he hates her but its part of the rules that all the sailors have to pretend to fancy the passengers. Who else is there? Well a lot of old ones. Papa is having a walk out with one called Lady Muriel something or other who knew uncle Ned. And there is a honeymoon couple very embarrassing. And a clergyman and a lovely pansy with a camera and white suit and lots of families from the industrial north.

So Bertie sends his love too. XXXXXX etc.

Mum bought a shawl and an animal made of lava.

POST-CARD

This is a picture of Taormina.[5] Mum bought a shawl here. V. funny because Miss P. got left as shed made chums only with second officer and he wasnt allowed ashore so when it came to getting into cars Miss P. had to pack in with a family from the industrial north.

S.S. *Glory of Greece*

Darling,

Hope you got P.C. from Sicily. The moral of that was not to make chums with sailors though who I've made a chum of is the purser who's different on account he leads a very cynical life with a gramophone in his cabin and as many cocktails as he likes and welsh rabbits[6] sometimes and I said but do you pay for all these drinks but he said no that's all right.

So we have three days at sea which the clergyman said is a good thing as it makes us all friendly but it hasn't made me friendly with Miss P. who won't leave poor Bill alone not taking any more chances of being left alone when she goes ashore. The purser says theres always someone like her on board in fact he says that about everyone except me who he says quite rightly is different goodness how decent.

---

3. Pompeii is being described, a city on the Bay of Naples buried by the eruption of Mount Vesuvius in A.D. 79. Much of the city has been excavated, including several erotic frescoes.

4. Lousy with money; rich.

5. Coastal town on the island of Sicily.

6. Welsh rabbit (or rarebit): English muffins covered with a sauce of melted cheese, beer, and mustard.

So there are deck games they are hell. And the day before we reach Haifa[7] there is to be a fancy dress dance. Papa is very good at the deck games expecially one called shuffle board and eats more than he does in London but I daresay its alright. You have to hire dresses for the ball from the barber I mean we do not you. Miss P. has brought her own. So I've thought of a v. clever thing at least the purser suggested it and that is to wear the clothes of one of the sailors I tried his on and looked a treat. Poor Miss P.

Bertie is madly unpop. he wont play any of the games and being plastered the other night too and tried to climb down a ventilator and the second officer pulled him out and the old ones at the captains table look *askance* at him. New word that. Literary yes? No?

So I think the pansy is writing a book he has a green fountain pen and green ink but I couldnt see what it was. XXXX Pretty good about writing you will say and so I am.

POST-CARD

This is a photograph of the Holyland and the famous sea of Gallillee. It is all v. Eastern with camels. I have a lot to tell you about the ball. *Such* goings on and will write very soon. Papa went off for the day with Lady M. and came back saying enchanting woman Knows the world.

S.S. Glory of Greece

Darling,

Well the Ball we had to come in to dinner in our clothes and everyone clapped as we came downstairs. So I was pretty late on account of not being able to make up my mind whether to wear the hat and in the end did and looked a corker. Well it was rather a faint clap for me considering so when I looked about there were about twenty girls and some women all dressed like me so how cynical the purser turns out to be. Bertie looked horribly dull as an apache. Mum and Papa were sweet. Miss P. had a ballet dress from the Russian ballet which couldnt have been more unsuitable so we had champagne for dinner and were jolly and they threw paper streamers and I threw mine before it was unrolled and hit Miss P. on the nose. Ha ha. So feeling matey I said to the steward isnt this fun and he said yes for them who hasnt got to clear it up goodness how Sad.

Well of course Bertie was plastered and went a bit far particularly in what he said to Lady M. then he sat in the cynical pursers cabin in the dark and cried so Bill and I found him and Bill gave him some drinks and what you do think he went off with Miss P. and we didnt see either of them again it only shows into what degradation the Demon Drink can drag you him I mean.

Then who should I meet but the young man who had steak and onions on the first morning and is called Robert and said I have been trying to meet you again all the voyage. Then I bitched him a bit goodness how Decent.

Poor Mum got taken up by Bill and he told her all about his wife and how she had disillusioned him with the foreigner so to-morrow we reach Port Said d.v.[8] which is latin in case you didn't know meaning God Willing and all go up the nile and to Cairo for a week.

---

7. Port city in Palestine, now Israel.   8. *Deo volente*: God willing.

Will send P.C. of Sphinx.
XXXXXX

POST-CARD

This is the Sphinx. Goodness how Sad.

POST-CARD

This is temple of someone. Darling I cant wait to tell you I'm engaged to Arthur. Arthur is the one I thought was a pansy. Bertie thinks egyptian art is v. inartistic.

POST-CARD

This is Tutankhamens v. famous Tomb. Bertie says it is vulgar and is engaged to Miss P. so hes not one to speak and I call her Mabel now. G how S. Bill wont speak to Bertie Robert wont speak to me Papa and Lady M. seem to have had a row there was a man with a snake in a bag also a little boy who told my fortune which was v. prosperous Mum bought a shawl.

POST-CARD

Saw this Mosque today. Robert is engaged to a new girl called something or other who is lousy.

S.S. *Glory of Greece*

Darling,

Well so we all came back from Egypt pretty excited and the cynical purser said what news and I said *news* well Im engaged to Arthur and Bertie is engaged to Miss P. and she is called Mabel now which is hardest of all to bear I said and Robert to a lousy girl and Papa has had a row with Lady M. and Bill has had a row with Bertie and Roberts lousy girl was awful to me and Arthur was sweet but the cynical purser wasnt a bit surprised on account he said people always get engaged and have quarrels on the Egyptian trip every cruise so I said I wasnt in the habit of getting engaged lightly thank you and he said I wasnt apparently in the habit of going to Egypt so I wont speak to him again nor will Arthur.

All love.

S.S. *Glory of Greece*

Sweet,

This is Algiers[9] *not* very eastern in fact full of frogs.[1] So it is all off with Arthur I was right about him at the first but who I am engaged to is Robert which is *much* better for all concerned really particularly Arthur on account of what I said originally first impressions always right. Yes? No? Robert and I drove about all day in the Botanic gardens and Goodness he was Decent. Bertie got plastered and had a row with Mabel—Miss P. again—so thats all right too and Robert's lousy girl spent all

9. Capital of Algeria, port city on the Mediterranean Sea.   1. Frenchmen.

day on board with second officer. Mum bought shawl. Bill told Lady M. about his dis-illusionment and she told Robert who said yes we all know so Lady M. said it was very unreticent of Bill and she had very little respect for him and didnt blame his wife or the foreigner.

Love.

POST-CARD

I forget what I said in my last letter but if I mentioned a lousy man called Robert you can take it as unsaid. This is still Algiers and Papa ate *dubious oysters* but is all right. Bertie went to a house full of tarts when he was plastered and is pretty unreticent about it as Lady M. would say.

POST-CARD

So now we are back and sang old lang syne is that how you spell it and I kissed Arthur but wont speak to Robert and he cried not Robert I mean Arthur so then Bertie apologised to most of the people hed insulted but Miss P. walked away pre-tending not to hear. Goodness what a bitch.

COMPANION READING

Monty Python:[1] Travel Agent

Fade up on close up of picture of Everest. Pull back to reveal travel agent's office.

BOUNDER Mount Everest, forbidding, aloof, terrifying. The highest place on earth. No I'm sorry we don't go there. No.
   By the time Bounder is saying his last sentence the camera has revealed the office and Bounder himself sitting at a desk. Bounder now replaces the telephone into which he has been speaking. After a pause the tourist—Mr Smoke-Too-Much—enters the office and approaches Mr Bounder's secretary.
TOURIST Good morning.
SECRETARY Oh good morning. (*Sexily.*) Do you want to go upstairs?
TOURIST What?
SECRETARY (*sexily*) Do you want to go upstairs? (*Brightly.*) Or have you come to arrange a holiday?
TOURIST Er . . . to arrange a holiday.
SECRETARY Oh, sorry.
TOURIST What's all this about going upstairs?
SECRETARY Oh, nothing, nothing. Now, where were you thinking of going?
TOURIST India.
SECRETARY Ah one of our adventure holidays!
TOURIST Yes!
SECRETARY Well you'd better speak to Mr Bounder about that. Mr Bounder, this gentleman is interested in the India Overland.

---

1. A popular British comedy troupe, made famous through their weekly BBC television series *Monty Python's Flying Circus* (1969–1974), as well as feature films such as *Monty Python and the Holy Grail* (1974) and *The Life of Brian* (1979). The performers in this skit, as presented on their television program, are Michael Palin (Bounder), Eric Idle (Tourist), and Carol Cleveland (Secretary).

Walks over to Bounder's desk where he is greeted by Bounder.

BOUNDER Ah. Good morning. I'm Bounder of Adventure.

TOURIST My name is Smoke-Too-Much.

BOUNDER What?

TOURIST My name is Smoke-Too-Much. Mr Smoke-Too-Much.

BOUNDER Well, you'd better cut down a bit then.

TOURIST What?

BOUNDER You'd better cut down a bit then.

TOURIST Oh I see! Cut down a bit, for Smoke-Too-Much.

BOUNDER Yes, ha ha . . . I expect you get people making jokes about your name all the time, eh?

TOURIST No, no actually. Actually, it never struck me before. Smoke . . . too . . . much!

BOUNDER Anyway, you're interested in one of our adventure holidays, eh?

TOURIST Yes. I saw your advert in the bolour supplement.

BOUNDER The what?

TOURIST The bolour supplement.

BOUNDER The colour supplement?[2]

TOURIST Yes. I'm sorry I can't say the letter "B."

BOUNDER C?

TOURIST Yes that's right. It's all due to a trauma I suffered when I was a spoolboy. I was attacked by a bat.

BOUNDER A cat?

TOURIST No a bat.

BOUNDER Can you say the letter "K."

TOURIST Oh yes. Khaki, king, kettle, Kuwait, Keble Bollege Oxford.

BOUNDER Why don't you say the letter "K" instead of the letter "C?"

TOURIST What you mean . . . spell bolour with a "K?"

BOUNDER Yes.

TOURIST Kolour. Oh, that's very good, I never thought of that.

BOUNDER Anyway, about the holiday.

TOURIST Well I saw your adverts in the paper and I've been on package tours several times, you see, and I decided that this was for me.

BOUNDER Ah good.

TOURIST Yes I quite agree with you, I mean what's the point of being treated like a sheep, I mean I'm fed up going abroad and being treated like sheep, what's the point of being carted round in buses, surrounded by sweaty mindless oafs from Kettering and Boventry in their cloth caps and their cardigans and their transistor radios and their "Sunday Mirrors," complaining about the tea, "Oh they don't make it properly here do they not like at home" stopping at Majorcan bodegas,[3] selling fish and chips and Watney's Red Barrel[4] and calamares[5] and two veg and sitting in cotton sun frocks squirting Timothy White's suncream all over their puffy raw swollen purulent flesh cos they "overdid it on the first day!"

BOUNDER *(agreeing patiently)* Yes. Absolutely, yes, I quite agree . . .

TOURIST And being herded into endless Hotel Miramars and Bellevueses and Bontinentals with their international luxury modern roomettes and their Watney's Red Barrel and their swimming pools full of fat German businessmen pretending

2. A photo insert in the Sunday newspaper.
3. Grocery stores on the island of Majorca, off the coast of Spain.
4. A popular English beer.
5. Squid.

to be acrobats and forming pyramids and frightening the children and barging in to the queues and if you're not at your table spot on seven you miss your bowl of Campbell's Cream of Mushroom soup, the first item on the menu of International Cuisine, and every Thursday night there's bloody cabaret in the bar featuring some tiny emaciated dago with nine-inch hips and some big fat bloated tart with her hair Brylcreemed down and a big arse presenting Flamenco for Foreigners.

BOUNDER (*beginning to get fed up*) Yes, yes, now . . .

TOURIST And then some adenoidal typists from Birmingham with diarrhoea and flabby white legs and hairy bandy-legged wop waiters called Manuel, and then, once a week there's an excursion to the local Roman ruins where you can buy cherryade and melted ice cream and bleedin' Watney's Red Barrel, and then one night they take you to a local restaurant with local colour and colouring and they show you there and you sit next to a party of people from Rhyl[6] who keeps singing "Torremolinos, Torremolinos," and complaining about the food, "Oh! It's so greasy isn't it?" and then you get cornered by some drunken greengrocer from Luton with an Instamatic and Dr Scholl sandals and Tuesday's "Daily Express" and he drones on and on and on about how Mr Smith should be running this country and how many languages Enoch Powell can speak and then he throws up all over the Cuba Libres.[7]

BOUNDER Will you be quiet please.

TOURIST And sending tinted postcards of places they don't know they haven't even visited, "to all at number 22, weather wonderful our room is marked with an "X". Wish you were here."

BOUNDER Shut up.

TOURIST "Food very greasy but we have managed to find this marvellous little place hidden away in the back streets."

BOUNDER Shut up!

TOURIST "Where you can even get Watney's Red Barrel and cheese and onion . . ."

BOUNDER Shut up!!!

TOURIST ". . . crisps[8] and the accordionist plays 'Maybe its because I'm a Londoner'" and spending four days on the tarmac at Luton[9] airport on a five-day package tour with nothing to eat but dried Watney's sandwiches . . .

BOUNDER Shut your bloody gob! I've had enough of this, I'm going to ring the police.

He dials and waits. Cut to a corner of a police station. One policeman is knitting, another is making a palm tree out of old newspapers. The phone rings.

KNITTING POLICEMAN Oh . . . take it off the hook. (*They do so.*)

Cut back to travel agent's office. The man is still going on, the travel agent looks crossly at the phone and puts it down. Then picks it up and dials again.

BOUNDER Hello operator, operator . . . I'm trying to get the police . . . the police yes, what? (*Takes his shoe off and looks inside.*) nine and a half, nine and a half, yes, yes . . . I see . . . well can you keep trying please . . .

Through all this the tourist is still going on:

TOURIST . . . and there's nowhere to sleep and the kids are vomiting and throwing up on the plastic flowers and they keep telling you it'll only be another hour although your plane is still in Iceland waiting to take some Swedes to Yugoslavia

---

6. A small town in Wales.
7. A drink made with rum and cola.

8. Potato chips.
9. Small city northwest of London.

before it can pick you up on the tarmac at 3 a.m. in the bloody morning and you sit on the tarmac till six because of "unforeseen difficulties," i.e. the permanent strike of Air Traffic Control in Paris, and nobody can go to the lavatory until you take off at eight, and when you get to Malaga airport everybody's swallowing Enterovioform tablets[1] and queuing for the toilets and when you finally get to the hotel there's no water in the taps, there's no water in the pool, there's no water in the bog and there's only a bleeding lizard in the bidet, and half the rooms are double-booked and you can't sleep anyway . . .

Graham Greene
1904–1991

In a 1945 essay on the French Catholic novelist François Mauriac, Graham Greene wrote that "a disaster overtook the English novel" with the death of Henry James; the cause of that disaster, Greene goes on to explain, was that "the religious sense was lost to the English novel, and with the religious sense went the sense of the importance of the human act." It is this importance of the human act that comprises the recurrent theme of Greene's own writing, and makes his voice a unique one in twentieth-century fiction.

Greene was one of six children born to Charles Henry Greene, the headmaster of Berkhamstead School, and his wife Marion R. Greene. Graham matriculated at his father's school in 1915 and graduated in 1921, when he went to Oxford, taking his degree in history. Like Evelyn Waugh, whom he would later befriend, Greene became a Roman Catholic convert in his twenties (he joined the church in 1926); after a few years as a literary journalist and an editor for the *Times* of London, Greene published his first novel, *The Man Within*, in 1929. His first self-consciously Catholic novel was *Brighton Rock* (1938); the religious framework through which Greene had come to view the world was now pressed into service as a framework for fictional narrative, and with impressive success. The novel makes clear the pattern that was to emerge in the majority of Greene's later fiction: that of "perfect evil walking the world where perfect good can never walk again"—a theme amply illustrated in his chilling 1936 story *A Chance for Mr Lever*.

Three novels of the 1940s and 1950s are today generally recognized as Greene's greatest: *The Power and the Glory* (1940), set in Mexico; *The Heart of the Matter* (1948), set, like *A Chance for Mr Lever*, in West Africa; and *The End of the Affair* (1951), which takes place back home in London during the Blitz. In all of Greene's most powerful work, his protagonist suffers a fall—a fall which, as the critic Richard Hauer Costa writes, often comes to seem a fortunate fall, stripping him of all disguises and pretense and hurling him headlong into a state of unmerited grace. The narrator who tells of Mr. Lever's fall, though, doubts that the hand of Providence has been at work.

A Chance for Mr Lever

Mr Lever knocked his head against the ceiling and swore. Rice was stored above, and in the dark the rats began to move. Grains of rice fell between the slats on to his Revelation suitcase, his bald head, his cases of tinned food, the little square box in which he kept his medicines. His boy had already set up the camp-bed and mosquito-net, and outside in the warm damp dark his folding table and chair. The thatched pointed huts streamed away towards the forest and a woman went from hut to hut carrying fire. The glow lit her old face, her sagging breasts, her tattooed diseased body.

1. Anti-diarrheal medicine.

It was incredible to Mr Lever that five weeks ago he had been in London.

He couldn't stand upright; he went down on hands and knees in the dust and opened his suitcase. He took out his wife's photograph and stood it on the chop-box; he took out a writing-pad and an indelible pencil: the pencil had softened in the heat and left mauve stains on his pyjamas. Then, because the light of the hurricane lamp disclosed cockroaches the size of black-beetles flattened against the mud wall, he carefully closed the suitcase. Already in ten days he had learnt that they'd eat anything—socks, shirts, the laces out of your shoes.

Mr Lever went outside; moths beat against his lamp, but there were no mosquitoes; he hadn't seen or heard one since he landed. He sat in a circle of light carefully observed. The blacks squatted outside their huts and watched him; they were friendly, interested, amused, but their strict attention irritated Mr Lever. He could feel the small waves of interest washing round him, when he began to write, when he stopped writing, when he wiped his damp hands with a handkerchief. He couldn't touch his pocket without a craning of necks.

Dearest Emily, he wrote, *I've really started now. I'll send this letter back with a carrier when I've located Davidson. I'm very well. Of course everything's a bit strange. Look after yourself, my dear, and don't worry.*

"Massa buy chicken," his cook said, appearing suddenly between the huts. A small stringy fowl struggled in his hands.

"Well," Mr Lever said, "I gave you a shilling, didn't I?"

"They no like," the cook said. "These low bush people."

"Why don't they like? It's good money."

"They want king's money," the cook said, handing back the Victorian shilling. Mr Lever had to get up, go back into his hut, grope for his money-box, search through twenty pounds of small change: there was no peace.

He had learnt that very quickly. He had to economize (the whole trip was a gamble which scared him); he couldn't afford hammock carriers. He would arrive tired out after seven hours of walking at a village of which he didn't know the name and not for a minute could he sit quietly and rest. He must shake hands with the chief, he must see about a hut, accept presents of palm wine he was afraid to drink, buy rice and palm oil for the carriers, give them salts and aspirin, paint their sores with iodine. They never left him alone for five minutes on end until he went to bed. And then the rats began, rushing down the walls like water when he put out the light, gambolling[1] among his cases.

I'm too old, Mr Lever told himself, *I'm too old,* writing damply, indelibly, *I hope to find Davidson tomorrow. If I do, I may be back almost as soon as this letter. Don't economize on the stout and milk, dear, and call in the doctor if you feel bad. I've got a premonition this trip's going to turn out well. We'll take a holiday, you need a holiday,* and staring ahead past the huts and the black faces and the banana trees towards the forest from which he had come, into which he would sink again next day, he thought, Eastbourne,[2] Eastbourne would do her a world of good; and he continued to write the only kind of lies he had ever told Emily, the lies which comforted. *I ought to draw at least three hundred in commission and expenses.* But it wasn't the sort of place where he'd been accustomed to sell heavy machinery; thirty years of it, up and down Europe and in the States, but never anything like this. He could hear his filter dripping in the hut, and somewhere somebody was playing something (he was so lost he hadn't

---

1. Frolicking.   2. A seaport in Sussex, England.

got the simplest terms to his hands), something monotonous, melancholy, superficial, a twanging of palm fibres which seemed to convey that you weren't happy, but it didn't matter, everything would always be the same.

Look after yourself, Emily, he repeated. It was almost the only thing he found himself capable of writing to her; he couldn't describe the narrow, steep, lost paths, the snakes sizzling away like flames, the rats, the dust, the naked diseased bodies. He was unbearably tired of nakedness. *Don't forget*—It was like living with a lot of cows.

"The chief," his boy whispered, and between the huts under a waving torch came an old stout man wearing a robe of native cloth and a battered bowler hat. Behind him his men carried six bowls of rice, a bowl of palm oil, two bowls of broken meat. "Chop for the labourers," the boy explained, and Mr Lever had to get up and smile and nod and try to convey without words that he was pleased, that the chop was excellent, that the chief would get a good dash[3] in the morning. At first the smell had been almost too much for Mr Lever.

"Ask him," he said to his boy, "if he's seen a white man come through here lately. Ask him if a white man's been digging around here. Damn it," Mr Lever burst out, the sweat breaking on the backs of his hands and on his bald head, "ask him if he's seen Davidson?"

"Davidson?"

"Oh, hell," Mr Lever said, "you know what I mean. The white man I'm looking for."

"White man?"

"What do you imagine I'm here for, eh? White man? Of course white man. I'm not here for my health." A cow coughed, rubbed its horns against the hut and two goats broke through between the chief and him, upsetting the bowls of meat scraps; nobody cared, they picked the meat out of the dust and dung.

Mr Lever sat down and put his hands over his face, fat white well-cared-for hands with wrinkles of flesh over the rings. He felt too old for this.

"Chief say no white man been here long time."

"How long?"

"Chief say not since he pay hut tax."

"How long's that?"

"Long long time."

"Ask him how far is it to Greh, tomorrow."

"Chief say too far."

"Nonsense," Mr Lever said.

"Chief say too far. Better stay here. Fine town. No humbug."

Mr Lever groaned. Every evening there was the same trouble. The next town was always too far. They would invent any excuse to delay him, to give themselves a rest.

"Ask the chief how many hours—?"

"Plenty, plenty." They had no idea of time.

"This fine chief. Fine chop. Labourers tired. No humbug."

"We are going on," Mr Lever said.

"This fine town. Chief say—"

He thought: if this wasn't the last chance, I'd give up. They nagged him so, and suddenly he longed for another white man (not Davidson, he daren't say anything to Davidson) to whom he could explain the desperation of his lot. It wasn't fair that a

3. Tip.

man, after thirty years' commercial travelling, should need to go from door to door asking for a job. He had been a good traveller, he had made money for many people, his references were excellent, but the world had moved on since his day. He wasn't streamlined; he certainly wasn't streamlined. He had been ten years retired when he lost his money in the depression.

Mr Lever walked up and down Victoria Street showing his references. Many of the men knew him, gave him cigars, laughed at him in a friendly way for wanting to take on a job at his age ("I can't somehow settle at home. The old warhorse you know . . . ."), cracked a joke or two in the passage, went back that night to Maidenhead silent in the first-class carriage, shut in with age and ruin and how bad things were and poor devil his wife's probably sick.

It was in the rather shabby little office off Leadenhall Street that Mr Lever met his chance. It called itself an engineering firm, but there were only two rooms, a typewriter, a girl with gold teeth and Mr Lucas, a thin narrow man with a tic in one eyelid. All through the interview the eyelid flickered at Mr Lever. Mr Lever had never before fallen so low as this.

But Mr Lucas struck him as reasonably honest. He put "all his cards on the table." He hadn't got any money, but he had expectations; he had the handling of a patent. It was a new crusher. There was money in it. But you couldn't expect the big trusts to change over their machinery now. Things were too bad. You'd got to get in at the start, and that was where—why, that was where this chief, the bowls of chop, the nagging and the rats and the heat came in. They called themselves a republic, Mr Lucas said, he didn't know anything about that, they were not as black as they were painted, he supposed (ha, ha, nervously, ha, ha); anyway, this company had slipped agents over the border and grabbed a concession: gold and diamonds. He could tell Mr Lever in confidence that the trust was frightened of what they'd found. Now an enterprising man could just slip across (Mr Lucas liked the word slip, it made everything sound easy and secret) and introduce this new crusher to them: it would save them thousands when they started work, there'd be a fat commission, and afterwards, with that start . . . There was a fortune for them all.

"But can't you fix it up in Europe?"

Tic, tic, went Mr Lucas's eyelid. "A lot of Belgians; they are leaving all decisions to the man on the spot. An Englishman called Davidson."

"How about expenses?"

"That's the trouble," Mr Lucas said. "We are only beginning. What we want is a partner. We can't afford to send a man. But if you like a gamble . . . Twenty per cent commission."

"Chief say excuse him." The carriers squatted round the basins and scooped up the rice in their left hands. "Of course. Of course," Mr Lever said absent-mindedly. "Very kind, I'm sure."

He was back out of the dust and dark, away from the stink of goats and palm oil and whelping bitches, back among the rotarians and lunch at Stone's, "the pint of old," and the trade papers; he was a good fellow again, finding his way back to Golders Green just a bit lit;[4] his masonic emblem rattled on his watch-chain, and he bore with him from the tube station to his house in Finchley Road a sense of companionship, of broad stories and belches, a sense of bravery.

4. Tipsy.

He needed all his bravery now; the last of his savings had gone into the trip. After thirty years he knew a good thing when he saw it, and he had no doubts about the new crusher. What he doubted was his ability to find Davidson. For one thing there weren't any maps; the way you travelled in the Republic was to write down a list of names and trust that someone in the villages you passed would understand and know the route. But they always said "Too far." Good fellowship wilted before the phrase.

"Quinine,"[5] Mr Lever said. "Where's my quinine?" His boy never remembered a thing; they just didn't care what happened to you; their smiles meant nothing, and Mr Lever, who knew better than anyone the value of a meaningless smile in business, resented their heartlessness, and turned towards the dilatory boy an expression of disappointment and dislike.

"Chief say white man in bush five hours away."

"That's better," Mr Lever said. "It must be Davidson. He's digging for gold?"

"Ya. White man dig for gold in bush."

"We'll be off early tomorrow," Mr Lever said.

"Chief say better stop this town. Fever humbug white man."

"Too bad," Mr Lever said, and he thought with pleasure: my luck's changed. He'll want help. He won't refuse me a thing. A friend in need is a friend indeed, and his heart warmed towards Davidson, seeing himself arrive like an answer to prayer out of the forest, feeling quite biblical and vox humana.[6] He thought: Prayer. I'll pray tonight, that's the kind of thing a fellow gives up, but it pays, there's something in it, remembering the long agonizing prayer on his knees, by the sideboard, under the decanters, when Emily went to hospital.

"Chief say white man dead."

Mr Lever turned his back on them and went into his hut. His sleeve nearly over-turned the hurricane lamp. He undressed quickly, stuffing his clothes into a suitcase away from the cockroaches. He wouldn't believe what he had been told; it wouldn't pay him to believe. If Davidson were dead, there was nothing he could do but return; he had spent more than he could afford; he would be a ruined man. He supposed that Emily might find a home with her brother, but he could hardly expect her brother—he began to cry, but you couldn't have told in the shadowy hut the difference between sweat and tears. He knelt down beside his camp-bed and mosquito-net and prayed on the dust of the earth floor. Up till now he had always been careful never to touch ground with his naked feet for fear of jiggers;[7] there were jiggers everywhere, they only waited an opportunity to dig themselves in under the toe-nails, lay their eggs and multiply.

"O God," Mr Lever prayed, "don't let Davidson be dead; let him be just sick and glad to see me." He couldn't bear the idea that he might not any longer be able to support Emily. "O God, there's nothing I wouldn't do." But that was an empty phrase; he had no real notion as yet of what he would do for Emily. They had been happy together for thirty-five years; he had never been more than momentarily unfaithful to her when he was lit after a rotarian dinner and egged on by the boys; whatever skirt he'd been with in his time, he had never for a moment imagined that he could be happy married to anyone else. It wasn't fair if, just when you were old and needed each other most, you lost your money and couldn't keep together.

---

5. Chemical compound taken to fight off malaria.
6. A type of pipe organ.

7. A tropical flea that burrows under the skin.

But of course Davidson wasn't dead. What would he have died of? The blacks were friendly. People said the country was unhealthy, but he hadn't so much as heard a mosquito. Besides, you didn't die of malaria; you just lay between the blankets and took quinine and felt like death and sweated it out of you. There was dysentery, but Davidson was an old campaigner; you were safe if you boiled and filtered the water. The water was poison even to touch; it was unsafe to wet your feet because of guinea worm,[8] but you didn't die of guinea worm.

Mr Lever lay in bed and his thoughts went round and round and he couldn't sleep. He thought: you don't die of a thing like guinea worm. It makes a sore on your foot, and if you put your foot in water you can see the eggs dropping out. You have to find the end of the worm, like a thread of cotton, and wind it round a match and wind it out of your leg without breaking; it stretches as high as the knee. I'm too old for this country, Mr Lever thought.

Then his boy was beside him again. He whispered urgently to Mr Lever through the mosquito-net. "Massa, the labourers say they go home."

"Go home?" Mr Lever asked wearily; he had heard it so often before. "Why do they want to go home? What is it now?" but he didn't really want to hear the latest squabble: that the Bande men were never sent to carry water because the headman was a Bande, that someone had stolen an empty treacle tin and sold it in the village for a penny, that someone wasn't made to carry a proper load, that the next day's journey was "too far." He said, "Tell 'em they can go home. I'll pay them off in the morning. But they won't get any dash. They'd have got a good dash if they'd stayed." He was certain it was just another try-on; he wasn't as green as all that.

"Yes, massa. They no want dash."

"What's that?"

"They frightened fever humbug them like white man."

"I'll get carriers in the village. They can go home."

"Me too, massa."

"Get out," Mr Lever said; it was the last straw; "get out and let me sleep." The boy went at once, obedient even though a deserter, and Mr Lever thought: sleep, what a hope. He lifted the net and got out of bed (barefooted again: he didn't care a damn about the jiggers) and searched for his medicine box. It was locked, of course, and he had to open his suitcase and find the key in a trouser pocket. His nerves were more on edge than ever by the time he found the sleeping tablets and he took three of them. That made him sleep, heavily and dreamlessly, though when he woke he found that something had made him fling out his arms and open the net. If there had been a single mosquito in the place, he'd have been bitten, but of course there wasn't one.

He could tell at once that the trouble hadn't blown over. The village—he didn't know its name—was perched on a hilltop; east and west the forest flowed out beneath the little plateau; to the west it was a dark unfeatured mass like water, but in the east you could already discern the unevenness, the great grey cotton trees lifted above the palms. Mr Lever was always called before dawn, but no one had called him. A few of his carriers sat outside a hut sullenly talking; his boy was with them. Mr Lever went back inside and dressed; he thought all the time, I must be firm, but he was scared, scared of being deserted, scared of being made to return.

---

8. A worm, growing up to several feet long, which lives under the skin.

When he came outside again the village was awake: the women were going down the hill to fetch water, winding silently past the carriers, past the flat stones where the chiefs were buried, the little grove of trees where the rice birds, like green and yellow canaries, nested. Mr Lever sat down on his folding chair among the chickens and whelping bitches and cow dung and called his boy. He took "a strong line"; but he didn't know what was going to happen. "Tell the chief I want to speak to him," he said.

There was some delay; the chief wasn't up yet, but presently he appeared in his blue and white robe, setting his bowler hat straight. "Tell him," Mr Lever said, "I want carriers to take me to the white man and back. Two days."

"Chief no agree," the boy said.

Mr Lever said furiously, "Damn it, if he doesn't agree, he won't get any dash from me, not a penny." It occurred to him immediately afterwards how hopelessly dependent he was on these people's honesty. There in the hut for all to see was his money-box; they had only to take it. This wasn't a British or French colony; the blacks on the coast wouldn't bother, could do nothing if they did bother, because a stray Englishman had been robbed in the interior.

"Chief say how many?"

"It's only for two days," Mr Lever said. "I can do with six."

"Chief say how much?"

"Sixpence a day and chop."

"Chief no agree."

"Ninepence a day then."

"Chief say too far. A shilling."

"All right, all right," Mr Lever said, "A shilling then. You others can go home if you want to. I'll pay you off now, but you won't get any dash, not a penny."

He had never really expected to be left, and it gave him a sad feeling of loneliness to watch them move sullenly away (they were ashamed of themselves) down the hill to the west. They hadn't any loads, but they weren't singing; they drooped silently out of sight, his boy with them, and he was alone with his pile of boxes and the chief who couldn't talk a word of English. Mr Lever smiled tremulously.

It was ten o'clock before his new carriers were chosen; he could tell that none of them wanted to go, and they would have to walk through the heat of the middle day if they were to find Davidson before it was dark. He hoped the chief had explained properly where they were going; he couldn't tell; he was completely shut off from them, and when they started down the eastward slope, he might just as well have been alone.

They were immediately caught up in the forest. Forest conveys a sense of wildness and beauty, of an active natural force, but this Liberian forest was simply a dull green wilderness. You passed, on the path a foot or so wide, through an endless back garden of tangled weeds; it didn't seem to be growing round you, so much as dying. There was no life at all, except for a few large birds whose wings creaked overhead through the invisible sky like an unoiled door. There was no view, no way out for the eyes, no change of scene. It wasn't the heat that tired, so much as the boredom; you had to think of things to think about; but even Emily failed to fill the mind for more than three minutes at a time. It was a relief, a distraction, when the path was flooded and Mr Lever had to be carried on a man's back. At first he had disliked the strong bitter smell (it reminded him of a breakfast food he was made to eat as a child), but he soon got over that. Now he was unaware that they smelt at all; any more than he was aware that the great swallow-tailed butterflies, which clustered at the water's edge and rose in green clouds round his waist, were beautiful. His senses were dulled and registered very little except his boredom.

But they did register a distinct feeling of relief when his leading carrier pointed to a rectangular hole dug just off the path. Mr Lever understood. Davidson had come this way. He stopped and looked at it. It was like a grave dug for a small man, but it went down deeper than graves usually do. About twelve feet below there was black water, and a few wooden props which held the sides from slipping were beginning to rot; the hole must have been dug since the rains. It didn't seem enough, that hole, to have brought out Mr Lever with his plans and estimates for a new crusher. He was used to big industrial concerns, the sight of pitheads, the smoke of chimneys, the dingy rows of cottages back to back, the leather armchair in the office, the good cigar, the masonic hand-grips, and again it seemed to him, as it had seemed in Mr Lucas's office, that he had fallen very low. It was as if he was expected to do business beside a hole a child had dug in an over-grown and abandoned back garden; percentages wilted in the hot damp air. He shook his head; he mustn't be discouraged; this was an old hole. Davidson had probably done better since. It was only common sense to suppose that the gold rift which was mined at one end in Nigeria, at the other in Sierra Leone, would pass through the republic. Even the biggest mines had to begin with a hole in the ground. The company (he had talked to the directors in Brussels) were quite confident: all they wanted was the approval of the man on the spot that the crusher was suitable for local conditions. A signature, that was all he had to get, he told himself, staring down into the puddle of black water.

Five hours, the chief had said, but after six hours they were still walking. Mr Lever had eaten nothing; he wanted to get to Davidson first. All through the heat of the day he walked. The forest protected him from the direct sun, but it shut out the air, and the occasional clearings, shrivelled though they were in the vertical glare, seemed cooler than the shade because there was a little more air to breathe. At four o'clock the heat diminished, but he began to fear they wouldn't reach Davidson before dark. His foot pained him; he had caught a jigger the night before; it was as if someone were holding a lighted match to his toe. Then at five they came on a dead black.

Another rectangular hole in a small cleared space among the dusty greenery had caught Mr Lever's eye. He peered down and was shocked to see a face return his stare, white eyeballs like phosphorus in the black water. The black had been bent almost double to fit him in; the hole was really too small to be a grave, and he had swollen. His flesh was like a blister you could prick with a needle. Mr Lever felt sick and tired; he might have been tempted to return if he could have reached the village before dark, but now there was nothing to do but go on; the carriers luckily hadn't seen the body. He waved them forward and stumbled after them among the roots, fighting his nausea. He fanned himself with his sun helmet; his wide fat face was damp and pale. He had never seen an uncared-for body before; his parents he had seen carefully laid out with closed eyes and washed faces; they "fell asleep" quite in accordance with their epitaphs, but you couldn't think of sleep in connexion with the white eyeballs and the swollen face. Mr Lever would have liked very much to say a prayer, but prayers were out of place in the dead drab forest; they simply didn't "come."

With the dusk a little life did waken: something lived in the dry weeds and brittle trees, if only monkeys. They chattered and screamed all round you, but it was too dark to see them; you were like a blind man in the centre of a frightened crowd who wouldn't say what scared them. The carriers too were frightened. They ran under their fifty-pound loads behind the dipping light of the hurricane lamp, their huge flat carriers' feet flapping in the dust like empty gloves. Mr Lever listened nervously for mosquitoes; you would have expected them to be out by now, but he didn't hear one.

Then at the top of a rise above a small stream they came on Davidson. The ground had been cleared in a square of twelve feet and a small tent pitched; he had dug another hole; the scene came dimly into view as they climbed the path; the chop-boxes piled outside the tent, the syphon of soda water, the filter, an enamel basin. But there wasn't a light, there wasn't a sound, the flaps of the tent were not closed, and Mr Lever had to face the possibility that after all the chief might have told the truth.

Mr Lever took the lamp and stooped inside the tent. There was a body on the bed. At first Mr Lever thought Davidson was covered with blood, but then he realized it was a black vomit which stained his shirt and khaki shorts, the fair stubble on his chin. He put out a hand and touched Davidson's face, and if he hadn't felt a slight breath on his palm he would have taken him for dead; his skin was so cold. He moved the lamp closer, and now the lemon-yellow face told him all he wanted to know: he hadn't thought of that when his boy said fever. It was quite true that a man didn't die of malaria, but an odd piece of news read in New York in '98 came back to mind: there had been an outbreak of yellow jack[9] in Rio and ninety-four per cent of the cases had been fatal. It hadn't meant anything to him then, but it did now. While he watched, Davidson was sick, quite effortlessly; he was like a tap out of which something flowed.

It seemed at first to Mr Lever to be the end of everything, of his journey, his hopes, his life with Emily. There was nothing he could do for Davidson, the man was unconscious, there were times when his pulse was so low and irregular that Mr Lever thought that he was dead until another black stream spread from his mouth; it was no use even cleaning him. Mr Lever laid his own blankets over the bed on top of David-son's because he was so cold to the touch, but he had no idea whether he was doing the right, or even the fatally wrong, thing. The chance of survival, if there were any chance at all, depended on neither of them. Outside his carriers had built a fire and were cooking the rice they had brought with them. Mr Lever opened his folding chair and sat by the bed. He wanted to keep awake: it seemed right to keep awake. He opened his case and found his unfinished letter to Emily. He sat by Davidson's side and tried to write, but he could think of nothing but what he had already written too often: *Look after yourself. Don't forget that stout and milk.*

He fell asleep over his pad and woke at two and thought that Davidson was dead. But he was wrong again. He was very thirsty and missed his boy. Always the first thing his boy did at the end of a march was to light a fire and put on a kettle; after that, by the time his table and chair were set up, there was water ready for the filter. Mr Lever found half a cup of soda water left in Davidson's syphon; if it had been only his health at stake he would have gone down to the stream, but he had Emily to remember. There was a typewriter by the bed, and it occurred to Mr Lever that he might just as well begin to write his report of failure now; it might keep him awake; it seemed disrespectful to the dying man to sleep. He found paper under some letters which had been typed and signed but not sealed. Davidson must have been taken ill very suddenly. Mr Lever wondered whether it was he who had crammed the black into the hole; his boy perhaps, for there was no sign of a servant. He balanced the typewriter on his knee and headed the letter "In Camp near Greh."

It seemed to him unfair that he should have come so far, spent so much money, worn out a rather old body to meet his inevitable ruin in a dark tent beside a dying man, when he could have met it just as well at home with Emily in the plush parlour. The thought of the prayers he had uselessly uttered on his knees by the camp-bed among the jiggers, the rats and the cockroaches made him rebellious. A mosquito, the first he had heard, went humming round the tent. He slashed at it savagely; he would-n't have recognized himself among the rotarians. He was lost and he was set free.

9. Yellow fever, a tropical disease transmitted by mosquitoes.

Moralities were what enabled a man to live happily and successfully with his fellows, but Mr Lever wasn't happy and he wasn't successful, and his only fellow in the little stuffy tent wouldn't be troubled by Untruth in Advertising or by Mr Lever coveting his neighbour's oxen. You couldn't keep your ideas intact when you discovered their geographical nature. The Solemnity of Death: death wasn't solemn; it was a lemon-yellow skin and a black vomit. Honesty is the Best Policy: he saw quite suddenly how false that was. It was an anarchist who sat happily over the typewriter, an anarchist who recognized nothing but one personal relationship, his affection for Emily. Mr Lever began to type: *I have examined the plans and estimates of the new Lucas crusher . . .*

Mr Lever thought with savage happiness: I win. This letter would be the last the company would hear from Davidson. The junior partner would open it in the dapper Brussels office; he would tap his false teeth with a Waterman pen and go in to talk to M. Golz. *Taking all these factors into consideration I recommend acceptance. . . .* They would telegraph to Lucas. As for Davidson, that trusted agent of the company would have died of yellow fever at some never accurately determined date. Another agent would come out, and the crusher . . . Mr Lever carefully copied Davidson's signature on a spare sheet of paper. He wasn't satisfied. He turned the original upside-down and copied it that way, so as not to be confused by his own idea of how a letter should be formed. That was better, but it didn't satisfy him. He searched until he found Davidson's own pen and began again to copy and copy the signature. He fell asleep copying it and woke again an hour later to find the lamp was out; it had burnt up all the oil. He sat there beside Davidson's bed till daylight; once he was bitten by a mosquito in the ankle and clapped his hand to the place too late: the brute went humming out. With the light Mr Lever saw that Davidson was dead. "Dear, dear," he said. "Poor fellow." He spat out with the words, quite delicately in a corner, the bad morning taste in his mouth. It was like a little sediment of his conventionality.

Mr Lever got two of his carriers to cram Davidson tidily into his hole. He was no longer afraid of them or of failure or of separation. He tore up his letter to Emily. It no longer represented his mood in its timidity, its secret fear, its gentle fussing phrases, *Don't forget the stout. Look after yourself.* He would be home as soon as the letter, and they were going to do things together now they'd never dreamt of doing. The money for the crusher was only the beginning. His ideas stretched farther now than Eastbourne, they stretched as far as Switzerland; he had a feeling that, if he really let himself go, they'd stretch as far as the Riviera. How happy he was on what he thought of as "the trip home." He was freed from what had held him back through a long pedantic career, the fear of a conscious fate that notes the dishonesty, notes the skirt in Piccadilly, notes the glass too many of Stone's special. Now he had said Boo to that goose . . . .

But you who are reading this, who know so much more than Mr Lever, who can follow the mosquito's progress from the dead swollen black to Davidson's tent, to Mr Lever's ankle, you may possibly believe in God, a kindly god tender towards human frailty, ready to give Mr Lever three days of happiness, three days off the galling chain, as he carried back through the forest his amateurish forgeries and the infection of yellow fever in the blood. The story might very well have encouraged my faith in that loving omniscience if it had not been shaken by personal knowledge of the drab forest through which Mr Lever now went so merrily, where it is impossible to believe in any spiritual life, in anything outside the nature dying round you, the shrivelling of the weeds. But of course, there are two opinions about everything; it was Mr Lever's favourite expression, drinking beer in the Ruhr, Pernod[1] in Lorraine, selling heavy machinery.

1936

---

1. A licorice-flavored liqueur.

P. G. Wodehouse
1881–1975

Pelham Grenville Wodehouse—"Plum" to his many friends—wrote ninety-eight books over a period of seventy-five years, virtually inventing the modern comic novel. He created a world of feckless aristocrats and energetic young adventurers, detailing their exploits in a rich and supple prose that blends classical rhythms with the latest British and American slang. Immensely popular as a novelist—with sales of over fifty million volumes at last count, in more than thirty languages—Wodehouse was equally active as a writer for Broadway and the London stage, and he became the first truly trans-Atlantic writer, shuttling back and forth between England and America in company with his productions. From 1915 through the 1930s, Wodehouse had a major influence on the development of musical theater; he had no fewer than five shows running at once on Broadway in 1917.

All these successes followed hard work under difficult circumstances. Born in England, Wodehouse spent several years in Hong Kong, where his father was a magistrate; his parents then sent him back to England for boarding school, and he saw little of his parents thereafter, often spending vacations with some of his twenty aunts—most of them (he later claimed) menaces to society. As he was completing high school, his father suffered sunstroke and returned to England on disability, unable to afford to send his son to college. Wodehouse went to work as a bank clerk, writing reams of stories in the evenings. He sold his first story in 1901, got a part-time job as a humor columnist in 1902, and quit his bank job on the spot.

His early stories centered on British boarding-school life, satirizing the students' jockeyings for popularity and the teachers'—always futile—efforts to project authority. In 1915 he had his first great commercial success with *Pigs Have Wings*, mining what would prove to be his lasting territory of choice, a half-imaginary world of eccentric minor nobility bumbling about in their country homes, surrounded by censorious servants, witty con artists, elderly aunts, and houseguests like the eminent looney-doctor Sir Roderick Glossop and his drippy daughter Honoria, who thinks the stars are God's daisy chain. Struggling for a foothold in this world are usually two young people, Wodehouse's typical hero and heroine: an amiable but somewhat passive young man and an energetic and imaginative young woman, in this instance Amelia Bassett, who must persuade her formidable mother Lady Bassett that her young swain is not the "pipsqueak" she believes him to be. Explorer, lion-hunter, and detective story fanatic, Lady Bassett has dozens of analogues in other Wodehouse stories, as well as a clear family resemblance to the "blocking characters" of stage comedies, like Wilde's Lady Bracknell and Shaw's Lady Britomart, who stand in the way of the young couple's desires.

Wodehouse's fiction drew on his extensive stage experience, and he composed his stories with an eye for staging and a keen ear for dialogue. He never tired of playing variations on the stock elements of popular farce, and as early as 1928 a reviewer accused him of plagiarizing his own work. Wodehouse countered this charge by admitting it, in the preface to his next book, *Fish Preferred*: "A certain critic—for such men, I regret to say, do exist—made a nasty remark about my last novel that it contained 'all the old Wodehouse characters under different names.' . . . With my superior intelligence I have outgeneraled the man this time by putting in all the old Wodehouse characters under the same names. Pretty silly it will make him feel, I rather fancy."

Strychnine in the Soup, from *Meet Mr. Mulliner* (1927), takes the pleasures of popular fiction as its own theme, its plot turning on the characters' mutual obsession with the latest tale by their favorite detective-story writer. The story is set in a frame of storytelling: it is one of a series of tales by Mr. Mulliner, a raconteur who regales his club companions (named for their favorite drinks) with the adventures of his many nieces and nephews. In Wodehouse's world, literary and social conventions intermingle, and the pleasures of storytelling can bridge the gaps between classes, genders, and generations. A master of convention and a mocker of conventionality, Wodehouse himself creates an artificial paradise, shot through with reality.

Strychnine in the Soup

From the moment the Draught Stout entered the bar parlor of the Anglers' Rest, it had been obvious that he was not his usual cheery self. His face was drawn and twisted, and he sat with bowed head in a distant corner by the window, contributing nothing to the conversation which, with Mr Mulliner as its center, was in progress around the fire. From time to time he heaved a hollow sigh.

A sympathetic Lemonade and Angostura, putting down his glass, went across and laid a kindly hand on the sufferer's shoulder.

"What is it, old man?" he asked. "Lost a friend?"

"Worse," said the Draught Stout. "A mystery novel. Got halfway through it on the journey down here, and left it in the train."

"My nephew Cyril, the interior decorator," said Mr Mulliner, "once did the very same thing. These mental lapses are not infrequent."

"And now," proceeded the Draught Stout, "I'm going to have a sleepless night, wondering who poisoned Sir Geoffrey Tuttle, Bart."

"The bart. was poisoned, was he?"

"You never said a truer word. Personally, I think it was the vicar who did him in. He was known to be interested in strange poisons."

Mr Mulliner smiled indulgently.

"It was not the vicar," he said. "I happen to have read *The Murglow Manor Mystery*. The guilty man was the plumber."

"What plumber?"

"The one who comes in Chapter Two to mend the shower bath. Sir Geoffrey had wronged his aunt in the year '96, so he fastened a snake in the nozzle of the shower bath with glue; and when Sir Geoffrey turned on the stream the hot water melted the glue. This released the snake, which dropped through one of the holes, bit the baronet in the leg, and disappeared down the waste pipe."

"But that can't be right," said the Draught Stout. "Between Chapter Two and the murder there was an interval of several days."

"The plumber forgot his snake and had to go back for it," explained Mr. Mulliner. "I trust that this revelation will prove sedative."

"I feel a new man," said the Draught Stout. "I'd have lain awake worrying about that murder all night."

"I suppose you would. My nephew Cyril was just the same. Nothing in this modern life of ours," said Mr Mulliner, taking a sip of his hot Scotch and lemon, "is more remarkable than the way in which the mystery novel has gripped the public. Your true enthusiast, deprived of his favorite reading, will stop at nothing in order to get it. He is like a victim of the drug habit when withheld from cocaine. My nephew Cyri—"

"Amazing the things people will leave in trains," said a Small Lager. "Bags . . . umbrellas . . . even stuffed chimpanzees, occasionally, I've been told. I heard a story the other day . . ."

My nephew Cyril (said Mr Mulliner) had a greater passion for mystery stories than anyone I have ever met. I attribute this to the fact that, like so many interior decorators, he was a fragile, delicate young fellow, extraordinarily vulnerable to any ailment that happened to be going the rounds. Every time he caught mumps or influenza or German measles or the like, he occupied the period of convalescence in reading mystery stories. And, as the appetite grows by what it feeds on, he had become, at the time at which this narrative opens, a confirmed addict. Not only did he devour every volume of this type on which he could lay his hands, but he was also to be found at any theater which was offering the kind of drama where skinny arms come unexpectedly out of the chiffonier and the audience feels a mild surprise if the lights stay on for ten consecutive minutes.

And it was during a performance of *The Gray Vampire* at the St James's that he found himself sitting next to Amelia Bassett, the girl whom he was to love with all the stored-up fervor of a man who hitherto had been inclined rather to edge away when in the presence of the other sex.

He did not know her name was Amelia Bassett. He had never seen her before. All he knew was that at last he had met his fate, and for the whole of the first act he was pondering the problem of how he was to make her acquaintance.

It was as the lights went up for the first intermission that he was aroused from his thoughts by a sharp pain in the right leg. He was just wondering whether it was gout or sciatica when, glancing down, he perceived that what had happened was that his neighbor, absorbed by the drama, had absent-mindedly collected a handful of his flesh and was twisting it in an ecstasy of excitement.

It seemed to Cyril a good *point d'appui*.

"Excuse me," he said.

The girl turned. Her eyes were glowing, and the tip of her nose still quivered.

"I beg your pardon?"

"My leg," said Cyril. "Might I have it back, if you've finished with it?"

The girl looked down. She started visibly.

"I'm awfully sorry," she gasped.

"Not at all," said Cyril. "Only too glad to have been of assistance."

"I got carried away."

"You are evidently fond of mystery plays."

"I love them."

"So do I. And mystery novels?"

"Oh, yes!"

"Have you read *Blood on the Banisters*?"

"Oh, *yes!* I thought it was better than *Severed Throats!*"

"So did I," said Cyril. "Much better. Brighter murders, subtler detectives, crisper clues . . . better in every way."

The two twin souls gazed into each other's eyes. There is no surer foundation for a beautiful friendship than a mutual taste in literature.

"My name is Amelia Bassett," said the girl.

"Mine is Cyril Mulliner. Bassett?" He frowned thoughtfully. "The name seems familiar."

"Perhaps you have heard of my mother. Lady Bassett. She's rather a well-known big-game hunter and explorer. She tramps through jungles and things. She's gone out to the lobby for a smoke. By the way"—she hesitated—"if she finds us talking, will you remember that we met at the Polterwoods'?"

"I quite understand."

"You see, Mother doesn't like people who talk to me without a formal introduction. And when Mother doesn't like anyone, she is so apt to hit them over the head with some hard instrument."

"I see," said Cyril. "Like the Human Ape in *Gore by the Gallon*."

"Exactly. Tell me," said the girl, changing the subject, "if you were a millionaire, would you rather be stabbed in the back with a paper knife or found dead without a mark on you, staring with blank eyes at some appalling sight?"

Cyril was about to reply when, looking past her, he found himself virtually in the latter position. A woman of extraordinary formidableness had lowered herself into the seat beyond and was scrutinizing him keenly through a tortoise-shell lorgnette. She reminded Cyril of Wallace Beery.[1]

"Friend of yours, Amelia?" she said.

"This is Mr Mulliner, Mother. We met at the Polterwoods'."

"Ah?" said Lady Bassett.

She inspected Cyril through her lorgnette.

"Mr Mulliner," she said, "is a little like the chief of the Lower Isisi—though, of course, he was darker and had a ring through his nose. A dear, good fellow," she continued reminiscently, "but inclined to become familiar under the influence of trade gin. I shot him in the leg."

"Er—why?" asked Cyril.

"He was not behaving like a gentleman," said Lady Bassett primly.

"After taking your treatment," said Cyril, awed, "I'll bet he could have written a Book of Etiquette."

"I believe he did," said Lady Bassett carelessly. "You must come and call on us some afternoon, Mr Mulliner. I am in the telephone book. If you are interested in man-eating pumas, I can show you some nice heads."

The curtain rose on Act Two, and Cyril returned to his thoughts. Love, he felt joyously, had come into his life at last. But then so, he had to admit, had Lady Bassett. There is, he reflected, always something.

I will pass lightly over the period of Cyril's wooing. Suffice it to say that his progress was rapid. From the moment he told Amelia that he had once met Dorothy Sayers,[2] he never looked back. And one afternoon, calling and finding that Lady Bassett was away in the country, he took the girl's hand in his and told his love.

For a while all was well. Amelia's reactions proved satisfactory to a degree. She checked up enthusiastically on his proposition. Falling into his arms, she admitted specifically that he was her Dream Man.

Then came the jarring note.

"But it's no use," she said, her lovely eyes filling with tears. "Mother will never give her consent."

"Why not?" said Cyril, stunned. "What is it she objects to about me?"

"I don't know. But she generally alludes to you as 'that pipsqueak.'"

"Pipsqueak?" said Cyril. "What *is* a pipsqueak?"

"I'm not quite sure, but it's something Mother doesn't like very much. It's a pity she ever found out that you are an interior decorator."

"An honorable profession," said Cyril, a little stiffly.

"I know; but what she admires are men who have to do with the great open spaces."

---

1. American film actor (1885–1949) specializing in blustery, rubber-faced palookas.   2. English writer of mystery stories (1893–1957).

"Well, I also design ornamental gardens."

"Yes," said the girl doubtfully, "but still—"

"And, dash it," said Cyril indignantly, "this isn't the Victorian age. All that business of Mother's Consent went out twenty years ago."

"Yes, but no one told Mother."

"It's preposterous!" cried Cyril. "I never heard such rot. Let's just slip off and get married quietly and send her a picture postcard from Venice or somewhere, with a cross and a 'This is our room. Wish you were with us' on it."

The girl shuddered.

"She would be with us," she said. "You don't know Mother. The moment she got that picture postcard, she would come over to wherever we were and put you across her knee and spank you with a hairbrush. I don't think I could ever feel the same toward you if I saw you lying across Mother's knee, being spanked with a hairbrush. It would spoil the honeymoon."

Cyril frowned. But a man who has spent most of his life trying out a series of patent medicines is always an optimist.

"There is only one thing to be done," he said. "I shall see your mother and try to make her listen to reason. Where is she now?"

"She left this morning for a visit to the Winghams in Sussex."

"Excellent! I know the Winghams. In fact, I have a standing invitation to go and stay with them whenever I like. I'll send them a wire and push down this evening. I will oil up to your mother sedulously and try to correct her present unfavorable impression of me. Then, choosing my moment, I will shoot her the news. It may work. It may not work. But at any rate I consider it a fair sporting venture."

"But you are so diffident, Cyril. So shrinking. So retiring and shy. How can you carry through such a task?"

"Love will nerve me."

"Enough, do you think? Remember what Mother is. Wouldn't a good, strong drink be more help?"

Cyril looked doubtful.

"My doctor has always forbidden me alcoholic stimulants. He says they increase the blood pressure."

"Well, when you meet Mother, you will need all the blood pressure you can get. I really do advise you to fuel up a little before you see her."

"Yes," agreed Cyril, nodding thoughtfully. "I think you're right. It shall be as you say. Good-bye, my angel one."

"Good-bye, Cyril, darling. You will think of me every minute while you're gone?"

"Every single minute. Well, practically every single minute. You see, I have just got Horatio Slingsby's latest book, *Strychnine in the Soup,* and I shall be dipping into that from time to time. But all the rest of the while . . . Have you read it, by the way?"

"Not yet. I had a copy, but Mother took it with her."

"Ah? Well, if I am to catch a train that will get me to Barkley for dinner, I must be going. Good-bye, sweetheart, and never forget that Gilbert Glendale in *The Missing Toe* won the girl he loved in spite of being up against two mysterious stranglers and the entire Black Mustache gang."

He kissed her fondly, and went off to pack.

. . .

Barkley Towers, the country seat of Sir Mortimer and Lady Wingham, was two hours from London by rail. Thinking of Amelia and reading the opening chapters of Horatio Slingsby's powerful story, Cyril found the journey pass rapidly. In fact, so preoccupied was he that it was only as the train started to draw out of Barkley Regis station that he realized where he was. He managed to hurl himself onto the platform just in time.

As he had taken the five-seven express, stopping only at Gluebury Peveril, he arrived at Barkley Towers at an hour which enabled him not only to be on hand for dinner but also to take part in the life-giving distribution of cocktails which preceded the meal.

The house party, he perceived on entering the drawing room, was a small one. Besides Lady Bassett and himself, the only visitors were a nondescript couple of the name of Simpson, and a tall, bronzed, handsome man with flashing eyes who, his hostess informed him in a whispered aside, was Lester Mapledurham (pronounced Mum), the explorer and big-game hunter.

Perhaps it was the oppressive sensation of being in the same room with two explorers and big-game hunters that brought home to Cyril the need for following Amelia's advice as quickly as possible. But probably the mere sight of Lady Bassett alone would have been enough to make him break a lifelong abstinence. To her normal resemblance to Wallace Beery she appeared now to have added a distinct suggestion of Victor McLaglen,[3] and the spectacle was sufficient to send Cyril leaping toward the cocktail tray.

After three rapid glasses he felt a better and a braver man. And so lavishly did he irrigate the ensuing dinner with hock, sherry, champagne, old brandy, and port that at the conclusion of the meal he was pleased to find that his diffidence had completely vanished. He rose from the table feeling equal to asking a dozen Lady Bassetts for their consent to marry a dozen daughters.

In fact, as he confided to the butler, prodding him genially in the ribs as he spoke, if Lady Bassett attempted to high-hat *him*, he would know what to do about it. He made no threats, he explained to the butler; he simply stated that he would know what to do about it. The butler said "Very good, sir. Thank you, sir," and the incident closed.

It had been Cyril's intention—feeling, as he did, in this singularly uplifted and dominant frame of mind—to get hold of Amelia's mother and start oiling up to her immediately after dinner. But, what with falling into a doze in the smoking room and then getting into an argument on theology with one of the underfootmen whom he met in the hall, he did not reach the drawing room until nearly half-past ten. And he was annoyed, on walking in with a merry cry of "Lady Bassett! Call for Lady Bassett!" on his lips, to discover that she had retired to her room.

Had Cyril's mood been even slightly less elevated, this news might have acted as a check on his enthusiasm. So generous, however, had been Sir Mortimer's hospitality that he merely nodded eleven times, to indicate comprehension, and then, having ascertained that his quarry was roosting in the Blue Room, sped thither with a brief "Tallyho!"

Arriving at the Blue Room, he banged heartily on the door and breezed in. He found Lady Bassett propped up with pillows. She was smoking a cigar and reading a book. And that book, Cyril saw with intense surprise and resentment, was none other than Horatio Slingsby's *Strychnine in the Soup.*

---

3. A character actor in films, specializing in military roles (1886–1959).

The spectacle brought him to an abrupt halt.

"Well, I'm dashed!" he cried. "Well, I'm blowed! What do you mean by pinching[4] my book?"

Lady Bassett had lowered her cigar. She now raised her eyebrows.

"What are you doing in my room, Mr Mulliner?"

"It's a little hard," said Cyril, trembling with self-pity. "I go to enormous expense to buy detective stories, and no sooner is my back turned than people rush about the place sneaking them."

"This book belongs to my daughter Amelia."

"Good old Amelia!" said Cyril cordially. "One of the best."

"I borrowed it to read in the train. Now will you kindly tell me what you are doing in my room, Mr Mulliner?"

Cyril smote his forehead.

"Of course. I remember now. It all comes back to me. She told me you had taken it. And, what's more, I've suddenly recollected something which clears you completely. I was hustled and bustled at the end of the journey. I sprang to my feet, hurled bags onto the platform—in a word, lost my head. And, like a chump, I went and left my copy of *Strychnine in the Soup* in the train. Well, I can only apologize."

"You can not only apologize. You can also tell me what you are doing in my room."

"What I am doing in your room?"

"Exactly."

"Ah!" said Cyril, sitting down on the bed. "You may well ask."

"I *have* asked. Three times."

Cyril closed his eyes. For some reason, his mind seemed cloudy and not at its best.

"If you are proposing to go to sleep here, Mr Mulliner," said Lady Bassett, "tell me, and I shall know what to do about it."

The phrase touched a chord in Cyril's memory. He recollected now his reasons for being where he was. Opening his eyes, he fixed them on her.

"Lady Bassett," he said, "you are, I believe, an explorer?"

"I am."

"In the course of your explorations, you have wandered through many a jungle in many a distant land?"

"I have."

"Tell me, Lady Bassett," said Cyril keenly, "while making a pest of yourself to the denizens of those jungles, did you notice one thing? I allude to the fact that Love is everywhere—aye, even in the jungle. Love, independent of bounds and frontiers, of nationality and species, works its spell on every living thing. So that, no matter whether an individual be a Congo native, an American song writer, a jaguar, an armadillo, a bespoke tailor, or a tsetse-tsetse fly, he will infallibly seek his mate. So why shouldn't an interior decorator and designer of ornamental gardens? I put this to you, Lady Bassett."

"Mr Mulliner," said his roommate, "you are blotto!"

Cyril waved his hand in a spacious gesture, and fell off the bed.

"Blotto I may be," he said, resuming his seat, "but, none the less, argue as you will, you can't get away from the fact that I love your daughter Amelia."

There was a tense pause.

"What did you say?" cried Lady Bassett.

4. Stealing.

"When?" said Cyril absently, for he had fallen into a daydream and, as far as the intervening blankets would permit, was playing This Little Pig Went to Market with his companion's toes.

"Did I hear you say . . . my daughter Amelia?"

"Gray-eyed girl, medium height, sort of browny red hair," said Cyril, to assist her memory. "Dash it, you *must* know Amelia. She goes everywhere. And let me tell you something, Mrs—I've forgotten your name. We're going to be married, if I can obtain her foul mother's consent. Speaking as an old friend, what would you say the chances were?"

"Extremely slight."

"Eh?"

"Seeing that I *am* Amelia's mother . . ."

Cyril blinked, genuinely surprised.

"Why, so you are! I didn't recognize you. Have you been there all the time?"

"I have."

Suddenly Cyril's gaze hardened. He drew himself up stiffly.

"What are you doing in my bed?" he demanded.

"This is not your bed."

"Then whose is it?"

"Mine."

Cyril shrugged his shoulders helplessly.

"Well, it all looks very funny to me," he said. "I suppose I must believe your story, but, I repeat, I consider the whole thing odd, and I propose to institute very strict inquiries. I may tell you that I happen to know the ringleaders. I wish you a very hearty good night."

It was perhaps an hour later that Cyril, who had been walking on the terrace in deep thought, repaired once more to the Blue Room in quest of information. Running over the details of the recent interview in his head, he had suddenly discovered that there was a point which had not been satisfactorily cleared up.

"I say," he said.

Lady Bassett looked up from her book, plainly annoyed.

"Have you no bedroom of your own, Mr Mulliner?"

"Oh, yes," said Cyril. "They've bedded me out in the Moat Room. But there was something I wanted you to tell me."

"Well?"

"Did you say I might or mightn't?"

"Might or mightn't what?"

"Marry Amelia?"

"No. You may not."

"No?"

"No!"

"Oh!" said Cyril. "Well, pip-pip once more."

It was a moody Cyril Mulliner who withdrew to the Moat Room. He now realized the position of affairs. The mother of the girl he loved refused to accept him as an eligible suitor. A dickens of a situation to be in, felt Cyril, somberly unshoeing himself.

Then he brightened a little. His life, he reflected, might be wrecked, but he still had two thirds of *Strychnine in the Soup* to read.

At the moment when the train reached Barkley Regis station, Cyril had just got to the bit where Detective Inspector Mould looks through the half-open cellar door and, drawing in his breath with a sharp hissing sound, recoils in horror. It was obviously going to be good. He was just about to proceed to the dressing table where, he presumed, the footman had placed the book on unpacking his bag, when an icy stream seemed to flow down the center of his spine and the room and its contents danced before him.

Once more he had remembered that he had left the volume in the train.

He uttered an animal cry and tottered to a chair.

The subject of bereavement is one that has often been treated powerfully by poets, who have run the whole gamut of the emotions while laying bare for us the agony of those who have lost parents, wives, children, gazelles, money, fame, dogs, cats, doves, sweethearts, horses, and even collar studs. But no poet has yet treated of the most poignant bereavement of all—that of the man halfway through a detective story who finds himself at bedtime without the book.

Cyril did not care to think of the night that lay before him. Already his brain was lashing itself from side to side like a wounded snake as it sought for some explanation of Inspector Mould's strange behavior. Horatio Slingsby was an author who could be relied on to keep faith with his public. He was not the sort of man to fob the reader off in the next chapter with the statement that what had made Inspector Mould look horrified was the fact that he had suddenly remembered that he had forgotten all about the letter his wife had given him to post. If looking through cellar doors disturbed a Slingsby detective, it was because a dismembered corpse lay there, or at least a severed hand.

A soft moan, as of something in torment, escaped Cyril. What to do? What to do? Even a makeshift substitute for *Strychnine in the Soup* was beyond his reach. He knew so well what he would find if he went to the library in search of something to read. Sir Mortimer Wingham was heavy and county-squire-ish. His wife affected strange religions. Their literature was in keeping with their tastes. In the library there would be books on Bahai-ism, volumes in old leather of the *Rural Encyclopedia*, *My Two Years in Sunny Ceylon*, by the Rev. Orlo Waterbury . . . but of anything that would interest Scotland Yard, of anything with a bit of blood in it and a corpse or two into which a fellow could get his teeth, not a trace.

What, then, coming right back to it, to do?

And suddenly, as if in answer to the question, came the solution. Electrified, he saw the way out.

The hour was now well advanced. By this time Lady Bassett must surely be asleep. *Strychnine in the Soup* would be lying on the table beside her bed. All he had to do was to creep in and grab it.

The more he considered the idea, the better it looked. It was not as if he did not know the way to Lady Bassett's room or the topography of it when he got there. It seemed to him as if most of his later life had been spent in Lady Bassett's room. He could find his way about it with his eyes shut.

He hesitated no longer. Donning a dressing gown, he left his room and hurried along the passage.

Pushing open the door of the Blue Room and closing it softly behind him, Cyril stood for a moment full of all those emotions which come to man revisiting some long-familiar spot. There the dear old room was, just the same as ever. How it all came back to him! The place was in darkness, but that did not deter him. He knew where the bed table was, and he made for it with stealthy steps.

In the manner in which Cyril Mulliner advanced toward the bed table there was much which would have reminded Lady Bassett, had she been an eyewitness, of the furtive prowl of the Lesser Iguanodon tracking its prey. In only one respect did Cyril and this creature of the wild differ in their technique. Iguanodons—and this applies not only to the Lesser but to the Larger Iguanodon—seldom, if ever, trip over cords on the floor and bring the lamps to which they are attached crashing to the ground like a ton of bricks.

Cyril did. Scarcely had he snatched up the book and placed it in the pocket of his dressing gown, when his foot became entangled in the trailing cord and the lamp on the table leaped nimbly into the air and, to the accompaniment of a sound not unlike that made by a hundred plates coming apart simultaneously in the hands of a hundred scullery maids, nose-dived to the floor and became a total loss.

At the same moment, Lady Bassett, who had been chasing a bat out of the window, stepped in from the balcony and switched on the lights.

To say that Cyril Mulliner was taken aback would be to understate the facts. Nothing like his recent misadventure had happened to him since his eleventh year, when, going surreptitiously to his mother's cupboard for jam, he had jerked three shelves down on his head, containing milk, butter, homemade preserves, pickles, cheese, eggs, cakes, and potted meat. His feelings on the present occasion closely paralleled that boyhood thrill.

Lady Bassett also appeared somewhat discomposed.

"You!" she said.

Cyril nodded, endeavoring the while to smile in a reassuring manner.

"Hullo!" he said.

His hostess's manner was now one of unmistakable displeasure.

"Am I not to have a moment of privacy, Mr Mulliner?" she asked severely. "I am, I trust, a broad-minded woman, but I cannot approve of this idea of communal bedrooms."

Cyril made an effort to be conciliatory.

"I do keep coming in, don't I?" he said.

"You do," agreed Lady Bassett. "Sir Mortimer informed me, on learning that I had been given this room, that it was supposed to be haunted. Had I known that it was haunted by you, Mr. Mulliner, I should have packed up and gone to the local inn."

Cyril bowed his head. The censure, he could not but feel, was deserved.

"I admit," he said, "that my conduct has been open to criticism. In extenuation, I can but plead my great love. This is no idle social call, Lady Bassett. I looked in because I wished to take up again this matter of my marrying your daughter Amelia. You say I can't. Why can't I? Answer me that, Lady Bassett."

"I have other views for Amelia," said Lady Bassett stiffly. "When my daughter gets married it will not be to a spineless, invertebrate product of our modern hothouse civilization, but to a strong, upstanding, keen-eyed, two-fisted he-man of the open spaces. I have no wish to hurt your feelings, Mr Mulliner," she continued, more kindly, "but you must admit that you are, when all is said and done, a pipsqueak."

"I deny it," cried Cyril warmly. "I don't even know what a pipsqueak is."

"A pipsqueak is a man who has never seen the sun rise beyond the reaches of the Lower Zambezi; who would not know what to do if faced by a charging rhinoceros. What, pray, would you do if faced by a charging rhinoceros, Mr Mulliner?"

"I am not likely," said Cyril, "to move in the same social circles as charging rhinoceri."

"Or take another simple case, such as happens every day. Suppose you are crossing a rude bridge over a stream in Equatorial Africa. You have been thinking of a hundred trifles and are in a reverie. From this you wake to discover that in the branches overhead a python is extending its fangs toward you. At the same time, you observe that at one end of the bridge is a crouching puma; at the other are two headhunters—call them Pat and Mike—with poisoned blowpipes to their lips. Below, half hidden in the stream, is an alligator. What would you do in such a case, Mr Mulliner?"

Cyril weighed the point.

"I should feel embarrassed," he had to admit. "I shouldn't know where to look."

Lady Bassett laughed an amused, scornful little laugh.

"Precisely. Such a situation would not, however, disturb Lester Mapledurham."

"Lester Mapledurham!"

"The man who is to marry my daughter Amelia. He asked me for her hand shortly after dinner."

Cyril reeled. The blow, falling so suddenly and unexpectedly, had made him feel boneless. And yet, he felt, he might have expected this. These explorers and big-game hunters stick together.

"In a situation such as I have outlined, Lester Mapledurham would simply drop from the bridge, wait till the alligator made its rush, insert a stout stick between its jaws, and then hit it in the eye with a spear, being careful to avoid its lashing tail. He would then drift downstream and land at some safer spot. That is the type of man I wish for as a son-in-law."

Cyril left the room without a word. Not even the fact that he now had *Strychnine in the Soup* in his possession could cheer his mood of unrelieved blackness. Back in his room, he tossed the book moodily onto the bed and began to pace the floor. And he had scarcely completed two laps when the door opened.

For an instant, when he heard the click of the latch, Cyril supposed that his visitor must be Lady Bassett, who, having put two and two together on discovering her loss, had come to demand her property back. And he cursed the rashness which had led him to fling it so carelessly upon the bed, in full view.

But it was not Lady Bassett. The intruder was Lester Mapledurham. Clad in a suit of pajamas which in their general color scheme reminded Cyril of a boudoir he had recently decorated for a society poetess, he stood with folded arms, his keen eyes fixed menacingly on the young man.

"Give me those jewels!" said Lester Mapledurham.

Cyril was at a loss.

"Jewels?"

"Jewels!"

"What jewels?"

Lester Mapledurham tossed his head impatiently.

"I don't know what jewels. They may be the Wingham Pearls or the Bassett Diamonds or the Simpson Sapphires. I'm not sure which room it was I saw you coming out of."

Cyril began to understand.

"Oh, did you see me coming out of a room?"

"I did. I heard a crash and, when I looked out, you were hurrying along the corridor."

"I can explain everything," said Cyril. "I had just been having a chat with Lady Bassett on a personal matter. Nothing to do with diamonds."

"You're sure?" said Mapledurham.

"Oh, rather," said Cyril. "We talked about rhinoceri and pythons and her daughter Amelia and alligators and all that sort of thing, and then I came away."

Lester Mapledurham seemed only half convinced.

"H'm!" he said. "Well, if anything is missing in the morning, I shall know what to do about it." His eye fell on the bed. "Hullo!" he went on, with sudden animation. "Slingsby's latest? Well, well! I've been wanting to get hold of this. I hear it's good. The Leeds *Mercury* says: 'These gripping pages . . .'"

He turned to the door, and with a hideous pang of agony Cyril perceived that it was plainly his intention to take the book with him. It was swinging lightly from a bronzed hand about the size of a medium ham.

"Here!" he cried vehemently.

Lester Mapledurham turned.

"Well?"

"Oh, nothing," said Cyril. "Just good night."

He flung himself face downwards on the bed as the door closed, cursing himself for the craven cowardice which had kept him from snatching the book from the explorer. There had been a moment when he had almost nerved himself to the deed, but it was followed by another moment in which he had caught the other's eye. And it was as if he had found himself exchanging glances with Lady Bassett's charging rhinoceros.

And now, thanks to this pusillanimity,[5] he was once more *Strychnine in the Soup* -less.

How long Cyril lay there, a prey to the gloomiest thoughts, he could not have said. He was aroused from his meditations by the sound of the door opening again.

Lady Bassett stood before him. It was plain that she was deeply moved. In addition to resembling Wallace Beery and Victor McLaglen, she now had a distinct look of George Bancroft.[6]

She pointed a quivering finger at Cyril.

"You hound!" she cried. "Give me that book!"

Cyril maintained his poise with a strong effort.

"What book?"

"The book you sneaked out of my room."

"Has someone sneaked a book out of your room?" Cyril struck his forehead. "Great heavens!" he cried.

"Mr Mulliner," said Lady Bassett coldly, "more book and less gibbering!"

Cyril raised a hand.

"I know who's got your book. Lester Mapledurham!"

"Don't be absurd."

"He has, I tell you. As I was on my way to your room just now, I saw him coming out, carrying something in a furtive manner. I remember wondering a bit at the time. He's in the Clock Room. If we pop along there now, we shall just catch him red-handed."

Lady Bassett reflected.

"It is impossible," she said at length. "He is incapable of such an act. Lester Mapledurham is a man who once killed a lion with a sardine opener."

5. Timidity.

6. Film actor (1882–1956), specializing in gangster roles and exuding a smooth villainy.

"The very worst sort," said Cyril. "Ask anyone."

"And he is engaged to my daughter." Lady Bassett paused. "Well, he won't be long, if I find that what you say is true. Come, Mr Mulliner!"

Together the two passed down the silent passage. At the door of the Clock Room they paused. A light streamed from beneath it. Cyril pointed silently to this sinister evidence of reading in bed, and noted that his companion stiffened and said something to herself in an undertone in what appeared to be some sort of native dialect.

The next moment she had flung the door open and, with a spring like that of a crouching zebu, had leaped to the bed and wrenched the book from Lester Mapledurham's hands.

"So!" said Lady Bassett.

"So!" said Cyril, feeling that he could not do better than follow the lead of such a woman.

"Hullo!" said Lester Mapledurham, surprised. "Something the matter?"

"So it was you who stole my book!"

"Your book?" said Lester Mapledurham. "I borrowed this from Mr Mulliner there."

"A likely story!" said Cyril. "Lady Bassett is aware that I left my copy of *Strychnine in the Soup* in the train."

"Certainly," said Lady Bassett. "It's no use talking, young man, I have caught you with the goods. And let me tell you one thing that may be of interest. If you think that, after a dastardly act like this, you are going to marry Amelia, forget it!"

"Wipe it right out of your mind," said Cyril.

"But listen—"

"I will not listen. Come, Mr Mulliner."

She left the room, followed by Cyril. For some moments they walked in silence.

"A merciful escape," said Cyril.

"For whom?"

"For Amelia. My gosh, think of her tied to a man like that. Must be a relief to you to feel that she's going to marry a respectable interior decorator."

Lady Bassett halted. They were standing outside the Moat Room now. She looked at Cyril, her eyebrows raised.

"Are you under the impression, Mr Mulliner," she said, "that, on the strength of what has happened, I intend to accept you as a son-in-law?"

Cyril reeled.

"Don't you?"

"Certainly not."

Something inside Cyril seemed to snap. Recklessness descended upon him. He became for a space a thing of courage and fire, like the African leopard in the mating season.

"Oh!" he said.

And, deftly whisking *Strychnine in the Soup* from his companion's hand, he darted into his room, banged the door, and bolted it.

"Mr Mulliner!"

It was Lady Bassett's voice, coming pleadingly through the woodwork. It was plain that she was shaken to the core, and Cyril smiled sardonically. He was in a position to dictate terms.

"Give me that book, Mr. Mulliner!"

"Certainly not," said Cyril. "I intend to read it myself. I hear good reports of it on every side. The Peebles *Intelligencer* says: 'Vigorous and absorbing.'"

A low wail from the other side of the door answered him.

"Of course," said Cyril suggestively, "if it were my future mother-in-law who was speaking, her word would naturally be law."

There was a silence outside.

"Very well," said Lady Bassett.

"I may marry Amelia?"

"You may."

Cyril unbolted the door.

"Come—Mother," he said, in a soft, kindly voice. "We will read it together, down in the library."

Lady Bassett was still shaken.

"I hope I have acted for the best," she said.

"You have," said Cyril.

"You will make Amelia a good husband?"

"Grade A," Cyril assured her.

"Well, even if you don't," said Lady Bassett resignedly, "I can't go to bed without that book. I had just got to the bit where Inspector Mould is trapped in the underground den of the Faceless Fiend."

Cyril quivered.

"*Is* there a Faceless Fiend?" he cried.

"There are two Faceless Fiends," said Lady Bassett.

"My gosh!" said Cyril. "Let's hurry."

W. H. Auden
1907–1973

Wystan Hugh Auden's fantastically wrinkled face is a familiar icon from photographs taken in his later years, showing a fissured map of lines across his features. These photographs, many depicting Auden posing with his ever-present cigarette against a cityscape or airport, reveal part of Auden's continuing allure, which is that he was a witness, in his writing and in his person, to the changing scene of life and letters in the middle decades of the twentieth century. Auden came to embody a British literary Golden Age that lived on after the conditions that had brought it into being had changed utterly. His imperturbable face, looking much older than it was, had a sagelike quality of wisdom and the measurement of time passing: a map of modern experience.

Born in York, England, Auden had a pampered childhood, and was too young to see service in World War I. He was of the post-War generation, a group of gifted poets and writers who sought to replace the terrible losses of the war, its literary as well as its human casualties. Auden attended Christ Church College, Oxford, where his precocious literary career began in 1928 with the private publication of his *Poems*, thirty copies of which were put together by his friend and fellow writer Stephen Spender at Oxford. Auden joined a number of his friends and peers in heading to Berlin; his friend Christopher Isherwood's *I Am a Camera* (later the basis for the musical *Cabaret*) documented the phenomenon of these expatriate British writers spending their youthful careers in a decadent and exciting Berlin. Like many of the rest—though some died fighting fascism in Spain—Auden returned to England; he became a teacher in Scotland and England while writing feverishly. The cultural ferment of the thirties led Auden in many directions: chiefly, he wrote poetry, but he also became a noted literary critic, and he collaborated with Isherwood and others on plays and screenplays.

Auden's literary and political wanderlust took him to Iceland in 1936, where he wrote *Letters from Iceland* with Louis MacNeice; to Spain, which resulted in much poetry and occasional writing; to China, Japan, and the United States, culminating in the book *On the Frontier*. In 1939 he took an epochal step: he settled in the United States, where he became a citizen in 1946. In this he was a reverse T. S. Eliot—Eliot was an American who became a British citizen and is usually included as a premier writer of British, not American, literature. Auden was an American citizen who is always included in British anthologies, and rarely, if ever, in American collections. Part of Auden's desire to live in America had to do with his need to escape a stifling set of expectations for him that obtained in England—social, literary, and even personal expectations. In 1935, he had married Thomas Mann's daughter Erika, largely to protect her from political persecution in Germany, since Auden was a homosexual and lived for most of his adult life with the poet Chester Kallman, whom he met in 1939.

It was during Auden's teaching and fellowship years in the United States that he began to produce the large oeuvre of his poetry and his criticism. He taught and lectured at many colleges and universities, and read widely, taking a particular interest in the existentialist theology of Søren Kierkegaard. Increasingly impatient with Marxist materialism, Auden found a renewed commitment to Christianity in his later decades. During these years he published such notable milestones as his *Collected Shorter Poems*, *The Age of Anxiety*, and the critical work *The Enchafèd Flood*. In 1958 his definitive *Selected Poetry* was published, followed in 1962 by his magisterial work of criticism, *The Dyer's Hand*, which contained his luminous essay *Writing*, included here. His peripatetic and sometimes difficult teaching life led him to accept an offer from Oxford in 1956, to spend summers in Italy and in Austria, and to make a final move to Oxford and Christ Church College in 1972. However, he died shortly thereafter in 1973, in Austria, where he shared the summer house with Kallman.

The title of one of Auden's major long poems, *The Age of Anxiety*, summons up a reigning motif of Auden's poetic writing. Auden's poetry is edgy, tense, worried, psychoanalytic and yet despondent of the powers of psychoanalysis to allay anxiety. Anxiety is in some ways Auden's muse. This arises from the seriousness with which Auden had gauged the world political situation. Having witnessed the depression, the rise of Nazism, totalitarianism, World War II, the Holocaust, the atomic bomb, and the Cold War, Auden's political realism is tinged inevitably with disillusionment. Modern history is one primary source for Auden's poetry; in poems like *Spain 1937* and *September 1, 1939*, he makes no retreat to purely aesthetic subject matter, or to the past, or to pure experimentation. Auden's is a poetry of waiting rooms, radio broadcasts, armed battalions, and of snatched pleasures treasured all the more for their fleeting magic.

Paradoxically, Auden's moral and political engagements coexist with an anarchic streak, a wry wit, and a love of leisure and play. Auden developed one of the most seductively varied voices in modern poetry, creating an endlessly inventive style that draws at will on Latin elegy, Anglo-Saxon alliterative verse forms, Norse runes and "kennings," technical scientific discourse, and the meters and language of British music hall songs and of American blues singers. All these elements can be present in a single stanza, to sometimes dizzying effect; in other poems, these radically different materials are blended and modulated into a deceptively plain style of great power.

A topic of special concern for Auden was the survival of literary language. How would poetry make claims for its relevance, given that it was now surrounded by so many other voices, from those of mass culture to the exigent rhetoric of war? Auden often compared himself poetically to William Butler Yeats, as another political poet in a time when poetry was seen as largely irrelevant or even antithetical to politics. The pithy, ironic paragraphs of Auden's essay *Writing* (1962) explore the essence of good writing and also the possibility for authentic life in modern society.

Auden's poetry remains a profoundly lyric poetry: that is, it celebrates the singular human voice that sings its lines. It is not surprising that he wrote opera librettos, notably *The Rake's Progress*, which he wrote with Chester Kallman for Igor Stravinsky. Auden was an intellectual inheritor of Freud and Marx—he knew the ways that the self could remain unknown to itself, and the ways that history could relentlessly rush on oblivious of the human lives swept up in its current. Still, the human voice of poetry goes on, even in the age of anxiety, framing its lyric songs. In the late phase of his poetry, Auden had despaired of systems, and returned even more to the meticulous versification he was so well versed in. His poems become almost defiant vehicles of traditional rhyme and meter, lodged in the modern, everyday world, where "in the deserts of the heart," Auden would "let the healing fountain start."

Musée des Beaux Arts [1]

About suffering they were never wrong,
The Old Masters: how well they understood
Its human position; how it takes place
While someone else is eating or opening a window or just walking dully along;
5   How, when the aged are reverently, passionately waiting
For the miraculous birth, there always must be
Children who did not specially want it to happen, skating
On a pond at the edge of the wood:
They never forgot
10 That even the dreadful martyrdom must run its course
Anyhow in a corner, some untidy spot
Where the dogs go on with their doggy life and the torturer's horse
Scratches its innocent behind on a tree.

In Brueghel's *Icarus*, for instance: how everything turns away
15 Quite leisurely from the disaster; the ploughman may
Have heard the splash, the forsaken cry,
But for him it was not an important failure; the sun shone
As it had to on the white legs disappearing into the green
Water; and the expensive delicate ship that must have seen
20 Something amazing, a boy falling out of the sky,
Had somewhere to get to and sailed calmly on.

1938   1940

In Memory of W. B. Yeats
(d. January 1939)

1

He disappeared in the dead of winter:
The brooks were frozen, the air-ports almost deserted,
And snow disfigured the public statues;

---

1. The Musées Royaux des Beaux-Arts in Brussels contain a collection of paintings by the Flemish painter Pieter Brueghel (1525–1569) that includes *The Fall of Icarus*; Brueghel is famous for his acute observation of ordinary life. A figure from Greek mythology, Icarus had wings of wax and feathers but flew too close to the sun, which melted the wax and caused him to fall into the sea.

The mercury sank in the mouth of the dying day.
5   O all the instruments agree
The day of his death was a dark cold day.

Far from his illness
The wolves ran on through the evergreen forests,
The peasant river was untempted by the fashionable quays;
10   By mourning tongues
The death of the poet was kept from his poems.

But for him it was his last afternoon as himself,
An afternoon of nurses and rumours;
The provinces of his body revolted,
15   The squares of his mind were empty,
Silence invaded the suburbs,
The current of his feeling failed: he became his admirers.

Now he is scattered among a hundred cities
And wholly given over to unfamiliar affections;
20   To find his happiness in another kind of wood
And be punished under a foreign code of conscience.
The words of a dead man
Are modified in the guts of the living.

But in the importance and noise of to-morrow
25   When the brokers are roaring like beasts on the floor of the Bourse,[1]
And the poor have the sufferings to which they are fairly accustomed,
And each in the cell of himself is almost convinced of his freedom;
A few thousand will think of this day
As one thinks of a day when one did something slightly unusual.

30   O all the instruments agree
The day of his death was a dark cold day.

2

You were silly like us: your gift survived it all;
The parish of rich women, physical decay,
Yourself; mad Ireland hurt you into poetry.
35   Now Ireland has her madness and her weather still,
For poetry makes nothing happen: it survives
In the valley of its saying where executives
Would never want to tamper; it flows south
From ranches of isolation and the busy griefs,
40   Raw towns that we believe and die in; it survives,
A way of happening, a mouth.

3

Earth, receive an honoured guest;
William Yeats is laid to rest:
Let the Irish vessel lie
Emptied of its poetry.

45   Time that is intolerant
Of the brave and innocent,

---

1. Stock exchange.

And indifferent in a week
To a beautiful physique,

Worships language and forgives
50   Everyone by whom it lives;
Pardons cowardice, conceit,
Lays its honours at their feet.

Time that with this strange excuse
Pardoned Kipling and his views,
55   And will pardon Paul Claudel,[2]
Pardons him for writing well.

In the nightmare of the dark
All the dogs of Europe bark,
And the living nations wait,
60   Each sequestered in its hate;

Intellectual disgrace
Stares from every human face,
And the seas of pity lie
Locked and frozen in each eye.

65   Follow, poet, follow right
To the bottom of the night,
With your unconstraining voice
Still persuade us to rejoice;

With the farming of a verse
70   Make a vineyard of the curse,
Sing of human unsuccess
In a rapture of distress;

In the deserts of the heart
Let the healing fountain start,
75   In the prison of his days
Teach the free man how to praise.

February 1939   1940

Spain 1937[1]

Yesterday all the past. The language of size
Spreading to China along the trade-routes; the diffusion
        Of the counting-frame and the cromlech;[2]
Yesterday the shadow-reckoning in the sunny climates.
5   Yesterday the assessment of insurance by cards,
The divination of water; yesterday the invention
        Of cart-wheels and clocks, the taming of
Horses; yesterday the bustling world of the navigators.

---

2. Rudyard Kipling (1865–1936), short-story writer, poet, and novelist remembered for his celebration of British imperialism; Paul Claudel (1868–1955), French poet and diplomat noted for his conservative views.
1. Auden visited Spain between January and March 1937, when the civil war between the Spanish govern-ment and military-backed Fascist insurgents was at its height. Many foreigners (the so-called "International Brigade") went to Spain at this time to aid the republican forces.
2. Prehistoric stone circle.

Yesterday the abolition of fairies and giants;
The fortress like a motionless eagle eyeing the valley,
      The chapel built in the forest;
Yesterday the carving of angels and of frightening gargoyles.

The trial of heretics among the columns of stone;
Yesterday the theological feuds in the taverns
      And the miraculous cure at the fountain;
Yesterday the Sabbath of Witches. But today the struggle.

Yesterday the installation of dynamos and turbines;
The construction of railways in the colonial desert;
      Yesterday the classic lecture
On the origin of Mankind. But today the struggle.

Yesterday the belief in the absolute value of Greek;
The fall of the curtain upon the death of a hero;
      Yesterday the prayer to the sunset,
And the adoration of madmen. But today the struggle.

As the poet whispers, startled among the pines
Or, where the loose waterfall sings, compact, or upright
      On the crag by the leaning tower:
"O my vision. O send me the luck of the sailor."

And the investigator peers through his instruments
At the inhuman provinces, the virile bacillus
      Or enormous Jupiter finished:
"But the lives of my friends. I inquire, I inquire."

And the poor in their fireless lodgings dropping the sheets
Of the evening paper: "Our day is our loss. O show us
      History the operator, the
Organiser, Time the refreshing river."

And the nations combine each cry, invoking the life
That shapes the individual belly and orders
      The private nocturnal terror:
"Did you not found once the city state of the sponge,

"Raise the vast military empires of the shark
And the tiger, establish the robin's plucky canton?
      Intervene. O descend as a dove or
A furious papa or a mild engineer: but descend."

And the life, if it answers at all, replies from the heart
And the eyes and the lungs, from the shops and squares of the city:
      "O no, I am not the Mover,
Not today, not to you. To you I'm the

"Yes-man, the bar-companion, the easily-duped:
I am whatever you do; I am your vow to be
      Good, your humorous story;
I am your business voice; I am your marriage.

"What's your proposal? To build the Just City? I will.
I agree. Or is it the suicide pact, the romantic

55   Death? Very well, I accept, for
I am your choice, your decision: yes, I am Spain."

Many have heard it on remote peninsulas,
On sleepy plains, in the aberrant fishermen's islands,
        In the corrupt heart of the city;
60   Have heard and migrated like gulls or the seeds of a flower.

They clung like burrs to the long expresses that lurch
Through the unjust lands, through the night, through the alpine tunnel;
        They floated over the oceans;
They walked the passes: they came to present their lives.

65   On that arid square, that fragment nipped off from hot
Africa, soldered so crudely to inventive Europe,
        On that tableland scored by rivers,
Our fever's menacing shapes are precise and alive.

Tomorrow, perhaps, the future: the research on fatigue
70   And the movements of packers; the gradual exploring of all the
        Octaves of radiation;
Tomorrow the enlarging of consciousness by diet and breathing.

Tomorrow the rediscovery of romantic love;
The photographing of ravens; all the fun under
75   Liberty's masterful shadow;
Tomorrow the hour of the pageant-master and the musician.

Tomorrow, for the young, the poets exploding like bombs,
The walks by the lake, the winter of perfect communion;
        Tomorrow the bicycle races
80   Through the suburbs on summer evenings: but today the struggle.

Today the inevitable increase in the chances of death;
The conscious acceptance of guilt in the fact of murder;
        Today the expending of powers
On the flat ephemeral pamphlet and the boring meeting.

85   Today the makeshift consolations; the shared cigarette;
The cards in the candle-lit barn and the scraping concert,
        The masculine jokes; today the
Fumbled and unsatisfactory embrace before hurting.

The stars are dead; the animals will not look:
90   We are left alone with our day, and the time is short and
        History to the defeated
May say Alas but cannot help or pardon.

                                                    1937

Lullaby

Lay your sleeping head, my love,
Human on my faithless arm;
Time and fevers burn away
Individual beauty from
5   Thoughtful children, and the grave

Proves the child ephemeral:
But in my arms till break of day
Let the living creature lie,
Mortal, guilty, but to me
10 The entirely beautiful.

Soul and body have no bounds:
To lovers as they lie upon
Her tolerant enchanted slope
In their ordinary swoon,
15 Grave the vision Venus sends
Of supernatural sympathy,
Universal love and hope;
While an abstract insight wakes
Among the glaciers and the rocks
20 The hermit's carnal ecstasy.

Certainty, fidelity
On the stroke of midnight pass
Like vibrations of a bell
And fashionable madmen raise
25 Their pedantic boring cry:
Every farthing of the cost,
All the dreaded cards foretell,
Shall be paid, but from this night
Not a whisper, not a thought,
30 Not a kiss nor look be lost.

Beauty, midnight, vision dies:
Let the winds of dawn that blow
Softly round your dreaming head
Such a day of welcome show
35 Eye and knocking heart may bless,
Find our mortal world enough;
Noons of dryness find you fed
By the involuntary powers,
Nights of insult let you pass
40 Watched by every human love.
1937   1940

September 1, 1939[1]

I sit in one of the dives
On Fifty-Second Street
Uncertain and afraid
As the clever hopes expire
5 Of a low dishonest decade:
Waves of anger and fear
Circulate over the bright

---

1. Auden arrived in New York City, where he was to spend World War II and much of the rest of his life, in January 1939. German forces marched into Poland on September 1, 1939; Britain and France declared war on September 3.

And darkened lands of the earth,
Obsessing our private lives;
10   The unmentionable odour of death
Offends the September night.

Accurate scholarship can
Unearth the whole offence
From Luther[2] until now
15   That has driven a culture mad,
Find what occurred at Linz,[3]
What huge imago made
A psychopathic god:[4]
I and the public know
20   What all schoolchildren learn,
Those to whom evil is done
Do evil in return.

Exiled Thucydides[5] knew
All that a speech can say
25   About Democracy,
And what dictators do,
The elderly rubbish they talk
To an apathetic grave;
Analysed all in his book,
30   The enlightenment driven away,
The habit-forming pain,
Mismanagement and grief:
We must suffer them all again.

Into this neutral air
35   Where blind skyscrapers use
Their full height to proclaim
The strength of Collective Man,
Each language pours its vain
Competitive excuse:
40   But who can live for long
In an euphoric dream;
Out of the mirror they stare,
Imperialism's face
And the international wrong.

45   Faces along the bar
Cling to their average day:
The lights must never go out,
The music must always play,

2. Martin Luther, German religious reformer (1483–1546), whose criticisms of Roman Catholic doctrine sparked the Protestant Reformation in Europe.
3. Linz, Austria, was Adolf Hitler's birthplace.
4. In the psychological terminology developed by C. G. Jung (1875–1961), an *imago* is an idealized mental image of self or others, especially parental figures.
5. Fifth-century Athenian historian and general in the Peloponnesian War between Athens and Sparta (431–404

B.C.). In his famous *History of the Peloponnesian War*, which follows events until 411 B.C., Thucydides records the Athenian statesman Pericles' *Funeral Oration*, given at the end of the first year of the war. In it, Pericles describes the benefits and possible dangers of democratic government as it was then practiced at Athens. Thucydides himself was exiled from Athens in 424 B.C., following a military defeat incurred under his leadership.

All the conventions conspire
50   To make this fort assume
The furniture of home;
Lest we should see where we are,
Lost in a haunted wood,
Children afraid of the night
55   Who have never been happy or good.

The windiest militant trash
Important Persons shout
Is not so crude as our wish:
What mad Nijinsky wrote
60   About Diaghilev
Is true of the normal heart;[6]
For the error bred in the bone
Of each woman and each man
Craves what it cannot have,
65   Not universal love
But to be loved alone.

From the conservative dark
Into the ethical life
The dense commuters come,
70   Repeating their morning vow,
"I *will* be true to the wife,
I'll concentrate more on my work,"
And helpless governors wake
To resume their compulsory game:
75   Who can release them now,
Who can reach the deaf,
Who can speak for the dumb?

All I have is a voice
To undo the folded lie,
80   The romantic lie in the brain
Of the sensual man-in-the-street
And the lie of Authority
Whose buildings grope the sky:
There is no such thing as the State
85   And no one exists alone;
Hunger allows no choice
To the citizen or the police;
We must love one another or die.

Defenceless under the night
90   Our world in stupor lies;
Yet, dotted everywhere,
Ironic points of light

6. Vaslav Nijinsky (1890–1950), principal male dancer in the Ballet Russes company under the direction of Sergei Pavlovich Diaghilev (1872–1929). The company revolutionized the world of dance, causing a sensation on its visit to Paris in 1909. Auden borrowed the following lines from Nijinsky's (1937) *Diary:* "Diaghilev does not want universal love, but to be loved alone."

Flash out wherever the Just
Exchange their messages:
95   May I, composed like them
Of Eros and of dust,
Beleaguered by the same
Negation and despair,
Show an affirming flame.

1939   1940

In Praise of Limestone[1]

If it form the one landscape that we, the inconstant ones,
    Are consistently homesick for, this is chiefly
Because it dissolves in water. Mark these rounded slopes
    With their surface fragrance of thyme and, beneath,
5   A secret system of caves and conduits; hear the springs
    That spurt out everywhere with a chuckle,
Each filling a private pool for its fish and carving
    Its own little ravine whose cliffs entertain
The butterfly and the lizard; examine this region
10   Of short distances and definite places:
What could be more like Mother or a fitter background
    For her son, the flirtatious male who lounges
Against a rock in the sunlight, never doubting
    That for all his faults he is loved; whose works are but
15   Extensions of his power to charm? From weathered outcrop
    To hill-top temple, from appearing waters to
Conspicuous fountains, from a wild to a formal vineyard,
    Are ingenious but short steps that a child's wish
To receive more attention than his brothers, whether
20   By pleasing or teasing, can easily take.

Watch, then, the band of rivals as they climb up and down
    Their steep stone gennels[2] in twos and threes, at times
Arm in arm, but never, thank God, in step; or engaged
    On the shady side of a square at midday in
25   Voluble discourse, knowing each other too well to think
    There are any important secrets, unable
To conceive a god whose temper-tantrums are moral
    And not to be pacified by a clever line
Or a good lay: for, accustomed to a stone that responds,
30   They have never had to veil their faces in awe
Of a crater whose blazing fury could not be fixed;
    Adjusted to the local needs of valleys
Where everything can be touched or reached by walking,
    Their eyes have never looked into infinite space
35   Through the lattice-work of a nomad's comb; born lucky,
    Their legs have never encountered the fungi
And insects of the jungle, the monstrous forms and lives

---

1. This poem is set in the landscape of Yorkshire, where   2. Channels.
Auden was born.

With which we have nothing, we like to hope, in common.
So, when one of them goes to the bad, the way his mind works
40   Remains comprehensible: to become a pimp
Or deal in fake jewellery or ruin a fine tenor voice
          For effects that bring down the house, could happen to all
But the best and worst of us . . .
                                        That is why, I suppose,
          The best and worst never stayed here long but sought
45   Immoderate soils where the beauty was not so external,
          The light less public and the meaning of life
Something more than a mad camp. "Come!" cried the granite wastes,
          "How evasive is your humour, how accidental
Your kindest kiss, how permanent is death." (Saints-to-be
50   Slipped away sighing.) "Come!" purred the clays and gravels.
"On our plains there is room for armies to drill; rivers
          Wait to be tamed and slaves to construct you a tomb
In the grand manner: soft as the earth is mankind and both
          Need to be altered." (Intendant Caesars rose and
55   Left, slamming the door.) But the really reckless were fetched
          By an older colder voice, the oceanic whisper:
"I am the solitude that asks and promises nothing;
          That is how I shall set you free. There is no love;
There are only the various envies, all of them sad."
60   They were right, my dear, all those voices were right
And still are; this land is not the sweet home that it looks,
          Nor its peace the historical calm of a site
Where something was settled once and for all: A backward
          And dilapidated province, connected
65   To the big busy world by a tunnel, with a certain
          Seedy appeal, is that all it is now? Not quite:
It has a worldly duty which in spite of itself
          It does not neglect, but calls into question
All the Great Powers assume; it disturbs our rights. The poet,
70   Admired for his earnest habit of calling
The sun the sun, his mind Puzzle, is made uneasy
          By these marble statues which so obviously doubt
His antimythological myth; and these gamins,[3]
          Pursuing the scientist down the tiled colonnade
75   With such lively offers, rebuke his concern for Nature's
          Remotest aspects: I, too, am reproached, for what
And how much you know. Not to lose time, not to get caught,
          Not to be left behind, not, please! to resemble
The beasts who repeat themselves, or a thing like water
80   Or stone whose conduct can be predicted, these
Are our Common Prayer, whose greatest comfort is music
          Which can be made anywhere, is invisible,
And does not smell. In so far as we have to look forward
          To death as a fact, no doubt we are right: But if
85   Sins can be forgiven, if bodies rise from the dead,

3. Street urchins.

These modifications of matter into
Innocent athletes and gesticulating fountains,
    Made solely for pleasure, make a further point:
The blessed will not care what angle they are regarded from,
90   Having nothing to hide. Dear, I know nothing of
Either, but when I try to imagine a faultless love
    Or the life to come, what I hear is the murmur
Of underground streams, what I see is a limestone landscape.
1948   1948

Writing

It is the author's aim to say once and emphatically, "He said."

—*H. D. Thoreau*

The art of literature, vocal or written, is to adjust the language so that it embodies what it indicates.

—*A. N. Whitehead*

All those whose success in life depends neither upon a job which satisfies some specific and unchanging social need, like a farmer's, nor, like a surgeon's, upon some craft which he can be taught by others and improve by practice, but upon "inspiration," the lucky hazard of ideas, live by their wits, a phrase which carries a slightly pejorative meaning. Every "original" genius, be he an artist or a scientist, has something a bit shady about him, like a gambler or a medium.

Literary gatherings, cocktail parties and the like, are a social nightmare because writers have no "shop" to talk. Lawyers and doctors can entertain each other with stories about interesting cases, about experiences, that is to say, related to their professional interests but yet impersonal and outside themselves. Writers have no impersonal professional interests. The literary equivalent of talking shop would be writers reciting their own work at each other, an unpopular procedure for which only very young writers have the nerve.

No poet or novelist wishes he were the only one who ever lived, but most of them wish they were the only one alive, and quite a number fondly believe their wish has been granted.

In theory, the author of a good book should remain anonymous, for it is to his work, not to himself, that admiration is due. In practice, this seems to be impossible. However, the praise and public attention that writers sometimes receive does not seem to be as fatal to them as one might expect. Just as a good man forgets his deed the moment he has done it, a genuine writer forgets a work as soon as he has completed it and starts to think about the next one; if he thinks about his past work at all, he is more likely to remember its faults than its virtues. Fame often makes a writer vain, but seldom makes him proud.

Writers can be guilty of every kind of human conceit but one, the conceit of the social worker: "We are all here on earth to help others; what on earth the others are here for, I don't know."

When a successful author analyzes the reasons for his success, he generally underestimates the talent he was born with, and overestimates his skill in employing it.

Every writer would rather be rich than poor, but no genuine writer cares about popularity as such. He needs approval of his work by others in order to be reassured that the vision of life he believes he has had is a true vision and not a self-delusion, but he can only be reassured by those whose judgment he respects. It would only be necessary for a writer to secure universal popularity if imagination and intelligence were equally distributed among all men.

When some obvious booby tells me he has liked a poem of mine, I feel as if I had picked his pocket.

Writers, poets especially, have an odd relation to the public because their medium, language, is not, like the paint of the painter or the notes of the composer, reserved for their use but is the common property of the linguistic group to which they belong. Lots of people are willing to admit that they don't understand painting or music, but very few indeed who have been to school and learned to read advertisements will admit that they don't understand English. As Karl Kraus[1] said: "The public doesn't understand German, and in Journalese I can't tell them so."

How happy the lot of the mathematician! He is judged solely by his peers, and the standard is so high that no colleague or rival can ever win a reputation he does not deserve. No cashier writes a letter to the press complaining about the incomprehensibility of Modern Mathematics and comparing it unfavorably with the good old days when mathematicians were content to paper irregularly shaped rooms and fill bathtubs without closing the waste pipe.[2]

To say that a work is inspired means that, in the judgment of its author or his readers, it is better than they could reasonably hope it would be, and nothing else.

All works of art are commissioned in the sense that no artist can create one by a simple act of will but must wait until what he believes to be a good idea for a work "comes" to him. Among those works which are failures because their initial conceptions were false or inadequate, the number of self-commissioned works may well be greater than the number commissioned by patrons.

The degree of excitement which a writer feels during the process of composition is as much an indication of the value of the final result as the excitement felt by a worshiper is an indication of the value of his devotions, that is to say, very little indication.

---

1. Austrian journalist, satirist, and critic (1874–1936).

2. Mathematics classes in British schools used such examples to teach the calculation of area, volume, etc.

The Oracle claimed to make prophecies and give good advice about the future; it never pretended to be giving poetry readings.

If poems could be created in a trance without the conscious participation of the poet, the writing of poetry would be so boring or even unpleasant an operation that only a substantial reward in money or social prestige could induce a man to be a poet. From the manuscript evidence, it now appears that Coleridge's account of the composition of "Kubla Khan" was a fib.[3]

It is true that, when he is writing a poem, it seems to a poet as if there were two people involved, his conscious self and a Muse whom he has to woo or an Angel with whom he has to wrestle, but, as in an ordinary wooing or wrestling match, his role is as important as Hers. The Muse, like Beatrice in Much Ado,[4] is a spirited girl who has as little use for an abject suitor as she has for a vulgar brute. She appreciates chivalry and good manners, but she despises those who will not stand up to her and takes a cruel delight in telling them nonsense and lies which the poor little things obediently write down as "inspired" truth.

> When I was writing the chorus in G Minor, I suddenly dipped my pen into the medicine bottle instead of the ink; I made a blot, and when I dried it with sand (blotting paper had not been invented then) it took the form of a natural, which instantly gave me the idea of the effect which the change from G minor to G major would make, and to this blot all the effect—if any—is due.
>
> (Rossini to Louis Engel.)

Such an act of judgment, distinguishing between Chance and Providence, deserves, surely, to be called an inspiration.

To keep his errors down to a minimum, the internal Censor to whom a poet submits his work in progress should be a Censorate. It should include, for instance, a sensitive only child, a practical housewife, a logician, a monk, an irreverent buffoon and even, perhaps, hated by all the others and returning their dislike, a brutal, foul-mouthed drill sergeant who considers all poetry rubbish.

In the course of many centuries a few laborsaving devices have been introduced into the mental kitchen—alcohol, coffee, tobacco, Benzedrine, etc.—but these are very crude, constantly breaking down, and liable to injure the cook. Literary composition in the twentieth century A.D. is pretty much what it was in the twentieth century B.C.: nearly everything has still to be done by hand.

Most people enjoy the sight of their own handwriting as they enjoy the smell of their own farts. Much as I loathe the typewriter, I must admit that it is a help in self-criticism. Typescript is so impersonal and hideous to look at that, if I type out a poem, I immediately see defects which I missed when I looked through it in manuscript.

---

3. Coleridge claimed that his poem Kubla Khan (1816) came to him while he was asleep under the influence of opium. Upon waking, he began to write out the poem but was interrupted by a "person from Porlock"; when he returned to his task, he found that the remainder of his poem had slipped from his memory.
4. Beatrice is the heroine of Shakespeare's Much Ado About Nothing.

When it comes to a poem by somebody else, the severest test I know of it is to write it out in longhand. The physical tedium of doing this ensures that the slightest defect will reveal itself; the hand is constantly looking for an excuse to stop.

Most artists are sincere and most art is bad, though some insincere (sincerely insincere) works can be quite good. (STRAVINSKY.) Sincerity is like sleep. Normally, one should assume that, of course, one will be sincere, and not give the question a second thought. Most writers, however, suffer occasionally from bouts of insincerity as men do from bouts of insomnia. The remedy in both cases is often quite simple: in the case of the latter, to change one's diet, in the case of the former, to change one's company.

The schoolmasters of literature frown on affectations of style as silly and unhealthy. Instead of frowning, they ought to laugh indulgently. Shakespeare makes fun of the Euphuists in *Love's Labour's Lost* and in *Hamlet*, but he owed them a great deal and he knew it.[5] Nothing, on the face of it, could have been more futile than the attempt of Spenser, Harvey and others to be good little humanists and write English verse in classical meters, yet, but for their folly, many of Campion's most beautiful songs and the choruses in *Samson Agonistes* would never have been written.[6] In literature, as in life, affectation, passionately adopted and loyally persevered in, is one of the chief forms of self-discipline by which mankind has raised itself by its own bootstraps.

A mannered style, that of Góngora[7] or Henry James, for example, is like eccentric clothing: very few writers can carry it off, but one is enchanted by the rare exception who can.

When a reviewer describes a book as "sincere," one knows immediately that it is (a) insincere (insincerely insincere) and (b) badly written. Sincerity in the proper sense of the word, meaning authenticity, is, however, or ought to be, a writer's chief preoccupation. No writer can ever judge exactly how good or bad a work of his may be, but he can always know, not immediately perhaps, but certainly in a short while, whether something he has written is authentic—in his hand-writing—or a forgery.

The most painful of all experiences to a poet is to find that a poem of his which he knows to be a forgery has pleased the public and got into the anthologies. For all he knows or cares, the poem may be quite good, but that is not the point; *he should not have written it.*

The work of a young writer—*Werther* is the classic example—is sometimes a therapeutic act.[8] He finds himself obsessed by certain ways of feeling and thinking of which his instinct tells him he must be rid before he can discover his authentic interests and sympathies, and the only way by which he can be rid of them forever is by surrendering to them. Once he has done this, he has developed the necessary antibodies which will make him immune for the rest of his life. As a rule, the disease is

5. *The Anatomy of Wit* (1578) and *Euphues and his England* (1580) are prose romances by John Lyly. Both are marked by a highly mannered style, which was much imitated.
6. The poet Edmund Spenser (c. 1552–1599) and his former tutor and friend Gabriel Harvey (c. 1550–1631) experimented with writing English verse in Greek and Latin meters, but without much success. Thomas Campion (1567–1620) was a lyric poet and musician; *Samson Agonistes* (1671) is by John Milton.
7. Luis de Góngora y Argote (1561–1627) used elaborate conceits in his poems.
8. *The Sorrows of Young Werther* (1774), by Johann Wolfgang von Goethe, depicts a melancholy artist at odds with society, who eventually commits suicide.

some spiritual malaise of his generation. If so, he may, as Goethe did, find himself in an embarrassing situation. What he wrote in order to exorcise certain feelings is enthusiastically welcomed by his contemporaries because it expresses just what they feel but, unlike him, they are perfectly happy to feel in this way; for the moment they regard him as their spokesman. Time passes. Having gotten the poison out of his system, the writer turns to his true interests which are not, and never were, those of his early admirers, who now pursue him with cries of "Traitor!"

> The intellect of man is forced to choose
> Perfection of the life or of the work. (YEATS)

This is untrue; perfection is possible in neither. All one can say is that a writer who, like all men, has his personal weaknesses and limitations, should be aware of them and try his best to keep them out of his work. For every writer, there are certain subjects which, because of defects in his character and his talent, he should never touch.

What makes it difficult for a poet not to tell lies is that, in poetry, all facts and all beliefs cease to be true or false and become interesting possibilities. The reader does not have to share the beliefs expressed in a poem in order to enjoy it. Knowing this, a poet is constantly tempted to make use of an idea or a belief, not because he believes it to be true, but because he sees it has interesting poetic possibilities. It may not, perhaps, be absolutely necessary that he believe it, but it is certainly necessary that his emotions be deeply involved, and this they can never be unless, as a man, he takes it more seriously than as a mere poetic convenience.

The integrity of a writer is more threatened by appeals to his social conscience, his political or religious convictions, than by appeals to his cupidity. It is morally less confusing to be goosed by a traveling salesman than by a bishop.

Some writers confuse authenticity, which they ought always to aim at, with originality, which they should never bother about. There is a certain kind of person who is so dominated by the desire to be loved for himself alone that he has constantly to test those around him by tiresome behavior; what he says and does must be admired, not because it is intrinsically admirable, but because it is *his* remark, *his* act. Does not this explain a good deal of avant-garde art?

Slavery is so intolerable a condition that the slave can hardly escape deluding himself into thinking that he is choosing to obey his master's commands when, in fact, he is obliged to. Most slaves of habit suffer from this delusion and so do some writers, enslaved by an all too "personal" style.

> "Let me think: was I the same when I got up this morning? . . . But if I'm not the same, the next question is 'Who in the world am I?' . . . I'm sure I'm not Ada . . . for her hair goes in such long ringlets and mine doesn't go in ringlets at all; and I'm sure I can't be Mabel, for I know all sorts of things, and she, oh! she knows such a very little! Beside she's she and I'm I and—oh dear, how puzzling it all is! I'll try if I know all the things I used to know . . . ." Her eyes filled with tears . . . : "I must be Mabel after all, and I shall have to go and live in that poky little house, and have next to no toys to play with, and oh!—ever so many lessons to learn! No, I've made up my mind about it: if I'm Mabel, I'll stay down here!"

> (Alice in Wonderland.)

> *At the next peg the Queen turned again and this time she said: "Speak in French when you can't think of the English for a thing—turn your toes out as you walk—and remember who you are."*
>
> (*Through the Looking-Glass.*)

Most writers, except the supreme masters who transcend all systems of classification are either Alices or Mabels. For example:

ALICE	MABEL
Montaigne	Pascal
Marvell	Donne
Burns	Shelley
Jane Austen	Dickens
Turgenev	Dostoievski
Valéry	Gide
Virginia Woolf	Joyce
E. M. Forster	Lawrence
Robert Graves	Yeats

"Orthodoxy," said a real Alice of a bishop, "is reticence."

Except when used as historical labels, the terms *classical* and *romantic* are misleading terms for two poetic parties, the Aristocratic and the Democratic, which have always existed and to one of which every writer belongs, though he may switch his party allegiance or, on some specific issue, refuse to obey his Party Whip.

The Aristocratic Principle as regards subject matter:
  No subject matter shall be treated by poets which poetry cannot digest. It defends poetry against didacticism and journalism.
The Democratic Principle as regards subject matter:
  No subject matter shall be excluded by poets which poetry is capable of digesting. It defends poetry against limited or stale conceptions of what is "poetic."
The Aristocratic Principle as regards treatment:
  No irrelevant aspects of a given subject shall be expressed in a poem which treats it. It defends poetry against barbaric vagueness.
The Democratic Principle as regards treatment:
  No relevant aspect of a given subject shall remain unexpressed in a poem which treats it. It defends poetry against decadent triviality.

Every work of a writer should be a first step, but this will be a false step unless, whether or not he realize it at the time, it is also a further step. When a writer is dead, one ought to be able to see that his various works, taken together, make one consistent *oeuvre.*

It takes little talent to see clearly what lies under one's nose, a good deal of it to know in which direction to point that organ.

The greatest writer cannot see through a brick wall but, unlike the rest of us, he does not build one.

Only a minor talent can be a perfect gentleman; a major talent is always more than a bit of a cad. Hence the importance of minor writers—as teachers of good manners. Now and again, an exquisite minor work can make a master feel thoroughly ashamed of himself.

The poet is the father of his poem; its mother is a language: one could list poems as race horses are listed—*out of L by P.*

A poet has to woo, not only his own Muse but also Dame Philology, and, for the beginner, the latter is the more important. As a rule, the sign that a beginner has a genuine original talent is that he is more interested in playing with words than in saying something original; his attitude is that of the old lady, quoted by E. M. Forster—"How can I know what I think till I see what I say?" It is only later, when he has wooed and won Dame Philology, that he can give his entire devotion to his Muse.

Rhymes, meters, stanza forms, etc., are like servants. If the master is fair enough to win their affection and firm enough to command their respect, the result is an orderly happy household. If he is too tyrannical, they give notice; if he lacks authority, they become slovenly, impertinent, drunk and dishonest.

The poet who writes "free" verse is like Robinson Crusoe on his desert island: he must do all his cooking, laundry and darning for himself. In a few exceptional cases, this manly independence produces something original and impressive, but more often the result is squalor—dirty sheets on the unmade bed and empty bottles on the unswept floor.

There are some poets, Kipling for example, whose relation to language reminds one of a drill sergeant: the words are taught to wash behind their ears, stand properly at attention and execute complicated maneuvers, but at the cost of never being allowed to think for themselves. There are others, Swinburne, for example, who remind one more of Svengali:[9] under their hypnotic suggestion, an extraordinary performance is put on, not by raw recruits, but by feeble-minded schoolchildren.

Due to the Curse of Babel, poetry is the most provincial of the arts, but today, when civilization is becoming monotonously the same all the world over, one feels inclined to regard this as a blessing rather than a curse: in poetry, at least, there cannot be an "International Style."

My language is the universal whore whom I have to make into a virgin. (KARL KRAUS.) It is both the glory and the shame of poetry that its medium is not its private property, that a poet cannot invent his words and that words are products, not of nature, but of a human society which uses them for a thousand different purposes. In mod-

9. The poetry of Algernon Charles Swinburne (1837–1909) is characterized by an emphasis on verbal effects arguably at the expense of sense; Svengali, a character in George du Maurier's novel *Trilby* (1894), exercises a mesmeric influence over the novel's protagonist.

ern societies where language is continually being debased and reduced to non-speech, the poet is in constant danger of having his ear corrupted, a danger to which the painter and the composer, whose media are their private property, are not exposed. On the other hand he is more protected than they from another modern peril, that of solipsist subjectivity; however esoteric a poem may be, the fact that all its words have meanings which can be looked up in a dictionary makes it testify to the existence of other people. Even the language of *Finnegans Wake* was not created by Joyce *ex nihilo* [out of nothing]; a purely private verbal world is not possible.

The difference between verse and prose is self-evident, but it is a sheer waste of time to look for a definition of the difference between poetry and prose. Frost's definition of poetry as the untranslatable element in language looks plausible at first sight but, on closer examination, will not quite do. In the first place, even in the most rarefied poetry, there are some elements which are translatable. The sound of the words, their rhythmical relations, and all meanings and association of meanings which depend upon sound, like rhymes and puns, are, of course, untranslatable, but poetry is not, like music, pure sound. Any elements in a poem which are not based on verbal experience are, to some degree, translatable into another tongue, for example, images, similes and metaphors which are drawn from sensory experience. Moreover, because one characteristic that all men, whatever their culture, have in common is uniqueness—every man is a member of a class of one—the unique perspective on the world which every genuine poet has survives translation. If one takes a poem by Goethe and a poem by Hölderlin and makes literal prose cribs of them, every reader will recognize that the two poems were written by two different people. In the second place, if speech can never become music, neither can it ever become algebra. Even in the most "prosy" language, in informative and technical prose, there is a personal element because language is a personal creation. *Ne pas se pencher au dehors* has a different feeling tone from *Nichthinauslehnen*.[1] A purely poetic language would be unlearnable, a purely prosaic not worth learning.

Valéry bases his definitions of poetry and prose on the difference between the gratuitous and the useful, play and work, and uses as an analogy the difference between dancing and walking. But this will not do either. A commuter may walk to his suburban station every morning, but at the same time he may enjoy the walk for its own sake; the fact that his walk is necessary does not exclude the possibility of its also being a form of play. Vice versa, a dance does not cease to be play if it is also believed to have a useful purpose like promoting a good harvest.

If French poets have been more prone than English to fall into the heresy of thinking that poetry ought to be as much like music as possible, one reason may be that, in traditional French verse, sound effects have always played a much more important role than they have in English verse. The English-speaking peoples have always felt that the difference between poetic speech and the conversational speech of everyday

---

1. "Do not lean out" [of the window] in French and German respectively; the words occur as a warning on European trains.

should be kept small, and, whenever English poets have felt that the gap between poetic and ordinary speech was growing too wide, there has been a stylistic revolution to bring them closer again. In English verse, even in Shakespeare's grandest rhetorical passages, the ear is always aware of its relation to everyday speech. A good actor must—alas, today he too seldom does—make the audience hear Shakespeare's lines as verse not prose, but if he tries to make the verse sound like a different language, he will make himself ridiculous.

But French poetry, both in the way it is written and the way it is recited, has emphasized and gloried in the difference between itself and ordinary speech; in French drama, verse and prose are different languages. Valéry quotes a contemporary description of Rachel's powers of declamation; in reciting she could and did use a range of two octaves, from F below Middle C to F in alt; an actress who tried to do the same with Shakespeare as Rachel did with Racine would be laughed off the stage.[2]

One can read Shakespeare to oneself without even mentally *hearing* the lines and be very moved; indeed, one may easily find a performance disappointing because almost anyone with an understanding of English verse can speak it better than the average actor and actress. But to read Racine to oneself, even, I fancy, if one is a Frenchman, is like reading the score of an opera when one can hardly play or sing; one can no more get an adequate notion of *Phèdre* without having heard a great performance, than one can of *Tristan und Isolde*[3] if one has never heard a great Isolde like Leider or Flagstad.

(Monsieur St. John Perse tells me that, when it comes to everyday speech, it is French which is the more monotonous and English which has the wider range of vocal inflection.)

I must confess that French classical tragedy strikes me as being opera for the unmusical. When I read the *Hippolytus*, I can recognize, despite all differences, a kinship between the world of Euripides and the world of Shakespeare, but the world of Racine, like the world of opera, seems to be another planet altogether. Euripides' Aphrodite is as concerned with fish and fowl as she is with human beings; Racine's Venus is not only unconcerned with animals, she takes no interest in the Lower Orders. It is impossible to imagine any of Racine's characters sneezing or wanting to go to the bathroom, for in his world there is neither weather nor nature. In consequence, the passions by which his characters are consumed can only exist, as it were, on stage, the creation of the magnificent speech and the grand gestures of the actors and actresses who endow them with flesh and blood. This is also the case in opera, but no speaking voice, however magnificent, can hope to compete, in expressiveness through sound, with a great singing voice backed by an orchestra.

Whenever people talk to me about the weather, I always feel certain that they mean something else. (OSCAR WILDE.) The only kind of speech which approximates to the symbolist's poetic ideal is polite tea table conversation,[4] in which the meaning of the banalities uttered depends almost entirely upon vocal inflections.

2. Jean Racine, French tragic dramatist and author of *Phèdre* (1677); his plays, in contrast to Shakespeare's, are classically conceived and executed.
3. An opera by the German composer Richard Wagner (1813–1883).

4. Symbolism was a late 19th-century, largely French movement in poetry, which stressed suggestion over description or narration in poetry, and awarded to the poetic "symbol" a preeminent, quasi-magical function.

Owing to its superior power as a mnemonic, verse is superior to prose as a medium for didactic instruction. Those who condemn didacticism must disapprove *a fortiori* [more conclusively] of didactic prose; in verse, as the Alka-Seltzer advertisements testify, the didactic message loses half its immodesty. Verse is also certainly the equal of prose as a medium for the lucid exposition of ideas; in skillful hands, the form of the verse can parallel and reinforce the steps of the logic. Indeed, contrary to what most people who have inherited the romantic conception of poetry believe, the danger of argument in verse—Pope's *Essay on Man*[5] is an example—is that the verse may make the ideas too clear and distinct, more Cartesian than they really are.

On the other hand, verse is unsuited to controversy, to proving some truth or belief which is not universally accepted, because its formal nature cannot but convey a certain skepticism about its conclusions.

Thirty days hath September,
April, June and November

is valid because nobody doubts its truth. Were there, however, a party who passionately denied it, the lines would be powerless to convince him because, formally, it would make no difference if the lines ran:

Thirty days hath September,
August, May and December.

Poetry is not magic. In so far as poetry, or any other of the arts, can be said to have an ulterior purpose, it is, by telling the truth, to disenchant and disintoxicate.

"The unacknowledged legislators of the world" describes the secret police, not the poets.[6]

Catharsis is properly effected, not by works of art, but by religious rites. It is also effected, usually improperly, by bullfights, professional football matches, bad movies, military bands and monster rallies at which ten thousand girl guides form themselves into a model of the national flag.

The condition of mankind is, and always has been, so miserable and depraved that, if anyone were to say to the poet: "For God's sake stop singing and do something useful like putting on the kettle or fetching bandages," what just reason could he give for refusing? But nobody says this. The self-appointed unqualified nurse says: "You are to sing the patient a song which will make him believe that I, and I alone, can cure him. If you can't or won't, I shall confiscate your passport and send you to the mines." And the poor patient in his delirium cries: "Please sing me a song which will give me sweet dreams instead of nightmares. If you succeed, I will give you a penthouse in New York or a ranch in Arizona."

---

5. Philosophical poem in heroic couplets by Alexander Pope.
6. A famous slogan from Shelley's *A Defence of Poetry* (1821), which describes the nature and social role of poetry.

PERSPECTIVES

World War II and the End of Empire

World War I had been a catastrophe of unprecedented proportions. Never before in world history had a preponderance of national powers joined together into two warring alliances; never before had the theater of war included such a wide expanse of the globe. But for Great Britain, at least, the war was foreign rather than domestic; as demoralizing and bleak as the fighting was, it was "over there," and never touched the British Isles. World War II would be a very different story.

World War II started, technically, with Hitler's invasion of Poland on September 1, 1939; as is the case with all world-historical conflicts, however, the war's genesis can be traced further back—in this case, back two decades to the peace treaties with which World War I was uneasily concluded. The victors of World War I never quite got what they hoped for, and the defeated nations had their defeat transformed into ritual diplomatic humiliation. Meanwhile, a worldwide economic depression had begun in the United States in 1929 and spread to Europe by the early 1930s, weakening democratic governments and lending a seductive edge to the rhetoric of political extremists. As a result, when Hitler began to rise to power in a beleaguered Germany during the 1930s, his message of empowerment was one that many Germans wanted to hear. Beginning with Poland, Hitler overran Denmark, Luxembourg, the Netherlands, Belgium, and Norway in quick succession, and by June 1940 had conquered even France. Britain was next on Hitler's list, as the major remaining obstacle to the domination of Europe.

Hitler hoped to paralyze and demoralize the British by a devastating series of attacks by air. This drew out to become the ten-month long Battle of Britain, in which the German Luftwaffe (air force) engaged Britain's Royal Air Force in the previously inviolable air space over England's green and pleasant land. The battle brought enormous costs—especially during the eight months of nightly air raids over British metropolitan centers known as the Blitz. The bombing caused great destruction to London, which was bombed every night between September 7 and November 2, 1940; more than 15,000 civilians were killed in London (30,000 nationwide), over half a million left homeless, and important cultural and architectural treasures, such as the House of Commons and Buckingham Palace, were damaged or destroyed. This violation of England's homeland was costly in psychological and emotional terms as well; one poignant register of the broad impact of the air raids can be seen in Virginia Woolf's final novel *Between the Acts*, where the sound of bombs falling on distant London unnerves the residents and guests of Pointz Hall. As Woolf's diaries and letters make clear, the sound of those bombs were also a crucial factor in her decision to take her own life in March 1941.

In May of 1941, Germany finally gave up its attempt to conquer Britain from the air. With the bombing of Pearl Harbor by the Japanese in December 1941, the United States entered the war on the side of the Allies; with their help, Britain was able to mount an offensive against Germany on the European mainland and retake land that had been invaded by Germany. In 1942, Britain and the United States began to plan an invasion across the English Channel. The first attempt, a raid staged at the French port of Dieppe in the summer of 1942, was a disappointing failure. The Allies regrouped, however, and planned the offensive known as D-Day. On June 6, 1944, Allied troops, under the command of General Dwight D. Eisenhower, crossed the channel with 2,700 ships and 176,000 soldiers and overcame German defenses; by the end of the month, about a million Allied troops were on the ground in France, and the tide of the war had turned. In April 1945 Hitler committed suicide; one week later, Germany signed a statement of unconditional surrender, with Japan following suit on September 2.

World War II was over; in some important arenas, however, its influence had just begun to be felt. With such a great proportion of its able-bodied young men going off to war, millions of women in both Britain and the United States took employment outside the home for the first time; that trend, once started, has only gained momentum in the years since. The economic and personal freedom ceded to women during the wartime emergency laid the groundwork for the contemporary women's movement in Great Britain; Margaret Thatcher, Britain's first woman Prime Minister (1979–1990), was a postwar inheritor of Winston Churchill's legacy.

At the same time, the United States and the Soviet Union emerged from the war as the preeminent world powers; Britain, while on the winning side, saw its global prestige in eclipse, and found itself in the midst of an economic crisis. At the height of the war, Britain was devoting 54 percent of its gross national product to the war effort; by the war's end it had expended practically all of its foreign financial resources and was several billion pounds in debt to its wartime allies. In short, Britain was bankrupt. As its colonial possessions increased their protests against British rule, Britain had neither the military nor the economic power to control them; India, which had begun its independence movement during World War I, finally won full independence on August 15, 1947, and Burma and Ceylon (now Sri Lanka) quickly followed suit in early 1948. At about the same time, Britain was forced to withdraw from Palestine, and from all of Egypt except for the Suez Canal; the Canal itself was nationalized by Egypt in the summer of 1956. The 1960s saw increased Irish Republican activity in Northern Ireland, degenerating into armed sectarian violence in 1968; recent years have seen periodic waves of IRA violence in support of independence for Ulster, alternating with largely unsuccessful diplomatic attempts to forge a lasting peace in Northern Ireland. In the spring of 1982 Prime Minister Thatcher sent British troops to liberate the Falkland Islands, a small self-governing British colony off the coast of Argentina, from an Argentinian occupying force; Thatcher won a resounding reelection the following year on the strength of the British success, suggesting that pride in the British Empire, while diminishing in importance, was by no means yet extinct.

+ —— ◄◆► —— +

Sir Winston Churchill
1874–1965

British historian A. J. P. Taylor has written of a unique paradox of World War II: though it was a time of unprecedented stress and anxiety for the British people, "Great Britain was never so free from political controversy." The reason? Winston Churchill's ability to forge a partnership between himself and the British people. "There have been many great British leaders," Taylor continues; "There has only been one whom everyone recognized as the embodiment of the national will." The pictures of Churchill—watch-chain draped across his waistcoat, cigar drooping from his jowly face (above his bow tie and beneath his homburg), index and middle fingers raised in the V of Victory—is perhaps the most familiar and bouyant icon of Allied victory in the war.

Winston Churchill was born at Blenheim Palace, the ancestral home of his grandfather, the seventh duke of Marlborough; his father, Lord Randolph Churchill, had a distinguished career as a Conservative member of Parliament. Young Winston proved not to be an outstanding scholar, however, and instead of university, was sent to the Royal Military Academy. This military training, and his subsequent combat experience on the Western Front and in the Sudan, was to prove invaluable as he led his country as Prime Minister through the darkest days of World War II. Equally important to Churchill the statesman was his early work as a journalist and essayist; the economist John Kenneth Galbraith suggested that Churchill's power as an orator derived from his "fearsome certainty that he was completely right," a certainty made manifest in "his use of language as a weapon." In Churchill's well-known phrases, like "blood, toil, tears and sweat," a nation at war found its rallying cries.

Winston Churchill, June 1943.
Returning to 10 Downing
Street after meeting with
American president Franklin
Roosevelt in Washington, D.C.,
and visiting Allied armies in
North Africa, the Prime Minis-
ter flashes his famous "V for
Victory" sign to reporters.

Two Speeches Before the House of Commons

["BLOOD, TOIL, TEARS AND SWEAT"][1]

I beg to move,

> That this House welcomes the formation of a Government representing the united
> and inflexible resolve of the nation to prosecute the war with Germany to a victorious
> conclusion.

On Friday evening last I received His Majesty's Commission to form a new
Administration. It was the evident wish and will of Parliament and the nation that
this should be conceived on the broadest possible basis and that it should include all
parties, both those who supported the late Government and also the parties of the
Opposition. I have completed the most important part of this task. A War Cabinet
has been formed of five Members, representing, with the Opposition Liberals, the
unity of the nation. The three party Leaders have agreed to serve, either in the War
Cabinet or in high executive office. The three Fighting Services have been filled. It

1. Delivered in the House of Commons, 13 May 1940.

was necessary that this should be done in one single day, on account of the extreme urgency and rigour of events. A number of other positions, key positions, were filled yesterday, and I am submitting a further list to His Majesty to-night. I hope to complete the appointment of the principal Ministers during to-morrow. The appointment of the other Ministers usually takes a little longer, but I trust that, when Parliament meets again, this part of my task will be completed, and that the administration will be complete in all respects.

I considered it in the public interest to suggest that the House should be summoned to meet to-day. Mr Speaker agreed, and took the necessary steps, in accordance with the powers conferred upon him by the Resolution of the House. At the end of the proceedings to-day, the Adjournment of the House will be proposed until Tuesday, 21st May, with, of course, provision for earlier meeting, if need be. The business to be considered during that week will be notified to Members at the earliest opportunity. I now invite the House, by the Motion which stands in my name, to record its approval of the steps taken and to declare its confidence in the new Government.

To form an Administration of this scale and complexity is a serious undertaking in itself, but it must be remembered that we are in the preliminary stage of one of the greatest battles in history, that we are in action at many other points in Norway and in Holland, that we have to be prepared in the Mediterranean, that the air battle is continuous and that many preparations, such as have been indicated by my hon. Friend below the Gangway, have to be made here at home. In this crisis I hope I may be pardoned if I do not address the House at any length to-day. I hope that any of my friends and colleagues, or former colleagues, who are affected by the political reconstruction, will make allowance, all allowance, for any lack of ceremony with which it has been necessary to act. I would say to the House, as I said to those who have joined this Government: "I have nothing to offer but blood, toil, tears and sweat."

We have before us an ordeal of the most grievous kind. We have before us many, many long months of struggle and of suffering. You ask, what is our policy? I can say: It is to wage war, by sea, land and air, with all our might and with all the strength that God can give us; to wage war against a monstrous tyranny, never surpassed in the dark, lamentable catalogue of human crime. That is our policy. You ask, what is our aim? I can answer in one word: It is victory, victory at all costs, victory in spite of all terror, victory, however long and hard the road may be; for without victory, there is no survival. Let that be realised; no survival for the British Empire, no survival for all that the British Empire has stood for, no survival for the urge and impulse of the ages, that mankind will move forward towards its goal. But I take up my task with buoyancy and hope. I feel sure that our cause will not be suffered to fail among men. At this time I feel entitled to claim the aid of all, and I say, "Come then, let us go forward together with our united strength."

["WARS ARE NOT WON BY EVACUATIONS"][1]

From the moment that the French defenses at Sedan and on the Meuse[2] were broken at the end of the second week of May, only a rapid retreat to Amiens[3] and the south could have saved the British and French Armies who had entered Belgium at the

---

1. Delivered in the Hosue of Commons 4 June 1940. This speech exemplifies Churchill's ability to rally his people amid the greatest difficulties—here, the disastrous defeat of the British and French armies in April–May 1940. What might have been seen as the humiliation of the British army becomes, in Churchill's stirring account, the

heroic achievement of a successful evacuation against all odds.
2. A river flowing through France, Belgium, and the Netherlands.
3. A city located on the Somme River in northern France.

appeal of the Belgian King; but this strategic fact was not immediately realized. The French High Command hoped they would be able to close the gap, and the Armies of the north were under their orders. Moreover, a retirement of this kind would have involved almost certainly the destruction of the fine Belgian Army of over 20 divisions and the abandonment of the whole of Belgium. Therefore, when the force and scope of the German penetration were realized and when a new French Generalissimo,[4] General Weygand, assumed command in place of General Gamelin, an effort was made by the French and British Armies in Belgium to keep on holding the right hand of the Belgians and to give their own right hand to the newly created French Army which was to have advanced across the Somme[5] in great strength to grasp it.

However, the German eruption swept like a sharp scythe around the right and rear of the Armies of the north. Eight or nine armored divisions, each of about four hundred armored vehicles of different kinds, but carefully assorted to be complementary and divisible into small self-contained units, cut off all communications between us and the main French Armies. It severed our own communications for food and ammunition, which ran first to Amiens and afterwards through Abbeville, and it shore its way up the coast to Boulogne and Calais, and almost to Dunkirk.[6] Behind this armored and mechanized onslaught came a number of German divisions in lorries, and behind them again there plodded comparatively slowly the dull brute mass of the ordinary German Army and German people, always so ready to be led to the trampling down in other lands of liberties and comforts which they have never known in their own.

I have said this armored scythe-stroke almost reached Dunkirk—almost but not quite. Boulogne and Calais were the scenes of desperate fighting. The Guards defended Boulogne for a while and were then withdrawn by orders from this country. The Rifle Brigade, the 60th Rifles, and the Queen Victoria's Rifles, with a battalion of British tanks and 1,000 Frenchmen, in all about four thousand strong, defended Calais to the last. The British Brigadier was given an hour to surrender. He spurned the offer, and four days of intense street fighting passed before silence reigned over Calais, which marked the end of a memorable resistance. Only 30 unwounded survivors were brought off by the Navy, and we do not know the fate of their comrades. Their sacrifice, however, was not in vain. At least two armored divisions, which otherwise would have been turned against the British Expeditionary Force, had to be sent to overcome them. They have added another page to the glories of the light divisions, and the time gained enabled the Graveline water lines to be flooded and to be held by the French troops.

Thus it was that the port of Dunkirk was kept open. When it was found impossible for the Armies of the north to reopen their communications to Amiens with the main French Armies, only one choice remained. It seemed, indeed, forlorn. The Belgian, British and French Armies were almost surrounded. Their sole line of retreat was to a single port and to its neighboring beaches. They were pressed on every side by heavy attacks and far outnumbered in the air.

When, a week ago today, I asked the House to fix this afternoon as the occasion for a statement, I feared it would be my hard lot to announce the greatest military disaster in our long history. I thought—and some good judges agreed with me—that perhaps 20,000 or 30,000 men might be re-embarked. But it certainly seemed that

4. Supreme commander of the French forces.
5. A river in northern France.
6. Seaports in northern France.

the whole of the French First Army and the whole of the British Expeditionary Force north of the Amiens-Abbeville gap would be broken up in the open field or else would have to capitulate for lack of food and ammunition. These were the hard and heavy tidings for which I called upon the House and the nation to prepare themselves a week ago. The whole root and core and brain of the British Army, on which and around which we were to build, and are to build, the great British Armies in the later years of the war, seemed about to perish upon the field or to be led into an ignominious and starving capacity.

That was the prospect a week ago. But another blow which might well have proved final was yet to fall upon us. The King of the Belgians[7] had called upon us to come to his aid. Had not this Ruler and his Government severed themselves from the Allies, who rescued their country from extinction in the late war, and had they not sought refuge in what was proved to be a fatal neutrality, the French and British Armies might well at the outset have saved not only Belgium but perhaps even Poland. Yet at the last moment, when Belgium was already invaded, King Leopold called upon us to come to his aid, and even at the last moment we came. He and his brave, efficient Army, nearly half a million strong, guarded our left flank and thus kept open our only line of retreat to the sea. Suddenly, without prior consultation, with the least possible notice, without the advice of his Ministers and upon his own personal act, he sent a plenipotentiary[8] to the German Command, surrendered his Army, and exposed our whole flank and means of retreat.

I asked the House a week ago to suspend its judgment because the facts were not clear, but I do not feel that any reason now exists why we should not form our own opinions upon this pitiful episode. The surrender of the Belgian Army compelled the British at the shortest notice to cover a flank to the sea more than 30 miles in length. Otherwise all would have been cut off, and all would have shared the fate to which King Leopold had condemned the finest Army his country had ever formed. So in doing this and in exposing this flank, as anyone who followed the operations on the map will see, contact was lost between the British and two out of the three corps forming the First French Army, who were still farther from the coast than we were, and it seemed impossible that any large number of Allied troops could reach the coast.

The enemy attacked on all sides with great strength and fierceness, and their main power, the power of their far more numerous Air Force, was thrown into the battle or else concentrated upon Dunkirk and the beaches. Pressing in upon the narrow exit, both from the east and from the west, the enemy began to fire with cannon upon the beaches by which alone the shipping could approach or depart. They sowed magnetic mines in the channels and seas; they sent repeated waves of hostile aircraft, sometimes more than a hundred strong in one formation, to cast their bombs upon the single pier that remained, and upon the sand dunes upon which the troops had their eyes for shelter. Their U-boats, one of which was sunk, and their motor launches took their toll of the vast traffic which now began. For four or five days an intense struggle reigned. All their armored divisions—or what was left of them—together with great masses of infantry and artillery, hurled themselves in vain upon the ever-narrowing, ever-contracting appendix within which the British and French Armies fought.

Meanwhile, the Royal Navy, with the willing help of countless merchant seamen, strained every nerve to embark the British and Allied troops; 220 light warships and 650 other vessels were engaged. They had to operate upon the difficult coast,

---

7. Leopold III (1901–1983).   8. Diplomatic agent.

often in adverse weather, under an almost ceaseless hail of bombs and an increasing concentration of artillery fire. Nor were the seas, as I have said, themselves free from mines and torpedoes. It was in conditions such as these that our men carried on, with little or no rest, for days and nights on end, making trip after trip across the dangerous waters, bringing with them always men whom they had rescued. The numbers they have brought back are the measure of their devotion and their courage. The hospital ships, which brought off many thousands of British and French wounded, being so plainly marked were a special target for Nazi bombs; but the men and women on board them never faltered in their duty.

Meanwhile, the Royal Air Force, which had already been intervening in the battle, so far as its range would allow, from home bases, now used part of its main metropolitan fighter strength, and struck at the German bombers and at the fighters which in large numbers protected them. This struggle was protracted and fierce. Suddenly the scene has cleared, the crash and thunder has for the moment—but only for the moment—died away. A miracle of deliverance, achieved by valor, by perseverance, by perfect discipline, by faultless service, by resource, by skill, by unconquerable fidelity, is manifest to us all. The enemy was hurled back by the retreating British and French troops. He was so roughly handled that he did not hurry their departure seriously. The Royal Air Force engaged the main strength of the German Air Force, and inflicted upon them losses of at least four to one; and the Navy, using nearly 1,000 ships of all kinds, carried over 335,000 men, French and British, out of the jaws of death and shame, to their native land and to the tasks which lie immediately ahead. We must be very careful not to assign to this deliverance the attributes of a victory. Wars are not won by evacuations. But there was a victory inside this deliverance, which should be noted. It was gained by the Air Force. Many of our soldiers coming back have not seen the Air Force at work; they saw only the bombers which escaped its protective attack. They underrate its achievements. I have heard much talk of this; that is why I go out of my way to say this. I will tell you about it.

This was a great trial of strength between the British and German Air Forces. Can you conceive a greater objective for the Germans in the air than to make evacuation from these beaches impossible, and to sink all these ships which were displayed, almost to the extent of thousands? Could there have been an objective of greater military importance and significance for the whole purpose of the war than this? They tried hard, and they were beaten back; they were frustrated in their task. We got the Army away; and they have paid fourfold for any losses which they have inflicted. Very large formations of German aeroplanes—and we know that they are a very brave race—have turned on several occasions from the attack of one-quarter of their number of the Royal Air Force, and have dispersed in different directions. Twelve aeroplanes have been hunted by two. One aeroplane was driven into the water and cast away by the mere charge of a British aeroplane, which had no more ammunition. All of our types—the Hurricane, the Spitfire and the new Defiant—and all our pilots have been vindicated as superior to what they have at present to face.

When we consider how much greater would be our advantage in defending the air above this Island against an overseas attack, I must say that I find in these facts a sure basis upon which practical and reassuring thoughts may rest. I will pay my tribute to these young airmen. The great French Army was very largely, for the time being, cast back and disturbed by the onrush of a few thousands of armored vehicles. May it not also be that the cause of civilization itself will be defended by the skill and devotion of a few thousand airmen? There never has been, I suppose, in all the world, in all the history of war, such an opportunity for youth. The Knights of the Round Table, the Crusaders, all fall back into the past—not only distant but prosaic; these young men, going forth every morn to guard their native land and all that we stand for, holding in their hands these instruments of colossal and shattering power, of whom it may be said that

> Every morn brought forth a noble chance
> And every chance brought forth a noble knight,[9]

deserve our gratitude, as do all the brave men who, in so many ways and on so many occasions, are ready, and continue ready to give life and all for their native land.

I return to the Army. In the long series of very fierce battles, now on this front, now on that, fighting on three fronts at once, battles fought by two or three divisions against an equal or somewhat larger number of the enemy, and fought fiercely on some of the old grounds that so many of us knew so well—in these battles our losses in men have exceeded 30,000 killed, wounded and missing. I take occasion to express the sympathy of the House to all who have suffered bereavement or who are still anxious. The President of the Board of Trade [Sir Andrew Duncan] is not here today. His son has been killed, and many in the House have felt the pangs of affliction in the sharpest form. But I will say this about the missing: We have had a large number of wounded come home safely to this country, but I would say about the missing that there may be very many reported missing who will come back home, some day, in one way or another. In the confusion of this fight it is inevitable that many have been left in positions where honor required no further resistance from them.

Against this loss of over 30,000 men, we can set a far heavier loss certainly inflicted upon the enemy. But our losses in materiel are enormous. We have perhaps lost one-third of the men we lost in the opening days of the battle of 21st March, 1918, but we have lost nearly as many guns—nearly one thousand—and all our transport, all the armored vehicles that were with the Army in the north. This loss will impose a further delay on the expansion of our military strength. That expansion had not been proceeding as far as we had hoped. The best of all we had to give had gone to the British Expeditionary Force, and although they had not the numbers of tanks and some articles of equipment which were desirable, they were a very well and finely equipped Army. They had the first-fruits of all that our industry had to give, and that is gone. And now here is this further delay. How long it will be, how long it will last, depends upon the exertions which we make in this Island. An effort the like of which has never been seen in our records is now being made. Work is proceeding everywhere, night and day, Sundays and week days. Capital and Labor have cast aside their interests, rights, and customs and put them into the common stock. Already the flow of munitions has leaped forward. There is no reason why we should not in a few months overtake the sudden and serious loss that has come upon us, without retarding the development of our general program.

Nevertheless, our thankfulness at the escape of our Army and so many men, whose loved ones have passed through an agonizing week, must not blind us to the fact that what has happened in France and Belgium is a colossal military disaster. The French Army has been weakened, the Belgian Army has been lost, a large part of those fortified lines upon which so much faith had been reposed is gone, many valuable mining districts and factories have passed into the enemy's possession, the whole

---

9. Churchill misquotes slightly Tennyson's poem *Morte d'Arthur*, lines 280–281.

of the Channel ports are in his hands, with all the tragic consequences that follow from that, and we must expect another blow to be struck almost immediately at us or at France. We are told that Herr Hitler has a plan for invading the British Isles. This has often been thought of before. When Napoleon lay at Boulogne for a year with his flat-bottomed boats and his Grand Army, he was told by someone. "There are bitter weeds in England." There are certainly a great many more of them since the British Expeditionary Force returned.

The whole question of home defense against invasion is, of course, powerfully affected by the fact that we have for the time being in this Island incomparably more powerful military forces than we have ever had at any moment in this war or the last. But this will not continue. We shall not be content with a defensive war. We have our duty to our Ally. We have to reconstitute and build up the British Expeditionary Force once again, under its gallant Commander-in-Chief, Lord Gort. All this is in train; but in the interval we must put our defenses in this Island into such a high state of organization that the fewest possible numbers will be required to give effective security and that the largest possible potential of offensive effort may be realized. On this we are now engaged. It will be very convenient, if it be the desire of the House, to enter upon this subject in a secret Session. Not that the government would necessarily be able to reveal in very great detail military secrets, but we like to have our discussions free, without the restraint imposed by the fact that they will be read the next day by the enemy; and the Government would benefit by views freely expressed in all parts of the House by Members with their knowledge of so many different parts of the country. I understand that some request is to be made upon this subject, which will be readily acceded to by His Majesty's Government.

We have found it necessary to take measures of increasing stringency, not only against enemy aliens and suspicious characters of other nationalities, but also against British subjects who may become a danger or a nuisance should the war be transported to the United Kingdom. I know there are a great many people affected by the orders which we have made who are the passionate enemies of Nazi Germany. I am very sorry for them, but we cannot, at the present time and under the present stress, draw all the distinctions which we should like to do. If parachute landings were attempted and fierce fighting attendant upon them followed, these unfortunate people would be far better out of the way, for their own sakes as well as for ours. There is, however, another class, for which I feel not the slightest sympathy. Parliament has given us the powers to put down Fifth Column[1] activities with a strong hand, and we shall use those powers subject to the supervision and correction of the House, without the slightest hesitation until we are satisfied, and more than satisfied, that this malignancy in our midst has been effectively stamped out.

Turning once again, and this time more generally, to the question of invasion, I would observe that there has never been a period in all these long centuries of which we boast when an absolute guarantee against invasion, still less against serious raids, could have been given to our people. In the days of Napoleon the same wind which would have carried his transports across the Channel might have driven away the blockading fleet. There was always the chance, and it is that chance which has excited and befooled the imaginations of many Continental tyrants. Many are the tales that are told. We are assured that novel methods will be adopted, and when we see

1. Traitorous: a term coined by a Spanish fascist general in 1936, who attacked Madrid with four columns of troops, and later boasted that he had been aided by a "fifth column" of secret fascist supporters inside the city.

the originality of malice, the ingenuity of aggression, which our enemy displays, we may certainly prepare ourselves for every kind of novel stratagem and every kind of brutal and treacherous maneuver. I think that no idea is so outlandish that it should not be considered and viewed with a searching, but at the same time, I hope, with a steady eye. We must never forget the solid assurances of sea power and those which belong to air power if it can be locally exercised.

I have, myself, full confidence that if all do their duty, if nothing is neglected, and if the best arrangements are made, as they are being made, we shall prove ourselves once again able to defend our Island home, to ride out the storm of war, and to outlive the menace of tyranny, if necessary for years, if necessary alone. At any rate, that is what we are going to try to do. That is the resolve of His Majesty's Government—every man of them. That is the will of Parliament and the nation. The British Empire and the French Republic, linked together in their cause and in their need, will defend to the death their native soil, aiding each other like good comrades to the utmost of their strength. Even though large tracts of Europe and many old and famous States have fallen or may fall into the grip of the Gestapo and all the odious apparatus of Nazi rule, we shall not flag or fail. We shall go on to the end, we shall fight in France, we shall fight on the seas and oceans, we shall fight with growing confidence and growing strength in the air, we shall defend our Island, whatever the cost may be, we shall fight on the beaches, we shall fight on the landing grounds, we shall fight in the fields and in the streets, we shall fight in the hills; we shall never surrender, and even if, which I do not for a moment believe, this Island or a large part of it were subjugated and starving, then our Empire beyond the seas, armed and guarded by the British Fleet, would carry on the struggle, until, in God's good time, the New World, with all its power and might, steps forth to the rescue and the liberation of the old.

✦ ✦ ✦

Stephen Spender
1909–1995

Stephen Spender was an important member of the group of poets writing in the wake of World War I and in the rising shadow of fascism and the approach of World War II. World War I, Spender said, "knocked the ballroom-floor from under middle-class English life"; his first important volume, *Poems*, was published in 1933—the year that Hitler rose to the chancellorship of the Third Reich. Thus the turn toward politics that characterizes the poetry of Spender and the other young Oxford poets who allied themselves with W. H. Auden—the so-called "Auden Generation"—seems in retrospect not so much a decision as an inevitability. Spender speaks this way, too, about his brief affiliation with communism, suggesting that the embrace of communism by British intellectuals in the 1930s was not a matter of economic theory but of conscience. For Spender, Auden, Cecil Day-Lewis and others, fascism was such an obvious, and obviously powerful, evil that only communism appeared strong enough to keep it at bay.

The complex energies and tensions of the 1930s drew forth from Spender his most idealistic and passionate poetry; he will be remembered primarily for the poetry he wrote in his twenties. Some of the energy of his writing derives from his sense of exclusion from English society; his mixed German-Jewish-English ancestry and his bisexuality led him to find, as he wrote, that "my feeling for the English was at times almost like being in love with an alien race." After World War II, Spender wrote little poetry, but continued to work in literary and cultural criticism. His *Collected Poems* was published in 1985.

Icarus[1]

He will watch the hawk with an indifferent eye
    Or pitifully;
Nor on those eagles that so feared him, now
    Will strain his brow;
5   Weapons men use, stone, sling and strong-thewed° bow   *strong-muscled*
    He will not know.

This aristocrat, superb of all instinct,
    With death close linked
Had paced the enormous cloud, almost had won
10   War on the sun;
Till now, like Icarus mid-ocean-drowned,
    Hands, wings, are found.

                                      1929

What I Expected

What I expected, was
Thunder, fighting,
Long struggles with men
And climbing.
5   After continual straining
I should grow strong;
Then the rocks would shake
And I rest long.

What I had not foreseen
10   Was the gradual day
Weakening the will
Leaking the brightness away,
The lack of good to touch,
The fading of body and soul
15   Smoke before wind,
Corrupt, unsubstantial.

The wearing of Time,
And the watching of cripples pass
With limbs shaped like questions
20   In their odd twist,
The pulverous° grief   *dusty*
Melting the bones with pity,
The sick falling from earth—
These, I could not foresee.

25   Expecting always
Some brightness to hold in trust
Some final innocence

---

1. In Greek mythology, Icarus was the son of Daedalus, the inventor. To escape from Crete, Daedalus fashioned wings for his son and himself out of wax. Daedalus warned Icarus not to fly too high, for the heat of the sun would melt the wax wings; but Icarus, intoxicated by the power of flight, ignored his father's warning and plunged to his death in the sea.

Exempt from dust,
That, hanging solid,
30   Would dangle through all
Like the created poem,
Or the faceted crystal.

1933

The Express

After the first powerful plain manifesto
The black statement of pistons, without more fuss
But gliding like a queen, she leaves the station.
Without bowing and with restrained unconcern
5   She passes the houses which humbly crowd outside,
The gasworks, and at last the heavy page
Of death, printed by gravestones in the cemetery.
Beyond the town, there lies the open country
Where, gathering speed, she acquires mystery,
10   The luminous self-possession of ships on ocean.
It is now she begins to sing—at first quite low
Then loud, and at last with a jazzy madness—
The song of her whistle screaming at curves,
Of deafening tunnels, brakes, innumerable bolts.
15   And always light, aerial underneath
Retreats the elate metre of her wheels.
Steaming through metal landscape on her lines,
She plunges new eras of white happiness
Where speed throws up strange shapes, broad curves
20   And parallels clean like trajectories from guns.
At last, further than Edinburgh or Rome,
Beyond the crest of the world, she reaches night
Where only a low stream-line brightness
Of phosphorus, on the tossing hills is white.
25   Ah, like a comet through flame, she moves entranced
Wrapt in her music no bird-song, no, nor bough,
Breaking with honey buds, shall ever equal.

1933

The Pylons

The secret of these hills was stone, and cottages
Of that stone made,
And crumbling roads
That turned on sudden hidden villages.
5   Now over these small hills, they have built the concrete
That trails black wire;
Pylons, those pillars
Bare like nude, giant girls that have no secret.

The valley with its gilt and evening look
10   And the green chestnut

Of customary root,
Are mocked dry like the parched bed of a brook.

But far above and far as sight endures
Like whips of anger
15   With lightning's danger
There runs the quick perspective of the future.

This dwarfs our emerald country by its trek
So tall with prophecy:
Dreaming of cities
20   Where often clouds shall lean their swan-white neck.

1933

+ ──≡✦≡── +

Elizabeth Bowen
1899–1973

Elizabeth Bowen was born into a world that was, at the turn of the century, on the verge of disappearing forever: the world of the Anglo-Irish ascendancy, the privileged world of the Protestant "big house" tradition. Bowen's Court, an estate in County Cork, had been in her family since an ancestor in the service of Oliver Cromwell had come to Ireland in 1749; the estate passed out of the family in 1960, when Elizabeth could no longer afford to maintain the property, and it was torn down by its new owner in 1963.

In stark contrast to her proud Anglo-Irish heritage, Bowen's childhood was rootless in the extreme. As a young child, the family's time was split between Bowen's Court, in the country, and Dublin, where her father was a barrister; in 1906, he suffered a nervous breakdown, and Elizabeth moved to London with her mother. Bowen's mother died of cancer in 1912, and Elizabeth was shuttled between various relatives. During World War I, she returned to neutral Ireland, where she worked in a hospital with veterans suffering from "shell shock"; she returned to London in 1918 to attend art school and lived primarily in London for the rest of her life.

Bowen was in London during the Blitz. She again volunteered her services to the victims of war, working for the Ministry of Information as an air-raid warden. She wrote a number of vivid, powerful stories about the ravages of war in London during the Blitz—among them *Mysterious Kôr* (1946), which the American novelist and short-story writer Eudora Welty has called the "most extraordinary story of those she wrote out of her life in wartime London."

Bowen's writing was not confined to short fiction; in addition to her more than eighty short stories, she was the author of ten novels—the most popular of which are *The Death of the Heart* (1938) and *The Heat of the Day* (1949)—as well as a great deal of newspaper and magazine writing and a history of her ancestral home, *Bowen's Court* (1964), published the year after it was demolished.

Mysterious Kôr

Full moonlight drenched the city and searched it; there was not a niche left to stand in. The effect was remorseless: London looked like the moon's capital—shallow, cratered, extinct. It was late, but not yet midnight; now the buses had stopped the polished roads and streets in this region sent for minutes together a ghostly unbroken reflection up. The soaring new flats and the crouching old shops and houses looked equally brittle under the moon, which blazed in windows that looked its way. The futility of the black-out[1] became laughable: from the sky, presumably, you could see

---

1. During the Blitz all lights were ordered concealed or extinguished at night so that enemy planes would have difficulty locating their targets.

every slate in the roofs, every whited kerb, every contour of the naked winter flowerbeds in the park; and the lake, with its shining twists and tree-darkened islands would be a landmark for miles, yes, miles, overhead.

However, the sky, in whose glassiness floated no clouds but only opaque balloons, remained glassy-silent. The Germans no longer came by the full moon. Something more immaterial seemed to threaten, and to be keeping people at home. This day between days, this extra tax, was perhaps more than senses and nerves could bear. People stayed indoors with a fervour that could be felt: the buildings strained with battened-down human life, but not a beam, not a voice, not a note from a radio escaped. Now and then under streets and buildings the earth rumbled: the Underground[2] sounded loudest at this time.

Outside the now gateless gates of the park, the road coming downhill from the north-west turned south and became a street, down whose perspective the traffic lights went through their unmeaning performance of changing colour. From the promontory of pavement outside the gates you saw at once up the road and down the street: from behind where you stood, between the gateposts, appeared the lesser strangeness of grass and water and trees. At this point, at this moment, three French soldiers, directed to a hostel[3] they could not find, stopped singing to listen derisively to the waterbirds wakened up by the moon. Next, two wardens coming off duty emerged from their post and crossed the road diagonally, each with an elbow cupped inside a slung-on tin hat. The wardens turned their faces, mauve in the moonlight, towards the Frenchmen with no expression at all. The two sets of steps died in opposite directions, and, the birds subsiding, nothing was heard or seen until, a little way down the street, a trickle of people came out of the Underground, around the antipanic brick wall. These all disappeared quickly, in an abashed way, or as though dissolved in the street by some white acid, but for a girl and a soldier who, by their way of walking, seemed to have no destination but each other and to be not quite certain even of that. Blotted into one shadow he tall, she little, these two proceeded towards the park. They looked in, but did not go in; they stood there debating without speaking. Then, as though a command from the street behind them had been received by their synchronized bodies, they faced round to look back the way they had come.

His look up the height of a building made his head drop back, and she saw his eyeballs glitter. She slid her hand from his sleeve, stepped to the edge of the pavement and said: "Mysterious Kôr."

"What is?" he said, not quite collecting himself.

"This is—

Mysterious Kôr thy walls forsaken stand,
Thy lonely towers beneath a lonely moon—

—this is Kôr."[4]

"Why," he said, "it's years since I've thought of that."
She said: "I think of it all the time—"

Not in the waste beyond the swamps and sand,
The fever-haunted forest and lagoon,
Mysterious Kôr thy walls———

2. The London subway system.
3. An inn.
4. Kôr is the lost city of H. Rider Haggard's 1887 adventure novel *She*. The central character Ayesha, whose name means *She-who-must-be-obeyed*, is incessantly described as "mysterious." One of Ayesha's statements—"My empire is of the imagination"—may have had an ironic resonance for Bowen, writing about the condition of England during World War II.

—a completely forsaken city, as high as cliffs and as white as bones, with no history———"

"But something must once have happened: why had it been forsaken?"

"How could anyone tell you when there's nobody there?"

"Nobody there since how long?"

"Thousands of years."

"In that case, it would have fallen down."

"No, not Kôr," she said with immediate authority. "Kôr's altogether different; it's
very strong; there is not a crack in it anywhere for a weed to grow in; the corners of
stones and the monuments might have been cut yesterday, and the stairs and arches
are built to support themselves."

"You know all about it," he said, looking at her.

"I know, I know all about it."

"What, since you read that book?"

"Oh, I didn't get much from that; I just got the name. I knew that must be the
right name; it's like a cry."

"Most like the cry of a crow to me." He reflected, then said: "But the poem
begins with 'Not'—'Not in the waste beyond the swamps and sand—' And it goes on, as
I remember, to prove Kôr's not really anywhere. When even a poem says there's no
such place—"

"What it tries to say doesn't matter: I see what it makes me see. Anyhow, that
was written some time ago, at that time when they thought they had got everything taped, because the whole world had been explored, even the middle of
Africa. Every thing and place had been found and marked on some map; so what
wasn't marked on any map couldn't be there at all. So *they* thought: that was why
he wrote the poem. 'The world is disenchanted,' it goes on. That was what set me off
hating civilization."

"Well, cheer up," he said; "there isn't much of it left."

"Oh, yes, I cheered up some time ago. This war shows we've by no means come
to the end. If you can blow whole places out of existence, you can blow whole places
into it. I don't see why not. They say we can't say what's come out since the bombing
started. By the time we've come to the end, Kôr may be the one city left: the abiding
city. I should laugh."

"No, you wouldn't," he said sharply. "*You* wouldn't—at least, I hope not. I hope
you don't know what you're saying—does the moon make you funny?"

"Don't be cross about Kôr; please don't, Arthur," she said.

"I thought girls thought about people."

"What, these days?" she said. "Think about people? How can anyone think
about people if they've got any heart? I don't know how other girls manage: I always
think about Kôr."

"Not about me?" he said. When she did not at once answer, he turned her hand
over, in anguish, inside his grasp. "Because I'm not there when you want me—is that
my fault?"

"But to think about Kôr *is* to think about you and me."

"In that dead place?"

"No, ours—we'd be alone here."

Tightening his thumb on her palm while he thought this over, he looked behind
them, around them, above them—even up at the sky. He said finally: "But we're
alone here."

"That was why I said 'Mysterious Kôr.'"

"What, you mean we're there now, that here's there, that now's then? . . . *I* don't mind," he added, letting out as a laugh the sigh he had been holding in for some time. "You ought to know the place, and for all I could tell you we might be anywhere: I often do have it, this funny feeling, the first minute or two when I've come up out of the Underground. Well, well: join the Army and see the world." He nodded towards the perspective of traffic lights and said, a shade craftily: "What are those, then?"

Having caught the quickest possible breath, she replied: "Inexhaustible gases; they bored through to them and lit them as they came up; by changing colour they show the changing of minutes; in Kôr there is no sort of other time."

"You've got the moon, though: that can't help making months."

"Oh, and the sun, of course; but those two could do what they liked; we should not have to calculate when they'd come or go.'

"We might not have to," he said, 'but I bet I should."

"I should not mind what you did, so long as you never said, 'What next?'"

"I don't know about 'next,' but I do know what we'd do first."

"What, Arthur?"

"Populate Kôr."

She said: "I suppose it would be all right if our children were to marry each other?"

But her voice faded out; she had been reminded that they were homeless on this his first night of leave. They were, that was to say, in London without any hope of any place of their own. Pepita shared a two-roomed flatlet with a girl friend, in a by-street off the Regent's Park Road, and towards this they must make their halfhearted way. Arthur was to have the sitting-room divan, usually occupied by Pepita, while she herself had half of her girl friend's bed. There was really no room for a third, and least of all for a man, in those small rooms packed with furniture and the two girls' belongings: Pepita tried to be grateful for her friend Callie's forbearance—but how could she be, when it had not occurred to Callie that she would do better to be away tonight? She was more slow-witted than narrow-minded—but Pepita felt she owed a kind of ruin to her. Callie, not yet known to be home later than ten, would be now waiting up, in her house-coat, to welcome Arthur. That would mean three-sided chat, drinking cocoa, then turning in: that would be that, and that would be all. That was London, this war—they were lucky to have a roof—London, full enough before the Americans came. Not a place: they would even grudge you sharing a grave—that was what even married couples complained. Whereas in Kôr . . .

In Kôr . . . Like glass, the illusion shattered: a car hummed like a hornet towards them, veered, showed its scarlet tail-light, streaked away up the road. A woman edged round a front door and along the area railings timidly called her cat; meanwhile a clock near, then another set further back in the dazzling distance, set about striking midnight. Pepita, feeling Arthur release her arm with an abruptness that was the inverse of passion, shivered; whereat he asked brusquely: "Cold? Well, which way?—we'd better be getting on."

Callie was no longer waiting up. Hours ago she had set out the three cups and saucers, the tins of cocoa and household milk and, on the gas-ring, brought the kettle to just short of the boil. She had turned open Arthur's bed, the living-room divan, in the neat inviting way she had learnt at home—then, with a modest impulse, replaced the cover. She had, as Pepita foresaw, been wearing her cretonne[5] housecoat, the nearest thing to a hostess gown that she had; she had already brushed her hair for the

---

5. Cotton fabric with a printed pattern.

night, rebraided it, bound the braids in a coronet round her head. Both lights and the wireless[6] had been on, to make the room both look and sound gay: all alone, she had come to that peak moment at which company should arrive—but so seldom does. From then on she felt welcome beginning to wither in her, a flower of the heart that had bloomed too early. There she had sat like an image, facing the three cold cups, on the edge of the bed to be occupied by an unknown man.

Callie's innocence and her still unsought-out state had brought her to take a proprietary pride in Arthur; this was all the stronger, perhaps, because they had not yet met. Sharing the flat with Pepita, this last year, she had been content with reflecting the heat of love. It was not, surprisingly, that Pepita seemed very happy—there were times when she was palpably on the rack, and this was not what Callie could understand. "Surely you owe it to Arthur," she would then say, "to keep cheerful? So long as you love each other————" Callie's calm brow glowed—one might say that it glowed in place of her friend's; she became the guardian of that ideality which for Pepita was constantly lost to view. It was true, with the sudden prospect of Arthur's leave, things had come nearer to earth: he became a proposition, and she would have been as glad if he could have slept somewhere else. Physically shy, a brotherless virgin, Callie shrank from sharing this flat with a young man. In this flat you could hear everything: what was once a three-windowed Victorian drawing-room had been partitioned, by very thin walls, into kitchenette, living-room, Callie's bedroom. The living-room was in the centre; the two others open off it. What was once the conservatory, half a flight down, was now converted into a draughty bathroom, shared with somebody else on the girl's floor. The flat, for these days, was cheap—even so, it was Callie, earning more than Pepita, who paid the greater part of the rent: it thus became up to her, more or less, to express good will as to Arthur's making a third. "Why, it will be lovely to have him here," Callie said. Pepita accepted the good will without much grace—but then, had she ever much grace to spare?—she was as restlessly secretive, as self-centred, as a little half-grown black cat. Next came a puzzling moment: Pepita seemed to be hinting that Callie should fix herself up somewhere else. "But where would I go?" Callie marvelled when this was at last borne in on her. "You know what London's like now. And, anyway"—here she laughed, but hers was a forehead that coloured as easily as it glowed—"it wouldn't be proper, would it, me going off and leaving just you and Arthur; I don't know what your mother would say to me. No, we may be a little squashed, but we'll make things ever so homey. I shall not mind playing gooseberry, really, dear."

But the hominess by now was evaporating, as Pepita and Arthur still and still did not come. At half-past ten, in obedience to the rule of the house, Callie was obliged to turn off the wireless, whereupon silence out of the stepless street began seeping into the slighted room. Callie recollected the fuel target and turned off her dear little table lamp, gaily painted with spots to make it look like a toadstool, thereby leaving only the hanging light. She laid her hand on the kettle, to find it gone cold again and sigh for the wasted gas if not for her wasted thought. Where are they? Cold crept up her out of the kettle; she went to bed.

Callie's bed lay along the wall under the window: she did not like sleeping so close up under glass, but the clearance that must be left for the opening of door and cupboards made this the only possible place. Now she got in and lay rigidly on the

6. Radio.

bed's inner side, under the hanging hems of the window curtains, training her limbs not to stray to what would be Pepita's half. This sharing of her bed with another body would not be the least of her sacrifice to the lovers' love; tonight would be the first night—or at least, since she was an infant—that Callie had slept with anyone. Child of a sheltered middle-class household, she had kept physical distances all her life. Already repugnance and shyness ran through her limbs; she was preyed upon by some more obscure trouble than the expectation that she might not sleep. As to *that*, Pepita was restless; her tossings on the divan, her broken-off exclamations and blurred pleas had been to be heard, most nights, through the dividing wall.

Callie knew, as though from a vision, that Arthur would sleep soundly, with assurance and majesty. Did they not all say, too, that a soldier sleeps like a log? With awe she pictured, asleep, the face that she had not yet, awake, seen— Arthur's man's eyelids, cheekbones and set mouth turned up to the darkened ceiling. Wanting to savour darkness herself, Callie reached out and put off her bedside lamp.

At once she knew that something was happening—outdoors, in the street, the whole of London, the world. An advance, an extraordinary movement was silently taking place; blue-white beams overflowed from it, silting, dropping round the edges of the muffling black-out curtains. When, starting up, she knocked a fold of the curtain, a beam like a mouse ran across her bed. A searchlight, the most powerful of all time, might have been turned full and steady upon her defended window; finding flaws in the blackout stuff, it made veins and stars. Once gained by this idea of pressure she could not lie down again; she sat tautly, drawn-up knees touching her breasts, and asked herself if there were anything she should do. She parted the curtains, opened them slowly wider, looked out—and was face to face with the moon.

Below the moon, the houses opposite her window blazed back in transparent shadow; and something—was it a coin or a ring?—glittered half-way across the chalk-white street. Light marched in past her face, and she turned to see where it went: out stood the curves and garlands of the great white marble Victorian mantelpiece of that lost drawing-room; out stood, in the photographs turned her way, the thoughts with which her parents had faced the camera, and the humble puzzlement of her two dogs at home. Of silver brocade, just faintly purpled with roses, became her housecoat hanging over the chair. And the moon did more: it exonerated and beautified the lateness of the lovers' return. No wonder, she said herself, no wonder—if this was the world they walked in, if this was whom they were with. Having drunk in the white explanation, Callie lay down again. Her half of the bed was in shadow, but she allowed one hand to lie, blanched, in what would be Pepita's place. She lay and looked at the hand until it was no longer her own.

Callie woke to the sound of Pepita's key in the latch. But no voices? What had happened? Then she heard Arthur's step. She heard his unslung equipment dropped with a weary, dull sound, and the plonk of his tin hat on a wooden chair. "Sssh-sssh!" Pepita exclaimed, "she *might* be asleep!"

Then at last Arthur's voice: "But I thought you said—"

"I'm not asleep; I'm just coming!" Callie called out with rapture, leaping out from her form in shadow into the moonlight, zipping on her enchanted house-coat over her nightdress, kicking her shoes on, and pinning in place, with a trembling firmness, her plaits in their coronet round her head. Between these movements of hers she heard not another sound. Had she only dreamed they were there? Her heart beat: she stepped through the living-room, shutting her door behind her.

Pepita and Arthur stood on the other side of the table; they gave the impression of being lined up. Their faces, at different levels—for Pepita's rough, dark head came only an inch above Arthur's khaki shoulder—were alike in abstention from any kind of expression; as though, spiritually, they both still refused to be here. Their features looked faint, weathered—was this the work of the moon? Pepita said at once: "I suppose we are very late?"

"I don't wonder," Callie said, "on this lovely night."

Arthur had not raised his eyes; he was looking at the three cups. Pepita now suddenly jogged his elbow, saying, "Arthur, wake up; say something; this is Callie—well, Callie, this is Arthur, of course."

"Why, yes of course this is Arthur," returned Callie, whose candid eyes since she entered had not left Arthur's face. Perceiving that Arthur did not know what to do, she advanced round the table to shake hands with him. He looked up, she looked down, for the first time: she rather beheld than felt his red-brown grip on what still seemed her glove of moonlight. "Welcome, Arthur," she said. "I'm so glad to meet you at last. I hope you will be comfortable in the flat."

"It's been kind of you," he said after consideration.

"Please do not feel that," said Callie. "This is Pepita's home, too, and we both hope—don't we, Pepita?—that you'll regard it as yours. Please feel free to do just as you like. I am sorry it is so small."

"Oh, I don't know," Arthur said, as though hypnotized; "it seems a nice little place."

Pepita, meanwhile, glowered and turned away.

Arthur continued to wonder, though he had once been told, how these two unalike girls had come to set up together—Pepita so small, except for her too-big head, compact of childish brusqueness and of unchildish passion, and Callie, so sedate, waxy and tall—an unlit candle. Yes, she was like one of those candles on sale outside a church; there could be something votive even in her demeanour. She was unconscious that her good manners, those of an old fashioned country doctor's daughter, were putting the other two at a disadvantage. He found himself touched by the grave good faith with which Callie was wearing that tartish house-coat, above which her face kept the glaze of sleep; and, as she knelt to relight the gas-ring under the kettle, he marked the strong, delicate arch of one bare foot, disappearing into the arty green shoe. Pepita was now too near him ever again to be seen as he now saw Callie—in a sense, he never *had* seen Pepita for the first time: she had not been, and still sometimes was not, his type. No, he had not thought of her twice; he had not remembered her until he began to remember her with passion. You might say he had not seen Pepita coming: their love had been a collision in the dark.

Callie, determined to get this over, knelt back and said: "Would Arthur like to wash his hands?" When they had heard him stumble down the half-flight of stairs, she said to Pepita: "Yes, I was so glad you had the moon."

"Why?" said Pepita. She added: "There was too much of it."

"You're tired. Arthur looks tired, too."

"How would you know? He's used to marching about. But it's all this having no place to go."

"But, Pepita, you——"

But at this point Arthur came back: from the door he noticed the wireless, and went direct to it. "Nothing much on now, I suppose?" he doubtfully said.

"No; you see it's past midnight; we're off the air. And, anyway, in this house they don't like the wireless late. By the same token," went on Callie, friendly smiling, "I'm afraid I must ask you, Arthur, to take your boots off, unless, of course, you mean to stay sitting down. The people below us——"

Pepita flung off, saying something under her breath, but Arthur, remarking, "No, I don't mind," both sat down and began to take off his boots. Pausing, glancing to left and right at the divan's fresh cotton spread, he said: "It's all right is it, for me to sit on this?"

"That's my bed," said Pepita. "You are to sleep in it."

Callie then made the cocoa, after which they turned in. Preliminary trips to the bathroom having been worked out, Callie was first to retire, shutting the door behind her so that Pepita and Arthur might kiss each other good night. When Pepita joined her, it was without knocking: Pepita stood still in the moon and began to tug off her clothes. Glancing with hate at the bed, she asked: "Which side?"

"I expected you'd like the outside."

"What are you standing about for?"

"I don't really know: as I'm inside I'd better get in first."

"Then why not get in?"

When they had settled rigidly, side by side, Callie asked: "Do you think Arthur's got all he wants?"

Pepita jerked her head up. "We can't sleep in all this moon."

"Why, you don't believe the moon does things, actually?"

"Well, it couldn't hope to make some of us *much* more screwy."

Callie closed the curtains, then said: "What do you mean? And—didn't you hear?—I asked if Arthur's got all he wants."

"That's what I meant—have you got a screw loose, really?"

"Pepita, I won't stay here if you're going to be like this."

"In that case, you had better go in with Arthur."

"What about me?" Arthur loudly said through the wall. "I can hear practically all you girls are saying."

They were both startled—rather that than abashed. Arthur, alone in there, had thrown off the ligatures[7] of his social manner: his voice held the whole authority of his sex—he was impatient, sleepy, and he belonged to no one.

"Sorry," the girls said in unison. Then Pepita laughed soundlessly, making their bed shake, till to stop herself she bit the back of her hand, and this movement made her elbow strike Callie's cheek. "Sorry," she had to whisper. No answer: Pepita fingered her elbow and found, yes, it was quite true, it was wet. "Look, shut up crying, Callie: what have I done?"

Callie rolled right round, in order to press her forehead closely under the window, into the curtains, against the wall. Her weeping continued to be soundless: now and then, unable to reach her handkerchief, she staunched her eyes with a curtain, disturbing slivers of moon. Pepita gave up marvelling, and soon slept: at least there is something in being dog-tired.

A clock struck four as Callie woke up again—but something else had made her open her swollen eyelids. Arthur, stumbling about on his padded feet, could be heard next door attempting to make no noise. Inevitably, he bumped the edge of the table.

7. Restrictions.

Callie sat up: by her side Pepita lay like a mummy rolled half over, in forbidding, tenacious sleep. Arthur groaned. Callie caught a breath, climbed lightly over Pepita, felt for her torch[8] on the mantelpiece, stopped to listen again. Arthur groaned again: Callie, with movements soundless as they were certain, opened the door and slipped through to the living-room. "What's the matter?" she whispered. "Are you ill?"

"No; I just got a cigarette. Did I wake you up?"

"But you groaned."

"I'm sorry; I'd no idea."

"But do you often?"

"I've no idea, really, I tell you," Arthur repeated. The air of the room was dense with his presence, overhung by tobacco. He must be sitting on the edge of his bed, wrapped up in his overcoat—she could smell the coat, and each time he pulled on the cigarette his features appeared down there, in the fleeting, dull reddish glow. "Where are you?" he said. "Show a light."

Her nervous touch on her torch, like a reflex to what he said, made it flicker up for a second. "I am just by the door; Pepita's asleep; I'd better go back to bed."

"Listen. Do you two get on each other's nerves?"

"Not till tonight," said Callie, watching the uncertain swoops of the cigarette as he reached across to the ashtray on the edge of the table. Shifting her bare feet patiently, she added: "You don't see us as we usually are."

"She's a girl who shows things in funny ways—I expect she feels bad at our putting you out like this—I know I do. But then we'd got no choice, had we?"

"It is really I who am putting you out," said Callie.

"Well, that can't be helped either, can it? You had the right to stay in your own place. If there'd been more time, we might have gone to the country, though I still don't see where we'd have gone there. It's one harder when you're not married, unless you've got the money. Smoke?"

"No, thank you. Well, if you're all right, I'll go back to bed."

"I'm glad she's asleep—funny the way she sleeps, isn't it? You can't help wondering where she is. You haven't got a boy, have you, just at present?"

"No. I've never had one."

"I'm not sure in one way that you're not better off. I can see there's not so much in it for a girl these days. It makes me feel cruel the way I unsettle her: I don't know how much it's me myself or how much it's something the matter that I can't help. How are any of us to know how things could have been? They forget war's not just only war; it's years out of people's lives that they've never had before and won't have again. Do you think she's fanciful?"

"Who, Pepita?"

"It's enough to make her—tonight was the pay-off. We couldn't get near any movie or any place for sitting; you had to fight into the bars, and she hates the staring in bars, and with all that milling about, every street we went, they kept on knocking her even off my arm. So then we took the tube to that park down there, but the place was as bad as daylight, let alone it was cold. We hadn't the nerve—well, that's nothing to do with you."

"I don't mind."

"Or else you don't understand. So we began to play—we were off in Kôr."

8. Flashlight.

"Core of what?"

"Mysterious Kôr—ghost city."

"Where?"

"You may ask. But I could have sworn she saw it, and from the way she saw it I saw it, too. A game's a game, but what's a hallucination? You begin by laughing, then it gets in you and you can't laugh it off. I tell you, I woke up just now not knowing where I'd been; and I had to get up and feel round this table before I even knew where I was. It wasn't till then that I thought of a cigarette. Now I see why she sleeps like that, if that's where she goes."

"But she is just as often restless; I often hear her."

"Then she doesn't always make it. Perhaps it takes me, in some way—Well, I can't see any harm: when two people have got no place, why not want Kôr, as a start? There are no restrictions on wanting, at any rate."

"But, oh, Arthur, can't wanting want what's human?"

He yawned. "To be human's to be at a dead loss." Stopping yawning, he ground out his cigarette: the china tray skidded at the edge of the table. "Bring that light here a moment—that is, will you? I think I've messed ash all over these sheets of hers."

Callie advanced with the torch alight, but at arm's length: now and then her thumb made the beam wobble. She watched the lit-up inside of Arthur's hand as he brushed the sheet; and once he looked up to see her white-nightgowned figure curving above and away from him, behind the arc of light. "What's that swinging?"

"One of my plaits of hair. Shall I open the window wider?"

"What, to let the smoke out? Go on. And how's your moon?"

"Mine?" Marvelling over this, as the first sign that Arthur remembered that she was Callie, she uncovered the window, pushed up the sash, then after a minute said: "Not so strong."

Indeed, the moon's power over London and the imagination had now declined. The siege of light had relaxed; the search was over; the street had a look of survival and no more. Whatever had glittered there, coin or ring, was now invisible or had gone. To Callie it seemed likely that there would never be such a moon again; and on the whole she felt this was for the best. Feeling air reach in like a tired arm round her body, she dropped the curtains against it and returned to her own room.

Back by her bed, she listened; Pepita's breathing still had the regular sound of sleep. At the other side of the wall the divan creaked as Arthur stretched himself out again. Having felt ahead of her lightly, to make sure her half was empty, Callie climbed over Pepita and got in. A certain amount of warmth had travelled between the sheets from Pepita's flank, and in this Callie extended her sword-cold body: she tried to compose her limbs; even they quivered after Arthur's words in the dark, words to the dark. The loss of her own mysterious expectation, of her love for love, was a small thing beside the war's total of unlived lives. Suddenly Pepita flung out one hand: its back knocked Callie lightly across the face.

Pepita had now turned over and lay with her face up. The hand that had struck Callie must have lain over the other, which grasped the pyjama collar. Her eyes, in the dark, might have been either shut or open, but nothing made her frown more or less steadily: it became certain, after another moment, that Pepita's act of justice had been unconscious. She still lay, as she had lain, in an avid dream, of which Arthur had been the source, of which Arthur was not the end. With him she looked this way, that way, down the wide, void, pure streets, between statues, pillars and shadows, through archways and colonnades. With him she went up the stairs down which nothing but moon came; with him trod the ermine[9] dust of the endless halls, stood on terraces, mounted the extreme tower, looked down on the statued squares, the wide, void, pure streets. He was the password, but not the answer: it was to Kôr's finality that she turned.

◆━◆◆◆━◆

George Orwell
1903–1950

The critic Irving Howe called George Orwell (pseudonym of Eric Arthur Blair) "the greatest moral force in English letters during the past several decades," as well as "the best English essayist since Hazlitt." He was one of the most consistently provocative British writers of the 1930s and 1940s; his characteristic mode was the polemic, whether that polemic was cloaked in the form of an essay or literary criticism, a novel or even travel writing.

Orwell was born in India into a lower-middle-class family, his father a British civil servant working as an administrator in the Opium Department of the Government of India. His mother managed to gain his entrance into Eton, an elite preparatory school, on a scholarship. The snobbism of his more affluent classmates was to leave a permanent mark. Unable to afford college, Orwell followed in his father's footsteps and enlisted in the Indian Imperial Police. Unlike his father, however, he was disgusted by the inhumanity of colonial rule that he witnessed while stationed in Burma; his revulsion is vividly depicted in essays like *Shooting an Elephant* and *A Hanging*, as well as in his early novel *Burmese Days* (1934). His distaste for police work caused Orwell to leave after five years, determined to establish himself as a writer; he became convinced of the importance of establishing an art of political writing. His 1945 political allegory *Animal Farm* is most specifically an indictment of the Soviet Union during the Cold War, but it conveys timeless larger lessons—that totalitarianism lurks just below the surface of every civil government, that absolute power in the hands of any government leads to the abolition of personal freedoms. Schoolchildren in both the United Kingdom and the United States are familiar with the novel's famous slogan: "All animals are equal . . . but some are more equal than others." These same themes are explored in Orwell's dystopian novel *Nineteen Eighty-Four* (1949), which has entered the contemporary imagination through its images of tyranny and oppression, through phrases like "newspeak" and "double-think," and through the foreboding, forbidding image of Big Brother, who is always "watching you."

Before his untimely death from tuberculosis, Orwell did important work in literary and cultural criticism. His criticism, Evelyn Waugh complained, insisted that the critic ask of every text: "What kind of man wrote or painted this? What were his motives, conscious or unconscious? What sort of people like his work? Why?" They were questions under which, as his disparaging mention of Waugh in *Inside the Whale* suggests, most of the fiction written during the 1930s did not fare well. He also became a defender of British popular culture in the 1940s; his essays on such "subliterary" forms as boys' magazines, seaside resort postcards, and personal ads, for instance, anticipate the recent interest in material culture at the center of British and American cultural studies. Almost half a century after his death, Orwell's enduring importance would seem to be his thoroughgoing distrust of "smelly little orthodoxies," be they literary, aesthetic, political, or linguistic.

9. White.

from **Inside the Whale**

By 1937 the whole of the intelligentsia was mentally at war. Left-wing thought had narrowed down to "anti-Fascism," *i.e.* to a negative, and a torrent of hate-literature directed against Germany and the politicians supposedly friendly to Germany was pouring from the Press. The thing that, to me, was truly frightening about the war in Spain[1] was not such violence as I witnessed, nor even the party feuds behind the lines, but the immediate reappearance in left-wing circles of the mental atmosphere of the Great War. The very people who for twenty years had sniggered over their own superiority to war hysteria were the ones who rushed straight back into the mental slum of 1915. All the familiar wartime idiocies, spy-hunting, orthodoxy-sniffing (Sniff, sniff. Are you a good anti-Fascist?), the retailing of atrocity stories, came back into vogue as though the intervening years had never happened. Before the end of the Spanish war, and even before Munich, some of the better of the left-wing writers were beginning to squirm. Neither Auden nor, on the whole, Spender wrote about the Spanish war in quite the vein that was expected of them. Since then there has been a change of feeling and much dismay and confusion, because the actual course of events has made nonsense of the left-wing orthodoxy of the last few years. But then it did not need very great acuteness to see that much of it was nonsense from the start. There is no certainty, therefore, that the next orthodoxy to emerge will be any better than the last.

On the whole the literary history of the 'thirties seems to justify the opinion that a writer does well to keep out of politics. For any writer who accepts or partially accepts the discipline of a political party is sooner or later faced with the alternative: toe the line, or shut up. It is, of course, possible to toe the line and go on writing—after a fashion. Any Marxist can demonstrate with the greatest of ease that "bourgeois" liberty of thought is an illusion. But when he has finished his demonstration there remains the psychological *fact* that without this "bourgeois" liberty the creative powers wither away. In the future a totalitarian literature may arise, but it will be quite different from anything we can now imagine. Literature as we know it is an individual thing, demanding mental honesty and a minimum of censorship. And this is even truer of prose than of verse. It is probably not a coincidence that the best writers of the 'thirties have been poets. The atmosphere of orthodoxy is always damaging to prose, and above all it is completely ruinous to the novel, the most anarchical of all forms of literature. How many Roman Catholics have been good novelists? Even the handful one could name have usually been bad Catholics. The novel is practically a Protestant form of art; it is a product of the free mind, of the autonomous individual. No decade in the past hundred and fifty years has been so barren of imaginative prose as the nineteen-thirties. There have been good poems, good sociological works, brilliant pamphlets, but practically no fiction of any value at all. From 1933 onwards the mental climate was increasingly against it. Anyone sensitive enough to be touched by the *zeitgeist* [spirit of the age] was also involved in politics. Not everyone, of course, was definitely *in* the political racket, but practically everyone was on its periphery and more or less mixed up in propaganda campaigns

---

1. The Spanish Civil War (1936–1939) pitted army officers under the leadership of General Francisco Franco (the Nationalists) against the forces that supported Spain's elected government (the Republicans). Republican sympathizers from all over the world volunteered to fight in Spain, but in the end the Nationalist forces prevailed on 1 April 1939, and Franco established a dictatorship in Spain.

A still from Alfred Hitchcock's *The Man Who Knew Too Much*. 1934. Hitchcock was among the great film-makers of the twentieth century. Nearly all of his fifty films were in the popular genre of the suspense-thriller, although their stylistic brilliance and cinematic daring elevate them to the highest levels of film art. The first half of Hitchcock's movie career was spent in his native Britain; after World War II he became a major Hollywood director. *The Man Who Knew Too Much* was his first international success, and the only film he ever remade (an American version in 1957). The film is a classical Hitchcockian parable of evil emerging in the midst of the everyday, as political violence erupts during a concert at the Royal Albert Hall, a London monument to Queen Victoria's husband.

and squalid controversies. Communists and near-Communists had a disproportion- ately large influence in the literary reviews. It was a time of labels, slogans, and eva- sions. At the worst moments you were expected to lock yourself up in a constipating little cage of lies; at the best a sort of voluntary censorship ("Ought I to say this? Is it pro-Fascist?") was at work in nearly everyone's mind. It is almost inconceivable that good novels should be written in such an atmosphere. Good novels are not written by orthodoxy-sniffers, nor by people who are conscience-stricken about their own unorthodoxy. Good novels are written by people who are *not frightened*. This brings me back to Henry Miller.[2]

If this were a likely moment for the launching of "schools" of literature, Henry Miller might be the starting-point of a new "school". He does at any rate mark an unexpected swing of the pendulum. In his books one gets right away from the "polit-

2. American writer (1891–1980) best known for his novels *Tropic of Cancer* and *Tropic of Capricorn*; both were banned because of their graphic sexuality and obscene language.

ical animal" and back to a viewpoint not only individualistic but completely passive—the view-point of a man who believes the world-process to be outside his control and who in any case hardly wishes to control it.

I first met Miller at the end of 1936, when I was passing through Paris on my way
to Spain. What most intrigued me about him was to find that he felt no interest in
the Spanish war whatever. He merely told me in forcible terms that to go to Spain at
that moment was the act of an idiot. He could understand anyone going there from
purely selfish motives, out of curiosity, for instance, but to mix oneself up in such
things *from a sense of obligation* was sheer stupidity. In any case my ideas about combating Fascism, defending democracy, etc., etc., were all baloney. Our civilisation
was destined to be swept away and replaced by something so different that we should
scarcely regard it as human—a prospect that did not bother him, he said. And some
such outlook is implicit throughout his work. Everywhere there is the sense of the
approaching cataclysm, and almost everywhere the implied belief that it doesn't matter. The only political declaration which, so far as I know, he has ever made in print
is a purely negative one. A year or so ago an American magazine, the *Marxist Quarterly*, sent out a questionnaire to various American writers asking them to define
their attitude on the subject of war. Miller replied in terms of extreme pacifism, an
individual refusal to fight, with no apparent wish to convert others to the same opinion—practically, in fact, a declaration of irresponsibility.

However, there is more than one kind of irresponsibility. As a rule, writers who do
not wish to identify themselves with the historical process at the moment either ignore
it or fight against it. If they can ignore it, they are probably fools. If they can understand
it well enough to want to fight against it, they probably have enough vision to realise
that they cannot win. Look, for instance, at a poem like "The Scholar Gipsy,"[3] with its
railing against the "strange disease of modern life" and its magnificent defeatist simile
in the final stanza. It expresses one of the normal literary attitudes, perhaps actually the
prevailing attitude during the last hundred years. And on the other hand there are the
"progressives," the yea-sayers, the Shaw-Wells[4] type, always leaping forward to embrace
the ego-projections which they mistake for the future. On the whole the writers of the
'twenties took the first line and the writers of the 'thirties the second. And at any given
moment, of course, there is a huge tribe of Barries and Deepings and Dells[5] who simply
don't notice what is happening. Where Miller's work is symptomatically important is
in its avoidance of any of these attitudes. He is neither pushing the world-process forward nor trying to drag it back, but on the other hand he is by no means ignoring it. I
should say that he believes in the impending ruin of Western Civilisation much more
firmly than the majority of "revolutionary" writers; only he does not feel called upon to
do anything about it. He is fiddling while Rome is burning, and, unlike the enormous
majority of people who do this, fiddling with his face towards the flames.

In *Max and the White Phagocytes* there is one of those revealing passages in which
a writer tells you a great deal about himself while talking about somebody else. The
book includes a long essay on the diaries of Anais Nin,[6] which I have never read,
except for a few fragments, and which I believe have not been published. Miller
claims that they are the only true feminine writing that has ever appeared, whatever

3. By Matthew Arnold (see page 1643)
4. Both Bernard Shaw and H. G. Wells used their writing
and their popularity to work for progressive political and
social causes.
5. Popular, apolitical writers like Sir James Barrie, author

of *Peter Pan* (1904).
6. American novelist (1903–1977) whose *Diary* tells the
story of a woman's development as an artist; she was a
longtime friend of Miller's.

that may mean. But the interesting passage is one in which he compares Anais Nin—evidently a completely subjective, introverted writer—to Jonah in the whale's belly. In passing he refers to an essay that Aldous Huxley wrote some years ago about El Greco's picture, *The Dream of Philip the Second*. Huxley remarks that the people in El Greco's pictures always look as though they were in the bellies of whales, and professes to find something peculiarly horrible in the idea of being in a "visceral prison." Miller retorts that, on the contrary, there are many worse things than being swallowed by whales, and the passage makes it clear that he himself finds the idea rather attractive. Here he is touching upon what is probably a very widespread fantasy. It is perhaps worth noticing that everyone, at least every English-speaking person, invariably speaks of Jonah and the *whale*. Of course the creature that swallowed Jonah was a fish, and was so described in the Bible (Jonah i.17), but children naturally confuse it with a whale, and this fragment of baby-talk is habitually carried into later life—a sign, perhaps, of the hold that the Jonah myth has upon our imaginations. For the fact is that being inside a whale is a very comfortable, cosy, homelike thought. The historical Jonah, if he can be so called, was glad enough to escape, but in imagination, in day-dream, countless people have envied him. It is, of course, quite obvious why. The whale's belly is simply a womb big enough for an adult. There you are, in the dark, cushioned space that exactly fits you, with yards of blubber between yourself and reality, able to keep up an attitude of the completest indifference, no matter *what* happens. A storm that would sink all the battleships in the world would hardly reach you as an echo. Even the whale's own movements would probably be imperceptible to you. He might be wallowing among the surface waves or shooting down into the blackness of the middle seas (a mile deep, according to Herman Melville), but you would never notice the difference. Short of being dead, it is the final, unsurpassable stage of irresponsibility. And however it may be with Anais Nin, there is no question that Miller himself is inside the whale. All his best and most characteristic passages are written from the angle of Jonah, a willing Jonah. Not that he is especially introverted—quite the contrary. In his case the whale happens to be transparent. Only he feels no impulse to alter or control the process that he is undergoing. He has performed the essential Jonah act of allowing himself to be swallowed, remaining passive, *accepting*.

It will be seen what this amounts to. It is a species of quietism,[7] implying either complete unbelief or else a degree of belief amounting to mysticism. The attitude is "*Je m'en fous*" [I don't give a damn] or "Though He slay me, yet will I trust in Him,"[8] whichever way you like to look at it; for practical purposes both are identical, the moral in either case being "Sit on your bum." But in a time like ours, is this a defensible attitude? Notice that it is almost impossible to refrain from asking this question. At the moment of writing we are still in a period in which it is taken for granted that books ought always to be positive, serious, and "constructive." A dozen years ago this idea would have been greeted with titters. ("My dear aunt, one doesn't write *about* anything, one just *writes*.") Then the pendulum swung away from the frivolous notion that art is merely technique, but it swung a very long distance, to the point of asserting that a book can only be "good" if it is founded on a "true" vision of life. Naturally the people who believe this also believe that they are in possession of the truth themselves. Catholic critics, for instance, tend to claim that books are only "good"

---

7. A philosophy counseling withdrawal from worldly interests.   8. Isaiah 13.16.

when they are of Catholic tendency. Marxist critics make the same claim more boldly for Marxist books. For instance, Mr Edward Upward ("A Marxist Interpretation of Literature", in *The Mind in Chains*):

> Literary criticism which aims at being Marxist must . . . proclaim that no book written *at the present time* can be "good" unless it is written from a Marxist or near-Marxist viewpoint.

Various other writers have made similar or comparable statements. Mr Upward italicises "at the present time" because he realises that you cannot, for instance, dismiss *Hamlet* on the ground that Shakespeare was not a Marxist. Nevertheless his interesting essay only glances very shortly at this difficulty. Much of the literature that comes to us out of the past is permeated by and in fact founded on beliefs (the belief in the immortality of the soul, for example) which now seem to us false and in some cases contemptibly silly. Yet it is "good" literature, if survival is any test. Mr Upward would no doubt answer that a belief which was appropriate several centuries ago might be inappropriate and therefore stultifying now. But this does not get one much farther, because it assumes that in any age there will be *one* body of belief which is the current approximation to truth, and that the best literature of the time will be more or less in harmony with it. Actually no such uniformity has ever existed. In seventeenth-century England, for instance, there was a religious and political cleavage which distinctly resembled the left-right antagonism of to-day. Looking back, most modern people would feel that the bourgeois-Puritan viewpoint was a better approximation to truth than the Catholic-feudal one. But it is certainly not the case that all or even a majority of the best writers of the time were puritans. And more than this, there exist "good" writers whose world-view would in *any* age be recognised as false and silly. Edgar Allan Poe is an example. Poe's outlook is at best a wild romanticism and at worst is not far from being insane in the literal clinical sense. Why is it, then, that stories like *The Black Cat, The Tell-tale Heart, The Fall of the House of Usher* and so forth, which might very nearly have been written by a lunatic, do not convey a feeling of falsity? Because they are true within a certain framework, they keep the rules of their own peculiar world, like a Japanese picture. But it appears that to write successfully about such a world you have got to believe in it. One sees the difference immediately if one compares Poe's *Tales* with what is, in my opinion, an insincere attempt to work up a similar atmosphere, Julian Green's *Minuit*.[9] The thing that immediately strikes one about *Minuit* is that there is no reason why any of the events in it should happen. Everything is completely arbitrary; there is no emotional sequence. But this is exactly what one does *not* feel with Poe's stories. Their maniacal logic, in its own setting, is quite convincing. When, for instance, the drunkard seizes the black cat and cuts its eye out with his penknife,[1] one knows exactly *why* he did it, even to the point of feeling that one would have done the same oneself. It seems therefore that for a creative writer possession of the "truth" is less important than emotional sincerity. Even Mr Upward would not claim that a writer needs nothing beyond a Marxist training. He also needs talent. But talent, apparently, is a matter of being able to *care*, of really *believing* in your beliefs, whether they are true or false. The difference between, for instance, Céline[2] and Evelyn Waugh is a difference of emotional intensity. It is the difference between genuine

---

9. In *Minuit* Green evokes the hallucinatory and nightmarish world of his protagonist.
1. In Poe's story *The Black Cat*.

2. Louis-Ferdinand Céline, French author of nihilistic fiction like *Death on the Installment Plan* (1936).

despair and a despair that is at least partly a pretence. And with this there goes another consideration which is perhaps less obvious: that there are occasions when an "untrue" belief is more likely to be sincerely held than a "true" one.

If one looks at the books of personal reminiscence written about the war of 1914–18, one notices that nearly all that have remained readable after a lapse of time are written from a passive, negative angle. They are the records of something completely meaningless, a nightmare happening in a void. That was not actually the truth about the war, but it was the truth about the individual reaction. The soldier advancing into a machine-gun barrage or standing waist-deep in a flooded trench knew only that here was an appalling experience in which he was all but helpless. He was likelier to make a good book out of his helplessness and his ignorance than out of a pretended power to see the whole thing in perspective. As for the books that were written during the war itself, the best of them were nearly all the work of people who simply turned their backs and tried not to notice that the war was happening. Mr E. M. Forster has described how in 1917 he read *Prufrock* and others of Eliot's early poems, and how it heartened him at such a time to get hold of poems that were "innocent of public-spiritedness":

> They sang of private disgust and diffidence, and of people who seemed genuine be-
> cause they were unattractive or weak. . . . Here was a protest, and a feeble one, and the
> more congenial for being feeble. . . . He who could turn aside to complain of ladies
> and drawing rooms preserved a tiny drop of our self-respect, he carried on the human
> heritage.

That is very well said. Mr MacNeice,[3] in the book I have referred to already, quotes this passage and somewhat smugly adds:

> Ten years later less feeble protests were to be made by poets and the human heritage car-
> ried on rather differently. . . . The contemplation of a world of fragments becomes boring
> and Eliot's successors are more interested in tidying it up.

Similar remarks are scattered throughout Mr. MacNeice's book. What he wishes us to believe is that Eliot's "successors" (meaning Mr. MacNeice and his friends) have in some way "protested" more effectively than Eliot did by publishing *Prufrock* at the moment when the Allied armies were assaulting the Hindenburg Line. Just where these "protests" are to be found I do not know. But in the contrast between Mr Forster's comment and Mr MacNeice's lies all the difference between a man who knows what the 1914–18 war was like and a man who barely remembers it. The truth is that in 1917 there was nothing that a thinking and a sensitive person could do, except to remain human, if possible. And a gesture of helplessness, even of frivolity, might be the best way of doing that. If I had been a soldier fighting in the Great War, I would sooner have got hold of *Prufrock* than *The First Hundred Thousand*[4] or Horatio Bottomley's *Letters to the Boys in the Trenches*. I should have felt, like Mr Forster, that by simply standing aloof and keeping touch with pre-war emotions, Eliot was carrying on the human heritage. What a relief it would have been at such a time, to read about the hesitations of a middle-aged highbrow with a bald spot! So different from bayonet-drill! After the bombs and the food-queues and the recruiting-posters, a human voice! What a relief!

3. Louis MacNeice (1907–1963), Ulster poet who wrote radio dramas and other programs for the BBC.
4. *The First Hundred Thousand, Being the Unofficial Chron-* *icle of a Unit "K (1)"* (1917), a personal narrative of the war by Ian Hay.

But, after all, the war of 1914–18 was only a heightened moment in an almost continuous crisis. At this date it hardly even needs a war to bring home to us the disintegration of our society and the increasing helplessness of all decent people. It is for this reason that I think that the passive, non-co-operative attitude implied in Henry Miller's work is justified. Whether or not it is an expression of what people *ought* to feel, it probably comes somewhere near to expressing what they do feel. Once again it is the human voice among the bomb-explosions, a friendly American voice, "innocent of public-spiritedness." No sermons, merely the subjective truth. And along those lines, apparently, it is still possible for a good novel to be written. Not necessarily an edifying novel, but a novel worth reading and likely to be remembered after it is read.

While I have been writing this essay another European war has broken out. It will either last several years and tear Western civilisation to pieces, or it will end inconclusively and prepare the way for yet another war which will do the job once and for all. But war is only "peace intensified." What is quite obviously happening, war or no war, is the break-up of *laissez-faire* capitalism and of the liberal-Christian culture. Until recently the full implications of this were not foreseen, because it was generally imagined that socialism could preserve and even enlarge the atmosphere of liberalism. It is now beginning to be realised how false this idea was. Almost certainly we are moving into an age of totalitarian dictatorships—an age in which freedom of thought will be at first a deadly sin and later on a meaningless abstraction. The autonomous individual is going to be stamped out of existence. But this means that literature, in the form in which we know it, must suffer at least a temporary death. The literature of liberalism is coming to an end and the literature of totalitarianism has not yet appeared and is barely imaginable. As for the writer, he is sitting on a melting iceberg; he is merely an anachronism, a hangover from the bourgeois age, as surely doomed as the hippopotamus. Miller seems to me a man out of the common because he saw and proclaimed this fact a long while before most of his contemporaries—at a time, indeed, when many of them were actually burbling about a renaissance of literature. Wyndham Lewis had said years earlier that the major history of the English language was finished, but he was basing this on different and rather trivial reasons. But from now onwards the all-important fact for the creative writer is going to be that this is not a writer's world. That does not mean that he cannot help to bring the new society into being, but he can take no part in the process *as a writer*. For *as a writer* he is a liberal, and what is happening is the destruction of liberalism. It seems likely, therefore, that in the remaining years of free speech any novel worth reading will follow more or less along the lines that Miller has followed—I do not mean in technique or subject matter, but in implied outlook. The passive attitude will come back, and it will be more consciously passive than before. Progress and reaction have both turned out to be swindles. Seemingly there is nothing left but quietism—robbing reality of its terrors by simply submitting to it. Get inside the whale—or rather, admit you are inside the whale (for you *are*, of course). Give yourself over to the world-process, stop fighting against it or pretending that you control it; simply accept it, endure it, record it. That seems to be the formula that any sensitive novelist is now likely to adopt. A novel on more positive, "constructive" lines, and not emotionally spurious, is at present very difficult to imagine.

But do I mean by this that Miller is a "great author," a new hope for English prose? Nothing of the kind. Miller himself would be the last to claim or want any such thing. No doubt he will go on writing—anybody who has once started always goes on writing—and associated with him there are a number of writers of approximately the same tendency, Lawrence Durrell, Michael Fraenkel and others, almost amounting to a "school." But he himself seems to me essentially a man of one book. Sooner or later I should expect him to descend into unintelligibility, or into charlatanism: there are signs of both in his later work. His last book, *Tropic of Capricorn*, I have not even read. This was not because I did not want to read it, but because the police and Customs authorities have so far managed to prevent me from getting hold of it. But it would surprise me if it came anywhere near *Tropic of Cancer* or the opening chapters of *Black Spring*. Like certain other autobiographical novelists, he had it in him to do just one thing perfectly, and he did it. Considering what the fiction of the nineteen-thirties has been like, that is something.

Miller's books are published by the Obelisk Press in Paris. What will happen to the Obelisk Press, now that war has broken out and Jack Kahane, the publisher, is dead, I do not know, but at any rate the books are still procurable. I earnestly counsel anyone who has not done so to read at least *Tropic of Cancer*. With a little ingenuity, or by paying a little over the published price, you can get hold of it, and even if parts of it disgust you, it will stick in your memory. It is also an "important" book, in a sense different from the sense in which that word is generally used. As a rule novels are spoken of an "important" when they are either a "terrible indictment" of something or other or when they introduce some technical innovation. Neither of these applies to *Tropic of Cancer*. Its importance is merely symptomatic. Here in my opinion is the only imaginative prose-writer of the slightest value who has appeared among the English-speaking races for some years past. Even if that is objected to as an overstatement, it will probably be admitted that Miller is a writer out of the ordinary, worth more than a single glance; and after all, he is a completely negative, unconstructive, amoral writer, a mere Jonah, a passive acceptor of evil, a sort of Whitman among the corpses. Symptomatically, that is more significant than the mere fact that five thousand novels are published in England every year and four thousand nine hundred of them are tripe. It is a demonstration of the *impossibility* of any major literature until the world has shaken itself into its new shape.

1940

Politics and the English Language

Most people who bother with the matter at all would admit that the English language is in a bad way, but it is generally assumed that we cannot by conscious action do anything about it. Our civilization is decadent and our language—so the argument runs—must inevitably share in the general collapse. It follows that any struggle against the abuse of language is a sentimental archaism, like preferring candles to electric light or hansom cabs to aeroplanes. Underneath this lies the half-conscious belief that language is a natural growth and not an instrument which we shape for our own purposes.

Now, it is clear that the decline of a language must ultimately have political and economic causes: it is not due simply to the bad influence of this or that individual writer. But an effect can become a cause, reinforcing the original cause and producing the same effect in an intensified form, and so on indefinitely. A man may take to drink because he feels himself to be a failure, and then fail all the more completely because he drinks. It is rather the same thing that is happening to the English language. It becomes ugly and inaccurate because our thoughts are foolish, but the slovenliness of our language makes it easier for us to have foolish thoughts. The point is that the process is reversible. Modern English, especially written English, is full of bad habits which spread by imitation and which can be avoided if one is willing to take the necessary trouble. If one gets rid of these habits one can think more clearly, and to think clearly is a necessary first step towards political regeneration: so that the fight against bad English is not frivolous and is not the exclusive concern of professional writers. I will come back to this presently, and I hope that by that time the meaning of what I have said here will have become clearer. Meanwhile, here are five specimens of the English language as it is now habitually written.

These five passages have not been picked out because they are especially bad—I could have quoted far worse if I had chosen—but because they illustrate various of the mental vices from which we now suffer. They are a little below the average, but are fairly representative samples. I number them so that I can refer back to them when necessary:

(1) I am not, indeed, sure whether it is not true to say that the Milton who once seemed not unlike a seventeenth-century Shelley had not become, out of an experience ever more bitter in each year, more alien [sic] to the founder of that Jesuit sect which nothing could induce him to tolerate.

Professor Harold Laski (Essay in Freedom of Expression)

(2) Above all, we cannot play ducks and drakes with a native battery of idioms which prescribes such egregious collocations of vocables as the Basic *put up with* for *tolerate* or *put at a loss* for *bewilder*.

Professor Lancelot Hogben (Interglossa)

(3) On the one side we have the free personality: by definition it is not neurotic, for it has neither conflict nor dream. Its desires, such as they are, are transparent, for they are just what institutional approval keeps in the forefront of consciousness; another institutional pattern would alter their number and intensity; there is little in them that is natural, irreducible, or culturally dangerous. But *on the other side*, the social bond itself is nothing but the mutual reflection of these self-secure integrities. Recall the definition of love. Is not this the very picture of a small academic? Where is there a place in this hall of mirrors for either personality or fraternity?

Essay on psychology in Politics (New York)

(4) All the "best people" from the gentlemen's clubs, and all the frantic fascist captains, united in common hatred of Socialism and bestial horror of the rising tide of the mass revolutionary movement, have turned to acts of provocation, to foul incendiarism, to medieval legends of poisoned wells, to legalize their own destruction of proletarian organizations, and rouse the agitated petty-bourgeoisie to chauvinistic fervor, on behalf of the fight against the revolutionary way out of the crisis.

Communist pamphlet

(5) If a new spirit is to be infused into this old country, there is one thorny and contentious reform which must be tackled, and that is the humanization and galvanization of the B.B.C. Timidity here will bespeak canker and atrophy of the soul. The heart of Britain may be sound and of strong beat, for instance, but the British lion's roar at present is like that of Bottom in Shakespeare's *Midsummer Night's Dream*—as gentle as any sucking dove. A virile new Britain cannot continue indefinitely to be traduced in the eyes or rather ears, of the world by the effete languors of Langham Place, brazenly masquerading as "standard

English." When the Voice of Britain is heard at nine o'clock, better far and infinitely less ludicrous to hear aitches honestly dropped than the present priggish, inflated, inhibited, school-ma'amish arch braying of blameless bashful mewing maidens!

Letter in Tribune

Each of these passages has faults of its own, but, quite apart from avoidable ugliness, two qualities are common to all of them. The first is staleness of imagery; the other is lack of precision. The writer either has a meaning and cannot express it, or he inadvertently says something else, or he is almost indifferent as to whether his words mean anything or not. This mixture of vagueness and sheer incompetence is the most marked characteristic of modern English prose, and especially of any kind of political writing. As soon as certain topics are raised, the concrete melts into the abstract and no one seems able to think of turns of speech that are not hackneyed: prose consists less and less of *words* chosen for the sake of their meaning, and more and more of *phrases* tacked together like the sections of a prefabricated hen-house. I list below, with notes and examples, various of the tricks by means of which the work of prose-construction is habitually dodged:

Dying metaphors. A newly invented metaphor assists thought by evoking a visual image, while on the other hand a metaphor which is technically "dead" (e.g. *iron resolution*) has in effect reverted to being an ordinary word and can generally be used without loss of vividness. But in between these two classes there is a huge dump of worn-out metaphors which have lost all evocative power and are merely used because they save people the trouble of inventing phrases for themselves. Examples are: *Ring the changes on, take up the cudgels for, toe the line, ride roughshod over, stand shoulder to shoulder with, play into the hands of, no axe to grind, grist to the mill, fishing in troubled waters, on the order of the day, Achilles' heel, swan song, hotbed.* Many of these are used without knowledge of their meaning (what is a "rift," for instance?), and incompatible metaphors are frequently mixed, a sure sign that the writer is not interested in what he is saying. Some metaphors now current have been twisted out of their original meaning without those who use them even being aware of the fact. For example, *toe the line* is sometimes written *tow the line.* Another example is *the hammer and the anvil,* now always used with the implication that the anvil gets the worst of it. In real life it is always the anvil that breaks the hammer, never the other way about: a writer who stopped to think what he was saying would be aware of this, and would avoid perverting the original phrase.

Operators or *verbal false limbs.* These save the trouble of picking out appropriate verbs and nouns, and at the same time pad each sentence with extra syllables which give it an appearance of symmetry. Characteristic phrases are *render inoperative, militate against, make contact with, be subjected to, give rise to, give grounds for, have the effect of, play a leading part (role) in, make itself felt, take effect, exhibit a tendency to, serve the purpose of, etc., etc.* The keynote is the elimination of simple verbs. Instead of being a single word, such as *break, stop, spoil, mend, kill,* a verb becomes a *phrase,* made up of a noun or adjective tacked on to some general-purposes verb such as *prove, serve, form, play, render.* In addition, the passive voice is wherever possible used in preference to the active, and noun constructions are used instead of gerunds (*by examination of* instead of *by examining*). The range of verbs is further cut down by means of the *-ize* and *de-* formations, and the banal statements are given an appearance of profundity by means of the *not un-* formation. Simple conjunctions and prepositions are replaced by such phrases as *with respect to, having regard to, the fact that, by dint of, in view of, in the interests of, on the hypothesis that*; and the ends of sentences are saved by anticlimax by such resounding common-places as *greatly to be desired, cannot be left out of account, a development to be expected in the near future, deserving of serious consideration, brought to a satisfactory conclusion*, and so on and so forth.

Pretentious diction. Words like *phenomenon, element, individual* (as noun), *objective, categorical, effective, virtual, basic, primary, promote, constitute, exhibit, exploit, utilize, eliminate, liquidate*, are used to dress up simple statement and give an air of scientific impartiality to biased judgments. Adjectives like *epoch-making, epic, historic, unforgettable, triumphant, age-old, inevitable, inexorable, veritable*, are used to dignify the sordid processes of international politics, while writing that aims at glorifying war usually takes on an archaic color, its characteristic words being: *realm, throne, chariot, mailed fist, trident, sword, shield, buckler, banner, jackboot, clarion*. Foreign words and expressions such as *cul de sac, ancien régime, deus ex machina, mutatis mutandis, status quo, gleichschaltung, weltanschauung*, are used to give an air of culture and elegance. Except for the useful abbreviations *i.e., e.g.*, and *etc.*, there is no real need for any of the hundreds of foreign phrases now current in English. Bad writers, and especially scientific, political and sociological writers, are nearly always haunted by the notion that Latin or Greek words are grander than Saxon ones, and unnecessary words like *expedite, ameliorate, predict, extraneous, deracinated, clandestine, subaqueous* and hundreds of others constantly gain ground from their Anglo-Saxon opposite numbers.[1] The jargon peculiar to Marxist writing (*hyena, hangman, cannibal, petty bourgeois, these gentry, lacquey, flunkey, mad dog, White Guard*, etc.) consists largely of words and phrases translated from Russian, German or French; but the normal way of coining a new word is to use a Latin or Greek root with the appropriate affix and, where necessary, the *-ize* formation. It is often easier to make up words of this kind (*deregionalize, impermissible, extramarital, non-fragmentary* and so forth) than to think up the English words that will cover one's meaning. The result, in general, is an increase in slovenliness and vagueness.

Meaningless words. In certain kinds of writing, particularly in art criticism and literary criticism, it is normal to come across long passages which are almost completely lacking in meaning.[2] Words like *romantic, plastic, values, human, dead, sentimental, natural, vitality*, as used in art criticism, are strictly meaningless, in the sense that they not only do not point to any discoverable object, but are hardly ever expected to do so by the reader. When one critic writes, "The outstanding feature of Mr. X's work is its living quality," while another writes, "The immediately striking thing about Mr. X's

1. An interesting illustration of this is the way in which the English flower names which were in use till very recently are being ousted by Greek ones, *snapdragon* becoming *antirrhinum, forget-me-not* becoming *myosotis*, etc. It is hard to see any practical reason for this change of fashion: it is probably due to an instinctive turning-away from the more homely word and a vague feeling that the Greek word is scientific [Orwell's note].
2. Example: "Comfort's catholicity of perception and

image, strangely Whitmanesque in range, almost the exact opposite in aesthetic compulsion, continues to evoke that trembling atmospheric accumulative hinting at a cruel, an inexorably serene timelessness. . . . Wrey Gardiner scores by aiming at simple bull's-eyes with precision. Only they are not so simple, and through this contented sadness runs more than the surface bitter-sweet of resignation." (*Poetry Quarterly*) [Orwell's note].

work is its peculiar deadness," the reader accepts this as a simple difference of opinion. If words like *black* and *white* were involved, instead of the jargon words *dead* and *living*, he would see at once that language was being used in an improper way. Many political words are similarly abused. The word *Fascism* has now no meaning except in so far as it signifies "something not desirable." The words *democracy, socialism, freedom, patriotic, realistic, justice,* have each of them several different meanings which cannot be reconciled with one another. In the case of a word like *democracy,* not only is there no agreed definition, but the attempt to make one is resisted from all sides. It is almost universally felt that when we call a country democratic we are praising it: consequently the defenders of every kind of régime claim that it is a democracy, and fear that they might have to stop using the word if it were tied down to any one meaning. Words of this kind are often used in a consciously dishonest way. That is, the person who uses them has his own private definition, but allows his hearer to think he means something quite different. Statements like *Marshal Pétain[3] was a true patriot, The Soviet Press is the freest in the world, The Catholic Church is opposed to persecution,* are almost always made with intent to deceive. Other words used in variable meanings, in most cases more or less dishonestly, are: *class, totalitarian, science, progressive, reactionary, bourgeois, equality.*

Now that I have made this catalogue of swindles and perversions, let me give another example of the kind of writing that they lead to. This time it must of its nature be an imaginary one. I am going to translate a passage of good English into modern English of the worst sort. Here is a well-known verse from *Ecclesiastes:*

> I returned and saw under the sun, that the race is not to the swift, nor the battle to the strong, neither yet bread to the wise, nor yet riches to men of understanding, nor yet favour to men of skill; but time and chance happeneth to them all.

Here it is in modern English:

> Objective considerations of contemporary phenomena compels the conclusion that success or failure in competitive activities exhibits no tendency to be commensurate with innate capacity, but that a considerable element of the unpredictable must invariably be taken into account.

This is a parody, but not a very gross one. Exhibit (3), above, for instance, contains several patches of the same kind of English. It will be seen that I have not made a full translation. The beginning and ending of the sentence follow the original meaning fairly closely, but in the middle the concrete illustrations—race, battle, bread—dissolve into the vague phrase "success or failure in competitive activities." This had to be so, because no modern writer of the kind I am discussing—no one capable of using phrases like "objective consideration of contemporary phenomena"—would ever tabulate his thoughts in that precise and detailed way. The whole tendency of modern prose is away from concreteness. Now analyse these two sentences a little more closely. The first contains forty-nine words but only sixty syllables, and all its words are those of everyday life. The second contains thirty-eight words of ninety syllables: eighteen of its words are from Latin roots, and one from Greek. The first sentence contains six vivid images, and only one phrase ("time and

---

3. Premier of the puppet government installed in France by the Nazis (1940–1944).

chance") that could be called vague. The second contains not a single fresh, arresting phrase, and in spite of its ninety syllables it gives only a shortened version of the meaning contained in the first. Yet without a doubt it is the second kind of sentence that is gaining ground in modern English. I do not want to exaggerate. This kind of writing is not yet universal, and outcrops of simplicity will occur here and there in the worst-written page. Still, if you or I were told to write a few lines on the uncertainty of human fortunes, we should probably come much nearer to my imaginary sentence than to the one from *Ecclesiastes*.

As I have tried to show, modern writing at its worst does not consist in picking out words for the sake of their meaning and inventing images in order to make the meaning clearer. It consists in gumming together long strips of words which have already been set in order by someone else, and making the results presentable by sheer humbug. The attraction of this way of writing is that it is easy. It is easier—even quicker, once you have the habit—to say *In my opinion it is not an unjustifiable assumption that* than to say *I think*. If you use ready-made phrases, you not only don't have to hunt about for words; you also don't have to bother with the rhythms of your sentences, since these phrases are generally so arranged as to be more or less euphonious. When you are composing in a hurry—when you are dictating to a stenographer, for instance, or making a public speech—it is natural to fall into a pretentious, Latinized style. Tags like *a consideration which we should do well to bear in mind* or *a conclusion to which all of us would readily assent* will save many a sentence from coming down with a bump. By using stale metaphors, similes and idioms, you save much mental effort, at the cost of leaving your meaning vague, not only for your reader but for yourself. This is the significance of mixed metaphors. The sole aim of a metaphor is to call up a visual image. When these images clash—as in *The Fascist octopus has sung its swan song, the jackboot is thrown into the melting pot*—it can be taken as certain that the writer is not seeing a mental image of the objects he is naming; in other words he is not really thinking. Look again at the examples I gave at the beginning of this essay. Professor Laski (1) uses five negatives in fifty-three words. One of these is superfluous, making nonsense of the whole passage, and in addition there is the slip *alien* for akin, making further nonsense, and several avoidable pieces of clumsiness which increase the general vagueness. Professor Hogben (2) plays ducks and drakes with a battery which is able to write prescriptions, and, while disapproving of the everyday phrase *put up with*, is unwilling to look *egregious* up in the dictionary and see what it means; (3), if one takes an uncharitable attitude towards it, is simply meaningless: probably one could work out its intended meaning by reading the whole of the article in which it occurs. In (4), the writer knows more or less what he wants to say, but an accumulation of stale phrases chokes him like tea leaves blocking a sink. In (5), words and meaning have almost parted company. People who write in this manner usually have a general emotional meaning—they dislike one thing and want to express solidarity with another—but they are not interested in the detail of what they are saying. A scrupulous writer, in every sentence that he writes, will ask himself at least four questions, thus: What am I trying to say? What words will express it? What image or idiom will make it clearer? Is this image fresh enough to have an effect? And he will probably ask himself two more: Could I put it more shortly? Have I said anything that is avoidably ugly? But you are not obliged to go to all this trouble. You can shirk it by simply throwing your mind open and letting the ready-made phrases come crowding in. They will construct your sentences for you—even think your thoughts for you, to a certain extent—and at need they will perform the important service of partially concealing your meaning even from yourself. It is at this point that the special connection between politics and the debasement of language becomes clear.

In our time it is broadly true that political writing is bad writing. Where it is not true, it will generally be found that the writer is some kind of rebel, expressing his private opinions and not a "party line." Orthodoxy, of whatever color, seems to demand a lifeless, imitative style. The political dialects to be found in pamphlets, leading articles, manifestos, White Papers and the speeches of under-secretaries do, of course, vary from party to party, but they are all alike in that one almost never finds in them a fresh, vivid, home-made turn of speech. When one watches some tired hack on the platform mechanically repeating the familiar phrases—*bestial atrocities, iron heel, bloodstained tyranny, free peoples of the world, stand shoulder to shoulder*—one often has a curious feeling that one is not watching a live human being but some kind of dummy: a feeling which suddenly becomes stronger at moments when the light catches the speaker's spectacles and turns them into blank discs which seem to have no eyes behind them. And this is not altogether fanciful. A speaker who uses that kind of phraseology has gone some distance towards turning himself into a machine. The appropriate noises are coming out of his larynx, but his brain is not involved as it would be if he were choosing his words for himself. If the speech he is making is one that he is accustomed to make over and over again, he may be almost unconscious of what he is saying, as one is when one utters the responses in church. And this reduced state of consciousness, if not indispensable, is at any rate favorable to political conformity.

In our time, political speech and writing are largely the defense of the indefensible. Things like the continuance of British rule in India, the Russian purges and deportations, the dropping of the atom bombs on Japan, can indeed be defended, but only by arguments which are too brutal for most people to face, and which do not square with the professed aims of political parties. Thus political language has to consist largely of euphemism, question-begging and sheer cloudy vagueness. Defenseless villages are bombarded from the air, the inhabitants driven out into the countryside, the cattle machine-gunned, the huts set on fire with incendiary bullets: this is called *pacification*. Millions of peasants are robbed of their farms and sent trudging along the roads with no more than they can carry: this is called *transfer of population* or *rectification of frontiers*. People are imprisoned for years without trial, or shot in the back of the neck or sent to die of scurvy in Arctic lumber camps: this is called *elimination of unreliable elements*. Such phraseology is needed if one wants to name things without calling up mental pictures of them. Consider for instance some comfortable English professor defending Russian totalitarianism. He cannot say outright, "I believe in killing off your opponents when you can get good results by doing so." Probably, therefore, he will say something like this:

> While freely conceding that the Soviet regime exhibits certain features which the humanitarian may be inclined to deplore, we must, I think, agree that a certain curtailment of the right to political opposition is an unavoidable concomitant of transitional periods, and that the rigors which the Russian people have been called upon to undergo have been amply justified in the sphere of concrete achievement.

The inflated style is itself a kind of euphemism. A mass of Latin words falls upon the facts like soft snow, blurring the outlines and covering up all the details. The great enemy of clear language is insincerity. When there is a gap between one's real and one's declared aims, one turns as it were instinctively to long words and exhausted idioms, like a cuttlefish squirting out ink. In our age there is no such thing as "keeping out of politics." All issues are political issues, and politics itself is a mass of lies, evasions, folly, hatred, and schizophrenia. When the general atmosphere is bad, language must suffer. I should expet to find—this is a guess which I have not sufficient knowledge to verify—that the German, Russian and Italian languages have all deteriorated in the last ten or fifteen years, as a result of dictatorship.

But if thought corrupts language, language can also corrupt thought. A bad usage can spread by tradition and imitation, even among people who should and do know better. The debased language that I have been discussing is in some ways very convenient. Phrases like *a not unjustifiable assumption, leaves much to be desired, would serve no good purpose, a consideration which we should do well to bear in mind,* are a continuous temptation, a packet of aspirins always at one's elbow. Look back through this essay, and for certain you will find that I have again and again committed the very faults I am protesting against. By this morning's post I have received a pamphlet dealing with conditions in Germany. The author tells me that he "felt impelled" to write it. I open it at random, and here is almost the first sentence that I see: "[The Allies] have an opportunity not only of achieving a radical transformation of Germany's social and political structure in such a way as to avoid a nationalistic reaction in Germany itself, but at the same time of laying the foundations of a co-operative and unified Europe." You see, he "feels impelled" to write—feels, presumably, that he has something new to say—and yet his words, like cavalry horses answering the bugle, group themselves automatically into the familiar dreary pattern. This invasion of one's mind by ready-made phrases (*lay the foundations, achieve a radical transformation*) can only be prevented if one is constantly on guard against them, and every such phrase anaesthetizes a portion of one's brain.

I said earlier that the decadence of our language is probably curable. Those who deny this would argue, if they produced an argument at all, that language merely reflects existing social conditions, and that we cannot influence its development by any direct tinkering with words and constructions. So far as the general tone or spirit of a language goes, this may be true, but it is not true in detail. Silly words and expressions have often disappeared, not through any evolutionary process but owing to the conscious action of a minority. Two recent examples were *explore every avenue* and *leave no stone unturned,* which were killed by the jeers of a few journalists. There is a long list of flyblown metaphors which could similarly be got rid of if enough people would interest themselves in the job; and it should also be possible to laugh the *not un-* formation out of existence, to reduce the amount of Latin and Greek in the average sentence, to drive out foreign phrases and strayed scientific words, and, in general, to make pretentiousness unfashionable. But all these are minor points. The defence of the English language implies more than this, and perhaps it is best to start by saying what it does *not* imply.

To begin with it has nothing to do with archaism, with the salvaging of obsolete words and turns of speech, or with the setting up of a "standard English" which must never be departed from. On the contrary, it is especially concerned with the scrapping of every word or idiom which has outworn its usefulness. It has nothing to do with correct grammar and syntax, which are of no importance so long as one makes one's meaning clear, or with the avoidance of Americanisms, or with having what is called a "good prose style." On the other hand it is not concerned with fake simplicity and the attempt to make written English colloquial. Nor does it even imply in every case preferring the

Saxon word to the Latin one, though it does imply using the fewest and shortest words that will cover one's meaning. What is above all needed is to let the meaning choose the word, and not the other way about. In prose, the worst thing one can do with words is to surrender to them. When you think of a concrete object, you think wordlessly, and then, if you want to describe the thing you have been visualizing you probably hunt about till you find the exact words that seem to fit it. When you think of something abstract you are more inclined to use words from the start, and unless you make a conscious effort to prevent it, the existing dialect will come rushing in and do the job for you, at the expense of blurring or even changing your meaning. Probably it is better to put off using words as long as possible and get one's meaning as clear as one can through pictures or sensations. Afterwards one can choose—not simply *accept*—the phrases that will best cover the meaning, and then switch round and decide what impression one's words are likely to make on another person. This last effort of the mind cuts out all stale or mixed images, all prefabricated phrases, needless repetitions, and humbug and vagueness generally. But one can often be in doubt about the effect of a word or a phrase, and one needs rules that one can rely on when instinct fails. I think the following rules will cover most cases:

(i) Never use a metaphor, simile or other figure of speech which you are used to seeing in print.
(ii) Never use a long word where a short one will do.
(iii) If it is possible to cut a word out, always cut it out.
(iv) Never use the passive where you can use the active.
(v) Never use a foreign phrase, a scientific word or a jargon word if you can think of an everyday English equivalent.
(vi) Break any of these rules sooner than say anything outright barbarous.

These rules sound elementary, and so they are, but they demand a deep change of attitude in anyone who has grown used to writing in the style now fashionable. One could keep all of them and still write bad English, but one could not write the kind of stuff that I quoted in those five specimens at the beginning of this article.

I have not here been considering the literary use of language, but merely language as an instrument for expressing and not for concealing or preventing thought. Stuart Chase and others have come near to claiming that all abstract words are meaningless, and have used this as a pretext for advocating a kind of political quietism. Since you don't know what Fascism is, how can you struggle against Fascism? One need not swallow such absurdities as this, but one ought to recognize that the present political chaos is connected with the decay of language, and that one can probably bring about some improvement by starting at the verbal end. If you simplify your English, you are freed from the worst follies of orthodoxy. You cannot speak any of the necessary dialects, and when you make a stupid remark its stupidity will be obvious, even to yourself. Political language—and with variations this is true of all political parties, from Conservatives to Anarchists—is designed to make lies sound truthful and murder respectable, and to give an appearance of solidity to pure wind. One cannot change this all in a moment, but one can at least change one's own habits, and from time to time one can even, if one jeers loudly enough, send some worn-out and useless phrase—some *jackboot, Achilles' heel, hotbed, melting pot, acid test, veritable inferno* or other lump of verbal refuse—into the dustbin where it belongs.

1946

➤➤ ⯈❖⯇ ⯇⯇

Salman Rushdie
b. 1947

Born in Bombay on the day India achieved independence from Britain, Rushdie was raised in Pakistan after the partition of the subcontinent. He then settled in England, where he soon became one of the most noted writers about the aftermath of empires. His magisterial novel *Midnight's Children* was awarded not only the prestigious Booker McConnell Prize for the best British novel of 1981 but later the "Booker of Bookers," as the best novel in the first twenty-five years of the prize's history. Like Saleem Sinai, the protagonist and narrator of *Midnight's Children*, Rushdie delights in telling its story, in a mixture of history, fantasy, fable, and sheer stylistic exuberance that has come to be known (through the works of Latin American writers like Gabriel Garcia Marquez) as magic realism. At once an Indian and a British writer, Rushdie enjoys a double status as both insider and outsider that allows him to comment both on the history of his native land and on the contemporary politics of Britain with savage and comic incisiveness.

Unfortunately, most who do not know Rushdie's writing well know his name from the publicity surrounding his 1988 novel *The Satanic Verses;* the novel was judged to be an affront to Islam, and on Valentine's Day in 1989 the late Iranian leader Ayatollah Ruhollah Khomeini issued a *fatwa,* or death threat, against both Rushdie and his publisher, carrying a multimillion dollar bounty. As a result, Rushdie was forced to go underground; for nearly ten years he moved from place to place protected by full-time bodyguards, making but unable to receive phone calls, and generally staying out of the public eye and out of harm's way. Under Islamic law, a *fatwa* can be lifted only by the man who imposed it; since Khomeini died with the *fatwa* still in effect, it technically will remain in effect until Rushdie's death, although subsequent Iranian leaders have suggested that the edict would not be enforced. Rushdie has, very recently, begun to make selective, unadvertised public appearances.

It is both appalling and intriguing that the written word still has this much power. The book that followed *The Satanic Verses* was *Haroun and the Sea of Stories,* a tale often (mistakenly) labeled "juvenile." It is in fact an allegory of the power of language—its power to liberate, and the desperate attempts of what political philosopher Louis Althusser calls the "ideological state apparatus" to silence this free, anarchic speech. The story did indeed begin as a bath-time entertainment for Rushdie's son Zafar; but as the affair over the *Satanic Verses* grew and festered, the story matured into a parable of the responsibility of the artist to speak from the heart and conscience, regardless of the political consequences. Rushdie's concerns with the politics of language are shown in his pointed rejoinder to Orwell, *Outside the Whale,* while his haunting story *Chekov and Zulu* mixes reality and fantasy, East and West, popular culture and high literary art.

Outside the Whale

Anyone who has switched on the television set, been to the cinema or entered a bookshop in the last few months will be aware that the British Raj,[1] after three and a half decades in retirement, has been making a sort of comeback. After the big-budget fantasy double-bill of *Gandhi* and *Octopussy* we have had the blackface minstrel-show of *The Far Pavilions* in its TV serial incarnation, and immediately afterwards the overpraised *Jewel in the Crown.* I should also include the alleged "documentary" about Subhas Chandra Bose, Granada Television's *War of the Springing Tiger,* which, in the finest traditions of journalistic impartiality, described India's second-most-revered independence leader as a "clown." And lest we begin to console ourselves that the

---

1. Period of British rule over India prior to 1947.

painful experiences are coming to an end, we are reminded that David Lean's film of *A Passage to India* is in the offing. I remember seeing an interview with Mr Lean in *The Times*, in which he explained his reasons for wishing to make a film of Forster's novel. "I haven't seen Dickie Attenborough's *Gandhi* yet," he said, "but as far as I'm aware, nobody has yet succeeded in putting India on the screen." The Indian film industry, from Satyajit Ray to Mr N. T. Rama Rao, will no doubt feel suitably humbled by the great man's opinion.

These are dark days. Having expressed my reservations about the *Gandhi* film elsewhere, I have no wish to renew my quarrel with Mahatma Dickie. As for *Octopussy*, one can only say that its portrait of modern India was as grittily and uncompromisingly realistic as its depiction of the skill, integrity and sophistication of the British secret services.

In defence of the Mahattenborough, he did allow a few Indians to be played by Indians. (One is becoming grateful for the smallest of mercies.) Those responsible for transferring *The Far Pavilions* to the screen would have no truck with such tomfoolery. True, Indian actors were allowed to play the villains (Saeed Jaffrey, who has turned the Raj revival into a personal cottage industry, with parts in *Gandhi* and *Jewel in the Crown* as well, did his hissing and hand-rubbing party piece; and Sneh Gupta played the selfish princess but, unluckily for her, her entire part consisted of the interminably repeated line, "Ram Ram"). Meanwhile, the good-guy roles were firmly commandeered by Ben Cross, Christopher Lee, Omar Sharif, and, most memorably, Amy Irving as the good princess, whose make-up person obviously believed that Indian princesses dip their eyes in black ink and get sun-tans on their lips.

Now of course *The Far Pavilions* is the purest bilge. The great processing machines of TV soap-opera have taken the somewhat more fibrous garbage of the M. M. Kaye book and puréed it into easy-swallow, no-chewing-necessary drivel. Thus, the two central characters, both supposedly raised as Indians, have been lobotomized to the point of being incapable of pronouncing their own names. The man calls himself "A Shock," and the woman "An Jooly." Around and about them there is branding of human flesh and snakery and widow-burning by the natives. There are Pathans who cannot speak Pushto. And, to avoid offending the Christian market, we are asked to believe that the child "A Shock," while being raised by Hindus and Muslims, somehow knew that neither "way" was for him, and instinctively, when he wished to raise his voice in prayer, "prayed to the mountains." It would be easy to conclude that such material could not possibly be taken seriously by anyone, and that it is therefore unnecessary to get worked up about it. Should we not simply rise above the twaddle, switch off our sets and not care?

I should be happier about this, the quietist option—and I shall have more to say about quietism[2] later on—if I did not believe that it matters, it always matters, to name rubbish as rubbish; that to do otherwise is to legitimize it. I should also mind less, were it not for the fact that *The Far Pavilions*, book as well as TV serial, is only the latest in a very long line of fake portraits inflicted by the West on the East. The creation of a false Orient of cruel-lipped princes and dusky slim-hipped maidens, of ungodliness, fire and the sword, has been brilliantly described by Edward Said in his classic study *Orientalism*, in which he makes clear that the purpose of such false portraits was to provide moral, cultural and artistic justification for imperialism and for

---

2. A philosophy counseling withdrawal from worldly interests. The critique of quietism figures prominently in Orwell's *Inside the Whale*.

its underpinning ideology, that of the racial superiority of the Caucasian over the Asiatic. Let me add only that stereotypes are easier to shrug off if yours is not the culture being stereotyped; or, at the very least, if your culture has the power to counterpunch against the stereotype. If the TV screens of the West were regularly filled by equally hyped, big-budget productions depicting the realities of India, one could stomach the odd M. M. Kaye. When praying to the mountains is the norm, the stomach begins to heave.

Paul Scott was M. M. Kaye's agent, and it has always seemed to me a damning indictment of his literary judgement that he believed *The Far Pavilions* to be a good book. Even stranger is the fact that *The Raj Quartet*[3] and the Kaye novel are founded on identical strategies of what, to be polite, one must call borrowing. In both cases, the central plot motifs are lifted from earlier, and much finer novels. In *The Far Pavilions*, the hero Ash ("A Shock"), raised an Indian, discovered to be a sahib,[4] and ever afterwards torn between his two selves, will be instantly recognizable as the cardboard cut-out version of Kipling's *Kim*.[5] And the rape of Daphne Manners in the Bibighar Gardens derives just as plainly from Forster's *A Passage to India*. But because Kaye and Scott are vastly inferior to the writers they follow, they turn what they touch to pure lead. Where Forster's scene in the Marabar caves retains its ambiguity and mystery, Scott gives us not one rape but a gang assault, and one perpetrated, what is more, by peasants. Smelly persons of the worst sort. So class as well as sex is violated; Daphne gets the works. It is useless, I'm sure, to suggest that if rape must be used as the metaphor of the Indo-British connection, then surely, in the interests of accuracy, it should be the rape of an Indian woman by one or more Englishmen of whatever class. But not even Forster dared to write about such a crime. So much more evocative to conjure up white society's fear of the darkie, of big brown cocks.

You will say I am being unfair; Scott is a writer of a different calibre to M. M. Kaye. What's more, very few of the British characters come at all well out of the *Quartet*—Barbie, Sarah, Daphne, none of the men. (Kaye, reviewing the TV adaptation, found it excessively rude about the British.)

In point of fact, I am not so sure that Scott is so much finer an artist. Like Kaye, he has an instinct for the cliché. Sadistic, bottom-flogging policeman Merrick turns out to be (surprise!) a closet homosexual. His grammar school origins give him (what else?) a chip on the shoulder. And all around him is a galaxy of chinless wonders, regimental *grandes dames*, lushes, empty-headed blondes, silly-asses, plucky young things, good sorts, bad eggs and Russian counts with eyepatches. The overall effect is rather like a literary version of Mulligatawny soup. It tries to taste Indian, but ends up being ultra-parochially British, only with too much pepper.

And yes, Scott is harsh in his portraits of many British characters; but I want to try and make a rather more difficult point, a point about *form*. The *Quartet*'s form tells us, in effect, that the history of the end of the Raj was largely composed of the doings of the officer class and its wife. Indians get walk-ons,[6] but remain, for the most part, bit-players in their own history. Once this form has been set, it scarcely matters that individual fictional Brits get unsympathetic treatment from their author. The form insists that *they are the ones whose stories matter*, and that is so much less than the whole truth that it must be called a falsehood. It will not do to argue that Scott was

3. Paul Scott's four novels about India during British rule: *The Jewel in the Crown* (1966), *The Day of the Scorpion* (1968), *The Towers of Silence* (1971), and *A Division of the Spoils* (1975). The television production *The Jewel in the*

Crown is an adaptation of the entire quartet.
4. A term of respect for a European (colonial) master.
5. The hero of Rudyard Kipling's 1901 novel *Kim*.
6. A brief, nonspeaking role in a film.

attempting to portray the British in India, and that such was the nature of imperialist society that the Indians *would* only have had bit-parts. It is no defence to say that a work adopts, in its structure, the very ethic which, in its content and tone, it pretends to dislike. It is, in fact, the case for the prosecution.

I cannot end this brief account of the Raj revival without returning to David Lean, a film director whose mere interviews merit reviews. I have already quoted his masterpiece in *The Times*; here now are three passages from his conversation with Derek Malcolm in the *Guardian* of 23 January, 1984:

(1) Forster was a bit anti-English, anti-Raj and so on. I suppose it's a tricky thing to say, but I'm not so much. I intend to keep the balance more. I don't believe all the English were a lot of idiots. Forster rather made them so. He came down hard against them. I've cut out that bit at the trial where they try to take over the court. Richard [Goodwin, the producer] wanted me to leave it in. But I said no, it just wasn't right. They wouldn't have done that.

(2) As for Aziz, there's a hell of a lot of Indian in him. They're marvellous people but maddening sometimes, you know . . . He's a goose. But he's warm and you like him awfully. I don't mean that in a derogatory way—things just happen. He can't help it. And Miss Quested . . . well, she's a bit of a prig and a bore in the book, you know. I've changed her, made her more sympathetic. Forster wasn't always very good with women.

(3) One other thing. I've got rid of that "Not yet, not yet" bit. You know, when the Quit India stuff comes up, and we have the passage about driving us into the sea? Forster experts have always said it was important, but the Fielding-Aziz friendship was not sustained by those sort of things. At least I don't think so. The book came out at the time of the trial of General Dyer[7] and had a tremendous success in America for that reason. But I thought that bit rather tacked on. Anyway I see it as a personal not a political story.

Forster's lifelong refusal to permit his novel to be filmed begins to look rather sensible. But once a revisionist enterprise gets under way, the mere wishes of a dead novelist provide no obstacle. And there can be little doubt that in Britain today the refurbishment of the Empire's tarnished image is under way. The continuing decline, the growing poverty and the meanness of spirit of much of Thatcherite Britain[8] encourages many Britons to turn their eyes nostalgically to the lost hour of their precedence. The recrudescence[9] of imperialist ideology and the popularity of Raj fictions put one in mind of the phantom twitchings of an amputated limb. Britain is in danger of entering a condition of cultural psychosis, in which it begins once again to strut and to posture like a great power while, in fact, its power diminishes every year. The jewel in the crown is made, these days, of paste.

Anthony Barnett has cogently argued, in his television essay *Let's Take the "Great" Out of Britain*, that the idea of a *great* Britain (originally just a collective term for the countries of the British Isles, but repeatedly used to bolster the myth of national grandeur) has bedevilled the actions of all post-war governments. But it was Margaret Thatcher who, in the euphoria of the Falklands victory,[1] most plainly nailed her

---

7. British General R. E. H. Dyer, in response to an Indian protest gathering at Jallianwalah Bagh (Garden) in the Sikh holy city of Amritsar, ordered his troops to fire into a crowd of 10,000 unarmed men, women, and children. About 400 were killed and 1,200 wounded; Dyer returned to a hero's welcome in England and was presented with a jeweled sword inscribed, "Saviour of the Punjab."

8. Britain under the conservative leadership of Prime Minister Margaret Thatcher (1979–1990).
9. New outbreak.
1. In 1982 Britain launched a successful military campaign to oust an Argentinian occupying force from the Falkland Islands.

colours to the old colonial mast, claiming that the success in the South Atlantic proved that the British were still the people "who had ruled a quarter of the world." Shortly afterwards she called for a return to Victorian values, thus demonstrating that she had embarked upon a heroic battle against the linear passage of Time.

I am trying to say something which is not easily heard above the clamour of praise for the present spate of British-Indian fictions: that works of art, even works of entertainment, do not come into being in a social and political vacuum; and that the way they operate in a society cannot be separated from politics, from history. For every text, a context; and the rise of Raj revisionism, exemplified by the huge success of these fictions, is the artistic counterpart of the rise of conservative ideologies in modern Britain. And no matter how innocently the writers and film-makers work, no matter how skilfully the actors act (and nobody would deny the brilliance of, for example, the performances of Susan Wooldridge as Daphne and Peggy Ashcroft as Barbie in the TV *Jewel*), they run the grave risk of helping to shore up the conservatism, by offering it the fictional glamour which its reality so grievously lacks.

The title of this essay derives, obviously, from that of an earlier piece (1940) by 1984's other literary phenomenon, Mr Orwell.[2] And as I'm going to dispute its assertions about the relationship between politics and literature, I must of necessity begin by offering a summary of that essay, *Inside the Whale*.

It opens with a largely admiring analysis of the writing of Henry Miller:

> On the face of it no material could be less promising. When *Tropic of Cancer* was published the Italians were marching into Abyssinia and Hitler's concentration camps were already bulging . . . It did not seem to be a moment at which a novel of outstanding value was likely to be written about American dead-beats cadging drinks in the Latin Quarter. Of course a novelist is not obliged to write directly about contemporary history, but a novelist who simply disregards the major public events of the moment is generally either a footler or a plain idiot. From a mere account of the subject matter of *Tropic of Cancer*, most people would probably assume it to be no more than a bit of naughty-naughty left over from the twenties. Actually, nearly everyone who read it saw at once that it was . . . a very remarkable book. How or why remarkable?

His attempt to answer that question takes Orwell down more and more tortuous roads. He ascribes to Miller the gift of opening up a new world "not by revealing what is strange, but by revealing what is familiar." He praises him for using English "as a spoken language, but spoken *without fear*, i.e., without fear of rhetoric or of the unusual or poetic word. It is a flowing, swelling prose, a prose with rhythms in it." And most crucially, he likens Miller to Whitman, "for what he is saying, after all, is 'I accept.'"

Around here things begin to get a little bizarre. Orwell quite fairly points out that to say "I accept" in life in the thirties "is to say that you accept concentration camps, rubber truncheons, Hitler, Stalin, bombs, aeroplanes, tinned food, machine-guns, *putsches*, purges, slogans, Bedaux belts, gas masks, submarines, spies, provocateurs, press censorship, secret prisons, aspirins, Hollywood films and political murders." (No, I don't know what a Bedaux belt is, either.) But in the very next paragraph he tells us that "precisely because, in one sense, he is passive to experience, Miller is able to get nearer to the ordinary man than is possible to more purposive writers. For the ordinary man is also passive." Characterizing the ordinary man as a

---

2. Rushdie here plays, of course, with the title of Orwell's best-known novel, *1984*; this essay was written in 1984.

victim, he then claims that only the Miller type of victim-books, "non-political, . . . non-ethical, . . . non-literary, . . . non-contemporary," can speak with the people's voice. So to accept concentration camps and Bedaux belts turns out to be pretty worthwhile, after all.

There follows an attack on literary fashion. Orwell, a thirty-seven-year-old patri-arch, tells us that "when one says that a writer is fashionable one practically always means that he is admired by people under thirty." At first he picks easy targets—A. E. Housman's "roselipt maidens" and Rupert Brooke's "Grantchester" ("a sort of accumulated vomit from a stomach stuffed with place-names"). But then the polemic is widened to include "the movement," the politically committed generation of Auden and Spender and MacNeice. "On the whole," Orwell says, "the literary histo-ry of the thirties seems to justify the opinion that a writer does well to keep out of politics." It is true he scores some points, as when he indicates the bourgeois, board-ing-school origins of just about all these literary radicals, or when he connects the popularity of Communism among British intellectuals to the general middle-class disillusion with all traditional values: "Patriotism, religion, the Empire, the family, the sanctity of marriage, the Old School Tie, birth, breeding, honour, discipline—anyone of ordinary education could turn the whole lot of them inside out in three minutes." In this vacuum of ideology, he suggests, there was still "the need for some-thing to believe in," and Stalinist Communism filled the void.

Returning to Henry Miller, Orwell takes up and extends Miller's comparison of Anaïs Nin to Jonah in the whale's belly.

> The whale's belly is simply a womb big enough for an adult . . . A storm that would sink all the battleships in the world would hardly reach you as an echo . . . Miller himself is inside the whale . . . a willing Jonah . . . He feels no impulse to alter or control the process that he is undergoing. He has performed the essential Jonah act of allowing himself to be swallowed, remaining passive, *accepting*. It will be seen what this amounts to. It is a species of quietism.

And at the end of this curious essay, Orwell—who began by describing writers who ignored contemporary reality as "usually footlers or plain idiots"—*embraces* and *espouses* this quietist philosophy, this cetacean[3] version of Pangloss's exhortation to "*cultiver notre jardin*".[4] "Progress and reaction," Orwell concludes, "have both turned out to be swindles. Seemingly there is nothing left but quietism—robbing reality of its terrors by simply submitting to it. Get inside the whale—or rather, admit you are inside the whale (for you *are*, of course). Give yourself over to the world-process . . . simply accept it, endure it, record it. That seems to be the formula that any sensitive novelist is now likely to adopt."

The sensitive novelist's reasons are to be found in the essay's last sentence, in which Orwell speaks of "the *impossibility* of any major literature until the world has shaken itself into its new shape."

And we are told that fatalism is a quality of Indian thought.

It is impossible not to include in any response to *Inside the Whale* the suggestion that Orwell's argument is much impaired by his choice, for a quietist model, of Henry Miller. In the forty-four years since the essay was first published, Miller's reputation has more or less completely evaporated, and he now looks to be very little more than

3. Whalelike.
4. This is the oft-repeated wisdom of the philosopher Dr.

Pangloss in Voltaire's *Candide:* "we must cultivate our garden." In context, the phrase is an apology for quietism.

the happy pornographer beneath whose scatological surface Orwell saw such improbable depths. If we, in 1984, are asked to choose between, on the one hand, the Miller of *Tropic of Cancer* and "the first hundred pages of *Black Spring*" and, on the other hand, the collected works of Auden, MacNeice and Spender, I doubt that many of us would go for old Henry. So it would appear that politically committed art can actually prove more durable than messages from the stomach of the fish.

It would also be wrong to go any further without discussing the senses in which Orwell uses the term "politics." Six years after *Inside the Whale*, in the essay *Politics and the English Language* (1946), he wrote: "In our age there is no such thing as 'keeping out of politics.' All issues are political issues, and politics itself is a mass of lies, evasions, folly, hatred and schizophrenia."

For a man as truthful, direct, intelligent, passionate and sane as Orwell, "politics" had come to represent the antithesis of his own world-view. It was an underworld-become-overworld, Hell on earth. "Politics" was a portmanteau term[5] which included everything he hated; no wonder he wanted to keep it out of literature.

I cannot resist the idea that Orwell's intellect, and finally his spirit, too, were broken by the horrors of the age in which he lived, the age of Hitler and Stalin (and, to be fair, by the ill health of his later years). Faced with the overwhelming evils of exterminations and purges and fire-bombings, and all the appalling manifestations of politics-gone-wild, he turned his talents to the business of constructing and also of justifying an escape-route. Hence his notion of the ordinary man as victim, and therefore of passivity as the literary stance closest to that of the ordinary man. He is using this type of logic as a means of building a path back to the womb, into the whale and away from the thunder of war. This looks very like the plan of a man who has given up the struggle. Even though he knows that "there is no such thing as 'keeping out of politics,'" he attempts the construction of a mechanism with just that purpose. Sit it out, he recommends; we writers will be safe inside the whale, until the storm dies down. I do not presume to blame him for adopting this position. He lived in the worst of times. But it is important to dispute his conclusions, because a philosophy built on an intellectual defeat must always be rebuilt at a later point. And undoubtedly Orwell did give way to a kind of defeatism and despair. By the time he wrote *Nineteen Eighty-Four*, sick and cloistered on Jura,[6] he had plainly come to think that resistance was useless. Winston Smith[7] considers himself a dead man from the moment he rebels. The secret book of the dissidents turns out to have been written by the Thought Police. All protest must end in Room 101. In an age when it often appears that we have all agreed to believe in entropy, in the proposition that things fall apart, that history is the irreversible process by which everything gradually gets worse, the unrelieved pessimism of *Nineteen Eighty-Four* goes some way towards explaining its status as a true myth of our times.

What is more (and this connects the year's parallel phenomena of Empire-revivalism and Orwellmania), the quietist option, the exhortation to submit to events, is an intrinsically conservative one. When intellectuals and artists withdraw from the fray, politicians feel safer. Once, the right and left in Britain used to argue about which of them "owned" Orwell. In those days both sides wanted him; and, as Raymond Williams[8] has said, the tug-of-war did his memory little honour. I have no

---

5. Lewis Carroll's term for an invented word that collapses different words together.
6. A mountain range between France and Switzerland.

7. The protagonist of *1984*.
8. British Marxist intellectual (1921–1988).

wish to reopen these old hostilities; but the truth cannot be avoided, and the truth is that passivity always serves the interests of the status quo, of the people already at the top of the heap, and the Orwell of *Inside the Whale* and *Nineteen Eighty-Four* is advocating ideas that can only be of service to our masters. If resistance is useless, those whom one might otherwise resist become omnipotent.

It is much easier to find common ground with Orwell when he comes to discuss the relationship between politics and language. The discoverer of Newspeak was aware that "when the general [political] atmosphere is bad, language must suffer." In *Politics and the English Language* he gives us a series of telling examples of the perversion of meaning for political purposes. "Statements like 'Marshal Pétain was a true patriot,' 'The Soviet Press is the freest in the world,' 'The Catholic Church is opposed to persecution' are almost always made with intent to deceive," he writes. He also provides beautiful parodies of politicians' metaphor-mixing: "The Fascist octopus has sung its swan song, the jackboot is thrown into the melting pot." Recently, I came across a worthy descendant of these grand old howlers: *The Times*, reporting the smuggling of classified documents out of Civil Service departments, referred to the increased frequency of "leaks" from "a high-level mole."

It's odd, though, that the author of *Animal Farm*, the creator of so much of the vocabulary through which we now comprehend these distortions—doublethink, thoughtcrime, and the rest—should have been unwilling to concede that literature was best able to defend language, to do battle with the twisters, *precisely by entering the political arena*. The writers of the Group 47 in post-war Germany, Grass, Böll and the rest,[9] with their "rubble literature" whose purpose and great achievement it was to rebuild the German language from the rubble of Nazism, are prime instances of this power. So, in quite another way, is a writer like Joseph Heller.[1] In *Good as Gold* the character of the presidential aide Ralph provides Heller with some superb satire at the expense of Washingtonspeak. Ralph speaks in sentences that usually conclude by contradicting their beginnings: "This administration will back you all the way until it has to"; "This President doesn't want yes-men. What we want are independent men of integrity who will agree with all our decisions after we make them." Every time Ralph opens his oxymoronic mouth he reveals the limitations of Orwell's view of the interaction between literature and politics. It is a view which excludes comedy, satire, deflation; because of course the writer need not always be the servant of some beetle-browed ideology. He can also be its critic, its antagonist, its scourge. From Swift to Solzhenitsyn,[2] writers have discharged this role with honour. And remember Napoleon the Pig.[3]

Just as it is untrue that politics ruins literature (even among "ideological" political writers, Orwell's case would founder on the great rock of Pablo Neruda[4]) so it is by no means axiomatic that the "ordinary man," *l'homme moyen sensuel*, is politically passive. We have seen that the myth of this inert commoner was a part of Orwell's logic of retreat; but it is nevertheless worth reminding ourselves of just a few instances in which the "ordinary man"—not to mention the "ordinary woman"—has been anything but inactive. We may not approve of Khomeini's Iran,

9. The German writers Günter Grass (1927–) and Heinrich Böll (1917–) have both written sophisticated novels dealing with the moral fallout of Nazism.
1. American writer best known for his novel *Catch-22* (1961).
2. Alexander Solzhenitsyn, Soviet dissident writer; author of *The Gulag Archipelago* (1973–1975), an indict-

ment of Soviet labor camps.
3. The totalitarian barnyard ruler in Orwell's *Animal Farm*, modeled on Soviet dictator Joseph Stalin.
4. Chilean poet and politically committed writer and diplomat (1904–1973); awarded the Nobel Prize for literature in 1971.

but the revolution there was a genuine mass movement. So is the revolution in Nicaragua. And so, let us not forget, was the Indian revolution. I wonder if independence would have arrived in 1947 if the masses, ignoring Congress and the Muslim League, had remained seated inside what would have had to be a very large whale indeed.

The truth is that there is no whale. We live in a world without hiding places; the missiles have made sure of that. However much we may wish to return to the womb, we cannot be unborn. So we are left with a fairly straightforward choice. Either we agree to delude ourselves, to lose ourselves in the fantasy of the great fish, for which a second metaphor is that of Pangloss's garden; or we can do what all human beings do instinctively when they realize that the womb has been lost for ever—that is, we can make the very devil of a racket. Certainly, when we cry, we cry partly for the safety we have lost; but we also cry to affirm ourselves, to say, here I am, I matter, too, you're going to have to reckon with me. So, in place of Jonah's womb, I am recommending the ancient tradition of making as big a fuss, as noisy a complaint about the world as is humanly possible. Where Orwell wished quietism, let there be rowdyism; in place of the whale, the protesting wail. If we can cease envisaging ourselves as metaphorical foetuses, and substitute the image of a new-born child, then that will be at least a small intellectual advance. In time, perhaps, we may even learn to toddle.

I must make one thing plain: I am not saying that all literature must now be of this protesting, noisy type. Perish the thought; now that we are babies fresh from the womb, we must find it possible to laugh and wonder as well as rage and weep. I have no wish to nail myself, let alone anyone else, to the tree of political literature for the rest of my writing life. Lewis Carroll and Laurence Sterne are as important to literature as Swift or Brecht. What I am saying is that politics and literature, like sport and politics, do mix, are inextricably mixed, and that that mixture has consequences.

The modern world lacks not only hiding places, but certainties. There is no consensus about reality between, for example, the nations of the North and of the South. What President Reagan says is happening in Central America differs so radically from, say, the Sandinista version,[5] that there is almost no common ground. It becomes necessary to take sides, to say whether or not one thinks of Nicaragua as the United State's "front yard." (Vietnam, you will recall, was the "back yard.") It seems to me imperative that literature enter such arguments, because what is being disputed is nothing less than *what is the case*, what is truth and what untruth. If writers leave the business of making pictures of the world to politicians, it will be one of history's great and most abject abdications.

Outside the whale is the unceasing storm, the continual quarrel, the dialectic of history. Outside the whale there is a genuine need for political fiction, for books that draw new and better maps of reality, and make new languages with which we can understand the world. Outside the whale we see that we are all irradiated by history, we are radioactive with history and politics; we see that it can be as false to create a politics-free fictional universe as to create one in which nobody needs to work or eat or hate or love or sleep. Outside the whale it becomes necessary, and even exhilarating, to grapple with the special problems created by the incorporation of political material, because politics is by turns farce and tragedy, and sometimes (e.g., Zia's

5. The Sandinistas were leftists who took control of Nicaragua in 1979; the United States supported the Contra rebels, whom Reagan characteristically referred to as "freedom fighters."

Pakistan[6]) both at once. Outside the whale the writer is obliged to accept that he (or she) is part of the crowd, part of the ocean, part of the storm, so that objectivity becomes a great dream, like perfection, an unattainable goal for which one must struggle in spite of the impossibility of success. Outside the whale is the world of Samuel Beckett's famous formula: *I can't go on, I'll go on.*[7]

This is why (to end where I began) it really is necessary to make a fuss about Raj fiction and the zombie-like revival of the defunct Empire. The various films and TV shows and books I discussed earlier propagate a number of notions about history which must be quarrelled with, as loudly and as embarrassingly as possible.

These include: The idea that non-violence makes successful revolutions; the peculiar notion that Kasturba Gandhi could have confided the secrets of her sex-life to Margaret Bourke-White; the bizarre implication that any Indians could look like or speak like Amy Irving or Christopher Lee; the view (which underlies many of these works) that the British and Indians actually understood each other jolly well, and that the end of the Empire was a sort of gentleman's agreement between old pals at the club; the revisionist theory—see David Lean's interviews—that *we, the British, weren't as bad as people make out;* the calumny, to which the use of rape-plots lends credence, that frail English roses were in constant sexual danger from lust-crazed wogs[8] (just such a fear lay behind General Dyer's Amritsar massacre); and, above all, the fantasy that the British Empire represented something "noble" or "great" about Britain; that it was, in spite of all its flaws and meannesses and bigotries, fundamentally glamorous.

If books and films could be made and consumed in the belly of the whale, it might be possible to consider them merely as entertainment, or even, on occasion, as art. But in our whaleless world, in this world without quiet corners, there can be no easy escapes from history, from hullabaloo, from terrible, unquiet fuss.

1984

Chekov and Zulu

1

On 4th November, 1984, Zulu disappeared in Birmingham, and India House sent his old schoolfriend Chekov to Wembley[1] to see the wife.

"Adaabarz, Mrs Zulu. Permission to enter?"

"Of course come in, Dipty sahib, why such formality?"

"Sorry to disturb you on a Sunday, Mrs Zulu, but Zulu-tho hasn't been in touch this morning?"

"With me? Since when he contacts me on official trip? Why to hit a telephone call when he is probably enjoying?"

"Whoops, sore point, excuse *me*. Always been the foot-in-it blunderbuss type."

"At least sit, take tea-shee."

"Fixed the place up damn fine, Mrs Zulu, wah-wah.[2] Tasteful decor, in spades, I must say. So much cut-glass! That bounder Zulu must be getting too much pay, more than yours truly, clever dog."

---

6. Mohammed Zia ul-Haq, Indian-born dictator, became President and Prime Minister of Pakistan in 1978; he was assassinated in 1988.
7. These are the closing words of the narrator in Beckett's *The Unnameable*.

8. Derogatory British slang for foreigners.
1. Birmingham is a city in West Midlands, central England; Wembley is a London suburb.
2. Excellent.

"No, how is it possible? Acting Dipty's tankha[3] must be far in excess of Security Chief."

"No suspicion intended, ji.[4] Only to say what a bargain-hunter you must be."

"Some problem but there is, na?"

"Beg pardon?"

"Arré,[5] Jaisingh! Where have you been sleeping? Acting Dipty Sahib is thirsting for his tea. And biscuits and jalebis, can you not keep two things in your head? Jump, now, guest is waiting."

"Truly, Mrs Zulu, please go to no trouble."

"No trouble is there, Diptyji, only this chap has become lazy since coming from home. Days off, TV in room, even pay in pounds sterling, he expects all. So far we brought him but no gratitude, what to tell you, noth-*thing*."

"Ah, Jaisingh; why not? Excellent jalebi, Mrs Z. Thanking you."

Assembled on top of the television and on shelf units around it was the missing man's collection of *Star Trek* memorabilia: Captain Kirk and Spock dolls, spaceship models—a Klingon Bird of Prey, a Romulan vessel, a space station, and of course the Starship *Enterprise*. In pride of place were large figurines of two of the series's supporting cast.

"These old Doon School nicknames," Chekov exclaimed heartily. "They stay put like stuck records. Dumpy, Stumpy, Grumpy, Humpy. They take over from our names. As in our case our intrepid cosmonaut aliases."

"I don't like. This 'Mrs Zulu' I am landed with! It sounds like a blackie."

"Wear the name with pride, begum[6] sahib. We're old comrades-in-arms, your husband and I; since boyhood days, perhaps he was good enough to mention? Intrepid diplomauts. Our umpteen-year mission to explore new worlds and new civilisations. See there, our alter egos standing on your TV, the Asiatic-looking Russky and the Chink. Not the leaders, as you'll appreciate, but the ultimate professional servants. 'Course laid in!' 'Hailing frequencies open!' 'Warp factor three!' What would that strutting Captain have been without his top-level staffers? Likewise with the good ship Hindustan.[7] We are servants also, you see, just like your fierce Jaisingh here. Never more important than in a moment like the present sad crisis, when an even keel must be maintained, jalebis must be served and tea poured, no matter what. We do not lead, but we enable. Without us, no course can be laid, no hailing frequency opened. No factors can be warped."

"Is he in difficulties, then, your Zulu? As if it wasn't bad enough, this terrible time."

On the wall behind the TV was a framed photograph of Indira Gandhi,[8] with a garland hung around it. She had been dead since Wednesday. Pictures of her cremation had been on the TV for hours. The flower-petals, the garish, unbearable flames.

"Hard to believe it. Indiraji! Words fail one. She was our mother. Hai, hai! Cut down in her prime."

"And on radio-TV, such-such stories are coming about Delhi goings-on. So many killings, Dipty Sahib. So many of our decent Sikh[9] people done to death, as if all were guilty for the crimes of one-two badmash guards."

---

3. Wages.
4. Term of respect added to ends of sentences or words.
5. Exclamation of surprise.
6. High-ranking muslim woman.
7. Persian name for India.

8. Indian prime minister between 1966–1977 and 1980–1984; assassinated in 1984.
9. Community in the Punjab whose religion attempts to combine Hindusim and Islam.

"The Sikh community has always been thought loyal to the nation," Chekov reflected. "Backbone of the Army, to say nothing of the Delhi taxi service. Super-citizens, one might say, seemingly wedded to the national idea. But such ideas are being questioned now, you must admit; there are those who would point to the comb, bangle, dagger et cetera as signs of the enemy within."

"Who would dare say such a thing about us? Such an evil thing."

"I know. I know. But you take Zulu. The ticklish thing is, he's not on any official business that we know of. He's dropped off the map, begum sahib. AWOL[1] ever since the assassination. No contact for two days plus."

"O God."

"There is a view forming back at HQ that he may have been associated with the gang. Who have in all probability long-established links with the community over here."

"O God."

"Naturally I am fighting strenuously against the proponents of this view. But his absence is damning, you must see. We have no fear of these tinpot Khalistan wallahs.[2] But they have a ruthless streak. And with Zulu's inside knowledge and security background . . . They have threatened further attacks, as you know. As you must know. As some would say you must know all too well."

"O God."

"It is possible," Chekov said, eating his jalebi, "that Zulu has boldly gone where no Indian diplonaut has gone before."

The wife wept. "Even the stupid name you could never get right. It was with S. 'Sulu.' So-so many episodes I have been made to see, you think I don't know? Kirk Spock McCoy Scott Uhura Chekov *Sulu*."

"But Zulu is a better name for what some might allege to be a wild man," Chekov said. "For a suspected savage. For a putative traitor. Thank you for excellent tea."

2

In August, Zulu, a shy, burly giant, had met Chekov off the plane from Delhi. Chekov at thirty-three was a small, slim, dapper man in grey flannels, stiff-collared shirt and a double-breasted navy blue blazer with brass buttons. He had bat's-wing eyebrows and a prominent and pugnacious jaw, so that his cultivated tones and habitual soft-spokenness came as something of a surprise, disarming those who had been led by the eyebrows and chin to expect an altogether more aggressive personality. He was a high flyer, with one small embassy already notched up. The Acting Number Two job in London, while strictly temporary, was his latest plum.

"What-ho, Zools! Years, yaar,[3] years," Chekov said, thumping his palm into the other man's chest. "So," he added, "I see you've become a hairy fairy." The young Zulu had been a modern Sikh in the matter of hair—sporting a fine moustache at eighteen, but beardless, with a haircut instead of long tresses wound tightly under a turban. Now, however, he had reverted to tradition.

"Hullo, ji," Zulu greeted him cautiously. "So then is it OK to utilise the old modes of address?"

"Utilise away! Wouldn't hear of anything else," Chekov said, handing Zulu his bags and baggage tags. "Spirit of the *Enterprise* and all that jazz."

---

1. Absent without leave.
2. Sikh military who call for a separate Sikh state called

Khalistan; *wallah* means boy or man.
3. Friend, buddy.

In his public life the most urbane of men, Chekov when letting his hair down in private enjoyed getting interculturally hot under the collar. Soon after his taking up his new post he sat with Zulu one lunchtime on a bench in Embankment Gardens and jerked his head in the direction of various passers-by.

"Crooks," he said, *sotto voce* [softly].

"Where?" shouted Zulu, leaping athletically to his feet. "Should I pursue?"

Heads turned. Chekov grabbed the hem of Zulu's jacket and pulled him back on to the bench. "Don't be such a hero," he admonished fondly. "I meant all of them, generally; thieves, every last one. God, I love London! Theatre, ballet, opera, restaurants! The Pavilion at Lord's on the Saturday of the Test Match![4] The royal ducks on the royal pond in royal St. James's Park! Decent tailors, a decent mixed grill when you want it, decent magazines to read! I see the remnants of greatness and I don't mind telling you I am impressed. The Athenaeum, Buck House, the lions in Trafalgar Square. *Damn* impressive. I went to a meeting with the junior Minister at the F. & C.O. and realised I was in the old India Office. All that John Company black teak, those tuskers rampant on the old bookcases. Gave me quite a turn. I applaud them for their success: hurrah! But then I look at my own home, and I see that it has been plundered by burglars. I can't deny there is a residue of distress."

"I am sorry to hear of your loss," Zulu said, knitting his brows. "But surely the culpables are not in the vicinity."

"Zulu, Zulu, a figure of speech, my simpleton warrior prince. Their museums are full of our treasures, I meant. Their fortunes and cities, built on the loot they took. So on, so forth. One forgives, of course; that is our national nature. One need not forget."

Zulu pointed at a tramp, sleeping on the next bench in a ragged hat and coat. "Did he steal from us, too?" he asked.

"Never forget," said Chekov, wagging a finger, "that the British working class collaborated for its own gain in the colonial project. Manchester cotton workers, for instance, supported the destruction of our cotton industry. As diplomats we must never draw attention to such facts; but facts, nevertheless, they remain."

"But a beggarman is not in the working class," objected Zulu, reasonably. "Surely this fellow at least is not our oppressor."

"Zulu," Chekov said in exasperation, "don't be so bleddy difficult."

Chekov and Zulu went boating on the Serpentine, and Chekov got back on his hobby-horse. "They have stolen us," he said, reclining boatered and champagned on striped cushions while mighty Zulu rowed. "And now we are stealing ourselves back. It is an Elgin marbles[5] situation."

"You should be more content," said Zulu, shipping oars and gulping cola. "You should be less hungry, less cross. See how much you have! It is enough. Sit back and enjoy. I have less, and it suffices for me. The sun is shining. The colonial period is a closed book."

"If you don't want that sandwich, hand it over," said Chekov. "With my natural radicalism I should not have been a diplomat. I should have been a terrorist."

---

4. A group of cricket games played between international all-star teams.
5. A group of sculptures removed from the Acropolis in Athens by Lord Elgin in 1801–1803 and purchased by the British Museum in 1816. Recent opinion polls have suggested that over 90 percent of the British public support the return of the marbles to Greece, though a 1996 resolution in the Parliament was tabled.

"But then we would have been enemies, on opposite sides," protested Zulu, and suddenly there were real tears in his eyes. "Do you care nothing for our friendship? For my responsibilities in life?"

Chekov was abashed. "Quite right, Zools old boy. Too bleddy true. You can't imagine how delighted I was when I learned we would be able to join forces like this in London. Nothing like the friendships of one's boyhood, eh? Nothing in the world can take their place. Now listen, you great lummox, no more of that long face. I won't permit it. Great big chap like you shouldn't look like he's about to blub. Blood brothers, old friend, what do you say? All for one and one for all."

"Blood brothers," said Zulu, smiling a shy smile.

"Onward, then," nodded Chekov, settling back on his cushions. "Impulse power only."

The day Mrs Gandhi was murdered by her Sikh bodyguards, Zulu and Chekov played squash in a private court in St John's Wood. In the locker-room after showering, prematurely-greying Chekov still panted heavily with a towel round his softening waist, reluctant to expose his exhaustion-shrivelled purple penis to view; Zulu stood proudly naked, thick-cocked, tossing his fine head of long black hair, caressing and combing it with womanly sensuality, and at last twisting it swiftly into a knot.

"Too good, Zulu yaar. Fataakh! Fataakh! What shots! Too bleddy good for me."

"You desk-pilots, ji. You lose your edge. Once you were ready for anything."

"Yeah, yeah, I'm over the hill. But you were only one year junior."

"I have led a purer life, ji—action, not words."

"You understand we will have to blacken your name," Chekov said softly.

Zulu turned slowly in Charles Atlas pose in front of a full-length mirror.

"It has to look like a maverick stunt. If anything goes wrong, deniability is essential. Even your wife must not suspect the truth."

Spreading his arms and legs, Zulu made his body a giant X, stretching himself to the limit. Then he came to attention. Chekov sounded a little frayed.

"Zools? What do you say?"

"Is the transporter ready?"

"Come on, yaar, don't arse around."

"Respectfully, Mister Chekov, sir, it's my arse. Now then: is the transporter ready?"

"Transporter ready. Aye."

"Then, energise."

Chekov's memorandum, classified top-secret, eyes-only, and addressed to 'JTK' (James T. Kirk):

> My strong recommendation is that Operation Startrek be aborted. To send a Federation employee of Klingon origin unarmed into a Klingon cell to spy is the crudest form of loyalty test. The operative in question has never shown ideological deviation of any sort and deserves better, even in the present climate of mayhem, hysteria and fear. If he fails to persuade the Klingons of his bona fides [good faith] he can expect to be treated with extreme prejudice. These are not hostage takers.

> The entire undertaking is misconceived. The locally settled Klingon population is not the central problem. Even should we succeed, such intelligence as can be gleaned about more important principals back home will no doubt be of dubious accuracy and limited value. We should advise Star Fleet Headquarters to engage urgently with the grievances and aspirations of the Klingon people. Unless these are dealt with fair and square there cannot be a lasting peace.

The reply from JTK:

Your closeness to the relevant individual excuses what is otherwise an explosively communalist document. It is not for you to define the national interest nor to determine what undercover operations are to be undertaken. It is for you to enable such operations to occur and to provide back-up as and when required to do so. As a personal favour to you and in the name of my long friendship with your eminent Papaji I have destroyed your last without keeping a copy and suggest you do the same. Also destroy this.

Chekov asked Zulu to drive him up to Stratford for a performance of *Coriolanus*.[6]

"How many kiddiwinks by now? Three?"

"Four," said Zulu. "All boys."

"By the grace of God. She must be a good woman."

"I have a full heart," said Zulu, with sudden feeling. "A full house, a full belly, a full bed."

"Lucky so and so," said Chekov. "Always were warm-blooded. I, by contrast, am not. Reptiles, certain species of dinosaur, and me. I am in the wife market, by the way, if you know any suitable candidates. Bachelordom being, after a certain point, an obstacle on the career path."

Zulu was driving strangely. In the slow lane of the motorway, as they approached an exit lane, he accelerated towards a hundred miles an hour. Once the exit was behind them, he slowed. Chekov noticed that he varied his speed and lane constantly. "Doesn't the old rattletrap have cruise control?" he asked. "Because, sport, this kind of performance would not do on the bridge of the flagship of the United Federation of Planets."

"Anti-surveillance," said Zulu. "Dry-cleaning." Chekov, alarmed, looked out of the back window.

"Have we been rumbled, then?"

"Nothing to worry about," grinned Zulu. "Better safe than sorry is all. Always anticipate the worst-case scenario."

Chekov settled back in his seat. "You liked toys and games," he said. Zulu had been a crack rifle shot, the school's champion wrestler, and an expert fencer. "Every Speech Day," Zulu said, "I would sit in the hall and clap, while you went up for all the work prizes. English Prize, History Prize, Latin Prize, Form Prize. Clap, clap, clap, term after term, year after year. But on Sports Day I got my cups. And now also I have my area of expertise."

"Quite a reputation you're building up, if what I hear is anything to go by."

There was a silence. England passed by at speed.

"Do you like Tolkien?" Zulu asked.

"I wouldn't have put you down as a big reader," said Chekov, startled. "No offence."

"J.R.R. Tolkien," said Zulu. "*The Lord of the Rings*."[7]

6. Shakespeare's bloodiest tragedy; its themes are civil unrest and revolt.
7. Tolkien's triology (1954–1955), written during and just after World War II, concerns a war for control of Middle Earth, in which men, elves, dwarves, and a few British-like hobbits band together to defeat the evil eastern empire of Sauron.

"Can't say I've read the gentleman. Heard of him, of course. Elves and pixies. Not your sort of thing at all, I'd have thought."

"It is about a war to the finish between Good and Evil," said Zulu intently. "And while this great war is being fought there is one part of the world, the Shire, in which nobody even knows it's going on. The hobbits who live there work and squabble and make merry and they have no fucking clue about the forces that threaten them, and those that save their tiny skins." His face was red with vehemence.

"Meaning me, I suppose," Chekov said.

"I am a soldier in that war," said Zulu. "If you sit in an office you don't have one small idea of what the real world is like. The world of action, ji. The world of deeds, of things that are done and maybe undone too. The world of life and death."

"Only in the worst case," Chekov demurred.

"Do I tell you how to apply your smooth-tongued musca-polish to people's behinds?" stormed Zulu. "Then do not tell me how to ply my trade."

Soldiers going into battle pump themselves up, Chekov knew. This chest-beating was to be expected, it must not be misunderstood. "When will you vamoose?" he quietly asked.

"Chekov ji, you won't see me go."

Stratford approached. "Did you know, ji," Zulu offered, "that the map of Tolkien's Middle-earth fits quite well over central England and Wales? Maybe all fairylands are right here, in our midst."

"You're a deep one, old Zools," said Chekov. "Full of revelations today."

Chekov had a few people over for dinner at his modern-style official residence in a private road in Hampstead: a Very Big Businessman he was wooing, journalists he liked, prominent India-lovers, noted Non-Resident Indians. The policy was business as usual. The dreadful event must not be seen to have derailed the ship of State: whose new captain, Chekov mused, was a former pilot himself. As if a Sulu, a Chekov had been suddenly promoted to the skipper's seat.

Damned difficult doing all this without a lady wife to act as hostess, he grumbled inwardly. The best golden plates with the many-headed lion at the centre, the finest crystal, the menu, the wines. Personnel had been seconded from India House to help him out, but it wasn't the same. The secrets of good evenings, like God, were in the details. Chekov meddled and fretted.

The evening went off well. Over brandy, Chekov even dared to introduce a blacker note. "England has always been a breeding ground for our revolutionists," he said. "What would Pandit Nehru[8] have been without Harrow?[9] Or Gandhiji without his formative experiences here? Even the Pakistan idea was dreamt up by young radicals at college in what we then were asked to think of as the Mother Country. Now that England's status has declined, I suppose it is logical that the quality of the revolutionists she breeds has likewise fallen. The Kashmiris![1] Not a hope in hell. And as for these Khalistan types, let them not think that their evil deed has brought their dream a day closer. On the contrary. On the contrary. We will root them out and smash them to—what's the right word?—to *smithereens*."

8. Jawaharlal Nehru, first Prime Minister of the Republic of India (1947–1964), father of Indira Gandhi.
9. An exclusive English preparatory school.

1. Residents of Kashmir, a territory in dispute between India and Pakistan since 1947.

To his surprise he had begun speaking loudly and had risen to his feet. He sat down hard and laughed. The moment passed.

"The funny thing about this blasted nickname of mine," he said quickly to his dinner-table neighbour, the septuagenarian Very Big Businessman's improbably young and attractive wife, "is that back then we never saw one episode of the TV series. No TV to see it on, you see. The whole thing was just a legend wafting its way from the US and UK to our lovely hill-station of Dehra Dun.

"After a while we got a couple of cheap paperback novelisations and passed them round as if they were naughty books like Lady C or some such. Lots of us tried the names on for size but only two of them stuck; probably because they seemed to go together, and the two of us got on pretty well, even though he was younger. A lovely boy. So just like Laurel and Hardy we were Chekov and Zulu."

"Love and marriage," said the woman.

"Beg pardon?"

"You know," she said. "Go together like is it milk and porridge. Or a car and garage, that's right. I love old songs. La-la-la-something-brother, you can't have fun without I think it's your mother."[2]

"Yes, now I do recall," said Chekov.

3

Three months later Zulu telephoned his wife.

"O my God where have you vanished are you dead?"

"Listen please my bivi. Listen carefully my wife, my only love."

"Yes. OK. I am calm. Line is bad, but."

"Call Chekov and say condition red."

"Arré! What is wrong with your condition?"

"Please. Condition red."

"Yes. OK. Red."

"Say the Klingons may be smelling things."

"Clingers-on may be smelly things. Means what?"

"My darling, I beg you."

"I have it all right here only. With this pencil I have written it, both."

"Tell him, get Scotty to lock on to my signal and beam me up at once."

"What rubbish! Even now you can't leave off that stupid game."

"Bivi. It is urgent. *Beam me up.*"

Chekov dropped everything and drove. He went via the dry-cleaners as instructed; he drove round roundabouts twice, jumped red lights, deliberately took a wrong turning, stopped and turned round, made as many right turns as possible to see if anything followed him across the stream of traffic, and, on the motorway, mimicked Zulu's techniques. When he was as certain as he could be that he was clean, he headed for the rendezvous point. "Roll over Len Deighton," he thought, "and tell le Carré the news."[3]

---

2. She is mangling the lyrics of Sammy Cahn's 1955 song *Love and Marriage:* "Love and marriage, love and marriage / Go together like a horse and carriage / This I tell you brother / You can't have one without the other."

3. Len Deighton and John le Carré are two popular contemporary writers of espionage fiction. The line refers to the popular song lyric, "Roll over, Beethoven."

He turned off the motorway and pulled into a lay-by. A man stepped out of the trees, looking newly bathed and smartly dressed, with a sheepish smile on his face. It was Zulu.

Chekov jumped out of the car and embraced his friend, kissing him on both cheeks. Zulu's bristly beard pricked his lips. "I expected you'd have an arm missing, or blood pouring from a gunshot wound, or some black eyes at least," he said. "Instead here you are dressed for the theatre, minus only an opera cloak and cane."

"Mission accomplished," said Zulu, patting his breast pocket. "All present and correct."

"Then what was that 'condition red' bakvaas?"

"The worst-case scenario," said Zulu, "does not always materialise."

In the car, Chekov scanned the names, places, dates in Zulu's brown envelope. The information was better than anyone had expected. From this anonymous Midlands lay-by a light was shining on certain remote villages and urban back-alleys in Punjab.[4] There would be a round-up, and, for some big badmashes at least, there would no longer be shadows in which to hide.

He gave a little, impressed whistle.

Zulu in the passenger seat inclined his head. "Better move off now," he said. "Don't tempt fate."

They drove south through Middle-earth.

Not long after they came off the motorway, Zulu said, "By the way, I quit."

Chekov stopped the car. The two towers of Wembley Stadium were visible through a gap in the houses to the left.

"What's this? Did those extremists manage to turn your head or what?"

"Chekov, ji, don't be a fool. Who needs extremists when there are the killings in Delhi? Hundreds, maybe thousands. Sikh men scalped and burned alive in front of their families. Boy-children, too."

"We know this."

"Then, ji, we also know who was behind it."

"There is not a shred of evidence," Chekov repeated the policy line.

"There are eyewitnesses and photographs," said Zulu. "We know this."

"There are those who think," said Chekov slowly, "that after Indiraji the Sikhs deserved what they got."

Zulu stiffened.

"You know me better than that, I hope," said Chekov. "Zulu, for God's sake, come on. All our bleddy lives."

"No Congress workers have been indicted," said Zulu. "In spite of all the evidence of complicity. Therefore, I resign. You should quit, too."

"If you have gone so damn radical," cried Chekov, "why hand over these lists at all? Why go only half the bleddy hog?"

"I am a security wallah," said Zulu, opening the car door. "Terrorists of all sorts are my foes. But not, apparently, in certain circumstances, yours."

"Zulu, get in, damn it," Chekov shouted. "Don't you care for your career? A wife and four kiddiwinks to support. What about your old chums? Are you going to turn your back on me?"

But Zulu was already too far away.

---

4. Province divided between India and Pakistan.

Chekov and Zulu never met again. Zulu settled in Bombay and as the demand for private-sector protection increased in that cash-rich boom-town, so his Zulu Shield and Zulu Spear companies prospered and grew. He had three more children, all of them boys, and remains happily married to this day.

As for Chekov, he never did take a wife. In spite of this supposed handicap, however, he did well in his chosen profession. His rapid rise continued. But one day in May 1991 he was, by chance, a member of the entourage accompanying Mr Rajiv Gandhi[5] to the South Indian village of Sriperumbudur, where Rajiv was to address an election rally. Security was lax, intentionally so. In the previous election, Rajivji felt, the demands of security had placed an alienating barrier between himself and the electorate. On this occasion, he decreed, the voters must be allowed to feel close.

After the speeches, the Rajiv group descended from the podium. Chekov, who was just a few feet behind Rajiv, saw a small Tamil[6] woman come forward, smiling. She shook Rajiv's hand and did not let go. Chekov understood what she was smiling about, and the knowledge was so powerful that it stopped time itself.

Because time had stopped, Chekov was able to make a number of private observations. "These Tamil revolutionists are not England-returned," he noted. "So, finally, we have learned to produce the goods at home, and no longer need to import. Bang goes that old dinner-party standby; so to speak." And, less dryly: "The tragedy is not how one dies," he thought. "It is how one has lived."

The scene around him vanished, dissolving in a pool of light, and was replaced by the bridge of the Starship *Enterprise*. All the leading figures were in their appointed places. Zulu sat beside Chekov at the front.

"Shields no longer operative," Zulu was saying. On the main screen, they could see the Klingon Bird of Prey uncloaking, preparing to strike.

"One direct hit and we're done for," cried Dr McCoy. "For God's sake, Jim, get us out of here!"

"Illogical," said First Officer Spock. "The degradation of our dilithium crystal drive means that warp speed is unavailable. At impulse power only, we would make a poor attempt indeed to flee the Bird of Prey. Our only logical course is unconditional surrender."

"Surrender to a Klingon!" shouted McCoy. "Damn it, you cold-blooded, pointy-eared adding-machine, don't you know how they treat their prisoners?"

"Phaser banks completely depleted," said Zulu. "Offensive capability nil."

"Should I attempt to contact the Klingon captain, sir?" Chekov inquired. "They could fire at any moment."

"Thank you, Mr Chekov," said Captain Kirk. "I'm afraid that won't be necessary. On this occasion, the worst-case scenario is the one we are obliged to play out. Hold your position. Steady as she goes."

"The Bird of Prey has fired, sir," said Zulu.

Chekov took Zulu's hand and held it firmly, victoriously, as the speeding balls of deadly light approached.

[END OF PERSPECTIVES: WORLD WAR II AND THE END OF EMPIRE]

---

5. Indian Prime Minister 1984–1989, assassinated in May 1991, son of Indira Gandhi.
6. Member of a people of South India and Sri Lanka. The government of India had been aiding the Sri Lankan government in suppressing violent protests by Tamil separatists in Sri Lanka.

Dylan Thomas

1914–1953

One of the most important facts of Dylan Thomas's biography is his birthplace: Swansea, South Wales. Thomas was Welsh first, English second. Although Wales is entirely contained within the borders of England, it is one of the areas of Gaeltacht, the places where forms of Gaelic language are or have been spoken. The Welsh language is a living and thriving one, and it is visible in Wales in place names, street signs, church music, and a host of other daily manifestations. Thomas uses the words of the English language in making his poems, plays, and stories, but these words are defamiliarized, are made strange, by virtue of their having been laid on top, as it were, of absent Welsh words and phrasings that echo nonetheless through the English lines. A common criticism made about Dylan Thomas's poetry by English critics who were his contemporaries was that the poetry was overly emotional and excessively musical, and that it lacked "rigor." These charges against the poems sound all too familiarly like the complaints against the Gaeltachts and their inhabitants— too emotional, too lyrical, too irrational. The innovative and densely lyrical patterns of Thomas's poetry and his prose style come partially out of his "Welshification" of English, a process that has effects on both the style and the subject matter of his work. In another register, he can be seen as the last of the Romantic poets, writing precocious lyrics infused with an intense sense of self.

Dylan Thomas's earliest volume, *18 Poems*, appeared in 1934 when Thomas was twenty years old, a suite of poems based on the cycle of life, birth, childhood, and death in Swansea. It caused a sensation for the magic of its wordplay and the intensely personal focus of the poems. The book was received ecstatically in Britain, but not so in Wales, whose provincial proprieties Thomas always viewed with a half-affectionate sarcasm. Like James Joyce, Thomas felt the necessity of escape; at the age of twenty-one he moved to the metropolitan center, to London, to pursue his hopes of a literary career. There he worked for the BBC as a writer and a performer on radio broadcasts. The short stories of his collection *Portrait of the Artist as a Young Dog* (1940) wittily recount, in obvious homage and parody of Joyce's *Portrait of the Artist as a Young Man*, the travails of the would-be writer who hopes to break through the barriers of class and nation. He spent the years of World War II in London as well, but as a conscientious objector, not a combatant, and, as a Welshman, to a certain degree as an outsider within. The war was traumatizing for him as for so many others, and Thomas's pacifism and despair led to the superb poetry of his volume *Deaths and Entrances*.

Poetry alone could not pay the bills and allow Thomas and his young family to live in London. After the war he turned to screenplays and to short stories. The haunting radio play *Return Journey* gives a medley of voices encountered by the poet returning to a Swansea inhabited by the ghost of his youthful self. It can be compared to some of Hardy's memory-filled poetic landscapes and to stories like *Ivy Day in the Committee Room* in Joyce's *Dubliners;* it also anticipates the spare, ironic dramas that Samuel Beckett would write in the 1960s and 1970s.

In the late 1940s, Thomas returned to his poetry, this time less as a poet than as a performer or public reader of his own work. His vibrant and sonorous Welsh-accented voice (akin to that of the Welsh actor Richard Burton), melded with the incantatory lyricism of his poetic language, proved to be irresistible to the public, both in England and in the United States. His brilliant poetry readings instigated a new popularity for poetry itself on both sides of the Atlantic, and his captivating talents as a reader and indeed an actor created for him the persona of Dylan Thomas, Bohemian poet, which he wore until his early death in New York City, after an overdose of whiskey following a poetry reading. He was on his way to California to stay with Igor Stravinsky, with whom he planned to write an epic opera.

The great American poet John Berryman described certain recurrent words as the "unmistakable signature" of Dylan Thomas's poetry. Berryman chose a list of forty "key words" in Thomas's work, including among them: blood, sea, ghost, grave, death, light, time, sun, night, wind, love, and rain. Berryman noted the symbolic value Thomas made these seemingly simple words carry across the span of many poems. Thomas's themes were agreed by most critics to be simple and elemental ones—related to the cycles of life, to nature and childhood, to life's meaning. Berryman argued fiercely that while these were simple themes on the surface, what a poem means *is* its imagery, the way its words are put into relation to one another: "A poem that works well demonstrates an insight, and the insight may consist, not in the theme, but in the image-relations or the structure-relations." Thomas himself aimed at using wordplay and fractured syntax to create sound as a "verbal music." The musicality of his poems and his prose is stunningly evident, and rarely more so than in his play *Under Milk Wood*, a kind of oratorio for disembodied voices. In the play, published posthumously in 1954, Thomas gives voice to the inhabitants of the Welsh village of Llaregyub, whose voices weave together the actions of nature and humans on one single rural day. There is no "plot," and the actors simply stand on stage and read, taking on many voices as these ebb and flow musically through them.

Oral speech and song are more important than written language in rural countries and cultures, especially when one's written language is officially discouraged or even forbidden. Social memory is passed on in story and song; tales and jokes and sermons and performances loom larger in the society of a country town than do written artifacts. Dylan Thomas was very much a writer, yet his poetry and prose are written to be heard, to exist in the ear of the listener as much as the eye of the reader. The lush richness of Thomas's poetic voice is a verbal music that passes on a tradition of oral culture and its precious gifts. The spoken or sung word is a word accompanied by breath; breath is related in most cultures, but certainly in those of Wales and Ireland, to the spirit. One collection of Dylan Thomas's poetry and sketches he titled *The World I Breathe*. This title could as easily be *The Word I Breathe*.

The Force That Through the Green Fuse Drives the Flower

The force that through the green fuse drives the flower
Drives my green age; that blasts the roots of trees
Is my destroyer.
And I am dumb to tell the crooked rose
5   My youth is bent by the same wintry fever.

The force that drives the water through the rocks
Drives my red blood; that dries the mouthing streams
Turns mine to wax.
And I am dumb to mouth unto my veins
10   How at the mountain spring the same mouth sucks.

The hand that whirls the water in the pool
Stirs the quicksand; that ropes the blowing wind
Hauls my shroud sail.
And I am dumb to tell the hanging man
15   How of my clay is made the hangman's lime.

The lips of time leech to the fountain head;
Love drips and gathers, but the fallen blood
Shall calm her sores.
And I am dumb to tell a weather's wind
20   How time has ticked a heaven round the stars.

And I am dumb to tell the lover's tomb
How at my sheet goes the same crooked worm.

1933

Do Not Go Gentle into That Good Night

Do not go gentle into that good night,
Old age should burn and rave at close of day;
Rage, rage against the dying of the light.

Though wise men at their end know dark is right,
5   Because their words had forked no lightning they
Do not go gentle into that good night.

Good men, the last wave by, crying how bright
Their frail deeds might have danced in a green bay,
Rage, rage against the dying of the light.

10   Wild men who caught and sang the sun in flight,
And learn, too late, they grieved it on its way,
Do not go gentle into that good night.

Grave men, near death, who see with blinding sight
Blind eyes could blaze like meteors and be gay,
15   Rage, rage against the dying of the light.

And you, my father, there on the sad height,
Curse, bless, me now with your fierce tears, I pray.
Do not go gentle into that good night.
Rage, rage against the dying of the light.

1951

Return Journey[1]

NARRATOR It was a cold white day in High Street, and nothing to stop the wind slicing up from the docks, for where the squat and tall shops had shielded the town from the sea lay their blitzed flat graves marbled with snow and headstoned with fences. Dogs, delicate as cats on water, as though they had gloves on their paws, padded over the vanished buildings. Boys romped, calling high and clear, on top of a levelled chemist's and a shoe-shop, and a little girl, wearing a man's cap, threw a snowball in a chill deserted garden that had once been the Jug and Bottle of the Prince of Wales.[2] The wind cut up the street with a soft sea-noise hanging on its arm, like a hooter in a muffler. I could see the swathed hill stepping up out of the town, which you never could see properly before, and the powdered fields of the roofs of Milton Terrace and Watkin Street and Fullers Row. Fish-frailed, net-bagged, umbrella'd, pixie-capped, fur-shoed, blue-nosed, puce-lipped, blinkered like drayhorses, scarved, mittened, galoshed, wearing everything but the cat's blanket, crushes of shopping-women crunched in the little Lapland of the once grey drab street, blew and queued and yearned for hot tea, as I began my search through Swansea town cold and early on that wicked February morning.[3] I went into the hotel. "Good morning."

1. Written in February 1947; broadcast by the BBC May 1947.
2. The name of a public house (pub).

3. Swansea, a city in South Wales on the mouth of the river Tawe, is the second largest city in Wales after Cardiff (the capital).

The hall-porter did not answer. I was just another snowman to him. He did not know that I was looking for someone after fourteen years, and he did not care. He stood and shuddered, staring through the glass of the hotel door at the snowflakes sailing down the sky, like Siberian confetti. The bar was just opening, but already one customer puffed and shook at the counter with a full pint of half-frozen Tawe water in his wrapped-up hand. I said Good morning, and the barmaid, polishing the counter vigorously as though it were a rare and valuable piece of Swansea china, said to her first customer:

BARMAID Seen the film at the Elysium Mr Griffiths there's snow isn't it did you come up on your bicycle our pipes burst Monday . . .

NARRATOR A pint of bitter,[4] please.

BARMAID Proper little lake in the kitchen got to wear your Wellingtons when you boil a egg one and four please[5] . . .

CUSTOMER The cold gets me just here . . .

BARMAID . . . and eightpence change that's your liver Mr Griffiths you been on the cocoa again . . .

NARRATOR I wonder whether you remember a friend of mine? He always used to come to this bar, some years ago. Every morning, about this time.

CUSTOMER Just by here it gets me. I don't know what'd happen if I didn't wear a band . . .

BARMAID What's his name?

NARRATOR Young Thomas.

BARMAID Lots of Thomases come here it's a kind of home from home for Thomases isn't it Mr Griffiths what's he look like?

NARRATOR He'd be about seventeen or eighteen . . .

(Slowly)

BARMAID . . . I was seventeen once . . .

NARRATOR . . . and above medium height. Above medium height for Wales, I mean, he's five foot six and a half. Thick blubber lips; snub nose; curly mouse-brown hair; one front tooth broken after playing a game called Cats and Dogs, in the Mermaid, Mumbles; speaks rather fancy; truculent; plausible; a bit of a shower-off; plus-fours and no breakfast, you know; used to have poems printed in the *Herald of Wales*; there was one about an open-air performance of *Electra* in Mrs Bertie Perkins's garden in Sketty; lived up the Uplands; a bombastic adolescent provincial Bohemian with a thick-knotted artist's tie made out of his sister's scarf, she never knew where it had gone, and a cricket-shirt dyed bottle-green; a gabbing, ambitious, mock-tough, pretentious young man; and mole-y, too.

BARMAID There's words what d'you want to find him for I wouldn't touch him with a barge-pole . . . would you, Mr Griffiths? Mind, you can never tell. I remember a man came here with a monkey. Called for 'alf for himself and a pint for the monkey. And he wasn't Italian at all. Spoke Welsh like a preacher.

NARRATOR The bar was filling up. Snowy business bellies pressed their watch-chains against the counter; black business bowlers, damp and white now as Christmas puddings in their cloths, bobbed in front of the misty mirrors. The voice of commerce rang sternly through the lounge.

FIRST VOICE Cold enough for you?

SECOND VOICE How's your pipes, Mr Lewis?

---

4. British beer.   5. One shilling and 4 pence.

THIRD VOICE Another winter like this'll put paid to me, Mr Evans. I got the 'flu . . .

FIRST VOICE Make it a double . . .

SECOND VOICE Similar . . .

BARMAID Okay, baby . . .

CUSTOMER I seem to remember a chap like you described. There couldn't be two like him let's hope. He used to work as a reporter. Down the Three Lamps I used to see him. Lifting his ikkle elbow.

(Confidentially)

NARRATOR What's the Three Lamps like now?

CUSTOMER It isn't like anything. It isn't there. It's nothing mun. You remember Ben Evans's stores? It's right next door to that. Ben Evans isn't there either . . .

(Fade)

NARRATOR I went out of the hotel into the snow and walked down High Street, past the flat white wastes where all the shops had been. Eddershaw Furnishers, Curry's Bicycles, Donegal Clothing Company, Doctor Scholl's, Burton Tailors, W. H. Smith, Boots Cash Chemists, Leslie's Stores, Upson's Shoes, Prince of Wales, Tucker's Fish, Stead & Simpson—all the shops bombed and vanished. Past the hole in space where Hodges & Clothiers had been, down Castle Street, past the remembered, invisible shops, Price's Fifty Shilling, and Crouch the Jeweller, Potter Gilmore Gowns, Evans Jeweller, Master's Outfitters, Style and Mantle, Lennard's Boots, True Form, Kardomah, R. E. Jones, Dean's Tailor, David Evans, Gregory Confectioners, Bovega, Burton's, Lloyd's Bank, and nothing. And into Temple Street. There the Three Lamps had stood, old Mac magisterial in his corner. And there the Young Thomas whom I was searching for used to stand at the counter on Friday paynights with Freddie Farr Half Hook, Bill Latham, Cliff Williams, Gareth Hughes, Eric Hughes, Glyn Lowry, a man among men, his hat at a rakish angle, in that snug, smug, select Edwardian holy of best-bitter holies . . .

(Bar noises in background)

OLD REPORTER Remember when I took you down the mortuary for the first time, Young Thomas? He'd never seen a corpse before, boys, except old Ron on a Saturday night. "If you want to be a proper newspaperman," I said, "you got to be well known in the right circles. You got to be *persona grata* [acceptable] in the mortuary, see." He went pale green, mun.

FIRST YOUNG REPORTER Look, he's blushing now . . .

OLD REPORTER And when we got there what d'you think? The decorators were in at the mortuary, giving the old home a bit of a re-do like. Up on ladders having a slap at the roof. Young Thomas didn't see 'em, he had his pop eyes glued on the slab, and when one of the painters up the ladder said "Good morning, gents" in a deep voice he upped in the air and out of the place like a ferret. Laugh!

BARMAID (off) You've had enough, Mr Roberts. You heard what I said.

(Noise of a gentle scuffle)

SECOND YOUNG REPORTER (casually) There goes Mr Roberts.

OLD REPORTER Well fair do's they throw you out very genteel in this pub . . .

FIRST YOUNG REPORTER Ever seen Young Thomas covering a soccer match down the Vetch and working it out in tries?

SECOND YOUNG REPORTER And up the Mannesman Hall shouting "Good footwork, sir," and a couple of punch-drunk colliers galumphing about like jumbos.

FIRST YOUNG REPORTER What you been reporting to-day, Young Thomas?

SECOND YOUNG REPORTER Two typewriter Thomas the ace news-dick . . .

OLD REPORTER Let's have a dekko[6] at your note-book. "Called at British Legion: Nothing. Called at Hospital: One broken leg. Auction at the Metropole. Ring Mr Beynon *re* Gymanfa Ganu. Lunch: Pint and pasty at the Singleton with Mrs Giles. Bazaar at Bethesda Chapel. Chimney on fire at Tontine Street. Walters Road Sunday School Outing. Rehearsal of the *Mikado* at Skewen'—all front page stuff . . . (*Fade*)

NARRATOR The voices of fourteen years ago hung silent in the snow and ruin, and in the falling winter morning I walked on through the white havoc'd centre where once a very young man I knew had mucked about as chirpy as a sparrow after the sips and titbits and small change of the town. Near the *Evening Post* building and the fragment of the Castle I stopped a man whose face I thought I recognized from a long time ago. I said: I wonder if you can tell me . . .

PASSER-BY Yes?

NARRATOR He peered out of his blanketing scarves and from under his snowballed Balaclava like an Eskimo with a bad conscience. I said: If you can tell me whether you used to know a chap called Young Thomas. He worked on the Post and used to wear an overcoat sometimes with the check lining inside out so that you could play giant draughts on him. He wore a conscious woodbine,[7] too . . .

PASSER-BY What d'you mean, conscious woodbine?

NARRATOR . . . and a perched pork pie with a peacock feather and he tried to slouch like a newshawk even when he was attending a meeting of the Gorseinon Buffalos[8] . . .

PASSER-BY Oh, *him!* He owes me half a crown. I haven't seen him since the old Kardomah days. He wasn't a reporter then, he'd just left the grammar school.[9] Him and Charlie Fisher—Charlie's got whiskers now—and Tom Warner and Fred Janes, drinking coffee-dashes and arguing the toss.

NARRATOR What about?

PASSER-BY Music and poetry and painting and politics. Einstein and Epstein, Stravinsky and Greta Garbo, death and religion, Picasso and girls . . .

NARRATOR And then?

PASSER-BY Communism, symbolism, Bradman, Braque, the Watch Committee, free love, free beer, murder, Michelangelo, ping-pong, ambition, Sibelius, and girls . . .

NARRATOR Is that all?

PASSER-BY How Dan Jones was going to compose the most prodigious symphony, Fred Janes paint the most miraculously meticulous picture, Charlie Fisher catch the poshest trout, Vernon Watkins and Young Thomas write the most boiling poems, how they would ring the bells of London and paint it like a tart . . .

NARRATOR And after that?

PASSER-BY Oh the hissing of the butt-ends in the drains of the coffee-dashes and the tinkle and the gibble-gabble of the morning young lounge lizards as they talked about Augustus John, Emil Jannings, Carnera, Dracula, Amy Johnson, trial marriage, pocket-money, the Welsh sea, the London stars, King Kong, anarchy, darts, T. S. Eliot, and girls. . . . Duw, it's cold!

---

6. British army slang for "a look" (from the Hindi word *dekho*).

7. A brand of cigarette.

8. A pork-pie hat takes its name from the circular shape of a pork pie; Gorseinon is a town near Swansea, apparently with a chapter of the Royal Antediluvian Order of Buffaloes (founded 1822), a men's club.

9. Secondary school, typically educating students of ages 11–18.

NARRATOR And he hurried on, into the dervish snow, without a good morning or good-bye, swaddled in his winter woollens like a man in the island of his deafness, and I felt that perhaps he had never stopped at all to tell me of one more departed stage in the progress of the boy I was pursuing. The Kardomah Café was razed to the snow, the voices of the coffee-drinkers—poets, painters, and musicians in their beginnings—lost in the willynilly flying of the years and the flakes.

Down College Street I walked then, past the remembered invisible shops, Langley's, Castle Cigar Co., T. B. Brown, Pullar's, Aubrey Jeremiah, Goddard Jones, Richards, Hornes, Marles, Pleasance & Harper, Star Supply, Sidney Heath, Wesley Chapel, and nothing. . . . My search was leading me back, through pub and job and café, to the School.

(Fade) (School bell)

SCHOOLMASTER Oh yes, yes, I remember him well,
    though I do not know if I would recognize him now:
    nobody grows any younger, or better,
    and boys grow into much the sort of men one would suppose
    though sometimes the moustaches bewilder
    and one finds it hard to reconcile one's memory of a small
    none-too-clean urchin lying his way unsuccessfully out of his homework
    with a fierce and many-medalled sergeant-major with three children or a
    divorced chartered accountant;
    and it is hard to realize
    that some little tousled rebellious youth whose only claim
    to fame among his contemporaries was his undisputed right
    to the championship of the spitting contest
    is now perhaps one's own bank manager.
    Oh yes, I remember him well, the boy you are searching for:
    he looked like most boys, no better, brighter, or more respectful;
    he cribbed, mitched,[1] spilt ink, rattled his desk and
    garbled his lessons with the worst of them;
    he could smudge, hedge, smirk, wriggle, wince,
    whimper, blarney, badger, blush, deceive, be
    devious, stammer, improvise, assume
    offended dignity or righteous indignation as though to the manner born;[2]
    sullenly and reluctantly he drilled, for some small
    crime, under Sergeant Bird, so wittily nicknamed
    Oiseau,° on Wednesday half-holidays,   *bird*
    appeared regularly in detention classes,
    hid in the cloakroom during algebra,
    was, when a newcomer, thrown into the bushes of the
    Lower Playground by bigger boys,
    and threw newcomers into the bushes of the Lower
    Playground when *he* was a bigger boy;
    he scuffled at prayers,
    he interpolated, smugly, the time-honoured wrong
    irreverent words into the morning hymns,
    he helped to damage the headmaster's rhubarb,
    was thirty-third in trigonometry,
    and, as might be expected, edited the School Magazine

(Fade)

---

1. Stole.   2. As though born into a high station in life.

NARRATOR The Hall is shattered, the echoing corridors charred where he scribbled and smudged and yawned in the long green days, waiting for the bell and the scamper into the Yard: the School on Mount Pleasant Hill has changed its face and its ways. Soon, they say, it may be no longer the School at all he knew and loved when he was a boy up to no good but the beat of his blood: the names are havoc'd from the Hall and the carved initials burned from the broken wood. But the names remain. What names did he know of the dead? Who of the honoured dead did he know such a long time ago? The names of the dead in the living heart and head remain for ever. Of all the dead whom did he know?

(Funeral bell)

VOICE

Evans, K. J.
Haines, G. C.
Roberts, I. L.
Moxham, J.
Thomas, H.
Baines, W.
Bazzard, F. H.
Beer, L. J.
Bucknell, R.
Tywford, G.
Vagg, E. A.
Wright, G.

(Fade)

NARRATOR Then I tacked down the snowblind hill, a cat-o'-nine-gales whipping from the sea, and, white and eiderdowned in the smothering flurry, people padded past me up and down like prowling featherbeds. And I plodded through the ankle-high one cloud that foamed the town, into flat Gower Street, its buildings melted, and along long Helen's Road. Now my search was leading me back to the seashore.

(Noise of sea, softly)

NARRATOR Only two living creatures stood on the promenade, near the cenotaph, facing the tossed crystal sea: a man in a chewed muffler and a ratting cap, and an angry dog of a mixed make. The man dithered in the cold, beat his bare blue hands together, waited for some sign from sea or snow; the dog shouted at the weather, and fixed his bloodshot eyes on Mumbles Head. But when the man and I talked together, the dog piped down and fixed his eyes on me, blaming me for the snow. The man spoke towards the sea. Year in, year out, whatever the weather, once in the daytime, once in the dark, he always came to look at the sea. He knew all the dogs and boys and old men who came to see the sea, who ran or gambolled on the sand or stooped at the edge of the waves as though over a wild, wide, rolling ashcan. He knew the lovers who went to lie in the sandhills, the striding masculine women who roared at their terriers like tiger tamers, the loafing men whose work it was in the world to observe the great employment of the sea. He said:

PROMENADE-MAN Oh yes, yes, I remember him well, but I didn't know what was his name. I don't know the names of none of the sandboys. They don't know mine. About fourteen or fifteen years old, you said, with a little red cap. And he used to play by Vivian's Stream. He used to dawdle in the arches, you said, and lark about on the railway-lines and holler at the old sea. He'd mooch about the dunes and watch the tankers and the tugs and the banana boats come out of the docks. He was going to run away to sea, he said. I know. On Saturday afternoon he'd go down to the sea when it was a long way out, and hear the foghorns though he couldn't see the ships. And on Sunday nights, after chapel, he'd be swaggering with his pals along the prom, whistling after the girls.

(*Titter*)

GIRL Does your mother know you're out? Go away now. Stop following us.

(*Another girl titters*)

GIRL Don't you say nothing, Hetty, you're only encouraging. No thank *you*, Mr Cheeky, with your cut-glass accent and your father's trilby![3] I don't want *no* walk on *no* sands. What d'you say? Ooh listen to him, Het, he's swallowed a dictionary. No, I don't want to go with nobody up no lane in the moonlight, see, and I'm not a baby-snatcher neither. I seen you going to school along Terrace Road, Mr Glad-Eye, with your little satchel and wearing your red cap and all. You seen me wearing my . . . no you never. Hetty, mind your glasses! Hetty Harris, you're as bad as them. Oh go away and do your homework, see. Cheek! Hetty Harris, don't you let him! Oooh, there's brazen! Well, just to the end of the prom, if you like. No further, mind . . .

PROMENADE-MAN Oh yes, I knew him well. I've known him by the thousands . . .

NARRATOR Even now, on the frozen foreshore, a high, far cry of boys, all like the boy I sought, slid on the glass of the streams and snowballed each other and the sky. Then I went on my way from the sea, up Brynmill Terrace and into Glanbrydan Avenue where Bert Trick had kept a grocer's shop and, in the kitchen, threatened the annihilation of the ruling classes over sandwiches and jelly and blancmange.[4] And I came to the shops and houses of the Uplands. Here and around here it was that the journey had begun of the one I was pursuing through his past.

(*Old piano cinema-music in background*)

FIRST VOICE Here was once the flea-pit picture-house where he whooped for the scalping Indians with Jack Basset and banged for the rustlers' guns.

NARRATOR Jackie Basset, killed.

THIRD VOICE Here once was Mrs Ferguson's, who sold the best gob-stoppers[5] and penny packets full of surprises and a sweet kind of glue.

FIRST VOICE In the fields behind Cwmdonkin Drive, the Murrays chased him and all cats.

SECOND VOICE No fires now where the outlaws' fires burned and the paradisiacal potatoes roasted in the embers.

THIRD VOICE In the Graig beneath Town Hill he was a lonely killer hunting the wolves (or rabbits) and the red Sioux tribe (or Mitchell brothers).

(*Fade cinema-music into background of children's voices reciting, in unison, the names of the counties of Wales*)

FIRST VOICE In Mirador School he learned to read and count. Who made the worst raffia doilies? Who put water in Joyce's galoshes, every morning prompt as prompt? In the afternoons, when the children were good, they read aloud from Struwelpeter.[6] And when they were bad, they sat alone in the empty classroom, hearing, from above them, the distant, terrible, sad music of the late piano lesson.

(*The children's voices fade. The piano lesson continues in background*)

---

3. With an upper-class accent and an elegant hat.
4. A pudding.
5. A kind of candy.

6. *Struwelpeter* ("Shock-head Peter") by the German Heinrich Hoffman (1809–1874) was a popular book for children.

NARRATOR And I went up, through the white Grove, into Cwmdonkin Park, the snow still sailing and the childish, lonely, remembered music fingering on in the suddenly gentle wind. Dusk was folding the Park around, like another, darker snow. Soon the bell would ring for the closing of the gates, though the Park was empty. The park-keeper walked by the reservoir, where swans had glided, on his white rounds. I walked by his side and asked him my questions, up the swathed drives past buried beds and loaded utterly still furred and birdless trees towards the last gate. He said:

PARK-KEEPER Oh yes, yes, I knew him well. He used to climb the reservoir railings and pelt the old swans. Run like a billygoat over the grass you should keep off of. Cut branches off the trees. Carve words on the benches. Pull up moss in the rockery, go snip through the dahlias. Fight in the bandstand. Climb the elms and moon up the top like a owl. Light fires in the bushes. Play on the green bank. Oh yes, I knew him well. I think he was happy all the time. I've known him by the thousands.

NARRATOR We had reached the last gate. Dusk drew around us and the town. I said: What has become of him now?

PARK-KEEPER Dead.

NARRATOR The Park-keeper said:

(*The park bell rings*)

PARK-KEEPER Dead . . . Dead . . . Dead . . . Dead . . . Dead . . . Dead.

Samuel Beckett
1906–1989

On January 5, 1953, *En Attendant Godot* (*Waiting for Godot*) premiered at the Théâtre de Babylone, Paris—and the shape of twentieth-century drama was permanently changed. *Godot* helped to strip the modern stage of everything but its essentials: two characters, seemingly without past or future or worldly possessions, and a spare stage: "A country road. A tree. Evening." Critics would subsequently find in Beckett's bleak stage suggestions of a postnuclear holocaust landscape, as they would in the later *Fin de partie* (*Endgame*, 1957); and for the remainder of his long and productive career, Beckett would continue to explore, with unparalleled honesty and courage, that realm of being that he called in one story *Sans*—"lessness."

April 13, 1906—Good Friday—is the date usually given for Samuel Barclay Beckett's birth, though the birth certificate shows May 13. He was born in the family home of Cooldrinagh in Foxrock, an upper-class Protestant suburb south of Dublin, to William Beckett, surveyor, and Mary (May) Roe, the daughter of a wealthy Kildare family. "You might say I had a happy childhood," Beckett later recalled; "my father did not beat me, nor did my mother run away from home." Beckett attended private academies in Dublin, then in 1920 was enrolled in Portora Royal School in Enniskillen, Northern Ireland, where he excelled more in sports than studies as star bowler on the cricket team, captain of rugby and swimming, and light-heavyweight champion in boxing. In 1923 Beckett entered Trinity College, Dublin, studying modern languages; he also enjoyed the freedom of the city, frequenting the Gate Theatre (for the drama of Pirandello and O'Casey), the music hall, and the movies (especially Charlie Chaplin, Laurel and Hardy, Buster Keaton, and the Marx Brothers). All would prove formative influences on his later drama and fiction.

In 1927 Beckett received his B.A. degree, first in his class in modern languages, and went off on fellowship to France to teach for two years at the École Normale Supérieure in Paris. While in Paris he became a friend of James Joyce, who influenced him profoundly. Besides aiding Joyce in various ways with his work, Beckett wrote an important essay, *Dante . . . Bruno . . . Vico . . . Joyce*, on *Finnegans Wake*—for a volume of critical writing published before the novel itself was completed. With characteristic understatement, Beckett has said that "Paris in the twenties was a good place for a young man to be"; at the same time, learning the craft of writing in Paris under the shadow of fellow Irish expatriate James Joyce would be enough to provoke the anxiety of influence in even the best of writers. However, Beckett's respect and admiration for Joyce were boundless and never wavered. In 1969 Beckett admitted that Joyce had become "an ethical ideal" for him: "Joyce had a moral effect on me. He made me realize artistic integrity."

The term of his fellowship in Paris having run out, Beckett returned to Dublin to assume teaching at Trinity College. That he was ill-suited to this role was immediately apparent to students, colleagues, and Beckett himself. "I saw that in teaching," Beckett later said, "I was talking of something I knew little about, to people who cared nothing about it. So I behaved very badly." The bad behavior to which Beckett refers was his resignation by mail while on spring holidays in Germany during his second year. Beckett returned briefly to Paris, where it became clear that the unwelcome attentions of Joyce's daughter Lucia were straining Beckett's relationship with the elder writer. He returned to the family home for a time in 1933, where he worked on his first published fiction, the Joycean collection of short stories *More Pricks than Kicks*.

The 1930s found Beckett shuttling back and forth between poverty in London and the frustrating comforts of home in Dublin; Paris seemed to him forbidden, owing to the break with Joyce. In spite of his difficult living circumstances, however, and occasional crippling attacks of clinical depression, Beckett managed to complete his first novel, *Murphy*. The manuscript was rejected by forty-one publishers before being accepted by Routledge in 1937. At the end of 1937, Beckett overcame his reluctance and moved back to Paris. From then on, he wrote largely in French. During the early years of World War II, he attempted to write but found it increasingly difficult to maintain the neutrality required of him by his Irish citizenship in light of the German invasion of France. He abandoned that neutrality in October 1940, when he joined one of the earliest French Resistance groups; he helped in Paris with Resistance activities until his group had been penetrated and betrayed, and just in the nick of time he and his lover Suzanne Deschevaux-Dumesnil (the two had met in 1938, and would eventually marry in 1961) were smuggled into Unoccupied France. At the end of the war Beckett returned to Paris, where he was awarded the *Croix de Guerre* and the *Médaille de la Résistance* by the French government.

While hiding from the Germans from 1942 to 1945 in the village of Roussillon in southeast France, Beckett wrote *Watt*, a complex and aridly witty novel that was never to enjoy the attention devoted to Beckett's other fiction. Meanwhile, Beckett continued his experiments with drama. Though it is drama for which Beckett is best known, he always put more stock in his fiction; "I turned to writing plays," he once said dismissively, "to relieve myself of the awful depression the prose led me into."

At an impasse in the writing of what would prove to be his greatest novels, the trilogy *Molloy*, *Malone Dies*, and *The Unnameable* (1951–1953), Beckett took off three months to write *Waiting for Godot*; it took four years to get the play produced. It is easy enough, in retrospect, to understand the producers' reservations: *Godot* breaks with the conventions of the well-made play at just about every turn, even down to its symmetrical, mirror-image two-act structure. The Irish critic Vivian Mercier wittily described *Godot* as a play in which "nothing happens, twice." Beckett's play *Krapp's Last Tape* (1960) uses a tape recorder (which, at the time of writing, Beckett had never seen) as a stage metaphor for the struggle over memory. In this play Beckett went farther than ever in stripping down his action, now involving just a single character. The play is less a monologue, though, than Krapp's dialogue with his past and future selves—and with the machine on which the selves of different years have recorded their fragmentary observations and memories.

After the success of his plays of the fifties and early sixties, Beckett turned to shorter and shorter forms, both in drama and fiction; he produced a number of very powerful, very short plays (*Not I*, 1973; *Footfalls*, 1976; *Rockabye*, 1981) and short, poetic texts that he called by a variety of self-deprecating names ("fizzles," "residua," "texts for nothing"). He sought an intensified power in the increasing economy of his works. In 1969 Beckett was awarded the Nobel Prize for literature, for "a body of work," as the citation declares, "that, in new forms of fiction and the theatre, has transmuted the destitution of modern man into exaltation."

Krapp's Last Tape

A late evening in the future.

Krapp's den.

Front centre a small table, the two drawers of which open towards the audience.

Sitting at the table, facing front, i.e. across from the drawers, a wearish old man: Krapp.

Rusty black narrow trousers too short for him. Rusty black sleeveless waistcoat, four capacious pockets. Heavy silver watch and chain. Grimy white shirt open at neck, no collar. Surprising pair of dirty white boots, size ten at least, very narrow and pointed.

White face. Purple nose. Disordered grey hair. Unshaven.

Very near-sighted (but unspectacled). Hard of hearing.

Cracked voice. Distinctive intonation.

Laborious walk.

On the table a tape-recorder with microphone and a number of cardboard boxes containing reels of recorded tapes.

Table and immediately adjacent area in strong white light. Rest of stage in darkness.

Krapp remains a moment motionless, heaves a great sigh, looks at his watch, fumbles in his pockets, takes out an envelope, puts it back, fumbles, takes out a small bunch of keys, raises it to his eyes, chooses a key, gets up and moves to front of table. He stoops, unlocks first drawer, peers into it, feels about inside it, takes out a reel of tape, peers at it, puts it back, locks drawer, unlocks second drawer, peers into it, feels about inside it, takes out a large banana, peers at it, locks drawer, puts keys back in his pocket. He turns, advances to edge of stage, halts, strokes banana, peels it, drops skin at his feet, puts end of banana in his mouth and remains motionless, staring vacuously before him. Finally he bites off the end, turns aside and begins pacing to and fro at edge of stage, in the light, i.e. not more than four or five paces either way, meditatively eating banana. He treads on skin, slips, nearly falls, recovers himself, stoops and peers at skin and finally pushes it, still stooping, with his foot over edge of stage into pit. He resumes his pacing, finishes banana, returns to table, sits down, remains a moment motionless, heaves a great sigh, takes keys from his pockets, raises them to his eyes, chooses key, gets up and moves to front of table, unlocks second drawer, takes out a second large banana, peers at it, locks drawer, puts back keys in his pocket, turns, advances to edge of stage, halts, strokes banana, peels it, tosses skin into pit, puts end of banana in his mouth and remains motionless, staring vacuously before him. Finally he has an idea, puts banana in his waistcoat pocket, the end emerging, and goes with all the speed he can muster backstage into darkness. Ten seconds. Loud pop of cork. Fifteen seconds. He comes back into light carrying an old ledger and sits down at table. He lays ledger on table, wipes his mouth, wipes his hands on the front of his waistcoat, brings them smartly together and rubs them.

KRAPP [*briskly*] Ah! [*He bends over ledger, turns the pages, finds the entry he wants, reads.*] Box . . . thrree . . . spool . . . five. [*He raises his head and stares front. With relish.*] Spool . . . [*Pause.*] Spooool! [*Happy smile. Pause. He bends over table, starts peering and poking at the boxes.*] Box . . . thrree . . . thrree . . . four . . . two . . . [*with surprise*] nine! good God! . . . seven . . . ah! the little rascal! [*He takes up box, peers at it.*] Box thrree. [*He lays it on table, opens it and peers at spools inside.*] Spool . . . [*he peers at ledger*] . . . five . . . [*he peers at spools*] . . . five . . . five . . . ah! the little scoundrel! [*He takes out a spool, peers at it.*] Spool five. [*He lays it on table, closes box three, puts it back with the others, takes up the spool.*] Box thrree, spool five. [*He bends over the machine, looks up. With relish.*] Spooool! [*Happy smile. He bends, loads spool on machine, rubs his hands.*] Ah! [*He peers at ledger, reads entry at foot of page.*] Mother at rest at last. . . . Hm. . . . The black ball. . . . [*He raises his head, stares blankly front. Puzzled.*] Black ball? . . . [*He peers again at ledger, reads.*] The dark nurse. . . . [*He raises his head, broods, peers again at ledger, reads.*] Slight improvement in bowel condition. . . . Hm. . . . Memorable . . . what? [*He peers closer.*] Equinox, memorable equinox. [*He raises his head, stares blankly front. Puzzled.*] Memorable equinox? . . . [*Pause. He shrugs his shoulders, peers again at ledger, reads.*] Farewell to—[*he turns page*]—love. [*He raises his head, broods, bends over machine, switches on and assumes listening posture, i.e. leaning forward, elbows on table, hand cupping ear towards machine, face front.*]

TAPE [*strong voice, rather pompous, clearly Krapp's at a much earlier time*] Thirty-nine today, sound as a—[*Settling himself more comfortably he knocks one of the boxes off the table, curses, switches off, sweeps boxes and ledger violently to the ground, winds tape back to beginning, switches on, resumes posture.*] Thirty-nine today, sound as a bell, apart from my old weakness, and intellectually I have now every reason to suspect at the . . . [*hesitates*] . . . crest of the wave—or thereabouts. Celebrated the awful occasion, as in recent years, quietly at the Winehouse. Not a soul. Sat before the fire with closed eyes, separating the grain from the husks. Jotted down a few notes, on the back of an envelope. Good to be back in my den, in my old rags. Have just eaten I regret to say three bananas and only with difficulty refrained from a fourth. Fatal things for a man with my condition. [*Vehemently.*] Cut'em out! [*Pause.*] The new light above my table is a great improvement. With all this darkness round me I feel less alone. [*Pause.*] In a way. [*Pause.*] I love to get up and move about in it, then back here to . . . [*hesitates*] . . . me. [*Pause.*] Krapp.

[*Pause.*]

The grain, now what I wonder do I mean by that, I mean . . . [*hesitates*] . . . I suppose I mean those things worth having when all the dust has—when all *my* dust has settled. I close my eyes and try and imagine them.

[*Pause. Krapp closes his eyes briefly.*]

Extraordinary silence this evening, I strain my ears and do not hear a sound. Old Miss McGlome always sings at this hour. But not tonight. Songs of her girlhood, she says. Hard to think of her as a girl. Wonderful woman though. Connaught,[1] I fancy. [*Pause.*] Shall I sing when I am her age, if I ever am? No. [*Pause.*] Did I sing as a boy? No. [*Pause.*] Did I ever sing? No.

[*Pause.*]

Just been listening to an old year, passages at random. I did not check in the book, but it must be at least ten or twelve years ago. At that time I think I was still living on and off with Bianca in Kedar Street. Well out of that, Jesus yes! Hopeless business. [*Pause.*] Not much about her, apart from a tribute to her eyes. Very warm. I suddenly saw them again. [*Pause.*] Incomparable! [*Pause.*] Ah well?

1. A province in northwestern Ireland.

[*Pause.*] These old P.M.s are gruesome, but I often find them—[*Krapp switches off, broods, switches on.*]—a help before embarking on a new . . . [*hesitates*] . . . retrospect. Hard to believe I was ever that young whelp. The voice! Jesus! And the aspirations! [*Brief laugh in which Krapp joins.*] And the resolutions! [*Brief laugh in which Krapp joins.*] To drink less, in particular. [*Brief laugh of Krapp alone.*] Statistics. Seventeen hundred hours, out of the preceding eight thousand odd, consumed on licensed premises[2] alone. More than 20 per cent, say 40 per cent of his waking life. [*Pause.*] Plans for a less . . . [*hesitates*] . . . engrossing sexual life. Last illness of his father. Flagging pursuit of happiness. Unattainable laxation.[3] Sneers at what he calls his youth and thanks to God that it's over. [*Pause.*] False ring there. [*Pause.*] Shadows of the opus . . . magnum.[4] Closing with a—[*brief laugh*]—yelp to Providence. [*Prolonged laugh in which Krapp joins.*] What remains of all that misery? A girl in a shabby green coat, on a railway-station platform? No?
[*Pause.*]
   When I look—
[*Krapp switches off, broods, looks at his watch, gets up, goes backstage into darkness. Ten seconds. Pop of cork. Ten seconds. Second cork. Ten seconds. Third cork. Ten seconds. Brief burst of quavering song.*]

KRAPP [*sings*] Now the day is over,
                Night is drawing nigh-igh,
                Shadows—
[*Fit of coughing. He comes back into light, sits down, wipes his mouth, switches on, resumes his listening posture.*]

TAPE —back on the year that is gone, with what I hope is perhaps a glint of the old eye to come, there is of course the house on the canal where mother lay a-dying, in the late autumn, after her long viduity [*Krapp gives a start*] and the—[*Krapp switches off, winds back tape a little, bends his ear closer to machine, switches on*]—a-dying, after her long viduity, and the—
[*Krapp switches off, raises his head, stares blankly before him. His lips move in the syllables of "viduity." No sound. He gets up, goes backstage into darkness, comes back with an enormous dictionary, lays it on table, sits down and looks up the word.*]

KRAPP [*reading from dictionary*] State—or condition—of being—or remaining—a widow—or widower. [*Looks up. Puzzled.*] Being—or remaining? . . . [*Pause. He peers again at dictionary. Reading.*] "Deep weeds of viduity." . . . Also of an animal, especially a bird . . . the vidua or weaver-bird. . . . Black plumage of male. . . . [*He looks up. With relish.*] The vidua-bird!
[*Pause. He closes dictionary, switches on, resumes listening posture.*]

TAPE —bench by the weir from where I could see her window. There I sat, in the biting wind, wishing she were gone. [*Pause.*] Hardly a soul, just a few regulars, nursemaids, infants, old men, dogs. I got to know them quite well—oh by appearance of course I mean! One dark young beauty I recollect particularly, all white and starch, incomparable bosom, with a big black hooded perambulator, most funeral thing. Whenever I looked in her direction she had her eyes on me. And yet when I was bold enough to speak to her—not having been introduced—she threatened to call a policeman. As if I had designs on her virtue! [*Laugh. Pause.*]

---

2. Pubs licensed to sell alcohol.
3. Movement of the bowels.

4. A "magnus opus" is a great work; a magnum is a large wine bottle.

The face she had! The eyes! Like . . . [hesitates] . . . chrysolite![5] [Pause.] Ah well.
. . . [Pause.] I was there when—[Krapp switches off, broods, switches on again.]—the
blind went down, one of those dirty brown roller affairs, throwing a ball for a little
white dog as chance would have it. I happened to look up and there it was. All
over and done with, at last. I sat on for a few moments with the ball in my hand
and the dog yelping and pawing at me. [Pause.] Moments. Her moments, my
moments. [Pause.] The dog's moments. [Pause.] In the end I held it out to him and
he took it in his mouth, gently, gently. A small, old, black, hard, solid rubber ball.
[Pause.] I shall feel it, in my hand, until my dying day. [Pause.] I might have kept
it. [Pause.] But I gave it to the dog.

[Pause.]

Ah well. . . .

[Pause.]

Spiritually a year of profound gloom and indigence until that memorable night
in March, at the end of the jetty, in the howling wind, never to be forgotten,
when suddenly I saw the whole thing. The vision at last. This I fancy is what I
have chiefly to record this evening, against the day when my work will be done
and perhaps no place left in my memory, warm or cold, for the miracle that . . .
[hesitates] . . . for the fire that set it alight. What I suddenly saw then was this, that
the belief I had been going on all my life, namely—[Krapp switches off impatiently,
winds tape forward, switches on again]—great granite rocks the foam flying up in the
light of the lighthouse and the wind-gauge spinning like a propeller, clear to me at
last that the dark I have always struggled to keep under is in reality my most—
[Krapp curses, switches off, winds tape forward, switches on again]—unshatterable
association until my dissolution of storm and night with the light of the understanding and the fire—[Krapp curses louder, switches off, winds tape forward, switches on again]—my face in her breasts and my hand on her. We lay there without
moving. But under us all moved, and moved us, gently, up and down, and from
side to side.

[Pause.]

Past midnight. Never knew such silence. The earth might be uninhabited.

[Pause.]

Here I end—

[Krapp switches off, winds tape back, switches on again.]

—upper lake, with the punt,[6] bathed off the bank, then pushed out into the
stream and drifted. She lay stretched out on the floorboards with her hands under
her head and her eyes closed. Sun blazing down, bit of a breeze, water nice and
lively. I noticed a scratch on her thigh and asked her how she came by it. Picking
gooseberries, she said. I said again I thought it was hopeless and no good going on
and she agreed, without opening her eyes. [Pause.] I asked her to look at me and
after a few moments—[Pause.]—after a few moments she did, but the eyes just
slits, because of the glare. I bent over her to get them in the shadow and they
opened. [Pause. Low.] Let me in. [Pause.] We drifted in among the flags[7] and stuck.
The way they went down, sighing, before the stem! [Pause.] I lay down across her
with my face in her breasts and my hand on her. We lay there without moving. But
under us all moved, and moved us, gently, up and down, and from side to side.

---

5. Green gemstone.   7. Reeds.
6. A small, flat-bottomed boat.

[*Pause.*]

Past midnight. Never knew—

[*Krapp switches off, broods. Finally he fumbles in his pockets, encounters the banana, takes it out, peers at it, puts it back, fumbles, brings out envelope, fumbles, puts back envelope, looks at his watch, gets up and goes backstage into darkness. Ten seconds. Sound of bottle against glass, then brief siphon. Ten seconds. Bottle against glass alone. Ten seconds. He comes back a little unsteadily into light, goes to front of table, takes out keys, raises them to his eyes, chooses key, unlocks first drawer, peers into it, feels about inside, takes out reel, peers at it, locks drawer, puts keys back in his pocket, goes and sits down, takes reel off machine, lays it on dictionary, loads virgin reel on machine, takes envelope from his pocket, consults back of it, lays it on table, switches on, clears his throat and begins to record.*]

KRAPP Just been listening to that stupid bastard I took myself for thirty years ago, hard to believe I was ever as bad as that. Thank God that's all done with anyway. [*Pause.*] The eyes she had! [*Broods, realizes he is recording silence, switches off, broods. Finally.*] Everything there, everything, all the—[*Realizes this is not being recorded, switches on.*] Everything there, everything on this old muckball, all the light and dark and famine and feasting of . . . [*hesitates*] . . . the ages! [*In a shout.*] Yes! [*Pause.*] Let that go! Jesus! Take his mind off his homework! Jesus! [*Pause. Weary.*] Ah well, maybe he was right. [*Pause.*] Maybe he was right. [*Broods. Realizes. Switches off. Consults envelope.*] Pah! [*Crumples it and throws it away. Broods. Switches on.*] Nothing to say, not a squeak. What's a year now? The sour cud and the iron stool.[8] [*Pause.*] Revelled in the word spool. [*With relish.*] Spoooool! Happiest moment of the past half million. [*Pause.*] Seventeen copies sold, of which eleven at trade price to free circulating libraries beyond the seas. Getting known. [*Pause.*] One pound six and something, eight I have little doubt. [*Pause.*] Crawled out once or twice, before the summer was cold. Sat shivering in the park, drowned in dreams and burning to be gone. Not a soul. [*Pause.*] Last fancies. [*Vehemently.*] Keep 'em under! [*Pause.*] Scalded the eyes out of me reading *Effie*[9] again, a page a day, with tears again. Effie. . . . [*Pause.*] Could have been happy with her, up there on the Baltic, and the pines, and the dunes. [*Pause.*] Could I? [*Pause.*] And she? [*Pause.*] Pah! [*Pause.*] Fanny came in a couple of times. Bony old ghost of a whore. Couldn't do much, but I suppose better than a kick in the crutch. The last time wasn't so bad. How do you manage it, she said, at your age? I told her I'd been saving up for her all my life. [*Pause.*] Went to Vespers[1] once, like when I was in short trousers. [*Pause. Sings.*]

> Now the day is over,
> Night is drawing nigh-igh,
> Shadows—[*coughing, then almost inaudible*]—of the evening
> Steal across the sky.

[*Gasping.*] Went to sleep and fell off the pew. [*Pause.*] Sometimes wondered in the night if a last effort mightn't—[*Pause.*] Ah finish your booze now and get to your bed. Go on with this drivel in the morning. Or leave it at that. [*Pause.*] Leave it at that. [*Pause.*] Lie propped up in the dark—and wander. Be again in

8. Indigestion and constipation.
9. Theodor Fontane's sentimental novel *Effi Briest* (1895).

1. Evening church service.

the dingle[2] on a Christmas Eve, gathering holly, the red-berried. [*Pause.*] Be again on Croghan[3] on a Sunday morning, in the haze, with the bitch, stop and listen to the bells. [*Pause.*] And so on. [*Pause.*] Be again, be again. [*Pause.*] All that old misery. [*Pause.*] Once wasn't enough for you. [*Pause.*] Lie down across her.

[*Long pause. He suddenly bends over machine, switches off, wrenches off tape, throws it away, puts on the other, winds it forward to the passage he wants, switches on, listens staring front.*]

TAPE —gooseberries, she said. I said again I thought it was hopeless and no good going on and she agreed, without opening her eyes. [*Pause.*] I asked her to look at me and after a few moments—[*Pause.*]—after a few moments she did, but the eyes just slits, because of the glare. I bent over to get them in the shadow and they opened. [*Pause. Low.*] Let me in. [*Pause.*] We drifted in among the flags and stuck. The way they went down, sighing, before the stem! [*Pause.*] I lay down across her with my face in her breasts and my hand on her. We lay there without moving. But under us all moved, and moved us, gently, up and down, and from side to side.

[*Pause. Krapp's lips move. No sound.*]

Past midnight. Never knew such silence. The earth might be uninhabited.

[*Pause.*]

Here I end this reel. Box—[*Pause.*]—three, spool—[*Pause.*]—five. [*Pause.*] Perhaps my best years are gone. When there was a chance of happiness. But I wouldn't want them back. Not with the fire in me now. No, I wouldn't want them back.

[*Krapp motionless staring before him. The tape runs on in silence.*]

CURTAIN

from Texts for Nothing[1]

4

Where would I go, if I could go, who would I be, if I could be, what would I say, if I had a voice, who says this, saying it's me? Answer simply, someone answer simply. It's the same old stranger as ever, for whom alone accusative I exist, in the pit of my inexistence, of his, of ours, there's a simple answer. It's not with thinking he'll find me, but what is he to do, living and bewildered, yes, living, say what he may. Forget me, know me not, yes, that would be the wisest, none better able than he. Why this sudden affability after such desertion, it's easy to understand, that's what he says, but he doesn't understand. I'm not in his head, nowhere in his old body, and yet I'm there, for him I'm there, with him, hence all the confusion. That should have been enough for him, to have found me absent, but it's not, he wants me there, with a form and a world, like him, in spite of him, me who am everything, like him who is nothing. And when he feels me void of existence it's of his he would have me void, and vice versa, mad, mad, he's mad. The truth is he's looking for me to kill me, to have me dead like him, dead like the living. He knows all that, but it's no help his knowing it, I don't know it, I know nothing. He protests he doesn't reason and does nothing but reason, crooked, as if that could improve matters. He thinks words fail

---

2. Valley.
3. Mountain in County Wicklow in Southeastern Ireland.
1. Having completed his *Molloy* trilogy in 1950, Beckett

wrote this series of short texts between 1950 and 1952 as "an attempt to get out of the attitude of disintegration" established in his trilogy—an attempt, Beckett later said, that failed.

him, he thinks because words fail him he's on his way to my speechlessness, to being speechless with my speechlessness, he would like it to be my fault that words fail him, of course words fail him. He tells his story every five minutes, saying it is not his, there's cleverness for you. He would like it to be my fault that he has no story, of course he has no story, that's no reason for trying to foist one on me. That's how he reasons, wide of the mark, but wide of what mark, answer us that. He has me say things saying it's not me, there's profundity for you, he has me who say nothing say it's not me. All that is truly crass. If at least he would dignify me with the third person, like his other figments, not he, he'll be satisfied with nothing less than me, for his me. When he had me, when he was me, he couldn't get rid of me quick enough, I didn't exist, he couldn't have that, that was no kind of life, of course I didn't exist, any more than he did, of course it was no kind of life, now he has it, his kind of life, let him lose it, if he wants to be in peace, with a bit of luck. His life, what a mine, what a life, he can't have that, you can't fool him, ergo it's not his, it's not him, what a thought, treat him like that, like a vulgar Molloy, a common Malone, those mere mortals, happy mortals, have a heart, land him in that shit, who never stirred, who is none but me, all things considered, and what things, and how considered, he had only to keep out of it. That's how he speaks, this evening, how he has me speak, how he speaks to himself, how I speak, there is only me, this evening, here, on earth, and a voice that makes no sound because it goes towards none, and a head strewn with arms laid down and corpses fighting fresh, and a body, I nearly forgot. This evening, I say this evening, perhaps it's morning. And all these things, what things, all about me, I won't deny them any more, there's no sense in that any more. If it's nature perhaps it's trees and birds, they go together, water and air, so that all may go on, I don't need to know the details, perhaps I'm sitting under a palm. Or it's a room, with furniture, all that's required to make life comfortable, dark, because of the wall outside the window. What am I doing, talking, having my figments talk, it can only be me. Spells of silence too, when I listen, and hear the local sounds, the world sounds, see what an effort I make, to be reasonable. There's my life, why not, it is one, if you like, if you must, I don't say no, this evening. There has to be one, it seems, once there is speech, no need of a story, a story is not compulsory, just a life, that's the mistake I made, one of the mistakes, to have wanted a story for myself, whereas life alone is enough. I'm making progress, it was time, I'll learn to keep my foul mouth shut before I'm done, if nothing foreseen crops up. But he who somehow comes and goes, unaided from place to place, even though nothing happens to him, true, what of him? I stay here, sitting, if I'm sitting, often I feel sitting, sometimes standing, it's one or the other, or lying down, there's another possibility, often I feel lying down, it's one of the three, or kneeling. What counts is to be in the world, the posture is immaterial, so long as one is on earth. To breathe is all that is required, there is no obligation to ramble, or receive company, you may even believe yourself dead on condition you make no bones about it, what more liberal regimen could be imagined, I don't know, I don't imagine. No point under such circumstances in saying I am somewhere else, someone else, such as I am I have all I need to hand, for to do what, I don't know, all I have to do, there I am on my own again at last, what a relief that must be. Yes, there are moments, like this moment, when I seem almost restored to the feasible. Then it goes, all goes, and I'm far again, with a far story again, I wait for me afar for my story to begin, to end, and again this voice cannot be mine. That's where I'd go, if I could go, that's who I'd be, if I could be.

8

Only the words break the silence, all other sounds have ceased. If I were silent I'd hear nothing. But if I were silent the other sounds would start again, those to which the words have made me deaf, or which have really ceased. But I am silent, it sometimes happens, no, never, not one second. I weep too without interruption. It's an unbroken flow of words and tears. With no pause for reflection. But I speak softer, every year a little softer. Perhaps. Slower too, every year a little slower. Perhaps. It is hard for me to judge. If so the pauses would be longer, between the words, the sentences, the syllables, the tears, I confuse them, words and tears, my words are my tears, my eyes my mouth. And I should hear, at every little pause, if it's the silence I say when I say that only the words break it. But nothing of the kind, that's not how it is, it's for ever the same murmur, flowing unbroken, like a single endless word and therefore meaningless, for it's the end gives the meaning to words. What right have you then, no, this time I see what I'm up to and put a stop to it, saying, None, none. But get on with the stupid old threne[2] and ask, ask until you answer, a new question, the most ancient of all, the question were things always so. Well I'm going to tell myself something (if I'm able), pregnant I hope with promise for the future, namely that I begin to have no very clear recollection of how things were before (I was!), and by before I mean elsewhere, time has turned into space and there will be no more time, till I get out of here. Yes, my past has thrown me out, its gates have slammed behind me, or I burrowed my way out alone, to linger a moment free in a dream of days and nights, dreaming of me moving, season after season, towards the last, like the living, till suddenly I was here, all memory gone. Ever since nothing but fantasies and hope of a story for me somehow, of having come from somewhere and of being able to go back, or on, somehow, some day, or without hope. Without what hope, haven't I just said, of seeing me alive, not merely inside an imaginary head, but a pebble sand to be, under a restless sky, restless on its shore, faint stirs day and night, as if to grow less could help, ever less and less and never quite be gone. No truly, no matter what, I say no matter what, hoping to wear out a voice, to wear out a head, or without hope, without reason, no matter what, without reason. But it will end, a desinence[3] will come, or the breath fail better still, I'll be silence, I'll know I'm silence, no, in the silence you can't know, I'll never know anything. But at least get out of here, at least that, no? I don't know. And time begin again, the steps on the earth, the night the fool implores at morning and the morning he begs at evening not to dawn. I don't know, I don't know what all that means, day and night, earth and sky, begging and imploring. And I can desire them? Who says I desire them, the voice, and that I can't desire anything, that looks like a contradiction, it may be for all I know. Me, here, if they could open, those little words, open and swallow me up, perhaps that is what has happened. If so let them open again and let me out, in the tumult of light that sealed my eyes, and of men, to try and be one again. Or if I'm guilty let me be forgiven and graciously authorized to expiate, coming and going in passing time, every day a little purer, a little deader. The mistake I make is to try and think, even the way I do, such as I am I shouldn't be able, even the way I do. But whom can I have offended so grievously, to be punished in this inexplicable way, all is inexplicable, space and time, false and inexplicable, suffering and tears, and even the old convulsive cry, It's not me, it can't be me. But am I in pain, whether it's me

---

2. Song of lamentation.   3. Termination.

or not, frankly now, is there pain? Now is here and here there is no frankness, all I say will be false and to begin with not said by me, here I'm a mere ventriloquist's dummy, I feel nothing, say nothing, he holds me in his arms and moves my lips with a string, with a fish-hook, no, no need of lips, all is dark, there is no one, what's the matter with my head, I must have left it in Ireland, in a saloon, it must be there still, lying on the bar, it's all it deserved. But that other who is me, blind and deaf and mute, because of whom I'm here, in this black silence, helpless to move or accept this voice as mine, it's as him I must disguise myself till I die, for him in the meantime do my best not to live, in this pseudo-sepulture[4] claiming to be his. Whereas to my certain knowledge I'm dead and kicking above, somewhere in Europe probably, with every plunge and suck of the sky a little more overripe, as yesterday in the pump of the womb. No, to have said so convinces me of the contrary, I never saw the light of day, any more than he, ah if no were content to cut yes's throat and never cut its own. Watch out for the right moment, then not another word, is that the only way to have being and habitat? But I'm here, that much at least is certain, it's in vain I keep on saying it, it remains true. Does it? It's hard for me to judge. Less true and less certain in any case than when I say I'm on earth, come into the world and assured of getting out, that's why I say it, patiently, variously, trying to vary, for you never know, it's perhaps all a question of hitting on the right aggregate. So as to be here no more at last, to have never been here, but all this time above, with a name like a dog to be called up with and distinctive marks to be had up with, the chest expanding and contracting unaided, panting towards the grand apnoea.[5] The right aggregate, but there are four million possible, nay probable, according to Aristotle, who knew everything. But what is this I see, and how, a white stick and an ear-trumpet, where, Place de la République, at pernod[6] time, let me look closer at this, it's perhaps me at last. The trumpet, sailing at ear level, suddenly resembles a steam-whistle, of the kind thanks to which my steamers forge fearfully through the fog. That should fix the period, to the nearest half-century or so. The stick gains ground, tapping with its ferrule[7] the noble bassamento of the United Stores, it must be winter, at least not summer. I can also just discern, with a final effort of will, a bowler hat which seems to my sorrow a sardonic synthesis of all those that never fitted me and, at the other extremity, similarly suspicious, a complete pair of brown boots lacerated and gaping. These insignia, if I may so describe them, advance in concert, as though connected by the traditional human excipient,[8] halt, move on again, confirmed by the vast show windows. The level of the hat, and consequently of the trumpet, hold out some hope for me as a dying dwarf or at least hunchback. The vacancy is tempting, shall I enthrone my infirmities, give them this chance again, my dream infirmities, that they may take flesh and move, deteriorating, round and round this grandiose square which I hope I don't confuse with the Bastille,[9] until they are deemed worthy of the adjacent Père Lachaise[1] or, better still, prematurely relieved trying to cross over, at the hour of night's young thoughts. No, the answer is no. For even as I moved, or when the moment came, affecting beyond all others, to hold out my hand, or hat, without previous song, or any other form of concession to self-respect, at the terrace of a café, or in the mouth of the underground, I would know it was not me, I would know I was

---

4. Tomb.
5. Cessation of breathing.
6. A licorice-flavored liqueur.
7. Metal-capped tip.

8. Glue.
9. Parisian prison destroyed during the French Revolution in 1789.
1. Parisian cemetery.

here, begging in another dark, another silence, for another alm, that of being or of ceasing, better still, before having been. And the hand old in vain would drop the mite and the old feet shuffle on, towards an even vainer death than no matter whose.

The Expelled

There were not many steps. I had counted them a thousand times, both going up and coming down, but the figure has gone from my mind. I have never known whether you should say one with your foot on the sidewalk, two with the following foot on the first step, and so on, or whether the sidewalk shouldn't count. At the top of the steps I fell foul of the same dilemma. In the other direction. I mean from top to bottom, it was the same, the word is not too strong. I did not know where to begin nor where to end, that's the truth of the matter. I arrived therefore at three totally different figures, without ever knowing which of them was right. And when I say that the figure has gone from my mind, I mean that none of the three figures is with me any more, in my mind. It is true that if I were to find, in my mind, where it is certainly to be found, one of these figures, I would find it and it alone, without being able to deduce from it the other two. And even were I to recover two, I would not know the third. No, I would have to find all three, in my mind, in order to know all three. Memories are killing. So you must not think of certain things, of those that are dear to you, or rather you must think of them, for if you don't there is the danger of finding them, in your mind, little by little. That is to say, you must think of them for a while, a good while, every day several times a day, until they sink forever in the mud. That's an order.

After all it is not the number of steps that matters. The important thing to remember is that there were not many, and that I have remembered. Even for the child there were not many, compared to other steps he knew, from seeing them every day, from going up them and coming down, and playing on them at knuckle-bones and other games the very names of which he has forgotten. What must it have been like then for the man I had overgrown into?

The fall was therefore not serious. Even as I fell I heard the door slam, which brought me a little comfort, in the midst of my fall. For that meant they were not pursuing me down into the street with a stick, to beat me in full view of the passers-by. For if that had been their intention they would not have shut the door, but left it open, so that the persons assembled in the vestibule might enjoy my chastisement and be edified. So, for once, they had confined themselves to throwing me out and no more about it. I had time, before coming to rest in the gutter, to conclude this piece of reasoning.

Under these circumstances nothing compelled me to get up immediately. I rested my elbow on the sidewalk, funny the things you remember, settled my ear in the cup of my hand and began to reflect on my situation, notwithstanding its familiarity. But the sound, fainter but unmistakable, of the door slammed again, roused me from my reverie, in which already a whole landscape was taking form, charming with hawthorn and wild roses, most dreamlike, and made me look up in alarm, my hands flat on the sidewalk and my legs braced for flight. But it was merely my hat sailing towards me through the air, rotating as it came. I caught it and put it on. They were most correct, according to their god. They could have kept this hat, but it was not theirs, it was mine, so they gave it back to me. But the spell was broken.

How describe this hat? And why? When my head had attained I shall not say its definitive but its maximum dimensions, my father said to me, Come, son, we are going to buy your hat, as though it had pre-existed from time immemorial in a pre-established place. He went straight to the hat. I personally had no say in the matter, nor had the hatter. I have often wondered if my father's purpose was not to humiliate me, if he was not jealous of me who was young and handsome, fresh at least, while he was already old and all bloated and purple. It was forbidden me, from that day forth, to go out bareheaded, my pretty brown hair blowing in the wind. Sometimes, in a secluded street, I took it off and held it in my hand, but trembling. I was required to brush it morning and evening. Boys my age with whom, in spite of everything, I was obliged to mix occasionally, mocked me. But I said to myself, It is not really the hat, they simply make merry at the hat because it is a little more glaring than the rest, for they have no finesse. I have always been amazed at my contemporaries' lack of finesse, I whose soul writhed from morning to night, in the mere quest of itself. But perhaps they were simply being kind, like those who make game of the hunchback's big nose. When my father died I could have got rid of this hat, there was nothing more to prevent me, but not I. But how describe it? Some other time, some other time.

I got up and set off. I forget how old I can have been. In what had just happened to me there was nothing in the least memorable. It was neither the cradle nor the grave of anything whatever. Or rather it resembled so many other cradles, so many other graves, that I'm lost. But I don't believe I exaggerate when I say that I was in the prime of life, what I believe is called the full possession of one's faculties. Ah yes, them I possessed all right. I crossed the street and turned back towards the house that had just ejected me, I who never turned back when leaving. How beautiful it was! There were geraniums in the windows. I have brooded over geraniums for years. Geraniums are artful customers, but in the end I was able to do what I liked with them. I have always greatly admired the door of this house, up on top of its little flight of steps. How describe it? It was a massive green door, encased in summer in a kind of green and white striped housing, with a hole for the thunderous wrought-iron knocker and a slit for letters, this latter closed to dust, flies and tits by a brass flap fitted with springs. So much for that description. The door was set between two pillars of the same colour, the bell being on that to the right. The curtains were in unexceptionable taste. Even the smoke rising from one of the chimney-pots seemed to spread and vanish in the air more sorrowful than the neighbours', and bluer. I looked up at the third and last floor and saw my window outrageously open. A thorough cleaning was in full swing. In a few hours they would close the window, draw the curtains and spray the whole place with disinfectant. I knew them. I would have gladly died in that house. In a sort of vision I saw the door open and my feet come out.

I wasn't afraid to look, for I knew they were not spying on me from behind the curtains, as they could have done if they had wished. But I knew them. They had all gone back into their dens and resumed their occupations.

And yet I had done them no harm.

I did not know the town very well, scene of my birth and of my first steps in this world, and then of all the others, so many that I thought all trace of me was lost, but I was wrong! I went out so little! Now and then I would go to the window, part the curtains and look out. But then I hastened back to the depths of the room, where the bed was. I felt ill at ease with all this air about me, lost before the confusion of innumerable prospects. But I still knew how to act at this period, when it was absolutely necessary. But first I raised my eyes to the sky, whence cometh our help, where there are no roads, where you wander freely, as in a desert, and where nothing obstructs your vision, wherever you turn your eyes, but the limits of vision itself. When I was younger I thought life would be good in the middle of a plain and went to the Lüneburg[1] heath. With the plain in my head I went to the heath. There were other heaths far less remote, but a voice kept saying to me, It's the Lüneburg heath you need. The element lüne must have had something to do with it. As it turned out the Lüneburg heath was most unsatisfactory, most unsatisfactory. I came home disappointed and at the same time relieved. Yes, I don't know why, but I have never been disappointed, and I often was in the early days, without feeling at the same time, or a moment later, an undeniable relief.

I set off. What a gait. Stiffness of the lower limbs, as if nature had denied me knees, extraordinary splaying of the feet to right and left of the line of march. The trunk, on the contrary, as if by the effect of a compensatory mechanism, was as flabby as an old ragbag, tossing wildly to the unpredictable jolts of the pelvis. I have often tried to correct these defects, to stiffen my bust, flex my knees and walk with my feet in front of one another, for I had at least five or six, but it always ended in the same way, I mean by a loss of equilibrium, followed by a fall. A man must walk without paying attention to what he's doing, as he sighs, and when I walked without paying attention to what I was doing I walked in the way I have just described, and when I began to pay attention I managed a few steps of creditable execution and then fell. I decided therefore to be myself. This carriage is due, in my opinion, in part at least, to a certain leaning from which I have never been able to free myself completely and which left its stamp, as was only to be expected, on my impressionable years, those which govern the fabrication of character, I refer to the period which extends, as far as the eye can see, from the first totterings, behind a chair, to the third form, in which I concluded my studies. I had then the deplorable habit, having pissed in my trousers, or shat there, which I did fairly regularly early in the morning, about ten or half past ten, of persisting in going on and finishing my day as if nothing had happened. The very idea of changing my trousers, or of confiding in mother, who goodness knows asked nothing better than to help me, was unbearable, I don't know why, and till bedtime I dragged on with burning and stinking between my little thighs, or sticking to my bottom, the result of my incontinence. Whence this wary way of walking, with legs stiff and wide apart, and this desperate rolling of the bust, no doubt intended to put people off the scent, to make them think I was full of gaiety and high spirits, without a care in the world, and to lend plausibility to my explanations concerning my nether rigidity, which I ascribed to hereditary rheumatism. My youthful ardour, in so far as I had any, spent itself in this effort, I became sour and mistrustful, a little before my time, in love with hiding and the prone position. Poor juvenile solutions, explaining nothing. No need then for caution, we may reason on to our heart's content, the fog won't lift.

The weather was fine. I advanced down the street, keeping as close as I could to the sidewalk. The widest sidewalk is never wide enough for me, once I set myself in motion, and I hate to inconvenience strangers. A policeman stopped me and said, The street for vehicles, the sidewalk for pedestrians. Like a bit of Old Testament. So I got back on the sidewalk, almost apologetically, and persevered there, in spite of an indescribable jostle, for a good twenty steps, till I had to fling myself to the ground to avoid crushing a child. He was wearing a little harness, I remember, with little bells,

---

1. City 25 miles southeast of Hamburg, Germany. Lüne means "moon."

he must have taken himself for a pony, or a Clydesdale, why not, I would have crushed him gladly, I loathe children, and it would have been doing him a service, but I was afraid of reprisals. Everyone is a parent, that is what keeps you from hoping. One should reserve, on busy streets, special tracks for these nasty little creatures, their prams, hoops, sweets, scooters, skates, grandpas, grandmas, nannies, balloons and balls, all their foul little happiness in a word. I fell then, and brought down with me an old lady covered with spangles and lace, who must have weighed about sixteen stone.[2] Her screams soon drew a crowd. I had high hopes she had broken her femur, old ladies break their femur easily, but not enough, not enough. I took advantage of the confusion to make off, muttering unintelligible oaths, as if I were the victim, and I was, but I couldn't have proved it. They never lynch children, babies, no matter what they do they are whitewashed in advance. I personally would lynch them with the utmost pleasure, I don't say I'd lend a hand, no, I am not a violent man, but I'd encourage the others and stand them drinks when it was done. But no sooner had I begun to reel on than I was stopped by a second policeman, similar in all respects to the first, so much so that I wondered whether it was not the same one. He pointed out to me that the sidewalk was for everyone, as if it was quite obvious that I could not be assimilated to that category. Would you like me, I said, without thinking for a single moment of Heraclitus,[3] to get down in the gutter? Get down wherever you want, he said, but leave some room for others. If you can't bloody well get about like everyone else, he said, you'd do better to stay at home. It was exactly my feeling. And that he should attribute to me a home was no small satisfaction. At that moment a funeral passed, as sometimes happens. There was a great flurry of hats and at the same time a flutter of countless fingers. Personally if I were reduced to making the sign of the cross I would set my heart on doing it right, nose, navel, left nipple, right nipple. But the way they did it, slovenly and wild, he seemed crucified all of a heap, no dignity, his knees under his chin and his hands anyhow. The more fervent stopped dead and muttered. As for the policeman he stiffened to attention, closed his eyes and saluted. Through the windows of the cabs I caught a glimpse of the mourners conversing with animation, no doubt scenes from the life of their late dear brother in Christ, or sister. I seem to have heard that the hearse trappings are not the same in both cases, but I never could find out what the difference consists in. The horses were farting and shitting as if they were going to the fair. I saw no one kneeling.

But with us the last journey is soon done, it is in vain you quicken your pace, the last cab containing the domestics soon leaves you behind, the respite is over, the bystanders go their ways, you may look to yourself again. So I stopped a third time, of my own free will, and entered a cab. Those I had just seen pass, crammed with people hotly arguing, must have made a strong impression on me. It's a big black box, rocking and swaying on its springs, the windows are small, you curl up in a corner, it smells musty. I felt my hat grazing the roof. A little later I leaned forward and closed the windows. Then I sat down again with my back to the horse. I was dozing off when a voice made me start, the cabman's. He had opened the door, no doubt despairing of making himself heard through the window. All I saw was his moustache. Where to? he said. He had climbed down from his seat on purpose to ask me that. And I who thought I was far away already. I reflected, searching in my memory for the name of a street, or a monument. Is your cab for sale? I said. I added, Without the horse. What would I do with a horse? But what would I do with a cab? Could I as much as stretch

2. 224 pounds.   3. Ancient Greek philosopher of flux.

out in it? Who would bring me food? To the Zoo, I said. It is rare for a capital to be without a Zoo. I added, Don't go too fast. He laughed. The suggestion that he might go too fast to the Zoo must have amused him. Unless it was the prospect of being cabless. Unless it was simply myself, my own person, whose presence in the cab must have transformed it, so much so that the cabman, seeing me there with my head in the shadows of the roof and my knees against the window, had wondered perhaps if it was really his cab, really a cab. He hastens to look at his horse, and is reassured. But does one ever know oneself why one laughs? His laugh in any case was brief, which suggested I was not the joke. He closed the door and climbed back to his seat. It was not long then before the horse got under way.

Yes, surprising though it may seem, I still had a little money at this time. The small sum my father had left me as a gift, with no restrictions, at his death, I still wonder if it wasn't stolen from me. Then I had none. And yet my life went on, and even in the way I wanted, up to a point. The great disadvantage of this condition, which might be defined as the absolute impossibility of all purchase, is that it compels you to bestir yourself. It is rare, for example, when you are completely penniless, that you can have food brought to you from time to time in your retreat. You are therefore obliged to go out and bestir yourself, at least one day a week. You can hardly have a home address under these circumstances, it's inevitable. It was therefore with a certain delay that I learnt they were looking for me, for an affair concerning me. I forget through what channel. I did not read the newspapers, nor do I remember having spoken with anyone during these years, except perhaps three or four times, on the subject of food. At any rate, I must have had wind of the affair one way or another, otherwise I would never have gone to see the lawyer, Mr Nidder, strange how one fails to forget certain names, and he would never have received me. He verified my identity. That took some time. I showed him the metal initials in the lining of my hat, they proved nothing but they increased the probabilities. Sign, he said. He played with a cylindrical ruler, you could have felled an ox with it. Count, he said. A young woman, perhaps venal,[4] was present at this interview, as a witness no doubt. I stuffed the wad in my pocket. You shouldn't do that, he said. It occurred to me that he should have asked me to count before I signed, it would have been more in order. Where can I reach you, he said, if necessary? At the foot of the stairs I thought of something. Soon after I went back to ask him where this money came from, adding that I had a right to know. He gave me a woman's name that I've forgotten. Perhaps she had dandled me on her knees while I was still in swaddling clothes and there had been some lovey-dovey. Sometimes that suffices. I repeat, in swaddling clothes, for any later it would have been too late, for lovey-dovey. It is thanks to this money then that I still had a little. Very little. Divided by my life to come it was negligible, unless my conjectures were unduly pessimistic. I knocked on the partition beside my hat, right in the cabman's back if my calculations were correct. A cloud of dust rose from the upholstery. I took a stone from my pocket and knocked with the stone, until the cab stopped. I noticed that, unlike most vehicles, which slow down before stopping, the cab stopped dead. I waited. The whole cab shook. The cabman, on his high seat, must have been listening. I saw the horse as with my eyes of flesh. It had not lapsed into the drooping attitude of its briefest halts, it remained alert, its ears pricked up. I looked out of the window, we were again in motion. I banged again on the partition, until the cab stopped again. The cabman got down cursing from his seat. I lowered

4. Able to be bribed.

the window to prevent his opening the door. Faster, faster. He was redder than ever, purple in other words. Anger, or the rushing wind. I told him I was hiring him for the day. He replied that he had a funeral at three o'clock. Ah the dead. I told him I had changed my mind and no longer wished to go to the Zoo. Let us not go to the Zoo, I said. He replied that it made no difference to him where we went, provided it wasn't too far, because of his beast. And they talk to us about the specificity of primitive peoples' speech. I asked him if he knew of an eating-house. I added, You'll eat with me. I prefer being with a regular customer in such places. There was a long table with two benches of exactly the same length on either side. Across the table he spoke to me of his life, of his wife, of his beast, then again of his life, of the atrocious life that was his, chiefly because of his character. He asked me if I realized what it meant to be out of doors in all weathers. I learnt there were still some cabmen who spent their day snug and warm inside their cabs on the rank, waiting for a customer to come and rouse them. Such a thing was possible in the past, but nowadays other methods were necessary, if a man was to have a little laid up at the end of his days. I described my situation to him, what I had lost and what I was looking for. We did our best, both of us, to understand, to explain. He understood that I had lost my room and needed another, but all the rest escaped him. He had taken it into his head, whence nothing could ever dislodge it, that I was looking for a furnished room. He took from his pocket an evening paper of the day before, or perhaps the day before that again, and proceeded to run through the advertisements, five or six of which he underlined with a tiny pencil, the same that hovered over the likely outsiders. He underlined no doubt those he would have underlined if he had been in my shoes, or perhaps those concentrated in the same area, because of his beast. I would only have confused him by saying that I could tolerate no furniture in my room except the bed, and that all the other pieces, and even the very night-table, had to be removed before I would consent to set foot in it. About three o'clock we roused the horse and set off again. The cabman suggested I climb up beside him on the seat, but for some time already I had been dreaming of the inside of the cab and I got back inside. We visited, methodically I hope, one after another, the addresses he had underlined. The short winter's day was drawing to a close. It seems to me sometimes that these are the only days I have ever known, and especially that most charming moment of all, just before night wipes them out. The addresses he had underlined, or rather marked with a cross, as common people do, proved fruitless one by one, and one by one he crossed them out with a diagonal stroke. Later he showed me the paper, advising me to keep it safe so as to be sure not to look again where I had already looked in vain. In spite of the closed windows, the creaking of the cab and the traffic noises, I heard him singing, all alone aloft on his seat. He had preferred me to a funeral, this was a fact which would endure forever. He sang, *She is far from the land where her young hero,* those are the only words I remember. At each stop he got down from his seat and helped me down from mine. I rang at the door he directed me to and sometimes I disappeared inside the house. It was a strange feeling, I remember, a house all about me again, after so long. He waited for me on the sidewalk and helped me climb back into the cab. I was sick and tired of this cabman. He clambered back to his seat and we set off again. At a certain moment there occurred this. He stopped. I shook off my torpor and made ready to get down. But he did not come to open the door and offer me his arm, so that I was obliged to get down by myself. He was lighting the lamps. I love oil lamps, in spite of their having been, with candles, and if I except the stars, the first lights I ever knew. I asked him if I might light the second lamp, since he had already lit the first himself. He gave me his box of matches, I swung open on its hinges the little convex glass, lit and closed at once, so that the wick might burn steady and bright, snug in its little house, sheltered from the wind. I had this joy. We saw nothing, by the light of these lamps, save the vague outlines of the horse, but the others saw them from afar, two yellow glows sailing slowly through the air. When the equipage turned an eye could be seen, red or green as the case might be, a bossy rhomb,[5] as clear and keen as stained glass.

After we had verified the last address the cabman suggested bringing me to a hotel he knew where I would be comfortable. That makes sense, cabman, hotel, it's plausible. With his recommendation I would want for nothing. Every convenience, he said, with a wink. I place this conversation on the sidewalk, in front of the house from which I had just emerged. I remember, beneath the lamp, the flank of the horse, hollow and damp, and on the handle of the door the cabman's hand in its woollen glove. The roof of the cab was on a level with my neck. I suggested we have a drink. The horse had neither eaten nor drunk all day. I mentioned this to the cabman, who replied that his beast would take no food till it was back in the stable. If it ate anything whatever, during work, were it but an apple or a lump of sugar, it would have stomach pains and colics that would root it to the spot and might even kill it. That was why he was compelled to tie its jaws together with a strap whenever for one reason or another he had to let it out of his sight, so that it would not have to suffer from the kind hearts of the passers-by. After a few drinks the cabman invited me to do his wife and him the honour of spending the night in their home. It was not far. Recollecting these emotions, with the celebrated advantage of tranquillity, it seems to me he did nothing else, all that day, but turn about his lodging. They lived above a stable, at the back of a yard. Ideal location, I could have done with it. Having presented me to his wife, extraordinarily full-bottomed, he left us. She was manifestly ill at ease, alone with me. I could understand her, I don't stand on ceremony on these occasions. No reason for this to end or go on. Then let it end, I said I would go down to the stable and sleep there. The cabman protested. I insisted. He drew his wife's attention to the pustule[6] on top of my skull, for I had removed my hat out of civility. He should have that removed, she said. The cabman named a doctor he held in high esteem who had rid him of an induration[7] of the seat. If he wants to sleep in the stable, said his wife, let him sleep in the stable. The cabman took the lamp from the table and preceded me down the stairs, or rather ladder, which descended to the stable, leaving his wife in the dark. He spread a horse blanket on the ground in a corner on the straw and left me a box of matches in case I needed to see clearly in the night. I don't remember what the horse was doing all this time. Stretched out in the dark I heard the noise it made as it drank, a noise like no other, the sudden gallop of the rats and above me the muffled voices of the cabman and his wife as they criticized me. I held the box of matches in my hand, a big box of safety matches. I got up during the night and struck one. Its brief flame enabled me to locate the cab. I was seized, then abandoned, by the desire to set fire to the stable. I found the cab in the dark, opened the door, the rats poured out, I climbed in. As I settled down I noticed that the cab was no longer level, it was inevitable, with the shafts resting on the ground. It was better so, that allowed me to lie well back, with my feet higher than my head on the other seat. Several times during the night I felt the horse looking at me through the win-

5. Round bulge.   7. Uncomfortable hardening of tissue.
6. Pus-filled blister.

dow and the breath of its nostrils. Now that it was unharnessed it must have been puzzled by my presence in the cab. I was cold, having forgotten to take the blanket, but not quite enough to go and get it. Through the window of the cab I saw the window of the stable, more and more clearly. I got out of the cab. It was not so dark now in the stable, I could make out the manger, the rack, the harness hanging, what else, buckets and brushes. I went to the door but couldn't open it. The horse didn't take its eyes off me. Don't horses ever sleep? It seemed to me the cabman should have tied it, to the manger for example. So I was obliged to leave by the window. It wasn't easy. But what is easy? I went out head first, my hands were flat on the ground of the yard while my legs were still thrashing to get clear of the frame. I remember the tufts of grass on which I pulled with both hands, in my effort to extricate myself. I should have taken off my greatcoat and thrown it through the window, but that would have meant thinking of it. No sooner had I left the yard than I thought of something. Weakness. I slipped a banknote in the match-box, went back to the yard and placed the box on the sill of the window through which I had just come. The horse was at the window. But after I had taken a few steps in the street I returned to the yard and took back my banknote. I left the matches, they were not mine. The horse was still at the window. I was sick and tired of this cabhorse. Dawn was just breaking. I did not know where I was. I made towards the rising sun, towards where I thought it should rise, the quicker to come into the light. I would have liked a sea horizon, or a desert one. When I am abroad in the morning I go to meet the sun, and in the evening, when I am abroad, I follow it, till I am down among the dead. I don't know why I told this story. I could just as well have told another. Perhaps some other time I'll be able to tell another. Living souls, you will see how alike they are.

V. S. Naipaul
b. 1932

V. S. Naipaul has been called "the world's writer." Naipaul is a British citizen, and he writes in English; he was educated at Oxford University, and he currently resides in Wiltshire, England. All the elements lend themselves to imagining an almost cozy British writer, happily ensconced within British society. And yet Naipaul's novels, stories, and essays are anything but complacent, rooted in place, or, for that matter, cozy. In major novels from *A House for Mr. Biswas* (1961) to *The Mimic Men* (1967), *In a Free State* (1971), *Guerrillas* (1973), and *The Enigma of Arrival* (1987), Naipaul has addressed the most volatile, violent, and despairing aspects of life in the developing world, from India to Africa to the Caribbean. Naipaul has referred to himself as "rootless," in spite of his present rootedness in the British countryside, and as "content to be a colonial, without a past, without ancestors."

Born in Chaguanas, Trinidad, Vidiadhar Surajprasad Naipaul grew up amid the complexities of a still-colonial environment, as the British government presided over the Caribbean islands of Trinidad and Tobago. His father was a journalist and writer; both his parents were part of the West Indian community in Trinidad, a community that was created as the British brought laborers from the then-British colony of India to work in other colonies in Africa and the Caribbean. Naipaul has always described himself as estranged from India where he has never lived, yet his family carried on many Indian traditions in Trinidad. Trinidad was and is a poor country, still suffering from the effects of its colonial dependence and underdevelopment.

As Naipaul's semiautobiographical novel *A House for Mr. Biswas* depicts it, jobs were almost nonexistent. Naipaul attended Queen's Royal College in Trinidad from 1943–1948; at that point, like many other intellectuals from Caribbean nations, he left for England and Oxford University, from which he received his B.A. in 1953.

Naipaul writes of places that are on the brink of national independence or experiencing its aftermath, places that must try to construct a national identity out of the flimsy leavings of colonial power and superiority. Part of Naipaul's force as a writer derives from his unsparing examination of such societies, whether Caribbean, Indian, African, or even, in his travel memoir *A Turn in the South* (1988), the southern United States. Naipaul is noteworthy for his refusal to exempt the developing world from criticism for the failures he detects in its societies, even though he fully grants the harsh struggles of these nations and regions emerging from colonial rule into independence. In fact, Naipaul has himself been criticized for the harshness of his judgments of the efforts of postcolonial societies, which his essays have excoriated for their corruption, ineptitude, and political oppressiveness. Even the drive for political justice Naipaul often represents as turning into a desperate and futile fanaticism—the tragedy of conquest having devolved into farcical attempts at revolution. He also extends this pessimism to Britain itself, tracing the bitter legacy of empire, and the permanent scars it caused in British culture and politics.

Naipaul can be compared to his great precursor Joseph Conrad, also a novelist of the world, an exile and a rootless man. Conrad was never fully part of British society, and his first language was Polish, yet he remains a consummate British writer. Naipaul is something of a reverse Conrad, in that, also a self-imposed exile, he came back to the heart of England from one of the "ends of the earth" Conrad writes about. Naipaul's prose style is as elegantly British as the most rooted of British native writers; he uses chiseled cadences to construct compelling narratives about the strangest thing of all—the ordinariness of the extraordinary in modern times. He deals with specific themes: the loss of home in postcolonial Britain, the loss of the past that is a consequence of these forced migrations, and the unalterable void that remains behind.

Naipaul's *In a Free State* was awarded the Booker Prize, England's major literary award, in 1971. The novella presents three intertwined stories of displacement and homelessness: the first, *One Out of Many*, describes a Bombay-born domestic servant who finds himself transplanted to Washington, D.C.; the middle story, *Tell Me Who to Kill*, focuses on a frustrated young West Indian man transported to London; and the final story, *In a Free State*, turns the tables, throwing two white Englishmen into the middle of an African state in upheaval. The novella is framed within two passages from Naipaul's journal writing, reprinted here; the tramp in the first selection, who considers himself "a citizen of the world," poses the question, "what's nationality these days?"—a question with real resonance for Naipaul's writing; the closing piece presents a circus as a symbol of postwar Europe, in which the old geopolitical and racial boundaries no longer make sense.

FROM IN A FREE STATE
Prologue, from a Journal
The Tramp at Piraeus

It was only a two-day crossing from Piraeus to Alexandria,[1] but as soon as I saw the dingy little Greek steamer I felt I ought to have made other arrangements. Even from the quay it looked overcrowded, like a refugee ship; and when I went aboard I found there wasn't enough room for everybody.

There was no deck to speak of. The bar, open on two sides to the January wind, was the size of a cupboard. Three made a crowd there, and behind his little counter the little Greek barman, serving bad coffee, was in a bad mood. Many of the chairs in

---

1. Piraeus is the port of Athens, Greece; Alexandria is a major port on Egypt's Mediterranean coast.

the small smoking-room, and a good deal of the floor space, had been seized by overnight passengers from Italy, among them a party of overgrown American school-children in their mid-teens, white and subdued but watchful. The only other public room was the dining-room, and that was being got ready for the first of the lunch sittings by stewards who were as tired and bad-tempered as the barman. Greek civility was something we had left on shore; it belonged perhaps to idleness, unemployment and pastoral despair.

But we on the upper part of the ship were lucky. We had cabins and bunks. The people on the lower deck didn't. They were deck passengers; night and day they required only sleeping room. Below us now they sat or lay in the sun, sheltering from the wind, humped figures in Mediterranean black among the winches and orange-coloured bulkheads.

They were Egyptian Greeks. They were travelling to Egypt, but Egypt was no longer their home. They had been expelled; they were refugees. The invaders had left Egypt; after many humiliations Egypt was free; and these Greeks, the poor ones, who by simple skills had made themselves only just less poor than Egyptians, were the casualties of that freedom.[2] Dingy Greek ships like ours had taken them out of Egypt. Now, briefly, they were going back, with tourists like ourselves, who were neutral, travelling only for the sights; with Lebanese businessmen; a troupe of Spanish night-club dancers; fat Egyptian students returning from Germany.

The tramp, when he appeared on the quay, looked very English; but that might only have been because we had no English people on board. From a distance he didn't look like a tramp. The hat and the rucksack, the lovat tweed jacket, the grey flannels and the boots might have belonged to a romantic wanderer of an earlier generation; in that rucksack there might have been a book of verse, a journal, the beginnings of a novel.

He was slender, of medium height, and he moved from the knees down, with short springy steps, each foot lifted high off the ground. It was a stylish walk, as stylish as his polka-dotted saffron neck-scarf. But when he came nearer we saw that all his clothes were in ruin, that the knot on his scarf was tight and grimy; that he was a tramp. When he came to the foot of the gangway he took off his hat, and we saw that he was an old man, with a tremulous worn face and wet blue eyes.

He looked up and saw us, his audience. He raced up the gangway, not using the hand-ropes. Vanity! He showed his ticket to the surly Greek; and then, not looking about him, asking no questions, he continued to move briskly, as though he knew his way around the ship. He turned into a passageway that led nowhere. With comical abruptness he swung right round on one heel and brought his foot down hard.

"Purser," he said to the deck-boards, as though he had just remembered something. "I'll go and see the purser."

And so he picked his way to his cabin and bunk.

Our sailing was delayed. While their places in the smoking-room were being watched over, some of the American schoolchildren had gone ashore to buy food; we were waiting for them to come back. As soon as they did—no giggles: the girls were

---

2. Since antiquity, there had been a strong Greek presence in Egypt, especially in Alexandria. In the 19th century, however, there was a renewed influx of Greek immigrants, most of whom retained their Greek nationality. This community played major roles in business, finance, shipping, and the professions, and Alexandria became noted for its flourishing Greek cultural life. From the 1930s on, however, with the rise of Egyptian nationalism and the end of many features of colonial rule, Greek numbers declined; following the 1952 revolution, the end of British colonial power in the region, and the later advent of "Arab Socialism," events to which Naipaul here refers, this decline became an exodus; today there are few Greeks in Egypt.

plain, pale and abashed—the Greeks became especially furious and rushed. The Greek language grated like the anchor chain. Water began to separate us from the quay and we could see, not far from where we had been, the great black hulk of the liner *Leonardo da Vinci*, just docked.

The tramp reappeared. He was without his hat and rucksack and looked less nervous. Hands in trouser-pockets already stuffed and bulging, legs apart, he stood on the narrow deck like an experienced sea-traveller exposing himself to the first sea breeze of a real cruise. He was also assessing the passengers; he was looking for company. He ignored people who stared at him; when others, responding to his own stare, turned to look at him he swivelled his head away.

In the end he went and stood beside a tall blond young man. His instinct had guided him well. The man he had chosen was a Yugoslav who, until the day before, had never been out of Yugoslavia. The Yugoslav was willing to listen. He was baffled by the tramp's accent but he smiled encouragingly; and the tramp spoke on.

"I've been to Egypt six or seven times. Gone around the world about a dozen times. Australia, Canada, all those countries. Geologist, or used to be. First went to Canada in 1923. Been there about eight times now. I've been travelling for thirty-eight years. Youth-hostelling, that's how I do it. Not a thing to be despised. New Zealand, have you been there? I went there in 1934. Between you and me, they're a cut above the Australians. But what's nationality these days? I myself, I think of myself as a citizen of the world."

His speech was like this, full of dates, places and numbers, with sometimes a simple opinion drawn from another life. But it was mechanical, without conviction; even the vanity made no impression; those quivering wet eyes remained distant.

The Yugoslav smiled and made interjections. The tramp neither saw nor heard. He couldn't manage a conversation; he wasn't looking for conversation; he didn't even require an audience. It was as though, over the years, he had developed this way of swiftly explaining himself to himself, reducing his life to names and numbers. When the names and numbers had been recited he had no more to say. Then he just stood beside the Yugoslav. Even before we had lost sight of Piraeus and the *Leonardo da Vinci* the tramp had exhausted that relationship. He hadn't wanted company; he wanted only the camouflage and protection of company. The tramp knew he was odd.

At lunch I sat with two Lebanese. They were both overnight passengers from Italy and were quick to explain that it was luggage, not money, that had prevented them travelling by air. They looked a good deal less unhappy with the ship than they said they were. They spoke in a mixture of French, English and Arabic and were exciting and impressing each other with talk of the money other people, mainly Lebanese, were making in this or that unlikely thing.

They were both under forty. One was pink, plump and casually dressed, with a canary pullover; his business in Beirut was, literally, money. The other Lebanese was dark, well-built, with moustached Mediterranean good looks, and wore a three-piece check suit. He made reproduction furniture in Cairo and he said that business was bad since the Europeans had left. Commerce and culture had vanished from Egypt; there was no great demand among the natives for reproduction furniture; and there was growing prejudice against Lebanese like himself. But I couldn't believe in his gloom. While he was talking to us he was winking at one of the Spanish dancers.

At the other end of the room a fat Egyptian student with thick-lensed glasses was being raucous in German and Arabic. The German couple at his table were laughing. Now the Egyptian began to sing an Arabic song.

The man from Beirut said in his American accent, "You should go modern."

"Never," the furniture-maker said. "I will leave Egypt first. I will close my factory. It is a horror, the modern style. It is grotesque, totally grotesque. *Mais le style Louis Seize, ah, voilà l'âme*[3]—" He broke off to applaud the Egyptian and to shout his congratulations in Arabic. Wearily then, but without malice, he said under his breath, "Ah, these natives." He pushed his plate from him, sank in his chair, beat his fingers on the dirty tablecloth. He winked at the dancer and the tips of his moustache flicked upwards.

The steward came to clear away. I was eating, but my plate went as well.

"You were dining, monsieur?' the furniture-maker said. 'You must be *calme*. We must all be *calme*."

Then he raised his eyebrows and rolled his eyes. There was something he wanted us to look at.

It was the tramp, standing in the doorway, surveying the room. Such was the way he held himself that even now, at the first glance, his clothes seemed whole. He came to the cleared table next to ours, sat on a chair and shifted about in it until he was settled. Then he leaned right back, his arms on the rests, like the head of a household at the head of his table, like a cruise-passenger waiting to be served. He sighed and moved his jaws, testing his teeth. His jacket was in an appalling state. The pockets bulged; the flaps were fastened with safety pins.

The furniture-maker said something in Arabic and the man from Beirut laughed. The steward shooed us away and we followed the Spanish girls to the windy little bar for coffee.

Later that afternoon, looking for privacy, I climbed some steep steps to the open railed area above the cabins. The tramp was standing there alone, stained trouser-legs swollen, turn-ups shredded, exposed to the cold wind and the smuts from the smoke-stack. He held what looked like a little prayer-book. He was moving his lips and closing and opening his eyes, like a man praying hard. How fragile that face was, worked over by distress; how frail that neck, below the tight knot of the polka-dotted scarf. The flesh around his eyes seemed especially soft; he looked close to tears. It was strange. He looked for company but needed solitude; he looked for attention, and at the same time wanted not to be noticed.

I didn't disturb him. I feared to be involved with him. Far below, the Greek refugees sat or lay in the sun.

In the smoking-room after dinner the fat young Egyptian shouted himself hoarse, doing his cabaret act. People who understood what he was saying laughed all the time. Even the furniture-maker, forgetting his gloom about the natives, shouted and clapped with the rest. The American schoolchildren lay in their own promiscuous seasick heap and looked on, like people helplessly besieged; when they spoke among themselves it was in whispers.

The non-American part of the room was predominantly Arab and German and had its own cohesion. The Egyptian was our entertainer, and there was a tall German girl we could think of as our hostess. She offered us chocolate and had a word for

---

3. "But in Louis XVI style—now there is the soul" (Fr.).

each of us. To me she said: "You are reading a very good English book. These Penguin books are very good English books." She might have been travelling out to join an Arab husband; I wasn't sure.

I was sitting with my back to the door and didn't see when the tramp came in. But suddenly he was there before me, sitting on a chair that someone had just left. The chair was not far from the German girl's, but it stood in no intimate relationship to that chair or any other group of chairs. The tramp sat squarely on it, straight up against the back. He faced no one directly, so that in that small room he didn't become part of the crowd but appeared instead to occupy the centre of a small stage within it.

He sat with his old man's legs wide apart, his weighted jacket sagging over his bulging trouser-pockets. He had come with things to read, a magazine, the little book which I had thought was a prayer-book. I saw now that it was an old pocket diary with many loose leaves. He folded the magazine in four, hid it under his thigh, and began to read the pocket diary. He laughed, and looked up to see whether he was being noticed. He turned a page, read and laughed again, more loudly. He leaned towards the German girl and said to her over his shoulder, "I say, do you read Spanish?"

She said, carefully, "No."

"These Spanish jokes are awfully funny."

But though he read a few more, he didn't laugh again.

The Egyptian continued to clown; that racket went on. Soon the German girl was offering chocolate once more. "*Bitte?*" [would you like some] Her voice was soft.

The tramp was unfolding his magazine. He stopped and looked at the chocolate. But there was none for him. He unfolded his magazine. Then, unexpectedly, he began to destroy it. With nervous jigging hands he tore at a page, once, twice. He turned some pages, began to tear again; turned back, tore. Even with the raucousness around the Egyptian the sound of tearing paper couldn't be ignored. Was he tearing out pictures—sport, women, advertisements—that offended him? Was he hoarding toilet paper for Egypt?

The Egyptian fell silent and looked. The American schoolchildren looked. Now, too late after the frenzy, and in what was almost silence, the tramp made a show of reason. He opened the tattered magazine wide out, turned it around angrily, as though the right side up hadn't been easy to find, and at last pretended to read. He moved his lips; he frowned; he tore and tore. Strips and shreds of paper littered the floor around his chair. He folded the loose remains of the magazine, stuffed it into his jacket pocket, pinned the flaps down, and went out of the room, looking like a man who had been made very angry.

"I will kill him," the furniture-maker said at breakfast the next morning.

He was in his three-piece suit but he was unshaven and the dark rings below his eyes were like bruises. The man from Beirut, too, looked tired and crumpled. They hadn't had a good night. The third bunk in their cabin was occupied by an Austrian boy, a passenger from Italy, with whom they were on good terms. They had seen the rucksack and the hat on the fourth bunk; but it wasn't until it was quite late, all three in their bunks, that they had discovered that the tramp was to be the fourth among them.

"It was pretty bad," the man from Beirut said. He felt for delicate words and added, "The old guy's like a child."

"Child! If the English pig comes in now"—the furniture-maker raised his arm and pointed at the door—"I will *kill* him. *Now.*"

He was pleased with the gesture and the words; he repeated them, for the room. The Egyptian student, hoarse and hungover after the evening's performance, said something in Arabic. It was obviously witty, but the furniture-maker didn't smile. He beat his fingers on the table, stared at the door and breathed loudly through his nose.

No one was in a good mood. The drumming and the throbbing and bucking of the ship had played havoc with stomachs and nerves; the cold wind outside irritated as much as it refreshed; and in the dining-room the air was stale, with a smell as of hot rubber. There was no crowd, but the stewards, looking unslept and unwashed, even their hair not well combed, were as rushed as before.

The Egyptian shrieked.

The tramp had come in, benign and rested and ready for his coffee and rolls. He had no doubts about his welcome now. He came without hesitation or great speed to the table next to ours, settled himself in his chair and began to test his teeth. He was quickly served. He chewed and drank with complete relish.

The Egyptian shrieked again.

The furniture-maker said to him, "I will send him to your room tonight."

The tramp didn't see or hear. He was only eating and drinking. Below the tight knot of his scarf his Adam's apple was very busy. He drank noisily, sighing afterwards; he chewed with rabbit-like swiftness, anxious to be free for the next mouthful; and between mouthfuls he hugged himself, rubbing his arms and elbows against his sides, in pure pleasure at food.

The fascination of the furniture-maker turned to rage. Rising, but still looking at the tramp, he called, "Hans!"

The Austrian boy, who was at the table with the Egyptian, got up. He was about sixteen or seventeen, square and chunky, enormously well-developed, with a broad smiling face. The man from Beirut also got up, and all three went outside.

The tramp, oblivious of this, and of what was being prepared for him, continued to eat and drink until, with a sigh which was like a sigh of fatigue, he was finished.

It was to be like a tiger-hunt, where bait is laid out and the hunter and spectators watch from the security of a platform. The bait here was the tramp's own rucksack. They placed that on the deck outside the cabin door, and watched it. The furniture-maker still pretended to be too angry to talk. But Hans smiled and explained the rules of the game as often as he was asked.

The tramp, though, didn't immediately play. After breakfast he disappeared. It was cold on the deck, even in the sunshine, and sometimes the spray came right up. People who had come out to watch didn't stay, and even the furniture-maker and the man from Beirut went from time to time to rest in the smoking-room among the Germans and Arabs and the Spanish girls. They were given chairs; there was sympathy for their anger and exhaustion. Hans remained at his post. When the cold wind made him go inside the cabin he watched through the open door, sitting on one of the lower bunks and smiling up at people who passed.

Then the news came that the tramp had reappeared and had been caught according to the rules of the game. Some of the American schoolchildren were already on deck, studying the sea. So were the Spanish girls and the German girl. Hans blocked the cabin door. I could see the tramp holding the strap of his rucksack; I could hear him complaining in English through the French and Arabic shouts of the furniture-maker, who was raising his arms and pointing with his right hand, the skirts of his jacket dancing.

In the dining-room the furniture-maker's anger had seemed only theatrical, an aspect of his Mediterranean appearance, the moustache, the wavy hair. But now, in the open, with an expectant audience and a victim so nearly passive, he was working himself into a frenzy.

"Pig! Pig!"

"It's not true," the tramp said, appealing to people who had only come to watch.

"Pig!"

The grotesque moment came. The furniture-maker, so strongly built, so elegant in his square-shouldered jacket, lunged with his left hand at the old man's head. The tramp swivelled his head, the way he did when he refused to acknowledge a stare. And he began to cry. The furniture-maker's hand went wide and he stumbled forward against the rails into a spatter of spray. Putting his hands to his breast, feeling for pen and wallet and other things, he cried out, like a man aggrieved and desperate, "Hans! Hans!"

The tramp stooped; he stopped crying; his blue eyes popped. Hans had seized him by the polka-dotted scarf, twisting it, jerking it down. Kicking the rucksack hard, Hans at the same time flung the tramp forward by the knotted scarf. The tramp stumbled over Hans's kicking foot. The strain went out of Hans's smiling face and all that was left was the smile. The tramp could have recovered from his throw and stumble. But he preferred to fall and then to sit up. He was still holding the strap of his rucksack. He was crying again.

"It's not true. These remarks they've been making, it's not true."

The young Americans were looking over the rails.

"Hans!" the furniture-maker called.

The tramp stopped crying.

"Ha-ans!"

The tramp didn't look round. He got up with his rucksack and ran.

The story was that he had locked himself in one of the lavatories. But he reappeared among us, twice.

About an hour later he came into the smoking-room, without his rucksack, with no sign of distress on his face. He was already restored. He came in, in his abrupt way, not looking to right or left. Just a few steps brought him right into the small room and almost up against the legs of the furniture-maker, who was stretched out in an upholstered chair, exhausted, one hand over his half-closed eyes. After surprise, anger and contempt filled the tramp's eyes. He started to swivel his head away.

"Hans!" the furniture-maker called, recovering from his astonishment, drawing back his legs, leaning forward. "Ha-ans!"

Swivelling his head, the tramp saw Hans rising with some playing cards in his hands. Terror came to the tramp's eyes. The swivelling motion of his head spread to the rest of his body. He swung round on one heel, brought the other foot down hard, and bolted. Entry, advance, bandy-legged swivel and retreat had formed one unbroken movement.

"Hans!"

It wasn't a call to action. The furniture-maker was only underlining the joke. Hans, understanding, laughed and went back to his cards.

The tramp missed his lunch. He should have gone down immediately, to the first sitting, which had begun. Instead, he went into hiding, no doubt in one of the lavatories, and came out again only in time for the last sitting. It was the sitting the Lebanese and Hans had chosen. The tramp saw from the doorway.

"Ha-ans!"

But the tramp was already swivelling.

Later he was to be seen with his rucksack, but without his hat, on the lower deck, among the refugees. Without him, and then without reference to him, the joke continued, in the bar, on the narrow deck, in the smoking-room. "Hans! Ha-ans!" Towards the end Hans didn't laugh or look up; when he heard his name he completed the joke by giving a whistle. The joke lived; but by nightfall the tramp was forgotten.

At dinner the Lebanese spoke again in their disinterested way about money. The man from Beirut said that because of certain special circumstances in the Middle East that year, there was a fortune to be made from the well-judged exporting of Egyptian shoes; but not many people knew. The furniture-maker said the fact had been known to him for months. They postulated an investment, vied with each other in displaying knowledge of hidden, local costs, and calmly considered the staggering profits. But they weren't really exciting one another any longer. The game was a game; each had taken the measure of the other. And they were both tired.

Something of the lassitude of the American schoolchildren had come over the other passengers on this last evening. The Americans themselves were beginning to thaw out. In the smoking-room, where the lights seemed dimmer, their voices were raised in friendly boy-girl squabbles; they did a lot more coming and going; especially active was a tall girl in a type of ballet-dancer's costume, all black from neck to wrist to ankle. The German girl, our hostess of the previous evening, looked quite ill. The Spanish girls were flirting with nobody. The Egyptian, whose hangover had been compounded by seasickness, was playing bridge. Gamely from time to time he croaked out a witticism or a line of song, but he got smiles rather than laughs. The furniture-maker and Hans were also playing cards. When a good card or a disappointing one was played the furniture-maker said in soft exclamation, expecting no response, "Hans, Hans." It was all that remained of the day's joke.

The man from Beirut came in and watched. He stood beside Hans. Then he stood beside the furniture-maker and whispered to him in English, their secret language. "The guy's locked himself in the cabin."

Hans understood. He looked at the furniture-maker. But the furniture-maker was weary. He played his hand, then went out with the man from Beirut.

When he came back he said to Hans, "He says that he will set fire to the cabin if we try to enter. He says that he has a quantity of paper and a quantity of matches. I believe that he will do it."

"What do we do?" the man from Beirut asked.

"We will sleep here. Or in the dining-room."

"But those Greek stewards sleep in the dining-room. I saw them this morning."

"That proves that it is possible," the furniture-maker said.

Later, the evening over, I stopped outside the tramp's cabin. At first I heard nothing. Then I heard paper being crumpled: the tramp's warning. I wonder how long he stayed awake that night, listening for footsteps, waiting for the assault on the door and the entry of Hans.

In the morning he was back on the lower deck, among the refugees. He had his hat again; he had recovered it from the cabin.

Alexandria was a long shining line on the horizon: sand and the silver of oil-storage tanks. The sky clouded over; the green sea grew choppier. We entered the breakwater in cold rain and stormlight.

Long before the immigration officials came on board we queued to meet them. Germans detached themselves from Arabs, Hans from the Lebanese, the Lebanese from the Spanish girls. Now, as throughout the journey since his meeting with the tramp, the tall blond Yugoslav was a solitary. From the lower deck the refugees came up with their boxes and bundles, so that at last they were more than their emblematic black wrappings. They had the slack bodies and bad skins of people who ate too many carbohydrates. Their blotched faces were immobile, distant, but full of a fierce, foolish cunning. They were watching. As soon as the officials came aboard the refugees began to push and fight their way towards them. It was a factitious frenzy, the deference of the persecuted to authority.

The tramp came up with his hat and rucksack. There was no nervousness in his movements but his eyes were quick with fear. He took his place in the queue and pretended to frown at its length. He moved his feet up and down, now like a man made impatient by officials, now like someone only keeping out the cold. But he was of less interest than he thought. Hans, mountainous with his own rucksack, saw him and then didn't see him. The Lebanese, shaved and rested after their night in the dining-room, didn't see him. That passion was over.

Epilogue, from a Journal
The Circus at Luxor

I was going to Egypt, this time by air, and I broke my journey at Milan. I did so for business reasons. But it was Christmas week, not a time for business, and I had to stay in Milan over the holidays. The weather was bad, the hotel empty and desolate.

Returning through the rain to the hotel one evening, after a restaurant dinner, I saw two Chinese men in dark-blue suits come out of the hotel dining-room. Fellow Asiatics, the three of us, I thought, wanderers in industrial Europe. But they didn't glance at me. They had companions: three more Chinese came out of the dining-room, two young men in suits, a fresh-complexioned young woman in a flowered tunic and slacks. Then five more Chinese came out, healthy young men and women; then about a dozen. Then I couldn't count. Chinese poured out of the dining-room and swirled about the spacious carpeted lobby before moving in a slow, softly chattering mass up the steps.

There must have been about a hundred Chinese. It was minutes before the lobby emptied. The waiters, serving-napkins in hand, stood in the door of the dining-room and watched, like people able at last to acknowledge an astonishment. Two more Chinese came out of the dining-room; they were the last. They were both short, elderly men, wrinkled and stringy, with glasses. One of them held a fat wallet in his small hand, but awkwardly, as though the responsibility made him nervous. The waiters straightened up. Not attempting style, puzzling over the Italian notes, the old Chinese with the wallet tipped, thanked and shook hands with each waiter. Then both the Chinese bowed and got into the lift. And the hotel lobby was desolate again.

"They are the circus," the dark-suited desk-clerk said. He was as awed as the waiters. "*Vengono dalla Cina rossa.* They come from Red China."

I left Milan in snow. In Cairo, in the derelict cul-de-sac behind my hotel, children in dingy jibbahs,[1] feeble from their day-long Ramadan fasting, played football in the white, warm dust.[2] In cafés, shabbier than I remembered, Greek and Lebanese busi-

---

1. A long outer garment, open at the front, with wide sleeves.

2. During the month of Ramadan in the Islamic calendar, Muslims fast from sunrise to sunset.

nessmen in suits read the local French and English newspapers and talked with sullen excitement about the deals that might be made in Rhodesian tobacco, now that it was outlawed. The Museum was still haunted by Egyptian guides possessing only native knowledge. And on the other bank of the Nile there was a new Hilton hotel.

But Egypt still had her revolution. Street signs were now in Arabic alone; people in tobacco kiosks reacted sharply, as to an insult, when they were asked for *Egyptian* cigarettes; and in the railway station, when I went to get the train south, there was a reminder of the wars that had come with the revolution. Sunburnt soldiers, back from duty in Sinai,[3] crouched and sprawled on the floor of the waiting-room. These men with shrunken faces were the guardians of the land and the revolution; but to Egyptians they were only common soldiers, peasants, objects of a disregard that was older and more rooted than the revolution.

All day the peasant land rolled past the windows of the train: the muddy river, the green fields, the desert, the black mud, the *shadouf*,[4] the choked and crumbling flat-roofed towns the colour of dust: the Egypt of the school geography book. The sun set in a smoky sky; the land felt old. It was dark when I left the train at Luxor. Later that evening I went to the temple of Karnak.[5] It was a good way of seeing it for the first time, in the darkness, separate from the distress of Egypt: those extravagant columns, ancient in ancient times, the work of men of this Nile Valley.

There was no coin in Egypt that year, only paper money. All foreign currencies went far; and Luxor,[6] in recent imperial days a winter resort of some style, was accommodating itself to simpler tourists. At the Old Winter Palace Hotel, where fat Negro servants in long white gowns stood about in the corridors, they told me they were giving me the room they used to give the Aga Khan.[7] It was an enormous room, overfurnished in a pleasing old-fashioned way. It had a balcony and a view of the Nile and low desert hills on the other bank.

In those hill were the tombs.[8] Not all were of kings and not all were solemn. The ancient artist, recording the life of a lesser personage, sometimes recorded with a freer hand the pleasures of that life: the pleasures of the river, full of fish and birds, the pleasures of food and drink. The land had been studied, everything in it categorized, exalted into design. It was the special vision of men who knew no other land and saw what they had as rich and complete. The muddy Nile was only water: in the paintings, a blue-green chevron: recognizable, but remote, a river in fairyland.

It could be hot in the tombs. The guide, who was also sometimes the watchman, crouched and chattered in Arabic, earning his paper piastres,[9] pointing out every symbol of the goddess Hathor, rubbing a grimy finger on the paintings he was meant to protect. Outside, after the darkness and the bright visions of the past, there was only rubbled white sand; the sunlight stunned; and sometimes there were beggar boys in jibbahs.

---

3. The Sinai Peninsula, stretching from the Suez Canal to the Israeli border, was occupied by Israel during the 1967 war between Israel and several Arab countries including Egypt; it was restored to Egypt in 1982 following almost a decade of negotiations.
4. A mechanism for raising irrigation water.
5. Luxor is a city in southern Egypt; north of it are ruins of the temple-complex of Karnak, which mostly dates back to the New Kingdom (1550–1069 B.C.).
6. A favorite winter resort for European tourists when the

Ottoman province and later Kingdom of Egypt was a British "protectorate" and British troops were stationed in the country. Following the coup d'etat in 1952, the subsequent declaration of a republic and British evacuation, their numbers dropped.
7. The *Imam*, or spiritual leader, of a sect within Islam.
8. Across from Luxor, on the western bank of the Nile, are the mountains that enclose the Valley of the Kings, where many Egyptian pharoahs were buried.
9. There are 100 piastres in one Egyptian pound.

To me these boys, springing up expectantly out of rock and sand when men approached, were like a type of sand animal. But my driver knew some of them by name; when he shooed them away it was with a languid gesture which also contained a wave. He was a young man, the driver, of the desert himself, and once no doubt he had been a boy in a jibbah. But he had grown up differently. He wore trousers and shirt and was vain of his good looks. He was reliable and correct, without the frenzy of the desert guide. Somehow in the desert he had learned boredom. His thoughts were of Cairo and a real job. He was bored with the antiquities, the tourists and the tourist routine.

I was spending the whole of that day in the desert, and now it was time for lunch. I had a Winter Palace lunchbox, and I had seen somewhere in the desert the new government rest-house where tourists could sit at tables and eat their sandwiches and buy coffee. I thought the driver was taking me there. But we went by unfamiliar ways to a little oasis with palm trees and a large, dried-up timber hut. There were no cars, no minibuses, no tourists, only anxious Egyptian serving-people in rough clothes. I didn't want to stay. The driver seemed about to argue, but then he was only bored. He drove to the new rest-house, set me down and said he would come back for me later.

The rest-house was crowded. Sunglassed tourists, exploring their cardboard lunch-boxes, chattered in various European languages. I sat on the terrace at a table with two young Germans. A brisk middle-aged Egyptian in Arab dress moved among the tables and served coffee. He had a camel-whip at his waist, and I saw, but only slowly, that for some way around the rest-house the hummocked sand was alive with little desert children. The desert was clean, the air was clean; these children were very dirty.

The rest-house was out of bounds to them. When they came close, tempted by the offer of a sandwich or an apple, the man with the camel-whip gave a camel-frightening shout. Sometimes he ran out among them, beating the sand with his whip, and they skittered away, thin little sand-smoothed legs frantic below swinging jibbahs. There was no rebuke for the tourists who had offered the food; this was an Egyptian game with Egyptian rules.

It was hardly a disturbance. The young Germans at my table paid no attention. The English students inside the rest-house, behind glass, were talking competitively about Carter and Lord Carnarvon.[1] But the middle-aged Italian group on the terrace, as they understood the rules of the game, became playful. They threw apples and made the children run far. Experimentally they broke up sandwiches and threw the pieces out onto the sand; and they got the children to come up quite close. Soon it was all action around the Italians; and the man with the camel-whip, like a man understanding what was required of him, energetically patrolled that end of the terrace, shouting, beating the sand, earning his paper piastres.

A tall Italian in a cerise jersey stood up and took out his camera. He laid out food just below the terrace and the children came running. But this time, as though it had to be real for the camera, the camel-whip fell not on sand but on their backs, with louder, quicker camel-shouts. And still, among the tourists in the rest-house and among the Egyptian drivers standing about their cars and minibuses, there was no disturbance. Only the man with the whip and the chil-

---

1. Funded by Lord Carnarvon, the British Egyptologist Howard Carter discovered the tomb of Tutankhamen in the Valley of the Kings at Luxor in 1922.

dren scrabbling in the sand were frantic. The Italians were cool. The man in the cerise jersey was opening another packet of sandwiches. A shorter, older man in a white suit had stood up and was adjusting his camera. More food was thrown out; the camel-whip continued to fall; the shouts of the man with the whip turned to resonant grunts.

Still the Germans at my table didn't notice; the students inside were still talking. I saw that my hand was trembling. I put down the sandwich I was eating on the metal table; it was my last decision. Lucidity, and anxiety, came to me only when I was almost on the man with the camel-whip. I was shouting. I took the whip away, threw it on the sand. He was astonished, relieved. I said, "I will report this to Cairo." He was frightened; he began to plead in Arabic. The children were puzzled; they ran off a little way and stood up to watch. The two Italians, fingering cameras, looked quite calm behind their sunglasses. The women in the party leaned back in their chairs to consider me.

I felt exposed, futile, and wanted only to be back at my table. When I got back I took up my sandwich. It had happened quickly; there had been no disturbance. The Germans stared at me. But I was indifferent to them now as I was indifferent to the Italian in the cerise jersey. The Italian women had stood up, the group was leaving; and he was ostentatiously shaking out lunch-boxes and sandwich wrappers onto the sand.

The children remained where they were. The man from whom I had taken the whip came to give me coffee and to plead again in Arabic and English. The coffee was free; it was his gift to me. But even while he was talking the children had begun to come closer. Soon they would be back, raking the sand for what they had seen the Italian throw out.

I didn't want to see that. The driver was waiting, leaning against the car door, his bare arms crossed. He had seen all that had happened. From him, an emancipated young man of the desert in belted trousers and sports shirt, with his thoughts of Cairo, I was expecting some gesture, some sign of approval. He smiled at me with the corners of his wide mouth, with his narrow eyes. He crushed his cigarette in the sand and slowly breathed out smoke through his lips; he sighed. But that was his way of smoking. I couldn't tell what he thought. He was as correct as before, he looked as bored.

Everywhere I went that afternoon I saw the pea-green Volkswagen minibus of the Italian group. Everywhere I saw the cerise jersey. I learned to recognize the plump, squiffy, short-stepped walk that went with it, the dark glasses, the receding hairline, the little stiff swing of the arms. At the ferry I thought I had managed to escape; but the minibus arrived, the Italians got out. I thought we would separate on the Luxor bank. But they too were staying at the Winter Palace. The cerise jersey bobbed confidently through bowing Egyptian servants in the lobby, the bar, the grand dining-room with fresh flowers and intricately folded napkins. In Egypt that year there was only paper money.

I stayed for a day or two on the Luxor bank. Dutifully, I saw Karnak by moonlight. When I went back to the desert I was anxious to avoid the rest-house. The driver understood. Without any show of triumph he took me when the time came to the timber hut among the palm trees. There were doing more business that day. There were about four or five parked minibuses. Inside, the hut was dark, cool and uncluttered. A number of tables had been joined together; and at this central dining-board there were about forty or fifty Chinese, men and women, chattering softly. They were part of the circus I had seen in Milan.

The two elderly Chinese sat together at one end of the long table, next to a small, finely made lady who looked just a little too old to be an acrobat. I had missed her in the crowd in Milan. Again, when the time came to pay, the man with the fat wallet used his hands awkwardly. The lady spoke to the Egyptian waiter. He called the other waiters and they all formed a line. For each waiter the lady had a hand-shake and gifts, money, something in an envelope, a medal. The ragged waiters stood stiffly, with serious averted faces, like soldiers being decorated. Then all the Chinese rose and, chattering, laughing softly, shuffled out of the echoing hut with their relaxed, slightly splayed gait. They didn't look at me; they appeared scarcely to notice the hut. They were as cool and well-dressed in the desert, the men in suits, the girls in slacks, as they had been in the rain of Milan. So self-contained, so handsome and healthy, so silently content with one another: it was hard to think of them as sightseers.

The waiter, his face still tense with pleasure, showed the medal on his dirty striped jibbah. It had been turned out from a mould that had lost its sharpness; but the ill-defined face was no doubt Chinese and no doubt that of the leader. In the envelope were pretty coloured postcards of Chinese peonies.

Peonies, China! So many empires had come here. Not far from where we were was the colossus on whose shin the Emperor Hadrian had caused to be carved verses in praise of himself, to commemorate his visit.[2] On the other bank, not far from the Winter Palace, was a stone with a rougher Roman inscription marking the southern limit of the Empire, defining an area of retreat.[3] Now another, more remote empire was announcing itself. A medal, a postcard; and all that was asked in return was anger and a sense of injustice.

Perhaps that had been the only pure time, at the beginning, when the ancient artist, knowing no other land, had learned to look at his own and had seen it as complete. But it was hard, travelling back to Cairo, looking with my stranger's eye at the fields and the people who worked in them, the dusty towns, the agitated peasant crowds at railway stations, it was hard to believe that there had been such innocence. Perhaps that vision of the land, in which the Nile was only water, a blue-green chevron, had always been a fabrication, a cause for yearning, something for the tomb.

The air-conditioning in the coach didn't work well; but that might have been because the two Negro attendants, still with the habits of the village, preferred to sit before the open doors to chat. Sand and dust blew in all day; it was hot until the sun set and everything went black against the red sky. In the dimly lit waiting-room of Cairo station there were more sprawled soldiers from Sinai, peasants in bulky woollen uniforms going back on leave to their villages. Seventeen months later these men, or men like them, were to know total defeat in the desert; and news pho-tographs taken from helicopters flying down low were to show them lost, trying to walk back home, casting long shadows on the sand.

August 1969–October 1970

2. The Roman emperor Hadrian (reigned 117–138 A.D.) was noted for his interest in Egypt, traveling extensively there.
3. Egypt became a personal estate of the Roman emperor following the defeat of Cleopatra at the hands of Roman forces in 30 B.C.; the border with Nubia was set some 50 miles south of the first cataract of the Nile (some distance south of Luxor).

Hanif Kureishi
b. 1954

Hanif Kureishi embodies the complexities of postwar British society. Born in Kent, England, and raised in a middle-class London suburb by a British mother and a father who worked as a journalist in both England and his native Pakistan, Kureishi is part of what is called "black Britain": the second generation, British-born children of returning colonials from the far-flung British empire in India and Pakistan, in Africa and the Caribbean. His electrifying screenplays, stage plays, and novels have delineated the melange of cultures, races, and histories that form the multicultural society of today's England.

Kureishi's contemporaneity is demonstrated by the fact that his most celebrated writing has been screenwriting; while major British writers from Graham Greene to Dylan Thomas have written for films, and many others have dabbled in them, Kureishi may be the first writer whose screenplays have been so compelling that he achieved his primary fame through the medium of cinema. Kureishi's vivid writing and his narrative skill, not to say the provocative subject matter of his screenplays, succeeded in drawing as much attention to the written dimension of the films *My Beautiful Laundrette* (1986) and *Sammy and Rosie Get Laid* (1988) as to their visual direction by Stephen Frears. Taken on their own as screenplays, separate from the films eventually made from them, the works resonate with the vibrancy of Kureishi's dramatic and novelistic writing. Furthermore, the screenplays and the films exemplify an important and innovative direction in contemporary British fiction.

Throughout his childhood, Kureishi was subjected to the racist taunts and even beatings that had become commonplace as nationalistic politicians such as Enoch Powell stirred up racial enmity among working-class and middle-class Britons. "Paki-bashing" became a sport of working-class white youths, especially as many cities developed large Pakistani communities. The Pakistanis drew together with Asian and Afro-Caribbean immigrants under the self-proclaimed banner of "Black Britain," a cultural solidarity movement that opposed all types of discrimination. Kureishi's writing is hardly demagogic, though, nor is it purely political in the sense of arguing in a systematic way against discrimination. It is instead antic and comic, filled with picaresque elements and absurdist humor drawn from everything from the Beatles to Monty Python and Beyond the Fringe. He models his narratives on satirical forebears—from Laurence Sterne in the eighteenth century to Joe Orton in the twentieth—developing a special mode of comedy predicated on self-deprecating yet also politically radical subversions.

Kureishi's works generally depict a semiautobiographical figure who, with a combination of naivete and passion, attempts to negotiate the twists and turns of urban existence, racial and class prejudice, sexual ambiguity, and the sheer comedy of manners that is Britain today. Somewhat like V.S. Naipaul—although not with his pessimism or misanthropy—Kureishi refuses to make simplistic analyses that would have the British always in the wrong, their former colonial subjects always right. Kureishi sees the shades of gray, rather than merely blacks and whites, and makes pointed yet hilarious comedy of the wild and inevitable conflicts of a society now filled with immigrants.

My Beautiful Laundrette is a case in point. Its story revolves around Omar, whose relatives wish to draw him firmly into the Pakistani community, safe from the insecurities of British society. What Omar wants, though, is to be a part of mainstream British society, to become an entrepreneur, an independent adult, and a man who chooses his soul mate from outside the tradition of arranged marriages still prevalent in Pakistani Britain. Omar achieves a certain reconciliation with British society on his own terms, when he and his boyhood friend Johnny establish a successful neighborhood laundromat, or "laundrette" in British parlance, and simul-

Omar (Gordon Warnecke) and Johnny (Daniel Day-Lewis) in a publicity still from *My Beautiful Laundrette*.

taneously discover their love for each other. Their interracial and same-sex romance cuts across many of the divisions of British society, as they struggle to make their way out of deadening social and familial constraints. Kureishi embodies this quest in a lively and many-layered language whose idioms are drawn from many worlds—from popular music and slang to film and television to great literature: a stew made up of all the disparate elements of a culture. Kureishi's tribute to the creative energies of the problematic society he calls home is symbolized in the title of his most recent novel, *The Black Album* (1995). Naming his book after The Beatles' *White Album*, the most mysterious and evocative of their recordings, Kureishi pays homage to a Britain he himself helps to name Black.

My Beautiful Laundrette[1]

1. EXT[ERIOR] OUTSIDE A LARGE DETACHED HOUSE. DAY.

Cherry and Salim get out of their car. Behind them, the four Jamaicans get out of their car.

Cherry and Salim walk towards the house. It is a large falling-down place, in South London. It's quiet at the moment—early morning—but the ground floor windows are boarded up.

On the boarded-up windows is painted: "Your greed will be the death of us all" and "We will defeat the running wogs of capitalism"[2] and "Opium is the opium of the unemployed".[3]

Cherry and Salim look up at the house. The four Jamaicans stand behind them, at a respectful distance.

---

1. Filmed by Stephen Frears, starring Daniel Day-Lewis as Johnny and Gordon Warnecke as Omar; the film was first shown at the Edinburgh and London Film Festivals in fall 1985.
2. Variant on a revolutionary slogan, "the running dogs of

capitalism"; *wog* is insulting British slang for a nonwhite foreigner.
3. Echoes Marx's dictum that religion is the opium of the masses.

CHERRY I don't even remember buying this house at the auction. What are we going to do with it?

SALIM Tomorrow we start to renovate it.

CHERRY How many people are living here?

SALIM There are no people living here. There are only squatters.[4] And they're going to be renovated—right now.

(*And Salim pushes Cherry forward, giving her the key. Cherry goes to the front door of the house. Salim, with two Jamaicans goes round the side of the house. Two Jamaicans go round the other side.*)

2. INT[ERIOR] A ROOM IN THE SQUAT. DAY.

Genghis and Johnny are living in a room in the squat. It is freezing cold, with broken windows. Genghis is asleep on a mattress, wrapped up. He has the flu. Johnny is lying frozen in a deck chair, with blankets over him. He has just woken up.

3. EXT. OUTSIDE THE HOUSE. DAY.

Cherry tries to unlock the front door of the place. But the door has been barred. She looks in through the letter box. A barricade has been erected in the hall.

4. EXT. THE SIDE OF THE HOUSE. DAY.

The Jamaicans break into the house through side windows. They climb in. Salim also climbs into the house.

5. INT. INSIDE THE HOUSE. DAY.

The Jamaicans and Salim are in the house now.

The Jamaicans are kicking open the doors of the squatted rooms.

The squatters are unprepared, asleep or half-awake, in disarray.

The Jamaicans are going from room to room, yelling for everyone to leave now or get thrown out of the windows with their belongings.

Some squatters complain but they are shoved out of their rooms into the hall; or down the stairs. Salim is eager about all of this.

6. INT. GENGHIS AND JOHNNY'S ROOM. DAY.

Johnny looks up the corridor to see what's happening. He goes back into the room quickly and starts stuffing his things into a black plastic bag. He is shaking Genghis at the same time.

GENGHIS I'm ill.

JOHNNY We're moving house.

GENGHIS No, we've got to fight.

JOHNNY Too early in the morning.

(*He rips the blankets off Genghis, who lies there fully dressed, coughing and shivering. A Jamaican bursts into the room.*)

All right, all right.

---

4. People living in unoccupied premises without authorization (hence, a *squat*).

(The Jamaican watches a moment as Genghis, too weak to resist, but cursing violently, takes the clothes Johnny shoves at him and follows Johnny to the window. Johnny opens the broken window.)

7. EXT. OUTSIDE THE HOUSE. DAY.

A wide shot of the house.

The Squatters are leaving through windows and the re-opened front door and gathering in the front garden, arranging their wretched belongings. Some of them are junkies. They look dishevelled and disheartened.

From an upper room in the house come crashing a guitar, a TV and some records. This is followed by the enquiring head of a Jamaican, looking to see these have hit no one.

One Squatter, in the front garden, is resisting and a Jamaican is holding him. The Squatter screams at Cherry: you pig, you scum, you filthy rich shit, etc.

As Salim goes to join Cherry, she goes to the screaming Squatter and gives him a hard backhander across the face.

8. EXT. THE BACK OF THE HOUSE. DAY.

Johnny and Genghis stumble down through the back garden of the house and over the wall at the end, Johnny pulling and helping the exhausted Genghis.

At no time do they see Cherry or Salim.

9. INT. BATHROOM. DAY.

Omar has been soaking Papa's clothes in the bath. He pulls them dripping from the bath and puts them in an old steel bucket, wringing them out. He picks up the bucket.

10. EXT. BALCONY. DAY.

Omar is hanging out Papa's dripping pyjamas on the washing line on the balcony, pulling them out of the bucket.

The balcony overlooks several busy railway lines, commuter routes into Charing Cross and London Bridge,[5] from the suburbs.

Omar turns and looks through the glass of the balcony door into the main room of the flat. Papa is lying in bed. He pours himself some vodka. Water from the pyjamas drips down Omar's trousers and into his shoes.

When he turns away, a train, huge, close, fast, crashes towards the camera and bangs and rattles its way past, a few feet from the exposed overhanging balcony. Omar is unperturbed.

11. INT. PAPA'S ROOM. DAY.

The flat Omar and his father, Papa, share in South London. It's a small, damp and dirty place which hasn't been decorated for years.

Papa is as thin as a medieval Christ: an unkempt alcoholic. His hair is long; his toenails uncut; he is unshaven and scratches his arse shamelessly. Yet he is not without dignity.

His bed is in the living room. Papa never leaves the bed and watches TV most of the time.

By the bed is a photograph of Papa's dead wife, Mary. And on the bed is an address book and the telephone.

---

5. Railway stations in Central London.

Papa empties the last of a bottle of vodka into a filthy glass. He rolls the empty bottle under the bed.

Omar is now pushing an old-fashioned and ineffective carpet sweeper across the floor. Papa looks at Omar's face. He indicates that Omar should move his face closer, which Omar reluctantly does. To amuse himself, Papa squashes Omar's nose and pulls his cheeks, shaking the boy's unamused face from side to side.

PAPA I'm fixing you with a job. With your uncle. Work now, till you go back to college. If your face gets any longer here you'll overbalance. Or I'll commit suicide.

12. INT. KITCHEN. DAY.

Omar is in the kitchen of the flat, stirring a big saucepan of dall.[6] He can see through the open door his father speaking on the phone to Nasser. Papa speaks in Urdu.[7] "How are you?" he says. "And Bilquis? And Tania and the other girls?"

PAPA *(into phone)* Can't you give Omar some work in your garage for a few weeks, yaar? The bugger's your nephew after all.
NASSER *(VO [voice-over] on phone)* Why do you want to punish me?

13. INT. PAPA'S ROOM. DAY.

Papa is speaking to Nasser on the phone. He watches Omar slowly stirring dall in the kitchen. Omar is, of course, listening.

PAPA He's on dole[8] like everyone else in England. What's he doing home? Just roaming and moaning.
NASSER *(VO on phone).* Haven't you trained him up to look after you, like I have with my girls?
PAPA He brushes the dust from one place to another. He squeezes shirts and heats soup. But that hardly stretches him. Though his food stretches me. It's only for a few months, yaar. I'll send him to college in the autumn.
NASSER *(VO).* He failed once. He has this chronic laziness that runs in our family except for me.
PAPA If his arse gets lazy—kick it. I'll send a certificate giving permission. And one thing more. Try and fix him with a nice girl. I'm not sure if his penis is in full working order.

14. INT. FLAT. DAY.

Later. Omar puts a full bottle of vodka on the table next to Papa's bed.

PAPA Go to your uncle's garage.

(And Papa pours himself a vodka. Omar quickly thrusts a bottle of tomato juice towards Papa, which Papa ignores.

Before Papa can take a swig of the straight vodka, Omar grabs the glass and adds tomato juice. Papa takes it.)

6. Lentil dish from India.
7. Official language of Pakistan; also spoken in northern
India.
8. On welfare.

If Nasser wants to kick you—let him. I've given permission in two languages. (*To the photograph.*) The bloody's doing me a lot of good. Eh, bloody Mary?

15. EXT. STREET. DAY.

Omar walks along a South London street, towards Nasser's garage. It's a rough area, beautiful in its own falling-down way.

A youngish white Busker is lying stoned in the doorway of a boarded-up shop, his guitar next to him. Omar looks at him.

Walking towards Omar from an amusement arcade across the street are Johnny and Genghis and Moose. Genghis is a well-built white man carrying a pile of right-wing newspapers, badges etc. Moose is a big white man, Genghis's lieutenant.

Johnny is an attractive man in his early twenties, quick and funny.

Omar doesn't see Johnny but Johnny sees him and is startled. To avoid Omar, in the middle of the road, Johnny takes Genghis's arm a moment.

Genghis stops suddenly. Moose charges into the back of him. Genghis drops the newspapers. Genghis remonstrates with Moose. Johnny watches Omar go. The traffic stops while Moose picks up the newspapers. Genghis starts to sneeze. Moose gives him a handkerchief.

They walk across the road, laughing at the waiting traffic.

They know the collapsed Busker. He could even be a member of the gang. Johnny still watches Omar's disappearing back.

Genghis and Moose prepare the newspapers.

JOHNNY (*indicating Omar*). That kid. We were like that.

GENGHIS (*sneezing over Moose's face*). You don't believe in nothing.

16. INT. UNDERGROUND GARAGE. DAY.

Uncle Nasser's garage. It's a small private place where wealthy businessmen keep their cars during the day. It's almost full and contains about fifty cars—all Volvos, Rolls-Royces, Mercedes, Rovers, etc.

At the end of the garage is a small glassed-in office. Omar is walking down the ramp and into the garage.

17. INT. GARAGE OFFICE. DAY.

The glassed-in office contains a desk, a filing cabinet, a typewriter, phone etc. With Nasser is Salim.

Salim is a Pakistani in his late thirties, well-dressed in an expensive, smooth and slightly vulgar way. He moves restlessly about the office. Then he notices Omar wandering about the garage. He watches him.

Meanwhile, Nasser is speaking on the phone in the background.

NASSER (*into phone*). We've got one parking space, yes. It's £25 a week. And from this afternoon we provide a special on the premises "clean-the-car" service. New thing.

(*From Salim's POV [point of view] in the office, through the glass, we see Omar trying the door of one of the cars. Salim goes quickly out of the office.*)

18. INT. GARAGE. DAY.

Salim stands outside the office and shouts at Omar. The sudden sharp voice in the echoing garage.

SALIM Hey! Is that your car? Why are you feeling it up then? (*Omar looks at him.*) Come here. Here, I said.

19. INT. GARAGE OFFICE. DAY.

Nasser puts down the phone.

20. INT. GARAGE OFFICE. DAY.

Nasser is embracing Omar vigorously, squashing him to him and bashing him lovingly on the back.

NASSER (*introducing him to Salim*) This one who nearly beat you up is Salim. You'll see a lot of him.

SALIM (*shaking hands with Omar*) I've heard many great things about your father.

NASSER (*to Omar*) I must see him. Oh God, how have I got time to do anything?

SALIM You're too busy keeping this damn country in the black. Someone's got to do it.

NASSER (*to Omar*) Your papa, he got thrown out of that clerk's job I fixed him with? He was pissed?[9]

(*Omar nods. Nasser looks regretfully at the boy.*)

Can you wash a car?

(*Omar looks uncertain.*)

SALIM Have you washed a car before?

(*Omar nods.*)

Your uncle can't pay you much. But you'll be able to afford a decent shirt and you'll be with your own people. Not in a dole queue.[1] Mrs Thatcher will be pleased with me.[2]

21. INT. GARAGE. DAY.

Salim and Omar walk across the garage towards a big car. Omar carries a full bucket of water and a cloth. He listens to Salim.

SALIM It's easy to wash a car. You just wet a rag and rub. You know how to rub, don't you?

(*The bucket is overfull. Omar carelessly bangs it against his leg. Water slops out. Salim dances away irritably. Omar walks on. Salim points to a car. Rachel swings down the ramp and into the garage, gloriously.*)

Hi, baby.

RACHEL My love.

(*And she goes into the garage office. We see her talking and laughing with Nasser.*)

SALIM (*indicating car*). And you do this one first. Carefully, as if you were restoring a Renaissance painting. It's my car.

(*Omar looks up and watches as Rachel and Nasser go out through the back of the garage office into the room at the back.*)

---

9. Drunk.
1. Welfare line.
2. Margaret Thatcher, Prime Minister and leader of the

Conservative Party, 1979–1990, whose administration promoted free-market economics and the cutting back of the welfare state.

22. INT. ROOM AT BACK OF GARAGE OFFICE. DAY.

Rachel and Nasser, half-undressed, are drinking, laughing and screwing on a bulging sofa in the wrecked room behind the office, no bigger than a large cupboard. Rachel is bouncing up and down on his huge stomach in her red corset and outrageous worn-for-a-joke underwear.

NASSER Rachel, fill my glass, darling.

  (*Rachel does so, then she begins to move on him.*)

RACHEL Fill mine.

NASSER What am I, Rachel, your trampoline?

RACHEL Yes, oh, je vous aime beaucoup[3] trampoline.

NASSER Speak my language, dammit.

RACHEL I do nothing else. Nasser, d'you think we'll ever part?

NASSER Not at the moment. (*Slapping her arse.*) Keep moving, I love you. You move . . . Christ . . . like a liner . . .

RACHEL And can't we go away somewhere?

NASSER Yes, I'm taking you.

RACHEL Where?

NASSER Kempton Park,[4] Saturday.

RACHEL Great. We'll take the boy.

NASSER No, I've got big plans for him.

RACHEL You're going to make him work?

23. INT. GARAGE OFFICE. DAY.

Omar has come into the garage office with his car-washing bucket and sponge. Salim has gone home. Omar is listening at the door to his uncle Nasser and Rachel screwing. He hears:

NASSER Work? That boy? You'll think the word was invented for him!

24. INT. COCKTAIL BAR/CLUB. EVENING.

Rachel and Nasser have taken Omar to Anwar's club/bar.

  Omar watches Anwar's son Tariq behind the bar. Tariq is rather contemptuous of Omar and listens to their conversation.

  Omar eats peanuts and olives off the bar. Tariq removes the bowl.

NASSER By the way, Rachel is my old friend. (*To her.*) Eh?

OMAR (*to Nasser*) How's Auntie Bilquis?

NASSER (*glancing at amused Rachel*). She's at home with the kids.

OMAR Papa sends his love. Uncle, if I picked Papa up—

NASSER (*indicating the club*). Have you been to a high-class place like this before? I suppose you stay in that black-hole flat all the time.

OMAR If I picked Papa up, uncle—

NASSER (*to Rachel*) He's one of those underprivileged types.

OMAR And squeezed him, squeezed Papa out, like that, uncle, I often imagine. I'd get—

NASSER Two fat slaps.

OMAR Two bottles of pure vodka. And a kind of flap of skin. (*To Rachel.*) Like a French letter.[5]

---

3. I love you a lot.   5. A condom.
4. A racetrack.

NASSER What are you talking, madman? I love my brother. And I love you.

OMAR I don't understand how you can . . . love me.

NASSER Because you're such a prick?

OMAR You can't be sure that I am.

RACHEL Nasser.

NASSER She's right. Don't deliberately egg me on to laugh at you when I've brought you here to tell you one essential thing. Move closer.

> (*Omar attempts to drag the stool he is sitting on near to Nasser. He crashes off it. Rachel helps him up, laughing. Tariq also laughs. Nasser is solicitous.*)

> In this damn country which we hate and love, you can get anything you want. It's all spread out and available. That's why I believe in England. You just have to know how to squeeze the tits of the system.

RACHEL (*to Omar*) He's saying he wants to help you.

OMAR What are you going to do with me?

NASSER What am I going to do with you? Make you into something damn good. Your father can't now, can he?

> (*Rachel nods at Nasser and he takes out his wallet. He gives Omar money. Omar doesn't want to take it. Nasser shoves it down Omar's jumper, then cuddles his confused nephew.*)

> Damn fool, you're just like a son to me. (*Looking at Rachel.*) To both of us.

25. INT. GARAGE. DAY.

Omar is vigorously washing down a car, the last to be cleaned in the garage. The other cars are gleaming. Nasser comes quickly out of the office and watches Omar squeezing a cloth over a bucket.

NASSER You like this work? (*Omar shrugs.*) Come on, for Christ's sake, take a look at these accounts for me.

> (*Omar follows him into the garage office.*)

26. INT. GARAGE OFFICE. NIGHT.

Omar is sitting at the office desk in his shirt-sleeves. The desk is covered with papers. He's been sitting there some time and it is late. Most of the cars in the garage have gone.

> *Nasser drives into the garage, wearing evening clothes. Rachel, looking divine, is with him. Omar goes out to them.*

27. INT. GARAGE. NIGHT.

NASSER (*from the car*) Kiss Rachel. (*Omar kisses her.*)

OMAR I'll finish the paperwork tonight, Uncle.

NASSER (*to Rachel*) He's such a good worker I'm going to promote him.

RACHEL What to?

NASSER (*to Omar*) Come to my house next week and I'll tell you.

RACHEL It's far. How will he get there?

NASSER I'll give him a car, dammit. (*He points to an old convertible parked in the garage. It has always looked out of place.*) The keys are in the office. Anything he wants. (*He moves the car off. To Omar.*) Oh yes, I've got a real challenge lined up for you.

> (*Rachel blows him a kiss as they drive off.*)

28. INT. PAPA'S FLAT. EVENING.

Papa is lying on the bed drinking. Omar, in new clothes, tie undone, comes into the room and puts a plate of steaming food next to Papa. Stew and potatoes. Omar turns away and looking in the mirror snips at the hair in his nostrils with a large pair of scissors.

PAPA You must be getting married. Why else would you be dressed like an undertaker on holiday?

OMAR Going to uncle's house, Papa. He's given me a car.

PAPA What? The brakes must be faulty. Tell me one thing because there's something I don't understand, though it must be my fault. How is it that scrubbing cars can make a son of mine look so ecstatic?

OMAR It gets me out of the house.

PAPA Don't get too involved with that crook. You've got to study. We are under siege by the white man. For us education is power.

    (Omar shakes his head at his father.)

    Don't let me down.

29. EXT. COUNTRY LANE. EVENING.

Omar, in the old convertible, speeds along a country lane in Kent.[6] The car has its roof down, although it's raining. Loud music playing on the radio.

    He turns into the drive of a large detached house. The house is brightly lit. There are seven or eight cars in the drive. Omar sits there a moment, music blaring.

30. INT. LIVING ROOM IN NASSER'S HOUSE. EVENING.

A large living room furnished in the modern style. A shy Omar has been led in by Bilquis, Nasser's wife. She is a shy, middle-aged Pakistani woman. She speaks and understands English, but is uncertain in the language. But she is warm and friendly.

    Omar has already been introduced to most of the women in the room.

    There are five women there: a selection of wives; plus Bilquis's three daughters. The eldest, Tania, is in her early twenties.

    Cherry, Salim's Anglo-Indian wife is there.

    Some of the women are wearing saris or salwar kamiz,[7] though not necessarily only the Pakistani women.

    Tania wears jeans and T-shirt. She watches Omar all through this and Omar, when he can, glances at her. She is attracted to him.

BILQUIS *(to Omar)* And this is Salim's wife, Cherry. And of course you remember our three naughty daughters.

CHERRY *(ebulliently to Bilquis)* He has his family's cheekbones, Bilquis. *(To Omar.)* I know all your gorgeous family in Karachi.[8]

OMAR *(This is a faux pas.)* You've been there?

CHERRY You stupid, what a stupid, it's my home. Could anyone in their right mind call this silly little island off Europe their home? Every day in Karachi, every day your other uncles and cousins are at our house for bridge, booze and VCR.

BILQUIS Cherry, my little nephew knows nothing of that life there.

---

6. A county in southeast England.
7. A *sari* is a length of cotton or silk worn draped around the body; *salwar kamiz* is an outfit of loose pants and shirt.

Both are traditionally worn by Indian or Pakistani women.
8. A city in Pakistan.

CHERRY Oh God, I'm so sick of hearing about these in-betweens. People should make up their minds where they are.

TANIA Uncle's next door. (*Leading him away. Quietly.*) Can you see me later? I'm so bored with these people.

(*Cherry stares at Tania, not approving of this whispering and cousin-closeness. Tania glares back defiantly at her.*
    Bilquis looks warmly at Omar.)

31. INT. CORRIDOR OF NASSER'S HOUSE. DAY.

Tania takes Omar by the hand down the corridor to Nasser's room. She opens the door and leads him in.

32. INT. NASSER'S ROOM. EVENING.

Nasser's room is further down the corridor. It's his bedroom but where he receives guests. And he has a VCR in the room, a fridge, small bar, etc. Behind his bed a window which overlooks the garden.
    Omar goes into the smoke-filled room, led by Tania. She goes.
    Nasser is lying on his bed in the middle of the room like a fat king. His cronies are gathered round the bed. Zaki, Salim, an Englishman and an American called Dick O'Donnell.
    They're shouting and hooting and boozing and listening to Nasser's story, which he tells with great energy. Omar stands inside the door shyly, and takes in the scene.

NASSER There'd been some tappings on the window. But who would stay in a hotel without tappings? My brother Hussein, the boy's papa, in his usual way hadn't turned up and I was asleep. I presumed he was screwing some barmaid somewhere. Then when these tappings went on I got out of bed and opened the door to the balcony. And there he was, standing outside. With some woman! They were completely without clothes! And blue with cold! They looked like two bars of soap. This I refer to as my brother's blue period.

DICK O'DONNELL What happened to the woman?

NASSER He married her.

(*When Nasser notices the boy, conversation ceases with a wave of his hand. And Nasser unembarrassedly calls him over to be fondled and patted.*)
    Come along, come along. Your father's a good man.

DICK O'DONNELL This is the famous Hussein's son?

NASSER The exact bastard. My blue brother was also a famous journalist in Bombay and great drinker. He was to the bottle what Louis Armstrong is to the trumpet.

SALIM But you are to the bookie what Mother Theresa is to the children.

ZAKI (*to Nasser*). Your brother was the clever one. You used to carry his typewriter.

(*Tania appears at the window behind the bed, where no one sees her but Omar and then Zaki. Later in the scene, laughing and to distract the serious-faced Omar, she bares her breasts. Zaki sees this and cannot believe his swimming-in-drink eyes.*)

DICK O'DONNELL Isn't he coming tonight?

SALIM (*to Nasser*). Whatever happened to him?

OMAR Papa's lying down.

SALIM I meant his career.

NASSER That's lying down too. What chance would the Englishman give a leftist communist Pakistani on newspapers?

OMAR Socialist. Socialist.

NASSER What chance would the Englishman give a leftist communist socialist?

ZAKI What chance has the racist Englishman given us that we haven't torn from him with our hands? Let's face up to it. (*And Zaki has seen the breasts of Tania. He goes white and panics.*)

NASSER Zaki, have another stiff drink for that good point!

ZAKI Nasser, please God, I am on the verge already!

ENGLISHMAN Maybe Omar's father didn't make chances for himself. Look at you, Salim, five times richer and more powerful than me.

SALIM Five times? Ten, at least.

ENGLISHMAN In my country! The only prejudice in England is against the useless.

SALIM It's rather tilted in favour of the useless I would think. The only positive discrimination they have here.

(*The Pakistanis in the room laugh at this. The Englishman looks annoyed. Dick O'Donnell smiles sympathetically at the Englishman.*)

DICK O'DONNELL (*to Nasser*) Can I make this nice boy a drink?

NASSER Make him a man first.

SALIM (*to Zaki*) Give him a drink. I like him. He's our future.

33. INT. THE VERANDAH. NIGHT.

Omar shuts the door of Nasser's room and walks down the hall, to a games room at the end. This is a verandah overlooking the garden. There's a table-tennis table, various kids' toys, an exercise cycle, some cane chairs and on the walls numerous photographs of India.

Tania turns as he enters and goes eagerly to him, touching him warmly.

TANIA It's been years. And you're looking good now. I bet we understand each other, eh?

(*He can't easily respond to her enthusiasm. Unoffended, she swings away from him. He looks at photographs of his Papa and Bhutto[9] on the wall.*)

Are they being cruel to you in their typical men's way? (*He shrugs.*) You don't mind?

OMAR I think I should harden myself.

TANIA (*patting seat next to her*). Wow, what are you into?

OMAR Your father's done well.

(*He sits. She kisses him on the lips. They hold each other.*)

TANIA Has he? He adores you. I expect he wants you to take over the businesses. He wouldn't think of asking me. But he is too vicious to people in his work. He doesn't want you to work in that shitty laundrette, does he?

OMAR What's wrong with it?

TANIA And he has a mistress, doesn't he?

(*Omar looks up and sees Auntie Bilquis standing at the door. Tania doesn't see her.*)

Rachel. Yes, I can tell from your face. Does he love her?

Yes. Families, I hate families.

BILQUIS Please Tania, can you come and help.

(*Bilquis goes. Tania follows her.*)

---

9. Z. A. Bhutto, Pakistani politician and prime minister in the 1970s. Overthrown by General Zia ul-Haq and executed in 1979.

34. INT. HALL OF NASSER'S HOUSE. DAY.

Omar is standing in the hall of Nasser's house as the guests leave their respective rooms and go out into the drive. Omar stands there. Nasser shouts to him from his bed.

NASSER Take my advice. There's money in muck.
  (*Tania signals and shakes her head.*)
  What is it the gora[1] Englishman always needs? Clean clothes!

35. EXT. NASSER'S DRIVE. NIGHT.

Omar has come out of the house and into the drive. A strange sight: Salim staggering about drunkenly. The Englishman, Zaki and Cherry try to get him into the car. Salim screams at Zaki.

SALIM Don't you owe me money? Why not? You usually owe me money! Here, take this! Borrow it! (*And he starts to scatter money about.*) Pick it up!
  (*Zaki starts picking it up. He is afraid.*)
CHERRY (*to Omar*). Drive us back, will you. Pick up your own car tomorrow. Salim is not feeling well.
  (*As Zaki bends over, Salim who is laughing, goes to kick him. Bilquis stands at the window watching all this.*)

36. INT. SALIM'S CAR, DRIVING INTO SOUTH LONDON. NIGHT.

Omar driving Salim's car enthusiastically into London. Cherry and Salim are in the back. The car comes to a stop at traffic lights.
  On the adjacent pavement outside a chip shop a group of lads are kicking cans about. The lads include Moose and Genghis.
  A lively street of the illuminated shops, amusement arcades and late-night shops of South London.
  Moose notices that Pakistanis are in the car. And he indicates to the others.
  The lads gather round the car and bang on it and shout. From inside the car this noise is terrifying. Cherry starts to scream.

SALIM Drive, you bloody fool, drive!

(*But Moose climbs on the bonnet of the car and squashes his arse grotesquely against the windscreen. Faces squash against the other windows.*
  Looking out of the side window Omar sees Johnny standing to one side of the car, not really part of the car-climbing and banging.
  Impulsively, unafraid, Omar gets out of the car.)

37. EXT. STREET. NIGHT.

Omar walks past Genghis and Moose and the others to the embarrassed Johnny. Cherry is yelling after him from inside the open-doored car.
  The lads are alert and ready for violence but are confused by Omar's obvious friendship with Johnny.
  Omar sticks out his hand and Johnny takes it.

---

1. White (Hindi, derogatory).

OMAR It's me.

JOHNNY I know who it is.

OMAR How are yer? Working? What you doing now then?

JOHNNY Oh, this kinda thing.

CHERRY (*yelling from the car*). Come on, come on!

  (*The lads laugh at her. Salim is hastily giving Moose cigarettes.*)

JOHNNY What are you now, chauffeur?

OMAR No. I'm on to something.

JOHNNY What?

OMAR I'll let you know. Still living in the same place?

JOHNNY Na, don't get on with me mum and dad. You?

OMAR She died last year, my mother. Jumped on to the railway line.

JOHNNY Yeah. I heard. All the trains stopped.

OMAR I'm still there. Got the number?

JOHNNY (*indicates the lads*). Like me friends?

  (*Cherry starts honking the car horn. The lads cheer.*)

OMAR Ring us then.

JOHNNY I will. (*Indicates car.*) Leave 'em there. We can do something. Now. Just us.

OMAR Can't.

  (*Omar touches Johnny's arm and runs back to the car.*)

38. INT. CAR. NIGHT.

They continue to drive. Cherry is screaming at Omar.

CHERRY What the hell were you doing?

  (*Salim slaps her.*)

SALIM He saved our bloody arses! (*To Omar, grabbing him round the neck and pressing his face close to his.*) I'm going to see you're all right!

39. INT. PAPA'S ROOM. NIGHT.

Omar has got home. He creeps into the flat. He goes carefully along the hall, fingertips on familiar wall.

  He goes into Papa's room. No sign of Papa. Papa is on the balcony. Just a shadow.

40. EXT. BALCONY. NIGHT.

Papa is swaying on the balcony like a little tree. Papa's pyjama bottoms have fallen down. And he's just about maintaining himself vertically. His hair has fallen across his terrible face. A train bangs towards him, rushing out of the darkness. And Papa sways precariously towards it.

OMAR (*screams above the noise*) What are you doing?

PAPA I want to pee.

OMAR Can't you wait for me to take you!

PAPA My prick will drop off before you show up these days.

OMAR (*pulling up Papa's bottoms*) You know who I met? Johnny. Johnny.

PAPA The boy who came here one day dressed as a fascist with a quarter inch of hair?

OMAR He was a friend once. For years.

PAPA There were days when he didn't deserve your admiration so much.
OMAR Christ, I've known him since I was five.
PAPA He went too far. They hate us in England. And all you do is kiss their arses
and think of yourself as a little Britisher!

41. INT. PAPA'S ROOM. NIGHT.

They are inside the room now, and Omar shuts the doors.

OMAR I'm being promoted. To uncle's laundrette.
   (*Papa pulls a pair of socks from his pyjama pockets and thrusts them at Omar.*)
PAPA Illustrate your washing methods!
   (*Omar throws the socks across the room.*)

42. EXT. SOUTH LONDON STREET. DAY.

*Nasser and Omar get out of Nasser's car and walk over the road to the laundrette. It's
called "Churchills." It's broad and spacious and in bad condition. It's situated in an area
of run-down second-hand shops, betting shops, grocers with their windows boarded-up,
etc.*

NASSER It's nothing but a toilet and a youth club now. A finger up my damn arse.

43. INT. LAUNDRETTE. DAY.

We are inside the laundrette. Some of the benches in the laundrette are church pews.

OMAR Where did you get those?
NASSER Church.

(*Three or four rough-looking kids, boys and girls, one of whom isn't wearing shoes, sitting
on the pews. A character by the telephone. The thunderous sound of running-shoes in a
spin-drier.*
   The kid coolly opens the spin-drier and takes out his shoes.)

   Punkey, that's how machines get buggered!

(*The kid puts on his shoes. He offers his hot-dog to another kid, who declines it. So the
kid flings it into a spin-drier. Nasser moves to throttle him. He gets the kid by the
throat.*
   *The other kids get up. Omar pulls his eager uncle away. The telephone character looks
suspiciously at everyone. Then makes his call.*)
TELEPHONE CHARACTER Hi, baby, it's number one here, baby. How's your foot
   now?

44. INT. BACK ROOM OF LAUNDRETTE. DAY.

Nasser stands at the desk going through bills and papers.

NASSER (*to Omar*) Get started. There's the broom. Move it!
OMAR I don't only want to sweep up.

NASSER What are you now, Labour Party?[2]

OMAR I want to be manager of this place. I think I can do it. (*Pause.*) Please let me. (*Nasser thinks.*)

NASSER I'm just thinking how to tell your father that four punks drowned you in a washing machine. On the other hand, some water on the brain might clear your thoughts. Okay. Pay me a basic rent. Above that—you keep. (*He goes quickly, eager to get out. The telephone character is shouting into the phone.*)

TELEPHONE CHARACTER (*into phone*). Was it my fault? But you're everything to me! More than everything. I prefer you to Janice—!

(*The telephone character indicates to Nasser that a washing machine has overflowed all over the floor, with soap suds. Nasser gets out. Omar looks on.*)

45. INT. BACK ROOM OF LAUNDRETTE. DAY.

Omar sitting gloomily in the back room. The door to the main area open. Kids push each other about. Straight customers are intimidated.

From Omar's POV through the laundrette windows, we see Salim getting out of his car. Salim walks in through the laundrette, quickly. Comes into the back room, slamming the door behind him.

SALIM Get up! (*Omar gets up. Salim rams the back of a chair under the door handle.*) I've had trouble here.

OMAR Salim, please. I don't know how to make this place work. I'm afraid I've made a fool of myself.

SALIM You'll never make a penny out of this. Your uncle's given you a dead duck. That's why I've decided to help you financially. (*He gives him a piece of paper with an address on it. He also gives him money.*) Go to this house near the airport. Pick up some video cassettes and bring them to my flat. That's all.

46. INT. SALIM'S FLAT. EVENING.

The flat is large and beautiful. Some Sindi music[3] playing. Salim comes out of the bathroom wearing only a towel round his waist. And a plastic shower cap. He is smoking a fat joint.

Cherry goes into another room.

Omar stands there with the cassettes in his arms. Salim indicates them.

SALIM Put them. Relax. No problems? (*Salim gives him the joint and Omar takes a hit on it. Salim points at the walls. Some erotic and some very good paintings.*) One of the best collections of recent Indian painting. I patronize many painters. I won't be a minute. Watch something if you like.

(*Salim goes back into the bedroom. Omar puts one of the cassettes he has brought into the VCR. But there's nothing on the tape. Just a screenful of static.*

Meanwhile, Omar makes a call, taking the number off a piece of paper.)

OMAR (*into phone*). Can I speak to Johnny? D'you know where he's staying? Are you sure? Just wanted to help him. Please, if you see him, tell him to ring Omo.

---

2. Out of power throughout the 1980s, the Labour Party opposed the Conservative government's free-market economic policies and its policy of returning state-owned industries to private ownership.
3. From the north-central provinces of India.

47. INT. SALIM'S FLAT. EVENING.

Dressed now, and ready to go out, Salim comes quickly into the room. He picks up the video cassettes and realizes one is being played. Salim screams savagely at Omar.

SALIM Is that tape playing? (*Omar nods.*) What the hell are you doing? (*He pulls the tape out of the VCR and examines it.*)
OMAR Just watching something, Salim.
SALIM Not these! Who gave you permission to touch these?
   (*Omar grabs the tape from Salim's hand.*)
OMAR It's just a tape!
SALIM Not to me!
OMAR What are you doing? What business, Salim?

(*Salim pushes Omar hard and Omar crashes backwards across the room. As he gets up quickly to react Salim is at him, shoving him back down, viciously. He puts his foot on Omar's nose.*
   Cherry watches him coolly, leaning against a door jamb.)

SALIM Nasser tells me you're ambitious to do something. But twice you failed your exams. You've done nothing with the laundrette and now you bugger me up. You've got too much white blood. It's made you weak like those pale-faced adolescents that call us wog. You know what I do to them? I take out this. (*He takes cut a pound note. He tears it to pieces.*) I say: your English pound is worthless. It's worthless like you, Omar, are worthless. Your whole great family—rich and powerful over there—is let down by you.
   (*Omar gets up slowly.*)
   Now fuck off.
OMAR I'll do something to you for this.
SALIM I'd be truly happy to see you try.

48. EXT. OUTSIDE LAUNDRETTE. EVENING.

Omar, depressed after his humiliation at Salim's, drives slowly past the laundrette. Music plays over this. It's raining and the laundrette looks grim and hopeless.
   Omar sees Genghis and Moose. He drives up alongside them.

OMAR Seen Johnny?
GENGHIS Get back to the jungle, wog boy.
   (*Moose kicks the side of the car.*)

49. INT. PAPA'S ROOM. EVENING.

Omar is cutting Papa's long toenails with a large pair of scissors. Omar's face is badly bruised. Papa jerks about, pouring himself a drink. So Omar has to keep grabbing at his feet. The skin on Papa's legs is peeling through lack of vitamins.

PAPA Those people are too tough for you. I'll tell Nasser you're through with them.
   (*Papa dials. We hear it ringing in Nasser's house. He puts the receiver to one side to pick up his drink. He looks at Omar who wells with anger and humiliation. Tania answers.*)
TANIA Hallo.

(*Omar moves quickly and breaks the connection.*)

PAPA (*furious*) Why do that, you useless fool?

(*Omar grabs Papa's foot and starts on the toe job again. The phone starts to ring. Papa pulls away and Omar jabs him with the scissors. And Papa bleeds. Omar answers the phone.*)

OMAR Hallo. (*Pause.*) Johnny.

PAPA (*shouts over*) I'll throw you out of this bloody flat, you're nothing but a bum liability!

(*But Omar is smiling into the phone and talking to Johnny, a finger in one ear.*)

50. INT. THE LAUNDRETTE. DAY.

Omar is showing Johnny round the laundrette.

JOHNNY I'm dead impressed by all this.

OMAR You were the one at school. The one they liked.

JOHNNY (*sarcastic*) All the Pakis liked me.

OMAR I've been through it. With my parents and that. And with people like you. But now there's some things I want to do. Some pretty big things I've got in mind. I need to raise money to make this place good. I want you to help me do that. And I want you to work here with me.

JOHNNY What kinda work is it?

OMAR Variety. Variety of menial things.

JOHNNY Cleaning windows kinda thing, yeah?

OMAR Yeah. Sure. And clean out those bastards, will ya?

(*Omar indicates the sitting kids playing about on the benches.*)

JOHNNY Now?

OMAR I'll want everything done now. That's the only attitude if you want to do anything big.

(*Johnny goes to the kids and stands above them. Slowly he removes his watch and puts it in his pocket. This is a strangely threatening gesture. The kids rise and walk out one by one. One kid resents this. He pushes Johnny suddenly. Johnny kicks him hard.*)

51. EXT. OUTSIDE THE LAUNDRETTE. DAY.

Continuous. The kicked kid shoots across the pavement and crashes into Salim who is getting out of his car. Salim pushes away the frantic arms and legs and goes quickly into the laundrette.

52. INT. LAUNDRETTE. DAY.

Salim drags the reluctant Omar by the arm into the back room of the laundrette. Johnny watches them, then follows.

53. INT. BACK ROOM OF LAUNDRETTE. DAY.

Salim lets go of Omar and grabs a chair to stuff under the door handle as before. Omar suddenly snatches the chair from him and puts it down slowly. And Johnny, taking Omar's lead, sticks his big boot in the door as Salim attempts to slam it.

SALIM Christ, Omar, sorry what happened before. Too much to drink. Just go on one little errand for me, eh? (*He opens Omar's fingers and presses a piece of paper into his hand.*) Like before. For me.

OMAR For fifty quid as well.

SALIM You little bastard.

(*Omar turns away. Johnny turns away too, mocking Salim, parodying Omar.*)
All right.

54. INT. HOTEL ROOM. DUSK.

Omar is standing in a hotel room. A modern high building with a view over London. He is with a middle-aged Pakistani who is wearing salwar kamiz. Suitcases on the floor.

The man has a long white beard. Suddenly he peels it off and hands it to Omar. Omar is astonished. The man laughs uproariously.

55. INT. LAUNDRETTE. EVENING.

Johnny is doing a service wash in the laundrette. Omar comes in quickly, the beard in a plastic bag. He puts the beard on.

JOHNNY You fool.

(*Omar pulls Johnny towards the back room.*)

OMAR I've sussed Salim's game. This is going to finance our whole future.

56. INT. BACK ROOM OF LAUNDRETTE. DAY.

Johnny and Omar sitting at the desk. Johnny is unpicking the back of the beard with a pair of scissors. The door to the laundrette is closed.

Johnny carefully pulls plastic bags out of the back of the beard. He looks enquiringly at Omar. Omar confidently indicates that he should open one of them. Johnny looks doubtfully at him. Omar pulls the chair closer. Johnny snips a corner off the bag. He opens it and tastes the powder on his finger. He nods at Omar. Johnny quickly starts stuffing the bags back in the beard.

Omar gets up.

OMAR Take them out. You know where to sell this stuff. Yes? Don't you?

JOHNNY I wouldn't be working for you now if I wanted to go on being a bad boy.

OMAR This means more. Real work. Expansion.

(*Johnny reluctantly removes the rest of the packets from the back of the beard.*)
We'll re-sell it fast. Tonight.

JOHNNY Salim'll kill us.

OMAR Why should he find out it's us? Better get this back to him. Come on. I couldn't be doing any of this without you.

57. INT. OUTSIDE SALIM'S FLAT. NIGHT.

Omar, wearing the beard, is standing outside Salim's flat, having rung the bell. Cherry answers the door. At first she doesn't recognize him. Then he laughs. And she pulls him in.

58. INT. SALIM'S FLAT. NIGHT.

There are ten people sitting in Salim's flat. Well-off Pakistani friends who have come round for dinner. They are chatting and drinking. At the other end of the room the table has been laid for dinner.

Salim is fixing drinks, and talking to his friends over his shoulder.

SALIM We were all there, yaar, to see Ravi Shankar.[4] But you all just wanted to talk about my paintings. My collection. That's why I said, why don't you all come round. I will turn my place into an art gallery for the evening . . . (*The friends are giggling at Omar, who is wearing the beard. Salim, disturbed, turns suddenly. Salim is appalled by Omar in the beard.*) Let's have a little private chat, eh?

59. INT. SALIM'S BEDROOM. EVENING.

Salim snatches the beard from Omar's chin. He goes into the bathroom with it. Omar moves towards the bathroom and watches Salim frantically examine the back of the beard. When Salim sees, in the mirror, Omar watching him, he kicks the door shut.

60. INT. SALIM'S BEDROOM. NIGHT.

Salim comes back into the bedroom from the bathroom. He throws down the beard.

SALIM You can go.
OMAR But you haven't paid me.
SALIM I'm not in the mood. Nothing happened to you on the way here? (*Omar shakes his head.*) Well, something may happen to you on the way back. (*Salim is unsure at the moment what's happened. Omar watches him steadily. His nerve is holding out.*) Get the hell out.

61. EXT. OUTSIDE SALIM'S FLAT. NIGHT.

As Omar runs down the steps of the flats to Johnny waiting in the revving car, Salim stands at the window of his flat, watching them. Music over. We go with the music into:

62. INT. CLUB/BAR. NIGHT.

Omar has taken Johnny to the club he visited with Nasser and Rachel.
   The club is more lively in the evening, with West Indian, English and Pakistani customers. All affluent. In fact, a couple of the Jamaicans from the opening scene are there.
   Omar and Johnny are sitting at a table. Tariq, the young son of the club's owner, stands beside them. He puts two menus down.

TARIQ (*to Omar*) Of course a table is always here for you. Your Uncle Nasser—a great man. And Salim, of course. No one touches him. No one. You want to eat?
OMAR Tariq, later. Bring us champagne first. (*Tariq goes. To Johnny.*) Okay?
JOHNNY I'm selling the stuff tonight. The bloke's coming here in an hour. He's testing it now.
OMAR Good. (*Smiles at a girl.*) She's nice.
JOHNNY Yes.

63. INT. CLUB/BAR. NIGHT.

Omar is sitting alone at the table, drinking. Tariq clears the table and goes. Johnny comes out of the toilet with the white dealer. The dealer goes. Johnny goes and sits beside Omar.

---

4. Popular Indian musician.

JOHNNY We're laughing.

64. INT. NASSER'S ROOM. EVENING.

Nasser is lying on his bed wearing salwar kamiz. One of the young Daughters is pressing his legs and he groans with delight. Omar is sitting across the room from him, well-dressed and relaxed. He eats Indian sweets. The other Daughter comes in with more sweets, which she places by Omar.

OMAR Tell me about the beach at Bombay, Uncle. Juhu beach.
   (*But Nasser is in a bad mood. Tania comes into the room. She is wearing salwar kamiz for the first time in the film. And she looks stunning. She has dressed up for Omar.*)
   (*Playing to Tania.*) Or the house in Lahore.[5] When Auntie Nina put the garden hose in the window of my father's bedroom because he wouldn't get up. And Papa's bed started to float.
   (*Tania stands behind Omar and touches him gently on the shoulder. She is laughing at the story.*)
TANIA Papa.
   (*But he ignores her.*)
OMAR (*to Tania*) You look beautiful.
   (*She squeezes his arm.*)
NASSER (*sitting up suddenly*). What about my damn laundrette? Damn these stories about a place you've never been. What are you doing, boy!
OMAR What am I doing?

65. INT. LAUNDRETTE. DAY.

Omar and Johnny in the laundrette. Johnny, with an axe, is smashing one of the broken-down benches off the wall while Omar stands there surveying the laundrette, pencil and pad in hand. Splinters, bits of wood fly about as Johnny, athletically and enthusiastically singing at the top of his voice, demolishes existing structures.

OMAR (*voice over*) It'll be going into profit any day now. Partly because I've hired a bloke of outstanding competence and strength of body and mind to look after it with me.

66. INT. NASSER'S ROOM. EVENING.

NASSER (*to young daughter*) Jasmine, fiddle with my toes. (*To Omar.*) What bloke?

67. INT. LAUNDRETTE. DAY.

Johnny is up a ladder vigorously painting a wall and singing loudly. The washing machines are covered with white sheets. Pots and paints and brushes lie about.
   Omar watches Johnny.

OMAR (*voice over*) He's called Johnny.
NASSER (*voice over*) How will you pay him?

---

5. A city in Pakistan.

68. INT. NASSER'S ROOM. EVENING.

Salim and Zaki come into the room. Salim carries a bottle of whisky. Zaki looks nervously at Tania who flutters her eyelashes at him.

Salim and Zaki shake hands with Nasser and sit down in chairs round the bed.

ZAKI (*to Nasser*) How are you, you old bastard?

NASSER (*pointing at drinks*). Tania.

(*Tania fixes drinks for everyone. Salim looks suspiciously at Omar through this. But Omar coolly ignores him.*)

Zaki, how's things now then?

ZAKI Oh good, good, everything. But . . .

(*He begins to explain about his declining laundrette business and how bad his heart is, in Urdu. Nasser waves at Omar.*)

NASSER Speak in English, Zaki, so this boy can understand.

ZAKI He doesn't understand his own language?

NASSER (*with affectionate mock anger*) Not only that. I've given him that pain-in-the-arse laundrette to run.

SALIM I know.

NASSER But this is the point. He's hired someone else to do the work!

ZAKI Typically English, if I can say that.

SALIM (*harshly*) Don't fuck your uncle's business, you little fool.

TANIA I don't think you should talk to him like that, Uncle.

SALIM Why, what is he, royalty?

(*Salim and Nasser exchange amused looks.*)

ZAKI (*to Nasser*) She is a hot girl.

TANIA I don't like it.

OMAR (*to Salim*) In my small opinion, much good can come of fucking.

(*Tania laughs. Zaki is shocked. Salim stares at Omar.*)

NASSER (*to Omar*) Your mouth is getting very big lately.

OMAR Well. (*And he gets up quickly, to walk out.*)

NASSER All right, all right, let's all take it easy.

SALIM Who is it sitting in the drive? It's bothering me. (*To Tania.*) Some friend of yours?

(*She shakes her head.*)

NASSER Zaki, go and check it for me please.

OMAR It's only Johnny. My friend. He works for me.

NASSER No one works without my permission. (*To Tania.*) Bring him here now.

(*She goes. Omar gets up and follows her.*)

69. EXT. NASSER'S FRONT DRIVE. EVENING.

Johnny is standing by the car, music coming from the car radio. Tania and Omar walk over to him. Tania takes Omar's arm.

TANIA I know why you put up with them. Because there's so much you want. You're greedy like my father. (*Nodding towards Johnny.*) Why did you leave him out here?

OMAR He's lower class. He won't come in without being asked. Unless he's doing a burglary.

(*They get to Johnny, Omar not minding if he overhears the last remark.*)

TANIA Come in, Johnny. My father's waiting for you.

(*She turns and walks away. Omar and Johnny walk towards the house. Bilquis is standing in the window of the front room, looking at them. Omar smiles and waves at her.*)

JOHNNY How's Salim today?

OMAR Wearing too much perfume as usual. (*Omar stops Johnny a moment and brushes his face.*) An eyelash.

(*Tania, waiting at the door, watches this piece of affection and wonders.*)

70. INT. NASSER'S ROOM. EVENING.

Nasser, Salim, Johnny, Zaki and Omar are laughing together at one of Nasser's stories. Johnny has been introduced and they are getting along well. Tania hands Salim another drink and checks that everyone else has drinks.

NASSER . . . So I said, in my street I am the law! You see, I make wealth, I create money.

(*There is a slight pause. Nasser indicates to Tania that she should leave the room. She does so, irritably. Salim tries to take her hand as she goes but she pulls away from him. She has gone now.*)

(*To Omar.*) You like Tania?

OMAR Oh yes.

NASSER I'll see what I can do.

(*Zaki laughs and slaps Omar on the knee. Omar is uncomprehending.*)

To business now. I went to see the laundrette. You boys will make a beautiful job of it, I know. You need nothing more from there. (*To Johnny.*) But in exchange I want you to do something. You look like a tough chap. I've got some bastard tenants in one of my houses I can't get rid of.

JOHNNY No, I don't do nothing rough no more.

NASSER I'm not looking for a mass murderer, you bloody fool.

JOHNNY What's it involve, please?

NASSER I tell you. Unscrewing. (*To Salim.*) We're on your favourite subject.

SALIM For Christ's sake!

JOHNNY What is unscrewing?

ZAKI You're getting into some family business, that's all.

SALIM What the hell else is there for them in this country now?

NASSER (*to Omar*) Send him to my garage. And call Tania to bring us champagne. And we'll drink to Thatcher and your beautiful laundrette.

JOHNNY Do they go together?

NASSER Like dall and chipatis![6]

71. EXT. OUTSIDE THE LAUNDRETTE. NIGHT.

Johnny and Omar have parked their car by the laundrette. They lean against the car, close together, talking.

JOHNNY The timber's coming tomorrow morning. I'm getting it cheap.

6. An Indian round bread.

(*They walk slowly towards the laundrette.*)

OMAR I've had a vision. Of how this place could be. Why do people hate laundrettes? Because they're like toilets. This could be a Ritz[7] among laundrettes.

JOHNNY A laundrette as big as the Ritz. Yeah.

(*Johnny puts his arm around Omar. Omar turns to him and they kiss on the mouth. They kiss passionately and hold each other.*

On the other side of the laundrette, Genghis, Moose and three other lads are kicking the laundrette dustbins[8] across the pavement. They can't see Omar and Johnny.

Johnny detaches himself from Omar and walks round the laundrette to the lads. Omar moves into a position from where he can see, but doesn't approach the lads.

Moose sees Johnny and motions to Genghis who is engrossed with the kicking. Genghis faces Johnny. Johnny controls himself. He straightens the dustbin and starts banging the rubbish back in. He gestures to a couple of the lads to help him. They move back, away from him.

Johnny grabs Moose by the hair and stuffs his head into a dustbin. Moose, suitably disciplined, then helps Johnny stuff the rubbish back in the bin, looking guiltily at Genghis.)

GENGHIS Why are you working for them? For these people? You were with us once. For England.

JOHNNY It's work. I want to work. I'm fed up of hanging about.

GENGHIS I'm angry. I don't like to see one of our men grovelling to Pakis. They came here to work for us. That's why we brought them over. OK?

(*And Genghis moves away. As he does so, he sees Omar. The others see him at the same time. Moose takes out a knife. Genghis indicates for him to keep back. He wants to concentrate on Johnny.*)

Don't cut yourself off from your own people. Because there's no one else who really wants you. Everyone has to belong.

72. EXT. SOUTH LONDON STREET. NIGHT.

They are in a street of desolate semi-detached houses in bad condition, ready for demolition. Johnny kisses Omar and opens the car door.

JOHNNY I can't ask you in. And you'd better get back to your father.

OMAR I didn't think you'd ever mention my father.

JOHNNY He helped me, didn't he? When I was at school.

OMAR And what did you do but hurt him?

JOHNNY I want to forget all of those things.

(*He gets out quickly and walks across the front of the car. He turns the corner of the street. Omar gets out of the car and follows him.*)

73. EXT. STREET. NIGHT.

Omar follows Johnny, making sure he isn't seen.

Johnny turns into a boarded-up derelict house. Omar watches him go round the side of the house and climb in through a broken door.

Omar turns away.

7. A fashionable London hotel.   8. Trash cans.

74. INT. PAPA'S FLAT. NIGHT.

Papa is asleep in the room, dead drunk and snoring. Omar has come in. He stands by Papa's bed and strokes his head.

> *He picks up an almost empty bottle of vodka and drinks from it, finishing it. He goes to the balcony door with it.*

75. EXT. BALCONY. NIGHT.

Omar stands on the balcony, looking over the silent railway line. Then, suddenly, he shouts joyfully into the distance. And throws the empty bottle as far as he can.

76. EXT. OUTSIDE THE LAUNDRETTE. DAY.

Omar and Johnny are working hard and with great concentration, painting the outside of the laundrette, the doors, etc. Although it's not finished, it's beginning to reach its final state. The new windows have been installed; but the neon sign isn't yet up.

> *Kids play football nearby. And various cynical locals watch, a couple of old men who we see in the betting shop later. Also Moose and another lad who are amused by all the effort. They lean against a wall opposite and drink from cans.*

> *Further up the street Salim is watching all this from his parked car.*

> *Johnny is up a ladder. He gets down the ladder, nods goodbye to Omar and puts his paint brush away. Salim reverses his car. Johnny walks away. Omar looks nervously across at Moose who stares at him.*

77. INT. GARAGE OFFICE. DAY.

Nasser and Salim in the glassed-in office of the garage. Nasser is going through various papers on his desk. Salim watches him and is very persistent.

SALIM I passed by the laundrette. So you gave them money to do it up? (*Nasser shakes his head.*) Where did they get it from, I wonder?

NASSER Government grant. (*Salim looks dubiously at Nasser.*) Oh, Omo's like us, yaar. Doesn't he fit with us like a glove? He's pure bloody family. (*Looks knowingly at Salim.*) So, like you, God knows what he's doing for money. (*Nasser looks up and sees Johnny squashing his face against the glass of the door of the office. He starts to laugh.*)

SALIM That other joker's a bad influence on Omo. I'm sure of it. There's some things between them I'm looking into.

> (*Johnny comes in.*)

(*To Johnny.*) So they let you out of prison. Too crowded, are they?

JOHNNY Unscrew.

> (*Salim reacts. Nasser quickly leads Johnny out of the office, while speaking to Salim through the open door.*)

NASSER (*in Urdu*) Don't worry, I'm just putting this bastard to work.

SALIM (*in Urdu*) The bastard, it's a job in itself.

NASSER (*in Urdu*) I'll have my foot up his arse at all times.

SALIM (*in Urdu*) That's exactly how they like it. And he'll steal your boot too.

> (*Johnny looks amusedly at them both.*)

78. INT. HOUSE. DAY.

This is one of Nasser's properties. A falling down four-storey place in South London, the rooms of which he rents out to itinerants and students.

Peeling walls, faded carpets, cat piss. Johnny and Nasser are on the top landing of the house, standing by a door. Johnny is holding a tool kit, which he starts to unpack.

NASSER He's changed the lock so you take off the whole door in case he changes it again. He's only a poet with no money.

JOHNNY I'm not hurting nobody, OK?

79. INT. TOP CORRIDOR OF HOUSE. DAY.

Later. Nasser has gone. Johnny has got through the lock and the door is open. He is un-screwing the hinges and singing to himself.

At the end of the hall a Pakistani in his fifties watches him.

Johnny lifts the door off the frame and leans it against the wall.

POET Now that door you've just taken off. Hang it back.

(With great grunting effort Johnny picks the door up. He tries hard to move past the poet with it. The poet shoves Johnny hard. Johnny almost balances himself again but not quite, does a kind of dance with the door before crashing over with it on top of him.

Johnny struggles to his feet. The poet advances towards him and Johnny retreats.)

I'm a poor man. This is my room. Let's leave it that way.

(And the poet shoves Johnny again.

Johnny, not wanting to resist, falls against the wall. At the end of the hall, at the top of the stairs, Nasser appears. The poet turns to Nasser and moves towards him, abusing him in Punjabi.[9] Nasser ignores him. As the poet goes for Nasser, Johnny grabs the poet from behind and twists his arm up behind him.)

NASSER Throw this bugger out!

(Johnny shoves the struggling poet along the corridor to the top of the stairs and then bundles him downstairs.)

80. INT. ROOM. DAY.

The room from which Johnny removed the door. A large badly furnished bedsit[1] with a cooker, fridge, double-bed, wardrobe, etc.

Nasser is giving Johnny money. Then Nasser opens the window and looks out down the street. The poet is walking away from the house. Nasser calls out after him in Punjabi. And he throws the poet's things out of the window. The poet scrabbles around down below, gathering his things.)

JOHNNY Aren't you giving ammunition to your enemies doing this kind of . . . unscrewing? To people who say Pakis just come here to hustle other people's lives and jobs and houses.

NASSER But we're professional businessmen. Not professional Pakistanis. There's no race question in the new enterprise culture. Do you like the room? Omar said you had nowhere to live. I won't charge.

JOHNNY Why not?

---

9. Language spoken in the Punjab, in west-central India.   1. One-room apartment.

NASSER You can unscrew. That's confirmed beautifully. But can you unblock and can you keep this zoo here under control? Eh?

81. EXT. LAUNDRETTE. EVENING.

Music.

Johnny is working on the outside of the laundrette. He's fixing up the neon sign, on his own, and having difficulty. Omar stands down below, expensively dressed, not willing to assist. Across the street Moose and a couple of lads are watching.

OMAR I wish Salim could see this.

JOHNNY Why? He's on to us. Oh yeah, he's just biding his time. Then he'll get us.

(He indicates to Moose. Moose comes over and helps him. The old men are watching wisely as Johnny and Moose precariously sway on a board suspended across two ladders, while holding the neon sign saying POWDERS.)

OMAR You taking the room in Nasser's place?

(A ball is kicked by the kids which whistles past Johnny's ear. Moose reacts.)

Make sure you pay the rent. Otherwise you'll have to chuck yourself out of the window.

(Genghis walks down the street towards the laundrette. Omar turns and goes.

Moose goes into a panic, knowing Genghis will be furious at this act of collaboration. Johnny glances at Moose.

Genghis is coming. The ladders sway. And the old men watch. Genghis stops. Moose looks at him.)

82. INT. LAUNDRETTE. DAY.

The day of the opening of the laundrette.

The laundrette is finished. And the place looks terrific: pot plants; a TV on which videos are showing; a sound system; and the place is brightly painted and clean.

Omar is splendidly dressed. He is walking round the place, drink in hand, looking it over.

Outside, local people look in curiously and press their faces against the glass. Two old ladies are patiently waiting to be let in. A queue of people with washing gradually forms.

In the open door of the back room Johnny is changing into his new clothes.

JOHNNY Let's open. The world's waiting.

OMAR I've invited Nasser to the launch. And Papa's coming.

They're not here yet. Papa hasn't been out for months. We can't move till he arrives.

JOHNNY What time did they say they'd be here?

OMAR An hour ago.

JOHNNY They're not gonna come, then.

(Omar looks hurt. Johnny indicates that Omar should go to him. He goes to him.)

83. INT. BACK ROOM OF LAUNDRETTE. DAY.

The back room has also been done up, in a bright high-tech style. And a two-way mirror has been installed, through which they can see into the laundrette.

Omar watches Johnny, sitting on the desk.

JOHNNY Shall I open the champagne then? (*He opens the bottle.*)

OMAR Didn't I predict this? (*They look through the mirror and through the huge windows of the laundrette to the patient punters waiting outside.*) This whole stinking area's on its knees begging for clean clothes. Jesus Christ.

(*Omar touches his own shoulders. Johnny massages him.*)

JOHNNY Let's open up.

OMAR Not till Papa comes. Remember? He went out of his way with you. And with all my friends. (*Suddenly harsh.*) He did, didn't he!

JOHNNY Omo. What are you on about, mate?

OMAR About how years later he saw the same boys. And what were they doing?

JOHNNY What?

OMAR What were they doing on marches through Lewisham?[2] It was bricks and bottles and Union Jacks.[3] It was immigrants out. It was kill us. People we knew. And it was you. He saw you marching. You saw his face, watching you. Don't deny it. We were there when you went past. (*Omar is being held by Johnny, in his arms.*) Papa hated himself and his job. He was afraid on the street for me. And he took it out on her. And she couldn't bear it. Oh, such failure, such emptiness.

(*Johnny kisses Omar then leaves him, sitting away from him slightly. Omar touches him, asking him to hold him.*)

84. INT. LAUNDRETTE. DAY.

Nasser and Rachel stride enthusiastically into the not yet open laundrette, carrying paper cups and a bottle of whisky. Modern music suitable for waltzing to is playing.

NASSER What a beautiful thing they've done with it! Isn't it? Oh, God and with music too!

RACHEL It's like an incredible ship. I had no idea.

NASSER He's a marvellous bloody boy, Rachel, I tell you.

RACHEL You don't have to tell me.

NASSER But I tell you everything five times.

RACHEL At least.

NASSER Am I a bad man to you then?

RACHEL You are sometimes . . . careless.

NASSER (*moved*) Yes.

RACHEL Dance with me. (*He goes to her.*) But we are learning.

NASSER Where are those two buggers?

85. INT. BACK ROOM OF LAUNDRETTE. DAY.

Omar and Johnny are holding each other.

JOHNNY Nothing I can say, to make it up to you. There's only things I can do to show that I am . . . with you.

(*Omar starts to unbutton Johnny's shirt.*)

86. INT. LAUNDRETTE. DAY.

Nasser and Rachel are waltzing across the laundrette. Outside, the old ladies are shifting about impatiently.

---

2. Working-class district of south London.   3. The flag of the United Kingdom.

NASSER Of course, Johnny did all the physical work on this.

RACHEL You're fond of him.

NASSER I wish I could do something more to help the other deadbeat children like him. They hang about the road like pigeons, making a mess, doing nothing.

RACHEL And you're tired of work.

NASSER It's time I became a holy man.

RACHEL A sadhu[4] of South London.

NASSER (*surprised at her knowledge*) Yes. But first I must marry Omar off.

87. INT. BACK ROOM OF LAUNDRETTE. DAY.

Omar and Johnny are making love vigorously, enjoying themselves thoroughly. Suddenly Omar stops a moment, looks up, sees Nasser and Rachel waltzing across the laundrette. Omar jumps up.

88. INT. LAUNDRETTE. DAY.

Nasser strides impatiently towards the door of the back room.

89. INT. BACK ROOM OF LAUNDRETTE. DAY.

Omar and Johnny are quickly getting dressed. Nasser bursts into the room.

NASSER What the hell are you doing? Sunbathing?

OMAR Asleep, Uncle. We were shagged out. Where's Papa?

(*Nasser just looks at Omar. Rachel appears at the door behind him.*)

90. INT. LAUNDRETTE. DAY.

The laundrette is open now. The ladies and other locals are doing their washing. The machines are whirring, sheets are being folded, magazines read, music played, video games played, etc.

Salim arrives with Zaki. They talk as they come in.

ZAKI Laundrettes are impossible. I've got two laundrettes and two ulcers. Plus . . . piles!

(*Genghis, Moose and the rest of the gang arrive. Moose goes into the laundrette, followed by Genghis. Genghis turns and forbids the rest of the gang from entering. They wait restlessly outside. Johnny is talking to Rachel.*)

RACHEL What's your surname?

JOHNNY Burfoot.

RACHEL That's it. I know your mother.

(*The telephone character is on the phone, talking eagerly to his Angela.*

Through the window, Omar, who is talking to Nasser, sees Tania. She is crossing the road and carrying a bouquet of flowers.)

OMAR I thought Papa just might make it today, Uncle.

NASSER He said he never visits laundrettes.

(*Tania comes in through the door.*)

4. Indian holy man or ascetic.

JOHNNY (*to Rachel*) Oh good, it's Tania.
RACHEL I've never met her. But she has a beautiful face.

(*Johnny leaves Rachel and goes to Tania, kissing her. He takes the flowers delightedly.*
    Nasser is disturbed by the sudden unexpected appearance of his daughter, since he is with his mistress, Rachel.)

NASSER (*to Omar*) Who invited Tania, dammit?
    (*Genghis and Moose shout out as they play the video game.*)
OMAR I did, Uncle.

(*They watch as Tania goes to Rachel with Johnny.*
    Johnny has no choice but to introduce Tania and Rachel.)

TANIA (*smiles at Rachel*) At last. After so many years in my family's life.
RACHEL Tania, I do feel I know you.
TANIA But you don't.
NASSER (*watching this*) Bring Tania over here.
TANIA (*to Rachel*) I don't mind my father having a mistress.
RACHEL Good. I am so grateful.
NASSER (*to Omar*) Then marry her. (*Omar looks at him.*) What's wrong with her? If
    I say marry her then you damn well do it!
TANIA (*to Rachel*) I don't mind my father spending our money on you.
RACHEL Why don't you mind?
NASSER (*to Omar*) Start being nice to Tania. Take the pressure off my fucking head.
TANIA (*to Rachel*) Or my father being with you instead of with our mother.
NASSER (*to Omar*) Your penis works, doesn't it?
TANIA (*to Rachel*) But I don't like women who live off men.
NASSER (*shoving Omar forward*) Get going then!
TANIA (*to Rachel*) That's a pretty disgusting parasitical thing, isn't it?
OMAR (*to Tania*) Tania, come and look at the spin-driers. They are rather interesting.
RACHEL But tell me, who do you live off? And you must understand, we are of dif-
    ferent generations, and different classes. Everything is waiting for you. The only
    thing that has ever waited for me is your father.
    (*Then, with great dignity, Nasser goes to Rachel.*)
NASSER We'd better get going. See you boys.

(*He shakes hands warmly with Omar and Johnny. And goes out with Rachel, ignoring Tania.*
    Outside in the street, Rachel and Nasser begin to argue bitterly. They are watched by the rest of the gang. Rachel and Nasser finally walk away from each other, in different directions, sadly.)

91. INT. LAUNDRETTE. DAY.

The laundrette is full now, mostly with real punters doing their washing and enjoying being there.
    Genghis and Moose are still drinking. Genghis talks across the laundrette to Johnny. Johnny is doing a service wash, folding clothes.
    Omar is saying goodbye to Tania at the door.
    Salim has hung back and is waiting for Omar, Zaki says goodbye to him and goes tentatively past the volatile breast-baring Tania.

TANIA (*to Omar*) I want to leave home. I need to break away. You'll have to help me financially.

(*Omar nods enthusiastically.*)

GENGHIS (*to Johnny*) Why don't you come out with us no more?

OMAR (*to Tania*) I'm drunk.

JOHNNY (*to Genghis*) I'm busy here full-time, Genghis.

OMAR (*to Tania*) Will you marry me, Tania?

TANIA (*to Omar*) If you can get me some money.

GENGHIS (*to Johnny*) Don't the Paki give you time off?

MOOSE (*to Johnny*) I bet you ain't got the guts to ask him for time off.

SALIM (*to Johnny, indicating Omar*) Omo's getting married.

(*Tania goes. Salim goes to Omar. He puts his arm round him and takes him outside. Omar is reluctant to go at first, but Salim is firm and strong and pulls him out. Johnny watches.*).

GENGHIS (*to Johnny*) You out with us tonight then?

92. EXT. STREET OUTSIDE LAUNDRETTE. DAY.

It is starting to get dark. Omar and Salim stand beside Salim's smart car.
Eager and curious customers are still arriving. Salim nods approvingly at them.
Above them the huge pink flashing neon sign saying "POWDERS."
Some kids are playing football in the street opposite the laundrette.
Johnny rushes to the door of the laundrette. He shouts at the kids.

JOHNNY You mind these windows!

(*Salim, being watched by Johnny, starts to lead Omar up the street, away from the laundrette.*)

SALIM (*to Omar*) I'm afraid you owe me a lot of money. The beard? Remember? Eh? Good. It's all coming back. I think I'd better have that money back, don't you?

OMAR I haven't got money like that now.

SALIM Because it's all in the laundrette?

(*Genghis and Moose have come out of the laundrette and walked up the street away from it, parallel with Omar and Salim. Genghis stares contemptuously at Salim and Moose spits on the pavement. Salim ignores them.*)

I'd better have a decent down payment then, of about half. (*Omar nods.*) By the time Nasser has his annual party, say. Or I'll instruct him to get rid of the laundrette. You see, if anyone does anything wrong with me, I always destroy them.

(*Johnny comes out of the laundrette and runs up behind Genghis and Moose, jumping on Moose's back. They turn the corner, away from Salim and Omar. Omar watches them go anxiously, not understanding what Johnny could be doing with them.*)

OMAR Took you a while to get on to us.

SALIM Wanted to see what you'd do. How's your Papa? (*Omar shrugs.*) So many books written and read. Politicians sought him out. Bhutto was his close friend. But we're nothing in England without money.

93. INT. BETTING SHOP. DAY.

There are only five or six people in the betting shop, all of them men.

And the men are mostly old, in slippers and filthy suits; with bandaged legs and stained shirts and unshaven milk-bottle-white faces and National Health [5] *glasses. Nasser looks confident and powerful beside them. He knows them. There's a good sense of camaraderie amongst them.*

When Omar goes into the betting shop, Nasser is sitting on a stool, a pile of betting slips in front of him, staring at one of the newspaper pages pinned to the wall. An old man is sitting next to Nasser, giving him advice.

Omar goes to Nasser.

OMAR (*anxiously*) Uncle. (*Nasser ignores him.*) Uncle.

NASSER (*scribbling on betting slip*) Even royalty can't reach me in the afternoons.

OMAR I've got to talk. About Salim.

NASSER Is he squeezing your balls?

OMAR Yes. I want your help, Uncle.

NASSER (*getting up*) You do it all now. It's up to you, boy.

(*Nasser goes to the betting counter and hands over his betting slips. He also hands over a thick pile of money.*

Over the shop PA we can hear that the race is beginning. It starts.

Nasser listens as if hypnotized, staring wildly at the others in the shop, for sympathy, clenching his fists, stamping his feet and shouting loudly as his horse, "Elvis," is among the front runners.

Omar has never seen Nasser like this before.)

(*To horse.*) Come on, Elvis, my son. (*To Omar.*) You'll just have to run the whole family yourself now. (*To horse.*) Go on, boy! (*To Omar.*) You take control. (*To horse and others in shop.*) Yes, yes, yes, he's going to take it, the little bastard black beauty! (*To Omar.*) It's all yours. Salim too. (*To horse.*) Do it, do it, do it, baby! No, no, no, no.

(*Nasser is rigid with self-loathing and disappointment as "Elvis" loses the race. The betting slip falls from his hand. And he hangs his head in despair.*)

OMAR Where's Rachel?

NASSER You can't talk to her. She's busy pulling her hair out. If only your damn father were sober. I'd talk to him about her. He's the only one who knows anything. (*Facetious.*) I'd ask him about Salim if I were you.

(*Omar stares at Nasser in fury and disgust. He storms out of the betting shop, just as the next race—a dog race—is about to start.*)

94. INT. LAUNDRETTE. EVENING.

The laundrette is fully functional now, busy and packed with customers. Music is playing—a soprano aria from Madame Butterfly. [6]

Customers are reading magazines. They are talking, watching TV with the sound turned down and one white man is singing along with the Puccini which he knows word for word.

The telephone character is yelling into the bright new yellow phone.

TELEPHONE CHARACTER (*into phone*) 'Course I'll look after it! I'll come round every other night. At least. Honest. I want children!

5. Government medical service.

6. Opera (1904) by Giacomo Puccini, about an interracial love affair.

(*Omar walks around the laundrette, watching over it, proud and stern. He helps people if the doors of the renovated machines are stiff.*

And he hands people baskets to move their washing about in. Shots of people putting money into the machines.

But Johnny isn't there. Omar doesn't know where he is and looks outside anxiously for him. He is worried and upset about Salim's demand for money.

Finally Omar goes out into the street and asks a kid if he's seen Johnny.)

95. INT. TOP HALL OF THE HOUSE JOHNNY'S MOVED INTO. NIGHT.

A party is going on in one of the rooms on this floor. The noise is tremendous and people are falling about the hall.

A Pakistani student, a man in his late twenties with an intelligent face, is bent over someone who has collapsed across the doorway between room and hall.

PAKISTANI STUDENT (*as Omar goes past*) There's only one word for your uncle. (*Omar walks on fastidiously, ignoring them, to Johnny's door. The student yells.*) Collaborator with the white man!
   (*Omar knocks on Johnny's door.*)

96. INT. JOHNNY'S ROOM. NIGHT.

Omar goes into Johnny's room. Johnny is lying on the bed, drinking, wearing only a pair of boxer shorts.
   Omar stands at the open door.
   Johnny runs to the door and screams up the hall to the Pakistani student.

JOHNNY Didn't I tell you, didn't I tell you 'bout that noise last night? (*Pause.*) Well, didn't I?

(*The Pakistani student stares contemptuously at him. The drunks lie where they are. Johnny slams the door of his room.*
   And Omar starts on him.)

OMAR Where did you go? You just disappeared!
JOHNNY Drinking, I went. With me old mates. It's not illegal.
OMAR 'Course it is. Laundrettes are a big commitment. Why aren't you at work?
JOHNNY It'll be closing time soon. You'll be locking the place up, and coming to bed.
OMAR No, it never closes. And one of us has got to be there. That way we begin to make money.
JOHNNY You're getting greedy.
OMAR I want big money. I'm not gonna be beat down by this country. When we were at school, you and your lot kicked me all round the place. And what are you doing now? Washing my floor. That's how I like it. Now get to work. Get to work I said. Or you're fired!
   (*Omar grabs him and pulls him up. Johnny doesn't resist. Omar throws his shirt and shoes at him. Johnny dresses.*)
JOHNNY (*touching him*) What about you?
OMAR I don't wanna see you for a little while. I got some big thinking to do.
   (*Johnny looks regretfully at him.*)

JOHNNY But today, it's been the best day!
OMAR Yeah. Almost the best day.

97. INT. TOP HALL. NIGHT.

Johnny, dressed now, walks past the party room. The Pakistani student is now playing a tabla[7] in the hall.
Johnny ignores him, though the student looks ironically at him.

98. INT. BOTTOM ENTRANCE HALL OF THE HOUSE. NIGHT.

Johnny stops by a wall box in the hall. He pulls a bunch of keys out of his pocket and unlocks the wall box.
He reaches in and pulls a switch.

99. EXT. OUTSIDE THE HOUSE. NIGHT.

Johnny walks away from the house. He has plunged the party room into darkness. In the room people are screaming.
The Pakistani student yells out of the window at Johnny.

PAKISTANI STUDENT You are not human! You are cold people, you English, the big icebergs of Europe!

(Omar stands at the next window along, looking out. This room is lighted.
Johnny chuckles to himself as he walks jauntily away.)

100. INT. LAUNDRETTE. NIGHT.

Nina Simone's smooth "Walk On By" playing in the laundrette.
And there are still plenty of people around.
The telephone character has turned to the wall, head down, to concentrate on his conversation.
A man is asleep on a bench. Johnny walks past him, notices he's asleep and suddenly pokes him. The man jumps awake. Johnny points at the man's washing.
A young black couple are dancing, holding each other sleepily as they wait for their washing.
A bum comes in through the door, slowly, with difficulty in walking. He's wearing a large black overcoat with the collar turned up. Johnny watches him.

JOHNNY Hey!
(The bum doesn't respond. Johnny goes to him and takes his arm, about to chuck him out. Then the bum turns to Johnny.)
PAPA I recognize you at least. Let me sit.

(Johnny leads Papa up the laundrette.
The telephone character throws down the receiver and walks out.)

JOHNNY *(deferential now)* We were expecting you today.
PAPA I've come.

---

7. Small Indian hand drums.

JOHNNY The invitation was for two o'clock, Mr Ali.

PAPA (*looking at his watch*) It's only ten past now. I thought I'd come to the wrong place. That I was suddenly in a ladies' hairdressing salon in Pinner,[8] where one might get a pink rinse. Do you do a pink rinse, Johnny? Or are you still a fascist?

JOHNNY You used to give me a lot of good advice, sir. When I was little.

PAPA When you were little. What's it made of you? Are you a politician? Journalist? A trade unionist? No, you are an underpants cleaner. (*Self-mocking.*) Oh dear, the working class are such a great disappointment to me.

JOHNNY I haven't made much of myself.

PAPA You'd better get on and do something.

JOHNNY Yes. Here, we can do something.

PAPA Help me. I want my son out of this underpants cleaning condition. I want him reading in college. You tell him: you go to college. He must have knowledge. We all must, now. In order to see clearly what's being done and to whom in this country. Right?

JOHNNY I don't know. It depends on what he wants.

PAPA No. (*Strongly.*) You must use your influence. (*Papa gets up and walks out slowly. Johnny watches him go, sadly. Papa turns.*) Not a bad dump you got here.

101. EXT. OUTSIDE THE LAUNDRETTE. NIGHT.

Papa walks away from the laundrette.

102. EXT. THE DRIVE OF NASSER'S HOUSE. DAY.

Johnny has come by bus to Nasser's house. And Omar opens the front door to him. Johnny is about to step into the house. Omar takes him out into the drive.

JOHNNY What you make me come all this way for?

OMAR Gotta talk.

JOHNNY You bloody arse. (*At the side of the house a strange sight. Tania is climbing a tree. Bilquis is at the bottom of the tree yelling instructions to her in Urdu. Johnny and Omar watch.*) What's going on?

OMAR It's heavy, man. Bilquis is making magical potions from leaves and bird beaks and stuff. She's putting them on Rachel.

   (*Johnny watches Tania groping for leaves in amazement.*)

JOHNNY Is it working?

OMAR Rachel rang me. She's got the vicar round. He's performing an exorcism right now. The furniture's shaking. Her trousers are walking by themselves.

103. INT. NASSER'S ROOM. DAY.

Omar and Johnny and Nasser are sitting at a table in Nasser's room, playing cards. Nasser is sulky. He puts his cards down.

NASSER I'm out.

(*He gets up and goes and lies down on the bed, his arm over his face.*

---

8. District of North London.

Omar and Johnny continue playing. They put their cards down. Johnny wins. He collects the money.)

OMAR Salim's gotta have money. Soon. A lot of money. He threatened me. (*They get up and walk out of the room, talking in low voices. Nasser lies there on the bed, not listening but brooding.*) I didn't wanna tell you before. I thought I could raise the money on the profits from the laundrette. But it's impossible in the time.

104. INT. HALL OUTSIDE NASSER'S ROOM. DAY.

They walk down the hall to the verandah.

JOHNNY This city's chock-full of money. When I used to want money—
OMAR You'd steal it.
JOHNNY Yeah. Decide now if you want it to be like that again.

105. INT. VERANDAH. DAY.

They reach the verandah. Outside, in the garden, the two younger daughters are playing.

At the other end of the verandah Bilquis and Tania are sitting on the sofa, a table in front of them. Bilquis is mixing various ingredients in a big bowl—vegetables, bits of bird, leaves, some dog urine, the squeezed eyeball of a newt, half a goldfish, etc. We see her slicing the goldfish.

At the same time she is dictating a letter to Tania, which Tania takes down on a blue airletter. Tania looks pretty fed-up.

Omar and Johnny sit down and watch them.

OMAR She's illiterate. Tania's writing to her sister for her. Bilquis is thinking of going back, after she's hospitalized Rachel. (*Bilquis looks up at them, her eyes dark and her face humourless.*) Nasser's embarked on a marathon sulk. He's going for the world record.
   (*Pause. Johnny changes the subject back when Tania—suspecting them of laughing at her—gives them a sharp look.*)
JOHNNY We'll just have to do a job to get the money.
OMAR I don't want you going back to all that.
JOHNNY Just to get us through, Omo. It's for both of us. If we're going to go on. You want that, don't you?
OMAR Yes. I want you.

(*Suddenly Nasser appears at the door and starts abusing Bilquis in loud Urdu, telling her that the magic business is stupid, etc. But Bilquis has a rougher, louder tongue. She says, among other things, in Urdu, that Nasser is a big fat black man who should get out of her sight for ever.*

Tania is very distressed by this, hands over face. Suddenly she gets up. The magic potion bowl is knocked over, the evil ingredients spilling over Bilquis' feet. Bilquis screams. Johnny starts laughing. Bilquis picks up the rest of the bowl and throws the remainder of the potion over Nasser.)

106. EXT. OUTSIDE A SMART HOUSE. NIGHT.

A semi-detached house. A hedge around the front of the house.

Johnny is forcing the front window. He knows what he's doing. He climbs in. He indicates to Omar that he should follow. And Omar follows.

107. INT. FRONT ROOM OF THE HOUSE. NIGHT.

They're removing the video and TV and going out the front door with them. Their car is parked outside.

Suddenly a tiny kid of about eight is standing behind them at the bottom of the stairs. He is an Indian kid. Omar looks at him, the kid opens his mouth to yell. Omar grabs the kid and slams his hand over his mouth. While he holds the kid, Johnny goes out with the stereo. Then the compact disc player.

108. INT. BACK ROOM OF LAUNDRETTE. NIGHT.

There are televisions, stereos, radios, videos, etc. stacked up in the back room. Omar stands there looking at them.

Johnny comes in struggling with a video. Omar smiles at him. Johnny doesn't respond.

109. INT. HALL. DAY.

The top hall of the house Johnny lives in. Johnny, wearing jeans and T-shirt, barefoot, only recently having woken up, is banging on the door of the Pakistani student's room.

Omar is standing beside him, smartly dressed and carrying a briefcase. He's spent the night with Johnny. And now he's going to the laundrette.

JOHNNY (*to door*) Rent day! Rent up, man!

(*Omar watches him. Johnny looks unhappy.*)

OMAR I said it would bring you down, stealing again. It's no good for you. You need a brand new life.

(*The Pakistani student opens the door. Omar moves away. To Johnny.*)

Party tonight. Then we'll be in the clear.

PAKISTANI STUDENT Unblock the toilet, yes, Johnny?

JOHNNY (*looking into the room*) Tonight. You're not doing nothing political in there, are you, man? I've gotta take a look.

(*Omar, laughing, moves away. Johnny shoves the door hard and the Pakistani student relents.*)

110. INT. PAKISTANI STUDENT'S ROOM. DAY.

Johnny goes into the room. A young Pakistani woman is sitting on the bed with a child.

A younger Pakistani boy of about fourteen is standing behind her. And across the room a Pakistani girl of seventeen.

PAKISTANI STUDENT My family, escaping persecution. (*Johnny looks at him.*) Are you a good man or are you a bad man?

111. EXT. COUNTRY LANE AND DRIVE OF NASSER'S HOUSE. EVENING.

Omar and Johnny are sitting in the back of a mini-cab.

Johnny is as dressed up as is Omar, but in fashionable street clothes rather than an expensive dark suit. Johnny will be out of keeping sartorially with the rest of the party.

The young Asian driver moves the car towards Nasser's house.

The house is a blaze of light and noise. And the drive is full of cars and Pakistanis and Indians getting noisily out of them. Looking at the house, the lights, the extravagance, Johnny laughs sarcastically.

Omar, paying the driver, looks irritably at Johnny.

JOHNNY What does he reckon he is, your uncle? Some kinda big Gatsby geezer?[9] (*Omar gives him a cutting look.*) Maybe this just isn't my world. You're right. Still getting married?

(*They both get out of the car. Omar walks towards the house. Johnny stands there a moment, not wanting to face it all.*

When Omar has almost reached the front door and Tania has come out to hug him, Johnny moves towards the house.

Tania hugs Johnny.

Omar looks into the house and sees Salim and Cherry in the crowd in the front room. He waves at Salim but Salim ignores him. Cherry is starting to look pregnant.

Bilquis is standing at the end of the hall. She greets Omar in Urdu. And he replies in rudimentary Urdu.

Johnny feels rather odd since he's the only white person in sight.)

112. INT/EXT. THE VERANDAH, PATIO AND GARDEN. EVENING.

The house, patio and garden are full of well-off, well-dressed, well-pissed, middle-class Pakistanis and Indians.

The American, Dick, and the Englishman are talking together.

DICK England needs more young men like Omar and Johnny, from what I can see.
ENGLISHMAN (*slightly camp*) The more boys like that the better.
(*We see Omar on the verandah talking confidently to various people. Occasionally he glances at Salim who is engrossed in conversation with Zaki and Zaki's wife. A snatch of their conversation.*)
SALIM Now Cherry is pregnant I will be buying a house. I am going to have many children . . .

(*Bilquis is there. She is alone but there is a fierceness and cheerfulness about her that we haven't noticed before.*

Johnny doesn't know who to talk to. Cherry goes up to him.)

CHERRY Please, can you take charge of the music for us?

(*Johnny looks at her. Then he shakes his head.*

Nasser, in drunken, ebullient mood, takes Omar across the room to Zaki, who is with Salim.)

ZAKI (*shaking hands with Omar*) Omar, my boy.
(*Salim moves away.*)
NASSER (*to Omar, of Zaki*) Help him. (*To Zaki.*) Now tell him, please.

---

9. Rich man. F. Scott Fitzgerald's novel *The Great Gatsby* (1925) satirizes wealth and social climbing.

ZAKI Oh God, Omo, I've got these two damn laundrettes in your area. I need big advice on them.

> (*We hear Omar's voice as we look at the party.*)

OMAR I won't advise you. If the laundrettes are a trouble to you I'll pay you rent for them plus a percentage of the profits.

NASSER How about it, Zaki? He'll run them with Johnny.

We see Tania talking to two interested Pakistani men in their middle twenties who see her as marriageable and laugh at everything she says. But Tania is looking at Johnny who is on his own, drinking. He also dances, bending his knees and doing an inconspicuous handjive. He smiles at Tania.

Tania goes across to Johnny. He whispers something in her ear. She leads Johnny by the hand out into the garden.

Bilquis looks in fury at Nasser, blaming him for this. He turns away from her.

Zaki is happily explaining to his wife about the deal with Omar.

113. EXT. GARDEN. EVENING.

Tania leads Johnny across the garden, towards the little garden house at the end. A bicycle is leaning against it. She takes off her shoes. And they hold each other and dance.

114. INT. THE HOUSE. EVENING.

Salim is on his own a moment. Omar moves towards him. Salim walks out and across the garden.

115. EXT. GARDEN. EVENING.

Omar follows Salim across the lawn.

OMAR I've got it. (*Salim turns to him.*) The instalment. It's hefty, Salim. More than you wanted.

> (*Omar fumbles for the money in his jacket pocket. At the end of the garden Johnny and Tania are playing around with a bicycle. Omar, shaking, drops some of the money. Salim raises his hand in smiling rejection.*)

SALIM Don't ever offer me money. It was an educational test I put on you. To make you see you did a wrong thing.

> (*Tania and Johnny are now riding the bicycle on the lawn.*)

Don't in future bite the family hand when you can eat out of it. If you need money just ask me. Years ago your uncles lifted me up. And I will do the same for you.

> (*Through this Omar has become increasingly concerned as Tania, with Johnny on the back of the bicycle, is riding at Salim's back. Omar shouts out.*)

OMAR Tania!

(*And he tries to pull Salim out of the way. But Tania crashes into Salim, knocking him flying flat on his face. Nasser comes rushing down the lawn.*

Tania and Johnny lie laughing on their backs.

Salim gets up quickly, furiously, and goes to punch Johnny. Omar and Nasser grabs an arm of Salim's each.

Johnny laughs in Salim's face.)

(*To Salim.*) All right, all right, he's no one.

(*Salim calms down quickly and just raises a warning finger at Johnny. The confrontation is mainly diverted by Nasser going for Tania.*)

NASSER (*to Tania*) You little bitch! (*He grabs at Tania to hit her. Johnny pulls her away.*) What the hell d'you think you're doing?

SALIM (*to Nasser*) Can't you control your bloody people? (*And he abuses Nasser in Urdu. Nasser curses and scowls in English:*) Why should you be able to? You've gambled most of your money down the toilet! (*Salim turns and walks away.*)

TANIA (*pointing after him*) That smooth suppository owns us! Everything! Our education, your businesses, Rachel's stockings. It's his!

NASSER (*to Omar*) Aren't you two getting married?

OMAR Yes, yes, any day now.

TANIA I'd rather drink my own urine.

OMAR I hear it can be quite tasty, with a slice of lemon.

NASSER Get out of my sight, Tania!

TANIA I'm going further than that.

(*Nasser turns and storms away. As he walks up the lawn we see that Bilquis has been standing a quarter of the way down the lawn, witnessing all this.*

Nasser stops for a moment beside her, not looking at her. He walks on.)

OMAR (*to Johnny*) Let's get out of here.

TANIA (*to Johnny*) Take me.

(*Omar shakes his head and takes Johnny's hand.*)

OMAR Salim'll give us a lift.

JOHNNY What?

OMAR I need him for something I've got in mind.

116. INT. SALIM'S CAR. NIGHT.

Salim is driving Johnny and Omar along a country lane, fast, away from Nasser's house.

Johnny is sitting in the back, looking out of the window.

Omar is sarcastic for Johnny's unheeding benefit and undetected by the humourless Salim.

OMAR Well, thanks, Salim, you know. For saving the laundrette and everything. And for giving us a lift. Our car's bust.

SALIM (*accelerating*) Got to get to a little liaison. (*To Johnny.*) He doesn't have to thank me. Eh, Johnny? What's your problem with me, Johnny?

JOHNNY (*eventually, and tough*) Salim, we know what you sell, man. Know the kids you sell it to. It's shit, man. Shit.

SALIM Haven't you noticed? People are shit. I give them what they want. I don't criticize. I supply. The laws of business apply.

JOHNNY Christ, what a view of people. Eh, Omo? You think that's a filthy shit thing, don't you, Omo?

(*Suddenly Salim steps on the brakes. They skid to a stop on the edge of a steep drop away from the road.*)

SALIM Get out!

(*Johnny opens the car door. He looks down the steep hill and across the windy Kent landscape. He leans back in his seat, closing the car door.*)

JOHNNY I don't like the country. The snakes make me nervous.
(*Salim laughs and drives off.*)

117. INT. SALIM'S CAR. NIGHT.

They've reached South London, near the laundrette.
Omar's been explaining to Salim about his new scheme.

OMAR . . . So I was talking to Zaki about it. I want to take over his two laundrettes.
He's got no idea.
SALIM None.
OMAR Do them up. With this money. (*He pats his pocket.*)
SALIM Yeah. Is it enough?
OMAR I thought maybe you could come in with me . . . financially.
SALIM Yeah. I'm looking for some straight outlets. (*Pause.*) You're a smart bastard.
(*Suddenly.*) Hey, hey, hey . . .
(*And he sees, in the semi-darkness near the football ground, a group of roaming laughing lads. They are walking into a narrow lane. Salim slows the car down and enters the street behind them, following them now, watching them and explaining. To Johnny.*)
These people. What a waste of life. They're filthy and ignorant. They're just nothing. But they abuse people. (*To Omar.*) Our people. (*To Johnny.*) All over England, Asians, as you call us, are beaten, burnt to death. Always we are intimidated. What these scum need—(*and he slams the car into gear and starts to drive forward fast*)—is a taste of their own piss.*

(*He accelerates fast, and mounting the pavement, drives at the Lads ahead of him. Moose turns and sees the car. They scatter and run. Another of the Lads is Genghis. Some of the others we will recognize as mates of his.*
Genghis gets in close against a wall, picking up a lump of wood to smash through the car windscreen. But he doesn't have time to fling it and drops it as Salim drives at him, turning away at the last minute. Genghis sees clearly who is in the front of the car.
As Salim turns the car away from Genghis, Moose is suddenly standing stranded in the centre of the road. Salim can't avoid him. Moose jumps aside but Salim drives over his foot. Moose screams.
Salim drives on.)

118. INT. JOHNNY'S ROOM. NIGHT.

Omar and Johnny have made love. Omar appears to be asleep, lying across the bed.
Johnny gets up, walks across the room and picks up a bottle of whisky. He drinks.

119. INT. ANOTHER LAUNDRETTE. DAY.

This is a much smaller and less splendid laundrette than Omar's.
Omar is looking it over "expertly." Zaki is awaiting Omar's verdict. This is Zaki's problem laundrette.
Salim is also there, striding moodily about.

OMAR I think I can do something with this. Me and my partner.
ZAKI Take it. I trust you and your family.
OMAR Salim?

SALIM I'd happily put money into it.
OMAR All right. Wait a minute.

120. EXT. OUTSIDE THIS SMALLER LAUNDRETTE. DAY.

Johnny is morosely sitting in the car, examining himself in the car mirror. In the mirror, at the far end of the street, he sees a figure on crutches watching them. This is Moose.
   Omar comes out of the laundrette and talks to Johnny through the car window.

OMAR You wanna look at this place? Think we could do something with it?
JOHNNY Can't tell without seeing it.
OMAR Come on, then.
JOHNNY Not if that scum Salim's there.
   (*Omar turns away angrily and walks back into the laundrette.*)

121. EXT. OUTSIDE OMAR AND JOHNNY'S BEAUTIFUL LAUNDRETTE. DAY.

Genghis is standing on the roof of the laundrette, a plank of wood studded with nails in his hand.
   Across the street, in the alley and behind cars, the lads are waiting and watching the laundrette. Moose is with them, hobbling. Inside, Johnny washes the floor. Tania, not seeing Genghis or the lads, walks down the street towards the laundrette.

122. INT. LAUNDRETTE. DAY.

Johnny is washing the floor of the laundrette. A white man opens a washing machine and starts picking prawns out of it, putting them in a black plastic bag. Johnny watches in amazement.
   Tania comes into the laundrette to say goodbye to Johnny. She is carrying a bag.

TANIA (*excited*) I'm going.
JOHNNY Where?
TANIA London. Away.
   (*Some kids are playing football outside, dangerously near the laundrette windows. Johnny goes to the window and bangs on it. He spots a lad and Moose watching the laundrette from across the street. Johnny waves at them. They ignore him.*)
   (*To him.*) I'm going, to live my life. You can come.
JOHNNY No good jobs like this in London.
TANIA Omo just runs you around everywhere like a servant.
JOHNNY Well. I'll stay here with my friend and fight it out.
TANIA My family, Salim and all, they'll swallow you up like a little kebab.
JOHNNY I couldn't just leave him now. Don't ask me to. You ever touched him?
   (*She shakes her head.*) I wouldn't trust him, though.
TANIA Better go. (*She kisses him and turns and goes. He stands at the door and watches her go.*)

123. EXT. OUTSIDE THE LAUNDRETTE. DAY.

From the roof Genghis watches Tania walk away from the laundrette.
   At the end of the street, Salim's car turns the corner. A lad standing on the corner signals to Genghis. Genghis nods at the lads in the alley opposite and holds his piece of wood ready.

124. INT. CLUB/BAR. DAY.

Nasser and Rachel are sitting at a table in the club/bar. They have been having an intense, terrible, sad conversation. Now they are staring at each other. Nasser holds her hand. She withdraws her hand.

Tariq comes over to the table with two drinks. He puts them down. He wants to talk to Nasser. Nasser touches his arm, without looking up. And Tariq goes.

RACHEL So . . . so . . . so that's it.

NASSER Why? Why d'you have to leave me now? (*She shrugs.*) After all these days.

RACHEL Years.

NASSER Why say you're taking from my family?

RACHEL Their love and money. Yes, apparently I am.

NASSER No.

RACHEL And it's not possible to enjoy being so hated.

NASSER It'll stop.

RACHEL Her work. (*She pulls up her jumper to reveal her blotched, marked stomach. If possible we should suspect for a moment that she is pregnant.*) And I am being cruel to her. It is impossible.

NASSER Let me kiss you. (*She gets up.*) Oh, Christ. (*She turns to go.*) Oh, love. Don't go. Don't, Rachel. Don't go.

125. EXT. OUTSIDE LAUNDRETTE. DAY.

Salim is sitting in his car outside the laundrette. Genghis stands above him on the roof, watching. Across the street the lads wait in the alley, alert.

Salim gets out of his car.

126. EXT. OUTSIDE ANWAR'S CLUB. DAY.

Rachel walks away from the club. Nasser stands at the door and watches her go.

127. EXT. OUTSIDE PAPA'S HOUSE. DAY.

Nasser gets out of his car and walks towards Papa's house. The door is broken and he pushes it, going into the hall, to the bottom of the stairs.

128. EXT. OUTSIDE THE LAUNDRETTE. DAY.

Salim walks into the laundrette.

129. INT. PAPA'S HOUSE. DAY.

Nasser sadly climbs the filthy stairs of the house in which Papa's flat is.

130. INT. LAUNDRETTE. DAY.

Salim has come into the busy laundrette. Johnny is working.

SALIM I want to talk to Omo about business.

JOHNNY I dunno where he is.

SALIM Is it worth waiting?

JOHNNY In my experience it's always worth waiting for Omo.

(*The telephone character is yelling into the receiver.*)

TELEPHONE CHARACTER No, no, I promise I'll look after it. I want a child, don't I? Right, I'm coming round now! (*He slams the receiver down. Then he starts to dial again.*)

131. INT. PAPA'S HOUSE. DAY.

Nasser has reached the top of the stairs and the door to Papa's flat. He opens the door with his key. He walks along the hall to Papa's room. He stops at the open door to Papa's room. Papa is lying in bed completely still. Nasser looks at him, worried.

132. EXT. OUTSIDE THE LAUNDRETTE. DAY.

The lads are waiting in the alley opposite. Genghis gives them a signal from the roof.

The lads run across the street and start to smash up Salim's car with big sticks, laying into the headlights, the windscreen, the roof, etc.

133. INT. LAUNDRETTE. DAY.

We are looking at the telephone character. He is holding the receiver in one hand. His other hand over his mouth. Salim sees him and then turns to see, out of the laundrette window, his car being demolished.

134. INT. PAPA'S ROOM. DAY.

Nasser walks into Papa's room. Papa hears him and looks up. Papa struggles to get to the edge of the bed, and thrusts himself into the air.

Nasser goes towards him and they embrace warmly, fervently. Then Nasser sits down on the bed next to his brother.

135. EXT. OUTSIDE THE LAUNDRETTE. DAY.

Salim runs out of the laundrette towards his car. He grabs one of the lads and smashes the lad's head on the side of the car.

Genghis is standing above them, on the edge of the roof.

GENGHIS (*yells*) Hey! Paki! Hey! Paki!

136. INT. PAPA'S ROOM. DAY.

Papa and Nasser sit side by side on the bed.

PAPA This damn country has done us in. That's why I am like this. We should be there. Home.
NASSER But that country has been sodomized by religion. It is beginning to interfere with the making of money. Compared with everywhere, it is a little heaven here.

137. EXT. OUTSIDE THE LAUNDRETTE. DAY.

Salim looks up at Genghis standing on the edge of the roof. Suddenly Genghis jumps down, on top of Salim, pulling Salim to the ground with him.

Genghis quickly gets to his feet. And as Salim gets up, Genghis hits him across the face with the studded piece of wood, tearing Salim's face.

Johnny is watching from inside the laundrette.

138. INT. PAPA'S ROOM. DAY.

Papa and Nasser are sitting on the bed.

PAPA Why are you unhappy?
NASSER Rachel has left me. I don't know what I'm going to do.
(*He gets up and goes to the door of the balcony.*)

139. EXT. OUTSIDE THE LAUNDRETTE. DAY.

Salim, streaming blood, rushes at Genghis. Genghis smashes him in the stomach with the piece of wood.

140. EXT. SOUTH LONDON STREET. DAY.

Omar and Zaki are walking along a South London street, away from Zaki's small laundrette. Across the street is the club/bar. Tariq is just coming out. He waves at Omar.

ZAKI So you're planning an armada of laundrettes?

OMAR What do you think of the dry-cleaners?

ZAKI They are the past. But then they are the present also. Mostly they are the past. But they are going to be the future too, don't you think?

141. EXT. OUTSIDE THE LAUNDRETTE. DAY.

Salim is on the ground. Moose goes to him and whacks him with his crutch. Salim lies still. Genghis kicks Salim in the back. He is about to kick him again.
  Johnny is standing at the door of the laundrette. He moves towards Genghis.

JOHNNY He'll die.

  (*Genghis kicks Salim again. Johnny loses his temper, rushes at Genghis and pushes him up against the car.*)

  I said: leave it out! (*One of the lads moves towards Johnny. Genghis shakes his head at the lad. Salim starts to pull himself up off the floor. Johnny holds Genghis like a lover. To Salim.*) Get out of here!

  (*Genghis punches Johnny in the stomach. Genghis and Johnny start to fight. Genghis is strong but Johnny is quick. Johnny tries twice to stop the fight, pulling away from Genghis.*)

  All right, let's leave it out now, eh?

  (*Salim crawls away. Genghis hits Johnny very hard and Johnny goes down.*)

142. EXT. STREET. DAY.

Zaki and Omar turn the corner, into the street where the fight is taking place. Zaki sees Salim staggering up the other side of the street. Zaki goes to him.
  Omar runs towards the fight. Johnny is being badly beaten now. A lad grabs Omar. Omar struggles.
  Suddenly the sound of police sirens. The fight scatters. As it does, Genghis throws his lump of wood through the laundrette window, showering glass over the punters gathered round the window.
  Omar goes to Johnny, who is barely conscious.

143. EXT. BALCONY OF PAPA'S FLAT. DAY.

Nasser is standing leaning over the balcony, looking across the railway track. Papa comes through the balcony door and stands behind him, in his pyjamas.

NASSER You still look after me, eh? But I'm finished.

PAPA Only Omo matters.

NASSER I'll make sure he's fixed up with a good business future.

PAPA And marriage?

NASSER I'm working on that.

PAPA Tania is a possibility?

  (*Nasser nods confidently, perhaps over-confidently.*)

144. INT. BACK ROOM OF LAUNDRETTE. DAY.

Omar is bathing Johnny's badly bashed up face at the sink in the back room of the laundrette.

OMAR All right?

JOHNNY What d'you mean all right? How can I be all right? I'm in the state I'm in. (*Pause.*) I'll be handsome. But where exactly am I?

OMAR Where you should be. With me.

JOHNNY No. Where does all this leave me?

OMAR Are you crying?

JOHNNY Where does it? Kiss me then.

OMAR Don't cry. Your hand hurts too. That's why.

JOHNNY Hey.

OMAR What?

JOHNNY I better go. I think I had, yeah.

OMAR You were always going, at school. Always running about, you. Your hand is bad. I couldn't pin you down then.

JOHNNY And now I'm going again. Give me my hand back.

OMAR You're dirty. You're beautiful.

JOHNNY I'm serious. Don't keep touching me.

OMAR I'm going to give you a wash.

JOHNNY You don't listen to anything.

OMAR I'm filling this sink.

JOHNNY Don't.

OMAR Get over here! (*Omar fills the sink. Johnny turns and goes out of the room.*) Johnny.

(*We follow Johnny out through the laundrette.*)

145. EXT. THE BALCONY. DAY.

Papa turns away from Nasser.

A train is approaching, rushing towards Nasser. Suddenly it is passing him and for a moment, if this is technically possible, he sees Tania sitting reading in the train, her bag beside her. He cries out, but he is drowned out by the train.

If it is not possible for him to see her, then we go into the train with her and perhaps from her POV in the train look at the balcony, the two figures, at the back view of the flat passing by.

146. INT. LAUNDRETTE. DAY.

Johnny has got to the door of the laundrette. Omar has rushed to the door of the back room.

The shattered glass from the window is still all over the floor. A cold wind blows through the half-lit laundrette.

Johnny stops at the door of the laundrette. He turns towards Omar.

147. INT. BACK ROOM OF LAUNDRETTE. DAY.

As the film finishes, as the credits roll, Omar and Johnny are washing and splashing each other in the sink in the back room of the laundrette, both stripped to the waist. Music over this.

END.

⊷⊰⊱⊷

Margaret Drabble
b. 1939

Margaret Drabble wrote her first novel, *A Summer Bird-Cage*, shortly after taking her degree at Newnham College, Cambridge, one of the colleges where Virginia Woolf had delivered the lectures that became *A Room of One's Own*. On some level Drabble took to heart Woolf's message about women's rights, and women writers; in the four decades since that first book, she has gone on to become one of the foremost women of English letters in the second half of the century.

Drabble's early books are essentially character studies; while a traditionalist in formal terms, she did pioneering work exploring the emotional and interpersonal conflicts faced by a new generation of college-educated women attempting to balance the demands of family and career. It was a set of conflicting demands that Drabble knew firsthand: the mother of three children, she wrote each of her first three novels during her pregnancies and while trying to establish herself as an actress (she was an understudy to Vanessa Redgrave in the Royal Shakespeare Company). After publishing *The Millstone* (1965), Drabble gave up her plans for a career in the theater, and devoted herself to her writing, working primarily at night after her children were asleep. With her fifth novel, *The Waterfall* (1969), Drabble came fully to the attention of both British and American readers; the story of a passionate love affair, the novel suggests both an urgency and a joy in sexual love for its protagonist Jane Grey that is still surprising in its candor. The novel was quite controversial; Drabble herself has called it "a wicked book" which stuck in the craw of those readers "who say that you should not put into people's heads the idea that one can be saved from fairly pathological conditions by loving a man." Her next novel, *The Needle's Eye* (1972), is considered by Drabble herself and by many of her critics to be her best. Asked by the London *Guardian* to write an article on child custody cases, Drabble began her characteristically thorough research; that research became, however, not an article, but *The Needle's Eye*. Her story *The Gifts of War* (1970), given here, explores in powerful, understated prose the tensions both between parents and children and between women of different classes.

In addition to her creative writing—recent novels include *A Natural Curiosity* (1989), *The Gates of Ivory* (1992), and *The Witch of Exmoor* (1996)—Drabble has written a good deal of literary criticism, including studies of William Wordsworth, Thomas Hardy, and Arnold Bennett, and an analysis of the relationship of literature to place (*A Writer's Britain*, 1979). She has also edited *The Oxford Companion to English Literature* (1995). Margaret Drabble was named Commander of the British Empire by the Queen Mother in 1980.

The Gifts of War
Timeo Danaos et dona ferentes.[1]

Aeneid 2.49

When she woke in the morning, she could tell at once, as soon as she reached consciousness, that she had some reason to feel pleased with herself, some rare cause for satisfaction. She lay there quietly for a time, enjoying the unfamiliar sensation, not bothering to place it, grateful for its vague comfortable warmth. It protected her from

---

1. "I fear the Greeks, even when they bear gifts"—spoken by a cautious Trojan soldier who urges his countrymen to refuse the gift of the Trojan horse—supposedly a peace offering, but secretly filled with enemy soldiers.

the disagreeable noise of her husband's snores, from the thought of getting breakfast, from the coldness of the linoleum when she finally dragged herself out of bed. She had to wake Kevin: he always overslept these days, and he took so long to get dressed and get his breakfast, she was surprised he wasn't always late for school. She never thought of making him go to bed earlier; she hadn't the heart to stop him watching the telly, and anyway she enjoyed his company, she liked having him around in the evenings, laughing in his silly seven-year-old way at jokes he didn't understand— jokes she didn't always understand herself, and which she couldn't explain when he asked her to. "You don't know *anything*, Mum," he would groan, but she didn't mind his condemnations: she didn't expect to know anything, it amused her to see him behaving like a man already, affecting superiority, harmlessly, helplessly, in an igno- rance that was as yet so much greater than her own—though she would have died rather than have allowed him to suspect her amusement, her permissiveness. She grumbled at him constantly, even while wanting to keep him there: she snapped at his endless questions, she snubbed him, she repressed him, she provoked him. And she did not suffer from doing this, because she knew that they could not hurt each other: he was a child, he wasn't a proper man yet, he couldn't inflict true pain, any more than she could truly repress him, and his teasing, obligatory conventional schoolboy complaints about her cooking and her stupidity seemed to exorcise, in a way, those other crueller onslaughts. It was as though she said to herself: if my little boy doesn't mean it when he shouts at me, perhaps my husband doesn't either: per- haps there's no more serious offence in my bruises and my greying hair than there is in those harmless childish moans. In the child, she found a way of accepting the man: she found a way of accepting, without too much submission, her lot.

She loved the child: she loved him with so much passion that a little of it spilled over generously onto the man who had misused her: in forgiving the child his dirty blazer and shirts and his dinner-covered tie, she forgave the man for his Friday nights and the childish vomit on the stairs and the bedroom floor. It never occurred to her that a grown man might resent more than hatred such second-hand forgiveness. She never thought of the man's emotions: she thought of her own, and her feelings for the child redeemed her from bitterness, and shed some light on the dark industrial terraces and the waste lands of the city's rubble. Her single-minded commitment was a wonder of the neighbourhood: she's a sour piece, the neighbours said, she keeps herself to herself a bit too much, but you've got to hand it to her, she's been a won- derful mother to that boy, she's had a hard life, but she's been a wonderful mother to that boy. And she, tightening her woolly headscarf over her aching ears as she walked down the cold steep windy street to join the queue at the post office or the butcher's, would stiffen proudly, her hard lips secretly smiling as she claimed and accepted and nodded to her role, her place, her social dignity.

This morning, as she woke Kevin, he reminded her instantly of her cause for satis- faction, bringing to the surface the pleasant knowledge that had underlain her wakening.

"Hi, Mum," he said, as he opened his eyes to her, "how old am I today?"

"Seven, of course," she said, staring dourly at him, pretending to conceal her instant knowledge of the question's meaning, assuming scorn and dismissal. "Come on, get up, child, you're going to be late as usual."

"And how old am I tomorrow, Mum?" he asked, watching her like a hawk, wait- ing for that delayed, inevitable break.

"Come on, come on," she said crossly, affecting impatience, stripping the blankets off him, watching him writhe in the cold air, small and bony in his striped pyjamas.

"Oh, go on, Mum," he said.

"What d'you mean, 'go on,'" she said, "don't be so cheeky, come on, get a move on, you'll get no breakfast if you don't get a move on."

"Just think, Mum," he said, "how old am I tomorrow?"

"I don't know what you're talking about," she said, ripping his pyjama jacket off him, wondering how long to give the game, secure in her sense of her own thing.

"Yes you do, yes you do," he yelled, his nerve beginning, very slightly, to falter. "You know what day it is tomorrow."

"Why, my goodness me," she said, judging that the moment had come, "I'd quite forgotten. Eight tomorrow. My goodness me."

And she watched him grin and wriggle, too big now for embraces, his affection clumsy and knobbly; she avoided the touch of him these days, pushing him irritably away when he leant on her chair-arm, twitching when he banged into her in the corridor or the kitchen, pulling her skirt or overall away from him when he tugged at it for attention, regretting sometimes the soft and round docile baby that he had once been, and yet proud at the same time of his gawky growing, happier, more familiar with the hostilities between them (a better cover for love) than she had been with the tender wide smiles of adoring infancy.

"What you got me for my birthday?" he asked, as he struggled out of his pyjama trousers: and she turned at the door and looked back at him, and said,

"What d'you mean, what've I got you? I've not got you anything. Only good boys get presents."

"I *am* good," he said: "I've been ever so good all week."

"Not that I noticed, you weren't," she said, knowing that too prompt an acquiescence would ruin the dangerous pleasure of doubtful anticipation.

"Go on, tell me," he said, and she could tell from his whining plea that he was almost sure that she had got what he wanted, almost sure but not quite sure, that he was, in fact, in the grip of an exactly manipulated degree of uncertainty, a torment of hope that would last him for a whole twenty-four hours, until the next birthday morning.

"I'm telling you," she said, her hand on the door, staring at him sternly, "I'm telling you, I've not got you anything." And then, magically, delightfully, she allowed herself and him that lovely moment of grace: "I've not got you anything— *yet*," she said: portentous, conspiratorial, yet very very faintly threatening.

"You're going to get it today," he shrieked, unable to restrain himself, unable to keep the rules: and as though annoyed by his exuberance she marched smartly out of the small back room, and down the narrow stairs to the kitchen, shouting at him in an excessive parade of rigour, "Come on, get moving, get your things on, you'll be late for school, you're always late—": and she stood over him while he ate his flakes, watching each spoonful disappear, heaving a great sigh of resigned fury when he spilled on the oilcloth,[2] catching his guilty glance as he wiped it with his sleeve, not letting him off, unwilling, unable to relax into a suspect tenderness.

He went out the back way to school: she saw him through the yard and stood in the doorway watching him disappear, as she always watched him, down the narrow alley separating the two rows of back-to-back cottages, along the ancient industrial cobbles, relics of another age: as he reached the Stephensons' door she called out to him, "Eight tomorrow, then," and smiled, and waved, and he smiled back, excited, affectionate, over the ten yards' gap, grinning, his grey knee socks pulled smartly up,

---

2. A cheap waterproof tablecloth.

his short cropped hair already standing earnestly on end, resisting the violent flattening of the brush with which she thumped him each morning: he reminded her of a bird, she didn't know why, she couldn't have said why, a bird, vulnerable, clumsy, tenacious, touching. Then Bill Stephenson emerged from his back door and joined him, and they went down the alley together, excluding her, leaving her behind, kicking at pebbles and fag[3] packets with their scuffed much-polished shoes.

She went back through the yard and into the house, and made a pot of tea, and took it up to the man in bed. She dumped it down on the corner of the dressing-table beside him, her lips tight, as though she dared not loosen them: her face had only one expression, and she used it to conceal the two major emotions of her life, resentment and love. They were so violently opposed, these passions, that she could not move from one to the other: she lacked flexibility; so she inhabited a grim inexpressive no-man's-land between them, feeling in some way that she thus achieved a kind of justice.

"I'm going up town today," she said, as the man on the bed rolled over and stared at her.

He wheezed and stared.

"I'm going to get our Kevin his birthday present," she said, her voice cold and neutral, offering justice and no more.

"What'll I do about me dinner?" he said.

"I'll be back," she said. "And if I'm not, you can get your own. It won't kill you."

He mumbled and coughed, and she left the room. When she got downstairs, she began, at last, to enter upon the day's true enjoyment: slowly she took possession of it, this day that she had waited for, and which could not now be taken from her. She'd left herself a cup of tea on the table, but before she sat down to drink it she got her zip plastic purse from behind the clock on the dresser, and opened it, and got the money out. There it was, all of it: thirty shillings, three ten-bob notes, folded tightly up in a brown envelope: twenty-nine and eleven, she needed, and a penny over. Thirty shillings, saved, unspoken for, to spend. She'd wondered, from time to time, if she ought to use it to buy him something useful, but she knew now that she wasn't going to: she was going to get him what he wanted—a grotesque, unjustifiable luxury, a pointless gift. It never occurred to her that the pleasure she took in doing things for Kevin was anything other than selfish: she felt vaguely guilty about it, she would have started furtively, like a miser, had anyone knocked on the door and interrupted her contemplation, she would bitterly have denied the intensity of her anticipation.

And when she put her overcoat on, and tied on her headsquare, and set off down the road, she tried to appear to the neighbours as though she wasn't going anywhere in particular: she nodded calmly, she stopped to gape at Mrs. Phillips' new baby (all frilled up, poor mite, in ribbons and pink crochet, a dreadful sight poor little innocent like something off an iced cake, people should know better than to do such things to their own children); she even called in at the shop for a quarter of tea as a cover for her excursion, so reluctant was she to let anyone know that she was going to town, thus unusually, on a Wednesday morning. And as she walked down the steep hillside, where the abandoned tram-lines still ran, to the next fare stage of the bus, she could not have said whether she was making the extra walk to save two pence, or whether she was, more deviously, concealing her destination until the last moment from both herself and the neighbourhood.

---

3. Cigarette.

Because she hardly ever went into town these days. In the old days she had come this way quite often, going down the hill on the tram with her girl friends, with nothing better in mind than a bit of window-shopping and a bit of a laugh and a cup of tea: penniless then as now, but still hopeful, still endowed with a touching faith that if by some miracle she could buy a pair of nylons or a particular blue lace blouse or a new brand of lipstick, then deliverance would be granted to her in the form of money, marriage, romance, the visiting prince who would glimpse her in the crowd, glorified by that seductive blouse, and carry her off to a better world. She could remember so well how hopeful they had been: even Betty Jones, fat, monstrous, ludicrous Betty Jones had cherished such rosy illusions, had gazed with them in longing at garments many sizes too small and far too expensive, somehow convinced that if she could by chance or good fortune acquire one all her flesh would melt away and reveal the lovely girl within. Time had taught Betty Jones: she shuffled now in shoes cracked and splitting beneath her own weight. Time had taught them all. The visiting prince, whom need and desire had once truly transfigured in her eyes, now lay there at home in bed, stubbly, disgusting, ill, malingering, unkind: she remembered the girl who had seen such other things in him with a contemptuous yet pitying wonder. What fools they all had been, to laugh, to giggle and point and whisper, to spend their small wages to deck themselves for such a sacrifice. When she saw the young girls today, of the age she had been then, still pointing and giggling with the same knowing ignorance, she was filled with a bitterness so acute that her teeth set against it, and the set lines of her face stiffened to resist and endure and conceal it. Sometimes she was possessed by a rash desire to warn them, to lean forward and tap on their shoulders, to see their astonished vacant faces, topped with their mad over-perfumed mounds of sticky hair, turn upon her in alarm and disbelief. What do you think you're playing at, she would say to them, what do you think you're at? Where do you think it leads you, what do you think you're asking for? And they would blink at her, uncomprehending, like condemned cattle, the sacrificial virgins, not yet made restless by the smell of blood. I could tell you a thing or two, she wanted to say, I could tell you enough to wipe those silly grins off your faces: but she said nothing, and she could not have said that it was envy or a true charitable pity that most possessed and disturbed her when she saw such innocents.

What withheld her most from envy, pure and straight and voracious, was a sense of her own salvation. Because, amazingly, she had been saved, against all probability: her life which had seemed after that bridal day of white nylon net and roses to sink deeply and almost instantly into a mire of penury and beer and butchery, had been so redeemed for her by her child that she could afford to smile with a kind of superior wisdom, a higher order of knowledge, at those who had not known her trials and her comforts. They would never attain, the silly teenagers, her own level of consolation; they would never know what it was like to find in an object which had at first appeared to her as a yet more lasting sentence, a death blow to the panic notions of despair and flight—to find in such a thing love, and identity, and human warmth. When she thought of this—which she did, often, though not clearly, having little else to think of—she felt as though she alone, or she one of the elected few, had been permitted to glimpse something of the very nature of the harsh, mysterious processes of human survival; and she could induce in herself a state of recognition that was almost visionary. It was all she had: her maternal role, her joy, her sorrow. She gazed out of the bus window now, as the bus approached the town centre and the shops, and as she thought of the gift she was going to buy him, her eyes lit on the bombed sites, and the rubble and decay of decades, and the exposed walls where dirty fading wallpapers had flapped in the wind for years, and she saw where the willowherb grew, green and purple, fields of it amongst the brick, on such thin soil, on the dust of broken bricks and stones, growing so tall in tenacious aspiration out of such shallow infertile ground. It was significant: she knew, as she looked at it, that it was significant. She herself had grown out of this landscape, she had nourished herself and her child upon it. She knew what it meant.

Frances Janet Ashton Hall also knew what it meant, for she too had been born and bred there; although, being younger, she had not lived there for so long, and, having been born into a different class of society, she knew that she was not sentenced to it for life, and was indeed upon the verge of escape, for the next autumn she was to embark upon a degree in economics at a southern University. Nevertheless, she knew what it meant. She was a post-war child, but it was not for nothing that she had witnessed since infancy the red and smoking skies of the steel-works (making arms for the Arabs, for the South Africans, for all those wicked countries)—it was not for nothing that she had seen the deep scars in the city's centre, not all disguised quite comfortably as car parks. In fact, she could even claim the distinction of having lost a relative in the air-raids: her great-aunt Susan, who had refused to allow herself to be evacuated to the Lake District, had perished from a stray bomb in the midst of a highly residential suburban area. Frances was not yet old enough to speculate upon the effect that this tale, oft-repeated, and with lurid details, had had upon the development of her sensibility; naturally she ascribed her ardent pacifism and her strong political convictions to her own innate radical virtue, and when she did look for ulterior motives for her faith she was far more likely to relate them to her recent passion for a newfound friend, one Michael Swaines, than to any childhood neurosis.

She admired Michael. She also liked him for reasons that had nothing to do with admiration, and being an intelligent and scrupulous girl she would spend fruitless, anxious and enjoyable hours trying to disentangle and isolate her various emotions, and to assess their respective values. Being very young, she set a high value on disinterest: standing now, for his sake, on a windy street corner in a conspicuous position outside the biggest department store in town, carrying a banner and wearing (no less) a sandwich-board, proclaiming the necessity for Peace in Vietnam, and calling for the banning of all armaments, nuclear or otherwise, she was carrying on a highly articulate dialogue with her own conscience, by means of which she was attempting to discover whether she was truly standing there for Michael's sake alone, or whether she would have stood there anyway, for the sake of the cause itself. What, she asked herself, if she had been solicited to make a fool of herself in this way merely by that disagreeable Nicholas, son of the Head of the Adult Education Centre? Would she have been prepared to oblige? No, she certainly would not, she would have laughed the idea of sandwich-boards to scorn, and would have found all sorts of convincing arguments against the kind of public display that she was now engaged in. But, on the other hand, this did not exactly invalidate her actions, for she *did* believe, with Michael, that demonstrations were necessary and useful: it was just that her natural reluctance to expose herself would have conquered her, had not Michael himself set about persuading her. So she was doing the right thing but for the wrong reason, like that man in *Murder in the Cathedral*.[4] And perhaps it was for a very wrong reason, because she could not deny that she even found a sort of corrupt pleasure in doing

---

4. Thomas à Becket, the 12th-century English churchman who is the hero of T. S. Eliot's 1935 drama.

things she didn't like doing—accosting strangers, shaking collection-boxes, being stared at—when she knew that it was being appreciated by other people: a kind of yearning for disgrace and martyrdom. Like stripping in public. Though not, surely, *quite* the same, because stripping didn't do any good, whereas telling people about the dangers of total war was a useful occupation. So doing the right thing for the wrong reason could at least be said to be better than doing the wrong thing for the wrong reason, couldn't it? Though her parents, of course, said it was the wrong thing any-way, and that one shouldn't molest innocent shoppers: Oh Lord, she thought with sudden gloom, perhaps my *only* reason for doing this is to annoy my parents: and bravely, to distract herself from the dreadful suspicion, she stepped forward and asked a scraggy thin woman in an old red velvet coat what she thought of the American policy in Vietnam.

"What's that?" said the woman, crossly, annoyed at being stopped in mid-stride, and when Frances repeated her question she gazed at her as though she were an idiot and walked on without replying. Frances, who was becoming used to such responses, was not as hurt as she had been at the beginning of the morning: she was even beginning to think it was quite funny. She wondered if she might knock off for a bit and go and look for Michael: he had gone into the store, to try to persuade the manager of the Toy Department not to sell toy machine-guns and toy bombs and toy battleships. She thought she would go and join him; and when a horrid man in a cloth cap spat on the pavement very near her left shoe and muttered something about bloody students bugger off ruining the city for decent folk, she made up her mind. So she ditched her sandwich-board and rolled her banner up, and set off through the swing doors into the cosy warmth: although it was Easter the weather was bitterly cold, spring seemed to reach them two months later than anywhere else in England. It was a pity, she thought, that there weren't any more Easter marches: she would have liked marching, it would have been more sociable; but Michael believed in isolated pockets of resistance. Really, what he meant was, he didn't like things that he wasn't organising himself. She didn't blame him for that, he was a marvellous organiser, it was amazing the amount of enthusiasm he'd got up in the Students' Union for what was after all rather a dud project: no, not dud, she hadn't meant that, what she meant was that it was no fun, and anyone with a lower sense of social responsibility than herself couldn't have been expected to find it very interesting. Very nice green stockings on the stocking counter, she wondered if she could afford a pair. This thing that Michael had about children and violence, it really was very odd: he had a brother who was writing a thesis on violence on the television and she supposed it must have affected him. She admired his faith. Although at the same time she couldn't help remembering a short story by Saki[5] that she had read years ago, called "The Toys of Peace," which had been about the impossibility of making children play with anything but soldiers, or something to that effect.

When she reached the toy department, she located Michael immediately, because she could hear his voice raised in altercation. In fact, as she approached, she could see that quite a scene was going on, and if Michael hadn't looked quite so impressive when he was making a scene she would have lost nerve and fled: but as it was she approached, discreetly, and hovered on the outskirts of the centre of activity. Michael was arguing with a man in a black suit, some kind of manager figure she

5. Pen name of H. H. Munro (1870–1916), Scottish novelist and short-story writer.

guessed (though what managers were or did she had no idea) and a woman in an overall: the man, she could see, was beginning to lose his patience, and was saying things like:

"Now look here, young man, we're not here to tell our customers what they ought to do, we're here to sell them what they want," and Michael was producing his usual arguments about responsibility and education and having to make a start somewhere and why not here and now; he'd already flashed around his leaflets on violence and delinquency, and was now offering his catalogue of harmless constructive wooden playthings.

"Look," he was saying, "look how much more attractive these wooden animals are, I'm sure you'd find they'd sell just as well, and they're far more durable"—whereat the woman in an overall sniffed and said since when had salesmen dressed themselves up as University students, if he wanted to sell them toys he ought to do it in the proper way; an interjection which Michael ignored, as he proceeded to pick up off the counter in front of him a peculiarly nasty piece of clockwork, a kind of car-cum-aeroplane thing with real bullets and knives in the wheels and hidden bomb-carriers and God knows what, she rather thought it was a model from some television puppet programme, it was called The Desperado Destruction Machine. "I mean to say, look at this horrible thing," Michael said to the manager, pressing a knob and nearly slicing off his own finger as an extra bit of machinery jumped out at him, "whatever do you think can happen to the minds of children who play with things like this?"

"That's a very nice model," said the manager, managing to sound personally grieved and hurt, "it's a very nice model, and you've no idea how popular it's been for the price. It's not a cheap foreign thing, that, you know, it's a really well-made toy. Look—" and he grabbed it back off Michael and pulled another lever, to display the ejector-seat mechanism. The driver figure was promptly ejected with such violence that he shot right across the room, and Michael, who was quite well brought up really, dashed off to retrieve it: and by the time he got back the situation had been increasingly complicated by the arrival of a real live customer who had turned up to buy that very object. Though if it really was as popular as the manager had said, perhaps that wasn't such a coincidence. Anyway, this customer seemed very set on purchasing one, and the overalled woman detached herself from Michael's scene and started to demonstrate one for her, trying to pretend as she did so that there was no scene in progress and that nothing had been going on at all: the manager too tried to hush Michael up by engaging him in conversation and backing him away from the counter and the transaction, but Michael wasn't so easy to silence: he continued to argue in a loud voice, and stood his ground. Frances wished that he would abandon this clearly pointless attempt, and all the more as he had by now noticed her presence, and she knew that at any moment he would appeal for her support. And finally the worst happened, as she had known it might; he turned to the woman who was trying to buy the Desperado Destruction Machine, and started to appeal to her, asking her if she wouldn't like to buy something less dangerous and destructive. The woman seemed confused at first, and when he asked her for whom she was buying it, she said that it was for her little boy's birthday, and she hadn't realised it was a dangerous toy, it was just something he'd set his heart on, he'd break his heart if he didn't get it, he'd seen it on the telly and he wanted one just like that: whereupon the manager, who had quite lost his grip, intervened and started to explain to her that there was nothing dangerous about the toy at all, on the contrary it was a well-made pure British product, with no lead paint or sharp edges, and that if Michael didn't shut up he'd call the police: whereupon Michael said that there was no law to stop customers discussing products in shops with one another, and he was himself a bona-fide customer, because look, he'd got a newly-purchased pair of socks in his pocket in a Will Baines bag. The woman continued to look confused, so Frances thought that she herself ought to intervene to support Michael, who had momentarily run out of aggression: and she said to the woman, in what she thought was a very friendly and reasonable tone, that nobody was trying to stop her buying her little boy a birthday present, they just wanted to point out that with all the violence in the world today anyway it was silly to add to it by encouraging children to play at killing and extermi-nating and things like that, and hadn't everyone seen enough bombing, particularly here (one of Michael's favourite points, this), and why didn't she buy her boy some-thing constructive like Meccano or a farmyard set: and as she was saying all this she glanced from time to time to the woman's face, and there was something in it, she later acknowledged, that should have warned her. She stood there, the woman, her woollen headscarf so tight round her head that it seemed to clamp her jaws together into a violently imposed silence; her face unnaturally drawn, prematurely aged; her thickly-veined hands clutching a zip plastic purse and that stupid piece of clockwork machinery: and as she listened to Frances's voice droning quietly and soothingly and placatingly away her face began to gather a glimmering of expression, from some depths of reaction too obscure to guess at: and as Frances finally ran down to a polite and only very faintly hopeful enquiring standstill, she opened her mouth and spoke. She said only one word, and it was a word that Frances had never heard before, though she had seen it in print in a once-banned book; and by some flash of insight, crossing the immeasurable gap of quality that separated their two lives, she knew that the woman herself had never before allowed it to pass her lips, that to her too it was a shocking syllable, portentous, unforgettable, not a familiar word casually dropped into the dividing spaces. Then the woman, having spoken, started to cry: incredibly, horribly, she started to cry. She dropped the clockwork toy on to the floor, and it fell so heavily that she could almost have been said to have thrown it down, and she stood there, staring at it, as the tears rolled down her face. Then she looked at them, and walked off. Nobody followed her: they stood there and let her go. They did not know how to follow her, nor what appeasement to offer for her unknown wound. So they did nothing. But Frances knew that in their innocence they had done some-thing dreadful to her, in the light of which those long-since ended air raids and even distant Vietnam itself were an irrelevance, a triviality: but she did not know what it was, she could not know. At their feet, the Destruction Machine buzzed and whirred its way to a broken immobility, achieving a mild sensation in its death-throes by shooting a large spring coil out of its complex guts; she and Michael, after lengthy apologies, had to pay for it before they were allowed to leave the store.

Philip Larkin
1922–1985

Philip Larkin's lifetime production of poems was quite small but highly influential; he is best known for his three last volumes, *The Less Deceived* (1955), *The Whitsun Weddings* (1964), and *High Windows* (1974), which together collect fewer than one hundred poems. During his lifetime, however, he fulfilled the role—a role that every society seems to require—of the crotchety traditionalist poet, becoming famous for what the poet and critic Donald Hall has called a "genuine, uncultivated, sincere philistinism."

Born in Coventry, Larkin completed a B.A. and M.A. at Oxford (where he was a friend of the novelist Kingsley Amis), and became a professional librarian, working at the University of Hull from 1955 until his death. After two modestly successful novels (*Jill* and *A Girl in Winter*) and two undistinguished volumes of poetry (*The North Ship* and *XX Poems*), Larkin established himself as a new and important voice in British poetry with his collection *The Less Deceived*. According to most critics, the influence of Thomas Hardy's poetry was decisive; Seamus Heaney writes that the "slips and excesses" of his first two volumes—consisting, primarily, of embarrassing echoes of W. B. Yeats—led Larkin "to seek the antidote of Thomas Hardy."

Larkin was attracted to Hardy's bleak outlook on life, as well as his skilled versification and spare language. Larkin's dark vision remained unremitting as late as *Aubade*, the last poem to be published during his lifetime:

> I work all day, and get half drunk at night.
> Waking at four to soundless dark, I stare.
> In time the curtain-edges will grow light.
> Till then I see what's really always there:
> Unresting death, a whole day nearer now,
> Making all thought impossible but how
> And where and when I shall myself die.

Like the most famous postwar British playwright, Samuel Beckett, the most important postwar British poet was not above having a laugh at his own despair; in an oft-repeated remark, Larkin told an interviewer that "deprivation is for me what daffodils were for Wordsworth."

Larkin is one of the most English of modern British poets; he refused to read "foreign" literature—including most American poetry—or to travel abroad; Hull became the center and circumference of his poetic world. He kept to himself to an extraordinary degree; he never married, nor did he maintain any longstanding intimate relationship. In his obituary for Larkin, Kingsley Amis described him as "a man much driven in upon himself, with increasing deafness from early middle age cruelly emphasizing his seclusion."

Even in his solitude, though, Larkin kept up a running dialogue with the outside world, not only as a poet but as a jazz reviewer for many years. His encyclopedic knowledge of jazz provides the basis for his probing, dyspeptic account of modernity in the opening essay of his collection *All What Jazz*. In this essay as in his verse, Larkin's writing is pointed, skeptical, acerbic—and always self-consciously English.

Church Going

Once I am sure there's nothing going on
I step inside, letting the door thud shut.
Another church: matting, seats, and stone,
And little books; sprawlings of flowers, cut
5   For Sunday, brownish now; some brass and stuff
Up at the holy end; the small neat organ;
And a tense, musty, unignorable silence,
Brewed God knows how long. Hatless, I take off
My cycle-clips in awkward reverence,

10   Move forward, run my hand around the font.
From where I stand, the roof looks almost new—
Cleaned, or restored? Someone would know: I don't.

Mounting the lectern, I peruse a few
Hectoring large-scale verses, and pronounce
15 "Here endeth" much more loudly than I'd meant.
The echoes snigger briefly. Back at the door
I sign the book, donate an Irish sixpence,
Reflect the place was not worth stopping for.

Yet stop I did: in fact I often do,
20 And always end much at a loss like this,
Wondering what to look for; wondering, too,
When churches fall completely out of use
What we shall turn them into, if we shall keep
A few cathedrals chronically on show,
25 Their parchment, plate and pyx[1] in locked cases,
And let the rest rent-free to rain and sheep.
Shall we avoid them as unlucky places?

Or, after dark, will dubious women come
To make their children touch a particular stone;
30 Pick simples° for a cancer; or on some   *medicinal plants*
Advised night see walking a dead one?
Power of some sort or other will go on
In games, in riddles, seemingly at random;
But superstition, like belief, must die,
35 And what remains when disbelief has gone?
Grass, weedy pavement, brambles, buttress, sky,

A shape less recognisable each week,
A purpose more obscure. I wonder who
Will be the last, the very last, to seek
40 This place for what it was; one of the crew
That tap and jot and know what rood-lofts[2] were?
Some ruin-bibber, randy for antique,
Or Christmas-addict, counting on a whiff
Of gown-and-bands and organ-pipes and myrrh?
45 Or will he be my representative,

Bored, uninformed, knowing the ghostly silt
Dispersed, yet tending to this cross of ground
Through suburb scrub because it held unspilt
So long and equably what since is found
50 Only in separation—marriage, and birth,
And death, and thoughts of these—for which was built
This special shell? For, though I've no idea
What this accoutred frowsty° barn is worth,   *stuffy*
It pleases me to stand in silence here;

55 A serious house on serious earth it is,
In whose blent air all our compulsions meet,
Are recognised, and robed as destinies.

---

1. The vessel in which the consecrated bread of the eucharist is kept.

2. Loft at the top of a carved wood or stone screen, separating the nave from the chancel of a church.

And that much never can be obsolete,
Since someone will forever be surprising
60   A hunger in himself to be more serious,
And gravitating with it to this ground,
Which, he once heard, was proper to grow wise in,
If only that so many dead lie round.

1954   1955

High Windows

When I see a couple of kids
And guess he's fucking her and she's
Taking pills or wearing a diaphragm,
I know this is paradise

5   Everyone old has dreamed of all their lives—
Bonds and gestures pushed to one side
Like an outdated combine harvester,
And everyone young going down the long slide

To happiness, endlessly. I wonder if
10   Anyone looked at me, forty years back,
And thought, *That'll be the life;*
No God any more, or sweating in the dark

About hell and that, or having to hide
What you think of the priest. He
15   *And his lot will all go down the long slide*
Like free bloody birds. And immediately

Rather than words comes the thought of high windows:
The sun-comprehending glass,
And beyond it, the deep blue air, that shows
20   Nothing, and is nowhere, and is endless.

1967   1974

Talking in Bed

Talking in bed ought to be easiest,
Lying together there goes back so far,
An emblem of two people being honest.

Yet more and more time passes silently.
5   Outside, the wind's incomplete unrest
Builds and disperses clouds about the sky,

And dark towns heap up on the horizon.
None of this cares for us. Nothing shows why
At this unique distance from isolation

10   It becomes still more difficult to find
Words at once true and kind,
Or not untrue and not unkind.

1960   1964

MCMXIV[1]

Those long uneven lines
Standing as patiently
As if they were stretched outside
The Oval or Villa Park,
5 The crowns of hats, the sun
On moustached archaic faces
Grinning as if it were all
An August Bank Holiday lark;

And the shut shops, the bleached
10 Established names on the sunblinds,
The farthings and sovereigns,
And dark-clothed children at play
Called after kings and queens,
The tin advertisements
15 For cocoa and twist, and the pubs
Wide open all day;

And the countryside not caring:
The place-names all hazed over
With flowering grasses, and fields
20 Shadowing Domesday[2] lines
Under wheat's restless silence;
The differently-dressed servants
With tiny rooms in huge houses,
The dust behind limousines;

25 Never such innocence,
Never before or since,
As changed itself to past
Without a word—the men
Leaving the gardens tidy,
30 The thousands of marriages
Lasting a little while longer:
Never such innocence again.

1960   1964

from **All What Jazz**
A Record Diary 1961–1971

Preface

[W]hen I was asked to write these articles I was patently unfitted to do so and should have declined. The reason I didn't was that I still thought of myself as a jazz lover, someone unquestionably on the wavelength of Congo Square, and although I knew things had been changing I didn't believe jazz itself could alter out of all recognition any more than the march or the waltz could. It was simply a question of hearing enough of the new stuff: I welcomed the chance to do so, feeling confident that once

---

1. 1914, in the style of a monument to the war dead.   2. The Domesday Book is the medieval record of the extent, value, and ownership of lands in England.

I got the feel of it all would be made clear. Secondly, I hadn't really any intention of being a jazz *critic*. In literature, I understood, there were several old whores who had grown old in the reviewing game by praising everything, and I planned to be their jazz equivalent. This isn't as venal as it sounds. Since my space was to be so limited, anything but praise would be wasteful; my readers deserved to be told of the best of all worlds, and I was the man to do it. It didn't really matter, therefore, whether I liked things at first or not, as I was going to call them all masterpieces.

But there came a hitch. When the records, in their exciting square packages, began obligingly to arrive from the companies, the eagerness with which I played them turned rapidly to astonishment, to disbelief, to alarm. I felt I was in some nightmare, in which I had confidently gone into an examination hall only to find that I couldn't make head or tail of the questions. It wasn't like listening to a kind of jazz I didn't care for—Art Tatum,[1] shall I say, or Jelly Roll Morton's Red Hot Peppers.[2] It wasn't like listening to jazz at all. Nearly every characteristic of the music had been neatly inverted: for instance, the jazz tone, distinguished from "straight" practice by an almost-human vibrato, had entirely disappeared, giving way to utter flaccidity. Had the most original feature of jazz been its use of collective improvisation? Banish it: let the first and last choruses be identical exercises in low-temperature unison. Was jazz instrumentation based on the hock-shop trumpets, trombones and clarinets of the returned Civil War regiments? Brace yourself for flutes, harpsichords, electronically-amplified bassoons. Had jazz been essentially a popular art, full of tunes you could whistle? Something fundamentally awful had taken place to ensure that there should be no more tunes. Had the wonderful thing about it been its happy, cakewalky syncopation that set feet tapping and shoulders jerking? Any such feelings were now regularly dispelled by random explosions from the drummer ("dropping bombs"), and the use of non-jazz tempos, $\frac{3}{4}$, $\frac{5}{8}$, $1\frac{1}{4}$. Above all, was jazz the music of the American Negro? Then fill it full of conga drums and sambas and all the tawdry trappings of South America, the racket of Middle East bazaars, the cobra-coaxing cacophonies of Calcutta.

But, deeper than this, the sort of emotion the music was trying to evoke seemed to have changed. Whereas the playing of Armstrong, Bechet, Waller and the Condon groups[3] had been relaxed and expansive, the music of the new men seemed to have developed from some of the least attractive characteristics of the late thirties—the tight-assed little John Kirby band, for instance, or the more riffladen Goodman[4] units. The substitution of bloodless note-patterns for some cheerful or sentimental popular song as a basis for improvisation (I'm thinking of some of the early Parkers[5]) was a retrograde step, but worse still was the deliberately-contrived eccentricity of the phrasing and harmonies. One of the songs I remember from my dance-music childhood was called "I'm Nuts About Screwy Music, I'm Mad About Daffy Tempos," and I've often meant to look it up in the British Museum to see whether the rest of the lyric forecast the rise of bop with such uncanny accuracy. This new mode seemed to have originated partly out of boredom with playing ordinary jazz six nights a week (admittedly a pretty gruelling way

1. Piano virtuoso (1910–1956), known for speed, tempo and key changes.
2. Early jazz pioneer (1885–1941), who combined many different styles of playing.
3. Louis Armstrong (1900–1971), considered one of the greatest vocalists and instrumentalists of jazz; Sidney Bechet (1897–1959), clarinet and soprano sax player; Fats Waller (1904–1943), pianist who wrote songs that

have become jazz standards; Albert Edwin Condon (1905–1973), guitarist and banjo player who helped to start the white Dixieland jazz school of players.
4. Kirby (1908–1952), was known for tight arrangements and quiet playing; Benny Goodman (1909–1986), preferred an expansive style with freely improvised riffs.
5. Charlie Parker (1920–1955), jazz saxophonist and composer.

of earning a living), and partly from a desire to wrest back the initiative in jazz from the white musician, to invent "something they can't steal because they can't play it." This motive is a bad basis for any art, and it isn't surprising that I found the results shallow and *voulu* [contrived]. Worst of all was the pinched, unhappy, febrile, tense nature of the music. The constant pressure to be different and difficult demanded greater and greater technical virtuosity and more and more exaggerated musical non-sequiturs. It wasn't, in a word, the music of happy men. I used to think that anyone hearing a Parker record would guess he was a drug addict, but no one hearing Beiderbecke[6] would think he was an alcoholic, and that this summed up the distinction between the kinds of music.

What I was feeling was, no doubt, a greatly-amplified version of the surprise many European listeners felt when, after the war, records of Parker and his followers began to arrive across the Atlantic. "America has gone mad!" wrote George Shearing[7] on reaching New York during this period (it didn't take him long to follow suit), and whereas Shearing was (presumably) taking only Parker and Gillespie[8] on the chin, I was taking everything up to 1961—Monk, Davis, Coltrane, Rollins, The Jazz Messengers, the lot. I was denied even the solace of liking this man and disliking that: I found them all equally off-putting. Parker himself, compulsively fast and showy, couldn't play four bars without resorting to a peculiarly irritating five-note cliché from a pre-war song called "The Woody Woodpecker Song." His tone, though much better than that of some of his successors, was thin and sometimes shrill. The impression of mental hallucination he conveyed could also be derived from the pianist Bud Powell, who cultivated the same kind of manic virtuosity and could sometimes be stopped only by the flashing of a light in his eyes. Gillespie, on the other hand, was a more familiar type, the trumpeter-leader and entertainer, but I didn't relish his addiction to things Latin-American and I found his sense of humour rudimentary. Thelonious Monk seemed a not-very-successful comic, as his funny hats proclaimed: his *faux-naif* elephant-dance piano style, with its gawky intervals and absence of swing, was made doubly tedious by his limited repertoire. With Miles Davis and John Coltrane a new inhumanity emerged. Davis had several manners: the dead muzzled slow stuff, the sour yelping fast stuff, and the sonorous theatrical arranged stuff, and I disliked them all. With John Coltrane metallic and passionless nullity gave way to exercises in gigantic absurdity, great boring excursions on not-especially-attractive themes during which all possible changes were rung, extended investigations of oriental tedium, long-winded and portentous demonstrations of religiosity. It was with Coltrane, too, that jazz started to be *ugly on purpose:* his nasty tone would become more and more exacerbated until he was fairly screeching at you like a pair of demoniacally-possessed bagpipes. After Coltrane, of course, all was chaos, hatred and absurdity, and one was almost relieved that severance with jazz had become so complete and obvious. But this is running ahead of my story.

The awkward thing was that it was altogether too late in the day to publicize this kind of reaction. In the late forties battle had been joined in the correspondence columns between the beret-and-dark-glasses boys and the mouldy figs; by the early sixties, all this had died down. Setting aside a qualification or two I should like to make later, one can say only that to voice such a viewpoint in 1961 would have

6. Bix Beiderbecke (1903–1931), whose alcoholism eventually killed him.
7. Blind British pianist who came to the United States in 1946.
8. Dizzy Gillespie (1917–1993), trumpet player who helped establish be-bop as a valid style.

been journalistically impossible. By then Parker was dead and a historical figure, in young eyes probably indistinguishable from King Oliver[9] and other founding fathers. There was nothing for it but to carry on with my original plan of undiscriminating praise, and I did so for nearly two years. During this time I blocked in the background by subscribing to *Down Beat* again (there were none of the FRISCO CHIRP'S VEGAS DEBUT headlines I remembered from my schooldays), and read a lot of books. I learned that jazz had now developed, socially and musically: the post-war Negro was better educated, more politically conscious and culturally aware than his predecessors, and in consequence the Negro jazz musician was more musically sophisticated. He knew his theory, his harmony, his composition: he had probably been to the Juilliard School of Music, and jazz was just what he didn't want to be associated with, in the sense of grinning over half a dozen chords to an audience all night. He had freed his music as a preliminary to freeing himself: jazz was catching up with the rest of music, becoming chromatic instead of diatonic (this was the something fundamentally awful), taking in other national musical characteristics as the American Negro looked beyond the confines of his own bondage. Practically everyone was agreed about all this. It was fearful. In a humanist society, art—and especially modern, or current, art—assumes great importance, and to lose touch with it is parallel to losing one's faith in a religious age. Or, in this particular case, since jazz is the music of the young, it was like losing one's potency. And yet, try as I would, I couldn't find anything to enjoy in the things I was sent, despite their increasing length— five, seven, nine minutes at a time, nothing like the brilliant three-minute cameos of the age of 78s. Something, I felt, had snapped, and I was drifting deeper into the silent shadowland of middle age. Cold death had taken his first citadel.

And yet again, there was something about the books I was now reading that seemed oddly familiar. This *development*, this *progress*, this *new language* that was more *difficult*, more *complex*, that required you to *work hard at appreciating it*, that you *couldn't expect to understand first go*, that needed *technical and professional knowledge* to evaluate it *at all levels*, this *revolutionary explosion that spoke for our time* while at the same time being *traditional* in the *fullest*, the *deepest* . . . Of course! This was the language of criticism of modern painting, modern poetry, modern music. *Of course!* How glibly I had talked of *modern* jazz, without realizing the force of the adjective: this was *modern* jazz, and Parker was a modern jazz player just as Picasso was a modern painter and Pound a modern poet. I hadn't realized that jazz had gone from Lascaux[1] to Jackson Pollock[2] in fifty years, but now I realized it relief came flooding in upon me after nearly two years' despondency. I went back to my books: "After Parker, you had to be something of a musician to follow the best jazz of the day." Of course! After Picasso! After Pound! There could hardly have been a conciser summary of what I don't believe about art.

The reader may here have the sense of having strayed into a private argument. All I am saying is that the term "modern," when applied to art, has a more than chronological meaning: it denotes a quality of irresponsibility peculiar to this century, known sometimes as modernism, and once I had classified modern jazz under this heading I knew where I was. I am sure there are books in which the genesis of modernism is set out in full. My own theory is that it is related to an imbalance between the two tensions from which art springs: these are the tension between the artist and his material, and between the artist and his audience, and that in the last seventy-

9. Joe "King" Oliver (1885–1938).
1. Site of the prehistoric cave paintings in Central France.
2. American abstract expressionist painter (1912–1956).

five years or so the second of these has slackened or even perished. In consequence
the artist has become over-concerned with his material (hence an age of technical
experiment), and, in isolation, has busied himself with the two principal themes of
modernism, mystification and outrage. Piqued at being neglected, he has painted
portraits with both eyes on the same side of the nose, or smothered a model with
paint and rolled her over a blank canvas. He has designed a dwelling-house to be
built underground. He has written poems resembling the kind of pictures typists
make with their machines during the coffee break, or a novel in gibberish, or a play
in which the characters sit in dustbins.[3] He has made a six-hour film of someone
asleep.[4] He has carved human figures with large holes in them.[5] And parallel to this
activity ("every idiom has its idiot," as an American novelist has written) there has
grown up a kind of critical journalism designed to put it over. The terms and the
arguments vary with circumstances, but basically the message is: don't trust your
eyes, or ears, or understanding. They'll tell you this is ridiculous, or ugly, or meaningless. Don't believe them. You've got to work at this: after all, you don't expect to
understand anything as important as art straight off, do you? I mean, this is pretty
complex stuff: if you want to know how complex, I'm giving a course of ninety-six
lectures at the local college, starting next week, and you'd be more than welcome.
The whole thing's on the rates,[6] you won't have to pay. After all, think what asses
people have made of themselves in the past by not understanding art—you don't
want to be like that, do you? And so on, and so forth. Keep the suckers spending.

The tension between artist and audience in jazz slackened when the Negro stopped
wanting to entertain the white man, and when the audience as a whole, with the end of
the Japanese war and the beginning of television, didn't in any case particularly want to
be entertained in that way any longer. The jazz band in the night club declined just as
my old interest, the dance band, had declined in the restaurant and hotel: jazz moved,
ominously, into the culture belt, the concert halls, university recital rooms and summer
schools where the kind of criticism I have outlined has freer play. This was bound to
make the re-establishment of any artist-audience nexus more difficult, for universities
have long been the accepted stamping-ground for the subsidized acceptance of art rather
than the real purchase of it—and so, of course, for this kind of criticism, designed as it is
to prevent people using their eyes and ears and understandings to report pleasure and
discomfort. In such conditions modernism is bound to flourish.

I don't know whether it is worth pursuing my identification of modern jazz with
other branches of modern art any further: if I say I dislike both in what seems to me
the same way I have made my point. Having made the connection, however, I soon
saw how quickly jazz was passing from mystification ("Why don't you get a piano
player? and what's that stuff he's playing?") to outrage. Men such as Ornette Coleman, Albert Ayler and Archie Shepp,[7] dispensing with pitch, harmony, theme, tone,
tune and rhythm, were copied by older (Rollins, Coltrane) and young players alike.
And some of them gave a keener edge to what they were playing by suggesting that it
had some political relation to the aspiration of the Black Power movement. From
using music to entertain the white man, the Negro had moved to hating him with it.
Anyone who thinks that an Archie ("America's done me a lot of wrong") Shepp

3. Larkin mocks Samuel Beckett's *Endgame*, in which the
protagonist's parents live in trash cans.
4. American pop artist Andy Warhol made such a film,
called *Sleep*.
5. Larkin is describing the work of British sculptor Henry
Moore (1898–1986).
6. Funded by public taxes.
7. "Free jazz" musicians, all born in the thirties, who
abstracted traditional jazz.

record is anything but two fingers extended from a bunched fist at him personally cannot have much appreciation of what he is hearing. Or, as LeRoi Jones[8] puts it, "Listening to Sonny Murray,[9] you can hear the primal needs of the new music. The heaviest emotional indentation it makes. From ghostly moans of spirit, let out full to the heroic marchspirituals and priestly celebrations of the new blackness."

By this time I was quite certain that Jazz had ceased to be produced. The society that had engendered it had gone, and would not return. Yet surely all that energy and delight could not vanish as completely as it came? Looking round, it didn't take long to discover what was delighting the youth of the sixties as jazz had delighted their fathers; indeed, one could hardly ask the question for the deafening racket of the groups, the slamming, thudding, whanging cult of beat music that derived straight from the Negro clubs on Chicago's South Side, a music so popular that its practitioners formed a new aristocracy that was the envy of all who beheld them, supported by their own radio stations throughout the world's waking hours. Perhaps I was mistaken in thinking that jazz had died; what it had done was split into two, intelligence without beat and beat without intelligence, and it was the latter which had won the kind of youthful allegiance that had led me to hammer an accompaniment to Ray Noble's "Tiger Rag" when I was 12 or 13. Beat was jazz gone to seed, just as "modern jazz" was: B. B. King[1] or Ornette Coleman? A difficult choice, and if I were to come down (as I should) on the side of the former, it wouldn't be under the illusion that I was listening to the latterday equivalent of Billie Holiday[2] and Teddy Wilson, Pee Wee Russell and Jess Stacy, or Fats Waller and his Rhythm.

My slow approximation through these articles to the position just stated is the story I promised lay in them, and the amusement—at least, for me—is watching truthfulness break in, despite my initial resolve. As I said, it's an ordinary tale, and perhaps hardly worth telling. On the other hand, once I had worked out to my own satisfaction what had happened to post-war jazz, I couldn't help looking round to see who, if anyone, had anticipated me. Jazz writers as a class are committed to a party line that presents jazz as one golden chain stretching from Buddy Bolden to Sun Ra,[3] and their task is facilitated by the practice jazz magazines have of employing several reviewers (the trad man, the mod man, the blues man) to ensure that nobody ever has to write about anything they really detest. This is good for trade, lessens the amount of ill-will flying about the business, and gives the impression that jazz is a happy and homogeneous whole. But was there no one among them who had realized what was going on, apart from myself?

I don't mean to suggest that there are not many knowledgeable critics to whom the party line is a sincere reality, nor to imply that they are given to mendacity. When a jazz writer says, "You can hear Bessie in Bird," or "Shepp's playing pure New Orleans street marches," I'm quite prepared to believe he means it, as long as I have permission to mark his mental competence below zero. I also take leave to reflect that most of them are, after all, involved with "the scene" on a commercial day-to-day basis, and that their protestations might be compared with the strictures of a bishop on immorality: no doubt he means it, but it's also what he draws his money for saying. Would any critic seriously try to convince his hearers that jazz was dead? "Jazz dead, you say, Mr Stickleback? Then we shan't be wanting next month's record stint, shall we? And don't bother

8. American poet and political activist (born 1934); he later changed his name to Imamu Amiri Baraka.
9. Drummer (born 1936) who helped build the bridge between traditional swing jazz and abstract free jazz.
1. American blues guitarist and singer (1925–).

2. The queen of jazz (1915–1959); considered to be the greatest jazz vocalist ever. Other famous musicians of her generation follow.
3. Bolden (1877–1931), was the first jazz trumpeter; Sun Ra helped begin improv jazz and free jazz.

to review "Pharaoh Sanders: Symbol and Synthesis" for the book page. And—let's see—we'd better cancel that New Wave Festival you were going to compare. Hope you make the pop scene, daddyo." And so they soldier on at their impossible task, as if trying to persuade us that a cold bath is in some metaphysical way the same as a hot bath, instead of its exact opposite ("But don't you see the evolutionary development?").

But of course there was Hugues Panassié, the venerable Frog, who matter-of-factly refused to admit that bop or any of its modernist successors was jazz at all; simply adducing their records as evidence. It was a shock to find myself agreeing with Panassié: back in 1940 I had considered him rather an ass, chiefly because he overvalued Negro players at the expense of white ones ("the natural bad taste of the Negro" was a favourite phrase of the time), in particular the forcible-feeble Ladnier.[4] But in appealing to the ear, rather than regurgitating the convoluted persuasions of the sleeves, he was producing the kind of criticism I liked, and I had to take back much of what I had thought of him in consequence. Then there was Brian Rust, authoritative discographer, who in his introduction to *Jazz Records 1932–42*, claimed that by 1944 "jazz had split, permanently, the followers of the bop cult demanding—and getting—music in an ever-freer form till (at least in the writer's opinion) it ceased even to be recognizable as jazz at all." He also said that if he played Charlie Parker records to his baby it cried. And it was amusing to find Benny Green,[5] who had made very merry with the bewilderment of old-style fans at the chromatic revolution, devoting the last pages of his book to sarcasms about Ornette Coleman and "some nebulous lunacy called Free Form": nothing is funnier than an upstaged revolutionary. Now and then, too, a reviewer got the wrong record, as in 1961 when the editor of *Down Beat*, Don DeMicheal, took off on Ornette in heartwarming style ("the resulting chaos is an insult to the listener"), ending "If Coleman is to be a standard of excellence in jazz, then other standards might as well be done away with." Only once (August 1967) did I let fly in this way, and then it was like hitting the stumps with a no-ball: the piece wasn't printed.

Such examples could indeed be multiplied, but might only seem added strokes to a self-portrait of the critic as ossified sensibility. To say I don't like modern jazz because it's modernist art simply raises the question of why I don't like modernist art: I have a suspicion that many readers will welcome my grouping of Parker with Picasso and Pound as one of the nicest things I could say about him. Well, to do so settles at least one question: as long as it was only Parker I didn't like, I might believe that my ears had shut up about the age of 25 and that jazz had left me behind. My dislike of Pound and Picasso, both of whom pre-date me by a considerable margin, can't be explained in this way. The same can be said of Henry Moore and James Joyce (a textbook case of declension from talent to absurdity). No, I dislike such things not because they are new, but because they are irresponsible exploitations of technique in contradiction of human life as we know it. This is my essential criticism of modernism, whether perpetrated by Parker, Pound or Picasso: it helps us neither to enjoy nor endure. It will divert us as long as we are prepared to be mystified or outraged, but maintains its hold only by being more mystifying and more outrageous: it has no lasting power. Hence the compulsion on every modernist to wade deeper and deeper into violence and obscenity: hence the succession of Parker by Rollins and Coltrane, and of Rollins and Coltrane by Coleman, Ayler and Shepp. In a way, it's a relief: if jazz records are to be one long screech, if painting is to be a blank canvas, if a play is to be two hours of sexual

4. Tommy Ladnier (1900–1939), jazz trumpeter.   5. Trombonist (1923–1977), who mixed be-bop and swing.

intercourse performed *coram populo* [in public], then let's get it over, the sooner the better, in the hope that human values will then be free to reassert themselves.

Whose Language?

Though Britain's last major overseas colony, Hong Kong, rejoined China in 1997, at least one important reminder of British rule remains in countries as far-flung as India, South Africa, and New Zealand: the English language itself. Twentieth-century linguists, following on the pioneering work of Benjamin Lee Whorf and Edward Sapir, are nearly unanimous in their belief that languages do not merely serve to describe the world but in fact help to create that world, establishing both a set of possibilities and a set of limits.

The politics of language thus becomes important for writers, especially writers in colonial and postcolonial cultures. In an episode from Joyce's A *Portrait of the Artist as a Young Man*, the Irish protagonist Stephen Dedalus converses with the English-born Dean of Studies at University College, Dublin, where Stephen is a student. In the course of the conversation it becomes clear that Stephen is already a more supple and cunning user of the English language than his teacher, and yet he feels himself at a disadvantage in having to use the language of the invader; he muses: "The language in which we are speaking is his before it is mine. How different are the words *home, Christ, ale, master*, on his lips and on mine! I cannot speak or write these words without unrest of spirit. His language, so familiar and so foreign, will always be for me an acquired speech. I have not made or accepted its words. My voice holds them at bay. My soul frets in the shadow of his language." The Penal Acts of 1695 and 1696 had made the Irish language illegal in Ireland; after 500 years of trying to subdue the "wild Irish," British lawmakers realized that the Irish natives would never be brought under English rule until their tongues were bound. In his poem *Traditions*, Seamus Heaney meditates on the enduring cost of what he has called elsewhere "the government of the tongue":

> Our guttural muse
> was bulled long ago
> by the alliterative tradition,
> her uvula grows
> vestigial, forgotten.

In much colonial and postcolonial writing, however, the confusion of tongues inflicted by British rule has been seen by the writers of Empire as a positive linguistic resource. Nadine Gordimer in South Africa and James Kelman in Scotland both mix local dialect with standard English to take the measure of reality a far cry from London. Salman Rushdie, explaining his decision to use English rather than his native Hindi, writes: "Those of us who do use English do so in spite of our ambiguity towards it, or perhaps because of that, perhaps because we can find in that linguistic struggle a reflection of other struggles taking place in the real world, struggles between the cultures within ourselves and the influences working upon our societies. To conquer English may be to complete the process of making ourselves free." Thus a great deal of contemporary English-language writing—especially in countries where English was once the language of the conqueror (such as Ireland, Scotland, Wales, South Africa, India, and Kenya)—meditates on the blindnesses and insights inherent in using English. Some writers, like the Irish poet Nuala Ní Dhomhnaill, write in defiance of English; if one's native tongue is a minority language like Irish, this decision necessarily narrows a writer's potential audience. More common is the decision made by Rushdie, and by James Joyce before him: to write English as an "outsider," attesting to an alien's perspective on the majority language.

Seamus Heaney
b. 1939

More prominently than any poet since Yeats, Heaney has put Irish poetry back at the center of British literary studies. His first full-length collection, *Death of a Naturalist* (1966), ushered in a period of renewed interest in Irish poetry generally, and Ulster poetry in particular; the subsequent attention to poets like Derek Mahon, Michael Longley, Medbh McGuckian, and Paul Muldoon owes a great deal to the scope of Heaney's popularity.

As a great number of Heaney's early poems bear poignant witness, he spent his childhood in rural County Derry, Northern Ireland; his family was part of the Catholic minority in Ulster, and his experiences growing up were for that reason somewhat atypical. The critic Irvin Ehrenpreis maps the matrix of Heaney's contradictory position as an Irish poet: "Speech is never simple, in Heaney's conception. He grew up as an Irish Catholic boy in a land governed by Protestants whose tradition is British. He grew up on a farm in his country's northern, industrial region. As a person, therefore, he springs from the old divisions of his nation." His experience was split not only along religious lines, then, but also national and linguistic ones; in some of his early poetry Heaney suggests the split through the paired names—"Mossbawn" (the very English name of his family's fifty-acre farm) and "Anahorish" (Irish *anach fhior uisce*, "place of clear water," where he attended primary school). As a result, Heaney's is a liminal poetry—a "door into the dark"—and Heaney stands in the doorway, with one foot in each world. Heaney makes brilliant use of the linguistic resources of both the traditions he inherited, drawing on the heritage of English Romanticism while also relying heavily on Irish-language assonance in lines like "There were dragon-flies, spotted butterflies, / But best of all was the warm thick slobber / of frogspawn that grew like clotted water / In the shade of the banks" (*Death of a Naturalist*).

When he was twelve, Heaney won a scholarship to a Catholic boarding school in Londonderry (now Derry) then went on to Queen's University, Belfast, which was the center of a vital new poetic movement in the 1960s. He was influenced by poets who were able to transform the local into the universal, especially Ted Hughes and Robert Frost. As an "Ulster poet," it has fallen to Heaney to use his voice and his position to comment on Northern Ireland's sectarian violence; ironically enough, however, his most explicitly "political" poems were published before the flare-up of the Troubles that began in 1969, and his most self-conscious response to Ulster's strife, the volume *North* (1975), uses historical and mythological frameworks to address the current political situation obliquely. The Irish critic Seamus Deane has written, "Heaney is very much in the Irish tradition in that he has learned, more successfully than most, to conceive of his personal experience in terms of his country's history"; for Heaney, as the popular saying has it, the personal is the political, and the political the personal. His most successful poems dealing with Ulster's political and religious situation are probably those treating neolithic bodies found preserved in peat bogs. Heaney was living in Belfast, lecturing at Queen's University, at the inception of the Troubles; as a Catholic, he felt a need to convey the urgency of the situation without falling into the easy Republican—or Unionist, for that matter—rhetoric. It was at this point that Heaney discovered the anthropologist P. V. Glob's *The Bog People* (1969), which documents (with riveting photographs) the discovery of sacrificial victims preserved in bogs for 2,000 years. Heaney intuitively knew that he had found his "objective correlative"—what he has called his "emblems of adversity"—with which to explore the Troubles.

Like Yeats, Heaney has, from the very start, enjoyed both popular and critical acclaim. His poems have a surface simplicity; his early poetry especially relishes the carefully observed detail of rural Irish life. As his luminous essay *Feeling into Words* shows, he has continued over the years to probe his debts to English literary tradition, and his distance from it. He has been the recipient of numerous awards, honors, and literary prizes, including in 1995 the Nobel Prize for literature.

Feeling into Words[1]

I intend to retrace some paths into what William Wordsworth called in *The Prelude* "the hiding places."

> The hiding places of my power
> Seem open; I approach, and then they close;
> I see by glimpses now; when age comes on,
> May scarcely see at all, and I would give,
> While yet we may, as far as words can give,
> A substance and a life to what I feel:
> I would enshrine the spirit of the past
> For future restoration.

Implicit in those lines is a view of poetry which I think is implicit in the few poems I have written that give me any right to speak: poetry as divination, poetry as revelation of the self to the self, as restoration of the culture to itself; poems as elements of continuity, with the aura and authenticity of archaeological finds, where the buried shard has an importance that is not diminished by the importance of the buried city; poetry as a dig, a dig for finds that end up being plants.

"Digging," in fact, was the name of the first poem I wrote where I thought my feelings had got into words, or to put it more accurately, where I thought my *feel* had got into words. Its rhythms and noises still please me, although there are a couple of lines in it that have more of the theatricality of the gunslinger than the self-absorption of the digger. I wrote it in the summer of 1964, almost two years after I had begun to "dabble in verses." This was the first place where I felt I had done more than make an arrangement of words: I felt that I had let down a shaft into real life. The facts and surfaces of the thing were true, but more important, the excitement that came from naming them gave me a kind of insouciance and a kind of confidence. I didn't care who thought what about it: somehow, it had surprised me by coming out with a stance and an idea that I would stand over:

> The cold smell of potato mould, the squelch and slap
> Of soggy peat, the curt cuts of an edge
> Through living roots awaken in my head.
> But I've no spade to follow men like them.
>
> Between my finger and my thumb
> The squat pen rests.
> I'll dig with it.

As I say, I wrote it down years ago; yet perhaps I should say that I dug it up, because I have come to realize that it was laid down in me years before that even. The pen/spade analogy was the simple heart of the matter and *that* was simply a matter of almost proverbial common sense. As a child on the road to and from school, people used to ask you what class you were in and how many slaps you'd got that day

1. Lecture given at the Royal Society of Literature, October 1974.

Heaney

2845

and invariably they ended up with an exhortation to keep studying because "learning's easy carried" and "the pen's lighter than the spade." And the poem does no more than allow that bud of wisdom to exfoliate, although the significant point in this context is that at the time of writing I was not aware of the proverbial structure at the back of my mind. Nor was I aware that the poem was an enactment of yet another digging metaphor that came back to me years later. This was the rhyme we used to chant on the road to school, though, as I have said before, we were not fully aware of what we were dealing with:

> "Are your praties dry
> And are they fit for digging?"
> "Put in your spade and try,"
> Says Dirty-Faced McGuigan.

There digging becomes a sexual metaphor, an emblem of initiation, like putting your hand into the bush or robbing the nest, one of the various natural analogies for uncovering and touching the hidden thing. I now believe that the "Digging" poem had for me the force of an initiation: the confidence I mentioned arose from a sense that perhaps I could do this poetry thing too, and having experienced the excitement and release of it once, I was doomed to look for it again and again.

I don't want to overload "Digging" with too much significance. It is a big coarse-grained navvy[2] of a poem, but it is interesting as an example—and not just as an example of what one reviewer called "mud-caked fingers in Russell Square," for I don't think that the subject-matter has any particular virtue in itself—it is interesting as an example of what we call "finding a voice."

Finding a voice means that you can get your own feeling into your own words and that your words have the feel of you about them; and I believe that it may not even be a metaphor, for a poetic voice is probably very intimately connected with the poet's natural voice, the voice that he hears as the ideal speaker of the lines he is making up.

In his novel The First Circle, Solzhenitsyn[3] sets the action in a prison camp on the outskirts of Moscow where the inmates are all highly skilled technicians forced to labour at projects dreamed up by Stalin. The most important of these is an attempt to devise a mechanism to bug a phone. But what is to be special about this particular bugging device is that it will not simply record the voice and the message but that it will identify the essential sound patterns of the speaker's voice; it will discover, in the words of the narrative, "what it is that makes every human voice unique," so that no matter how the speaker disguises his accent or changes his language, the fundamental structure of his voice will be caught. The idea was that a voice is like a fingerprint, possessing a constant and unique signature that can, like a fingerprint, be recorded and employed for identification.

Now one of the purposes of a literary education as I experienced it was to turn the student's ear into a poetic bugging device, so that a piece of verse denuded of name and date could be identified by its diction, tropes and cadences. And this secret policing of English verse was also based on the idea of a style as a signature. But what I wish to suggest is that there is a connection between the core of a poet's speaking voice and the core of his poetic voice, between his original accent and his discovered

---

2. Manual laborer.

3. Alexander Solzhenitsyn (1918–), dissident Soviet writer and political activist.

style. I think that the discovery of a way of writing that is natural and adequate to your sensibility depends on the recovery of that essential quick which Solzhenitzyn's technicians were trying to pin down. This is the absolute register to which your proper music has to be tuned.

How, then, do you find it? In practice, you hear it coming from somebody else, you hear something in another writer's sounds that flows in through your ear and enters the echo-chamber of your head and delights your whole nervous system in such a way that your reaction will be, "Ah, I wish I had said that, in that particular way." This other writer, in fact, has spoken something essential to you, something you recognize instinctively as a true sounding of aspects of yourself and your experience. And your first steps as a writer will be to imitate, consciously or unconsciously, those sounds that flowed in, that in-fluence.

One of the writers who influenced me in this way was Gerard Manley Hopkins. The result of reading Hopkins at school was the desire to write, and when I first put pen to paper at university, what flowed out was what had flowed in, the bumpy alliterating music, the reporting sounds and ricochetting consonants typical of Hopkins's verse. I remember lines from a piece called "October Thought" in which some frail bucolic images foundered under the chainmail of the pastiche:

> Starling thatch-watches, and sudden swallow
> Straight breaks to mud-nest, home-rest rafter
> Up past dry dust-drunk cobwebs, like laughter
> Ghosting the roof of bog-oak, turf-sod and rods of willow . . .

and then there was "heaven-hue, plum-blue and gorse-pricked with gold" and "a trickling tinkle of bells well in the fold."

Looking back on it, I believe there was a connection, not obvious at the time but, on reflection, real enough, between the heavily accented consonantal noise of Hopkins's poetic voice, and the peculiar regional characteristics of a Northern Ireland accent. The late W. R. Rodgers, another poet much lured by alliteration, said in his poem "The Character of Ireland" that the people from his (and my) part of the world were

> an abrupt people
> who like the spiky consonants of speech
> and think the soft ones cissy; who dig
> the k and t in orchestra, detect sin
> in sinfonia, get a kick out of
> tin-cans, fricatives, fornication, staccato talk,
> anything that gives or takes attack
> like Micks, Teagues, tinker's gets, Vatican.

It is true that the Ulster accent is generally a staccato consonantal one. Our tongue strikes the tangent of the consonant rather more than it rolls the circle of the vowel— Rodgers also spoke of "the round gift of the gab in southern mouths." It is energetic, angular, hard-edged, and it may be because of this affinity between my dialect and Hopkins's oddity that those first verses turned out as they did.

I couldn't say, of course, that I had found a voice but I had found a game. I knew the thing was only word-play, and I hadn't even the guts to put my name to it. I called myself *Incertus*, uncertain, a shy soul fretting and all that. I was in love with words themselves, but had no sense of a poem as a whole structure and no experience of how the successful achievement of a poem could be a stepping stone in your life. Those verses were what we might call "trial-pieces," little stiff inept designs in imitation of the master's fluent interlacing patterns, heavy-handed clues to the whole craft.

I was getting my first sense of crafting words and for one reason or another, words as bearers of history and mystery began to invite me. Maybe it began very early when my mother used to recite lists of affixes and suffixes, and Latin roots, with their English meanings, rhymes that formed part of her schooling in the early part of the century. Maybe it began with the exotic listing on the wireless dial: Stuttgart, Leipzig, Oslo, Hilversum. Maybe it was stirred by the beautiful sprung rhythms of the old BBC weather forecast: Dogger, Rockall, Malin, Shetland, Faroes, Finisterre; or with the gorgeous and inane phraseology of the catechism; or with the litany of the Blessed Virgin that was part of the enforced poetry in our household: Tower of Gold, Ark of the Covenant, Gate of Heaven, Morning Star, Health of the Sick, Refuge of Sinners, Comforter of the Afflicted. None of these things were consciously savoured at the time but I think the fact that I still recall them with ease, and can delight in them as verbal music, means that they were bedding the ear with a kind of linguistic hardcore that could be built on some day.

That was the unconscious bedding, but poetry involves a conscious savouring of words also. This came by way of reading poetry itself, and being required to learn pieces by heart, phrases even, like Keats's, from "Lamia":

> and his vessel now
> Grated the quaystone with her brazen prow,

or Wordsworth's:

> All shod with steel,
> We hiss'd along the polished ice,

or Tennyson's:

> Old yew, which graspest at the stones
> That name the underlying dead,
> Thy fibres net the dreamless head,
> Thy roots are wrapped about the bones.

These were picked up in my last years at school, touchstones of sorts, where the language could give you a kind of aural goose-flesh. At the university I was delighted in the first weeks to meet the moody energies of John Webster—"I'll make Italian cut-works in their guts / If ever I return"—and later on to encounter the pointed masonry of Anglo-Saxon verse and to learn about the rich stratifications of the English language itself. Words alone were certain good.[4] I even went so far as to write these "Lines to myself":

> In poetry I wish you would
> Avoid the lilting platitude.
> Give us poems humped and strong,
> Laced tight with thongs of song,
> Poems that explode in silence
> Without forcing, without violence
> Whose music is strong and clear and good
> Like a saw zooming in seasoned wood.

4. Cf. W. B. Yeats, *The Song of the Happy Shepherd*: "For words alone are certain good."

> You should attempt concrete expression,
> Half-guessing, half-expression.

Ah well. Behind that was "Ars Poetica," MacLeish's and Verlaine's, Eliot's "objective correlative" (half understood) and several critical essays (by myself and others) about "concrete realization." At the university I kept the whole thing at arm's length, read poetry for the noise and wrote about half a dozen pieces for the literary magazine. But nothing happened inside me. No experience. No epiphany.[5] All craft—and not much of that—and no technique.

I think technique is different from craft. Craft is what you can learn from other verse. Craft is the skill of making. It wins competitions in the *Irish Times* or the *New Statesman*. It can be deployed without reference to the feelings or the self. It knows how to keep up a capable verbal athletic display; it can be content to be *vox et praeterea nihil*—all voice and nothing else—but not voice as in "finding a voice." Learning the craft is learning to turn the windlass at the well of poetry. Usually you begin by dropping the bucket halfway down the shaft and winding up a taking of air. You are miming the real thing until one day the chain draws unexpectedly tight and you have dipped into waters that will continue to entice you back. You'll have broken the skin on the pool of yourself. Your praties will be "fit for digging."

At that point it becomes appropriate to speak of technique rather than craft. Technique, as I would define it, involves not only a poet's way with words, his management of metre, rhythm and verbal texture; it involves also a definition of his stance towards life, a definition of his own reality. It involves the discovery of ways to go out of his normal cognitive bounds and raid the inarticulate: a dynamic alertness that mediates between the origins of feeling in memory and experience and the formal ploys that express these in a work of art. Technique entails the watermarking of your essential patterns of perception, voice and thought into the touch and texture of your lines; it is that whole creative effort of the mind's and body's resources to bring the meaning of experience within the jurisdiction of form. Technique is what turns, in Yeats's phrase, "the bundle of accident and incoherence that sits down to breakfast" into "an idea, something intended, complete."

It is indeed conceivable that a poet could have a real technique and a wobbly craft—I think this was true of Alun Lewis and Patrick Kavanagh—but more often it is a case of a sure enough craft and a failure of technique. And if I were asked for a figure who represents pure technique, I would say a water diviner. You can't learn the craft of dowsing or divining—it is a gift for being in touch with what is there, hidden and real, a gift for mediating between the latent resource and the community that wants it current and released. As Sir Philip Sidney notes in his *Apologie for Poetry*: "Among the Romans a Poet was called *Vates*, which is as much as a Diviner . . ."

The poem was written simply to allay an excitement and to name an experience, and at the same time to give the excitement and the experience a small *perpetuum mobile* in language itself. I quote it here, not for its own technique but for the image of technique contained in it. The diviner resembles the poet in his function of making contact with what lies hidden, and in his ability to make palpable what was sensed or raised.

The Diviner

> Cut from the green hedge a forked hazel stick
> That he held tight by the arms of the V:

---

5. A moment of transcendent vision and insight, crucial in the poetics of modernists like Joyce and Woolf.

> Circling the terrain, hunting the pluck
> Of water, nervous, but professionally
>
> Unfussed. The pluck came sharp as a sting.
> The rod jerked with precise convulsions,
> Spring water suddenly broadcasting
> Through a green hazel its secret stations.
>
> The bystanders would ask to have a try.
> He handed them the rod without a word.
> It lay dead in their grasp till nonchalantly
> He gripped expectant wrists. The hazel stirred.

What I had taken as matter of fact as a youngster became a matter of wonder in memory. When I look at the thing now I am pleased that it ends with a verb, "stirred," the heart of the mystery; and I am glad that "stirred" chimes with "word," bringing the two functions of *vates* into the one sound.

Technique is what allows that first stirring of the mind round a word or an image or a memory to grow towards articulation: articulation not necessarily in terms of argument or explication but in terms of its own potential for harmonious self-reproduction. The seminal excitement has to be granted conditions in which, in Hopkins's words, it "selves, goes itself . . . crying / What I do is me, for that I came." Technique ensures that the first gleam attains its proper effulgence. And I don't just mean a felicity in the choice of words to flesh the theme—that is a problem also but it is not so critical. A poem can survive stylistic blemishes but it cannot survive a still-birth. The crucial action is pre-verbal, to be able to allow the first alertness or come-hither, sensed in a blurred or incomplete way, to dilate and approach as a thought or a theme or a phrase. Robert Frost put it this way: "a poem begins as a lump in the throat, a homesickness, a lovesickness. It finds the thought and the thought finds the words." As far as I am concerned, technique is more vitally and sensitively connected with that first activity where the "lump in the throat" finds "the thought" than with "the thought" finding "the words." That first emergence involves the divining, vatic, oracular function; the second, the making function. To say, as Auden did, that a poem is a "verbal contraption" is to keep one or two tricks up your sleeve.

Traditionally an oracle speaks in riddles, yielding its truths in disguise, offering its insights cunningly. And in the practice of poetry, there is a corresponding occasion of disguise, a protean, chameleon moment when the lump in the throat takes protective colouring in the new element of thought. One of the best documented occasions in the canon of English poetry, as far as this process is concerned, is a poem that survived in spite of its blemish. In fact, the blemish has earned it a peculiar fame:

> High on a mountain's highest ridge,
> Where oft the stormy winter gale
> Cuts like a scythe, while through the clouds
> It sweeps from vale to vale;
> Not five yards from the mountain path,
> This thorn you on your left espy;
> And to the left, three yards beyond,
> You see a little muddy pond
> Of water never dry;
> I've measured it from side to side:
> 'Tis three feet long and two feet wide.

Those two final lines were probably more ridiculed than any other lines in *The Lyrical Ballads* yet Wordsworth maintained "they ought to be liked." That was in 1815, seventeen years after the poem had been composed; but five years later he changed them to "Though but of compass small, and bare / To thirsting suns and parching air." Craft, in more senses than one.

Yet far more important than the revision, for the purposes of this discussion, is Wordsworth's account of the poem's genesis. "The Thorn," he told Isabella Fenwick in 1843,

> arose out of my observing on the ridge of Quantock Hills, on a stormy day, a thorn which I had often passed in calm and bright weather without noticing it. I said to myself, "Cannot I by some invention do as much to make this thorn permanently an impressive object, as the storm has made it to my eyes at this moment?" I began the poem accordingly, and composed it with great rapidity.

The storm, in other words, was nature's technique for granting the thorn-tree its epiphany, awakening in Wordsworth that engendering, heightened state which he describes at the beginning of *The Prelude*—again in relation to the inspiring influence of wind:

> For I, methought, while the sweet breath of Heaven
> Was blowing on my body, felt within
> A corresponding, mild, creative breeze,
> A vital breeze which travell'd gently on
> O'er things which it had made, and is become
> A tempest, a redundant energy
> Vexing its own creation.

This is exactly the kind of mood in which he would have "composed with great rapidity"; the measured recollection of the letter where he makes the poem sound as if it were written to the thesis propounded (retrospectively) in the Preface of 1800—"cannot I by some invention make this thorn permanently an impressive object?"—probably tones down an instinctive, instantaneous recognition into a rational procedure. The technical triumph was to discover a means of allowing his slightly abnormal, slightly numinous vision of the thorn to "deal out its being."

What he did to turn "the bundle of accident and incoherence" of that moment into "something intended, complete" was to find, in Yeats's language, a mask. The poem as we have it is a ballad in which the speaker is a garrulous superstitious man, a sea captain, according to Wordsworth, who connects the thorn with murder and distress. For Wordsworth's own apprehension of the tree, he instinctively recognized, was basically superstitious: it was a standing over, a survival in his own sensibility of a magical way of responding to the natural world, of reading phenomena as signs, occurrences requiring divination. And in order to dramatize this, to transpose the awakened appetites in his consciousness into the satisfactions of a finished thing, he needed his "objective correlative." To make the thorn "permanently an impressive object," images and ideas from different parts of his conscious and unconscious mind were attracted by almost magnetic power. The thorn in its new, wind-tossed aspect had become a field of force.

Into this field were drawn memories of what the ballads call "the cruel mother'" who murders her own baby:

> She leaned her back against a thorn
> All around the loney-o

> And there her little babe was born
> Down by the greenwood side-o

is how a surviving version runs in Ireland. But there have always been variations on this pattern of the woman who kills her baby and buries it. And the ballads are also full of briars and roses and thorns growing out of graves in symbolic token of the life and death of the buried one. So in Wordsworth's imagination the thorn grew into a symbol of tragic, feverish death, and to voice this the ballad mode came naturally; he donned the traditional mask of the tale-teller, legitimately credulous, entering and enacting a convention. The poem itself is a rapid and strange foray where Wordsworth discovered a way of turning the "lump in the throat" into a "thought," discovered a set of images, cadences and sounds that amplified his original visionary excitement into "a redundant energy / Vexing its own creation":

> And some had sworn an oath that she
> Should be to public justice brought;
> And for the little infant's bones
> With spades they would have sought.
> But then the beauteous hill of moss
> Before their eyes began to stir;
> And for full fifty yards around
> The grass it shook upon the ground.

"The Thorn" is a nicely documented example of feeling getting into words, in ways that paralleled much in my own experience; although I must say that it is hard to discriminate between feeling getting into words and words turning into feeling, and it is only on posthumous occasions like this that the distinction arises. Moreover, it is dangerous for a writer to become too self-conscious about his own processes: to name them too definitively may have the effect of confining them to what is named. A poem always has elements of accident about it, which can be made the subject of inquest afterwards, but there is always a risk in conducting your own inquest: you might begin to believe the coroner in yourself rather than put your trust in the man in you who is capable of the accident. Robert Graves's "Dance of Words" puts this delightfully:

> To make them move, you should start from lightning
> And not forecast the rhythm: rely on chance
> Or so-called chance for its bright emergence
> Once lightning interpenetrates the dance.
>
> Grant them their own traditional steps and postures
> But see they dance it out again and again
> Until only lightning is left to puzzle over—
> The choreography plain and the theme plain.

What we are engaged upon here is a way of seeing that turns the lightning into "the visible discharge of electricity between cloud and cloud or between cloud and ground" rather than its own puzzling, brilliant self. There is nearly always an element of the bolt from the blue about a poem's origin.

When I called my second book *Door into the Dark* I intended to gesture towards this idea of poetry as a point of entry into the buried life of the feelings or as a point of exit for it. Words themselves are doors; Janus is to a certain extent their deity, looking back to a ramification of roots and associations and forward to a clarification of sense and meaning. And just as Wordsworth sensed a secret asking for release in the thorn, so in *Door into the Dark* there are a number of poems that arise out of the almost unnameable energies that, for me, hovered over certain bits of language and landscape.

The poem "Undine," for example. It was the dark pool of the sound of the word that first took me: if our auditory imaginations were sufficiently attuned to plumb and sound a vowel, to unite the most primitive and civilized associations, the word "undine" would probably suffice as a poem in itself. *Unda*, a wave, *undine*, a water-woman—a litany of undines would have ebb and flow, water and woman, wave and tide, fulfilment and exhaustion in its very rhythms. But, old two-faced vocable that it is, I discovered a more precise definition once, by accident, in a dictionary. An undine is a water-sprite who has to marry a human being and have a child by him before she can become human. With that definition, the lump in the throat, or rather the thump in the ear, *undine*, became a thought, a field of force that called up other images. One of these was an orphaned memory, without a context, obviously a very early one, of watching a man clearing out an old spongy growth from a drain between two fields, focusing in particular on the way the water, in the cleared-out place, as soon as the shovelfuls of sludge had been removed, the way the water began to run free, rinse itself clean of the soluble mud and make its own little channels and currents. And this image was gathered into a more conscious reading of the myth as being about the liberating, humanizing effect of sexual encounter. Undine was a cold girl who got what the dictionary called a soul through the experience of physical love. So the poem uttered itself out of that nexus—more short-winded than "The Thorn," with less red*undant* energy, but still escaping, I hope, from my incoherence into the voice of the undine herself:

> He slashed the briars, shovelled up grey silt
> To give me right of way in my own drains
> And I ran quick for him, cleaned out my rust.
>
> He halted, saw me finally disrobed,
> Running clear, with apparent unconcern.
> Then he walked by me. I rippled and I churned
>
> Where ditches intersected near the river
> Until he dug a spade deep in my flank
> And took me to him. I swallowed his trench
>
> Gratefully, dispersing myself for love
> Down in his roots, climbing his brassy grain—
> But once he knew my welcome, I alone
>
> Could give him subtle increase and reflection.
> He explored me so completely, each limb
> Lost its cold freedom. Human, warmed to him.

I once said it was a myth about agriculture, about the way water is tamed and humanized when streams become irrigation canals, when water becomes involved with seed. And maybe that is as good an explanation as any. The paraphrasable extensions of a poem can be as protean as possible as long as its elements remain firm. Words can allow you that two-faced approach also. They stand smiling at the audience's way of reading them and winking back at the poet's way of using them.

Behind this, of course, there is a good bit of symbolist theory. Yet in practice, you proceed by your own experience of what it is to write what you consider a successful poem. You survive in your own esteem not by the corroboration of theory but by the trust in certain moments of satisfaction which you know intuitively to be moments of extension. You are confirmed by the visitation of the last poem and threatened by the elusiveness of the next one, and the best moments are those when your mind seems to implode and words and images rush of their own accord into the vortex. Which happened to me once when the line "We have no prairies" drifted into my head at bedtime, and loosened a fall of images that constitute the poem "Bogland," the last one in *Door into the Dark.*

I had been vaguely wishing to write a poem about bogland, chiefly because it is a landscape that has a strange assuaging effect on me, one with associations reaching back into early childhood. We used to hear about bog-butter, butter kept fresh for a great number of years under the peat. Then when I was at school the skeleton of an elk had been taken out of a bog nearby and a few of our neighbours had got their photographs in the paper, peering out across its antlers. So I began to get an idea of bog as the memory of the landscape, or as a landscape that remembered everything that happened in and to it. In fact, if you go round the National Museum in Dublin, you will realize that a great proportion of the most cherished material heritage of Ireland was "found in a bog." Moreover, since memory was the faculty that supplied me with the first quickening of my own poetry, I had a tentative unrealized need to make a congruence between memory and bogland and, for the want of a better word, our national consciousness. And it all released itself after "We have no prairies . . ."—but we have bogs.

At that time I was teaching modern literature in Queen's University, Belfast, and had been reading about the frontier and the west as an important myth in the American consciousness, so I set up—or rather, laid down—the bog as an answering Irish myth. I wrote it quickly the next morning, having slept on my excitement, and revised it on the hoof, from line to line, as it came:

> We have no prairies
> To slice a big sun at evening—
> Everywhere the eye concedes to
> Encroaching horizon,
>
> Is wooed into the cyclops' eye
> Of a tarn. Our unfenced country
> Is bog that keeps crusting
> Between the sights of the sun.
>
> They've taken the skeleton
> Of the great Irish Elk
> Out of the peat, set it up
> An astounding crate full of air.
>
> Butter sunk under
> More than a hundred years
> Was recovered salty and white.
> The ground itself is kind, black butter
>
> Melting and opening underfoot,
> Missing its last definition

> By millions of years.
> They'll never dig coal here,
>
> Only the waterlogged trunks
> Of great firs, soft as pulp.
> Our pioneers keep striking
> Inwards and downwards,
>
> Every layer they strip
> Seems camped on before.
> The bogholes might be Atlantic seepage.
> The wet centre is bottomless.

Again, as in the case of "Digging," the seminal impulse had been unconscious. What generated the poem about memory was something lying beneath the very floor of memory, something I only connected with the poem months after it was written, which was a warning that older people would give us about going into the bog. They were afraid we might fall into the pools in the old workings so they put it about (and we believed them) that *there was no bottom* in the bog-holes. Little did they—or I— know that I would filch it for the last line of a book.

There was also in that book a poem called "Requiem for the Croppies" which was written in 1966 when most poets in Ireland were straining to celebrate the anniversary of the 1916 Rising. That rising was the harvest of seeds sown in 1798, when revolutionary republican ideals and national feeling coalesced in the doctrines of Irish republicanism and in the rebellion of 1798 itself—unsuccessful and savagely put down. The poem was born of and ended with an image of resurrection based on the fact that some time after the rebels were buried in common graves, these graves began to sprout with young barley, growing up from barley corn which the "croppies" had carried in their pockets to eat while on the march. The oblique implication was that the seeds of violent resistance sowed in the Year of Liberty had flowered in what Yeats called "the right rose tree" of 1916. I did not realize at the time that the original heraldic murderous encounter between Protestant yeoman and Catholic rebel was to be initiated again in the summer of 1969, in Belfast, two months after the book was published.

From that moment the problems of poetry moved from being simply a matter of achieving the satisfactory verbal icon to being a search for images and symbols adequate to our predicament. I do not mean liberal lamentation that citizens should feel compelled to murder one another or deploy their different military arms over the matter of nomenclatures such as British or Irish. I do not mean public celebrations or execrations of resistance or atrocity—although there is nothing necessarily unpoetic about such celebration, if one thinks of Yeats's "Easter 1916." I mean that I felt it imperative to discover a field of force in which, without abandoning fidelity to the processes and experience of poetry as I have outlined them, it would be possible to encompass the perspectives of a humane reason and at the same time to grant the religious intensity of the violence its deplorable authenticity and complexity. And when I say religious, I am not thinking simply of the sectarian division. To some extent the enmity can be viewed as a struggle between the cults and devotees of a god and a goddess. There is an indigenous territorial numen, a tutelar of the whole island, call her Mother Ireland, Kathleen Ni Houlihan, the poor old woman, the Shan Van Vocht, whatever; and her sovereignty has been temporarily usurped or infringed by a new male cult whose founding fathers were Cromwell, William of Orange and

Edward Carson, and whose godhead is incarnate in a rex or caesar resident in a palace in London. What we have is the tail-end of a struggle in a province between territorial piety and imperial power.

Now I realize that this idiom is remote from the agnostic world of economic interest whose iron hand operates in the velvet glove of "talks between elected representatives," and remote from the political manoeuvres of power-sharing; but it is not remote from the psychology of the Irishmen and Ulstermen who do the killing, and not remote from the bankrupt psychology and mythologies implicit in the terms Irish Catholic and Ulster Protestant. The question, as ever, is "How with this rage shall beauty hold a plea?" And my answer is, by offering "befitting emblems of adversity."

Some of these emblems I found in a book that was published in English translation, appositely, the year the killing started, in 1969. And again appositely, it was entitled *The Bog People*. It was chiefly concerned with preserved bodies of men and women found in the bogs of Jutland, naked, strangled or with their throats cut, disposed under the peat since early Iron Age times. The author, P. V. Glob, argues convincingly that a number of these, and in particular the Tollund Man, whose head is now preserved near Aarhus[6] in the museum at Silkeburg, were ritual sacrifices to the Mother Goddess, the goddess of the ground who needed new bridegrooms each winter to bed with her in her sacred place, in the bog, to ensure the renewal and fertility of the territory in the spring. Taken in relation to the tradition of Irish political martyrdom for that cause whose icon is Kathleen Ni Houlihan, this is more than an archaic barbarous rite: it is an archetypal pattern. And the unforgettable photographs of these victims blended in my mind with photographs of atrocities, past and present, in the long rites of Irish political and religious struggles. When I wrote this poem, I had a completely new sensation, one of fear. It was a vow to go on pilgrimage and I felt as it came to me—and again it came quickly—that unless I was deeply in earnest about what I was saying, I was simply invoking dangers for myself. It is called "The Tollund Man":

I

Some day I will go to Aarhus
To see his peat-brown head,
The mild pods of his eye-lids,
His pointed skin cap.

In the flat country nearby
Where they dug him out,
His last gruel of winter seeds
Caked in his stomach,

Naked except for
The cap, noose and girdle,
I will stand a long time.
Bridegroom to the goddess,

She tightened her torc[7] on him
And opened her fen,[8]
Those dark juices working
Him to a saint's kept body,

6. A county in East Jutland, in Denmark.
7. A twisting or rotating force.

8. Low land covered with shallow water.

Trove of the turfcutters'
Honeycombed workings.
Now his stained face
Reposes at Aarhus.

II

I could risk blasphemy,
Consecrate the cauldron bog
Our holy ground and pray
Him to make germinate

The scattered, ambushed
Flesh of labourers,
Stockinged corpses
Laid out in the farmyards,

Tell-tale skin and teeth
Flecking the sleepers
Of four young brothers, trailed
For miles along the lines.

III

Something of his sad freedom
As he rode the tumbril
Should come to me, driving,
Saying the names

Tollund, Grauballe, Nebelgard,[9]
Watching the pointing hands
Of country people,
Not knowing their tongue.

Out there in Jutland
In the old man-killing parishes
I will feel lost,
Unhappy and at home.

And just how persistent the barbaric attitudes are, not only in the slaughter but in the psyche, I discovered, again when the *frisson* of the poem itself had passed, and indeed after I had fulfilled the vow and gone to Jutland, "the holy blisful martyr for to seek."[1] I read the following in a chapter on "The Religion of the Pagan Celts" by the Celtic scholar, Anne Ross:

> Moving from sanctuaries and shrines . . . we come now to consider the nature of the actual deities. . . . But before going on to look at the nature of some of the individual deities and their cults, one can perhaps bridge the gap as it were by considering a symbol which, in its way, sums up the whole of Celtic pagan religion and is as representative of it as is, for example, the sign of the cross in Christian contexts. This is the symbol of the severed human head; in all its various modes of iconographic representation and verbal presentation, one may find the hard core of Celtic religion. It is indeed . . . a kind of shorthand symbol for the entire religious outlook of the pagan Celts.[2]

9. Locations in Jutland.
1. The goal of the storytelling pilgrims in Chaucer's *Canterbury Tales*.

2. *Pagan Celtic Britain: Studies in Iconography and Tradition* (1967).

My sense of occasion and almost awe as I vowed to go to pray to the Tollund Man and assist at his enshrined head had a longer ancestry than I had at the time realized.

I began by suggesting that my point of view involved poetry as divination, as a restoration of the culture to itself. In Ireland in this century it has involved for Yeats and many others an attempt to define and interpret the present by bringing it into significant relationship with the past, and I believe that effort in our present circumstances has to be urgently renewed. But here we stray from the realm of technique into the realm of tradition; to forge a poem is one thing, to forge the uncreated conscience of the race, as Stephen Dedalus put it,[3] is quite another and places daunting pressures and responsibilities on anyone who would risk the name of poet.

Medbh McGuckian
b. 1950

Medbh McGuckian's debut as a poet was a high-profile one: even before her first full-length collection was published, her poem *The Flitting* won the Poetry Society Competition, in Britain in 1979, thrusting McGuckian and her writing into the spotlight. An early reviewer called her "a contemporary, Irish Emily Dickinson." Such comparisons are always something of a blessing and a curse; but to date, McGuckian seems to have lived up to the high expectations laid early upon her.

McGuckian was born in Belfast, Northern Ireland. At Queen's University, Belfast, she was a student of Seamus Heaney, and was a classmate of other gifted young poets like Paul Muldoon and Ciarán Carson. Her poetry, however, has little in common with an older generation of Ulster poets whose work meditates on the social, religious, and political unrest in Northern Ireland; McGuckian's poetry, by contrast, is militantly domestic, even—in her own words—"womanly." It is a private poetry, woven of dense rhythms and personal symbols; the critic Tim Dooley fastens on another phrase from McGuckian's verse, "curtainings and cushionings," to describe the way in which her poetry differs from the masculine logic of most poetry. McGuckian's tone and imagery are frequently called "feminine," as opposed to strictly feminist; while clearly animated, and agitated, by many of the questions raised by the women's movement, McGuckian clings to a vision both more global and more essentially mystical than any politics would allow. "I believe wholly in the beauty and power of language," McGuckian has said, "the music of words, the intensity of images to shadow-paint the inner life of the soul." The result is an associative and highly suggestive poetry. As such, it is a poetry rich in possibility, and a poignant, if soft-spoken, response to the angry rhetoric and political violence of her native land. And it makes possible, as the critic Neil Corcoran has written, "a marvelously realized register of desire—desire, in particular, for a privacy, a domestic interior . . . made fully and properly one's own."

Mr. McGregor's Garden[1]

Some women save their sanity with needles.
I complicate my life with studies
Of my favourite rabbit's head, his vulgar volatility,
Or a little ladylike sketching

---

3. The protagonist of Joyce's *A Portrait of the Artist as a Young Man* describes his ambition in these terms at the novel's close.

1. Mr. McGregor is the farmer who chases Peter Rabbit from his garden in Beatrix Potter's stories.

5   Of my resident toad in his flannel box;
       Or search for handsome fungi for my tropical
       Herbarium, growing dry-rot in the garden,
       And wishing that the climate were kinder,
       Turning over the spiky purple heads among the moss
10   With my cheese-knife to view the slimy veil.
       Unlike the cupboard-love of sleepers in the siding,
       My hedgehog's sleep is under his control
       And not the weather's; he can rouse himself
       At half-an-hour's notice in the frost, or leave at will
15   On a wet day in August, by the hearth.
       He goes by breathing slowly, after a large meal,
       A lively evening, very cross if interrupted,
       And returns with a hundred respirations
       To the minute, weak and nervous when he wakens,
20   Busy with his laundry.

       On sleepless nights while learning
       Shakespeare off by heart,
       I feel that Bunny's at my bedside
       In a white cotton nightcap,
25   Tickling me with his whiskers.

                                                        1982

The Dream-Language of Fergus[1]

                            1
       Your tongue has spent the night
       In its dim sack as the shape of your foot
       In its cave. Not the rudiment
       Of half a vanquished sound,
5   The excommunicated shadow of a name,
       Has rumpled the sheets of your mouth.

                            2
       So Latin sleeps, they say, in Russian speech,
       So one river inserted into another
       Becomes a leaping, glistening, splashed
10   And scattered alphabet
       Jutting out from the voice,
       Till what began as a dog's bark
       Ends with bronze, what began
       With honey ends with ice;
15   As if an aeroplane in full flight
       Launched a second plane,
       The sky is stabbed by their exits
       And the mistaken meaning of each.

                            3
       Conversation is as necessary
20   Among these familiar campus trees
       As the apartness of torches;

1. In Irish legend, Fergus was one of the great warrior kings of Ulster.

And if I am a threader
Of double-stranded words, whose
Quando° has grown into now,   *when*
25   No text can return the honey
In its path of light from a jar,
Only a seed-fund, a pendulum,
Pressing out the diasporic snow.

1988

Coleridge

In a dream he fled the house
At the Y of three streets
To where a roof of bloom lay hidden
In the affectation of the night,
5   As only the future can be. Very tightly,
Like a seam, she nursed the gradients
Of his poetry in her head,
She got used to its movements like
A glass bell being struck
10   With a padded hammer.
It was her own fogs and fragrances
That crawled into the verse, the
Impression of cold braids finding
Radiant escape, as if each stanza
15   Were a lamp that burned between
Their beds, or they were writing
The poems in a place of birth together.
Quietened by drought, his breathing
Just became audible where a little
20   Silk-mill emptied impetuously into it,
Some word that grew with him as a child's
Arm or leg. If she stood up, easy,
Easy, it was the warmth that finally
Leaves the golden pippin for the
25   Cider, or the sunshine of fallen trees.

1988

—— ⇥✦⇤ ——

Nuala Ní Dhomhnaill
b. 1952

Ní Dhomhnaill was born in a coal mining region in England, to Irish parents; she was sent at the age of five, however, to live with relatives in the Gaeltacht (Irish-speaking area) on the Dingle Peninsula in West Kerry—"dropped into it cold-turkey," she says. She thus grew up bilingual, speaking English in the home, Irish out of it. Ní Dhomhnaill quickly learned that translation always picks up and leaves behind meaning; she tells this story: "I recall as a child someone asking my name in Irish. The question roughly translates as 'Who do you belong to?' Still most fluent in English, I replied, 'I don't belong to anybody. I belong to myself.' That became quite a joke in the village." In some ways, Ní Dhomhnaill's poetic career has been the process of discovering who, and whose, she is—and making those discoveries through the medium of the Irish language; her name itself, pronounced *nu-AH-la ne GOE-ne*, sounds different than it looks to English eyes.

"The individual psyche is a rather puny thing," she has said; "One's interior life dries up without the exchange with tradition." Ní Dhomhnaill's fruitful exchange with the Irish literary tradition has resulted in a poetry rich in the imagery of Irish folklore and mythology, and pregnant with the sense of contradiction and irony that undergirds Irish writing ("We [Celts] are truly comfortable only with ambiguity," she says). Ní Dhomhnaill's poetry in Irish includes the prize-winning volumes *An Dealg Droighin* (1981) and *Féar Suaithinseach* (1984), as well as a selection of poems from her volume *Feis* translated into English by the poet Paul Muldoon. The *Irish Literary Supplement* has called her "the most widely known and acclaimed Gaelic poet of the century"; by continuing to write in Irish, she has helped make it a viable language for modern poetry. Ní Dhomhnaill lives in Dublin and teaches at University College, Cork.

Feeding a Child[1]

From honey-dew of milking
from cloudy heat of beestings
the sun rises up the back
of bare hills,
5   a guinea gold
to put in your hand,
my own.
You drink your fill from my breast
and fall back asleep
10   into a lasting dream
laughter in your face.
What is going through your head
you who are but
a fortnight on earth?

15   Do you know day from night
that the great early ebb
announces spring tide?
That the boats
are on deep ocean,
20   where live the seals and fishes
and the great whales,
and are coming hand over hand
each by seven oars manned?
That your small boats swims
25   óró[2] in the bay
with the flippered peoples
and the small sea-creatures
she slippery-sleek
from stem to bow
30   stirring sea-sand up
sinking sea-foam down.

Of all these things are you
ignorant?
As my breast is explored
35   by your small hand
you grunt with pleasure

---

1. Translated by Michael Hartnett.   2. Soothing nonsense sound in Irish.

smiling and senseless.
I look into your face child
not knowing if you know
40   your herd of cattle
graze in the land of giants
trespassing and thieving
and that soon you will hear
the fee-fie-fo-fum
45   sounding in your ear.

You are my piggy
who went to market
who stayed at home
who got bread and butter
50   who got none.
There's one good bite in you
but hardly two—
I like your flesh
but not the broth thereof.
55   And who are the original patterns
of the heroes and giants
if not you and I?

1986

Parthenogenesis[1]

Once, a lady of the Ó Moores
(married seven years without a child)
swam in the sea in summertime.
She swam well, and the day
5   was fine as Ireland ever saw
not even a puff of wind in the air
all the bay calm, all the sea smooth—
a sheet of glass—supple, she struck out
with strength for the breaking waves
10   and frisked, elated by the world.
She ducked beneath the surface and there saw
what seemed a shadow, like a man's.
And every twist and turn she made
the shadow did the same
15   and came close enough to touch.
Heart jumped and sound stopped in her mouth
her pulses ran and raced, sides near burst.
The lower currents with their ice
pierced her to the bone
20   and the noise of the abyss numbed all her limbs
then scales grew on her skin . . .
the lure of the quiet dreamy undersea . . .
desire to escape to sea and shells . . .
the seaweed tresses where at last
25   her bones changed into coral
and time made atolls of her arms,

1. Translated by Michael Hartnett. "Parthenogenesis" is the scientific term for virgin birth.

pearls of her eyes in deep long sleep,
at rest in a nest of weed,
secure as feather beds . . .
30   But stop!
Her heroic heritage was there,
she rose with speedy, threshing feet
and made in desperation for the beach:
with nimble supple strokes she made the sand.
35   Near death until the day,
some nine months later
she gave birth to a boy.
She and her husband so satisfied,
so full of love for this new son
40   forgot the shadow in the sea
and did not see what only the midwife saw—
stalks of sea-tangle in the boy's hair
small shellfish and sea-ribbons
and his two big eyes
45   as blue and limpid as lagoons.
A poor scholar passing by
who found lodging for the night
saw the boy's eyes never closed
in dark or light and when all the world slept
50   he asked the boy beside the fire
"Who are your people?" Came the prompt reply
"Sea People."

This same tale is told in the West
but the woman's an Ó Flaherty
55   and tis the same in the South
where the lady's called Ó Shea:
this tale is told on every coast.
But whoever she was I want to say
that the fear she felt
60   when the sea-shadow followed her
is the same fear that vexed
the young heart of the Virgin
when she heard the angels' sweet bell
and in her womb was made flesh
65   by all accounts
the Son of the Living God.

1986

Labasheedy (The Silken Bed)[1]

I'd make a bed for you
in Labasheedy
in the tall grass
under the wrestling trees
5   where your skin
would be silk upon silk

---

1. Translated by the author.

in the darkness
when the moths are coming down.

Skin which glistens
10   shining over your limbs
like milk being poured
from jugs at dinnertime;
your hair is a herd of goats
moving over rolling hills,
15   hills that have high cliffs
and two ravines.

And your damp lips
would be as sweet as sugar
at evening and we walking
20   by the riverside
with honeyed breezes
blowing over the Shannon
and the fuchsias bowing down to you
one by one.

25   The fuchsias bending low
their solemn heads
in obeisance to the beauty
in front of them
I would pick a pair of flowers
30   as pendant earrings
to adorn you
like a bride in shining clothes.

O I'd make a bed for you
in Labasheedy,
35   in the twilight hour
with evening falling slow
and what a pleasure it would be
to have our limbs entwine
wrestling
40   while the moths are coming down.

1986

As for the Quince[1]

There came this bright young thing
with a Black & Decker
and cut down my quince-tree.
I stood with my mouth hanging open
5   while one by one
she trimmed off the branches.

When my husband got home that evening
and saw what had happened
he lost the rag,
10   as you might imagine.
"Why didn't you stop her?
What would she think

---

1. Translated by Paul Muldoon.

if I took the Black & Decker
round to her place
15   and cut down a quince-tree
belonging to her?
What would she make of that?"

Her ladyship came back next morning
while I was at breakfast.
20   She enquired about his reaction.
I told her straight
that he was wondering how she'd feel
if he took a Black & Decker
round to her house
25   and cut down a quince-tree of hers,
etcetera etcetera.

"O," says she, "that's very interesting."
There was a stress on the "very."
She lingered over the "ing."
30   She was remarkably calm and collected.

These are the times that are in it, so,
all a bit topsy-turvy.
The bottom falling out of my belly
as if I had got a kick up the arse
35   or a punch in the kidneys.
A fainting-fit coming over me
that took the legs from under me
and left me so zonked
I could barely lift a finger
40   till Wednesday.

As for the quince, it was safe and sound
and still somehow holding its ground.

1988

Why I Choose to Write in Irish,
The Corpse That Sits Up and Talks Back[1]

Not so long ago I telephoned my mother about some family matter. "So what are you writing these days?" she asked, more for the sake of conversation than anything else. "Oh, an essay for *The New York Times*," I said, as casually as possible. "What is it about?" she asked. "About what it is like to write in Irish," I replied. There was a good few seconds' pause on the other end of the line; then, "Well, I hope you'll tell them that it is mad." End of conversation. I had got my comeuppance. And from my mother, who was the native speaker of Irish in our family, never having encountered a single word of English until she went to school at the age of 6, and well up in her teens before she realized that the name they had at home for a most useful item was actually two words—"safety pin"—and that they were English. Typical.

But really not so strange. Some time later I was at a reception at the American Embassy in Dublin for two of their writers, Toni Morrison and Richard Wilbur. We

1. Published in *The New York Times Book Review*, January 1995.

stood in line and took our buffet suppers along to the nearest available table. An Irishwoman across from me asked what I did. Before I had time to open my mouth her partner butted in: "Oh, Nuala writes poetry in Irish." And what did I write about? she asked. Again before I had time to reply he did so for me: "She writes poems of love and loss, and I could quote you most of them by heart." This was beginning to get up my nose, and so I attempted simultaneously to deflate him and to go him one better. "Actually," I announced, "I think the only things worth writing about are the biggies: birth, death and the most important thing in between, which is sex." "Oh," his friend said to me archly, "and is there a word for sex in Irish?"

I looked over at the next table, where Toni Morrison was sitting, and I wondered if a black writer in America had to put up with the likes of that, or its equivalent. Here I was in my own country, having to defend the official language of the state from a compatriot who obviously thought it was an accomplishment to be ignorant of it. Typical, and yet maybe not so strange.

Let me explain. Irish (as it is called in the Irish Constitution; to call it Gaelic is not P.C. at the moment, but seen as marginalizing) is the Celtic language spoken by a small minority of native speakers principally found in rural pockets on the western seaboard. These Irish-speaking communities are known as the "Gaeltacht," and are the last remnants of an earlier historical time when the whole island was Irish-speaking, or one huge "Gaeltacht." The number of Irish speakers left in these areas who use the language in most of their daily affairs is a hotly debated point, and varies from 100,000 at the most optimistic estimate to 20,000 at the most conservative. For the sake of a round number let us take it to be 60,000, or about 2 percent of the population of the Republic of Ireland.

Because of the effort of the Irish Revival movement, and of the teaching of Irish in the school system, however, the language is also spoken with varying degrees of frequency and fluency by a considerably larger number of people who have learned it as a second language. So much so that census figures over the last few decades have consistently indicated that up to one million people, or 30 percent of the population of the Republic, claim to be speakers of Irish. To this can be added the 146,000 people in the Six Counties of Northern Ireland who also are competent in Irish. This figure of one million speakers is, of course, grossly misleading and in no way reflects a widespread use of the language in everyday life. Rather it can be seen as a reflection of general good will toward the language, as a kind of wishful thinking. Nevertheless that good will is important.

The fact that the Irish language, and by extension its literature, has a precarious status in Ireland at the moment is a development in marked contrast to its long and august history. I believe writing in Irish is the oldest continuous literary activity in Western Europe, starting in the fifth century and flourishing in a rich and varied manuscript tradition right down through the Middle Ages. During this time the speakers of any invading language, such as Norse, Anglo-Norman and English, were assimilated, becoming "more Irish than the Irish themselves." But the Battle of Kinsale in 1601, in which the British routed the last independent Irish princes, and the ensuing catastrophes of the turbulent 17th century, including forced population transfers, destroyed the social underpinning of the language. Its decline was much accelerated by the great famine of the mid-19th century; most of the one million who died of starvation and the millions who left on coffin ships for America were Irish speakers. The fact that the fate of emigration stared most of the survivors in the eye further speeded up the language change to English—after all, "What use was Irish to you over in Boston?"

The indigenous high culture became the stuff of the speech of fishermen and small farmers, and this is the language that I learned in West Kerry in the 1950's at the age of 5 in a situation of total immersion, when I was literally and figuratively farmed out to my aunt in the parish of Ventry. Irish is a language of enormous elasticity and emotional sensitivity; of quick and hilarious banter and a welter of references both historical and mythological; it is an instrument of imaginative depth and scope, which has been tempered by the community for generations until it can pick up and sing out every hint of emotional modulation that can occur between people. Many international scholars rhapsodize that this speech of ragged peasants seems always on the point of bursting into poetry. The pedagogical accident that had me learn this language at an early age can only be called a creative one.

The Irish of the Revival, or "book Irish," was something entirely different, and I learned it at school. Although my first literary love affair was with the Munster poets, Aodhagán Ó Rathaille and Eoghan Rua Ó Suilleabháin, and I had learned reams and reams of poetry that wasn't taught at school, when I myself came to write it didn't dawn on me that I could possibly write in Irish. The overriding ethos had got even to me. Writing poetry in Irish somehow didn't seem to be intellectually credible. So my first attempts, elegies on the deaths of Bobby Kennedy and Martin Luther King published in the school magazine, were all in English. They were all right, but even I could see that there was something wrong with them.

Writing Irish poetry in English suddenly seemed a very stupid thing to be doing. So I switched language in mid-poem and wrote the very same poem in Irish, and I could see immediately that it was much better. I sent it in to a competition in *The Irish Times*, where it won a prize, and that was that. I never looked back.

I had chosen my language, or more rightly, perhaps, at some very deep level, the language had chosen me. If there is a level to our being that for want of any other word for it I might call "soul" (and I believe there is), then for some reason that I can never understand, the language that my soul speaks, and the place it comes from, is Irish. At 16 I had made my choice. And that was that. It still is. I have no other.

But if the actual choice to write poetry in Irish was easy, then nothing else about it actually is, especially the hypocritical attitude of the state. On the one hand, Irish is enshrined as a nationalistic token (the ceremonial *cúpla focal*—"few words"—at the beginning and end of speeches by politicians, broadcasters and even airline crews is an example). On the other hand, it would not be an exaggeration to speak of the state's indifference, even downright hostility, to Irish speakers in its failure to provide even the most basic services in Irish for those who wish to go about their everyday business in that language.

"The computer cannot understand Irish" leads the excuses given by the state to refuse to conduct its business in Irish, even in the Gaeltacht areas. Every single service gained by Irish speakers has been fought for bitterly. Thus the "Gaelscoileanna," or Irish schools, have been mostly started by groups of parents, often in the very teeth of fierce opposition from the Department of Education. And the only reason we have a single Irish radio station is that a civil rights group started a pirate station 20 years ago in the West and shamed the Government into establishing this vital service. An Irish television channel is being mooted[2] at present, but I'll believe it when I see it.

---

2. Debated.

You might expect at least the cultural nationalists and our peers writing in English to be on our side. Not so. A recent television documentary film about Thomas Kinsella begins with the writer intoning the fact that history has been recorded in Irish from the fifth century to the 19th. Then there is a pregnant pause. We wait for a mention of the fact that life, experience, sentient consciousness, even history is being recorded in literature in Irish in the present day. We wait in vain. By an antiquarian sleight of hand it is implied that Irish writers in English are now the natural heirs to a millennium and a half of writing in Irish. The subtext of the film is that Irish is dead.

So what does that make me, and the many other writers of the large body of modern literature in Irish? A walking ghost? A linguistic specter?

Mind you, it is invidious of me to single out Thomas Kinsella; this kind of insidious "bad faith" about modern literature in Irish is alive and rampant among many of our fellow writers in English. As my fellow poet in Irish, Biddy Jenkinson, has said, "We have been pushed into an ironic awareness that by our passage we would convenience those who will be uneasy in their Irishness as long as there is a living Gaelic tradition to which they do not belong." Now let them make their peace with the tradition if they wish to, I don't begrudge them a line of it. But I'll be damned if their cultural identity is procured at the expense of my existence, or of that of my language.

I can well see how it suits some people to see Irish-language literature as the last rictus[3] of a dying beast. As far as they are concerned, the sooner the language lies down and dies, the better, so they can cannibalize it with greater equanimity, peddling their "ethnic chic" with nice little translations "from the Irish." Far be it from them to make the real effort it takes to learn the living language. I dare say they must be taken somewhat aback when the corpse that they have long since consigned to choirs of angels, like a certain Tim Finnegan,[4] sits up and talks back to them.

The fault is not always one-sided. The Gaels (Irish-language writers) often fell prey to what Terence Browne, a literary historian, has called an "atmosphere of national self-righteousness and cultural exclusiveness," and their talent did not always equal the role imposed on them. Nevertheless, long after the emergence of a high standard of literature in Irish with Seán Ó Riordáin, Máirtín Ó Direáin and Máire Mhac an tSaoi in poetry, and Máirtín Ó Cadhain in prose, writing in Irish was conspicuously absent from anthologies in the 1950's and 60's. Even as late as the 70's one of our "greats," Seán Ó Riordáin, could hear on the radio two of his co-writers in English saying how "poetry in Ireland had been quiescent in the 50's," thus consigning to nothingness the great work that he and his fellow poets in Irish had produced during that very decade. After a lifetime devoted to poetry, is it any wonder that he died in considerable grief and bitterness?

As for the cultural nationalists, Irish was never the language of nationalist mobilization. Unlike other small countries where nationalism rose throughout the 19th century, in Ireland it was religion rather than language that mostly colored nationalism. Daniel O'Connell, the Liberator, a native-Irish-speaking Kerryman, used to address his monster mass meetings from the 1820's to the 40's in English, even though this language was not understood by 70 percent of the people he was addressing. Why? Because it was at the reporters over from *The Times* of London and their readers that his words were being primarily directed. It is particularly painful to recall

3. Gasp.
4. In the vaudeville song *Tim Finnegan's Wake*, the hero takes a drunken fall and dies. At his wake, however, whiskey is spilled over his body and he comes back to life. James Joyce uses this story as the central structure for *Finnegans Wake*.

that while nationalism was a major motivator in developing modern literary languages out of such varied tongues as Norwegian, Hungarian, Finnish and Estonian, during that very same period the high literary culture of Irish was being reduced to the language of peasants. By the time the revival began, the damage had already been done, and the language was already in irreversible decline (spoken by only 14.5 percent in 1880). The blatant myopia of the cultural nationalists is still alive and glaringly obvious in the disgraceful underrepresentation of Irish in the recently published three-volume *Field Day Anthology of Irish Writing.*

It should not be surprising, then, that we poets and fiction writers in Irish who are included in the anthology feel as if we are being reduced to being exotic background, like Irish Muzak. Thus the cultural nationalists, without granting Irish the intellectual credibility of rational discourse or the popular base of the oral tradition, enshrine it instead as the repository of their own utopian fantasies; pristine, changeless, "creative," but otherwise practically useless.

How does all this affect me, as a poet writing in Irish? Well, inasmuch as I am human and frail and prone to vanity and clamoring for attention, of course it disturbs me to be misunderstood, misrepresented and finally all but invisible in my own country. I get depressed, I grumble and complain, I stand around in rooms muttering darkly. Still and all, at some very deep and fundamental level it matters not one whit. All I ever wanted was to be left alone so that I could go on writing poetry in Irish. I still remember a time when I had an audience I could count on the fingers of one hand. I was perfectly prepared for that. I still am.

But it has been gratifying to reach a broader audience through the medium of translations, especially among the one million who profess some knowledge of Irish. Many of them probably had good Irish when they left school but have had no chance of using it since for want of any functional context where it would make sense to use the language. I particularly like it when my poetry in English translation sends them back to the originals in Irish, and when they then go on to pick up the long-lost threads of the language that is so rightly theirs. I also find it pleasant and vivifying to make an occasional trip abroad and to reach a wider audience by means of dual-language readings and publications.

But my primary audience is those who read my work in Irish only. A print run for a book of poems in Irish is between 1,000 and 1,500 copies. That doesn't sound like much until you realize that that number is considered a decent run by many poets in English in Ireland, or for that matter even in Britain or America, where there's a much larger population.

The very ancientness of the Irish literary tradition is also a great source of strength to me as a writer. This works at two levels, one that is mainly linguistic and prosodic and another that is mainly thematic and inspirational. At the linguistic level, Old Irish, though undoubtedly very difficult, is much closer to Modern Irish than, say, Anglo-Saxon is to Modern English. Anyone like me with a basic primary degree in the language and a bit of practice can make a fair job of reading most of the medieval texts in the original.

Thematically too, the older literature is a godsend, though I am only now slowly beginning to assess its unique possibilities to a modern writer. There are known to be well over 4,000 manuscripts in Ireland and elsewhere of material from Old to Modern Irish. Apart from the great medieval codices, only about 50 other manuscripts date from before 1650. Nevertheless, the vast majority of the manuscripts painstakingly copied down after this time are exemplars of much earlier manuscripts that have since been lost. A lot of this is catalogued in ways that are unsatisfactory for our time.

Many items of enormous psychological and sexual interest, for example, are described with the bias of the last century as "indecent and obscene tales, unsuitable for publication." On many such manuscripts human eye has not set sight since they were so described. In addition, most scholarly attention has been paid to pre-Norman-Conquest material as the repository of the unsullied wellsprings of the native soul (those cultural nationalists again!), with the result that the vast area of post-Conquest material has been unfairly neglected. The main advantage of all this material to me is that it is proof of the survival until even a very late historical date of a distinct *Weltanschauung* [worldview] radically different from the Anglo mentality that has since eclipsed it.

Because of a particular set of circumstances, Irish fell out of history just when the modern mentality was about to take off. So major intellectual changes like the Reformation, the Renaissance, the Enlightenment, Romanticism and Victorian prudery have never occurred in it, as they did in the major European languages.

One consequence is that the attitude to the body enshrined in Irish remains extremely open and uncoy. It is almost impossible to be "rude" or "vulgar" in Irish. The body, with its orifices and excretions, is not treated in a prudish manner but is accepted as *an nádúir*, or "nature," and becomes a source of repartee and laughter rather than anything to be ashamed of. Thus little old ladies of quite impeccable and unimpeachable moral character tell risqué stories with gusto and panache. Is there a word for sex in Irish, indeed! Is there an Eskimo word for snow?

By now I must have spent whole years of my life burrowing in the department of folklore at University College, Dublin, and yet there are still days when my hands shake with emotion holding manuscripts. Again, this material works on me on two levels. First is when I revel in the well-turned phrase or nuance or retrieve a word that may have fallen into disuse. To turn the pages of these manuscripts is to hear the voices of my neighbors and my relatives—all the fathers and grandfathers and uncles come to life again. The second interest is more thematic. This material is genuinely ineffable, like nothing else on earth.

Indeed, there is a drawer in the index entitled "Neacha neamhbeo agus nithe nach bhfuil ann" ("Unalive beings and things that don't exist"). Now I am not the greatest empiricist in the world but this one has even me stumped. Either they exist or they don't exist. But if they don't exist why does the card index about them stretch the length of my arm? Yet that is the whole point of this material and its most enduring charm. Do these beings exist? Well, they do and they don't. You see, they are beings from *an saol eile*, the "otherworld," which in Irish is a concept of such impeccable intellectual rigor and credibility that it is virtually impossible to translate into English, where it all too quickly becomes fey and twee and "fairies-at-the-bottom-of-the-garden."

The way so-called depth psychologists go on about the subconscious nowadays you'd swear they had invented it, or at the very least stumbled on a ghostly and ghastly continent where mankind had never previously set foot. Even the dogs in the street in West Kerry know that the "otherworld" exists, and that to be in and out of it constantly is the most natural thing in the world.

This constant tension between reality and fantasy, according to Jeffrey Gantz, the translator of *Early Irish Myths and Sagas,* is characteristic of all Celtic art, but manifests itself particularly in the literature of Ireland. Mr Gantz believes that it is not accidental to the circumstances of the literary transmission but is rather an innate characteristic, a gift of the Celts. It means that the "otherworld" is not simply an anticipated joyful afterlife; it is also—even primarily—an alternative to reality.

This easy interaction with the imaginary means that you don't have to have a raving psychotic breakdown to enter the "otherworld." The deep sense in the language that something exists beyond the ego-envelope is pleasant and reassuring, but it is also a great source of linguistic and imaginative playfulness, even on the most ordinary and banal of occasions.

Let's say I decide some evening to walk up to my aunt's house in West Kerry. She hears me coming. She knows it is me because she recognizes my step on the cement pavement. Still, as I knock lightly on the door she calls out, "An de bheoaibh nó de mhairbh thu?" ("Are you of the living or of the dead?") Because the possibility exists that you could be either, and depending on which category you belong to, an entirely different protocol would be brought into play. This is all a joke, of course, but a joke that is made possible by the imaginative richness of the language itself.

I am not constructing an essentialist argument here, though I do think that because of different circumstances, mostly historical, the strengths and weaknesses of Irish are different from those of English, and the imaginative possibilities of Irish are, from a poet's perspective, one of its greatest strengths. But this is surely as true of, say, Bengali as it is of Irish. It is what struck me most in the Nobel Prize acceptance speech made by the Yiddish writer Isaac Bashevis Singer. When often asked why he wrote in a dead language, Singer said he was wont to reply that he wrote mostly about ghosts, and that is what ghosts speak, a dead language.

Singer's reply touched a deep chord with his Irish audience. It reminded us that the precariousness of Irish is not an Irish problem alone. According to the linguist Michael Krause in *Language* magazine, minority languages in the English language sphere face a 90 percent extinction rate between now and some time in the next century. Therefore, in these days when a major problem is the growth of an originally Anglo-American, but now genuinely global, pop monoculture that reduces everything to the level of the most stupendous boredom, I would think that the preservation of minority languages like Irish, with their unique and unrepeatable way of looking at the world, would be as important for human beings as the preservation of the remaining tropical rain forests is for biological diversity.

Recently, on a short trip to Kerry with my three daughters, I stayed with my brother and his wife in the old house he is renovating on the eastern end of the Dingle peninsula, under the beetling brow of Cathair Chonroi promontory fort. My brother said he had something special to show us, so one day we trooped up the mountain to Derrymore Glen. Although the area is now totally denuded of any form of growth other than lichens and sphagnum moss, the name itself is a dead giveaway: Derrymore from *Doire Mór* in Irish, meaning "Large Oak Grove."

A more desolate spot you cannot imagine, yet halfway up the glen, in the crook of a hanging valley, intricate and gnarled, looking for all the world like a giant bonsai, was a single survivor, one solitary oak tree. Only the top branches were producing leaves, it was definitely on its last legs and must have been at least 200 to 300 years old. How it had survived the massive human and animal depredation of the countryside that occurred during that time I do not know, but somehow it had.

It was very much a *bile,* a sacred tree, dear to the Celts. A fairy tree. A magic tree. We were all very moved by it. Not a single word escaped us, as we stood in the drizzle. At last Ayse, my 10-year-old, broke the silence. "It would just give you an idea," she said, "of what this place was like when it really was a '*Doire Mór*' and covered with oak trees." I found myself humming the air of *Cill Cais*, that lament for both the great woods of Ireland and the largess of the Gaelic order that they had come to symbolize:

> Cad a dhéanfaimid feasta gan adhmad?
> Tá deireadh na gcoillte ar lár.
> Níl trácht ar Chill Cais ná a theaghlach
> is ní chlingfear a chling go brách.

> What will we do now without wood
> Now that the woods are laid low?
> Cill Cais or its household are not mentioned
> and the sound of its bell is no more.

A week later, back in Dublin, that question is still ringing in the air. I am waiting for the children to get out of school and writing my journal in Irish in a modern shopping mall in a Dublin suburb. Not a single word of Irish in sight on sign or advertisement, nor a single sound of it in earshot. All around me are well-dressed and articulate women. I am intrigued by snatches of animated conversation, yet I am conscious of a sense of overwhelming loss. I think back to the lonely hillside, and to Ayse. This is the answer to the question in the song. This is what we will do without wood.

At some level, it doesn't seem too bad. People are warm and not hungry. They are expressing themselves without difficulty in English. They seem happy. I close my notebook with a snap and set off in the grip of that sudden pang of despair that is always lurking in the ever-widening rents of the linguistic fabric of minority languages. Perhaps my mother is right. Writing in Irish is mad. English is a wonderful language, and it also has the added advantage of being very useful for putting bread on the table. Change is inevitable, and maybe it is part of the natural order of things that some languages should die while others prevail.

And yet, and yet . . . I know this will sound ridiculously romantic and sentimental. Yet not by bread alone. . . . We raise our eyes to the hills. . . . We throw our bread upon the waters.[5] There are mythical precedents. Take for instance Moses' mother, consider her predicament. She had the choice of giving up her son to the Egyptian soldiery, to have him cleft in two before her very eyes, or to send him down the Nile in a basket, a tasty dinner for crocodiles. She took what under the circumstances must have seemed very much like *rogha an dá dhiogha* ("the lesser of two evils") and Exodus and the annals of Jewish history tell the rest of the story, and are the direct results of an action that even as I write is still working out its inexorable destiny. I know it is wrong to compare small things with great, yet my final answer to why I write in Irish is this:

Ceist 'na Teangan

> Curirim mo dhóchas ar snámh
> i mbáidín´ teangan
> faoi mar a leagfá naíonán

---

5. Echoing three biblical affirmations of the need to look beyond immediate material wants (Matthew 4.4, Psalm 121.1, Ecclesiastes 11.1). In the first passage cited, Jesus is fasting in the wilderness and rejects Satan's tempting suggestion that he turn stones into bread: "he answered, 'It is written, "Man shall not live by bread alone, but by every word that proceeds from the mouth of God."'"

i gcliabhán
a bheadh fite fuaite
de dhuilleoga feileastraim
is bitiúman agus pic
bheith cuimilte lena thóin

ansan é a leagadh síos
i measc na ngiolcach
is coigeal na mban sí
le taobh na habhann,
féachaint n'fheadaráis
cá dtabharfaidh an sruth é,
féachaint, dála Mhaoise,
an bhfóirfidh iníon Fharoinn?

The Language Issue

I place my hope on the water
in this little boat
of the language, the way a body might put
an infant

in a basket of intertwined
iris leaves,
its underside proofed
with bitumen and pitch,

then set the whole thing down amidst
the sedge
and bulrushes by the edge
of a river

only to have it borne hither and thither,
not knowing where it might end up;
in the lap, perhaps,
of some Pharaoh's daughter.[6]

━━━━ ⋝◆⋜ ━━━━

Nadine Gordimer
b. 1923

Nadine Gordimer was born in South Africa to Jewish emigrant parents from London. Thus her childhood, like those of the children of countless middle-class colonial families, was somewhat complex and contradictory. In an interview, Gordimer offers this explanation: "I think when you're born white in South Africa, you're peeling like an orange. You're sloughing off all the conditioning that you've had since you were a child." In Gordimer's case, that "sloughing off" of white, British prejudices and habits of mind has been thorough; the novelist Paul Theroux,

---

6. As happened with Moses when the Israelites were enslaved in Egypt (Exodus 2). Fearing their growing numbers, Pharaoh had ordered all male Hebrew infants to be drowned in the Nile; Moses's mother instead set him adrift in a reed basket, which was found by the Pharaoh's daughter, who adopted him and raised him as an Egyptian. As an adult, Moses led the Israelites out of Egypt to the Promised Land.

for instance, suggests that "Gordimer's vision of Africa is the most complete one we have, and in time to come, when we want to know everything there is to know about a newly independent black African country, it is to this white South African woman . . . that we will turn."

Since Gordimer published her first collection of short stories in 1949 her writing has been praised for its evenhanded and scrupulously honest treatment of the political terrain of South Africa; and over the years she has become, in the words of one critic, "the literary voice and conscience of her society." Among her gifts are an ear sensitive to the cadences and idiosyncrasies of spoken English, and a gift for social satire in service of a finally moral purpose. The longstanding subject of Gordimer's writing—her great theme—is, as critic Michiko Kakutani describes it, "the consequences of apartheid on the daily lives of men and women, the distortions it produces in relationships among both blacks and whites." In Gordimer's writing, these distortions are always shown rather than explained; her presentation is essentially dramatic, a trait she shares with modern masters of short fiction like Chekhov and Joyce.

Gordimer has been faulted for the emphasis in politics in her writing. Her response to this charge is eloquent: "The real influence of politics on my writing is the influence of politics on people. Their lives, and I believe their very personalities, are changed by the extreme political circumstances one lives under in South Africa. I am dealing with people; here are people who are shaped and changed by politics. In that way my material is profoundly influenced by politics." To date, Gordimer has published more than ten novels, including the celebrated *A Guest of Honour* (1970) and *The Conservationist* (1974; cowinner of the Booker McConnell Prize), and more than a dozen collections of short stories. *Jump and Other Stories*, which includes *What Were You Dreaming?*, was published in 1991, the same year Gordimer was awarded the Nobel Prize for Literature. In this story, the disjunction between black and white South African English is the starting-point for an exploration of blocked communication between races and genders alike.

What Were You Dreaming?

I'm standing here by the road long time, yesterday, day before, today. Not the same road but it's the same—hot, hot like today. When they turn off where they're going, I must get out again, wait again. Some of them they just pretend there's nobody there, they don't want to see nobody. Even go a bit faster, *ja*. Then they past, and I'm waiting. I combed my hair; I don't want to look like a *skollie* [ruffian]. Don't smile because they think you being too friendly, you think you good as them. They go and they go. Some's got the baby's napkin hanging over the back window to keep out this sun. Some's not going on holiday with their kids but is alone; all alone in a big car. But they'll never stop, the whites, if they alone. Never. Because these *skollies* and that kind've spoilt it all for us, sticking a gun in the driver's neck, stealing his money, beating him up and taking the car. Even killing him. So it's buggered up for us. No white wants some guy sitting behind his head. And the blacks—when they stop for you, they ask for money. They want you must pay, like for a taxi! The blacks!

But then these whites: they stopping; I'm surprised, because it's only two—empty in the back—and the car it's a beautiful one. The windows are that special glass, you can't see in if you outside, but the woman has hers down and she's calling me over with her finger. She ask me where I'm going and I say the next place because they don't like to have you for too far, so she say get in and lean into the back to move along her stuff that's on the back seat to make room. Then she say, lock the door, just push that button down, we don't want you to fall out, and it's like she's joking with someone she know. The man driving smiles over his shoulder and say something—I can't hear it very well, it's the way he talk English. So anyway I say what's all right to say, yes master, thank you

master, I'm going to Warmbad. He ask again, but man, I don't get it—*Ekskuus?* Please?
And she chips in—she's a lady with grey hair and he's a young chap—My friend's from
England, he's asking if you've been waiting a long time for a lift. So I tell them—A long
time? Madam! And because they white, I tell them about the blacks, how when they
stop they ask you to pay. This time I understand what the young man's saying, he say,
And most whites don't stop? And I'm careful what I say, I tell them about the blacks,
how too many people spoil it for us, they robbing and killing, you can't blame white people. Then he ask where I'm from. And she laugh and look round where I'm behind her. I
see she know I'm from the Cape, although she ask me. I tell her I'm from the Cape Flats[1]
and she say she suppose I'm not born there, though, and she's right, I'm born in Wynberg, right there in Cape Town. So she say, And they moved you out?

Then I catch on what kind of white she is; so I tell her, yes, the government
kicked us out from our place, and she say to the young man, You see?

He want to know why I'm not in the place in the Cape Flats, why I'm so far away
here. I tell them I'm working in Pietersburg.[2] And he keep on, why? Why? What's my
job, everything, and if I don't understand the way he speak, she chips in again all the
time and ask me for him. So I tell him, panel beater.[3] And I tell him, the pay is very
low in the Cape. And then I begin to tell them lots of things, some things is real and
some things I just think of, things that are going to make them like me, maybe they'll
take me all the way there to Pietersburg.

I tell them I'm six days on the road. I not going to say I'm sick as well, I been
home because I was sick—because *she's* not from overseas, I suss that, she know that
old story. I tell them I had to take leave because my mother's got trouble with my
brothers and sisters, we seven in the family and no father. And s'true's God, it seem
like what I'm saying. When do you ever see him except he's drunk. And my brother
is trouble, trouble, he hangs around with bad people and my other brother doesn't
help my mother. And that's no lie, neither, how can he help when he's doing time;
but they don't need to know that, they only get scared I'm the same kind like him, if
I tell about him, assault and intent to do bodily harm. The sisters are in school and
my mother's only got the pension. *Ja.* I'm working there in Pietersburg and every
week, madam, I swear to you, I send my pay for my mother and sisters. So then he
say, Why get off here? Don't you want us to take you to Pietersburg? And she say, of
course, they going that way.

And I tell them some more. They listening to me so nice, and I'm talking, talking. I talk about the government, because I hear she keep saying to him, telling about
this law and that law. I say how it's not fair we had to leave Wynberg and go to the
Flats. I tell her we got sicknesses—she say what kind, is it unhealthy there? And I
don't have to think what, I just say it's *bad, bad,* and she say to the man, *As I told you.*
I tell about the house we had in Wynberg, but it's not my grannie's old house where
we was all living together so long, the house I'm telling them about is more the kind
of house they'll know, they wouldn't like to go away from, with a tiled bathroom,
electric stove, everything. I tell them we spend three thousand rands fixing up that
house—my uncle give us the money, that's how we got it. He give us his savings,
three thousand rands. (I don't know why I say three; old Uncle Jimmy never have
three or two or one in his life. I just say it.) And then we just kicked out. And panel
beaters getting low pay there; it's better in Pietersburg.

1. A small town near Cape Town.   3. A person who does body work on automobiles.
2. A city in northeastern South Africa.

He say, but I'm far from my home? And I tell her again, because she's white but she's a woman too, with that grey hair she's got grown-up kids—Madam. I send my pay home every week, s'true's God, so's they can eat, there in the Flats. I'm saying, *six days on the road*. While I'm saying it, I'm thinking; then I say, look at me, I got only these clothes, I sold my things on the way, to have something to eat. *Six days on the road*. He's from overseas and she isn't one of those who say you're a liar, doesn't trust you—right away when I got in the car, I notice she doesn't take her stuff over to the front like they usually do in case you pinch something of theirs. Six days on the road, and am I tired, tired! When I get to Pietersburg I must try borrow me a rand to get a taxi there to where I live. He say, Where do you live? Not in town? And she laugh, because he don't know nothing about this place, where whites live and where we must go—but I know they both thinking and I know what they thinking; I know I'm going to get something when I get out, don't need to worry about that. They feeling bad about me, now. Bad. Anyhow it's God's truth that I'm tired, tired, that's true.

They've put up her window and he's pushed a few buttons, now it's like in a super-market, cool air blowing, and the windows like sunglasses: that sun can't get me here.

The Englishman glances over his shoulder as he drives.

"Taking a nap."

"I'm sure it's needed."

All through the trip he stops for everyone he sees at the roadside. Some are not hitching at all, never expecting to be given a lift anywhere, just walking in the heat outside with an empty plastic can to be filled with water or paraffin or whatever it is they buy in some country store, or standing at some point between departure and des-tination, small children and bundles linked on either side, baby on back. She hasn't said anything to him. He would only misunderstand if she explained why one doesn't give lifts in this country; and if she pointed out that in spite of this, she doesn't mind him breaking the sensible if unfortunate rule, he might misunderstand that, as well— think she was boasting of her disregard for personal safety weighed in the balance against decent concern for fellow beings.

He persists in making polite conversation with these passengers because he doesn't want to be patronizing; picking them up like so many objects and dropping them off again, silent, smelling of smoke from open cooking fires, sun and sweat, there behind his head. They don't understand his Englishman's English and if he gets an answer at all it's a deaf man's guess at what's called for. Some grin with pleasure and embarrass him by showing it the way they've been taught is acceptable, invoking him as *baas* and *mas-ter* when they get out and give thanks. But although he doesn't know it, being too much concerned with those names thrust into his hands like whips whose purpose is repug-nant to him, has nothing to do with him, she knows each time that there is a moment of annealment[4] in the air-conditioned hired car belonging to nobody—a moment like that on a no-man's-land bridge in which an accord between warring countries is signed—when there is no calling of names, and all belong in each other's presence. He doesn't feel it because he has no wounds, neither has inflicted, nor will inflict any.

This one standing at the roadside with his transistor radio in a plastic bag was actually thumbing a lift like a townee; his expectation marked him out. And when her companion to whom she was showing the country inevitably pulled up, she read the face at the roadside immediately: the lively, cajoling, performer's eyes, the

4. Tempering by heating.

salmon-pinkish cheeks and nostrils, and as he jogged over smiling, the unselfconscious gap of gum between the canines.

A sleeper is always absent; although present, there on the back seat.

"The way he spoke about black people, wasn't it surprising? I mean—he's black himself."

"Oh no he's not. Couldn't you see the difference? He's a Cape Coloured. From the way he speaks English—couldn't you hear he's not like the Africans you've talked to?"

But of course he hasn't seen, hasn't heard: the fellow is dark enough, to those who don't know the signs by which you're classified, and the melodramatic, long-vowelled English is as difficult to follow if more fluent than the terse, halting responses of blacker people.

"Would he have a white grandmother or even a white father, then?"

She gives him another of the little history lessons she has been supplying along the way. The Malay slaves brought by the Dutch East India Company[5] to their supply station, on the route to India, at the Cape in the seventeenth century; the Khoikhoi who were the indigenous inhabitants of that part of Africa; add Dutch, French, English, German settlers whose back-yard progeniture with these and other blacks began a people who are all the people in the country mingled in one bloodstream. But encounters along the road teach him more than her history lessons, or the political analyses in which they share the same ideological approach although he does not share responsibility for the experience to which the ideology is being applied. She has explained Acts, Proclamations, Amendments. The Group Areas Act, Resettlement Act, Orderly Movement and Settlement of Black Persons Act. She has translated these statute-book euphemisms: people as movable goods. People packed onto trucks along with their stoves and beds while front-end loaders scoop away their homes into rubble. People dumped somewhere else. Always somewhere else. People as the figures, decimal points and multiplying zero-zero-zeros into which individual lives—Black Persons Orderly-Moved, -Effluxed, -Grouped—coagulate and compute. Now he has here in the car the intimate weary odour of a young man to whom these things happen.

"Half his family sick . . . it must be pretty unhealthy, where they've been made to go."

She smiles. "Well, I'm not too sure about that. I had the feeling, some of what he said . . . they're theatrical by nature. You must take it with a pinch of salt."

"You mean about the mother and sisters and so on?"

She's still smiling, she doesn't answer.

"But he couldn't have made up about taking a job so far from home—and the business of sending his wages to his mother? That too?"

He glances at her.

Beside him, she's withdrawn as the other one, sleeping behind him. While he turns his attention back to the road, she is looking at him secretly, as if somewhere in his blue eyes registering the approaching road but fixed on the black faces he is trying to read, somewhere in the lie of his inflamed hand and arm that on their travels have been plunged in the sun as if in boiling water, there is the place through which the worm he needs to be infected with can find a way into him, so that he may host it and become its survivor, himself surviving through being fed on. Become like her. Complicity is the only understanding.

"Oh it's true, it's all true . . . not in the way he's told about it. Truer than the way he told it. All these things happen to them. And other things. Worse. But why burden

5. Occupied South Africa from 1652–1795 while it was a Dutch Cape Colony.

us? Why try to explain to us? Things so far from what we know, how will they ever explain? How will we react? Stop our ears? Or cover our faces? Open the door and throw him out? They don't know. But sick mothers and brothers gone to the bad—these are the staples of misery, mmh? Think of the function of charity in the class struggles in your own country in the nineteenth century; it's all there in your literature. The lord-of-the-manor's compassionate daughter carrying hot soup to the dying cottager on her father's estate. The "advanced" upper-class woman comforting her cook when the honest drudge's daughter takes to whoring for a living. *Shame,* we say here. Shame. You must've heard it? We think it means, what a pity; we think we are expressing sympathy—for them. *Shame.* I don't know what we're saying about ourselves." She laughs.

"So you think it would at least be true that his family were kicked out of their home, sent away?"

"Why would anyone of them need to make that up? It's an everyday affair."

"What kind of place would they get, where they were moved?"

"Depends. A tent, to begin with. And maybe basic materials to build themselves a shack. Perhaps a one-room prefab. Always a tin toilet set down in the veld,[6] if nothing else. Some industrialist must be making a fortune out of government contracts for those toilets. You build your new life round that toilet. His people are Coloured, so it could be they were sent where there were houses of some sort already built for them; Coloureds usually get something a bit better than blacks are given."

"And the house would be more or less as good as the one they had? People as poor as that—and they'd spent what must seem a fortune to them, fixing it up."

"I don't know what kind of house they had. We're not talking about slum clearance, my dear; we're talking about destroying communities because they're black, and white people want to build houses or factories for whites where blacks live. I told you. We're talking about loading up trucks and carting black people out of sight of whites."

"And even where he's come to work—Pietersburg, whatever-it's-called—he doesn't live in the town."

"Out of sight." She has lost the thought for a moment, watching to make sure the car takes the correct turning. "Out of sight. Like those mothers and grannies and brothers and sisters far away on the Cape Flats."

"I don't think it's possible he actually sends all his pay. I mean how would one eat?"

"Maybe what's left doesn't buy anything he really wants."

Not a sound, not a sigh in sleep behind them. They can go on talking about him as he always has been discussed, there and yet not there.

Her companion is alert to the risk of gullibility. He verifies the facts, smiling, just as he converts, mentally, into pounds and pence any sum spent in foreign coinage. "He didn't sell the radio. When he said he'd sold all his things on the road, he forgot about that."

"When did he say he'd last eaten?"

"Yesterday. He said."

She repeats what she has just been told: "Yesterday." She is looking through the glass that takes the shine of heat off the landscape passing as yesterday passed, time measured by the ticking second hand of moving trees, rows of crops, country-store stoeps,[7] filling stations, spiny crook'd fingers of giant euphorbia.[8] Only the figures by the roadside waiting, standing still.

Personal remarks can't offend someone dead-beat in the back. "How d'you think such a young man comes to be without front teeth?"

6. Plains.
7. Verandas.
8. An African shrub.

She giggles whisperingly and keeps her voice low, anyway. "Well, you may not believe me if I tell you . . . ."

"Seems odd . . . I suppose he can't afford to have them replaced."

"It's—how shall I say—a sexual preference. Most usually you see it in their young girls, though. They have their front teeth pulled when they're about seventeen."

She feels his uncertainty, his not wanting to let comprehension lead him to a conclusion embarrassing to an older woman. For her part, she is wondering whether he won't find it distasteful if—at her de-sexed age—she should come out with it: for cock-sucking. "No one thinks the gap spoils a girl's looks, apparently. It's simply a sign she knows how to please. Same significance between men, I suppose ? A form of beauty. So everyone says. We've always been given to understand that's the reason."

"Maybe it's just another sexual myth. There are so many."

She's in agreement. "Black girls. Chinese girls. Jewish girls."

"And black men?"

"Oh my goodness, you bet. But we white ladies don't talk about that, we only dream, you know! Or have nightmares."

They're laughing. When they are quiet, she flexes her shoulders against the seat-back and settles again. The streets of a town are flickering their text across her eyes. "He might have had a car accident. They might have been knocked out in a fight."

They have to wake him because they don't know where he wants to be set down. He is staring at her lined white face (turned to him, calling him gently), stunned for a moment at this evidence that he cannot be anywhere he ought to be; and now he blinks and smiles his empty smile caught on either side by a canine tooth, and gulps and gives himself a shake like someone coming out of water. "Sorry! Sorry! Sorry madam!"

What about, she says, and the young man glances quickly, his blue eyes coming round over his shoulder: "Had a good snooze?"

"Ooh I was finished, master, finished, God bless you for the rest you give me. And with an empty stummick, you know, you dreaming so real. I was dreaming, dreaming, I didn't know nothing about I'm in the car!"

It comes from the driver's seat with the voice (a real Englishman's from overseas) of one who is hoping to hear something that will explain everything. "What were you dreaming?"

But there is only hissing, spluttery laughter between the two white pointed teeth. The words gambol. "Ag, nothing, master, nothing, all non-sunce—"

The sense is that if pressed, he will produce for them a dream he didn't dream, a dream put together from bloated images on billboards, discarded calendars picked up, scraps of newspapers blown about—but they interrupt, they're asking where he'd like to get off.

"No, anywhere. Here it's all right. Fine. Just there by the corner. I must go look for someone who'll praps give me a rand for the taxi, because I can't walk so far, I haven't eaten nothing since yesterday . . . just here, the master can please stop just here—"

The traffic light is red, anyway, and the car is in the lane nearest the kerb. Her thin, speckled white arm with a skilled flexible hand, but no muscle with which to carry a load of washing or lift a hoe, feels back to release the lock he is fumbling at. "Up, up, pull it up." She has done it for him. "Can't you take a bus?"

"There's no buses Sunday, madam, this place is ve-ery bad for us for transport, I must tell you, we can't get nowhere Sundays, only work-days." He is out, the plastic bag with the radio under his arm, his feet in their stained, multi-striped jogging sneakers drawn neatly together like those of a child awaiting dismissal. "Thank you madam, thank you master, God bless you for what you done."

The confident dextrous hand is moving quickly down in the straw bag bought from a local market somewhere along the route. She brings up a pale blue note (the Englishman recognizes the two-rand denomination of this currency that he has memorized by colour) and turns to pass it, a surreptitious message, through the open door behind her. *Goodbye master madam.* The note disappears delicately as a tit-bit finger-fed. He closes the door, he's keeping up the patter, *goodbye master, goodbye madam,* and she instructs—"No, bang it. Harder. That's it." *Goodbye master, goodbye madam*—but they don't look back at him now, they don't have to see him thinking he must keep waving, keep smiling, in case they should look back.

She is the guide and mentor; she's the one who knows the country. She's the one—she knows that too—who is accountable. She must be the first to speak again. "At least if he's hungry he'll be able to buy a bun or something. And the bars are closed on Sunday."

James Kelman
b. 1946

Though his first collection of stories was published (in a very limited edition) back in 1970, it was not until the 1990s that James Kelman emerged as one of the most distinctive voices in British literature. His development as a writer does not fit any of the usual patterns. He was born in Glasgow, Scotland, one of five sons of a frame-maker; he left school at fifteen to apprentice as a compositor. He worked at various manual jobs in Glasgow, London, and Manchester, peppered with regular bouts of unemployment and living "on the giro" (collecting unemployment).

At age twenty-eight, Kelman enrolled at Strathclyde University, where he studied English and philosophy; he left during his third year, however. In the meantime, he continued to write short stories while working at jobs including that of bus driver, which provided material for his grittily realistic first novel, *The Busconductor Hines* (1984). The novel's stark language and lack of dramatic events were ridiculed, however, by London-based critics; and his next novel, *A Chancer* (1985), was largely ignored. His writing, as Kelman well knows, is a slap in the face of the English literary establishment; he describes his work as both "political" and "anti-imperialist." The raw power of his writing could not be overlooked forever, though, and his 1989 novel *A Disaffection* was a finalist for the Booker Prize. Full recognition of Kelman's gifts seems to have come when he won the Booker Prize for his 1994 novel *How Late It Was, How Late;* this award provoked sharp controversy in England over the literary merits of the obscenity-laced musings of Kelman's shiftless, blind protagonist Sammy. The best of Kelman's writing regularly occasions comparisons with the bleak and brutal prose of Samuel Beckett, and has earned him the label "Scotland's Kafka"—a paradoxical term of praise for such a resolutely local writer.

Other writers (notably James Joyce, in his short story collection *Dubliners*) have attempted to chronicle the weary lives of the downtrodden working class on the fringes of the British Empire; unlike Joyce and Beckett, Kelman foreswore exile, choosing to remain a member of the local culture he depicts. "I don't earn much money," Kelman has said, "so I'm involved in the culture I write about." His 1987 story *Home for a Couple of Days* shows Kelman's powers of close observation and his keen ear for the vernacular style of Scottish English. The bitten-off cadences of Glasgow dialect at once unite and separate the characters, in a story of estrangement and return.

Home for a Couple of Days

Three raps at the door. His eyes opened and blinked as they met the sun rays streaming in through the slight gap between the curtains. "Mister Brown?" called somebody—a girl's voice.

"Just a minute." He squinted at his wristwatch. 9 o'clock. He walked to the door and opened it, poked his head out from behind it.

"That's your breakfast." She held out the tray as if for approval. A boiled egg and a plate of toast, a wee pot of tea.

"Thanks, that's fine, thanks." He took it and shut the door, poured a cup of tea immediately and carried it into the bathroom. He was hot and sweaty and needed a shower. He stared at himself in the mirror. He was quite looking forward to the day. Hearing the girl's accent made it all even more so. After the shower he started on the grub, ate all the toast but left the egg. He finished the pot of tea then shaved. As he prepared to leave he checked his wallet. He would have to get to a bank at some point.

The Green Park was a small hotel on the west side of Sauchiehall Street. Eddie had moved in late last night and taken a bed and breakfast. Beyond that he was not sure, how long he would be staying. Everything depended.

He was strolling in the direction of Partick, glancing now and then at the back pages of the *Daily Record*, quite enjoying the novelty of Scottish football[1] again. He stopped himself from smiling, lighted a cigarette. It was a sunny morning in early May and maybe it was that alone made him feel so optimistic about the future. The sound of a machine, noisy—but seeming to come from far away. It was just from the bowling greens across the street, a loud lawn-mower or something.

He continued round the winding bend, down past the hospital and up Church Street, cutting in through Chancellor Street and along the lane. The padlock hung ajar on the bolt of the door of the local pub he used to frequent. Farther on the old primary school across the other side of the street. He could not remember any names of teachers or pupils at this moment. A funny feeling. It was as if he had lost his memory for one split second. He had stopped walking. He lighted another cigarette. When he returned the lighter and cigarette packet to the side pockets of his jacket he noticed a movement in the net curtains of the ground floor window nearby where he was standing. It was Mrs McLachlan. Who else. He smiled and waved but the face disappeared.

His mother stayed up the next close.[2] He kept walking. He would see her a bit later on. He would have to get her something too, a present, she was due it.

Along Dumbarton Road he entered the first cafe and he ordered a roll and sausage and asked for a cup of tea right away. The elderly woman behind the counter did not look twice at him. Why should she? She once caught him thieving a bar of Turkish Delight, that's why. He read the *Daily Record* to the front cover, still quite enjoying it all, everything, even the advertisements with the Glasgow addresses, it was good reading them as well.

At midday he was back up the lane and along to the old local. He got a pint of heavy,[3] sat in a corner sipping at it. The place had really changed. It was drastic—new curtains!

There were not many customers about but Eddie recognized one, a middle-aged man of average build who was wearing a pair of glasses. He leaned on the bar with his

1. Soccer.
2. Alley.
3. Stout or porter.

arms folded, chatting to the bartender. Neilie Johnston. When Eddie finished his beer he walked with the empty glass to the counter. "Heavy," he said and he pointed at Neilie's drink. The bartender nodded and poured him a whisky. Neilie looked at it and then at Eddie.

"Eddie!"

"How's it going Neilie?"

"Aw no bad son no bad." Neilie chuckled. The two of them shook hands. "Where've you been?"

"London."

"Aw London; aw aye. Well well."

"Just got back last night."

"Good . . ." Neilie glanced at Eddie's suit. "Prospering son eh?"

"Doing alright."

"That's the game."

"What about yourself? still marking the board?"[4]

"Marking the board! Naw. Christ son I've been away from that for a while!" Neilie pursed his lips before lifting the whisky and drinking a fairly large mouthful. He sniffed and nodded. "With Sweeney being out the game and the rest of it."

"Aye."

"You knew about that son?"

"Mm."

"Aye well the licence got lost because of it. And they'll no get it back either neither they will. They're fucking finished—caput! Him and his brother."

Both of them were silent for a time. The bartender had walked farther along and was now looking at a morning paper. Neilie nudged the glasses up his nose a bit and he said, "You and him got on okay as well son, you and Sweeney, eh?"

Eddie shrugged. "Aye, I suppose." He glanced at the other men ranged about the pub interior, brought his cigarettes and lighter out. When they were both smoking he called the bartender: "Two halfs!"

"You on holiday like?" said Neilie.

"Couple of days just, a wee break . . ." he paused to pay for the two whiskies.

Neilie emptied the fresh one into the tumbler he already had. "Ta[5] son," he said, "it's appreciated."

"You skint?"[6]

"Aye, how d'you guess! Giro[7] in two days."

"Nothing doing then?"

"Eh well . . ." Neilie sniffed. "I'm waiting the word on something, a wee bit of business. Nothing startling right enough." He pursed his lips and shrugged, swallowed some whisky.

"I hope you're lucky."

"Aye, ta."

"Cheers." Eddie drank his own whisky in a gulp and chased it down with a mouthful of heavy beer. "Aw Christ," he said, glancing at the empty tumbler.

"You should never rush whisky son!" Neilie chuckled, peering along at the bartender.

"I'm out the habit."

4. Taking bets.
5. Thanks.

6. Broke.
7. Unemployment check.

"Wish to fuck I could say the same!"

Eddie took a long drag on the cigarette and he kept the smoke in his lungs for a while. Then he drank more beer. Neilie was watching him, smiling in quite a friendly way. Eddie said, "Any of the old team come in these days?"

"Eh . . ."

"Fisher I mean, or Stevie Price? Any of them? Billy Dempster?"

"Fisher drinks in T. C.'s."

"Does he? Changed days."

"Och there's a lot changed son, a lot."

"Stevie's married right enough eh!"

"Is that right?"

"He's got two wee lassies."

"Well well."

"He's staying over in the south side."

"Aw."

A couple of minutes later and Eddie was swallowing the last of his beer and returning his cigarettes and lighter to the side pockets. "Okay Neilie, nice seeing you."

Neilie looked as if he was going to say something but changed his mind.

"I'm taking a walk," said Eddie.

"Fair enough son."

"I'll look in later." Eddie patted him on the side of the shoulder, nodded at the bartender. He glanced at the other customers as he walked to the exit but saw nobody he knew.

It was good getting back out into the fresh air. The place was depressing and Neilie hadnt helped matters. A rumour used to go about that he kept his wife on the game.[8] Eddie could believe it.

There was a traffic jam down at Partick Cross. The rear end of a big articulated lorry[9] was sticking out into the main road and its front seemed to be stuck between two parked cars near to The Springwell Tavern. The lines of motors stretched along the different routes at the junction. Eddie stood at the Byres Road corner amongst a fair crowd of spectators. Two policemen arrived and donned the special sleeves they had for such emergencies and started directing operations. Eddie continued across the road.

In T. C.'s two games of dominoes were in progress plus there was music and a much cheerier atmosphere. It was better and fitted in more with the way Eddie remembered things. And there was Fisher at the other end of the bar in company with another guy. Eddie called to him: "Hey Tam!"

"Eddie!" Fisher was delighted. He waved his right fist in the air and when Eddie reached the other end he shook hands with him in a really vigorous way. "Ya bastard," he said, "it's great to see ye!" And then he grinned and murmured, "When did you get out!"[1]

"Out—what d'you mean?"

Fisher laughed.

"I'm being serious," said Eddie.

"Just that I heard you were having a holiday on the Isle of Wight."

"That's garbage."

"If you say so."

"Aye, fuck, I say so." Eddie smiled.

8. Forced his wife to work as a prostitute.   1. Of prison.
9. Semi truck.

"Well, I mean, when Sweeney copped it . . . Then hearing about you . . . Made me think it was gen."[2]

"Ah well, there you are!"

"That's good," said Fisher and he nodded, then jerked his thumb at the other guy. "This is Mick . . ."

After the introductions Eddie got a round of drinks up and the three of them went to a table at the wall, the only one available. An elderly man was sitting at it already; he had a grumpy wizened face. He moved a few inches to allow the trio more space.

There was a short silence. And Eddie said, "Well Tam, how's Eileen?"

"Dont know. We split."

"Aw. Christ."

"Ah," Fisher said, "she started . . . well, she started seeing this other guy, if you want to know the truth."

"Honest?" Eddie frowned.

Fisher shook his head. "A funny lassie Eileen I mean you never really fucking knew her man I mean." He shook his head again. "You didnt know where you were with her, that was the fucking trouble!"

After a moment Eddie nodded. He lifted his pint and drank from it, waiting for Fisher to continue but instead of continuing Fisher turned and looked towards the bar, exhaled a cloud of smoke. The other guy, Mick, raised his eyebrows at Eddie who shrugged. Then Fisher faced to the front again and said, "I was surprised to hear that about Sweeney but, warehouses, I didnt think it was his scene."

Eddie made no answer.

"Eh . . . ?"

"Mm."

"Best of gear right enough," Fisher added, still gazing at Eddie.

Eddie dragged on his cigarette. Then he said, "You probably heard he screwed the place well he never, he just handled the stuff."

"Aw."

"It was for screwing the place they done him for, but . . ." Eddie sniffed, drank from his pint.

"Aye, good." Fisher grinned. "So how you doing yourself then Eddie?"

"No bad."

"Better than no bad with that!" He gestured at Eddie's clothes. He reached to draw his thumb and forefinger along the lapel of the jacket. "Hand stitched," he said, "you didnt get that from John Collier's. Eh Mick?"

Mick smiled.

Eddie opened the jacket, indicated the inner pocket. "Look, no labels."

"What does that mean?"

"It means it was fucking dear."

"You're a bastard," said Fisher.

Eddie grinned. "Yous for another? A wee yin?"[3]

"Eh . . . Aye." Fisher said, "I'll have a doctor."

"What?"

"A doctor." Fisher winked at Mick. "He doesnt know what a doctor is!"

"What is it?" asked Eddie.

"A doctor, a doctor snoddy, a voddy."

---

2. Genuine.   3. One.

"Aw aye. What about yourself?" Eddie asked Mick.

"I'll have one as well Eddie, thanks."

Although it was busy at the bar he was served quite quickly. It was good seeing as many working behind the counter as this. One of things he didnt like about England was the way sometimes you could wait ages to get served in their pubs—especially if they heard your accent.

He checked the time of the clock on the gantry[4] with his wristwatch. He would have to remember about the bank otherwise it could cause problems. Plus he was wanting to get a wee present for his mother, he needed a couple of quid[5] for that as well.

When he returned to the table Fisher said, "I was telling Mick about some of your exploits."

"Exploits." Eddie laughed briefly, putting the drinks on the table top and sitting down.

"It's cause the 2,000 Guineas is coming up. It's reminding me about something!"

"Aw aye." Eddie said to Mick. "The problem with this cunt[6] Fisher is that he's loyal to horses."

"Loyal to fucking horses!" Fisher laughed loudly.

"Ah well if you're thinking about what I think you're thinking about!"

"It was all Sweeney's fault!"

"That's right, blame a guy that cant talk up for himself!"

"So it was but!"

Eddie smiled. "And Dempster, dont forget Dempster!"

"That's right," said Fisher, turning to Mick, "Dempster was into it as well."

Mick shook his head. Fisher was laughing again, quite loudly.

"It wasnt as funny as all that," said Eddie.

"You dont think so! Every other cunt does!"

"Dont believe a word of it," Eddie told Mick.

"And do you still punt?"[7] Mick asked him.

"Now and again."

"Now and again!" Fisher laughed.

Eddie smiled.

"There's four races on the telly this afternoon," said Mick.

"Aye," said Fisher, "we were thinking of getting a couple of cans and that. You interested?"

"Eh, naw, I'm no sure yet, what I'm doing."

Fisher nodded.

"It's just eh . . ."

"Dont worry about it," said Fisher, and he drank a mouthful of the vodka.

"How's Stevie?"

"Alright—as far as I know, I dont see him much; he hardly comes out. Once or twice at the weekends, that's about it."

"Aye."

"What about yourself, you no married yet?"

"Eh . . ." Eddie made a gesture with his right hand. "Kind of yes and no."

Fisher jerked his thumb at Mick. "He's married—got one on the way."

"Have you? Good, that's good." Eddie raised his tumbler of whisky and saluted him. "All the best."

---

4. Panelling.
5. Pounds sterling.
6. Often used in Scottish slang to refer to men, not sexu-

ally but as equivalent to "guy" or "bastard."
7. Bet.

"Thanks."

"I cant imagine having a kid," said Eddie, and to Fisher he said: "Can you?"

"What! I cant even keep myself going never mind a snapper!"

Mick laughed and brought out a 10-pack of cigarettes. Eddie pushed it away when offered. "It's my crash,"[8] he said.

"Naw," said Mick, "you bought the bevy."

"I know but . . ." He opened his own packet and handed each of them a cigarette and he said to Fisher: "You skint?"

Fisher paused and squinted at him, "What do you think?"

"I think you're skint."

"I'm skint."

"It's a fucking dump of a city this, every cunt's skint."

Fisher jerked his thumb at Mick. "No him, he's no skint, a fucking millionaire, eh!"

Mick chuckled, "That'll be fucking right."

Eddie flicked his lighter and they took a light from him. Fisher said, "Nice . . ."

Eddie nodded, slipping it back into his pocket.

"What you up for by the way?"

"Och, a couple of things."

"No going to tell us?"

"Nothing to tell."

Fisher winked at Mick: "Dont believe a word of it."

"It's gen," said Eddie, "just the maw and that. Plus I was wanting to see a few of the old faces. A wee while since I've been away, three year."

"Aye and no even a postcard!"

"You never sent me one!"

"Aye but I dont know where the fuck you get to man I mean I fucking thought you were inside!"

"Tch!"

"He's supposed to be my best mate as well Mick, what d'you make of it!"

Mick smiled.

Not too long afterwards Eddie had swallowed the last of his whisky and then the heavy beer. "That's me," he said, "better hit the road. Aw right Tam! Mick, nice meeting you." Eddie shook hands with the two of them again.

Fisher said, "No bothering about the racing on the telly then . . ."

"Nah, better no—I've got a couple of things to do. The maw as well Tam, I've got to see her."

"Aye how's she keeping? I dont see her about much."

"Aw she's fine, keeping fine."

"That's good. Tell her I was asking for her."

"Will do . . ." Eddie edged his way out. The elderly man shifted on his chair, made a movement towards the drink he had lying by his hand. Eddie nodded at Mick and said to Fisher, "I'll probably look in later on."

A couple of faces at the bar seemed familiar but not sufficiently so and he continued on to the exit, strolling, hands in his trouser pockets, the cigarette in the corner of his mouth. Outside on the pavement he glanced from right to left, then the pub door banged behind him. It was Fisher. Eddie looked at him. "Naw eh . . ." Fisher sniffed. "I was just wondering and that, how you're fixed, just a couple of quid."

Eddie sighed, shook his head. "Sorry Tam but I'm being honest, I've got to hit the bank straight away; I'm totally skint."

8. Treat.

"Aw. Okay. No problem."

"I mean if I had it . . . I'm no kidding ye, it's just I'm skint."

"Naw dont worry about it Eddie."

"Aye but Christ!" Eddie held his hands raised, palms upwards. "Sorry I mean." He hesitated a moment then said, "Wait a minute . . ." He dug out a big handful of loose change from his trouser pockets and arranged it into a neat sort of column on his left hand, and presented it to Fisher. "Any good?"

Fisher gazed at the money.

"Take it," said Eddie, giving it into his right hand.

"Ta Eddie. Mick's been keeping me going in there."

"When's the giro due?"

"Two more days."

"Garbage eh." He paused, nodded again and patted Fisher on the side of the shoulder. "Right you are then Tam, eh! I'll see ye!"

"Aye."

"I'll take a look in later on."

"Aye do that Eddie. You've actually just caught me at a bad time."

"I know the feeling," said Eddie and he winked and gave a quick wave. He walked on across the street without looking behind. Farther along he stepped sideways onto the path up by the Art Galleries.

There were a lot of children rushing about, plus women pushing prams. And the bowling greens were busy. Not just pensioners playing either, even young boys were out. Eddie still had the *Record* rolled in his pocket and he sat down on a bench for a few minutes, glancing back through the pages again, examining what was on at all the cinemas, theatres, seeing the pub entertainment and restaurants advertised.

No wind. Hardly even a breeze. The sun seemed to be beating right down on his head alone. Or else it was the alcohol; he was beginning to feel the effects. If he stayed on the bench he would end up falling asleep. The hotel. He got up, paused to light a cigarette. Along Sauchiehall Street there was a good curry smell coming for somewhere. He was starving. He turned into the entrance to The Green Park, walking up the wee flight of stairs and in to the lobby, the reception lounge. Somebody was hoovering carpets. He pressed the buzzer button, pressed it again when there came a break in the noise.

The girl who had brought him breakfast. "Mrs Grady's out the now," she told him.

"Aw."

"What was it you were wanting?"

"Eh well it was just I was wondering if there's a bank near?"

"A bank. Yes, if you go along to Charing Cross. They're all around there."

"Oh aye. Right." Eddie smiled. "It's funny how you forget wee details like that."

"Mmhh."

"Things have really changed as well. The people . . ." He grinned, shaking his head.

She frowned. "Do you mean Glasgow people?"

"Aye but really I mean I'm talking about people I know, friends and that, people I knew before."

"Aw, I see."

Eddie yawned. He dragged on his cigarette. "Another thing I was wanting to ask her, if it's okay to go into the room, during the day."

"She prefers you not to, unless you're on full board."

"Okay."

"You can go into the lounge though."

He nodded.

"I dont know whether she knew you were staying tonight . . ."

"I am."

"I'll tell her."

"Eh . . ." Eddie had been about to walk off; he said, "Does she do evening meals as well like?"

"She does." The girl smiled.

"What's up?"

"I dont advise it at the moment," she said quietly, "the real cook's off sick just now and she's doing it all herself."

"Aw aye. Thanks for the warning!" Eddie dragged on the cigarette again. "I smelled a curry there somewhere . . ."

"Yeh, there's places all around."

"Great."

"Dont go to the first one, the one further along's far better—supposed to be one of the best in Glasgow."

"Is that right. That's great. Would you fancy coming at all?"

"Pardon?"

"It would be nice if you came, as well, if you came with me." Eddie shrugged. "It'd be good."

"Thanks, but I'm working."

"Well, I would wait."

"No, I dont think so."

"It's up to you," he shrugged, "I'd like you to but."

"Thanks."

Eddie nodded. He looked towards the glass-panelled door of the lounge, he patted his inside jacket pocket in an absent-minded way. And the girl said, "You know if it was a cheque you could cash it here. Mrs Grady would do it for you."

"That's good." He pointed at the lounge door. "Is that the lounge? Do you think it'd be alright if I maybe had a doze?"

"A doze?"

"I'm really tired. I was travelling a while and hardly got any sleep last night. If I could just stretch out a bit . . ."

He looked about for an ashtray, there was one on the small half-moon table closeby where he was standing; he stubbed the cigarette out, and yawned suddenly.

"Look," said the girl, "I'm sure if you went up the stair and lay down for an hour or so; I dont think she would mind."

"You sure?"

"It'll be okay."

"You sure but I mean . . ."

"Yeh."

"I dont want to cause you any bother."

"It's alright."

"Thanks a lot."

"Your bag's still there in your room as well you know."

"Aye."

"Will I give you a call? about 5?"

"Aye, fine. 6 would be even better!"

"I'm sorry, it'll have to be 5—she'll be back in the kitchen after that."
"I was only kidding."
"If it could be later I'd do it."
"Naw, honest, I was only kidding."
The girl nodded.
After a moment he walked to the foot of the narrow, carpeted staircase.
"You'll be wanting a cheque cashed then?"
"Aye, probably."
"I'll mention it to her."

Up in the room he unzipped his bag but did not take anything out, he sat down on the edge of the bed instead. Then he got up, gave a loud sigh and took off his jacket, draping it over the back of the bedside chair. He closed the curtains, lay stretched out on top of the bedspread. He breathed in and out deeply, gazing at the ceiling. He felt amazingly tired, how tired he was. He had never been much of an afternoon drinker and today was just proving the point. He raised himself up to unknot his shoelaces, lay back again, kicking the shoes off and letting them drop off onto the floor. He shut his eyes. He was not quite sure what he was going to do. Maybe he would just leave tomorrow. He would if he felt like it. Maybe even tonight! if he felt like it. Less than a minute later he was sleeping.

<hr />

Derek Walcott
b. 1930

Over the last five decades, Derek Walcott has articulated the tensions of living between two worlds—the competing claims and traditions of the West Indies, his home, and Europe. A concern with issues of national identity runs throughout Walcott's large body of poetry and drama; his poetry exploits the resources of a European literary tradition in the service of Caribbean themes and concerns. No poet, as T. S. Eliot insisted, can write important poetry without tapping into some cultural or literary tradition; in the poem *Forest of Europe*, Walcott puts the question this way:

> What's poetry, if it is worth its salt,
> but a phrase men can pass from hand to mouth?
> From hand to mouth, across the centuries,
> the bread that lasts when systems have decayed.

Walcott was born in Castries, Saint Lucia, an isolated, volcanic island in the West Indies. Saint Lucia is a former British colony, and Walcott's education there was thoroughly British. In the introduction to *Dream on Monkey Mountain and Other Plays* (1970), Walcott writes, "The writers of my generation were natural assimilators. We knew the literature of Empires, Greek, Roman, British, through their essential classics; and both the patois of the street and the language of the classroom hid the elation of discovery." Empire and slavery left their impress on the Walcott family; both of his grandmothers were said to be descended from slaves. Walcott attended University College of the West Indies in Jamaica on a British government scholarship; he completed a degree in English in 1953, and from 1954 until 1957 taught in West Indian schools. In 1958 a Rockefeller Fellowship allowed him to spend a year in New York studying theater; the following year he moved to Trinidad and founded the Little Carib Theatre Workshop. It was in his playwriting that Walcott first accomplished the fusion of native and European elements he sought; his 1958 play *Drums and Colours*, for instance, employs calypso music, mime, and carnival masks to "carnivalize" the smooth surface of European drama, creating a literary form which, while written in English, is uniquely Caribbean in character. *O Babylon!* (1976), his most popular play, focuses on the Rastafarians of Jamaica. He is also a talented painter, and his poems are notable for the vivid clarity of their images.

Walcott has written more than fifteen volumes of poetry as well as a dozen plays. His first important poetry collection was *In a Green Night* (1962), which includes his best-known poem, *A Far Cry from Africa*. Africa and Britain serve as the double setting for his trenchant portrait of a foreign aid bureaucrat in *The Fortunate Traveller*. Walcott himself has never settled in one place for long, and for many years he has split his time between his home in Trinidad and a teaching post at Boston University. Walcott's poems create a landscape of historical and personal memory, overlaying empires, centuries, continents, and stages of his own life. He developed his themes most expansively in his verse novel *Omeros* (1991), which rewrites Homer's *Iliad* as a Caribbean story, interspersed with scenes of the poet's own life and travels in Boston, London, and Dublin. Walcott was awarded the Nobel Prize for literature in 1992, "for a poetic oeuvre of great luminosity, sustained by a historical vision, the outcome of a multicultural commitment."

A Far Cry from Africa

A wind is ruffling the tawny pelt
Of Africa. Kikuyu,[1] quick as flies,
Batten° upon the bloodstreams of the veldt.°   *fasten/open country*
Corpses are scattered through a paradise.
5 Only the worm, colonel of carrion, cries:
"Waste no compassion on these separate dead!"
Statistics justify and scholars seize
The salients of colonial policy.
What is that to the white child hacked in bed?
10 To savages, expendable as Jews?

Threshed out by beaters, the long rushes break
In a white dust of ibises[2] whose cries
Have wheeled since civilization's dawn
From the parched river or beast-teeming plain.
15 The violence of beast on beast is read
As natural law, but upright man
Seeks his divinity by inflicting pain.
Delirious as these worried beasts, his wars
Dance to the tightened carcass of a drum,
20 While he calls courage still that native dread
Of the white peace contracted by the dead.

Again brutish necessity wipes its hands
Upon the napkin of a dirty cause, again
A waste of our compassion, as with Spain,
25 The gorilla wrestles with the superman.
I who am poisoned with the blood of both,
Where shall I turn, divided to the vein?
I who have cursed
The drunken officer of British rule, how choose
30 Between this Africa and the English tongue I love?

---

1. Indigenous people of Kenya.   2. Wading birds resembling storks.

Betray them both, or give back what they give?
How can I face such slaughter and be cool?
How can I turn from Africa and live?

1962

Wales

for Ned Thomas

Those white flecks cropping the ridges of Snowdon[1]
will thicken their fleece and come wintering down
through the gap between alliterative hills,
through the caesura[2] that let in the Legions,
5   past the dark disfigured mouths of the chapels,
till a white silence comes to green-throated Wales.
Down rusty gorges, cold rustling gorse,[3]
over rocks hard as consonants, and rain-vowelled shales
sang the shallow-buried axe, helmet, and baldric°   sword belt
10   before the wet asphalt sibilance of tires.
A plump raven, Plantagenet,[4] unfurls its heraldic
caw over walls that held the cult of the horse.
In blackened cottages with their stony hatred
of industrial fires, a language is shared
15   like bread to the mouth, white flocks to dark byres°.   sheds

1981

The Fortunate Traveller[1]

for Susan Sontag

And I heard a voice in the midst of the four beasts say,
A measure of wheat for a penny,
and three measures of barley for a penny;
and see thou hurt not the oil and the wine.

—*Revelation 6.6*[2]

1

It was in winter. Steeples, spires
congealed like holy candles. Rotting snow
flaked from Europe's ceiling. A compact man,
I crossed the canal in a grey overcoat,
5   on one lapel a crimson buttonhole
for the cold ecstasy of the assassin.
In the square coffin manacled to my wrist:
small countries pleaded through the mesh of graphs,
in treble-spaced, Xeroxed forms to the World Bank
10   on which I had scrawled the one word, MERCY;

I sat on a cold bench
under some skeletal lindens.

---

1. The highest peak in Wales.
2. A break or pause in the middle of a line of verse.
3. Spiny shrub with yellow leaves.
4. English royal house between 1154 and 1485.
1. Walcott's title invokes Thomas Nashe's tale *The Unfor-*

tunate Traveller (1594). Susan Sontag (b. 1933) is an
American cultural critic and novelist.
2. One of the Four Horsemen of the Apocalypse is
decreeing the famine and inflation that accompany wars
as the end of the world approaches.

Two other gentlemen, black skins gone grey
as their identical, belted overcoats,
15   crossed the white river.
They spoke the stilted French
of their dark river,
whose hooked worm, multiplying its pale sickle,
could thin the harvest of the winter streets.
20   "Then we can depend on you to get us those tractors?"
"I gave my word."
"May my country ask you why you are doing this, sir?"
Silence.
"You know if you betray us, you cannot hide?"
25   A tug. Smoke trailing its dark cry.

At the window in Haiti, I remember
a gecko[3] pressed against the hotel glass,
with white palms, concentrating head.
With a child's hands. Mercy, monsieur. Mercy.
30   Famine sighs like a scythe
across the field of statistics and the desert
is a moving mouth. In the hold of this earth
10,000,000 shoreless souls are drifting.
Somalia: 765,000, their skeletons will go under the tidal sand.
35   "We'll meet you in Bristol to conclude the agreement?"
Steeples like tribal lances, through congealing fog
the cries of wounded church bells wrapped in cotton,
grey mist enfolding the conspirator
like a sealed envelope next to its heart.

40   No one will look up now to see the jet
fade like a weevil through a cloud of flour.
One flies first-class, one is so fortunate.
Like a telescope reversed, the traveller's eye
swiftly screws down the individual sorrow
45   to an oval nest of antic numerals,
and the iris, interlocking with this globe,
condenses it to zero, then a cloud.
Beetle-black taxi from Heathrow[4] to my flat.
We are roaches,
50   riddling the state cabinets, entering the dark holes
of power, carapaced in topcoats,
scuttling around columns, signalling for taxis,
with frantic antennae, to other huddles with roaches;
we infect with optimism, and when
55   the cabinets crack, we are the first
to scuttle, radiating separately
back to Geneva, Bonn, Washington, London.

Under the dripping planes of Hampstead Heath,
I read her letter again, watching the drizzle
60   disfigure its pleading like mascara. Margo,

---

3. A small lizard.   4. London's primary airport.

I cannot bear to watch the nations cry.
Then the phone: "We will pay you in Bristol."
Days in fetid bedclothes swallowing cold tea,
the phone stifled by the pillow. The telly
65   a blue storm with soundless snow.
I'd light the gas and see a tiger's tongue.
I was rehearsing the ecstasies of starvation
for what I had to do. *And have not charity.*[5]

I found my pity, desperately researching
70   the origins of history, from reed-built communes
by sacred lakes, turning with the first sprocketed
water-driven wheels. I smelled imagination
among bestial hides by the gleam of fat,
seeking in all races a common ingenuity.
75   I envisaged an Africa flooded with such light
as alchemized the first fields of emmer wheat and barley,
when we savages dyed our pale dead with ochre,
and bordered our temples
with the ceremonial vulva of the conch
80   in the grey epoch of the obsidian adze.
I sowed the Sahara with rippling cereals,
my charity fertilized these aridities.

What was my field? Late sixteenth century.
My field was a dank acre. A Sussex don,
85   I taught the Jacobean anxieties: *The White Devil.*[6]
Flamineo's torch startles the brooding yews.
The drawn end comes in strides. I loved my Duchess,
the white flame of her soul blown out between
the smoking cypresses. Then I saw children pounce
90   on green meat with a rat's ferocity.

I called them up and took the train to Bristol,
my blood the Severn's[7] dregs and silver.
On Severn's estuary the pieces flash,
Iscariot's salary,[8] patron saint of spies.
95   I thought, who cares how many million starve?
Their rising souls will lighten the world's weight
and level its gull-glittering waterline;
we left at sunset down the estuary.

England recedes. The forked white gull
100   screeches, circling back.
Even the birds are pulled back by their orbit,
even mercy has its magnetic field.
                                        Back in the cabin,
I uncap the whisky, the porthole

---

5. "Though I speak with the tongues of men and of angels, and have not charity, I am become as sounding brass, or a tinkling cymbal" (1 Corinthians 13.1).
6. Revenge tragedy (c. 1612) by John Webster.

7. A river running through Wales and England.
8. For betraying Jesus Christ, Judas Iscariot was paid 30 pieces of silver by the Roman authorities.

105 mists with glaucoma. By the time I'm pissed,[9]
England, England will be
that pale serrated indigo on the sea-line.
"You are so fortunate, you get to see the world—"
Indeed, indeed, sirs, I have seen the world.
110 Spray splashes the portholes and vision blurs.

Leaning on the hot rail, watching the hot sea,
I saw them far off, kneeling on hot sand
in the pious genuflections of the locust,
as Ponce's armoured knees crush Florida
115 to the funereal fragrance of white lilies.

II

Now I have come to where the phantoms live,
I have no fear of phantoms, but of the real.
The Sabbath benedictions of the islands.
Treble clef of the snail on the scored leaf,
120 the Tantum Ergo[1] of black choristers
soars through the organ pipes of coconuts.
Across the dirty beach surpliced with lace,
they pass a brown lagoon behind the priest,
pale and unshaven in his frayed soutane,[2]
125 into the concrete church at Canaries;
as Albert Schweitzer[3] moves to the harmonium
of morning, and to the pluming chimneys,
the groundswell lifts Lebensraum, Lebensraum.[4]

Black faces sprinkled with continual dew—
130 dew on the speckled croton,[5] dew
on the hard leaf of the knotted plum tree,
dew on the elephant ears of the dasheen.[6]
Through Kurtz's teeth, white skull in elephant grass,
the imperial fiction sings. Sunday
135 wrinkles downriver from the Heart of Darkness.
The heart of darkness is not Africa.
The heart of darkness is the core of fire
in the white center of the holocaust.
The heart of darkness is the rubber claw
140 selecting a scalpel in antiseptic light,
the hills of children's shoes outside the chimneys,
the tinkling nickel instruments on the white altar;
Jacob, in his last card, sent me these verses:
"Think of a God who doesn't lose His sleep
145 if trees burst into tears or glaciers weep.
So, aping His indifference, I write now,
not Anno Domini: After Dachau."[7]

9. Drunk.
1. A hymn sung after the Blessed Sacrament has been exposed in the mass.
2. Black robe.
3. German physician, missionary, and musician in Africa; winner of the Nobel Peace Prize in 1952.
4. Space to live in; the term is especially associated with Nazi Germany's territorial expansion.
5. A tropical plant.
6. The taro plant of tropical Asia.
7. Site of the notorious Nazi concentration camp.

III

The night maid brings a lamp and draws the blinds.
I stay out on the verandah with the stars.
150   Breakfast congealed to supper on its plate.

There is no sea as restless as my mind.
The promontories snore. They snore like whales.
Cetus, the whale, was Christ.
The ember dies, the sky smokes like an ash heap.
155   Reeds wash their hands of guilt and the lagoon
is stained. Louder, since it rained,
a gauze of sand flies hisses from the marsh.

Since God is dead,[8] and these are not His stars,
but man-lit, sulphurous, sanctuary lamps,
160   it's in the heart of darkness of this earth
that backward tribes keep vigil of His Body,
in deya, lampion,[9] and this bedside lamp.
Keep the news from their blissful ignorance.
Like lice, like lice, the hungry of this earth
165   swarm to the tree of life. If those who starve
like these rain-flies who shed glazed wings in light
grew from sharp shoulder blades their brittle vans
and soared towards that tree, how it would seethe—
ah, Justice! But fires
170   drench them like vermin, quotas
prevent them, and they remain
compassionate fodder for the travel book,
its paragraphs like windows from a train,
for everywhere that earth shows its rib cage
175   and the moon goggles with the eyes of children,
we turn away to read. Rimbaud[1] learned that.
                              Rimbaud, at dusk,
idling his wrist in water past temples
the plumed dates still protect in Roman file,
180   knew that we cared less for one human face
than for the scrolls in Alexandria's ashes,
that the bright water could not dye his hand
any more than poetry. The dhow's[2] silhouette
moved through the blinding coinage of the river
185   that, endlessly, until we pay one debt,
shrouds, every night, an ordinary secret.

IV

The drawn sword comes in strides.
It stretches for the length of the empty beach;
the fishermen's huts shut their eyes tight.
190   A frisson[3] shakes the palm trees.
and sweats on the traveller's tree.

---

8. So the German philosopher Friedrich Nietzsche
declared in his 1882 text *The Gay Science.*
9. A small oil lamp with tinted glass.
1. Arthur Rimbaud (1854–1891), French poet. After abandoning poetry at the age of 20, he travelled in Egypt and the
Sudan, later settling in Ethiopia as a trader and arms dealer.
2. A sailing vessel used by Arabs.
3. Sudden passing excitement.

They've found out my sanctuary. Philippe, last night:
"It had two gentlemen in the village yesterday, sir,
asking for you while you was in town.
195   I tell them you was in town. They send to tell you,
there is no hurry. They will be coming back."

In loaves of cloud, *and have not charity,*
the weevil will make a sahara of Kansas,
the ant shall eat Russia.
200   Their soft teeth shall make, *and have not charity,*
the harvest's desolation,
and the brown globe crack like a begging bowl,
and though you fire oceans of surplus grain,
and have not charity,

205   still, through thin stalks,
the smoking stubble, stalks
grasshopper: third horseman,
the leather-helmed locust.[4]

1981

from **Midsummer**
50

I once gave my daughters, separately, two conch shells
that were dived from the reef, or sold on the beach, I forget.
They use them as doorstops or bookends, but their wet
pink palates are the soundless singing of angels.
5   I once wrote a poem called "The Yellow Cemetery,"
when I was nineteen. Lizzie's age. I'm fifty-three.
These poems I heaved aren't linked to any tradition
like a mossed cairn;[1] each goes down like a stone
to the seabed, settling, but let them, with luck, lie
10   where stones are deep, in the sea's memory.
Let them be, in water, as my father, who did watercolours,
entered his work. He became one of his shadows,
wavering and faint in the midsummer sunlight.
His name is Warwick Walcott. I sometimes believe
15   that his father, in love or bitter benediction,
named him for Warwickshire.[2] Ironies
are moving. Now, when I rewrite a line,
or sketch on the fast-drying paper the coconut fronds
that he did so faintly, my daughters' hands move in mine.
20   Conches move over the sea-floor. I used to move
my father's grave from the blackened Anglican headstones
in Castries[3] to where I could love both at once—
the sea and his absence. Youth is stronger than fiction.

---

4. The locust, eater of crops, is here identified with the horseman of the Apocalypse quoted in the poem's epigraph.
1. A heap of stones marking a trail.
2. Birthplace of Shakespeare. Warwick Walcott, journal-

ist, occasional poet, and printer, died when his son was a young child.
3. Port and capital of Saint Lucia.

52

I heard them marching the leaf-wet roads of my head,
the sucked vowels of a syntax trampled to mud,
a division of dictions, one troop black, barefooted,
the other in redcoats bright as their sovereign's blood;
5   their feet scuffled like rain, the bare soles with the shod.
One fought for a queen, the other was chained in her service,
but both, in bitterness, travelled the same road.
Our occupation and the Army of Occupation
are born enemies, but what mortar can size
10   the broken stones of the barracks of Brimstone Hill
to the gaping brick of Belfast? Have we changed sides
to the moustached sergeants and the horsy gentry
because we serve English, like a two-headed sentry
guarding its borders? No language is neutral;
15   the green oak of English is a murmurous cathedral
where some took umbrage,[4] some peace, but every shade, all,
helped widen its shadow. I used to haunt the arches
of the British barracks of Vigie.[5] There were leaves there,
bright, rotting like revers of epaulettes[6], and the stenches
20   of history and piss. Leaves piled like the dropped aitches
of soldiers from rival shires, from the brimstone trenches
of Agincourt to the gas of the Somme.[7] On Poppy Day[8]
our schools bought red paper flowers. They were for Flanders.[9]
I saw Hotspur cursing the smoke through which a popinjay
25   minced from the battle. Those raging commanders
from Thersites to Percy,[1] their rant is our model.
I pinned the poppy to my blazer. It bled like a vowel.

54

The midsummer sea, the hot pitch road, this grass, these shacks that made me,
jungle and razor grass shimmering by the roadside, the edge of art;
wood lice are humming in the sacred wood,
nothing can burn them out, they are in the blood;
5   their rose mouths, like cherubs, sing of the slow science
of dying—all heads, with, at each ear, a gauzy wing.
Up at Forest Reserve, before branches break into sea,
I looked through the moving, grassed window and thought "pines,"
or conifers of some sort. I thought, they must suffer
10   in this tropical heat with their child's idea of Russia.
Then suddenly, from their rotting logs, distracting signs

---

4. In two senses: offence, shade.
5. Vigie Beach near Castries, Saint Lucia.
6. Turned-up edges of ornamental shoulder pieces worn on uniforms.
7. French sites of important battles in 1415 and in World War I.
8. Veterans Day.

9. Scene of a disastrous World War I offensive—"the battle of the mud"—in which the British lost 324,000 soldiers.
1. The headstrong Sir Henry Percy (1364–1403) became known as "Hotspur"; he serves as rival to Prince Hal in Shakespeare's Henry IV. Thersites accuses Achilles of cowardice in Homer's Iliad.

of the faith I betrayed, or the faith that betrayed me—
yellow butterflies rising on the road to Valencia[2]
stuttering "yes" to the resurrection; "yes, yes is our answer,"
15   the gold-robed Nunc Dimittis[3] of their certain choir.
Where's my child's hymnbook, the poems edged in gold leaf,
the heaven I worship with no faith in heaven,
as the Word turned toward poetry in its grief?
Ah, bread of life, that only love can leaven!
20   Ah, Joseph, though no man ever dies in his own country,[4]
the grateful grass will grow thick from his heart.

1984

[END OF PERSPECTIVES: WHOSE LANGUAGE?]

2. A seaport in Eastern Spain.
3. "Lord, now let thy servant depart in peace," sung at the end of Mass.
4. The line echoes Jesus's comment that no prophet is honored in his own country (Mark 6.4). On one level, Joseph may be Jesus's father, mourning his son's early death. Midsummer as a whole is addressed to Walcott's friend Joseph Brodsky, the exiled Russian poet.

POLITICAL AND RELIGIOUS ORDERS

One political order that cannot be ignored by readers of British literature and history is the monarchy, since it provides the terms by which historical periods are even today divided up. Thus much of the nineteenth century is often spoken of as the "Victorian" age or period, after Queen Victoria (reigned 1837–1901), and the writing of the period is given the name Victorian literature. By the same token, writing of the period 1559–1603 is often called "Elizabethan" after Elizabeth I, and that of 1901–1910 "Edwardian" after Edward VII. This system however is based more on convention than logic, since few would call the history (or literature) of late twentieth-century Britain "Elizabethan" any more than they would call the history and literature of the eighteenth century "Georgian," though four king Georges reigned between 1714 and 1820. Where other, better terms exist these are generally adopted.

As these notes suggest, however, it is still common to think of British history in terms of the dates of the reigning monarch, even though the political influence of the monarchy has been strictly limited since the seventeenth century. Thus, where an outstanding political figure has emerged it is he or she who tends to name the period of a decade or longer; for the British, for example, the 1980s was the decade of "Thatcherism" as for Americans it was the period of "Reaganomics." The monarchy, though, still provides a point of common reference and has up to now shown a remarkable historical persistence, transforming itself as occasion dictates to fit new social circumstances. Thus, while most of the other European monarchies disappeared early in the twentieth century, if they had not already done so, the British institution managed to transform itself from imperial monarchy, a role adopted in the nineteenth century, to become the head of a welfare state and member of the European Union. Few of the titles gathered by Queen Victoria, such as Empress of India, remain to Elizabeth II (reigns 1952–), whose responsibilities now extend only to the British Isles with some vestigial role in Australia, Canada, and New Zealand among other places.

The monarchy's political power, like that of the aristocracy, has been successively diminished over the past several centuries, with the result that today both monarch and aristocracy have only formal authority. This withered state of today's institutions, however, should not blind us to the very real power they wielded in earlier centuries. Though the medieval monarch King John had famously been obliged to recognize the rule of law by signing the Magna Carta ("Great Charter") in 1215, thus ending arbitrary rule, the sixteenth- and seventeenth-century English monarchs still officially ruled by "divine right" and were under no obligation to attend to the wishes of Parliament. Charles I in the 1630s reigned mostly without summoning a parliament, and the concept of a "constitutional monarchy," being one whose powers were formally bound by statute, was introduced only when King William agreed to the Declaration of Right in 1689. This document, together with the contemporaneous Bill of Rights, while recognizing that sovereignty still rests in the monarch, formally transferred executive and legislative powers to Parliament. Bills still have to receive Royal Assent, though this was last denied by Queen Anne in 1707; the monarch still holds "prerogative" powers, though these, which include the appointment of certain officials, the dissolution of Parliament and so on, are, in practice wielded by the prime minister. Further information on the political character of various historical periods can be found in the period introductions.

Political power in Britain is thus held by the prime minister and his or her cabinet, members of which are also members of the governing party in the House of Commons. As long as the government is able to command a majority in the House of Commons, sometimes by a coalition of several parties but more usually by the absolute majority of one, it both makes the laws and carries them out. The situation is therefore very different from the American doctrine of the "Separation of Powers," in which Congress is independent of the President and can even be controlled by the opposing party. The British state of affairs has led to the office of prime minister being compared to that of an "elected dictatorship" with surprising frequency over the past several hundred years.

British government is bicameral, having both an upper and a lower house. Unlike other bicameral systems, however, the upper house, the House of Lords, is not elected, its membership being largely hereditary. Membership can come about in four main ways: (1) by birth, (2) by appointment by the current prime minister often in consultation with the Leader of the Opposition, (3) by virtue of holding a senior position in the judiciary, and (4) by being a bishop of the Established Church (the Church of England). In the House of Commons, the lower house, the particular features of the British electoral system have meant that there are never more than two large parties, one of which is in power. These are, together, "Her Majesty's Government and Opposition." Local conditions in Northern Ireland and Scotland have meant that these areas sometimes send members to Parliament in London who are members neither of the Conservative nor of the Labour parties; in general, however, the only other group in the Commons is the small Liberal Party.

Taking these categories in turn, all members of the hereditary aristocracy (the "peerage") have a seat in the House of Lords. The British aristocracy, unlike those of other European countries, was never formally dispossessed of political power (for example by a revolution), and though their influence is now limited, nevertheless all holders of hereditary title—dukes, marquesses, earls, viscounts and barons, in that order of precedence—sit in the Lords. Some continue to do political work and may be members of the Government or of the Opposition, though today it would be considered unusual for a senior member of government to sit in the House of Lords. The presence of the hereditary element in the Lords tends to give the institution a conservative tone, though the presence of the other members ensures this is by no means always the case. Secondly there are "life peers," who are created by the monarch on the prime minister's recommendation under legislation dating from 1958. They are generally individuals who have distinguished themselves in one field or another; retiring senior politicians from the Commons are generally elevated to the Lords, for example, as are some senior civil servants, diplomats, business and trade union leaders, academics, figures in the arts, retiring archbishops, and members of the military. Some of these take on formal political responsibilities and others do not. Finally, senior members of the judiciary sit in the Lords as Law Lords, while senior members of the Church of England hierarchy also sit in the Lords and frequently intervene in political matters. It has been a matter of some controversy whether senior members of other religious denominations, or religions, should also sit in the House of Lords. Within the constitution (by the Parliament Act of 1911 and other acts) the powers of the House of Lords are limited mostly to the amendment and delay of legislation; from time to time the question of its reform or abolition is raised.

In addition, there are minor orders of nobility that should be mentioned. A baronet is a holder of a hereditary title, but he is not a member of the peerage; the style is Sir (followed by his first and last names), Baronet (usually abbreviated as Bart. or Bt.). A knight is a member of one of the various orders of British knighthood, the oldest of which dates back to the Middle Ages (the Order of the Garter), the majority to the eighteenth or nineteenth centuries (the Order of the Thistle, the Bath, Saint Michael, and Saint George, etc.). The title is nonhereditary and is given for various services; it is marked by various initials coming after the name. K.C.B., for example, stands for "Knight Commander of the Bath," and there are many others.

In the House of Commons itself, the outstanding feature is the dominance of the party system. Party labels, such as "Whigs" and "Tories," were first used from the late seventeenth century, when groups of members began to form opposing factions in a Parliament now freed of much of the power of the king. The "Tories," for example, a name now used to refer to the modern Conservative Party, were originally members of that faction that supported James II (exiled in 1689); the word "Tory" comes from the Irish (Gaelic) for outlaw or thief. The "Whigs," on the other hand, supported the constitutional reforms associated with the 1689 Glorious Revolution; the word "whig" is obscurely related to the idea of regicide. The Whig faction largely dominated the political history of the eighteenth century, though the electorate was too small, and politics too controlled by the patronage of the great aristocratic families, for much of a party system to develop. It was only in the middle decades of the nineteenth century that the familiar party system in parliament and the associated electioneering organization in the country at large came into being. The Whigs were replaced by the Liberal Party around the mid-century, as the Liberals were to be replaced by the Labour Party in the early decades of the twentieth century; the Tories had become firm Conservatives by the time of Lord Derby's administrations in the mid-nineteenth century.

The party system has always been fertile ground for a certain amount of parliamentary theater, and it has fostered the emergence of some powerful personalities. Whereas the eighteenth-century Whig prime minister Sir Robert Walpole owed his authority to a mixture of personal patronage and the power made available through the alliances of powerful families, nineteenth-century figures such as Benjamin Disraeli (Conservative prime minister 1868, 1874–1880) and William Ewart Gladstone (Liberal prime minister 1868–1874; 1880–1885; 1885; 1892–1894), were at the apex of their respective party machines. Disraeli, theatrical, personable and with a keen eye for publicity (he was, among other things, a close personal friend of Queen Victoria), formed a great contrast to the massive moral appeals of his parliamentary opponent Gladstone. One earlier figure, William Pitt (1759–1806), prime minister at twenty-four and leader of the country during the French Revolution and earlier Napoleonic wars, stands comparison with these in the historical record; of twentieth-century political figures, David Lloyd-George, Liberal prime minister during World War I, and Winston Churchill, Conservative, during World War II, deserve special mention.

Though political power in the United Kingdom now rests with Parliament at Westminster in London, this has not always been the only case. Wales, which is now formally a principality within the political construction "England and Wales," was conquered by the English toward the end of the thirteenth century—too early for indigenous representative institutions to have fallen into place. Scotland, on the other hand, which from 1603 was linked with England under a joint monarchy but only became part of the same political entity with the Act of Union in 1707, did develop discrete institutions. Recent votes in both Scotland and Wales are leading toward greater local legislative control over domestic issues in both Scotland and Wales. Many Scottish institutions—for example, the legal and educational systems—are substantially different from those of England, which is not true in the case of Wales. The Church of Scotland in particular has no link with the Church of England, having been separately established in 1690 on a Presbyterian basis; this means that authority in the Scottish church is vested in elected pastors and lay elders and not in an ecclesiastical hierarchy of priests and bishops. But the most vexed of the relationships within the union has undoubtedly been that between England and Ireland.

There has been an English presence in Ireland from the Middle Ages on, and this became dominant in the later sixteenth century when English policy was deliberately to conquer and colonize the rest of the country. The consequence of this policy, however, was that an Irish Protestant "Ascendancy" came to rule over a largely dispossessed Catholic Irish peasantry; in 1689 at the Battle of the Boyne this state of affairs was made permanent, as Irish Catholic support for the exiled and Catholic-sympathizing James II was routed by the invading troops of the new Protestant king, William III. An Irish parliament met in Dublin, but this was restricted to Protestants; the Church of Ireland was the established Protestant church in a country where most of the population was Catholic. Irish political representation was shifted to Westminster by Pitt in 1800 under the formal Act of Union with Ireland; the Church of Ireland was disestablished by Gladstone later in the century. In the twentieth century, continuing agitation in the Catholic south of the country first for Home Rule and subsequently for independence from Britain—agitation that had been a feature of almost the whole nineteenth century at greater or lesser levels of intensity—led to the establishment first of the Irish Free State (1922) and later of the Republic (1948). In the Protestant North of the country, a local parliament met from 1922 within the common framework of the United Kingdom, but this was suspended in 1972 and representation returned to Westminster, as renewed violence in the province threatened local institutions. In Northern Ireland several hundred years of conflict between Protestants, who form the majority of the population in the province, and Catholics have led to continuing political problems.

Since the Reformation in the sixteenth century Britain has officially been a Protestant country with a national church headed by the monarch. This "Established Church," the Church of England or Anglican Church, has its own body of doctrine in the Thirty-Nine Articles and elsewhere, its own order of services in the Book of Common Prayer, and its own translation of the Bible (the "Authorized Version"), commissioned by James I (reigned 1603–1625) as Head of the Church. There is an extensive ecclesiastical hierarchy and a worldwide communion that includes the American Episcopalian Church.

The Reformation in England was not an easy business, and it has certain negative consequences even today. Some of these have been touched upon above in the case of Ireland. Those professing Roman Catholicism were excluded from political office and suffered other penalties until 1829, and a Catholic hierarchy parallel to that of the Church of England only came into being in Britain in the later nineteenth century. Though many of the restrictions on Roman Catholics enacted by Act of Parliament at the end of the seventeenth century were considerably softened in the course of the eighteenth, nevertheless they were very real.

English Protestantism, however, is far from being all of a piece. As early as the sixteenth century, many saw the substitution of the King's authority and that of the national ecclesiastical hierarchy for that of the Pope to be no genuine Protestant Reformation, which they thought demanded local autonomy and individual judgment. In the seventeenth century many "dissenting" or "Non-Conformist" Protestant sects thus grew up or gathered strength (many becoming "Puritans"), and these rejected the authority of the national church and its bishops and so the authority of the king. They had a brief moment of freedom during the Civil War and the Commonwealth (1649–1660) following the execution of Charles I, when there was a flowering of sects from Baptists and Quakers, which still exist today, to Ranters, Shakers, Anabaptists, Muggletonians, etc., which in the main do not (except for some sects in the United States). The monarchy and the Church were decisively reestablished in 1660, but subsequent legislation, most importantly the Act of Toleration (1689), suspended laws against dissenters on certain conditions.

Religious dissent or nonconformity remained powerful social movements over the following centuries and received new stimulus from the "New Dissenting" revivalist movements of the eighteenth century (particularly Methodism, though there was also a growth in the Congregationalist and Baptist churches). By the nineteenth century, the social character and geographical pattern of English dissent had been established: religious nonconformity was a feature of the new working classes brought into being by the Industrial Revolution in the towns of the Midlands and North of England. Anglicanism, which was associated with the pre-industrial traditional order, was rejected also by many among the rising bourgeoisie and lower middle classes; almost every major English novel of the mid-nineteenth century and beyond is written against a background of religious nonconformity or dissent, which had complex social and political meanings. Nonconformity was also a particular feature of Welsh society.

Under legislation enacted by Edward I in 1290, the Jews were expelled from England, and there were few of them in the country until the end of the seventeenth century, when well-established Jewish communities began to appear in London (the medieval legislation was repealed under the Commonwealth in the 1650s). Restrictions on Jews holding public office continued until the mid-nineteenth century, and at the end of the century large Jewish communities were formed in many English cities by refugees from Central and Eastern European anti-Semitism.

Britain today is a multicultural country and significant proportions of the population, many of whom came to Britain from former British Empire territories, profess Hinduism or Islam, among other religions. The United Kingdom has been a member of the European Union since the early 1970s, and this has further loosened ties between Britain and former empire territories or dominions, many of which are still linked to Britain by virtue of the fact that the British monarch is Head of the "Commonwealth," an organization to which many of them belong. In some cases, the British monarch is also Head of State. Most importantly, however, British membership of the European Union has meant that powers formerly held by the national parliament have been transferred either to the European Parliament in Strasbourg, France, or to the European Commission, the executive agency in Brussels, Belgium, or, in the case of judicial review and appeal, to the European Court of Justice. This process seems set to generate tensions in Britain for some years to come.

David Tresilian

English Monarchs

Before the Norman conquest (1066), these included:

Alfred the Great	871–899
Edmund I	940–946
Ethelred the Unready	948–1016
Edward the Confessor	1042–1066
Harold II	1066

The following monarchs are divided by the dynasty ("House") to which they belong:

Normandy

William I the Conqueror	1066–1087
William II, Rufus	1087–1100
Henry I	1100–1135

Blois

Stephen	1135–1154

Plantagenet

Henry II	1154–1189
Richard I "Coeur de Lion"	1189–1199
John	1199–1216
Henry III	1216–1272
Edward I	1272–1307
Edward II	1307–1327
Edward III	1327–1377
Richard II	1377–1400

Lancaster

Henry IV	1399–1413
Henry V	1413–1422
Henry VI	1422–1471

York

Edward IV	1461–1483
Edward V	1483
Richard III	1483–1485

Tudor

Henry VII	1485–1509
Henry VIII	1509–1547
Edward VI	1547–1553
Mary I	1553–1558
Elizabeth I	1558–1603

Kings of England and of Scotland:
Stuart

James I (James VI of Scotland)	1603–1625
Charles I	1625–1649

Commonwealth (Republic)

Council of State	1649–1653
Oliver Cromwell, Lord Protector	1653–1658
Richard Cromwell	1658–1660

Stuart

Charles II	1660–1685
James II	1685–1688
(Interregnum 1688–1689)	
William III and Mary II	1685–1701 (Mary dies 1694)
Anne	1702–1714

Hanover

George I	1714–1727
George II	1727–1760
George III	1760–1820
George IV	1820–1830
William IV	1830–1837
Victoria	1837–1901

Saxe-Coburg and Gotha

Edward VII	1901–1910

Windsor

George V	1910–1936
Edward VIII	1936
George VI	1936–1952
Elizabeth II	1952–

MONEY, WEIGHTS, AND MEASURES

The possibility of confusion by the British monetary system has considerably decreased since 1971, when decimalization of the currency took place. There are now 100 pence to a pound (worth about $1.60 in the late 1990s). Prior to this date the currency featured a gallery of other units as well. These coins—shillings, crowns, half-crowns, florins, threepenny-bits, and far-things—were contemporary survivals of the currency's historical development. As such they had a familiar presence in the culture, which was reflected in the slang terms used to refer to them in the spoken language. At least one of these terms, that of a "quid" for a pound, is still in use today.

The old currency divided the pound into 20 shillings, each of which contained 12 pence. There were, therefore, 240 pence in 1 pound. Five shillings made a crown, a half-crown was 2½ shillings, and a florin was 2 shillings; there was also a sixpence, a threepenny-bit, and a far-thing (a quarter of a penny). In slang, a shilling was a "bob," a sixpence a "tanner," and a pen-ny a "copper." Sums were written as, for example, £12. 6s. 6d. or £12/6/6 (12 pounds, 6 shillings, and 6 pence; the "d." stands for "denarius," from the Latin). Figures up to £5 were often expressed in shillings alone: the father of the novelist D. H. Lawrence, for instance, who was a coal miner, was paid around 35 shillings a week at the beginning of the twentieth centu-ry—i.e., 1 pound and 15 shillings, or £1/15/–. At this time two gold coins were also still in cir-culation, the sovereign (£1) and the half-sovereign (10s.), which had been the principal coins of the nineteenth century; the largest silver coin was the half-crown (2 / 6). Later all coins were composed either of copper or an alloy of copper and nickel. The guinea was £1/1/– (1 pound and 1 shilling, or 21 shillings); though the actual coin had not been minted since the beginning of the nineteenth century, the term was still used well into the twentieth to price luxury items and to pay professional fees.

The number of dollars that a pound could buy has fluctuated with British economic for-tunes. The current figure has been noted above; in 1912 it was about $5.00. To get a sense of how much the pound was worth to those who used it as an everyday index of value, however, we have to look at what it could buy within the system in which it was used. To continue the Lawrence example, a coal miner may have been earning 35 shillings a week in the early years of the twentieth century, but of this he would have to have paid six shillings as rent on the family house; his son, by contrast, could command a figure of £300 as a publisher's advance on his novel *The Rainbow* (pub. 1915), a sum which alone would have placed him somewhere in the middle class. In *A Room of One's Own* (1928) Virginia Woolf recommended the figure of £500 a year as necessary if a woman were to write; at today's values this would be worth around £25,000 ($41,000)—considerably more than the pay of, for example, a junior faculty member at a British university, either then or now.

In earlier periods an idea of the worth of the currency, being the relation between wages and prices, can similarly be established by taking samples from across the country at specific dates. Toward the end of the seventeenth century, for example, Poor Law records tell us that a family of five could be considered to subsist on an annual income of £13/14/–, which included £9/14/– spent on food. At the same time an agricultural laborer earned around £15/12/– annu-ally, while at the upper end of the social scale, the aristocracy dramatically recovered and increased their wealth in the period after the restoration of the monarchy in 1660. By 1672 the early industrialist Lord Wharton was realizing an annual profit of £3,200 on his lead mine and smelting plant in the north of England; landed aristocratic families such as the Russells, spon-sors of the 1689 Glorious Revolution and later dukes of Bedford, were already worth £10,000 a year in 1660. Such details allow us to form some idea of the value of the £10 the poet John Milton received for *Paradise Lost* (pub. 1667), as well as to see the great wealth that went into building the eighteenth-century estates that now dot the English countryside.

By extending the same method to the analysis of wage-values during the Industrial Revolution over a century and a half later, the economic background to incidents of public disorder in the period, such as the 1819 "Peterloo Massacre," can be reconstructed, as can the background to the poems of Wordsworth, for example, many of which concern vagrancy and the lives of the rural poor. Thus the essayist William Cobbett calculated in the 1820s that £1/4/– a week was needed to support a family of five, though actual average earnings were less than half this sum. By contrast, Wordsworth's projection of "a volume which consisting of 160 pages might be sold at 5 shillings" (1806)—part of the negotiations for his *Poems in Two Volumes* (1807)—firmly establishes the book as a luxury item. Jane Austen's contemporaneous novel *Mansfield Park* (1814), which gives many details about the economic affairs of the English rural gentry, suggests that at least £1000 a year is a desirable income.

Today's pound sterling, though still cited on the international exchanges with the dollar, the deutsche mark, and the yen, decisively lost to the dollar after World War I as the central currency in the international system. At present it seems highly likely that, with some other European national currencies, it will shortly cease to exist as the currency unit of the European Union is adopted as a single currency in the constituent countries of the Union.

British weights and measures present less difficulty to American readers since the vast inertia permeating industry and commerce following the separation of the United States from Britain prevented the reform of American weights and measures along metric lines, which had taken place where the monetary system was concerned. Thus the British "Imperial" system, with some minor local differences, was in place in both countries until decimalization of the British system began in stages from the early 1970s on. Today all British weights and measures, with the exception of road signs, which still generally give distances in miles, are metric in order to bring Britain into line with European Union standards. Though it is still possible to hear especially older people measuring area in acres and not in hectares, distances in miles and not in kilometers, or feet and yards and not centimeters and meters, weight in pounds and ounces and not in grams and kilograms, and temperature in Fahrenheit and not in centigrade, etc., it is becoming increasingly uncommon. Measures of distance that might be found in older texts— such as the league (three miles, but never in regular use), the furlong (220 yards), and the ell (45 inches)—are now all obsolete; the only measure still heard in current use is the stone (14 pounds), and this is generally used for body weight.

David Tresilian

LITERARY AND CULTURAL TERMS*

Absolutism. In criticism, the belief in irreducible, unchanging values of form and content that underlie the tastes of individuals and periods and arise from the stability of an absolute hierarchical order.

Accent. Stress or emphasis on a syllable, as opposed to the syllable's length of duration, its quantity. *Metrical accent* denotes the metrical pattern (⌣ –) to which writers fit and adjust accented words and rhetorical emphases, keeping the meter as they substitute word-accented feet and tune their rhetoric.

Accentual Verse. Verse with lines established by counting accents only, without regard to the number of unstressed syllables. This was the dominant form of verse in English until the time of Chaucer.

Acrostic. Words arranged, frequently in a poem or puzzle, to disclose a hidden word or message when the correct combination of letters is read in sequence.

Aestheticism. Devotion to beauty. The term applies particularly to a 19th-century literary and artistic movement celebrating beauty as independent from morality, and praising form above content; art for art's sake.

Aesthetics. The study of the beautiful; the branch of philosophy concerned with defining the nature of art and establishing criteria of judgment.

Alexandrine. A six-foot iambic pentameter line.

Allegorical Meaning. A secondary meaning of a narrative in addition to its primary meaning or literal meaning.

Allegory. A story that suggests another story. The first part of this word comes from the Greek *allos*, "other." An allegory is present in literature whenever it is clear that the author is saying, "By this I also mean that." In practice, allegory appears when a progression of events or images suggests a translation of them into conceptual language. Allegory is thus a technique of aligning imaginative constructs, mythological or poetic, with conceptual or moral models. During the Romantic era a distinction arose between allegory and symbol. With Coleridge, symbol took precedence: "an allegory is but a translation of abstract notions into picture-language," but "a symbol always partakes of the reality which it makes intelligible."

Alliteration. "Adding letters" (Latin *ad* + *littera*, "letter"). Two or more words, or accented syllables, chime on the same initial letter (*lost love alone; after apple-picking*) or repeat the same consonant.

Alliterative Revival. The outburst of alliterative verse that occurred in the second half of the 14th century in west and northwest England.

Alliterative Verse. Verse using alliteration on stressed syllables for its fundamental structure.

Allusion. A meaningful reference, direct or indirect, as when William Butler Yeats writes, "Another Troy must rise and set," calling to mind the whole tragic history of Troy.

Amplification. A restatement of something more fully and in more detail, especially in oratory, poetry, and music.

Analogy. A comparison between things similar in a number of ways; frequently used to explain the unfamiliar by the familiar.

Anapest. A metrical foot: ⌣ ⌣ –.

Anaphora. The technique of beginning successive clauses or lines with the same word.

*Adapted from *The Harper Handbook to Literature* by Northrop Frye, Sheridan Baker, George Perkins, and Barbara M. Perkins, 2d edition (Longman, 1997).

Anatomy. Greek for "a cutting up": a dissection, analysis, or systematic study. The term was popular in titles in the 16th and 17th centuries.

Anglo-Norman (Language). The language of upper-class England after the Norman Conquest in 1066.

Anglo-Saxon. The people, culture, and language of three neighboring tribes—Jutes, Angles, and Saxons—who invaded England, beginning in 449, from the lower part of Denmark's Jutland Peninsula. The Angles, settling along the eastern seaboard of central and northern England, developed the first literate culture of any Germanic people. Hence England (Angle-land) became the dominant term.

Antagonist. In Greek drama, the character who opposes the protagonist, or hero: therefore, any character who opposes another. In some works, the antagonist is clearly the villain (Iago in *Othello*), but in strict terminology an antagonist is merely an opponent and may be in the right.

Anthropomorphism. The practice of giving human attributes to animals, plants, rivers, winds, and the like, or to such entities as Grecian urns and abstract ideas.

Antithesis. (1) A direct contrast or opposition. (2) The second phase of dialectical argument, which considers the opposition—the three steps being *thesis, antithesis, synthesis.* (3) A rhetorical figure sharply contrasting ideas in balanced parallel structures.

Aphorism. A pithy saying of known authorship, as distinguished from a folk proverb.

Apology. A justification, as in Sir Philip Sidney's *The Apology for Poetry* (1595).

Apostrophe. (Greek, "a turning away"). An address to an absent or imaginary person, a thing, or a personified abstraction.

Archaism. An archaic or old-fashioned word or expression—for example, *o'er, ere,* or *darkling.*

Archetype. (1) The first of a genre, like Homer's *Iliad,* the first heroic epic. (2) A natural symbol imprinted in human consciousness by experience and literature, like dawn symbolizing hope or an awakening; night, death or repose.

Assonance. Repetition of middle vowel sounds: *fight, hive; pane, make.* Assonance, most effective on stressed syllables, is often found within a line of poetry; less frequently it substitutes for end rhyme.

Aubade. Dawn song, from French *aube,* for dawn. The aubade originated in the Middle Ages as a song sung by a lover greeting the dawn, ordinarily expressing regret that morning means parting.

Avant-Garde. Experimental, innovative, at the forefront of a literary or artistic trend or movement. The term is French for *vanguard,* the advance unit of an army. It frequently suggests a struggle with tradition and convention.

Ballad. A narrative poem in short stanzas, with or without music. The term derives by way of French *ballade* from Latin *ballare,* "to dance," and once meant a simple song of any kind, lyric or narrative, especially one to accompany a dance. As ballads evolved, most lost their association with dance, although they kept their strong rhythms. Modern usage distinguishes three major kinds: the anonymous *traditional ballad* (popular ballad or *folk ballad*), transmitted orally; the *broadside ballad,* printed and sold on single sheets; and the *literary ballad* (or art ballad), a sophisticated imitation of the traditional ballad.

Ballad Stanza. The name for common meter as found in ballads: a quatrain in iambic meter, alternating tetrameter and trimeter lines, usually rhyming *abcb.*

Bard. An ancient Celtic singer of the culture's lore in epic form; a poetic term for any poet.

Baroque. (1) A richly ornamented style in architecture and art. Founded in Rome by Frederigo Barocci about 1550, and characterized by swirling allegorical frescoes on ceilings and walls, it flourished throughout Europe until 1700. (2) A chromatic musical style with strict forms containing similar exuberant ornamentation, flourishing from 1600 to 1750. In literature, Richard Crashaw's bizarre imagery and the conceits and rhythms of John Donne and other metaphysical poets are sometimes called baroque, sometimes mannerist.

Some literary historians designate a Baroque Age from 1580 to 1680, between the Renaissance and the Enlightenment.

Bathos. (1) A sudden slippage from the sublime to the ridiculous. (2) Any anticlimax. (3) Sentimental pathos. (4) Triteness or dullness.

Blank Verse. Unrhymed iambic pentameter. *See also* Meter. In the 1540s Henry Howard, earl of Surrey, seems to have originated it in English as the equivalent of Virgil's unrhymed dactylic hexameter. In *Gorboduc* (1561), Thomas Sackville and Thomas Norton introduced blank verse into the drama, whence it soared with Marlowe and Shakespeare in the 1590s. Milton forged it anew for the epic in *Paradise Lost* (1667).

Bloomsbury Group. An informal social and intellectual group associated with Bloomsbury, a London residential district near the British Museum, from about 1904 until the outbreak of World War II. Virginia Woolf was a principal member. With her husband, Leonard Woolf, she established the Hogarth Press, which published works by many of their friends. The group was loosely knit, but famed, especially in the 1920s, for its exclusiveness, aestheticism, and social and political freethinking.

Broadside. A sheet of paper printed on one side only. Broadsides containing a ballad, a tract, a criminal's gallows speech, a scurrilous satire, and the like were once commonly sold on the streets like newspapers.

Burden. (1) A refrain or set phrase repeated at intervals throughout a song or poem. (2) A bass accompaniment, the "load" carried by the melody, the origin of the term.

Burlesque. (1) A ridicule, especially on the stage, treating the lofty in low style, or the low in grandiose style. (2) A bawdy vaudeville, with obscene clowning and stripteasing.

Caesura. A pause in a metrical line, indicated by punctuation, momentarily suspending the beat (from Latin "a cutting off"). Caesuras are *masculine* at the end of a foot, and *feminine* in mid-foot.

Canon. The writings accepted as forming a part of the Bible, of the works of an author, or of a body of literature. Shakespeare's canon consists of works he wrote, which may be distinguished from works attributed to him but written by others. The word derives from Greek *kanon*, "rod" or "rule," and suggests authority. Canonical authors and texts are those taught most frequently, noncanonical are those rarely taught, and in between are disputed degrees of canonicity for authors considered minor or marginalized.

Canto. A major division in a long poem. The Italian expression is from Latin *cantus*, "song," a section singable in one sitting.

Caricature. Literary cartooning, depicting characters with exaggerated physical traits such as huge noses and bellies, short stature, squints, tics, humped backs, and so forth. Sir Thomas Browne seems to have introduced the term into English in 1682 from the Italian *caricatura*.

Catalog. In literature, an enumeration of ancestors, of ships, of warriors, of a woman's beauties, and the like; a standard feature of the classical epic.

Celtic Revival. In the 18th century, a groundswell of the Romantic movement in discovering the power in ancient, primitive poetry, particularly Welsh and Scottish Gaelic, as distinct from that of the classics.

Chiasmus. A rhetorical balance created by the inversion of one of two parallel phrases or clauses; from the Greek for a "placing crosswise," as in the Greek letter χ (chi).

Chronicle. A kind of history, with the emphasis on *time* (Greek *chronos*). Events are described in order as they occurred. The chronicles of the Middle Ages provided material for later writers and serve now as important sources of knowledge about the period. Raphael Holinshed's *Chronicle* (1577) is especially famous as the immediate source of much of Shakespeare's knowledge of English history.

Chronicle Play. A play dramatizing historical events, as from a chronicle. Chronicle plays tend to stress time order, presenting the reign of a king, for example, with much emphasis on pageantry and little on the unity of action and dramatic conflict necessary for a tragedy.

Classical Literature. (1) The literature of ancient Greece and Rome. (2) Later literature reflecting the qualities of classical Greece or Rome. *See also,* Classicism; Neoclassicism. (3) The classic literature of any time or place, as, for example, classical American literature or classical Japanese literature.

Classicism. A principle in art and conduct reflecting the ethos of ancient Greece and Rome: balance, form, proportion, propriety, dignity, simplicity, objectivity, rationality, restraint, unity rather than diversity. In English literature, classicism emerged with Erasmus (1466–1536) and his fellow humanists. In the Restoration and 18th century, classicism, or neoclassicism, expressed society's deep need for balance and restraint after the shattering Civil War and Puritan commonwealth. Classicism continued in the 19th century, after the Romantic period, particularly in the work of Matthew Arnold. T. E. Hulme, Ezra Pound, and T. S. Eliot expressed it for the 20th century.

Cliché. An overused expression, once clever or metaphorical but now trite and timeworn.

Closed Couplet. The heroic couplet, especially when the thought and grammar are complete in the two iambic pentameter lines.

Closet Drama. A play written for reading in the "closet," or private study. Closet dramas were usually in verse, like Percy Shelley's *Prometheus Unbound* (1820) and Robert Browning's *Pippa Passes* (1841).

Cockney. A native of the East End of central London. The term originally meant "cocks' eggs," a rural term of contempt for city softies and fools. Cockneys are London's ingenious street peddlers, speaking a dialect rich with an inventive rhyming slang, dropping and adding aitches.

Comedy. One of the typical literary structures, originating as a form of drama and later extending into prose fiction and other genres as well. Comedy, as Susanne Langer says, is the image of Fortune; tragedy, the image of Fate. Each sorts out for attention the different facts of life. Comedy sorts its pleasures. It pleases our egos and endows our dreams, stirring at once two opposing impulses, our vindictive lust for superiority and our wishful drive for success and happiness ever after. The dark impulse stirs the pleasure of laughter; the light, the pleasure of wish fulfillment.

Comedy of Humors. Comedy based on the ancient physiological theory that a predominance of one of the body's four fluids (humors) produces a comically unbalanced personality: (1) blood—sanguine, hearty, cheerful, amorous; (2) phlegm—phlegmatic, sluggish; (3) choler (yellow bile)—angry, touchy; (4) black bile—melancholic.

Comedy of Manners. Suave, witty, and risqué, satire of upper-class manners and immorals, particularly that of Restoration masters like George Etherege and William Congreve.

Common Meter. The ballad stanza as found in hymns and other poems: a quatrain (four-line stanza) in iambic meter, alternating tetrameter and trimeter, rhyming *abcb* or *abab*.

Complaint. A lyric poem, popular in the Middle Ages and the Renaissance, complaining of unrequited love, a personal situation, or the state of the world.

Conceit. Any fanciful, ingenious expression or idea, but especially one in the form of an extended metaphor.

Concordia Discors. "Discordant harmony," a phrase expressing for the 18th century the harmonious diversity of nature, a pleasing balance of opposites.

Concrete Poetry. Poetry that attempts a concrete embodiment of its idea, expressing itself physically apart from the meaning of the words. A recent relative of the much older *shaped poem,* the concrete poem places heavy emphasis on the picture and less on the words, so that the visual experience may be more interesting than the linguistic.

Connotation. The ideas, attitudes, or emotions associated with a word in the mind of speaker or listener, writer or reader. It is contrasted with the *denotation,* the thing the word stands for, the dictionary definition, an objective concept without emotional coloring.

Consonance. (1) Repetition of inner or end consonant sounds, as, for example, the *r* and *s* sounds from Gerard Manley Hopkins's *God's Grandeur*: "broods with warm breast." (2) In a broader sense, a generally pleasing combination of sounds or ideas; things that sound well together.

Couplet. A pair of rhymed metrical lines, usually in iambic tetrameter or pentameter. Sometimes the two lines are of different length.

Covenanters. Scottish Presbyterians who signed a covenant in 1557 as a "godly band" to stand together to resist the Anglican church and the English establishment.

Cynghanedd. A complex medieval Welsh system of rhyme, alliteration, and consonance, to which Gerard Manley Hopkins alluded to describe his interplay of euphonious sounds, actually to be heard in any rich poet, as in the Welsh Dylan Thomas: "The force that through the green fuse drives the flower / Drives my green age."

Dactyl. A three-syllable metrical foot: $-\smile\smile$. It is the basic foot of dactylic hexameter, the six-foot line of Greek and Roman epic poetry.

Dactylic Hexameter. The classical or heroic line of the epic. A line based on six dactylic feet, with spondees substituted, and always ending $-\smile\smile \mid --$.

Dead Metaphor. A metaphor accepted without its figurative picture: "a jacket," for the paper around a book, with no mental picture of the human coat that prompted the original metaphor.

Decasyllabic. Having ten syllables. An iambic pentameter line is decasyllabic.

Deconstruction. The critical dissection of a literary text's statements, ambiguities, and structure to expose its hidden contradictions, implications, and fundamental instability of meaning. Jacques Derrida originated deconstruction in *Of Grammatology* (1967) and *Writing and Difference* (1967). Because no understanding of any text is stable, as each new reading is subject to the deconstruction of any meaning it appears to have established, it follows that criticism can be a kind of game, either playful or serious, as each critic ingeniously deconstructs the meanings established by others.

Decorum. Propriety, fitness, the quality of being appropriate. George Puttenham, in his *Arte of English Poesie* (1589), chides a translator of Virgil for his indecorum of having Aeneas "trudge," like a beggar, from Troy.

Defamiliarization. Turning the familiar to the strange by disrupting habitual ways of perceiving things. Derived from the thought of Victor Shklovsky and other Russian formalists, the idea is that art forces us to see things differently as we view them through the artist's sensibility, not our own.

Deism. A rational philosophy of religion, beginning with the theories of Lord Herbert of Cherbury, the "Father of Deism," in his *De Veritate* (1624). Deists generally held that God, the supreme Artisan, created a perfect clock of a universe, withdrew, and left it running, not to return to intervene in its natural works or the life of humankind; that the Bible is a moral guide, but neither historically accurate nor divinely authentic; and that reason guides human beings to virtuous conduct.

Denotation. The thing that a word stands for, the dictionary definition, an objective concept without emotional coloring. It is contrasted with the *connotation*, ideas, attitudes, or emotions associated with the word in the mind of user or hearer.

Dénouement. French for "unknotting": the unraveling of plot threads toward the end of a play, novel, or other narrative.

Determinism. The philosophical belief that events are shaped by forces beyond the control of human beings.

Dialect. A variety of language belonging to a particular time, place, or social group, as, for example, an 18th-century cockney dialect, a New England dialect, or a coal miner's dialect. A language other than one's own is for the most part unintelligible without study or translation; a dialect other than one's own can generally be understood, although pronunciation, vocabulary, and syntax seem strange.

Dialogue. Conversation between two or more persons, as represented in prose fiction, drama, or essays, as opposed to *monologue*, the speech of one person. Good dialogue characterizes each speaker by idiom and attitude as it advances the dramatic conflict. The dialogue as a form of speculative exposition, or dialectical argument, is often less careful to distinguish the diction and character of the speakers.

Diatribe. Greek for "a wearing away": a bitter and abusive criticism or invective, often lengthy, directed against a person, institution, or work.

Diction. Word choice in speech or writing, an important element of style.

Didactic. Greek for "teaching": instructive, or having the qualities of a teacher. Since ancient times, literature has been assumed to have two functions, instruction and entertainment, with sometimes one and sometimes the other dominant. Literature intended primarily for instruction or containing an important moralistic element is didactic.

Dirge. A lamenting funeral song.

Discourse. (1) A formal discussion of a subject. (2) The conventions of communication associated with specific areas, in usages such as "poetic discourse," "the discourse of the novel," or "historical discourse."

Dissenter. A term arising in the 1640s for a member of the clergy or a follower who dissented from the forms of the established Anglican church, particularly Puritans. Dissenters generally came from the lower middle classes, merchants who disapproved of aristocratic frivolity and ecclesiastical pomp.

Dissonance. (1) Harsh and jarring sound; discord. It is frequently an intentional effect, as in the poems of Robert Browning. (2) Occasionally a term for half rhyme or slant rhyme.

Distich. A couplet, or pair of rhymed metrical lines.

Dithyramb. A frenzied choral song and dance to honor Dionysus, Greek god of wine and the power of fertility. Any irregular, impassioned poetry may be called *dithyrambic*. The irregular ode also evolved from the dithyramb.

Doggerel. (1) Trivial verse clumsily aiming at meter, usually tetrameter. (2) Any verse facetiously low and loose in meter and rhyme.

Domesday Book. The recorded census and survey of landholders that William the Conqueror ordered in 1085; from "Doomsday," the Last Judgment.

Dramatic Irony. A character in drama or fiction unknowingly says or does something in ironic contrast to what the audience or reader knows or will learn.

Dramatic Monologue. A monologue in verse. A speaker addresses a silent listener, revealing, in dramatic irony, things about himself or herself of which the speaker is unaware.

Eclogue. A short poem, usually a pastoral, and often in the form of a dialogue or soliloquy. During the Renaissance, in the works of Spenser and others, the eclogue became a major form of verse, with shepherds exchanging verses of love, lament, or eulogy.

Edition. The form in which a book is published, including its physical qualities and its content. A *first edition* is the first form of a book, printed and bound; a *second edition* is a later form, usually with substantial changes in content. Between the two, there may be more than one printing or impression of the first edition, sometimes with minor corrections. The term *edition* also refers to the format of a book. For example, an *illustrated edition* or a *two-volume edition* may be identical in verbal content to one without pictures or bound in a single volume.

Edwardian Period (1901–1914). From the death of Queen Victoria to the outbreak of World War I, named for the reign of Victoria's son, Edward VII (1901–1910), a period generally reacting against Victorian propriety and convention.

Elegiac Stanza. An iambic pentameter quatrain rhyming *abab*. Taking its name from Thomas Gray's *Elegy Written in a Country Churchyard* (1751), it is identical to the heroic quatrain.

Elegy. Greek for "lament": a poem on death or on a serious loss; characteristically a sustained meditation expressing sorrow and, frequently, an explicit or implied consolation.

Elision. Latin for "striking out": the omission or slurring of an unstressed vowel at the end of a word to bring a line of poetry closer to a prescribed metrical pattern, as in John Milton's *Lycidas:* "Tempered to th'oaten flute." *See also* Meter; Syncope.

Elizabethan Drama. English drama of the reign of Elizabeth I (1558–1603). Strictly speaking, drama from the reign of James I (1603–1625) belongs to the Jacobean period and that from the reign of Charles I (1625–1642) to the Caroline period, but the term *Elizabethan* is sometimes extended to include works of later reigns, before the closing of the theaters in 1642.

Elizabethan Period (1558–1603). The years marked by the reign of Elizabeth I; the "Golden Age of English Literature," especially as exemplified by the lyric poetry and dramas of Christopher Marlowe, Edmund Spenser, Sir Philip Sidney, and William Shakespeare, as well as the early Ben Jonson and John Donne.

Ellipsis. The omission of words for rhetorical effect: "*Drop dead*" for "You drop dead."

Emblem. (1) A didactic pictorial and literary form consisting of a word or phrase (*mot* or *motto*), a symbolic woodcut or engraving, and a brief moralistic poem (*explicatio*). Collections of emblems in book form were popular in the 16th and 17th centuries. (2) A type or symbol.

Emendation. A change made in a literary text to remove faults that have appeared through tampering or by errors in reading, transcription, or printing from the manuscript.

Empathy. Greek for "feeling with": identification with the feelings or passions of another person, natural creature, or even an inanimate object conceived of as possessing human attributes. Empathy suggests emotional identification, whereas sympathy may be largely an intellectual appreciation of another's situation.

Emphasis. Stress placed on words, phrases, or ideas to show their importance, by *italics*, **boldface,** and punctuation "!!!"; by figurative language, meter, and rhyme; or by strategies of rhetoric, like climactic order, contrast, repetition, and position.

Empiricism. Greek for "experience": the belief that all knowledge comes from experience, that human understanding of general truth can be founded only on observation of particulars. Empiricism is basic to the scientific method and to literary naturalism. It is opposed to rationalism, which discovers truth through reason alone, without regard to experience.

Enclosed Rhyme. A couplet, or pair of rhyming lines, enclosed in rhyming lines to give the pattern *abba*.

Encomium. Originally a Greek choral song in praise of a hero; later, any formal expression of praise, in verse or prose.

End Rhyme. Rhyme at the end of a line of verse (the usual placement), as distinguished from *initial rhyme*, at the beginning, or *internal rhyme*, within the line.

Enjambment. Run-on lines in which grammatical sense runs from one line of poetry to the next without pause or punctuation. The opposite of an end-stopped line.

Enlightenment. A philosophical movement in the 17th and 18th centuries, particularly in France, characterized by the conviction that reason could achieve all knowledge, supplant organized religion, and ensure progress toward happiness and perfection.

Envoy (or **Envoi**). A concluding stanza, generally shorter than the earlier stanzas of a poem, giving a brief summary of theme, address to a prince or patron, or return to a refrain.

Epic. A long narrative poem, typically a recounting of history or legend or of the deeds of a national hero. During the Renaissance, critical theory emphasized two assumptions: (1) the encyclopedic knowledge needed for major poetry, and (2) an aristocracy of genres, according to which epic and tragedy, because they deal with heroes and ruling-class figures, were reserved for major poets. Romanticism revived both the long mythological poem and the verse romance, but the prestige of the encyclopedic epic still lingered. In his autobiographical poem *The Prelude,* Wordsworth self-consciously internalized the heroic argument of the epic.

Epic Simile. Sometimes called a *Homeric simile:* an extended simile, comparing one thing with another by lengthy description of the second, often beginning with "as when" and concluding with "so" or "such."

Epicurean. Often meaning hedonistic (*see also* Hedonism), devoted to sensual pleasure and ease. Actually, Epicurus (c. 341–270 B.C.) was a kind of puritanical Stoic, recommending detachment from pleasure and pain to avoid life's inevitable suffering, hence advocating serenity as the highest happiness, intellect over the senses.

Epigram. (1) A brief poetic and witty couching of a home truth. (2) An equivalent statement in prose.

Epigraph. (1) An inscription on a monument or building. (2) A quotation or motto heading a book or chapter.

Epilogue. (1) A poetic address to the audience at the end of a play. (2) The actor performing the address. (3) Any similar appendage to a literary work, usually describing what happens to the characters in the future.

Epiphany. In religious tradition, the revelation of a divinity. James Joyce adapted the term to signify a moment of profound or spiritual revelation, when even the stroke of a clock or a noise in the street brings sudden illumination, and "its soul, its whatness leaps to us from the vestment of its appearance." For Joyce, art was an epiphany.

Episode. An incident in a play or novel; a continuous event in action and dialogue. Originally the term referred to a section in Greek tragedy between two choric songs.

Episodic Structure. In narration, the incidental stringing of one episode upon another, as in *Don Quixote* or *Moll Flanders*, in which one episode follows another with no necessary causal connection or plot.

Epistle. (1) A letter, usually a formal or artistic one, like Saint Paul's Epistles in the New Testament, or Horace's verse *Epistles*, widely imitated in the late 17th and 18th centuries, most notably by Alexander Pope. (2) A dedication in a prefatory epistle to a play or book.

Epitaph. (1) An inscription on a tombstone or monument memorializing the person, or persons, buried there. (2) A literary epigram or brief poem epitomizing the dead.

Epithalamium (or **Epithalamion**). A lyric ode honoring a bride and groom.

Epithet. A term characterizing a person or thing: e.g., *Richard the Lion-Hearted*.

Epitome. (1) A summary, an abridgment, an abstract. (2) One that supremely represents an entire class.

Essay. A literary composition on a single subject; usually short, in prose, and nonexhaustive. The word derives from French *essai* "an attempt," first used in the modern sense by Michel de Montaigne, whose *Essais* (1580–1588) are classics of the genre. Francis Bacon's *Essays* (1597) brought the term and form to English.

Estates. The "three estates of the realm," recognized from feudal times onward: the clergy (Lords Spiritual), the nobility (Lords Temporal), and the burghers (the Commons). In *Heroes and Hero-Worship*, Thomas Carlyle says that Edmund Burke (member of Parliament from 1766 to 1794) added to Parliament's three estates "the Reporters' Gallery" where "sat a fourth Estate more important than they all" (Lecture V). The Fourth Estate is now the press and other media.

Eulogy. A speech or composition of praise, especially of a deceased person.

Euphemism. Greek for "good speech": an attractive substitute for a harsh or unpleasant word or concept; figurative language or circumlocution substituting an indirect or oblique reference for a direct one.

Euphony. Melodious sound, the opposite of cacophony. A major feature of verse, but also a consideration in prose, euphony results from smooth-flowing meter or sentence rhythm as well as attractive sounds.

Euphuism. An artificial, highly elaborate affected style that takes its name from John Lyly's *Euphues: The Anatomy of Wit* (1578). Euphuism is characterized by the heavy use of rhetorical devices such as balance and antithesis, by much attention to alliteration and other sound patterns, and by learned allusion.

Excursus. (1) A lengthy discussion of a point, appended to a literary work. (2) A long digression.

Exegesis. (1) A detailed analysis, explanation, and interpretation of a difficult text, especially the Bible. (2) A rhetorical figure, also called *explicatio*, which clarifies a thought.

Exemplum. Latin for "example": a story used to illustrate a moral point. *Exempla* were a characteristic feature of medieval sermons. Chaucer's *Pardoner's Tale* and *Nun's Priest's Tale* are famous secular examples.

Existentialism. A philosophy centered on individual existence as unique and unrepeatable, hence rejecting the past for present existence and its unique dilemmas. Existentialism rose to prominence in the 1930s and 1940s, particularly in France after World War II in the work of Jean-Paul Sartre.

Expressionism. An early 20th-century movement in art and literature, best understood as a reaction against conventional realism and naturalism, and especially as a revolt against conventional society. The expressionist looked inward for images, expressing in paint, on stage, or in prose or verse a distorted, nightmarish version of reality, things dreamed about rather than actually existing.

Eye Rhyme. A rhyme of words that look but do not sound the same: *one, stone; word, lord; teak, break*.

Fable. (1) A short, allegorical story in verse or prose, frequently of animals, told to illustrate a moral. (2) The story line or plot of a narrative or drama. (3) Loosely, any legendary or fabulous account.

Falling Meter. A meter beginning with a stress, running from heavy to light.

Farce. A wildly comic play, mocking dramatic and social conventions, frequently with satiric intent.

Feminine Ending. An extra unstressed syllable at the end of a metrical line, usually iambic.

Feminine Rhyme. A rhyme of both the stressed and the unstressed syllables of one feminine ending with another.

Feudalism. The political and social system prevailing in Europe from the ninth century until the 1400s. It was a system of independent holdings (*feud* is Germanic for "estate") in which autonomous lords pledged fealty and service to those more powerful in exchange for protection, as did villagers to the neighboring lord of the manor.

Fiction. An imagined creation in verse, drama, or prose. Fiction is a thing made, an invention. It is distinguished from nonfiction by its essentially imaginative nature, but elements of fiction appear in fundamentally nonfictional constructions such as essays, biographies, autobiographies, and histories. Fictional anecdotes and illustrations abound in the works of politicians, business leaders, the clergy, philosophers, and scientists. Although any invented person, place, event, or condition is a fiction, the term is now most frequently used to mean "prose fiction," as distinct from verse or drama.

Figurative Language. Language that is not literal, being either metaphorical or rhetorically patterned.

Figure of Speech. An expression extending language beyond its literal meaning, either pictorially through metaphor, simile, allusion, and the like, or rhetorically through repetition, balance, antithesis, and the like. A figure of speech is also called a *trope*.

Fin de Siècle. "The end of the century," especially the last decade of the 19th. The term, acquired with the French influence of the symbolists Stéphane Mallarmé and Charles Baudelaire, connotes preciosity and decadence.

First-Person Narration. Narration by a character involved in a story.

Flyting. Scottish for "scolding": a form of invective, or violent verbal assault, in verse; traditional in Scottish literature, possibly Celtic in origin. Typically, two poets exchange scurrilous and often exhaustive abuse.

Folio. From Latin for "leaf." (1) A sheet of paper, folded once. (2) The largest of the book sizes, made from standard printing sheets, folded once before trimming and binding.

Folk Song. A song forming part of the folklore of a community. Like the folktale and the legend, a folk song is a traditional creative expression, characteristically shaped by oral tradition into the form in which it is later recorded in manuscript or print.

Folktale. A story forming part of the folklore of a community, generally less serious than the stories called *myths*. In preliterate societies, virtually all narratives were either myths or folktales: oral histories of real wars, kings, heroes, great families, and the like accumulating large amounts of legendary material.

Foot. The metrical unit; in English, an accented syllable with accompanying light syllable or syllables.

Foreshadowing. The technique of suggesting or prefiguring a development in a literary work before it occurs.

Formula. A plot outline or set of characteristic ingredients used in the construction of a literary work or applied to a portion of one. Formula fiction is written to the requirements of a particular market, usually undistinguished by much imagination or originality in applying the formula.

Foul Copy. A manuscript that has been used for printing, bearing the marks of the proofreader, editor, and printer, as well as, frequently, the author's queries and comments.

Four Elements. In ancient and medieval cosmology, earth, air, fire, and water—the four ultimate, exclusive, and eternal constituents that, according to Empedocles (c. 493–c. 433 B.C.) made up the world.

Four Senses of Interpretation. A mode of medieval criticism in which a work is examined for four kinds of meaning. The *literal meaning* is related to fact or history. The *moral* or *tropological meaning* is the lesson of the work as applied to individual behavior. The *allegorical meaning* is the particular story in its application to people generally, with emphasis on their beliefs. The *anagogical meaning* is its spiritual or mystical truth, its universal significance. After the literal, each of the others represents a broader form of what is usually called allegory, moving from individual morality to social organization to God.

Fourteeners. Lines of 14 syllables—7 iambic feet, popular with the Elizabethans.

Frame Narrative. A narrative enclosing one or more separate stories. Characteristically, the frame narrative is created as a vehicle for the stories it contains.

Free Verse. French *vers libre*; poetry free of traditional metrical and stanzaic patterns.

Genre. A term often applied loosely to the larger forms of literary convention, roughly analogous to "species" in biology. The Greeks spoke of three main genres of poetry—lyric, epic, and drama. Within each major genre, there are subgenres. In written forms dominated by prose, for example, there is a broad distinction between works of fiction (e.g., the novel) and thematic works (e.g., the essay). Within the fictional category, we note a distinction between novel and romance, and other forms such as satire and confession. The object of making these distinctions in literary tradition is not simply to classify but to judge authors in terms of the conventions they themselves chose.

Georgian. (1) Pertaining to the reigns of the four Georges—1714–1830, particularly the reigns of the first three, up to the close of the 18th century. (2) The literature written during the early years (1910–1914) of the reign of George V.

Georgic. A poem about farming and annual rural labors, after Virgil's *Georgics*.

Gloss. An explanation (from Greek *glossa* "tongue, language"); originally, Latin synonyms in the margins of Greek manuscripts and vernacular synonyms in later manuscripts as scribes gave the reader some help.

Glossary. A list of words, with explanations or definitions. A glossary is ordinarily a partial dictionary, appended to the end of a book to explain technical or unfamiliar terms.

Gothic. Originally, pertaining to the Goths, then to any Germanic people. Because the Goths began warring with the Roman empire in the 3rd century A.D., eventually sacking Rome itself, the term later became a synonym for "barbaric," which the 18th century next applied to anything medieval, of the Dark Ages.

Gothic Novel. A type of fiction introduced and named by Horace Walpole's *Castle of Otranto, A Gothic Story* (1764). Walpole introduced supernatural terror, with a huge mysterious helmet, portraits that walk abroad, and statues with nosebleeds. Matthew Gregory Lewis, "Monk Lewis," added sexual depravity to the murderous supernatural mix (*The Monk*, 1796). Mary Shelley's *Frankenstein* (1818) transformed the Gothic into moral science fiction.

Grotesque. Anything unnaturally distorted, ugly, ludicrous, fanciful, or bizarre; especially, in the 19th century, literature exploiting the abnormal.

Hedonism. A philosophy that sees pleasure as the highest good.

Hegelianism. The philosophy of G. W. F. Hegel (1770–1831), who developed the system of thought known as Hegelian dialectic, in which a given concept, or *thesis*, generates its opposite, or *antithesis*, and from the interaction of the two arises a *synthesis*. The synthesis then forms a thesis for a new cycle. Hegelian dialectic suggests that history is not static but contains a rational progression, an idea influential on many later thinkers.

Heroic Couplet. The closed and balanced iambic pentameter couplet typical of the heroic plays of John Dryden; hence, any closed couplet.

Heroic Quatrain. A stanza in four lines of iambic pentameter, rhyming *abab* (*see also* Meter). Also known as the *heroic stanza* and the *elegiac stanza*.

Hexameter. Six-foot lines.

Historicism. (1) Historical relativism. (2) An approach to literature that emphasizes its historical environment, the climate of ideas, belief, and literary conventions surrounding and influencing the writer.

Homily. A religious discourse or sermon, especially one emphasizing practical spiritual or moral advice.

Hubris. From Greek *hybris*, "pride": prideful arrogance or insolence of the kind that causes the tragic hero to ignore the warnings that might turn aside the action that leads to disaster.

Humors. The *cardinal humors* of ancient medical theory: blood, phlegm, yellow bile (choler), black bile (melancholy). From ancient times until the 19th century, the humors were believed largely responsible for health and disposition. Hippocrates (c. 460–c. 370 B.C.) thought an imbalance produced illness. Galen (c. A.D. 130–300) suggested that character types are produced by dominance of fluids: *sanguine*, or kindly, cheerful, amorous; *phlegmatic*, or sluggish, unresponsive; *choleric*, or quick-tempered; and *melancholic*, or brooding, dejected. In literature, especially during the early modern period, characters were portrayed according to the humors that dominated them, as in the comedy of humors.

Hyperbole. Overstatement to make a point, as when a parent tells a child "I've told you a thousand times."

Iambus (or Iamb). A metrical foot: ⏑ – .

Idealism. (1) In philosophy and ethics, an emphasis on ideas and ideals, as opposed to the sensory emphasis of materialism. (2) Literary idealism follows from philosophical precepts, emphasizing a world in which the most important reality is a spiritual or transcendent truth not always reflected in the world of sense perception.

Idyll. A short poem of rustic pastoral serenity.

Image. A concrete picture, either literally descriptive, as in "Red roses covered the white wall," or figurative, as in "She is a rose," each carrying a sensual and emotive connotation. A figurative image may be an analogy, metaphor, simile, personification, or the like.

Impressionism. A literary style conveying subjective impressions rather than objective reality, taking its name from the movement in French painting in the mid-19th century, notably in the works of Manet, Monet, and Renoir. The Imagists represented impressionism in poetry; in fiction, writers like Virginia Woolf and James Joyce.

Industrial Revolution. The accelerated change, beginning in the 1760s, from an agricultural-shopkeeping society, using hand tools, to an industrial-mechanized one.

Influence. The apparent effect of literary works on subsequent writers and their work, as in Robert Browning's influence on T. S. Eliot.

Innuendo. An indirect remark or gesture, especially one implying something derogatory; an insinuation.

Interlocking Rhyme. Rhyme between stanzas; a word unrhymed in one stanza is used as a rhyme for the next, as in terza rima: *aba bcb cdc* and so on.

Internal Rhyme. Rhyme within a line, rather than at the beginning (*initial rhyme*) or end (*end rhyme*); also, rhyme matching sounds in the middle of a line with sounds at the end.

Intertextuality. (1) The relations between one literary text and others it evokes through such means as quotation, paraphrase, allusion, parody, and revision. (2) More broadly, the relations between a given text and all other texts, the potentially infinite sum of knowledge within which any text has its meaning.

Inversion. A reversal of sequence or position, as when the normal order of elements within a sentence is inverted for poetic or rhetorical effect.

Irony. In general, irony is the perception of a clash between appearance and reality, between *seems* and *is*, or between *ought* and *is*. The myriad shadings of irony seem to fall into three categories: (1) *Verbal irony*—saying something contrary to what it means; the appearance is what the words say, the reality is their contrary meaning. (2) *Dramatic irony*—saying or doing something while unaware of its ironic contrast with the whole truth; named for its frequency in drama, dramatic irony is a verbal irony with the speaker's awareness erased. (3) *Situational irony*—events turning to the opposite of what is expected or what should be. The ironic situation turns the speaker's unknowing words ironic. Situational irony is the essence of both comedy and tragedy: the young lovers run into the worst possible luck, until everything clears up happily; the most noble spirits go to their death, while the featherheads survive.

Italian Sonnet (or **Petrarchan Sonnet**). A sonnet composed of an octave and sestet, rhyming *abbaabba cdecde* (or *cdcdcd* or some variant, without a closing couplet).

Italic (or **Italics**). Type slanting upward to the right. *This sentence is italic.*

Jacobean Period (1603–1625). The reign of James I, *Jacobus* being the Latin for "James." A certain skepticism and even cynicism seeped into Elizabethan joy. The Puritans and the court party, the Cavaliers, grew more antagonistic. But it was in the Jacobean period that Shakespeare wrote his greatest tragedies and tragi-comedies, and Ben Jonson did his major work.

Jargon. (1) Language peculiar to a trade or calling, as, for example, the jargon of astronauts, lawyers, or literary critics. (2) Confused or confusing language. This kind of jargon does not communicate to anybody.

Jeremiad. A lament or complaint, especially one enumerating transgressions and predicting destruction of a people, of the kind found in the Book of Jeremiah.

Juvenilia. Youthful literary products.

Kenning. A compound figurative metaphor, a circumlocution, in Old English and Old Norse poetry: hronrād, "whale-road," for the sea.

Lament. A grieving poem, an elegy, in Anglo-Saxon or Renaissance times. *Deor's Lament* (c. 980) records the actual grief of a scop, or court poet, at being displaced in his lord's hall.

Lampoon. A satirical, personal ridicule in verse or prose. The term probably derives from the French *lampons*, "Let's guzzle," a refrain in 17th-century drinking songs.

Lay (or **Lai**). (1) A ballad or related metrical romance originating with the Breton lay of French Brittany and retaining some of its Celtic magic and folklore.

Lexicon. A word list, a vocabulary, a dictionary.

Libretto. "The little book" (Italian): the text of an opera, cantata, or other musical drama.

Litany. A prayer with phrases spoken or sung by a leader alternated with responses from congregation or choir. *The Litany* is a group of such prayers in the Book of Common Prayer.

Literal. According to the letter (of the alphabet): the precise, plain meaning of a word or phrase in its simplest, original sense, considered apart from its sense as a metaphor or other figure of speech. Literal language is the opposite of figurative language.

Literature. Strictly defined, anything written. Therefore the oral culture of a people—its folklore, folk songs, folktales, and so on—is not literature until it is written down. The movies are not literature except in their printed scripts. By the same strict meaning, historical records, telephone books, and the like are all literature because they are written in letters of the alphabet, although they are not taught as literature in schools. In contrast to this strict, literal meaning, literature has come to be equated with *creative writing* or works of the imagination: chiefly poetry, prose fiction, and drama.

Lollards. From Middle Dutch, literally, "mumblers": a derisive term applied to the followers of John Wyclif (c. 1328–1384), the reformer behind the Wyclif Bible (1385), the first in English. Lollards preached against the abuses of the medieval church, setting up a standard of poverty and individual service as against wealth and hierarchical privilege.

Lyric. A poem, brief and discontinuous, emphasizing sound and pictorial imagery rather than narrative or dramatic movement.

Macaronic Verse. (1) Strictly, verse mixing words in a writer's native language with endings, phrases, and syntax of another language, usually Latin or Greek, creating a comic or burlesque effect. (2) Loosely, any verse mingling two or more languages.

Mannerism, Mannerist. (1) In architecture and painting, a style elongating and distorting human figures and spaces, deliberately confusing scale and perspective. (2) Literary or artistic affectation; a stylistic quality produced by excessively peculiar, ornamental, or ingenious devices.

Manners. Social behavior. In usages like comedy of manners and novel of manners, the term suggests an examination of the behavior, morals, and values of a particular time, place, or social class.

Manuscript. Literally, "written by hand": any handwritten document, as, for example, a letter or diary; also, a work submitted for publication.

Marginalia. Commentary, references, or other material written by a reader in the margins of a manuscript or book.

Masculine Ending. The usual iambic ending, on the accented foot: $\smile$ –.

Masculine Rhyme. The most common rhyme in English, on the last syllable of a line.

Masque. An allegorical, poetic, and musical dramatic spectacle popular in the English courts and mansions of the 16th and early 17th centuries. Figures from mythology, history, and romance mingled in a pastoral fantasy with fairies, fauns, satyrs, and witches, as masked amateurs from the court (including kings and queens) participated in dances and scenes.

Materialism. In philosophy, an emphasis upon the material world as the ultimate reality. Its opposite is *idealism*. Thomas Hobbes was an early materialist in 17th-century England. In the 19th century, materialism had evolved into naturalism, which emerged as an especially materialistic form of realism.

Melodrama. A play with dire ingredients—the mortgage foreclosed, the daughter tied to the railroad tracks—but with a happy ending. The typical emotions produced here result in romantic tremors, pity, and terror.

Menippean Satire. Satire on pedants, bigots, rapacious professional people, and other persons or institutions perceiving the world from a single framework. The focus is on intellectual limitations and mental attitudes. Typical ingredients include a rambling narrative; unusual settings; displays of erudition; and long digressions.

Metaphor. Greek for "transfer" (*meta* and *trans* meaning "across"; *phor* and *fer* meaning "carry"): to carry something across. Hence a metaphor treats something as if it were something else. Money becomes a *nest egg*; a sandwich, a *submarine*.

Metaphysical Poetry. Seventeenth-century poetry of wit and startling extended metaphor.

Meter. The measured pulse of poetry. English meters derive from four Greek and Roman quantitative meters (*see* also Quantitative Verse), which English stresses more sharply, although the patterns are the same. The unit of each pattern is the *foot*, containing one stressed syllable and one or two light ones. *Rising meter* goes from light to heavy; *falling meter*, from heavy to light. One meter—iambic—has dominated English poetry, with the three others lending an occasional foot, for variety, and producing a few poems.

Rising Meters

Iambic:　⏑ – (the iambus)

Anapestic:　⏑ ⏑ – (the anapest)

Falling Meters

Trochaic:　– ⏑ (the trochee)

Dactylic:　– ⏑ ⏑ (the dactyl)

The number of feet in a line also gives the verse a name:

1 foot: monometer

2 feet: dimeter

3 feet: trimeter

4 feet: tetrameter

5 feet: pentameter

6 feet: hexameter

7 feet: heptameter

All meters show some variations, and substitutions of other kinds of feet, but three variations in iambic writing are virtually standard:

Inverted foot:　– ⏑ (a trochee)

Spondee:　– –

Ionic double foot:　⏑ ⏑ – –

The *pyrrhic foot* of classical meters, two light syllables (⏑ ⏑), lives in the English line only in the Ionic double foot, although some prosodists scan a relatively light iambus as pyrrhic.

Examples of meters and scansion:

Iambic Tetrameter

An-ni- | hil-a- | ting all | that's made |

To a | green thought | in a | green shade. |

Andrew Marvell, "The Garden"

Iambic Tetrameter

(*with two inverted feet*)

Close to | the sun | in lone- | ly lands, |

Ringed with | the az- | ure world, | he stands. |

Alfred, Lord Tennyson, "The Eagle"

Iambic Pentameter

Love's not | Time's fool, | though ros- | y lips | and cheeks |
Within | his bend- | ing sick- | le's com- | pass come |

William Shakespeare, Sonnet 116

When to | the ses- | sions of | sweet si- | lent thought |

William Shakespeare, Sonnet 30

Anapestic Tetrameter

(trochees substituted)
The pop- |lars are felled; | farewell | to the shade |
And the whis- | pering sound | of the cool | colonnade |

William Cowper, "The Popular Field"

Trochaic Tetrameter

Tell me | not in | mournful | numbers |

Henry Wadsworth Longfellow, "A Psalm of Life"

Dactylic Hexameter

This is the | forest prim- | eval. The | murmuring | pines and the | hemlocks |
Bearded with | moss . . . .

Henry Wadsworth Longfellow, "Evangeline"

Metonymy. "Substitute naming." A figure of speech in which an associated idea stands in for the actual item: "The *pen* is mightier than the *sword*" for "Literature and propaganda accomplish more and survive longer than warfare," or "The *White House* announced" for "The President announced." *See also* synecdoche.

Metrics. The analysis and description of meter; also called *prosody*.

Middle English. The language of England from the middle of the 12th century to approximately 1500. English began to lose its inflectional endings and accepted many French words into its vocabulary, especially terms associated with the new social, legal, and governmental structures (*baron, judge, jury, marshal, parliament, prince*), and those in common use by the French upper classes (*mansion, chamber, veal, beef*).

Mimesis. A term meaning "imitation." It has been central to literary criticism since Aristotle's *Poetics*. The ordinary meaning of *imitation* as creating a resemblance to something else is clearly involved in Aristotle's definition of dramatic plot as *mimesis praxeos*, the imitation of an action. But there are many things that a work of literature may imitate, and hence many contexts of imitation. Works of literature may imitate other works of literature: this is the aspect of literature that comes into such conceptions as convention and genre. In a larger sense, every work of literature imitates, or finds its identity in, the entire "world of words," in Wallace Stevens's phrase, the sense of the whole of reality as potentially literary, as finding its end in a book, as Stéphane Mallarmé says.

Miracle Play. A medieval play based on a saint's life or story from the Bible.

Miscellany. A collection of various things. A literary miscellany is therefore a book collecting varied works, usually poems by different authors, a kind of anthology. The term is applied especially to the many books of this kind that appeared in the Elizabethan period.

Mock Epic. A poem in epic form and manner ludicrously elevating some trivial subject to epic grandeur.

Modernism. A collective term, generally associated with the first half of the 20th century, for various aesthetic and cultural attempts to place a "modern" face on experience. Modernism arose from a sense that the old ways were worn out. The new century opened with broad social, philosophical, religious, and cultural discussion and reform. For creative artists, the challenges of the new present meant that art became subject to change in every way, that the content, forms, and techniques inherited from the 19th century existed to be challenged, broken apart, and re-formed.

Monodrama. (1) A play with one character. (2) A closet drama or dramatic monologue.

Monody. (1) A Greek ode for one voice. (2) An elegiac lament, a dirge, in poetic soliloquy.

Monologue. (1) A poem or story in the form of a soliloquy. (2) Any extended speech.

Motif (or **Motive**). (1) A recurrent thematic element—word, image, symbol, object, phrase, action. (2) A conventional incident, situation, or device like the unknown knight of mysterious origin and low degree in the romance, or the baffling riddle in fairy tales.

Muse. The inspirer of poetry, on whom the poet calls for assistance. In Greek mythology the Muses were the nine daughters of Zeus and Mnemosyne ("Memory") presiding over the arts and sciences.

Mystery Play. Medieval religious drama; eventually performed in elaborate cycles of plays acted on pageant wagons or stages throughout city streets, with different guilds of artisans and merchants responsible for each.

Mysticism. A spiritual discipline in which sensory experience is expunged and the mind is devoted to deep contemplation and the reaching of a transcendental union with God.

Myth. From Greek *mythos*, "plot" or "narrative." The verbal culture of most if not all human societies began with stories, and certain stories have achieved a distinctive importance as being connected with what the society feels it most needs to know: stories illustrating the society's religion, history, class structure, or the origin of peculiar features of the natural environment.

Narrative Poem. One that tells a story, particularly the epic, metrical romance, and shorter narratives, like the ballad.

Naturalism. (1) Broadly, according to nature. In this sense, naturalism is opposed to idealism, emphasizing things accessible to the senses in this world in contrast to permanent or spiritual truths presumed to lie outside it. (2) More specifically, a literary movement of the late 19th century; an extension of realism, naturalism was a reaction against the restrictions inherent in the realistic emphasis on the ordinary, as naturalists insisted that the extraordinary is real, too.

Neoclassical Period. Generally, the span of time from the restoration of Charles II to his father's throne in 1660 until the publication of William Wordsworth and Samuel Taylor Coleridge's *Lyrical Ballads* (1798). Writers hoped to revive something like the classical Pax Romana, an era of peace and literary excellence.

Neologism. A word newly coined or introduced into a language, or a new meaning given to an old word.

New Criticism. An approach to criticism prominent in the United States after the publication of John Crowe Ransom's *New Criticism* (1941). Generally, the New Critics were agreed that a poem or story should be considered an organic unit, with each part working to support the whole. They worked by close analysis, considering the text as the final authority, and were distrustful, though not wholly neglectful, of considerations brought from outside the text, as, for example, from biography or history.

New Historicism. A cross-disciplinary approach fostered by the rise of feminist and multicultural studies as well as a renewed emphasis on historical perspective. Associated in particular with work on the early modern and the romantic periods in the United States and England, the approach emphasizes analysis of the relationship between history and literature, viewing writings in both fields as "texts" for study. New Historicism has tended to note political influences on literary and historical texts, to illuminate the role of the writer against the backdrop of social customs and assumptions, and to view history as changeable and interconnected instead of as a linear progressive evolution.

Nocturne. A night piece; writing evocative of evening or night.

Nominalism. In the Middle Ages, the belief that universals have no real being, but are only names, their existence limited to their presence in the minds and language of humans. This belief was opposed to the beliefs of medieval realists, who held that universals have an independent existence, at least in the mind of God.

Norman Conquest. The period of English history in which the Normans consolidated their hold on England after the defeat of the Saxon King Harold by William, Duke of Normandy, in 1066. French became the court language and Norman lords gained control of English lands, but Anglo-Saxon administrative and judicial systems remained largely in place.

Novel. The extended prose fiction that arose in the 18th century to become a major literary expression of the modern world. The term comes from the Italian *novella*, the short "new" tale of intrigue and moral comeuppance most eminently disseminated by Boccaccio's *Decameron* (1348–1353). The terms *novel* and *romance*, from the French *roman*, competed interchangeably for most of the 18th century.

Novella. (1) Originally, a short tale. (2) In modern usage, a term sometimes used interchangeably with short novel or for a fiction of middle length, between a short story and a novel. See Novel, above.

Octave. (1) The first unit in an Italian sonnet: eight lines of iambic pentameter, rhyming *abbaabba. See also* Meter. (2) A stanza in eight lines.

Octavo (Abbreviated 8vo). A book made from sheets folded to give signatures of eight leaves (16 pages), a book of average size.

Octet. An octastich or octave.

Octosyllabic. Eight-syllable.

Ode. A long, stately lyric poem in stanzas of varied metrical pattern.

Old English. The language brought to England, beginning in 449, by the Jute, Angle, and Saxon invaders from Denmark; the language base from which modern English evolved.

Old English Literature. The literature of England from the Anglo-Saxon invasion of the mid-5th century until the beginning of the Middle English period in the mid-12th century.

Omniscient Narrative. A narrative account untrammeled by constraints of time or space. An omniscient narrator perspective knows about the external and internal realities of characters as well as incidents unknown to them, and can interpret motivation and meaning.

Onomatopoeia. The use of words formed or sounding like what they signify—*buzz, crack, smack, whinny*—especially in an extensive capturing of sense by sound.

Orientalism. A term denoting Western portrayals of Oriental culture. In literature it refers to a varied body of work beginning in the 18th century that described for Western readers the history, language, politics, and culture of the area east of the Mediterranean.

Oxford Movement. A 19th-century movement to reform the Anglican church according to the high-church and more nearly Catholic ideals and rituals of the later 17th-century church.

Oxymoron. A pointed stupidity: *oxy*, "sharp," plus *moron*. One of the great ironic figures of speech—for example, "a fearful joy," or Milton's "darkness visible."

Paleography. The study and interpretation of ancient handwriting and manuscript styles.

Palimpsest. A piece of writing on secondhand vellum, parchment, or other surface carrying traces of erased previous writings.

Panegyric. A piece of writing in praise of a person, thing, or achievement.

Pantheism. A belief that God and the universe are identical, from the Greek words *pan* ("all") and *theos* ("god"). God is all; all is God.

Pantomime. A form of drama presented without words, in a dumb show.

Parable. (1) A short tale, such as those of Jesus in the gospels, encapsulating a moral or religious lesson. (2) Any saying, figure of speech, or narrative in which one thing is expressed in terms of another.

Paradox. An apparently untrue or self-contradictory statement or circumstance that proves true upon reflection or when examined in another light.

Paraphrase. A rendering in other words of the sense of a text or passage, as of a poem, essay, short story, or other writing.

Parody. Originally, "a song sung beside" another. From this idea of juxtaposition arose the two basic elements of parody, comedy and criticism. As comedy, parody exaggerates or distorts the prominent features of style or content in a work. As criticism, it mimics the work, borrowing words or phrases or characteristic turns of thought in order to highlight weaknesses of conception or expression.

Passion Play. Originally a play based on Christ's Passion; later, one including both Passion and Resurrection. Such plays began in the Middle Ages, performed from the 13th century onward, often as part of the pageants presented for the feast of Corpus Christi.

Pastiche. A literary or other artistic work created by assembling bits and pieces from other works.

Pastoral. From Latin *pastor*, a shepherd. The first pastoral poet was Theocritus, a Greek of the 3rd century B.C. The pastoral was especially popular in Europe from the 14th through the 18th centuries, with some fine examples still written in England in the 19th century. The pastoral mode is self-reflexive. Typically the poet echoes the conventions of earlier pastorals in order to put "the complex into the simple," as William Empson observed in *Some Versions of Pastoral* (1935). The poem is not really about shepherds, but about the complex society the poet and readers inhabit.

Pathetic Fallacy. The attribution of animate or human characteristics to nature, as, for example, when rocks, trees, or weather are portrayed as reacting in sympathy to human feelings or events.

Pathos. The feeling of pity, sympathy, tenderness, compassion, or sorrow evoked by someone or something that is helpless.

Pedantry. Ostentatious book learning: an accusation frequently hurled in scholarly disagreements.

Pentameter. A line of five metrical feet. (*See* Meter.)

Peripeteia (or **Peripetia, Peripety**). A sudden change in situation in a drama or fiction, a reversal of luck for good or ill.

Periphrasis. The practice of talking around the point; a wordy restatement; a circumlocution.

Peroration. (1) The summative conclusion of a formal oration. (2) Loosely, a grandiloquent speech.

Persona. A mask (in Latin); in poetry and fiction, the projected speaker or narrator of the work—that is, a mask for the actual author.

Personification. The technique of treating abstractions, things, or animals as persons. A kind of metaphor, personification turns abstract ideas, like love, into a physical beauty named Venus, or conversely, makes dumb animals speak and act like humans.

Petrarchan Sonnet. Another name for an Italian sonnet.

Philology. The study of ancient languages and literatures; also more broadly interpreted from its basic meaning, "love of the word," to include all literary studies. In the 19th century, the field of historical linguistics.

Phoneme. In linguistics, the smallest distinguishable unit of sound. Different for each language, phonemes are defined by determining which differences in sound function to signal a difference in meaning.

Phonetics. (1) The study of speech sounds and their production, transmission, and reception. (2) The phonetic system of a particular language. (3) Symbols used to represent speech sounds.

Picaresque Novel. A novel chronicling the adventures of a rogue (Spanish: *picaro*), typically presented as an autobiography, episodic in structure and panoramic in its coverage of time and place.

Picturesque, The. A quality in landscape, and in idealized landscape painting, admired in the second half of the 18th century and featuring crags, flaring and blasted trees, a torrent or winding stream, ruins, and perhaps a quiet cottage and cart, with contrasting light and shadow. It was considered an aesthetic mean between the poles of Edmund Burke's *A Philosophical Inquiry into the Sublime and the Beautiful* (1756).

Plagiarism. Literary kidnapping (Latin *plagiarius*, "kidnapper")—the seizing and presenting as one's own the ideas or writings of another.

Plain Style. The straightforward, unembellished style of preaching favored by 17th-century Puritans as well as by reformers within the Anglican church, as speaking God's word directly from the inspired heart as opposed to the high style of aristocratic oratory and courtliness, the vehicle of subterfuge. Plain style was simultaneously advocated for scientific accuracy by the Royal Society.

Platonism. Any reflection of Plato's philosophy, particularly the belief in the eternal reality of ideal forms, of which the diversities of the physical world are but transitory shadows.

Poetics. The theory, art, or science of poetry. Poetics is concerned with the nature and function of poetry and with identifying and explaining its types, forms, and techniques.

Poet Laureate. Since the 17th century, a title conferred by the monarch on English poets. At first, the laureate was required to write poems to commemorate special occasions, such as royal birthdays, national celebrations, and the like, but since the early 19th century the appointment has been for the most part honorary.

Poetry. Imaginatively intense language, usually in verse. Poetry is a form of fiction—"the supreme fiction," said Wallace Stevens. It is distinguished from other fictions by the compression resulting from its heavier use of figures of speech and allusion and, usually, by the music of its patterns of sounds.

Postmodernism. A term first used in relation to literature in the late 1940s by Randall Jarrell and John Berryman to proclaim a new sensibility arising to challenge the reigning assumptions and practices of modernism. The attitudes and literary devices of the modernists—stream of consciousness, for example—had taken on the patina of tradition. For many of the postmodernists, disillusionment seemed to have reached its fullest measure. Life had little meaning, art less, and a neat closure to expectations raised by the artist seemed impossible. Intruding into one's own fiction to ponder its powers became a hallmark of the 1960s and 1970s.

Poststructuralism. A mode of literary criticism and thought centered on Jacques Derrida's concept of deconstruction. Structuralists see language as the paradigm for all structures. Poststructuralists see language as based on differences—hence the analytical deconstruction of what seemed an immutable system. What language expresses is already absent. Poststructuralism challenges the New Criticism, which seeks a truth fixed within the "verbal icon," the text, in W. K. Wimsatt's term. Poststructuralism invites interpretations through the spaces left by the way words operate.

Pragmatism. In philosophy, the idea that the value of a belief is best judged by the acts that follow from it—its practical results.

Preciosity. Since the 19th century, a term for an affected or overingenious refinement of language.

Predestination. The belief that an omniscient God, at the Creation, destined all subsequent events, particularly, in Calvinist belief, the election for salvation and the damnation of individual souls.

Pre-Raphaelite. Characteristic of a small but influential group of mid-19th-century painters who hoped to recapture the spiritual vividness they saw in medieval painting before Raphael (1483–1520).

Presbyterianism. John Calvin's organization of ecclesiastical governance not by bishops representing the pope but by elders representing the congregation.

Proscenium. Originally, in Greece, the whole acting area ("in front of the scenery"); now, that part of the stage projecting in front of the curtain.

Prose. Ordinary writing patterned on speech, as distinct from verse.

Prose Poetry. Prose rich in cadenced and poetic effects like alliteration, assonance, consonance, and the like, and in imagery.

Prosody. The analysis and description of meters; metrics (*see also* Meter). Linguists apply the term to the study of patterns of accent in a language.

Protagonist. The leading character in a play or story; originally the leader of the chorus in the agon ("contest") of Greek drama, faced with the antagonist, the opposition.

Pseudonym. A fictitious name adopted by an author for public use, like George Eliot (Mary Ann/Marian Evans), and George Orwell (Eric Arthur Blair).

Psychoanalytic Criticism. A form of criticism that uses the insights of Freudian psychology to illuminate a work.

Ptolemaic Universe. The universe as perceived by Ptolemy, a Greco-Egyptian astronomer of the 2nd century A.D., whose theories were dominant until the Renaissance produced the Copernican universe. In Ptolemy's system, the universe was world-centered, with the sun, moon, planets, and stars understood as rotating around the earth in a series of concentric spheres, producing as they revolved the harmonious "music of the spheres."

Puritanism. A Protestant movement arising in the mid-16th century with the Reformation in England. Theocracy—the individual and the congregation governed directly under God through Christ—became primary, reflected in the centrality of the Scriptures and their exposition, direct confession through prayer and public confession to the congregation rather than through priests, and the direct individual experience of God's grace.

Quadrivium. The more advanced four of the seven liberal arts as studied in medieval universities: arithmetic, geometry, astronomy, and music.

Quantitative Verse. Verse that takes account of the quantity of the syllables (whether they take a long or short time to pronounce) rather than their stress patterns.

Quarto (Abbreviated 4to, 4o). A book made from sheets folded twice, giving signatures of four leaves (eight pages). Many of Shakespeare's plays were first printed individually in quarto editions, designated First Quarto, Second Quarto, etc.

Quatrain. A stanza of four lines, rhymed or unrhymed. With its many variations, it is the most common stanzaic form in English.

Rationalism. The theory that reason, rather than revelation or authority, provides knowledge, truth, the choice of good over evil, and an adequate understanding of God and the universe.

Reader-Response Theory. A form of criticism that arose during the 1970s; it postulates the essential active involvement of the reader with the text and focuses on the effect of the process of reading on the mind.

Realism (in literature). The faithful representation of life. Realism carries the conviction of true reports of phenomena observable by others.

Realism (in philosophy). (1) In the Middle Ages, the belief that universal concepts possess real existence apart from particular things and the human mind. They exist either as entities like Platonic forms or as concepts in the mind of God. Medieval realism was opposed to nominalism. (2) In later epistemology, the belief that things exist apart from our perception of them. In this sense, realism is opposed to idealism, which locates all reality in our minds.

Recension. (1) A process of editorial revision based on an examination of the various versions and sources of a literary text. (2) The text produced as a result of reconciling variant readings.

Recto. The right-hand page of an open book; the front of a leaf as opposed to the *verso* or back of a leaf.

Redaction. (1) A revised version. (2) A rewriting or condensing of an older work.

Refrain. A set phrase, or chorus, recurring throughout a song or poem, usually at the end of a stanza or other regular interval.

Relativism. The philosophical belief that nothing is absolute, that values are relative to circumstances. In criticism, relativism is either personal or historical.

Revenge Tragedy. The popular Elizabethan mode, initiated by Thomas Kyd's *Spanish Tragedy* (c. 1586), wherein the hero must revenge a ruler's murder of father, son, or lover.

Reversal. The thrilling change of luck for the protagonist at the last moment in comedy or tragedy—the *peripeteia*, which Aristotle first described in his *Poetics*, along with the discovery that usually sparks it.

Rhetoric. From Greek *rhetor*, "orator": the art of persuasion in speaking or writing. Since ancient times, rhetoric has been understood by some as a system of persuasive devices divorced from considerations of the merits of the case argued.

Rhetorical Figure. A figure of speech employing stylized patterns of word order or meaning for purposes of ornamentation or persuasion.

Rhetorical Question. A question posed for rhetorical effect, usually with a self-evident answer.

Rhyme (sometimes **Rime,** an older spelling). The effect created by matching sounds at the ends of words. The functions of rhyme are essentially four: pleasurable, mnemonic, structural, and rhetorical. Like meter and figurative language, rhyme provides a pleasure derived from fulfillment of a basic human desire to see similarity in dissimilarity, likeness with a difference.

Rhyme Royal. A stanza of seven lines of iambic pentameter, rhyming *ababbcc* (*see also* Meter).

Rhythm. The measured flow of repeated sound patterns, as, for example, the heavy stresses of accentual verse, the long and short syllables of quantitative verse, the balanced syntactical arrangements of parallelism in either verse or prose.

Romance. A continuous narrative in which the emphasis is on what happens in the plot, rather than on what is reflected from ordinary life or experience. Thus a central element in romance is adventure; at its most primitive, romance is an endless sequence of adventures.

Romanticism. A term describing qualities that colored most elements of European and American intellectual life in the late 18th and early 19th centuries, from literature, art, and music, through architecture, landscape gardening, philosophy, and politics. Within the social, political, and intellectual structures of society, the Romantics stressed the separateness of the person, celebrated individual perception and imagination, and embraced nature as a model for harmony in society and art. Their view was an egalitarian one, stressing the value of expressive abilities common to all, inborn rather than developed through training.

Roundheads. Adherents of the Parliamentary, or Puritan, party in the English Civil War, so called from their short haircuts, as opposed to the fashionable long wigs of the Cavaliers, supporters of King Charles I.

Rubric. From Latin *rubrica*, "red earth" (for coloring): in a book or manuscript, a heading, marginal notation, or other section distinguished for special attention by being printed in red ink or in distinctive type.

Run-on Line. A line of poetry whose sense does not stop at the end, with punctuation, but runs on to the next line.

Satire. Poking corrective ridicule at persons, types, actions, follies, mores, and beliefs.

Scop. An Anglo-Saxon bard, or court poet, a kind of poet laureate.

Semiotics. In anthropology, sociology, and linguistics, the study of signs, including words, other sounds, gestures, facial expressions, music, pictures, and other signals used in communication.

Senecan Tragedy. The bloody and bombastic tragedies of revenge inspired by Seneca's nine closet dramas, which had been discovered in Italy in the mid-16th century and soon thereafter translated into English.

Sensibility. Sensitive feeling, emotion. The term arose early in the 18th century to denote the tender undercurrent of feeling in the neoclassical period, continuing through Jane Austen's *Sense and Sensibility* (1811) and afterward.

Sequel. A literary work that explores later events in the lives of characters introduced elsewhere.

Serial. A narration presented in segments separated by time. Novels by Charles Dickens and other 19th-century writers were first serialized in magazines.

Seven Liberal Arts. The subjects studied in medieval universities, consisting of the *trivium* (grammar, logic, and rhetoric), for the B.A., and the *quadrivium* (arithmetic, geometry, astronomy, and music), for the M.A.

Shakespearean Sonnet (or English Sonnet). A sonnet in three quatrains and a couplet, rhyming *abab cdcd efef gg*.

Signified, Signifier. In structural linguistics, the *signified* is the idea in mind when a word is used, an entity separate from the *signifier*, the word itself.

Simile. A metaphor stating the comparison by use of *like*, *as*, or *as if*.

Slang. The special vocabulary of a class or group of people (as, for example, truck drivers, jazz musicians, salespeople, drug dealers), generally considered substandard, low, or offensive when measured against formal, educated usage.

Sonnet. A verse form of 14 lines, in English characteristically in iambic pentameter and most often in one of two rhyme schemes: the *Italian* (or *Petrarchan*) or *Shakespearean* (or *English*). An Italian sonnet is composed of an octave, rhyming *abbaabba*, and a sestet, rhyming *cdecde* or *cdcdcd*, or in some variant pattern, but with no closing couplet. A Shakespearean sonnet has three quatrains and a couplet, and rhymes *abab cdcd efef gg*. In both types, the content tends to follow the formal outline suggested by rhyme linkage, giving two divisions to the thought of an Italian sonnet and four to a Shakespearean one.

Sonnet Sequence. A group of sonnets thematically unified to create a longer work, although generally, unlike the stanza, each sonnet so connected can also be read as a meaningful separate unit.

Spondee. A metrical foot of two long, or stressed, syllables: – –.

Sprung Rhythm. Gerard Manley Hopkins's term to describe his variations of iambic meter to avoid the "same and tame." His feet, he said, vary from one to four syllables, with one stress per foot, on the first syllable.

Stanza. A term derived from an Italian word for "room" or "stopping place" and used, loosely, to designate any grouping of lines in a separate unit in a poem: a verse paragraph. More strictly, a stanza is a grouping of a prescribed number of lines in a given meter, usually with a particular rhyme scheme, repeated as a unit of structure. Poems in stanzas provide an instance of the aesthetic pleasure in repetition with a difference that also underlies the metrical and rhyming elements of poetry.

Stereotype. A character representing generalized racial or social traits repeated as typical from work to work, with no individualizing traits.

Stichomythia. Dialogue in alternate lines, favored in Greek tragedy and by Seneca and his imitators among the Elizabethans—including William Shakespeare.

Stock Characters. Familiar types repeated in literature to become symbolic of a particular genre, like the strong, silent hero of the western or the hard-boiled hero of the detective story.

Stoicism. (1) Generally, fortitude, repression of feeling, indifference to pleasure or pain. (2) Specifically, the philosophy of the Stoics, who, cultivating endurance and self-control, restrain passions such as joy and grief that place them in conflict with nature's dictates.

Stress. In poetry, the accent or emphasis given to certain syllables, indicated in scansion by a *macron* (–). In a trochee, for example, the stress falls on the first syllable: *sŭmmĕr*. *See also* Meter.

Structuralism. The study of social organizations and myths, of language, and of literature as structures. Each part is significant only as it relates to others in the total structure, with nothing meaningful by itself.

Structural Linguistics. Analysis and description of the grammatical structures of a spoken language.

Sublime. In literature, a quality attributed to lofty or noble ideas, grand or elevated expression, or (the ideal of sublimity) an inspiring combination of thought and language. In nature or art, it is a quality, as in a landscape or painting, that inspires awe or reverence.

Subplot. A sequence of events subordinate to the main story in a narrative or dramatic work.

Syllabic Verse. Poetry in which meter has been set aside and the line is controlled by a set number of syllables, regardless of stress.

Symbol. Something standing for its natural qualities in another context, with human meaning added: an eagle, standing for the soaring imperious dominance of Rome.

Symbolism. Any use of symbols, especially with a theoretical commitment, as when the French Symbolists of the 1880s and 1890s stressed, in Stéphane Mallarmé's words, not the thing but the effect, the subjective emotion implied by the surface rendering.

Snycopation. The effect produced in verse or music when two stress patterns play off against one another.

Synecdoche. The understanding of one thing by another—a kind of metaphor in which a part stands for the whole, or the whole for a part: *a hired hand* meaning "a laborer."

Synesthesia. Greek for "perceiving together": close association or confusion of sense impressions. The result is essentially a metaphor, transferring qualities of one sense to another, as in common phrases like "blue note" and "cold eye."

Synonyms. Words in the same language denoting the same thing, usually with different connotations: *female, woman, lady, dame; male, masculine, macho*.

Synopsis. A summary of a play, a narrative, or an argument.

Tenor and **Vehicle.** I. A. Richards's terms for the two aspects of metaphor, *tenor* being the actual thing projected figuratively in the *vehicle*. "She [tenor] is a rose [vehicle]."

Tercet (or **Triplet**). A verse unit of three lines, sometimes rhymed, sometimes not.

Terza Rima. A verse form composed of tercets with interlocking rhyme (*aba bcb cdc*, and so on), usually in iambic pentameter. Invented by Dante for his *Divine Comedy*.

Third-Person Narration. A method of storytelling in which someone who is not involved in the story, but stands somewhere outside it in space and time, tells of the events.

Topos. A commonplace, from Greek *topos* (plural *topoi*), "place." (1) A topic for argument, remembered by the classical system of placing it, in the mind's eye, in a place within a building and then proceeding mentally from one place to the next. (2) A rhetorical device, similarly remembered as a commonplace.

Tragedy. Fundamentally, a serious fiction involving the downfall of a hero or heroine. As a literary form, a basic mode of drama. Tragedy often involves the theme of isolation, in which a hero, a character of greater than ordinary human importance, becomes isolated from the community. Then there is the theme of the violation and reestablishment of order, in which the neutralizing of the violent act may take the form of revenge. Finally, a character may embody a passion too great for the cosmic order to tolerate, such as the passion of sexual love. Renaissance tragedy seems to be essentially a mixture of the heroic and the ironic. It tends to center on heroes who, though they cannot be of divine parent-

2930 Literary and Cultural Terms

age in Christianized Western Europe, are still of titanic importance, with an articulateness and social authority beyond anything in our normal experience.

Tragic Irony. The essence of tragedy, in which the most noble and most deserving person, because of the very grounds of his or her excellence, dies in defeat. *See also* Irony.

Tragicomedy. (1) A tragedy with happy ending, frequently with penitent villain and romantic setting, disguises, and discoveries.

Travesty. Literally a "cross-dressing": a literary work so clothed, or presented, as to appear ludicrous; a grotesque image or likeness.

Trivium. The first three of the seven liberal arts as studied in medieval universities: grammar, logic, and rhetoric (including oratory).

Trochee. A metrical foot going – ⌣.

Trope. Greek *tropos* for "a turn": a word or phrase turned from its usual meaning to an unusual one; hence, a figure of speech, or an expression turned beyond its literal meaning.

Type. (1) A literary genre. (2) One of the type characters. (3) A symbol or emblem. (4) In theology and literary criticism, an event in early Scriptures or literatures that is seen as prefiguring an event in later Scriptures or in history or literature generally.

Type Characters. Individuals endowed with traits that mark them more distinctly as representatives of a type or class than as standing apart from a type: the typical doctor or rakish aristocrat, for example. Type characters are the opposite of individualized characters.

Typology. The study of types. Typology springs from a theory of literature or history that recognizes events as duplicated in time.

Utopia. A word from two Greek roots (*outopia*, meaning "no place," and *eutopia*, meaning "good place"), pointing to the idea that a utopia is a nonexistent land of social perfection.

Verisimilitude (*vraisemblance* in French). The appearance of actuality.

Verso. The left-hand page of an open book; the back of a leaf of paper.

Vice. A stock character from the medieval morality play, a mischief-making tempter.

Vignette. (1) A brief, subtle, and intimate literary portrait, named for *vignette* portraiture, which is unbordered, shading off into the surrounding color at the edges, with features delicately rendered. (2) A short essay, sketch, or story, usually fewer than five hundred words.

Villanelle. One of the French verse forms, in five tercets, all rhyming *aba*, and a quatrain, rhyming *abaa*. The entire first and third lines are repeated alternately as the final lines of tercets 2, 3, 4, and 5, and together to conclude the quatrain.

Virgule. A "little rod"—the diagonal mark or slash used to indicate line ends in poetry printed continuously in running prose.

Vulgate. (1) A people's common vernacular language (Latin *vulgus*, "common people"). (2) The Vulgate Bible, translated by St. Jerome c. 383–405; the official Roman Catholic Bible.

Wit and **Humor.** *Wit* is intellectual acuity; *humor*, an amused indulgence of human deficiencies. Wit now denotes the acuity that produces laughter. It originally meant mere understanding, then quickness of understanding, then, beginning in the 17th century, quick perception coupled with creative fancy. Humor (British *humour*, from the four bodily humors) was simply a disposition, usually eccentric. In the 18th century, *humour* came to mean a laughable eccentricity and then a kindly amusement at such eccentricity.

Zeugma. The technique of using one word to yoke two or more others for ironic or amusing effect, achieved when at least one of the yoked is a misfit, as in Alexander Pope's "lose her Heart, or Necklace, at a Ball."

BIBLIOGRAPHY

General Background • Shari Benstock, *Women of the Left Bank: Paris, 1900–1940*, 1986. • Joseph Bristow, *Effeminate England: Homoerotic Writing after 1885*, 1995. • Carol T. Christ, *Victorian and Modern Poetics*, 1984. • Valentine Cunningham, *British Writers of the Thirties*, 1988. • Alistair Davies, ed., *An Annotated Critical Bibliography of Modernism*, 1982. • Marianne DeKoven, *Rich and Strange: Gender, History, Modernism*, 1991. • Kevin J. H. Dettmar, ed., *Rereading the New: A Backward Glance at Modernism*, 1992. • Maud Ellmann, *The Poetics of Impersonality: T. S. Eliot and Ezra Pound*, 1987. • David Gervais, *Literary Englands: Versions of "Englishness" in Modern Writing*, 1993. • Sandra Gilbert and Susan Gubar, *No Man's Land: The Place of the Woman Writer in the Twentieth Century*, 3 vols., 1988–. • John Halperin, *Eminent Georgians: The Lives of King George V, Elizabeth Bowen, St. John Philby, and Nancy Astor*, 1995. • Robert Hogan et al., *Dictionary of Irish Literature*, 1996. • Robert Hughes, *The Shock of the New*, 1981. • Hugh Kenner, *The Pound Era*, 1971. • Michael H. Levenson, *A Genealogy of Modernism: A Study of English Literary Doctrine, 1908–1922*, 1984. • James Longenbach, *Stone Cottage: Pound, Yeats, and Modernism*, 1988. • Perry Meisel, *The Myth of the Modern: A Study in British Literature and Criticism after 1850*, 1987. • Peter Nicholls, *Modernisms: A Literary Guide*, 1995. • Michael North, *The Political Aesthetic of Yeats, Eliot, and Pound*, 1991. • Herbert N. Schneidau, *Waking Giants: The Presence of the Past in Modernism*, 1991. • Sanford Schwartz, *The Matrix of Modernism: Pound, Eliot, and Early Twentieth-Century Thought*, 1985. • Bonnie Kime Scott, ed., *The Gender of Modernism: A Critical Anthology*, 1990. • John L. Somer and Barbara Eck Cooper, *American and British Literature, 1945–1975: An Annotated Bibliography of Contemporary Scholarship*, 1980. • C. K. Stead, *The New Poetic: Yeats to Eliot*, 1964. • C. K. Stead, *Pound, Yeats, Eliot, and the Modernist Movement*, 1986. • George Watson, *British Literature since 1945*, 1991.

Perspectives: The Great War: Confronting the Modern • Allyson Booth, *Postcards from the Trenches: Negotiating the Space between Modernism and the First World War*, 1996. • Paul Fussell, *The Great War and Modern Memory*, 1975. • Dorothy Goldman, ed., *Women and World War I: The Written Response*, 1993. • Klein-Holger, *The First World War in Fiction: A Collection of Critical Essays*, 1976. • John Onions, *English Fiction and Drama of the Great War, 1918–1939*, 1990. • William C. Wees, *Vorticism and the English Avant-Garde*, 1972.

Perspectives: Whose Language? • Eugene Benson and L. W. Conolly, eds., *Encyclopedia of Post-Colonial Literatures in English*, 1994. • Elleke Boehmer, *Colonial and Postcolonial Literature: Migrant Metaphors*, 1995. • Michael Edward Gorra, *After Empire: Scott, Naipaul, Rushdie*, 1997. • Bruce King, ed., *New National and Post-Colonial Literatures: An Introduction*, 1996. • Judie Newman, *The Ballistic Bard: Postcolonial Fictions*, 1995. • Jonathan White, ed., *Recasting the World: Writing after Colonialism*, 1993.

Perspectives: World War II and the End of Empire • Bill Ashcroft, Gareth Griffiths, and Helen Tiffin, *The Empire Writes Back: Theory and Practice in Post-Colonial Literatures*, 1989. • Bernard Bergonzi, *Wartime and Aftermath: English Literature and its Background, 1939–1960*, 1993. • Patrick Brantlinger, *Rule of Darkness: British Literature and Imperialism, 1830–1914*, 1988. • George Richard Esenwein, *Spain at War: The Spanish Civil War in Context, 1931–1939*, 1995. • Robert Hewison, *Under Siege: Literary Life in London, 1939–1945*, 1977. • Karen R. Lawrence, ed., *Decolonizing Tradition: New Views of Twentieth-Century "British" Literary Canons*, 1992. • David Leavitt, *While England Sleeps* [novel], 1993. • David Lloyd, *Anomalous States: Irish Writing and the Post-Colonial Moment*, 1993. • Robert H. MacDonald, *The Language of Empire: Myths and Metaphors of Popular Imperialism, 1880–1918*, 1994. • David Morgan, *The Battle for Britain: Citizenship and Ideology in the Second World War*, 1993. • John M. Muste, *Say That We Saw Spain Die: Literary Consequences of the Spanish Civil War*, 1966. • Andrew Sinclair, *War Like a Wasp: The Lost Decade of the 'Forties*, 1989. • Hugh Thomas,

The Spanish Civil War, 1986. • Keith Williams, British Writers and the Media, 1930–1945, 1996.

Speeches on Irish Independence • Seamus Deane, Celtic Revivals: Essays in Modern Irish Literature, 1880–1980, 1985. • Tom Garvin, 1922, The Birth of Irish Democracy, 1996. • Michael Hopkinson, Green against Green: The Irish Civil War, 1988. • Declan Kiberd, Inventing Ireland, 1996. • Julian Moynahan, Anglo-Irish: The Literary Imagination in a Hyphenated Culture, 1995.

W. H. Auden • George W. Bahlke, ed., Critical Essays on W. H. Auden, 1991. • John G. Blair, The Poetic Art of W. H. Auden, 1965. • Harold Bloom, ed., W. H. Auden, 1986. • John R. Boly, Reading Auden: The Returns of Caliban, 1991. • Frederick Buell, W. H. Auden as a Social Poet, 1973. • John Fuller, A Reader's Guide to W. H. Auden, 1970. • John Haffenden, ed., W. H. Auden: The Critical Heritage, 1983. • Anthony Hecht, The Hidden Law: The Poetry of W. H. Auden, 1993. • Richard Davenport Hines, Auden, 1995. • Lucy McDiarmid, Saving Civilization: Yeats, Eliot, and Auden between the Wars, 1984. • Lucy McDiarmid, Auden's Apologies for Poetry, 1990. • Edward Mendelson, ed., W. H. Auden: A Tribute, 1974. • Edward Mendelson, Early Auden, 1981. • Charles Osborne, W. H. Auden: The Life of a Poet, 1979. • Monroe K. Spears, The Poetry of W. H. Auden: The Disenchanted Island, 1963. • George T. Wright, W. H. Auden, 1969. • George T. Wright, W. H. Auden, 1981.

Samuel Beckett • Biographies. Lois Gordon, The World of Samuel Beckett, 1906–1946, 1996. • James Knowlson, Damned to Fame: The Life of Samuel Beckett, 1996.

Criticism. H. Porter Abbott, Beckett Writing Beckett: the Author in the Autograph, 1996. • James Acheson, Samuel Beckett's Artistic Theory and Practice: Criticism, Drama, and Early Fiction, 1997. • Richard Begam, Samuel Beckett and The End of Modernity, 1996. • Linda Ben-Zvi, Samuel Beckett, 1986. • Bob Cochran, Samuel Beckett: A Study of the Short Fiction, 1992. • Ruby Cohn, Back to Beckett, 1974. • Ruby Cohn, Just Play: Beckett's Theater, 1980. • J. E. Dearlove, Accommodating the Chaos: Samuel Beckett's Nonrelational Art, 1982. • S. E. Gontarski, ed., The Beckett Studies Reader, 1993. • S. E. Gontarski, ed., On Beckett: Essays and Criticism, 1986. • Lawrence Graver and Raymond Federman, eds., Samuel Beckett: The Critical Heritage, 1979. • Mel Gussow, ed., Conversations With and About Beckett, 1996. • Hugh Kenner, Flaubert, Joyce, and Beckett: The Stoic Comedians, 1962. • Hugh Kenner, A Reader's Guide to Samuel Beckett, 1973. • Hugh Kenner, Samuel Beckett: A Critical Study, 1968. • Charles R. Lyons, Samuel Beckett, 1990. • Patrick A. McCarthy, ed., Critical Essays on Samuel Beckett, 1986. • Vivian Mercier, Beckett/Beckett, 1977. • Kristin Morrison, Canters and Chronicles: The Use of Narrative in the Plays of Samuel Beckett and Harold Pinter, 1983. • Eoin O'Brien, The Beckett Country: Samuel Beckett's Ireland, 1993. • John Piling, ed., The Cambridge Companion to Beckett, 1994. • Christopher B. Ricks, Beckett's Dying Words: The Clarendon Lectures, 1990, 1993.

Elizabeth Bowen • Biographies. Elizabeth Bowen, Bowen's Court and Seven Winters: Memories of a Dublin Childhood, 1984. • Patricia Craig, Elizabeth Bowen, 1986.

Criticism. Allan E. Austin, Elizabeth Bowen, 1989. • Andrew Bennett and Nicholas Royle, Elizabeth Bowen and the Dissolution of the Novel: Still Lives, 1995. • Harold Bloom, ed., Elizabeth Bowen, 1987. • Renée Hoogland, Elizabeth Bowen: A Reputation in Writing, 1994. • Heather B. Jordan, How Will the Heart Endure: Elizabeth Bowen and the Landscape of War, 1992. • Phyllis Lassner, Elizabeth Bowen: A Study of Short Fiction, 1991.

Rupert Brooke • Biographies. John Lehmann, Rupert Brooke: His Life and His Legend, 1980.

Criticism. Rupert Brooke, The Letters of Rupert Brooke, ed. Geoffrey Keynes, 1968. • Adrian Caesar, Taking It Like a Man: Suffering, Sexuality, and the War Poets: Brooke, Sassoon, Owen, Graves, 1993. • Paul Delany, The Neo-Pagans: Rupert Brooke and the Ordeal of Youth, 1987. • Pippa Harris, Song of Love: The Letters of Rupert Brooke and Noel Oliver, 1991. • William E. Laskowski, Rupert Brooke, 1994.

Sir Winston Churchill • Biographies. William Manchester, The Last Lion: Winston Spencer Churchill Visions of Glory, 1874–1932, 1983. • William Manchester, The Last Lion: Winston Spencer Churchill: Alone, 1932–1940, 1989.

Criticism. Winston S. Churchill, Memoirs of The Second World War, 1990. • Victor Feske, From Belloc to Churchill: Private Scholars, Public Culture, and the Crisis of British Liberalism, 1900–1939, 1996. • James Humes, Wit and

Wisdom of Winston Churchill, 1995. • Warren F. Kimball, *Churchill and Roosevelt, the Complete Correspondence*, 3 vols, 1984. • Warren F. Kimball, *Forged in War: Roosevelt, Churchill, and the Second World War*, 1997. • Sheila Lawlor, ed., *Churchill and the Politics of War, 1940–1941*, 1994. • Keith Robbins, *Churchill*, 1993. • Manfred Weidhorn, *Churchill's Rhetoric and Political Discourse*, 1988.

Michael Collins • *Biographies*. Tim P. Coogan, *Michael Collins: The Man Who Made Ireland*, 1996. • James Mackay, *Michael Collins: A Life*, 1997.

Criticism. P. S. Beaslai, *Michael Collins and the Making of a New Ireland*, 2 vols., 1985. • Eoin Neeson, *The Life and Death of Michael Collins*, 1968. • Leon O'Broin, ed., *In Great Haste: The Letters of Michael Collins and Kitty Kiernan*, 1996. • Frank O'Connor, *The Big Fellow: Michael Collins and the Irish Revolution*, 1965. • Ulick O'Connor, *Michael Collins and the Troubles: The Struggle for Irish Freedom, 1912–1922*, 1996.

Joseph Conrad • Chinua Achebe, "An Image of Africa." • John Batchelor, *The Life of Joseph Conrad: A Critical Biography*, 1993. • Ted Billy, ed., *Critical Essays on Joseph Conrad*, 1987. • Harold Bloom, ed., *Joseph Conrad's "Heart of Darkness,"* 1987. • Harold Bloom, ed., *Joseph Conrad*, 1986. • Harold Bloom, *Marlow*, 1992. • Keith Carabine, ed., *Joseph Conrad: Critical Assessments*, 4 vols., 1992. • Avrom Fleishman, *Conrad's Politics: Community and Anarchy in the Fiction of Joseph Conrad*, 1967. • Ford Madox Ford, *Joseph Conrad: A Personal Remembrance*, 1989. • Christopher L. GoGwilt, *The Invention of the West: Joseph Conrad and the Double-Mapping of Europe and Empire*, 1995. • Albert J. Guerard, *Conrad the Novelist*, 1958. • Geoffrey Harpham, *One of Us: The Mastery of Joseph Conrad*, 1996. • Fredric Jameson, *The Political Unconscious: Narrative as a Socially Symbolic Act*, 1981. • Frederick Karl, *Joseph Conrad: The Three Lives: A Biography*, 1979. • Frederick R. Karl and Laurence Davies, eds., *The Collected Letters of Joseph Conrad*, 1983- . • Jeffrey Meyers, *Joseph Conrad: A Biography*, 1991. • Vincent P. Pecora, *Self and Form in Modern Narrative*, 1989. • Martin Ray, ed., *Joseph Conrad: Interviews & Recollections*, 1990. • Edward W. Said, *Joseph Conrad and the Fiction of Autobiography*, 1966. • Edward W. Said, *The World, the Text, and the Critic*, 1983. • Norman Sherry, ed., *Conrad: The Critical Heritage*, 1973. • J. H. Stape, ed., *The*

Cambridge Companion to Joseph Conrad, 1996. • Bruce Teets, *Joseph Conrad: An Annotated Bibliography*, 1990. • Ian Watt, *Joseph Conrad: A Critical Biography*, 1979. • Cedric P. Watts, *A Preface to Conrad*, 1993. • Mark A. Wollaeger, *Joseph Conrad and the Fictions of Skepticism*, 1990.

Nuala Ní Dhomhnaill. M. Louise Cannon, "The Extraordinary Within the Ordinary: The Poetry of Eavan Boland and Nuala Ni Dhomhnaill," *South Atlantic Review* 60 (1995). • Deborah McWilliams Consalvo, "The Lingual Ideal in the Poetry of Nuala Ni Dhomhnaill," *Eire-Ireland: A Journal of Irish Studies*, 30 (1995). • Patricia Boyle Haberstroh, *Women Creating Women: Contemporary Irish Women Poets*, 1996.

Margaret Drabble • Joanne V. Creighton, *Margaret Drabble*, 1985. • John Hannay, *The Intertextuality of Fate: A Study of Margaret Drabble*, 1986. • Valerie G. Myer, *Margaret Drabble: A Reader's Guide*, 1991. • Valerie G. Myer, *Margaret Drabble: Puritanism and Permissiveness*, 1974. • Ellen Cronan Rose, *The Novels of Margaret Drabble: Equivocal Figures*, 1980. • Ellen Cronan Rose, ed., *Critical Essays on Margaret Drabble*, 1985. • Lynn Veach Sadler, *Margaret Drabble*, 1986.

T. S. Eliot • *Biographies*. Peter Ackroyd, *T. S. Eliot: A Life*, 1984. • Lyndall Gordon, *Eliot's Early Years*, 1977. • Lyndall Gordon, *Eliot's New Life*, 1988.

Criticism. Harold Bloom, ed., *T. S. Eliot*, 1985. • Harold Bloom, ed., *T. S. Eliot's "The Waste Land,"* 1986. • Jewel Spears Brooker and Joseph Bentley, *Reading "The Waste Land": Modernism and the Limits of Interpretation*, 1990. • Ronald Bush, *T. S. Eliot: The Modernist in History*, 1991. • T. S. Eliot, *The Letters of T. S. Eliot*, ed. Valerie Eliot, 1988- . • T. S. Eliot, *"The Waste Land": A Facsimile and Transcript of the Original Drafts Including the Annotations of Ezra Pound*, ed. Valerie Eliot, 1971. • Maud Ellmann, *The Poetics of Impersonality: T. S. Eliot and Ezra Pound*, 1987. • Nancy K. Gish, *"The Waste Land": A Poem of Memory and Desire*, 1988. • Michael Grant, ed., *T. S. Eliot: The Critical Heritage*, 1982. • Frank Lentricchia, *Modernist Quartet*, 1994. • James Longenbach, *Modernist Poetics of History: Pound, Eliot, and the Sense of the Past*, 1987. • Lucy McDiarmid, *Saving Civilization: Yeats, Eliot, and Auden Between the Wars*, 1984. • Gail McDonald, *Learning to Be Mod-*

ern: *Pound, Eliot, and the American University*, 1993. • Louis Menand, *Discovering Modernism: T. S. Eliot and His Context*, 1986. • Anthony David Moody, ed., *The Cambridge Companion to T. S. Eliot*, 1994. • Anthony David Moody, *Thomas Stearns Eliot, Poet*, 1979. • Jeffrey M. Perl, *Skepticism and Modern Enmity: Before and After Eliot*, 1989. • Christopher B. Ricks, *T. S. Eliot and Prejudice*, 1988. • John Paul Riquelme, *Harmony of Dissonances: T. S. Eliot, Romanticism and Imagination*, 1990. • Sanford Schwartz, *The Matrix of Modernism: Pound, Eliot, and Early Twentieth-Century Thought*, 1985. • Grover Cleveland Smith, *The Waste Land*, 1983. • Stanley Sultan, *Eliot, Joyce, and Company*, 1987. • Stanley Sultan, *"Ulysses," "The Waste Land," and Modernism: A Jubilee Study*, 1977.

E. M. Forester • Nicola Beauman, *Morgan: A Biography of the Novelist E. M. Forster*, 1994. • Calvin Bedient, *Architects of the Self: George Eliot, D. H. Lawrence, and E. M. Forster*, 1972. • Harold Bloom, ed., *E. M. Forster*, 1987. • G. K. Das, *E. M. Forster's India*, 1977. • P. N. Furbank, *E. M. Forster: A Life*, 1994. • Philip Gardner, *E. M. Forster: The Critical Heritage*, 1973. • Christopher Gillie, *A Preface to Forster*, 1983. • B. J. Kirkpatrick, *A Bibliography of E. M. Forster*, 1986. • Mary Lago, *E.M. Forster: A Literary Life*, 1995. • Mary Lago and P. N. Furbank, eds., *Selected Letters of E. M. Forster*, 1983-85. • J. H. Stape, ed., *E. M. Forster: Interviews and Recollections*, 1993. • Lionel Trilling, *E. M. Forster*, 1965. • Alan Wilde, *Critical Essays on E. M. Forster*, 1985.

Roger Fry • David Dowling, *Bloomsbury Aesthetics and the Novels of Forster and Woolf*, 1985. • Frances Spalding, *Roger Fry: Art and Life*, 1980. • Denys Sutton, *Collected Letters of Roger Fry*, 1972. • Virginia Woolf, *Roger Fry: A Biography*, 1940.

Nadine Gordimer • *Biographies*. Nadine Gordimer, *Writing and Being*, 1995.

Criticism. Nancy T. Bazin and Marilyn D. Seymour, *Conversations with Nadine Gordimer*, 1990. • Stephen Clingman, *The Novels of Nadine Gordimer: History from the Inside*, 1986. • Andrew V. Ettin, *Betrayals of the Body Politic: The Literary Commitments of Nadine Gordimer*, 1993. • Dominic Head, *Nadine Gordimer*, 1995. • Christopher Heywood, *Nadine Gordimer*, 1983. • Bruce King, ed., *The Later Fiction of Nadine Gordimer*, 1993. • Judie Newman, *Nadine Gordimer*, 1988. • Rowland Smith, ed., *Critical*

Essays on Nadine Gordimer, 1990. • Kathrin Wagner, *Rereading Nadine Gordimer*, 1994.

Robert Graves • *Biographies*. Richard Perceval Graves, *Robert Graves: The Assault Heroic, 1895–1926*, 1986. • Richard Perceval Graves, *Robert Graves: The Years with Laura, 1926–1940*, 1990.

Criticism. Harold Bloom, ed., *Robert Graves*, 1987. • Adrian Caesar, *Taking It Like a Man: Suffering, Sexuality, and the War Poets: Brooke, Sassoon, Owen, Graves*, 1993. • Robert H. Canary, *Robert Graves*, 1980. • Diane DeBell, "Strategies of Survival: David Jones, In Parenthesis, and Robert Graves, Goodbye to All That," in *The First World War in Fiction: A Collection of Critical Essays*, ed. Klein-Holger, 1976. • Robert Graves, *Between Moon and Moon: Selected Letters of Robert Graves, 1946–1972*, ed. Paul O'Prey, 1984. • Robert Graves, *In Broken Images: Selected Letters of Robert Graves, 1914–1946*, ed. Paul O'Prey, 1982. • John Hildebidle, "Neither Worthy nor Capable: The War Memoirs of Graves, Blunden, and Sassoon," in *Modernism Reconsidered*, eds., Robert Kiely and John Hildebidle, 1983. • Frank L. Kersnowski, ed., *Conversations with Robert Graves*, 1989. • Patrick J. Quinn, *The Great War and the Missing Muse: The Early Writings of Robert Graves and Siefried Sassoon*, 1994. • Katherine Snipes, *Robert Graves*, 1979.

Graham Greene • *Biographies*. Michael Shelden, *Graham Greene: The Enemy Within*, 1994. • Norman Sherry, *The Life of Graham Greene*, 1989–1995.

Criticism. Harold Bloom, ed., *Graham Greene*, 1987. • Henry J. Donaghy, *Conversations with Graham Greene*, 1992. • Haim Gordon, *Fighting Evil: Unsung Heroes in the Novels of Graham Greene*, 1997. • Rosemary Kelly, *Graham Greene: A Study of the Short Fiction*, 1992. • Neil McEwan, *Graham Greene*, 1988. • Jeffrey Meyers, ed., *Graham Greene: A Revaluation: New Essays*, 1989. • R. H. Miller, *Understanding Graham Greene*, 1990. • Paul O'Prey, *A Reader's Guide to Graham Greene*, 1988. • Grahame Smith, *The Achievement of Graham Greene*, 1986. • Cedric T. Watts, *A Preface to Greene*, 1997.

Thomas Hardy • Harold Bloom, ed., *Thomas Hardy*, 1987. • Graham Clarke, ed., *Thomas Hardy: Critical Assessments*, 4 vols., 1993. • Reginald Gordon Cox, *Thomas Hardy: The Critical Heritage*, 1970. • Ronald P. Draper,

An Annotated Critical Bibliography of Thomas Hardy, 1989. • Simon Gatrell, Hardy, the Creator: A Textual Biography, 1988. • James Gibson, Thomas Hardy: A Literary Life, 1996. • Dale Kramer, Critical Essays on Thomas Hardy: The Novels, 1990. • Robert Langbaum, Thomas Hardy in Our Time, 1995. • C. Day Lewis, The Lyrical Poetry of Thomas Hardy, 1970. • Perry Meisel, Thomas Hardy: The Return of the Repressed: A Study of the Major Fiction, 1972. • J. Hillis Miller, Thomas Hardy: Distance and Desire, 1970. • Michael Millgate, ed., Selected Letters, 1990. • Michael Millgate, Thomas Hardy: A Biography, 1982. • Charles P. C. Pettit, ed., New Perspectives on Thomas Hardy, 1994. • Richard L. Purdy and Michael Millgate, eds., The Collected Letters of Thomas Hardy, 1978-88. • Merryn Williams, A Preface to Hardy, 1993. • Paul Zietlow, Moments of Vision: The Poetry of Thomas Hardy, 1974.

Seamus Heaney • Biographies. Michael Parker, Seamus Heaney: The Making of the Poet, 1993.

Criticism. Elmer Andrews, The Poetry of Seamus Heaney, 1988. • Harold Bloom, ed., Seamus Heaney, 1986. • Sidney Burris, ed., The Poetry of Resistance: Seamus Heaney and the Pastoral Tradition, 1990. • Neil Corcoran, Seamus Heaney: A Faber Student Guide, 1986. • Tony Curtis, ed., The Art of Seamus Heaney, 1994. • Michael J. Durkan and Rand Brandes, Seamus Heaney: A Reference Guide, 1996. • Thomas C. Foster, Seamus Heaney, 1989. • Robert F. Garratt, Critical Essays on Seamus Heaney, 1995. • Henry Hart, Seamus Heaney, Poet of Contrary Progressions, 1992. • Catherin Malloy and Phyllis Carey, eds., Seamus Heaney: The Shaping Spirit, 1996. • Michael R. Molino, Questioning Tradition, Language, and Myth: The Poetry of Seamus Heaney, 1994. • Blake Morrison, Seamus Heaney, 1982. • Bernard O'Donoghue, Seamus Heaney and the Language of Poetry, 1994.

David Jones • Biographies. René Hague, ed., Dai Great-Coat: A Self-Portrait of David Jones in His Letters, 1980.

Criticism. Thomas Dilworth, The Shape of Meaning in the Poetry of David Jones, 1988. • Thomas Dilworth, ed., Inner Necessities: The Letters of David Jones to Desmond Chute, 1984. • René Hague, David Jones, 1975. • Jeremy Hooker, David Jones: An Exploratory Study of the Writings, 1975. • David Jones, David Jones: Letters to Vernon Watkins, ed. Ruth Pryor, 1976. • Jonathan Miles and Derek Shiel,

David Jones: The Maker Unmade, 1996. • Kathleen Raine, David Jones, Solitary Perfectionist, 1974. • Kathleen Staudt, ed., At the Turn of a Civilization: David Jones and Modern Poetics, 1993.

James Joyce • Edition. Ulysses, ed. Hans Walter Gabler, 1984.

Biographies. Richard Ellmann, James Joyce, 1982. • Herbert S. Gorman, James Joyce, 1948.

Criticism. Derek Attridge, ed., The Cambridge Companion to James Joyce, 1990. • Richard Brown, James Joyce and Sexuality, 1989. • Frank Budgen, James Joyce and the Making of "Ulysses," 1960. • Kevin J. H. Dettmar, The Illicit Joyce of Postmodernism: Reading Against the Grain, 1996. • Enda Duffy, The Subaltern "Ulysses," 1994. • Don Gifford, Ulysses Annotated: Notes for Joyce's "Ulysses," 1988. • Stuart Gilbert, James Joyce's "Ulysses": A Study, 1930. • Clive Hart and David Hayman, eds., James Joyce's "Ulysses": Critical Essays, 1974. • Hugh Kenner, Joyce's Voices, 1978. • Hugh Kenner, Ulysses, 1987. • R. B. Kershner, Joyce, Bakhtin, and Popular Literature: Chronicles of Disorder, 1989. • Karen Lawrence, The Odyssey of Style in "Ulysses," 1981. • A. Walton Litz, The Art of James Joyce: Method and Design in "Ulysses" and "Finnegans Wake," 1961. • Vicki Mahaffey, Reauthorizing Joyce, 1988. • Dominic Manganiello, Joyce's Politics, 1980. • E. H. Mikhail, James Joyce: Interviews and Recollections, 1990. • Margot Norris, Joyce's Web: The Social Unraveling of Modernism, 1992. • Richard Pearce, The Politics of Narration: James Joyce, William Faulkner, and Virginia Woolf, 1991. • David Pierce, James Joyce's Ireland, 1992. • Arthur Power, Conversations with James Joyce, 1974. • Mary T. Reynolds, ed., James Joyce: A Collection of Critical Essays, 1993. • Bonnie K. Scott, Joyce and Feminism, 1984. • Robert E. Spoo, James Joyce and the Language of History: Dedalus's Nightmare, 1994. • Jennifer Wicke, Advertising Fictions: Literature, Advertising, and Social Reading, 1988.

James Kelman • Ian Bell, "James Kelman," in The New Welsh Review 3 (1990). • Cairns Craig, "Resisting Arrest: James Kelman," in The Scottish Novel Since the Seventies: New Visions, Old Dreams, eds. Gavin Wallace and Randall Stevenson, 1993. • James Kelman, Some Recent Attacks: Essays, Cultural and Political, 1992. • Drew Milne, "James Kelman: Dialectics of Urbanity," Swansea Review (1994).

Hanif Kureishi • Alamgir Hashmi, "Hanif Kureishi and the Tradition of the Novel," 1993. • Radhika Mohanram, "Postcolonial Spaces and Deterritorialized (Homo)Sexuality: The Films of Hanif Kureishi." In Gita Rajan and Radhika Mohanram, eds., *Postcolonial Discourse and Changing Cultural Contexts: Theory and Criticism*, 1995.

Philip Larkin • *Biographies*. Andrew Motion, *Philip Larkin: A Writer's Life*, 1993.

Criticism. James Booth, *Philip Larkin: Writer*, 1992. • Richard Hoffpauir, *The Art of Restraint: English Poetry from Hardy to Larkin*, 1991. • Philip Larkin, *Selected Letters: 1940–1985*, ed. Anthony Thwaite, 1993. • Bruce K. Martin, *Philip Larkin*, 1978. • Janice Rossen, *Philip Larkin: His Life's Work*, 1990. • Dale Salwak, ed., *Philip Larkin: The Man and His Work*, 1988. • Andrew Swarbrick, *Out of Reach: The Poetry of Philip Larkin*, 1995. • Anthony Thwaite, *Larkin at Sixty*, 1982. • David Timms, *Philip Larkin*, 1973.

D. H. Lawrence. • James T. Boulton, ed., *The Letters of D. H. Lawrence*, 6 vols., 1979- . • Henry Coombes, *D. H. Lawrence: A Critical Anthology*, 1973. • James C. Cowan, *D. H. Lawrence: An Annotated Bibliography of Writings about Him*, 1982. • Paul Delany, *D. H. Lawrence's Nightmare: The Writer and His Circle in the Years of the Great War*, 1978. • R. P. Draper, *D. H. Lawrence: The Critical Heritage*, 1970. • Sandra Gilbert, *Acts of Attention: The Poems of D. H. Lawrence*, 1972. • Leo Hamalian, *D. H. Lawrence: A Collection of Criticism*, 1973. • Philip Hobsbaum, *A Reader's Guide to D.H. Lawrence*, 1981. • Mark Kinkead-Weekes, *D. H. Lawrence: Triumph to Exile, 1912-1922*, 1996. • Dennis Jackson and Fleda Brown Jackson, eds., *Critical Essays on D.H. Lawrence*, 1988. • Thomas Rice Jackson, *D. H. Lawrence: A Guide to Research*, 1983. • F. R. Leavis, *D. H. Lawrence, Novelist*, 1970. • Henry Miller, *The World of Lawrence: A Passionate Appreciation*, 1980. • Kate Millet, *Sexual Politics*, 1970. • Harry T. Moore, *The Priest of Love: A Life of D. H. Lawrence*, 1974. • Ross C. Murfin, *The Poetry of D. H. Lawrence: Texts and Contexts*, 1983. • Joyce Carol Oates, *The Hostile Sun: The Poetry of D.H. Lawrence*, 1973. • F. B. Pinion, *A D. H. Lawrence Companion: Life, Thought, and Works*, 1979. • Tony Pinkney, *D.H. Lawrence and Modernism*, 1990. • Paul Poplawski, *D. H. Lawrence: A Reference Companion*, 1996. • Peter Preston and Peter Hoare, eds., *D.H. Lawrence in the Modern World*, 1989. • Warren Roberts, *A Bibliography of D. H. Lawrence*, 1982. • Keith Sagar, ed., *A D. H. Lawrence Handbook*, 1982. • Keith M. Sagar, *The Art of D.H. Lawrence*, 1975. • Carol Siegel, *Lawrence among the Women: Wavering Boundaries in Women's Literary Traditions*, 1991. • Stephen Spender, *D. H. Lawrence: Novelist, Poet, Prophet*, 1973. • John Worthen, *D. H. Lawrence: A Literary Life*, 1989.

T. E. Lawrence • *Biographies*. Phillip Knightley, and Colin Simpson, *The Secret Lives of Lawrence of Arabia*, 1969. • Jeremy Wilson, *Lawrence of Arabia: The Authorized Biography of T. E. Lawrence*, 1989.

Criticism. Frank Clements, *T. E. Lawrence: A Reader's Guide*, 1972. • Richard Perceval Graves, *Lawrence of Arabia and His World*, 1928. • T. E. Lawrence, *The Letters of T. E. Lawrence*, ed. Malcolm Brown, 1988. • Jeffrey Meyers, ed., *T. E. Lawrence: Soldier, Writer, Legend: New Essays*, 1989. • Jeffrey Meyers, *The Wounded Spirit: T. E. Lawrence's "Seven Pillars of Wisdom,"* 1989. • Desmond Stewart, *T. E. Lawrence*, 1977. • Stephen E. Tabachnick, ed., *The T. E. Lawrence Puzzle*, 1984. • Stephen E. Tabachnick, *T. E. Lawrence*, 1978. • Lowell Thomas, *With Lawrence in Arabia*, 1924. • Stanley Weintraub, *Lawrence of Arabia: The Literary Impulse*, 1975.

Doris Lessing • *Biographies*. Doris Lessing, *Under My Skin: Volume One of My Autobiography, to 1949*, 1995.

Criticism. Harold Bloom, ed., *Doris Lessing*, 1986. • Judith K. Gardiner, *Rhys, Stead, Lessing, and the Politics of Empathy*, 1989. • Gayle Greene, *Doris Lessing: The Poetics of Change*, 1994. • Molly Hite, *The Other Side of the Story: Structures and Strategies of Contemporary Feminist Narrative*, 1989. • Elizabeth Maslen, *Doris Lessing*, 1994. • Margaret M. Rowe, *Doris Lessing*, 1994. • Ruth Saxon and Jean Tobin, *Woolf and Lessing: Breaking the Mold*, 1994. • Claire Sprague, *Rereading Doris Lessing: Narrative Patterns of Doubling and Repetition*, 1987. • Claire Sprague and Virginia Tiger, eds., *Critical Essays on Doris Lessing*, 1986. • Claire Sprague, ed., *In Pursuit of Doris Lessing: Nine Nations Reading*, 1990.

Katherine Mansfield • *Biographies*. Gillian Boddy, *Katherine Mansfield: The Woman and the Writer*, 1988. • Claire Tomalin, *Katherine Mansfield: A Secret Life*, 1987.

Criticism. Mary Burgan, *Illness, Gender, and Writing: The Case of Katherine Mansfield*, 1994.

• Saralyn R. Daly, *Katherine Mansfield*, 1994. • Ian A. Gordon, *Undiscovered Country: The New Zealand Stories of Katherine Mansfield*, 1974. • Sydney J. Kaplan, *Katherine Mansfield and the Origins of Modernist Fiction*, 1990. • Jasper F. Kobler, *Katherine Mansfield: A Study of the Short Fiction*, 1990. • Patricia Moran, *Word of Mouth: Body Language in Katherine Mansfield and Virginia Woolf*, 1996. • Patrick D. Morrow, *Katherine Mansfield's Fiction*, 1993. • Rhoda B. Nathan, ed., *Critical Essays on Katherine Mansfield*, 1993. • Vincent O' Sullivan and Margaret Scott, *The Collected Letters of Katherine Mansfield*, 1984–1996. • Jan Pilditch, ed., *The Critical Response to Katherine Mansfield*, 1996. • Roger Robinson, ed., *Katherine Mansfield: In from the Margin*, 1994.

Medbh McGuckian • Molly Bendall, "Flower Logic: The Poems of Medbh McGuckian," *The Antioch Review* 48 (1990). • Patricia Boyle Haberstroh, *Women Creating Women: Contemporary Irish Women Poets*, 1996. • Peggy O'Brien, "Reading Medbh McGuckian: Admiring What We Cannot Understand," *Colby Quarterly* 28 (1992). • Mary O'Connor, "'Rising Out': Medbh McGuckian's Destabilizing Poetics," *Eire-Ireland: A Journal of Irish Studies* 30 (1996). • Susan Shaw Sailer, "An Interview with Medbh McGuckian," *Michigan Quarterly Review* 32 (1993).

V.S. Naipaul. Selwyn Reginald Cudjoe, *V. S. Naipaul: A Materialist Reading*, 1988. • Michael Edward Gorra, *After Empire: Scott, Naipaul, Rushdie*, 1997. • Robert D. Hamner, *V. S. Naipaul*, 1973. • Peter Hughes, *V. S. Naipaul*, 1988. • Kelvin Jarvis, *V. S. Naipaul: A Selective Bibliography with Annotations, 1957-1987*, 1989. • Richard Kelly, *V. S. Naipaul*, 1989. • Bruce Alvin King, *V. S. Naipaul*, 1993. • Judith Levy, *V. S. Naipaul: Displacement and Autobiography*, 1995. • Fawzia Mustafa, *V. S. Naipaul*, 1995. • Timothy F. Weiss, *On the Margins: The Art of Exile in V. S. Naipaul*, 1992. • Landeg White, *V. S. Naipaul: A Critical Introduction*, 1975.

George Orwell • *Biographies.* Peter Hobley Davison, *George Orwell: A Literary Life*, 1996. • Michael Shelden, *Orwell: The Authorized Biography*, 1991.

Criticism. Harold Bloom, ed., *George Orwell*, 1987. • Peter Buitenhuis and Ira B. Nadel, *George Orwell, A Reassessment*, 1988. • Roger Fowler, *The Language of George Orwell*, 1995.

• Jeffrey Meyers, ed., *George Orwell: The Critical Heritage*, 1975. • Valerie Meyers, *George Orwell*, 1991. • Bernard Oldsey and Joseph Browne, eds., *Critical Essays on George Orwell*, 1986. • Alok Rai, *Orwell and the Politics of Despair: A Critical Study of the Writings of George Orwell*, 1990. • John Rodden, *The Politics of Literary Reputation: The Making and Claiming of "St. George" Orwell*, 1991. • Raymond Williams, *George Orwell*, 1971. • David Wykes, *A Preface to Orwell*, 1987.

Wilfred Owen • *Biographies.* Harold Owen, *Journey from Obscurity; Wilfred Owen, 1893–1918*, 1963–1965. • Jon Stallworthy, *Wilfred Owen*, 1974.

Criticism. Sven Bäckman, *Tradition Transformed: Studies in the Poetry of Wilfred Owen*, 1979. • Adrian Caesar, *Taking It Like a Man: Suffering, Sexuality, and the War Poets: Brooke, Sassoon, Owen, Graves*, 1993. • Desmond Graham, *The Truth of War: Owen, Rosenberg and Blunden*, 1984. • Dominic Hibberd, *Owen the Poet*, 1988. • Douglas Kerr, *Wilfred Owen's Voices: Language and Community*, 1993. • Arthur E. Lane, *An Adequate Response: The War Poetry of Wilfred Owen and Siegfried Sassoon*, 1972. • Stephen MacDonald, *Not About Heroes: The Friendship of Siegfried Sassoon and Wilfred Owen*, 1983. • Wilfred Owen, *Wilfred Owen: Collected Letters*, eds. William H. Owen and John Bell, 1967.

Charles Stewart Parnell • *Biographies.* Robert Kee, *The Laurel and the Ivy: The Story of Charles Stewart Parnell and Irish Nationalism*, 1993. • F. S. L. Lyons, *Charles Stewart Parnell*, 1977.

Criticism. Jules Abels, *The Parnell Tragedy*, 1966. • D. George Boyce and Alan O'Day, eds., *Parnell in Perspective*, 1991. • Noel Kissane, *Parnell: A Documentary History*, 1991. • Emmet Larkin, *The Roman Catholic Church in Ireland and the Fall of Parnell, 1888–1891*, 1979. • F. S. L. Lyons, *The Fall of Parnell, 1890–1891*, 1960. • Conor Cruise O'Brien, *Parnell and His Party, 1880–90*, 1968. • Alan O'Day, *Parnell and the First Home Rule Episode 1884–87*, 1986. • Michael Steinman, *Yeats's Heroic Figures: Wilde, Parnell, Swift, Casement*, 1983.

Padraic Pearse • Ruth Dudley Edwards, *Patrick Pearse: The Triumph of Failure*, 1977. • Sean Farrell Moran, *Patrick Pearse and the Politics of Redemption: The Mind of the Easter Rising, 1916*, 1994. • Padraic Pearse, *The Letters of P. H. Pearse*, ed. Seamus O Buachalla, 1980. • Raymond J. Porter, *P.H. Pearse*, 1973.

Ezra Pound • *Biographies*. Humphrey Carpenter, *A Serious Character: The Life of Ezra Pound*, 1988. • Noel Stock, *The Life of Ezra Pound*, 1970.

Criticism. Harold Bloom, ed., *Ezra Pound*, 1987. • Michael Coyle, *Ezra Pound, Popular Genres, and the Discourse of Culture*, 1995. • Reed Way Dasenbrock, *The Literary Vorticism of Ezra Pound and Wyndham Lewis: Towards the Condition of Painting*, 1985. • Eric Homberger, ed., *Ezra Pound: The Critical Heritage*, 1972. • Hugh Kenner, *The Poetry of Ezra Pound*, 1968. • Hugh Kenner, *The Pound Era*, 1971. • Gail McDonald, *Learning to Be Modern: Pound, Eliot, and the American University*, 1993. • Ezra Pound, *The Letters of Ezra Pound, 1907–1941*, ed. D. D. Paige, 1974. • Ezra Pound, *Pound/Lewis: The Letters of Ezra Pound and Wyndham Lewis*, 1985. • K. K. Ruthven, *A Guide to Ezra Pound's "Personae," 1926*, 1969.

Issac Rosenberg • *Biographies*. Joseph Cohen, *Journey to the Trenches: The Life of Isaac Rosenberg: 1890–1918*, 1975. • Jean Moorcroft Wilson, *Isaac Rosenberg, Poet and Painter: A Biography*, 1975.

Criticism. Desmond Graham, *The Truth of War: Owen, Rosenberg and Blunden*, 1984.

Salman Rushdie • Anouar Abdallah, ed., *For Rushdie: A Collection of Essays by 100 Arabic and Muslim Writers*, 1994. • Fawzia Afzal-Khan, *Cultural Imperialism and the Indo-English Novel: Genre and Ideology in R. K. Narayan, Anita Desai, Kamala Markandaya, and Salman Rushdie*, 1993. • Lisa Appignanesi and Sara Maitland, eds., *The Rushdie File*, 1990. • Timothy Brennan, *Salman Rushdie and the Third World: Myths of the Nation*, 1989. • Catherine Cundy, *Salman Rushdie*, 1997. • Michael Edward Gorra, *After Empire: Scott, Naipaul, Rushdie*, 1997. • James Harrison, *Salman Rushdie*, 1991. • Steve MacDonogh, ed., *The Rushdie Letters: Freedom to Speak, Freedom to Write*, 1993. • Daniel Pipes, *The Rushdie Affair: The Novel, the Ayatollah, and the West*, 1990. • Malise Ruthven, *A Satanic Affair: Salman Rushdie and the Rage of Islam*, 1990.

Siegfried Sassoon • *Biographies*. Sanford V. Sternlicht, *Siegfried Sassoon*, 1993.

Criticism. Adrian Caesar, *Taking It Like a Man: Suffering, Sexuality, and the War Poets: Brooke, Sassoon, Owen, Graves*, 1993. • Felicitas Corrigan, ed., *Siegfried Sassoon: Poet's Pilgrimage*, 1973. • John Hildebidle, "Neither Worthy Nor Capable: The War Memoirs of Graves, Blunden, and Sassoon," in *Modernism Reconsidered*, eds. Robert Kiely and John Hildebidle, 1983. • Arthur E. Lane, *An Adequate Response: The War Poetry of Wilfred Owen and Siegfried Sassoon*, 1972. • Stephen MacDonald, *Not About Heroes: The Friendship of Siegfried Sassoon and Wilfred Owen*, 1983. • Paul Moeyes, *Siegfried Sassoon, Scorched Glory: A Critical Study*, 1997. • Sigfried Sassoon, *Diaries*, 3 vols., ed. Rupert Hart-Davis, 1981–1985. • Michael Thorpe, *Siegfried Sassoon: A Critical Study*, 1966.

Bernard Shaw • *The Bodley Head Bernard Shaw: Collected Plays and Their Prefaces*, Vol. 7. London : Reinhardt, Bodley Head, 1972. • Harold Bloom, ed., *George Bernard Shaw's "Major Barbara,"* 1987. • Ian Britain, *Fabianism and Culture: A Study in British Socialism and the Arts c. 1884-1918*, 1982. • T. F. Evans, ed., *Shaw and Politics*, 1991. • J. Ellen Gainor, *Shaw's Daughters: Dramatic and Narrative Constructions of Gender*, 1991. • A. M. Gibbs, ed., *Shaw: Interviews and Recollections*, 1990. • Gareth Griffith, *Socialism and Superior Brains: The Political Thought of Bernard Shaw*, 1992. • Michael Holroyd, *Bernard Shaw*, 4 vols., 1988-93. • Michael Holroyd, *The Genius of Shaw: A Symposium*, 1979. • Dan H. Laurence and James Rambeau, eds., *Agitations: Letters to the Press, 1875-1950*, 1985. • Dan H. Laurence, ed., *Collected Letters, 1965-* . • Dan H. Laurence, *Bernard Shaw: A Bibliography*, 1983. • Sally Peters, *Bernard Shaw: The Ascent of the Superman*, 1996. • J. P. Wearing, Elsie B. Adams, & Stanley Weintraub, eds., *G. B. Shaw: An Annotated Bibliography of Writings about Him*, 3 vols., 1986-87. •Stanley Weintraub, *Bernard Shaw: A Guide to Research*, 1992. • Stanley Weintraub, ed., *Shaw: An Autobiography, Selected from His Writings*, 2 Vols., 1969-70. • Robert F. Whitman, *Shaw and the Play of Ideas*, 1977. • Rose A. Zimbardo, ed., *Twentieth Century Interpretations of "Major Barbara": A Collection of Critical Essays*, 1970.

Stephen Spender • *Biographies*. Hugh David, *Stephen Spender: A Portrait with Background*, 1992.

Criticism. Hemant Balvantrao Kulkarni, *Stephen Spender: Poet in Crisis*, 1970. • Michael O'Neill, *Auden, MacNeice, Spender: The Thirties Poetry*, 1992. • Surya Nath Pandey, *Stephen Spender: A Study in Poetic Growth*, 1982. • Stephen Spender, *Journals, 1939–1983*, 1986. • Stephen Spender, *Letters* to Christopher: Stephen Spender's Letters to Christopher Isherwood, 1929–1939, with "The Line of the Branch"—Two Thirties Journals, ed. Lee Bartlett, 1980. • Sanford Sternlicht, Stephen Spender, 1992. • A. K. Weatherhead, Stephen Spender and the Thirties, 1975.

Lytton Strachey • Max Beerbohm, Lytton Strachey, 1974. • John Ferns, Lytton Strachey, 1988. • Michael Holroyd, Lytton Strachey by Himself: A Self-Portrait, 1971. • Michael Holroyd, Lytton Strachey and the Bloomsbury Group: His Work, Their Influence, 1971. • Michael Holroyd, Lytton Strachey: The New Biography, 1995.

Dylan Thomas • John Ackerman, Thomas: His Life and Work, 1996 • Walford Davies, Dylan Thomas: New Critical Essays, 1972. • Paul Ferris, ed., The Collected Letters, 1985. • Paul Ferris, Dylan Thomas, 1977. • Constantine Fitzgibbon, Selected Letters of Dylan Thomas, 1966. • Georg Gaston, ed., Critical Essays on Dylan Thomas, 1989. • R. B. Kershner, Dylan Thomas, 1976. • Ruskworth M. Kidder, Dylan Thomas: The Country of the Spirit, 1973. • Jacob Korg, Dylan Thomas, 1992. • William T. Moynihan, The Craft and Art of Dylan Thomas, 1966. • Andrew Sinclair, Dylan Thomas: No Man More Magical, 1975. • Caitlin Thomas, Leftover Life to Kill, 1957. • William York Tindall, A Reader's Guide to Dylan Thomas, 1962.

Derek Walcott • William Baer, ed., Conversations with Derek Walcott, 1996. • Edward Baugh, Derek Walcott: Memory as Vision: Another Life, 1978. • Stewart Brown, ed., Art of Derek Walcott, 1991. • Robert D. Hamner, Derek Walcott, 1993. • Robert D. Hamner, ed., Critical Perspectives on Derek Walcott, 1993. • Bruce King, Derek Walcott and West Indian Drama: Not Only a Playwright But a Company: The Trinidad Theatre Workshop 1959–1993, 1995. • Tejumola Olaniyan, Scars of Conquest—Masks of Resistance: The Invention of Cultural Identities in African, African-American, and Caribbean Drama, 1995. • Michael Parker and Roger Starkey, eds., Postcolonial Literatures: Achebe, Ngugi, Desai, Walcott, 1995. • Rei Terada, Derek Walcott's Poetry: American Mimicry, 1992.

Evelyn Waugh • Biographies. Selina Hastings, Evelyn Waugh: A Biography, 1995. • Martin Stannard, Evelyn Waugh: The Early Years, 1903–1939, 1987. • Martin Stannard, Evelyn Waugh: The Later Years, 1939–1966, 1992.

Criticism. Alain Blayac, ed., Evelyn Waugh: New Directions, 1991. • James F. Carens, ed., Critical Essays on Evelyn Waugh, 1987. • Robert Murray Davis, Evelyn Waugh and the Forms of His Time, 1989. • Paul A. Doyle, A Reader's Companion to the Novels and Short Stories of Evelyn Waugh, 1989. • George McCartney, Confused Roaring: Evelyn Waugh and the Modernist Tradition, 1987. • Jacqueline McDonnell, Evelyn Waugh, 1988. • William Myers, Evelyn Waugh and the Problem of Evil, 1991. • Martin Stannard, ed., Evelyn Waugh: The Critical Heritage, 1984. • Evelyn Waugh, The Diaries of Evelyn Waugh, ed. Michael Davie, 1976. • Evelyn Waugh, The Letters of Evelyn Waugh, 1980.

Rebecca West • Biographies. Victoria Glendinning, Rebecca West: A Life, 1987. • J. R. Hammond, H. G. Wells and Rebecca West, 1991.

Criticism. Motley F. Deakin, Rebecca West, 1980. • Gordon N. Ray, H. G. Wells and Rebecca West, 1974. • Bonnie Kime Scott, Refiguring Modernism. Vol. I: The Women of 1928. Vol. II: Postmodern Feminist Readings of Woolf, West, and Barnes, 1995. • Peter Wolfe, Rebecca West: Artist and Thinker, 1971.

P. G. Wodehouse • Biographies. Lady Frances Lonsdale Donaldson, P. G. Wodehouse: A Biography, 1982.

Criticism. Robert A. Hall Jr., The Comic Style of P.G. Wodehouse, 1974. • Robert F. Kiernan, Frivolity Unbound: Six Masters of the Camp Novel—Thomas Love Peacock, E. F. Benson, Max Beerbohm, P. G. Wodehouse, Ronald Firbank, Ivy Compton-Burnett, 1990. • Barry Phelps, P. G. Wodehouse: Man and Myth, 1992. • Iain Sproat, Wodehouse Redeemed, 1994. • Richard Usborne, After Hours with P. G. Wodehouse, 1991. • Richard J. Voorhees, P. G. Wodehouse, 1966. • P. G. Wodehouse, Yours, Plum: The Letters of P. G. Wodehouse, ed. Frances Donaldson, 1990.

Virginia Woolf • Anne O. Bell, ed., A Moment's Liberty: The Shorter Diary, 1992. • Alison Booth, Greatness Engendered: George Eliot and Virginia Woolf, 1992. • Rachel Bowlby, ed., Virginia Woolf, 1993. • Thomas C. Caramagno, The Flight of the Mind: Virginia Woolf's Art and Manic-Depressive Illness, 1992. • Pamela L. Caughie, Virginia Woolf and Postmodernism: Literature in Quest and Question of Itself, 1991. • Mary A. Caws, Women of Bloomsbury: Virginia, Vanessa and Carrington,

1991. • Lyndall Gordon, *Virginia Woolf: A Writer's Life*, 1993. • Margaret Homans, ed., *Virginia Woolf: A Collection of Critical Essays (20th Century Views)*, 1992. • Mark Hussey, *Virginia Woolf A to Z: A Comprehensive Reference for Students, Teachers, and Common Readers to Her Life, Work, & Critical Reception*, 1996. • Mitchell A. Leaska, ed., *A Passionate Apprentice: The Early Journals, 1897-1909*, 1992. • Eleanor McNees, ed., *Virginia Woolf: Critical Assessments*, 4 vols., 1994. • Andrew McNeillie, ed., *Essays of Virginia Woolf*, 4 vols. • John Mepham, *Virginia Woolf: A Literary Life*, 1991. • Kathy J. Phillips, *Virginia Woolf Against Empire*, 1994. • Panthea Reid, *Art and Affection: A Life of Virginia Woolf*, 1996. • S. P. Rosenbaum, ed., *Women and Fiction: The Manuscript Versions of "A Room of One's Own,"* 1992. • Bonnie Kime Scott, *Refiguring Modernism*, 2 vols., 1995. • Peter Stansky, *On Or about December 1910: Early Bloomsbury and Its Intimate World*, 1996. • J. H. Stape, *Virginia Woolf: Interviews and Recollections*, 1995. • J. H. Stape, *Congenial Spirits: The Selected Letters of Virginia Woolf*, 1991. • Jeanette Winterson, *Art Objects: Essays on Ecstasy and Effrontery*, 1996. • Alex Zwerdling, *Virginia Woolf and Real Life*, 1987.

William Butler Yeats • *Edition. The Poems of W. B. Yeats: A New Edition*, ed. Richard J. Finneran, 1983.

Biographies. Richard Ellmann, *Yeats, the Man and the Masks*, 1948. • R. F. Foster, *W. B. Yeats: A Life*, 1997–.

Criticism. Harold Bloom, *Yeats*, 1970. • Elizabeth B. Cullingford, *Gender and History in Yeats's Love Poetry*, 1993. • Una Mary Ellis-Fermor, *The Irish Dramatic Movement*, 1954. • Richard Ellmann, *Eminent Domain: Yeats among Wilde, Joyce, Pound, Eliot, and Auden*, 1967. • Richard J. Finneran, *Critical Essays on W.B. Yeats*, 1986. • Adrian Frazier, *Behind the Scenes: Yeats, Horniman, and the Struggle for the Abbey Theatre*, 1990. • Maud Gonne, *The Gonne-Yeats Letters 1893–1938*, eds. Anna MacBride White and A. Norman Jeffares, 1993. • A. Norman Jeffares, *A New Commentary on the Poems of W. B. Yeats*, 1984. • A. Norman Jeffares, *W. B. Yeats: The Critical Heritage*, 1977. • A. Norman Jeffares, *W. B. Yeats, Man and Poet*, 1996. • Frank Kermode, *Romantic Image*, 1961. • Louis MacNeice, *The Poetry of W. B. Yeats*, 1941. • Edward Greenway Malins, *A Preface to Yeats*, 1974. • Lucy McDiarmid, *Saving Civilization: Yeats, Eliot, and Auden Between the Wars*, 1984. • E. H. Mikhail, ed., *W. B. Yeats: Interviews and Recollections*, 2 vols, 1977. • David Pierce, *Yeats's Worlds: Ireland, England and the Poetic Imagination*, with photographs by Dan Harper, 1995. • John Quinn, *The Letters of John Quinn to William Butler Yeats*, ed. Alan Himber, with George Mills Harper, 1983. • Jahan Ramazani, *Yeats and the Poetry of Death: Elegy, Self-Elegy, and the Sublime*, 1990. • M. L. Rosenthal, *Running to Paradise: Yeats's Poetic Art*, 1994. • Michael J. Sidnell, *Yeats's Poetry and Poetics*, 1996. • Jon Stallworthy, *Between the Lines: Yeats's Poetry in the Making*, 1963. • William York Tindall, *W. B. Yeats*, 1966. • John Eugene Unterecker, *A Reader's Guide to William Butler Yeats*, 1959. • William Butler Yeats, *Collected Letters of W. B. Yeats*, eds. Warwick Gould, John Kelly, and Dierdre Toomey, 1986–.

ACKNOWLEDGMENTS

Throughout the extended collaborative process that has produced these volumes, the editors have benefited enormously from advice and counsel of many kinds. Our first and greatest debt is to our editor, Lisa Moore, who inspired us to begin this project, and whose enthusiasm and good judgment have seen us through. She and her associates Roth Wilkofsky, Richard Wohl, and Patricia Rossi have supported us in every possible way throughout the process, ably assisted by Lynn Huddon and Christopher Narozny. We have also been fortunate to enjoy the constant aid of Mark Getlein, the Platonic ideal of a developmental editor, whose literary and visual sensitivity have benefited every page of this anthology.

The best table of contents in the world would be of little use without actual texts following it. For these we are first of all indebted to the eloquence and cajolery of permissions wizards Kathy Smeilis and Robert Ravas, who negotiated hundreds of permissions with often recalcitrant publishers and occasionally unbalanced heirs. Julie Tesser traced and cleared our illustrations. Kevin Bradley, Candice Carta, and the staff of York Production Services then performed miracles in producing a beautiful and highly accurate text out of incredible masses of tearsheets, sometimes involving semilegible texts of works that hadn't been republished for centuries. The canny copyediting of Stephanie Argeros-Magean and her colleagues did much to bring clarity and consistency to the work of a dozen editors across thirteen thousand pages of copyedited manuscript. Through these stages and as the book went to press, Valerie Zaborski, Paula Soloway, and Patti Brecht oversaw a production process of Joycean complexity, with an edgy good humor that kept everyone focused on a constantly endangered schedule.

At every stage of the project, our plans and our prose were thoughtfully reviewed and assessed by colleagues at institutions around the country. Their advice helped us enormously in selecting our materials and in refining our presentation of them. We owe hearty thanks to Lucien Agosta (California State University, Sacramento), Anne W. Astell (Purdue University), Derek Attridge (Rutgers University), Linda Austin (Oklahoma State University), Joseph Bartolomeo (University of Massachusetts, Amherst), Todd Bender (University of Wisconsin, Madison), Bruce Boehrer (Florida State University), Joel J. Brattin (Worcester Polytechnic Institute), James Campbell (University of Central Florida), J. Douglas Canfield (University of Arizona), Paul A. Cantor (University of Virginia), George Allan Cate (University of Maryland, College Park), Eugene R. Cunnar (New Mexico State University), Earl Dachslager (University of Houston), Elizabeth Davis (University of California, Davis), Andrew Elfenbein (University of Minnesota), Margaret Ferguson (University of California, Davis), Sandra K. Fisher (State University of New York, Albany), Allen J. Frantzen (Loyola University, Chicago), Kate Garder Frost (University of Texas), Leon Gottfried (Purdue University), Mark L. Greenberg (Drexel University), James Hala (Drew University), Wayne Hall (University of Cincinnati), Wendell Harris (Pennsylvania State University), Richard H. Haswell (Washington State University), Susan Sage Heinzelman (University of Texas, Austin), Standish Henning (University of Wisconsin, Madison), Jack W. Herring (Baylor University),

Maurice Hunt (Baylor University), Colleen Juarretche (University of California, Los Angeles), R. B. Kershner (University of Florida), Lisa Klein (Ohio State University), Rita S. Kranidis (Radford University), Elizabeth B. Loizeaux (University of Maryland), John J. Manning (University of Connecticut), Michael B. McDonald (Iowa State University), Celia Millward (Boston University), Thomas C. Moser, Jr. (University of Maryland), Jude V. Nixon (Baylor University), Violet O'Valle (Tarrant County Junior College, Texas), Richard Pearce (Wheaton College), Renée Pigeon (California State University, San Bernardino), Tadeusz Pioro (Southern Methodist University), Deborah Preston (Dekalb College), Elizabeth Robertson (University of Colorado), Deborah Rogers (University of Maine), Brian Rosenberg (Allegheny College), Charles Ross (Purdue University), Harry Rusche (Emory University), Kenneth D. Shields (Southern Methodist University), Clare A. Simmons (Ohio State University), Sally Slocum (University of Akron), Phillip Snyder (Brigham Young University), Isabel Bonnyman Stanley (East Tennessee University), Margaret Sullivan (University of California, Los Angeles), Herbert Sussmann (Northeastern University), Ronald R. Thomas (Trinity College), Theresa Tinkle (University of Michigan), William A. Ulmer (University of Alabama), Jennifer A. Wagner (University of Memphis), Anne D. Wallace (University of Southern Mississippi), Jackie Walsh (McNeese State University, Louisiana), John Watkins (University of Minnesota), Martin Wechselblatt (University of Cincinnati), Arthur Weitzman (Northeastern University), Bonnie Wheeler (Southern Methodist University), Dennis L. Williams (Central Texas College), and Paula Woods (Baylor University).

Other colleages brought our developing book into the classroom, teaching from portions of the work-in-progress while it was still in page proof. Our thanks for classroom testing to Lisa Abney (Northwestern State University), Charles Lynn Batten (University of California, Los Angeles), Brenda Riffe Brown (College of the Mainland, Texas), John Brugaletta (California State University, Fullerton), Dan Butcher (Southeastern Louisiana University), Lynn Byrd (Southern University at New Orleans), David Cowles (Brigham Young University), Sheila Drain (John Carroll University), Lawrence Frank (University of Oklahoma), Leigh Garrison (Virginia Polytechnic Institute), David Griffin (New York University), Rita Harkness (Virginia Commonwealth University), Linda Kissler (Westmoreland County Community College, Pennsylvania), Brenda Lewis (Motlow State Community College, Tennessee), Paul Lizotte (River College), Wayne Luckman (Green River Community College, Washington), Arnold Markely (Pennsylvania State University, Delaware County), James McKusick (University of Maryland, Baltimore), Eva McManus (Ohio Northern University), Manuel Moyrao (Old Dominion University), Kate Palguta (Shawnee State University, Ohio), Paul Puccio (University of Central Florida), Sarah Polito (Cape Cod Community College), Meredith Poole (Virginia Western Community College), Tracy Seeley (University of San Francisco), Clare Simmons (Ohio State University), and Paul Yoder (University of Arkansas, Little Rock).

As if all this help weren't enough, the editors also drew directly on friends and colleagues in many ways, for advice, for information, sometimes for outright contributions to headnotes and footnotes, even (in a pinch) for aid in proofreading. In particular, we wish to thank James Cain, Michael Coyle, Pat Denison, Andrew Fleck, Laurie Glover, Lisa Gordis, Joy Hayton, Jean Howard, David Kastan, Stanislas Kemper, Ron Levao, Carol Levin, David Lipscomb, Denise MacNeil, Jackie Maslowski, Richard Matlak, Anne Mellor, James McKusick, Michael North, David Paroissien, Stephen M. Parrish, Peter Platt, Cary Plotkin, Gina Renee, Alan Richardson, Esther Schor, Catherine Siemann, Glenn Simshaw, David Tresilian, Shasta Turner, Nicholas Watson, Michael Winckleman, and Gillen Wood for all their guidance and assistance.

The pages on the Restoration and the eighteenth century are the work of many collaborators, diligent and generous. Michael F. Suarez, S. J. (Campion Hall, Oxford) edited the Swift and Pope sections; Mary Bly (Washington University) edited Etherege and Sheridan; Michael Caldwell (University of Chicago) edited the portions of "Reading Papers" on *The Craftsman* and the South Sea Bubble. Steven N. Zwicker (Washington University) co-wrote the period introduction, and the headnotes for the Dryden section. Bruce Redford (Boston University) crafted the footnotes for Dryden, Gay, Johnson, and Boswell. Susan Brown, Christine Coch, and Paige Reynolds helped with texts, footnotes, and other matters throughout; William Pritchard gathered texts, wrote notes, and prepared bibliography. To all, abiding thanks.

It has been a pleasure to work with all of these colleagues, and this is, after all, only the beginning of what we hope will be a long-term collaboration with those who use this anthology, as teachers, students, and general readers. This book exists for its readers, whose reactions and suggestions we warmly welcome, as these will in turn reshape this book for later users in the years to come.

CREDITS

ILLUSTRATION CREDITS

INDEX